LOGARITHMIC SPEED SCALE

To find SPEED, place one point of dividers on n[...]
right point on 60 and left point will then indicate spe[...]

DANGER
CABLE CROSSING
DO NOT DRAG ANCHOR

Bridge clearances at high tide are shown either next to the bridge or in a separate note (left). Tide gauge (above, right) shows actual height of bridge.

NOTE B

The channels at the entrances to many of the inlets on this chart are subject to changes. Big Sarasota Pass buoy No. 3 is not charted because it is frequently shifted in position.

Black daybeacons, like black buoys, are kept to port entering. Green area in chart indicates shoal that's above the surface at low tide.

Red daybeacons, like red buoys, are kept to starboard entering port.

Special hazard near some inlets: breaking seas in shallows.

Black lighted buoy marks beginning of entrance. It has a flashing white light.

Red buoys have conical tops. They're called nuns, have even numbers and are kept to starboard when entering port.

Lighted buoy marks beginning of entrance channel. This one has a 4 second, flashing red light.

'Note B' refers to uncharted buoys moved to mark changing channel. They can be black and white (center of channel), red, or black as shown.

CHAPMAN

CHARLES F. CHAPMAN

PILOTING
SEAMANSHIP AND
SMALL BOAT HANDLING

By ELBERT S. MALONEY

55th EDITION

HEARST BOOKS
New York

MOTOR BOATING
& SAILING

ELBERT S. MALONEY

ELBERT S. MALONEY spent his boyhood at Virginia Beach, Virginia, where quite literally, his family home's front yard was the Atlantic Ocean. Ever since, he has rarely been happy at any distance from salt water. Colonel Maloney retired from the Marine Corps after 28 years' service, principally in communications and electronics. He has engineering degrees from Virginia Polytechnic Institute and The George Washington University. He is a member of the Institute of Navigation and its governing council.

"Mack," as he is best known, is an active boatman of wide experience and has been a boating educator for many years. He has been a member of the National Educational Staff of United States Power Squadrons for many years, and was Director of Education from 1971 to 1976. He is an active member of the Coast Guard Auxiliary and serves or has served in Flotilla, Division, and National staff offices. Mack, and his wife, Mary, are a true boating family, having lived afloat more than ten years and cruised many thousands of miles on board "Trident."

Mack has written for *Motor Boating & Sailing,* and other publications, since 1959. He started his work on "Chapman's" in 1965 with the addition of a new chapter on electronic equipment and in subsequent years has dedicated himself to keeping *Piloting, Seamanship and Small Boat Handling* current and authoritative. He revises and adds to the book for each edition and printing so that it is always the last word in boating information.

MOTOR BOATING & SAILING BOOKS
224 W. 57th St., New York., N.Y. 10019

Printed in the United States of America by
AMERICAN BOOK-STRATFORD PRESS, Inc., New York

CHAPMAN

PILOTING
SEAMANSHIP AND
SMALL BOAT HANDLING

The Story of a Famous Book

Few books in today's world are used by father, son and grandson. Few books grow with the changing technology of an age-old art. Few books are loved, respected—and at the same time are so authoritative that they can be called upon like an expert witness in a court of law. One of these rare books is Chapman's "Piloting, Seamanship & Small Boat Handling," now in its sixth decade.

The story of the book began during World War I when Franklin Delano Roosevelt, Assistant Secretary of the Navy, asked Charles F. Chapman, editor of Motor Boating magazine, to write a manual of instruction in small boat seamanship for young men who were aiming for the Navy, the Coast Guard, or the Merchant Marine. This small volume was published in several forms and sizes, and in 1922 first appeared with its present title, just ten years after Chapman became editor of Motor Boating.

The early editions of "Piloting, Seamanship & Small Boat Handling" consisted of 120 pages. With each new edition new material was added—and the book became a combination compendium of nautical lore and a home instruction course in boat operation. Some of the information, as in today's editions, was from government sources. Part was a fascinating excerpt from the Cunard Line's instructions to the deck officers of its crack Atlantic steamships. A good deal, of course, was a paste-up of instructional articles from what was already one of the world's leading boating magazines.

The book grew. The United States Power Squadrons (which Chapman had helped start in 1912), used it for free courses for the public, as well as for more advanced courses. The Coast Guard Auxiliary used the book for courses given by various flotillas around the country. Yachtsmen whose navigating skills were part of their lives took pride in having a copy of the book aboard their boats. The book also acquired nicknames: "the bible of boating," "the blue book," "Volume Five" (because it was one of the series of books published by Motor Boating), and just plain "Piloting" or "Chapman's."

The man who created and developed this nautical best seller was born in Connecticut in 1881. He majored in Mechanical and Marine Engineering at Cornell University. Settling in Manhattan, he joined the New York Motor Boat Club and was later elected Commodore. This club was active in the new American Power Boat Association, and Chapman became chairman of the APBA's racing commission, sanctioning body for motor boat races in the U.S. He was secretary of the APBA for 25 years. He wrote the first power boat racing rules.

But it wasn't all on paper. Chap drove speedboats, finishing second in the Gold Cup classics of 1924 and 1927, and in the Duke of York race in England in 1926. To dramatize the speed potential of motor boats, he organized long distance races—Gar Wood's hydroplane against the Twentieth Century Limited. Chap served as navigator when the speedboat beat the train from Albany to New York in 1925. Another such boat vs. train race was from Miami to New York; there is still a Motor Boating & Sailing Trophy for the fastest time in a power boat between Miami and New York or for other appropriate on-the-water accomplishments.

The U.S. Power Squadrons provided another area of Chap's service to pleasure boating. He was for many years chairman of the flag and etiquette committee and designed the USPS ensign. At various times he was Treasurer, Vice Commander and for two terms Chief Commander. He administered the first national boating tests. The organization, in recognition of his service and because he was one of the first organizers, gave him USPS Certificate #1.

Another honor that came in 1955 was from the Ole Evinrude Boating Foundation—a silver bowl with a citation reading "No other man deserves so much from so many of us in the World of Boating." Perhaps it was fitting that twenty-two years later Motor Boating & Sailing magazine presented the Charles F. Chapman Award to Ralph Evinrude, son of Ole, for his 50 years of service to boating. The Charles F. Chapman Award, administered by the

National Association of Engine & Boat Manufacturers, is given annually for service to boating. It has been won by organizations such as the American Red Cross as well as by individuals.

"Piloting" continued to grow with each new edition in the fifties and sixties—but the country's most widely known boating book was also getting to be more of a hodgepodge scrapbook. After William Koelbel was detached from his associate editorship on the magazine to become a full-time book editor, he proposed to Mr. Chapman that a complete revision be undertaken. This was begun in 1966, on a chapter-by-chapter basis.

Two years later, at the age of 86, Mr. Chapman was preparing to retire as publisher. The revision process was well started, and Chap held a series of planning meetings in 1968 with John Whiting, his successor. Their publishing plan became one for a "living book" that could adapt to the technological and governmental changes that were happening to boating.

"Piloting" was redesigned typographically, under the guiding hand of designer Merrill Lauck. Additional outside contributors were recruited. Each new edition (approximately every two years) would be timed and edited to take care of major changes in the Federal laws, as well as the gradual but inevitable changes in boating technology. The marlinespike chapter, for example, has changed as nylon and Dacron cordage, as well as braided rope, came on the scene.

All this called for a constant review of details on every page as well as major subjects to get into the ever-changing editions of Chapman's. One of the key persons for more than a dozen years has been Elbert S. Maloney. An experienced boat owner and long a leading member of the Power Squadrons educational organization, and one who is in constant touch with the bureaucracies in Washington, "Mack" Maloney has most often been the man at the typewriter . . . adding chapters, rewriting specialists' contributions where necessary, making the book work well as a text book, keeping track of hundreds of necessary small changes, and of course working with the Editors in the planning. Maloney is now in fact the author of "Piloting."

Besides those already mentioned, the following have been key contributors or workers: Thomas Bottomley, who took over as "in-house" editor for eight years after Bill Koelbel's retirement, Morris and Stanley Rosenfeld, Gardner Emmons, Robert Ogg, Dr. John Wilde, and particularly Jeff Hammond, now editor of Motor Boating & Sailing. The cooperation of the Educational Officers of the U.S. Power Squadrons has been important. The Army Engineers and their U.S. Lake Survey, the Coast & Geodetic Survey (now combined in the National Ocean Survey), the U.S. Navy and most of all the U.S. Coast Guard have been both able and necessary contributors to this book. Scores of manufacturers of equipment, boats, instruments and other nautical gear aid the staff in checking technical information and providing illustrations for every new edition. Ruth B. Smith (Mrs. Harold McCann) called upon her wide acquaintanceship in boating, and her knowledge from many years as Chap's assistant, to help make the transition to the new "Piloting."

Even in retirement, Chap kept his eyes upon the book. In his home, Bylandorsea, on the Connecticut River near Essex, he welcomed visitors from the staff. He deferred, saying "You are closer to it all today"—but the staff had in mind keeping up the standards with the new book that he had set with the original volume, sixty years and nearly two million copies ago. Mr. Chapman died at Essex on March 21, 1976.

He would have been proud to know that his blue book had become a part of one of the largest adult education programs in the United States. More than two hundred thousand persons take serious, well-planned courses in pleasure boat operation every year. Many of them use Chapman's as their textbook and as their keep-aboard book afterward.

As with any important book that has a long life, it is not surprising that professional boat captains, airplane pilots, amateur sailors, cruising boatmen, and many others who love the sea are constantly making suggestions for the improvement of "Piloting, Seamanship & Small Boat Handling." Many of them start their letters: "I knew Chap, and he would have . . ."

—The Editors
Motor Boating & Sailing Books
November, 1981

The safety of life and property on America's waterways is a proud tradition in the U.S. Coast Guard; it also should be the primary concern of each individual boater. The Coast Guard strongly encourages all boaters to acquire the knowledge and skills which will ensure their boating activities are safe and enjoyable.

Common sense, education, knowledge and experience are all key elements to the prevention of boating accidents. As a "Skipper", you must assure not only the safety of your craft and passengers, but also the safety of fellow boaters. By educating yourself to the ways of safe boating you make our job easier and guarantee that boating will continue to be a pleasurable sport.

Chapman's contains vital boating information and is one source which can aid you in attaining the knowledge and skills of a good "skipper". Safe boating is everyone's responsibility.

J. B. HAYES
Admiral, U. S. Coast Guard

CONTENTS

COMPLETE INDEX
ON PAGE 623

SEE PAGE 623 FOR INDEX OF COLOR PLATES

THE METRIC SYSTEM

The Metric Conversion Act of 1975 declared the policy of the United States to increase the use of the metric system of measurement on a voluntary basis with the goal of "a nation predominantly, although not exclusively, metric." Accordingly, this Edition is including metric equivalents for all measurements in customary (English) units. (English) units.

The proper name is the International System of Units, abbreviated (from the French) as SI. This is a modernized version of the metric system which traces its origins back more than three centuries. SI provides a logical and inter-related framework for measurements in science, industry, commerce, and other forms of human endeavor.

The modern metric system is built upon a foundation of seven base units, plus two supplementary units. Multiples and submultiples are expressed in a decimal system using various prefixes.

The units

The base units and their symbols are:

Length	meter—m
Mass (weight)	kilogram—kg
Temperature	Kelvin—K*
Time	second—s
Electric current	Ampere—A
Amount of substance	mole—mol
Luminous intensity	candela—cd

The supplementary units and their symbols are:

Plane angle	radian—rad
Solid angle	steradian—sr

*The commonly-used unit of temperature is the degree Celsius, °C (formerly called "centigrade"); the size of the unit is the same, the zero point is different.

Note that the units for time and electric current are the same in both the customary and metric systems.

Most *symbols* (they are not abbreviations) are written in lower-case letters; exceptions are units named after persons for which the symbol is capitalized. Periods are *not* used with any symbols.

Derived units

Other units in the SI (metric) system are *derived* from the *base* units. Typical of those expressed in combinations of base units are

Area	square meter—m²
Volume	cubic meter—m³
Speed, veliocity	meter per second—m/s
Acceleration	meter per second squared—m/s²
Density	kilogram per cubic meter—kg/m³

Typical of derived units with special names are:

Frequency	hertz = Hz	s⁻¹
Force	newton = N	kg·m/s²
Pressure, stress	pascal = Pa	N/m²
Energy, work	Joule = J	N·m
Temperature	°Celsius = °C	K − 273.15

Multiples and submultiples

Units larger and smaller than the base units are formed by adding prefixes decimally to make multiples and sub-

multiples. Symbols for the prefixes are added to the symbols for the base units.

1,000,000,000	10⁹	giga	G
1,000,000	10⁶	mega	M
1,000	10³	kilo	k
100	10²	hecto	h
10	10¹	deka	da
0.1	10⁻¹	deci	d
0.01	10⁻²	centi	c
0.001	10⁻³	milli	m
0.000,001	10⁻⁶	micro	μ

There are others, both larger multiples and smaller sub-multiples, but those are of lesser interest to boatmen.

Retained customary units

Certain units that are not a part of the metric system are so widely used that it is impractical to abandon them.

> day, hour, minute (time)
> degree, minute, second (time)
> liter

Other customary units to be continued "for a limited time, subject to future review" include:

> nautical mile, knot
> bar, millibar (atmospheric pressure)

CONVERSION

The conversion factors given below have been rounded-off for practical use and do not, in most cases, yield exact results.

Customary units to metric

	Known value	Multiply by	To find	
in	inches	25.4	millimeters	mm
ft	feet	0.3048	meters	m
yd	yards	0.9144	meters	m
s mi	statute miles	1.609	kilometers	km
n mi	nautical miles	1.852	kilometers	km
oz	ounces (weight)	28.35	grams	g
lb	pounds	0.4536	kilograms	kg
oz	ounces (liquid)	30.28	milliliters	ml
qt	quarts	0.9464	liters	l
gal	gallons	3.785	liters	l
°F	Fahrenheit temperature	5/9 after subtracting 32	Celsius temperature	°C
°(angle)	degree	0.01745	radian	rad

Metric units to customary

cm	centimeters	0.3937	inches	in
m	meters	3.281	feet	ft
m	meters	1.094	yards	yd
km	kilometers	0.6214	statute miles	s mi
km	kilometers	0.5400	naut. miles	n mi
g	grams	0.03527	ounce (weight)	oz
kg	kilograms	2.205	pounds	lb
ml	milliliters	0.03302	ounces (liquid)	oz
l	liters	1.057	quarts	qt
l	liters	0.2642	gallon	gal
°C	Celsius temperature	9/5 then add 32	Fahrenheit temperature	°F
rad	radian	57.30	degree	°

NAUTICAL TERMS

FIG. 101 Both of the above watercraft are "boats"—the term encompasses a wide variety of sizes. They are also both "vessels" in the language of the law.

The language of Boats and Boating—it's different from that of the land and landsmen, having developed over centuries of use by men who go down to the sea in ships, yet flavored by terms invented in our generation. When you speak of the "stern" of a boat you are using a word that goes back centuries through several languages; yet when you say that in the stern is an "inboard-outboard" engine, you are using a perfectly correct. term that has been in existence only a relatively few years.

No, a boatman doesn't have to be excessively "salty" in his speech, nor should he be, but there are strong reasons for knowing and using the right terms for objects and activities and the like around boats. It shows a degree of interest and knowledge, a desire to call things by their right names. In times of emergency, many seconds of valuable time may be saved when correct, precise terms are used for needed tools or actions. In correspondence and other written material, the right word often shortens long explanations and eliminates doubt or confusion.

So learn and use the proper nautical terms for the parts of your boat, her equipment, and activities aboard her—to do so will mark you as one who is truly interested in his boating and who cares enough to learn about it. But above all, form the habit of *thinking directly* in nautical terms, not in "shore" terms with subsequent mental translation—use the proper words consistently and you will soon find them coming naturally.

BASIC BOATING TERMS

The terms to be discussed in this chapter are not all-inclusive for the field of boating. No two "experts" would agree on what constituted a "complete" list, and any such list would far exceed the available space. What follows is intended as a basic nautical vocabulary, to prepare you for the various boating topics presented in detail in succeeding chapters. Many terms will be repeated and covered more fully later in the book, and more specialized words and phrases will be introduced at that time. Terms in this chapter will be described in simple, brief remarks rather than comprehensively defined as in dictionaries. Glossaries are available for those who need or desire exhaustive definitions.

FIG. 102 A motorsailer combines features of the motorboat and powered sailboat. This design includes many of the advantages of each type and is excellent for certain applications, but also suffers from the deficiencies of any compromise.

General Terms

What is a *boat*? The term has no really precise definition. It is a water-borne vehicle smaller than a *ship*, which is usually thought of as being used for ocean travel. Indeed, one definition of a boat is a small craft carried aboard a ship, such as a lifeboat. Many consider a boat as a craft not over 65 feet (19.8 meters)* in length —this being the maximum length of vessels subject to certain federal boating laws. The term *small craft* is often used interchangeably with boat.

Vessel is a broad term for water-borne vehicles and is used *without* reference to size, particularly in laws and regulations relating to all water traffic. A *yacht* is a vessel used for recreation and pleasure, as opposed to work or business. Usually it is not used for boats under approximately 40 feet (12.2 m) in length, but there are no established limits in this respect. This term is also applied to government craft used by officials and dignitaries, such as a presidential yacht or a state governor's yacht.

Although more and more people are coming to refer to boats with the neuter pronoun "it," the traditional "she" remains fully correct in speaking or writing about any size of vessel.

Categories of boats

Boats may be subdivided into *powerboats (motorboats)*, *sailboats*, and *rowboats* as determined by their basic means of propulsion. Remember, however, that sailboats may have *auxiliary engines* in which case they are often called *auxiliaries*; they are considered legally to be motorboats when propelled either by engine alone or by the engine and the sails. A *motor sailer* is a subcategory in which sails can still be used but their area has been reduced and the engine power has been increased. Like most compromises, motor sailers are somewhat less

efficient under sail than sailboats and slower under power than motorboats—they do, however, have desirable features taken from both major categories. There are no precise rules to differentiate between auxiliary-powered sailboats and motor sailers. Some pure motorboats used offshore will have a *steadying sail*; this is not for propulsion but rather for an easier ride in rough seas. See fig. 913.

The term "cruiser" indicates a type of boat with at least minimum accommodations and facilities for overnight trips. The type of propulsion may be added so as to form the terms *outboard cruiser* and *inboard cruiser*. The term is also applied to many sailboats to distinguish them from others designed primarily for racing. Other types of boats include *runabouts* for day fishing or recreational outings on the water and *utility boats* for general service applications.

A *dinghy* is a small open boat carried on or towed by a larger boat or yacht; it may be propelled by oars, sails, or a low-power outboard motor. The slangy contraction, "dink" is often used. *Prams* are small craft with square bows which serve as dinghies and are frequently used for youth program instruction and competitions. *Tenders* include dinghies and larger boats employed to carry persons and supplies to and from large yachts or ships.

Houseboats include both cruising yachts whose superstructure is larger and more designed for living aboard, and many smaller vessels that appear to have evolved from land trailers and mobile homes. Houseboats offer more living space than cruisers, but generally at some sacrifice of seaworthiness and rough water cruising ability.

Hydrofoil boats have structures called *foils* extending below the normal hull that are scientifically designed to give lift, like the wings of an airplane, when moving through the water at high speeds. The submerged foils permit the boat to "fly" just above the water surface with little drag and at much increased cruising speeds.

Boatmen and yachtsmen

The owner-operators of recreational small craft can be referred to as *yachtsmen* or *boatmen*, the usage often depending on the size of the craft involved, but again without any clear line of demarcation in boat length. The term *boater* is often heard, but it is generally less acceptable than the two just mentioned—perhaps because a "boater" is also an old-fashioned straw hat with a flat top and a broad brim! The term "rag men" and "stink potter" are applied in many areas to the skippers of sail-

FIG. 103 Large cruising houseboats have nearly disappeared from today's boating scene, but they have been more than replaced by the modern high-speed design in the 30 to 50 foot size. These are excellent for all but the most exposed boating waters.

*In anticipation of the increased use of the metric system of measurement in the United States, approximate metric equivalents are given in parentheses following customary units.

FIG. 104 Hydrofoil craft "fly" on subsurface structures contoured much like the wings of an airplane. The foils may be of the "surface piercing" type, as above, or of the "fully submerged" style.

boats and motorboats respectively—sometimes good-naturedly, and sometimes not. A *Corinthian* is any non-professional in the field of boating.

Directions Aboard a Boat

The front end of a boat is of course its *bow;* the other end is its *stern. Port* and *starboard* (pronounced starb'd) are lateral terms—port designating the left side and starboard the right when on the vessel and facing the bow, or, to express it differently, when facing *forward.* Turning around and facing the stern, one is looking *aft.*

The bow is the *forward* part of the boat; the stern is the *after* part. When one point on a boat is aft of another it is said to be *abaft* it; when nearer the bow; it is *forward* of the other. When an object lies on a line or in a plane parallel to the centerline of the vessel it is referred to as lying *fore-and-aft,* as distinguished from *athwartships,* which means right angles to the centerline.

The term *amidships* has a double meaning. In one sense, it refers to an object or area midway between the boat's sides. On the other hand, it can relate to something midway between the bow and the stern. *Inboard* and *outboard,* as directional terms, draw a distinction between objects near or toward amidships and those

away from the centerline or beyond the sides.

To express the idea of overhead in the rigging, one says *aloft. Below* means the opposite direction. Note, though, that *abovedeck* means on deck, and not actually above it as does "aloft." We should not say that a person is in or on a boat—rather he is *aboard,* or *on board.*

Terms Relating to the Boat

The basic part of a boat is its *hull,* usually consisting of a major central structural member, the *keel,* with *frames* (also called *ribs*) set into it at right angles; this skeleton is covered with skin—*planks* in the case of a planked wooden boat; *plates* for a metal boat—to make a water-tight vessel that provides buoyancy to float the weight of the craft and its load. Boats may be of the *open* type or the hull may be covered over with a *deck;* some boats are partially open, partially decked. As boats get above the smallest sizes, they may have a *superstructure* above the main deck level, variously referred to as a *deckhouse* or *cabin* (cabins also extend below the level of the deck). Small, relatively open boats may have only a *shelter cabin,* or *cuddy,* forward.

The hulls of boats made of metal—usually aluminum or steel—or of fiberglass-reinforced plastics, will differ in some respects from wooden boats, but the basic components of keel, frames, and covering normally will be retained in at least modified form.

Terms denoting shape

Sheer is the term used to designate the curve or sweep of the deck of a vessel as viewed from the side. The side skin of a boat between the waterline and deck is called the *topsides.* If these are drawn in toward the centerline away from a perpendicular as they go upward, as they often do near the stern of a boat, they are said to *tumble home.* Forward, they are more likely to incline outward to make the bow more buoyant and to keep the deck drier by throwing spray aside; this is *flare.* See Fig. 108.

The bottom of a boat may be one of three basic shapes—*flat, round,* or *vee*—or it may be a combination of two shapes, one forward gradually changing to the other toward the stern. There are also more complex modern shapes such as *cathedral-hull, deep-vee, multi-step,* and others.

A *displacement* hull is one that achieves its buoyancy or flotation capability by displacing a volume of water equal in weight to the hull and its load, whether under way or at rest. A *planing hull,* on the other hand, is one that achieves the major part of its load-carrying ability by the dynamic action of its underside with the surface of the water over which it is rapidly traveling; at rest, a planing hull reverts to displacement buoyancy. A *semiplaning* (or *semi-displacement)* hull is one that gets a

FIG. 105 Port and starboard. To help keep the terms "port" and "starboard" straight in your mind, remember that "port" is the shorter word and that "left" is shorter than "right."

FIG. 106 Flare is the outward curvature of the sides near the bow. It is a characteristic of modern designs, providing more usable forward deck area and making for a "drier" boat by turning aside spray. Tumble-home is the inward curving of topsides near the stern.

FIG. 107 Different bottom designs are used for various types of boats. A flat-bottom craft is inexpensive to build; a vee-bottom is used on fast craft. The "cathedral" hull is used on many small craft for speed and stability.

FIG. 108 A planing hull at high speeds rides more "on" the water than "in" it. Hydrodynamic forces support the craft rather than displacement. Friction is reduced and higher speeds are achieved with the same horsepower.

portion of its weight-carrying capability from dynamic action, but which does not travel at a fast enough speed for full planing action. It is often a hull that is round-bottomed forward gradually flattening out toward the stern to provide a planing surface.

Two main types of *multi-hull* craft are the *catamaran* with two hulls of equal size held apart by rigid structural members, and the *trimaran* with a principal central hull flanked on either side by smaller outboard hulls.

Bow and sterns

The *stem* is the extreme leading edge of a hull; on wooden craft it is the major structural member at the bow. A stem is common to all boats with a conventional bow; the *pram* or *punt* type has a bow resembling its square stern. The stem of a boat is *plumb* if it is perpendicular to the waterline, or *raked* if inclined at an angle for better appearance. The term *overhang* describes the projection of the upper part of the bow or stern beyond a perpendicular from the waterline. *Eye bolts* or *ring bolts* are frequently fitted through the stems of small boats for towing or for pulling aboard trailers.

The flat area across the stern is called the *transom*. If, however, the stern is pointed, resembling a conventional bow, there is no transom and the boat is called a *double-ender*. The *quarter* of a boat is the after portion of her sides, particularly the furthermost aft portion where the sides meet the transom.

Terms relating to the keel

The *keel* is the major longitudinal member of a hull. An extra wooden piece fastened externally to the keel to protect it is a *worm shoe* or *false keel*. A metal fitting extending back from the underside of the keel for protection of the rudder and propeller is called a *skeg*.

The *rudder* of a craft is the flat surface at or near the stern that is pivoted about a vertical or near-vertical axis so as to turn to either side and thus change the direction of movement of the vessel through the water. The upward extension of the rudder through which force is applied to turn the rudder is the *rudderpost* (or *rudderstock*). A *stuffing* box keeps the hull watertight where the rudderpost enters. A stuffing box is also used where a propellor shaft goes through the hull.

Fiberglass construction

The modern marine material for small craft undoubtedly is *fiberglass*. The full name is "fiber reinforced plastic" which properly describes the material as glass fibers embedded in a thermosetting plastic.

The advantages of fiberglass construction are many. Surfaces can be of any desired compound curvature; multiple identical hulls, superstructures, and lesser components can be made economically from reusable molds; and plastic hulls underwater completely resist attack by marine organisms, although they do require anti-fouling paint.

The reinforcing material is glass fiber, usually in the form of *mat, roving* or *cloth,* which is *laid up* in alternate layers with *polyester resin* which has been mixed with a *catalyst* that causes the resin to harden in a few minutes. The *working time* can be controlled by the proportion of catalyst added and the working temperature. Sometimes a *chopper gun* is used which sprays into the mold resin and catalyst mixed with the proper proportion of *chopped glass fiber*. The smooth and bright, shining color of the surface of a fiberglass boat comes from the *gel coat,* a thin finish layer of pigmented plastic which is laid in the mold as *layup* commences.

Fiberglass is useful also in covering wood, either in new construction or in the repair of older boats, where

FIG. 109 Multihull sailing craft have become very popular. The catamaran, above, is seen in all sizes from small day sailers to large ocean racers. Trimarans, left, are generally found in sizes from 30 feet upward.

its properties of *adhesion* are important. *Epoxy* is another resin whose adhesive properties are superior to polyester but it is more expensive.

Fiberglass construction has added few new terms to the vocabulary of hull construction. Overhead surfaces are protected by *headliners*; *high-hat sections* are used as stiffeners, playing the role of frame or stringers according to the direction in which they are run. *Balsa core* and *foam core* refer to methods of stiffening the otherwise extremely flexible panels of glass fiber and resin by separating two of them by perhaps an inch of the core material, producing a light, strong, and stiff structure.

Deck openings

Hatches (sometimes *hatchways*) are openings in the deck of a vessel to provide access below. *Companion ladders* or steps lead downward from the deck; these are also termed *companionways*.

Cockpits are open wells in the deck of a boat outside of deckhouses and cabins. *Coamings* are vertical pieces around the edges of cockpit, hatches, etc., to prevent water on deck from running below.

Scuppers are holes permitting water to drain overboard from decks and cockpits. A cockpit is said to be *self-bailing* when it has scuppers to drain it.

Interior terms

Vertical partitions, corresponding to walls in a house, are called *bulkheads*. *Watertight bulkheads* are solid or are equipped with doors that can be secured so tightly as to be leak-proof. The interior areas divided off by bulkheads are termed *compartments*—such as an engine compartment—or cabins—such as the main cabin, aft cabin, etc. Some areas are named by their use; the "kitchen" aboard a boat is its *galley*. The toilet area is the *head* (the same name is also given to the toilet itself).

Overhead is the nautical term for what would be the ceiling of a room in a house; the nautical use of the term ceiling has been explained above.

The *forepeak* of a boat is the compartment furthest forward in the bow, usually used for the storage of line and/or chain, sometimes for sails. The *forecastle* (pronounced fo'c's'l), if any small craft can be said to have one, is the cabin furthest forward. The term is generally used today to mean the crew's quarters forward.

Cabin styles

A *trunk cabin* is one that extends above the main deck level, but less than the full width of the boat so that walkways—side decks—are left on either side; such a

TRUNK CABIN   RAISED DECK CABIN

FIG. 110 The cabins of some motorboats and sailing craft are of the "raised deck" type extending the full width of the hull. Other boats have "trunk cabins" with a smaller superstructure set above the level of the deck.

FIG. 111 The principal external dimensions of a boat are shown above. Don't confuse "draft" with "depth"—an internal measurement used in connection with the documentation of vessels.

BEAM · OVERALL LENGTH · FREEBOARD · DRAFT · WATERLINE LENGTH · WATERLINE

boat is referred to as a *trunk cabin cruiser*. Conversely, a *raised deck* cruiser is one in which the cabin is formed by extending the topsides above the normal deck level—it extends for the full width of the hull, thus eliminating side decks. A *sedan cruiser* has the main cabin on the same level as an aft cockpit and opening out into it. A *sport fisherman* is a motorboat, usually fast, with special equipment for off-shore trolling for large game fish.

The *bridge* of a vessel is the location from which it is steered and its speed controlled. On small craft, the term *control station* is perhaps more appropriate; *helm* is often used aboard sailboats. Many modern motorboats have a *flying bridge*, an added set of controls above the level of the normal control station for better visibility and more fresh air. These, also called *fly bridges*, are usually open, but may have a collapsible top for shade.

Portholes and portlights

On a boat, a port (or *porthole*) is an opening in the hull to admit light and air. The glass used in it to keep the hull weathertight is termed a *portlight* if it can be opened.

The dimensions of a vessel

The length of a boat is often given in two forms. *Overall length* (l.o.a.) is measured from the fore part of the stem to the after part of the stern. The *waterline* of a boat is the plane where the surface of the water touches the hull when she is loaded normally; *length on the waterline* (l.w.l.) is measured along this plane. The greatest width of a vessel is her *beam*; boats of greater than normal beam are described as *beamy*. A vessel's *draft* is the depth of water required to float her. Draft should not be confused with the term *depth*, which is used in connection with larger vessels and documented boats and is measured inside the hull from the underside of the deck to the top of the keel.

The height of a boat's topsides from the waterline to the deck is called her *freeboard*. *Headroom* is the vertical distance between the deck and the cabin or canopy top, or other overhead structure.

Other terms aboard a boat

The lower interior areas of the hull of a vessel are called her *bilge* (or *bilges*). It is here that water that leaks in, or is blown aboard as spray, collects as *bilge water*, to be later pumped overboard by a *bilge pump*.

When something is put away in its proper place on a vessel, it is *stowed*. The opposite of stowing, to *break out*, is to take a needed article from its locker or other secure place. To *unship* an item of equipment is to re-

FIG. 112(a) A wharf is a facility along and parallel to a shore to which vessels may be made fast for loading, fueling, etc.

FIG. 112(b) Left, piers extend outward from the shoreline and craft may be made fast alongside the main structure or in slips separated by catwalks.

FIG. 113(a) Marine railways are widely used for hauling out craft of all sizes. A cradle is pulled down into the water deep enough for the boat to be floated onto it. She is then blocked in place and the cradle is slowly pulled up rails until it is clear of the water.

FIG. 113(b) Craft up to 60 feet or more in length are now being taken out of the water by travelling lifts that straddle a wet slip. Broad slings are lowered, passed under the hull, and then raised. When the boat is high enough, the lift moves back on shore under tow or its own power.

move it from its normal working location or position.

Berths and *bunks* are seagoing names for beds aboard a boat. Closets are termed *lockers,* and a *hanging locker* is one tall enough for full-length garments. Chests and boxes may also be called lockers. A *rope* or *chain locker* is often found in the bow of a boat for stowing the anchor line or chain. *Lazarettes* are compartments in the stern of a vessel used for general storage.

Helm is a term relating to the steering mechanism of a craft. An individual is *at the helm* when he is at the controls of the boat; he is then the *helmsman.*

Terms Used in Boating Activities

In addition to the numerous terms for the boat itself, there are many others to be learned in connection with boating in general and the use of craft of all sizes. The list of these is virtually endless, and those that follow are only the more basic and often-used ones.

Docks, piers, and harbors

There is a difference between the strict definition and popular usage for the term "dock." Most properly speaking, a *dock* is the *water* area in which a boat lies when she is *made fast* to shore installations (and "made fast" is the proper term rather than "tied up"). A *drydock* is

one that can be shut off from the surrounding water and pumped out in order to make repairs on the vessel's bottom. *To dock* a vessel is to bring her to the shore installation and make her fast.

In boating, however, the term "dock" is usually applied to structures bordering the water area in which boats lie. A *wharf* is properly a structure generally parallel to the shore, while a *pier* projects out from the shoreline. *Piles* are substantial stakes driven into the bottom to which craft may be made fast; a *dolphin* is a group of piles driven close together and bound with wire cables into a single structure. (The name dolphin is also given to the species of sea mammal often called porpoises, and quite separately to a species of ocean game fish.) Piles are often used to form *slips* out from a pier or wharf in which boats can be *berthed;* short *catwalks* (or *finger piers*) may extend out between the slips for easier access to the boats. A boat is made fast to a pile, *in* a slip, and *alongside* a pier or wharf.

A *harbor* is an anchorage which affords reasonably good protection for a vessel, with shelter from wind and sea. Strictly speaking, it applies to the water area only. *Port* is a more comprehensive term, including not only the harbor but, collectively, all the facilities for freight, passengers, and services as well, such as wharves, piers, warehouses, etc. A *yacht basin* or *marina* is a protected facility primarily for recreational small craft.

Jetties are dikes or embankments connected to the shore; when these are used to protect a harbor, and have no connection to the land, they are generally referred to as *breakwaters*. *Groins* are jetty-like dikes built out at roughly a 90° angle from the shore to prevent erosion of the beach.

Boats are *hauled out* of the water on inclined planes at the water's edge called *ways* (also *marine ways* or *marine railways*). The framework which supports a boat as she is hauled out is termed a *cradle*. Small and medium sized boats are also lifted bodily out of the water and set on shore for storage or work with *slings*, which are lowered, passed under the hull, and raised by *cranes* or *traveling lifts*.

Ropes and lines

Generally speaking, the word *rope* is used but little aboard a boat; the correct general term is *line*. "Rope" may be bought ashore at the store, but when it comes aboard and is put to use it becomes "line." *Marlinespike seamanship* is the term applied to that portion of the art related to the use of line and the making of *knots, bends, hitches,* and *splices.* Chapter 11 is devoted to this important subject.

Lines used to make a boat fast to a shore structure are usually called *docking lines. Bow lines* and *stern lines* lead forward and aft from these respective parts of the craft. *Spring lines* lead from the bow aft or from the stern forward to prevent the boat from moving ahead or astern. See fig. 827.

A *painter* is a line at the bow of a small boat, such as a dinghy, for towing or making fast. The line by which a boat is made fast to a mooring buoy is called a *pennant* (sometimes *pendant*).

Heave is a nautical term for throw or pull. One *heaves in* on a line when he pulls in the slack and *takes a strain* on it. When a line is let out, one *pays it out;* to lessen the strain on a line or let it out slightly or slowly, one *eases* it. A line is *snubbed* when its outward run is *checked;* it is *cast off* when it is let go. (A boat is cast off when all lines have been taken off the pier or other object to which it has been made fast.)

The *bitter end* of a line is the extreme end, the end made fast when all line has been paid out. The middle part of a line not including either end is the *bight,* particularly when formed into a loop. If a strain is put on a line heavy enough to break it, it *parts.*

Heaving lines are light lines, usually with a knot or weight at one end which makes it easier to throw them far and accurately. The knot that encloses a weight at the end of a heaving line is called a *monkey's fist. Belay* has two meanings—a line is belayed when it is made fast without knotting to a *cleat* or *belaying pin; belay* as a command signifies "stop" or "cease."

Ends of lines are *whipped* or *seized* when twine or thread is wrapped around them to prevent strands from untwisting or *unlaying.* Ragged ends of lines are said to be *fagged. Hawsers* are very heavy lines, in common use on tugboats and larger vessels but rarely found on boats.

Tackle is a broad, general term applied to equipment and *gear* used aboard a boat. It has a specific use, however, to mean a combination of line and *blocks* (pulleys)

FIG. 114 A set of blocks and some line can be used to increase lifting or pulling power. The set shown here has a theoretical "mechanical advantage" of 3—actually less due to friction in the blocks.

used to increase a pulling or hoisting force. The wheels or rollers of the blocks are the *sheaves* (pronounced shivs). When a line is passed through a block or hole it is *reeved;* to *render* is to ensure that the line will pass freely through the block or hole.

Lines have *standing parts* and *hauling parts.* The standing part is the fixed part, the one which is made fast; the hauling part is the one that is taken in or let out as the tackle is used. Lines are *foul* when tangled, *clear* when in order to run freely.

Anchors and moorings

An *anchor* is a specially shaped metal device designed to dig efficiently into the bottom under a body of water and hold a vessel in place despite winds and currents. Chapter 6 is devoted to anchors and their use. Figs. 602 and 604 show several different kinds of anchors. *Ground tackle* is a general term embracing anchors, lines, and other gear used in anchoring. On boats, the anchor line may be referred to as a *rode.* A *mooring* is a semipermanent anchorage installation, consisting of a heavy anchor (usually of the *mushroom* type), chain, a mooring buoy, and pennant of nylon or manila. See fig. 652.

The anchor carried on a boat for most normal uses is its *working anchor.* A heavier model carried for emergencies is termed a *storm anchor,* and a smaller, lighter anchor for brief daytime stops when the craft will not be left unattended is popularly called a *lunch hook.*

Anchors come in many styles—*kedge, stockless, grapnel,* and modern *light-weight* types such as the *Danforth, Northill,* and *plow.* More on this subject will be found in Chapter 6.

FIG. 115 There are many types of anchors used on boats. The old-fashioned, or yachtsman's type, left, and the modern patent (Danforth), right are only two; many others are illustrated in Chapter 8.

FIG. 116 A boat must always be anchored with adequate "scope." This is the ratio of the length of the anchor line in use to the distance from the bow chocks to the bottom of the water (not just the depth of the water!) See also fig. 631.

The term *kedge* is also applied to an anchor of any type that is used for getting a boat off when it has run aground. The kedge is carried out by a dinghy or other means and set so that a pull on the line will help get the boat off or at least keep it from being driven harder aground; this process is called *kedging*.

When a boat is anchored, the ratio of the length of line in use to the distance to the bottom of the water as measured from the deck is termed *scope*. An *anchorage* is an area specifically designated by governmental authorities in which vessels may anchor; special regulations may prevail in these areas.

Motions of a boat

A vessel *grounds* when she touches bottom, and if stuck there she is *aground*. When a boat moves through the water, she is said to be *underway* (or *under weigh*). According to government laws and regulations, a vessel is underway at any time that she is not aground, at anchor, or made fast to the shore. The direction in which she is moving may be made more specific by stating that she makes *headway* (moving forward), *sternway* (backwards), or *leeway* (to one side or the other, as when pushed by a beam wind). A boat is said to be *underway with no way on* when she is free of the bottom or shore but is making no motion through the water (*adrift*). A vessel has *steerageway* if she is making enough speed through the water for her rudder to be effective. A vessel's anchor is said to be *aweigh* when it has broken out of the bottom and has been lifted clear.

FIG. 117 Nearly all boats leave an area of disturbed water— wake—behind them as they move forward through the water. Each skipper must be careful that the waves caused by this motion do not disturb or damage others.

The disturbed water that a boat leaves astern as a result of her motion is her *wake*. *Wash* is the flow of water that results from the action of her propeller or propellers. Both of these effects are commonly lumped together as "wake."

Sidewise rotational motion in rough water is called *roll*; vertical motion as the bow rises and falls is termed *pitching*. A craft *yaws* when she runs off her course to either side as she might if she didn't steer properly. If she yaws too widely and is thrown broadside into the *trough* of the sea (between the crests and parallel to them), she *broaches to,* a dangerous situation that should be carefully avoided. In very rough seas a small boat can be thrown end-over-end; this is *pitchpoling*.

FIG. 118 The three basic motions of a boat are roll, pitch, and yaw. At sea, these are often combined with uncomfortable results!

A boat may *capsize* without *foundering*—in the first instance she turns over, in the latter she fills with water and sinks. If a boat fills with water from over the side, she *swamps*. Before his vessel is reduced to such straits, the wise skipper *heaves to,* reducing headway and generally lying with the bow slightly off from meeting the waves head on. He may put out a *sea anchor (drogue)* that will hold the bow at the most favorable angle; a sea anchor does not go to the bottom, it merely serves as a drag.

Trim

Trim relates to the way a boat floats in the water. When she floats properly as designed, she is on an *even keel*; but if she inclines to port or starboard, she *lists*. *Heel* conveys the same idea as list, a sideward inclination from the vertical. If a vessel is too heavily loaded forward, she *trims by the head*; if her draft is excessive aft, she *trims by the stern*.

Directions from the boat

Dead ahead refers to any point which the vessel is approaching directly on a straight course. *Dead astern* is, of course, the opposite direction. To convey the idea of opposite, or at right angles, we say *abreast*. An object that is at right angles (90°) to the centerline (keel) of a craft is *abeam*, or *broad on the beam*. If the boat passes near to it, it is said to be *close aboard*. (Vessels are *abreast* of one another when they are side-by-side.)

If we look ahead from abeam to a direction that is midway between abeam and dead ahead, this is *broad on the bow*, port or starboard as the case may be. Going in the other direction, an object seen midway between abeam and dead astern is *broad on the (port or starboard) quarter*.

To express the direction of another vessel or object relative to our boat, we say that it *bears* so-and-so, using the phraseology above. For intermediate directions through a circle centered on the observer's boat, the *point* system can be used, with 32 points making a complete circle. Each direction in the point system is named. A ship or other object seen from your craft might be said to bear *two points abaft the port beam, one point on the starboard bow*, etc. See fig. 119. Half-points and quarter points exist but are rarely used. The direction of a remote object is its *bearing*.

Windward (pronounced wind'ard) means toward the direction from which the wind is blowing. A boat goes to windward, but in speaking of the side of a vessel and the parts on that side on which the wind is blowing, it is better to refer to the *weather* side.

Opposite to windward is *leeward* (pronounced *loo-ard*), the direction away from the wind, toward which it is blowing. The *lee* side of a boat is the side away from the wind, and a boat makes *leeway* when blown sideways off her course. The lee and weather sides are sometimes referred to as *hands*, thus a *lee shore* is the shore on the *lee hand*, one toward which the vessel is blown by the wind. However, the vessel finds shelter in the *lee* of the land when she is under a *weather shore*.

FIG. 120 Cleats, bitts, and chocks are found on both motorboats and sailboats. Their shape and size may vary with the craft that they are on, but all are basic forms of deck hardware.

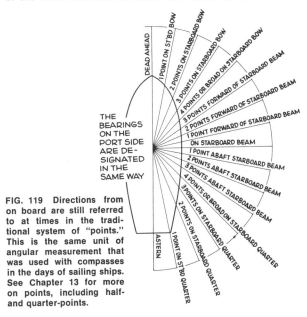

FIG. 119 Directions from on board are still referred to at times in the traditional system of "points." This is the same unit of angular measurement that was used with compasses in the days of sailing ships. See Chapter 13 for more on points, including half- and quarter-points.

Terms Relating to Equipment

Chocks are deck fittings, usually of metal, with inward curving arms through which lines such as mooring or anchor lines are passed so as to lead them in the proper direction both on board and off the boat; they should be smooth so as to prevent excess wearing of the line. *Cleats* are fittings of metal or wood with outward curving arms or horns on which lines can be made fast *(belayed)*.

While cleats are generally satisfactory for most purposes on a boat, wooden or metal *bitts* are often preferred where heavy strains are to be taken. These are stout vertical posts, either single or double. They may take the form of a fitting bolted securely (never screwed) to the deck, but more often, as in the case of a wooden

samson post, passing through the deck and *stepped* at the keel or otherwise strongly fastened. Sometimes a round metal pin is fitted horizontally through the head of a post or bitt to aid in belaying the line; this is a *norman pin*.

Fenders are relatively soft objects of rubber or plastic (older models were canvas cases filled with cork) used between boats and piles, pier sides, seawalls, etc. to protect the topsides from scarring and to cushion any shock of the craft striking the fixed object. Fenders, sometimes referred to in a landlubberly fashion as "bumpers," are also used between boats when they are tied, or *rafted*, together. *Fender boards* are short lengths of stout planking, often with cushion material or metal rubbing strips on one side. They may be used with two fenders hung vertically, or occasionally by themselves, to provide a wider bearing surface against a single pile.

Life preservers provide additional buoyancy to keep a person afloat when he is in the water. They take the form of cushions, belts, vests, jackets, and ring buoys. Life preservers must be of a Coast Guard-approved type to meet the legal requirement as set forth in Chapter 2.

FIG. 121 For protection against rough piers or other boats, a skipper will often need to hang fenders (don't call them "bumpers") over the side. Modern ones are made of rubber or plastic. Where necessary, fenders may be hung horizontally, or two of them may be used vertically behind a fenderboard; see fig. 855.

FIG. 122 A boarding ladder can either be hung over the gunwales of a small boat or fitted into brackets on the topsides of a larger craft to make easier boarding from a low float or dinghy. A longer ladder reaching down into the water is used for swimming.

A *boathook* is a short shaft of wood or metal with a fitting at one end shaped to aid in extending one's effective reach from the side of a boat, such as when putting a line over a pile or picking up an object dropped overboard. It can also be used for pushing or fending off.

A *boarding ladder* is a set of steps temporarily fitted over the side of a boat to assist persons coming aboard from a low pier or float. A *swimming ladder* is much the same except that it extends down into the water. A *swimming platform* is a narrow wooden shelf attached to a boat's transom just above the waterline.

Grab rails are hand-hold fittings mounted on cabin tops or sides for personal safety when moving around the boat, both on deck and below. Whenever these or other fittings such as cleats and chocks are installed, *bedding compound* should be smeared on the surface of the fitting that will be in contact with the hull, deck, etc., to seal out moisture.

Magnetic *compasses* are mounted near the control station in boxes or other protective casings known as *binnacles*. Compasses are swung in *gimbals*, pivoted rings that permit the compass *bowl* and *card* to remain relatively level regardless of the boat's motion. To enable the helmsman to steer a compass course, a *lubber's line* is marked on the inside of the compass bowl to indicate direction of the vessel's bow. Much more on compasses will be found in Chapters 13 and 14.

A *lead* (pronounced led) *line* is a length of light rope with a weight (the lead) at one end and markers at accurately measured intervals from that end. It is used for determining the depth of water alongside a vessel. A *depth sounder* is an electronic device for determining depths; often such devices are referred to as "fathometers"—this is incorrect as that term is the trademark of one particular manufacturer of electronic depth sounders. Boats used frequently in shallow waters may be equipped with a long slender *sounding pole* with depth in feet and fractions marked off from its lower end.

A *barometer* is often carried aboard a boat; it measures and indicates (in some cases, records) atmospheric pressure. Knowledge of the amount and direction of change in atmospheric pressure is useful in predicting changes in the weather.

Binoculars are hand-held optical devices that aid in detecting and identifying distant objects. Separate sets of lenses and prisms enable the user to see with both eyes at the same time.

A *winch* is a mechanical device, either hand or power operated, for exerting an increased pull on a line or chain, such as an anchor line.

Flags

Strictly speaking, a vessel's *colors* are the flag or flags that she flies to indicate her nationality, but the term is often expanded to include all flags flown. An *ensign* is a flag to denote the nationality of a vessel or her owner, or on a boat to denote the membership of her owner in an organization (other than a yacht club).

The *hoist* of a flag is its inner vertical side; also its vertical dimension. The *fly* is its length from the hoist out to the free end. The *union* is the upper portion near the hoist—in the U.S. national flag, the blue area with the white stars. The *union jack* is a flag consisting solely of the union of the national flag.

A *burgee* is a triangular, rectangular, or swallow-tailed flag usually denoting yacht club or similar unit membership. A *pennant* is a flag, most often triangular in shape, used for general designating or decorative purposes. See Chapter 22 for additional information on flags and how they should be flown.

FIG. 123 The principal parts and dimensions of a flag are shown at left. For boat flags the usual ratio between the fly and the hoist is 3:2. This may vary in the case of some pennants.

Terms of Distance and Speed

On salt water, distances are measured in *nautical miles*, a unit about 1/7th longer than the land or *statute* mile with which we all are more familiar. The international nautical mile is slightly more than 6076 feet; the statute mile used on shore and fresh water bodies is 5280 feet.

Where nautical miles are used for distance, the unit of speed is the *knot*, one nautical mile per hour. Note carefully that the "per hour" is included in the definition—to say "knots per hour" is incorrect. *Miles per hour* is the correct term for most inland fresh water bodies, as it is on shore. A *speed curve* is a plot of speed through the water versus engine speed in revolutions per minute (RPM).

In boating, depths are usually measured in feet, but offshore the unit *fathom* may be used—it is six feet.

Increasingly, metric units are coming into use—*meters* and *kilometers* (1000 meters) for distance; *meters* and *decimeters* (1/10 of a meter) for depths and heights.*

*1 nautical mile=1.852 km 1 statute mile=1.609 km 1 fathom (6 feet)=1.83 m

Miscellaneous Terms

When any part of the vessel's gear or equipment breaks or gives way, it *carries away;* an object goes *by the board* when it goes *overboard.* If a boat is *stove* (planking broken in from outside), the craft *springs a leak* or *makes water.* When water is dipped out of a small boat the process is called *bailing.*

The term *clear* has many meanings. Before leaving for a foreign port, a ship must clear through Customs authorities. She clears the land when she leaves it, clears a shoal when she passes it by safely. The bilges are cleared of water when they are pumped out. Tangled *(foul)* lines are cleared by straightening them out and getting them ready for use.

A boat *stands by* when she remains with another craft to give her assistance if necessary. When used as an order, stand by means to be prepared to carry out an instruction. *Aye,* or *aye aye,* is a properly nautical (if somewhat military) way of acknowledging an order or instruction, indicating that it has been heard and understood, and will be obeyed.

Entries are made in a *log* (book) to record all events occurring aboard; more on this in Chapter 30. A *patent log* is a device to record distance traveled. One *raises* a light or landmark when it first becomes visible; he makes a *landfall* when the shore is first sighted on coming in from sea. *Passage* is generally construed to mean a run from one port to another; *voyage* includes both the outward and homeward passages. *Watches* are periods of duty, usually four hours long, aboard a vessel; *dog watches* are shorter, two-hour periods between 4:00 and 8:00 pm (1600 and 2000 in the 24-hour system of time, see page 376). A period of duty at the helm is a *trick.*

Tides and currents

The word *tide* is almost certainly one of the most misused of nautical terms, so much so that its misapplication has come to be widely accepted even though incorrect. Properly speaking, it means only the rise and fall, the vertical movement, of bodies of water as a result of the interacting gravitational pulls of the moon and sun. Commonly, but wrongly, "tide" is also used to refer to the inflow and outflow as a result of changes in tidal level. *Current* is the proper term for a horizontal flow of water, *tidal current* for flows resulting from tidal influences. It is proper to say a two-knot current, but not a two-knot tide.

The incoming tidal current running toward the shore, or upstream in a river, is the *flood;* the retreating, or downstream, current is the *ebb.* The *range* of the tide (difference between the height of *high water* and *low water* (or *high tide* and *low tide)* is not always the same as the days go by. *Spring tides* occur when the moon is new or full and have a greater range than those at other times. *Neap tides* are those occurring at quarter moons; and these have a less than average range.

Water movements and conditions

Various terms are used to describe specific water movements or conditions of the surface. A broad term, *waves,* is frequently used for disturbed conditions on a body of water; these actually represent vertical move-

FIG. 124 The horizontal motion of water is current, not tide, although it is termed tidal current if it results from tidal influences. Such currents "flood" (flow in from sea) and "ebb" (flow out). Tides, vertical changes in water level, do not "come in" and "go out"; they "rise" and "fall."

FIG. 125 Waves result from local wind action on the water surface. Large deep-water swells may come from great distances away; they crest over and become breakers as they move into shallower water near shore.

U.S. Coast Guard Photo

ment of water particles regardless of their apparent forward motion. *Sea* is a general term often used to describe waves and water action on the surface, but properly it should be applied only to waves produced by wind. *Rips* are short, steep waves caused by the meeting of currents. The confused water action found at places where tidal currents meet is also called a *chop,* but this term is more often applied to small, closely spaced waves resulting from wind action on inland bodies of water.

Swells (ground swells) are long heavy undulations of the surface resulting from disturbances some distance away on oceans and sea. *Surf* is produced when waves leave deep water forming *breakers* on the shore as they *crest* and curl over. A *following sea* is one that comes up from astern, running in the same direction as the boat is going. A *head sea* is just the opposite; one where the progress of the waves is against that of the craft which must meet them head on. *Beam seas* come from either side. *Cross* or *confused seas* are irregular ones with components from two or more directions.

Powerboat Terms

A number of basic boating terms are applicable specifically to boats equipped with some form of engine, whether *inboard* (mounted within the hull) or *outboard* (mounted on the transom and detachable).

Propulsion

Thrust for the movement of the boat through the water is achieved by the rotation of a *propeller* (or *screw)* which draws in water from ahead and pushes it out

FIG. 126 Some small craft are "jet-propelled." The engine drives a multistage pump and the reaction from the high-speed stream of water coming out of the stern provides the forward propulsion. Such systems are excellent for very shallow water but are less efficient overall than conventional drives.

FIG. 127 On displacement-type hulls of heavy construction, the propeller shaft normally runs through a "deadwood" above the keel. On higher-speed hulls, struts extend downward from the bottom of the craft to support the exposed shaft. Long shafts on larger craft may have two or more struts.

FIG. 128 inboard-outboard drives combine the advantages of using conventional inboard engines with the flexibility of outside drive units much like an outboard motor. Steering is accomplished without rudders by pivoting the drive units; these can also be tilted up for service.

astern. Boats with two engines and propellers are referred to as *twin-screw* craft. An often-used slang term for a propeller is *wheel*. A very few boats achieve their thrust from the reaction of a *water jet*.

A more recent development is the *inboard-outboard* (or *I-O*, or *stern-drive*, or *outdrive*). Here the motor is of the inboard type mounted within the hull at the stern with an external driving unit closely resembling the *lower unit* of an outboard motor, even to the extent of being capable of being tilted up. Power is applied to the propeller through two right-angle sets of gears resulting in another name sometimes used, *Z-drive*.

Engine mountings

An inboard engine is mounted on *engine beds,* stout structural members running fore-and-aft across the floor timbers. On single-screw boats, the *deadwood* is a heavy fore-and-aft timber that lies above the keel and may extend beyond it. (On sailboats the deadwood may be beneath the keel timbers of the hull.) *Shaft logs* are timbers through which the *propeller shaft* passes; a *stuffing box* prevents water from entering at this point. The *propeller post*, if one is used, stands vertically behind the deadwood and is joined to it and to the keel. On many boats, the propeller shaft is supported externally under the hull by one or more *struts*.

In some designs of boats, the engine is turned about so that the shaft leads forward to a gear box which reverses its direction to come out under the hull in a normal manner; this *V-drive* permits a compact engine-in-the-stern arrangement.

Reverse and reduction gears

Reverse gears change the direction of rotation of the propeller to give a thrust in the opposite direction for stopping the craft or giving it sternway. *Reduction gears* are often combined with the reversing function so that the propeller, turning at a slower rate than the engine, will have increased efficiency.

The gears of outdrive and V-drive units include the reversing capability and a reduction ratio if required.

Engine accessories

A complete engine normally includes a *fuel pump* to feed fuel under pressure (to the *carburetor* if gasoline is used), an *oil pump* to supply lubricating oil where needed within the engine, and one or more *water pumps* for circulating cooling water. An engine is *raw water cooled* if water for cooling is drawn in through a hull fitting, circulated in the engine, and then discharged overboard. A *closed cooling system* uses a separate quantity of fresh water to circulate solely within the engine; heat picked up by this water is transferred to raw cooling water in a *heat exchanger,* or is dissipated to the water in which the boat is floating by means of a *keel cooler.*

Engine instruments usually include gauges for indicating oil pressure, cooling water temperature, and battery charging or discharging (ammeter). Speedometers and odometers (distance traveled indicators) are not normally used on powerboats although they do exist; instead a *tachometer* indicates the speed of the engine in revolutions per minute (RPM) and may indicate the total revolutions or operating hours as a guide for the performance of routine maintenance. Gasoline engines are fitted with *flame arresters*, screen-like metal fittings over the air intakes of carburetors so that any flame from a backfire will not come out dangerously into the *engine compartment.*

On many small outboard motors a *shear pin* is part of the propeller assembly. This small pin of relatively soft metal breaks apart—shears—when the propeller strikes a hard underwater object, thus saving the motor from more serious damage; the pin is easily replaced.

Sailboat Terms

Although some powerboat terms will also be applicable to many sailboats (especially those with auxiliary engines), "ragmen" have a language of their own. All boatmen, including powerboat skippers, should have a working knowledge of the basic terminology of sailing and sailboats.

Basic sailboat components

The principal components of a sailboat are its *hull*, *spars*, and *sails*. The hull is essentially as described before in this chapter, with certain modifications and additions resulting from the use of the wind as a means of propulsion. A portion of the wind force on the sails drives the boat forward, but another portion tends to make it move sideways. To counteract this, the exterior keel is much enlarged in area, or the craft is fitted with a *centerboard*, a relatively thin plate that can be put down vertically through the keel for greater lateral area, but which can be raised when it is desired to lessen the boat's draft. To permit this raising and lowering action, the centerboard is normally pivoted on a pin near the lower forward corner.

To maintain the watertight integrity of the hull, the centerboard is housed in a *centerboard trunk* which extends internally to above the waterline. On some very small sailboats, a *daggerboard* is forced down vertically in lieu of a pivoted centerboard.

Ballast

The sideward thrust of the wind, besides making leeway, also causes the sailboat to heel to leeward. To lessen such heeling and to increase stability, many larger sailing craft carry *ballast*, additional weight either *external* in the form of a heavy mass (usually lead) on

FIG. 130 Square-rigged vessels no longer sail in great numbers as they did before the days of steam, but some are still seen as training ships or cruise vessels. There are many types of rigs for these ships.

the bottom of the keel, or *internal* ballast within the hull. In smaller sailboats, the crew shifts its weight about within the craft, or just over the side, as a form of readily movable internal ballast.

Spars

The term *spars* is used broadly to cover masts, booms, gaffs, etc. *Masts* are, of course, the principal vertical spars from which sails are *set*. They are *stepped* when put in position and are *raked* if the mast is inclined aft at an angle rather than being exactly vertical.

The horizontal spar along the lower edge of a fore-and-aft sail is a *boom*.

When a four-sided sail has its upper edge laced to a fore-and-aft spar, that spar is a *gaff* and the sail is *gaff-rigged*.

Rigging

All of the various lines about a vessel that secure the sails, masts, and other spars are collectively referred to as *rigging*. Lines or wires bracing the mast and certain other fixed spars comprise the *standing* rigging; those used for hoisting and adjusting the sails make up the *running rigging*.

The standing rigging—usually wire—from the mast to the sides of the boat are called *shrouds*. Those commonly used to support the mast in a fore-and-aft plane are *stays*—*forestays* run to the bow and *backstays*, if used, support the mast from aft.

The slack is usually taken out of a stay or shrouds by the use of a *turnbuckle*, a metal sleeve threaded right-handed in one end and left-handed in the other so that when turned in one direction eyebolts in both ends are drawn in so as to shorten the fitting; turning the sleeve in the other direction increases its overall length and provides slack.

FIG. 129 The principal components of a basic small sailboat are identified above. Every boatman, even those only active with motorboats, should be familiar with these terms.

Sails

Canvas is a general term for a boat's sails, although most modern sails are made of lighter synthetic materials. Sails *draw* when they fill with wind and provide power to drive the craft through the water. One *makes sail* when the sails are hoisted; he *shortens* sail when the area of sails in use is reduced. A sail is *reefed* by partly lowering it and securing it so that it continues to draw, but with reduced area and power. The sail is *dowsed* (or *doused)* when it is lowered quickly, *furled* when it is folded and rolled and then secured to a boom or yard. One *looses sail* when *unfurling* it.

Most recreational sailing craft are now fitted with triangular-shaped sails and are said to be *Marconi rigged* (or *jib-headed*). If a four-sided sail with gaff is used, the boat is described as *gaff-rigged.*

A *suit of sails* is a complete set for any particular boat.

Sailing rigs

Rig is the general term applied to the arrangement of a vessel's masts and sails. The principal sail of a boat is its *mainsail.* If the boat has only this one sail, it is a *catboat,* and may be either Marconi- or gaff-rigged.

A sail forward of the mast, or ahead of the most forward mast if there are more than one, is a *headsail;* a single headsail is usually termed a *jib.* A boat having a single mast, with a mainsail and a jib, is a *sloop.* On some boats additional headsails are set from a *bowsprit,* a spar projecting forward over the craft's bow. A sloop without a bowsprit, on which the jib is set from a stay to the stem, is sometimes called a *knockabout,* but this term has fallen into relative disuse.

A modern *cutter* is a variation of the sloop rig in which the mast is stepped further aft, resulting in a larger area for headsails. A cutter normally sets two headsails, a *forestay-sail* and a jib ahead of it.

Yawls have two masts, the after one of which is much smaller and is stepped abaft the rudder post. A *ketch* likewise has two masts with the after one smaller, but here the difference in height is not so marked and the after mast is stepped forward of the rudder post. The taller mast is the *mainmast;* the shorter mast of both rigs is the *mizzenmast,* and the sail is the *mizzen* (may be either jib-headed or with a gaff).

Schooners are *fore-and-aft rigged* (as distinguished from square-rigged) and have two or more masts. Unlike yawls and ketches, the after mast of a two-masted schooner is taller than the forward one (in rare designs, the two masts may be the same height). Thus the after mast becomes the mainmast and the other the *foremast.* Additional names are used if there are more than two masts.

Square-rigged vessels

Vessels on which the principal sails are set generally athwartships are referred to as *square-rigged.* These four-sided sails are hung from horizontal spars known as *yards.* Headsails are carried as on other rigs, forward of the foremost mast. Staysails may be used, and the aftermost mast of square-rigged vessels normally carry a fore-and-aft sail.

Sailing terms

As sailboats cannot sail directly into the wind, the wind is almost always coming over one side or the other. If the wind is coming over the starboard side, the boat is said to be on a *starboard tack;* the *port tack* is, of course, just the opposite. A boat *tacks* when she *comes up* (heads) into the wind and changes the side over which it blows. In tacking, a boat *goes (comes) about.* Changing tacks with the wind passing astern rather than ahead of the boat is called *jibing* (pronounced with a long *i* as in ice), or *wearing ship;* jibes (also spelled gibes or gybes) sometimes occur accidentally when sailing downwind (the wind nearly dead astern) and can be dangerous.

FIG. 132 A sailboat normally changes direction by bringing her bow through the wind—this is "tacking." If the wind passes astern, she "jibes," a maneuver that can be dangerous if not carefully controlled.

FIG. 131 The various rigs of modern sailing craft are shown above. Careful attention is sometimes necessary to differentiate between sloops and cutters; yawls and ketches are more easily distinguished from one another.

After the sails have been *hoisted* by their *halyards,* they are trimmed with their *sheets* (*jibsheets, mainsheets,* etc.), lines used to control their lateral position and movement. To *trim* is to haul in and tighten up on the sheet attached to a jib, mainsail, etc. Sheets are *eased* when they are let out. Headsails normally have two sheets so that they can be trimmed on either tack; other sails have only one sheet.

Although a detailed discussion of sailing techniques is beyond the scope of this chapter, all boatmen should know that a sailboat is *close hauled (full and by)* when she is sailing with the wind as far ahead as possible, about 45° off the bow in most boats (this is also termed

Miscellaneous Basic Terms

There are many other basic boating terms that do not fit neatly into one of the above categories. Among these are words and phrases relating to the operation of a vessel, navigation, etc.

FIG. 133(a) A sailing craft pointing as close to the wind as possible is "beating."

(b) As the wind moves more aft, she is "reaching." **(c) With the wind astern or nearly so, she is "running."**

Navigation and piloting

Navigation is the art and science of safely directing the movements of a vessel from one point to another. The basic boatman is primarily interested in one of its subdivisions, *piloting,* which is navigation using visible references, the depth of the water, etc. Other forms of navigation include *celestial,* taking *sights* by *sextant* on the sun, moon, planets, and stars, used for long offshore passages; and *electronic,* which may be used in varying degrees by inshore and offshore boatmen.

Courses

A *course* is the direction of movement prescribed for a vessel from one place to another. A *true course* is one taken from the chart with reference to true (geographic) north—it is the angle between the boat's keel and the geographic meridian when she is on course. The *magnetic course* is the angle between her keel and the magnetic meridian passing through that position; it is almost always different from the true course. A *compass course* is the course indicated by the vessel's compass—it is the angle between the vessel's keel and the direction indicated by the north point on the compass card when she is on course. The *heading* is the direction a vessel's bow points at any given time.

Bearings

A *bearing* is the direction of a terrestrial object from the observer and may be stated in terms of true, magnetic, or compass values. A *relative bearing* is the direction of a terrestrial object from the observer measured from the vessel's heading clockwise from 000° to 360°.

Variation and deviation

Variation is the angular difference between true north and the direction of magnetic north at a given point on earth. It is the direction indicated by a magnetic compass that is unaffected by local influences. Variation is "easterly" if the north mark of a compass card points to the east of true north, "westerly" if the opposite.

Deviation is the error in a magnetic compass caused by local magnetic influences on the boat. It is easterly or

FIG. 134 A skipper makes a plot on his chart to record his position at various times and his craft's movements, past and projected, through the water. This is important should an emergency arise as he must be able to quickly and accurately determine his location.

Lights (not "flashers") are aids consisting of a light source mounted on a fixed object (as distinguished from lighted buoys). Each light will have a characteristic color and on-off pattern; most light structures will also have a daymark for daytime identification. The term "light" covers all such aids from the relatively weak minor light on a single pile to the largest seacoast lighthouses.

Detailed information on aids to navigation will be found in Chapters 15 and 16.

FIG. 135 Relative bearings are measured as angles from dead ahead clockwise around the starboard side, past the stern, and back up the port side to the bow. Directions are always described in three-digit groups using zeroes as necessary, i.e. 050°, not 50°.

RELATIVE BEARINGS

westerly as the compass points east or west of magnetic north. *Compass error* is the algebraic sum of variation and deviation.

Plotting and charting

In navigation, one *plots* various data on a *chart* (never map), takes *bearings* to determine his *position (fix)*, and takes a *departure* to establish an exact point from which to commence his *dead reckoning* (a plot of courses steered and distances travelled through the water). *To chart*, a verb, is to record information, usually additional information, on an existing chart of the area.

Aids to navigation

Various governmental authorities establish and maintain *aids to navigation*, artificial objects to supplement natural landmarks. These may be used to indicate both safe and unsafe waters; the boatman must know the meanings and use of each.

Buoys are floating aids to navigation of characteristic shapes and colors. They may be lighted or unlighted; they may or may not have audible signals such as bells, gongs, whistles, etc.

Daybeacons (not "markers") are fixed aids normally consisting of a distinctive sign, the *daymark*, mounted on a pile or group of piles driven into the bottom. Daymarks will have a characteristic shape and color or colors.

Lubberly is used to describe the doing of any task aboard a boat or ship in an ignorant or sloppy manner.

In nautical terminology, *hard* means fully or completely as in turning a steering wheel *hard aport* (fully to the left) or *hard over* (in either direction).

A *beach* is the land immediately in from the water's edge. In tidal regions, it includes the area between the high- and low-water lines. To go *to the beach* is a nautical expression meaning to go ashore, even if not to an actual beach.

A *bar* is a build-up, usually of sand, that reduces the depth of water; it may or may not be partially exposed above the surface of the water and it usually has an elongated shape. Bars frequently form across the openings *(mouths)* of rivers, creeks, harbors, etc. Larger, broader areas of shallow water are often termed *flats*.

FIG. 136 Aids to navigation are among a boatman's best friends. Unlighted buoys and daybeacons are the most numerous types of aids; these and many others are described and discussed in Chapters 15 and 16.

Advanced Boating Terminology

Once a boatman has mastered the basic "language" of this field of interest, he is ready to go further into the subject, learning terms perhaps not necessary to every-day operation of his boat, but rather words and phrases that will expand and broaden his knowledge. The terms discussed here will by no means exhaust the possibilities, but they will add to the skipper's understanding of his craft and its use.

These additional terms occur in many areas of boating; they are, however, perhaps most noticeable in those relating to boat construction and sailing—these fields of interest have extensive vocabularies all their own.

Additional Boat Construction Terms

Vessels, including boats, are normally designed by a *naval architect*. In so doing, he prepares detailed *plans* and *specifications*, including the *lines* (shape) of her hull. *Clean* is a term applied, not to a boat's condition, but rather to her lines. If the lines are *fine,* so that she slips easily through the water, the lines are said to be clean.

A *marine surveyor* is a person whose job it is to make detailed inspections—the *survey*—of boats and ships to determine the condition of their hull, equipment, machinery, etc.

Hull shape terms

In addition to being used for the lower interior portions of a vessel, the term *bilge* is also applied to the area of the hull of a round-bottom craft where the bottom gradually becomes the topsides; a somewhat longer but perhaps more descriptive term for this is *turn of the bilge.* If the boat is flat or vee-bottomed, the bottom and the topsides meet at a well-defined angle rather than a gradual curve—this is the *chine* of the boat. The smaller the angle of intersection of these planes, the *harder* the chine. *Soft* chine craft have a lesser angle; this term is sometimes applied to round-bottom boats, but this is not correct. Some modern boats are designed with *multiple chines (longitudinal steps)* for a softer ride at high speeds in rough water.

Larger round-bottom vessels may be built with *bilge keels,* secondary keels at the turn of the bilge to reduce their tendency to roll in beam seas.

The significance of the term *deadrise* can be appreciated by visualizing a transverse section across a hull. If the bottom were flat, extending horizontally from the keel, there would be no deadrise. In a round- or vee-bottom boat, where the bottom rises at an angle to a horizontal line outward from the keel, the amount of such rise is the deadrise, expressed in inches per foot or as an angle.

With normal sheer, the bow of a boat, as viewed from the side, rises and the stern is at least level with amidships. *Reverse sheer,* however, has the deck sloping downward at the bow, or stern, or both.

Flam is that part of the flare of the topsides just below the deck. If it curves outward sharply, it will both increase deck width and reduce the amount of bow spray that blows aboard. The *cutwater* is, naturally enough, the forward edge of the stem, particularly near the waterline. *Stem bands* of metal are frequently fitted over the

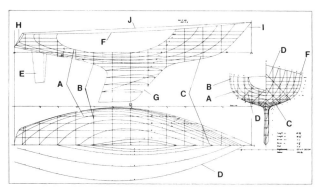

FIG. 137 Line drawing of a 24-foot sloop from the board of E. G. van de Stadt, Naval Architect. The four basic sections are labelled as follows: A, buttocks; B, sections; C, waterlines; D, diagonals. Other labelled parts are; E, spade rudder; F, sheer line; G, fin keel; H, reverse transom; I, stem; J, crown of deck.

stem for protection from debris in the water, ice, pier edges, etc. The *forefoot* of a boat is where the stem joins the keel.

If the boat has an *overhanging* stern, this part of the hull is the *counter.* Her lines aft to her stern are her *run;* lines forward to the stem are her *entrance* (or *entry*). The descriptions "fine" and "clean" are often applied to the entrance and run. The term *bluff* is applied to bows that are broader and blunter than normal.

Planking terms

Each continuous line of planking along the hull from bow to stern is called a *strake.* The lowest strake, next to the keel, is termed the *garboard strake.* The *ʒunwale* (pronounced gun'l) is the upper part of the *sheer strake,* the top plank of the topsides.

When the topsides are carried substantially above the level of the deck, they are called *bulwarks,* and at the top of the bulwarks is the *rail.* More common than bulwarks are *toe rails,* narrow strips placed on top of the gunwale to finish it·off and provide some safety for personnel on deck. *Lifelines* are used on larger craft at the edges of the side decks to aid in preventing people from falling overboard. These lines usually consist of wire, often plastic-covered, supported above the deck on *stanchions.* If made of solid material—wood or metal—they are called *liferails.* Boats may also have waist-high *bow rails* of solid tubing for the same safety purpose. A *pulpit* is an extension, usually a heavy plank with rails extending up from it, beyond the bow of a sport-fishing boat used for spearing or harpooning large game fish. Bow rail installations on sailboats are also often called pulpits, whether they extend forward of the stem or not.

Floors and ceilings

There are two terms that have different meanings afloat than ashore. *Floors,* nautically speaking, are not laid as in a house to be walked upon. In a boat they are important transverse structural members, tying together the keel and the lower ends of the frames. *Ceiling* is not overhead, as ashore; it is light planking or plywood sheeting on the inside of the frames.

Reinforcing pieces

Various kinds of *knees* are used throughout the hull to connect members joined at an angle to each other. These

FIG. 138 Reinforcing pieces are often used where two structural members meet. This "transom knee" strengthens the stern and adds rigidity to the craft.

may be of metal, but often a natural growth of wood is selected in which the grain runs in the desired direction for maximum strength.

When another timber is fastened along the top of the keel to strengthen it, or as a necessary part of the construction, this is the *keelson*, sometimes *apron*. On some boats an extra piece is fastened externally to the bottom of the keel to protect it. This is termed a *false keel* or *worm shoe*. A metal fitting extending back from the under side of the keel to provide additional protection for the boat is called a *skeg*.

Planking details

On a planked wooden hull, the sheer (or uppermost) strake is sometimes thicker than other lines of planking. When a second plank, next below the sheer strake, is also thicker than the others it is called a *binding strake*. *Bilge strakes* are those fitted at the turn of the bilge and these, too, may be heavier than others in the topsides.

A heavier strake in the topsides extending beyond the exposed face of the planking is termed a *rubbing strake* and is intended to protect the topsides from the roughness of piles, pier faces, etc. A strip of wood for the same purpose added externally to the planking is generally called a *rubrail* or *guard*. Both of these may be faced with metal strips for their own better protection.

Many hulls are fitted with a *spray rail* external to the planking just above the waterline. Such a rail usually

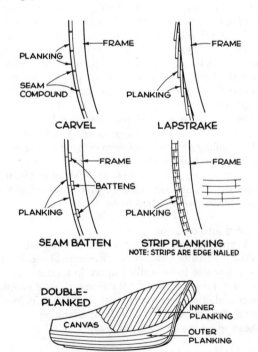

CARVEL

LAPSTRAKE

SEAM BATTEN

STRIP PLANKING
NOTE: STRIPS ARE EDGE NAILED

DOUBLE-PLANKED

FIG. 139 Despite the increase in popularity of fiberglass and other modern boat construction materials, many craft are still made of wood using one of the traditional planking methods.

extends about halfway aft from the stem and deflect downward any spray from the bow wave.

Frame members such as the keel and stem are *rabbeted* to receive the ends and edges of the planks. This *rabbet* is merely a longitudinal recess cut into the wood in the proper size to take the plank. Plank ends at the stem and stern are the *hood ends*.

The term *fastening* is applied to the screws or specially-designed nails which hold the planks to the frames. It may also be applied to screws, bolts, and similar items used to hold down equipment, cleats, chocks, etc. *Through fastenings* are bolts that go all the way through the hull or other base timbers and are secured with a washer and nut on the inside; a *backing block* is generally advisable to spread the stress for additional strength.

Waterways are gutters along the edge of a boat's deck to aid in draining off water through the *scuppers*. (This same term is also applied to water areas suitable for navigation, particularly improved channels in rivers, lakes, etc.)

Wedges are sometimes placed on the underside of a boat's hull at the transom to provide additional "lift" to the stern, preventing *squat* and so improving running trim. Wedges provide a fixed action; more sophisticated electrical-mechanical-hydraulic devices can be built in or installed to provide adjustable amounts of wedge action.

Interior details

For strengthening the hull, there are *bosom* knees and *carling* knees, *dagger* knees and *hanging* knees, *lodging* knees, *panting* knees, *thwart* knees, and many others. The name of each is derived from its location in the boat. They are strength members used wherever two structural members meet at an angle and reinforcing is required.

A *breasthook* is a triangular reinforcing member, usually of wood but sometimes of metal, placed horizontally behind the stem of a boat to strengthen her bow.

On a boat whose stern extends beyond the end of her keel, the *horn timber* is the backbone structural member to which the after frames are fastened. One-piece timbers running the full length of the keel are often not available. In such cases, shorter pieces are bevelled and bolted together in a joint called a *scarph* (scarf); similar joints may be used elsewhere, such as in the stem. A *stopwater* is a dowel (round rod or pin) of soft wood driven into a hole drilled through the joint line of a scarph; it swells when wet and prevents water from entering.

Sister frames are additional frames added at a later date next to original frames that may have cracked or split. Such a frame is not fastened to the broken frame but to the planking.

Limber holes are passages cut into the lower edges of floors and frames next to the keel to allow bilge water to flow to the lowest point of the hull from whence it can be pumped out. These limber holes must be kept clean so that drainage to the lowest point can occur; on some larger vessels a *limber chain* is run through these holes so that it can be pulled back and forth a short distance to clean them out.

FIG. 140 Limber holes are notches cut into frames or floor timbers where they join the keel so that bilge water can run to the lowest point to be pumped out. These must be periodically checked to make sure that they are free of any obstructions.

Some boats are severely damaged by "dry rot," a fungus attack on wooden areas. The name is incorrect, as moisture is essential for the growth and spread of the fungus. The wood is greatly weakened by the action of the fungus. Prevention of standing water in corners and pockets, and adequate ventilation, are the best defenses against dry rot; chemical treatments can be used to attack existing rot infestations.

A *collision bulkhead* is sometimes found in larger craft; it is a solid one near the bow intended to preserve flotation in case of a bow-on accident.

Stringers, beams and carlines

Stringers are longitudinal members fastened inside the hull for additional structural strength. If they run along the turn of the bilge (the turn of the hull below the waterline) they are termed *bilge stringers*. Stringers fastened inside the gunwale are referred to as *clamps*.

Deck beams are the athwartships members that support the deck. Their outer ends usually rest on the clamps, although a horizontal *shelf* may be used above the clamp in which case the beams rest upon this on either side.

A *carline* (also spelled *carlin* or *carling*) is a short timber running fore-and-aft between deck beams. These will be found, for example, at the port and starboard sides of any opening in the deck.

Open boats often have a *finishing piece* which runs along the gunwale, lying on the top of the *clamp* or *inwale* and covering the top edge of the planking and the heads of the frames. This is *capping*. In many boats, however, capping is omitted so that there is nothing to catch dirt and water when the boat is heeled over on its side to be emptied, instead of being bailed out. Such a boat would be said to have *open gunwales*.

Deck terms

The sheer plank has been defined as the topmost strake of the topsides, where the sides join the deck. The *plank sheer,* on the other hand, means the outermost plank of the deck. Sometimes called a *covering board*, it covers the tops of frames and the upper edge of the sheer strake on a decked boat, just as capping does in an open boat. Covering boards are usually wider than any of the other deck planks. The center plank of a deck is the *king plank*. If a deck is arched to aid in the draining off of water, it is said to be *cambered*. Similarly, camber occurs on the tops of cabins, deckhouses, etc.

The deck over the forward part of a vessel, or the forward part of the total deck area, is termed a *foredeck*. Similarly, the *afterdeck* is located in the after part of the vessel. The deck of a cockpit or interior cabin is often called a *sole*.

Other construction terms

Composite construction is the use of two or more materials in the hull of a vessel. Often this consists of wood planking over iron or steel frames.

Sea cocks are valves installed just inside *through-hull fittings* and ahead of the piping or hose running from the fittings. They are important safety devices. See fig. 1010.

The *boot top* is that portion of the exterior hull at the waterline. It is usually finished with special paint—*boot-topping*—of a color to contrast with the *anti-fouling paint* of the bottom and the paint of the topsides.

Areas that are varnished to a high gloss are termed *brightwork*. (In naval usage, this term may be applied to polished brass.) A *tack rag* is a slightly sticky cloth that is wiped over surfaces that are to be varnished just before the brush is applied in order to remove all dust and grit.

When the rudder of a boat is exactly centered, one spoke of the steering wheel should be vertical; this is the *king spoke* and is usually marked with special carving or wrapping so that it can be recognized by feel alone.

FIG. 141 A balanced rudder has a portion of its blade surface—much less than half—forward of the axis of rotation. This design considerably reduces the force required to turn the rudder against the pressure of the passing flow of water.

A boat's rudder is said to be *balanced* when a portion of its blade area extends forward of the axis of rotation. Such a rudder is easier to turn than one that is not so designed.

Many motorboats will have a small *signal mast* from which flags can be flown—see Chapter 22. These flags are hoisted on signal halyards. When partially hoisted they are said to be *at the dip;* when fully hoisted, they are termed *two-blocked.*

Sailboat and Sailing Terms

An *offshore wind* blows from the land; an *onshore* wind, towards it. A *weather shore* is one from which wind is blowing toward a vessel. A *lee shore* is a good one to *give a wide berth* (keep well clear of). Many use this term in the opposite, erroneous, sense, thinking that there is protection under the lee shore. But since this is the shore on the lee side of the vessel, it is the one onto which the wind is blowing, and thus it is a dangerous one. When a sailboat is caught on a lee shore and has to work her way clear, she is *clawing off*. To be *under the lee* of an island is to be on the sheltered side, the safe side in stormy weather.

Wind *veers* when it shifts by changing its direction clockwise as would be seen looking down from above the earth. It *backs* when it shifts in a counter-clockwise direction, such as going from southerly to more easterly.

Measurement and classes

One-design class sailboats are virtually identical craft built and equipped to the same set of plans for racing.

Measurement-rule boats are not identical, but the total effect of design variations theoretically cancel out differences in performance so that they can compete without handicaps. Other racing sailboats are individually *measured* and *rated* to determine the *time allowance* (handicap) to be used in any given competition.

Details of sails

The forward edge of a triangular (Marconi or Bermuda) sail is its *luff*; its after edge is its *leech* (also spelled *leach*); and the lower edge is the *foot*. The foot is normally attached to a boom, but if it is not, or is attached only at the ends, the sail is said to be *loose-footed*.

The upper corner of such a sail is the *head*; the lower forward corner, as where the boom and the mast meet, is the *tack*; and the after lower corner, at the outer end of the boom if there is one, is the *clew*. The same terms apply to the sides and corners of all triangular fore-and-aft sails.

For four-sided (gaff-rig) sails, the term "head" is applied to the upper edge, with the upper forward corner, where the gaff and the mast meet, being the *throat*; the upper after corner, at the outer, higher end of the gaff, is the *peak*.

A *bolt rope* is often sewed into the edges of a sail to strengthen it. *Tabling* is the reinforced part of a sail to which the bolt rope is sewed. The leech of a fore-and-aft sail is usually cut with an outward curve called the *roach* of the sail. To support the roach and preserve its shape by flattening the leech, *battens* (thin flat strips of wood or plastic) are inserted in *batten pockets* in the sail along its after edge. This flattening results in a more efficient sail. A few designs use *full battens* extending across the sail from luff to leech.

Most sails are *bent* (attached or fastened) to the mast by the use of *slides* attached to the luff which ride on or in a track attached to the mast. A similar arrangement holds the foot of the sail to the boom. Headsails are fastened to the *headstay* with *hanks*.

On some small sailboats the sail is held to the mast by sliding the bolt rope of the luff up an internal groove in the mast. If gaff-rigged, *hoops* encircling the mast are used to hold the luff in place with respect to the mast.

FIG. 142 A spinnaker is a foresail of very light material that is full in shape. It is set in light or moderate breezes that come from well astern, usually in lieu of a regular jib. This ketch is also flying a fore staysail, mainsail, and mizzen staysail.

Jibs are headsails set forward of the foremost mast, but they often *overlap* and extend aft of this mast. Large overlapping jibs are called *Genoas*, in slang terms, "gennies," and *reaching jibs* or *reachers*. In coming about, care must be taken that the clew of an overlapping jib gets around the mast without fouling so that the new tack can be assumed smoothly. Smaller, non-overlapping jibs lack the "power" of larger jibs, but these can be self-trimming when tacking; to make them so, a light spar, called a *club*, not a boom, may be attached to the foot of such a jib.

Spinnakers are large, three-sided sails of very light material set from booms called *spinnaker poles* on the opposite side of the main or fore boom when running before a *fair wind*.

Staysails are triangular jib-like sails set from the stays which support the masts, including the stays between the masts of yawls, ketches, and other multi-masted sailing craft.

Plain sails are the ordinary working sails, not including the lighter jibs and staysails. *Storm canvas*, on the other hand, includes jibs, staysails, and *trysails* of extra heavy material for use in strong winds.

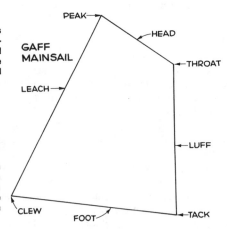

FIG. 143 The marconi style of sail is by far the most popular design for sailboats today. The major parts are labeled in the sketch, left. Such sails may be made of cotton canvas, or of dacron and other synthetic materials.

FIG. 144 Gaff-rig sails are still seen but not so often as formerly. They are usually found on larger or older sailing craft. Note that the term "head" here applies to a side of the sail rather than to a corner as on the marconi rig.

FIG. 145 The tall masts of sailboats must be braced to withstand the side and fore-and-aft forces placed on them. The complexity of standing rigging increases with the height of the mast and the sail area.

FIG. 146 Larger sailboats usually have a bowsprit to extend further forward the lower end of the forestay. The bowsprit in turn needs its stays and shrouds for bracing. Trailboards are merely decorative.

FIG. 147(a) Sail area must be reduced by "reefing" when the wind blows too hard for safety. The sail is lowered slightly and the reef points are tied around the foot of the sail, never around the boom. Many larger sails have two or more rows of reef points.

(b) Many modern jibs are reefed by rolling them up windowshade-fashion around their luff. Modern mainsails are often roller-reefed around the boom.

Masts and booms

The foot of a mast, its lower end, is called the *heel*; it fits into a *step* in the keel. Masts are often secured in place where they pass through the deck or cabin top with *mast wedges* which bear against the *mast partners* (or *mast bench*), the heavier framing around the opening, the *mast hole*, through which the mast passes. In some sailing craft, the mast ends in a *tabernacle*, a pair of side-by-side vertical timbers, or equivalent metal fitting, on the deck or cabin top, this fitting often has a pin so that the mast is in effect hinged and can easily be lowered for passing under bridges, trailering, etc.

The top end of the mast is the *masthead*, sometimes referred to as the *truck*, the traditional name for the highest point on the mast at which a signal flag can be displayed by hoisting it on a *signal halyard*. *Truck to keel* describes the whole vessel from top to bottom. At the masthead there will be a *masthead fitting*, or *masthead crane*, a metal fitting for the attachment of shrouds and stays and the support of sheaves and blocks for halyards.

A *jury mast* is any spar rigged temporarily as a mast in the event that the mast itself has carried away. If such an accident occurs, the vessel is said to have been *dismasted*. A *jury rig* is any device or arrangement fashioned from available materials in an emergency as a substitute for regular gear that has broken.

The *jaws* of a boom or gaff are the extensions at the forward end that partially encircle the mast.

Standing and running rigging

Horizontal spars fitted on a mast to spread the shrouds for more effective bracing are called *spreaders*. *Tangs* are metal plates attached to a mast where standing rigging is to be made fast; they distribute the strain over a wider area of the mast. The lower ends of shrouds are attached to *chainplates*, metal fittings in the form of straps that extend downward on the topsides across several strakes to distribute the load.

Jumper stays are short stays on the forward side of a mast that come down from the masthead and back into the upper part of the mast rather than extending down to the deck. The *jumper strut* holds these stays out from the mast so that bracing action is achieved.

A *topping lift* is a portion of the running rigging used to support or hoist the outer end of a boom. A *peak halyard* is used on a gaff-rigged sailboat to hoist the peak end of the gaff and the head of the sail. A separate *throat halyard* is used to hoist the throat end of the gaff.

A *clew outhaul* is a short length of line attached to the clew of the sail which is led outward to the end of the boom, around the sheave, and back to a cleat or small winch; it is used to stretch the foot of the sail.

A *boom vang* (or *boom jack*) is a line or tackle used to hold a boom down in a more effective position when reaching or running before the wind.

Lazy jacks are light lines run down from the masthead to the boom on either side of a sail. Their purpose is to contain the sail when it is lowered, keeping it from spilling onto the deck or over the side, and thus making it easier to furl.

Bowsprits and boomkins

While a mast is stayed in a vertical position, bowsprits are *guyed* horizontally (or at a slight angle) by *bowsprit shrouds* at the sides and in a vertical plane by a *bobstay*—often chain—from below. A short, downward spreader to the bobstay is a *dolphin-striker*.

A bowsprit projects forward from the stem, and on quite large sailing vessels a *jib-boom* may be rigged out beyond the bowsprit. A jib-boom is thus a fixed spar and not like the other "booms" (remember, too, a spar along the foot of a jib is not a boom either, but a "club").

Short spars sometimes project aft from the stern, particularly on yawls, where the mizzen boom overhangs the stern considerably; these are *boomkins*.

Trailboards are added pieces of wood on either side of the bow of a sailboat, often elaborately carved and painted or gilded. They sometimes lead forward to a *figurehead*.

Pin rails and fife rails

Belaying pins are short bars or pins, usually of wood, about which the lines of a sailboat's running rigging may be made fast. The same line is always *belayed* to the same pin for quick and easy identification at night or in an emergency. Belaying pins are mounted in *pin rails*, racks at a boat's side, usually at the shrouds, and in *fife rails* around the lower part of a mast at a handy height above deck level. See fig. 132.

Cleats are more often used for securing sheets and halyards of modern sailing boats, but pin rails and fife rails will be found on larger and more tradition-minded vessels.

Reefing

To permit reefing a sail when the wind increases beyond a safe strength, there are usually strips of additional material, *reef bands*, sewed to the sail parallel to the foot. Short lengths of line, *reef points*, are attached at intervals along these bands; these are tied around the foot of the sail—never around the boom—to reduce the sail area.

A *reef cringle* is an eye in the leech or luff of a fore-and-aft sail in line with the reef points. *Reef earings* (or *pendants*) are short pieces of line spliced into the cringles to permit the latter to be secured to the boom when the sail is reefed.

Many modern sailing rigs use *roller reefing* in which the *gooseneck* fitting where the boom attaches to the mast is designed with a swivel to permit the boom to be rotated and thus roll up the foot of the sail like a window shade as the halyard is slacked off. In a few smaller rigs, the mainsail is reefed by winding it around the mast.

Jibs are sometimes roller furled around the stay upon which they are set; a single jib can have its effective area varied so widely that it will eliminate the need for carrying and setting various sizes of jibs for many different wind conditions when cruising.

Construction details

A metal rod called a *horse* (or *deck horse* or *boom horse*) is sometimes bolted to the deck and on it the ring of a *sheet block* can travel from side to side as the boom swings over on a change of tack. This is the *traveller*. A more modern rig uses a section of metal track instead of a horse; the sheet block is attached to a *slide* or *car* that rides the track. On small boats, a wire bridle often takes the place of the metal rod type of horse or track. Often, but inaccurately, the deck fitting or wire bridle is itself called the "traveller."

A *tiller* is a horizontal arm extending forward from the top of the rudder or rudderstock and which is moved from side to side for steering. It is much used on sailboats as it is said to provide a better "feel" of the boat's performance than a wheel, and is also cheaper.

FIG. 148 Many sailboats are fitted with a traveller across the deck near the stern. With this device, the trim of the mainsail on each tack can be more closely controlled. Stops may be used to limit the movement to either side of the lower block on the mainsheet.

On small sailing craft, the rudder is often detachable from the transom or stern post. Ordinarily, the rudder is fitted with downward pointing hooks or pins, called *pintles*, which fit into metal eyes, *gudgeons*, on the hull of the boat.

A *fin keel* is one in the form of a relatively thin plate extending below the hull to give a sailboat greater *lateral resistance*; it may have a concentrated weight of metal on its lower edge for increased stability effectiveness, this is a *bulb keel*.

A *boom crutch* is an upright strut temporarily put in place to support a boom when the sails have been lowered.

Small, shallow-draft sailboats, such as sailing canoes, are sometimes equipped with *leeboards* in lieu of a centerboard or daggerboard. These are a pair of flat surfaces extended over each side of the boat, normally pivoted at the top for easy lowering and raising. Only the leeward board is lowered when underway. They are also used on certain types of foreign sailing craft of considerable size.

Sailing terms

A sailboat *carries weather helm* if she has a tendency to *head up* into the wind and the tiller must be kept to windward to hold her on course. Lee helm is the opposite with a tendency to *fall off* the wind and a need to hold the tiller to leeward. A boat with *balanced helm* shows neither of these tendencies.

Generally speaking, it is well for a sailboat to carry a small amount of weather helm. Then if the tiller is accidentally let go, the boat will *round up* into the wind, a

FIG. 149 Daysailers often have easily detachable rudders. Pintles on the rudder fit into brackets—"gudgeons"—on the transom. The boat may be more easily beached or trailered with the rudder removed.

FIG. 150 When a sailboat's objective is more nearly upwind than the craft can sail, a series of tacks, or boards, must be used. These will be a combination of long and short legs if the objective is not directly upwind.

A Yacht Club Burgee
B Masthead Crane
C Jib Halyard
D Head of Mainsail
E Headstay
F, AA Topping Lift
G Mast
H Batten Pocket
I, R Upper Shroud
J Staysail Halyard
K Leach of Mainsail
L Spreader
M Bow Light
N Permanent Backstay
O, X, Y Lazyjacks
P Forestay
Q Genoa Jib
R, I Upper Shroud
S Reefing Band
T Forward Lower Shroud
U Running Backstay
V After Lower Shroud
W Patch for Reef Earing
X, O, Y Lazyjacks
Y, O, X Lazyjacks
Z Tabling at Leach of Sail

AA, F Topping Lift
BB Foot of Mainsail
CC Tack of Mainsail
DD Miter of Staysail
EE Clew of Mainsail
FF Clew Outhaul Slide
GG Boom
HH Staysail Sheet
II Staysail Club
JJ Pulpit
KK Mainsheet Tackle
LL Boom Crutch
MM Jib Sheet
NN Gooseneck
OO Staysail Traveller
PP Grab Rail
QQ Flagstaff
RR Mainsheet Traveller
SS Steering Wheel
TT Binnacle
UU Backstay Tackle
VV Cowl Ventilator
WW Roller Chock
XX Plow Anchor
YY Sheet Winch

FIG. 151 Outboard profile and sail plan of the cutter-rigged "Motor Boating & Sailing '35," designed by Edward S. Brewer. The staysail is bent to a club, permitting a single sheet so that the sail will "tend itself" when coming about. The lowest batten pocket on the main is parallel to the boom so that the batten can remain in place when the sail is reefed. The spreader is seen end-on about halfway up the mast, and Mr. Brewer has drawn it so as to suggest that it is slightly canted upward at the outboard end so as to bisect the angle formed by the upper shroud, as it should be.

relatively safe action, instead of falling off into what might become a dangerous jibe. Too much weather helm, however, is undesirable as the constant rudder angle creates drag and slows the boat down. The angle of rake of the mast and the trim of the boat, determined by the distribution of the weight of the crew and ballast, have much to do with what helm and how much of it the boat will carry.

A *stiff* vessel returns quickly to her normal upright position from a rolled or heeled position. If she rolls in a seaway without quick action or sudden movements, her roll is *easy*. When a boat's center of gravity is too high

and stability is low, she is *tender*; *crank* conveys the same idea.

A skipper *fetches* a given objective if he is sailing a course to windward and reaches the mark without tacking. When working to windward, each *leg* or tack may be called a *board*, and, depending upon the length of each leg, there may be *long boards* and *short boards*.

If a sailboat attempts to come about and the bow does not fall off on the other tack, she is *caught in* (or *misses*) *stays*, or is said to be *in irons*. A sailboat is *pinched* when she is steered so close to the wind that the sails shiver. A vessel is said to *luff* when she is brought up into the

LATEEN SAIL   SPRIT SAIL   LUG SAIL

GUNTER RIG

FIG. 152 Minor sailing rigs are often encountered on some types of small catamarans and sailing boards. They are rarely used on conventional sailboats.

FIG. 153(a) (left)   A two-speed winch of the sort used on 30-foot cruising sailboats to adjust and belay sheets. Turning the crank one way turns the winch drum clockwise at high speed; turning in the opposite direction advances the drum clockwise at low speed. The drums will not turn counter-clockwise.   FIG. 153(b) (right) shows a riding turn. The winch is now jammed and cannot be cleared until the tension is somehow removed from the sheet that is wrapped around it.

wind so as to spill some of it out of the sails, thus relieving the pressure and *easing* her.

Sailing before the wind, sails are sometimes set on opposite sides of the boat; this is called *wing and wing*. A light *whisker pole* may be used to wing out the jib so that it will draw more effectively.

One boat *blankets* another when, being just to windward, she takes the wind out of the other's sails. She *outfoots* another craft by sailing faster, *outpoints* her by sailing closer to the wind.

Minor sailing rigs

A *lateen* rig consists of a single mast and a triangular sail whose forward edge is sharply raked aft at an angle of roughly 45°. This edge is attached to a light spar, or yard, which in turn is attached to the mast, the near midpoint of the yard to the near top of the mast. A boom is used which extends forward of the mast to the lower end of the yard. This rig is widely used for small catamarans and, in modified form, for *sailboards*, small sailing craft whose hulls resemble surfboards.

A *sprit* rig is used on some dinghies and other small craft. In this type of rig the upper aft corner (peak) of the four-sided fore-and-aft sail is held aloft by a light spar known as a *sprit* inserted in an eye in the sail called a grommet. The *sprit* at its lower end is supported by a *snotter* or *becket* consisting of a light line about the mast with an eye in the lower end to take the sprit. Although the sail is four-sided, no gaff at the head or boom at the foot is required, although a boom is sometimes used with its forward end held in a becket as the sprit above it.

Lug rigs are of various types and their use is also confined to small craft. The *standing lug* has a yard which crosses the mast obliquely while the tack of the four-sided sail (forward lower corner) is made fast to the mast. In a *dipping lug* the tack is made fast to the stem, ahead of the mast, so that the yard must be *dipped* around the mast when tacking.

A *gunter* (or *sliding gunter*) rig uses a triangular sail whose luff is attached to a spar which is hoisted much like a gaff except that it is hoisted to a fully vertical position where it becomes an extension of the short mast. A jib may also be used.

Rowboats and Rowing

Although this book is primarily for the skippers of motorboats and sailing craft, the well-informed boatman knows the essential facts about boats propelled by muscle-power. Dinghies are often rowed, and light mo-

 SAILBAG   **Running Backstays**

Fig. 151, page 23, illustrates some points about backstays. Unless a yawl or ketch carries a boomkin, a permanent (more precisely, standing) backstay will interfere with the mizzen boom, so *running backstays* must be depended on to support the mizzen from aft. Because the boom interferes with the lee backstay, only the weather one is usually set, and the crew must hand the backstay tackles or levers when the yacht comes about. In jibing the mizzen, the boom must first be hauled in so that the lee backstay can be set before the jibe is executed. Unless mizzen backstays are smartly handled the mizzenmast may go by the board. Furthermore, their lead aft is limited by the available space on deck, so even when they are well-handled there is not much margin of support for the mast. They are always a cause for some concern.

torboats are at times rowed or paddled to safety when the engine fails. The technique of paddling and rowing is an art unto itself and is best learned by practice under proper instruction, but the terms involved can be made familiar here.

Rowboats and oars

Rowboat is the term generally applied to a light craft propelled by one or more persons using *oars*. These are long slender wooden shafts shaped into a round *handle* (or *grip*) at one end and a flat *blade* at the other; between these ends the shaft of the oar is termed the *loom*.

The transverse seats in rowing craft are called *thwarts*. The ends of thwarts land on *risers* (or *risings*) which are fore-and-aft pieces or stringers fastened to the inside of the frames. To support the thwart, a vertical piece is often fitted amidships, called a *thwart stanchion*. *Stretchers* (also called *foot boards*, although this creates confusion with an alternate term for bottom boards) are sometimes fitted athwartships against which the *oarsman* can brace his feet.

The terms *rowlock* and *oarlock* are synonymous. These are the fittings in the gunwale which hold the oars when rowing. There are many styles of rowlocks; some open,

FIG. 154 Engines do fail and gas tanks do run dry! Every boatman should know at least the fundamentals of oars and rowing. Small outboards should be equipped with oars or paddles as determined by their design.

others closed; some mounted permanently, others removable; some attached to the oars. In place of rowlocks, wooden *thole pins* are sometimes driven into holes or sockets.

Where the loom of the oar bears against the rowlock, it is often protected from excess wear by a *leather* (which may be of leather or rubber). On the side of the leather toward the handle, there may be a *button*, a ring around the oar to keep it from slipping outward through the rowlock. Where the loom becomes the blade is the *neck* (or *throat*) of the oar. The *tip* of the blade, its outer end, may be metal sheathed for protection from wear, but this is not common on oars used with light rowboats.

A man who is *sculling* would stand in the stern and propel the boat by working a single oar back and forth, using either one or two hands.

Canoes and paddles

Canoe is the term applied to very lightly built open craft of narrow beam and shallow draft that are *paddled* rather than rowed; they are normally double-ended. A *paddle* is much like an oar except that it is shorter. The various parts of a paddle are named the same as for an oar. The grip is shaped differently as the paddle is used vertically rather than horizontally; the blade will normally be somewhat wider for its length in comparison with an oar.

Some paddles are *double-ended* (double-bladed) so that they may be more conveniently dipped alternately on either side of the canoe, an advantage when one person is propelling the boat rather than two.

Documentation and Tonnage

Large ships and many commercial vessels are *documented* by the United States government (and foreign vessels by their governments). This procedure can also be used for medium and large size recreational craft. Such documentation is in lieu of *registration* (number-

ing) with state authorities. Before documentation can be considered, however, a discussion of "tonnage" is in order. The procedures and effects of documentation are covered in Chapter 2.

Admeasurement and tonnage

The *tonnage* of ships and boats is determined in several different ways; it may be a measurement of either (1) weight, or (2) size without regard to weight. Persons unfamiliar with the term as it is used in connection with vessels are likely, in error, to think only of the common ton which is a measure of weight—either 2000 pounds in a short ton or 2240 pounds in a long ton.* This as a part, but only a part, of the situation when ships are considered.

The determination of the "tonnage" of a vessel is called *measurement* or *admeasurement*, the latter term being found mainly in legal documents. (This measurement should not be confused with the measurement of racing sailboats for rating purposes, a quite different process.)

Gross and net tonnage

The documentation law repeatedly refers to vessels of a certain tonnage, as for example when it states that a yacht of 5 net tons or over may be documented. *Net tons* are derived from gross tonnage which is a measurement of volume rather than weight.

Gross tonnage is the total enclosed space or internal capacity of a vessel, calculated in terms of "tons" of 100 cubic feet each. This was agreed upon many years ago as the average space or volume required by a ton (by weight) of general merchandise. Gross tonnage includes all spaces below the upper deck as well as permanently closed-in spaces on that deck.

Net (or *registered*) tonnage is a measurement of the earning power of a vessel when carrying cargo. Thus to arrive at a net tonnage figure it is necessary to deduct from the gross the volume of such spaces as would have no earning capacity or room for cargo. For example, on a ship there would be deducted the volume of the fuel compartments, engine room, crew's quarters, bridge, etc. In the case of recreational boats and yachts, deductions would mainly be for engine compartments and control

FIG. 155 Canoes are light, easily propelled craft for protected inland waters. Paddles are sometimes double-ended for convenience in solo operation.

FIG. 162 Large vessels are measured in various kinds of tonnage —gross and net, displacement and register. See text for differences and how each is measured.

*1 metric ton=1,000 kilograms=2,204.6 pounds.

25

FIG. 157 The lines of any craft should be protected from chafing and wear wherever they come in contact with abrasive surfaces, other lines, etc. Modern devices such as shown above may be slipped over the line, or in an emergency the line may be wrapped with old rags.

FIG. 158 A shackle permits the attachment of a line or chain to an anchor or any sort of ring. The pin of the shackle should be secured with safety wire to prevent its accidental loosening. The thimble in the eye splice prevents excessive wear on the line at a point of high stress.

stations. Many charges against vessels, such as canal tolls, harbor dues, etc., are based on net tonnage.

Displacement and deadweight tonnage

Although not closely related to documentation or boats, a yachtsman should have some knowledge of several other forms of "tonnage" used in connection with ships.

Displacement tonnage is the actual weight, in tons of 2240 pounds, which a vessel displaces when floating at any given draft, such as "light" or "loaded." The displacement is calculated by figuring the volume of the vessel under the water in cubic feet and dividing by 35, as 35 cubic feet of sea water weighs one long ton.

Deadweight tonnage is the carrying capacity of a vessel figured by weight in terms of tons of 2240 pounds. If her displacement were calculated when the vessel was "light" (with fuel and supplies but no cargo) and again when she was loaded (with the same fuel and supplies aboard), the difference would express the deadweight tonnage.

FIG. 159 Ocean cruising, and particularly ocean racing, sailboats usually are fitted with a horseshoe type of life preserver mounted aft near the helmsman's position so that it can be quickly thrown to a man overboard. For nighttime use, an automatic waterlight is attached to the life preserver.

Miscellaneous Terms

The meaning of the word *lay* depends on its usage. One *lays aft* when he goes to the stern of the vessel. The lines of a boat are *laid down* before she is built. A boat is *laid up* when she is decommissioned for the winter in northern climates. A sailboat *lays her course* when she can make her objective without tacking. When an oarsman stops rowing, he *lays on his oars*. Referring to rope, *lay* is the direction of the twist (right or left hand) and its tightness (hard or soft).

When a vessel is hauled out of the water she is *shored up* with supports to hold her upright. If she is not supported properly, so that she is held amidships while the bow and stern settle, the boat will assume a shape that is described as *hogged*. Contrariwise, if the amidships portion of the keel is not adequately supported and droops, she is said to be *sagged*.

A vessel is said to *hail* from her home port; one *hails* another vessel at sea to get her attention, *speaks* to her when communicating with her.

The direction in which a current flows is its *set* and its velocity is its *drift*. (The amount of leeway that a vessel makes is also its drift.) *Slack* is the period of time between flood and ebb currents when there is no flow in either direction. *Stand* is the period when there is no rise or fall in the tidal level; slack and stand usually do not occur simultaneously at any given place.

FIG. 160 Bollards are massive metal fittings placed along wharves and piers to which the heavy lines of large vessels are made fast.

Chafing occurs when a line or sail rubs against a rough surface and wears excessively. To prevent this, line is usually encased in *chafing gear* made of plastic or rubber tubing. To protect sails from chafing and wearing, *baggy-wrinkle*, consisting of short lengths of old line matted together, is placed on shrouds, spreaders, etc.

A *shackle*, or *clevis*, is a roughly U-shaped metal fitting with a pin that can be inserted through a hole in one arm of the U and screwed or pinned in the other arm to close the link. Some special-purpose shackles close with a hinged *snap* or have a *swivel* built in. A *thimble* is a round or heart-shaped metal fitting with a deep outer groove around which line or wire can be eye-spliced. It protects the line

FIG. 161 The anchors for large yachts and ships become too heavy to be hoisted on deck. They are drawn up into hawse pipes with power-operated winches.

from wearing on a shackle where it is joined to a chain, fastened to a deck fitting, etc.

A *fid* is a smooth, tapered pin, usually of wood, used to open up the strands of a rope for splicing.

A *waterlight* is an electric light, often automatically operated, that is attached to a life ring with a short length of line. It is intended for use in man-overboard accidents at night.

The term "charter" has usage both as a verb and a noun. *To charter* a craft is to lease her from the owner for a temporary period of time. She may be chartered on a *bare boat* basis, without crew, or as a *time charter* with crew. The contract covering the use of the boat is termed the *charter*.

Ships and large vessels may have compartments below deck used solely for carrying cargo, these are *holds*. The hatch giving access through the deck to such a hold is covered over with canvas and *battened down* with wooden strips around the edges *(battens)* to secure it against storms and water across the deck. The same term is used for the general securing of a boat against adverse weather conditions.

Another vessel is said to be seen *hull down* when she is at such a distance that her superstructure and/or masts are visible but the hull is not seen due to the curvature of the earth.

Flotsam is material floating on the surface of the water after a vessel has broken up and sunk. Larger pieces may be dangerous to the hull or shaft and propeller of small craft. *Jetsam* consists of items of equipment or cargo that have been deliberately *jettisoned* (thrown overboard) to lighten a vessel endangered by heavy seas.

A *bollard* is a heavy single or double post set into the edge of a wharf or pier to which the lines of a ship may be made fast.

Cavitation occurs when a high-speed propeller loses its "bite" on the water, creating a partial vacuum, loss of thrust, and excessive shaft speed; continued cavitation can result in blade wear. On outboard motors where the propeller is relatively near the surface of the water and aft of the transom, there may be a *cavitation plate* mounted above the propeller to deflect downward the water discharge from the blades—a more correct term might be "anti-cavitation plate" but this is not used.

If the galley stove is of the type that requires its own vent above deck, the pipe for this is sometimes referred to as a *Charlie Noble*.

A boat is *ship-shape* when everything is in good order; *well-found* when it is well equipped. *Bristol*-fashion is a term used to describe an especially well-cared-for vessel. One *swabs* (or *swabs down*) the deck when he washes it down with a mop, called a *swab* in nautical language.

A task aboard a boat—such as lowering the dinghy—is done *handsomely* when it is done slowly and carefully. To do something *smartly* is to do it in a quick and lively manner.

The term *gangway* is applied both to the area of a ship's side where people *come aboard (board)* and *disembark*, and to the temporary ramp or platform used between the vessel and the wharf or pier. In the latter case, the terms *gangplank* and *brow* are also used.

A *windlass* is a particular form of winch with its *drum* on which the line is wrapped turning on a horizontal axis. If the drum's axis is vertical, the device may be called a *capstan*.

When an anchor line or chain is brought through the topsides rather than over the rail, it enters through a *hawse hole* and runs upward through a *hawse pipe*. An *anchor chock* is a fitting for holding an anchor securely on a deck.

Small boats, such as dinghies and runabouts, are hoisted aboard larger craft by *davits*, mechanical arms extending over the side or stern, or which can be swung over the side, plus the necessary lines and blocks.

FIG. 162 Dinghies and small speedboats may be hoisted to the upper decks of large yachts with hand or power operated davits. On smaller yachts, dinghies are often carried on stern davits.

FIG. 158 Marine sanitation devices are coming into widespread use aboard all types of boats large enough to have one or more installed toilets. A number of different designs are available, but not all are acceptable on specific bodies of water.

Pollution Control Systems

Boatmen on almost all waters have been faced with a rising tide of water pollution control laws. State and local regulations have varied widely as to the restrictions imposed and the type of device, if any, that will be accepted. Standards have been set by the Environmental Protection Agency and regulations have been issued by the Coast Guard covering the certification and use of *marine sanitation devices*. Various types of MSDs are described below.

The *macerator-chlorinator* device takes the discharge of a marine toilet, grinds up all solids to very fine particles, and treats the resultant waste with a disinfectant to reduce the bacteria to a safe count. This chemical is usually a chlorine compound which may be introduced either as a liquid (such as the household bleach, sodium hypochlorite, bought as "Clorox" or the equivalent), or in tablet form. The mixture of waste and treatment chemical is retained in a small tank until the next time the "head" is used, at which time it is pumped overboard and a fresh batch is taken in from the toilet. These units may be added to an existing toilet, or may be installed as a complete, self-contained device.

Holding tanks are simply what their name says, additional tanks installed on a boat to take the waste fluids and solids from the toilet and retain them temporarily. Some models provide the option of overboard discharge—for use when in waters where this is permitted—as well as pumping-out to a shore facility, but many states withhold approval of a system that would allow overboard discharge. Tanks are available in various sizes such as 10 and 20 gallons which will permit a few days' use of the head (with restraint!) before pump-out is necessary. A chemical is usually added to the tank for partial disinfecting action and to deodorize the contents. A vent over the side is required.

Self-contained toilets are closely related to holding tanks. These devices are "charged" with a few gallons of water and special chemicals. The internal mechanism recirculates this treated water plus the wastes that are added each time the head is used. The toilet can be used a number of times over a period of several days before pump-out is required. This is the type of facility used on modern airliners.

Incinerators dry liquid wastes pumped into them from marine toilets and reduce the resultant solids to ash. This final product is of low volume and need be removed only at infrequent intervals, roughly monthly. Heat is obtained from either bottled LP gas or electricity.

When subjected to heavy strains in working her way through high seas, a vessel is said to *labor*. If she takes the large waves easily, she is said to be *sea kindly*. A boat that takes head seas heavily and comes down hard on successive waves is said to *pound;* this is more likely to occur with a hard-chined hull. If she takes little spray aboard when running into a choppy sea, she is termed *dry*.

To *flemish down* a line is to secure it on deck in a tight, flat coil roughly resembling a mat. When a line is laid down in loose, looping figure-eights it is said to be *faked* (or *flaked*) down; each loop is a *fake*, see pages 229-230.

To *put* is to take action, as to *put about, put into port*, etc.

A boat is said to be *off-soundings* when she is so far out from the shore (*offshore*) that depths (*soundings*) cannot be conveniently measured nor are used in navigation; this is commonly taken as the 100-fathom line.* Contrary-wise, a boat is *on-soundings* when she is within this line.

Admiralty law is the body of law pertaining to ships and to navigation and commerce on the seas.

But Don't Overdo It!

There is literally no end to the list of boating terms that could be included here, but practical limitations of space must prevail. What has been covered in this chapter will serve as a framework for the remainder of the book. As the boatman gains experience in this form of recreation, his vocabulary will broaden proportionately and naturally. It is hoped, however, that his enthusiasm for boating will not cause him to toss indiscriminate *Avasts, Ahoys*, and *Belays* into every conceivable nook and corner of his conversation. The natural, proper use of correct terms is much to be desired; strained efforts to effect a salty lingo are conspicuously inappropriate.

*On metric charts, the 200 meter curve is sometimes taken as the delineation.

BOATING LAWS and REGULATIONS

FIG. 201 All boating, commercial and recreational, is subject to certain laws and regulations for the safety of the craft involved and all on board. Federal rules are often supplemented by state and local requirements and restrictions.

Although boating is certainly not an inherently unsafe form of recreation, there are dangers and hazards for ignorant and careless individuals. To protect such persons, and "innocent bystanders," too, there has arisen a body of federal, state, and local laws and regulations. The basic intent of such restrictions is the safety of persons and property; to a much lesser degree do such factors enter as registration and taxation.

Boating laws and regulations can be roughly divided into two major categories. The first subdivision includes those that relate to the craft and its equipment; the second group covers the operator of the boat and his use of it. Formerly, the first category was greatly predominant, but in recent years regulations regarding boat operation have expanded rapidly.

Comparison of boating and motor vehicle laws

A quick comparison may be made between recreational boating and the field of ownership and operation of automobiles, an activity so much a part of our everyday lives. Here the trend has been rather in the reverse direction. Some years ago motor vehicle laws focused almost entirely on operational matters such as driving and parking, with a minimum of attention to details of equipment. In more recent times we have seen a considerable push toward legislated standards for safety equipment and design features. The obvious comparisons can be drawn in such areas as the requirements for headlights and turn signals on cars with the need for navigation lights on boats; and the necessity for both types of vehicles to observe rules as to relative right-of-way in congested areas. The principal point of difference at the present time is the lack of any requirement for an operator license or permit for the noncommercial skipper; the duration of this difference is a matter of some doubt. Some states are now requiring operator licenses on wholly inland bodies of water, but as yet there is no overall federal requirement.

In both boating and automobile operation the goals are essentially the same—the prevention of accidents insofar as possible, and the minimization of death and injury in those that regrettably do occur. Restrictive laws and regulations are irksome to all of us, but they should be known, understood, and accepted as proper guidance for our self-protection and the protection of others' lives and property.

Registration and numbering

A third category of boating laws and regulations includes those relating to registration and assignment of identification numbers to craft. This may perhaps be considered a minor category as compared with rules for safety

FIG. 202 Water traffic must be subject to "Rules of the Road" which prescribe relative right-of-way between boats encountering each other. They are especially important in congested waters.

equipment and boat operation, but still these must be known and obeyed.

Again a close comparison can be drawn with motor vehicles, although in the case of boats it is probable that regulation is rather more related to taxation and revenue-raising than it is to identification—not many watercraft get "tickets" for overtime parking. The regulations relating to numbering must be followed by boatmen even though they have little to do with his safety or that of others.

FEDERAL VS. STATE JURISDICTION

This book will concentrate on federal laws and regulations relating to boating rather than state and local ordinances, rules, etc., due to the obviously wider applicability of the former. State and municipal regulations will be touched upon later in this chapter, but only in broad terms because of the wide variations between different jurisdictions. Each conscientious boatman must individually familiarize himself with the local requirements and restrictions for the waters that he uses.

Limits of federal jurisdiction

"Navigable waters of the United States"—where federal law prevails—are defined in broad terms by law and are specifically delineated by Coast Guard regulations. These include waters off the beaches along the coast and all bodies of water open to the sea or connected to the open sea by navigable rivers and channels. Typical of this category are all harbors and bays as well as major rivers as far

as they can be navigated continuously from the sea, often a considerable distance for such great waterways as the Mississippi, Missouri, Ohio, and Tennessee Rivers.

Also subject to federal jurisdiction are some bodies of water that overlap or separate two or more states, even though not connected with the ocean. Certain inland lakes and rivers fit into this category when it is possible for persons or goods to be moved by water from one state to another; this is "interstate commerce" and subject to regulation by the U.S. Congress. A typical example is Lake Mead that borders both Nevada and Arizona. A third qualification places waters under federal jurisdiction if they can be used for travel to or from a foreign nation.

FIG. 204 The construction of dams, and locks for the passage of vessels around them, have extended far inland the limits of navigable waters subject to Federal jurisdiction. These limits are set forth in official publications.

The construction of a dam does not change the navigable status of a river. In fact, the building of a dam and lock system may serve to extend the river's navigability. The Coast Guard makes determinations of the bodies of water that do or do not fall under federal jurisdiction; such rulings are subject to challenge in Federal courts. The determinations will be found in Part 2 of Title 33, Code of Federal Regulations; changes are published in the daily Federal Register.

An understanding of federal jurisdiction over navigable waters is essential for all boatmen, especially those far from the coasts of our nation. Federal jurisdiction means the

FIG. 203 Boats entering inland waters through an inlet from the open ocean will pass from one set of Rules of the Road to another. Skippers must know both sets of rules and be alert for the change.

applicability of federal laws and regulations, aids to navigation by the Coast Guard, and charting by the Coast & Geodetic Survey or Army Corps of Engineers. It does *not* deprive state and local authorities of their rights to regulate certain aspects of the use of the waters that are *not in conflict* with an applicable federal law or regulation; local rules might relate to speed limits, restrictions on water skiing, etc. Many state boating laws also require safety equipment on boats in excess of that called for by Acts of Congress and Coast Guard Regulations.

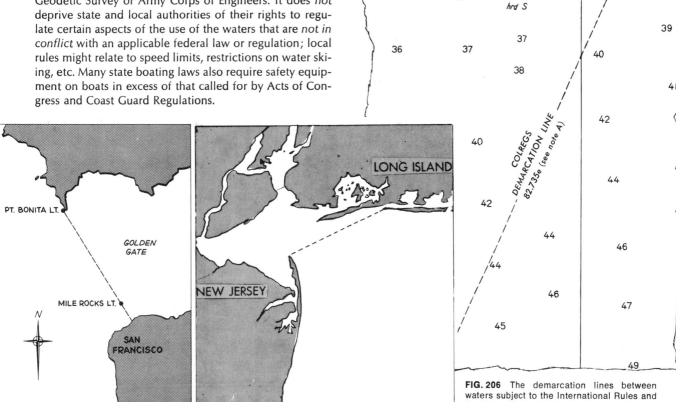

FIG. 205 At the entrances to harbors, rivers, bays, sounds, etc., there have been established "COLREGS Demarcation Lines" to separate waters governed by the International Rules of the Road from those subject to the Inland Rules. These lines are generally defined in terms of aids to navigation and prominent geographic features.

FIG. 206 The demarcation lines between waters subject to the International Rules and the Inland Rules of the Road are marked on charts by a broken line in nautical purple with an appropriate label.

BOUNDARY LINES

The United States uses a number of boundary lines to indicate the seaward limits of its authority, each for one or more regulatory purposes. There is a "base line" running generally along the shore and from headland to headland across the entrances to harbors, rivers, bays, etc. The waters for three nautical miles seaward are termed the "territorial sea." Waters extending another nine miles out, to the 12-mile limit," are designated the "contiguous zone." Waters out to 200 miles from the base line comprise a "Fishery Conservation Zone" within which the Coast Guard enforces strict control over all catches.

All of the above lines are now being added to nautical charts as they are reprinted in new editions.

Demarcation lines for Rules of the Road

Of greatest interest to boatmen are the lines that separate waters governed by the International Rules of the Road and those subject to the U.S. Inland Rules. (These Rules are discussed in Chapters 4 and 5.) When the 1972 International Rules—termed "72 COLREGS" by the Coast Guard as a contraction of their formal name, International Regulations for Preventing Collisions at Sea, 1972—came into effect, it was necessary for legal reasons to re-define the separation lines in many areas. (The "boundary lines" used with the 1960 Rules remain in existence, but only for regulatory purposes of no concern to boatmen.) The new

"COLREGS Demarcation Lines" generally extend the coverage of the International Rules shoreward into waters formerly subject to the Inland Rules. Boatmen should ignore the boundary lines printed on older editions of charts; the new COLREGS demarcation lines will replace them when new editions are printed as the old boundary lines no longer have any significance for navigation.

In establishing the COLREGS demarcation lines, it was found neither desirable nor practical to have an overall general line. Individual lines are defined, wherever practicable, by physical objects readily discernable by eye rather than by instrument; for example, fixed aids to navigation, prominent points on land, ranges, etc. The lines were set to be as short and direct as feasible, and as perpendicular as possible to vessel traffic flow.

Although COLREGS demarcation lines were established for many more specific locations than had been with the previous boundary lines, the new lines are individually simpler and more direct, with fewer delineation points per line. The general trend is from headland to headland, with highly visible objects used to clearly define the line. *In a number of instances, whole bays, harbors and inlets are now subject to the International Rules*, waters that were formerly governed by the Inland Rules. *A boatman should at all times know which set of Rules of the Road govern the waters on which is then operating.* The demarcation lines are defined in detail in the 1981 edition of Coast Guard Publication CG-169; see fig. 1708 and page 332.

3 nautical miles = 5.56 km; 12 n. mi. = 22.2 km; 200 n. mi. = 370 km.

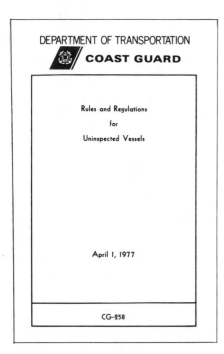

DEPARTMENT OF TRANSPORTATION

COAST GUARD

Rules and Regulations
for
Uninspected Vessels

April 1, 1977

CG-258

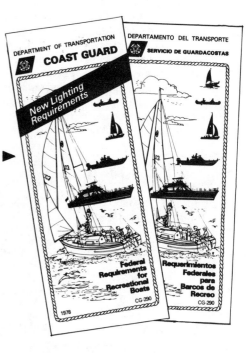

◄ **FIG. 207 Coast Guard Publication CG-258 contains the full text of regulations that were issued to implement the Motorboat Act of 1940, now repealed for recreational small craft. These rules do, however, remain in effect until specifically superseded by regulations implementing the Federal Boat Safety Act of 1971.**

FIG. 208 This small and convenient USCG pamphlet summarizes in simple language the basic federal requirements for recreational craft. It is available without charge from most Coast Guard offices. The number is CG-290. ▶

Federal Laws and Regulations

Recreational boating—and commercial boating and shipping, too—is subject to "laws" and "regulations." The former consist of Acts of Congress and provide basic policies and rules upon which more specific and detailed regulations may be promulgated. Regulations have the advantage of greater flexibility, being more easily created, modified, or revoked than laws which are subject to the full legislative process for any changes.

Coast Guard regulations

Most federal boating regulations are issued by the United States Coast Guard under authority given by Congress to the "Secretary of the Department in which the Coast Guard is operating." This rather cumbersome wording is necessary as federal laws make possible the transfer of this armed service from its normal peacetime Department (now Transportation, but formerly Treasury until 1967) to its wartime Department (Navy). The authority given by Congress to the Departmental Secretary is, in most instances, routinely delegated to the Commandant of the Coast Guard.

Coast Guard regulations cover a wide variety of matters including boat equipment and operation, lights for special-purpose vessels, aids to navigation, inland water boundary lines as mentioned above, and many other topics.

Other regulatory agencies

Boatmen on some waters will also be affected by regulations issued by other federal agencies such as the Corps of Engineers, U.S. Army; and the National Park Service. The operation of radio and radar transmitters on boats on all waters is subject to the rules and regulations of the Federal Communications Commission as explained in Chapter 25.

FEDERAL BOAT SAFETY ACT OF 1971

The Federal Boat Safety Act of 1971 (see pp. 611–614) differs in philosophy from the 1940 and 1958 Laws, which formerly regulated boating, by giving authority to "The Secretary of the Department in which the Coast Guard is operating" to make regulations, from time to time. Where regulations are not yet issued, provisions of the earlier acts remain in effect. When conditions require change, regulations are far easier to modify than laws, which require action by Congress. *

Scope

The FBSA/71 authorizes the "Secretary" to establish minimum safety standards for boats and "associated equipment," provides for numbering of all undocumented vessels equipped with propulsion machinery, directs that a "Boating Safety Advisory Council" be established, and authorizes financial assistance to the States for boating safety programs. The new law essentially repeals the 1958 Federal Boating Act and so amends the Motorboat Act of 1940 as to virtually exclude recreational boats and small passenger-carrying craft; the 1940 Act remains on the books, applicable to commercial craft, such as fishing vessels.

Definition of terms

The FBSA/71 contains a number of definitions that must be clearly understood, as they directly affect its applicability.

The word "vessel" includes every description of watercraft, other than a seaplane on the water, used or capable of being used as a means of transportation on the water.

The term "boat" is limited to the following categories of vessels—

---

*As of January, 1976, a few regulations had been issued and more were in the proposal stage; boatmen should be alert for new rules and requirements.

(1) Those manufactured or used primarily for non-commercial use.

(2) Those leased, rented, or chartered to another for the latter's noncommercial use.

(3) Those engaged in the carrying of six or fewer passengers for hire.

The distinction between "vessels" and "boats" is necessary because certain aspects of the bill (notably those sections dealing with safety standards and equipment) pertain *only* to the category called "boats." Other sections (those dealing with numbering) pertain to a broader category, all undocumented vessels equipped with propulsion machinery. Still other provisions of the Act (the prohibition of negligent operation) pertain to *all* vessels. Note that there is *no upper size limit* in the definition of "boat" as used in the FBSA/71.

Despite its general aim toward the regulation of non-commercial boats and boating, craft carrying six or less passengers for hire are included as these are not covered by existing laws regulating vessels carrying a greater number of passengers for hire. Livery and charter boats are included in the FBSA/71 as their operation is closely akin to noncommercial recreational use even though they are a part of a commercial enterprise.

The term "associated equipment" means—

(1) Any system, part, or component of a boat as originally manufactured, or any similar part, or component manufactured or sold for replacement, repair, or improvement of such system, part, or component.

(2) Any accessory or equipment for, or appurtenance to a boat.

(3) Any marine safety article, accessory, or equipment intended for use by a person on a boat.

The term "associated equipment" does *not* include radio equipment.

The word "State" means a State of the United States, the Commonwealth of Puerto Rico, the Virgin Islands, Guam, American Samoa, and the District of Columbia.

Applicability

The FBSA/71 applies to vessels and associated equipment used, or to be used, or carried on vessels on waters subject to the jurisdiction of the United States. This Act *also* applies to every vessel owned in a "State" and *used*

FIG. 211 Boating accidents must be reported if they involve more than specified levels of damage or personal injury. This is true whether one or more craft are concerned. In many areas, reports are made to state authorities rather than the Coast Guard.

on the high seas, the waters beyond the territorial jurisdiction of the United States.

Certain limited categories of vessels are excluded from coverage by the FBSA/71; these include foreign vessels, military or public vessels of the United States (except for recreational-type craft which are included), vessels owned by a State or political subdivision thereof and used primarily for governmental purposes, and ships' lifeboats.

Regulations

Although the Motorboat Act of 1940 (MBA/40) is no longer applicable to the "boats" of the 1971 Act, the Coast Guard regulations which implemented the MBA/40 are retained and remain in effect until replaced.

Classes of boats

For the purpose of applying graduated requirements for equipment as the size of the craft increases, the regulations of the MBA/40 divide all motorboats into four "classes" based on length. This is "overall length" as measured in a straight line parallel to the keel from the foremost part of the vessel to the aftermost part, excluding sheer and excluding bowsprits, boomkins, rudders aft of the transom, outboard motor brackets, etc.

Class A—less than 16 feet in length

Class 1—16 feet and over, but less than 26 feet in length

Class 2—26 feet and over, but less than 40 feet in length

Class 3—40 feet and over, but not more than 65 feet*

(Note: The new regulations will not have an upper limit on length of boats.)

Required Equipment

The regulations of the MBA/40, applicable until superceded by new rules, contain many provisions for required equipment, including fire extinguishers, whistles, bells, and other items. It is specifically stated in the FBSA/71 that

FIG. 210 Federal law does not require the registration and numbering of sailboats with no mechanical power, but some states do make this requirement. All boats, including such sailboats, are subject to Coast Guard requirements for equipment such as personal flotation devices.

*16 ft.=4.9 m   26 ft.=7.9 m   40 ft.=12.2 m   65 ft.=19.8 m

33

FIG. 213 In addition to their frequent rescue missions, Coast Guard patrol craft have enforcement powers for the Federal Boat Safety Act and other federal laws and regulations. They are always clearly marked, fly the Coast Guard Ensign, and are manned by uniformed personnel.

regulations will be issued covering items not now required on board, such as ground tackle and navigation equipment. The new requirements will not become effective without considerable study and wide publicity. Because of the importance of equipment, this topic is covered separately in Chapter 3.

The MBA/40 regulations also prescribe navigation lights for boats, but as these are also included in the Rules of the Road, they are considered separately in Chapter 4.

Numbering of Boats

Although the Federal Boat Safety Act of 1971 repeals the Federal Boating Act of 1958 (FBA/58), it continues the numbering provisions of that law with one major and several minor changes. States were allowed until August 1974 to bring their boat registration systems into conformity with the 1971 Act, but many acted sooner.

The FBSA/71 provides for a system of boat numbering that is uniform throughout the "States" although the actual process of issuing certificates and number assignments may be done individually by the States. As of late 1975 all but three had elected to perform this function within their jurisdiction; in the states of New Hampshire and Washington, boats are registered by the Coast Guard.

The FBSA/71 establishes broad standards for the numbering of vessels and provides for the issuance of more detailed and specific regulations by the "Secretary." The individual States prepare their boat numbering laws and regulations in accordance with Federal standards and then submit them to the Secretary for approval. The Act provides for the withdrawal of approval if the State does not administer its system in accordance with the Federal requirements.

Vessels subject to numbering

The 1971 Act requires the numbering of all vessels used on waters subject to Federal jurisdiction, or on the high seas if owned in the U.S., which are equipped with propulsion machinery *regardless* of horsepower. Exempted are foreign boats temporarily in U.S. waters, documented vessels, ships' lifeboats, and governmental vessels other than recreational type craft.*

A state numbering system may require the numbering of other craft (sailboats, rowboats, etc.) unless prohibited by Federal legislation.

Special provisions are made for tenders (dinghies) carried aboard for other than lifesaving purposes.

"State of principal use"

It is important to note that the FBSA makes it mandatory for the owner of a boat subject to the Act to secure a number "in the State in which the vessel is principally used." This has been interpreted literally—where the boat is most often used on the water, not the state of residence of the owner nor the state in which the boat might set on land on a trailer for a far greater proportion of the time. The term "used" is taken as meaning the time that the vessel is "on" the navigable waters of the United States whether in motion, at anchor, or moored.

Certificate of number

The identification number issued for a vessel is shown on a *Certificate of Number*. This Certificate must be on board whenever the vessel is in use (with exceptions for small rental boats). The FBSA/71 specifies that the certificate of number must be of "pocket size." Each person using a boat must present its Certificate for inspection at the request of any law enforcement officer.

The Federal law states that a certificate may not be valid for more than three years; many states are issuing registrations for shorter periods. All certificates, may, of course, be renewed at or prior to their expiration date.

Numbering systems

The specific details of the numbering of boats are now covered by regulations originally issued under the FBA/58 and still in effect. These will be replaced in due time, but no significant differences are anticipated.

The number pattern is divided into two parts. The first part consists of a two-letter symbol identifying the state of principal use. This is followed by a second part consisting of a combination of numerals and letters for individual identification. The list of state designators appears on page 620.

The individual vessel's identification consists of not more than four arabic numerals and two capital letters, or not more than three such numerals and three such letters. The

*States may require the registration of documented boats (and payment of fees) even though they are not numbered.

letters "I," "O," and "Q" might be mistaken for the numerals one and zero, and therefore they are not used as part of individual boat identification suffixes.

Numbers for dinghies

If used with a numbered vessel, a dinghy equipped with a motor of less than 10 horsepower need not be individually registered and numbered *if* "used as a tender for direct transportation between that vessel and the shore and for no other purpose." It must display the number of the parent boat followed by the suffix "1" separated from the last letter by a space or hyphen as used in the basic number; for example, DC-4567-ED-1 or DC 4567 EF 1.

A dinghy used with a vessel not having a number, such as a documented boat, must be registered and have its own number as for any other craft if it is propelled by a motor of *any* horsepower.

Size and style of numbers

The regulations require that boat numbers provide good legibility and contain certain specifications as to their style and size. The letters and numerals must be plain (no border or trim), vertical block characters not less than three inches in height. They must *not* be of slanting or script style; see Fig. 218. The numbers and letters should all be of one color.

Contrast

Numbers must provide good contrast with their background—black on white or white on black best meets this requirement.

A backing or mounting plate may be used. If so, it must be of sufficient size to provide good contrast, and thus good legibility, for the numbers without regard to the hull.

Display of numbers

The identification number must be painted on, or attached to, either side of the forward half of the vessel, and no other number may be displayed there. (This does not apply to serial numbers on small validation stickers that some states and the Coast Guard issues as a visual indication of payment of current fees.) In most cases, the numbers are quite near the bow, but since they have only to be displayed on the "forward half" of the boat, it is frequently desirable, in the case of boats with considerable flare to their bows, to place the numbers well aft from the stem so that they will be on a more nearly vertical surface and so will be more easily seen and read.

Numbers are placed on a boat so as to read normally from left to right on both sides of the bow. They may be on the hull or on a permanent superstructure. The group of digits appearing between the two sets of letters in the total number *must be separated* from those letters by hyphens or spaces. The hyphen or blank space must be equal to the width of any letter other than "I" or any numeral other than "1"; see Fig. 217.

Identification numbers must be maintained properly to ensure legibility at all times.

Names or insignia may be displayed on the bow of a boat, but only in such a manner that they will not detract from the legibility of the registration numbers. Only one set of numbers may be displayed at any time. If transferred to a new state, the old numbers must be removed.

FIG. 214 A boat must be registered in, and receive its numbers from, "the state of principal use" even though this is not the owner's state of residence nor where the boat is stored on a trailer and out of the water for more days than it is used in the water.

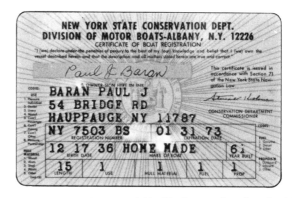

FIG. 215 The assignment of identification numbers to a boat by a state or by the Coast Guard is made on a "Certificate of Number" which must be on board whenever the craft is in use (except for small rental boats).

Applications for numbers

The addresses of State and other authorities to whom application for a Certificate of Number must be made are listed on page 640.

The same numbers are assigned by a regular renewal Certificate. Upon transfer of ownership, if the boat continues in the same state of principal use, the old numbers stay on the craft and are assigned to the new owner.

Numbers may not be transferred from one boat to another, except for special dealers' and manufacturers' numbers issued for demonstrating, transporting, or testing boats.

Fees

Under the FBSA/71, States may set their own fees to be charged for registration and numbering of boats The fees vary widely from state to state—and in some jurisdictions, these merely cover the cost of administering the numbering program; in others, they are used as sources of revenue for the state.

The 1971 law specifically provides that a State may require proof of payment of State and local taxes before issuing a Certificate of Number. Withholding of certification on any other grounds is *not* authorized, except that a title or proof of ownership may be required.

Reciprocity

When a vessel is numbered in the State of principal use, it will be considered as in compliance with the numbering system of any State in which it is *temporarily* used. There is no specific time limit stated if such use is truly "temporary." This is of considerable advantage to boatmen who may cruise or trailer their craft to other state waters for vacation periods.

When a vessel is taken to a *new* "State of principal use," that state must recognize the validity of the number issued by the authority for a period of at least 60 days before requiring new registration.

Notification of changes

If a boat is destroyed or abandoned, or it is sold, or it is used for more than 60 days in a state other than the one where its Certificate of Number was issued, or it is documented, a report must be made to the issuing office within 15 days. The Certificate is invalid and must be surrendered. The numbers (and validation stickers, if any) must be removed from the craft. A report must also be made if the boat is stolen or recovered.

A change of address of the owner must be reported to the issuing office within 15 days. If the state of principal use is changed, application must be made for a number in the new state within 60 days. A change of motor only is not required to be reported.

Operators' "Safety Certificates"

The Federal Boat Safety Act of 1971 continues the provision in the 1958 law that gives States optional authority to require the operator of a vessel that comes within the scope of the numbering provisions of the Act to "hold a valid safety certificate issued under terms and conditions set by the issuing authority."

No Coast Guard regulations have been issued for this purpose, and little use of the authority has been made by the States except in the case of young persons.

Termination of Unsafe Use

The Federal Boat Safety Act of 1971 includes a provision that is entirely new to the general concept of boating laws and regulations If a Coast Guard boarding officer observes a boat being used without sufficient lifesaving or fire fighting devices, or in an overloaded or otherwise unsafe condition as defined in regulations (lack of proper navigation lights when required, fuel system leakage or fuel in the bilges or elsewhere outside of tanks, ventilation of engine and fuel tank areas, or flame arrestors, that do not meet requirements), and which in his judgement such use creates an especially hazardous condition, he may direct the operator to take whatever immediate and reasonable steps would be necessary for the safety of those aboard the vessel. This may include directing the operator to return to mooring and remain there until the situation creating the hazard is corrected or ended. Failure to comply with an order to terminate unsafe use of a vessel could result in the arrest of the operator.

MI 2345 AB

OR

MI-2345-AB

CORRECT

MI2345AB

INCORRECT

FIG. 217 Undoubtedly the most widespread violation of boating regulations is the faulty application of numbers. There must be either a space or a hyphen (dash) before and after the block of numerals to set them off from the letters that precede and follow them. In some areas, as much as a majority of boats will be seen with the letters and numerals run together.

ME 456 R

AND

ME 456 R

INCORRECT

ME 456 R

CORRECT

FIG. 218 The regulations that govern the shape of boat's numbers specify "block letters in good proportion." This phrase has been officially interpreted to mean vertical characters of plain style — script, slanting, or other "fancy" style characters are not acceptable.

Federal regulations designate certain portions of the Washington-Oregon coast as "regulated boating areas." When wave heights or surface currents exceed set limits, conditions are considered "unsafe" and the Coast Guard is authorized to terminate boating in the area concerned.

The Coast Guard has authority to forbid use of a craft officially designated as "manifestly unsafe for a specific voyage on a specific body of water." This covers unsuitable design, improper construction or condition, or improper or inadequate operational or safety equipment.

Negligent Operation

The FBSA/71 clearly states that "no person may use any vessel in a negligent manner so as to endanger the life, limb, or property of any person." Foreign vessels, governmental vessels, and other craft normally excluded from coverage under this Act are *not* exempted from the prohibition against negligent operations.

The endangerment of "any person" is so phrased as to *include* the operator of the vessel, no other person need be involved.

Boating Accidents

Sometimes, despite the best of care, boating accidents of one kind or another do occur. This may involve only a single craft, or two or more vessels may be concerned. In any case, there are obligations imposed on the skippers at the scene and afterwards.

Duties in case of accident

In case of collision, accident, or other casualty involving a vessel subject to the FBSA/71 (including such exempted vessels as foreign or governmental craft), it is the duty of the operator, to the extent that he can do so without serious danger to his vessel or those on board, to render such assistance as may be necessary and practicable to other persons affected by the incident in order to save them from danger as a result thereof. The operator must also give his name and address, and the identification of his vessel, to any person injured and to the owner of any property damaged.

FIG. 218 A common misconception is that the numbers must be on the "bow" of a boat. The legal requirement is that they must be on the "forward half of the vessel" and actually they should be sufficiently aft from the stem to ensure ease of readability despite any pronounced flare of the forward hull.

FIG. 219 Coast Guard regulations now require that manufacturers now place a "hull identification number" on all boats in a specified size and format. This "HIN" must be on the transom above the waterline and so permanently a part of the hull that removal or alteration would be obvious.

The duties described above for the operator of a vessel are applicable whether or not the incident was the result of apparent negligence. They are also in addition to any other duties provided by law.

"Good Samaritan" provision

Any person who complies with the duties described above, or any other person who gratuitously and in good faith renders assistance at the scene of an accident or other boating casualty without the objection of any person being assisted, is protected by a provision of the FBSA/71. He cannot be held liable for any civil damages as a result of the rendering of assistance or for any act or omission in providing or arranging salvage, towage, medical treatment, or other assistance where the assisting person acts as an ordinary, reasonably prudent man would have done under the same or similar circumstances.

Accident Reporting

In case of collision, accident, or other casualty involving a vessel subject to the Boat Safety Act of 1971, the operator must make a report under certain circumstances. A report is required if the incident results in death, an injury requiring medical treatment beyond first aid, the disappearance of a person from a vessel under circumstances that indicate death or injury, or if there is property damage totaling more than $200.

If death occurs within 24 hours of the accident, or a person has a reportable injury or disappears from the boat, a formal report must be made within 48 hours, otherwise, within 10 days.

Most state boating laws require that reports of boating accidents be made to a designated state office or official. If, however, there is no state provision for reporting such incidents, a report must be made to the Coast Guard Officer in Charge, Marine Inspection, nearest to the place where the accident occurred.

The Coast Guard regulations on boating accident reporting (see pages 619–621) list the information that must be furnished. The Boating Accident Report — CG-3865 — may be used in reports to the Coast Guard. States normally use this form or one of their own patterned after it. See fig. 222.

Accident Statistics

The 1971 Federal Boat Safety Act provides that as a part of an approved state registering and numbering system there shall be a casualty reporting plan in accordance with regulations issued by the Secretary. The recording, compilation, and forwarding of accident statistics is, for the time being, covered by regulations from the 1958 Act.

National statistics

The Coast Guard, in turn, is charged with the responsibility of combining state reports with its own to form national statistics as to the number of registered boats by classes; accidents by type, cause, surrounding circumstances, etc.; and other related data. Reports are compiled on the basis of calendar years.

Privacy of information

Information as to the identity and ownership of vessels numbered under the Act will be made available to Federal and local officials as needed in any enforcement or assistance program.

In general, files relating to the numbering of boats are considered "public records," and information from them may be released to anyone, subject only to reasonable restrictions necessary to carry on the work of the records office.

On the other hand, individual "Boating Accident Reports" or extracts therefrom are *not* releasable. These are intended to furnish information necessary for the Coast Guard to make findings as to the cause of accidents and recommendations for their prevention, and to compile appropriate statistics. Their privacy permits the filing of full and accurate reports without the possibility of their contents being used against the individual in civil suits.

Enforcement Authority

Federal boating regulations in general are enforced by the Coast Guard. USCG boarding vessels are identified by the Coast Guard ensign (see pages P, T) and uniformed personnel. A vessel underway upon being hailed by a Coast Guard vessel or patrol boat is required to stop immediately and lay to, or maneuver in such a way as to permit the boarding officer to come aboard.

Many state and local governmental units have navigation regulations backed up with patrol boats. Skippers should be alert for posted signs or regulatory buoys indicating speed limits, "no wake," etc., and should stop immediately upon being hailed by an official craft.

Many law-enforcement vessels—Coast Guard and state or local—are now equipped with a characteristic blue revolving light like those seen on police cars in many areas; see page 64(n) and Fig. 430.

Boat and Equipment Standards

The Federal Boat Safety Act of 1971 authorized minimum safety standards for "boats" and "associated equipment." Each standard must be reasonable, must meet the need for boating safety, and must be stated, insofar as practicable, in terms of performance. Under the 1971 Act's provisions, it will be the duty of the manufacturer to deliver to purchasers boats and associated equipment meeting all safety standards.

Penalties

The Federal Boat Safety Act of 1971 provides for both civil and criminal penalties for various violations of its provisions. It allows for variable penalties to meet situations of different degrees of seriousness, and provides for a flexible system of assessment and collection.

Civil penalties

A basic civil penalty of not more than $500 may be assessed for *any* violation of the FBSA/71 or any regulation issued thereunder. If the violation involves a vessel, that vessel may be liable and may be proceeded against in the Federal courts. The basic penalty may be assessed by administrative action; no trial in court is required, but procedures are established for appeals.

Criminal penalties

Any person who uses a vessel in a "grossly" negligent manner so as to endanger the life, limb, or property of any person (including himself) may be subjected to a criminal penalty of a fine of not more than $1,000 or imprisonment for not more than one year, or both. ("Simple" negligence comes under the civil penalty noted above.)

Written warnings

Coast Guard boarding officers may issue a *written warning* for certain minor violations of boating regulations; these are awarded in lieu of a citation that would lead to a monetary penalty. Written warnings are *not* issued for any violation involving danger to the occupants of a craft, or where three or more violations of any type are found in a single boarding.

Written warnings are issued for the first offense only of any calendar year; subsequent offenses will be subject to more severe penalties. Appeal procedures are provided if it is felt that the warning was not warranted.

Boating Safety Advisory Council

The FBSA/71 establishes the *Boating Safety Advisory Council* of 21 members, each of whom it is expected will have special knowledge and experience in boating safety. Membership of the Council will consist equally of representatives from State and local governments, boat and associated equipment manufacturers, and boating organizations and the general public. All boating safety standards and other major safety matters will be referred to the Council prior to being issued.

State Boating Safety Programs

The Federal Boat Safety Act of 1971 contains extensive provisions for State participation in boating safety programs. These State programs will include registration and numbering systems, boating safety educational programs, and patrol and other enforcement activities.

The initial Federal financial support in the FBSA/71 expired after five years. In 1980 Congress passed the Recreational Boating Safety and Facilities Improvement Act—the "Biagi Act"—which authorizes the use of a portion of the funds collected by the Federal tax on motor fuels used by boats for the purposes named in the

FIG. 222 Boating accident reports must contain all information required by regulations. The use of an official form will aid in ensuring completeness. States will either use the Coast Guard form shown above or one much like it.

title of the Act. A total of $10 million would be divided among the States for each of the two functions. These funds are not assured, however, as they are subject to specific appropriation action by Congress each year.

RULES OF THE ROAD

The "Rules of the Road" are sets of statutory requirements enacted by Congress to promote safety of navigation. The rules consist of requirements for navigation lights and day shapes, steering and sailing rules, sound signals for both good and restricted visibility situations, rules for conduct in restricted visibility, and distress signals.

There are different sets of Rules for various bodies and areas of waters.

International rules

International Regulations for Preventing Collisions at Sea—generally referred to as the International Rules of the Road—have been adopted at international conferences from time to time; changes often came at intervals of 12 years. The current International Rules bear the designation of "1972," the year that they were agreed upon, but only became effective on 15 July 1977 after ratification by the required number of maritime nations; there were many changes from the 1960 Rules. The International Rules were made effective for all vessels in U.S. waters, and for U.S. vessels in all international waters, by Presidential Proclamation and Act of Congress.

The International Rules of the Road are effective outside the demarcation lines discussed on page 31. Boatmen who go offshore along the coast must be familiar with their provisions, and especially with the differences in such waters from the rules for inland waters.

Rules for U.S. waters

On 24 December 1981 the U.S. adopted a single set of rules of the road for all waters inside the demarcation lines.* The new "Inland Navigational Rules" replaced the former three sets of rules—Inland, Great Lakes, and Western Rivers—that varied considerably from the International Rules and often differed among themselves.

* Implementation on the Great Lakes was delayed slightly to effect coordination with Canada.

FIG. 223 The penalties for violation of the Rules of the Road make no distinction between ships and small craft. Although the maximum of $5,000 is not likely to be assessed against the skipper of a recreational boat, it could be. Know and obey the Rules!

Provisions of the Rules

The four sets of Rules of the Road are of such importance and contain such extensive information that two chapters in this book are devoted to them and their implementing regulations.

Matters relating to navigation lights and day shapes are covered in Chapter 4 for all sets of Rules. Chapter 5 covers other topics of the Rules such as the steering and sailing rules, whistle signals, etc.

Official publication

The Coast Guard has published an excellent booklet on the rules of the road. CG-169 covers both the 1972 International Rules and the new U.S. Inland Navigational Rules. It provides a basis for ready comparison of the two sets of rules, and offers comments on them. Included are very clear illustrations, in color, of many various light and dayshape configurations. Other sections of this booklet contain extracts from other Acts and Federal Regulations relating to marine navigation.

A copy of this publication is not legally required to be on a recreational boat, but it is definitely a desirable document to have at hand for ready reference. Don't, however, depend on having time to look up the applicable Rule when a possibly dangerous situation develops—know at least the basic rules for the waters that you are on, and be able to act without delay!

Although previous editions of CG-169 were available from the Coast Guard without charge, budgetary restrictions have now made it necessary that the revised 1981 edition be sold through the Superintendent of Documents, Government Printing Office, Washington, DC 20402

Additional regulations

The Inland Navigational Rules Act of 1980 requires that the Secretary "of the Department in which the Coast Guard is operating" (this language is necessary as the Coast Guard can at times be operating in the Department of the Navy rather than Transportation) establish four Annexes to the U.S. Inland Rules corresponding to the four Annexes of the International Rules. The Secretary (actually the Commandant of the Coast Guard) may also issue other regulations as required, and under this authority Annex V to the Inland Rules was promulgated to replace portions of the former "Pilot Rules" (much of the content of the former Pilot Rules has now been incorporated into the basic U.S. Inland Rules). The five Annexes to the new Inland Rules are discussed in detail in Chapters 4 and 5.

Penalties against persons

The Inland Navigational Rules Act of 1980 provides that any person "who operates a vessel" in violation of that Act or any regulation issued thereunder—and this includes the various Annexes—is liable to a civil penalty of not more than $5,000 for each violation.

It should be noted that this penalty is not a "fine" such as would require conviction in a Federal court. Rather it is a civil forfeiture imposed by the Secretary, or a person to whom he has delegated that authority. No such penalty may be assessed until the person charged has been given notice of the violation involved and an opportunity for a hearing. The Secretary, or other delegated official, may remit, mitigate, or compromise any penalty assessed. If a penalty, as finally determined, is not paid, the matter can be taken to a Federal District Court for collection and/or other appropriate action.

A portion of the Act also provides for the withholding of customs clearance for any vessel the owner or operator of which is subject to penalties that have not been paid. This provision is especially important in cases concerning violations by foreign vessels in U.S. waters; clearance is normally granted following the posting of a bond where the final result of penalty proceedings has not been reached before the vessel's scheduled sailing date.

Penalties against vessels

In maritime law, a vessel itself can be held to be in violation and be subjected to penalties if operated contrary to any provision of the Inland Navigational Rules Act of 1980 or regulations issued thereunder, including the Annexes to the Rules. The same maximum penalty, $5,000 for each violation can be assessed, and in this case the vessel may be seized and proceeded against in any Federal District Court. The same procedures for due notice and hearings are available to the owner of a vessel charged with a violation as are available to individuals as described above. Withholding of a required customs clearance is particularly appropriate in the case of a vessel charged with violations.

International Rules penalties

The 1972 International Rules of the Road do not in themselves contain any penalties for violation of their provisions. However, the Navigational Rules Act of 1977, which made these international regulations effective in U.S. waters and for U.S. ships, provides for civil penalties of not more than $5,000 (increased from $500 in 1980). Procedures are generally the same as for violations and penalties under the U.S. Inland Rules as described above.

Individuals and vessels can also be sued for damages resulting from violations of the International Rules as well as the U.S. Inland Rules of the Road.

Penalty for failure to give aid

As noted before, the master or person in charge of a vessel in collision has duties to the other vessel and her crew and passengers (see page 36). A specific penalty is provided for failure, without reasonable cause, to meet these responsibilities. Such a person may be found guilty of a misdemeanor and subjected to a fine of $1000, or imprisonment for not more than two years, or both. The vessel may be proceeded against in Federal court with the penalty assessed being divided equally between the informer and the United States.

Use of searchlights

Annex V to the new U.S. Inland Navigational Rules now contains a specific regulation prohibiting the flashing of a searchlight or other blinding light onto the bridge or into the pilothouse of another vessel while underway. Violation may lead to the suspension or revocation of the offending person's license or certificate.

FIG. 225 All sets of Pilot Rules contain specific prohibitions against the use of a searchlight in such a way as to flash its rays onto the bridge or into the pilothouse of any vessel underway.

the pilothouse of another vessel while underway. Violation may lead to the suspension or revocation of the offending person's license or certificate.

Penalties

The penalties for violation of the Pilot Rules are the same as for offenses against the basic Rules of the Road; see page 39.

BILGE VENTILATION REGULATIONS

Of particular interest to the owners of motorboats using *gasoline* as a fuel are the Coast Guard regulations relating to the ventilation of engine and fuel tank compartments. The regulations are discussed and illustrated on pages 604-607.

REGATTAS AND MARINE PARADES

The Coast Guard has established a set of regulations covering the holding of regattas and marine parades. In some areas, the authority to regulate such events has been passed on to State authorities, but under the same general requirements and procedures.

The term "regattas and marine parades" includes all organized water events of limited duration conducted on a prearranged schedule; this covers races of all types.

An application must be submitted to the Commander of the Coast Guard District in which the event is to be held no less than 30 days prior to the start of the proposed event; late applications are normally rejected. The application must contain a number of items of information as specified

in Coast Guard regulations; see CG-169, 172, or 184.

Approved events will often result in the promulgation of "special local regulations" governing the conduct of the event, spectator craft restrictions, patrolling plans, etc. These are usually issued with Local Notices to Mariners and carry specific penalties for violations.

PARK REGULATIONS

The use of boats on many natural lakes and man-made reservoirs are subject to regulations issued by the National Park Service of the Department of the Interior. Other such bodies of water are controlled by state or local authorities. These rules and restrictions will vary from one body of water to another and each area must be individually checked to ensure that laws are not inadvertently violated.

State Boating Laws and Regulations

Federal laws and regulations now preempt State controls in the area of boat and equipment safety standards, but the Federal Boat Safety Act of 1971 does allow States to impose requirements for safety equipment beyond Federal rules if needed to meet uniquely hazardous local circumstances. The Act does *not* preempt State or local laws and regulations directed at safe boat operation. In addition, there are usually laws and regulations relating to boat trailers and their use.

The old saying that "Ignorance of the law is no excuse" is quite applicable to skippers of recreational boats. Each should know the requirements and restrictions of his state, and should take steps as appropriate to expand his knowledge if he plans to cruise in other states. He should particularly be alert to varying state laws about boat trailering on highways.

Information on applicable state laws and regulations may be obtained from each state, usually from the same office that handles registration and numbering; see page 504. The Outboard Boating Club of America publishes four regional handbooks that are thorough compilations of laws and regulations relating to boats of all sizes, trailers, boating activities, and taxation. These are up-dated when necessary by supplements. These may be ordered from OBC at 333 N. Michigan Avenue, Chicago, Ill. 60601.

TEMPORARY SUSPENSION
OF FEDERAL PREEMPTION

Immediately following the enactment of the Federal Boat Safety Act of 1971, the Secretary of Transportation exercised his authority under Section 9 of the Act which allows him to grant exemptions to its provisions. He granted a blanket exemption to all States and political subdivisions thereof from Section 10 which sets forth the Federal preemption over State and local regulations in the area of boat and equipment safety standards and requirements.

This action was taken to avoid a temporary "vacuum" of regulation. The new Federal boat safety program will be implemented by regulations to be issued under the authority of the Act, rather than by specific provisions of the basic law. Time will be required to prepare, coordinate, and publish these regulations, and for them to become effective. To avoid the cancellation of State and local laws and regulations before rules come in, the exemption was granted, allowing them to temporarily continue in effect in the interim.

FIG. 227 State boating laws and regulations vary widely. The Outboard Boating Club has prepared sectional compilations of these requirements and restrictions, with supplements published as required by changes.

requirements of the 1971 Federal Boat Safety Act do not apply to documented vessels; other provisions of this Act, however, do apply to "boats" as defined therein.

Documentation of a craft used solely for non-commercial recreational purposes is *optional,* and certain requirements must be met. The vessel must be owned by a citizen of the United States (or a corporation 51% or more owned by U.S. citizens) and it must be of a specified minimum size, 5 net tons as explained below. The captain of a documented vessel, if other than the owner, must be a U.S. citizen.

Tonnage

Before a vessel can be documented it must be *measured* for its tonnage. ("Admeasured" is the more formal term, but it means the same and is gradually being dropped in favor of the simpler language.) The details of gross and net tonnage are explained on page 25.

Types of Documents

The documents that are issued to vessels are of five forms—register, enrollment and license, license, yacht enrollment and license, and yacht license. Only the latter two are of interest to the owners of noncommercial craft, but all should be generally understood.

Yacht documents

A **yacht enrollment and license** may be issued to a vessel used *exclusively for pleasure* of 20 net tons or more. A **yacht license** may be issued to such a vessel of 5 net tons or over but less than 20 net tons.

Other types of documents

An **enrollment and license** may be issued to a vessel of 20 net tons or more and, if the vessel meets certain qualifications, may authorize it to engage in the coasting trade, the mackerel fishery, the cod fishery, the whale fishery, or

Miscellaneous Regulatory Matters

Boatmen will have need of knowledge of other regulatory matters in varying degrees as determined by the size of their craft, their cruising area, etc. Skippers should be alert to changes in these factors which may require additional knowledge in matters previously of no interest to them.

DOCUMENTATION

Not all boats are numbered—many are "documented." This is a process whereby official papers on the craft are issued by the Coast Guard in much the same manner as for large ships. (Formerly this was done by the Bureau of Customs of the Treasury Department, but the function was transferred to the Coast Guard in 1966.) The *numbering*

FIG. 228 Craft over a specified minimum size may be "documented" in much the same way as are large ships. This action, in lieu of state or Coast Guard registration and numbering, has both advantages and disadvantages.

the coasting trade and mackerel fishery. A vessel authorized to engage in the "mackerel fishery" may be used in the taking of fish of any description.

If a vessel is to be used for towing, dredging, freight or passenger carrying, or a combination of any of these functions, its document must so state.

Special enrollments and licenses are issued on the frontiers, authorizing vessels to engage in the foreign and coasting trades. Vessels of 5 net tons or more may be granted an enrollment and license for navigating the waters of the northern, northeastern, or northwestern frontiers.

A **license** may be issued to a vessel of 5 net tons or over but of less than 20 net tons and, if the vessel meets certain qualifications, may authorize the vessel to engage in any one of the employments for which an enrollment and license may be issued as discussed above.

A vessel under a **register** which is not limited by a prohibitive endorsement on its face may engage in any trade, including the foreign trade, the coastwise trade, and the American fisheries. Registered vessels, however, may be required upon arrival in a port of the United States to pay certain pilotage fees and other charges from which other documented vessels are generally exempted.

Temporary and permanent documents

Marine documents are also described as "permanent"—issued to vessels at their home ports, or "temporary"—granted to vessels at ports other than their home port.

Advantages of Yacht Documentation

Important privileges extended by documentation of vessels as yachts include (1) legal authority to fly the yacht ensign, which authority is not formally granted to other boats; and (2) the privilege of recording bills of sale, mortgages, and other instruments of title for the vessel with federal officials at her home port, giving constructive legal notice to all persons of the effect of such instruments and permitting the attainment of a preferred status for mortgages so recorded. This gives additional security to the purchaser or mortgagee and facilitates financing and transfer of title for such vessels.

The former advantages of documented yachts over registered (numbered) non-commercial motorboats when returning to the U.S. from a foreign port have now been eliminated in the general simplification of procedures that has occurred in recent years; see pages 48-49.

Obtaining Documentation

A procedure has been established under which the owner of a boat used *exclusively for pleasure* may file an "Application for Simplified Admeasurement" with the Officer in Charge, Marine Inspection in his local Coast Guard District.

In brief, the simplified measurement method uses the numerical product of three dimensions—the overall length (L), overall breadth (B), and depth (D)—note that this is "depth," an internal dimension, and not the boat's "draft." The **gross tonnage** of a vessel designed for sailing is assumed to be $\frac{1}{2}(LBD/100)$; for vessels not designed for sailing it is calculated to be $2/3(LBD/100)$.

The gross tonnage of a catamaran or a trimaran is determined by adding the gross tonnages of each hull as calculated above.

Where the volume of the deckhouse is disproportionate to the volume of the hull—as in some designs of houseboats—the volume of the deckhouse, calculated by appropriate geometric formulas and expressed in tons of 100 cubic feet each, is added to the gross tonnage of the hull as calculated with L, B, and D.

The **net tonnage** of a sailing vessel is recorded as 9/10 of the gross tonnage; for a non-sailing vessel, the multiplying factor is 8/10. If there is no propelling machinery in the hull, the net tonnage will be the same as the gross tonnage.

Application for simplified admeasurement is by letter; there is no standard form of application unless one has been prepared by the local Officer in Charge, Marine Inspection. The owner may take his own length, breadth, and depth measurements and complete the transaction by mail, quickly and without cost.

Considerable information on documentation can be obtained from the Coast Guard pamphlet "Yacht Admeasurement and Documentation"—CG-177, available without charge from Coast Guard offices.

Formal measurement

The owner of a boat may elect to have formal measurement rather than use the simplified method; this is *required* if the vessel is to be used *commercially*.

If an owner is contemplating formal admeasurement, it is suggested that he first make an estimate of the tonnage by using the simplified method. If the resulting net tonnage is less than 5 tons, it is not likely that the vessel will be 5 net tons or more when formally measured.

An application for formal measurement should be prepared in writing and submitted to the Officer in Charge,

FIG. 229 Much useful information on documentation requirements and procedures can be obtained from this free Coast Guard pamphlet. A copy should be obtained and studied before any decision is made regarding the possible documentation of a boat.

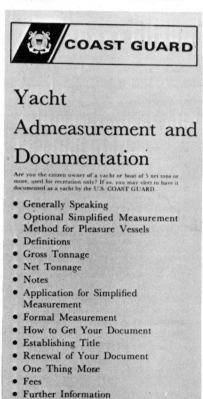

COAST GUARD

Yacht Admeasurement and Documentation

Are you the citizen owner of a yacht or boat of 5 net tons or more, used for recreation only? If so, you may elect to have it documented as a yacht by the U.S. COAST GUARD.

- Generally Speaking
- Optional Simplified Measurement Method for Pleasure Vessels
- Definitions
- Gross Tonnage
- Net Tonnage
- Notes
- Application for Simplified Measurement
- Formal Measurement
- How to Get Your Document
- Establishing Title
- Renewal of Your Document
- One Thing More
- Fees
- Further Information

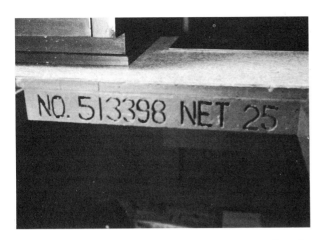

FIG. 230 A documented vessel, including a boat, must have its "official number" and "net tonnage" deeply carved or permanently marked on her "main beam." Special provisions have been made for fiberglass boats.

Marine Inspection, for the area in which the vessel is located. The information that must be submitted is listed in CG-177.

Under formal measurement procedures, a definite date and place should be agreed upon between the measuring officer and the owner, or his agent, so that the vessel may be physically measured and examined by the measuring officer.

Application for document

The measuring officer who calculates the tonnages by the simplified method, or who visits the vessel for formal measurement, will provide the necessary forms which must be filled out to receive the document. Further assistance may be obtained by writing, calling, or visiting the nearest Documentation Office, U.S. Coast Guard.

Establishing title

A vessel may be documented only in the name of the holder of legal title. It is necessary therefore for the owner

FIG. 231 A craft documented for pleasure only—no commercial use—must have her name and hailing port marked "on some conspicuous place on the hull." This is normally done on the stern, but such is not mandatory. Detailed specifications must be met regarding the lettering.

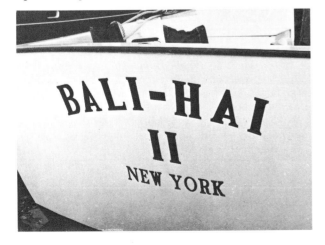

to present adequate title papers with his application.

If the vessel was built for the present owner and has never been owned by anyone else, that person should have the builder furnish a "Builder's Certificate" on Form 1261 to establish title.

If there were previous owners, the proper documents are the Builder's Certificate and bills of sale in recordable form from each of the previous owners, preferably on Form 1346, available without charge from the Documentation Office. If these steps are impracticable, consult the Officer in Charge, Marine Inspection, for alternative procedures.

Fees

The fee for documentation of a yacht is $75; a change of name adds another $75. Renewal of a document, or a change in master, costs $15. There is a $10 penalty for late renewal. There are no fees for the measurement of a yacht, except that if the presence of a measuring officer is required outside specific local limits, a charge is made to cover his travel expenses. There are substantial overtime charges for work on Saturdays and Sundays; it is suggested that a convenient weekday be proposed in the application to avoid the additional costs.

A small charge is made for recording each bill of sale or other recordable title instrument; the average cost of recording a bill of sale is approximately $2.

Markings of a Documented Boat

The owner or master of a vessel to be documented must file a certification with the Coast Guard Documentation Officer that the boat is properly *marked*. He must arrange for an official inspection of the marking if this is requested by the Coast Guard.

Official number and net tonnage

Every documented vessel, as a prerequisite to documentation, must have its official number and net tonnage carved or permanently marked on the *main beam* of the vessel.

The main beam is the beam at the forward end of the largest hatch on the weather deck and is usually located forward of amidships. If the vessel has no hatch on the weather deck, the main beam is any structural member integral to the hull.

The *official number* must be preceded by the abbreviation "NO." and the net tonnage must be preceded by the word "NET"; see fig. 230.

In a wooden vessel, the legend must be carved or cut on the main beam in arabic or block type letters three inches high, or as high as the width of the main beam will permit In a vessel built of metal, the legend must be outlined by punch marks and painted over with oil paint using a color that contrasts with the background.

On fiberglass boats, the legend can be carved into a plastic plate as in a wooden beam and this plate then is permanently bonded to a structural member integral to the hull or to the hull itself where one might expect to find a main beam. The plate will usually be six inches high by as long as necessary to show the required information.

Name and hailing port

All documented yachts are required to have their name and home port or hailing port marked on *some conspicu-*

---

*In some instances where overtime is involved, a small "after-hours" fee is charged for the issuance of a document.

ous place on their hull; this is usually done on the stern. The letters must be Roman type and not less than four inches in height. They may be painted, gilded, cut, or cast letters, and must be in a color that provides adequate contrast with the background surface.

The *home port* is the port where the craft is permanently documented. The *hailing port* is the port or place in the same Marine Inspection Zone where the vessel was built or where one or more of the owners reside. The state name, in full or abbreviated form, must be included in the home or hailing port.*

Documented commercial vessels must have the name and home or hailing port marked in full on the stern, plus the name in full marked on both bows.

Block letters required

For documented vessels, whether used for pleasure only or commercially, *the use of script or italic lettering is not acceptable.* It is *not* permissible to place the name or hailing port, on a board and attach the board to the hull, or to use cut or carved letters joined in one continuous piece. (For boats that are numbered rather than documented, there is no requirement that a name be shown nor specifications as to how one may or must be displayed.)

Use of Documented Boats

If a vessel is given a document as a yacht, that paper will authorize its use for *pleasure only.* A yacht document does *not* permit the transporting of merchandise or the carrying of passengers for hire, such as the taking out of fishing parties for a fee charged directly or indirectly. Any violation of this limitation may result in the imposition of severe penalties against the craft and its owner. See also section below on "Commercial Operation."

The documentation of a vessel as a yacht *does not exempt* it from any applicable State or Federal taxes. Further, the fact that a boat is federally documented will not excuse the owner from complying with safety and equipment regulations of the state or states in which it is operated.

Vessels that are documented are not required nor permitted to have a number issued under the 1971 Federal Boat Safety Act.

Renewal of Documents

A yacht license or enrollment and license must be renewed each year; this is probably the only disadvantage to documentation. The owner will ordinarily be notified by mail and will be sent the required renewal form and instructions several weeks in advance of the expiration date. Failure to receive this notice, however, will not affect the requirement for renewal.

For vessels under simplified measurement

At the discretion of the Officer in Charge, Marine Inspection, concerned, a document issued under the simplified measurement procedures *may* not be renewed, or another document issued, until the Coast Guard has verified the overall dimensions given in the application for such measurement.

Any correction of the stated overall dimensions of a vessel as a result of the above verification is deemed to be a change in the description of the vessel and the outstanding document will no longer be in force.

*Having the name and port on the bottom of a dinghy carried on its side across the transom, as is often done, especially in the Pacific Northwest, is *not* a legally acceptable

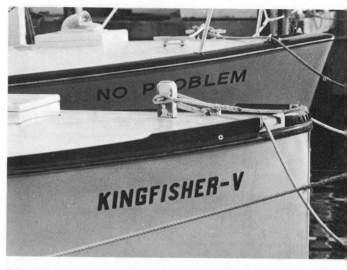

FIG. 232 A craft documented for any commercial use must be marked with her name and hailing port on the stern, and additionally must have her name on both sides of the vessel's bow. The style, size, and colors of the lettering are specified by regulation.

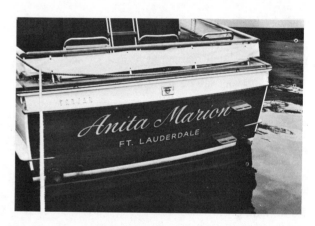

FIG. 233 The name in script-style letters on the stern of this boat is legal as she is numbered rather than documented. Such style of lettering is not acceptable on any documented boat or ship.

COMMERCIAL OPERATION

The Federal Government does not require that the owner of a motorboat or yacht of any size whatever have any knowledge of his boat or navigation or the handling of his vessel. Neither does the Government require that a *motorboat* or motor yacht under 300 gross tons not engaged in trade or carrying passengers for hire should have on board a licensed officer.

No licensed officers are required on *motor vessels documented as yachts* except on those of 200 gross tons and over when navigating the high seas.

Carrying Passengers For Hire

Persons wishing to operate a motorboat carrying passengers for hire must have a license. There are two categories of licensing as determined by the number of persons carried—six passengers and less, or more than six. Neither

substitute for a name and port *clearly* visible on the boat itself.

of these should be confused with the licenses required to be held by pilots and engineers on vessels of more than 15 gross tons or 65 feet length engaged in trade. Motorboats under 65 feet in length carrying freight for hire are not required to have licensed pilots and engineers.

Definition of "passenger"

Of particular interest to boatmen who use their craft exclusively for recreation is the definition of a "passenger" in the Federal Boat Safety Act of 1971. A person on board a vessel is *not* considered by law to be a passenger if he is in any of the following categories: (1) the owner or his representative; (2) the operator; (3) bona fide members of the crew who have contributed no consideration for their carriage and who are paid for their services; or (4) any guest on board a vessel which is being used exclusively for pleasure purposes who has not contributed any consideration, directly or indirectly, for his carriage.

The last exception noted above is the most troublesome. It is emphasized that to avoid being in a "passenger" status—which would subject the craft and its skipper to special requirements—the guest must not contribute *any* consideration, directly or indirectly, for his passage.

When is a boat carrying passengers for hire?

It is of considerable importance that a skipper have some understanding of circumstances that might be considered by the authorities as "carrying passengers for hire." Some situations are obvious—such as taking persons on a fishing trip for a specified amount of money for each individual or for the group as a whole—but other cases are more borderline and must be examined carefully.

It has been held that when the owner is a businessman who takes associates or customers aboard for the purpose of creating good-will or negotiating business matters not related to the trip this *does not* put the vessel and operator in the category of carrying passengers for hire.

On the other hand, the Coast Guard has ruled that the following situations *do* constitute instances of carrying passengers for hire.

1. When the boat owner invites guests aboard and one or more of them brings a gift of food or drink to be used on the trip.

2. Where the cruise guest takes the skipper ashore for dinner and entertainment.

3. Where during a cruise one of the guests aboard buys a tankful of fuel, or some similar action.

4. If there is a prearranged plan or agreement in advance that the guests are to pay their proportionate share, or any specific amount, of the cruise expenses. The operator of the craft would have to be properly licensed and the vessel would have to be equipped in accordance with the requirements for those carrying passengers for hire.

If the participants in an expense-sharing cruise are members of a *bona-fide* "joint venture," they are then all considered under the law to be "owners" and not "passengers" and thus no licensed operator would be required. It is essential, however, that this joint venture be legally sufficient and in writing. *Each person* must have *all* the incidents of ownership—the right to full possession, control, and navigation of the craft. A mere "share-the-expenses" agreement is not sufficient to establish a joint venture; rights of ownership and liability in case of accident and suit are necessary.

If a boat is chartered with the crew furnished by the owner, it has been held that the craft is then carrying passengers for hire and must be in charge of a licensed operator.

Licenses for Six or Less Passengers

Vessels equipped with propulsion machinery of any type, while carrying *not more than six* passengers for hire, must be "in the charge of" a person licensed for such service in accordance with regulations issued under the authority of the Federal Boat Safety Act of 1971.

Application for licenses

Licenses are issued by Officers in Charge, Marine Inspection, U.S. Coast Guard. These officers are located in many ports; check a nearby Coast Guard unit for the nearest Marine Inspection Office.

An applicant must submit a sworn application to one of these officers who will examine him concerning his character and fitness to hold such a license. The Officer in Charge, or his representative, investigates the proofs submitted concerning the applicant's character and ability, and determines whether his "capacity, knowledge, experience, character, and habits of life" qualify him for licensing as a Motorboat Operator.

The applicant must submit documentary evidence of at least one year's experience in operating motorboats.

FIG. 234 A craft carrying passengers for hire must be operated by a person possessing a valid Coast Guard license for the number of passengers on board and the waters navigated.

FIG. 235 The circumstances which distinguish between a "guest" on board and a "passenger for hire" are quite complex, but have been established with reasonable clarity. All boat operators should study the situation with some care to avoid law violations.

SAILBAG Sailboat Racing Rules

Formal sailboat racing in the United States of America is organized under the auspices of the United States Yacht Racing Union whose headquarters are in Newport, Rhode Island. The racing rules have no legal force except in the adjudication of disputes that may arise between competitors on the course, but some knowledge of them may aid power boatmen and non-racing sailors who find themselves suddenly surrounded on the water by racing sailboats.

The starting sequence, signalled by hoists and gunfire from the Committee Boat, usually takes ten minutes per class. Unless the race is a distance race for cruising sailboats the course will either be triangular or windward-leeward. When racing, yachts show no colors but usually have a wind sock or similar fly at the masthead and may, if the sailing instructions issued by the race committee so specify, show an international code flag to aid the Committee in distinguishing the competitors from other yachts.

If possible the committee, working from their flag-bedecked committee boat, will arrange the course so that the first leg is a thrash to windward. The secrets to success on a windward leg are boat speed and clear air, so there will be a great deal more tacking by the racers than would be done by a relaxed cruiser sailing over the course, and the competitors, whether rightly or wrongly, will generally expect non-combatants to stay out of the way and avoid hampering them, not because

Examination

An examination is given which is based on subjects any person operating a passenger-carrying vessel should know. The content of the exam, and whether it will be oral or written, varies with the issuing office and the waters concerned.

Questions deal generally with regulations governing motorboats, Rules of the Road and Pilot Rules for local waters, fire protection, lifesaving equipment, safe operation of gasoline engines, methods of operating and navigating boats carrying passengers for hire, and elementary first-aid.

As the Rules of the Road and Pilot Rules differ in various parts of the country, the holder of a license has the duty to familiarize himself with the prevalent rules if he should shift his operations to other waters.

Licenses to operate motorboats carrying passengers for hire are not issued to persons under 18 years of age. The applicant must be able to read and write.

Physical fitness required

Applicants must be physically fit or a license will not be granted. Normally, they must be examined by a U.S. Public Health Service surgeon or a reputable physician. Bad hearing or eye-sight, color blindness, use of narcotics, insanity, or presence of certain diseases are grounds for rejection of the applicant.

License issuance and renewal

Licenses are issued and signed by Officers in Charge, Marine Inspection; see fig. 237. Every license or certificate of lost license, see below) must be signed by the person to whom it is issued, who also places his thumbprint on the back. It is valid for five years, after which it can be renewed. There is no fee. Motorboat Operator Licenses may have geographical limits based on the area of the individual's boating experience.

To renew the license, the individual must present it to an Officer in Charge, Marine Inspection, together with a

they have a legal right to such treatment but because it is polite.

Although it is not true that sailboats will necessarily be disqualified for running their engines in gear during a race, there is a natural reluctance on the part of a racing skipper to do this (running in neutral to charge batteries, is always permissible). If he moves under engine power during a race the skipper must justify it to the Race Committee after the race and he may be penalized. Don't expect a racing sailboat to get out of your way, even if his boat is bigger than yours and he is drifting squarely in your path, unless you are a competitor with rights or a commercial vessel with right of way. There is one exception. Where failure to do so would seriously hamper large vessels confined by their draft to narrow channels, the racing instructions undoubtedly encourage him to start his engine and get out of the way, securing his engine the moment he is clear and reporting the time of use and the circumstances to the Race Committee after the finish.

FIG. 237 To legally carry from one to six passengers for hire, a "Motorboat Operator's License" is required. To legally carry more than six passengers for hire, a skipper must have either an "Operator" or an "Ocean Operator" license. The form shown above is used to issue all of these licenses.

certificate of color vision, within one year after its expiration date. If more than a year has elapsed since the license expired, the person must take another examination. In most situations, a brief test on the Rules of the Road will be a part of the renewal process. Except under extraordinary circumstances, renewal cannot be made more than 90 days before the expiration date.

Re-examination

An applicant who fails his examination may come before the same Officer-in-Charge, Marine Inspection for another examination at a later date set by that officer, but not earlier than 10 days following the failure.

Lost licenses

In the case of loss of license, except where it has been revoked or suspended, a certificate can be obtained from an Officer in Charge, Marine Inspection, on presentation of satisfactory evidence of the loss. This certificate is then as valid as the license for the unexpired term.

Suspension or revocation

If any operator is found guilty of incompetence, misbehavior, negligence, endangering life, or willfully violating any safety law or regulation, his license may be suspended or revoked. If revoked or suspended, the license must be surrendered to the official before whom the hearing was held. If an appeal is made, the license must still be surrendered but a certificate will be issued covering the period during which the appeal is pending.

Licenses for More Than Six Passengers

Rules and regulations for small passenger vessels are prescribed in an Act of 10 May 1956, frequently called the "Ray Act." Under this Act, a "passenger-carrying vessel" means any vessel which carries *more than six passengers* and which falls into one of the below categories.

1. Propelled in whole or in part by steam or by any form of mechanical or electrical power and is of 15 gross tons or less.

2. Propelled in whole or in part by steam or any form of mechanical or electrical power and is of more than 15 but less than 100 gross tons and is not more than 65 feet (19.8 m) in length.

3. Propelled by sail and is of 700 gross tons or less.

A few exceptions are made, including: foreign vessels, vessels operating on non-navigable waters of the U.S., vessels laid up and out of commission, public vessels, and lifeboats.

Operator licenses

A person holding only a license under the 1971 Boat Act, as described above, is not authorized to operate passenger-carrying vessels under the Ray Act. A separate license issued under the terms of this Act is required and its scope varies according to the waters navigated. For offshore waters, an "Ocean Operator's License" is issued. Within the coastline and on the Great Lakes, it is an "Operator's License"; see fig. 237. In both cases, specific geographic limits are normally prescribed. Licenses are issued for a specified maximum gross tonnage, in multiples of 10, and are valid for five years.

Application is made to the nearest Officer in Charge, Marine Inspection. Physical fitness must be established and a written examination must be passed. Proof of appropriate experience is required.

Vessel Inspection

Vessels subject to the Ray Act must be inspected by an Officer in Charge, Marine Inspection, from whom applications for inspection may be obtained. These are among the vessels generally referred to in Coast Guard regulations and publications as "inspected vessels"; ordinary motorboats are categorized as "uninspected vessels."

Certificates of inspection are valid for three years. They describe the area in which the vessel may be operated, the maximum number of passengers that can be carried, the minimum crew required, minimum lifesaving and firefighting equipment to be carried, etc.

FIG. 238 A boat returning to the United States from foreign waters must report to the proper authorities at the first port touched. In some areas, a single Federal agency has been assigned to handle all forms and reports for all authorities concerned.

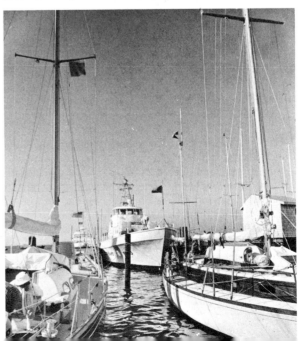

INTERNATIONAL VOYAGES

When an American boat crosses the national boundaries of the United States to visit a foreign port, or a foreign yacht visits an American port, certain customs, immigration, and other regulations must be obeyed. As a result of various provisions and exemptions applying to yachts, not engaged in trade, the procedure has been so simplified that there is nothing in these legal requirements to deter a recreational craft from enjoying a cruise outside the limits of U.S. waters. Severe penalties, however, are provided for failure to observe the applicable regulations.

Clearing and Entering

The terms "clearing" and "entering" are commonly used in connection with a vessel's voyage between ports of two nations. **Clearing** involves the obtaining of permission to sail by presenting the ship's papers to a customs official. **Entering** relates to arrival, when the owner or master "enters" his vessel by having his ship's papers accepted by customs authorities. Thus a U.S. vessel might be required to clear from an American port and enter on arrival at a foreign port. Then for the return passage, the vessel would clear from the foreign port and enter upon reaching an American harbor.

If desired, *bills of health* may be secured free of charge before leaving for a foreign port. This is not compulsory, but may make entry into the foreign port quicker and easier.

Report on arrival

There are four separate legal aspects to entering this country from a foreign nation, each involving its own government agency and officials. These are (1) **Customs,** relating to the bringing in of dutiable merchandise; (2) **Immigration,** relating to the eligibility for entry of persons; (3) **Public Health Service,** for the prevention of importation of human diseases; and (4) **Animal and Plant Quarantine,** for the prevention of entry of contaminated plants, fruits, and vegetables, or infected animals.

On arrival at a foreign port, the owner or captain of a yacht (any size) should report to the authorities mentioned above, or to such of them as exist for this port. The "Q" flag (plain yellow) should be flown where it can be easily seen—starboard spreader, radio antenna, fishing outrigger, etc.—to indicate that the vessel desires to be boarded by customs and other government authorities. When reporting, the crew and guests must remain aboard the boat until permission has been granted to land. Any additional or local regulations to be complied with, including details in connection with clearing from that port, will be supplied by the authorities.

Every vessel, whether documented or not, arriving in the United States from a foreign port or place must come into a *port of entry* and, within 24 hours, must report to the customhouse at that port. The crew and guests must remain aboard (one person may get off for the sole purpose of telephoning or otherwise notifying the authorities of the vessel's arrival), and no baggage or merchandise should be removed until the customs, immigration, and other officials have given their approval.

FIG. 239 Cruising with pets may introduce new problems into international voyages. Be sure to check the laws and regulations of all countries to be visited before departing from the United States. Investigate, too, any problems that may arise on your return to the U.S. from foreign shores with animals aboard.

All boats, regardless of size, must report to the immigration authorities on return to a United States port. Any alien passengers aboard must be reported and a heavy penalty may be imposed for failure to detain passengers and crew if ordered to do so by the authorities. A report giving names, nationalities, and other information concerning any paid crew aboard must be made on a crew manifest.

In many U.S. ports a "one-stop" service has been established whereby for the simple situations of a noncommercial craft from nearby foreign waters a single government official from one of the agencies will represent all of the authorities and bring all necessary forms to be filled in by the skipper.

Exemptions for non-commercial craft

Neither a licensed yacht nor an undocumented American pleasure vessel (not engaged in trade nor in any way violating the customs or navigation laws of the U.S.) is required to clear upon departure from the United States for a foreign port or place. Similarly a licensed yacht of any size or an undocumented American pleasure vessel (not engaged in trade nor in any way violating the customs or navigation laws of the U.S., and not having visited any other vessel "hovering" off the coast) is exempted from *formal* entry. These craft, however, *must* make a report to the proper authorities to cover such matters as the importation of items purchased while outside the United States.

At the Canadian border

U.S. yachts going into Canada may secure *cruising permits* with the right of free entry and clearance from 1 May to 1 October. These are issued without charge by the Canadian customs authorities at the Canadian port where the yacht first reports and must be surrenderd when leaving the country. Provided that the boat does not leave Canadian waters, she is then free to visit other Canadian ports until the permit is surrendered, though reports must be made at any port called where a custom officer is located.

Canadian boatmen with craft of less than 5 tons can enter the border waters of the United States for a day's outing without applying for admission at a U.S. port of entry. The Canadian Border Landing Card doesn't require advance application and is good for repeated 24-hour visits throughout the navigation season. It is good only for border waters; if the Canadian boatman wants to go farther into the U.S., he must apply at a port of entry and submit to inspection.

Arrival from coastwise cruises

There is a little-known law on the books that requires foreign vessels and documented vessels of the United States (but not numbered boats) navigating the "high seas" on coastwise cruises to give 24 hour's notice of their time of arrival to the Captain of the Port at their next intended port of call.

Bodies of water like Long Island Sound and Chesapeake Bay are excluded from the Act's definition of "high seas" but waters of the open sea below the low-water mark—as, for example, offshore along the Florida coast—are included.

This is basically a safety and security measure to control the entrance of commercial vessels into U.S. ports. For a time, the law was occasionally invoked against documented yachts, but now, however, these are specifically exempted in an amendment which excludes, among several types of vessels, "United States yachts, arriving at a U.S. port or place from a port or place outside the United States, or destined from one port or place in the United States to another port or place in the U.S."

Miscellaneous Provisions

Foreign yachts meeting certain requirements may receive from customs authorities in the United States a *cruising license* granting them special treatment while in United States waters.

Yacht "commission"

A documented yacht, belonging to a regularly organized and incorporated yacht club, may be issued a *commission*

to sail for pleasure on a foreign voyage. Application for this document may be made to any Collector of Customs in the United States. The commission serves mainly as an identification of the vessel and her owner. It must be surrendered upon return from the foreign country.

Additional information

A boatman who *leaves* this country with foreign-made articles—such as cameras made in Japan or Germany—will find their reintroduction into the United States facilitated if these are registered with the U.S. Customs officials *prior to departure*. Take such articles to a customs office at a port, airport, etc., and get a Form 4457 filled out and signed. Show this upon reporting in on your return and there will be no question of duty on such articles.

For further detailed information with regard to customs requirements, the boat owner should consult the nearest customs office. Likewise, for information regarding immigration, public health, etc., he should contact any convenient office of the applicable government agency. Information on the legal aspects of visiting a specific foreign country can best be obtained from that nation's consular offices in various major cities of the U.S. or its embassy in Washington, D.C.

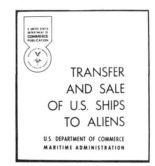

FIG. 240 There are legal restrictions on the sale of American vessels to foreigners. Some blanket exceptions have been made for smaller **numbered**, but **not** documented, boats. An owner should carefully check the laws and regulations before completing such a transaction.

Federal Water Pollution Law

The basic law covering water pollution is the "Federal Water Pollution Control Act" as amended and extended by the "Water Quality Improvement Act of 1970" which was in turn amended in 1972. These cover far more than discharges from vessels, but they form the basis for all implementing standards and regulations.

BASIC PROVISIONS

The newly-added section relates to all watercraft, large and small, commercial and recreational. The law does, however, permit enforcing authorities to distinguish among classes, types, and sizes of vessels (a boat is a vessel), as well as between new and existing vessels. There are provisions for waivers for groups of vessels, and for individual cases, where warranted, but it has been officially stated that very few waivers may be expected and only on the strongest justification for each situation.

Performance standards

The general approach of this federal legislation is the establishment of "standards of performance" for marine sanitation devices. These include all equipment on a vessel to "receive, retain, treat, or discharge sewage, and any process to treat such sewage." The term "sewage" is defined to mean human body wastes and the waste from

toilets and other receptacles intended to receive or retain human body wastes."

The law states that performance standards must be consistent with maritime safety standards and marine laws and regulations. It specifically notes that in the development of standards consideration must be given to "the economic costs involved" and "the available limits of technology."

Effective date

The Act initially became effective for all "new" boats, those whose construction started after 30 January 1979. Then on 30 January 1980 it became the law for all boats. There were several delays and modifications to the requirements, but "the day of reckoning" finally came!

Initial standards

Standards have been developed by the Environmental Protection Agency (EPA) in consultation with the Coast Guard and other agencies; members of the public, including boatmen, have opportunity to comment on proposals before they are issued in final form. Initial performance standards were issued in June 1972. These specified "no discharge"; thus requiring the use of holding tanks and shore pumpout facilities. There was, however an "escape clause" added to encourage the early installation of flow-through treatment devices which, while not as effective as desired, were better than no treatment at all. The installation of such discharge-type MSDs (provided they are certified as meeting the initial standard which is not too severe) was accepted for existing boats. On craft 65 feet or less in length such a device can continue in use indefinitely and even be replaced with a similar unit if that becomes necessary. On larger vessels such an MSD can be used only for the life of the device and must be replaced with a no-discharge unit or a discharge-type MSD that can meet higher standards.

Revised standards

The "initial" standards were replaced on 29 January 1976 with a set of "revised" standards. In general terms, these newer regulations eliminated the total "no discharge" concept for all waters, but at the same time considerably tightened up the allowable standards for the effluent from discharge-type devices.

The revised regulations divide waters into two categories: (1) freshwater lakes and reservoirs that have no inlet or outlet capable of navigation, and (2) other waters, including coastal waters and tributary rivers, the Great Lakes, and freshwater bodies accessible through locks.

Freshwater bodies in the first category above are still subject to "no discharge" rules by the 1977 (or 1980) dates for new (or existing) vessels. It should be noted, however, that craft equipped with a discharge-type MSD may be used on "no discharge" waters provided the device "has been secured so as to prevent discharge."

Type I marine sanitation devices are those that meet the initial standards—no more than 1000 fecal coliform per 100 ml of discharge and "no visible floating solids." A Type II device must conform to the revised higher standard—no more than 200 fecal coliform per 100 ml and no more than 150 mg per liter of "total suspended solids." (Manufacturers are having a greater difficulty in meeting the requirement for suspended solids than that for reduced coliform count.) All no-discharge MSDs are Type III; these include holding tanks and incinerator units.

On waters of the second category above, Type III no-discharge devices may, of course, be used. Originally it was planned that all discharge-type MSDs installed after 30 January 1980 would have to be models of Type II. Problems developed, however, in the design and manufacture of these higher-standard devices and it became necessary to issue a waiver. On 5 July 1978 the requirements were loosened to allow the installation of Type I MSDs, as well as units of Types II and III, on both new and existing small craft, boats of 65 feet or less length.

Enforcement

The law specifically authorizes Coast Guard and other enforcement personnel to board and inspect any vessel upon the navigable waters of the United States to check compliance with the provisions of this section.

The Coast Guard has stated as a general policy that its units will not board vessels solely to check for the absence of a legal MSD. They will, however, make such an inspection whenever a boat is boarded for any other reason. Thus if your craft is boarded for a minor safety violation—such as improper navigation lights or suspected

overloading—or as a routine procedure after receiving Coast Guard assistance, you can expect to be cited if you are not in compliance with the MSD requirements.

Penalties

The penalty for operation of a boat without an operable marine sanitation device of "certified" type is a civil penalty of not more than $2,000 for each violation. Note that this is an administrative type of penalty and one that does not require trial and conviction in court. No penalty will be assessed until the alleged violator has been given an opportunity for a hearing.

The penalty rises to $5,000 per violation for manufacturers and dealers in such devices and vessels.

PREEMPTION

A most important aspect of this federal anti-pollution law is "preemption." The Act provides that after the *effective* date of the initial standards and regulations "no state or political subdivision thereof shall adopt or enforce any statute or regulation with respect to the design, manufacture, installation, or use of any marine sanitation device on any vessel subject to the provisions of this Section."

Allowable State restrictions

The 1972 amendments added a provision that, after the effective date of the initial standards and regulations, a State may completely prohibit all sewage discharges, whether treated or not, but that such prohibition will not become effective until the EPA has determined that *adequate pumpout and treatment* facilities exist; this determination must be made within 90 days after a State's request. The prohibition may apply to all or any part of a State's waters.

There is a further clause that allows EPA to prohibit the discharge of any sewage, treated or not, if a State can establish that such action is necessary to preserve water quality. This is expected to be applied only to special situations such as swimming areas, drinking water intakes, shellfish beds, etc.

DISCHARGE OF OIL

Federal Regulations now provide that "no person may operate a vessel, except a foreign vessel or a vessel less than 26' in length, unless it has a placard at least 5" x 8", made of durable material, fixed in a conspicuous place in the machinery spaces, or at the bilge and ballast pump control station, stating the following:

> ### DISCHARGE OF OIL PROHIBITED
> The Federal Water Pollution Control Act prohibits the discharge of oil or oily waste into or upon the navigable waters and contiguous zone of the United States if such discharge causes a film or sheen upon, or discoloration of, the surface of the water, or causes a sludge or emulsion beneath the surface of the water. Violators are subject to a penalty of $5,000."

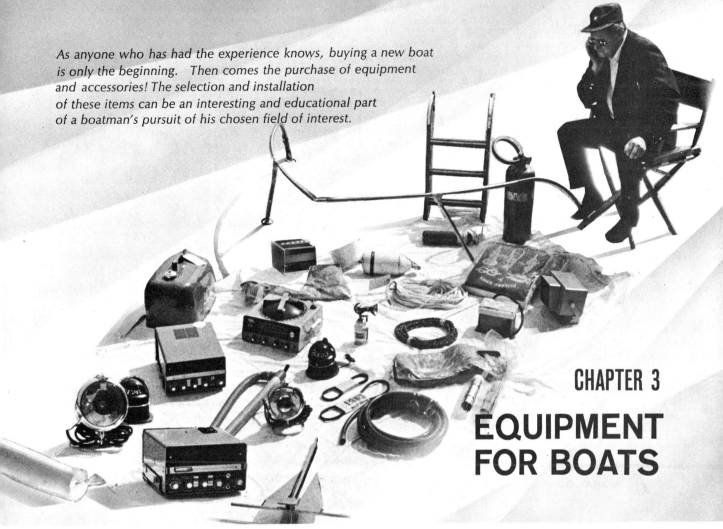

As anyone who has had the experience knows, buying a new boat is only the beginning.   Then comes the purchase of equipment and accessories! The selection and installation of these items can be an interesting and educational part of a boatman's pursuit of his chosen field of interest.

CHAPTER 3

EQUIPMENT FOR BOATS

FIG. 301 Many items of equipment are required for any boat. Some are needed to meet legal requirements, others for safety in basic operations, and still others for the general comfort and convenience of the crew and guests.

Categories of equipment

Equipment for a boat can be conveniently divided into three categories for separate consideration. These major groupings are—

1. **Equipment required by law—federal, state, or local.** This list is rather surprisingly limited. It has little flexibility; items are strictly specified and usually must be of an "approved" type.

2. **Additional equipment for safety and basic operations.** This list is less limited and greater flexibility is possible in the selection of individual items.

3. **Equipment for convenience and comfort.** Here the skipper can turn loose his imagination and be limited only by his financial resources.

Factors affecting selection

In all of the above categories, the items and quantities will vary with the size of the craft involved and the use that is made of her. The legally required items will be determined in most cases by the "class" of the boat as set by regulations issued under the Act of 1940; see page 615*. The equipment in the other categories will be governed by size generally, the waters boated upon, and the type of boating activities, together with other factors such as the amount of electrical power available on board, cost, etc.

*See page 33 for metric equivalents of the lengths of classes of boats.

Legally Required Equipment

The Federal Boat Safety Act of 1971 (FBSA/71) is· the basic source of authority for the requirement for various items of equipment aboard boats. The specific details are to be spelled out in regulations rather than appearing in the Act itself. The types of vessels subject to this Act are listed in Chapter 2, page 33.

Federal equipment regulations

Pending the issuance of regulations under the 1971 Act, the requirements of the regulations stemming from the Motorboat Act of 1940 remain in effect for such boats. These are a part of the Code of Federal Regulations, Title 46, Parts 24, 25, and 26. They also appear in a small pamphlet "Rules and Regulations for Undocumented Vessels" —Publication CG-258, see page 609. The new FBSA/71 regulations for recreational craft will appear in Title 33 of the Code of Federal Regulations.

Craft to be considered

It should be noted that the FBSA/71 will regulate the equipment of all "boats" *including sailboats without mechanical propulsion.* This is true even though the regulations temporarily retained from the MBA/40 are in terms of "motorboats."

The 1940 Act and its regulations will remain effective for commercial vessels such as fishing boats and diesel tugboats which are not subject to the 1971 law.

State Equipment Requirements

Although the Federal Boat Safety Act of 1971 provides for federal preemption over state controls regarding requirements for equipment on boats (and certain other aspects of boating safety), a blanket exemption has been granted which allows all State and local regulations in effect when the FBSA/71 became law to remain in force for the time being. When Federal requirements have been expanded beyond the regulations of the MBA/40, this exemption will be lifted and Federal rules will prevail.

The FBSA/71 allows States and political subdivisions thereof to have requirements for additional equipment beyond Federal requirements if needed to meet "uniquely hazardous conditions or circumstances" in a State or local area. The Federal government retains a veto over such additional State or local requirements.

Required Equipment as a Minimum

Skippers should regard the legal requirements as a minimum. If a particular boat is required to have two fire ex-

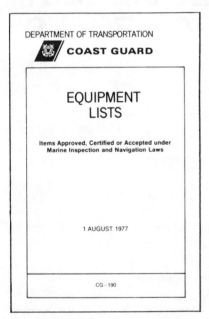

FIG. 302 Coast Guard publication CG-190 lists "Items Approved, Certified or Accepted under Marine Inspection and Navigation Laws" by category, acceptance number, manufacturer and model number. Over eighty categories of equipment are included. The pamphlet is free.

tinguishers, for example, its owner should carefully consider if this number will give adequate protection for *his* craft. Two may satisfy the authorities, but a third might be desirable, even necessary, to ensure that one is available at each location on board where it might be needed in a hurry. Two bilge vents may satisfy the regulations, but four would certainly give greater safety. Think "safety," not just compliance with the minimum in order to be "legal"!

Chocks

FIG. 303

Most modern cruising class sailboats are designed with high sides and light displacement. When anchored, the wind or current tends to make them charge around constantly chafing the anchor rode against the bow chock. When towing, a dinghy's painter also takes a lot of wear where it runs through a stern chock. Even if you wrap and tie canvas around the line at the point of chafe, a poorly designed chock—one with sharp edges and acute angles—can chafe the line through.

The bow chock to the left in Figure 303, has quite sharp edges. The stern chock, shown next to it, is well-shaped and smooth.

Non-approved items as excess

Some boatmen carry items of equipment no longer approved—older, superseded types, or items never approved, as "excess" equipment in addition to the legal minimum, or more, of approved items. This is not prohibited by regulations, but such action may give a false sense of protection and security. The danger of reaching for one of these sub-standard items in an emergency, rather than the proper item, must be recognized and positively guarded against. Some obsolete items of safety equipment, such as certain types of vaporizing-liquid fire extinguishers, see below, are actually hazardous on a boat and should not be on board even as "excess" equipment.

LIFESAVING EQUIPMENT

USCG regulations issued in 1973 under the authority of the Federal Boat Safety Act of 1971 require that *all* recreational boats subject to their jurisdiction, regardless of means of propulsion—motor, sails, or otherwise—must have on board an approved *personal flotation device (PFD)* for each person on board. (There are a few quite minor excep-

FIG. 305 The skipper of any craft must also know state and local laws that relate to his boating. These may differ in some details from Coast Guard regulations. Florida's Motorboat Law, for example, does not stop at 65 feet in length, and "FL" numbers may be seen on vessels quite large enough to be termed "ships."

FLORIDA MOTORBOAT LAW

FLORIDA BOARD OF CONSERVATION
Randolph Hodges, *Director*

tions such as racing shells, rowing sculls, and racing kay- aks; foreign boats temporarily in U.S. waters are also ex- empted.) "Persons on board" includes those in tow, such as water-skiers. The PFDs must be in serviceable condition and so stowed or located as to be readily available in an emergency.

More stringent requirements are placed on craft carry- ing passengers for hire (any number) than are applied to recreational boats.

TYPES OF PERSONAL FLOTATION DEVICES

Each approved personal flotation device manufactured under the regulations of 1973 must be marked with a PFD "Type" designation to indicate to the user the perform- ance level that the device is intended to provide. There are five PFD Type designations.

A *Type I PFD* is designed to turn an unconscious person from a face downward position in the water to a vertical or slightly backward position, and to have more than 20 pounds (9.07 kg) of buoyancy. A Type I PFD is, however, somewhat less "wearable" than other types of devices.

A *Type II PFD* is designed to turn an unconscious person in the same manner as a Type I, and to have at least 15½ pounds (7.03 kg) of buoyancy. A Type II device is more comfortable for wearing than a Type I PFD.

A *Type III PFD* is designed to keep a conscious person in a vertical or slightly backward position and to have at least 15½ pounds of buoyancy. Note that the Type III PFD has the same buoyancy as the Type II, but no turning re- quirement nor protection for a person who becomes un- conscious while in the water. These factors make it pos- sible to design a comfortable and wearable device for activities where it is especially desirable to wear a PFD because of the likelihood that the wearer will enter the water.

A *Type IV PFD* is designed to be thrown to a person in the water and to be grasped rather than worn; it must have at least 16½ pounds (7.48 kg) of buoyancy.

A *Type V PFD* is any approved device designed for a specific and restricted use.

APPROVED PERSONAL FLOTATION DEVICES

Coast Guard regulations recognize a number of different styles of personal flotation devices and contain specifica-

FIG. 307 **The Type III personal flotation device being worn by this skier is an approved model and may be counted toward the required number of PFDs, one for each person including the skier. Ski belts are not approved PFDs and cannot be counted.**

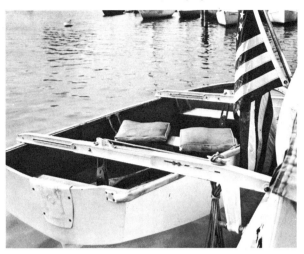

FIG. 306 **This Class 3 boat carries several buoyant cushions for use as lifesaving equipment in the dinghy. Such cushions, however, are not acceptable toward meeting the requirements for life pre- servers on a craft of this size.**

tions that must be met or exceeded if each is to be ap- proved. Each device must be marked with its approval number and all other information, such as limitations on its use, required by the specifications.

Life preservers—Type I PFDs consist of life preservers of various styles; see figs. 308 and 311. The flotation material of the jacket type will be pads of kapok or fibrous glass material; these are inserted in a cloth cover fitted with the necessary straps and ties. Kapok or fibrous glass *must* be encased in sealed plastic film covers; older life preservers without plastic inner containers are no longer acceptable. Old style cork and balsa wood life preservers manufactured as approved items before 1 July 1965 may still be accepted as initial or replacement equipment if they are in good and serviceable condition.

Life preservers of the "bib" type may be of cloth con- taining unicellular plastic foam sections of specified shape, or they may be of uncovered plastic foam material with a vinyl dip coating. The bib type must have a slit all the way down the front and have adjustable body straps.

Life preservers come in two sizes—*adult,* for persons 90 pounds (40.8 kg) or more in weight, and *child,* for individuals weighing less than 90 pounds—and are so marked in large letters.

Approved life preservers will also be marked with the type, manufacturer's name and address, and USCG ap- proval number, plus a date and place of individual inspection together with the inspector's initials. All USCG- approved life preservers are now required to be interna- tional orange in color.

Life preservers are distinguishable from other lifesaving gear by the words "Approved for Use on All Vessels and Motorboats" which appear near the other markings. (Life preservers manufactured before 1 July 1966 may not have this marking.)

Buoyant vests—Type II PFDs include *buoyant vests* which come in many styles and colors. They use the same flota- tion materials as life preservers and have the same require- ment for plastic inner cases, but vests are smaller and

FIG. 308 The most desirable type of lifesaving equipment for a boat is the "life preserver." It is produced in two styles, one of which is the "jacket" type shown above. Such devices are individually inspected at the factory by a representative of the Coast Guard.

FIG. 310 Ring buoys are classed as Type IV personal flotation devices under the 1973 regulations. Standard sizes of 20, 24, and 30 inch diameters will bear a USCG inspector's markings. The smaller 18½-inch rings are approved as "special purpose" devices and are marked accordingly. These are all acceptable as "throwable" PFDs.

Fig. 309 Buoyant vests are smaller and less expensive devices than life preservers, and provide less buoyancy. They may be of any color. Inflatable vests of any type are **not** acceptable for boats of any class or use.

provide less buoyancy, hence somewhat less safety for a person in the water. Their design must be such as to float the wearer in the same safe position as required for life preservers.

Buoyant vests are made in three sizes—one for adults and two for children, medium and small; weight ranges for children's sizes are marked on each vest. Each PFD must be of the proper size for its intended user.

Buoyant vests are marked with the model number, manufacturer's name and address, approval number, and other information. These water safety items are approved by lot and are *not* individually inspected and marked.

Special purpose devices—Personal flotation devices in this category may be either Type II or Type III if they are designed to be worn; they are Type IV if designed to be thrown.

The design of *special purpose water safety buoyant devices* is examined and approved by recognized laboratories, such as Underwriters Laboratories, see page 193; this approval is accepted by the Coast Guard. These devices are labeled with information as to the use for which intended, the size or weight category of the user, instructions as necessary for use and maintenance, and an approval number. Devices to be grasped rather than worn will also be marked "Warning: Do not Wear on Back."

Buoyant cushions—The most widely used style of Type IV PFD is the *buoyant cushion.* Although adequate buoyancy is provided, actually more than by a buoyant vest, the design of cushions does *not* provide safety for an exhausted or unconscious person.

This device consists of kapok, fibrous glass material, or unicellular plastic foam in a cover of fabric or coated cloth fitted with grab straps. Kapok or fibrous glass material pads must be encased in sealed plastic film covers.

Buoyant cushions are approved in various shapes and sizes, and may be of any color. Approval is indicated on a label on one side carrying generally the same information as for buoyant vests. Cushions are approved by lot number and are not individually inspected. All cushions manufactured since 1961 will carry the warning, "Do not wear on back."

Life rings—Another style of Type IV personal flotation device is the *life ring buoy* which may be of cork, balsa wood, or unicellular plastic foam. The ring is surrounded by a light grabline fastened at four points and used to obtain a better grasp of it; see fig. 310.

Standard sizes are 20, 24, and 30 inches in diameter. Life rings of 18½-inch diameter have been approved under the "special purpose water safety buoyant device" category and are authorized for use on boats of any size that are not carrying passengers for hire.*

Balsa wood or cork life ring buoys will be covered with cloth after the core material has been coated with a waterproof glue. These will be marked as Type IV personal flotation devices and with other data general similar to life preservers. They may be either orange or white in color.

Rings of plastic foam with special surface treatment will carry a small metal plate with approval information including the inspector's initials. Ring buoys of this style may be either international orange or white in color.

Some skippers paint the name of the craft on their ring buoys; this is not prohibited by the regulations.

Work vests—Buoyant *work vests* are classed as Type V personal flotation devices. These are items of safety equipment for crew members and workmen when employed over or near water under favorable conditions and properly supervised. Such PFDs are not normally approved for use on recreational boats, but may be so authorized in limited specific circumstances; when so authorized, they may be carried in lieu of other type devices.

*18½ in.=47.0 cm   20 in.=50.8 cm   24 in.=61.0 cm   30 in.=76.2 cm

PFD REQUIREMENTS BY BOAT SIZES

Recreational boats *less than 16 feet in length* (and canoes and kayaks of any length) must have on board at least one approved personal flotation device of Type I, II, III, or IV for each person on board.

Recreational boats *16 feet or more in length* (except canoes and kayaks) must have on board at least one approved personal flotation device of Type I, II, or III for each person on board. Note that *buoyant cushions are no longer acceptable* as the basic type of PFD for craft of this size.

Recreational boats *16 feet or more in length* must comply with the above paragraph and *in addition* must have on board at least one Type IV "throwable" PFD.

Size of PFD

Where the style of PFD that is carried comes in sizes, such as adult and children's life preservers, and the three sizes of buoyant vests, the PFD used to meet the requirements of the regulations must be of an "appropriate" size for the person for whom it is intended.

Stowage of PFDs

The regulations are very specific about the stowage of personal flotation devices. Any required Type I, II, or III PFD must be "readily accessible." Any Type IV PFD that is required to be on board must be "immediately available." These rules are strictly enforced.

The PFDs must also be "in serviceable condition."

Equivalents

Personal flotation devices manufactured before the 1973 regulations will not be marked as to PFD Type. The equivalents in older terminology which are acceptable to the regulations are as follows:

Type I—Life preserver
Type II—Buoyant vest or wearable special purpose water safety buoyant device.
Type III—Wearable special purpose water safety buoyant device.
Type IV—Buoyant cushion, life ring buoy, or throwable special purpose water safety buoyant device.

Cold weather areas

Boatmen who use colder northern waters should consider the purchase of a life raft to supplement other lifesaving gear and increase the chances of survival offshore. A raft with a canopy provides the best protection.

A life raft is not intended for use until an emergency occurs—but then it *must* work! It is of the utmost importance that life rafts be properly stored and protected, and that they be serviced periodically at an authorized facility.

PFD lights and reflective material

In order to better locate persons in the water at night, boats in commercial operation on certain waters must

FIG. 311 The "bib" style of life preserver of approved design is acceptable on all classes of motorboats used for any purpose. Certain older models without the slit down the front may no longer be counted toward the legal requirements.

FIG. 312 Buoyant cushions have been the most widely used personal flotation devices on smaller boats. It is expected, however, that these will be eliminated as primary lifesaving equipment, but will be allowed on larger craft as a "throwable" item in addition to the required "wearable" devices.

FIG. 313 Special purpose water safety buoyant devices are produced in a wide variety of designs, including sport vests, water skiing vests, hunters' jackets, and others. Check carefully for a USCG approval number before purchasing any such device for use on a boat.

FIG. 314 This buoyant cushion is not in "good and serviceable condition" as required by Coast Guard regulations. It will not be counted toward the legal minimum requirements. Items such as this generally cannot be repaired and must be replaced.

FIG. 316 Hand-portable fire extinguishers using a dry powdered chemical as the extinguishing agent are widely used on boats. Such units must have a pressure indicator to show their readiness for use. (Certain exceptions permit the continued use of some older models without pressure gauges.) Peter Smyth Photo

FIG. 317 Larger craft powered by inboard engines, particularly those using gasoline as a fuel, are often fitted with a built-in CO-2 fire extinguishing system. This is actuated automatically by temperature-rise detectors or it may be operated manually.

FIG. 318 Small outboard craft (not carrying passengers for hire) may or may not be required to have a fire extinguisher. Any one or more of the above construction features, see text for identification, will require one B-I fire extinguisher on board.

FIG. 319 The construction features identified above, see text for explanation of numbers, do **not**, in themselves, require that a fire extinguisher be carried—but one is still desirable for safety.

now carry personal flotation devices that are equipped with a light and retroreflective material on both front and back sides that will show up in the beam of a searchlight. Although such PFDs are not required for recreational boats, it's a good idea for increased safety!

FIRE EXTINGUISHERS

All hand-portable fire extinguishers and semiportable and fixed fire extinguishing systems must be of a type that has been approved by the Coast Guard. Such approvals are published in the pamphlet "Equipment Lists"—CG-190—with changes in the daily Federal Register.

All fire extinguishers and extinguishing systems approved for use on boats will have a metallic nameplate attached with information as to the manufacturer, type, and capacity. For those manufactured between 1962 and 1965, the nameplate must contain the wording "Marine Type USCG Type _____ Size _____"; those made since 1965 must have the above label plus "Approval No. 162.068/ _____." (See below for information on "type" and "size").

Kinds of extinguishers

Fire extinguishers for boats are described in terms of their contents, the actual extinguishing agent.

Dry Chemical—This type of extinguisher is widely used because of its convenience and relative low cost. These have an advantage over other types in that they may be quickly "recharged" by screwing another cylinder onto the discharge nozzle and valve assembly. Spare cylinders may be carried on board for increased safety.

The cylinder contains a dry chemical in powdered form together with a propellant gas under pressure. Coast Guard regulations now require that such extinguishers be equipped with a gauge or indicator to show that normal gas pressure exists within the extinguisher. (Some older models do not have indicators and must be checked by very careful weighing. Such extinguishers must have been manufactured before 1 June 1965 to be acceptable, but may continue to be carried if they are in good and serviceable condition.)

Carbon dioxide—Some boats carry portable carbon dioxide (CO_2) extinguishers; such units are advantageous as they are the only type to leave no messy residue to clean

up after use, and they cannot cause harm to the interior of engines as other types may do. This type may be used where a fixed system is installed in an engine compartment. Such a system may be operated either manually or automatically by heat-sensitive detectors.

Carbon dioxide extinguishers consist of a cylinder containing this gas under high pressure, a valve, and a properly designed discharge nozzle at the end of a short hose. The state of charge of a CO_2 extinguisher can only be checked by weighing the cylinder and comparing this figure with the one stamped on or near the valve. See page 210 for further details on the maintenance of CO_2 extinguishers.

Vapor systems—Other chemical vapors with a fire extinguishing action are available. Halon 1301 is a colorless, odorless gas that stops fire instantly by chemical action. It is heavier than air and sinks to lower parts of the bilge. Humans can tolerate a 7% concentration, more than enough to fight fire, for several minutes. It is used in built-in systems actuated manually or automatically; additional tanks can be carried to restore protection after use.

Foam—Fire extinguishers using chemical foam are legally acceptable on boats, but this type is rarely used as they leave a residue that is difficult to clean up after use and may require a partial engine disassembly.

Foam extinguishers are not pressurized before use and do not require tests for leakage. Such units contain water and must be protected from freezing. Foam extinguishers should be discharged and recharged annually.

Non-acceptable types—Vaporizing-liquid extinguishers, such as those containing carbontetrachloride and chlorobromomethane, are effective in fighting fires but produce highly toxic gases. They are *not* approved for use on motorboats and should NOT be carried as excess equipment because of their danger to the health or even life of a user in a confined space.

Classification of extinguishers

Fires are classified in three categories, A, B, and C, according to the general type of material being burned; see page 178. Fire extinguishers are similarly classified as to "type" and in addition are placed in size groups, I (the smallest) through V.*

The primary fire hazard on boats results from flammable liquids and so type "B" extinguishers are specified. (Some "B" extinguishers have adequate or limited effectiveness on other classes of fires; some should *not* be used on other types of fires, such as foam extinguishers on class "C" electrical fires.) Only the two smaller sizes, I and II, are hand portable, size III is a semi-portable fire extinguishing system, and sizes IV and V are too large for consideration here.

The type and size classifications for various extinguishing agents are shown in Table 3-1, page 64(a).

Requirements on Boats

Fire extinguisher requirements are prescribed in terms of the four "classes" of boats as established in the regulations which implemented the Motorboat Act of 1940.

Class A and 1 boats must have at least one type B-I hand portable fire extinguisher, except that boats of these classes propelled by outboard motors, not carrying passengers for hire *and* of such open construction that there can be no entrapment of explosive or flammable gases or vapors, need not carry an extinguisher.

A fire extinguisher is required on outboard boats under 26 feet in length if *one or more* of the following conditions exist, see fig. 318.

    1. Closed compartment under thwarts or seats in which portable fuel tanks may be stored.

    2. Double bottoms *not* sealed to the hull, or which are not *completely* filled with flotation material.

    3. Closed living spaces.

    4. Closed storage compartments in which combustible or flammable materials are stowed.

    5. Permanently installed fuel tanks. (To avoid being considered as "permanently installed", tanks must not be physically attached in such a manner that they cannot be lifted out with reasonable ease for filling off the boat; the size of the tank in gallons is *not* a specific criteria for determining whether it is a "portable" or a "permanently installed" tank.)

The following conditions do *not,* of themselves, require that fire extinguishers be carried, see fig. 319.

    1. Bait wells.

    2. Glove compartments.

    3. Buoyant flotation material.

    4. Open slatted flooring.

    5. Ice chests.

Class 2 boats must carry at least *two B-I* approved hand-portable fire extinguishers, *or* at least *one B-II* unit.

Class 3 craft must carry at least *three B-I* approved hand extinguishers, *or* at least *one B-II* unit *plus* one B-I unit.

Boats with fixed extinguisher systems in the engine compartment may have the above minimum requirement for their size reduced by one B-I unit. The fixed system must meet Coast Guard specifications.

Exemptions—Motorboats propelled by outboard motors, while engaged in a previously arranged and announced race (and such boats designed solely for racing, while engaged in operations incidental to preparing for racing) are exempted by Coast Guard regulations from any requirements to carry fire extinguishers.

Keeping Safe

Don't merely purchase and mount fire extinguishers, and then forget all about them. All types require some maintenance and checking; see page 210 for guidance in keeping up the level of fire protection you gain when first installing new extinguishers.

All members of your regular "crew," and to a lesser extent any guests that may be aboard, should know both the location and operation of all fire extinguishers.

BACKFIRE FLAME CONTROL

Every inboard gasoline engine installed in a motorboat must be equipped with an acceptable means of backfire flame control (with certain quite limited exceptions to be discussed below). Such a device is commonly called a

FIG. 320 With certain quite minor and technical exceptions, a gasoline engine used on a boat must be equipped with a "flame arrestor." This metal grid over the air intake to the carburetor prevents the exit of backfire flames into the engine compartment.

"flame arrestor" and must meet specific Coast Guard specifications to be approved. Accepted models will be listed by manufacturer's number in equipment lists or will have an approval number marked on the grid housing.

In use, flame arrestors must be secured to the air intake of the carburetor with an air-tight connection, have clean elements, and have no separation of the grids that would permit flames to pass through.

Exceptions

There are four categories of engine installations that are not required to have an approved flame arrestor, but these will actually include very few craft. The exempted situations are (1) Engines installed prior to 25 April 1940. (2) Installations made prior to 19 November 1952 which meet

*These USCG classifications B-I, B-II, etc., are not to be confused with Underwriters Laboratories classification 1-B, 2-B, 10-B, etc., which may also appear on extinguishers. The UL classification provides a better guide to extinguisher capacity, but they have not been written into USCG regulations as yet.

the lesser requirements then in effect and which are still in a good and serviceable condition. (3) Engines of a design inherently free from any backfire flames; each design must be tested and specifically approved by the Coast Guard. (4) Installations such that any backfire flames would be vented outside the vessel in such a manner as to not be dangerous to the craft; no formal inspection and specific approval is required.

VENTILATION REQUIREMENTS

All motorboats, except open boats, which use fuel having a flashpoint of 110°F. or less—gasoline but not diesel—must have at least two ventilation ducts for every engine and fuel tank compartment. These ducts must be fitted with cowls or the equivalent for the efficient removal of explosive or flammable vapors. Power exhaust blowers are desirable for all motorboats and are legally required in addition to natural ventilation on all craft built after 31 July 1980. See also pages 604–607.

OTHER REQUIRED EQUIPMENT

Additional items of equipment required by law or Coast Guard regulations to be on board a boat include a whistle, a bell, navigation lights, and, in some instances, one or more day shapes. As with other equipment, these devices are graduated with the size of the craft, and may vary with the waters on which they are used.

Since 24 December 1981, requirements for these items for craft on internal waters have been contained in the new Inland Rules of the Road. Requirements of the International Rules govern on waters outside demarcation lines (see page 31), or where there are no such lines, and the International Rules apply within bays, harbors, and inlets, and up connecting rivers.

Whistles

Boats on waters subject to the 1980 Inland Rules must carry a whistle meeting the technical specifications of Annex III if they are 12 meters (39.4 ft) in length or longer. The fundamental frequency must be between 250 and 525 Hz. The required range of audibility is ½ mile for boats 12 to 20 meters (39.4–65.7 ft) in length, and 1 mile for craft 20 to 75 meters (65.7–246.1 ft) long. Longer vessels must have whistles of lower-pitched tones, audible for greater distances.

Bells

Boats on inland waters must carry a bell meeting the technical characteristics of Annex III if they are 12

FIG. 322 If a bell is normally carried inside the bridge, cockpit, or cabin, there should be a second bracket for it mounted well out in the clear, usually forward. A bell is rung at anchor in fog for safety, not merely for compliance with the Rules of the Road!

meters (39.4 ft) or more in length. The Annex specifies that bells must be made of corrosion-resistant material and give a clear tone. For craft 12 to 20 meters (39.4–65.7 ft) long, the mouth of the bell must be at least 200 m (7.9 inches) in diameter; for larger vessels the minimum diameter is 300 mm (11.8 in).

Smaller craft

Boats less than 12 meters (39.4 ft) in length need not carry a whistle or bell meeting the technical requirements of Annex III; they need only have "some means of making an efficient sound signal."

Exemptions for Existing Boats

Boats the keel of which was laid, or which were at a corresponding stage of construction, before 24 December 1980, and which are equipped to the requirements of the Motor Boat Act of 1940, are exempted from the requirements of Annex III until 24 December 1990. This does not exempt such older boats from carrying the required equipment, only from the technical details. Newer boats must meet all requirements of Annex III.

International Rules Requirements

Boats having sound signalling equipment meeting the requirements of the International Rules of the Road are "legal" when on inland waters, but *not* vice versa. The

FIG. 321 The 1980 Rules of the Road do not specify whether a horn need be mouth, hand, or power operated. Boats under 12 meters (39.4 ft) in length need only have an "efficient means" of making a sound signal audible for at least ½ mile. Craft 12 to 20

meters (39.4–65.7 ft) long must have a sound producing device meeting specific technical specifications, but with the same minimum audible range.

FIG. 324 Some boats use liquified petroleum (LP) gas for cooking, and possibly for heating. Such installations are acceptable on recreational craft (strict safety precautions in installation and use must be observed), but these are prohibited on boats carrying passengers for hire.

FIG. 323 Navigation lights are part of the equipment requirements from the implementing regulations of the Motorboat Act. These are covered in Chapter 4 together with the lights for all types of vessels.

differences between the two sets of rules are quite minor. See Chapter 5 for details.

Visual distress signals

All boats of any type 16 feet or more in length, and all craft of any size carrying six or less passengers for hire, must be equipped with approved visual distress signals at all times when operated on coastal waters. Boats less than 16 feet in length must carry such signals when operating at night. There are a few limited exceptions.

Coastal waters are defined as the Great Lakes and the territorial seas (out to the "three-mile limit"), plus the bays and sounds that open directly onto such waters. Rivers are included only if the mouth is more than two miles in width, and then only upriver to the point where the width first narrows to less than two miles.

Visual distress signals are classified for day (D), or night (N) use, or for both (D/N). Acceptable types of devices include an orange flag with special square-and-disc markings in black (D); an S–O–S electric light (N); three orange smoke signals, hand-held or floating (D); or three red flares, hand-held, meteor, or parachute (D/N). Each signal must be legibly marked with a Coast Guard approval number or certification statement.* It must be serviceable and not past any expiration date. All distress signals must be stowed so as to be readily available.

Visual distress signals must not be displayed except

---

* Certain limited types of non-approved signals are acceptable until 1 July 1982.

where assistance is needed because of immediate or potential danger to the persons on board the boat.

Navigation Lights and Day Shapes

The 1980 Inland Rules of the Road contain the requirements for navigation lights and day shapes for boats; the Motor Boat Act of 1940 no longer applies. Details for boats, and for larger vessels, are in Chapter 4.

Motorboats are permitted to carry the lights prescribed for them by the International Rules of the Road while operating in inland waters, but *not* vice versa. The International lights for small craft will also be found in Chapter 4.

EQUIPMENT FOR COMMERCIAL OPERATION

Boats used for carrying six or fewer passengers for hire, or for commercial fishing, are subject to different requirements for lifesaving equipment than recreational craft. These "commercial uninspected vessels" are subject to the Motorboat Act of 1940 and Coast Guard regulations issued under the authority of that Act. Also covered by these regulations are sailing and non-self-propelled vessels carrying six or fewer passengers for hire.

All non-recreational craft less than 40 feet in length, *not* carrying passengers for hire, such as commercial fishing boats, must have on board at least one life preserver, buoyant vest, or special purpose water safety buoyant device of a suitable size for each person on board. "Suitable size" means that sufficient children's lifesaving devices (medium or small, as appropriate) must be carried in addition to adult sizes.

All vessels carrying passengers for hire (six or fewer), and all other vessels subject to the MBA/40 which are over 40 feet in length, must have at least one life preserver of a suitable size for each person on board.

Each vessel 26 or more feet in length must also carry at least one life ring buoy in addition to the life preservers or other wearable lifesaving devices required.

All lifesaving equipment must be in serviceable condition; wearable devices must be readily accessible and devices to be thrown must be immediately available.

Use of LP gas fuel

Vessels carrying passengers for hire are prohibited from using liquidified petroleum gases and certain other flammable liquids for cooking, heating, or lighting purposes.

FIG. 325 A sailboat without installed mechanical power and no detachable motor mounted need not be registered and numbered, but is subject to the various equipment requirements of the Federal Boat Safety Act of 1971 and its regulations.

FIG. 327 The Courtesy Marine Examination program of the Coast Guard Auxiliary lists equipment requirements over and above the legal minimums. These requirements are an excellent guide to all boat owners in equipping their craft for full safety.

FIG. 330 Small electric bilge pumps are found on most boats, but these should be backed-up with a hand-operated pump for emergency use. Larger craft may also be fitted with a high-capacity pump belt-driven from a main engine.

FIG. 328 Visual distress signals must be carried by all boats on coastal waters at night, and by craft 16 feet or more in length by day. Approved flares are acceptable for day and night use; orange smoke for day use only. Other acceptable signals include a distress flag and an S-O-S light.

FIG. 331 Coast Guard regulations do not require any lengths of line aboard a boat for use in docking, anchoring, etc., but these are essential for the operation of any craft. The number and length will vary with the size and use of the boat. Some state laws require an anchor and line of appropriate size and length.

More than six passengers

Motorboats carrying more than six passengers for hire are subject to a separate Act and set of Coast Guard regulations. These craft must be "inspected" and the certificate resulting from such action will specify minimum equipment such as lifesaving gear and fire extinguishers; see page 47.

EQUIPMENT FOR SAILBOATS

Sailboats, including those without any mechanical propulsion, are subject to the FBSA/71 and its regulations relating to equipment; they must also carry lights, fog horns, and bells to comply with the Rules of the Road.

SUMMARY

The federal equipment requirements for non-commercial motorboats are summarized, by class of boat, in Table 3-2, page 64(a).

Additional Equipment for Safety

In view of the May federal regulations for mandatory safety equipment on boats, any newcomer to this activity might be excused for thinking that he would be fully set to go if he ordered his new craft with "all equipment required by regulations." Actually, such is far from the real situation if one considers only the existing federal requirements. The problem may be ameliorated somewhat if state requirements are added in, but their lack of uniformity clouds the picture.

No quarrel can be made with the federal statutory and regulatory requirements; the sole problem is that

they stop too soon. Even the smallest rowboat requires at least one length of line with which to make fast to a pier or mooring or anchor; and a 40-footer will need some six to eight dock and anchor lines—yet none is required by Coast Guard regulations. Only the most foolhardy and ignorant would venture far from shore without an anchor—but again none is required by federal law or regulation.

Possible liability

Another factor that cannot be ignored in considering what equipment is truly needed is the possibility of liability in case of an accident. It is a mistake to think that the boating equipment specified by the government is the only equipment that you are *legally* bound to have aboard. The boatman must consider as well the far-reaching rules of negligence, as developed over the years in court cases. Technically, negligence is the unintentional breach of a legal duty to exercise a reasonable standard of care, thereby causing damage to someone. More simply stated, it is the failure to conduct oneself as a *reasonable* person would have under the circumstances. If, for example, a reasonable person would have carried charts, you may be liable to an injured party for an accident arising out of not having them available. If he would have had an anchor, compass, flares, lines, tools, and spare parts, etc., you may be held liable for not having them when needed. It is no defense to argue that no regulations require you to carry them.

Safety Harnesses

Although they are not required by any law or regulation, safety harnesses should be provided for every member of the crew of any boat which spends much time offshore. A few good commercial patterns are to be found, but many are clumsy, hard to adjust, uncomfortable to wear and to lie down in. The photographs above and below show a very simple design that consists of ½ inch nylon rope, formed by short splices to custom-fit the wearer, whose permanent property it becomes. The safety line of ⅜″ nylon has an eye splice at each end. One end is hitched through both loops, as shown above, right, and a stainless steel carabiner, of the sort used by mountaineers, is hitched to the other end. Do not trust your life to a snap of the pattern shown on the left in the picture below right.

ITEMS REQUIRED FOR USCGAUX DECAL

For a boat to receive the Auxiliary's Courtesy Motorboat Examination (CME) decal, it must, of course, first meet all of the legal requirements of the Coast Guard regulations derived from the 1971 Boat Safety Act. Also, some of the legal requirements are "beefed up" and made more stringent; additional items and conditions are imposed.

Personal flotation devices

An approved personal flotation device of the appropriate type is required for *each berth* on the boat; this may be more than the legal requirement of one PFD for each person on board at the time of a check. In addition, a boat with no bunks, or with only one, must still have a minimum of two lifesaving devices aboard.

Fire extinguishers

The Auxiliary standards for fire extinguishers on smaller boats are likewise more demanding than the law or regulations. Although a boat under 26 feet in length that is of "open construction," or one which has a built-in fire extinguisher system, need not carry an additional hand portable extinguisher to meet the legal minimum, it must have one for award of a CME decal.

FIG. 332 Despite the convenience and widespread use of modern electronic depth sounders, an old-fashioned hand-held lead line is often handy to have aboard, such as for checking depths all around the sides of a craft that has gone aground.

Additional fire extinguishers—The prudent skipper considers whether he will be adequately safe with only the minimum required number of fire extinguishers. An important safety factor is the ready availability of an extinguisher close at hand when a fire emergency suddenly bursts forth. An extinguisher should be considered for *each* of the following locations: (1) the helm, where there is always someone when underway; (2) the engine compartment; (3) the galley; and (4) adjacent to the skipper's bunk, for quick reach at night. On smaller craft, the legally required minimum, or even the USCG Aux requirements, may not be enough to provide one at all desirable locations.

Navigation lights

The law does not require that a boat operated only in the daylight have navigation lights, but these must be fitted and in good working order to meet the Auxiliary's standards for all craft 16 feet or more in length. Proper lights for use both underway and at anchor must be shown. The decal will not be awarded if lights are grossly misplaced even if they are operable.

Marine sanitation devices

The Courtesy Examination focuses on safety aspects of the boat. No check will be made for the presence or operating condition of an MSD, although the Examiner will be glad to provide information on legal requirements.

Anchor and line

An anchor of suitable type and weight together with line of appropriate size and length is required for the CME decal. This is a valuable safety item should the engine fail and the craft be in danger of drifting or being blown into hazardous waters.

Smaller craft requirements

All Class A boats must have an oar or paddle, a manual pump or bailer, and a whistle meeting the legal requirements for Class 1 boats.

Installation standards

In addition to requiring the above items of equipment, the CG Aux program has established standards for the installation of fuel systems, electrical systems, and galley stoves. Information on gasoline fuel systems and electrical systems will be found in pages 196-201.

FIG. 333 As determined by their normal use and area of operations, all craft should carry an emergency supply of drinking water, and possibly some emergency food supplies. These should be checked periodically and replaced if they show signs of deterioration.

FIG. 334 The set of tools and spare parts carried on board must be individually tailored to the craft, her equipment, her use, and the capabilities of her crew. An item for all boats is a spare bulb of each type used in the navigation lights.

The Auxiliary requires that a galley stove be of a marine type and be installed so as to present no hazard to the craft and its occupants. Any common fuel is acceptable except gasoline and derivatives or distillates of naphtha and benzene. LP gas stoves or heaters which use an integral fuel container or one which fastens directly to the appliance are not acceptable for award of the decal.

Equipment Recommended by the USCGAux

The CME checklist also contains a number of items recommended for the proper operation of a craft or for its safety, items beyond those required for award of the decal. The actual selections of items from this list will vary with the size and use of the particular boat involved.

This list of generally recommended items includes many that are required for "Facilities" and "Operational Facilities," the boats of members of the Auxiliary that have been brought to higher standards for use in their programs of search and rescue, regatta patrolling, etc.

Anchors

The carrying of a second anchor is recommended in addition to the one required to pass the CME check. This additional anchor may be a lighter one for non-emergency daytime use. Chapter 6 of this book in general, and page 99 in particular, provide guidance as to the selection of the proper size of anchor in several varying styles.

It is recommended that a length of chain be used between the anchor and the nylon line. Shackles used on either end of this chain should have their pins secured with safety wire.

Bilge pumps

One or more mechanical or electrical bilge pumps are recommended for all boats, and these should, of course, always be in good working order. Motorboats more than 26 feet in length should have at least two means of pumping bilges; and their bilges must be clean and free of any oil or grease; wood chips or any other debris that could clog pumps and limber holes must be removed.

Lines

Every boat should have mooring (dock) lines suitable in length and size to that particular craft. These should be of

FIG. 335 Windshield wipers, manually or electrically operated, are essential for the good vision of the helmsman despite rain or spray. When spray, especially that from salt water, is intermittent, fresh water washers (arrow) on the windshield help in keeping it clean.

several different lengths for convenience in use. No generalization can be made as to the lengths, but the diameter should roughly correspond to that of storm or working anchor rodes.

A heaving line of light construction is desirable if the craft is large enough to require the use of heavy mooring lines. The use of polypropylene line, or other material that is brightly colored and will float, is recommended for this purpose.

Life rings

A ring life buoy with a length of light line attached is recommended for rendering assistance to swimmers or accident victims in the water. This can also be used to float a heavier line across to a stranded boat. If of an approved type, this ring buoy may count as the required "throwable" PFD for all boats of Classes 1, 2, and 3. A water light (a device that automatically lights up in contact with the water) enhances the use of a ring buoy at night.

Operational equipment

Recommended operational equipment includes fenders in appropriate sizes and numbers for the craft involved. Not only will these be used in normal berthing, they are also necessary if two craft must make fast to each other while underway or at anchor. A boathook will be found very useful for fending off, placing lines over piles, picking up pennants of mooring buoys, recovering articles dropped over the side, and many other uses.

A searchlight—installed on larger craft, hand-held on smaller boats—serves both as a routine aid in night piloting and as an emergency signalling device. A multicell flashlight or electric lantern can serve these functions, but not so well as a searchlight.

Navigation publications and charts should be carried aboard boats in accordance with their use; see Chapters 17 and 18 for further details. Compasses are discussed in detail in Chapters 13 and 14; here we need merely to note that one is desirable on almost any boat for emergency if not regular use. Piloting and plotting instruments are covered in Chapter 19.

A hand-held lead line is a useful back-up to the more complicated electronic depth sounder; one is particularly handy when one must probe around a stranded boat in search of deeper water.

An emergency supply of drinking water—and perhaps food, too—should be carried on all craft. It may never be used, but when needed it can literally be a "lifesaver." Supplies of this nature should be periodically freshened or replaced to ensure acceptable quality when needed. Distilled water should be carried for periodic replenishment of any storage batteries on board; this can, of course, serve as an emergency source of drinking water.

A first aid kit is an essential item of safety equipment; see pages 211-214. The kit should be accompanied with a manual or separate book of instructions.

The list of tools and spare parts to be carried aboard must be developed by each skipper individually for his craft. The items will be governed by the type of boat, its normal use, and the capabilities of the crew to use them. An item required on USCGAux Facilities is one or more spare bulbs for the navigation lights. Items for all craft include simple tools, plugs, cloth, screws, nails, wire, tape, and other objects for the execution of emergency repairs at sea. Mechanical and electrical spares will be highly individualized by the particular boat and skipper.

Further Operational and Safety Items

A sea anchor or drogue, see pages 165-166, is an essential item of safety equipment for boats operating in many areas, but one is not legally required. As noted above, life rafts, preferably with a canopy, are much needed safety items in many waters.

Electric windshield wipers are excellent items of equipment when running into rainy or rough weather; safety is often much improved by their availability and use. The installation of washers that squirt fresh water on windshields will help greatly when spray, particularly of salt

FIG. 336 Electric-motor-driven blowers for bilge vents are now legally required on most new boats and are actually essential for safety on all boats, especially when starting up engines with no wind across the deck to provide natural ventilation.

Cowl Ventilators

FIG. 337 Cowl ventilators, mounted on "Dorade" boxes (named for the yacht on which they first appeared) allow air below but prevent water from reaching the cabin. They can be turned to face forward to let air in or aft to exhaust it. These are usually made of soft vinyl and are very durable. Handy places to stow winch handles or other gear temporarily.

water, is intermittently received over the bow.

Many electronic items that will add to operational safety are described in Chapter 25. These include radiotelephones, electronic depth sounders, radio direction finders (RDFs), and fuel vapor detectors for engine rooms and bliges of gasoline-powered craft. Alarm systems are available to alert the skipper of dangerous conditions of engine overheating, low oil pressure, or high water in the bilge. Electric bilge exhaust blowers will add to the safety of the required ventilation systems for all engine and fuel tank compartments. All of these are in the "desirable," or even "necessary," category. Less vital items are discussed in the next major subdivision of this chapter.

Pollution control equipment is rapidly moving from the operationally desirable to the necessary category. All skippers should be looking forward to their needs and problems in this area; see pages 49–50.

Cleaning gear may not be "glamorous," but it is certainly operational. Specific lists will vary from boat to boat, but all may be expected to contain a swab (mop), bucket, sponges, chamois, metal polish and rags, and similar items.

Sailboats

Sailboats without mechanical power, either installed or detachable, are now required to have personal flotation devices for each person on board; the type of PFD varies with the size of the boat. Such craft may be given a check under the Courtesy Marine Examination program. Sailboats longer than 16 feet, however, are eligible to become Auxiliary Facilities and must meet certain prescribed standards. These requirements can serve as a guide to all owners of sailing craft as to desirable safety equipment.

Sailing Facilities under 26 feet in length are required to have one B-I hand fire extinguisher and larger craft must have on board two such units. These sailboats must meet the CME standard of one approved lifesaving device on board for each berth, with a minimum of two such devices. Further, such craft must meet all standards for motorboats other than those relating to propulsion machinery, fuel systems, and ventilation of related compartments. This would leave in the requirements such items as an anchor with line, distress flare, galley stove installation and general electrical system—all matters appropriate to the safe operation of any sailboat.

Pumping the Bilge

Small boat sailors and power boatmen seldom encounter the sort of bilge pump that is best suited for a cruising sailboat. Pumps used in day sailers throw too small a stream and are too tiring to operate, as they are usually mounted vertically and require repeated flexing of upper arm muscles, and many power boatmen rely on the engine or battery to power the pump, relying on emergency manual pumps that are often no larger or more convenient than those found on day sailers.

There is an old saying that the most effective bilge pump is a frightened man with a bucket. Don't leave the bucket home, for there is much truth in the saying, but don't rely solely on the bucket, either. You should be prepared to keep yourself afloat indefinitely, without engine or batteries or incurring excessive fatigue from physical effort, with the boat leaking several gallons per minute. With the right pump this is easily accomplished with the pump going no more than five minutes in every hour. To do this hour after hour you need a pump that throws at least half a gallon per stroke and can be operated using the larger body muscles.

One excellent arrangement is a large diaphragm pump mounted on a floor timber below the cabin sole and operated by a rocking lever that stows nearby when not in use and engages the pump through a slotted plate in the sole. (The plate should have a cover or

things will fall through into the bilge.) The pumper can sit well-braced on the sole and use all his upper body muscles to take several hundred strokes in a few minutes.

A diaphragm pump can pass fairly large objects, so the intake screen at the bilge pump can be coarse—say a piece of 1″ copper pipe with the end closed over and a lot of ¼″ holes bored in the sides—and still be easily kept clear, provided the intake hose is flexible and accessible and the bilge and limber holes are kept clear. Limber chains help.

Pump until the intake sucks air, counting the strokes, and record the count in the log. In normal circumstances pump once a day at a regular time. When sailing watch-and-watch the Watch Captain should sound the bilge on each watch and record the results.

An automatic bilge pump should have an audible alarm or a bright indicator light where it will be seen. Tanks or hoses may spring leaks. Should this happen a running pump must be noticed promptly so that the cause can be determined and corrective action taken.

FIG. 341 A neat installation of a manual bilge pump under a cockpit seat, with a weatherproof cover. It is important that a manual pump be accessible from the cockpit by the helmsman, but this pattern is a tiring one to operate for long.

TABLE 3-1

Hand Portable types	Foam (minimum gallons)	Carbon Dioxide (minimum pounds)	Dry Chemical (minimum pounds)	Freon (minimum pounds)
B–I	1¼	4	2	2½
B–II	2½	15	10	(none)

TABLE 3-2

	Minimum Required Equipment			
EQUIPMENT	CLASS A (Less than 16 feet)	CLASS 1 (16 feet to less than 26 feet)	CLASS 2 (26 feet to less than 40 feet)	CLASS 3 (40 feet to not more than 65 feet)
PERSONAL FLOTATION DEVICES	One Type I, II, III, or IV for each person.	One Type I, II, or III for each person on board or being towed on water skiis, etc., plus one Type IV available to be thrown.		
FIRE EXTINGUISHER—PORTABLE When NO fixed fire extinguishing system is installed in machinery space(s).	At least One B-1 type approved hand portable fire extinguisher. (Not required on outboard motorboat less than 26 feet in length and not carrying passengers for hire if the construction of such motorboats will not permit the entrapment of explosive or flammable gases or vapors.)		At least Two B-1 type approved hand portable fire extinguishers; OR At least One B-II type approved hand portable fire extinguisher.	At least Three B-1 type approved hand portable fire extinguishers; OR At least One B-1 type Plus One B-II type approved hand portable fire extinguisher.
BACK-FIRE FLAME ARRESTER	One approved device on each carburetor of all gasoline engines installed after April 25, 1940, except outboard motors.			
VENTILATION	At least two ventilator ducts fitted with cowls or their equivalent for the purpose of properly and efficiently ventilating the bilges of every engine and fuel-tank compartment of boats constructed or decked over after April 25, 1940, using gasoline or other fuel having a flashpoint less than 110° F. Boats built after 31 July 1981 must have operable power blowers; see page 607			
WHISTLE	Boats up to 12 meters (39.4 ft) —any device capable of making an "efficient sound signal" audible ½ mile.	Boats up to 12 meters (39.4 ft) —any device capable of making an "efficient sound signal" audible ½ mile.	Boats up to 12 meters (39.4 ft) —any device capable of making an "efficient sound signal" audible ½ mile.	Boats 12 to 20 meters (39.4-65.7 ft)—device meeting technical specifications of Inland Rules Annex III audible ½ mile.
BELL	Boats up to 12 meters (39.4 ft) —any device capable of making an "efficient sound signal."	Boats up to 12 meters (39.4 ft) —any device capable of making an "efficient sound signal."	Boats up to 12 meters (39.4 ft) —any device capable of making an "efficient sound signal."	Boats 12 to 20 meters (39.4-65.7 ft)—bell meeting technical specifications of Inland Rules Annex III; mouth diameter of at least 200 m (7.9 inches).
When fixed fire extinguishing system is installed in machinery space(s).	None.	None.	At least One B-1 type approved hand portable fire extinguisher.	At least Two B-1 type approved hand portable fire extinguishers; OR At least One B-II type approved hand portable fire extinguisher.
	Note: Dry Chemical and Carbon Dioxide (CO₂) are the most widely used types, in that order. The others, while acceptable, are seldom seen on boats.			
	Fire extinguishers manufactured after 1 January 1965 will be marked, "Marine Type ____ Size ____ Approval No. 162.028/EX . . ." **			

* NOTE.—Not required by the Motorboat Act of 1940; however, the "Rules of the Road" require these vessels to sound proper signals.
** NOTE.—Toxic vaporizing-liquid type fire extinguishers, such as those containing carbon tetrachloride or chlorobromomethane, are not accepted as required approved extinguishers on uninspected vessels (private pleasure craft).

See page 33 for metric equivalents of the lengths of classes of boats.

RULES OF THE ROAD

Lights and Day Shapes

FIG. 401 The navigation lights shown by a vessel at night identify her as a water craft and give some indication of her type, size, and relative heading. (left) Lights are also used at night to indicate the status of a vessel. The single white light shown above signifies to another vessel that the boat is at anchor. This is often called a "riding light" to distinguish it from a "running light."

Nautical Rules of the Road are somewhat broader than their land counterparts. On the water, such sets of rules include not only the expected "keep to the right" and "the vessel to your right has the right-of-way" provisions, but they also cover many other matters related to safety of operations, principally through the avoidance of collisions.

The 1972 International Rules

The **International Regulations for Preventing Collisions at Sea, 1972,** were adopted at a conference in London on October 20th of that year, following four years of study and discussion by representatives of 46 nations and numerous non-governmental bodies. These are commonly termed the "International Rules of the Road" by mariners and boatmen, and the "72 COLREGS" by the Coast Guard. Following ratification by the necessary number of countries, they became effective in most U.S. coastal waters for all vessels, and for U.S. vessels in all international waters, on 15 July 1977.

The 1980 U.S. Inland Rules

The 1972 International Rules were unique for the U.S., since for the first time such rules had the status of an international *treaty*; previous sets of International Rules had the status of an international *agreement*. A treaty is more binding on a country, offering less flexibility and requiring stricter compliance with its terms. A key provision of the 1972 International Rules was the requirement in Rule 1(b) that national rules for internal waters "shall conform as closely as possible" to the International Rules. The first result of this requirement was that the U.S. Inland Rules no longer applied out to the offshore "boundary lines," but were effective only behind new "demarcation lines" that did not venture into offshore waters. The longer term effect of the 1972 International Rules was the passage by Congress of the **Inland Navigational Rules Act of 1980,** the long-desired unification of the Inland, Great Lakes, and Western Rivers Rules and their respective Pilot Rules. These became effective on all U.S. waters, except the Great Lakes, on 24 December 1981, and on the Great Lakes a few months later, following coordination with Canada.

Sequence of Consideration

The International Rules of the Road now apply to all vessels once they clear the jetties or headlands at a harbor entrance; indeed, the rules even intrude into harbors, bay, inlets, etc., in some areas, such as along the upper Maine Coast, and the lower Florida Keys. (More on the demarcation lines that separate what the Coast Guard calls "COLREGS Waters" from "Inland Rules Waters" will be found on page 31.) The majority of recreational boatmen, however, use their craft on

FIG. 402 A single set of navigational rules now governs craft and ships of all sizes on most inland waters, including the Great Lakes and the Western Rivers.

waters of rivers, lakes, bays, and sounds that are governed by the U.S. Inland Navigational Rules, and for this reason primary consideration will be given to these rules, with the International Rules being presented in terms of their differences with the Inland Rules. *Note carefully:* the term "Inland Rules" used in Chapters 4 and 5 refers to the 1980 U.S. rules, effective on and after 24 December 1981 (except later on the Great Lakes), *not* to the Inland Rules that previously existed along with the now-repealed Great Lakes and Western Rivers Rules; the similarity of terms is regrettable, but that's the way the Act of Congress was written.

The consideration of the rules of the road in this chapter and Chapter 5 is not complete; it focuses primarily on points of greatest concern to boatmen.

Numbered "Rules"

Both the U.S. Inland Rules and the International Rules consist of major subdivisions: Part A—General, Part B—Steering and Sailing Rules, Part C—Lights and Shapes, Part D—Sound and Light Signals, and Part E—Exemptions. (Part E provides specific temporary and permanent exemptions for existing vessels to permit a smooth transition from the previous requirements for lights and sound signals.)

Within both sets, the Rules are numbered from 1 to 38, with subparagraphs such as (a), (b), (c), etc., and still lower levels indicated as (i), (ii), (iii), etc. The same numbers are used in both sets for Rules that are identical, or nearly so; the Inland Rules omit a rule 28, which is on a topic not desired for inclusion, in order that the parallel numbering can be carried on in the following Rules.

Indication of references

Numbers and letters shown in brackets are references to the applicable Rule. References to Annexes are indicated by a Roman numeral, since the annexes to both sets are so designated; specific paragraphs and subparagraphs are noted by numbers and letters as appropriate. References are shown to facilitate looking up the exact language of the Rules and Annexes in Coast Guard publication CG-169, or in other sources.

WHY NAVIGATION LIGHTS AND DAY SHAPES

On a vessel, navigation lights are lights shown that are of specified color (white, red, green, yellow, blue), arc and range of visibility, and location, as required by law and regulations. Their basic purpose is the prevention of collision by alerting each vessel to the other's presence, and providing identification that gives some information about current activities. Lights indicate the relative heading of one vessel as seen from the other, and may give some clues as to her size, special characteristics, and/or current operations. Most important is her orientation with respect to your craft—a fact that must be known to determine who has the right-of-way.

Navigation lights are sometimes referred to as *running lights* (those shown under way) and *riding lights* (those shown while at anchor or moored), but this terminology is unofficial and does not appear in the Rules of the Road.

Day shapes are objects of specified shape, size, and placement on a vessel, as required by rules and regulations; all are black in color. They serve some of the same purposes by day that navigation lights do by night. In normal visibility situations, no day shapes are required, the relative aspect and motions of two vessels can be determined by observation. However, day shapes are used to indicate special situations, such as being anchored or engaged in fishing, and some conditions not detectable by eye, such as a sailboat with her sails up but with her engine also in use (as will be noted in Chapter 5, such a craft is regarded as a power-driven vessel and is not entitled to any of the right-of-way privileges of sailing craft merely because her sails are up).

FIG. 403 During the day, when lights would be ineffective, "day shapes" are used to indicate the special status of vessels. Other information provided at night by lights—type, size, and relative heading—can be determined by direct observation in daylight.

Importance of knowledge

Knowledge of navigation lights is important to a small-craft skipper for two separate, but both important, reasons. First, he is legally responsible that his craft is displaying lights of the proper color, intensity, location, and visibility. Unfortunately, he cannot assume that the manufacturer of his boat has installed proper and adequate lights; he must know the requirements of the applicable rules of the road and check that his craft fully complies; if it doesn't, it is he, not the boat builder, who will be cited by the Coast Guard and possibly fined. He must also know which lights to turn on (and which not to turn on) and when.

Second, and perhaps even more important, he will have to depend on his knowledge of navigation lights for the safety of his boat when operating at night. Quite often, all of the information available as to the presence, size, type, relative course, and any special status of another vessel, is obtained from an interpretation of her navigation lights. There are many lights and possible combinations; often a quick decision is needed, with no time to go "look it up in the book." *Know* the lights shown on both boats and ships. Even in the daytime with good visibility, the carrying of one or more day shapes by another vessel will give you information as to her activities or limitations that could not possibly be determined from simple observation. *Know* day shapes as well as lights.

The Inland Rules

The **U.S. Inland Navigational Rules** are applicable inside *demarcation* lines, where such lines have been established at entrances to bays, sounds, rivers, inlets, etc. They are not applicable to all waters of harbors that have been specifically designated, such as along coasts with many small harbors (New England Coast especially), and in the harbors of off-shore land masses, such as Block Island and Catalina Island. The demarcation lines are delineated in Coast Guard regulations published in CG-169 (formerly in CG-169-1, now discontinued) and on charts of the area.

Only those Rules and Annexes* applicable to navigation lights and day shapes will be covered in this chapter; the balance of the Inland Rules will be discussed in Chapter 5.

FIG. 404 The term "vessel" in the Inland Navigation Rules is all-inclusive, covering the smallest boat to the largest ship.

* The material in this chapter on the Annexes was prepared from drafts before the final promulgation; differences may exist.

FIG. 405 A sailboat is *not* a "sailing vessel" if she is using any mechanical power for propulsion even if her sails are hoisted.

General

The Inland Rules are applicable to all vessels, regardless of nationality, on the inland waters of the United States, as described above. They are also applicable to U.S. vessels on the Canadian waters of the Great Lakes, to the extent that they are not in conflict with Canadian laws or regulations. [1(a)]

Basic definitions

Rule 3 contains general definitions that are used throughout the U.S. Inland Rules.

Vessel—every description of water craft, including nondisplacement craft (air-cushion vehicles) and seaplanes, used or capable of being used as a means of transportation on water. The term "vessel" includes all sizes without limit, from your dinghy to a supertanker.

Power-driven vessel—any vessel propelled by machinery.

Sailing vessel—any vessel under sail, provided that propelling machinery, if fitted, is *not* then being used. A sailboat or motor sailer using both sail and engine simultaneously is a *power-driven* vessel for purposes of the rules of the road.

Underway—a vessel not at anchor, made fast to the shore, or aground. This term applies whether or not the vessel is moving ("making way") through the water.

Vessel engaged in fishing—any vessel fishing with nets, lines, trawls, or other fishing apparatus that restricts maneuverability. It does *not* include vessels with trolling lines, or drift fishing with hand rods and lines.

Vessel not under command—a vessel which through some exceptional circumstances is unable to maneuver as required by the Rules, and therefore is unable to keep out of the way of another vessel. Typically, this category would apply to a boat drifting with an inoperative engine or steering system.

Vessel restricted in her ability to maneuver—a vessel which from the nature of her work is restricted in her ability to maneuver as required by the Rules, and therefore is unable to keep out of the way of another vessel. Typically, this term is applied to dredges, vessels engaged in laying or repairing submarine cables or pipelines, and vessels engaged in a towing operation that severely restricts the towing vessel and her tow in their ability to deviate from their course.

Visibility—vessels are deemed to be "in sight of one another" only when one can be observed from the other.

Restricted visibility—any condition in which visibility is reduced by fog, mist, falling snow, heavy rain, sandstorms, or any other similar cause.

Rule 3 also contains other technical definitions of lesser interest to boatmen. The term "Secretary" means the Secretary of the Department of the Federal Government in which the Coast Guard is operating. This is normally the Department of Transportation, but in times of war or national emergency it could become the Department of the Navy, by Presidential Executive Order.

FIG. 406 The 1980 Inland Rules are basically the same for all U.S. waters, but they do contain a few special provisions for the Western Rivers and Great Lakes.

Although separate sets of rules of the road for the Great Lakes and the Western Rivers no longer exist, these terms are still defined in the 1980 Inland Rules, because of certain exceptions and special provisions for specified waters. The "Great Lakes" are defined as the lakes and their connecting and tributary waters, including the Calumet River as far as the Thomas J. O'Brien Lock and Controlling Works (between mile 326 and 327), the Chicago River as far as the east side of the Ashland Avenue Bridge (between mile 321 and 322), and the St. Lawrence River as far east as the lower exit of the St. Lambert Lock. (These are essentially the same waters as defined in the former Great Lakes Rules, but the limits are stated differently and more explicitly.) "Western Rivers" means the Mississippi River, its tributaries, South Pass, and Southwest Pass to the demarcation lines for COLREGS waters; the Port Allen-Morgan City Alternate Route; and that part of the Atchafalaya River above its junction with the Port Allen-Morgan City Alternate Route, including the Old River and the Red River. [3(l)] (This, too, is a revision of the former Western Rivers Rules: coverage is now extended down the Mississippi River below New Orleans to demarcation lines in the vicinity of its mouth.) It should be noted carefully that the term "Western Rivers" does not apply to rivers on the West Coast of the United States—such rivers as the Sacramento or the Columbia; the Inland Rules are in effect for all rivers emptying into the Pacific Ocean.

Units of measurement

Except for distances in nautical miles, linear units of measurement in the 1980 U.S. Inland Rules are in the metric system. Lengths of vessels, spacing and height of lights, etc., in this Chapter and Chapter 5, will be in meters, with the corresponding length or distance in customary (English) units following in parentheses.

NAVIGATION LIGHTS

Navigation lights will be discussed for various categories and sizes of vessels in the sub-sections below; they are also summarized in Table 4-1 of this chapter.

When lights and shapes are shown

Vessels are required to show the proper navigation lights from *sunset* to *sunrise* in all weather conditions, good and bad. During these times, no other lights that could be mistaken for lights specified in the rules can be displayed, nor any lights that impair the visibility or distinctive character of navigation lights, or interfere with the keeping of a proper lookout. [20(a) and (b)]

The Inland Rules also state that navigation lights *must* be shown from sunrise to sunset in conditions of reduced visibility, and *may* be shown at any other time considered necessary. [20(c)]

Day shapes specified in the rules must be displayed by day; although not specifically so stated, it would appear that this means from sunrise to sunset. [20(d)]

Definitions

A **masthead light** is a white light placed over the fore-and-aft centerline of the vessel, showing an unbroken light over an arc of 225°, from dead ahead to 22.5° abaft the beam on both sides of the vessel. On craft less than 12 meters (39.4 ft) in length, the masthead light may be off the fore-and-aft centerline, but must be as near thereto as practicable. [21(a)]

As will be seen later, the term "masthead light" is something of a misnomer. More often than not, this light is *not at the top* of a mast. In the case of motorboats, it is often on a short fixture on the top of the cabin; on sailboats, it is usually part of the way up the mast; another light, the anchor light, is actually at the masthead.

Sidelights are colored lights—red on port and green on starboard—showing over an unbroken arc of the horizon of 112.5°, from dead ahead to 22.5° abaft the beam on each side. On a vessel of less than 20 meters (65.7 ft) length, the sidelights may be combined in a single fixture carried on the centerline of the vessel, except that on craft less than 12 meters (39.4 ft) in length, this *combination light* need be carried only as close to the centerline as practicable. [21(b)] Note that the sum of the arcs of the two side-lights is exactly the same as that for the white masthead light.

A **sternlight** is a white light showing over an unbroken arc of the horizon of 135°, centered on dead astern. [21(c)]

A **towing light** is a yellow light having the same arc as a sternlight, showing 67.5° to either side of dead astern. [21(d)]

Numbers and letters shown in brackets are references to the applicable Rule.

An **all-round light** is a light, the color determined by its use, showing over an unbroken arc of the horizon of 360°. [21(e)]

A **flashing light** is a light flashing at regular intervals, at a rate of 120 or more flashes per minute. [21(g)] This high flashing rate is used to lessen any possibility of confusion with "quick flashing lights" on aids to navigation; see page 306.

A **special flashing light** is a yellow light flashing at a rate of 50 to 70 flashes per minute, placed as far forward and as nearly a practicable on the centerline of the tow, and showing an unbroken light over a horizontal arc of not less than 180° nor more than 225° centered on dead ahead. [21(g)]

Lights for Power-driven Vessels Underway

The basic navigation lights for a power-driven vessel underway are one or two masthead lights, a pair of sidelights, and a sternlight. [23(a)]

Forward lights

The forward "masthead" light need not actually be at the masthead, but must meet placement requirements given in Annex I. On a vessel 20 meters (65.7 ft) or more in length, it must be not less than 5 meters (16.4 ft) above the hull, except that if the breadth (beam) of the vessel is greater than 5 meters, then the height must be not less than the breadth, but need not in any case be greater than 8 meters (26.2 ft). [I, 84.03(a) (i)] The term "height above the hull" is defined in Annex I, 84.01(a). The forward masthead light must be in the forward half of the vessel, except that in craft of less than 20 meters (65.7 ft) length, it need only be as far forward as practicable. [23(a) (i)] When two masthead lights are carried, the horizontal distance between them must be at least one-fourth of the length of the vessel, except that this distance need not in any case exceed 50 meters (164.1 ft). [I, 84.05(a)]

A second masthead light is required on vessels 50 meters (164.1 ft) or more in length, and may be carried on vessels of lesser length [23(a) (ii)]. This light must be at least 2 meters (6.5 ft) higher than the forward light. [I, 84.03(a)(2)]

The masthead light of a vessel 12 meters (39.4 ft) or more, but less than 20 meters (65.7 ft) in length, must be at least 2.5 meters (8.2 ft) above the gunwale. [I, 84.03(c)] On craft less than 12 meters (39.4 ft) long, the masthead light need only be at least 1 meter (3.3 ft) higher than the sidelights; it must be screened if necessary to prevent interference with the helmsman's vision. [I, 84.03(d)]

Masthead lights must have a range of visibility as follows: Vessels over 50 meters (164.1 ft) in length—6 miles; vessels of 12 to 50 meters length (39.4–164.1 ft)—5 miles, except 3 miles for vessels less than 20 meters (65.4 ft) in length; and craft less than 12 meters (39.4 ft) long—2 miles. [22]

In all cases, masthead lights must be placed so as to be clear of all other lights or obstructions. [I, 84.03(f)]

Value of range lights. When two masthead lights are carried they form a *range*, a valuable aid in determining the relative heading of another vessel when she is first

FIG. 407 The after masthead light, which forms a range with the forward light, is mandatory for vessels 50 meters (164.1 ft) or more in length, and is optional for smaller vessels. Both lights cover an arc of 225°. The required stern light is not visible in this view.

sighted at night. Since these white lights are both brighter and higher than the sidelights, they will normally be seen well before the colored light or lights can be detected and read for their meaning.

The relative location of the two range lights will be the key. Should they be seen one directly over the other, the other vessel is headed *directly toward* you and danger of collison may exist. Should the lower (forward) range light be seen to the right or left of the higher (aft) white light, the other vessel is on an oblique course and the angle can be roughly gauged by the horizontal separation between the lights.

Sidelights

Sidelights on a vessel of any length must be at a height above the hull at least 1 meter (3.3 ft) less than the (forward) masthead light. [I, 84.03(g)] On vessels of 20 meters (65.4 ft) or more in length, the sidelights must not be forward of the forward masthead light; they must be placed at or near the sides of the vessel. [I, 84.05(b)] On such vessels, the sidelights must be provided with black inboard screens to make the necessary cut-off of light at the ahead limit of each arc of visibility. Sidelights on smaller craft also must have these screens if needed to meet the cut-off requirements and to prevent excessive light spillover from sidelights. A combination light using a single *vertical filament* bulb and a very narrow division between sectors need not have a screen.

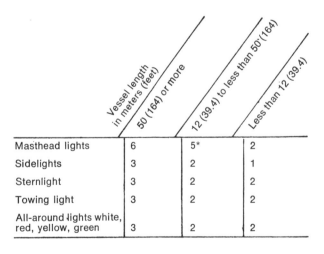

	Vessel length in meters (feet) 50 (164) or more	12 (39.4) to less than 50 (164)	Less than 12 (39.4)
Masthead lights	6	5*	2
Sidelights	3	2	1
Sternlight	3	2	2
Towing light	3	2	2
All-around lights white, red, yellow, green	3	2	2

TABLE 4-1 Required distance of visibility (in nautical miles) for navigation lights of vessels of various sizes under the 1980 Inland Rules of the Road. *3 miles for craft under 20 meters (65.7 ft).

Numbers and letters shown in brackets are references to the applicable Rule.

Sidelights must have a range of visibility as follows: Vessels over 50 meters (164.1 ft) in length— 3 miles; vessels of 12 to 50 meters (39.4–164.1 ft) length—2 miles; and craft less than 12 meters (39.4 ft) long—1 mile. [22]

Sternlights

The required range of visibility of a stern light is as follows: Vessels over 50 meters (164.1 ft) in length—3 miles; and vessels of lesser length—2 miles. [22]

The Rules and Annex I do not specify a vertical or horizontal placement for a sternlight, except that it be as nearly as practicable "at the stern."

Exceptions. A power-driven vessel of less than 12 meters (39.4 ft) length may carry, in place of the masthead light and sternlight described above, a white all-round light, visible at 2 miles; sidelights, visible at 1 mile, would continue to be shown. [23(c)]

A power-driven vessel operating on the Great Lakes *may* show an all-round white light in place of the normal after-masthead light and sternlight. This must be carried in the same position and have the same visibility range as a second masthead light. [23(d)]

An air-cushion vehicle, when operating in the non-displacement mode ("flying"), must show the normal navigation lights for a vessel of her length, plus an all-round flashing yellow light where it can best be seen. [23(b)] There are no special lights for hydrofoil craft.

Lights for Sailing Vessels Underway

A sailing vessel underway—remember that if any propelling machinery is in use she is *not* a sailing vessel— will carry the same sidelights and sternlight as a power-driven vessel of the same length, but will *not* carry a forward white masthead light. [25(a)]

A sailing vessel *may* additionally carry at or near the masthead two all-round lights in a vertical line, with the same visibility range as sternlight, the upper being red and the lower green. [25(c)]

Sailboats under 20 meters

If a sailboat is less than 20 meters (65.7 ft) in length, the sidelights and sternlight may be combined into a single fixture at or near the top of the mast where it can best be seen (although not so stated, it can be presumed that "the mast" would be the mainmast if there were more than two masts). [25(b)] The use of a combination masthead light, however is *not* permitted when any mechanical power is being used, since there is no way to carry a white forward light higher than the colored

FIG. 408 Vessels 50 meters (164 ft) or more in length at anchor must show two anchor lights with the after one lower. Smaller vessels may show the after light, but are not required to do so.

side lights. The carrying of a three-color combination light also eliminates any use of the red-over-green optional light for sailboats.

A sailboat less than 7 meters (23.0 ft) long *should* carry normal sidelights and sternlight; but if this is not practicable, it is sufficient to have an electric flashlight or lighted lantern ready at hand to be shown in sufficient time to prevent collision. [25(d) (i)]

Rowboats

Small craft propelled by oars may show the lights of a sailboat, or have handy an electric flashlight or lighted lantern to show to prevent a collision. [28(d)]

Lights for Vessels at Anchor

The Inland Rules basically require a white all-round light in the fore part of a vessel at anchor, plus a second all-round white light at or near the stern, and lower than the forward light. [30(a)] The forward anchor light, when two are shown, must be at least 4.5 meters (14.8 ft) above the other one. If the vessel is 50 meters (164.1 ft) or more in length, the minimum height is increased to not less than 6 meters (19.7 ft). Vessels less than 50 meters (164.1 ft) in length may show both anchor lights as above, or may show only a single all-round white light wherever it can best be seen: [30(b)]

Any vessel at anchor may, and a vessel of 100 meters (328.1 ft) and more in length must, also use the available working or equivalent lights to illuminate her decks. [30(c)]

Small craft

A boat less than 7 meters (23.4 ft) in length, when at anchor *not* in or near a narrow channel, fairway, or anchorage, or where other vessels normally navigate, need not show an anchor light as described above. [30(e)]

Special anchorage areas

There are, however, locations on the inland waters designated as "special anchorage areas," where anchor lights are not required for vessels less than 20 meters (65.7 ft) long. [30(g)]

These special anchorage areas are frequently found off yacht clubs and similar facilities. For the boatman, they offer the possibility of legally leaving his craft unattended at a mooring for extended times, without having an anchor light burning continuously or turning one on each sunset.

Lights for Vessels Aground

A vessel that is aground must show the normal anchor light(s), plus two all-round red lights arranged vertically. [30(d)] A vessel less than 12 meters (39.4 ft) in length is exempted from this requirement.

Lights for Towing

Vessels which are either towing another or are being towed have, because of this condition, much less

Numbers and letters shown in brackets are references to the applicable Rule.

maneuverability than vessels proceeding singly. To indicate this situation at night, special navigation lights are prescribed for vessels towing or being towed.

Towing alongside or pushing ahead

A power-driven vessel, when towing another alongside, must carry, in addition to her normal sidelights, two masthead white lights in a vertical line with standard spacing and positioning. These lights must be shown, but may be carried at *either* the position of the normal forward masthead light or that of the after masthead light, if used. She must also carry two towing lights in a vertical line. [24(c)] The reason for these special towing lights showing astern is to ensure that an

POWER-DRIVEN VESSELS 12 but less than 20 meters (39.4-65.6 ft) in length—Option 1

A 135° white light visible 2 miles

A 225° white masthead light visible 3 miles and located not less than 2.5 meters (8.2 ft) above the gunwale

Green starboard and red port 112½° sidelights visible 2 miles and located above the hull (gunwale) not more than ¾ of the height of the masthead light

POWER-DRIVEN VESSELS 12 but less than 20 meters (39.4-65.6 ft) in length—Option 2

A 225° white masthead light visible 3 miles and located not less than 2.5 meters (8.2 ft) above the gunwale

A 135° white light visible 2 miles

A combination red-and-green light visible 2 miles from dead ahead to 22½° abaft the beam, and located above the hull (gunwale) not less than 1 meter (3.3 ft) lower than the masthead light

POWER-DRIVEN VESSELS less than 12 meters (39.4 ft) in length—Option 1

A 135° white light visible 2 miles

A 225° white masthead light visible 2 miles; permitted to be mounted less than 2.5 meters above the gunwale, but not less than 1 meter (3.3 ft) higher than the sidelights

Green starboard and red port 112½° sidelights visible 1 mile, and mounted above the hull (gunwale) not more than ¾ of the height of the masthead light

POWER-DRIVEN VESSELS less than 12 meters (39.4 ft) in length—Option 2

A 135° white light visible 2 miles

A 225° white masthead light visible 2 miles; permitted to be mounted less than 2.5 meters above the gunwale, but not less than 1 meter (3.3 ft) above the combination light

A combination red-and-green light visible 1 mile from dead ahead to 22½° abaft each beam, and located above the hull not less than 1 meter (3.3 ft) lower than the masthead light

Note: A power-driven vessel less than 7 meters (23.0 ft) in length whose maximum speed does not exceed 7 knots need show only an all-around white light visible 2 miles, but should also show sidelights

SAILING CRAFT under 20 meters (65.6 ft)

Green starboard and red port 112½° sidelights visible 2 miles and located above the hull (gunwale) OR a combination red-and-green light located on the centerline, visible 2 miles

A 135° white light visible 2 miles

SAILING CRAFT less than 12 meters (39.4 ft)

In lieu of sidelights (or combination red-and-green light) and sternlight, a triple combination light at or near masthead showing red and green sidelight and white sternlight sectors (Red over green optional lights not permitted)

A 135° white light visible 2 miles

Green starboard and red port 112½° sidelights visible 2 miles and located above the hull (gunwale) OR a combination red-and-green light located on the centerline, visible 1 mile

Note: Sailing craft less than 7 meters (23.0 ft) in length need not show side and stern lights but rather can have an electric flashlight or lighted lantern with white light ready to be shown in sufficient time to prevent collision

FIG. 409 The 1972 International Rules provide several options for small craft, power-driven or sail, under 20 meters (65.7 ft) in length. These lights are also acceptable in waters subject to the Inland Rules, which have slightly lesser requirements in some details and allow a single white all-round light for boats under 12 meters (39.4 ft) long.

Numbers and letters shown in brackets are references to the applicable Rule.

LIGHTS FOR VARIOUS TYPES OF VESSELS—1980 INLAND RULES
TABLE 4-1
(Effective 24 December 1981)

	Vessel	Masthead (forward)	Side	Stern	Additional lights or Remarks
1	Power-driven vessel 12 m but less than 20 m in length	White, 225°, Vis. 3 mi. At least 2.5 m above gunwale[1]	Separate red and green 112½° or combination, vis. 2 mi. Above hull at least 1 m below masthead light[2]	White 135°, vis. 2 mi.	[1]After masthead light may be shown but not required. (Exception allowed on Great Lakes) [2]Fitted with inboard screens if necessary to prevent being seen across bow
2	Power-driven vessel less than 12 m in length	White, 225°, vis. 2 mi. Can be less than 2.5 m above gunwale, but at least 1 m above side lights[1,3]	Separate red and green, 112½°, or combination, vis. 1 mi. Above hull at least 1 m below masthead light[2,3]	White 135°, vis. 2 mi.	[3]Less than 12 m in length, need only have all-round white light, vis. 2 mi. but should have side lights
3	Sailing vessel under 20 m in length	None	Separate red and green, 112½°, or combination, vis. 2 mi.[2,4]	White 135°, vis. 2 mi.	Optional—two all-round lights at or near top of mast, red over green, separated at least 1 m, vis. 2 mi.
4	Sailing vessel under 12 m in length	None	Separate red and green, 112½°, or combination, vis. 1 mi.[2,4,5]	White, 135°, vis. 2 mi.[4,5]	[4]May be combined into triple combination light at masthead [5]Less than 7 m, need only have flashlight or lantern to show
5	Vessel propelled by oars	None	May show separate red and green, 112½°, or combination, vis. 1 mi.[6]	May show white, 135°, vis. 2 mi.[6]	[6]Need only have flashlight or lantern to show white light
6	Power-driven vessel 20 m but less than 50 m in length	White, 225°, vis. 5 mi. Not more than ½ of length aft from stem; 6 m, or beam (up to 10 m) above hull	Red and green, 112½°, vis. 2 mi. At or near sides of vessel; above hull at least 1 m below masthead light	White, 135°, vis. 2 mi.	After masthead light may be shown; at least 4.5 m higher than forward masthead light
7	Power-driven vessel 50 m or more in length	White, 225°, vis. 6 mi. Not more than ½ of length aft from stem; 6 m or beam (up to 10 m) above hull	Red and green, 112½°, vis. 3 mi. At or near sides of vessel; above hull at least 1 m below masthead light	White, 135°, vis. 3 mi.	After masthead light required; at least 4.5 m higher and ¼ of vessel length (up to 50 m) aft of forward masthead light
8	Vessel towing; tow less than 200 m overall from stern of towing vessel. (Also towing alongside or pushing ahead)	Two white, arranged vertically, 225°, vis. determined by length of vessel (not required pushing ahead or towing alongside on Western Rivers)	Normal for size of vessel	Normal for size of vessel	Towing astern: Towing light[7] over stern light. Pushing ahead or towing alongside: Two towing lights[7] vertically [7]Vis. 3 mi. for vessels 50 m or more in length; 2 mi. for shorter vessels
9	Vessel towing; tow 200 m or more overall length	Three white, arranged vertically, 225°, vis. determined by length of vessel	Normal for size of vessel	Normal for size of vessel	Towing light: yellow, 135°, above sternlight[7]
10	Vessel being towed astern, if manned	None	Normal for size of vessel	Normal for size of vessel	
11	Vessel being towed alongside or pushed ahead	None	Normal for size of vessel; at forward end	Normal for size of vessel (not used for pushed ahead)	Also "special flashing light" at center or forward end. A group of vessels is lighted as a single vessel
12	Vessel engaged in trolling or drift fishing	[8]	[8]	[8]	[8]Show only normal lights of power-driven or sailing vessel
13	Vessel engaged in trawling	None[12]	When making way through the water, normal for size of vessel	When making way through the water, normal for size of vessel	Underway or at anchor, two all-round lights, green over white[7,9,10,11] [9]Vertical spacing 1 m [10]Lower light not less than 4 m (2 m if under 20 m in length) above hull [11]Lower light above sidelights at least twice vertical spacing
14	Vessel engaged in fishing, other than trawling (or trolling)	None[12]	When making way through the water, normal for size of vessel	When making way through the water, normal for size of vessel	Underway or at anchor, two all-round lights, red over white[7,9,10,11] [12]When not actually fishing, show normal masthead lights for vessel its size
15	Vessel at anchor, less than 50 m in length	None	None	None	White, all-round light where can best be seen. Vis. 2 mi. (not required if less than 7 m in length and not anchored in a narrow channel or where vessels normally navigate)
16	Vessel at anchor; 50 m or more in length	None	None	None	White, all-round light in fore part of vessel not less than 6 m above hull. A second white, all-round light in after part, not less than 4.5 m lower than forward anchor light. Vis. 3 mi.
17	Vessel aground	None	None		Anchor light(s) as line 15 or 16, plus two red all-round lights of same visibility range[7,9,10] (not required if less than 12 m in length)
18	Pilot vessel	None if on pilot duty; normal if underway and not on pilot duty	When underway, normal for size of vessel	When underway, normal for size of vessel	Two all-round lights, white over red, at masthead[7,9,10] If at anchor, normal anchor light(s); line 15 or 16
19	Vessel not under command	None	If making way through the water, normal for size of vessel	If making way through the water, normal for size of vessel	Two red all-round lights vertically where best can be seen[7,9,10]
20	Vessel restricted in ability to maneuver	None	When making way through the water, normal for size of vessel	When making way through the water, normal for size of vessel	Three all-round lights vertically, red-white-red.[7,9] If at anchor, normal anchor light(s). (Not required if less than 12 m in length)

Equivalent measurements in customary units: 50 m—164 ft 7 m—23.0 ft 2. m—6.6 ft 200 m—656 ft 20 m—65.6 ft 4.5m—14.8 ft
6 m—19.7 ft 1. m—3.3 ft 100 m—328 ft 12 m—39.4 ft 2.5 m—8.2 ft
Numbers and letters shown in parentheses are references to the applicable Article or Rule.

8 and 11

2

6

2

3 and C

14

5

A

LIGHTS FOR VARIOUS TYPES OF VESSELS—1972 INTERNATIONAL RULES
TABLE 4-2
(Effective 15 July 1977)

	Vessel	Masthead (forward)	Side	Stern	Additional lights or Remarks
A	Power-driven vessel 12 m but less than 20 m in length	White, 225°, vis. 3 mi. At least 2.5 m above gunwale[1]	Separate red and green, 112½°, or combination, vis. 2 m. Above hull at least 1 m below masthead light[2]	White, 135°, vis. 2 mi.	[1]After masthead light may be shown but not required [2]Fitted with inboard screens if necessary to prevent being seen across bow
B	Power-driven vessel less than 12 m in length	White, 225°, vis. 2 mi. Can be less than 2.5 m above gunwale, but at least 1 m above side lights[3]	Separate red and green, 112½°, or combination, vis. 1 mi. Above hull at least 1 m below masthead light[2]	White, 135°, vis. 2 mi.	[3]Less than 7 m and less than 7 kt max speed need only have all-round white light, vis. 2 mi. but should have sidelights
C	Sailing vessel under 20 m in length	None	Separate red and green, 112½°, or combination, vis. 2 mi.	White, 135°, vis. 2 mi.	Optional—two all-round lights at or near top of mast, red over green, separated at least 1 m, vis. 2 mi.
D	Sailing vessel under 12 m in length	None	Separate red and green, 112½°, or combination, vis. 1 mi.[2,4]	White,[5] 135°, vis. 2 mi.[4,5]	[4]May be combined into triple combination light at masthead [5]Less than 7 m need only have flashlight or lantern to show
E	Vessel propelled by oars	None	May show separate red and green, 112½°, or combination, vis. 1 mi.[6]	May show white, 135°, vis. 2 mi.[6]	[6]Need only have flashlight or lantern to show white light
F	Power-driven vessel 20 but less than 50 m in length	White, 225°, vis. 5 mi. Not more than ¼ of length aft from stem; 6 m or beam (up to 12 m) above hull	Red and green, 112½°, vis. 2 mi. At or near sides of vessel; not more than ¾ height of masthead light	White, 135°, vis. 2 mi.	After masthead light may be shown; at least 4.5 m higher than forward masthead light
G	Power-driven vessel 50 m or more in length	White, 225°, vis. 6 mi. Not more than ¼ of length aft from stem; 6 m or beam (up to 12 m) above hull	Red and green, 112½°, vis. 3 mi. At or near sides of vessel; not more than ¾ height of forward masthead light	White, 135°, vis. 3 mi.	After masthead light required; at least 4.5 m higher and half of vessel length (up to 100 m) aft of forward masthead light
H	Vessel towing; tow from stern of towing less than 200 m overall vessel. (Also towing alongside or pushing ahead)	Two white, arranged vertically, 225°, vis. determined by length of vessel	Normal for size of vessel	Normal for size of vessel	Towing light[7] over sternlight (not shown when towing alongside or pushing ahead) [7]Vis. 3 mi. for vessels 50 m or more in length; 2 mi. for shorter vessels
I	Vessel towing; tow 200 m or more overall length	Three white, arranged vertically, 225°, vis. determined by length of vessel	Normal for size of vessel	Normal for size of vessel	Towing light[7] over stern light
J	Vessel being towed astern, if manned	None	Normal for size of vessel	Normal for size of vessel	
K	Vessel being towed alongside or pushed ahead	None	Normal for size of vessel; at forward end	Normal for size of vessel (not used for pushed ahead)	A group of vessels is lighted as a single vessel
L	Vessel engaged in trolling or drift fishing	[8]	[8]	[8]	[8]Show only normal lights of power-driven or sailing vessel
M	Vessel engaged in trawling	None[12]	When making way through the water, normal for size of vessel	When making way through the water, normal for size of vessel	Underway or at anchor, two all-round lights, green over white[7,9,10,11] [9]Vertical spacing 2 m for vessels 20 m or more in length, 1 m for shorter vessels [10]Lower light not less than 4 m (2 m if under 20 m in length) above hull [11]Lower light above sidelights at least twice vertical spacing
N	Vessel engaged in fishing, other than trawling (or trolling)	None[12]	When making way through the water, normal for size of vessel	When making way through the water, normal for size of vessel	Underway or at anchor, two all-round lights, red over white[7,9,10,11] [12]When not actually fishing, show normal masthead lights for vessel its size
O	Vessel at anchor, less than 50 m in length	None	None	None	White, all-round light where can best be seen. Vis. 2 mi. (Not required if less than 7 m in length and not anchored in a narrow channel where vessels normally navigate)
P	Vessel at anchor; 50 m or more in length	None	None	None	White, all-round light in fore part of vessel not less than 6 m above hull. A second white all-round light in after part, not less than 4.5 m lower than forward anchor light. Vis. 3 mi.
Q	Vessel aground	None	None		Normal anchor light(s) plus two red all-round lights of same visibility range
R	Pilot vessel	None if on pilot duty; normal if underway and not on pilot duty	When underway, normal for size of vessel	When underway, normal for size of vessel	Two all-round lights, white over red, at masthead[7,9,10] If at anchor, normal anchor light(s)
S	Vessel not under command	None	If making way through the water, normal for size of vessel	If making way through the water, normal for size of vessel	Two red all-round lights vertically where best can be seen[7,9,10]
T	Vessel constrained by her draft	Normal for size of vessel	Normal for size of vessel	Normal for size of vessel	Three red all-round lights, arranged vertically and equally spaced[7,9,10]

Equivalent measurements in customary units: 50 m—164 ft 7 m—23.0 ft 2. m—6.6 ft 200 m—656 ft 20 m—65.6 ft 4.5m—14.8 ft
6 m—19.7 ft 1. m—3.3 ft 100 m—328 ft 12 m—39.4 ft 2.5 m—8.2 ft
Numbers and letters shown in parentheses are references to the applicable Article or Rule.

B

8 and 10

112.5° LT

135° LT

225° LT

360° LT

8 and 11

16 and P

15 and 0

H and J
8 and 10

C

4 and D

1 and A

3 and C

H and J
8 and 10

19 and S

14 and N

13 and M

7 and G

D

FIG. 410 A barge being pushed ahead will carry sidelights on each outside corner of the bow; these must be fitted with suitable inboard screens. If there are several barges being pushed as a unit, the sidelights will be on the outside bow of the outside leading barges of the group. An additional quick flashing yellow light is required at the forward center point of the barge or barges.

FIG. 411 If the height of the tow alongside is such as to obscure the tug's sidelight, then that colored light must be shown from the barge. The lower masthead light may be shown either forward or aft.

overtaking vessel is adequately warned of the task in which the overtaken vessel is engaged, and the possible complications in passing around.

Exception. On the Western Rivers and on waters specified by the Secretary, the prescribed lights for a vessel pushing ahead or towing alongside are only sidelights and two towing lights carried one above the other. [24(i)] It is said that masthead lights are not required on Western Rivers because of the number of low bridges which towboats must pass under.

Vessels towed alongside or being pushed ahead are considered as a unit. On a vessel being pushed ahead, sidelights must be shown at the forward end plus a "special flashing light" as defined in Rule 21(g). When towed alongside, a vessel shows sidelights at the forward end and a sternlight. [24(f)]

Standard vertical positioning. When two or three lights are required to be carried in a vertical line, they must be spaced and positioned as follows: The vertical spacing must be at least 1 meter (3.3 ft); where three lights are carried vertically, the spacings must be equal.

The lowest light on vessels more than 20 meters (65.7 ft) in length must be not less than 4 meters (13.1 ft) above the hull; on craft of lesser length, the lowest light need only be a minimum of 2 meters (6.6 ft) above the hull. [I, 8403(i)] This standard spacing and positioning is applicable for all lights arranged vertically, except towing lights; this includes fishing vessels, vessels aground, pilot vessels, vessels restricted in their ability to maneuver or not under command, and the forward lights of towing vessels. The lower of the two all-round lights required on a vessel engaged in fishing must be at a height above her sidelights not less than twice the distance between the two vertically arranged lights. [I, 80.03(j)]

When a pushing vessel and a vessel being pushed ahead are "rigidly connected" as a *composite unit*, they are considered to be a single power-driven vessel and carry the Rule 23 lights of such a vessel. This is *not* the same as a tug lashed to a barge ahead, no matter how tight the fastening cables are pulled in. [24(b)]

Towing astern

If the length of a tow astern, measured from the stern of the towing vessel to the after end of the tow, is 200 meters (656.2 ft) or less, the towing vessel must carry *two* "masthead" lights in the same manner as for pushinging ahead or towing alongside, plus sidelights, a sternlight, and one towing light above the sternlight. If the length of the tow is greater than 200 meters (656.2 ft), *three* "masthead" lights are carried in a vertical line, rather than two. [24(a)]

A vessel towed astern carries sidelights and a sternlight, but no white forward lights. [24(e)] An inconspicuous, partially submerged vessel or object must carry special lights, rather than those just described. If it is less than 25 meters (82.0 ft) in *breadth*, it must carry one all-round white light at or near each end; if it is 25 meters (82.0 ft) or more in breadth, four all-round white lights at or near corners. If it exceeds 100 meters (328.1 ft) in length, it must have additional all-round white lights, placed so that the distance between such lights is not more than 100 meters (328.1 ft). These white lights must be visible for 3 miles. This rule exists to provide for the proper lighting of large liquid-filled bags (called dracones), log rafts, and other nearly-awash objects. Vessels or objects towed alongside each other are lighted as a single vessel or object. [24(g)]

FIG 412 Towing lights distinguish between tows shorter (shown above) or longer than 200 meters (656 ft); length is measured from the stern of the towing vessel to the stern of the last vessel towed.

FIG. 413 Tows longer than 200 meters (656 ft) are identified by the three white forward lights of the towing vessel. The after masthead light shown above is optional rather than required, as this tug is less than 50 meters (164 ft) in length.

Numbers and letters shown in brackets are references to the applicable Rule.

When it is impracticable for a towed vessel to carry the prescribed lights, Rule 24(h) directs that all possible measures be taken to light the vessel or object being towed, or at least to indicate the presence of that vessel or object.

Small craft towing

Although the 1980 Inland Rules make no special provisions for small craft when towing, Rule 24(j) covers situations where towing is not the normal function of a vessel engaged in such work, and the towed vessel is in distress or otherwise in need of assistance. In this instance, if it is not practicable to show the usual special lights of a towing vessel, all possible measures must be taken to indicate the relationship between the two craft, including the use of a searchlight to illuminate the towed vessel.

Lights for Special Purpose Vessels

Specific lights or combinations of lights are prescribed for various categories of vessels, so that they may be more easily and quickly identified as such at night.

Fishing vessels

A vessel engaged in fishing, whether underway or at anchor, must show *only* the lights specified in Rule 26. Remember, however, that the definition of "fishing" does *not* include trolling lines.

A vessel engaged in trawling—the dragging through the water of a dredge net or "other apparatus used as a fishing appliance"—must show two all-round lights vertically, green over white, plus sidelights and a sternlight when making way through the water. She must also carry a white masthead light abaft of and higher than the green light, if she is 50 meters (164.1 ft) or more in length; shorter vessels may, but do not have to, carry this light.

A vessel engaged in fishing other than trawling shows red over white all-round lights, again with sidelights and sternlight, if making way. If there is outlying gear more than 150 meters (492.2 ft) horizontally from the vessel, an all-round white light must be shown in that direction. This light must be not less than 2 meters (6.6 ft) nor more than 6 meters (19.7 ft) horizontally away from the all-round red and white lights.

FIG. 415 A vessel is "not under command" when it is underway but incapable of maneuvering, as might result from a steering system failure or breakdown in propulsion machinery. Such a ship shows two red lights at night; sidelights are shown only if she is making way through the water.

In both of the cases above, the lower of the two vertical lights must be at a height above the sidelights not less than twice the spacing between the two vertical lights. The required visibility range is the same as for sternlights.

A vessel engaged in fishing in close proximity to other vessels engaged in fishing *may* exhibit the additional signals described in Annex II. These signals would aid trawlers and purse seiners working in groups to coordinate their movements. [26(d)]

A fishing vessel, when *not* engaged in fishing, will show the normal navigation lights for a vessel of her length. [26(a)]

Pilot vessels

A pilot vessel, when on pilotage duty, does not show normal lights for a vessel of her size, but rather two all-round lights in a vertical line, white over red, at or near the masthead. These lights have the same visibility distance requirement as a sternlight, which, together with sidelights, must be shown when underway. When at anchor, normal anchor lights are shown, in addition to the white-over-red lights. [29(a)]

A pilot vessel *not* on pilotage duty carries only the normal lights for a vessel of her length. [29(b)]

Vessels with limited maneuverability

The U.S. Inland Rules prescribe special lights for various types of vessels that are limited in their maneuverability by virtue of their condition or their operations.

Vessels not under command

A vessel "not under command"—such as one with disabled engines and unable to direct her movements—will show two red all-round lights vertically spaced where they can best be seen. If making way through the water, sidelights and a sternlight will be shown, but not masthead lights. [27(a)]

Vessels restricted in maneuverability

A vessel restricted in her ability to maneuver, except one engaged in minesweeping, will show three all-round lights with standard vertical separation, red-white-red. If underway or at anchor, the vessel will show the usual lights for that status. [27(b)]

FIG. 414 Fishing lights are of two types. Vessels trawling show a green-over-white combination; vessels other than trawlers (but not trolling) show red-over-white lights. When making way through the water, sidelights and sternlights are shown. When gear extends more than 150 meters (492 ft) from the vessel, a white all-around light is shown in the direction of the gear.

Numbers and letters shown in brackets are references to the applicable Rule.

FIG. 416 Vessels that have restricted maneuverability because they are working on submarine cables or pipelines, or other forms of sub-surface construction work, must show special lights or day shapes as appropriate to indicate their status.

A vessel engaged in a towing operation that severely restricts the towing vessel and her tow in their ability to deviate from their course will show normal towing lights, plus the red-white-red vertical lights. [27(c)] It is *not* intended, however, that vessels engaged in *routine* towing operations can declare that they are restricted in their ability to deviate from their course.

In addition to the red-white-red lights, a vessel engaged in dredging or underwater operations that involve an obstruction to navigation will also show two vertically spaced red all-round lights on the side on which the obstruction exists and two green all-round lights, one above the other, on the side on which it is safe to pass; these lights shall be at the maximum practical horizontal distance, but never less than 2 meters (6.6 ft) from the red-white-red lights, and the upper light of these pairs must not be higher than the lower red light. A vessel of this category will not show anchor light(s), but will show underway lights, if applicable. [27(d)]

Diving operations

Whenever the size of a vessel engaged in diving operations makes it impracticable to exhibit all the lights prescribed in Rule 27(d) (above), she shall instead, show three all-round lights placed vertically, red-white-red. [27(e)]

Minesweepers

A vessel engaged in minesweeping will show, in addition to all normal underway lights for a power-driven vessel, three green all-round lights. One of these will be at the foremast head and one at each end of the foreyard. These lights indicate that it is dangerous to approach closer than 1000 meters (1094 yds) astern or 500 meters (547 yds) on either side. [27(f)]

Smaller craft

Boats less than 12 meters (39.4 ft) in length are not required to show the lights of Rule 27, but larger boats must comply. [27(g)]

Not distress signals

The various lights of Rule 27, especially those for vessels not under command, should be understood by other vessels as signals of limited maneuverability, not as signals of vessels in distress and requiring assistance. [27(h)]

Miscellaneous Provisions of the Rules

Rule 1(b) (ii) continues the practice of allowing vessels equipped with lights meeting the requirements of the International Rules of the Road to use such lights on inland waters *in lieu of* the lights specified by the 1980 Inland Rules. Lights must be complete for one set of Rules or the other—no mixtures. See pages 71 to 73 for the applicable provisions of the International Rules.

This option is of value to the owners of boats that may be operated outside the Inland Rules demarcation lines at night, since it eliminates any need for making a change in lights when going from one body of water to the other. The navigation lights of the International Rules are permitted on inland waters, *but not vice versa;* a boat lighted for the Inland Rules may be in violation when proceeding seaward of the demarcation lines.

Exemptions for Government Vessels

Any requirements regarding lights and shapes—their number, placement, range or arc of visibility—do not apply to those displayed on vessels of the Navy or Coast Guard if the Secretary of the Department concerned certifies that this is not possible, due to the special construction of these vessels—for example, submarines and aircraft carriers. In such cases, however, their lights must comply as closely as the Secretary finds to be feasible. [1(e)]

Rule 1(c) allows the use of special station or signal lights by naval ships and vessels proceeding under convoy. These additional lights shall, so far as possible, be such that they cannot be mistaken for any lights of the rules of the road.

Special submarine lights. Because of their low height and close spacing, the normal navigation lights of submarines have been found to be easily mistaken for those of small craft, although submarines are large, deep-draft vessels with limited maneuverability on the surface. The Rules do not provide for any special lights for submarines at the surface, but under the authority of Rule 1(e), the United States has established a special distinctive light for its submarines; this light is in addition to all other required lights.

The distinctive light characteristic is an amber beacon with a sequence of one flash per second for three seconds, followed by three seconds of darkness. The light is located where it can be best seen, as nearly as practicable all around the horizon; it will be not less than two feet above or below the masthead light.

FIG. 417 U.S. submarines shown normal navigation lights but with vertical and horizontal placement and separations modified as made necessary by their special design. A special amber light with a sequence of one flash per second for three seconds followed by three seconds of darkness is carried above the forward masthead light

Numbers and letters shown in brackets are references to the applicable Rule.

67

Signals to attract attention

The new Inland Rules authorize a vessel to make light or sound signals to attract the attention of another vessel, provided that such actions cannot be mistaken for one of the normal lights or signals. A vessel may also direct the beam of her searchlight toward a danger, but not in such a way as to embarrass the navigation of any other vessel. [36]

Lights for seaplanes

The definition of a "vessel" specifically includes a seaplane, which in turn is defined as including any aircraft designed to maneuver on the water. [3(a) and (e)] Seaplanes, while on the water, are thus required, in theory at least, to show the same lights as a ship of the same size. Recognizing that this will probably be impractical, there is an exception which allows them to show lights "as closely similar in characteristics and position as is possible." [31]

Technical details for lights

Annex I to the 1980 Inland Rules also contains highly technical specifications for the "chromaticity" (color specifications) of navigation lights, and for the necessary luminous intensity to achieve the various ranges of visibility specified in the Rules. Specifications are also included for horizontal and vertical sectors, so that adequate light brightness will be maintained fully over the specified arc, yet rapidly decrease outside the set limits. The requirements for horizontal sectors are the same for all vessels, but the vertical sector specifications for sailing vessels differ from the requirements for power-driven vessels. When purchasing navigation lights, know for what type and size of vessels they are intended.

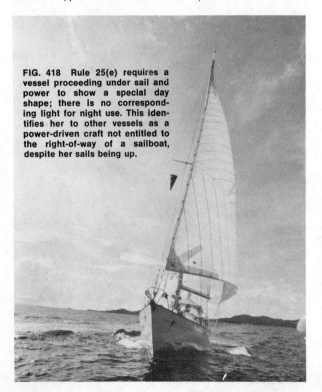

FIG. 418 Rule 25(e) requires a vessel proceeding under sail and power to show a special day shape; there is no corresponding light for night use. This identifies her to other vessels as a power-driven craft not entitled to the right-of-way of a sailboat, despite her sails being up.

Day Shapes

In the interests of collision prevention and greater overall safety on the water, the Rules of the Road prescribe a number of day shapes for certain situations and categories of vessels. Objects of specified shape, color, and minimum size are necessary in the daytime, when lights would be ineffective. The general requirements for the display of shapes are given in the numbered rules, with the details as to configuration, size, and placement being set forth in Annex I.

All day shapes of the new Inland Rules are black. The basic shapes are:

Ball—diameter of not less than 0.6 meter (2.0 ft).

Cone—base diameter not less than 0.6 meter (2.0 ft).

Cylinder—diameter not less than 0.6 meter (2.0 ft) and height twice the diameter.

Diamond—two cones, each as above, base to base.

If more than one shape is hoisted, they shall be spaced at least 1.5 meters (4.9 ft).

Small craft. Vessels less than 20 meters (65.7 ft) in length may display smaller shapes scaled down commensurate with the vessel's size; the vertical separation may be correspondingly reduced.

Vessels under sail and power

A vessel preceeding under sail in the daytime, when also being propelled by machinery, must carry forward, where it can best be seen, a black conical shape, point downward. A vessel of less than 12 meters (39.4 ft) length is not required to exhibit this shape, but may do so. [25(e)] This rule establishes a signal to indicate that such a vessel, although it has sails set, also has mechanical propulsion, and thus is *not* entitled to the right-of-way privileges of a sailing vessel specified in Rule 18.

Vessels at anchor or aground

A vessel at anchor must hoist a ball-shape daymark forward where it can best be seen. [30(a)] A vessel aground must display three ball shapes in a vertical line. [30(d)]

FIG. 419 A vessel anchored in a channel or fairway is required to hoist a day shape of one black ball not less than 0.6 meter (2 ft) in diameter. Some exceptions are made for small craft, but only in certain circumstances; see text.

Vessels towing and being towed

Between sunrise and sunset, a power-driven vessel having a tow astern, the length of which exceeds 200 meters (656.2 ft), must carry a diamond shape where it can best be seen. [24(a)]

Numbers and letters shown in brackets are references to the applicable Rule.

In such cases, the vessel being towed must also show a diamond shape where it can best be seen. [24(e)]

Vessels engaged in fishing

Vessels engaged in fishing by day must indicate their occupation by displaying, where it can best be seen, a shape consisting of two cones in a vertical line with their points together (in this case only, no vertical separation between the two shapes). If the vessel is less than 20 meters (65.7 ft) in length, a basket may be substituted for the two-cone shape. [26(b) and (c)] These shapes are used on vessels engaged in trawling or in fishing other than trawling (but not by vessels trolling or drift fishing).

If its outlying gear extends more than 150 meters horizontally from the vessel, a vessel engaged in fishing, other than trawling, will show a day shape of a single cone, point up, in the direction of the outlying gear. [26(c)]

FIG. 420 A day shape of two cones, points together without spacing, indicates a fishing vessel. Craft less than 20 meters (65.7 ft) in length may hoist a basket in lieu of the cones.

Vessels with limited maneuverability

A vessel not under command will show as a day signal two black balls one above the other. [27(a)]

A vessel "restricted in her ability to maneuver" will hoist three shapes in a vertical line, ball-diamond-ball. [27(b)]

A vessel engaged in a towing operation, which severely restricts the towing vessel and her tow in their ability to deviate from their course, will show the ball-diamond-ball shapes, in addition to any other required day shapes. It is not intended, however, that vessels engaged in routine towing operations can declare that they are restricted in their ability to deviate from their course.

FIG. 421 By day, a vessel not under command indicates her situation by hoisting two black ball shapes similar to the one used when at anchor. A vessel aground hoists three such shapes. Craft less than 12 meters (39.4 ft) in length need not show these shapes.

A vessel engaged in dredging or underwater operations when an obstruction to navigation exists will hoist two balls vertically on the side on which the obstruction exists, and two diamond shapes on the side on which another vessel may pass. [27(d)] If the size of a vessel engaged in diving operations makes it impracticable to exhibit these shapes, it shall show instead a rigid replica of the International Code flag "A" (white and blue, swallow-tailed) not less than 1 meter (3.3 ft) in height, arranged to ensure all-round visibility. [27(e)] This requirement for visibility in any direction will normally require multiple "flags" in a criss-cross or square arrangement. There is no recognition in the Rules or Annex I of the red flag with single white diagonal stripe so widely used in sport diving.

A vessel engaged in minesweeping will show three balls, one at the foremast head and one at each end of the foreyard; these have the same significance as the green lights shown at these positions at night. [27(f)]

Smaller craft

Vessels under 7 meters (23.0 ft) in length, not at anchor in or near a narrow channel, fairway, anchorage, or where vessels normally navigate, need not show an anchor ball.

Vessels under 20 meters (65.7 ft) in length, when at anchor in a "special anchorage area" need not have an anchor ball hoisted.

Vessels less than 12 meters (39.4 ft) in length are not required to show day shapes when aground or when operating with limited maneuverability, except for diving operations. [27(g) and 30(f)]

Exemptions

The 1980 Inland Rules provide for temporary and permanent exemptions to the requirements for the characteristics and positioning of lights, in order to ease the impact of changes from the old Inland, Great Lakes, and Western Rivers Rules to the 1980 Inland Navigational Rules. These exemptions apply to "any vessel or class of vessels, the keel of which was laid, or which was at a corresponding stage of construction" before 24 December 1980; newer vessels are not exempt and must comply with the new requirements. (Due to the delay in publication of effective Annexes to the Inland Rules, the actual date will probably be December 1981 rather than 1980. Where such exemptions are for a limited time, they are stated in terms of "years after the effective date of these rules"; this date was 24 December 1981. [38]

Craft less than 20 meters (65.7 ft) in length that have lights as specified in the Motor Boat Act of 1940 are permanently exempt from meeting the new visibility ranges and color specifications. For all vessels, any repositioning of lights because of the change of specifications in customary units to metric units and rounding off of measurement units need not be done at all, since there is a permanent exemption. The horizontal repositioning of masthead lights need not be done until 24 December 1990 for vessels over 150 meters (492.2 ft) in length, and shorter vessels are given a permanent exemption. An exemption until 24 December 1990 is also granted for the restructuring or repositioning of all lights to meet

Numbers and letters shown in brackets are references to the applicable Rule.

69

FIG. 421 A pipeline extending from a dredge must be properly lighted at night to prevent its being a hazard to the safe navigation of vessels. The pipeline must be lighted along its length and have special lights at the discharge end or any point of opening for the passage of vessels.

the specifications of Annex I. Power-driven vessels 12 meters (39.4 ft) or more in length, but less than 20 meters (65.7 ft), are permanently exempt from the provisions of showing a masthead light forward, plus a sternlight aft, provided they show an all-round white light aft in place of the new requirements.

PILOT RULES FOR INLAND WATERS

The **Pilot Rules** for inland waters under the 1980 Inland Rules are found in Annex V; their scope is much less than under the former Inland Rules, since many of the old Pilot Rules now appear as numbered Rules, and others have been shifted to other sections of Coast Guard regulations. Technically, they appear as Part 88 of Title 33, Code of Federal Regulations. The Pilot Rules require that a copy of the Inland Navigation Rules be carried on board every "self-propelled vessel" 12 meters (39.4 ft) or more in length. [88.05] They are most conveniently found in Coast Guard publication CG-169, which is available for purchase from the Superintendent of Documents, Government Printing Office, Washington, D.C. 20402, or from local sales agents for charts and nautical publications.

Law enforcement vessels

Law enforcement vessels of the United States, and the States and their political subdivisions, may display a flashing *blue* light when engaged in direct law enforcement activities. This light must be located so as to not interfere with the visibility of the vessel's navigation lights. [88.11]

Lights on dredge pipelines

Dredge pipelines that are floating or supported on trestles must display lights at night and in periods of restricted visibility. There must be yellow lights along the pipeline, approximately equally spaced and no more than 10 meters (32.8 ft) apart, where the pipeline crosses a navigable channel; where the pipeline does not cross a navigable channel, the lights must be sufficient to

clearly show the pipeline's length and course. Each light must be visible all around the horizon, flash 50 to 70 times per minute, and be located not less than 2 meters (6.6 ft) nor more than 3.5 meters (11.4 ft) above the water. There must also be two all-round red lights (not flashing) at each end of the pipeline, 1 meter (3.3 ft) apart vertically, with the lower red light at the same height above the water as the flashing yellow lights. [88.15]

Lights on barges at bank or dock

Section 88.13 of Annex V describes the circumstances requiring lights on barges moored at banks or docks, and the characteristics of such lights. Basically, the rules require white lights visible for 1 miles on a clear, dark night.

Modifications while passing under bridges

Any vessel, when passing under a bridge, may lower any light or day shape if required to do so by the available vertical clearance. When clear of the bridge, such lowered lights or day shapes must be raised immediately to the positions or heights required by law or regulations. [88.09]

FIG. 423 When necessary to pass under a bridge, a vessel may lower any navigation light or day shape. After passing under the bridge, the light or shape must be promptly restored to its required height or position.

Numbers and letters shown in brackets are references to the applicable Rule.

PENALTIES

The penalties for violation of the Inland Rules or Pilot Rule for Inland Waters are described in Chapter 2; see page 39.

General Cautions

Although not strictly a part of the Inland Rules or their Annexes, there are several other matters relating to navigation lists that should be considered by every skipper.

Misuse of navigation lights

Boats are often seen underway at night showing both running lights and the anchor light. This presents a confusing picture to another boat approaching from astern of the first craft—two white lights such as would be seen from ahead of a larger vessel under the Inland Rules. This illegal situation is usually caused by carelessness on the part of the skipper—he turned on one too many switches! Check your lights each time after you have turned them on.

Another problem is the small Class A or 1 boat at anchor that shows her combination red and green light as well as her all-round white light aft. Here the illegal situation is caused by the manufacturer who installed only one switch for all navigation lights, making it impossible for the boat to show only the white light as an anchor light, without simultaneously showing the red and green sidelights. The solution is for the skipper to install a second switch, so that the colored and white lights may be controlled independently.

Maintenance of navigation lights

Many boats are used only in the daytime, but the wise skipper checks his navigation lights once a month, whether they have been used or not. In this way, he can be sure that they are ready when needed. He also carries one or more spare bulbs and fuses, each of the proper type and size.

International Rules of the Road

Careful study of the 1980 U.S. Inland Rules of the Road provides an excellent basis for an understanding of the **"International Regulations for Preventing Collisions at Sea, 1972"**—the formal name for what are generally called the International Rules of the Road or "72 COLREGS." The current regulations carry a date of 1972 —the year that they were adopted at an international conference—but did not come into effect until 15 July 1977, following ratification by the necessary number of maritime nations. The International Rules of the Road (IntRR) are made applicable to U.S. waters and U.S. vessels by Presidential Proclamation and subsequent Act of Congress. The 1972 IntRR consist of 38 numbered "Rules" (organized into "Sections" which in turn are grouped together into "Parts"), plus four "Annexes" (the IntRR do not have Pilot Rules, the fifth annex of the U.S. Inland Rules). Some of these rules and annexes re-

late to lights and day shapes, and will be discussed in this chapter. Other rules and annexes are concerned with right-of-way, whistle signals, and distress signals; these are considered in Chapter 5.

The 1972 International Rules use metric measurements, except for visibility distances, which remain in nautical miles. For this reason, the following consideration of the IntRR will be in metric terms, with the approximate equivalent in customary units following in parentheses.

Applicability

The International Rules, as established under U.S. authority, are applicable to vessels in two situations:

1. To all vessels in waters within United States sovereignty, outside the prescribed demarcation lines at entrances to bays, rivers, harbors, etc.; see page 31. In the absence of demarcation lines, they are also applicable *within* bays, harbors, and inlets, along specified stretches of coasts and up the connecting rivers to their limits of continuous navigation.

2. To all U.S. vessels on the high seas, not subject to another nation's geographic jurisdiction.

Although the IntRR state that they are applicable "upon the high seas and in all waters connected therewith navigable by seagoing vessels" [1(a)], there is a provision for a nation to prescribe its own rules for harbors, rivers, and inland waterways [1(b)]; this is the basis for the U.S. Inland Rules.

FIG. 424 The International Rules of the Road are much like the 1980 Inland Rules, but skippers who venture outside "demarcation lines" must know the differences.

Manner of presentation

The 1980 U.S. Inland Rules of the Road were derived from the 1972 International Rules, and match them rule for rule, and annex for annex in format. Considerable effort was taken to make the language exactly identical wherever practicable, and this has been achieved to a great extent; the wide variances between the IntRR and the three former sets of U.S. Rules has now been eliminated, to the vast relief of both those who teach and those who must use them. Where there are differences, they exist because different operating conditions on the inland waters of the United States require rules for safety of navigation different from those applicable on the high seas. On inland waters, vessels are generally smaller in size and distances less. The International Rules, of course, do not contain the several special provisions for the Great Lakes or Western Rivers.

Thus, the consideration of the IntRR for lights and day shapes can be limited to the relatively few points of difference. *Where a difference is not noted, the International and 1980 U.S. Inland Rules are identical*, except for minor editorial modifications of no significance to vessel operation.

NAVIGATION LIGHTS

The requirement for showing navigation lights and day shapes is the same for waters governed by the International Rules as for those where the U.S. Inland Rules apply. See Table 4-2

Definitions

The IntRR definition of a **masthead** light *does not contain the exception* that permits a vessel of *less than 12 meters* (39.4 ft) length to place such a light off the fore-and-aft centerline; all vessels must have their masthead light(s) on the centerline.

The IntRR definitions *do not include* a "special flashing light"—the yellow light used at the bow of barges pushed ahead on inland waters.

The IntRR *do include* a definition not used in the Inland Rules. A "vessel constrained by her draft" is a power-driven vessel which, because of her draft in relation to the available depth of water, is severely restricted in her ability to deviate from the course she is following.

Lights for Power-driven Vessels Underway

International Rule 23(a) (i) *does not contain the exception* in the location of the forward masthead light for vessels *under 20 meters* (65.7 ft) in length; such a light thus *must* be in the forward half of the vessels length.

Permission for a vessel to carry an all-round white light, in place of a masthead and a stern light, is *limited* to vessels *less than 7 meters* (23.0 ft) in length whose maximum speed does not exceed 7 knots. [23(c)] This International Rule does not require sidelights if not "practicable."

Lights for Sailing Vessels Underway

The International Rules *limit the use* of a combination red-green-white light at or near the masthead to sailboats *less than 12 meters* (39.4 ft) in length. [25(b)] Thus, a sailboat between 12 and 20 meters (39.4 to 65.7 ft) in length carrying such a light would be "legal" on inland waters, but "illegal" when she was taken offshore.

Lights for Vessels Anchored or Aground

The International Rules contain *no provision* for "special anchorage areas" as established in inland waters. The *only exception* to the requirement for an anchor light is for vessels *under 7 meters* (23.0 ft) in length anchored in areas free of water-borne traffic. Such vessels are also the *only exceptions* to the requirement for showing two red all-round lights when aground. [30(e

FIG. 425 On inland waters, the white light on small boats may be off the centerline, but this provision does not appear in the International Rules, which also require separate forward and stern lights on craft over 7 meters (23.0) ft) in length.

Lights for Towing

The International Rules require that the two or three white masthead lights shown as an indication of towing status be on the *forward* mast (rather than either forward or aft, as permitted by the Inland Rules). [24(a) and (c)]

A vessel pushing a tow ahead or towing alongside must show a normal white stern light (rather than the two yellow towing lights in a vertical line, as required by the Inland Rules.) [24(c)] A vessel pushed ahead will *not* carry the special flashing yellow light used at the bow of such barges on inland waters.

The IntRR *do not include* any special requirements for "an inconspicuous, partially submerged vessel or object being towed." There is *no exception* to the requirement for different lights when towing for vessels not normally used for such work, but which are temporarily towing, while rendering assistance to a vessel in distress or otherwise needing assistance.

Lights for Vessels with Limited Maneuverability

International Rule 27(d) provides *additionally* that a vessel engaged in dredging or underwater operations and restricted in her ability to maneuver must, when underway, show masthead light(s), sidelights, and a sternlight, together with the prescribed white, red, and green all-round lights required by other paragraphs of that Rule.

The exception for the special lights required by Rule 27 is *limited* to vessels *less than 12 meters* (39.4 ft) in length; *all* vessels over this length must comply. [27(g)]

International Rule 28 *permits* a vessel "constrained by her draft" to show three red all-round lights in a vertical line wherever they can best be seen. (This is the Rule which is omitted from the U.S. Inland Rules.)

DAY SHAPES OF THE INTERNATIONAL RULES

International Rule 25(e) *requires* the use of a cone, with point downward, as a day shape on *all* sailing craft, when using machinery for propulsion while her sails are up. There are *no exceptions* in this rule for smaller sailboats.

The exception for showing an "anchor ball" is *limited* to vessels *under 7 meters* (23.0 ft) in length, when anchored in waters not subject to water-borne traffic. A similar exception applies to the requirement for showing three balls in a vertical line if aground in such a traffic-free area. [30(e)]

International Rule 24 has *no requirements* for day shapes on an inconspicuous, partly submerged vessel or object being towed.

International Rule 28 *permits* a vessel "constrained by her draft" to show a day shape consisting of a cylinder.

EXEMPTIONS

International Rule 38 provides for temporary and permanent exemptions to the requirements for the characteristics and positioning of lights, in order to ease the transition from the 1960 Rules to the 1972 Rules. Where such exemptions are of a limited duration, they are stated in terms of years "after the date of entry into force of these Regulations"; this date was 15 July 1977.

Vessels in existence on 15 July 1977 have four years to install lights meeting the required range of visibility and color specifications. [38(a) and (b)] Any repositioning of lights because of the change from specifications in customary units to metric units need not be done at all, since there is a permanent exemption. [38(c)] Repositioning of masthead lights and sidelights to meet the requirements of Annex 1 to the 1972 International Rules need not be accomplished until 15 July 1986, except that a permanent exemption is granted vessels 150 meters (492.2 ft) or less in length with respect to the requirement for the location of the forward masthead light and the horizontal separation of the after-masthead light, if carried. [38(d)]

PENALTIES

Although the International Regulations for Preventing Collisions at Sea, 1972, contain no provisions for penalties for violations, such provisions are included in the International Navigation Rules Act of 1977.

The penalties for violation of the International Rules of the Road by any vessel in U.S. waters or by a U.S. vessel in international waters are now the same as for violations of the U.S. Inland Rules; the maximum fine was increased from $500 to $5,000 in 1981. Vessels may be seized and proceeded against, or the required customs clearance denied, in the same manner as for Inland Rules violations.

INTERNATIONAL RULES CHANGES PENDING

At the time this chapter was written, there were a number of small changes pending to the International Rules of the Road. These included provisions for carrying the two or three masthead lights for towing either forward or aft, use by vessels 12 meters or less in length of a single all-round white light in place of a masthead light plus a sternlight, exemption from special lights for vessels performing emergency towing service, use of the tricolor masthead light on sailboats up to 20 meters in length, and the exemption of vessels under 12 meters in length from the requirement to show special lights and shapes when aground. The effect of these changes, expected to become effective in mid-1983, will be to reduce still further the differences between the International and Inland Rules. It seems that the drafters of the 1980 U.S. Inland Rules had a copy of the pending IntRR changes, and jumped the gun to get in there first!

CHAPTER 5

RULES OF THE ROAD / *Right-of-Way*
Whistle Signals
Fog Signals
Distress Signals

MOST OF US have had the experience, when walking down a street, of meeting another pedestrian, giving way to the right and having him turn to our right, then turning to the left and having him dodge to the same side, and finally bumping into him. To pedestrians on a sidewalk, such actions and subsequent collision are merely comical; between vessels on the water, it is very serious. Yet the skippers of ships and boats are human and might do the very same thing if there were not rules to guide them.

In the case of pedestrians on sidewalks, and even cars and trucks on highways, it is a fairly simple matter to keep clear of approaching danger. Both individuals and vehicles follow well-defined paths or lanes, and by keeping to their right, the danger of collision is nearly eliminated.

On the water, however, it is often a far different matter. Except in a limited number of areas, there are no narrow paths or channels to follow. Boats generally have a wide and open expanse of water on which to navigate, with their courses constantly crossing the tracks of other craft and vessels that may be in the vicinity. Thus the caution that must be observed on the water, even though the total traffic is much less than on land, is just as important as on sidewalks, streets, and highways.

RULES AND REGULATIONS

With the objective of preventing collisions, very carefully considered rules have been laid down so that the duty of the skipper of any vessel at the time of an encounter with another vessel is quite definitely prescribed. These rules are of three general classes. First, there are the International Regulations for Preventing Collisions at Sea, 1972, generally referred to by mariners as the International Rules of the Road, but by the Coast Guard as the "72 COLREGS." These were established as a multinational treaty and ratified by the United States for its vessels and waters. Second, there are the 1980 U.S. Inland Navigational Rules, enacted by Congress as laws of this country; these replaced three sets of rules—Inland, Great Lakes, and Western Rivers—that had been in effect for many decades. On the third level are regulations issued by various departments and agencies of the federal government. Most of these are promulgated by "the Secretary of the Department in which the Coast Guard is operating" (see page 32), or by the Commandant of the Coast Guard, under authority delegated to him by the Secretary. The principal regulations are the five annexes to the Inland Rules, including Annex V, Pilot Rules. State and local authorities may also issue

regulations covering matters related to the topics of this chapter, but these are too diverse to be considered in this book. In general, these regulations conform to the Inland Rules and Coast Guard regulations, but elaborate on certain minor details. Skippers should obtain knowledge of any such regulations that apply to the waters they use.

Numbered "Rules"

The International Rules and the U.S. Inland Rules contain sections which are designated as "Rules," numbered from 1 to 38. (The Inland Rules omit number 28.) These are grouped into five lettered "Parts," with Part B being further subdivided into three "Subparts" in the Inland Rules (called "Sections" in the International Rules). The rules of the road considered in this chapter concern the right-of-way between two vessels encountering each other, the general conduct of vessels in reduced visibility situations, whistle signals, fog signals, and distress signals. Annex III of both sets of Rules provides technical details of sound signalling equipment; Annex IV lists distress signals and regulations regarding their use.

74

FIG. 501 Many boating areas are relatively open expanses of water without specific channels. Craft may approach from one or more directions, often several at the same time. Knowledge of the right-of-way rules and whistle signals is important to every skipper.

These "rules of the nautical road" for both inland and offshore waters also prescribe navigation lights to be carried at night and certain shapes to be displayed by vessels during daylight; these are covered in Chapter 4.

Sequence of consideration

The 1980 U.S. Inland Navigational Rules will be considered in detail first. These are applicable on waters *inside* of demarcation lines at the entrances to most, but not all, harbors, bays, rivers, and inlets (see page 31). These also govern waters that were under the former Great Lakes and Western Rivers rules. Thus, the Inland Rules probably are applicable to a majority of our country's recreational boatmen.

The 1972 International Rules of the Road will be discussed in detail only where their provisions differ significantly from the 1980 U.S. Inland Rules. The International Rules are applicable *outside* the demarcation lines and in *all* waters along certain stretches of the U.S. coast —primarily New England waters, the Florida Keys, and the Gulf Coast—where there are no demarcation lines. The Inland Rules were derived from the 1972 International Rules and closely parallel them. The various provisions are matched rule for rule and annex for annex. Many rules are identical, but in a number of instances the content and language has been changed to reflect the generally smaller size of vessels and shorter distances involved in inland waters; in a few places an editorial change has been made for greater clarity. Annexes II and IV are identical; Annexes I and III have minor differences; and Annex V of the Inland Rules has no counterpart, since there are no Pilot Rules for the International Rules of the Road.

The consideration of the rules of the road in this chapter and Chapter 4 is not complete; it focuses primarily on points of greatest interest to boatmen.

Definition of Terms

The definitions of the Inland and International Rules that were discussed in Chapter 4 on pages 64(c) and 72 are also equally applicable in this Chapter. Additional definitions are as follows:

Whistle—any sound-signalling equipment capable of producing the prescribed blasts, and which complies with the specifications in Annex III. [32(a)]

Short blast—a blast of about one second's duration.

Prolonged blast—a blast of from four to six second's duration. (The term "long blast" is no longer used in the rules of the road.)

"Privileged" and "burdened" vessels

For decades and generations, skippers of ships and boats have used the terms "burdened" and "privileged" to define the status of two vessels encountering each other. The "privileged" vessel is the one that has the right-of-way—the right to proceed unhindered by the other. The "burdened" vessel is the one that does *not* have the right-of-way, the one that must take any necesssary action to keep out of the way of the privileged vessel.

These terms do not appear in the 1972 International Rules and the 1980 Inland Rules—but the concept remains. Officially, the privileged vessel is now the "stand-on" vessel; the burdened vessel is the "give-way" vessel. Although these terms are used in the titles of Rules 16 and 17, they are not included in the definitions of either set of rules. The new terms were adopted as being more descriptive of the required actions, but for years, many years, the terms "privileged" and "burdened" will surely remain in the vocabulary of mariners and boatmen.

The U.S. Inland Rules

The new Inland Rules were created by the "Inland Navigational Rules Act of 1980" (Public Law 96-591). The effective date was 24 December 1981 for all applicable waters except the Great Lakes, where a delay of several months was required to effect coordination with Canada. The annexes were authorized by the Act of Congress and promulgated as parts of Title 33, Code of Federal Regulations.*

STEERING AND SAILING RULES

The basic purpose of any set of rules of the nautical road is the prevention of collisions (indeed, this is the

FIG. 502 The 1980 Inland Rules now include the waters that formerly were governed by the Great Lakes and Western Rivers Rules.

75

* The material in this chapter on the Annexes was prepared from drafts before the final promulgation; differences may exist.

title of the International Rules). A major subdivision, Part B, termed "Steering and Sailing Rules," is particularly aimed at that goal with three subparts covering conduct of vessels in any visibility, [4–10] conduct when in sight of each other, [11–18] and conduct in restricted visibility. [19] Part D, Sound and Light Signals, is also largely focused on collision prevention.

Technically, the right-of-way rules do not come into effect between two vessels until the possibility of a collision exists—they are not applicable otherwise. Privilege and burden are not necessarily established when vessels first sight each other, as many seem to feel, but rather at the moment when a "risk of collision" develops. If, however, a collision does result, the rules must have been applicable—a "risk of collision" obviously existed before the event itself occurred. Although not a "rule," a basic principle of collision prevention is that, where the depth of the water permits, two vessels should not get so close to each other that the risk of a collision can materialize. A collision between two vessels is almost an impossibility if each skipper fully and properly obeys the applicable rules of the nautical road.

Determining risk of collision

Every vessel shall use all available means appropriate to the prevailing circumstances and conditions *to determine if risk of collision exists. If there is any doubt, such risk shall be deemed to exist.* [7(a)]

Every vessel must at all times maintain a proper lookout by sight *and hearing,* as well as all available means appropriate in the prevailing circumstances and conditions so as to make a full appraisal of the situation and of the risk of collision. [5]

An excellent method (and prescribed by the Rules) of determining whether your craft is on a collision course with another is to watch the relative bearing of the other vessel. If this bearing does not change appreciably, either forward or astern, a risk of collision exists. [7(d)] Then, the rules of the road apply, and appropriate action should be taken. More on this subject will be found on pages 449 and 450.

Boatmen are cautioned, however, against presuming there is no risk, when there *is* an appreciable change in bearing. The courts have held (112 F. 161) that such a presumption might, under some circumstances, be unwarranted. Each situation must be considered on its own merits. [7(d)]

In reduced visibility, proper use must be made of any radar equipment with which a vessel is equipped, if it

is operational, including long-range scanning to obtain early warning of risk of collision, and radar plotting or equivalent *systematic* observation of detected objects. [7(b)]

Assumptions must not be made on the basis of scanty information, especially scanty radar information. [7(c)]

Safe speed

Every vessel must proceed at a safe speed *at all times.* [6] (This replaces the former rule specifying moderate speed under conditions of reduced visibility.)

Rule 6(a) lists specific factors to be considered in determining a "safe speed," including but not limited to:

The state of visibility.

The traffic density, including concentration of fishing or other vessels.

The maneuverability of the vessel, with special reference to stopping distance and turning ability.

At night, the presence of background lights such as those from shore, or from the back-scatter of her own lights.

The state of wind, sea, and current, and the proximity of navigational hazards.

The draft in relation to the available depth of water.

Rule 6(b) provides *additional* guidance for determining a safe speed for a ship or boat fitted with an operational radar.

FIG. 504 All changes of course in the presence of a ship or another boat should be so pronounced and definite that they will be noticed and properly evaluated by the other skipper. Slight changes may be technically enough, but may fail to make intentions clear.

Actions to avoid collision

The Rules specifically require that any action taken to avoid collision, if the circumstances allow, will be positive, made in ample time, and with due regard to the observance of good seamanship. Any change of course or speed should be large enough to be readily apparent to the other vessel visually or by radar; a series of small changes should be avoided. Your judgment—your "seaman's eye"—may tell you that only a slight change will be sufficient, but such might well go undetected, leaving the other skipper in doubt as to your assessment of the situation and reaction to it. Make your actions both timely and boldly!

FIG. 503 When you are on a possible collision course with another vessel, keep a close check on her relative bearing. To be safe, there should be a distinct change in either direction; this will indicate that she will pass either ahead or astern of you. A constant or slowly changing bearing indicates probable danger.

Action taken to avoid collision must be sufficient to result in passing at a safe distance; its effectiveness must be checked until the other vessel is past and clear. If necessary to avoid collision, a vessel must slow down or take all way off by stopping or reversing her means of propulsion. [8]

Whistle Signals

One- and two-blast whistle signals to be used between power-driven vessels encountering each other will be discussed in this section, along with the determination of right-of-way and the necessary actions to be taken by the vessels. These signals are to be used only when the vessels are within sight of each other and are meeting or crossing at a distance within half a mile of each other. [34] These signals must never be used in fog or other condition of reduced visibility, if the vessels are not visible (by eye, not radar) to each other; only the fog signals of Rule 35 may be sounded at such a time.

Danger signal

If in any situation where two vessels—power-driven or sail—are approaching each other, either one fails to understand the actions or intentions of the other, or is in doubt as to whether sufficient action is being taken by the other vessel to avoid collision, the vessel in doubt must give the **danger signal**—*five or more* short and rapid blasts on her whistle. [34(d)]

This signal is also used by a skipper as an indication that he considers the actions of the other vessel dangerous to either vessel—such as a negative reply to a proposal to pass in a certain manner. *The giving of a danger signal does not relieve a vessel of her obligations or responsibilities under any rule.*

Although not specifically covered in the rules, it is prudent for a skipper hearing a danger signal, as well as he who sounds it, to *at once* slow or stop his vessel until the situation is clarified.

FIG. 505 In a confused situation—here caused by a boat backing into a dangerous encounter—it is important that the "danger signal" of five or more blasts be sounded promptly by a skipper uncertain of the other's intentions.

Equipment for sound signals

A vessel of 12 meters (39.4 ft) or more in length must have a *whistle* and a *bell;* a vessel of 100 meters (328.1 ft) or more in length must also have a *gong,* the tone and sound of which cannot be confused with those of the bell. [33(a)]

A vessel of less than 12 meters (39.4 ft) in length need not carry the sound-signaling equipment required on larger vessels, but if she does not, she must have "some other means of making an efficient sound signal." [33(b)] The regulations stemming from the Motor Boat Act of 1940 relating to "mouth, hand, or power operated" whistles have been repealed. There are now no requirements for small boats in terms of range (½ mile would be a reasonable minimum) or source of power—only in terms of efficiency—and sailboats have the same requirements as motorboats; the foghorn is no longer permitted.

Annex III contains detailed specifications for sound-signaling equipment, including different whistle tones, and ranges of audibility for various sizes of vessels over 12 meters (39.4 ft) in length. Higher-pitched tones are used for smaller vessels; for those of less than 75 meters (246.1 ft) length, the band of frequencies is 250–525 Hz. Required ranges of audibility gradually increase, from ½ mile for vessels 12 but less than 20 meters (39.4–54.7 ft) in length, to 2 miles; all distances are coordinated with specific sound pressure levels. [86.05] A vessel which is normally used for pushing ahead or towing alongside *may* carry a whistle with characteristics matched to the length of the longest towed-and-towing combination customarily operated, and use it even when operating singly. [86.15] Directional properties for whistles are specified, as well as their positioning, and a limitation on the sound pressure level at the vessel's own "listening posts" (lookout or helm position) [86.07 and 86.09]

Specifications for bells and gongs include different sizes for smaller and larger vessels, and a minimum sound-pressure level. A bell on a craft under 20 meters (65.7 ft) in length must be not less than 200 mm (7.9 inches) in diameter at the mouth. Bells on larger vessels must be at least 300 mm (11.8 inches) in diameter. The mass of the striker must not be less than 3% of the mass of the bell. [86.21 and 86.23] The bell or gong, or both, on a vessel may be replaced by "other equipment" (electronic?) having the same sound characteristics, provided that manual sounding of the prescribed signals is always possible. [33(a)]

Maneuvering lights

Whistle signals *may* be supplemented by a light signal synchronized with the whistle. This is a single all-round light, white or yellow, visible for at least two miles regardless of the size of the vessel. [34(b)] This *maneuvering light* must be placed in the same vertical plane as the "masthead" light(s), at least 1 meter (3.3 ft) *above* the forward masthead light, and at least 1 meter (3.3 ft) *above or below* the after masthead light. If a vessel carries only one masthead light, as will be the case for nearly all boats, the maneuvering light can be carried where it can best be seen, but not less than 1 meter (3.3 ft) above or below the masthead light; remember that a maneuvering light is an all-round light and should not be significantly obscured in any direction. [I, 84.23]

Rules for Power-driven Vessels

The rules of the road recognize three types of encounters between two approaching vessels—meeting,

---

Numbers and letters shown in brackets are references to the applicable Rule.

crossing, and overtaking. These may be collectively referred to as "passing situations"; see fig. 506. The rules governing right-of-way, whistle signals to be given, and actions to be taken with regard to course and speed changes, are given below for power-driven vessels. Remember that a boat being propelled by both machinery and sails is treated as a power-driven vessel.

Meeting situation

When two power-driven vessels are approaching one another head on, or nearly head on, this is a *meeting* situation. In this situation, it is the duty of each to pass on the *port* side of the other. [14(a)] Neither vessel has the right of way over the other, and both must alter course to starboard, if necessary, to provide sufficient clearance for safe passage. This is exactly the same, it will be noted, as for two cars meeting on a narrow road.

For the rule of the meeting situation to be applicable, both of two requirements must be met. First, the vessels must be meeting in such a manner as to involve risk of collision. Secondly, they must be on reciprocal or nearly-reciprocal courses. Such a situation is deemed to exist by day when a vessel sees the other ahead or nearly ahead, and by night when she can see the masthead lights of the other in a line or nearly in a line, or sees both sidelights. [14(b)] Although the rules do not set mathematical limits for the meeting situation, court interpretations and decisions over the years have established one point (11¼°) on either side of the bow as the practical boundaries within which vessels will be considered as meeting each other.

This rule does not apply to two vessels that will, if both keep on their respective courses without change of heading or speed, pass clear of each other. It also does not apply to situations by day, in which a vessel sees another ahead crossing her own course; nor by night to cases where the red light of one vessel is opposed to the red light of the other, or where the green light of one vessel is opposed to the green light of the other. It does not apply to situations where a red light without a green light, or a green light without a red light, is seen ahead; nor where both the red and green lights of another vessel are seen anywhere but ahead.

FIG. 507 In a nearly head-on meeting situation, both vessels must give way to starboard and sound one blast; neither has the right-of-way. If their projected courses are such that they will pass clear of each other, port-to-port, then neither must change course, but either signals one blast and the other answers similarly.

When a vessel has any doubt that a meeting situation exists, she must assume that it does exist and act accordingly; that is, change course to starboard [14(c)]

The 1980 Inland Rules no longer deal with a meeting situation in which the courses of the two vessels are in opposite directions, but their tracks are so far to starboard of each other that they cannot be considered as meeting "head-to-head." Such circumstances do not meet the "risk of collision" requirement.

In a winding channel, a vessel may first sight the other at an oblique angle rather than "head on, or nearly head on." Nevertheless, the situation is to be regarded as a meeting situation since such will be the case when the actual passing occurs. Each should keep to her own right side of the channel and neither has the right-of-way over the other.

Signals. When power-driven vessels are within sight of each other and meeting at a distance of one-half mile or less, each vessel *must* sound whistle signals as follows:

One short blast, meaning "I intend to leave you on my port side."

Two short blasts, meaning "I intend to leave you on my starboard side."

Three short blasts, meaning "I am operating astern propulsion" (engines in reverse gear).

Upon hearing the one- or two-blast signal from the other, a vessel will, if in agreement, sound the same signal and take any steps necessary to effect a safe passage. If, however, she doubts the safety of the proposed maneuver for any reason, she must sound the danger signal of five or more short, rapid blasts *and* take appropriate precautionary action until a safe passage agreement is made. [34(a)] The rule does not state which vessel should signal first—both craft are on an equal basis and either can make the first signal to the other.

Note that a vessel must **never** answer a one-blast signal with two blasts, or a two-blast signal with one blast. This is known as "cross signals," and is strictly prohibited. [V, 88.07]

FIG. 506 The Inland Rules of the Road recognize three types of "passing" situations—meeting, crossing, and overtaking. Specific procedures are established to govern the actions and signals of both vessels in such encounters.

Numbers and letters shown in brackets are references to the applicable Rule.

When one vessel sounds the danger signal in a meeting situation, both vessels should immediately reduce their forward speed to bare steerageway or stop. [8(e)] Neither vessel should attempt to proceed or pass until agreement is reached through the exchange of the same whistle signal, either one blast or two.

Crossing situations

When two vessels are not meeting head on, or nearly so, and each has the other forward of a direction 22½° abaft the beam, a crossing situation exists.

When two power-driven vessels are crossing, so as to involve risk of collision, the vessel that has the other on her own starboard side must keep out of the way of the other. [15] See fig. 508.

This leads to the unofficial definition of a craft's "danger zone"—a concept not explicitly stated in the rules of the road, but one very valuable for safety. This is the arc from nearly dead ahead to 22½° abaft the *starboard* beam; see fig. 509. If you see another vessel within this danger zone, she most likely is the stand-on (privileged) vessel; yours is the give-way (burdened) vessel and must change course or speed to avoid collision.

Exception. On the Great Lakes, Western Rivers, and any other waters specified by the Secretary, a vessel crossing a river must keep out of the way of a power-driven vessel proceeding up or down that river. [15(b)] This situation might be considered analagous to a road intersection on land, where the side street or minor road has a "Stop" sign to prevent interference with traffic proceeding on the main street or highway. This exception is now limited geographically, but it may later be extended to other waters.

Signals. The 1980 Inland Rules now *require* whistle signals in a meeting or crossing situation, if the vessels are in sight of each other and will pass within a distance of a half-mile. [34(a)] One, two, and three short blasts are used with the same meanings as described above for meeting situations. Again, the rules do not state which vessel should signal first, but by custom it is most often the vessel which is privileged, or believes herself to be privileged. A one- or two-blast signal is answered with the same number of blasts, if the other vessel is in agreement and will take the steps necessary to effect a safe passage. The danger signal of five or more short rapid blasts is used in the same way to indicate doubt as to the safety of the actions taken or the signalled intentions of the other vessel.

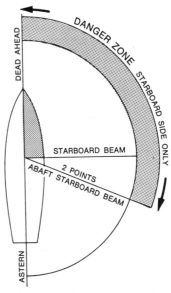

FIG. 509 A vessel in a crossing situation that has the other to starboard is the "give-way" (burdened) vessel. The other is the "stand-on" (privileged) vessel. Hence, a "danger zone" exists from dead ahead to two points (112½°) abaft the starboard beam, within which a crossing vessel has the right-of-way.

A maneuvering light *may* show one, two, three, or five or more flashes synchronized with the whistle blasts.

Note that this rule is applicable only if there is risk of collision. If the situation is such that the vessels will pass free and clear of each other, there is no privileged or burdened vessel, and whistle signals are not appropriate. In case of doubt, however, the safe procedure is to assume that the rules do apply, and exchange signals to be sure that the intentions of each are known to the other.

Although the rules do not explicitly so state, it is logical that when one vessel in a meeting or crossing situation sounds the danger signal, *both* vessels should immediately take such action as slowing, stopping, or backing, until signals for passing safely have been made and understood.

Use of radio communication

The 1980 Inland Rules state that vessels which have reached agreement in a meeting, crossing, or overtaking situation by using VHF-FM radiotelephone (Channel 13), as prescribed by the Bridge-to-Bridge Radiotelephone Act (see page 493), need not sound whistle signals, but may do so. If agreement is not reached, then whistle signals must be exchanged "in a timely manner," and these will govern the actions taken. [34(h)]

Overtaking situation

If one vessel is coming up on another, from astern of a direction 22½° abaft the beam of the other vessel, and making greater speed so as to close the distance between them, the vessel astern is said to be overtaking the slower vessel; fig. 500. At night, this situation would exist when the vessel astern could not see either of the navigation side lights of the vessel ahead. By day, the overtaking vessel cannot always know with certainty whether she is forward or abaft a direction 22½° abaft

FIG. 508 Vessels are "crossing" if they are not meeting head-on, or nearly so, and each has the other on a relative bearing forward of two points abaft either beam, port or starboard. The Rules of the Road determine relative right-of-way if there is risk of collision.

Numbers and letters shown in brackets are references to the applicable Rule.

FIG. 510 The overtaking boat is here coming up on the larger craft's starboard quarter. This is the less-than-usual overtaking situation, but it is not illegal. The larger craft is privileged and holds her course and speed.

FIG. 511 Although the smaller craft has moved up into the overtaken vessel's "danger zone," the relative right-of-way has not changed and she is still burdened and must make any necessary course and/or speed changes to pass safely.

the other vessel's beam; if in doubt, she should assume that she is an overtaking vessel. [13(b) and (c)]

Notwithstanding any other provision in the Rules of Road, every vessel overtaking another must keep out of the way of the overtaken vessel. The overtaking vessel is burdened; the overtaken vessel is privileged. [13(a)]

The rules state specifically that once a vessel is in an overtaking status, she remains so for the remainder of the encounter; no subsequent alteration of the bearing between the two vessels will serve to make the overtaking vessel a crossing vessel within the meaning of the rules, or relieve her of her duty to keep clear of the overtaken vessel until she is finally past and clear. In other words, should the overtaking vessel come up on the starboard side of the overtaken vessel, and move into the latter's danger zone, she does not by this movement become the privileged vessel with the right-of-way over the overtaken craft. [13(d)]

Signals. If the overtaking vessel desires to pass on the port side of the vessel ahead—as would be normal if the slower vessel were keeping to the right of a channel (see fig. 512)—she must sound a two-short-blast signal. If the privileged vessel agrees with such a passing, she should immediately sound the same two-blast signal. The faster vessel then directs her course to port and passes as proposed and agreed.

Should the vessel astern desire to pass on the other's starboard side—not normal, but legal (see fig. 512)—she must sound a one-short-blast signal, which is returned in kind by the privileged vessel if she consents. [34(c) and 9(e)]

If in either of the above situations, the vessel ahead does not consider that the passing can take place safely as proposed by the burdened vessel, she must immediately sound the danger signal of five or more short, rapid blasts. (The danger signal should also be sounded if the overtaking craft attempted an unsafe passing without first giving a whistle signal of her intentions.)

An overtaking vessel that receives a danger signal in reply to her stated intention to pass should immediately cease all actions related to passing and reduce speed so

as to not close further on the overtaken vessel; fig. 512. No attempt should be made to pass until the proper signals have been given and answered. Although not provided for in the rules, it is reasonable for a privileged vessel to give the danger signal, pause, and then give the *other* passing signal to the burdened vessel—saying in effect, "The side that you proposed is unsafe, but the other is OK." This initiation of the proposal and agreement for passing by the privileged vessel is not normal, but often it is logical, considering that the leading vessel has a better view of the conditions ahead.

As in the meeting situation, "cross signals"—answering one blast with two, or two blasts with one—are prohibited. Answer a signal *only* with the same signal as given by the other vessel, or with the danger signal. [I, 88.07]

Although the slower vessel ahead is privileged, she must in no case attempt to cross the bow or crowd upon the course of the passing vessel.

OVERTAKING CRAFT REDUCES SPEED & REMAINS BEHIND

A   B   C

FIG. 512 a, b, c The overtaking craft (1, above) signals first as indicated by numbers above. The overtaken (privileged) vessel (2, above) replies with the same signal (and the passing occurs normally) or with the danger signal (and the overtaking craft must not attempt to pass until the proper signals have been exchanged).

Numbers and letters shown in brackets are references to the applicable Rule.

Narrow channels

A vessel in a narrow channel must keep to the right and as close to the outer limit of the channel as is safe and practicable. This places a burden on a vessel on the left side of a channel to (1) be there only if she must, and (2) to establish agreement for a starboard-to-starboard passage. **Exception.** On the Great Lakes, Western Rivers, and any other waters specified by the Secretary, a power-driven vessel operating in a narrow channel or fairway and proceeding *downbound with a following current* has the right-of-way over an upbound vessel and shall initiate maneuvering signals as appropriate. The vessel proceeding upbound against the current must hold as necessary to permit safe passing. [19(a)] The geographic coverage is limited so as to avoid tidal areas where the normal reversing current could cause confusion as to which vessel had the right-of-way.

A vessel less than 20 meters (65.7 ft) in length, or a sailing vessel, must not impede the passage of a vessel that can navigate safely only within a narrow channel or fairway. [9(b)]

A vessel engaged in fishing must not impede the passage of any other vessel navigating within a narrow channel or fairway. [9(c)]

A vessel must not cross a narrow channel or fairway in such a manner as to impede the progress of a vessel that must stay within that channel or fairway. The latter vessel must use the danger signal if in doubt as to the intentions of the crossing vessel. [9(d)]

If the circumstances allow, a vessel must not anchor in a narrow channel. [9(g)]

Rounding bends in a channel

A special signal is provided for a situation in which a vessel, power-driven or sail, approaches a bend or area of a channel where other vessels may be obscured from view by an intervening obstruction such as the height of the banks, vegetation, or structures. In such a situation, the vessel sounds one prolonged blast. This signal will be answered with one prolonged blast by any approaching vessel that may be within hearing around the bend or behind the obstructions. [34(e)] If such an answer is received, normal whistle signals must be exchanged when the vessels come within sight of one another. If no reply to her signal is heard, the vessel may consider

FIG. 514 Vessels, including boats, approaching a bend in a river, where craft approaching from the other direction cannot be seen at a distance of a half-mile, must sound a special signal of one prolonged blast of 4 to 6 seconds duration.

the channel ahead to be clear and govern herself accordingly. All vessels in such situations must be navigated "with particular alertness and caution." [9(f)]

Leaving a berth

A power-driven vessel leaving a dock or berth must sound a warning signal of one prolonged blast. [34(g)]

Note that, although it is not explicitly so stated in the Rules of the Road, it may be inferred that a craft just emerging from a slip or berth does not have the right-of-way over another vessel passing in the channel or nearby open water, even though she is in the other's danger zone. Her privileged status in a crossing situation is not established until she is "fully in sight."

Ferry boats

Although there are no express provisions in the Inland Rules of the Road that give any special privileges to ferry boats, the courts have repeatedly ruled that ferries are entitled to a reasonable degree of freedom of entrance to and exit from their slips. The same is true in regard to other craft using slips and piers. Boats should avoid passing unnecessarily close to piers, wharves, etc., where they may be caught unawares by the movements of other craft.

Rules for Sailing Vessels

The provisions of Inland Rule 12 are applicable only to situations involving two sailing vessels; neither may be under power or a combination of sail and power.

When two sailing vessels are approaching one another so as to involve risk of collision, one of them must keep out of the way of the other in accordance with the following conditions:

(a) When each has the wind on a different side, the vessel which has the wind on the port side must keep out of the way of the other.

FIG. 513 A boat leaving its slip in a marina, or exiting from between parallel piers, should sound a long blast of 8 to 10 seconds duration. She does not have right-of-way until out in the clear.

Numbers and letters shown in brackets are references to the applicable Rule.

(b) When both have the wind on the same side, the vessel which is to windward must keep out of the way of the vessel that is to leeward.

(c) If a vessel with the wind on her port side sees a vessel to windward and cannot determine with certainty whether the other vessel has the wind on her port or on her starboard side, she must keep out of the way of that other vessel.

For the purpose of Rule 12, the windward side is considered to be the side opposite to that on which the mainsail is carried (or in the case of a square-rigged vessel, the side opposite to that on which the largest fore-and-aft sail is carried).

Signals. Sound signals are not used in passing situations between two sailing vessels.

Encounters between sailing and power vessels

In general, a sailing vessel has the right-of-way over a vessel propelled by machinery or by both sail and machinery. The power-driven vessel must keep out of the way of the sailing vessel. [18(a)] There are, however, some exceptions and they should be thoroughly understood.

FIG. 516 Rule 12 covers the relative right-of-way between sailboats encountering each other on either Inland or International Rules waters. The "give-way" (burdened) craft is shown with shaded sails.

Should a sailing vessel overtake a power-driven vessel —not likely, but possible—the overtaking situation rule prevails and the sailing vessel is the burdened one, regardless of the means of propulsion.

Likewise, a sailing vessel is not the privileged vessel in an encounter with certain vessels engaged in fishing, a vessel not under command, or a vessel restricted in her ability to maneuver. [18(b)]

General Right-of-Way Provisions

Except for vessels specifically designated otherwise— such as vessels in narrow channels and when overtaking —vessels may be "ranked" for right-of-way as follows:
Vessels not under command
Vessels restricted in ability to maneuver
Vessels engaged in fishing
Sailing vessels
Power-driven vessels
Each type of vessel in this list must yield right-of-way to vessels listed higher, and will be privileged with respect to those lower on the list. [18]

Vessel Traffic Services

New Rule 10 directs, simply, that all vessels required to participate in a "Vessel Traffic Service" (VTS) shall comply with all applicable regulations. A VTS normally provides traffic advisories to large vessels and may, at times, control their movements. Small craft are not normally subject to VTS regulations, but should be aware of the restrictions placed on the movement of larger vessels.

FIG. 515 a In any encounter between a sailing vessel and a power-driven vessel, the former has the right-of-way unless she is overtaking the other. Whistle signals are not sounded by a motorboat in such a situation as the sailboat is not equipped to reply.

FIG. 515 b The right-of-way of a sailboat over a power-driven vessel does not prevail if the latter cannot navigate outside the limits of the channel she is using.

Numbers and letters shown in brackets are references to the applicable Rule.

FIG. 517 A boat underway in reduced visibility must sound proper fog signals and proceed at a "safe speed." This is not precisely defined in the Rules, but numerous court interpretations exist.

Conduct in Restricted Visibility

Rule 19 applies to vessels *not* in sight of each other in or near areas of restricted visibility. They must procede at a "safe speed adapted to the prevailing circumstances and conditions"; a power-driven vessel must have her engine ready for immediate maneuvers. Vessels must also have due regard for the steering and sailing rules that prevail under *all* conditions of visibility; see Subpart I of Part B, Rules 4 through 10. See also section on safe speed, Rule 6, on page 76.

Sound Signals in Restricted Visibility

Rule 35 prescribes sound signals to be given by different types of vessels in various conditions when in *or near* an area of restricted visibility. These are often termed "fog signals," but are equally applicable in any of the conditions included in the definition of restricted visibility in Rule 3(k); see page 64(d). They are equally applicable by day or night. The same equipment is used for making these signals as is used for maneuvering and warning signals, and is the same for power-driven and sailing vessels.

Courts have held that fog signals should be sounded when visibility is reduced to the distance at which sidelights are required to be seen. These sound signals serve two purposes. Basically, they alert other vessels to the presence in their vicinity of the vessel sounding the signal, and give a rough indication of her position. Secondly, the signals may provide an indication of her status (underway or not) or limitations of maneuverability (towing, being towed, sailing, fishing, etc.)

FIG. 518 A power-driven vessel underway in reduced visibility sounds one prolonged blast—4 to 6 seconds duration—at intervals of not more than two minutes.

Power-driven vessels

A power-driven vessel making way through the water must sound one prolonged blast at intervals of *not more than two minutes*. [35(a)] Such a vessel underway but stopped and making no way through the water must sound, at the same intervals, a signal of two prolonged blasts separated by an interval of about two seconds. [35(b)]

A vessel towing or pushing another ahead, a vessel not under command, a vessel restricted in her ability (whether underway or at anchor), and a fishing vessel (whether underway or anchored), all sound the same signal—one prolonged blast followed by two short blasts. [35(c)]

Sailing vessels underway

A sailing vessel underway makes the *same* sound signal in restricted visibility conditions as a towing vessel, fishing vessel, etc., as just described above—one prolonged blast on her whistle followed by two short blasts. [35(c)] (The former Inland Rules had different signals for different tacks, and required a "foghorn" rather than whistle; these no longer are used.

FIG. 519 A vessel at anchor in fog or other conditions reducing visibility must ring her bell rapidly for about five seconds at intervals of not more than one minute. A craft of 20 meters (65.7 ft) or less anchored or moored in a "special anchorage area" is not required to sound this signal.

Vessels at anchor

A vessel at anchor *must*, at intervals of *not more than one* minute, ring the bell rapidly for about five seconds. If she is 100 meters (328.1 ft) or more in length, the bell must be sounded in the forepart of the vessel and immediately thereafter the gong must be sounded rapidly in the after part of the vessel. [35(f)]

A vessel at anchor *may* additionally sound a three-blast whistle signal—one short, one prolonged, one short—to give warning of her position, and the possibility of collision with an approaching vessel. [35(f)]

Vessels aground

A vessel aground must sound the bell signal of a vessel at anchor (and the gong signal, if applicable) and additionally give three separate and distinct strokes on the bell immediately *before and after* the rapid ringing of the bell. [35(g)]

A vessel aground *may* also sound an appropriate whistle signal on detecting the approach of another vessel, if there is the possibility of collision. [35(g)] This rule does not specify what signal might be "appropriate," but it would appear logical to use the five-blast danger signal especially when the vessels come into sight of each other.

Numbers and letters shown in brackets are references to the applicable Rule.

FIG. 520 A vessel towed astern (the last vessel if more than one is being towed in tandem) must, if manned, sound a signal of one prolonged blast followed by three short blasts; this should be sounded immediately following the tug's fog signal.

Vessels being towed

If manned, a vessel being towed (or the last vessel if several are being towed in a string) must sound a fog signal of four blasts—one prolonged and three short blasts—at intervals of not more than two minutes. When practicable, this signal should be sounded immediately after the signal of the towing vessel. [35(e)] (A vessel being towed now sounds her fog signals or a whistle; the term "foghorn" is no longer used.)

Pilot vessels

A pilot vessel, when engaged on pilot duties in restricted visibility conditions, *may* sound an "identity signal" of four short blasts. This would be in addition to the normal signals of a vessel underway, underway with no way on, or at anchor. [35(i)]

Small craft

Craft less than 12 meters (39.4 ft) in length need not sound the fog signals as described above; but if they do not, they must make some other efficient sound signal at intervals of not more than two minutes. [35(h)]

Special anchorage areas

Inland Rule 35(j) permits the omission of fog signals for vessels in a "special anchorage area" [see page 64(f)], if they are less than 20 meters (65.7 ft) in length, or are a barge, canal boat, scow, or "other nondescript craft."

Not too often!

The rules prescribe an interval of "not more than two minutes" (one minute for bell and gong signals) between the successive soundings of fog signals from a vessel. The timing, if not done by automatic means, should be measured to reasonable accuracy by the second hand on a watch or clock. Two minutes is a relatively brief interval and normally should not be further reduced by skippers concerned over the risk of collision. The interval between your blasts should be used for listening for other vessel's blasts, and is as valuable for safety as the actual blowing of your own whistle or horn. If your signals are sounded automatically, interrupt this procedure from time to time to make sure that you are not signaling in synchronization with another vessel and thus masking his blasts with the sound of your own.

BASIC RESPONSIBILITIES

There are two rules of the road that are of such primary importance that every skipper should know them by heart and be able to discuss them intelligently.

The Rule of Good Seamanship

Rule 2(a) is the broad, summing-up "rule of good seamanship." It provides that nothing in the rules shall exonerate any vessel, or the owner, master, or crew thereof, from the consequences of any failure to comply with the rules, or of the neglect of any precaution that may be required by the ordinary practice of seamen, or by the special circumstances of the case. Whatever you can do to avoid a collision, you must do!

Lookouts

Every vessel—and this includes boats of all sizes—must at *all* times maintain a proper lookout by *sight and hearing,* as well as by all other available and appropriate means, so as to make a full appraisal of the situation and the risk of collision. [5]

The need for a proper lookout is often taken rather too lightly by the skippers of boats and yachts, and this is a serious mistake. Under normal circumstances, the helmsman will satisfy this need, but he must be qualified, alert, and have no other responsibilities. The use of an automatic steering mechanism (a so-called "autopilot"; see page 522) is no justification for the absence of a human helmsman at the controls, observing all around the horizon and ready to take over immediately if needed. The use of radar at night or in fog is no justification for the absence of an additional person as a lookout, stationed outside the bridge, usually forward, where he can hear as well as see. The noise level of most motorboats renders the helmsman totally ineffective as a listening watch.

It is not the intent of Rule 5 to require additional personnel forward if none is needed for safety. The burden of proof, however, will continue to be on each vessel involved in a collision to establish that a proper lookout could not have prevented the accident.

FIG. 521 A good listening as well as visual lookout is essential in reduced visibility situations. On power-driven boats, this normally means sending a man to the bow, away from the noise of the craft's own engines.

Numbers and letters shown in brackets are references to the applicable Rule.

The General Prudential Rule

Rule 2(b) is often termed the "general prudential rule" and is of great importance because of its wide applicability.

In obeying and construing the Rules of the Road, due regard must be given to all dangers of navigation and collision, and to any special circumstances, including the limitations of the vessels involved, which may render a departure from the rules necessary to avoid immediate danger. No vessel is given the right of way *through* another vessel!

Interpretation of "immediate danger"

Courts have placed considerable emphasis on the words "immediate danger" of Rule 2(b) in rendering their decisions. The basic principle is that the rules must not be abandoned whenever perceptible risk of collision exists, but only when imperatively required by special circumstances in order to avoid such danger or the actions of one vessel alone will not avoid a collision.

Other Rules and Procedures

There are a number of other, somewhat unrelated, rules and procedures with which a skipper should be familiar.

Signals to attract attention

In order to attract the attention of another vessel, any vessel may make light and/or sound signals that cannot be mistaken for any signal authorized in the rules, or may direct the beam of his searchlight in the direction of the danger in such a way as to not embarrass any vessel. [36]

High-intensity flashing ("strobe") lights have been widely used for this purpose in the past. Their continued use for this purpose, however, has been objected to by some persons and there is the possibility that in the future such a light will become a distress signal, rather than a signal to attract attention.

Signals for drawbridges

For many years, a diverse range of signals was used throughout the United States in connection with the opening of drawbridges. Perhaps the most common whistle signal was three short blasts—a signal that had another, and very different, basic meaning, namely, that the vessel was operating her engine(s) in reverse.

Now, however, new Coast Guard regulations—not a part of the Inland Rules or Pilot Rules—prescribe uniform and unmistakable whistle signals for drawbridge operation. A vessel desiring that a closed drawbridge be opened for her passage will sound one prolonged blast of her whistle followed by one short blast; this signal has no other meaning in any set of rules of the road. The regulations also provide for making "these blasts" —meaning the opening signal—by horn, bell, or by shouting, or by any other similar device producing a sound that can be clearly heard.

If the bridge tender will open the draw immediately, he responds with a similar one-prolonged, one-short blast signal. If the draw cannot be opened immediately, the bridge tender will sound five short blasts. When this signal has been sounded from the bridge, a vessel is specifically prohibited from attempting to pass through the closed draw. When a draw is open and is to be closed immediately, the bridge tender must first sound the same five-short-blast signal.

FIG. 522 Signals for the opening of a drawbridge are being standardized as one prolonged blast followed by one short blast. The signal for canal locks may be the same or may be different; see the appropriate Coast Pilot volume for details.

Visual signals are also prescribed for alternate use, if weather conditions may prevent sound signals from being heard, or if sound-producing devices are not functioning properly. (Sound signals may also be used together with visual signals.) A vessel signals with a white flag of sufficient size as to be readily visible for one-half mile by day, or a white light bright enough to be seen at the same distance at night. This signal is raised and lowered vertically, in full sight of the bridge tender, until acknowledged. This person signals that the bridge will open immediately by repeating the same signal. The signal from the bridge that it cannot be opened immediately, or if open must be closed immediately, is a red flag waved horizontally by day, or a red light swung back and forth horizontally at night, in full sight of the vessel. (Some bridges may have mechanical devices and/or flashing electrical lights to signify the same meanings.)

Radio communications may be used to request a bridge opening and to receive information as to the bridge's status and the actions to be taken. If agreement is reached by radio, sound or visual signals are not required; both the vessel and the bridge must continue to monitor the selected channel—often 16, occasionally 13 or 12—until the vessel has cleared the draw. If radio contact cannot be maintained, sound or visual signals must be used.

When a vessel wishes to pass through two or more bridges close together, the opening signal is given for the first bridge, and after it has acknowledged that it will

Numbers and letters shown in brackets are references to the applicable Rule.

85

open promptly, the opening signal for the second bridge is given, and so on until all bridges have acknowledged that they will be opening promptly.

If two or more vessels approach the same drawbridge at nearly the same time, from the same or opposite directions, *each vessel must signal independently* for the opening of the draw, and the draw tender must reply in turn to the signal of each vessel.

Signals for the operation of canal locks are often the same as those for bridges nearby, but not always! Consult the appropriate volume of the Coast Pilot or Navigation Regulations for the proper signals to use before approaching any lock.

PILOT RULES FOR INLAND WATERS

The statutory Inland Navigational Rules of the Road provide authority for the issuance of regulations known as **Pilot Rules.** These are now in Annex V to the 1980 Inland Rules, and are much reduced in scope and length from their former edition. The Pilot Rules require that a copy of the Inland Navigational Rules be kept on board every self-propelled vessel 12 meters (39.4 ft) or more in length. [88.05]

The other five current Pilot Rules have been discussed in Chapter 4 and this chapter, in connection with related material of the rules.

EXEMPTIONS

The intent of the Act is that any vessel, or class of vessels, the keel of which was laid, or which was at an equivalent stage of construction, on 24 December 1981, and which complied with older requirements, is exempted from the Annex III technical requirements for sound-signalling equipment until 24 December 1990. Vessels constructed since 24 December 1980 must comply with all the requirements of the 1980 Inland Rules, including the technical details of Annex III.

PENALTIES

The penalties for violation of the Inland Rules are described in Chapter 2; see page 39.

International Rules of the Road

The "International Regulations for Preventing Collisions at Sea, 1972"—the full and formal name for what is generally called the International Rules of the Road (IntRR)—were created by an international conference and made applicable to U.S. waters and vessels by Presidential Proclamation and Act of Congress; they came into effect on 15 July 1977. The 1972 IntRR consist of "Rules" numbered from 1 to 38, plus four Annexes. The rules are grouped into five lettered "Parts," with Part B being further subdivided into three numbered "Sections."

Certain of the rules relate to navigation lights and shapes; these were discussed in Chapter 4. This chapter will consider only those rules and annexes relating to right-of-way, conduct of vessels in restricted visibility, sound signals and distress signals.

Applicability

The International Rules are applicable on various waters as discussed on page 71. Some foreign nations do not have their own "inland rules" and the IntRR are used on all their internal waters often with some local modifications or Pilot Rules.

Manner of consideration

Study of the 1980 U.S. Inland Rules provides an excellent base for learning the International Rules of the Road. Hence, the International Rules will be considered in detail here only where they differ from the 1980 U.S. Inland Rules. Topics will be discussed in the same sequence.

Definitions

The International Rules contain one definition that is not used in the U.S. Inland Rules. "A vessel constrained by her draft" is a power-driven vessel, which, because of her draft in relation to the available depths of water, is severely restricted in her ability to deviate from the course that she is following. [3(h)]

The International Rules do not, of course, contain certain definitions which are applicable only to U.S. internal waters, such as "Great Lakes" and "Western Rivers," and "Inland Waters."

STEERING AND SAILING RULES

The rules in Part B are very nearly identical in the two sets, but where they do differ, the difference can be considerable and significant.

Whistle Signals

The one- and two-short blast whistle signals in the Inland Rules under conditions of good visibility are "sig-

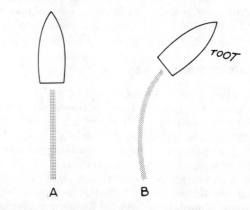

FIG. 523 a, b Under the International Rules, a power-driven vessel starting a change of course within sight of another vessel must sound a whistle signal. This is not returned by the other vessel, and thus there is no "exchange" of signals.

nals of intent and agreement," whereas those of the International Rules are indications of *taking action to alter course.* The IntRR signals are often termed "rudder signals"; they do *not* require a reply, although in some instances the other vessel will take similar action and so sound the same signal. The three- and five-or-more short blast signals have the same meaning in both sets of Rules. The 1980 Inland Rules retained the former U.S. signals, rather than adopting those of the 1972 International Rules, because of their long established use, plus the belief that they were simpler, clearer, and more suitable for confined inland waters.

Equipment for sound signals

Annex III of the International Rules presently differs from that of the Inland Rules, but proposals have been made that may result, in several years, in changes to the former that will eliminate many or all of these differences that are technical in nature; these proposals result primarily from experience gained in the years between the writing of the two sets of rules. The International Rules allow somewhat higher-pitched whistles on vessels between 12 and 75 meters (39.4 and 246.1 ft) in length; the new Inland Rules may bar the use of small hand-held air- or freon-operated horns on craft 12 meters (39.4 ft) or more in length, because of their high-frequency sound; there are no frequency limits for shorter craft.

The International Rules *do not contain* the provision allowing a vessel normally used for towing alongside or pushing ahead to carry and use a whistle matched to the length of the customary combination of towed and towing vessels.

Sound signaling equipment that is acceptable to the International Rules can also be used on inland waters, as provided for in Inland Rule 2(b) (ii).

Rules for Power-driven Vessels

The rules for meeting and crossing situations are the same in both sets, except for whistle signals. The International Rules *do not have* the one-half mile closest point of approach requirement for signaling of intent as to which side each will pass the other on, or the reply signals of agreement. They *do require* a whistle signal for each change of course, without reply signals from the other vessel. (Except that on winding rivers where the vessel's course follows the waterway, no whistle signals are used for the many necessary changes of course.)

Overtaking vessels

International Rule 9(e) prescribing procedures for vessels in an overtaking situation are *applicable* only in a narrow channel or fairway and only if the vessel being overtaken has to take some action to permit safe passing. [9(e)(i)], not in all waters, as in the Inland Rules. The whistle signals are very different, and quite complex. [34(c)]

A vessel overtaking another will signal her intention by two prolonged blasts, followed by one short blast ("I intend to overtake you on your starboard side") or by two prolonged followed by two short blasts ("I intend to overtake you on your port side"). The vessel about to be overtaken signals her agreement with one prolonged, one short, one prolonged, and one short blast—this is the letter "C" in Morse code and the international signal for "yes." In case of doubt, the vessel about to be overtaken will sound the five-or-more short and rapid blasts.

FIG. 524 **The International Rules require whistle signals in an overtaking situation** *only* **in a narrow channel where the overtaken vessel must take some action for a safe passage. The signals are much more complex than those of the Inland Rules; see text for details.**

Use of radio communication

The International Rules *do not contain* provisions for the use of radiotelephone communications in place of whistle signals. This does not mean, however, that such procedures are not an excellent means of ensuring a safe passing.

Narrow channels

International Rule 9(d) *differs* from its Inland Rules counterpart in that the sounding of a danger signal by a vessel that observes another crossing a narrow channel or fairway is optional, rather than mandatory.

Leaving a berth

The International Rules *do not include* a signal for a power-driven vessel leaving a berth, as does Inland Rule 34(g). Such a signal, however, is not prohibited and would be a good idea, even on those U.S. coastal waters subject to the IntRR.

General Right-of-Way Provisions

The International Rules *contain* the same general "ranking" of type of vessels for right-of-way as is found in the Inland Rules (see page 82), *plus* a provision that any vessel other than one not under command or one restricted in her ability to maneuver must avoid impeding the safe passage of a vessel constrained by her draft, a category not included in the Inland Rules. [18(d)]

Traffic Separation Schemes

International Rule 10 *contains many more details* as to the actions of vessels operating in a Traffic Separation Scheme (TSS). This rule applies only to internationally recognized TSSs. All TSSs adjacent to the United States are plotted on charts. The use of a TSS is optional, but if a vessel uses it, the provisions of Rule 10 must be adhered to. (Inland Rule 10 relates to Vessel Traffic Services, which are not the same as TSSs.)

Sound Signals in Restricted Visibility

The International Rules *prescribe* a fog signal for a vessel constrained by her draft; this is the same "one prolonged blast followed by two short blasts," as prescribed for a sailing vessel, a towing vessel, a vessel engaged in fishing, and a vessel restricted in her ability to maneuver. [35(c)]

The IntRR *do not provide* for "special anchorage areas," where fog signals need not be sounded by small craft, and by barges, scows, and the like.

EXEMPTIONS

International Rule 38(g) exempts all vessels built before 15 July 1977 from the technical requirements in Annex III for sound signalling equipment until 15 July 1986; newer ships and boats must meet these requirements.

PENALTIES

The International Rules of the Road do not contain any provisions for penalties for violation of the rules or requirements of the annexes. For all vessels in U.S. waters, and all U.S. vessels in any waters, the implementing action by Congress—the International Navigational Rules Act of 1977—does provide stiff penalties. These are the same as for violation of the 1980 U.S. Inland Rules; details are given on page 86.

Know the Rules

It cannot be emphasized too strongly that: (1) the skipper of any boat must know the rules of the road relating to his craft and waters; and (2) it is too late to start learning them when he gets into a tight situation! Rules must be studied carefully and thoroughly, and they should be periodically reviewed as a refresher.

Table 5–1   DISTRESS SIGNALS
Continuous sounding with any fog-signal apparatus
Firing of a gun or other explosive signal
Flames on the vessel (as from a burning tar or oil barrel, etc.)
A signal consisting of a square flag having either above or below it a ball or some object resembling a ball
Slowly and repeatedly raising and lowering arms outstretched to each side
Rockets or shells, throwing stars of any color or description, fired one at a time at short intervals
The International Code signal of distress indicated by NC
The signal SOS sent in the Morse Code (. . . — — — . . .) sent by any means
The spoken word "Mayday" by radiotelephone
A rocket parachute flare or a hand flare showing a red light
A smoke signal giving off a volume of orange colored smoke

The above signals can be used singly or in any combination.

Distress Signals

Because of their great importance, the accepted forms of **distress signals** have been written into both the International and U.S. Inland Rules of the Road. These are contained in Annex IV which is identical in both sets of rules.

Table 5-1 lists the *officially* recognized signals, but in an emergency a skipper can, and should, use any means within his capabilities to summon help.

Supplemental Signals

In the category of "supplemental signals," Annex IV lists a piece of orange-colored canvas, with either a black square and circle or other appropriate symbol, for identification from the air. (Actually, the circle should be solid, more properly termed a "disc"; and although "other appropriate symbol" is not defined, the word "HELP" in large black, block letters is often used.) Another supplemental signal is a dye marker; this will greatly enhance the spotting of a small object, such as a person, floating in rough waters.

Unofficial distress symbols

An unofficial, but well-recognized signal, especially in inland and coastal waters, is a red-orange flag of any size, waved from side-to-side.

Most American boatmen would recognize the flying of an inverted U.S. national or yacht ensign as a signal of distress. It should be carefully noted, however, that such a signal has no official sanction. This stems from the fact that the national flags of many maritime nations have no "top" or "bottom" and would appear exactly the same if turned upside down.

FIG. 525 The distress signals listed in Annex IV to both the Inland and International Rules are the same in both cases. Typical are the square flag and ball shape or the code flags "NC." It is proposed that the Inland Rules list also include a strobe light flashing 50 to 70 times per minute.

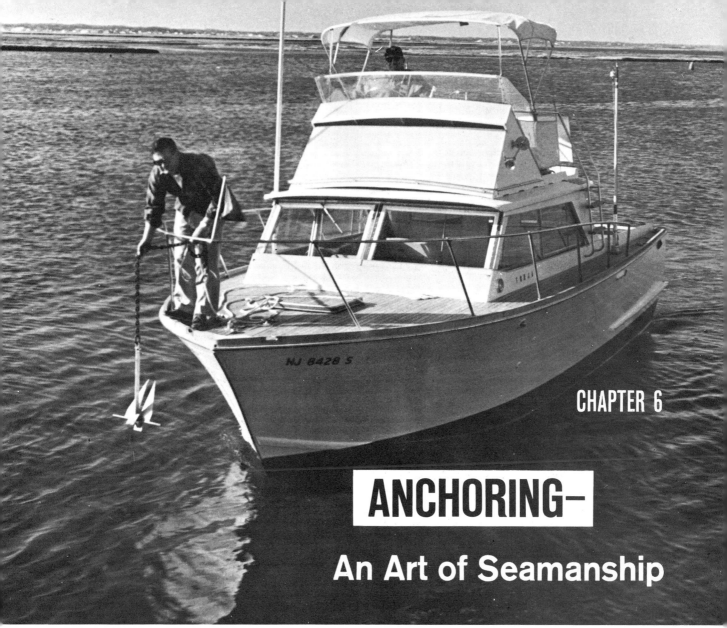

Photograph by Peter Smyth

ANCHORING—

An Art of Seamanship

CHAPTER 6

Of all the skills involved in seamanship, the art of anchoring is one the boatman must master if he is to cruise with an easy mind. Perhaps he is just getting by with inadequate gear, despite bad practices acquired in home waters. Sooner or later, carelessness and ignorance will lead to difficulty—probably inconvenience, possibly danger.

The essence of successful anchoring is to "stay put," without dragging, whenever the anchor is let go. Corollary to this is the need to respect the rights of nearby boats which could be fouled or damaged by your dragging.

Though the art may not be learned from the printed page alone, this chapter should help the tyro to get off to a good start, the seasoned boatman to round out and update his technique.

In quiet anchorages, in familiar surroundings, *ground tackle* (the gear we use) and the methods used are seldom put to test. Cruising into strange waters, find inadequate shelter in an exposed anchorage during a hard blow, and the elements will surely take the measure of both tackle and technique. The ultimate test, of course, would come in deep water on a lee shore with nothing between you and breakers on the beach except dependable gear. Ask yourself *now,* in a situation like that, would I hold . . . or hope?

The problem, then, breaks down into two principal parts—(1) the equipment we should carry, and (2) knowledge of how to use it. It is in this sequence that we treat the subject here, however anxious the reader may be to plunge headlong into the "how" aspect before he is quite familiar with the "what."

Conditions vary

In approaching the subject, it is imperative to have a sense of perspective, impossible to achieve if one is so wedded to the lore of one locality (no matter how good or effective) as to be blinded to practices proved in other areas. Lay down universal rules based on experience solely with one type of anchor in one kind of bottom, and the gale that would test your "rules" would be but a breeze compared to the storm of controversy you might raise in other knowledgeable quarters.

When we realize that the gear we see aboard that visiting boat from a distant port may have been dictated by proved and practical experience foreign to our own, we will have gone a long way toward broadening that perspective we need . . . and, who knows, perhaps improving our own anchoring skill as well.

Some of the variables

The man who has cruised in many areas, over many years, knows he can list nine or ten important variables. To cite a few: the size and type of boat; whether she is of light or heavy draft; the size and design of anchor; the nature of the bottom in which the anchor is bedded; the protection afforded by the anchorage; and the amount of sea running.

To say that any one kind of ground tackle would be ideal under all conceivable conditions for all boats of a given length is to discount the combined knowledge of the saltiest boatmen in waters all up and down our coastline. To rule out completely the value of certain specialized equipment is to overlook the fact that many a seasoned skipper has his own well-founded preferences . . . or prejudices.

FIG. 601 A century ago, wooden stock anchors were still in use. This one snagged the net of a dragger in the late 1940's, off Chatham, Cape Cod, offshore of Pollock Rip Lightship. It's likely that it was lost by a four- or five-masted coastal cargo schooner.
(From Kodachrome by Wm. H. Koelbel)

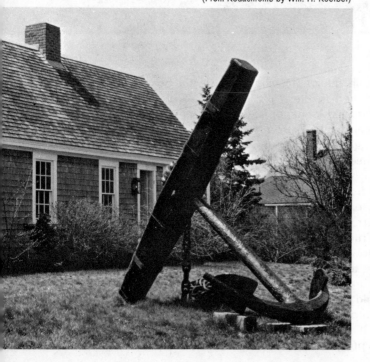

Evolution of the modern anchor

It is beyond the scope of this chapter to delve deeply into the history of anchors, interesting though that may be. Touching on it briefly, however, we get an insight into the evolution from ancient to modern design, and what lies behind the quest for an anchor that will *bury,* not drag. At this point it will be helpful to refer to the sketches, fig. 602, and labeled diagram, fig. 604, which, later, will clarify the meaning of terms used to describe the anchor's parts.

Going back to primitive times, the earliest "anchor" of which we have record was a simple stone used with a crude rope. Though it may have served under ideal conditions to prevent the drift of an ancient watercraft, dragging at times was inevitable, when sheer weight was unable to hold against the pull of wind and current.

Obviously what was needed was a device to engage the bottom, giving rise to the addition of simple wooden (and later, iron) hooks, forerunner of the arms and flukes found in later developments. To this day, survivors of this early anchor concept may be found Down East in Nova Scotia, where fishermen still fashion by hand their "killicks" of wood, stone and manila. Colloquially, we drop a "hook" when we lower an anchor.

Modifications of the hooking type of anchor evolved and, roughly 4,000 years ago, the Chinese added a stock at the crown end of the shank, perpendicular to the plane of the hooking arms, to put them in position to get a bite in the bottom. Junks still use this type today. In an ancient Greek design (about 750 B.C.) the stock had moved to the ring end of the shank.

In due course, in an effort to increase holding power, broad triangular flukes were added to the arms, giving rise to the old-fashioned kedge, fig. 603, often with a wooden stock, fig. 601, at the ring end of the shank, as used on naval vessels well into the 19th century. In 1821 the first of a series of stockless (patent) Navy anchors was invented Elimination of the stock permitted the shank to be drawn up into the hawsepipe of a vessel, flukes lying flat against the topsides.

Toward the middle of the 19th century, the mushroom anchor appeared, its design restricting its principal value to use in permanent moorings. Though their holding power is low, very small craft often use them for brief stops in light weather.

The principle of placing the stock at the crown end was brought to a relatively high state of development in the Northill design (now marketed as the Danforth Utility), where short, broad, thin flukes provided better penetration and a folding stock improved stowage characteristics.

In 1933, a radical innovation in design was introduced in England—the plow, a stockless type in which conventional flukes were replaced by a casting resembling a plow, pivoted at its point of attachment to the shank.

Supplanting mass and weight with scientific design, R. S. Danforth in 1939 developed what has been referred to by the U.S. Navy as the *lightweight-type* anchor in which broad pivoted flukes, stabilized by a stock, not only penetrate the bottom but bury completely until firm holding ground is reached. It is this feature, primarily, which distinguishes the *burying* anchor from a type that is prone to drag.

So much for history.

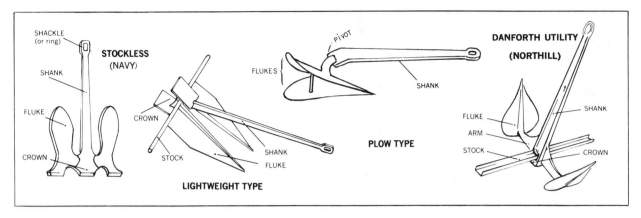

FIG. 602 How several anchor types differ. Principal parts of each are shown. All have shanks; not all have stocks.

Ground Tackle

Some terms and definitions

To prevent possibility of confusion in the use of terms, refer again to the labeled illustration of the parts of an anchor, fig. 604, and the more general definitions in Table 6-1. A popular version of the kedge was chosen to illustrate the parts, because it is a type frequently visualized as a conventional anchor. Subsequently we shall see how the proportioning and placement of parts have varied with the introduction of later designs. Many otherwise well-informed boatmen have often spoken of the shank and

stock as though the terms were interchangeable. In fact, however, most anchors (with few exceptions) have shanks, but some are stockless.

To illustrate graphically the basic fundamentals in anchoring, one authority sketches, in fig. 605, what has been referred to as *the anchoring system.* Though *scope* has been defined in Table 6-1 as the ratio between the length of the anchor line and the distance from the bow chocks to the bottom, there are other important factors, such as the range of any tidal rise and fall. This will be dealt with more fully later, as scope is one of the most important of all factors in determining holding power.

Finally, to forestall argument as to the validity of the term *rode,* it should be noted that the word has, on rare occasions, been challenged. Without going to its defense here, we can say that our best boating authorities have long accepted its usage in nautical jargon, and it is unlikely that it will ever be lost to the language.

TYPES OF ANCHORS IN USE

Lightweight type (LWT)

Scan a marine hardware catalog and, without experience, you may be confused by the diversity of designs offered today. What you should be buying, essentially, is holding power; sheer weight is no index of that. On the contrary, scientific design is the key to efficiency and a lightweight type, *if properly manufactured,* unquestionably stands at the top of the list today on a holding power-to-weight basis.

The lightweight type was originated just prior to World War II by R. S. Danforth. Its efficiency in war service was so high that it made possible the retraction of amphibious craft in assaults on enemy-held beachheads. After the war, models were developed specifically for recreational and small commercial craft and these are widely used. Such an anchor is excellent in mud and sand, and, with caution, can be used on rocky bottoms; however, it often does not hold well in grassy bottoms.

In this type of anchor, flukes are long and sharp, designed so that heavy strains bury the anchor completely. Tests have proved that it tends to work down through soft bottoms to firmer holding ground below, burying part of

---

TABLE 6-1. SOME BASIC DEFINITIONS

Anchor—A device designed to engage the bottom of a waterway and through its resistance to drag maintain a vessel within a given radius.

Anchor Chocks—Fittings on the deck of a vessel used to stow an anchor when it is not in use.

Anchor Rode—The line connecting an anchor with a vessel.

Bow Chocks—Fittings, usually on the rail of a vessel near its stem, having jaws that serve as fairleads for anchor rodes and other lines.

Ground Tackle—A general term for the anchor, anchor rodes, fittings, etc., used for securing a vessel at anchor.

Hawsepipe—A cylindrical or elliptical pipe or casting in a vessel's hull through which the anchor rode runs.

Horizontal Load—The horizontal force placed on an anchoring device by the vessel to which it is connected.

Mooring Bitt—A post or cleat through or on the deck of a vessel used to secure an anchor rode or other line to the vessel.

Scope—The ratio of the length of the anchor rode to the vertical distance from the bow chocks to the bottom (depth plus height of bow chocks above water).

Vertical Load—The lifting force placed on the bow of a vessel by its anchor rode.

Definitions (except scope) are from a code of standards and recommended practices adopted by the American Boat & Yacht Council.

FIG. 603 Old-fashioned kedges survived into the 20th century. This one, with iron stock, aboard the Joseph Conrad, is shown *catted* (hoisted up to the cathead).

the rode as well, fig. 609(b).

In place of a stock through the head, the lightweight type has a round rod at the crown end to prevent the anchor from rolling or rotating. This placement of the stock does not interfere with its being drawn into the hawsepipes of larger craft for stowage. (Many skippers place protective rubber tips over the stock ends; others merely plug the ends of the rod, which is hollow, to prevent mud and sand from entering and so being brought on deck.)

A key element in the high performance of Danforth Anchors is the design of the crown. The two flat, inwardsloping surfaces force the thin, sharp flukes to dig into the bottom and penetrate deeply. The surfaces of the crown are placed away from the plane of the flukes in order to help reduce clogging with mud, grass, or bottom debris that might possibly interfere with the penetration of the anchor and its holding power.

For recreational and commercial small craft, Standard Danforth anchors are made in approximate weights from 2-1/2 to 180 pounds, the Hi-Tensile model in sizes from 5 to 90 pounds. For comparable weights, Hi-Tensile models provide roughly 20% to 30% more holding power.

A number of other manufacturers produce anchors of the light-weight, burying type. The development of suitable alloys has made possible anchors of this style in aluminum (Viking) with considerable savings in dead weight.

In selecting an anchor, remember that all manufacturers have their own concepts of design, and "look-alikes" do not necessarily hold alike; data on holding power under similar conditions should be carefully compared.

The plow

The plow anchor is unique in design, resembling none of the other types. It was invented in England by Professor G. I. Taylor of Cambridge University; he called it the CQR (secure). It found wide acceptance because of its demonstrated efficiency in a variety of bottoms. Opinions vary as to its effectiveness in heavy weed, which is not surprising in that certain weed growths resist penetration by any anchor. The Plowright, fig. 608, is a model since developed and manufactured in the United States.

When a plow is lowered, the anchor first lies on its side

Note: For conversion to metric units, see page 99 or 115.

on the bottom. See fig. 609(a). Then when a pull is put on the rode, it rights itself, driving the point of the plow in, and finally burying the plow completely. The Plowright is claimed to hold up to 300 times its weight, depending naturally on the kind of bottom. CQR suggested catalog weights vary from 10 pounds for a 20-footer to 75 pounds for 75–125-footers.

Because of the pivoting feature of the shank, the tendency of the plow is to remain buried when the angle of pull is changed by wind or current. There is no projecting fluke to foul the rode and it breaks out easily when the pull is vertical, in position to bring the anchor up on deck.

Kedges

In discussing kedges it is important to make a sharp distinction between the more massive ancient types and later versions which have been designed for yacht use. In glossaries, "kedge anchors" as a rule are light anchors (of any design) carried out from a vessel aground to free her by winching in on the rode. Here, however, we refer to the kedge as an anchor with the more conventional type of

FIG. 604 Wilcox Crittenden's Yachtsman anchor, with parts labeled. The stock can be folded to lie along the shank.

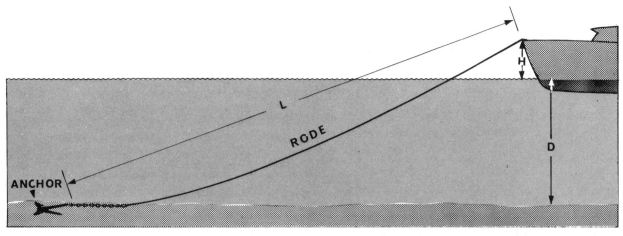

FIG. 605 The anchoring system includes not only the anchor but also the rode, the length of which is referred to in terms of "scope" (the ratio of L to D + H). It is important that the depth, D, be considered as that at high tide for it is at this time that the scope will be least.

FIG. 606 Two models of Danforth lightweight anchor — (a) the Standard and (b) Hi-Tensile. Both are burying types, with high holding power.

FIG. 607 The Danforth Utility anchor, a modification of the Northill design, is shown (a) with the stock folded and (b) with the stock set up in position for use.

arms, flukes and stocks as distinguished from newer light-weight types.

The earliest kedges, aside from their mass, were characterized by roughly triangular flukes and relatively dull bills. See fig. 601. The shoulders on the flukes, being nearly square with the arm, invited fouling of the rode as a vessel swung at her anchorage with shifts in wind and current. The dull bills made it difficult to bite in hard bottoms. Other kedges, like sand and trawl anchors, designed for use primarily on hard bottoms, had very small flukes and sharp bills. Both of these types left much to be desired for general yacht use, though often right for special purposes.

Yachtsman and Herreshoff anchors

Types of anchor which evolved from earlier kedges include the Yachtsman, fig. 604, and Herreshoff, fig. 611(b), designs. Though varying in details of construction, the principle used in both was a redistribution of the weight, a different proportioning of the length of stock to the chord measured from bill to bill, and a drastic change in the shape and size of fluke relative to the arm.

A major distinguishing feature of these modified kedges is the diamond-shaped fluke, embodied in the design to

reduce risk of fouling, on the theory that the rode would slip off an exposed fluke where no squared shoulder was presented. At the same time, sharpening of the bill permitted better penetration in hard bottoms.

Neither of these kedges is claimed to be a "burying" type, as the shank lies on the bottom and one fluke remains exposed. On the other hand, its "hook" design recommends it, probably above all other types, on rocky bottoms where one fluke can find a crevice, and retrieval, with proper precautions, is not too difficult. (More about this later.)

Northill-type anchors

The concept of light weight was first brought to kedge-type anchors with the introduction of the Northill design. Originally made in stainless steel, the current model, called the Danforth Utility, is made of malleable iron, hot-dip galvanized for resistance to corrosion.

The Northill design is unique, resembling the kedge only to the extent that it is a "hooking" type. Here, however, the stock has been placed at the other end of the shank, square with the arms, but moveable to fold along the shank or across the arms for better stowage.

Patterned after a principle utilized on wooden anchors in Malaysia through thousands of years, the Northill stock adds to the anchor's holding power when the fluke is buried. Arms are at right angles to the shank, and the broad reinforced flukes with sharp bills are set at a carefully computed angle to assure a quick bite. See fig. 613. Narrow fluke arms allow the anchor to penetrate well.

The Northill has demonstrated its efficiency in sand and mud, and has performed well even in heavy kelp and on rocky bottoms.

Other types

All the anchors discussed thus far have been of the so-called *stock-type,* though the stock, as we have seen, may be placed at either the ring or crown end of the shank. Although some stock anchors are made with a fast stock, for pleasure boat use they are more likely to have a loose stock which can be folded for better stowage. Frequently, a key is required to pin the stock of a kedge in its open position when set up ready for use, the key in turn being lashed in its slot to hold it in place.

Some anchors, however, are *stockless.* Frequently these are cataloged as Navy-type anchors. Inexperienced boatmen, seeing them on large ships, sometimes conclude that they are best for all vessels, including boats—this is not so. Ships use them because stockless anchors can be hauled up into hawsepipes. On boats the ratio of weight to holding power is so great that, if the anchor is heavy enough to hold, it is a back-breaker to haul up; if weight is held within reason, holding power is far below safe limits. The *Bruce* anchor, fig. 614, is designed to right itself no matter how it lands on the bottom while digging in within two shank lengths. Recommended sizes are roughly the same as for plow anchors; see Table 6–3.

Grapnels, though used more extensively by some commercial fishermen than many boatmen realize, are not recommended for general anchoring service aboard pleasure boats. These are also stockless models with, as a rule, five curved sharp-billed claw-like prongs symmetrically arranged around the crown end of the shank. Eyes may be cast in both ends of the shank—at the head in lieu of a ring for attachment of a rode (if used as an anchor) and at the crown end for a buoyed trip line. By dragging a small grapnel back and forth, a boatman may *grapple* for a piece of equipment lost on the bottom. See fig. 615.

When we speak of *folding anchors,* we think not so much in terms of a Yachtsman's kedge with movable stock as a highly specialized design in which, at some sacrifice of holding power, all parts fold against the shank into the smallest possible space for most convenient stowage. In one stockless type, the Norwegian SAV (imported by Canor Plarex) there are two pairs of flukes at right angles to each

FIG. 608 Woolsey's Plowright anchor has plow-shaped flukes, causing the anchor to bury deep. The shank is pivoted.

FIG. 609 How burying anchors work when an anchoring strain is put on the rode. In (a) below, a plow lands on the bottom on its side (1) gets a quick bite (2) and rights itself (3), digging deep. In (b) a lightweight anchor lands with flukes flat (1), penetrating (2) as the strain comes on the rode, and (3) burying in the holding position.

FIG. 610 Modern light-weight "burying" anchors depend on design and fluke area for holding power, rather than weight. This Viking anchor has excellent holding power although it is made of aluminum, and thus is much lighter and easier to handle than a steel anchor.

FIG. 611 (a) Flukes of this sand anchor are relatively small, the bills sharp, to penetrate hard bottoms. In soft bottoms holding power is low. (b) The Herreshoff version of the kedge. Note difference in fluke area.

FIG. 612 (a) This four-prong grapnel anchor is excellent for use in grassy bottoms. or in coral or rocks; a buoyed trip line is usually fastened to the eye in the crown. (b) The shank is square as is the hole in the moveable arm. By sliding this arm up to the other end of the stock, which is smaller and rounded, the moveable arm can be rotated 90° so that when it slides back down it nests inside the fixed arm and the anchor stows flat.

FIG. 613 Pitch of the flukes of a Northill-type anchor causes it to penetrate and dig in quickly. Here the anchor is turning to its ultimate horizontal position. Such an anchor can also be used to "hook" a hold on rocks.

other, almost in the manner of a grapnel. In rocky bottoms, they hook readily and may be rigged to pull out easily, crown first. See fig. 646.

Discussion of *mushroom* anchors, fig. 652, will be reserved till later as, properly, their principal use is in conjunction with permanent moorings, at anchorages. Modified versions of the mushroom are manufactured for small craft like canoes and rowboats, but their efficiency as "anchors" is at the lowest end of the scale.

All the anchors under discussion in this chapter are devices designed to keep a boat from drifting, by engagement with the bottom. *Sea anchors* do not fall in this category. These are intended to float at or just below the surface, serving merely as a drag to hold a boat's bow (or stern) up toward the seas to prevent her from lying in the trough. Sea anchors are rarely used aboard pleasure boats, and then only in the heaviest weather offshore, where there is room to drift to leeward. See chapter 9, Seamanship (pages 165-166) for a discussion of sea anchors and their use. *Drogues,* like the highly effective Fenger-type, are devices made up with planks, chain, weights and rode, to serve the purpose of a conventional sea anchor which, in some cases, they are reported to have bettered in efficiency.

THE RODE

All of the gear, taken collectively, that lies between a boat and her anchor is called the *rode*—whether it be synthetic fiber (like nylon), vegetable fiber (like manila), chain, wire, or a combination of fiber and chain. When his rode is nylon or manila, a knowledgeable boatman will not refer to his anchor "rope," as rope in a coil becomes "line" when cut for specific uses. Thus, with fiber rodes, it is quite appropriate to refer to the "anchor line."

Nylon

Since the introduction of synthetics, a quiet revolution has been taking place in the choice of material for anchor rodes. Good quality manila was once the accepted type of line. Synthetics, however, have brought new properties that make them even better adapted to the boatman's use.

Because other synthetics, such as dacron, polypropylene, polyethylene, etc., have little elasticity, they are not recommended for anchoring and towing. Nylon, on the other hand, has high elasticity and is the outstanding choice today.

Any differential in cost between nylon and manila is more than made up by differences in strength and longer life, both on the side of nylon. (See Table 11-1, breaking strengths, page 216.) Several times the strength of manila, nylon can be used in smaller diameters, light and easy to handle. See fig. 616. Though it can be damaged by rust from iron fittings or rusty chain, it is highly resistant to the rot, decay and mildew that attack vegetable fibers.

For anchoring purposes, nylon's greatest asset is its elasticity, stretching a third or more under load. Its working elasticity of 15 to 25% is several times greater than that of manila. When a boat surges at anchor in steep seas, there is a heavy shock load on fittings and ground tackle unless provision is made to absorb it gradually. Nylon's elasticity does exactly that.

Some boatmen unwittingly lose part or most of the advantage inherent in nylon by buying too strong a line. Within the limits of safe working loads, the smaller the diameter the better the elasticity for given conditions. A

95

Page 96

FIG. 614 The Bruce anchor is of one-piece construction shaped so that the direction of pull can change through 360° without breaking out, yet intentional breakout is easy on short scope. It is well-suited for use on mud or sand bottoms and hooks readily on rocks.

FIG. 615 A grapnel, shown here as it might be used in grappling to recover a mooring chain.

FIG. 616 Nylon (a) and manila (b). Nylon's great elasticity makes it popular for anchor rodes. A 3/8-inch diameter nylon line (breaking strength 3650 lbs.) will replace 9/16-inch manila (3450 lbs.).
(Gordon S. Smith photo)

BRAIDED OUTER ROPE

BRAIDED INNER ROPE

FIG. 617 Because of its construction, braided synthetic line has no tendency to twist. Braided nylon, for anchor rodes, retains high elasticity; braided polyester, with little stretch, is better for sheets and halyards.

FIG. 617 (a) Braided line coils best when faked (or flaked) down in a figure 8.

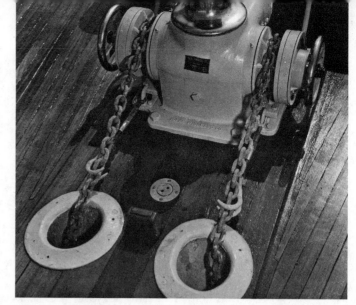

FIG. 618 On this large yacht, *wildcats* in the winch engage the links of the all-chain rodes. Chain, leading down to the anchors through hawsepipes, is shown here *stoppered*, held by split-hook *devil's claws*.

practical limit is reached when small diameters (though rated high enough for breaking strength) are not convenient to handle. Some of the most experienced boatmen use nylon as light as 3/8-inch diameter on the working anchors of their 30- to 40-foot cruisers.

Braided synthetic line

Most of the nylon currently in use today for anchor rodes is the type that is laid up by twisting three strands, in the same manner as manila. Synthetics, however, may also be laid up by braiding. For anchoring, mooring and towing, a braided outer cover of nylon surrounds a braided inner synthetic core. See fig. 617. The result is a line of exceptional stability with no inherent tendency to twist because of the nature of its lay. Consequently, it can be fed down into rope lockers without fear of kinking.

When braided nylon is handled on deck, it is advisable to fake it down in figure-8 pattern, rather than the conventional clockwise coil used with twisted fibers to prevent kinking. Because of the relatively smoother surface of braid, with more fibers exposed, chafe is less of a problem than it is with the twisted three-strand lay. Braided nylon retains a high degree of elasticity (14% at working loads, as against 25% for twisted nylon).

For sheets and halyards, where it is preferable to eliminate the stretch, an outer cover of polyester is used. Double-braided nylon is becoming increasingly popular for mooring pennants.

Double-braided synthetic rope is a quality product, its smooth, soft handling characteristics recommending it highly as a "yacht" line. Obviously it requires a special splicing technique; step-by-step instructions will be found in figs. 1108a through 1108h.

Manila

Most of the arguments that could once have been advanced for the selection of manila have quite generally been settled with the increasing trend toward nylon. It is a fact that manila is still in common use on many lighter anchors and in some areas it survives among boatmen of

FIG. 619 Manila line, badly chafed on a rough coral bottom. A fathom of chain, shackled between the anchor and fiber rode, would have prevented this.

FIG. 620 A thimble, shackle, and eye splice are commonly used to secure fiber rodes to the anchor ring or to a shackle in a short length of chain between the line and the anchor.

the old school who are not yet ready to give up the line they've grown up with. They find it easy to handle, light in weight (for required strength), comparatively inexpensive, and capable of enough stretch to absorb some shock load. Above all, it holds knots and splices better than the more slippery synthetics. Even at that, the experience of some of the hardest working commercial craft, like the charter fishermen who anchor day in and day out in open water in all weathers, is hard to deny. They've turned to nylon.

Chain

Nylon in diameters up to 1 inch is used on boats up to 50 or 60 feet in length—even larger, under normal conditions. Any fiber line, however, more than 1½ inches in diameter, is hard to handle, so chain is often chosen for larger craft. BBB chain is recommended (its size designated by the diameter of material in the links). To handle it, the boat should be equipped with a winch having a *wildcat* to fit the chain. See fig. 618.

From this it should not be inferred that chain is not also in use on smaller craft. On boats that cruise extensively and have occasion to anchor on sharp rock or coral, chain is often preferred—in cases, regarded as indispensable, as it stands chafing where fiber won't. Some boatmen with wide cruising experience have used one or more fathoms of chain shackled between the anchor and fiber line. Others prefer chain throughout.

In the larger diameters, the weight of chain tends to produce a sag in the rode which cushions shock loads due to surging. Once the sag is out, it is quite generally agreed that the shock on both boat and anchor is greater than with nylon or even manila. Too much emphasis should not be placed on the cushioning effect of a chain's sag, in small sizes. One test made in a moderate wind with generous scope of 10-to-1 revealed not a single link of chain resting on the bottom. On the other hand, in larger sizes, exhaustive tests on a 104-footer with ½-inch and ⅝-inch chain showed the weight of chain to be beneficial, reducing the maximum load on the anchor to as little as 5% of that recorded in a similar test with wire rope. Wire cable has

been used on some larger craft; though strong, it has no elasticity.

Nylon-and-chain

Today the concensus appears to be that for most average conditions, the ideal rode consists of a combination of nylon and short length (a fathom, more or less) of chain between the nylon and anchor. The only exception to this is in the very softest bottoms where one authority claims that the lightweight anchor bites best without chain.

The effect of chain in a combination rode is to lower the angle of pull, because chain tends to lie on the bottom. Of equal, perhaps greater, significance is the fact that modern lightweight anchors often bury completely, taking part of the rode with them. Chain stands the chafe, fig. 619, and sand has less chance to penetrate strands of the fiber line higher up. Sand doesn't stick to the chain, and mud is easily washed off. Without chain, nylon gets very dirty in mud.

Chain used in this manner may vary roughly from ¼-inch diameter for 20-footers up to ⅞₆-inch for 50-footers. It should be galvanized, of course, to protect against rust. Neoprene-coated chain is an added refinement, as it will not mar the boat.

SECURING THE RODE

Eyesplice, thimble, and shackle

Various methods are used in securing the rode to the anchor ring. With fiber line, the preferred practice is to work an eye splice around a thimble and use a galvanized shackle to join the thimble and ring. See fig. 620. Using manila, the common galvanized wire-rope thimble is satisfactory; with nylon more care must be taken to keep the thimble in the eye. A tight, snug splice will help and seizings around the line and the legs of the thimble, near the V, will keep the thimble in the eye splice when the line comes under loads that stretch the eye. A better thimble, fig. 621, is available in bronze alloy or plastic for use with synthetic rope. This is designed to hold and protect the line.

Note: For conversion to metric units, see page 99 or 115.

FIG. 621 Improved types of Newco thimble in plastic or bronze alloy for use with synthetic rope prevent line from jumping out of the thimble when an eye splice stretches under load.

TABLE 6-2 ANCHOR WEIGHT* (pounds)			
BOAT LENGTH (Maximum)	Lunch hook	Working anchor	Storm anchor
20'	4 (10)	5 (20)	12 (40)
30'	5 (15)	12 (30)	18 (60)
40'	12 (20)	18 (40)	28 (80)

*Bold-face figures based on modern lightweight burial-type anchors of efficient design. Figures in parentheses show how weights would be increased, using a formula of 1/2, 1 lb. and 2 lbs. per foot for certain kedges.

With this kind of rig, it is a good idea to put a bit of silicone spray, Lubriplate or graphite grease on threads of the shackle pin. This will keep the threads from seizing. Wire the pin to prevent its working out accidentally. For convenience, and to prevent loss of the pin, many prefer to bend a piece of marline to the eye of the pin, so that it can be lashed to a link of the chain. Watch for corrosion if different metals are used in thimbles, shackles and rings. Also beware of rust stains on nylon; cut out and resplice on new thimbles if the line is rust-stained.

With a thimble and shackle, a ready means is provided of backing up your line with a length of chain, if desired, shackling the chain in turn to the anchor ring. Shackles should be large enough so as not to bind the fiber against the ring and cause chafing.

When an anchor has an eye cast into the head of the shank, but no ring, it is generally convenient to use a shackle in the eye, even if the rode is to be bent to the anchor without an intermediate length of chain.

Anchor bends and bowlines

Some boatmen would rather bend their line directly to the ring using an anchor bend, fig. 622, seizing the free end to the rode. In the Chesapeake, and elsewhere, they use a bowline with an extra round turn around the ring, fig. 623, pointing out that this makes it easy to turn the line end-for-end occasionally or to remove the line from the anchor for easy handling when stowing.

Turning a line end-for-end greatly extends its useful life, as the lower end which has chafed on the bottom becomes the inboard end. Shackles and eye splices may be used at both ends of the rode, or may be added as necessary when the rode is turned.

Another convenient rig on small craft is merely to work a big eye splice in the end of the line, pass it through the ring, over the anchor while the stock (on stock types) is folded along the shank and then tighten the eye by hauling it up on itself at the ring.

Even where the regular working anchor is kept made-up with a combination of line and chain, it is well to know how to bend a line directly to the anchor. Often this is the handiest way to drop a light "lunch hook" for a brief stop, or to make up a second anchor when a bridle or stern anchor is needed.

Shackles, fig. 624, must be used to secure chain cables to the anchor, stout swivels, fig. 625, being an added re-

FIG. 622 Some boatmen prefer to make the rode fast to the anchor ring with an anchor bend. For added security, the free end may be seized to the rode. Line illustrated is braided nylon.

finement on combination rodes. As swivels are a weak point, they must be large. On an all-chain rode, they are a *must*. Swivels, however, should *not* be used with twisted soft-laid synthetic lines; a hockle, fig. 626, may be the result. Double-braided synthetic lines will not hockle, even though subjected to very heavy strains.

At the bitter end

To guard against loss in case the anchor goes by the board accidentally, the bitter (inboard) end of an anchor cable should preferably be made fast to some part of the boat. Sometimes this is accomplished by leading the line below, perhaps through a deck pipe, and securing to a Samson post or other strong timber. On sailboats, it may be secured to a mast. On small boats where the entire length of rode is carried on deck, it is usually feasible to have an eye splice in the bitter end to fit the post. Run this down close to the deck and use a clove hitch above the eye splice to adjust the scope.

HOW MANY—AND HOW HEAVY?

The number of anchors to be carried aboard will be conditioned upon several things—the size of boat, whether she is used only in sheltered waters or cruises extensively offshore and, to some extent, the type of anchor.

Though some small boats, like runabouts and utilities, are occasionally found with only a single anchor, this can by no stretch of the imagination be considered adequate. Even discounting the possibility of fouling one anchor so badly that it cannot be retrieved, there are many occasions when it is desirable to lie to two. Again, one anchor heavy enough for extreme conditions could be a nuisance in ordinary weather.

Many boats carry two anchors, proportioning the weight in the ratio of about 40 percent in one, 60 percent in the other. For cruising boats, three are undoubtedly better. This allows for two to be carried on deck—a light *lunch hook* for brief stops while some one is aboard, and a *working anchor* for ordinary service, including anchorages at night in harbor. The third might well be a big spare *storm anchor,* carried below, selected with an eye to its holding no matter what else lets go, even under extreme conditions of wind and weather. Break this out when you find it necessary to anchor overnight in an exposed anchorage, and you will sleep better. On long cruises, some experienced yachtsmen carry four.

Anchor size and holding power

Down through the years there have been repeated attempts to reduce anchor weights to a simple formula or table based on boat length or tonnage. Recommendations varied widely, up to as high as 3 or 4 pounds per foot for the heavy spare on cruising boats, assuming this would be a kedge type.

With the introduction of new anchors of lightweight design, it becomes obvious that the older figures no longer apply. Recognizing further that inefficient copies of a well

FIG. 623 The anchor bowline, an alternate method of bending the rode to the anchor ring. Note the extra round turn around the ring.

FIG. 624 This shackle, used to connect a short length of chain in a nylon-chain rode, should be secured in place with a short piece of non-corroding wire through the eye in the pin and around the side of the shackle.

TABLE 6-3   SUGGESTED RODE AND ANCHOR SIZES*

For Storm Anchor (Winds up to 60 knots)

| L.O.A. | BEAM | | RODE | | ANCHOR | | |
	SAIL	POWER	NYLON	CHAIN	NORTHILL	STANDARD	HI-TENSILE
10'	5'	5'	100'-1/4"	3'-3/16"	12 lb. (6-R)	8-S	5-H
15'	7'	7'	125'-1/4"	3'-3/16"	12 lb. (6-R)	8-S	5-H
20'	8'	9'	150'-3/8"	4'-1/4"	27 lb. (12-R)	13-S	12-H
25'	9'	10'	200'-3/8"	4'-1/4"	27 lb. (12-R)	22-S	12-H
30'	10'	11'	250'-7/16"	5'-5/16"	46 lb. (20-R)	22-S	20-H
35'	12'	13'	300'-1/2"	6'-3/8"	46 lb. (20-R)	40-S	35-H
40'	13'	14'	400'-5/8"	8'-7/16"	80 lb. (30-R)	65-S	60-H
50'	14'	16'	500'-5/8"	8'-7/16"	105 lb. (50-R)	130-S	60-H
60'	16'	19'	500'-3/4"	8'-1/2"	105 lb. (50-R)	180-S	90-H

For Working Anchor (Winds up to 30 knots)

| L.O.A. | BEAM | | RODE | | ANCHOR | | |
	SAIL	POWER	NYLON	CHAIN	NORTHILL	STANDARD	HI-TENSILE
10'	5'	5'	80'-1/4"	3'-3/16"	6 lb. (3-R)	4-S	5-H
15'	7'	7'	100'-1/4"	3'-3/16"	6 lb. (3-R)	8-S	5-H
20'	8'	9'	120'-1/4"	3'-3/16"	12 lb. (6-R)	8-S	5-H
25'	9'	10'	150'-3/8"	3'-3/16"	12 lb. (6-R)	8-S	5-H
30'	10'	11'	180'-3/8"	4'-1/4"	27 lb. (12-R)	13-S	12-H
35'	12'	13'	200'-3/8"	4'-1/4"	27 lb. (12-R)	22-S	12-H
40'	13'	14'	250'-7/16"	5'-5/16"	46 lb. (20-R)	22-S	20-H
50'	14'	16'	300'-1/2"	6'-3/8"	46 lb. (20-R)	40-S	35-H
60'	16'	19'	300'-1/2"	6'-3/8"	80 lb. (30-R)	65-S	35-H

For Lunch Hook

| L.O.A. | BEAM | | RODE | | ANCHOR | | |
	SAIL	POWER	NYLON	CHAIN	NORTHILL	STANDARD	HI-TENSILE
10'	5'	5'	70'-1/4"	3'-3/16"	6 lb. (3-R)	2½-S	5-H
15'	7'	7'	80'-1/4"	3'-3/16"	6 lb. (3-R)	2½-S	5-H
20'	8'	9'	90'-1/4"	3'-3/16"	6 lb. (3-R)	2½-S	5-H
25'	9'	10'	100'-1/4"	3'-3/16"	6 lb. (3-R)	4-S	5-H
30'	10'	11'	125'-1/4"	3'-3/16"	6 lb. (3-R)	4-S	5-H
35'	12'	13'	150'-1/4"	3'-3/16"	12 lb. (6-R)	4-S	5-H
40'	13'	14'	175'-3/8"	4'-1/4"	12 lb. (6-R)	8-S	5-H
50'	14'	16'	200'-3/8"	4'-1/4"	12 lb. (6-R)	8-S	12-H
60'	16'	19'	200'-3/8"	4'-1/4"	27 lb. (12-R)	13-S	12-H

*Suggested sizes assume fair holding ground, scope of at least 7-to-1 and moderate shelter from heavy seas.
PLOW ANCHORS—Woolsey, manufacturer of the Plowright anchor, makes the following recommendations for winds up to 30 knots: for working anchors, 10'-21', 6 lbs.—22'-32', 12 lbs.—32'-36', 18 lbs.—36'-39', 22 lbs.—39'-44', 35 lbs. For lunch hooks, they advise stepping down one size. For storm anchors, up one size.
KEDGES—Holding powers vary widely with the type. Best to consult manufacturer for individual recommendations.

FIG. 625 Swivels are required on all-chain rodes to prevent snarls.

Note—For conversion to metric units: 1 inch = 2.54 cm. 1 foot = 30.48 cm or 0.3048 m. 1 pound = 0.4536 kg.

designed anchor may vary tremendously in holding power, it is equally evident that a hard-and-fast table of anchor weights could easily be an over-simplification. With this caution, Table 6-2 is offered, merely as a point of departure, to be modified as necessary in individual cases. This same caution applies to Table 6-3, giving suggested rode and anchor sizes for boats from 10 to 60 feet in length.

Horizontal loads as criteria for anchor sizes

In a recent project to establish an advisory code of safety standards for all kinds of small craft up to 65 feet in length, the equipment division of the American Boat and Yacht Council took a different tack in recommending practices and standards for ground tackle. They have set up a Table (6-4) specifying, for boats of 10 to 60 feet in length, typical minimum *horizontal loads* (in pounds) which an anchor should be able to hold, assuming freedom to swing and moderate shelter from seas proportionate to hull size. This, too, is broken down into three sizes of anchor—lunch hooks, working anchors, and storm anchors. Armed with these figures, you can consult the recommendations of the manufacturer of the particular anchor you prefer.

STOWAGE

The boatman's seamanship is often measurable by the amount of common sense and foresight he displays in every-day boating practice. It shows up, for example, in the attention he gives to stowage of his ground tackle. Exactly how he goes about it depends to some extent on the kind of boating he does, the size of his boat, and the way it is equipped. In any case, unless his deck is uncluttered, with gear ready for immediate use, yet secured so that it cannot shift, he will never rate high as a seaman.

Ordinarily a cruising boat will carry one, sometimes two, anchors on deck, made up ready for use. On some small boats, where it is not feasible to leave anchors on deck at all times, or in cases where lines are stowed below at the home anchorage, one anchor and line at least should be prepared and made ready before getting under way from the dock or mooring. Engines have been known to fail and, when they do, it's likely to be at an embarrassing moment, with wind or current setting you down on a shoal or reef. Then it's too late to think about breaking out gear that should have been ready at hand.

An anchor lying loose on deck is a potential hazard. If the boat happens to roll deep in a seaway or be caught by the heavy wash of a passing boat, it may slide across the deck, leaving in its wake scars on woodwork and damage

TABLE 6-4 TYPICAL HORIZONTAL LOADS (pounds)

Length over all	Lunch hook	Working anchor	Storm anchor
10'	40	160	320
15'	60	250	500
20'	90	360	720
25'	125	490	980
30'	175	700	1,400
35'	225	900	1,800
40'	300	1,200	2,400
50'	400	1,600	3,200
60'	500	2,000	4,000

to equipment, conceivably going over the side, and taking line with it, at the risk of fouling a propeller. To forestall this, every anchor on deck should be stowed in chocks. See fig. 627. These are available at marine supply stores to fit standard anchors. Lashings hold them down to prevent their jumping out of the chocks. Hardwood blocks, prop-

FIG. 627 Anchors stowed on deck should be lashed down in chocks.

FIG. 628 A short "pulpit" on this motor sailer provides for the housing of a plow anchor.

FIG. 626 To avoid a hockle, swivels should not be used with twisted soft-laid synthetic lines.

Note: For conversion to metric units, see page 99 or 115.

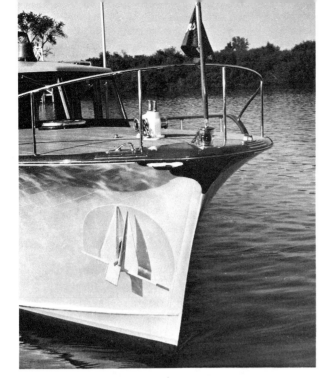

FIG. 629 Hawsepipes are commonly seen on large vessels, and may also be used on some yachts. The planking is protected by a circular pad.

erly notched, have often been used in lieu of metal chock fittings. Rubber caps should be fitted over the round stock ends of lightweight type anchors.

As an alternate to chocking on deck, anchors carried aboard auxiliaries may be lashed to shrouds, off the deck, where there is no risk of their getting underfoot, and less risk of their fouling running rigging. In one Dutch yacht, a foreign-built lightweight type anchor is carried in hooks provided in the bow rail. Some cruisers and motor sailers equipped with bowsprits or pulpits have a roller at the outboard end so that a plow can be carried in this outboard position as a regular working anchor. See fig. 628. There are devices that combine the anchor with a kind of well fixture to be let in flush with the deck. In considering such equipment, be sure the anchor weight and design are such as to meet the boat's requirements as to holding power. On some yachts provision is made to haul the anchor into a hawsepipe fitted into the topsides forward. See fig. 629.

Stowing the storm anchor

As the big spare storm anchor is used only on rare occasions, it is customary to carry it in some convenient location below. Frequently this will be a lazarette or in stowage space below a cockpit deck, accessible through a hatch. Chocks here should be arranged to carry the weight on floors or frames, never on the planking. If the big anchor gets adrift, it could easily loosen a bottom plank and start a leak.

The big risk in stowing a spare anchor away in some out-of-the-way corner is the possibility that other gear may be allowed to accumulate over and around it. Guard against that. Its sole value may some day depend upon your being able to get that big hook over quickly, bent to a long and strong spare rode that must be equally accessible.

Lunch hooks are small and seldom needed in a hurry, so there's justification for stowing them in some convenient

locker. Keep them away from the compass, however, as they can be a potent cause of deviation. That goes for all anchors and any ferrous metal that might inadvertently be left too close to the compass.

Rope and chain lockers

Though small craft frequently, carry their lines coiled on a forward deck or in an open cockpit, many cruising boats are built with rope lockers in the forepeak. Nylon dries quickly and can be fed down into lockers almost as soon as it comes aboard. Manila, on the other hand, must be thoroughly dried on deck before stowing below. Gratings are sometimes provided as an aid to drying lines on deck before stowage. Lockers must be well ventilated and arranged to assure good air circulation at all times. See fig. 630. Dark, wet lockers are an invitation to dry rot. A hatch over the rope locker will permit exposure to sun and air.

The rode should always be ready to run without fouling. Line is often passed below through a deck pipe, slotted so that it can be capped even when the line is in use. Slots must face aft to prevent water on deck from finding its way below. Caps are usually connected with a length of chain, preferably of brass, as galvanized chains may rust out too quickly. Some cast mooring bitts are also made with an opening on the after face, through which line can be passed below.

Chain won't soak up moisture like manila and is easy to stow in lockers. Where weight of chain in the bow of a small offshore cruising boat is objectionable, this can be overcome by splitting a long cable into two or three shorter lengths, stowed where convenient and shackled together as necessary. The chain portion of a combination nylon-and-chain rode is ordinarily shackled in place for regular use, but small-diameter nylon, if left on deck, should preferably be shaded from the sun to protect surface fibers from damage by ultraviolet rays.

SCOPE

Later, in a discussion of anchoring techniques, we will go into the matter of holding power but at this point it seems appropriate to cover, in advance, the subject of *scope*. See fig. 631. Once an anchor of suitable design and size has

FIG. 630 Lightweight anchors chocked on deck, their round stock-ends fitted with rubber tips. A grating provides ventilation to the forepeak. Inboard ends of the nylon dock lines are *flemished* in spiral mats.

$$\text{SCOPE} = \frac{L}{D}$$

FIG. 631 Scope, the ratio of L to D in the sketch above, is critically important in safe anchoring. At (1) length of rode just equals depth of water plus height of bow above water. At (2) rode length is twice distance D, but still much too short. At (4) note how the greater scope has decreased the angle between the rode and the bottom. At (8) the scope is 8:1 and the short length of chain at the anchor lies flat on the bottom for a horizontal pull.

been chosen to provide adequate holding power, scope is the factor that will determine whether you will, in fact, hold or drag. Too short a scope can destroy the efficiency of the best anchor.

Although some books use the term "scope" to refer to the "length of cable from hawsepipe to anchor", more often it is recognized as the *ratio* of the length of the anchor line to the height of the bow above the bottom of the body of water as shown in fig. 631. Two important factors must not be overlooked: the height of the bow chocks above the surface, and the range of the tide.

Let's assume we anchor in 10 feet of water with 60 feet of rode paid out. Theoretically, one might suppose this is a reasonable scope of 6:1. Our bow chock, however, is 5 feet above the surface. Immediately the ratio is cut to 4:1 (60:15). Six hours later the tide has risen another 5 feet. So now we have an actual scope of 3:1 (60:20), exactly half of the original theoretical ratio.

What is a proper scope? Under favorable conditions, 5:1 might be considered a *minimum*; under average conditions, 7 or 8:1 is regarded as satisfactory. Government tests have indicated that proper scope ratios will range between 5:1 and 10:1, the latter for heavy weather. Even in a very hard blow, in an exposed anchorage, the chances are that you will never need a scope of more than 15:1 with an anchor of suitable holding power. Boatmen who carry more than one kind of anchor have found that effective scope required under a given set of conditions may vary with the type.

In our hypothetical example above, the length of rode paid out should have been 140 (7:1) to 160 (8:1) feet; 100 feet (5:1) might be regarded as a minimum.

To provide maximum efficiency, all anchors require a low angle of pull—preferably less than 8 degrees from the horizontal. With short scope, holding power is reduced because the angle of pull is too high, tending to break the anchor out. As the pull is brought down more nearly parallel with the bottom, flukes dig in deeper with heavier strains on the line. Surging, as a boat pitches in a sea, throws a great load on the anchor, particularly on short scope. With long scope, the angle of pull is not only better, but the elasticity of a long nylon line cushions the shock loads materially.

FIG. 632 A plastic marker used to indicate the scope of anchor line paid (or veered) out.

Marking a rode for scope

Granting that we know how much scope is required, how do we know when we have paid out enough? Estimates are risky. Plastic cable markers, fig. 632, may be bought in sets to mark various lengths such as 25, 50, 75, 100, 125, 150, and 200 feet, or generally similar lengths. These are attached by inserting them under a strand of the line. In daylight, when the figures can be read, such markers are fine. In the dark, however, the traditional markers of strips of leather, bits of cotton or flannel cloth, and pieces of marline with knots have the advantage of being able to be "read" by feel.

For all practical purposes, five or six marks at intervals of 20 feet (say 60-140 feet) should be adequate. One practical method would be to paint wide and narrow bands of a red vinyl liquid called Whip-End Dip at significant points, calling wide bands 50 feet, narrow ones 10. On chain rodes, as a measure of scope, some boatmen have painted links white at intervals.

One method that has proved successful on a 150-foot line with an additional 8 feet of chain is to whip the line at 50 and 100 feet from the chain with red sail twine. This gives an exact measure of 58 and 108 feet; other lengths can easily be estimated with sufficient accuracy.

Anchoring Techniques

HOW TO ANCHOR

Thus far we have discussed only equipment, or ground tackle. Let's consider now the technique—the art of anchoring. As a matter of fact, good equipment is more than half the battle; anyone can easily learn to use his gear correctly.

If, on the other hand, your anchors are of doubtful holding power, and your lines too short, then you can never escape the uneasy feeling associated with wondering whether, some day, you'll find yourself dragging on a lee shore. No part of your boat's equipment is more important, so don't stint here.

Before you can think about *how* to anchor, you must decide *where* you'll anchor, and here, as in all other phases of seamanship, a little foresight pays off handsomely.

Selecting an anchorage

There will be times, of course, when you will stop briefly in open water, coming to anchor for lunch, a swim, to fish, or perhaps to watch a regatta—but, in the main, the real problem of finding an anchorage comes down to choice of some spot where there's good holding bottom, protection from the wind, and water of suitable depth. Such an anchorage is the kind you'd look for in which to spend the night, free from anxiety about the weather.

Use the chart

The chart is the best guide in selecting such a spot. Sometimes you will be able to find a harbor protected on all sides, regardless of wind shifts. If not, the next best choice would be a cove, offering protection at least from the direction of the wind, or the quarter from which it is expected. As a last resort, anchorage may be found under a windward bank or shore—that is, where the wind blows from the bank toward the boat. In this case, watch for wind shifts, which could leave you in a dangerous berth on a lee shore.

Anchorages are sometimes designated on charts by means of an anchor symbol. Areas delineated on the chart by solid magenta lines, marked perhaps by white buoys, are often shown as special anchorage areas, where lights are not required on vessels less than 65 feet in length. See fig. 633. Never anchor in cable areas or channels, both indicated by broken parallel lines.

Shallow depths are preferred for an anchorage, because a given amount of scope will then provide better holding and reduce the diameter of the circle through which the boat will swing. Consideration, however, must be given to the range of tide, so that a falling level does not leave you aground, impaled perhaps on the exposed fluke of your own anchor, or bottled up behind a shoal with not enough water to get out at low tide.

Characteristics of the bottom

Character of the bottom is of prime importance. While the type and design of anchor fluke has a direct bearing on its ability to penetrate, as already noted, it may be stated broadly that mixtures of mud and clay, or sandy mud, make excellent holding bottom for most anchors; firm sand is

FIG. 633 In special anchorage areas shown on the chart, lights are not required on boats less than 65 feet in length.

Bottom characteristics:				
Cl. clay	M. mud	Oys oyster	stk. sticky	gn. green
Co. coral	Rk. rock	hrd. hard	bk. black	gy. gray
G. gravel	S. sand	rky. rocky	br. brown	wh. white
Grs. grass	Sh. shells	sft. soft	bu. blue	yl. yellow

FIG. 634 Abbreviations of some bottom characteristics as shown on charts.

FIG. 635 How ranges may be used to select an anchorage by lining up visible charted objects. At the intersection of one range through the tank and flagpole, and another through two towers, the boat has 14 feet of water (at low tide) in hard bottom, clear of rocks, with room to swing outside of shoal water.

good *if* your anchor will bite deep into it; loose sand is bad. Soft mud should be avoided if possible; rocks prevent an anchor from getting a bite except when a fluke is lodged in a crevice; grassy bottoms, while they provide good holding for the anchor that can get through to firm bottom, often prevent a fluke from taking hold.

Sometimes bottoms which ordinarily provide reasonably good holding will be covered with a thick cabbage-like

103

FIG. 636 In this crowded anchorage, there's risk that the swinging circles of boats may overlap.

growth that positively destroys the holding power of any anchor. Even if you happen to carry one of the fisherman's sand-anchor types, with its thin spidery arm and small flukes, expect it to pick up half a bushel of this growth. All you can do is clean it off and try elsewhere.

Characteristics of the bottom are always shown on charts. By making a few casts with the hand lead, a check can be had on the depth, and if the lead is armed with a bit of hard grease or tallow, samples of the bottom will be brought up as a further check. Abbreviations for some bottom characteristics are shown in fig. 634.

Approaching the anchorage

Having selected a suitable spot, try to run in *slowly* on some range ashore, selected from marks identified on the chart, crossing ranges, fig. 635, or referring your position to visible buoys and landmarks to aid you in locating the spot. Later these aids will also be helpful in determining whether you are holding or dragging, especially if the marks are visible at night and it comes on to blow after dark.

If there are rocks, shoals, reefs or other boats to consider, give them all as wide a berth as possible, keeping in mind a possible swing of 360 degrees about the anchor with wind shifts or current changes.

Remember, too, that large yachts nearby may swing to a much longer scope than you allow—and, conversely, that you may swing much further than a smaller boat nearby lying on short scope. See fig. 636. Such conditions bring about an overlapping of the swinging circles.

The risk of fouling a neighboring craft is aggravated when, in a current, the deep-draft vessel holds her position while a light-draft boat swings to a shift of wind not strong enough to influence the other. Keel sailboats may lie one way in a light current, power boats another.

The boat that has already established her location in an anchorage has a prior claim to the spot and can't be expected to move if you later find yourself in an embarrassing position. Consequently, allow room enough so that you

can pay out more scope if necessary in case of a blow, without being forced to change your anchorage, perhaps at night.

The way other boats lie, together with the set of nearby buoys, will help to determine how you should round up to the chosen spot. Estimate the relative effects of wind and current on your own boat and come up, *slowly*, against the stronger of these forces—in other words, heading as you expect to lie after dropping back on the anchor. Running through the anchorage, take care that your way is reduced to a point where your wake cannot disturb other boats.

FIG. 637 With its stock set up, this anchor can be let go quickly by casting off the lashing. Chain leads outboard through a hawsepipe up to the ring. Davit tackle can be hooked into the ring of the balancing band on the shank. On the port side of the winch a gipsy is provided for use with fiber rode.

Letting the anchor go

These preliminaries disposed of, you are ready to let the anchor go. Unless you are forced to work single-handed, one man should be stationed on the forward deck. Enough line should be hauled out of the locker and coiled down so as to run freely without kinking or fouling. If previously detached, the line must be shackled to the ring, stock set up (if of the stock type) and keyed. See fig. 637. Many an anchor has been lost for failure to attach the rode properly. Rodes, too, have gone with the anchor when not secured at the bitter end. Lightweight anchors are always ready for use and do not have to be set up, but always check to see that the shackle is properly fastened.

Despite the fact that in certain localities some experienced boatmen have adopted the practice of letting go while the boat has headway, depending on way to snub the anchor and give it a bite, the small-craft skipper would do well to make it a standing rule to *never* let go the anchor while his boat has any forward way on.

In a motorboat, or auxiliary under power, the bow should be brought *slowly* up to the spot where the anchor is to lie, and headway checked with the reverse gear if necessary. Then, just as the boat begins to gather sternway slowly in reverse, the anchor is lowered easily over the side till it hits bottom, crown first.

Never stand in the coils of line on deck and don't attempt to "heave" the anchor by casting it as far as possible from the side of the boat. Occasionally, with judgment, a light anchor in a small boat can be carefully thrown a short distance—taking care that it lands in its holding position—but the best all-around rule is to *lower* it as described. That way, the possibility of fouling is minimized.

Setting the anchor

An anchor must be *set* properly if it is to yield its full holding power. The best techniques for setting an anchor will vary from type to type; only general guidelines can be given here, and a skipper should experiment to determine the best procedures for his boat, his anchors, and his cruising waters.

With the anchor on the bottom and the boat backing down slowly, line should be paid out (sometimes spoken of as veering) as the boat takes it, preferably with a turn of line around the bitt. When the predetermined scope has been paid out, the line is quickly snubbed and the anchor

will probably get a quick bite into the bottom. A lightweight, burial type, such as a Danforth, is frequently set with a scope as short as 2 or 3, especially in a soft bottom. Anchors such as a kedge or grapnel seem to set better with a scope of 5 to 8.

Sometimes the anchor may become shod with a clod of mud or botton grass adhering to the flukes; in these cases, it is best to lift it, wash it off, and try again.

After the anchor is set, rode can be paid out or taken in to the proper length for the anchorage being used and the prevailing and expected weather conditions. Scope must be adequate for holding, but in a crowded anchorage consideration must be given to other craft.

When you must work single-handed, you can get your ground tackle ready to let go, long before you arrive at the anchorage, bring the boat up to the chosen spot, and then lower the anchor as the boat settles back with wind and current, paying out line as she takes it.

Regardless of the type of anchor, after full scope ha been paid out, a back-down load in excess of any anticipated loads should be applied. This is particularly important if the boat is to be left unattended.

Making fast

After the anchor has gotten a good bite, with proper scope paid out, the line can be made fast and the motor shut off.

On boats equipped with a forward bitt (sampson post), an excellent way to secure the anchor line is to make two or three full turns around the bitt and finish off with a half-hitch around each end of the pin through the bitt; see fig. 638. The bitt takes the load and the pin secures the line; this is more easily taken off the bitt than a clove hitch or any other hitch.

Where a stout cleat is used to make fast, take a full turn around the base, one turn over each horn crossing diagonally over the center of the cleat, and finish with a half-hitch around one horn; see fig. 1103h. Clove hitches should not be used on cleats as they may jam.

The fundamental idea in making fast is to secure in such a manner that the line can neither slip nor jam. If the strain comes on top of a series of turns on a cleat, fig. 1103(i), then it will be practically impossible to free if you want to change the scope, without first taking the strain off it by using power.

If it becomes necessary to shorten scope, clear the bitt

FIG. 638 Although a clove hitch can be used, a better way to make a line fast to a bitt or mooring post is to take two turns around it (to bear the load) and then finish with a half-hitch around each end of the pin (to secure the line). This is easily unfastened or slacked even under considerable strain.

first of old turns or hitches. Don't throw new ones over the old.

A trick worth using when the sea is so rough that it is difficult to go forward on deck—especially if you are single-handed—is to set up the anchor in the aft cockpit, lead the line forward on deck through a closed chock, and back aft to the cockpit. If there are stanchions for life lines, the lead of the rode from chock to anchor must obviously be outside any such obstructions. When you're ready to let go it can be dropped on the weather side from the cockpit, and the line secured on a bitt or cleat aft.

Anchoring without power

When anchoring under sail you don't have the same maneuverability that power supplies and, of course, there is no positive way to dig your anchor in. Here it is best to approach your anchorage with wind abeam so that you can spill most of the wind out of your sails, thereby slowing the boat down. If necessary trim your sail in to gain more headway as needed. Approach the anchorage with all sails down except the mainsail and with enough headway to keep the boat under control. Just before you are ready to let the anchor go, you should have steerageway, but no more. Let your sheet run and, with tiller hard-alee, shoot your bow directly into the wind and drop the mainsail. As your boat loses headway her bow will fall off and the boat will begin to drift to leeward; now lower your anchor.

Pay out scope as the boat drifts back and, occasionally, give a few jerks on the line. This usually helps to set the anchor. Hand-test the line by pulling it. You will be holding when the boat is drawn toward the anchor. Then pay out the usual scope of 7 or 8:1.

Hand signals

Anchoring, like docking, is one of the situations where it's a great help to have another hand aboard. The problem is communication between the anchor man on deck and the skipper at the wheel. With engine and exhaust noise, it's usually difficult for the skipper to hear, even though the man on deck can. Wind often aggravates the problem. If the skipper is handling the boat from a flying

bridge, he can usually hear better and, from his higher position, can see the trend of the anchor line.

In any case, it helps to have a pre-arranged set of hand signals. There is no need for standardization on this, as long as the helmsman clearly understands the crew's instructions. Keep the signals as simple as possible. Motion of the hands, calling for the helmsman to come ahead a little, or back down, can take the most obvious form. Pointing ahead or aft accomplishes the same purpose. A simple vertical wave of the hand may be used to signal "stop."

WHEN THE ANCHOR DRAGS

Let's assume now that you have anchored with a scope of 8:1, have inspected the rode, and taken bearings, if possible, as a check on your position. Though the wind has picked up, you turn in, only to be awakened at midnight by the boat's roll. Before you reach the deck you know what has happened—the anchor's dragging and the bow no longer heads up into the wind.

This calls for instant action—not panic. A quick check on bearings confirms what the roll indicated. You're dragging, with the wind abeam. Sizing the situation up swiftly, you note that danger is not imminent; there is still plenty of room to leeward and no boats down-wind to be fouled. Otherwise you would have to get under way, immediately.

The first step in trying to get the anchor to hold is to pay out more scope. Don't just throw over several more fathoms of line; pay it out, with an occasional sharp pull to try to give it a new bite. If you're dragging badly and can't handle the rode with your hands, take a turn around the bitt and snub the line from time to time. If this doesn't work, start the engine and hold the bow up into the wind

FIG. 639 Two schools of thought on the use of sentinels (kellets). In (a) below, the traditional use of a weight (about 25 pounds) or light anchor sent down the rode by means of a shackle over the rode, with light line to control the scope between sentinel and boat. In (b) below, a buoy rather than a weight has been proposed as a superior method, utilizing the principle commonly found in permanent mooring systems.

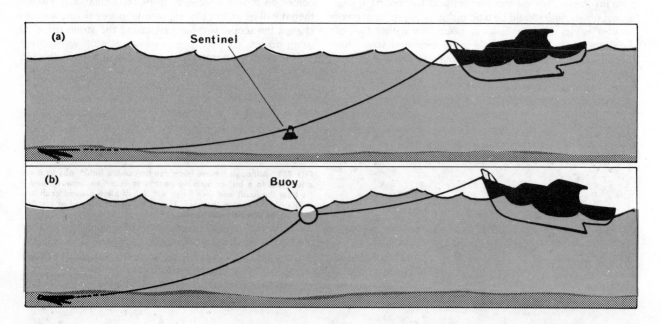

with just enough power to take the strain off the rode. This gives the anchor a chance to lie on the bottom and perhaps get a new bite as you ease the throttle and let the boat drift back slowly. If you haven't held when the scope is 10:1, get the anchor back aboard and try again with your larger storm anchor.

Sentinel—or buoy?

Suppose, now, that we have no spare storm anchor to fall back on. Can anything be done to increase our holding power? Here we enter an area of controversy with weight of experience on two opposing sides. We'll present both views.

For generations, seasoned cruising boatmen have known of the device known as a *sentinel,* or kellet. See fig. 639(a). Many have reported using it successfully; few have challenged its effectiveness. In principle, the sentinel is nothing more than a weight sent more than half-way down the rode to lower the angle of pull on the anchor and put a sag in the rode that must be straightened out before a load is thrown on the anchor. Working only with what came readily to hand in such a case, boatmen have shackled or snapped their light anchor to the main anchor rode, and sent it down the main rode with a line attached to the ring of the lunch hook, to be stopped at a suitable distance. A pig of ballast or other weight would do as well, provided it could be readily attached.

The other school of thought claims that when this principle is used with short scope in order to limit swinging room, it has proved inadvisable and dangerous, on the theory that, under storm conditions, a resonant condition

FIG. 640 A plastic foam buoy. Note how the strain is transmitted by solid rod through the buoy.

may be encountered which could quickly snap the line. Their alternative would be to use a buoy, fig. 639(b) rather than a weight, claiming that, properly used, the buoy can carry most of the vertical load in an anchoring or mooring system, limiting the basic load on the boat to the horizontal force required to maintain the boat's position. The argument is advanced that the buoy permits the boat's bow to ride up easily over wave crests, rather than being pulled down into them, with excessive loads on both rode and anchor.

What to watch

From these opposing views, certain conclusions may be drawn. To be most effective, a buoy, if used, should preferably be of the type found in a permanent mooring system, fig. 640, where its efficiency is undoubted. Its connection into the system should be as positive as it would be in a

mooring buoy, all strain being carried directly by the rode—in short, no "weak link" here! Provision should be made for carrying it as part of the "emergency" equipment, rather than trusting to a makeshift device improvised under stress of weather.

On the other side of the picture, if the sentinel is to be used, it should be done *with ample scope,* and every precaution taken to avoid a chafing condition on the main rode.

In support of advocates of the sentinel, we cite the scientific test made under controlled conditions aboard a 104-footer in which a *30-pound* weight, suspended from $^5/_8$-inch wire cable used as the main rode, cut the maximum anchor load practically in half. Obviously, wire rope is less suited to the average pleasure boat than it was to this test boat, it has no stretch and stands chafe of the sentinel's shackle, but figures on reduction of the load are irrefutable.

An alternate system

We offer a compromise. Carry a boat-length of substantial chain and a 25-pound pig of lead with a ring bolt cast in it. Stow them away somewhere in lieu of ballast. When the chips are down, with breakers to leeward, shackle the chain to your biggest and best anchor, and the chain in turn to your best and longest nylon rode, with the ring of the pig lead shackled in where chain and nylon join. It cannot be anything but an improvement over the same long scope of nylon without benefit of the extra scope of chain and added weight. This would seem to eliminate the twin problems of chafe (at the sentinel) and any tendency to hold the boat's bow down in the surge of pitching seas.

GETTING UNDER WAY

When you are ready to *weigh anchor* and get under way, run up to the anchor slowly under power, so that the line can be taken in easily without hauling the boat up to it. Ordinarily the anchor will break out readily when the line stands vertically.

As the line comes in, it can be whipped up and down to free it of any grass or weed it may have picked up. This clears the line before it comes on deck. If the anchor is not too heavy, mud can be washed off by swinging it back and forth near the surface as it leaves the water. With care, the line can be snubbed around a bitt and the anchor allowed to wash off as the boat gathers way, preferably astern. Two things must be watched: don't allow the flukes to hit the topsides, and be careful that water flowing past the anchor doesn't get too good a hold and take it out of your hands.

Manila, if used, must be coiled loosely on deck and allowed to dry thoroughly before stowing below. When the anchor is on deck, the stock (if there is one) can be folded and the anchor lashed down securely in its chocks.

On larger craft, equipped with a davit, the anchor is brought up with the winch to a point where a light tackle can be hooked into a ring in the balancing band on the anchor's shank. With the anchor suspended over the side, mud can be washed off with a hose.

In all this anchor handling, try to avoid letting the anchor hit the hull at any time as planking is soft and will get badly gouged and dented. Fiberglass finishes and metal hulls can also be marred. Guests often are eager to "help" by getting the anchor up, but unless they have had some experience, it's better to handle this part of the job your-

Note: For conversion to metric units, see page 99 or 115.

FIG. 641   In rocky bottoms when an anchor fouls, the first attempt to clear it should be made by reversing the original angle of pull (a), with moderate scope, so as to draw it out as shown in (b).

self. Handle and stow lines carefully. If a bight or end of line slips over the side it is almost certain to run back under the bottom and get hopelessly fouled in the propeller.

In a boat under sail alone, have your mainsail up before you break the anchor loose. The same procedure is used as stated above but there is no motor to help. However, it is possible to use your sails to assist.

Clearing a fouled anchor

If an anchor refuses to break out when you haul vertically on the line, snub it around the bitt and go ahead with the engine a few feet. If it doesn't respond to this treatment, it's an indication that the anchor may have fouled under some obstruction. To clear it, try making fast to the bitt and running slowly in a wide circle on a taut line. Changing the angle of pull may free it, or a turn of line may foul an exposed fluke (if it's a kedge) and draw it out.

Sometimes a length of chain can be run down the anchor line, rigged so that another boat can use her power to haul in a direction opposite to that in which the anchor line tends, thus changing the angle of pull 180 degrees. With kedges, if one fluke is exposed, a chain handled between two dinghies can occasionally be worked down the rode to catch the upper arm and draw the anchor out, crown first.

If the anchor is not fouled in something immovable, it may be broken out by making the line fast at low water and allowing a rising tide to exert a steady strain. Or, if there is a considerable ground swell, the line may be snubbed when the bow pitches low in a trough. There's some risk of parting the line this way, in case the fluke is fouled worse than you think.

In rocky bottoms, the first thing to try is reversing the direction of pull, opposite to that in which the anchor was originally set, using a moderate amount of scope. See fig. 641.

There is a type of anchor in which the ring is free to slide the full length of the shank. Properly rigged, it is claimed to be virtually snag-proof. More about this later.

If you have been anchored for a day or two in a brisk wind, the anchor may be dug in deep. Don't wait till you're ready to sail; 20 minutes before departure shorten the scope—*but keep a sharp watch.* Motion of the boat will tend to break the anchor out and save a lot of work.

HOLDING POWER

Before getting into some of the special techniques of anchor use, some understanding of holding power is in order. We have already seen how important anchor design and scope are in determining relative holding power, assuming of course that we are comparing anchors of equal weight. To understand just how critical design can be, remember that a change of as little as 1 degree in fluke angle may cause as much as a 50 percent reduction in efficiency. Lacking equipment to make individual scientific tests, one can readily appreciate how essential it is to rely on the reputability of the manufacturer.

Some factors involved

Tests have shown that the normal strain on an anchor due to wind and current in average weather is comparatively small. Current is a relatively small factor as compared with the pressure exerted by wind on exposed surfaces. Surge when a boat pitches in a seaway may throw a tremendous strain on the boat and all her ground tackle. Weight of the boat is also significant.

In calculating holding power required under average conditions, manufacturers have taken into account all of these factors, including such boat dimensions as length, beam, hull depth, draft, displacement, and height of superstructure. One has tabulated it as a percentage of gross

TABLE 6-5   HORIZONTAL HOLDING POWER DANFORTH ANCHORS (pounds)

Hi-Tensile	Soft Mud	Hard Sand	Standard	Soft Mud	Hard Sand
5-H	400	2,700	2½-S	140	800
12-H	900	6,000	4-S	230	1,600
20-H	1,250	8,750	8-S	480	3,200
35-H	1,600	11,000	13-S	720	4,900
60-H	2,400	17,000	22-S	1,200	8,000
90-H	2,900	20,000	40-S	1,500	10,000
200-H	5,000	35,000	65-S	2,300	15,000
500-H	7,500	50,000	85-S	2,700	19,000
3000-H	21,000	140,000	130-S	3,100	21,000

Note: 1 pound = 0.4536 kg

weight—for centerboard sailboats 5%; small motorboats 6%; larger cruisers 7%; keel-type sailboats 10%. As wind pressure varies as the square of the velocity, the same manufacturer has suggested another formula for extreme conditions where a boat is anchored in a gale. For sailboats, the formula says that pull (in pounds) = $AV^2/186$, for motorboats $AV^2/220$.*(V is wind velocity in miles per hour, A is a factor derived by multiplying height, from waterline to deckhouse top, by overall beam.) An added safety factor of one-third should be allowed.

Varies with bottom

In preparing tables of holding power for specific anchor sizes, the manufacturer must give proper consideration to the kind of bottom in which his tests are run. Table 6-5 illustrates how wide the discrepancy can be between results in soft mud and hard sand. The figures also bring into sharp focus the variation in holding power between different models of equal weight offered by the same manufacturer.

One test the boatman can make

A simple test that any boatman can make has been suggested by the owner of a 40-foot auxiliary sloop. He found that a well-powered boat can use her engine to throw a load on an anchor greater than she will normally register when riding to that anchor.

The pull of an engine can be approximated by multiplying the horsepower by 20, a value that works out about right for a fairly heavy-duty propeller. With a high-speed propeller of small diameter, the pull is reduced somewhat.

FIG. 642 Using two anchors out ahead, it is better to have the rodes form an angle as at (a), instead of in line as at (b).

FIG. 643 Anchoring in a narrow waterway with reversing tidal current, two anchors should be used, but they must be set properly. Two anchors, both from the bow and set as shown in the sketch, are better than one from the bow and one from the stern. Adequate scope should be used, but the lines must be pulled tight against each other with the boat's bow on the line between them.

The anchor to be tested is let go astern and scope of 7 or 8:1 paid out before making fast. Then the engine is speeded up till the anchor drags. Sufficient speed is maintained to drag the anchor at one or two knots, meanwhile noting the engine rpm. Testing other anchors the same way provides a basis for comparison in the varying rates of rpm required to move each.

Actual test readings of the load can be made by using spring scales in the line, rigged if necessary to permit a small scale to register heavy loads. If a lever-operated winch is available, the scale can be attached at the end of the lever. The scale's reading is then multiplied by the ratio of the radius of the lever arm to the radius of the drum on which the chain or rope is carried.

The originator of this idea determined that his 40-footer, powered with a 52 hp engine driving a 20-by-12 propeller through 2:1 reduction, under full power pulled about 1,000 pounds. Under normal conditions of anchoring, he found that the boat would rarely surge to a value higher than 400 pounds, especially if generous scope were paid out.

When making a comparison of holding powers it is interesting to note that holding power is proportional to the area of buried fluke multiplied by the distance it is buried in the bottom. Consequently, for given areas of fluke, the design which permits deepest penetration is the most effective.

USING TWO ANCHORS

Two anchors are sometimes laid for increased holding power in a blow. If your working anchor drags, you can run out your spare storm anchor, without picking up the working anchor. The important thing to remember is to lay them out at an angle, not in line, to reduce the risk of having one that drags cut a trough in the bottom for the other to follow. See fig. 642.

To stop yawing

Deep-draft sailboats lie well head to the wind but motorboats often "tack" back and forth at anchor. Skiffs, with high freeboard and little draft forward, are among the worst offenders in this respect.

You can stop this yawing by laying two anchors, lines leading out from either bow, making an angle of about 45 degrees between them. To do this, get one anchor down first and have a man tend the line carefully as you maneuver the bow off to one side before letting the other go. Then you can settle back on both lines, adjusting scope as

*For wind in km/hr, and pull in kg, the factors are 120 and 141, respectively.

necessary. *Fouling the wheel in slack line under the boat in maneuvers like this is disastrous.*

With good handling, it is possible to get two anchors down single-handed. The easiest way is to settle back on one anchor, making fast when the proper scope has been paid out. Then go ahead easily with the propeller, rudder over enough to hold the line out taut so you can keep an eye on it at all times. When the line stands out abeam, stop your headway, go forward and let the other anchor go, then drop back and adjust the lines to equal scope.

If a dinghy is available, the second anchor can be carried out in it, lines being adjusted as required after both anchors are set.

To guard against wind or current shifts

It is sometimes necessary to anchor where tidal currents reverse or wide wind shifts are likely. Here it is wise to set two anchors as security against an anchor breaking out and failing to set itself again.

The anchors are set 180° apart with the bow of the boat at the midpoint between them; see fig. 643. With both lines drawn up tight, the bow remains over essentially the same spot and swinging is limited to the boat's length.

When setting a second anchor for use as described above, set the up-wind anchor in the conventional way and then back down till double the normal scope is out. After the down-wind anchor is set, adjust the scope at the bow chocks until both are equal. Going ahead, with a rode tending aft, use great care not to foul the propeller.

If the two-anchor technique is used in a crowded anchorage to limit swinging radius, remember that other nearby boats may lie to one anchor only, so risk of having the swinging circles overlap is increased.

Stern anchors

In some anchorages, boats lie to anchors bow and stern. The easiest way to get these down is to let the bow anchor go first, and then drop back with wind or current on an extra long scope (15-18 times the depth), drop the stern anchor, and then adjust the scope on both as necessary, taking in line forward. In tidal waters make allowance for increasing depth as the tide rises. The value of this arrangement is pretty well restricted to areas where permanent moorings are set explicitly for this purpose, as in narrow streams, or on occasions where there is no risk of getting a strong wind or current abeam. Under such conditions, the strain on ground tackle could be tremendous.

Sometimes a stern anchor will be useful if you seek shelter under a windward bank. The stern anchor can be let go aft, carefully estimating the distance off as it is dropped, and scope paid out as the boat is run up toward the bank or beach. A second anchor can then be bedded securely in the bank, or a line taken to a dock or tree ashore.

The stern anchor will keep the stern off and prevent the boat from ranging ahead. But, again, *watch that stern line, while the propeller is turning!*

At piers and wharves

A berth on the weather side of a dock is a bad one, as considerable damage can be done to a boat pounding heavily against piles, even with fenders out. Anchors can help to ease the situation in a case where such a berth is unavoidable. Keeping well up to windward, angling into

FIG. 644 When a boat swings with wind or current about an anchor, fouling a line around an exposed arm, holding power is destroyed.

FIG. 645 A buoyed trip line to the crown will permit an anchor fouled in rocky bottom to be hauled up fluke first.

the wind as much as is practicable, have a man let one anchor go on a long scope off the quarter (the port quarter, if you'll lie starboard side to the pier). As he pays out scope, run ahead and get another off the port bow, judging positions of both so you can drop down to leeward toward the pier on equal scope, with lines tending off at a 45-degree angle. Properly executed, this maneuver will prevent you from hitting the pier, and the lines you then carry ashore will be needed only to prevent the boat from moving ahead or astern.

RAFTING

At rendezvous several boats frequently lie to a single anchor. As many as ten boats have been observed rafted together, too many for safety even in a quiet cove. After one boat is anchored, the second pulls alongside with plenty of fenders out on both. Stay six to ten feet away from the anchored boat and heave bow and stern lines. If this can't be done, run up to the anchored boat's bow at an angle of about 45° and pass a bow line first, then your stern line. Make sure you have no headway when lines are passed. As soon as the bow line is aboard the anchored boat, stop your engine so that there will be no chance of going ahead, breaking the anchor out.

Allow your boat to drift astern until transoms align. Then let the bow swing off and pull the sterns in close so it will be easier to step from one boat to another. To keep the transoms in line and fenders in position a spring line

FIG. 646 Scowing an anchor. The rode to this Norwegian SAV folding anchor is attached to the crown and led back along the shank, to be lashed at the ring. When it fails to release at (1), an upward strain (2) parts the lashing and the anchor is drawn out as shown at (3).

must be run from the stern of the second boat forward to the anchored boat.

If a third boat ties up, the anchored boat should be in the middle; if more tie up always alternate them, port and starboard of the anchored boat. Each succeeding boat should use the same technique, always with a spring from the stern of the outboard boat forward to the one next inboard. Keels of all boats in the group should be nearly parallel. Naturally boats should raft only when there is little wind and a relatively smooth surface. When four or more are tied together, it is a good precaution for the outboard boats to carry anchors out at a 45° angle. When it's time to turn in for the night, every boat should have its own separate anchorage.

OTHER TECHNIQUES

On rocky bottoms

Earlier we spoke of certain steps that could be taken to clear a fouled anchor. Hazardous at best, rocky bottoms should preferably be avoided, regardless of the type of anchor used. Before leaving a boat unattended, a load should be applied to the anchor, after setting, well in excess of any expected load.

If you normally anchor in rocky bottoms or suspect that the bottom is foul in the area where you must anchor, it is better to forestall trouble. One time-tested device is the *buoyed trip line*. See fig. 645. Make a light line fast to the crown (in some anchors an eye is provided). This trip line should be long enough to reach the surface (with allowance for a rising tide) where it is buoyed with any convenient float—a block of wood, ring buoy or plastic disposable bottle. If the anchor doesn't *trip* readily at the first pull on the rode, haul in the trip line and the anchor will be withdrawn, crown first.

An alternate scheme is to *scow* the anchor, fig. 646, by bending the rode to the crown, leading it back along the shank, and stopping it to the ring with a light lashing of marline. With sufficient scope, the strain is on the crown and not on the lashing. When hove up short, the strain is on the lashing. When this parts, the anchor comes up crown first.

There are anchors (the Sure-Ring, fig. 647, is typical) that have a slotted shank in which the ring can travel freely from end to end. If the anchor should snag, the theory is that when the boat is brought back over the anchor, the sliding ring can slip down the shank so the anchor will be drawn out backwards. The Sure-Ring has an added refinement—a unique ring design that permits the rode to be

bent to an eye in the shank for overnight or unattended anchoring. A general similar design is the Benson "Snag Proof" anchor; here, too, the ring can slide up to the crown end if the anchor must be backed out.

Kedging off a bar

The term *kedging* is often, and properly, applied to the use of a light anchor (not necessarily kedge-type) carried out to deep water in a dinghy to haul a stranded boat off a shoal. If you ever have to resort to this, coil the line down carefully in the dinghy, so that it pays out freely from the stern as you row. The dink might well become unmanageable in a wind or strong current if an attempt is made to pay the line out from the deck of the stranded boat.

Anchoring at night

Anchoring at night, you must display a white 32-point light, visible at least 2 miles, rigged forward where it can be best seen. Vessels over 150 feet in length show a white light forward at least 20 feet above the hull, and another aft at least 15 feet lower than the forward light. Vessels over 65 feet at anchor display a black ball as a day mark.

FIG. 647 In the Danforth Sure-Ring anchor, a ring slides in a slot down the shank so the anchor can be drawn out backwards if it snags. For overnight use, the line can be shackled through the eye in the shank.

In certain specially designated anchorage areas, fig. 633, no lights need be displayed at night on vessels less than 65 feet in length.

When anchoring overnight, if you have no ranges to check your position (or if those you have are unlighted) you can rig a *drift lead* (the lead line will do). Lower it to the bottom, leave some slack for swinging, and make fast. If it comes taut, you've dragged. Don't forget to pick it up before getting under way.

FIG. 648 Salisbury plastic Chafe-Gard protects mooring lines from abrasion at the bobstay of this auxiliary.

FIG. 649 Chafe-Gard is lashed by thongs to the rode to hold it in place to protect against chafe at the chock.

SOME CAUTIONS

Guard against chafe

Every possible precaution must be taken to avoid chafe on fiber lines. Wherever the line comes in contact with chocks or rails and rubs back and forth under continuous strain, outer fibers may be worn to such an extent as to seriously weaken the line. Mooring pennants, fig. 648, are particularly susceptible to this.

When lying at anchor, you can *freshen the nip* by paying out a little more scope from time to time, or parcel the line at the point of chafe with strips of canvas wrapped around it. Modern chafing gear is available in the form of plastic or rubber sleeves, fig. 649, which can be snapped over the line, centered in a chock and seized with thongs to prevent shifting. Chafing gear also comes in the form of a white waterproof tape, to be applied around the line at bitts, chocks and other points of contact.

The increasing use of relatively light anchor rodes of small diameter (frequently $3/8$ inch) points up the necessity of preventing chafe. The chafe that a $3/4$-inch line could tolerate might render a $3/8$-inch line unsafe.

Chocks, bitts, cleats and other fittings

Chafe is aggravated wherever a fitting has a rough surface to accelerate abrasion of the fiber. Even small nicks and scratches in a chock can damage a line by cutting fibers progressively, one at a time. Serious weakening of a line develops when it is forced to pass around any fitting with relatively sharp corners, such as a square bitt with only a minimum chamfering of the edges, especially when the bitts are too small for the job they have to do. Theoretically the ideal bitt is round, of generous diameter. The best chocks are those of special design with the largest possible radius at the arc where the line passes over it.

Mooring bitts especially must be fastened securely. The best bitt is the old-fashioned wooden bitt, fig. 650, long enough to have its heel fastened deep in the boat's frame. If a cast fitting must be used on deck, it should be through-bolted, the deck below reinforced with husky partners. Bitts have been torn completely off the decks of boats anchored in open water with chain rode.

All fittings playing a part in the use, handling or stowage of ground tackle should be designed and installed not with

Note: For conversion to metric units, see page 99 or 115.

112

FIG. 650 The drum of an electric windlass and, behind it, a substantial well-rounded wooden Samson post. The horizontal Norman pin keeps line from slipping off the top. At lower left, a deck pipe through which the rode is passed below.

Ultraviolet Ray Exposed

FIG. 651 Small-diameter nylon line must be protected from damage by exposure to ultraviolet rays of the sun.

an eye to just getting by in fair weather, but proof against failure in the worst blow the vessel will ever encounter.

Damage from ultraviolet rays

The outer layers of all types of rope are subject to some degree of damage from ultraviolet rays of the sun. See figure 651. With nylon line of relatively large diameter (upwards of $3/4$ inch) damage from this cause is probably negligible. As the diameter decreases, the problem becomes proportionally more serious. In $3/8$-inch nylon it is an important factor to be reckoned with. Every possible precaution should be taken to shield such lines from unnecessary exposure to direct sunlight. Often the rode can be fed down into a locker. If it must be carried on deck, it pays to shade it.

CARE AND INSPECTION

Anchors and chain

Galvanized anchors are usually coated by the hot-dip process which leaves a tough protective finish, normally requiring no care except ordinary washing off of mud that may be picked up in use. Occasionally, they are freshened up in appearance by a coat of aluminum paint.

On soft bottoms chain may come up fouled with mud

FIG. 653 This mushroom anchor has a heavy bulb cast into the shank at the shackle end.

FIG. 652 A small permanent mooring system consisting of mushroom anchor, chain, buoy and pennant, with necessary swivels, shackles, thimble and eye splices. Rigged as shown, no strain is carried by the buoy.

because its weight has caused it to lie on the bottom, where even a light strain would keep all but a few feet of fiber line from touching bottom. Obviously, the chain needs thorough cleaning and on some larger yachts a hose is carried on deck for the purpose.

Fiber Lines

Fiber lines should be kept free from sand and grit; manila must be dried before stowing. A low-pressure hose can be used to wash off grit or you can slosh the line overboard, tied in a loose coil. Throwing a strain on a kinked fiber or wire line can be fatal. To a lesser degree, short bends are injurious.

Good practice dictates the need for one long spare rode in good condition. Too often this is an "old but new" unused manila line, which has rotted in its locker. This might fail in the emergency for which it is broken out.

Lengths of line in regular use may be turned end-for-end periodically, as most of the chafe and wear come on the anchor end. If one size is used for all lines, a new spare anchor line could be put aboard each spring, the former spare put into regular use, and the oldest anchor line made into dock lines, cutting out any chafed sections.

Nylon should be unreeled from the coil like wire, not up through the coil like manila. Neither should it be towed like manila when new to take out the kinks. When splicing, tape and fuse the ends with a hot knife or flame. Strands should be kept twisted, and an extra tuck taken, the ends to be left a little longer, when trimming, until the splice is well set under strain. Use synthetic rope thimbles or splice thimbles in tightly to prevent them from dropping out when the nylon stretches. On deep-sea tugs the "legs" of thimbles are seized to the line. All whipping and seizings should be made tightly so they cannot slip.

Periodic inspection

Periodic inspection of all lines, particularly anchor lines, pays big dividends. Look for and appraise the effect of abrasion, cuts, rust on nylon, broken or frayed yarns, variations in strand size or shape, burns, rot and/or acid stains, and fiber "life." Rotten manila fibers have little or

FIG. 654 Diagram of mooring practice recommended by the Lake Michigan Yachting Association and approved by the U.S. Coast Guard. A weight added at the shackle between lengths of heavy and light chain would increase holding power.

no strength when broken individually. Nylon line may fuzz on the surface although the yarns are not broken. This seems to act as a cushion, reducing further outside abrasion.

Consider the remaining cross-sectional area as compared to new rope. Untwist and examine the inside of strands. They should be clean and bright as in new rope. If powder or broken fibers appear, the line has been overloaded or subject to excessive bending. Nylon may be fused or melted, either inside or out, from overloads.

Most old-timers in yachting know cordage. If you are in doubt, replace your line or get an expert's opinion. For a more detailed discussion of marlinespike seamanship, see Chapter 11.

Permanent Moorings

Permanent moorings, as distinguished from ordinary ground tackle in daily use, consist of the gear used when boats are to be left unattended for long periods, at yacht club anchorages, for example. See fig. 652. The traditional system has often consisted of a mushroom anchor, chain from the anchor to a buoy and a pennant of stainless steel or nylon from the buoy to a light pick-up float at the pennant's end.

Mushroom anchors, especially the type with a heavy bulb cast in the shank, fig. 653, have been able through suction to develop great holding power under ideal conditions if they are allowed time enough to bury deep in bottoms that will permit such burying. Unfortunately ideal bottom conditions are not always present.

Complicating the problem is the fact that anchorages are becoming increasingly crowded so that adequate scope cannot be allowed each boat because of overlapping swinging circles. Add to this the threat of abnormally high hurricane tides, reducing scope to a ratio allowing no safety factor and you have the explanation for devastation wrought by several hurricanes along the Atlantic Coast, beginning in 1938.

Systems used by typical yacht clubs

The problem faced by the Manhasset Bay Yacht Club at Port Washington, N. Y., is typical of that existing in numerous anchorages. Here about 200 boats are moored in a limited space. If it were possible to permit each boat to use a length of chain equal to 5 to 7 times the depth of water (maximum 30 feet), safety would be assured, but this would require a swinging radius of several hundred feet for each boat, which is not possible. After exhaustive study, they prepared a set of recommended standards, given in Table 6-6.

FIG. 655 A modern permanent mooring system scientifically designed as a vast improvement over single-mushroom systems. Three lightweight anchors are bridled 120 degrees apart. From the intersection a relatively short rode limits swing.

A similar system was adopted by the Lake Michigan Yachting Association, their standards approved by the U.S. Coast Guard. See figure 654.

Guest moorings are often available at yacht clubs. The launch man will know which of those not in use for the night will be heavy enough to hold your boat. As a rule, it's easier and safer to pick up such a mooring. In some places, a charge may be made.

A multiple anchor system

One hurricane that ravaged the North Atlantic Coast swept through an anchorage in the New York area and tore almost every boat from her moorings. Only two survived. What these two had in common was an "unconventional" mooring system—multiple (3) anchors bridled to a common center, with chain and pennant leading from that point to the boat. The principle is diagrammed in fig. 655.

TABLE 6-6   **SUGGESTIONS FOR PERMANENT YACHT MOORINGS**
For Wind Velocities Up to 75 M.P.H.

Boat Length Overall	Mushroom Anchor (Min. Wt.)	Heavy Chain		Light Chain		Length (Minim.)	Pennant			Total Length (Chocks to Mushroom)
		Length	Diameter	Length	Diameter		Diameter			
							Manila	Nylon	Stainless Steel	
—FOR MOTOR BOATS—										
25	225	30	7/8	20	3/8	20	1	7/8	9/32	70
35	300	35	1	20	7/16	20	1-1/4	1	11/32	75
45	400	40	1	20	1/2	20	1-1/2	1-1/4	3/8	80
55	500	50	1	20	9/16	20	2	1-1/2	7/16	90
—FOR RACING TYPE SAILBOATS—										
25	125	30	5/8	20	5/16	20	1	7/8	9/32	70
35	200	30	3/4	20	3/8	20	1-1/4	1	11/32	70
45	325	35	1	20	7/16	20	1-1/2	1-1/4	3/8	75
55	450	45	1	20	9/16	20	2	1-1/2	7/16	85
—FOR CRUISING TYPE SAILBOATS—										
25	175	30	3/4	20	5/16	20	1	7/8	9/32	70
35	250	30	1	20	3/8	20	1-1/4	1	11/32	70
45	400	40	1	20	7/16	20	1-1/2	1-1/4	3/8	80
55	550	55	1	20	9/16	20	2	1-1/2	7/16	95

NOTE:—Heavy chain to be shackled to mushroom anchor, light chain shackled to end of heavy chain.
With stainless steel pennants, use special bow chocks and mooring bitts to eliminate sharp bends.

TABLE 6-7   SUGGESTED ANCHOR SYSTEMS FOR PERMANENT MOORINGS — (Winds up to 75 knots)

| LENGTH O.A. | BEAM | | PENNANT NYLON | *RODE (COMBINATION) | | RODE CHAIN⊕ ONLY | ANCHOR | | DANFORTH | |
	SAIL	POWER		NYLON	CHAIN		†MUSHROOM	NORTHILL	STANDARD	HI-TENSILE
10'	5'	5'	4'-³⁄₈"	³⁄₈"	5'-¹⁄₄"	¹⁄₄"	250 lb.	12 lb. (6-R)	8-S	5-H
15'	7'	7'	6'-³⁄₈"	³⁄₈"	6'-⁵⁄₁₆"	⁵⁄₁₆"	400 lb.	27 lb. (12-R)	13-S	12-H
20'	8'	9'	8'-³⁄₈"	³⁄₈"	6'-⁵⁄₁₆"	⁵⁄₁₆"	550 lb.	27 lb. (12-R)	22-S	12-H
25'	9'	10'	10'-⁷⁄₈"	⁷⁄₁₆"	8'-³⁄₈"	³⁄₈"	750 lb.	46 lb. (20-R)	40-S	20-H
30'	10'	11'	12'-⁷⁄₁₆"	⁷⁄₁₆"	8'-³⁄₈"	³⁄₈"	1050 lb.	80 lb. (30-R)	65-S	35-H
35'	12'	13'	14'-¹⁄₂"	¹⁄₂"	10'-⁷⁄₁₆"	⁷⁄₁₆"	1350 lb.	105 lb. (50-R)	85-S	60-H
40'	13'	14'	16'-¹⁄₂"	¹⁄₂"	10'-⁷⁄₁₆"	⁷⁄₁₆"	1800 lb.	105 lb. (50-R)	130-S	60-H
50'	14'	16'	18'-³⁄₄"	³⁄₄"	12'-¹⁄₂"	¹⁄₂"	2400 lb.	—	180-S	90-H
60'	16'	19'	20'-1"	1"	14'-⁵⁄₈"	⁵⁄₈"	3000 lb.	—	300-S	90-H

NOTE: *Total scope with combination rode to be a minimum of 7:1. ⊕Scope with chain only to be a minimum of 5:1. Buoy with each system to have lifting power (in pounds) of 1½ times the submerged weight of total rode. †Suggestions offered (by Danforth) in table above may sound excessive to those accustomed to lighter tackle. Experience, however, under storm conditions has proved the wisdom of providing for loads of unexpected severity. Sizes suggested assume fair holding ground, scopes as recommended, and moderate shelter from heavy seas.

A casual inspection of figure 655 reveals the obvious advantages of the system. Regardless of how the wind shifts, the boat swings through a small circle, despite the advantage of a relatively long total scope from boat to anchor. The short rode up from the three-way bridle minimizes any "tacking" tendency. Always there will be one or two anchors to windward, the strain tending in the same direction. Using modern lightweight anchors instead of mushrooms, the greater the load the deeper they bury. Mushrooms often need a relatively long period to bed in securely, but lightweight anchors will dig in almost immediately. Using a safety factor of 1.5, each anchor in the 3-anchor system should have a holding power equal to the design holding power of the moorings.

A scientific 3-anchor system of this kind overcomes all of the weaknesses inherent in poor systems using inadequate scope and concrete blocks, railroad car wheels and old engines, all categorized as "dragging" types of "anchor."

Mooring buoys

To comply with new uniform state waterway regulations (applicable on waters under state control), mooring buoys should be white with a horizontal blue band. Buoys used in any mooring system should be of a type that transmits strain directly through chain or rod. See fig. 640. Buoys perform a useful function in removing much of the vertical load, the pennant is under a more nearly horizontal load, and the boat's bow is freer to lift to heavy seas.

Pennants of stainless steel have often been preferred because failures frequently were traceable to chafing of fiber pennants. When fiber is used for the pennant, it should be carefully protected with chafing gear, especially if there is a bobstay against which it can saw. See figure 648.

Note—For conversion to metric units:
  1 inch = 2.54 cm
  1 foot = 30.48 cm or 0.3048 m
  1 pound = 0.4536 kg

FIG. 656 The Rubbermaid snubber, bent into a mooring line with clove hitches as shown, leaving a loop of slack, absorbs heavy shock loads on line and fittings. Tensile strength is 2000 pounds.

Annual inspection necessary

Because ordinary moorings often depend for holding power on a period of time to silt in, annual inspection of chain, links, shackles and pins should be made early in the season—never disturbed just about the time storm warnings are issued. On the other hand, it is also wise to give the pennant from buoy to boat a double-check in midseason, just before the August-September months when hurricanes most often strike.

Table 6-7 includes figures suggested for Danforth and Northill anchors when used in place of mushroom anchors in a permanent mooring system.

THE SKIPPER

His Duties and Responsibilities

The yachtsman is properly interested in the pleasure and comradeship that he obtains with his boat; the rigorous routine of a battleship has little, if any, place on the bridge of a 40-foot cruiser. However, we amateurs can learn from Navy practices. As many of these practices have as their sole purpose insurance of the safety of the ship and her personnel, it is especially appropriate for us to know something of them and apply to our own cruising those that will contribute to our own safety. *The first responsibility of a skipper is the safety of his ship and his people.*

LEADERSHIP AND DISCIPLINE

Suppose we think first about leadership and discipline. These are subjects that are rarely considered by the yachtsman but in them we find much that can be of value in that sudden emergency for which all of us who cruise must always be prepared.

Discipline; shades of a hickory stick. But, discipline is not subservience, discipline is self-control. It means prompt and cheerful obedience to necessary laws and regulations, laws and regulations designed for the sole purpose of our safety. It also means a square deal to our shipmates; the skipper who expects discipline of his crew must likewise discipline himself. A well-disciplined boat is a secure and safe boat.

Discipline does not mean a long string of commands with a crew constantly scurrying about the deck. Gold braid is not necessary to discipline. Discipline does not mean that all the joy is gone out of the job. There can be discipline on board the smallest yacht without there being any apparent show of it. Real discipline is a function of leadership and leadership can be exercised in dungarees on board a 20-foot (6.1 m) sailboat; it is a characteristic that all of us should cultivate and practice.

Leadership is based on three things: (1) each man must know himself, his abilities and his limitations; (2) he must know his job, know it so well that he doesn't have to think about the details of doing it; (3) he must know his men and his boat and what he can reasonably expect of them in an emergency.

Authority and obligations

From the lowest third class Petty Officer to the Admiral of the Fleet, every man of the Navy charged with authority has two functions to perform: (1) his function as a military leader; (2) his function as a specialist in some technical phase of his profession. It is relatively easy for any of us to become technically skilled in shaping a course, making

FIG. 701   The primary responsibility of every skipper is the safety of his boat and crew.

a mooring, even swabbing a deck. All of these have to do with our technical ability and are equally applicable in the Navy and in amateur cruising.

But there usually comes a time, and it is always an emergency when seconds count, when there are too many jobs for even the most skillful of us to handle them all. This is the time when our capacity for leadership will bring us to port or put us aground. In one way, leadership on a motor cruiser is even more important than it is on an aircraft carrier; our friends on board may not be skilled in the operation of a boat. We have to make up for their lack of technical ability.

Let's look at it another way. There is an old saying that you get more out of a job when you have to work at it; the average guest on board should more quickly feel at home and should have pleasanter memories of his cruise if he has some of the boat's work to perform, if he must coordinate his efforts with those of his shipmates. As skippers, we all welcome the guest who is eager to turn to and do his share.

Assignment of tasks

A good skipper will privately catalog in his own mind the abilities of his guests and think ahead to the tasks that he will request them to do should an emergency arise. See fig. 702. He may and should go one step further; without making it obvious, he should see to it that all on board are given various jobs to do not only so that he can find the best spot for each but also so that they are able to do more than one thing. *Our first obligation is the safety of our boat and her people.*

One good U. S. Power Squadron skipper makes it a practice to have "informal formal" watches, which amount to Navy watch, quarter, and station bills. From the stories told of cruises in his schooner, everyone on board has a bang-up good time, as well as a safe cruise. This man is a real leader and he doesn't hesitate to work at it.

Let's not try to define leadership; there have been as many definitions of this word as there have been writers. Any intelligent man thoroughly understands the meaning and significance of the term. Taking honesty and integrity for granted, it is the first characteristic that a man should develop. Out of leadership comes confidence, pride, emulation on the part of our associates; out of it will come the pleasant cruise that all of us want.

FORESIGHT

Next to leadership comes forehandedness or foresightedness. A first class skipper doesn't wait for an emergency to arise; he has long before formulated several solutions to any emergency with which he may be faced. Commander Frost, one of the foremost destroyer captains in the Navy, put it something like this: "The most expert captain is the first to admit how often he has been fooled by some trick of wind or current. Dangerous situations develop with startling suddenness so even when things look easiest, watch out. Have an answer to every threat and a trick to take you out of every danger." An officer must always look ahead, a minute, an hour or a day as the circumstances of his situation dictate. And, whether we like it or not, a yacht skipper is an officer, good or bad.

VIGILANCE

Next in importance to forehandedness is vigilance. In no position more than that of the skipper is "eternal vigilance the price of safety." He must see intelligently all that comes within his vision, outside and inside the ship. And his vigilance must extend beyond this to the faculty of foreseeing situations as well as seeing them. The rule of the airlines that a pilot must be able to get into alternate fields as well as the airport of his destination holds meaning for the boat skipper too.

COMMON SENSE

One more check point; it is common sense. The successful skipper has a sense of proportion and of the fitness of things; let us adjust ourselves to our situation. For example, it is obviously ridiculous to dress in white flannels and blue coat when kedging off, although we might do so when the ladies are on board of a quiet Sunday afternoon. Yet we all probably can recall cases where, through a failure to exercise common sense, we did things as silly as that suggested above. The old adage "use your head" applies equally well on shipboard.

One more quotation from Commander Frost. He has defined the art of handling a ship: "Systematic application of knowledge and skill, acquired by study, observation and experience, in effecting the safe, smart, effective and economical operation of your ship." Think it over.

COURTESY

There is a courtesy extended by large ships that is worthy of attention: dipping the ensign when passing a ship of the Navy. Pleasure craft frequently do not do this but it is a mark of respect that is highly desirable for all to show. As your bridge draws abeam the bridge of the Naval vessel, dip the Yacht Ensign and immediately hoist it two-blocks. All persons on board, except the helmsman, should face the warship and stand at attention; any in uniform should salute.

DUTIES AND RESPONSIBILITIES

We come now to the duties and responsibilities of a skipper, of those activities with which you must be familiar while on the bridge.

Approximately in the order of their importance, the responsibilities of the skipper or of the man having the watch are as follows:

- Safe navigation of his boat.
- Safe and efficient handling of the boat in company with or in the presence of other boats. See fig. 703.
- Safety of personnel and materiel on board.
- Rendering assistance to all in danger or distress.
- Smart handling and smart appearance of the boat.
- Comfort and contentment on board.
- A good log.

These are some of the instructions that the U. S. Navy gives to watch officers, men who are charged with the

FIG. 702 The good skipper will catalog in his mind the abilities of guests and crew, assigning tasks accordingly.

responsibility for the ship. They form a pattern that all of us, whatever the size of our craft, can follow with benefit. They presuppose that a man know himself, his job, his crew, and his ship. Let's see what they mean in terms of actual practice.

Check of equipment

Before a boat can be gotten under way, it is important that a check-up be made to determine if she is ready to sail. Not alone should the equipment required by law be on board and in proper condition for use but all navigational and other equipment should be at hand. See fig. 704. Water and gasoline tanks should be sounded, the ground tackle inspected, stores checked, and all those other little odd jobs that can be done at the mooring, but not at sea in an emergency, completed. These things sound elementary and worthy of little consideration but all of us can recall results that might have been different had the proper attention been given in advance to such minor details.

The Navy provides each ship with a check list that the officer must use before he takes charge or gets the ship under way. The yachtsman could profitably make up his own check list and either actually or mentally go over it as he steps from the dock to the deck. The whole subject of safety is so important that every yachtsman should consider himself disqualified until he so thoroughly knows the requirements that he executes them as second nature.

Physical condition of the skipper

Another point in the safe navigation of a ship has to do with the physical condition of the skipper. The constant vigil which is necessary requires the complete possession of all faculties as well as a sense of physical well-being. No man should expose his boat or his people to danger, except in an extreme emergency, unless he is in good physical and mental condition.

Avoidance of risk

The good skipper will not permit any of his personnel to take needless risks. If a dangerous job that may result in a man's being swept overboard has to be done, he will insist that that man wear a life jacket. This may not be customary in yachting circles but that omission does not justify contempt for danger. In this connection, the state of the weather should be carefully observed and every effort made before getting under way to ascertain what the weather will be for the period of the cruise. A little foresight in this regard may save a ship or a life.

In conclusion, for those of us who wish to cruise tomorrow as well as today, let us think first of the things that spell safety; then the fun will take care of itself.

IMPORTANT THINGS TO DO

Here is a short check list of things to do:

• Frequently check and plot the boat's position when in sight of land or aids to navigation; be certain of the identification of the objects used to fix position.

• Take soundings and heed their warning.

• Note the effect on the boat of wind and current, especially in close waters or when maneuvering with other boats.

• Do not follow other boats blindly; steer a safe course and do not assume that the other fellow is on a safe course.

• When in doubt as to position, slow down promptly; do not wait until the last minute.

• Remember that the other fellow may not see us and always be alert immediately to take such steps as will prevent a collision.

FIG. 703 One of the major responsibilities of a skipper is the safe and efficient handling of his boat in the presence of other craft.

Maintenance of a lookout

A small cruiser cannot readily utilize the lookout routine of the large vessel but the implication of vigilance and caution of that routine should be acknowledged. We should make it a matter of pride that we, as skippers, will observe any danger before any other person on board sights it; this is definitely our responsibility.

Regarding Refuse The admonition (see item below) against throwing refuse overboard is more than a matter of etiquette alone—it is based on law. Complaints received by both the Coast Guard and Army Engineers concerning refuse in coastal waters have fostered an official appeal by both agencies to the public. While asking each citizen to do his part voluntarily the appeal pointed out that "throwing, discharging, or depositing either from or out of any floating craft or from the shore refuse matter of any kind into any navigable waters of the U.S. or into any tributary of any navigable waters from which the same shall float or be carried into such navigable water is a violation of federal law (33 USC 407)." And for any who might take the warning lightly the appeal adds that such violation is punishable by a fine not exceeding $2500, not less than $500 or by imprisonment for not more than one year nor less than 30 days, or by both fine and imprisonment.

Official U.S. Coast Guard photo.

FIG. 704 The skipper must take full responsibility for seeing that all essential equipment, including that required by law, is aboard (and in proper condition for use) before casting off.

YACHT_____

Glad To Have You On Board

The Skipper and Mate welcome you on board. We look forward to your company during our cruise and ask

Please

DO make yourself at home. The mate will show you your locker. There is no lock on the refrigerator and the berths are said to be comfortable. Decks are usually swabbed down at 0900.

DO be informal. Old clothes are fit companions for swabbing decks, weighing anchor, and securing from chow.

DO ask us all the questions you wish—while we are not handling the boat. If you have a yen for rope-work or other ship's business, let us know. Too, you may find a helpful magazine or book on board.

DO locate your life-belt and learn how to use it. We will show you how to toss a life-ring, if you do not know. Not looking for trouble, but we want to be ready for it.

DO the same for the fire extinguishers. In case of fire, the Skipper will tell you what to do—and not to do.

DO report any danger or unusual occurrence to the Skipper at once: what it is, where it is, what it is doing.

DO go swimming at every opportunity. Swim upstream, keeping an eye on your shipmates and on the boat.

DO fish too, if you wish. But watch out for fouling the propeller and mooring lines, watch out for that fish-hook.

DO conserve fresh water. Use all that you need but remember, the supply is limited.

DO likewise conserve electricity. Lights out on the bridge when under way at night.

DO learn to work the "head." The Skipper or Mate will gladly show you.

DO stand clear of dock lines and anchor rode, of all boat controls.

DO remember that sound carries far over the water especially late at night.

Please

DO NOT smoke or strike a match or cigarette lighter or touch off the galley stove while fueling or starting the engines.

DO NOT take chances on deck, especially if the sea kicks up. Remember, rubber-soled shoes often slip on a wet deck.

DO NOT fall overboard or cause another to do so, while under way or at anchor.

DO NOT use any equipment with which you are not familiar. See the Skipper or Mate.

DO NOT jump from deck to dock without watching your footing. Landing on a rope-end usually results in a sprained ankle.

DO NOT jump into the dinghy; it isn't built to "take it."

DO NOT let go the dinghy painter until you are ready to clear.

DO NOT jump over the side while wearing a life-belt; your chin may be the worse for wear.

DO NOT throw refuse overboard without instructions from the Mate. Puncture cans at both ends; fill bottles with sea water and jettison only in deep water.

DO NOT use the "head" for cigarettes, matches, chewing gum or bulky articles; plumbers are scarce afloat.

DO NOT wear hard-soled or high-heeled shoes on deck; a good varnish job is too hard to come by.

DO NOT use the Skipper's binoculars or chart without permission; he may need them in a hurry.

DO NOT intrude on the privacy of others.

Morning colors at 0800—Evening colors at sunset—Recognition Signal—COOPERATION

_____Mate   _____SKIPPER

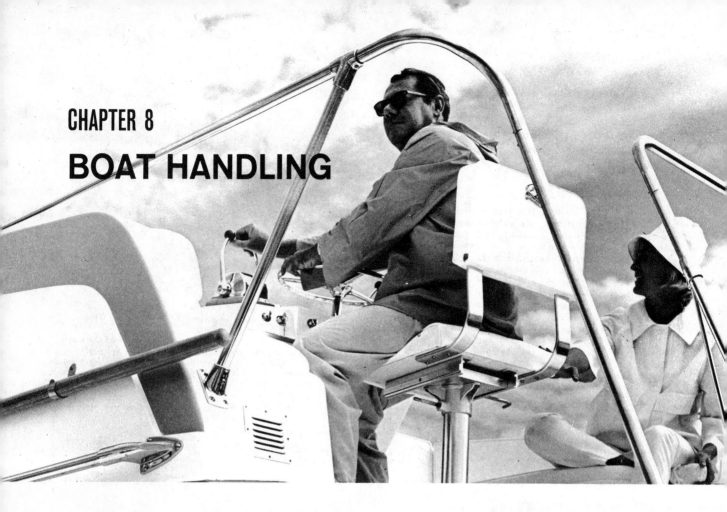

CHAPTER 8
BOAT HANDLING

Without a doubt some of the finest exhibitions of skill in the art of handling motor boats are often given by men who may never have read a printed page on the subject of seamanship. Their facility at the helm of a motor boat is their sheepskin from the sea's school of experience — in which the curriculum, admittedly, may be tough.

Witness, for example, the consummate skill some commercial fisherman might display in maneuvering his skiff into a tight berth under adverse weather conditions, finally to bring her up against the wharf in a landing that wouldn't crack an egg. Such proficiency, developed over long years of meeting every conceivable kind of situation, eventually manifests itself almost as an instinct, prompting the boatman to react right whether he has time to think the problem out in advance or not.

Sometimes the old-timer's methods might appear, to a novice, to verge on carelessness, but that's probably be-cause the old salt in a practical way understands exactly what the minimum requirements are for the safety of his craft and therefore doesn't waste any time on non-essentials. Consequently if he uses three lines where the text book says six, don't jump to the conclusion that he wouldn't know how to use more if they were needed.

So, in approaching a study of the principles of boat handling, it's helpful to keep in mind that the goal is not so much to be able to repeat verbatim definitions or the prescribed answers to a set of questions for the sake of passing a quiz as it is to understand the "why" of some of the curious capers your boat may cut when you're out there handling her. If she stubbornly refuses to make a turn under a given set of conditions, or persistently backs one way when you want her to go the other, you will be less likely to make the same mistake twice when you understand the reasons behind her behavior.

The Basic Principles

The paragraphs above lead up to a very fundamental thought. Learn all you possibly can about the principles according to which average boats respond under normal conditions; supplement this with all the experience you can get aboard your own boat and other types as well, and then learn to act so that controlling elements aid you rather than oppose you.

In consideration of boat handling, there are three primary types of powerboats — single-screw, inboard, twin-screw inboard, and outboard (including inboard-outboard propulsion). The first two of these use a rudder, or rudders in combination with a constant direction of thrust from the propeller or propellers; the latter type uses directed thrust without a rudder. The handling characteristics of each type is different from the others, but as the single-screw, single rudder inboard is the basic type, it will be given first consideration. An understanding of its principles is necessary to a study of the other types.

Although you may develop boat handling skills for your own present craft without knowing the "whys" (through the "school of hard knocks"—and that's no pun!), an understanding of the basic principles is very desirable when you change to your next, and probably larger, boat, or when at the helm of a strange craft.

No two boats will behave in identical manner in every situation, so great is their individuality. Just how a boat performs depends on many things—among them the design; the form and shape of the hull's underbody; the construction; the shape, position and area of the rudder; the trim; speed; the weight; load; strength and direction of wind and current; and the nature of the sea, if any.

EFFECT OF WIND AND CURRENT

Wind and current are particularly important factors in analyzing a boat's behavior as they may cause her to respond precisely opposite to what you would expect without these factors to reckon with. As a case in point, many motor boats have a tendency to back into the wind despite anything that can be done with the helm.

Given two boats of roughly the same size, one of which (A) has considerable draft forward but little aft, and another (B), with relatively greater draft aft but more superstructure forward—you will find radical differences in their handling qualities. What governs is the relative area presented above water to the wind as compared with the areas exposed to the water, both fore and aft.

The former (A), with wind abeam, might hold her course reasonably well when the bow of the latter (B) would persistently pay off, requiring considerable rudder angle to hold her up. On the other hand, with wind and sea aft, B might go along about her business with little attention to the helm while A insisted on "rooting" at the bow and yawing off her course despite the best efforts of the helmsman.

As a general rule, the boat with low freeboard and superstructure but relatively deep draft tending toward the sailboat type, fig. 801, will be less affected by wind and more by current than the light draft motor boat, fig. 802, with high freeboard and deckhouses. The latter floats relatively high in the water and has little below the waterline to hold her against wind pressures acting on areas exposed above water to drive her to leeward.

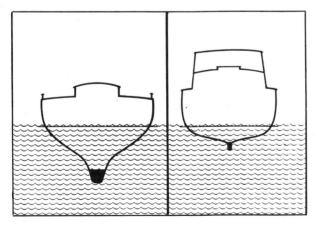

FIG. 801 Section of a deep-draft sailboat with relatively low freeboard, as compared with a typical motorboat.

FIG. 802 In this motorboat the draft is small compared to the height of superstructure exposed to windage.

In the type of motorboat where the greatest draft and least freeboard are aft, the greatest exposure to windage is presented by the relatively higher bow and cabin forward. Obviously her bow will be affected by wind pressures more than the stern. With wind abeam, the tendency would be for her bow to be driven to leeward more than the stern. To offset that, she would need a certain amount of rudder angle to hold her on her course and compensate for leeway.

For the same reason if she is drifting in a smooth sea with engine stopped, wind pressure on her bow will make the bow pay off so that the wind finally is brought abaft the beam. The action might also be compared to that of a sailboat in which a flattened jib, but no other canvas, is set.

But, just as an illustration to show how boat behavior may vary, suppose it is raining and cockpit curtains are buttoned down on that same cruiser. Here a new factor is introduced and the windage aft is increased to such an extent that it may more than offset the effect of the windage forward. Under such conditions she might be very hard to handle in close quarters because of the great amount of total windage compared to her draft.

Although flying bridges, fig. 803, on modern cruisers tend to add to the windage, they have an undeniable ad-

FIG. 803 A modern cruiser being brought up to a finger pier. The flying bridge and twin screws are a great advantage in handling, from the standpoint of visibility and control. Crew tends bow line.

vantage in better visibility when maneuvering, and running at night or in strange waters.

Some boats require humoring under certain conditions. For example, because of a combination of excessive superstructure forward and little draft at the bow, it may be practically impossible to turn a boat in close quarters by the conventional technique.

HELMSMAN MUST DEVELOP JUDGMENT

From these and many other variations in boat behavior it begins to be evident that the boatman must develop judgment, based on understanding of the individual boat he is handling and the forces acting upon her. Combina-

FIG. 804 Approaching a bridge. At this point the helmsman waits for the span to open. When about to enter the opened span, he will square away parallel with the center line.

tions of conditions are infinite, so he must be able to appraise the situation and act promptly, with decision.

A good helmsman will be prudent and try to foresee possibilities, having a solution in mind for the problem before it presents itself. On that basis, it's likely that he'll never meet an "emergency." To cite a simple example, if you're running down a narrow channel with a strong wind abeam, and you have a choice as to which side to take, the windward side is the better bet. If the engine should stop, you'll probably then have a chance to get an anchor down before going aground on the leeward side.

By the same token, you wouldn't skirt the windward side of a shoal too closely. To leeward, in case of engine failure, you would drift clear, but to windward you'd be driven down on the shoal. A strong current might have the same effect, and would have to be taken into account.

As another example of how the helmsman should try always to be prepared for possibilities, suppose you are approaching a bridge, fig. 804, having a narrow draw opening with a strong wind or current setting you down rapidly on it. If you were to approach the opening at an angle,

and power or steering gear failed, you'd be in a jam. On the other hand, if you are prepared and straighten out your course while still some distance off so you will be shooting down the center of the opening in alignment with it, the chances of doing any damage are practically nil because her straight course will tend to carry her through in the clear in any case.

In developing your boat sense, draw from as many sources as possible. Observe the way experienced yachtsmen, fishermen and Coast Guardsmen handle their boats, making due allowance for differences in your own boat when you try similar maneuvers.

TERMINOLOGY OF BOAT HANDLING

Before getting too deep into discussion of actual problems of maneuvering it is necessary in advance to get some of the correct terminology fixed in mind.

The *port* side of a boat is the *left* side facing forward; the *starboard* is the *right* side. This is easy to visualize while the boat has headway but when the boat is reversing the operator may face aft and get all mixed up when the terms right, left, starboard and port are used.

Therefore, bear in mind that the port side is the port side *no matter which way the boat is going.* When we speak of the boat's going to port it means that her bow turns to port when she has headway and her stern to port when she has sternway. Figure 805 makes this clear. At A the boat has headway and her bow is turning to port. At B she is going astern and her stern is going to port.

The old terms of port helm and starboard helm have now given way to new terms which prevent misunderstanding. In Figure 805 the boat has *left rudder* in both cases and with headway, as at A, her bow goes to port. *Right rudder,* which is not illustrated, is just the opposite. The rudder is then on the starboard side of the boat's centerline and her bow goes to starboard when the boat has headway.

A *balanced rudder,* fig. 806, is one in which the area of the blade surface is distributed so that part of it lies ahead of the rudder stock. An unbalanced rudder would have the stock attached at the edge of the blade.

While the proportion of this balanced area may be only

GOING AHEAD

A   B

PORT   STARBOARD   PORT   STARBOARD

LEFT RUDDER

GOING ASTERN

FIG. 805 With left rudder in a boat going ahead (A) the stern is thrown to starboard, bow to port. Going astern, left rudder throws stern to port.

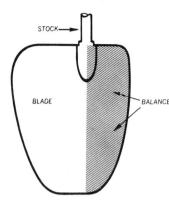

FIG. 806 A balanced rudder, in which part of the blade area (shaded section) projects a-head of the rudder stock.

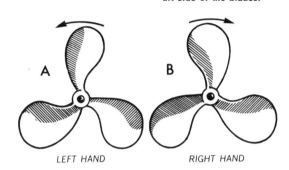

FIG. 807 Left-hand and right-hand propellers. This is how they turn when you stand astern of them, looking forward at the aft side of the blades.

LEFT HAND   RIGHT HAND

20 per cent of the total rudder area, it exerts considerable effect in taking strain off the steering gear and making steering easier, though it may slow the boat on a turn more than the unbalanced type.

RIGHT- AND LEFT-HAND PROPELLERS

Propellers are right-handed or left-handed, depending on the direction of their rotation. It is vital that the difference be understood because this has a great bearing on how a boat maneuvers, especially when reversing. To determine the hand, stand outside the boat, astern of the propeller, and look forward at the driving face of the blades, fig. 807. *If the top of the propeller turns clockwise when driving the boat ahead, it is right-handed; if counter-clockwise, left-handed.* A is left-handed; B, right-handed.

Most propellers on marine engines in single-screw installations are right-handed although some are left-handed. In any maneuvering problems which follow, the assumption is that the propeller on a single-screw boat under dis-

cussion is right-handed unless specifically noted to the contrary.

In twin-screw installations the ideal arrangement is to have the *tops of the blades turn outward* for better maneuvering qualities. In fig. 807 the port engine swings a left-hand 'wheel,' the starboard engine a right-hand wheel.

Don't be confused by the term right- and left-hand as applied to the engines that are driving the propellers. If you stand inside the boat, facing aft toward the engine, fig. 808, and the flywheel turns *counter-clockwise* (as in most marine engines) it is a *left-handed engine* and requires a *right-hand propeller.* A right-hand engine takes a left-hand wheel.

HOW THE PROPELLER ACTS

Motor boats are driven through the water by the action of their propellers which act almost like a pump, drawing in a stream of water from forward (when going ahead) and throwing it out astern. This stream moving astern reacts on the water around it to provide the power for propulsion. Sometimes an analogy is drawn between propeller action and a screw thread working in a nut, but this fails to give a correct picture of what really is happening at the propeller.

Actually all of the water drawn into the propeller does not flow from directly ahead like a thin column of water but for our purposes here it can be considered as coming in generally parallel to the propeller shaft. The propeller ejects it and as it does so imparts a twist or spiral motion to the water, fig. 809, its direction of rotation dependent on the way the propeller turns. This flow of water set up by the propeller is called *screw current.*

Suction and discharge screw currents

Regardless of whether the propeller is going ahead or reversing that part of the current which flows into the propeller is called the *suction screw current.* The part ejected from the propeller is the *discharge current,* fig. 811. The latter is not only spiral in motion but is also a more compact stream than the suction current and exerts a greater pressure than the suction current.

By locating the rudder behind the propeller in this discharge current a greater steering effect is possible than if it were to be placed elsewhere, to be acted upon only by water moving naturally past the hull. For that reason a

FIG. 808 Direction of rotation is marked on this marine engine flywheel housing. This is a left-hand engine, as shown by the counterclockwise direction of the arrow. It takes a right-hand propeller.

FIG. 809 The discharge screw current from a propeller is given a spiral twist by the propeller blades, as this view of an outboard lower unit shows. A left-handed inboard engine, driving a right-hand propeller, would create an opposite (clockwise) spiral.

FIG. 810 Boats under sail only have no propeller discharge current to increase the rudder's effect in steering. Their maneuverability is limited, and there are many tight places into which a motor boat could be worked where the sailboat (without power) could not.

FIG. 812 Regardless of differences in size or the number of blades, the same basic principles of propeller action apply and should be understood by all skippers.

twin-screw cruiser is likely to have twin rudders, one behind each propeller, thus keeping their blades at all times more directly in the propeller's discharge current. Exactly what the effect of each part of the screw current on the boat's behavior will be depends upon what part of the boat it is acting upon.

There is also a *wake current*. This is a body of water carried along by a vessel with her as she moves through the water due to friction on her hull. This has its maximum effect near the surface, is practically of no consequence at the keel.

Unequal blade thrust

Finally, there is another factor of some moment that needs to be understood in analyzing a boat's reaction to propeller rotation. While this has been sometimes referred to as sidewise blade pressure, it is more properly an unequal thrust exerted by the ascending and descending blades of the propeller, fig. 813.

Here we are looking at the starboard side of a propeller shaft, inclined, as most shafts are, at a considerable angle to the water's surface and to the flow of water past the propeller blades. The actual pitch of the blades as manufactured, of course, is the same, but the water flows diagonally across the plane in which the blades revolve.

Figure 813 shows clearly how the effect of this is to increase the pitch of the descending starboard blade as compared with the ascending port blade, when considered relative to the direction of water flow past the propeller.

The importance of this factor is reduced as the shaft angle is decreased, and naval architects, taking cognizance of this, sometimes take pains to have the engine installed as low as possible to keep the propeller shaft nearly parallel to the water's surface and the flow of water past the blades. This naturally contributes to propeller efficiency, and is a worth-while factor to be considered wherever consistent with other requirements of the design. Limitations in some designs, however, make it necessary for the engine and shaft to be installed at a considerable angle.

Effect of unequal blade thrust

The relatively greater pitch of the blade on the starboard side has the effect of creating a stronger thrust on this side with the result that the bow of the boat tends to turn to port. Putting it another way, insofar as this single factor is concerned, there is a natural tendency for the stern of a single-screw boat with right-hand propeller to go to starboard when the propeller is going ahead, and for the stern to go to port when it is reversing.

FIG. 811 The screw current which drives a boat through the water. Here the boat has headway. Suction current is shown leading into the propeller, the discharge current driven out astern.

FIG. 813 With rudder amidships, bow of boat with right-hand propeller may swing to port. Angularity of the propeller shaft has the effect of increasing the pitch of the descending blade relative to that of the ascending blade, so greater thrust is exerted on starboard side.

Again, when such a boat has headway, the bow apparently wants to turn to port if the rudder is held amidships, so a certain amount of right rudder may be necessary to maintain a straight course. To correct it, a small trimming tab may be attached to the after edge of the rudder and bent to an angle that provides the proper correction.

The effect is a great variable, so small in some cases as to be negligible; quite pronounced in others.

HOW THE RUDDER ACTS

The conventional arrangement for steering on most inboard boats a vertical rudder blade at the stern pivoted in hangers or on its own stock so that movement of the steering wheel or tiller throws it to port or starboard.

Steering gears on motor boats are almost invariably rigged today so that they turn with the rudder, that is, turning the top of the wheel to port throws the rudder to port. Consequently, with the usual rig, the boat having headway, putting the wheel over to port gives her left rudder which kicks the stern to starboard so that the bow, in effect, moves to port. Conversely, turning the wheel to starboard gives her right rudder, throwing the stern to port so that the boat turns to starboard.

Sailboat rudder action

In a sailboat, or auxiliary, fig. 810, when the engine is not driving a propeller, when the boat has headway water flows past the hull and if the rudder is moved to one side of the keel a resistance on that side is created together with a current at an angle to the keel. The combined effect is to throw the stern to port with right rudder, to starboard with left rudder.

But note that any control from the rudder is dependent on the boat's motion through the water. Even if she is drifting, with motion relative to the bottom, but none so far as the surrounding water is concerned, her rudder has no effect. Only when the water flows past the rudder and strikes it at an angle does the boat respond. The faster she is moving, the stronger the rudder effect. It makes no difference how her headway has been produced—she may even be in tow—there is control as long as there is motion relative to the water.

FIG. 815 With an outboard motor, the basic principles do not apply. Directed thrust from the pivoting lower unit is used for steering; there is no rudder.

Propeller current's action on rudder

In a motor boat the situation is different from that encountered in a sailboat. Here the rudder blade is almost invariably directly in the discharge current of the propeller which is pumping a strong stream of water astern. Moving the rudder to one side of the keel deflects the stream to that side. The reaction which pushes the stern in the opposite direction is much stronger than it would be in the absence of that powerful jet.

At very slow propeller speeds the boat's headway may not be sufficient to give good control over the boat if other forces are acting upon her at the time. For example, with a strong wind on the port beam, even with rudder hard over to port, it may not be possible to make a turn into the wind until the propeller is speeded up enough to exert a more powerful thrust against the offset rudder blade.

Here is a fundamental principle to remember in handling motor boats. In close quarters a motor boat can often be turned in a couple of boat lengths by judicious use of the power. If, for example, the rudder is set hard to starboard (that is, right rudder) while the boat has no headway and the throttle is suddenly opened, the stern can be kicked around to port before the boat has a chance to gather headway. The exact technique of turning in limited space will be described in detail further along.

FIG. 814 On inland waterways, boats may get into shoal water. This reduces the speed and also affects their handling qualities, response to the rudder being sluggish.

FIG. 816 The inboard-outboard, like the inboard boat, has an inboard engine. Unlike the inboard, it has an outboard drive unit which pivots like the outboard. This boat has twin engines.

TURNING CIRCLES

When the boat has headway and the rudder is put over to make a turn (to starboard, let us say), the stern is first kicked to port and the boat then tends to slide off obliquely, "crab-wise." Due to its momentum through the water it will carry some distance along the original course before settling into a turn, in which the bow describes a smaller circle than the stern, fig. 818. The pivoting point about which she turns may be between one-fourth and one-third of the boat's length from the bow, varying with different boats and changing for any given boat with the trim.

The distance a vessel moves in the direction of her original course, after the helm has been put over, is called the *advance*.

While there is always a loss of speed in making a turn, the size of a boat's turning circle will vary but little with changes in speed, assuming a given rudder angle. Whether she makes it at slow speed or at wide open throttle, the actual diameter of the turn is about the same.

There is, however, a great difference in the size of turning circles for single-screw inboards as compared with outboards or inboard-outboards because, as has been noted, the shaft and propeller of the inboard are fixed on the center line and cannot be rotated. This is dramatically illustrated in fig. 818. The twin-screw inboard, on the other hand, provides excellent maneuverability, as will be seen later.

Stops are invariably put on a rudder to limit its maximum angle. Beyond that point an increase of rudder angle would result, not in a smaller turning circle, but a larger one. That's why Naval vessels usually have a maximum rudder angle of 35 degrees.

When the boat has sternway (reversing) the rudder normally would be turned to port (left rudder) to turn the stern of the boat to port, while right rudder should normally tend to turn the stern to starboard in backing. However, the subject cannot be dismissed as easily as that and we shall see later how, under certain circumstances, the effect of the reversing propeller may more than offset the steering effect of the rudder.

Just as the speed of a boat is cut down in shallow water, fig. 814, so the depth has an effect on a boat's steering. Even though the keel may not actually be touching the bottom, it will be noticed that the boat's response to rudder action in shallow water is almost always sluggish.

KEEP STERN FREE TO MANEUVER

As soon as the boatman understands the underlying difference between the steering of a boat and a car, he will always be conscious of the need to keep the stern free to maneuver in close quarters. Furthermore, when he lies alongside a dock, a float or another boat, and wants to pull away, he will never, automobile-fashion, throw the wheel over until the stern is clear.

To set the rudder to starboard, for example, while lying port side to a dock and then attempt to pull away by going ahead, fig. 817, would only throw the port quarter against the dock piles and pin it there, to slam successively into one pile after the other as the boat moves ahead, with the likelihood of doing damage.

FIG. 817 With right rudder, as boat moves from A to B to C, stern is driven against piles, with risk of damage. Rudder should be amidships until boat is clear (or the craft should be backed away from the pier).

FIG. 818 When a boat's rudder is put over to make a turn, her stern is kicked away from the direction in which the rudder moves. Then, after sliding obliquely along the course (as shown from A to B) she settles into a turning circle in which the bow describes a smaller circle (solid line) than the stern (dotted line).

FIG. 819 A dramatic comparison of the turning circles of two boats at high speed. At "B" (left) the outdrive unit permits a tight turn in less than two boat lengths. At "A" (right) the inboard's propeller is fixed, and she responds only to rudder angle for steering.

HOW INDIVIDUAL BOATS DIFFER

We have seen how the helmsman has many things to consider when handling boats, due partly to individual characteristics which cause them to respond differently under identical conditions of wind, weather and current.

We have dealt too with the effect which draft and freeboard have on a boat's behavior, showing how high freeboard creates windage which acts to drive a boat to leeward whereas deep draft gives her a grip on the water with which to oppose that tendency.

The general principle is easily observed in the case of a deep keel sailboat, where deep draft acts to hold her on her course, and minimum freeboard is designed into her to reduce the windage factor.

Not only the draft, but the trim, has a bearing on a boat's handling qualities. Later we will see how the effect of rudder action in steering is to cause a boat to pivot about a point near the bow. But if she trims by the stern, that is, deeper than normal aft, the tendency is for that pivoting point to move aft.

The tendency to stray off course

Different boats require varying degrees of rudder angle to compensate for any tendency to fall off from a straight course. Depending on differences in construction, arrangement of rudder blade, and the hand of the propeller, the bow may tend to fall off to port or starboard. These are all factors that the helmsman should understand before attempting maneuvers with a boat.

Using a concrete example to make the significance of the last point more clear, a certain group of boats of almost identical design were found to have a strong tendency to pull off course to port. In some of these, the condition was corrected by the simple expedient of lowering the rudder blade, without changing its size or shape but merely by lengthening the stock an inch or two.

Before correcting that condition, these boats would make a quick and easy turn to port but would be obstinate in turning to starboard. As a matter of fact, unless steering controls were rigged with worm and gear to hold the wheel against pressure on the rudder, the boat would immediately swing into a short circle to port the instant the wheel was left unattended. While this is an exaggerated condition, far from normal, it does illustrate the handling characteristics the helmsman must pay attention to, especially in an unfamiliar boat.

Then again, the state of the sea will have an effect on a boat's performance. A heavy, deep draft boat or one which is heavily loaded will carry her way through the water longer than a light one when the propeller is disengaged by throwing the reverse gear lever into neutral. This is likely to be even more marked in a seaway, the light displacement boat losing her way against the sea much sooner than a heavier craft would.

Response of Boat to Propeller and Rudder

Let us consider now a number of typical situations to see how the average inboard motor boat will respond to propeller and rudder action *(assuming a single-screw boat with right-hand propeller).*

NO WAY ON, PROPELLOR NOT TURNING

When a boat is "dead in the water"—making no way forward or sternward through the water, although she may be drifting with respect to the bottom—and her propeller is not in gear, turning the rudder has no more effect than turning a car's front wheels while it is parked. There must be a flow of water past the rudder for it to be effective, from either the boat's motion through the water or the propeller's discharge current, or both.

NO WAY ON, PROPELLER TURNING AHEAD

Picture her first without any way on, engine idling and rudder amidships. Being dead in the water there is no wake current to act on the propeller blades. Now the clutch is engaged and the propeller starts to turn ahead.

Until she gathers headway, the unequal blade thrust (refer back to fig. 813) tends to throw her stern to starboard. As she gets headway, wake current enters the picture, increasing pressure against the upper blades (remember wake current is strongest at the surface, has little effect at the bottom of the keel) and this tends to offset the effect of unequal blade thrust.

What happens under identical conditions, except that the rudder is hard over at the time the propeller is engaged? In this case the propeller's discharge current strikes the rudder and exerts its normal effect of kicking the stern to port with right rudder, or stern to starboard with left rudder. With right rudder the kick to port would be much stronger than the effect of unequal blade thrust.

WITH HEADWAY, PROPELLER GOING AHEAD

After the boat has gathered normal headway, with rudder amidships, the average boat tends to hold her course in a straight line fairly well. From a purely theoretical standpoint, the unequal blade thrust, with a right-hand wheel, should tend to move the stern to starboard, and bow to port. On most boats, however, the effect is quite slight. Only in a comparatively few cases will unequal blade thrust have a pronounced effect on steering, and in these it can be corrected by a small rudder tab.

Now, the boat having headway, assume the rudder is put to starboard. The water flowing past the hull hits the rudder on its starboard side, forcing the stern to port. The propeller's discharge current intensifies this effect by acting on the same side and the boat's bow turns to starboard, the same side on which the rudder is set. With rudder to port the action would naturally be just the opposite.

WITH HEADWAY, PROPELLER REVERSING

A boat has no brakes as does a car, so she depends on reversing the propeller to bring her to a stop. Assuming that the boat has headway, rudder amidships, and the propeller is reversed, the effect is to throw the stern to port as the boat loses headway. The rudder has no steering effect in this case, and unequal blade thrust of the pro-

peller (which, remember, is reversing) tends to throw the stern to port. At the same time the propeller blades on the starboard side are throwing their discharge current in a powerful column forward against the starboard side of the keel and bottom of the boat, with nothing on the port side to offset this pressure. The stern, of necessity, is thrown to port.

This principle explains why a boatman will bring his boat up to a landing port side to the dock, if he has a choice. The stern then is thrown in toward the dock by the reversing propeller instead of away from it.

With rudder to port

Going back now to the case where the boat has headway and the propeller is reversed—this time with rudder over to port, let us say. Here the situation is more complicated. As before, we have the unequal blade thrust and propeller discharge current both driving the stern to port.

In addition there are two opposing factors. If the boat has much way on (ahead) her left rudder tends to throw the stern to starboard. However, her propeller suction current is being drawn in from astern in such a manner that it strikes the back of the rudder blade, tending to drive the stern to port.

Which combination of factors will be strongest depends on the amount of headway that the boat is carrying. If she has been running at some speed, the steering effect of left rudder will probably be the dominant factor and her stern would be thrown to starboard at first. As this steering effect weakens with reduced headway, the propeller slowing her down, then the effect of the suction current is added to help the tendency of the stern to port until eventually, with all headway killed, even the steering tendency to starboard is lost and all factors combine to throw the stern to port.

NO WAY ON, PROPELLER REVERSING

Now if the boat is lying dead in the water with no headway, rudder amidships, and the propeller is reversed, we again have that strong tendency of the stern to port as the

FORWARD-RIGHT HAND WHEEL
RUDDER DEAD AHEAD

PIVOT POINT

Boat lying dead in water. When controls are set for forward motion, the first movement is a kick to starboard. The amount of side kick will depend on the boat and the amount of throttle given.

PIVOT POINT FORWARD MOTION

With forward motion when the helm is put over, the boat pivots around a point about ⅓ aft of the stem.
Note that the stern swings through twice as wide an arc as the bow.

When backing down:

PIVOT POINT WITH STERNWAY

Pivot point is about ⅓ forward of stern, so bow describes twice as wide an arc as the stern.

FIG. 820 In the above series of sketches, the solid figure "A" represents the position of the boat before the action starts, and the broken outline "B" indicates its position afterwards.

discharge current strikes the starboard side of the hull. You see, in each of the cases where the discharge current of the reversing propeller is a factor, the strong current on the starboard side is directed generally toward the boat's bow but upward and inward in a spiral movement. The descending blade on the port side, on the other hand, tends to throw its stream downward at such an angle that its force is largely spent below the keel. Therefore, the two forces are never of equal effect.

Until the boat gathers sternway from her backing propeller it would not matter if the rudder were over to port or starboard. The discharge current against the starboard side is still the strong controlling factor and the stern is thrown to port. (Come back to this later when we discuss the matter of turning in a limited space.)

WITH STERNWAY, PROPELLER REVERSING

Now visualize the boat gathering sternway as the propeller continues to reverse. Here arises one of the seemingly mystifying conditions that baffle many a helmsman during his first trick at the wheel. The novice assumes that if he wants to back in a straight line his rudder must be amidships, just as it must be when he goes ahead on a straight course. Under certain conditions his boat may even respond to *right* rudder as he reverses by going to *port,* which is exactly what he doesn't expect, and if he is learning by trial-and-error he comes to the conclusion that it depends on the boat's fancy, while rudder position has nothing to do with control.

Let's analyze the situation, however, to see if he's right and whether there is anything that can be done about it. Fortunately, there is.

Backing with left rudder

At the outset we can rule out any effect of wake current as that force now is spent at the bow. Considering first the most obvious case, let's assume we have left rudder. Here there are four factors all working together to throw the stern to port. Unequal blade thrust is pushing the stern to port; the discharge current of the propeller is adding its powerful effect; and now we add the steering effect of the rudder acting on the aft side of the rudder blade, against which the suction current of the propeller is also working.

Remember this condition well for it is the answer to why *practically every single-screw vessel with right-hand propeller naturally backs to port* easily when she may be obstinate about going to starboard when reversing, fig. 821.

Backing with rudder amidships

Now, while backing to port, let's bring the rudder amidships and see what happens. Here we have eliminated the effects of suction current and steering from the rudder, leaving unequal blade thrust and the discharge current to continue forcing the stern to port.

Backing with right rudder

Assuming further that we have not yet gathered much sternway, let's put the rudder to starboard and see if we can't possibly make the boat back to starboard as you might expect she should with right rudder. The forces of unequal blade thrust and discharge current still tend to drive her stern to port, but the suction current of the pro-

Boat Backing, Propeller Reversing, Left Rudder — Boat's stern goes rapidly to port

Boat Backing, Propeller Reversing, Rudder Amidships — Boat's stern still goes to port

Boat Backing, Propeller Reversing, Right Rudder — Boat's stern may still go to port though with sufficient sternway and Full right rudder, she should back to starboard

FIG. 821 Three different situations where a boat is backing, her propeller reversing, with rudder set in various positions. Some boats back to port no matter how the rudder is set, but usually with right rudder and good sternway, they can be turned to starboard, though the turn to port is much better.

peller wants to offset this. The effect of the discharge current is stronger than the suction so the tendency is still to port. Now, with sternway, the steering effect of right rudder is to starboard, but as yet we haven't way enough to make this offset the stronger factors.

STEERING WHILE BACKING

Just about the time we are about to give it up on the assumption that she can't be made to back to starboard, we try opening the throttle to gain more sternway. This finally has the desired effect and with full right rudder we find that the steering effect at considerable backing speed is enough (probably) to turn her stern to starboard against all the opposing forces. How well she will back to starboard—in fact, whether she will or not—depends on the design.

All of this means that if the boat will back to starboard with full right rudder, she may also be made to go in a straight line—but not with rudder amidships. There's no use trying. She will need a certain amount of right rudder depending both on her design and the speed. Some boats, while their backing to port is always much better than to starboard, can be controlled with a reasonable degree of precision by one who understands the particular boat he is handling.

In cases, boats may even be steered backwards out of crooked slips or channels—not, however, without a lot of backing and filling if there is much wind to complicate the situation. Generally the trick is to keep the boat under control, making the turns no greater than necessary so as to prevent the boat from swinging too much as a result of momentum and making it correspondingly difficult to get her straightened out again.

In maneuvers of this kind it is best to set the rudder first and then get added maneuvering power by speeding up the propeller in the desired direction, instead of trying to swing the rudder after the propeller is turning fast either ahead or astern.

WITH STERNWAY, PROPELLER TURNING AHEAD

There is one other situation to be considered, where we wish to kill our sternway by engaging the propeller to turn ahead. Regardless of rudder position, unequal blade thrust with the propeller going ahead now tends to throw the stern to starboard while the suction current is of no consequence. Unequal blade thrust may or may not be offset by the steering effect and the discharge current.

With rudder amidships, there is no steering effect and the discharge current does not enter our calculations. Therefore the stern will go to starboard. Now if you throw the rudder to port the discharge current of the propeller hits the rudder and drives the stern to starboard—even though the normal steering effect of left rudder would be to send the stern to port, with sternway. The powerful discharge current from the propeller going ahead is the determining factor.

If the rudder is put to starboard, the steering effect works with the unequal blade thrust tending to move the stern to starboard but the discharge current strikes the starboard side of the rudder and acts to kick the stern to port. Application of enough power so that the force of the discharge current outweighs the other factors will result in the stern's going to port.

PROPELLER ACTION GOVERNS

From this analysis it will be seen that in a single-screw inboard boat one must constantly keep in mind what the propeller is doing in order to know how to use the rudder to best advantage. What the propeller is doing is even more important than whether the boat at the time may have headway or sternway.

To cite an example to make this clear, let's suppose you are backing in a direction that brings your port quarter up toward a dock. The tendency if you were to try to steer away from it would be to use right rudder. But the efficacy of that would be doubtful, because of the boat's inclination to back to port.

Therefore, we plan to kick the stern away by going ahead with the propeller so we set the rudder to port (left rudder, *toward* the dock), throw the reverse gear lever into the forward position and go ahead strong with the engine. The discharge current checks the sternway and, striking the rudder, throws the stern to starboard, clear of the dock.

It takes a lot of experience with any given boat to learn all her whims and traits—to know her strong points and use them wisely to overcome the weak ones. But boats, like individuals, do respond to understanding treatment.

Applying the Principles _____

Proficiency in motor boat handling is a matter of 10 percent principles, 90 percent application of these principles in practice. Therefore, the sooner we get afloat and start experimenting, the better. We've absorbed enough of the theory to have a broad idea of what to expect in practice; the next step is to get at the helm of a boat and actually learn by doing.

POINTS TO REMEMBER

Here are a few basic ideas to keep in mind, summarized from what has gone before.
• Remember that *the boat is always under better control with headway* than when she has sternway, because of the effect of the propeller's discharge current on the rudder when steering.
• Until the boat has gathered headway the stern has a tendency to swing (to starboard, with right-hand propeller) even with rudder amidships, as the propeller starts to turn ahead. *With good headway, rudder angle is the principal factor affecting control.*

• *Backing, there is a strong tendency to go to port* regardless of rudder angle, except (ordinarily) with full right rudder and considerable sternway. To back in a straight line you need a certain amount of right rudder varying, probably, with the speed.
• *With no way on there is no rudder control,* yet the stern can be kicked rapidly to port or starboard by putting the rudder over and applying plenty of power before the boat has a chance to gather way.
• *With left-hand propeller, the boat's reaction will be contrary to that outlined for the right-hand propeller.*

THE FIRST TIME OUT

The first step in applying these principles will be to take the boat out in open water—preferably on a day when there is little wind and no current. These factors should be ruled out at first and studied separately later, after the boat's normal reactions are fully understood.

With unlimited room to maneuver and no traffic to worry about, try putting the boat through all the maneuvers already discussed. Practice with every combination of

FIG. 822 In channels like this, speed must be held down to avoid damage to other craft and discomfort to their passengers. A boat is liable for damage caused by her wake.

conditions—with headway, sternway, and no way on; with right-rudder, left rudder and rudder amidships; with propeller turning in the direction of the boat's way, and also those cases where the propeller is turning opposite to the direction of the boat's way.

In each of these maneuvers note whether the rudder or propeller has the greater effect; note, too, how changing the speed alters the boat's response. Put the rudder hard over each way and see what happens when considerable power is applied before the boat has any way on.

Practice turns to determine the size of the boat's turning circle and the space required to bring the boat to a full stop with varying amounts of way, up to full speed.

GAINING EXPERIENCE

Later, when these fundamentals are mastered, go out again and observe how wind and current and sea alter the situation. Note how she tends to back into the wind until good steerageway is reached. How, if she is lying in the trough in a seaway, she tends to stay there with rudder amidships, because wave action is stronger than her natural tendency in smooth water to back to port.

Watch too how her stern starts to settle, and the bow comes up, when you get into shoal water. If there's just enough water to permit her to run without grounding, a wave will pile up on her quarter, steepest on the shallower side, as the natural formation of the wake is disturbed.

You should, of course, pick your maneuvering grounds from the chart to avoid danger of grounding, but if you see the first wave of your wake stretching away on the quarter in a sharp inverted V, tending to break at the top, beware of shoal water on that side.

GETTING UNDER WAY

Whenever you are about to get under way, assuming that you are starting a cold motor, don't spend too much time at the dock or mooring "warming up." There are a few things to check before getting under way and by the time these have been taken care of you will be ready to cast off and let the warming up of the motor be accomplished under load, at about half speed. Long periods of idling are bad for the clutch and the motor will warm up

better and quicker with the propeller engaged.

Before casting off, check the oil pressure and see that the cooling water is circulating. Whether your engine is "raw-water cooled" or "fresh-water cooled" with a heat exchanger, there should be a visible flow of water overboard, usually through the exhaust line. Until this water flows, it is unsafe to get underway.

If the water doesn't circulate, investigate at once as overheating can cause much damage, especially in a raw-water cooled engine if the cold water is suddenly picked up and pumped into the hot cylinder block. Cracking of the block could result.

Never race the motor as it idles, especially when cold. If the propeller is the right size and the throttle stop properly set, the motor should be able to take the propeller when the clutch is engaged at idling speeds. Boats don't require transmissions with a change of speeds as in cars, because the propeller slip automatically takes care of picking up the load gradually as the clutch is engaged.

After the clutch is in, the throttle (which almost invariably is hand-operated) can be opened gradually. Roughly speaking, normal cruising should be done at about two-thirds or three-quarters throttle. The extra few hundred revolutions available at wide open throttle seldom yield an increase in speed proportionate to the extra power required and the corresponding increase in fuel consumption. In congested waterways speed should be moderate, taking care that no damage is done by the wake, fig. 822.

One caution to observe when first learning to maneuver the boat is to avoid operating at too high a speed. Later, after you have become more familiar with the boat and its response to wheel and throttle, you will be able to use more power in certain situations—to accomplish a quick turn, for example—without getting into a jam.

CHECKING HEADWAY

Before attempting the maneuver of picking up a mooring you will want to experiment with the technique of checking the boat's headway while she is out in open water. Having no brakes, you must reverse the propeller to bring the boat to a stop. Caution must be exercised, *and docks or other craft must be approached at a very slow speed.* Unexpected failure of the clutch and reverse gears, or an unintentional killing of the engine, can result in embarrassing situations, if not actual damage, as you are unable to check your boat's forward motion.

Your experiments will show how effective the propeller is in killing the boat's headway. Generally speaking the larger diameter propellers, acting on a large volume of water, will exert the greatest effect. Small propellers, poorly matched to heavy hulls, may churn up much water before they are able to overcome the boat's momentum.

Many fast boats can be stopped in an incredibly short distance. When their throttles are closed, the boat changes her trim suddenly and headway is quickly lost, even before the propellers are reversed.

Whenever it is necessary to go from forward into reverse or vice versa, close the throttle to slow the engine down while going through neutral. If you make a practice of shifting the reverse gear from full ahead to full astern, look out for trouble. This is hard on the gear even if it doesn't fail—which it might do just when you're counting on it most.

FIG. 823A

Boat starts turn at left side of channel (1) making sure to allow room for stern to swing to port. Headway is checked (2) by reversing the propeller.

FIG. 823B

Rudder is kept to starboard (right rudder) throughout the maneuver. Unequal blade thrust and propeller discharge current force stern to port as boat backs from (2) to (3), propeller reversing.

FIG. 823C

Going ahead again, sternway is checked at (3) and propeller turning ahead kicks stern to port as shown at (4) before the boat has had a chance to gather headway.

FIG. 823D

Reversing once more, headway is checked at (4) and boat backs to (5). If necessary, alternate going ahead and backing can be repeated. Space available for the turn governs this. Turning in two boat lengths is easy.

FIG. 823E

At (5) boat is in a position to go ahead with right rudder, bringing it amidships at (6), where she is ready to proceed, having reversed her course 180° from her original position at (1).

TURNING IN CLOSE QUARTERS

Turning a boat in a waterway not much wider than the boat's length often seems a bugbear to the novice but, once he has mastered the technique, it's no more difficult than turning a car on a narrow road.

Take a look at fig. 823. The situation sketched might apply in many cases. Perhaps you've run to the head of a dead-end canal and must turn around. Or possibly the waterway is a narrow channel, flanked by shoals. In the former case you must allow room so the swinging stern doesn't hit the canal bulkhead; in the latter, a similar allowance must be made to avoid throwing the stern up on shoal water.

Referring to fig. 823A, we start at (1), on the left side of the channel, running at slow speed. Putting the rudder hard over to starboard, the boat swings toward position (2), her headway being checked by reversing. *Always* execute this maneuver (if the propeller is right-handed) by going ahead to starboard, backing to port, to take advantage of the boat's natural tendency, as explained before.

Now (see 823B) *leave the wheel hard over to starboard* (right rudder). Normally you would expect to use left rudder in backing from (2) to (3), but this is unnecessary as the boat has no chance to gather sternway. As the reversing propeller stops the boat at (2), open the throttle for an instant and the stern will be kicked around to port to position (3).

Any attempt to shift from right rudder while going ahead to left rudder while going astern only results in extra gymnastics at the wheel at a time when you want your hands free for the throttle and reverse gear lever.

Throttling while we engage the clutch to go ahead, the sternway is checked at (3). Opening the throttle again, just for an instant, keeps the stern swinging to port toward position (4)—see fig. 823C. Now the operation described in 823B is repeated, backing from position (4) to (5) as shown in 823D.

If this happens to be a bulkheaded slip you are maneuvering in, allow plenty of room so that the port quarter is not thrown against the head of the slip as you go ahead

again at (5)—see 823E. The stern will continue to swing to port as the boat straightens away toward (6). At this point the rudder can be brought amidships, the boat having executed a 180-degree turn.

Backing around a turn

Fig. 824 illustrates the successive steps required to work out another practical problem in boat handling. Suppose (see 824A) you are in a narrow slip or canal at position (1) and want to back around a sharp turn, to starboard.

Reversing with full right rudder, you will not be able to turn short enough to steer around the 90-degree angle. Most likely you will back to a position about as indicated at (2), gaining a little to starboard. Now (see 824B) by going ahead with left rudder the stern is kicked over to starboard, placing the boat at (3).

Reversing once more, with full right rudder, the boat backs to (4), necessitating our going ahead once more with left rudder. This puts the boat at (5) (824D) in a position to back down on the new course.

Note that if she is expected to back down in a straight line from (5) she will need right rudder, though not necessarily hard over.

Backing to port from a slip

Fig. 825 illustrates a variation of the maneuver just described. Suppose the boat is lying in a slip, at A, and wishes to back out into the channel, space being limited. Fig. 824 showed how it would be necessary to work her around if the turn were to starboard. In fig. 825 her problem would be exactly the same if she had to back around in the direction of C.

However, if there is a choice, and she can back out to port, the probability is that with left rudder she will work around from A to B without any special maneuvering. To do it, her initial position in the slip must be about as shown at A with some clearance on her port side, but considerably more on the starboard side.

Clearance on the port side is needed because in reversing her stern immediately starts to move to port. More clearance on the starboard side is necessary because the

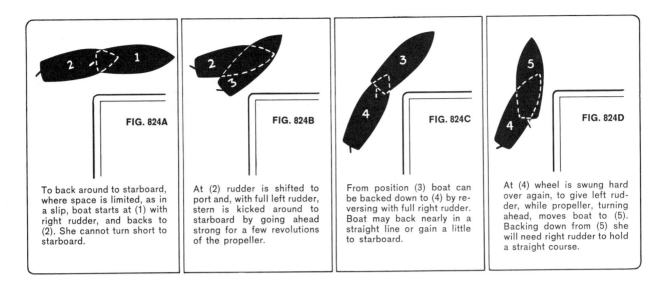

FIG. 824A

To back around to starboard, where space is limited, as in a slip, boat starts at (1) with right rudder, and backs to (2). She cannot turn short to starboard.

FIG. 824B

At (2) rudder is shifted to port and, with full left rudder, stern is kicked around to starboard by going ahead strong for a few revolutions of the propeller.

FIG. 824C

From position (3) boat can be backed down to (4) by reversing with full right rudder. Boat may back nearly in a straight line or gain a little to starboard.

FIG. 824D

At (4) wheel is swung hard over again, to give left rudder, while propeller, turning ahead, moves boat to (5). Backing down from (5) she will need right rudder to hold a straight course.

FIG. 825

Boat should make a short turn to port from A to B, when reversing with left rudder, but watch points X and Y.

bow will swing over toward point (x) as she backs.

In fact, points (x) and (y) are the ones to watch in executing this maneuver. If the boat shouldn't turn as short as expected, and doesn't swing directly from A to B, but takes a position as shown by the dotted lines at A', the starboard bow is in danger of touching at (x) and the starboard quarter at (y). This could be corrected at A' by going ahead with the propeller a few revolutions, using right rudder, to kick the stern over to port. This must be done carefully as there is no latitude here for much headway.

Having straightened her up, you could then back with left rudder to B and finally square away with rudder amidships to proceed toward C.

LEAVING A MOORING

Many yacht clubs have anchorages for members' boats, using mushroom anchors or heavy concrete blocks and mooring buoys to which the boat is secured by a pennant or mooring line over the forward bitt. Boats at moorings are reached from shore by dinghy or the club launch.

Getting away from the mooring when you are about to start a cruise is among the simplest of maneuvers, yet there is a right and a wrong way to go about it. The principal hazard in doing it wrong is the possibility of getting either the mooring line or dinghy painter fouled in the propeller. Handling of the boat is dictated by whatever is necessary

to accomplish this with a minimum of fuss.

If a dinghy was used to reach the boat, shorten up its painter so that the reversing propeller cannot pull any slack down into it, to be hopelessly fouled around the shaft and wheel. See that any boarding ladders, fenders or boat booms are aboard and send a man forward to let the mooring line go. The pennant usually has a small block of wood or metal buoy to float the end, making it easy to pick up again on return to the mooring.

In a river or stream where there is a current, the boat will lie head to that current (unless the wind is stronger). But in a bay on a calm day there may be neither wind nor current to move the boat even when the mooring line is let go. To go ahead under such conditions would almost certainly result in fouling the propeller.

To avoid this, back away a few boat lengths, far enough so you can keep the buoy in sight and allow sufficient room to clear it when you go ahead, with particular regard for any swinging of the stern. Whether you back away straight or turn as you reverse depends largely on the position of neighboring boats in the anchorage.

Until you are clear of the anchorage, run well throttled so as not to create a nuisance with your wake. Then, as you open up to cruising speed, the dinghy can be dropped back near the crest of the second wave astern. If she is astern of that crest, she will tow too hard, running "uphill" with bow too high. Shorten the painter from this point until the pull on it lessens as she flattens out to a better trim, but don't have her run "down-hill" either, if there is any tendency for her to yaw off the course. Exactly how you trim the dinghy by the length of the painter will depend largely on boat speed and sea conditions, fig. 826.

When there is wind or current

When your mooring is in a stream or if a tidal current flows past it, the boat will be set back when the mooring line has been let go. This usually simplifies the problem of getting away; reversing may not be necessary.

In a wind (assuming the current is not stronger) the boat will be lying head to the wind. As she drops back from the mooring, whether or not the reverse gear is used, the bow will pay off to one side and shape the boat up to get away without additional maneuvering.

All boats with considerable freeboard have a strong tendency to "tack" back and forth as they lie at anchor in a wind, and the same is true to an extent at permanent moorings unless the gear is so heavy as to retard this action.

If the bow is "tacking" this way and you want to shape the boat up to leave the buoy on one side or the other, wait till the boat reaches the limit of her swing in the right direction and then let the pennant go. The bow will pay off rapidly as she catches the wind on that side.

Sometimes, if the boat isn't too big or the wind too strong, you can help to cast the bow in the right direction by holding the pennant to one side so that the wind will catch that side and cause her to pay off toward the other.

PICKING UP A MOORING

Returning to the anchorage when the cruise is finished, approach your mooring at slow speed, noting carefully how other boats are lying at their buoys. They are heading into the wind or current (whichever is stronger) and your course in approaching the buoy should be roughly parallel to the way they align up-wind or against the current. Shorten the dinghy painter as necessary.

Now slip the clutch into neutral when you estimate that you have just way enough to carry you up to the buoy. A man should be stationed on the bow with a boathook to pick up the pennant float when it comes within reach. If you see that you are about to overshoot the mark, reverse enough to check the headway as the bow comes up to the buoy. If you fall short, a few extra kicks ahead with the propeller should suffice.

FIG. 826   Length of the dinghy painter will determine how well she tows.

Don't expect the man forward to do the work that the engine should accomplish in holding the boat in position until the signal is given that the pennant eye has been secured on the bitt. Watch especially that the boat doesn't tend to drop astern while the man forward tries to hang on with the boathook. Also try to avoid having the buoy chafe unnecessarily against the hull.

When running through an anchorage keep an eye peeled for other moorings so as not to foul or cut them. If yours is the only mooring in the anchorage, you will have to gauge the effect of wind and current on your own boat as best you can so as to approach up-wind or against the current or directly against any combination of these factors. Don't try to execute this maneuver with wind abeam or astern. When the pennant is secure forward, and only then, the motor can be stopped.

Dock Lines and Their Use

Lines play an important part in the handling of vessels at a dock. Obviously, the larger the craft the more lines are likely to be called into play. It would be absurd for the skipper of a 30-footer to burden his craft with a spider web of breasts, springs, and other lines that would be appropriate only on a large ship.

TERMINOLOGY

Nevertheless, it is well to be familiar with correct terms and the functions of lines that may be used. They may come in handy some time—though not necessarily all at once.

Most boat owners speak quite loosely of bow and stern lines—and little else—depending on whether the line is made fast forward or aft and regardless of the direction in which it leads or the purpose it serves. To be strictly correct, according to nautical terminology, there is *only one bow line*. This is made fast to the forward bitt and run along the dock as far as practicable to prevent the boat from moving astern.

Conversely, a *stern line*, properly, leads from the after bitt to a distant pile or bollard on the dock astern of the boat, to check her from going ahead. The special virtue of such lines as applied to small boats is the fact that, with but little slack, they may allow for considerable rise and fall of the tide.

Breast lines, on the other hand, lead athwartships nearly at right angles to the vessel and to the dock, to

keep her from moving sidewise away from her berth. Large craft may use bow, waist or quarter breasts, depending on where they are made fast.

Naturally breasts on large vessels are more important than on small craft. If a vessel has a 100-foot beam, her bow is 50 feet from the dock and the bow breast must be somewhat longer than that. On a small boat with 10-foot beam, the bow is only 5 feet from the dock, and other lines keep her from moving away from the dock.

Smaller recreational boats will frequently have only one bitt or cleat forward and one or two aft to which dock lines may be made fast. Additional cleats along the sides, properly through bolted, are desirable to provide flexibility in using dock lines.

FIG. 827   Shown above are most of the possible docking lines for a vessel with the identification of each. These are (1) bow line, (2) forward bow spring, (3) forward (bow) breast, (4) after bow spring, (5) forward quarter spring, (6) after (quarter) breast, (7) after spring, (8) stern line. Don't try to use them all on a small boat! Aboard ships, mooring lines are numbered from the bow aft, depending on where they are secured aboard the vessel.

MOORING A BOAT

Eight mooring lines that might be used to make fast a ship or boat are illustrated in fig. 827. They are *not* all used at the same time! What might be considered a typical satisfactory arrangement of mooring lines for a boat or yacht— 20 to 65 feet—is illustrated in fig. 828. The two spring lines are shown crossed and running to separate dock cleats or piles. This provides longer springs which can be drawn up rather snugly and yet allow for a rise and fall of tide. If only one pile or cleat is available, position the craft so that this point is opposite amidships and run both springs to it; see fig. 829.

The bow and stern lines should make roughly a 45° angle with the dock face. The stern line is most easily run to the near-shore quarter cleat, but a better tie-up is made if it is run to the off-shore quarter cleat, as shown by the dotted line in fig. 828.

Breast lines here would be superfluous and should be omitted. An exception might be a slack line to the near-shore quarter cleat used solely for pulling the boat in against an offshore wind for easier and safer boarding.

As we shall see later, a small boat might be adequately moored with springs alone, using no breasts. Sometimes boatmen attempt to make fast to a dock with bow and stern breasts only and get into trouble because slack must be left in the line to allow for tide. If adjusted right for low water, they may be entirely too slack at high water and the boat gets a chance to catch in some stringer or projection of the dock when her bow or stern swings in.

If lines are doubled

If two lines are used anywhere with the idea of getting double the strength of one, they must be of equal length when strain is put upon them. Otherwise one carries the load first and parts, and then the other follows suit.

Two lines on one bollard

Frequently, mooring lines may have an eye splice of suitable size in the end which goes ashore, to be dropped over the pile or bollard. Fig. 829 shows both the after bow spring and the forward quarter spring secured to a single bollard about amidships. If these are dropped one over the other, the upper one must first be cleared in order to get the lower one free.

Inasmuch as one or the other of these springs may be needed to get clear of the dock, depending on wind and current conditions at the time, it is well to rig these so that either can be freed without disturbing the other.

Assuming that the eye of the forward quarter spring is placed on the pile first, take the eye of the after box spring and run it up from below through the first eye, and then drop it down over the pile, fig. 829.

This way either line can be cleared without disturbing the other, though it may be necessary to use a little power to ease the strain on one if its eye happens to nip the other line between itself and the pile.

If a boat has much freeboard, the tide is high, and dock piles are relatively short, so that a mooring line leads down at a fairly sharp angle from deck to dock, there may be some risk of its slipping up over the top of the pile. An extra round turn of the eye splice taken over the pile will prevent this, fig. 830.

Note: For conversion to metric units, see page 99 or 115.

FIG. 828 Spring lines (3) and (4) are often crossed to gain a greater length for them, especially where significant rise and fall of tide occurs. The stern line (2) is often run to the off-shore quarter cleat. cleat.

FIG. 829 Where two spring lines must be placed on the same pile or cleat. Note that eye splice of after bow spring (A) is run up through eye (B) of forward quarter spring. Either can be cleared without removing the other.

Dock or Mooring Lines

On recreational boats, mooring lines are generally of nylon, either the usual twisted rope or the newer type with a braided core and a braided cover. The size of the line will vary with the size of the craft. Typically, a 30- to 40-footer will use lines of 5/8″ nylon, with larger yachts going to 3/4″ lines, and smaller boats to 1/2″ or even 3/8″ nylon for under-20-footers. Manila lines are rather infrequently used these days—1″ manila would not be as strong as 5/8″ nylon, yet it would be 2½ times heavier and correspondingly harder to handle. Nylon also has desirable properties of stretch, longer life, and softness in one's hands.

Heaving lines and monkey's fists

Part of the essence of good seamanship lies in knowing when a certain method of procedure is applicable to the size of vessel one is handling. Use of big ship technique on small motor boats is amusing to a seasoned boatman. Application of small boat principles aboard a big vessel may be distressing to a ship captain.

An excellent example of this is in the technique used to get the mooring lines from the ship or boat to the dock.

FIG. 830 An extra round turn in the eye splice of a mooring line should be taken around a pile if the lead is high from dock to deck. This prevents it from slipping up.

After Bow Spring

FIG. 831 Bow swung sharply in toward dock by going ahead on after bow spring.

spring, the *after bow spring*, the *forward quarter spring*, and the *after quarter spring;* see fig. 827.

Bow springs are made fast to the vessel at or near the bow, quarter springs at or near the stern. Forward springs lead forward from the vessel to the pier or wharf, and thus check any movement sternward. After springs lead aft from the vessel and check any movement ahead.

Remember that the terms *forward* and *after* relate to the *direction* in which the spring line runs from the vessel, and not to where it is made fast on board, this being indicated by the terms *bow* and *quarter*.

The lines of a big vessel are heavy hawsers, hard to handle, and impossible to heave. Therefore they make use of heaving lines, which are light lines weighted at the end by a "monkey's fist" (an intricate woven knot which encloses the weight). This heaving line is bent to the hawser near the eye splice—not in the loop where it might be jammed when a strain is thrown on the hawser—and the line is sent from ship to dock, dock to ship, or ship to ship as soon as possible as a messenger, fig. 832.

Small craft practices

On boats, heaving lines are more of a technique to be learned and then filed away in your memory for possible emergency use. Normally your crew can simply step ashore with the necessary lines or hand them to someone there.

Even if necessary to heave your regular mooring lines on a small boat, they will carry some distance if properly coiled, half held loosely in the left hand and the remaining half heaved by the right, fig. 833, all uncoiling naturally in the air, without fouling up into a knot and falling short. If necessary, a weight can be added at times to carry a line but this is seldom used.

If, in passing a line for towing purposes, for example, you had to send a heavier line a long distance, then break out the heaving line principle and use it to good advantage.

SPRING LINES

Springs are especially useful lines in preventing undesired movement ahead or astern in a berth. They are also useful in keeping a craft in position where it is made fast to a fixed structure and there is a significant rise and fall of tide. There may be four spring lines—the *forward bow*

Going Ahead on a Spring

We will see later on, fig. 841, how, by means of an after bow spring, the stern can be brought in to a dock by going ahead with the rudder set away from the dock; it is more easily done with line made fast farther aft. This technique is especially useful when a boat must be gotten in to a dock against a stiff offshore wind.

Now if the boat lay parallel to the dock but some distance off, she could be breasted in bodily by hauling in on bow and stern breasts, but with the wind off the dock and a sizable craft this might require much effort.

Again with an after bow spring, but with the rudder set amidships, let's see what would happen; fig. 831. This will cause the bow to be swung abruptly in toward the dock, as the bitt describes an arc of a circle, the length of the spring its radius. With left rudder, the bow turns in even faster as the stern is thrown to starboard further away from the dock.

Ahead on a quarter spring

If it were possible to secure an after spring at the boat's center of gravity, she could be sprung in bodily to the dock and her parallel alignment (or any other position) could be held by means of the rudder as the propeller goes ahead, because the stern would be free to swing as the discharge current acts on the rudder.

Actually this is more theoretical than practical on many boats as we will normally have only the bow and stern (or quarter) cleats to make any spring lines fast to, while the center of gravity may be nearly amidships. Now if we rig an after quarter spring, and go ahead with rudder amidships, the combination of forces is such that the boat will be sprung in nearly parallel to the dock. Her stern will

---

FIG. 832 A monkey's fist carries this light heaving line to a lightship from a Coast Guard cutter. The end will be bent to a heavier line or hawser.

FIG. 833 Mooring lines on pleasure boats are usually light enough to heave, if held properly coiled.

be sprung in nearly parallel to the dock. Her stern will come in till the quarter touches the dock, while the bow may stand off somewhat, fig. 834.

If the rudder were put to port at position (1) in fig. 834, in the expectation that the bow would thus be thrown to port, it would be seen that the effect is negligible, as the stern is prevented from being kicked to starboard by the taut spring. Putting the rudder to starboard would throw the stern in to port fast, however.

Reversing on a Spring

The action is just the opposite if we reverse on a spring. Turning to fig. 835, note how the stern is swung sharply in toward the dock by the action of the forward quarter spring when reversing. Compare this action with that illustrated in fig. 831, picturing the boat turned end for end.

Now note what happens, as in fig. 836, when backing on a forward bow spring. The turning effect of the spring on the boat is not important here, and she springs in nearly parallel to the dock in an action which might be compared with that in fig. 834—once again considering the boat turned end for end.

Allow for Tidal Range

Boatmen located on fresh water streams and lakes have no tidal problem confronting them when securing to a dock with mooring lines, but failure to take this action into account in tidal waters can part lines, and even sink the boat.

Springs provide an effective method of leaving a boat free to rise and fall, while preventing her from going ahead or astern or twisting in such a way as to get caught on dock projections.

The longer a mooring line can be, the more of a rise and fall of tide it can take care of with minimum of slack, fig. 837. Yet every line must be allowed slack enough so that all do not come taut together at either extreme stage of the tide.

Manila lines are left slack, too, to allow for shrinkage when wet or, if "made up" wet, must be checked when dry for excessive stretch. When nylon is used, generally the lines are "made up" taut, as they don't change much with the weather and will stretch to take up changes in wind strength. This point must be carefully observed in

FIG. 834 Boat sprung in to dock by going ahead on after quarter spring.

FIG. 835 Stern swings in when backing on forward quarter spring.

FIG. 836 Reversing on forward bow spring, the boat comes in nearly parallel to the dock.

narrow slips or close quarters. Better tight than so loose the boat will move too far.

As a general rule, where space permits, a bow line should be run well ahead of the boat to the dock, and a stern line well aft. If these two lines are run off at an angle of about 45 degrees to the centerline of the boat, they will often prove sufficient for small pleasure boats, breasts being entirely unnecessary and the springs (one or two) resorted to only if the necessary slack of bow and stern lines allows the boat to move about too much at her berth.

HOLDING WITH ONE SPRING

While we are talking of springs there is another trick worth remembering that deserves to be used more often, fig. 838.

In the illustration we assume that you have run up along the leeward side of a dock, to remain there for a short time while you pick up guests or perhaps put some one ashore. Instead of getting lines out to make fast fore and aft as you would for a longer stop, or expect the crew to hold the boat against the wind's pressure, try using one line as an after bow spring, as illustrated.

After coming alongside, rig the line and go ahead easily till it takes a strain; then go ahead, with left rudder, with power enough to hold the stern up against the dock. This is a maneuver that you can accomplish single-handed without too much difficulty, by having your spring fast to the forward bitt as you come in, with the end ready to pass ashore for someone on the dock to drop over a pile.

FIG. 837 How long spring lines act with great changes in tidal level. If water level drops 11' from E to D, a 32-foot spring line (A to B) would cause the boat to move astern to the position shown; cleat C would be at F at the higher level. Principle is a right triangle ($32^2 = 30^2 + 11^2$ approximately). Advantage of long spring lines is obvious.

Doubling the spring

Single-handed, you might prefer to use the spring double, with the bight of line around the pile and both ends of the line fast to your bitt. Then, when your guests are all aboard, you can slip the engine into neutral, cast off one end and haul the spring back aboard without leaving the deck. This would be helpful if the wind were of some force, the bollard well back from the dock edge, and no one ashore to assist. This way there would be no risk of the boat's being blown off as you step ashore to cast off the line.

In any case, when the line has been cast off forward, the wind will cause the boat to drift clear of the dock, the bow ordinarily paying off faster than the stern. Whether you go ahead or reverse to get under way will be depend-

FIG. 838 Making a brief stop on the leeward side of a dock, boat can be held in postion by going ahead on an after bow spring with rudder hard over (in this case, to port).

ent on the proximity of other docks and boats, etc., and whether your course is to be up- or down-stream. The same maneuver would be applicable if current were setting in the direction that the wind is blowing in the illustration.

Landing at a Dock

The knowledge you have already acquired in turning a boat where space for maneuvering is limited will stand you in good stead when you tackle the next problem of bringing her in neatly to a dock or float.

The factors involved here are, in part, the same as in coming to a mooring, with certain modifications. For example, when you pick up a mooring you have wind and current to consider, generally determining the angle of your approach. Wind and current must also be reckoned with at docks, but there are many occasions when the angle of approach to a dock is not a matter of choice.

With no wind or current to complicate the situation, landing, with a right-handed propeller, can be accomplished most effectively by bringing the boat in port side to the dock. Our previous analysis of propeller action when reversing makes the reason for this clear.

Keep boat under control

Don't come in with a grand flourish at high speed but throttle down gradually to keep the boat under control, fig. 839. When you see that you have enough to reach the dock, slip the clutch into neutral and use the reverse

gear as and when necessary to check headway as the boat goes into her berth.

If your speed has been properly estimated you will be several boat lengths from the dock when the clutch is thrown into neutral. Coming in at too high a speed you will be forced to go into neutral a long way from the dock (losing maneuverability with the propeller disengaged) or face the alternative of trusting the reverse gear to check excessive headway.

This is a good time to exercise judgment, keeping the way necessary for good maneuverability, yet using no more

FIG. 840 When landing port side to a dock, approach at an angle of 10 to 20 degrees as shown. Discharge current of the reversing propeller (if R.H.) will set the stern to port, as at (2), even though rudder is amidships.

than required. If you have been running at any speed, it is desirable to hold off briefly and let your own stern wave catch up with and pass your boat. It is embarrassing to "cuss" about being rocked by a wake just as you are coming alongside—and then find out that it was your own wake that upset your smooth approach and docking.

As the reversing propeller throws its discharge current against the starboard side aft, the stern is carried to port. For this reason it is customary to approach, not exactly parallel with the dock, but at a slight angle—say 10 to 20 degrees. Then as she comes up to the dock her stern will be brought alongside, fig. 840, with the boat parallel to the dock, properly berthed.

In docking, lines should be kept ready to run fore and aft and fenders placed if necessary to keep the boat from chafing against unprotected piles.

FIG. 839 This boat, properly, is being maneuvered near her berth at slow speed.

WIND OR CURRENT PARALLEL TO DOCK

When a berth happens to be on the shore of a river or bank of a tidal stream so that the current flows parallel to it, it is best to govern the direction of approach by the current flow, even though this puts the starboard side toward the dock. Heading into the current will enable you to keep the propeller turning over slowly—right up to the moment of reaching the dock, if the current is strong enough.

The same is true if wind is the force you are opposing. If your course puts the wind over the stern you will have to make a wide swing, starting far enough from the dock to permit you to round up to leeward of it, coming in against the wind. To miscalculate here by not allowing room enough for the turn would be embarrassing, as you head for the bank with wind or current sweeping you downstream. Hence the importance of preliminary practice in open water, noting the size of turning circles under various conditions, before attempting the actual docking maneuvers.

In starting a turn like this, even at some distance from the dock, it will be necessary to throttle down long before the dock comes abeam. Otherwise the wash the boat throws may carry along and leave you wallowing in your own wake just when you're trying to come alongside.

In coming up against wind or current, you use that force to check your headway, instead of the reverse. Therefore, allowance usually need not be made for the effect of a reversing propeller.

LANDINGS DOWN-WIND OR WITH CURRENT

Avoid, if you can, the landing in which wind or current is setting you down towards the dock in the direction of your course. In cases of this kind you are dependent on your reverse gear and even though they are practically 100 percent dependable an error in judgment or minor motor ailment would put you on the spot.

However, you will meet such situations, where space does not permit a turn before docking. For example, suppose you are coming in to a canal lock with a strong wind astern. Hold the speed down to a minimum consistent with adequate control and by all means take the port side of the lock, unless there is no choice.

Plan to get a line out from the stern or port quarter as soon as headway is checked. If necessary, the boat would lie well enough temporarily to this line alone, whereas to get a bow line fast first and then miss making the stern line fast would be to risk being turned end-for-end by the wind. This has happened repeatedly to inexperienced boatmen on their first cruise through canals, to the embarrassment of other boats already berthed along the lock walls.

Handling the lines

If you have a couple of hands aboard, assign one to the bow and one to the stern to handle lines, with instructions not to make fast until headway is checked. The seriousness of checking the boat's way by means of a snubbed bow line instead of reversing the propeller is only too obvious. If single-handed, you will have to work smartly, with a stern line fast to the after bitt coiled ready to carry ashore, and a bow line, preferably run in advance along the deck back to the cockpit. Such lines of course would have to be led outboard of all stanchions, to be clear when taken ashore.

The problem is no different if you are making your landing with a following current. In either case, be ready with the reverse on the approach, using it as strongly as necessary to hold the boat against its momentum and the push of wind or current. The propeller ordinarily should be turning over slowly in reverse for the last boat length or two of headway, the throttle being opened gradually and as needed to kill all headway at the right instant.

WHEN BOATS LIE AHEAD AND ASTERN

Let's vary the problem by assuming that boats are already lying at a wharf, leaving you little more than a boat length to squeeze into your berth. The technique is decidedly not the one you are accustomed to in parking a car at a curb.

Referring to fig. 841, boats A and B are already in their berths astern and ahead, respectively, of the berth we, in boat C, want to slip into. The position of boat A necessitates our going in at a greater angle than if the dock were clear, and there is no room to go either ahead or astern once we have nosed up to position C-2.

Consequently a man is stationed forward to take a line (in this case technically called an after bow spring) leading aft from the forward bitt to a pile or bollard on the dock. He takes a turn around the pile and holds fast while we go ahead with the propeller, setting the rudder to starboard. The spring prevents the boat from going ahead and the stern is thrown in toward the dock until she assumes her final position against the dock, as at C-3.

As the boat swings in, the spring must be slacked off a little and often a fender or two will be necessary at the point of contact.

USING WIND OR CURRENT

In a case such as that covered by fig. 841, with conditions the same except for a wind from the south (assume boats A and B are headed east) we could have used the wind to advantage in bringing the boat in.

Under such conditions the boat could be brought up parallel to her final position at C-3, allowing the wind to set her in to her berth at the dock. The bow, probably, would come in faster than the stern, but this would not matter.

During this maneuver, the engine would be idling and, if there were any tendency for the boat to go ahead or

FIG. 841 Landing at a dock between boats (A) and (B), C approaches at an angle. At (C-2), a spring line is run aft to dock from forward bitt. Going ahead with propeller and right rudder, boat swings into berth at (C-3).

astern, it could be offset by a turn or two of the propeller as needed, to maintain her position midway between A and B.

Balancing current against propeller action

A variation of this problem is sketched in fig. 842, where a current is flowing east. Here the boat is brought up to a position C-1 parallel to her berth at C-2. The propeller will have to be turning over very slowly in reverse (perhaps at the engine's idling speed) to hold her at C-1 against the current.

Now if the rudder is turned slightly to port the boat will tend to move bodily in toward the wharf, but the stern is likely to come in first. An after quarter spring should be

FIG. 842   The boat can be worked into her berth, using the current by setting the rudder to port and using just enough power to offset drift of the current. In this case, propeller must be reversed to hold her against the current.

run first, to hold the boat against the current as the propeller stops turning.

Only enough rudder and power should be used to work the boat slowly sidewise. Too much power will put her out of control and too much rudder may cause her stern to go to port too fast, permitting the current to act on the boat's starboard side.

Under identical conditions, except for a current setting west instead of east, the propeller would be allowed to turn slowly ahead, just enough to hold the boat against the current. Then, with rudder slightly to port, the boat would edge off sidewise to port, the bow coming in slightly ahead of the stern. The forward bow spring would be the first of the mooring lines to make fast in this case.

LANDING ON THE LEEWARD SIDE

Sometimes you will run into situations where a pier juts out into the water, with wind blowing at right angles to it, giving you a choice of sides on which to land. If there is much wind and sea, the windward side can be uncomfortable as the boat will pound against the piles.

The rougher it is, the more important it becomes to take the leeward side. The wind will then hold her clear, at the length of her mooring lines. If there is much wind you will have to work smartly when bringing the boat up to such a berth and it will help to have men ready at both bow and stern to run the mooring lines.

Bow line first

The bow line of course must be run first and made fast. The stern line may present more of a problem since the boat has had to approach at an angle to allow for the wind's tendency to blow the bow off. The stern line can be heaved ashore by the man aft to the other on the dock,

after the latter has made his bow line fast. The bow line, if necessary, can be used as a spring to bring the stern in by going ahead with rudder to starboard, on the principle sketched in fig. 841.

This maneuver, single-handed, would be difficult. It could be accomplished by getting a bow line off to use as a spring, working the stern up to the dock with the power, and lashing the wheel (unless you have a worm-and-gear steerer) to keep the rudder to starboard while you get a stern line fast.

Often it is a question of just how smartly the boatman works as to how much maneuvering he must go through. If he knows his boat and his crew know their job, he probably will get his lines ashore fast enough so that the spring line may not be needed to get the stern in.

STERN ANCHOR TO LEEWARD

Fig. 843 illustrates a method by which boats often line up at a pier beam to beam. Each has a secure berth on the leeward side of the pier and a maximum number of boats are accommodated for a given amount of dock space. The principal objection is the difficulty of stepping ashore from the bow.

The arrangement shown makes a snug berth even in a hard blow but a shift of wind might necessitate a shift of berth if the wind came abeam, throwing a heavy strain on the stern line and anchor.

The principle of getting into a berth like this is obvious from the sketch. Simply run up against the wind or current, propeller turning over just fast enough to give steerageway, and have a man let the anchor go over the stern, paying out line until the bow is close enough to get a line on the dock. The stern line is available as a check though the helmsman should make it his business to bring the bow up as required without over-shooting his mark and hitting the dock.

After passengers have been discharged the bow line can be slacked and the stern anchor line shortened, though this means that one person must be aboard. If all are to go ashore, adjust the stern line so that it just checks the boat from touching the dock. Then if there is room, carry the bow line off at an angle to another pile. This increases the clearance at the bow, and the wind or current acting on one side will help to hold her clear.

FIG. 843   A berth at the leeward side of a pier, using a stern anchor.

The sketch is not to scale. Often the scope of the anchor line astern will need to be much greater than that indicated to provide holding power in a given depth. Seven times the depth of water is a rough-and-ready rule to determine the scope of anchor lines though this is qualified by dozens of factors.

USING ANCHORS TO WINDWARD

If you see that a berth on the windward side of a dock is inevitable and there is reason to believe that the hull will suffer even with fenders strategically placed, plan in advance to get anchors out to windward. This trick is not used nearly as often as it should be, especially if the boat is to occupy such a berth for a considerable time.

You will need a man on the bow and another on the stern to handle anchor lines, though in a pinch the helmsman can handle the stern line if he takes every precaution to keep slack lines from fouling the propeller. Referring to fig. 844, the stern anchor is let go from the quarter when the boat is at A, moving slowly ahead to be checked at B, when the man forward lets his anchor go. If someone is tending the line aft, the helmsman can back a little as necessary to place the boat as the wind carries her down to her berth at C.

Tend lines carefully

On the other hand, if the helmsman must leave his wheel and tend the stern line, then the boat can be jockeyed into position merely by adjusting the length of the various lines. This probably will necessitate hauling in some of the stern line while the bow line is slacked away. Throughout, the lines should be carefully tended. Dock lines can be run from the port bow and quarter.

Note that at A and B the boat is not parallel to the dock, but has been headed up somewhat into the wind. As she drifts in, after the engine is put in neutral at B, the bow will come in faster than the stern.

This plan should be used with a full understanding of the great strain the anchor lines are carrying with the wind hitting the boat abeam, especially if there is some sea running as well. The stronger the wind and the rougher the sea, the longer the scope required if the anchors are to hold without dragging.

If you plan to land on the windward side of the dock without using anchors to hold her off, make due allowance for leeway on the approach and keep the bow somewhat up to windward if possible, checking headway while abreast of the berth you will occupy. Then have fenders handy as she drifts in.

WHEN CURRENT SETS TOWARD DOCK

Let's suppose now a situation in which the boat must find a berth off a pier in such a position that the current will be flowing from the boat toward the pier, fig. 845.

In this hypothetical case it may be assumed that the outside of the dock, which ordinarily would be the natural choice for landing, must be kept clear for ferries, perhaps, or other boats, while the lower side of the dock is also restricted for some reason. The only remaining berth is above it, at A in the illustration.

This situation should be sized up to determine exactly where the anchor is to be let go, with certainty that you will have sufficient scope. If your anchor drags here, you

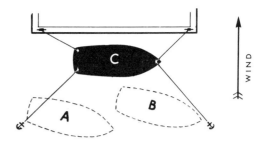

FIG. 844 Laying anchors to windward from the bow and quarter to keep a boat from pounding on the windward side of a pier or wharf.

will be in a bad spot as the current will set the boat down on the dock. Therefore make sure that the anchor really gets a bite.

The spot where the anchor is to be let go may be approached from any direction as long as the boat is rounded up into the current. The procedure, if we wish to land bow to the dock with a stern anchor out, has already been outlined in fig. 843. This, however, is not feasible above the dock because of the difficulty of backing away into the current when leaving.

Tending scope of anchor line

After the anchor has been let go, the boat can be dropped back toward her berth at A, simply by paying out more scope on the anchor line. The current will do the work though the engine could be used to help control the boat's position if wind tended to throw her out of line.

Just before the stern reaches the dock, a stern line can be made fast to a pile, after which the boat's position can be adjusted by the lines as desired. If the anchor is holding securely (and the berth should be left if it isn't) the stern can be brought close enough to the dock for passengers to step comfortably ashore.

The boat should not be left unattended in this position as she may safely be if berthed as in fig. 843. In fig. 845, where a convenient wing of the dock is available alongside the boat, a breast line could be run as shown. Then, before leaving the boat, the anchor line could be shortened to give ample clearance at the stern. Slacking the stern line would permit stepping ashore at B, after which the stern line could be adjusted from the dock.

FIG. 845 A situation where an anchor is let go and the boat drops back with the current to berth stern to dock.

The breast line is left slack but is available to haul the boat back in to B when boarding again after slacking the stern line. If the breast line is made fast too far aft it would be difficult to haul the stern in because of the "tacking" action of the boat in the current. Made fast forward of amidships, the boat will come in readily.

LANDING STARBOARD SIDE TO DOCK

Though a dock on the port side is preferable, as already explained, a good landing at a dock on the starboard side can be made, if care is exercised.

Referring to fig. 846, the boat is approaching the dock at (A), nearly parallel to it, engine idling or turning over just enough to insure control.

Just before it is necessary to reverse to check the headway, the rudder is shifted to full left (at B) to swing the stern in toward the dock. If she does not respond, give the propeller a kick ahead while the rudder is full left. This definitely kicks the stern in and, as she swings, the reverse can be used to kill the headway.

FIG. 846 Making a landing with starboard side of the boat toward the dock. Approaching slowly at (A), nearly parallel with the dock, rudder is shifted to full left at (B), swinging stern to starboard. At this point, give the boat a kick ahead with the propeller (if necessary) to swing the stern. Then reverse to check headway.

Getting Clear of a Dock

As a matter of strict terminology, you should never refer to a "dock" when you actually mean "pier" or "wharf." A pier projects out from the shoreline. A wharf is a structure generally parallel to and not far from the shore. Technically, a dock is the adjacent water area, but in boating it is customarily applied to the structure itself.

When the master of a ship takes her out of a berth, he calls it "undocking," a term applicable to all vessels but which may seem inappropriate to some for small boats. For a 20-footer, "undocking" may sound affected.

WIND OR CURRENT AHEAD

Probably the first situation to consider is with the wind or current parallel to the face of the dock to which the boat is made fast and in the opposite direction than that in which she is headed. This is the result of making a landing against the current, the easiest and "basic" technique of coming alongside.

A safe way of getting clear of the dock is to go ahead on an after bow spring with the rudder turned in toward the dock. The natural propeller action plus rudder action will swing the stern clear of the dock. The boat can then be backed down a short distance and will have sufficient clearance to go ahead and away, but don't try to cut away too sharply lest your stern come back in and your port quarter strike the dock face.

Another technique for the same situation is shown in fig. 848. If all lines were cast off, the boat might drift back along the dock, or if she went ahead, the helmsman would have to exercise care that the boat was kept exactly parallel in order to pull away without damage.

Again, it is more seamanlike to use a spring (unless the boat is so small that a person stepping aboard at the bow can merely push her bow out enough). This time we need a forward quarter spring on the port side. It is likely that this is already in use as one of the dock mooring lines, so all other lines can be cast off.

If the bow does not swing out at once with the effect of wind or current, backing easily on the spring will pull the stern in toward the dock, probably necessitating use of a fender on the port quarter to protect the hull.

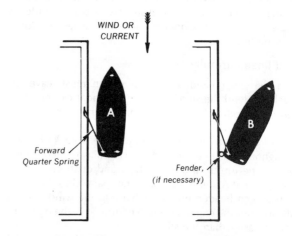

FIG. 848 When wind or current is ahead, backing on a forward quarter spring turns the stern in and bow out, shaping the boat up to get clear by going ahead.

In maneuvers where the bow swings in toward the dock, the fender is not always important if the bow has a good metal rub strip and the topsides are well flared. On the other hand, in cases like the one under discussion, the stern comes in against the dock and a fender is usually in order, especially if the topsides tumble home. Good stout metal-shod rubrails are a fine thing on any boat that has occasion to maneuver much around docks.

In fig. 848, when the bow has swung out as sketched at (B), the boat has been shaped up to pull directly away by casting off the spring and going ahead with rudder amidships.

FROM A WINDWARD BERTH

When either wind or current tends to set the boat off the dock, there is little difficulty in getting clear when you are ready to get underway. In fig. 849, however, we have assumed a situation in which the wind (or current) tends to hold the boat in her berth against the windward side of the dock. This is a bad berth if there is wind enough to raise much of a sea.

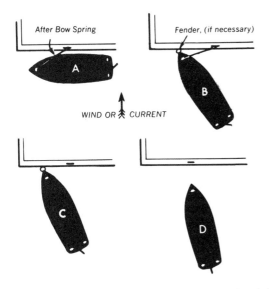

FIG. 849 How an after bow spring is used to leave the windward side of a dock. Boat goes ahead on the spring with rudder set toward dock, then backs away into the wind.

FIG. 850   Rigging an after bow spring.

If the principle of the spring is not used in a case like this there may be a great deal of effort expended with boat hooks and manpower doing a lubberly job, with the possibility, even, of damage to the boat. Correct use of an after bow spring is the seamanlike solution.

Referring to fig. 849 (A), all mooring lines have been cast off except the after bow spring. If the boat has been lying to bow and stern lines only, the stern line can be cast off and the bow line transferred to a position on the dock as shown in fig. 850 to convert it into a spring.

Going ahead easily on the spring with right rudder tends to nose the bow in and throw the stern up into the wind away from the dock. If it does not respond with the rudder hard over, open the throttle to provide the kick necessary to work the stern around against wind pressure. Depending on the nature of the dock and type of boat, you may need a fender or two at the critical spots between dock and boat.

Ease the spring

At (B), fig. 849, it is evident that the continued turning of the stern would throw a great strain on the spring. Therefore, it is generally necessary to ease the spring, yet keep the stem from slipping along the dock. One of the best ways to accomplish this is to have the spring made fast on the bitt by means of several round turns and a half hitch. With the half hitch cast off, the turns can be allowed to slip a little to ease the spring as necessary.

Here, again, remember the stretch of nylon with the possible reversal of direction when power is removed. In addition, if sufficient load is placed on a nylon line wound around a cleat or bitt the first turn or two may seize and grab the cleat so the line cannot be eased or slipped if there is a strain or load on the line. It may "jump" loose when turns are removed, causing a rapid and sudden change in control of the vessel by the line.

At (C), the boat has turned far enough so that the stem is not likely to slip, though the boat could be allowed to turn further till her stern was squarely into the wind. At

this point the spring and fender can be gotten aboard and the boat backed away with rudder amidships.

When single-handed

This is another of those maneuvers that can be accomplished single-handed with little effort if done in a seamanlike manner. If single-handed, the rudder must be set amidships when the stern has worked up into the wind, giving the helmsman a chance to go forward and cast off the spring. Furthermore, it will not be easy for him to go forward and ease his spring, but this can sometimes be done by momentarily going into neutral, which allows the spring to pull the stem toward the bollard. This, however, may not be expedient with much wind, requiring the help of a man forward to handle it properly.

When the boat lies with head to the dock and rudder amidships, there may be a natural tendency for her to work her stern around to starboard, because of the effect of unequal blade thrust (with a right-handed wheel). This usually is of little consequence as it takes but a moment to get forward and cast off.

With a worm-and-gear type steerer, which holds its position against pressure on the rudder, or any other type of control that will maintain rudder angle without a hand on the wheel, it can be set in a case like this for just enough right rudder to compensate for the effect of unequal blade thrust.

WITH WIND OR CURRENT ASTERN

The procedure just outlined can be used in getting away from a dock if the wind or current comes from astern.

Instead of merely casting off all lines and going ahead in such a situation, it is better to get the maneuverable stern out away from the dock, shaping the boat up to go astern first, before going ahead on the course. Let us look again at fig. 849, but now assuming that the wind is east or that the current sets westward (top of diagram being north) the after bow spring allows her stern to go out into the stream, to be kicked out if necessary by power, going ahead with right rudder. Often in such a case the stern swings out without aid from the power.

When the boat has swung anywhere from 45 to 90 degrees, depending on circumstances of the particular case, the spring is cast off and the boat reverses far enough to clear the dock nicely when you go ahead with left rudder.

BACKING AROUND

Elsewhere we have discussed the technique of backing a boat out of her slip, turning either to port or starboard, preparatory to getting under way. A variation of this is illustrated in fig. 851, where the boat is pictured lying in a slip at right angles to the outer side of a dock.

The problem may be to back her around so as to have her lying along the outside of the dock, or the principle might be used as a method of backing clear of the slip, preliminary to getting under way, especially if there is little room for maneuvering. The idea in this case is to use a forward quarter spring.

Forward Quarter Spring

FIG. 851 Use of a forward quarter spring when backing a boat out around the end of a dock. When spring is taut, boat reverses with full right rudder.

At (A) in the illustration, the boat is shown lying starboard side to the dock. The first step is to make the spring ready from a point near the corner of the dock to the after bitt, either amidships if there is only one, or the bitt on the starboard quarter, if there are two.

With the spring ready, but left slack and tended, the bow line is cast off, or slacked away and tended by a man on the dock and the boat is backed easily with full right rudder. At (B), a strain is taken on the spring to prevent her from backing further and this causes her to pivot as the stern is pulled around to starboard, as at (C). As she continues to back toward (D), the boat assumes a position parallel to the outer face of the dock.

At (D), the spring can be cast off the bollard and carried further up the dock to be made fast elsewhere as a stern line, if the boat is to remain in this new berth. The bow line in turn can be used to control the bow and prevent the boat's swinging too far; then made fast as necessary, perhaps to the bollard formerly used to secure the spring.

This method is especially useful when there is a breeze off the dock that would tend to blow her away if maneuvering without lines. No manpower is required and it can be accomplished leisurely in a seamanlike manner.

Getting under way

In the event that the maneuver is used preparatory to getting under way, the bow line is not required. When the boat has pivoted far enough, with starboard quarter near the corner of the dock, the engine can be idled while the spring is cast off the bollard and brought aboard. Getting under way from such a position, the rudder must be set amidships till the quarter clears the dock, then full left rudder turns her bow out into the stream.

Spring lines used this way should have a loop of convenient size in the end, formed either by an eye splice or a bowline so as to slip quickly and easily off the pile, bollard, or cleat, yet stand the strain of holding the boat against application of power, without slipping. The eye splice is best; the bowline is quickly turned into the end of a line having no splice.

In this or any other maneuver involving the application of engine power against the spring, it is obvious that strain must be taken up slowly, easily. A sudden surge of power puts a shock load on deck fittings that they were never designed to carry—may even tear cleats right out by the roots, so to speak. If the fastenings hold, the line may part —perhaps with a dangerous snap, as the parted ends lash out.

Once the strain has been taken up easily, proper deck fittings and good line of adequate size will stand the application of plenty of power, in those cases where the power is really needed. Bear this principle in mind when you are preparing to tow or in passing a line to a stranded boat with a view toward hauling her off.

TURNING AT A DOCK

Turning a boat at a dock—called *winding ship* in the case of a large vessel—is easy if wind or current is used as an aid, or if the engine is used in the absence of these factors.

FIG. 852 Turning a boat at a dock, using the current and springs.

Fig. 852 illustrates a boat lying, at position (1), with her stern toward the current and the problem is to turn her to head into the current. The first step is to let all lines go except the after bow spring.

Normally the effect of the current will then be sufficient to throw her bow in toward the dock and her stern out into the stream toward the position sketched at (2). If any factor, such as a beam wind, tends to keep her stern pinned against the dock, the stern can be kicked out by going ahead easily with right rudder. A fender should be kept handy as a protection to the starboard bow.

Some steps should be taken to prevent the bow from catching on the dock as she swings, thus exerting a great leverage on the spring. A small boat may roll the fender a little and the boat can be eased off by hand, but in larger craft it is customary to reverse the engine just enough to keep the bow clear, as shown at (3).

As she swings in with the current, the fender should be made ready near the port bow as shown at (4). At this point she may tend to lie in this position, depending on just how much strain there is on the bow spring. If she does not come alongside readily, perhaps helping her by going ahead a little with right rudder, a forward quarter spring can be rigged. Then, by taking a strain on the quarter spring, and easing the bow spring, she will set in to her new berth.

Larger vessels executing this maneuver would get a forward bow spring out on the port bow when the ship reaches position (3), rigging it not from the extreme bow but a point further aft. Going ahead easily with right rudder on this spring alone (the first one having been cast off), the ship could be kept under control and eased in nicely.

In turning a boat this way it is always easier and better to make the turn with the bow to the dock rather than the stern. The procedure would be the same as outlined in a case where wind is blowing in the direction in which the current sets in the illustration.

Turning with power

Considering a problem similar to that sketched in fig. 852, except that we assume there is neither wind nor current to assist in turning, the power of the engine can be used to swing her.

Going ahead on an after bow spring with right rudder (starboard side being toward the dock as in the figure) would throw the stern out away from the dock, a fender being used as in the previous illustration to protect the bow. In this case the stem is allowed to nose up against the dock, using another fender if necessary to cushion it.

As the boat swings toward a position at right angles to the dock, the spring will have to be eased. With the bow against the dock, engine going ahead slowly, and rudder amidships, the boat can be held in this position while the bow spring is cast off from the dock and re-rigged as an after bow spring on the port side. With right rudder again, the stern will continue to swing all the way around, fenders being shifted once more to protect the port bow.

[CAUTION: If nylon springs and lines are used, remember that they stretch and can store energy enough to snap the boat back when power is removed. If nylon is stretched to the breaking point, it can snap back with lethal effect.]

This principle has many applications and will be found useful in dozens of situations when the theory is understood. In a berth only inches wider than the overall length of the boat, without room to go ahead and astern, she can be turned end for end with no line-hauling or manual effort of any kind.

If there happens to be wind or current holding her against the dock, the first half of this maneuver may be used to get the stern out into the stream, preliminary to backing away when ready to get clear of the dock.

MAKE USE OF FENDERS

We have noted from time to time in the foregoing illustrations the necessity of protecting the hull with fenders in maneuvering around rough dock piles, or in lying alongside other craft, fig. 853. Articles on equipment have repeatedly pointed out the desirability of carrying plenty of good fenders, but often the equipment actually provided falls far short of being adequate.

The standard types of yacht fenders are satisfactory if large enough and provided in sufficient number. When a boat lies at a dock with no motion, except the rise and fall of tide and the flow of current, even the lightest of guardrails may be alright. But you can't count on these ideal conditions to prevail at all times.

The combination of topsides that are heavily flared forward, tumble home aft, high superstructure that reaches out practically to the deck edge, and comparatively light guard moldings, possibly of wood not even metal-shod with half-oval, all make for potential damage when the boat starts to roll and pound against piles, either as a result of the swell created by passing craft or wave action from the wind or a ground swell.

The ordinary fenders (not "bumpers") for pleasure boats are of several types of construction—canvas covers filled with ground cork for small craft; woven manila or cotton covers, also cork-filled; and all manila rope, braided so that no central core or filler is required. Newer types, fig. 854, include those of synthetic or rubber construction containing air or minute gas-filled cells; others have canvas covers enclosing sponge rubber, shredded rubber or cork and rubber. Kapok is also used as a filling.

FIG. 853 Rafted boats properly protected by substantial fenders.

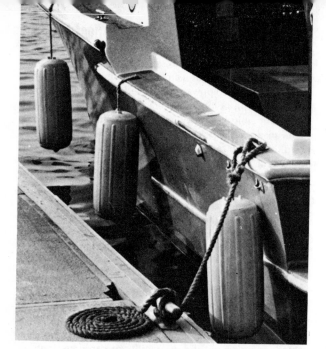

FIG. 854 Light-weight pneumatic fenders which can be inflated to various pressures for the service required. Lines may be run through them lengthwise to hang them horizontally.

The smallest of these fenders sometimes have a grommet, eye or rope ring at one end only, to take the pennant by which it is suspended from fender hooks on the boat. Better practice is to have an eye at each end so that the fender can be rigged horizontally as well as vertically, sometimes by hanging it over the pile, instead of from the boat where it moves as the boat moves. Some modern fenders have a longitudinal hole through which a line can be run, especially convenient when the fender is used horizontally.

Half a dozen substantial fenders are not too many to carry and if the boat is equipped with few, or no, hooks, go over it with a critical eye to see that stout fender hooks are placed where needed.

Fenderboards

If fender's are hung vertically from the boat's side, they give protection in cases where there is a vertical dock face to bear against as the craft moves fore and aft. If there are vertical piles to lie against, vertical fenders cannot be expected to stay in place. Movement of boat fore and aft shifts them between the piles and their protection is eliminated. Hanging a fender horizontally by both ends sometimes is satisfactory against piles; this is most effective when the fender is attached to the pile, but don't go off and forget it!

The solution to protecting the hull in many situations has been found in the use of *fenderboards*. These are short

FIG. 855 A side board or plank used in conjunction with ordinary fenders proves invaluable in cases where adequate protection to the hull cannot be provided by fenders alone. The rubber cushion-board illustrated is encased in a thick cover of tough white Nordel rubber with two rubber cushions to absorb the shock of impact.

lengths (approximately 4 to 6 feet) of heavy boards (2" by 6" is a common size) faced on one side with metal rub strips or rubber cushions.* Holes are drilled and lines attached so that the board may be hung horizontally behind two fenders with the wider face vertical, see fig. 855.

Fenderboards are excellent for providing the necessary cushioning between two or more craft "rafted" together as in fig. 853. One boat should put over the usual two fenders behind a fenderboard; the other puts over only its own two fenders. A second fenderboard should not be used as one board could tangle with the other as the "nest" of boats was rocked by waves, wash from other craft, etc.

Maneuvering at Slips in Tight Quarters

Many marinas and yacht clubs provide "slips" in which boats are berthed at right angles to a pier or wharf and made fast to piles as shown in figs. 827 and 856. Normally, a short secondary pier, or "catwalk," extends out between each slip or pair of slips.

A BERTH BETWEEN PILES

Figure 856 illustrates a problem where a boat must be backed into such a berth in a basin. Complicating the situation is a bulkhead along the east (leeward) and south sides, which prevents approach from any direction except west, down-wind.

If the space between piles and the south bulkhead is sufficient to allow the boat to make a turn, going ahead with right rudder, as in 2-3-4-5, she may round up this way, until, as in (5), she has headed partly into the wind.

If space, turning power, or wind prevent her from getting around any further than the position sketched at (4), her position is awkward as the wind will tend to blow her bow down to leeward faster than the stern so that her angle of approach will not conform with the path sketched

*1.2 to 1.8 m; 5 by 15 cm.

at 6-7-8. In that case, she would have to work out another technique.

Assuming that she can round up under power to position (5) with right rudder, she has been placed so that she

FIG. 856 Backing into a berth in a basin between piles, where space allows a turn ahead under power to maneuver the bow partly up into the wind.

WIND

146

FIG. 857 A variation of the situation sketched in Fig. 856. Here springs are used on the piles, on the assumption that the boat has insufficient room to maneuver to get into position (5), figure 856.

FIG. 858 In this case, arrangement of bulkheads in the basin permits approach against the wind, varying the technique employed to back into the slip.

FIG. 859 How to get clear of a pile when pinned against it by wind or current.

can back along the line 6-7-8 without shifting her rudder. Remembering that the stern normally tends to port, and that with full right rudder she might back practically in a straight line, it can be seen how her position at (5) allows for the wind to blow the bow down to leeward.

At (7) her bow should still be somewhat up into the wind, and her starboard quarter close to the pile (F). Having her head up into the wind more than is shown at (7) is alright as a kick ahead with left rudder will straighten her out to exactly the right angle. If that kick throws her stern too close to the pile (F), idling a moment allows the wind to carry her down into position.

As she passes pile (F), a line should be passed to it—or picked up if one is attached to the pile—and made fast forward when a man at the stern has been able to get another line on cleat (I). Lines to cleats (G) and (H) can be run at leisure.

Before the line to (G) is fast, backing easily draws the stern close enough for a man to step ashore from the stern. Adjusting and securing the line at (G) after all are ashore prevents the boat from going too far astern.

Using springs to the piles

With a good breeze, it might be impossible to get the bow around as shown at (5). In that case there is an alternative, using springs. You might approach close to the line of piles A B C D with the intent of bringing her up alongside piles (C) and (D), heading east, as at position (1), fig. 857. Now run an after bow spring, doubled, from the bitt around pile (D) and back to the bitt. Going ahead easily with left rudder will cause the stern to swing around to the south as at (2). Engine idling, she will swing completely around and if the spring is slacked a little she will lie starboard side against piles (E) and (F), as at (3). It may be necessary to back a little between positions (2) and (3).

Next rig a forward quarter spring on the starboard side to pile (F) and cast off the bow line to (D). The reason why this was doubled is now evident, as you can get the line back aboard by casting off the second hitch.

Reversing on the quarter spring throws her bow to the south and her stern in toward her berth as at (4). This spring can be carried forward by a crewman walking along the starboard side to the bow, where it becomes the forward bow spring to (F) when secured to the forward bitt.

Approaching up-wind

In fig. 856 and 857, if this were not a closed basin, so

that approach could be made against the wind, heading west, it would be comparatively easy to swing up into a position approximately as shown at (7) in fig. 856, heading perhaps more closely into the wind—say a 45-degree angle from the line of piles—with starboard quarter close to pile (F). This would have been accomplished by turning with left rudder as the berth came abeam.

Fig. 858 illustrates such a case. At (2) left rudder, while the boat is still moving ahead, throws the stern in toward the slip and pile (F) as at (3). Backing with right rudder brings her down to position (4), the bow sagging off to leeward somewhat, while the rudder is set to port and the propeller given a strong kick ahead. This throws the stern up to windward as at (5), shaping the boat up to back in with right rudder.

Between positions (4) and (6) it may be necessary to go ahead and back several times but in any case the combination of the engine kicking the stern to windward while the wind blows the bow to leeward can be used effectively to work her in neatly.

Another alternative, at (3), would be to pass a line around the pile (F) and hold on while the wind blew the bow to leeward just enough to shape the boat up, as at (5), to back in. A little reversing between positions (3) and (5) might be indicated. At (5), of course, the line from the starboard quarter is cast off and carried forward to become the forward bow spring on the starboard side, secured to pile (F) for mooring.

Getting clear of a pile

In maneuvering around piles, there is a possibility that you may be caught in a position where the wind or current, or both, will act to pin the boat against the pile and hold her there so that she cannot maneuver.

The solution is to rig a forward spring from the pile to a cleat aft, preferably on the side of the boat away from the pile, as shown in fig. 859. Then, by reversing with left rudder, the boat can be wound around the pile and her bow brought into the wind or against the current as in position (2), properly shaped up to draw clear by going ahead with power as the spring is cast off.

In getting clear from this point, it may be necessary to use a little left rudder to keep the stern clear of the pile, but not enough to throw her stern so far over that the starboard quarter is in danger of hitting the other pile.

As a matter of fact, at position (2) the wind may catch the bow on the port side, easing the boat away from the pile, so that you will be in a position to pull directly away with rudder amidships—always alert, however, to throw the stern one way or the other if needed by proper use of the rudder.

MAKING A TIGHT TURN

There are situations in which a burst of engine power for a short period may help the boat to turn within the limits of a channel or restricted waterway where she couldn't turn at low engine speeds.

Consider the following case in point. In fig. 860, we have a boat bound south in a narrow canal or stream with a strong northerly wind, her dock being on the west side. The south end of the illustration may represent the dead end of a canal or the stream may continue further. This is irrelevant except that if the stream widens further on it would be wise to go on down-stream and take advantage of the greater width for turning, then come back upstream against the wind to dock.

Preferably, if there is room, the helmsman should wait till he is beyond the dock before he starts his turn as this would allow more room for straightening out at the dock. Referring to the illustration, he has slowed down, the boat is under control and he gauges his distance from the east bank so that there is just sufficient room for the stern to swing to port with right rudder at (B) without hitting the bank.

From experience in this maneuver he knows that in the absence of wind he can round up nicely through track A-B-C-D-E-F with full right rudder at low speed. Now if he tries the same thing at low engine speed with the northerly wind, instead of moving from (C) to (D), the wind catches him abeam and tends to hold the bow down to leeward as at (D').

Using power at slow speed

At (D') he would be in a bad way, forced to reverse to avoid hitting the west bank and fortunate if he could back out quickly enough to prevent his bow from being driven down by the wind on the south bank, if this is a dead end.

Therefore at (B), if the boat is moving slowly, a sudden

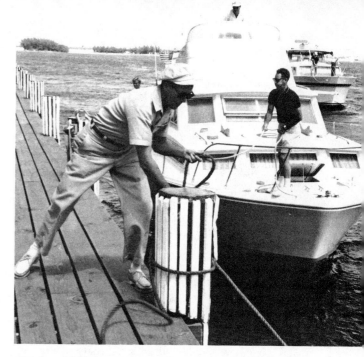

FIG. 861   A boatman's skill is often quickly revealed by the way he handles his lines.

burst of power at the propeller acting on the full right rudder will bring her around quickly. At (D) the helmsman must be ready to close his throttle in order to prevent the boat from gathering so much way that landing at the dock is difficult.

This is not a maneuver to be guessed at, but if you have occasion to make the same one repeatedly in bringing her in to her usual berth, you will soon get to know whether the strength of the wind will allow you to use these tactics or whether you must resort to some other procedure such as landing down-wind and allowing her to turn at the dock on a spring.

PLAN MANEUVERS IN ADVANCE

In previous pages we have outlined most of the basic ideas or principles by means of which the average single-screw motor boat can be handled when maneuvering around docks and moorings. Obviously the number of possible situations, considering the differences in boats, and the strength, direction, and effect of wind and current is almost infinite. Usually, however, the application of one of the principles we have mentioned, modified perhaps to suit conditions, will permit a seamanlike handling of the problem.

Understanding these principles as a background, you will be less likely to work in opposition to the forces of the elements and will use the control you have over the boat with propeller, rudder, and lines to best advantage. The seamanlike solution usually requires the least manpower and is accomplished with a minimum of confusion, fuss, shouting of orders, and other unnecessary hindrances to an orderly accomplishment of the task.

Even though you know the principles you are to use in executing a maneuver, you will find that it pays to think out in advance the steps you will take, and their succession. With a plan of action clearly worked out, you can take each step slowly and easily, and have time to keep the boat under perfect control. This does not conflict in

FIG. 860   Turning downwind in close quarters with wind astern. As boat approaches slowly at (B), a sudden short burst of power will turn her, when she may not be able to get around at slow speed.

any way with the truth that there will be occasions that call for bold, swift, and decisive action. Rather, under such circumstances, the need for calm ordered judgment is accentuated.

The lubberly handling of a situation may eventually achieve the end that is sought, but often at the expense of strained lines, fittings, and equipment, not to mention the nerves, muscles, and temper of both skipper and crew.

Common sense in executing the plan

If your planned line of action requires amendment or even complete abandonment because of unforeseen conditions, don't hesitate to act accordingly. If, for example, your plan for a clean approach to a dock has been upset by a freak current you couldn't calculate, back off and square away for another attempt. That in itself is good seamanship and good judgment regardless of how others may judge your apparent "miss" on the first try.

Common sense, if you act with deliberation, will enable you to work out a solution for any combination of conditions. Sometimes, understanding the idiosyncrasies of your own boat, you may put it through evolutions never mentioned in the books but if it achieves your end better than conventional practice, it's still good seamanship.

When you are at the helm and you have men on deck handling lines, fig. 861, issue the necessary orders to each so that all action is coordinated and under your control, instead of having two or three acting independently to cross purposes. This is especially imperative when your crew is not familiar with boats or your method of handling one.

Easy does it

As previously explained, the procedure is so simplified on a small boat that docking may involve only the stepping ashore of one man each at bow and stern with their respective lines, others to be passed as and if required after these are secured.

One mistake that crewmen often make in helping to handle lines on a small boat is that, in their eagerness to assist, they insist on snubbing them immediately when as a matter of fact the skipper wants them merely to be tended and left slack so that his boat is free to be maneuvered further with the power. A case in point is where the

boat is coming in to a landing at a dock and the bow man snubs his line instead of allowing the boat to ease up and draw alongside as the skipper intended.

One caution that cannot be emphasized too strongly is that, in handling lines, whether they are mooring lines, anchor lines, or any other kind, they must not be allowed to get over the side in such a way that they will be sucked down into the propeller and wrapped around the shaft and wheel.

 The Dinghy

A generation ago the ideal dinghy was thought to be

"Easy to row, easy to tow,
Easy to take aboard in a blow."

Today you can buy an eight-foot fiberglass dinghy which weighs only about seventy pounds, rows easily even when carrying three adults in a chop, and comes with a sailing rig that not only performs great service when supplies must be fetched from a distant point, but can provide hours of entertainment for the crew when in harbor. When the weather gets bad it can be brought aboard by two people easily and, in a pinch, can be managed by a strong man alone. If there are no chocks for the dink it can be lashed down on the cabin top or foredeck, or even rested on its gunwale leaning against the mast inside the shrouds, and lashed in place there.

Under way, tow it by a long painter so adjusted that the load imposed by the dinghy is small. Usually the best place is the forward face of the second wave astern.

At anchor, if it bumps up alongside try hoisting the dinghy's bow right up to the stern chock through which the painter is lead. If that doesn't work, hang a bucket down below the surface from the dinghy's stern so the current will have something to take hold of and keep the dinghy up against the breeze.

A wooden dinghy is usually heavier than a fiberglass one and requires more maintenance time. Inflatable rubber dinghies are far lighter—hence easier to ship aboard. They are also unsinkable if properly designed. They are hard to row though, and most cannot be sailed.

Handling Twin-Screw Boats _____

Practically everything that has been said thus far in this chapter has been related to a single-screw inboard boat. Although this permits a better study of the basic factors of boat handling, attention must now be given to twin-screw craft. These are increasingly popular, partly because of their superior maneuverability. In the twin-screw boat, the propellers are usually arranged so that the tops of the blades turn outward, so that the starboard wheel is right-hand, the port wheel is left-hand. The effect of this is to give a maximum of maneuverability.

Going ahead with the starboard wheel for a turn to port, the offset of the propeller from the center line is adding its effect by throwing the stern to starboard. Similarly, offset of the port wheel going ahead helps the steering

FIG. 862 For maximum maneuverability, twin rudders are placed behind propellers of twin-screw boats, in the discharge currents.

effect when the port propeller is turning ahead for a turn to starboard.

When reversing, the starboard wheel throws its discharge current against the starboard side of the hull to help the turn of the stern to port. Likewise, the port propeller reversing throws its stream against the port side of the hull to help the swing of the stern to starboard.

The important factors in turning and steering are thus combined by the outward-turning wheels. The steering effect is exerted in the same direction as the turning moment caused by the off-center location of the propellers.

Twin rudders for twin screws

Almost all twin-screw craft have two rudders, one directly behind each propeller in the discharge current, fig. 862. This provides much greater effectiveness than would a single center rudder not behind either propeller.

BASIC TURNING MANEUVERS

It can be readily seen that having two propellers, one each on the port and starboard sides at some distance from the centerline, gives a skipper the means of throwing one side or the other ahead or astern, independent of rudder control. In fact, much of a boat's maneuvering at low speed is done without touching the steering wheel as the two throttles are the key to the boat's control.

One propeller going ahead or backing

The stern of a boat may be put to one side or the other by going ahead or backing on one propeller only without turning the other. Some headway or sternway in these cases accompanies the turn.

Referring to (A), fig. 864, a kick on the port propeller throws the stern to port, bow to starboard, as in a single-screw boat with right rudder. If there are twin rud-

FIG. 863 Twin-screws give control independent of rudder position. Helmsman here is backing on his port engine, throwing his stern to starboard. Photo, courtesy of Vermont Development Department.

ders, right rudder helps this kick. A kick ahead with the starboard wheel throws the stern to starboard, bow to port, as shown at (B). Reversing the port wheel only, pulls the stern around to starboard and vice versa. See sketches (C) and (D).

When reversing with one propeller, the other being stopped, unequal blade thrust, discharge screw current and the offset of the working propeller from the center line all combine to throw the stern in a direction away from the reversing propeller.

A Typical Docking Maneuver with a Twin-screw Cruiser

1 FIG. 866-a In this case, the slip is on the starboard side of a canal. The helmsman turns to port to place his boat in position to back into the berth.

2 FIG. 866-b With his boat aligned as carefully as wind and current permit, the helmsman starts to back easily. With rudders amidships, he tends the throttles.

A	B	C	D

Port propeller only, going ahead | Starboard only, going ahead | Port propeller only, reversing | Starboard only, reversing

FIG. 864 What happens in a twin-screw boat when one propeller is thrown ahead or astern.

Response to rudder while backing

A twin-screw vessel starting from a position dead in the water, with both propellers backing at the same speed, is at a great advantage over the single-screw vessel as she can be made to take any desired course by steering with her rudders whereas the single-screw vessel, it will be remembered, is obstinate about backing her stern to starboard. In the twin-screw vessel opposite rotation of the propellers means that the forces which normally throw the single-screw vessel off course are balanced out.

In addition to use of the rudders, the twin-screw vessel offers the possibility of using her throttles to speed up one motor or the other as an aid to steering while maintaining her sternway or she can even stop one propeller or go ahead on it for maximum control in reverse, fig. 865.

While the twin-screw vessel backs as readily to starboard as to port, she is still subject to the effect of wind, waves, and current though the helmsman is in a better position to exercise control over them as we have seen in the case

of leeway, offset by different engine speeds instead of holding the rudder offset from the midships line.

Steering with the Throttles

In maintaining a straight course with a twin-screw vessel, the speed of the motors can be adjusted so that the leeward engine compensates for the effect of leeway. That is, the leeward engine can be turned a little faster to hold the bow up into the wind.

FIG. 865 Maneuvering his twin-screw boat, the helmsman can leave his rudders amidships, may even set his throttles, and handle the boat with a touch of one or both of his reverse gear controls.

If she happens to sustain some damage to her steering gear, whether it be the rudder(s) or any part of the gear inboard, she can still make port by steering with the throttles. One motor can be allowed to turn at a constant speed—the starboard one, let us say. Then opening the throttle of the port motor will speed up the port propeller

3 **FIG. 866-c** Here he goes ahead easily with the starboard engine, his port engine backing. He turns without making headway and watches clearance at the stern.

4 **FIG. 866-d** Now the transom is centered at the entrance to the slip and the boat is making neither headway nor sternway. Crewman stands ready in the cockpit.

and cause a turn to starboard. Closing the throttle of the port motor slows down the port propeller and allows the starboard wheel to push ahead, causing a turn to port. And we have also shown that she is at no great disadvantage when she finally maneuvers into her berth after getting into port as the throttle and reverse gears are adequate for complete control here too.

A disadvantage of this technique is that you must run the engine out of synchronism, with the accompanying audible "beat" sound which may be annoying.

Turning in a Boat's Length

With practice, a twin-screw boat can easily be made to turn in a circle the diameter of which is only a little greater than her length, fig. 868. The turn to port is accomplished as readily as a turn to starboard, since such effects as unequal blade thrust on two propellers rotating in opposite directions offset each other.

Turning bow to starboard, the rudder can be set amidships, while the port engine goes ahead and the starboard engine reverses, fig. 868. The engines will probably be turning at nearly, not exactly, the same speed. The boat drives forward more easily than it goes astern and the propeller at a given r.p.m. has more propelling power ahead than astern. Therefore the r.p.m. on the reversing starboard wheel may be somewhat higher than that on the port propeller, to prevent her from making some headway as she pivots.

By setting the throttle for the reversing starboard engine this can be left alone and the port throttle is adjusted till the size of the turning circle is established. A rate of r.p.m. can be found where she is actually turning in her own length. If the port engine is then speeded up a little, the circle is larger and she makes some headway. If the port engine is slowed down, the circle is also larger but she

FIG. 868 Turning twin-screw boat, bow to starboard, stern to port, in her own length. Rudder amidships, port propeller going ahead, starboard propeller reversing (probably at somewhat higher r.p.m. than port propeller). Changing r.p.m. can give her headway or sternway as she turns.

makes some sternway as the reversing starboard wheel pulls her around, stern to port.

DOCKING A TWIN-SCREW BOAT

Landing at a dock, a twin-screw vessel will approach at slow speed at an angle of 10 to 20 degrees, as is the case with a single-screw boat. When she has just way enough to carry her in nicely, the rudder is swung over to the side away from the dock to bring the stern in as the engines are thrown into neutral. To check headway as she comes up parallel to the dock, the outboard engine is reversed.

Landing either port or starboard side to the dock is accomplished with equal ease because of the starboard propeller turning counter-clockwise as it reverses in a port-side landing, or the port propeller turning clockwise in reverse on a landing starboard side to the dock.

USING SPRINGS WITH TWIN SCREWS

When a twin-screw vessel is lying at a dock and a spring is used to throw the bow or stern out as an aid to getting clear, one engine may be used. For example, with an after bow spring, going ahead on the outside engine only,

A Typical Docking Maneuver . . . (continued)

5 FIG. 866-e With barely enough clearance on both sides, the helmsman is alert to keep his alignment parallel with the dock, the boat centered as closely as possible.

6 FIG. 866-f As he backs gently into his berth, the helmsman keeps a sharp eye on his starboard quarter, prepared to kick the stern a little to port if necessary.

throws the stern out away from the dock. Or propellers can be turned in opposite directions.

Sometimes a twin-screw vessel is gotten clear of a dock by rigging a forward bow spring and reversing the propeller on the dock side to throw the propeller discharge current on that side forward between the boat and dock as a "cushion." Naturally this is most effective if the dock under water is solidly bulkheaded rather than built on open piling. The discharge current from the inside wheel forces the boat away from the dock and the line is then cast off. Further reversing on the propeller nearest the dock while the other propeller turns ahead, as necessary, shapes the boat up to get the stern clear. The speed of the two motors will vary with conditions of wind and current and the rudder is left amidships till the boat is clear and ready to pull away.

OTHER TWIN-SCREW MANEUVERS

If one propeller is stopped while the boat has headway, the bow necessarily turns in the direction of the propeller that is dead. Consequently, if one engine of a twin-screw power plant fails, and the boat is brought in on the other, a certain amount of rudder angle on the side of the operating propeller is necessary in order to maintain a straight course, or some kind of drag must be towed on the side of the working propeller.

A basic principle in the maneuvering of a twin-screw vessel is to use the rudder primarily in relation to the direction of the vessel's movement through the water (that is, whether she had headway or sternway). Elsewhere, it will be recalled, the principle as given for the single-screw vessel was that the rudder should be considered in relation to the direction in which the propeller happens to be turning, regardless of whether the vessel has headway or sternway.

When a twin-screw vessel has headway, both propellers turning ahead, and a quick turn to starboard is desired, the starboard engine is reversed with right rudder. The fact that the vessel has headway in this instance means that the right rudder adds its steering effect to shorten the turn.

With sternway, both propellers reversing, if a quick turn to port is wanted, the port engine is thrown ahead, with left rudder. Again, due to the vessel's sternway, the rudder's effect is added to that of the propellers in causing a short turn to port.

If a twin-screw vessel has considerable headway and her engines are reversed with rudder hard over, the stern will normally swing away from the rudder (to port with right rudder and vice versa) until the headway is overcome by the reversing engines. After she has gathered sternway, her stern tends to work toward the side on which her rudder is set. Then the vessel's stern in the illustration just cited would eventually move to starboard with right rudder, after her headway had changed to sternway.

HANDLING A LARGE YACHT

As a rule, most of our average sized pleasure boats are handled by their owners; the larger yachts are frequently in charge of professional skippers. It's of interest, nevertheless, to note an instruction technique regarded as applicable to craft in the 100-foot category when leaving and returning to a berth alongside other vessels.

In fig. 869 this vessel is the middle one of three tied abreast lying port side to a dock headed toward the beach. Let's call the boats A, B, and C. Our boat is B, the middle one; A is at the dock; C is the outside boat.

The engines are warmed up preliminary to getting under way and when they are ready lines are cleared as follows:

FIG. 866-g Settled in her berth, the crewman makes fast with docklines, giving attention first to the spring that will prevent the boat's ranging too far astern.

8 FIG. 866-h As the boat eases astern, the helmsman keeps his eye on the transom, using his controls to turn his propellers ahead just enough to check the sternway.

Leek Pacemaker photographs by Rosenfeld

153

FIG. 869 Large twin-screw vessel leaving berth between two others in a slip. At (1) stern has been sprung out by going ahead on bow spring to (A), starboard engine going ahead, port engine reversing. At (2) spring having been cast off, she has backed clear with both engines reversing. At (3) sternway is checked and stern kicked around to (4) by going ahead on the starboard engine. At (5) she is straightened out and, after headway is gained, responds to her rudder which has been left amidships during the maneuver.

With B clear, C heaves to A the line she has already prepared. At this point she can either run a stern breast to A and heave in on it or else rig an after bow spring to draw alongside A by using power. In the latter case, she will go ahead on the inside (port) engine and reverse the outside (starboard) engine. If the bow breast to A tends to check the swing of C's bow, it must be slacked. Back alongside A, C rigs all mooring lines to A as she was formerly secured to B.

B, in the meantime, has backed out into the slip and backs the port engine 2/3 while the starboard engine continues to back at 1/3. The effect of this will be to give her better clearance from the dock and swing her while backing.

Checking sternway and turning

The boat draws well clear of the dock under this maneuver but presently gathers too much sternway so that the starboard engine is thrown ahead 2/3 which checks the sternway and causes her to turn more rapidly, throwing the bow around to port.

When finally straightened out in the slip, both engines are run at 1/3 ahead to gather steerage-way. Then both are stopped (idled in neutral in the case of a boat with reverse gears) while steering with the rudder and a long blast is blown on the whistle as a warning prior to leaving the slip.

Moving out of the slip, the current catches the port bow and tends to set the vessel back toward the dock so she is given a short kick ahead on the starboard engine to offset it. Clear of the dock, she goes ahead 2/3 on both engines.

Returning to her berth

The same craft is now ready to return to her berth alongside another vessel. Keeping well out in the stream till the slip is almost abeam, she turns and passes into the slip about midway between the piers, favoring one side a little to allow for current. No abrupt changes of course will be needed.

Engines are stopped (or, with reverse gears, idling in neutral) passing the pier heads while the vessel is steered

First, C's bow breast is cast off from B's bow and run to A, forward of B's stem, with some slack to allow B to maneuver a little.

C now casts off all lines except the bow breast which has been transferred to A and gets a heaving line ready for use after B has pulled out.

B then casts off all lines securing her to A except an after bow spring which is slacked a little to allow B, going ahead, to get the bulge of her bow past that of A's bow and thus permit B to pivot better.

B now goes ahead 1/3 on the outside (starboard) engine and back 1/3 on the inside (port) engine. Two men are standing by with fenders. As B moves slowly ahead a few feet, the spring line takes the strain and the stern works out, to starboard.

Backing clear

C is being swung along with B but no lines secure the two vessels and there is nothing to prevent B from drawing clear as she backs both engines 1/3 after having swung her stern far enough around to starboard.

FIG. 870 In tight quarters, the twin-screw boat can turn in her own length. Here she backs on the port engine. Under perfect control, she could be made to complete a 180° turn, with starboard engine going ahead. With starboard engine idling, her reversing port engine would probably bring her up to the bulk-head, stern toward the transom of the docked cruiser. (Photo courtesy Palm Beach Isles Sales Corp.)

to a point just ahead of the other vessel's pilot house. The angle of approach to the other vessel should be small. If it appears that the angle is too wide the helm should be used decisively to place her in position in plenty of time to straighten out.

With reduced speed, the helmsman handles the wheel smartly, using considerably more helm to achieve a given response than he would need if the vessel had good headway. What he does is to get the bow to swing, then shifts the rudder smartly for a moment, then shifts back to the midships position.

Engines are kept stopped (or idling, as the case may be) as she comes in at a moderate angle, her bow about six feet from that of the other vessel. A bow spring is passed, slack taken up and secured. Now the outside (starboard in this case) engine is backed 1/3 while the inside (port) engine goes ahead 1/3. This is just a momentary kick to be repeated if necessary.

The effect of the reversing outside engine is to kill the headway and swing the stern to port toward the other vessel, assisted by the kick ahead on the inside engine. The last of the headway, acting on the spring, also contributes to the same effect. No heaving lines have been used during this maneuver and, under ideal conditions, only the outside engine will be called on for a short kick astern while the inside engine may not be needed at all.

Outboard and I-O Handling

Boat handling with outboard motors or inboard outboard (I-O) drives in Class A and Class I craft is quite different from the procedures and techniques discussed earlier in this chapter for inboard craft. The skipper who makes a too quick and brash change from inboards to outboards may find himself severely embarrassed. This is true whether he had a single- or a twin-screw inboard boat, and whether he has one or two outboard motors or outdrives. (Boats propelled by outboard motors and I-O drives have essentially the same handling characteristics; for the balance of this chapter, the two types will be considered together with the terms used interchangably.)

Major Differences

In a way, boat handling with outboard drives is easier than it is with inboard propulsion, but different, too! There are two differences, each of major importance. First, the direction of propeller discharge current of an inboard boat is always parallel to the craft's keel, although it may be forward or reverse; thrust is parallel to the direction that the boat is *headed,* regardless of the direction that it may momentarily be *traveling.* With a single-screw inboard craft, the thrust line is coincident with the boat's centerline (although angled down somewhat); with a twin-screw inboard, the thrust line of each engine is not coincident with the centerline, but each is parallel to it. On the other hand, with outboard propelled boats the situation is radically different. The thrust line of the propulsion is easily changed from dead ahead or astern to either side. On quite small motors not having reverse gears, thrust can be pointed in any direction through a full 360° circle; on other motors, those with reverse gears, the angle of thrust is limited to perhaps 40° either side of the centerline. It should be noted that the pivot point around which the thrust is rotated is *outside* the boat, just aft of the transom (this ignores a very few specialized boats with interior motor wells). This external turning point of the thrust will combine with the natural turning point of the hull to result in a pivot point for a craft that is highly individualized and must be learned from experience.

No rudder

The second major point of difference between inboard and outboard boats is the *absence of a rudder* on the latter. A rudder is unnecessary for the normal steering of outdrive craft as the change of direction of thrust very efficiently changes the heading of the boat, and consequently its direction of travel. When, however, the outdrive propeller is giving little or no thrust, as when the motor is idling or is stopped, the absence of rudder blade area deprives the skipper of control that he would have with an inboard boat from the flow of water past the rudder as the boat "coasts" along. The lower unit of the outboard does in a small measure act as a rudder, but it is a very inefficient and ineffective one. This lack of positive steering action without engine power is something that must be kept in mind; it is not a major problem, but it can't be overlooked or forgotten.

Torque effect

The propeller shaft of an outboard motor or outdrive is horizontal, and thus this form of propulsion is free of the side-turning tendencies which result from unequal blade pressures as described earlier in this chapter for inboard boats with inclined propeller shafts. Large outboard motors and I-O units do, however, tend to have a *torque effect* from their high rotational power. To correct for this, many such underwater units have a small tab or adjustable exhaust nozzle which can be offset from center to correct for torque effect. Properly adjusted, even the largest motors can be run at high speeds with little or no tendency of the boat to pull to one side.

FIG. 871 **Boats propelled by outboard motors and those with inboard-outboard drives handle in generally the same manner. Both of these types, however, with their directed thrust and lack of rudders maneuver quite differently than inboard craft.**

FIG. 872 Smaller outboard motors frequently have no reverse gears, but pivot in a full circle so that their propeller thrust may be "aimed" in any direction.

BASIC PRINCIPLES

The thrust of an outboard motor is parallel to the fore-and-aft axis of the powerhead, but remember that the steering handle is on the opposite side of the pivot point from the propeller—the handle must be moved to the side that is *opposite* to the direction in which you wish the craft to head. When you are going ahead, the motor handle must go to the left if you wish to turn to the right, and vice versa. (If the boat is equipped with a remote steering wheel, the connecting cables or other mechanism will turn the motor so as to make the boat go in the direction that the wheel is turned.) Just as with inboards, the new heading will be attained by having the stern initially swing out in the other direction; watch out for this action when maneuvering in close quarters.

When backing down, the reversed outdrive propeller can be thought of as moving itself through the water, pulling the hull after it. The craft will both build up sternway and at the same time head off in a new direction as the motor is turned to either side. Again, the motor's steering handle is moved to the opposite side to that in which it is desired that the stern go.

FUNDAMENTAL MANEUVERS

The essential maneuvers of outboard handling are the same as for inboard craft, and relate to getting away from alongside a pier or wharf ("undocking") and coming back in to such a position. The basic aspects of outboard boat handling while underway in open waters are covered in Chapter 28.

Leaving a Pier

In many instances it is possible to get away from the face of a pier in a small, light outboard boat by merely pushing off, waiting a moment until space opens up between the hull and the pierface, and then going ahead slowly with a very gentle outward turn. Care must be taken not to turn so sharply that the quarter of the boat strikes the pierface or piles, but with reasonable caution this maneuver can be executed without problems.

Backing out

If the wind or current is tending to pin the craft against

the pier, it is wiser to back out. The outboard motor, or I-O drive unit, is turned *away* from the pier, power in reverse is applied slowly, and the propeller draws the boat smoothly and safely away. (This is a good way to leave a pier in any circumstaances and is often taken as the sign of a prudent skipper.) Care must be exercised to get far enough out from the pier so that when forward thrust is applied the boat does not come right back in to the pier and strike it—it is better to err on the safe side and back out farther than necessary than to back out too little and have to repeat the whole procedure.

FIG. 873 When an outboard motor is centered, its thrust drives the boat straight ahead. When the motor is turned to one side, the thrust is to the opposite side and the stern swings in that direction, turning the craft onto a new course.

Docking

Bringing an outboard safely in to a pier or wharf is relatively easy with the directed thrust of this type of propulsion, but as with all kinds of vessels, any favorable influences of wind or current should be used to help you.

Against the wind or current

If there is wind and/or current, or a net effect of the two if they both exist but oppose each other, it is advisable to head into this opposing force as this allows the most positive control of the boat. Approach the pier in a gradual turn, bring the boat up parallel with the face of the

FIG. 874 Light outboard craft can be gotten clear of a pier by simply pushing off parallel and then going ahead under power with a slow gentle curve away from the pier. Don't attempt to turn away too sharply lest the stern of the boat come in and strike the pier.

pier, and stop with a touch of reverse power. If the stern of the boat is not quite in to the pier, the motor should be turned in toward the pier when reversed so as to complete the docking process. A bow line can be gotten across as the boat comes parallel with the pier, but under favorable conditions it is often possible not to use any lines until the boat is snug against the pier; this is helpful if the skipper is alone in his craft.

Other conditions of wind and current

If the wind or current is off the pier, the approach should be made at a relatively steep angle to the pier which will be nearly into the wind or current. Then with a sharp, but smooth, turn just as the pier is reached, the boat is brought around parallel to the face of the pier. Lines must be gotten across quickly so as to prevent the boat from being blown away. Reverse is used to check headway and to bring the stern in as required.

If there is no wind or current acting on the craft, the skipper has his choice of approach methods, but usually the best technique is to approach at a moderate angle, 30° to 60°, to the pier, checking forward motion with reverse power and pulling the stern in at the same time.

In all of these maneuvers, it is essential that the pier be approached at a slow speed with the boat fully under control. Any reverse, or forward, power should be applied positively but smoothly to avoid any risk of stalling the motor. Reverse power must be applied gently if the anti-tilt latch has not been locked; otherwise, the lower unit will pull itself up and out of the water, and the motor will race without effect.

TWIN-SCREW OUTBOARDS

Small boats with twin outboard motors or I-O drives are generally handled in the same manner as single installations. Because of the principle of steering by directed thrust, there is *not* the difference in handling characteristics between single and twin outboards that exists between single- and twin-screw inboard craft.

With larger outboard and I-O craft, the horsepower of the motors is frequently considerable. Although there is not the problem of unequal blade thrust, there is consid-

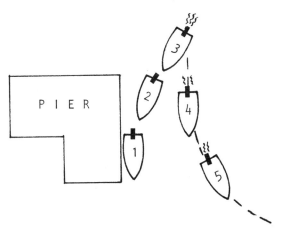

FIG. 875 A better way for clearing from a pier or wharf is backing out; this will be necessary with larger and heavier outboard and I-O craft. Be sure to back clear far enough that you can go ahead without bumping into the pier.

erable torque. It is highly desirable that the propellers rotate in opposite directions for balance of torque. Without opposite rotation, the skipper may find himself constantly fighting a tendency of the boat to turn off to one side, usually port. Adjustable tabs on the after end of the cavitation plate of an outboard motor will help, especially in the high speed range. Opposite rotation will give the best balance and is preferred for out-drives.

Larger I/O boats

Stern drives come in a variety of sizes and different gear ratios. Their steering characteristics vary somewhat for a variety of reasons. Shaft angle is said by some to have more bearing on a boat's steering behavior than the direction of rotation of the propeller. Another factor that plays a prominent part, but is usually overlooked, is the diameter-pitch ratio; various manufacturers and models have different limitations on propeller sizes. These three factors play a dominant part in the steering characteristics and maneuverability of larger I/O boats, especially those with twin engines, and large houseboats in particular.

Directional stability

The ability of a boat to hold its course, to travel in a straight line without constant attention to steering, is

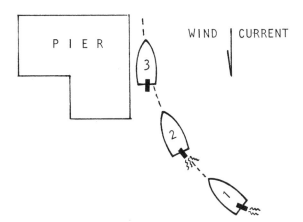

FIG. 876 If possible, approach a pier with your boat headed into the wind or current as this gives you the best control. If the elements oppose each other, head into the stronger of the two, the one having the greater effect on your boat.

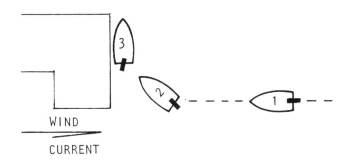

FIG. 877 When the wind (or current) is off the pier, approach at a steep angle to the pierface; this will make the wind nearly dead ahead to your movement through the water. When very close, turn and come in parallel; check your headway with a touch of reverse with the motor turned in toward the pier.

FIG. 878 If twin outboard motors or I-O drive units are used, the propellers should turn in opposite directions, the starboard propeller being right-hand and the port left-hand. This will provide a balance of torque and the greatest ability in maneuvering.

termed *directional stability*. This can be affected by shaft angle, direction of rotation of the propeller, or the diameter-pitch ratio. The torque effect with relation to shaft angle was discussed earlier in this chapter for inboard boats with inclined propeller shafts.

Houseboats

Most modern houseboats are of shallow draft. The large "sail area" of their cabins makes for windage problems. Anything that will prove helpful to steering one of these craft is certainly desirable. All houseboats do not, of course, handle in the same manner. Without going into technical considerations, it is sufficient to note that hull configuration can change the steering characteristics of an engine-sterndrive-propeller combination. Two houseboats with generally similar lines could have different handling characteristics even though both boats had identical propulsion packages.

"Walking" a boat in

A skipper's main concern is to take advantage of any factors that will ease his steering and maneuvering problems. In this respect, it is well to remember that a right-hand propeller is one that turns clockwise (going ahead) as you look at it when the boat is hauled out and you are standing at the stern facing the transom. A right-hand propeller causes the boat to turn toward the port. When you are going ahead, the bow veers to port; when you are in reverse, the stern will veer to port. Conversely, a left-hand propeller will make the boat turn to starboard. A propeller tends to "walk" toward the direction in which it is rotating. For example, when going ahead, a right-hand turning propeller moves the transom to the right, or starboard; when it is turning in the opposite direction, going astern, it moves the transom to the left (port). This "walking" action can be put to good use when docking. If you know which direction the propeller is turning, you can use this factor to the degree that is available in your particular craft. The amount of walking that one can expect depends on a number of conditions that cannot be precisely predicted; this must be learned for each boat by thorough, cautious trials. One element that affects phenomenon is the diameter-pitch ratio. By way of illustration, let us assume that you are turning a single 17 x 12 propeller and notice a slight walking effect

as you come in to a pier. Were you to change propellers and install a 17 x 15 and repeat the approach, you would notice a definite increase in the walking tendency of a typical boat. Generally speaking, the more shallow the draft of the boat, the more transverse walking action there will be.

Torque effect and its correction

At high speeds, the walking effect, also termed torgue, can be compensated for by adjusting tabs usually located on the after end of the cavitation plate; these tabs will vary in effectiveness from one manufacturer of outdrives to another, and from one model to another, but all will be of some help. In general terms, most of them are effective to some degree at any given speed. Their greatest effectiveness seems to be within a range of 600 or so RPMs of your choosing; in other words, you can adjust the tabs to perform best in the speed range which you use the most. Let us assume that you prefer to run your boat with a slow cruising speed of 2800 RPM and a high cruising speed of 3400 RPM. Through trial and error, you adjust the tabs to achieve "hands off" steering. Starting at 2800 RPM, you could speed up to 2900, 3000, etc., all the way up to 3400 and never have to make steering corrections of any magnitude. As you leave the 2800-3400 RPM range, however, you would notice that the boat's behavior pattern changes—it begins to veer, it becomes necessary to hold a constant pressure on the wheel to maintain a straight course.

Diameter-pitch ratio effects

The effect of diameter-pitch ratio was previously mentioned with relation to its action at the dead slow speeds of docking—but it makes a difference at high speeds, too! Using the 17 x 12 propeller as an example with a light, fast Class 2 boat running flat out, you might find a rim load on the steering wheel of one-half to one pound. Change to a 17 x 15 propeller and the rim load could very easily increase to four or five pounds. The engine might turn more slowly, but the torque rises sharply.

Thrust line adjustment

When setting up large twin-engine I/O boats for best handling characteristics, it is advisable to cant the stern drives out about five degrees toward the outsides of the boat. This set-up will help to break the suction at the transom, especially when coming out of a turn.

FIG. 879 Twin sterndrives are used on many larger houseboats to help counteract "windage" problem created by the shallow draft and large "sail area" of these craft.

Jet Drives

The jet-drive boat has unique handling characteristics and a skipper used to inboards or outdrives will get some surprises in his first experiences in operating one. The major feature is almost instantaneous response, whether in accelerating, stopping, or turning. There is a "jack rabbit reaction" to an increase in RPM, most obvious from dead in the water through lower planing speeds. Jet drive responds to the wheel with thrust rather than drag.

Instant reverse

The reverse mechanism for jet drives is a simple clam shell that diverts the water jet under the transom and toward the bow. If done suddenly, it stops the boat in its own length; it should not be done at high speed without a warning to any passengers aboard.

A skipper can shift instantly from full ahead to full astern with no strain on the engine. The direction of the water stream is the only thing that is altered in stopping or reversing.

No torque effect

Most small boat skippers have felt the torque or twist associated with the sudden acceleration of an I/O or outboard. A right-hand drive twists the hull to the right as the system has sufficient tension to hold the lower unit in an in-line position and the right-hand propeller causes the boat to veer to port. Pressure must be applied to the steering wheel and corrections made.

Not so with jet drive! Torque is contained within the pump housing and does not affect boat handling or heading. You can gun the engine without being thrown off course; there is no strain if the throttle is opened wide.

Getting a skier up

The five to ten second delay experienced with an I/O or outboard before adequate forward speed is achieved is not characteristic of jet drives. Acceleration is more directly proportional to the RPM. The throttle must be handled with a lighter touch, taking care not to strain the skier's arms with a too-rapid advance of RPMs. The "wobble period" for the skier is much reduced.

Turning

The pivot point of a jet driven boat is roughly 14 to 20 inches forward of the engine. Without rudder or strut drag, much sharper turns can be made; course can be reversed in little more than the boat's length.

Docking by "walking"

Getting into a tight space at a pier can be accomplished by "walking" a jet boat in sideways. With short bursts of power alternately in forward and reverse, it is possible to walk a boat into a berth with virtually no longitudinal movement. The instant, full-power, no-clutch operation in either direction makes this maneuver practicable.

Disadvantages

Although much has been done to eliminate it by improved design, jet-drive boats in general do suffer from some handling deficiencies at low speeds. On many mod-

els, the basic steering action of directed thrust is supplemented by a small fin or rudder.

Jet-drive boats with the best handling characteristics are those with a hull designed specifically for this means of propulsion. A deep-V hull is inherently better suited to water jet drive than is a flat, or nearly flat, bottom design craft.

FIG. 880 Jet drive allows this 19-foot deep-V boat to accelerate rapidly; as there is no torque effect, there is no tendency for the boat to be thrown off course.

TO SUM UP . . .

- Try to visualize just what conditions will be at the dock *before* you get there.
- Use fenders generously and pad your slip or dock well.
- Keep your engine, controls, and steering gear in good shape.
- Keep your mooring lines healthy and use chafing gear whenever possible.
- Favor a bight of line around a pile as the last line to let go (as it is an easy matter, when casting off, to let go the end on the vessel.
- Use your "amidship" or "springline" cleat for securing the first line when docking, and for the last line to let go when casting off.
- Watch lines to see that they don't foul your propeller.
- Remember that a boat will pivot about a point about 1/3 of her length aft from the bow and will not "follow the front wheels" as does a car. When the bow goes to starboard *the stern will also swing out to port* so that, when turning, a boat cuts a considerably wider path than its beam. It goes around a turn "crab-fashion."

Try the maneuvers (in easy weather first) and see how they treat you. I believe you'll find them kind to your boat, safe under most conditions, and easy to learn and use.

CHAPTER 9 SEAMANSHIP

The term "seamanship" is a broad one. It encompasses many topics and probably would be defined differently by various persons qualified in the subject. In its broadest scope, *seamanship* for the recreational craft skipper may be considered to cover such areas as knowledge of his craft, its construction and maintenance, its handling under favorable and adverse weather conditions, and the actions to be taken in emergencies. It also covers such subjects as nautical terms and language, and the use of lines, knots, and splices.

Several topics that fall under the general heading of "seamanship" are of such major importance that they are presented as separate chapters. Typical of these are boat handling, anchoring, and marlinespike seamanship. Other subject areas, highly specialized, are also covered separately—seamanship in breaking inlets and outboard seamanship. This chapter will include topics that are not considered elsewhere and thus complete the coverage of this broad but most essential subject area, seamanship.

THE CREW

Recreational boating is usually a family affair—indeed, one of its most pleasing aspects is that essentially the whole family can share in the activities.

One aspect of boating that should not be overlooked is the *training* of the crew. No boat of any appreciable size should depart its slip or mooring for an afternoon's run or a cruise measured in days without an adequately trained crew, especially an alternate for the skipper. The first mate, usually the skipper's wife, should be fully competent to take the helm under all normal conditions of wind and

FIG. 901 In a family crew, the "First Mate"—the Skipper's wife—should be qualified to take the helm and make simple maneuvers, such as coming alongside a pier or anchoring. (Gordon Manning photo)

waves, and hopefully to do so under adverse weather conditions. The mate should be capable of bringing the boat alongside a pier or of anchoring it. A sudden incapacitating illness (heart attack, stroke, etc.) or accident such as a broken arm or leg or blow on the head, may thrust heavy responsibilities upon the mate completely without warning. If that person has been trained ahead of time, the emergency will be significantly less drastic and much more easily handled.

Training the crew

A training program need not be either onerous or unpleasant. It should be planned and carried out on a formal basis so that the skipper can be *sure* that everyone knows what he has to know. The secret to a successful family crew training program is to make it *fun,* and not let it take the pleasure out of pleasure boating. This is not an impossible task; it is not even a difficult one.

With just a little imagination a man-overboard drill can be made into a game without losing one bit of its effectiveness. With patience and adequate opportunities for practice, the mate and older children can be developed into skillful helmsmen. Every member of the crew should know where the fire extinguishers are located *and should have had actual experience in using them.* It is well worth the small price of recharging one or two extinguishers to have had the experience of having put out a fire with one. (By the way, skipper, have *you* ever actually put out a fire with an extinguisher of the type now on your boat?) This practice should not, of course, be carried out on the boat, but it is easily done ashore.

The mate, at least, and preferably several others of the crew, should know how to place the radio set in operation,

how to change channels, which channel is to be used for emergencies, and what to say. All persons aboard, crew or guests, should know where the life preservers are stowed *and how they should properly be worn.*

Instruction plus practice

A proper training program consists of two parts—instruction and practice. The skipper first learns for himself what should be done and how, and then passes this information on to his crew. For routine matters such as boat handling, ample opportunity should be given each crew member to acquire proficiency—it may be quicker and easier on the nerves for the skipper always to bring the boat alongside a pier, but he must have the patience to let others learn how by doing. For emergency procedures, there should be both planned and snap, unannounced drills.

All aboard, *including the skipper,* can be trained to do the right thing instinctively, quickly and unquestioningly should a real emergency ever occur. Not only can they be trained, they must be—this is part of "seamanship" for the crew.

Boat Handling Under Adverse Conditions

Perhaps the greatest test of a skipper's seamanship abilities comes in his handling of his boat under adverse conconditions of wind and waves.

The size of his craft will have little bearing on its seaworthiness. This is fixed more by design and construction. The average power cruiser or sailboat is fully seaworthy enough for all of the conditions that she is likely to encounter in the use for which she is intended. Note carefully that qualifying phrase—"for which she is intended." Don't venture into water areas or weather conditions beyond those for which your boat was obviously designed. It is only good common sense that a craft designed for lake and river use should not be expected to be suitable in all weather offshore.

FIG. 902 Boating is usually a family affair and all members of the "crew" should be given informal training in their duties. Guests should be given a few of the essential "do's" and "don'ts" soon after coming aboard.

FIG. 903 "Rough" seas is a relative term. This ocean-racing sail-boat can weather almost any condition of wind and waves if her skipper and crew are good seamen. (Rosenfeld photo)

It is a fact, however, that just what a boat will do is governed to a great extent by the skill of the man at the helm. Thus a good seaman will bring a poor craft through a blow that a novice might not be able to weather in a larger, more seaworthy craft.

"Rough" weather

Rough weather is purely a relative term and what seems a terrible storm to the fair-weather man may be nothing more than a good breeze to the man who has known the sea in all its tantrums.

On large, shallow bodies of water, such as Long Island's Great South Bay, Delaware Bay and River, or Lake Erie, even a moderate wind will cause a steep, uncomfortable sea with crumbling crests because the depth of water is not great enough to permit waves to assume their natural form. Offshore, or in a deeper inland body of water, the same wind force might result in a moderate sea, but the slow, rolling swells would be no menace to a small craft.

 SAILBAG ### Self Reliance in Bad Weather

One of the worst places to be in truly violent weather can be an inlet or narrow harbor entrance where shoal water builds up treacherous surf that often cannot be seen from seaward. Inexperienced yachtsmen, nevertheless, often run for shelter rather than remain safe, if somewhat uncomfortable, at sea in a blow because they lack confidence in themselves and their boats.

A man learns as much about himself in his first storm at sea as he is likely to learn from any single experience in his life. If he is fortunate in his ship and his shipmates he learns a great deal about them, too; he learns that a well-found sailing yacht, given only a little help from her crew, will largely do the job herself when the going gets rough, and he learns that prudence and optimism will sustain the crew despite the awesome disparity between the storm's resources and their own.

If you aspire to spend much time afloat in a cruising sailboat, you will meet a storm at sea sooner or later. If you are in charge of the vessel your shipmates will look to you for leadership and will take their cue from you. The experience will be much pleasanter for all of you if you have, at some earlier time, taken the measure of your first storm at sea as a crew member on some other, more experienced, yachtsman's boat. You will be more confident and your judgement will be better if you can meet the storm as an old and familiar adversary rather than a new and unknown one.

Know your boat

Boat handling under adverse conditions is quite a flexible and individual matter, since no two boats are exactly alike in the same sea conditions. When the going begins to get heavy, each different hull design reacts differently—and even individual boats of the same class will behave differently because of such factors as the way they are loaded and trimmed.

Each skipper must learn his own boat to determine the precise application of general principles to be covered in the following section. Reading this book and taking courses are important first steps, but they won't be enough when the chips are down. You can pick up the basics of good seamanship by absorbing factual data and principles, but you'll have to pick up the remainder—the elusive quality that makes the "real" skipper—by applying your book and classroom learning on the spot when the wind blows.

Preparations for rough weather

In anticipation of high winds and rough seas, there are certain precautions and preparations that a prudent skipper takes. No single list will fit all boats or all weather conditions, but among the actions that should be considered are these:

1. Secure all hatches; close all ports and windows.
2. Pump the bilges dry and repeat this action as often as required. ("Free" water in bilges adversely affects the

FIG. 904 Each skipper must learn the individual traits of his own boat—how she handles under good and adverse conditions, and what weather she can safely take. Study seamanship, but learn by doing.

craft's stability.)

3. Secure all loose gear; put away small items and lash down the larger ones.
4. Break out life preservers and have all on board wear them if the situation worsens; don't wait too long.
5. Break out emergency gear that might be needed, such as hand pumps or bailers, sea anchor, etc.
6. Get a good check of your position if possible and update the plot on your chart.
7. Prepare plans for altering course to a protected harbor or sheltered waters if necessary.
8. Reassure your crew and guests; instruct them in what to do and not to do; give them something to do if possible to take their minds off the situation.

HEAD SEAS

Little difficulty should be experienced by the average well-designed power cruiser when running generally into head seas. Spray will be thrown, and in some hull designs there may be a tendency to pound against the waves. If the seas get too steep-sided, or if pounding is encountered, it will be necessary to slow down. This will give the bow a chance to rise in meeting each wave rather than being driven hard into it.

Match speed to sea conditions

Should the conditions get really bad, and there be any danger of "starting" leaks in the planking or tearing loose heavy objects in the bilge, slow down until you're making bare headway, holding your bow at an angle of about forty-five degrees to the swells. The more headway is reduced in meeting heavy seas, the less will be the strain on the hull.

Avoid propeller "racing"

You must reduce speed to avoid damage to either the hull or powerplant for your propeller will "race" as the seas lift the screw clear of the water. It sounds dangerous —and it may be. First, there's a rapidly increasing crescendo of sound as the engine winds up. Then an excessive vibration as the screw bites the water again. Don't panic—simply slow down and change your course till these effects are minimized. Keep headway so that you can maneuver her readily.

Adjust trim

It is possible to swamp your boat if you drive her ahead too fast or if she is poorly trimmed. In a head sea, a vessel with too much weight forward will plunge rather than rise. Under the same conditions, too much weight aft will cause her to fall off. You must give the bow time to rise as she meets the swells instead of driving straight into them. The ideal speed will vary with different boats and power plants —experiment with your craft and discover her best riding speed before you have to utilize the knowledge under storm conditions.

Change the weight aboard if necessary. On outboards, you can shift your tanks and other heavy gear. In any boat, you can direct your passengers and crew to remain where you place them. Under dire emergency situations, you can tow a pail or other form of sea anchor behind you, helping to steer a straight course, slowing your speed forward while enabling you to keep the throttle open wide enough to maneuver. Be careful, however, that you don't foul the line in your propeller.

Meet each wave as it comes

You will be able to make reasonable progress by carefully nursing the wheel—spotting the steep-sided combers coming in and varying your course, slowing or even stopping momentarily for the really big ones. If the man at the wheel is able to see clearly so he can act before dangerous conditions develop, you should be able to weather moderate gales with little discomfort. *Make sure the most experienced seaman aboard acts as helmsman!*

FIG. 905 Close-hauled, with lee rail awash, this yawl is being driven hard. Wind pressure on sails keeps her from rolling as a motor boat would in a beam sea. (Rosenfeld photo)

IN THE TROUGH

If the course to be made good is such that it will require you to run broadside to the swells, bouncing from crest to trough and back up again, you will be rolling heavily, perhaps dangerously. It would probably be wise to resort to what might be called a series of "tacks" much like a sailboat.

Tacking across the troughs

Change course and take the wind and waves at roughly a 45° angle, first broad on your bow and then broad on your quarter. This results in a zig-zag course that makes good the desired objective, while the boat is in the trough for only brief intervals while turning. With the wind broad on the bow, the behavior should be satisfactory; on the quarter, the motion will be less comfortable but at least it it will be better than running in the trough. Make each tack as long as possible for the waters that you are in so as to minimize the number of times that you must pass through the trough when changing tacks.

If you want to turn sharply, allow your powerboat to lose headway for a few seconds, throw the wheel hard over, then suddenly apply power. She will wheel quickly as a powerful stream of water strikes the rudder, kicking you to port or starboard, *without making any considerable headway.* You won't be broadside for more than a minimum length of time. This is the same technique as used in docking in close quarters with adverse current or wind conditions; it is particularly effective with single-screw powerboats.

RUNNING BEFORE THE SEA

Your course may be such that the swells are coming from directly behind you. Running directly before the sea is well enough if the stern of your craft can be kept reasonably up to the seas without being thrown around off course. This is known as *yawing.* But when the seas get too heavy, the boat tends to rush down a slope from crest to trough, and, stern high, the propeller comes out of the water and races. The rudder, also partly out of water, loses its grip, and the sea may take charge of the stern. At this stage, the boat may yaw so badly as to *broach,* to be thrown broadside into the trough out of effective control. This must be avoided through every possible action. Unfortunately, modern cruiser design emphasizes beam at the stern so as to provide a large, comfortable cockpit or afterdeck—this added width at the transom increases the tendency to yaw and possibly broach.

Reducing yawing

Slowing down so as to let the swells pass under the boat usually will reduce the tendency to yaw, or at least will reduce the extent of yawing and so lessen the chances of broaching. While seldom necessary, consideration can be given to towing a heavy line or small sea anchor astern to help check the boat's speed and keep her running straight.

FIG. 906 Sharp lines at the stern of this double-ender make for easier handling in a following sea. Motorboats with wide transoms are much more difficult to keep from yawing as heavy seas pass under the stern. (Rosenfeld photo)

Obviously the line must be carefully handled and not allowed to foul the propeller. Do not tow soft-laid nylon lines which may unlay—even though seized—and cause hockles (strand kinks).

Cutting down the engine speed will reduce the strain imposed on the motor by alternate laboring with stern deep down before an overtaking sea and racing as the head goes down and the propeller comes out at the crest.

Pitchpoling

The ordinary swell off shore is seldom troublesome on this point of running, but the steep wind sea of the lakes and shallow bays makes steering difficult and reduced speed imperative. Excessive speed down a steep slope may cause a boat to *pitchpole,* that is, drive her head under in the trough, tripping the bow, while the succeeding crest catches the stern and throws her end over end. When the going is bad enough to result in risk of this, it helps to keep the stern down and the bow light and buoyant, by shifting weight if necessary.

Shifting any considerable amount of weight aft will reduce a boat's tendency to yaw but too much might cause her to be "pooped" by a following sea breaking into the cockpit. *Do everything in moderation rather than in excess.* Find out if she acts more stable, adjusting her trim bit by bit rather than doing it all at once. Too much speed forward with the incorrect weight distribution might cause a small boat to pitchpole.

Tacking before the seas

Previously, a form of tacking was suggested for avoiding the necessity of running dead into heavy seas or with them directly abeam. This same technique of alternately heading to either side of the base course can also be used when it is desired to avoid large swells directly astern.

Try a zig-zag track so that the swells are off your quarter, minimizing their effects—experiment with slightly different headings to determine the angle at which the waves will have the least tendency to cause your boat to yaw off course. Be careful at all times to keep your craft under control and prevent an unexpected broach.

RUNNING AN INLET

When offshore swells run into shallower water along the beach, they build up a steeper ground swell because of resistance created by the bottom. Natural inlets on sandy beaches, unprotected by breakwaters, usually build up a bar across the mouth. When the ground swell reaches the bar, its form changes rapidly, and a short steep-sided wave is produced which may break where the water is shallowest.

This fact should be taken into consideration when approaching from offshore. A few miles off, the sea may be relatively smooth while the inlet from seaward may not look as bad as it actually is. The breakers may extend clear across the mouth, even in a buoyed channel.

The shoals shift so fast with the moving sand that it is not always feasible to keep buoys in the best water. Local boatmen often leave the buoyed channel and are guided by appearance of the sea, picking the best depth by the smoothest surface and absence of breakers. A stranger is handicapped in such a situation because he may not have knowledge of uncharted obstructions and so may not care to risk leaving the buoyed channel. In a case of this kind,

FIG. 907 Boats that must cross a bar with breaking waves must avoid "pitchpoling"—being thrown end over end if caught driving hard down the face of a steep sea, burying the bow. This double-ended fisherman just misses being caught on the forward face of a breaker. This is no place for pleasure boats.

he should have a local pilot if possible. Otherwise it will sometimes be well to anchor off, if necessary, until you can follow a local boat in.

If it becomes necessary to pick a way through without local help, there are several suggestions which may help to make things more comfortable. Don't run directly in but wait outside the bar until you have had a chance to watch the action of waves as they pile up at the most critical spot in the channel, which will be the shallowest. Usually they will come along in groups of three, sometimes more, but always three at least. The last sea will be bigger than the rest and by careful observation it can be picked out of the successive groups.

When you are ready to enter, stand off until a big one has broken or spent its force on the bar and then run through behind it. Watch the water both ahead *and behind* your craft; control your speed carefully and match it to that of the waves. Ebb tide builds up a worse sea on the bars than the flood, due to the rush of water out against and under the incoming ground swell. If the sea looks too bad on the ebb, it may be better to keep off a few hours until the flood has had a chance to begin.

This section has concentrated on entering inlets rather than departing through them. This latter action is less hazardous as the boat is on the safe side of the dangerous area and usually has the option of staying there. If the skipper does decide to go out, dangerous areas are more easily spotted from the inside, and a boat heading into surf is more easily controlled than one running with the swells. On the other hand, the skipper of a boat outside an inlet may have little option as to whether or not he can remain in the open sea indefinitely; he may have to enter and can only attempt to do it in the safest possible manner.

HEAVING TO

When conditions get so bad offshore that a boat cannot

make headway and begins to take too much punishment, it is time to *heave to,* a maneuver that varies in its execution with the type of craft under consideration. Motor boats, both single and twin screw, will usually be most comfortable if brought around head to the seas, or a few points off, using just enough power to make bare steerageway while conserving fuel.

Sailing craft traditionally *heave-to* with the helm lashed *down* (tiller *down* wind, to make the boat head up), a *storm jib* (small and made very strongly) sheeted *aback* (to windward, so as to hold the bow off the wind) and a *storm trysail* (small, strong triangular sail with a low clew to which a single sheet is permanently bent. It is not bent to the boom, which is secured in its crutch when the trysail is used) sheeted flat. This combination balances the tendency of trysail and rudder to head the vessel into the wind against the effect of the jib to head her off, and the effect is, ideally, to lay her about 45 degrees from the wind making very slow headway.

Lying ahull is the next step down as the wind increases. All sail is dropped and secured, the helm lashed to prevent damage to the rudder, and the vessel left to find her own way.

Care must be taken to avoid a heading on which waves might set the vessel back against the rudder, as rudders are not designed to withstand such shocks for long.

THE SEA ANCHOR

In extreme cases, a *sea anchor* is occasionally used. Normally, this will consist of a canvas cone-shaped bag having an iron hoop to keep it open at the mouth. To this hoop, a bridle and a heavy line is attached which is paid out from the bow and made fast to the forward bitt. A trip line is

FIG. 908 A sea anchor. Tow line is made fast to the ring at left; trip line is bent to the ring at apex of the cone. This end is often open, to allow water to flow through. Oil is allowed to drip slowly from the bag.

attached to a ring at the end of the cone. This is used to spill the bag and make it easier to haul the anchor back aboard. In use, the theory of the anchor is not to go to the bottom and hold, but merely to present a drag or resistance which will keep the boat's head up within a few points of the wind as she drifts off to leeward. A sea anchor, sometimes called a *drogue,* will usually float a short distance beneath the water's surface.

There are also available on the market, sea anchors made up of a series of plastic floats of a more modern design. These fold compactly for storage and are said to be more effective in holding a boat's head to the sea.

Whatever style of sea anchor is carried on your boat, make sure that it is of sufficient size to be effective. A small one may be easier to stow, but there's no point to having it if it won't do the job.

Improvised sea anchors

In the absence of a regular sea anchor, any form of drag rigged from spars, planks and canvas or other material at hand that will float just below the surface and effectively keep the boat from lying in the trough, would be worth trying. If it could be launched successfully and swamped, with a stout line securely attached, a dinghy could be tried in lieu of the sea anchor, but such procedure is easier to talk about than to accomplish when conditions are bad enough to justify the attempt.

Use of oil with sea anchors

Sea anchors are sometimes equipped with an *oil can* which permits oil to ooze out slowly and form a slick on the surface, thus preventing seas from breaking. The oil might be distributed from a bag punctured with a few holes and stuffed with oakum or waste saturated with oil. (See also the following section on the use of oil.)

Make sure this equipment—sea anchors, trip lines, oil bag lines, lead lines, etc.—is in good condition and not rotten from long disuse or old age. Cotton and manila emergency equipment should be discarded in favor of synthetics.

Sea anchors and lee shores

Sea anchors can be used only if there is sufficient sea room as there is naturally a steady drift to leeward. When a vessel is driven down onto a lee shore and is forced to use her regular ground tackle to ride out a gale, it is imperative that a constant watch be maintained to guard against dragging. Engines may have to be used to ease the strain during the worst of the blow, and a long scope will give the anchor its best chance to hold. Don't confuse

"lee shore"—a shore onto which the wind is blowing, a dangerous shore—with being "in the lee" of an island or point of land which is being on the sheltered side.

THE USE OF OIL ON ROUGH WATER*

Many years of experience at sea have established the value of using oil for the purpose of modifying the effect of breaking seas. Oil is easily dispensed and quickly dispersed; the effect of even small amounts is significant.

The following summary of information on the use of oil on rough waters can guide the small craft skipper should he ever be in a situation requiring its use.

1. On free waves, *i.e.,* waves in deep water, the effect is greatest.

2. In a surf, or waves breaking on a bar, where a mass of liquid is in actual motion in shallow water, the effect of the oil is uncertain, as nothing can prevent the larger waves from breaking under such circumstances, but even here it is of some value.

3. The heaviest and thickest oils are most effectual. Kerosene is of little use; crude petroleum is serviceable when nothing else is obtainable; but all animal and vegetable oils, and waste oil from the engines, will have a useful effect.

4. A small quantity of oil suffices, if applied in such a manner as to spread to windward.

5. In cold water, the oil, being thickened by the lower temperature and not being able to spread freely, will have its effect much reduced. This will vary with the type of oil used.

6. For a boat at sea, the best method of application appears to be to hang over the side, in such a manner as to be in the water, small canvas bags, capable of holding 1 to 2 gallons (3.8-7.6 liters) of oil; the bags are pricked with a sail needle to facilitate leakage of oil.

The position of these bags should vary with the circumstances. Running before the wind, they should be hung on either bow and allowed to tow in the water.

With the wind on the quarter, the effect seems to be

FIG. 909 The skipper of this sailboat is a good seaman. Note lifelines around the decks for safety. Note, too, the absence of any clutter of lines or gear on deck.

*The discharge of oil will be a technical violation of Coast Guard anti-pollution regulations. Oil should be used only in emergency situations involving immediate danger to life or property.

less than in any other position, as the oil goes astern while the waves come up on the quarter.

Lying-to, the weather bow, and another position farther aft, seem the best places from which to hang the bags, using sufficient line to permit them to draw to windward while the vessel drifts.

7. Crossing a bar with a flood tide, to pour oil overboard and allow it to float in ahead of the boat, which would follow with a bag towing astern, would appear to be the best plan. As noted before, however, under these circumstances, the effectiveness of oil can not always be depended upon.

On a bar, with the tidal current ebbing, it is probably useless to try to use oil for the purpose of entering.

8. For approaching a stranded boat, it is recommended that oil be poured overboard to windward of her before going alongside or close. The effect in this case will greatly depend upon the set of any current and depth of water.

9. For a boat riding in rough water from a sea anchor, it is recommended that the oil bag be fastened to an endless line rove through a block on the sea anchor. By this means, the oil can be diffused well ahead of the boat and the bag can be readily hauled on board for refilling whenever necessary.

10. The general principle involved is to get the oil slick to spread to windward if possible and around the boat in such a way that she stays in the slick. If the oil goes off to leeward or astern, it is of no use.

SEAMANSHIP IN "THICK" WEATHER

Another form of "adverse condition" that will require special skills in seamanship is "thick" weather—conditions of reduced visibility. The cause for this lessoned range of vision may be fog, heavy rain or snow, haze, etc. Of all these, fog is probably the most often encountered and most severe. The general rules and procedures to be considered here are, however, applicable whatever the situation.

Avoiding collisions

Seamanship in fog is primarily a matter of safety, avoiding collisions. Piloting and position determination, the legal requirements for sounding fog signals, and the meterological aspects of fog are all covered elsewhere in this book. Here we will consider only the aspects of boat handling and safety.

The primary needs of safety in fog or other conditions of reduced visibility are to *see and be seen*—to *hear and be heard.* The wise skipper takes every possible action to see or otherwise detect other craft and hazards, and simultaneously takes all steps to ensure that the presence of his boat will be most surely and easily detected by others.

Reduce speed

Detection of other vessels by sight, sound, or radar must be made early enough to allow for proper corrective action. All Rules of the Road require reduced speed for vessels in low visibility—Inland Rules require a "moderate speed"; International Rules specify a "safe speed." Court decisions have generally established "moderate speed" as that at which a vessel can come to a complete stop in one half of the existing range of visibility. This obviously is subject to varying interpretation rather than precise definition, but it should always be conservatively considered from the point of safety.

It is preferable to be able to stop short in time, rather than having to resort to violent evasive maneuvers. Inland Rules require a power-driven vessel hearing the fog signal of another vessel forward of her beam, and not knowing the position of that other vessel, insofar as circumstances permit, stop her engines and then navigate with caution until the danger of collision is past. The International Rules require that she "shall reduce her speed to the minimum at which she can be kept on her course"—a more reasonable requirement.

Lookouts

Equally important with a reduction in speed is the posting of *lookouts.* This, too, is a requirement of the Rules of the Road, but it is also simple common sense. Many, if not most, modern motor and sail boats are designed in a manner such that the helmsman is *not* so located as to be an effective lookout, and thus one or two additional persons are required for this function in thick weather.

Look . . . and listen

Despite the "look" in "lookout," such a person is as much for *listening* as he is for seeing. A person assigned as a lookout should have this duty as his sole responsibility while on watch. A skipper should certainly post a lookout as far forward as possible when in fog, and, if his helmsman is at inside controls, another lookout for the aft sector is desirable. Lookouts should be relieved as often as nec-

FIG. 910 The primary needs of safety in fog are to see and be seen—to hear and be heard. (Bob Ruskauff photo)

essary to ensure their alertness. If the crew is small, an exchange of bow and stern duties will provide some change in position and relief from monotony. If there are enough persons on board a larger craft, a double lookout forward is not wasted manpower. Care should be taken that they do not distract each other from their duties.

A bow lookout should keep alert for other vessels, sound signals from aids to navigation, and hazards in general. In the latter category are rocks and piles, breakers, and buoys—in thick weather, aids to navigation without audible signals can indeed become hazards. A lookout aft should be primarily alert for overtaking vessels, but he may also hear fog signals missed by the man on the bow.

The transmission of sound in fog is uncertain and tricky. It may seem to come from directions other than that toward the true source, and it may not be heard at all at ranges which would be expected as normal. See the discussion of fog signals in Chapter 16.

Stop your engine

When underway in fog in a powerboat, consideration should be given to slowing the engines to idle, or shutting them off entirely, at intervals in order to aid in hearing the fog signals of other vessels and aids to navigation. This is not a legal requirement of the Rules of the Road, but it is an excellent, practical action to take.

During these periods, silence should be maintained on the boat so that even the faintest signal will be heard. These periods of listening should be at least one minute in length in inland waters and two minutes on the high seas to conform with the legally required maximum intervals between the sounding of fog signals. Don't forget to continue to sound your own signal during the listening period —you may get an answer from close-by!

When proceeding in fog at a moderate speed, any time your lookout indicates that he has heard something, immediately cut your engines to idle, or stop them altogether, in order that the lookout may have the most favorable conditions for verifying and identifying what he believes he has heard.

Radar and radar reflectors

Radar comes into its greatest value in thick weather conditions. If you are so equipped, be sure to turn it on and use it; but not at the expense of posting a proper lookout.

Even if you do not have a radar set, you should have a passive radar reflector (see page 519); then is the time to open it and hoist it as high as possible.

Cruising with other boats

If you are cruising with other boats and fog closes in, you may be able to take advantage of a procedure used by wartime convoys. Tie onto the end of a long, light line some object that will float and make a wake as it moves through the water. A life ring, or a glass or plastic bottle with a built-in handle, will do quite well. This object is towed astern with the boats traveling in column, one object behind each craft except the last.

When the object is kept in sight by the bow lookout on the next boat in column, he knows just where the boat ahead of him is located even though he cannot see her and perhaps cannot even hear her fog signal.

Anchoring and laying-to

If the weather, depth of water, and other conditions are favorable, consideration should be given to anchoring rather than proceeding through conditions of low visibility; but do not anchor in a heavily-traveled channel or traffic lane.

If you cannot anchor, then perhaps laying-to—underway with no way on—may be safer than proceeding at even a much reduced speed. Added quiet will provide increased safety.

Remember that different fog signals are required when you are underway, with or without way on, and when you are at anchor. By all means, sound the proper fog signal and keep your lookouts posted to *look* and *listen* for other craft and hazards.

Helmsmanship

One of the characteristics of a good seaman is the ability to steer well. This is called *helmsmanship*. Here is another quality that cannot be learned entirely from the book, or in a classroom, but there are basic principles that can and should be studied. Knowledge of these, coupled with experience, can make a skipper a better man at the helm than one who has not taken the time and trouble to develop his ability.

Boat's individuality

When considering the general principles of helmsmanship, it must always be borne in mind that these are truly "general" principles. Boats are nearly as individualistic as people, and nowhere is this more noticeable than in their steering characteristics.

Deep-draft and shallow-draft vessels will handle differently. Boats that steer by changing their thrust direction— outboards and inboard-outboards—will respond entirely different than boats steered by rudders. Heavy, displacement hulls will react to helm changes quite unlike light, planing hulls.

FIG. 911 Handling characteristics of various boats are nearly as different as personalities of people. Not all boats will turn as sharply as this fast runabout. A good helmsman knows well the response to the helm of his own craft.

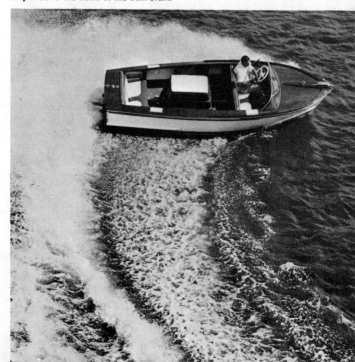

The secret of good helmsmanship is to "know the boat." If you are the skipper of your own craft, this will come relatively quickly as you gain experience with her. If you are invited to take the wheel or tiller of a friend's boat, take it easy at first with helm changes, and make a deliberate effort to get the "feel" of the craft's response.

Steering by compass

At sea and in many larger inland bodies of water, steering is often done by compass. The helmsman must keep the lubberline of the compass (also referred to as the lubber's line; see Chapter 13) on that mark of the card that indicates the course to be steered. If the course to be steered is 100 degrees, and the lubberline is at 95 degrees, the helmsman must *swing the boat's head,* with right rudder, 5 degrees to the right, so that the lubberline is brought around to 100. **Remember, the card stands still while the lubberline swings around it.** Any attempt to bring the desired course on the card up to the lubberline will produce exactly the *wrong* result.

FIG. 912 Steering by compass is a skill that must be acquired by practice. The compass card remains in essentially the same position with relation to the earth and the boat is moved about it.

As a vessel swings with a change in course, there is a tendency for the inexperienced helmsman to allow her to swing too far, due to the momentum of the turn and the lag between turning of the wheel and the craft's response to rudder action. That's why it is necessary to "meet her" so that the vessel comes up to, and steadies on, the new course without over-swinging. This often requires, partic-

ularly in larger and heavier cruisers, that the helmsman return the rudder to the neutral, amidships position noticeably before the craft reaches the intended new heading. It may even be necessary to use a slight amount of opposite rudder to check the boat's swinging motion.

A crooked course, yawing from side to side, brands the inexperienced helmsman. A straight course is the goal to shoot at; this can be achieved, after the boat has steadied, by only slight movements of the wheel. It calls for anticipation of the vessel's swing and correction with a little rudder instead of letting her get well off the course before the rudder is applied. A zig-zag course is an inefficient course. The mileage is longer and any offset of the rudder from the center-line tends to retard the craft's progress.

A good helmsman will not only use small amounts of rudder, but he will also turn the wheel slowly and deliberately. The actual manner of steering is again a characteristic of each individual boat and can only be learned by experience with that particular craft.

In piloting small craft, it is often better to pick out a distant landmark, if there is one, or a star at night, to steer by. This helps to maintain a straight course as the compass is smaller and less steady than aboard a larger vessel. The helmsman can then drop his eye periodically to the compass to check his course. Avoid steering on a particular cloud formation as these move with the wind and change shape. In some situations, a boat may be steered for a short time with reference to reflections on the water from the sun or moon, but always remember that these are moving rather than fixed reference points.

EFFECT OF WIND AND SEA

A beam wind will have considerable effect on the steering as the bow, with its relatively greater proportion of freeboard to draft, tends to be driven off more than the stern, and the rudder angle must be sufficient to compensate for this. In a heavy sea, the direction from which the seas are coming will have an effect on the steering. A head sea will be less troublesome than a following sea.

Driving into a head sea, a boat will probably be slowed down to prevent unnecessary pounding, and the swing of the bow will have to be corrected with *slight* rudder changes. In a following sea, the tendency for the stern to be thrown around by overtaking waves (yawing) must be anticipated and checked as much as possible. When the stern is tossed high before an overtaking sea, if it tends to be thrown to starboard, the helmsman must meet her by applying right rudder; a considerable amount of rudder may be required.

Broaching should be avoided at all costs. Ordinarily, if the seas are not too bad, it is possible in handling a small boat to watch astern for the big seas that might cause the boat to yaw excessively. Then by speeding up the engine, with rudder set against the direction of the yaw, the corrective effect of the rudder will be enough to straighten her out and keep the stern up to the sea. As the wave passes the bow, the throttle can be closed again to its previous setting and the rudder brought back to amidships.

SHALLOW WATER

Small craft in heavy following seas such as are built up on inlet bars and in big shallow bodies of water sometimes tend to broach despite anything that can be done by the

FIG. 913 A small steadying sail may be used to advantage to damp the rolling action of a motor cruiser in a beam sea. (F. Raymond Photo)

helmsman. Rudder hard over one way, the boat may run in the opposite direction. When conditions are as serious as that, a drag astern, consisting of a small sea anchor or length of heavy line has been recommended as an aid in keeping the stern up to the sea. The great risk in speeding up too much when the boat has acquired considerable momentum down the descending side of a wave is that of pitchpoling. If she is allowed to trip by running the bow under in the trough between steep seas, the next sea astern may throw her end over end.

Shallow water, besides tending to create a more bothersome steep-sided sea when the wind blows hard, also has a decided effect on the speed and steering of a vessel. A suction is created, the stern settles, and speed is decreased because of the change in the vessel's trim. Propeller and rudder action are both sluggish, so that response to the wheel is not as good as it will be in deep water.

In a small motor boat with exhaust at the stern near the waterline, warning of shallow water is often had before actual grounding, as the exhaust starts to bury under water and a difference in its sound is detected. This happens without any change in the throttle setting.

BEAM SEAS

All craft have what is known as a "natural" period of oscillation, or rolling period, which is the time required by a vessel to roll from one side to the other. If this period happens to coincide with the period of the waves in which she is running, as in a beam sea, the synchronism should be broken by a change of course (and speed, if necessary), to avoid excessive rolling. It is seldom necessary, in such a case, to meet the seas squarely bow-on.

Slight changes of course often damp the rolling enough to make the vessel comfortable. If the craft is disabled, with power not available, then the only way to prevent heavy rolling is to get out a sea anchor or drogue to hold the bow up to the sea, used perhaps in conjunction with storm oil if the waves are breaking.

Occasions may arise, as in preparing to heave to, when a vessel that has been running before a following sea must be brought around head to sea. This calls for skill and judgment and a knowledge of the steering qualities of the particular craft involved. By watching carefully the procession of waves as they pass, taking into consideration their height and the distance between them and space required for the turn, it will usually be possible to avoid having her caught broadside to a dangerous swell.

Invariably a boat is under better control when her engine is going ahead rather than in reverse. The propeller, in the first instance, is throwing a stream of water past the rudder blade. In general, if left to her own devices, with engines stopped, the bow of the average boat will fall off until the wind comes somewhat abaft the beam, because of the relative height of bow and superstructure forward as compared with that aft where the draft is normally greater.

Stranding, Assisting, and Towing

It is an unwritten law of the sea that one should never pass an opportunity to render assistance to any vessel in need of aid. Of course this is one of the primary functions of the Coast Guard, but there are plenty of occasions when a little timely help on the part of a fellow boatman may save hours of labor later after the tide has fallen or wind and sea have had a chance to make up.

As often as not, assistance is likely to take the form of a tow line passed to another skipper to get him out of a position of temporary embarrassment or perhaps to get him to a Coast Guard station or back to port in case of failure of any of his gear.

Or perhaps the situation will be the other way around. If you do a normal amount of boating, and poke your bow into a number of strange places, the chances are that some day *you* may go aground. It is equally possible that some day a balky motor may force you to ask a tow from a passing boat, or you may be on the passing boat from which a tow is requested.

In either case, you should know what to do, and why. Let us consider the problem and possible solutions from each of two points of view—being in need of help yourself, and being the boat that assists another.

STRANDING

Simple stranding, running aground, is more often an inconvenience than a danger and, with a little "know how" and some fast work, the period of stranding may be but a matter of minutes.

If it should happen in that before-mentioned strange harbor, the very fact that it is strange presupposes that you have been feeling your way along and so, probably, have just touched bottom lightly, in which case you should be off again with a minimum of difficulty, *provided* that your immediate actions do not tend to put you aground more firmly.

Right and wrong actions

One's first instinctive act on going aground is to throw one's engines into reverse and gun them to the limit in an effort to pull off; this may be the one thing that you should *not* do.

If in tidal waters, the first thing to consider is, of course, the stage of the tide.

If the tide is rising, and the sea quiet enough so that the hull is not pounding, time is working for you, and whatever you do to assist yourself and the boat will be much more effective after a little time has passed. If, on the other hand, you grounded on a falling tide, you will have to work quickly and do exactly the right things or you will be fast for several hours or more.

About the only thing you know offhand is the shape of the hull, its point of greatest draft, and consequently the part most apt to be touching, but bottom contours may be such that this premise will not be true. If, however, the hull shows any tendency to swing, due to the action of wind or waves, the point about which it pivots is most apt to be the part grounded.

Cautions in getting off

The type of bottom requires immediate consideration. If it is sandy, and you reverse hard, you will be apt to wash a quantity of sand from astern and throw it directly under the keel, with the obvious result of bedding the boat more firmly to the bottom. Always exercise discretion in reversing while aground due to the risk of pumping sand or mud into the engine. If the bottom is rocky and you insist on trying to reverse off, you may drag the hull and do more damage than with the original grounding. Also, if grounded forward, the well known tendency of

the stern to swing to port, when reversing with a single-screw boat having a right-hand wheel, may swing the hull broadside onto exposed pinnacles or to a greater contact with a soft bottom.

How to use a kedge

The one *right* thing to do immediately after grounding is to take out an anchor and set it firmly; this is called a *kedge;* the act of using it is *kedging.*

Unless the boat has really been driven on, the service anchor should be heavy enough. Put the anchor *and* the line in the dinghy, make the bitter end fast to the stern bitts or to something solid and row out as far as possible, letting the line run from the stern of the dinghy as it uncoils. Taken out this way, the oarsman's task will be much easier than if he tries to drag the line from the large boat through the water.

FIG. 914 The most important thing to do after going aground is to get out a *kedge*—an anchor to keep you from being driven further aground and possibly a means of pulling yourself free as waves or the wake from another boat lifts your craft.

If you do not carry a dinghy, it is often possible to swim out with an anchor provided that the sea and weather conditions do not make it hazardous to go into the water. Life preservers or buoyant cushions—one or two of either —can be used to support the anchor out to where you wish to set it. Be sure to wear a life jacket or buoyant vest yourself so as to save your energy for the work to be done.

If there is *no* other way to get a kedge anchor out, you may consider throwing it out as far as possible. Although this is, of course, contrary to the basic principle that an anchor is never thrown over the side, the importance of getting a kedge set is sufficient to warrant the use of this technique under the circumstances. It may be necessary to pull in the anchor and throw again one or more times to get it set firmly.

When setting out the kedge, consider again the sideways turning effect of a reversing single screw and, unless the boat has twin screws, set the kedge at a compensating angle from the stern. If the propeller is right hand, as those of most boats are, set the anchor slightly to starboard of the stern. This will give two desirable effects. When pulling together with kedge line and reverse the boat will have practically a straight pull on it, and when used alternately, first pulling on the line and then giving a short surge with the reverse, the action may give a sort of wiggling action to the stern and the keel, which will be a real help in starting the boat moving.

Getting added pulling power

If you can find a couple of double-sheave blocks (pulleys) and a length of suitable line on board, make up a handy-billy or fall and fasten it to the kedge line. Then you can really pull! Such a handy-billy should be a part of the boat's regular equipment, anyhow.

Whatever else you may do, during the entire period of grounding, persist in keeping that kedge-line as taut as the combined strength of those on board can make it. You may be agreeably surprised by having the boat yield suddenly to that continued pull, especially if a passing boat throws a wake to help lift the keel off the bottom.

Two kedges set out at an acute angle from either side of the stern and pulled upon alternately may give that desired stern wiggle that will help you work clear.

Working off

If the bottom is sandy, that same pull, with the propeller going *ahead* may result in washing some sand *away* from under the keel, with the desired result. If the kedge line is kept taut, you may try it with a clear mind. At least you will not do any harm.

Move your crew and passengers quickly from side to side to roll the boat and make the keel work in the bottom. If you have spars, swing the booms outboard and put men on them to heave the boat down, thus raising the keel line. Shift ballast or heavy objects from over the portion grounded to lighten that section and if you can, remove some internal weight by loading it into the dinghy or by taking it ashore if that is possible.

When to stay aground

All of the above is predicated on the assumption that the boat is grounded, but not holed or strained open. If either of these last has happened, you may be far better off where she lies than you would be if she were in deep water again. If she is badly stove, you may want to take an anchor ashore, to hold her on or pull her further up until temporary repairs can be made. Perhaps, as the tide falls, the damaged portion may be exposed far enough to allow some outside patching, always presupposing that you have something aboard to patch with! A piece of canvas, cushions, bedding, these are all illustrative of items that can be used in an emergency as temporary hull patches.

What to do while waiting

While waiting for the tide to rise, or for the Coast Guard to come, you do not need to sit idle. Take soundings all around the position where the boat lies aground. It is possible that a swing of the stern to starboard or port may do more for you than any amount of straight backward pulling; soundings will reveal any additional depth that may exist to either side to help you out.

If there is another boat present, she may be able to help you even if she is not suitable for pulling. Have the other skipper run his craft back and forth at a speed that will make as much wake as possible. The rise and fall of his wash may lift your boat just enough to permit you to back clear.

Even though the hull is unharmed, and you are left with a falling tide to sit it out for a few hours, you may as well be philosophical and get over the side and make good use of those hours. Undoubtedly you would prefer to do it under happier circumstances, but this may be your chance to get a good check on the condition of the bottom, or do any one of a number of little jobs that you could not do otherwise, short of a haulout.

FIG. 915 If you go aground on a falling tide, you may find yourself "high and dry." If so, try to brace the boat so that she will stay upright; she will refloat easier if you do. While you are out of water, make an inspection of the bottom.   (Photo by Charles True)

If she is going to be left high and dry, keep an eye on her layover condition. If there is anything to get a line to, even another kedge, you can make her lie over on whichever side you choose, as she loses buoyancy. If she is deep and narrow she may need some assistance in standing up again, particularly if she lies over in soft mud. Both the suction of the mud and her own deadweight will work against her in that case.

ASSISTING

If, rather than being stranded, you are in a position to render assistance to another skipper who has been so unlucky as to go aground, it is just as important that you know what to do, and what not to do, in the circumstances.

It is of *primary* importance to see that the assisting boat does not join the other craft in its trouble! Consider the probable draft of the stranded vessel in comparison with the draft of your boat. Consider also the size and weight of the boat that is aground in comparison with the power of your engines—don't tackle an impossible job; there are other ways of rendering assistance.

Getting a line over

It may seem easiest to bring a line in to a stranded boat by coming in under engine power, bow on, passing the line and then backing out again, but the maneuver should not be attempted unless one is sure that there will be water enough under the assisting boat, and also, unless the boat backs well, without too much stern crabbing due to the action of the reversed screw. Wind and current direction will greatly affect the success of this maneuver. If all conditions are adverse and tend to swing the boat broadside to the shallows as she backs, it will be best to try to pass the line in some other manner.

Perhaps the assisting boat may back in, with wind or current compensating for the reversed screw, thus keeping her straight and leaving the bow headed out with consequent better maneuverability. In any case, after the line is once passed and made fast, the assisting boat should do the actual pulling with engines going ahead, to get full power into the pull.

If conditions are such that a close approach is unwise, it will be far better for the second boat to drop anchor, or even two anchors, well off the stranded boat and then send the line over in a dinghy, or else buoy the line and attempt to float it in to the grounded boat.

Making the pull

If wind or current or both are broadside to the direction of the pull, the assisting boat would best stay anchored even while pulling. Otherwise, as soon as she takes the strain (particularly if the line is fast to her stern) she will have lost her own maneuverability, and will gradually make leeway, which could eventually put her aground broadside.

If the pulling must be done with the assisting boat under way, the line should be made fast well forward of the stern so that while hauling, she can angle into the wind and current and still hold her own position.

Tremendous strains can be set up, particularly on the stranded boat, by this sort of action, even to the point of carrying away whatever the tow-line is made fast to. Ordi-

nary recreational craft are *not* designed as tug boats! It is probable that the cleats or bitts available for making the line fast are not strong enough for such pulling, and even more likely that they are not located advantageously for such work.

It is far better to run a bridle around the whole hull and pull against this bridle rather than to risk starting some part of the stern by such straining. The assisting boat should also be bridled if there is any doubt of her ability to withstand such concentrated strains.

When operating in limited areas, the stranded craft should have a kedge out for control when she comes off. She should also have another anchor ready to be put over the side if necessary; this may be required to keep her from going back aground if she is without power.

Through all of this maneuvering, it is imperative to see that all lines are kept clear so as not to foul the propeller and that no sudden surge is put on a slack line.

FIG. 917 Most small craft must make the pull with the line made fast near the stern. This restricts maneuverability and, for safe control, a bow anchor should be put out. Slack of the anchor line should be taken up as the stranded boat comes free to prevent the pulling boat from being carried around into shoal water.

FIG. 918 To aid in maneuverability if a bow anchor cannot be set, the tow line may be made fast to a cleat forward of the stern on the up-wind or up-current side. This cleat *must* be capable of taking heavy strain.

FIG. 916 If a line is to be sent to another boat, you can heave a light line which can then be used to pull the heavier towing line across. A weighted end on the light line will make it easier to throw —this can be a "monkey's fist," as shown.

FIG. 919 Tremendous strains are set up when trying to free a stranded boat. Most bitts and cleats on recreational small craft cannot take such a load. It is safer to put a bridle around the superstructure of both boats. Pad pressure points to protect against chafing and scarring.

TOWING

Somewhere in the course of your boating experience you are likely to run up against a situation where you wish to take another vessel in tow. In good weather with no sea running, the problem is comparatively easy, involving little more than the maneuvering of your boat into position in line with, and ahead of, the other boat and the passing of a tow line.

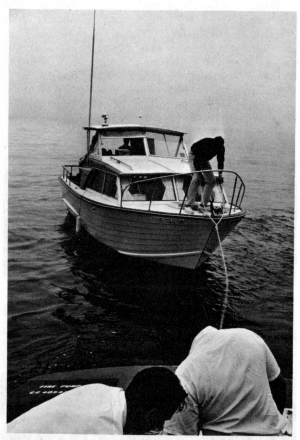

FIG. 920 It is generally desirable to pass a line from the assisting boat to the one being aided. If the weather is rougher than as shown here, or for any reason the other boat cannot be approached, the rescuing boat can float a line over, using a life ring or buoyant cushion.

Generally speaking, it is best for the towing boat to pass her tow-line to the other craft. It may be desirable to emulate large-ship practice and first send over a light line, using that to haul over the actual towing line. Plastic water ski tow lines that float are excellent for use as this initial ("messenger") line to the other boat.

When approaching a boat, dead in the water, with the intention of passing a line, if there is any kind of sea running, do not be dramatic and try to run in too close. Just buoy a long line with several life preservers, tow it astern and take a turn about the stern of the disabled one, but don't foul their propeller in so doing. The occupants will be able to pick it up with a boathook from the cockpit with far less fuss than by any heave-and-catch method.

The forward bitts are usually rugged and so the towed one may make the line fast at that point; then, with someone at the wheel to assist by steering, there is little more to do than to have an anchor ready to drop if, for any reason, the tow-line parts or is cast loose.

Handling the towing boat

The tow boat, however, requires some real handling!

The worst possible place to make the tow-line fast is to the stern of the lead boat, because the pull of the tow prevents the stern from swinging properly in response to rudder action and thus interferes with the boat's maneuvering ability. The tow-line should be made fast as far forward as practicable, as in tug and tow boat practice. If no suitable place is provided, it is best to make a bridle from the forward bitts, running around the superstructure to a point in the forward part of the cockpit. Such a bridle will have to be wrapped with chafing gear wherever it bears on the superstructure or any corners, and even then, some chafing of the finish is almost bound to occur.

Towing lines

Three-strand twisted nylon has excessive stretch and dangerous snap-back action if broken under load; it should not be used if it can be avoided. Polypropylene line floats and, being bright yellow, is highly visible. On the other hand, it has little elasticity and shock loads are heavily transferred to fittings on both the towed and towing craft. Further, it has less strength (requiring larger sizes), and is stiff, making it difficult to stow and handle; it is also very subject to abrasion damage. This line, in sizes up to ½-inch, is suitable only for light towing loads in protected waters.

The preferred line for towing is double-braided nylon. It has sufficient elasticity to cushion shock loads, but not so much as to create a snap-back hazard. Braid-on-braid line is stronger than three-strand twisted nylon and will not kink. Its disadvantage is that it does not float and must be watched to avoid entanglement in the towing vessel's propellor(s). It is the most expensive type of line, but for moderate- and heavy-duty towing it is well worth the difference.

Cautions in towing

The tow-line should be made fast so that it can be cast loose if necessary or, failing that, have a knife or hatchet ready to cut it. This line is a potential danger to anyone near if it should break and come whipping forward. Nylon, when it breaks or lets go, acts like a huge rubber band and there have been some bad accidents. In one case a cleat pulled loose from the deck and came through the air like a projectile. Never stand near or in line with a highly strained line and keep a wary eye out at all times.

If for any reason you have to approach a burning vessel, be sure to approach it in such a manner that the flames are blowing away from you. If there are reasons it must be towed (for instance, to prevent it from endangering other boats or property) your light anchor with its length of chain thrown into the cockpit or through a window could act as a good grappling hook.

Never at any time in the process of towing have people on deck to fend off with hands or feet as even the smallest boats coming together under these condition can cause broken bones or severed fingers. Also never allow anybody to be caught between two large vessels where they will be exposed to this danger. The risk here could be the loss of a whole limb.

Never allow anyone to hold a towing line while towing

another vessel regardless of size. Badly torn tendons and muscles could make them cripples for life, or they could be dragged overboard.

Starting the tow

Start off easy! Don't try to dig up the whole ocean with your screw, and merely end up with a lot of cavitation and vibration without getting anywhere in particular. A steady pull at a reasonable speed will get you there just as fast and with far less strain on boats, lines, and crews.

Towing principles

When towing, boats should be kept "in step," as it were, by adjusting the length of the tow line so that the towing craft and the towed boat are both on the crest or in the trough of seas at the same time. Sometimes, as with a contused sea, this may be largely a theoretical consideration, but the general principle is to prevent, if possible, a situation where the tow is shouldering up against the back of one sea, presenting a maximum of resistance, while the towing boat is trying to run down the forward slope of another sea. Then when this condition is reversed, the tow alternately runs ahead and surges back on the tow line with a heavy strain. If there is any degree of uniformity to the waves, the strain on the hawser will be minimized by adjusting it to the proper length.

As the tow gets into protected, quiet waters, shorten up on the line to allow better handling in close quarters. Swing as wide as possible around buoys, channel turns, etc., so that the tow will have room to follow.

A small boat in tow should preferably be trimmed a little by the stern because trimming by the head causes her to yaw. In a seaway this condition is aggravated and it becomes increasingly important to keep the bow relatively light.

In smooth water motor boats may at times borrow an idea from tugs which often, in harbor or sheltered waters, take their tow alongside for better maneuverability. If

FIG. 922 A boatman should always be ready to render assistance. In some cases, the best that can be done is to call for assistance and stand by. The Coast Guard 40-footer shown is well equipped to pull a stranded boat free and take her in tow; her crew, too, is better trained and more experienced. (U.S. Coast Guard photo)

the tow is a big one the tug will make fast on the other craft's quarter.

It is easy for a larger boat to tow a smaller vessel too fast, causing it to yaw and capsize. Always tow at a moderate speed and make full allowance for adverse conditions of wind and waves.

When not to tow

Towing can be a dangerous undertaking, as well as an expensive one, if not properly done. If you are not equipped to do a proper towing job, stand by the disabled vessel. It may, however, be feasible to put a line across and assist by holding the other craft's bow into the sea at a comfortable angle while waiting for a more suitable towing vessel.

Call the Coast Guard or other salvage agency and turn the job over to them when they arrive. Don't try to be a hero, as you are more than likely not experienced or trained for this type of work. No boat is worth a life.

Emergency Procedures

The best seaman is the one who is prepared for any emergency, before the need arises to meet it.

Value of planning and drills

An emergency is, by definition, not a planned event, but actions to cope with foreseeable ones can be pre-planned and rehearsed. Any emergency will be much less severe and much more easily countered if there is a routine to be executed almost instantly when needed.

The best plans are of little value if they have not been tried out and evaluated to the best extent practicable short of having a full occurrence of the emergency.

When the plans have been tried out and modified as needed, the next step is to have periodic drills. Every boating family should run through its emergency procedures at the beginning of each boating season, and once again on a staggered schedule later in the season. Include any guests who may be aboard. You may not be able to drill them as effectively as the regular crew but some of it may rub off on them to your and their benefit.

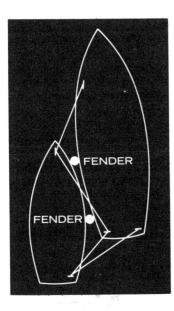

FIG. 921 How springs are used when a boat takes a larger vessel in tow alongside. Fenders are rigged at points of contact, springs made up with no slack. When the towing boat puts her rudder to port or starboard for a turn, both boats respond as a unit.

SAILBAG Wind Awareness

Probably the most useful instrument for warning of an imminent but unintended jibe is the hair on the back of the helmsman's neck as he stands at the wheel. The human nervous system easily detects changes in sounds, pressures on cheek or neck, strains in gear and many other significant precursors of change which you must train yourself to recognize and respond to.

This art can be developed to some degree by conscious effort. Close your eyes occasionally when you are on deck in broad daylight and not at the helm. Imagine you are standing watch on a dark night and relying on all senses except sight. When you "feel" the boat is not being sailed on her best course, open your eyes and check the accuracy of your other senses. If you can repeat this several times on different points of sailing and wind speeds, it will plant in your mind the association of auditory, kinesthetic and visual clues which, once recognized, becomes part of your sailor's instinct.

To aid in cultivating your wind awareness as you steer downwind, tie a yarn telltale to the backstay over your head and glance up at it from time to time as you concentrate on the sensations the wind creates on your cheek and the back of your neck.

MAN OVERBOARD

Preliminary planning for a "Man Overboard" emergency may include some of the following preparations:

1. Equip all life preservers with whistles, attached by short pieces of small stuff, and encourage crew members to carry whistles in their pockets or attached to the lanyard on which each keeps his pocket knife.

2. Make up a flag float. These are required equipment on offshore racing sailboats. They consist of a bamboo pole six or eight feet long with a flag at one end, a buoy near the other and a lead weight to hold the flag aloft. Ideally the float should be permanently attached to a whistle-equipped life preserver, a water light and a small drogue to prevent strong wind from carrying the assembly downwind faster than a man can swim to catch it. If stowing so much gear handy to your cockpit requires it, use your ingenuity to modify the proportions, but have *something* prepared in advance to throw to the person in the water that can easily be seen by him and by you in good weather, allows him to make a loud noise to guide you in poor visibility and can show a light at night.

3. Carry as a standard piece of rescue gear, in a spot known to the crew, an old magazine with many pages. Sometimes a paper trail in the water can lead you back to the scene of the accident when all else fails.

4. Think out the problems of getting a possibly unconscious person to the deck from the water and carry the necessary gear aboard at all times.

Immediate actions

If the helmsman has seen the victim fall from the bow, he should take the engine out of gear and swing the stern clear if possible.

A lookout should be posted immediately to keep an

SAILBAG The Power of a Boom

An unintended jibe in a large boat can be a true disaster. When the boom is sheeted far out, at a wide angle to the hull, and the helmsman steers so the wind can sneak around behind the *outboard* end of the sail, the boom will lift up and can silently, without warning, swing across the boat and crash to the other side with such speed and weight that it can kill humans and carry away the rigging.

If you are running in a boisterous sea and unsteady winds, it is prudent to rig a *preventer*, which can be simply a dock line made fast to the boom, as near as possible to its free end, then led forward outside the shrouds to the deck, usually to a mooring cleat on the foredeck. If the helmsman, though alert and attentive, has trouble sensing the wind direction when steering downwind, tie a yarn telltale on the upper shrouds, about 7 feet above the deck.

In bad weather the boom may be the most dangerous part of the ship's gear. It is controlled only at the forward end and can bounce up and down as well as swing back and forth, as the seas rock and toss the hull of the boat. Be quick to drop the mainsail and secure the boom in its crutch if you become concerned about this, and before you buy the boat, satisfy yourself that the boom crutch is strong enough to support the boom well if a heavy crewman falls against it. Experiment sailing your new boat on various points of sailing in winds of various strengths under the jib alone, so that when the chips are down, you will know what she can do with the boom lashed down.

eye on the victim or where he was last seen.

The helmsman should throw overboard whatever piece of gear is provided for use in this emergency. Ideally this would be a flag float of the sort described above, but absent such a rig any buoyant object is better than nothing, since the person in the water may have been injured in the fall or may panic in the water. Whatever is thrown should hit the water close to the victim, if possible, in case he is incapacitated.

Another crewman, if available, should tear pages from a magazine or newspaper, or from a roll of paper towels to provide a trail along which to return in circumstances of poor visibility. In a pinch, the helmsman can do this, too.

At night a light, if available, should be trained on the victim in the water, and held there to guide the helmsman, unless a water light was thrown over at the time of the accident.

No "heroes"

Don't let a would-be "hero" jump over the side immediately to rescue the victim—then you would only have two persons rather than one to fish out of the water. The only exception to this would be in the case of a small child or an elderly or handicapped adult. If this must be done, be sure that the rescuer takes with him a life ring or cushion; never let a person enter the water without some added buoyancy.

Maneuvering to return

Whether you turn to port or starboard had best be decided by experiment in advance. Ordinarily a boat with a right-handed propeller turns quickest to port, but practical experience shows that some boats behave otherwise. By this maneuver you should be able to get back to the scene, with boat under perfect control, in less than a minute. You might find that reversing and backing will be more effective for your boat, but the odds are against it. At any rate make a few tests. Throw a paper or cardboard box overboard and experiment in recovering it until you know precisely what to do if the need should ever arise.

Under sail

If under sail at the time of the accident, *start the engine*, whether racing or not. If a spinnaker is up it must come down before you can return for the pickup, which will be accomplished most quickly under power, unless you are carried far downwind before the spinnaker is off and you can sail upwind faster than you can motor.

The crewman who is watching the victim should keep the helmsman informed of the relative bearing of the point to which he should return. As the dust settles the skipper or watch captain should take over the job of directing the helmsman.

Use additional markers

In some circumstances, particularly at night, it may be desirable to throw overboard additional small objects that will float while the boat maneuvers so as to ensure that the path back to the victim can be retraced. A single marker may be lost to sight; multiple objects increase the probability of returning to the proper location.

Maneuvering for the pick-up

Circumstances will dictate best procedure as to how to approach the man in the water. Although the boat can best be kept under control by approaching from leeward, maneuvering into a position to windward of him will provide a lee as the boat drifts toward him.

The particular maneuver that you use in approaching the victim depends upon common sense and good judgment based on existing conditions such as the sea condition, the temperature of the water, physical condition and ability of the man in the water, boat maneuverability, and the availability of other assistance.

A good procedure is to stop the boat a short distance from the victim in the water, throwing him a light line (such as a skiing tow line of material that floats), and pulling him over to the boat. This will be considerably less hazardous than trying to maneuver the boat right up to him.

Getting the victim on board

While the boat is being maneuvered back to the victim in the water, make all preparations for getting him back on board. Have a member of the crew, who is physically capable, prepare to go into the water, *if necessary*. He should remove any excess clothing and shoes and *always* put on a life jacket. He will need the added buoyancy in order to save his strength to aid the victim. The rescuer should also have a light safety line; it may be useful in transferring it to the accident victim.

Assisting the unlucky victim back into the boat is a highly individualized matter determined by the craft, the person, and the prevailing sea conditions. The availability of a transom boarding platform if the boat is so equipped will be most helpful. A swimming ladder can usually be quickly rigged if one is carried aboard. Lines with a loop in one end tied with a bowline may be hung over the side for handholds or footholds in climbing back aboard.

Obviously, the propeller should be stopped whenever there is a person in the water near the stern of the boat.

Call for help if needed

If the victim is not immediately rescued, get on the radio with the urgent communications signal "Pan-Pan"—pronounced "Pahn-Pahn"—spoken three times before the call to get help from the Coast Guard and nearby boats. (Do *not* use "Mayday" as your craft is not in distress.) Continue the search until released by competent authority.

Importance of drills

Man overboard drills are most important. It is not necessary for an individual to go over the side, any floating object about the size of a human head can be used as the "victim." For such drills, one crew member should be told to stand aside and take no part in the "rescue" just as if it were he who was in the water. And don't forget that for some drills this non-participant should be the skipper—some day it just might be he who was the "man overboard" and his rescue had to be effected by the rest of the crew without his guidance.

Always hold a "critique" after each drill. Discuss what was done right and what was done wrong, how the procedures could be done better. Learn from your mistakes, and don't repeat them.

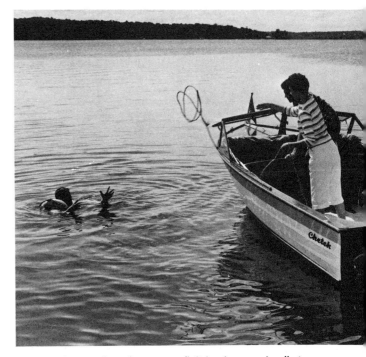

FIG. 924 On every boat, large or small, it is wise occasionally to conduct a "man-overboard" drill. The exact techniques may vary with conditions, but the essence of the idea is: be prepared.

FIRE EMERGENCIES

Fire on a boat can be a serious experience. A person's surroundings are burning, and he is faced with nowhere to go except into the water. In a sense, he is trapped.

Keep in mind that most fires are preventable. A skipper who keeps his boat in shipshape condition, which includes clean bilges and proper stowage of fuel and gear, will probably never be faced with the emergency condition of fighting a fire. This requires constant attention; whenever a condition is observed that might contribute to a fire, it should be corrected at once.

Despite the skipper's best efforts, fires are a possibility and do occur. Every boatman should be foresighted in this regard. Shipshape conditions include the proper stowage and maintenance of firefighting gear. Having this equipment handy and in good working condition is the first step in combating fire.

Explosions and fires

Fires may start with either a "bang"—an explosion—or on a much smaller scale. Should your craft have a gasoline explosion, there usually is little that you can do except grab a life preserver, if possible, and go over the side.

When clear of danger, check about and account for all those who were aboard. Render such assistance as you can to those who may be in the water without a buoyant device and those who may have been burned or injured in the blast. Keep all individuals in the water together in a group for their morale and to aid rescue operations.

Fires and extinguishment

Fires require four elements for their existence—fuel, oxygen (air), heat, and uninhibited chemical chain reactions; remove or interrupt any of these and the fire will go out. Many fires are fought by smothering (shutting off the flow of air) or by cooling them below the temperature that will support combustion. Others are extinguished by interrupting the chain reactions of the combustion process —this is the action of dry-chemical extinguishers so widely used on small boats.

FIG. 926 Risk of explosion or fire is greatest when the engines are being started or are running. The helmsman should have an extinguisher within easy reach.

Classes of fires

Fires are classified into three categories:

Class A—fires in ordinary combustible materials such as wood, paper, cloth, etc., where the "quenching-cooling" effect of quantities of water or solutions containing large percentages of water is most effective in reducing the temperature of the burning material below the ignition temperature, and is, therefore, of first importance.

Class B—fires in flammable petroleum products or other flammable liquids, greases, etc., where the "blanketing-smothering" effect of oxygen-excluding media is most effective.

Class C—fires involving electrical equipment where the electrical conductivity of the extinguishing media is of first importance.

Fire extinguishers

Fire extinguishers are classified on the same "A", "B", "C" system as are fires. Some types of extinguishers, however, have a suitability greater than their basic classification. Extinguishers required by law on boats are in the "B" category, but a carbon-dioxide or dry-chemical extinguisher will also have value in fighting an electrical ("C") fire and *some* dry-chemical units contain a different powder that is effective on Class "A" fires. The newest type of B/C extinguisher contains Halon gas under pressure; it leaves no residue. Boatmen should remember that the most effective extinguisher on typical "A" fires in paper, wood, and bedding is a bucket of water!

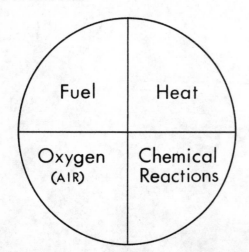

FIG. 925 Shown above are the four essential elements of a fire. If any one is removed or interrupted, the fire will go out. Different types of extinguishers attack different elements—water cools, CO_2 smothers (cuts off the air), and dry-chemicals or chemical vapors disrupt the chain reactions of the combustion process. Fires may also be fought by shutting off the flow of liquid or gaseous fuel.

Fire extinguishers should be distributed around the boat in relation to potential hazards. One should also be near the boat's control station where it can be grabbed quickly by the helmsman. Another should be mounted near the skipper's bunk so that he can roll out at night with it in his hand. Other locations include the galley (but remember that water is best on a stove alcohol fire!) and any other compartment at some distance from the location of other extinguishers. Fire extinguishers should be mounted where they are clearly visible to all on board as they move about the boat.

Fighting fires

Burning items such as wood, mattresses, and rags are best extinguished by the cooling effect of an agent such as water. For this reason a bailer or bucket can be a most valuable piece of equipment. Throwing burning materials over the side should not be overlooked.

If a fire occurs in a relatively confined space, the closing of hatches, doors, vents, and ports will tend to keep oxygen from fanning the flames. The hatch or door should not be reopened until fire-fighting equipment is ready for use. In addition, should the fire be in a machinery space, shut off the fuel supply and activate the fixed fire-extinguishing system, if your boat is so equipped.

It is *very important* to note that small fire extinguishers typically found on boats have a discharge time of *only 8 to 20 seconds*. They must be used effectively from the very start of discharge. *Aim at the base of the fire, not the smoke;* don't just trigger the extinguisher and drop it.

Maneuvering the boat

Now let us consider vessel maneuvers that will assist in extinguishing fires. When underway, wind caused by the boat's motion fans the flames; stopping or reducing speed helps to reduce the wind effect. Also it would make sense to keep the fire downwind—that is, if the fire is aft, head the bow of the boat into the wind; if the fire is forward, put the stern of the boat into the wind. Such action helps to reduce any tendency of the fire to spread to other parts of the boat, and may reduce the hazard of smoke enveloping persons on board.

Stow some life preservers well forward in case of fire aft or the necessity of abandoning ship over the bow.

Summary of actions

The following suggested steps are listed and may be performed, not necessarily in the order shown:
1. If possible, apply the extinguishing agent by:
   a. Using a fire extinguisher,
   b. Discharging fixed smothering system, or
   c. Applying water to wood or materials of this type.
2. If practical, burning materials should be jettisoned (thrown over the side).
3. Reduce the air supply by:
   a. Maneuvering the vessel to reduce the effect of wind, and
   b. Closing hatches, ports, vents, doors, etc. if the fire is in an area where this action will be effective.
4. Make preparation for abandoning ship, which include:
   a. Putting on lifesaving devices, and
   b. Signaling for assistance by radio or any other means available.

LEAKS AND DAMAGE CONTROL

A boat floats so long as the water is pumped out faster than it leaks in. Modern fiberglass boats leak almost not at all (although a slow drip from the propeller shaft stuffing box insures that the gland is not drawn up too tight), but should a through-hull fitting fail, or should you have the misfortune to hit a submerged, waterlogged "tidewalker," a broken-off piling which floats just below the surface in an upright position, while you are traveling at a rate of knots, your fiberglass boat will leak.

Planning ahead

Among provisions you should consider taking in contemplation of such an accident are:
1. Install a diaphragm pump, manually operated, as large as possible (you can get them with a capacity of a gallon per stroke), so arranged that you can operate it continuously for five or ten minutes without excessive fatigue.
2. Prepare an intake screen to fit in the end of the engine cooling water intake hose so that the engine's pumping capacity can be added to the bilge pump's should need arise. Keep this with your emergency gear.
3. Get a small, very strong tarpaulin with grommets at the corners to which dock lines can be attached to maneuver it to cover a damaged hull area from the outside and secure it there. Keep this with your emergency gear.
4. Fashion soft wooden plugs that will fit each of the through-hull openings in your hull, tapered so they can be driven into place from the inside. Keep them with your emergency gear.

Standard procedure

At the first suspicion of damage that might cause serious leaking, switch on all electric bilge pumps *before* investigating. In a few seconds, if inspection reveals that your fears were groundless, switch them off again. They will not be damaged by a very brief run while dry.

FIG. 927 In addition to electrical bilge pumps, a boat should be equipped with at least one manually-operated pump. This can be used even if rising water in the bilge shorts out the boat's batteries.

Crew action

Depending on how many helpers you have aboard, assign someone to man your manual bilge pump and someone else to investigate the extent of the damage by pulling up floorboards and checking conditions in the bilge. Better still, if conditions permit, conduct this investigation yourself. If leaking is rapid form a bucket brigade, assuming you have manpower enough. If there are three available bailers and only one bucket, break out a couple of cooking pots.

Emergency pumping

If conditions warrant, close the engine water intake seacock, disconnect the water intake line, connect your previously prepared intake screen, making sure there is enough water in the bilge to cover the intake well. Start the engine and *check* to be sure it is discharging water through the wet exhaust or other discharge line. Assign someone to frequently check the intake screen and be sure it is not obstructed.

Two precautions must be observed. First, there must be enough water already in the bilge and flowing in to meet the engine's needs for cooling. Secondly, caution must be exercised to keep bilge dirt and trash from being sucked into the engine's intake. To lose power if the engine over-heats might be disastrous. These two precautions will usually require that the intake hose be watched and tended at all times by a crew member assigned to that specific duty.

Operating USCG droppable pumps

Coast Guard aircraft are equipped with pumps that can be dropped in floating containers to boats that need them. The following operating instructions are applicable:
1. Make sure suction hose is tight—connect discharge hose.
2. Fill gas tank.
3. Pull stop switch away from spark plug.
4. Close carburetor choke—turn lever in direction of arrow.
5. Open throttle at base of engine.
6. Attach starting cord and spin engine.
7. After engine starts, open choke.
8. Normally, pumps are self-priming—if difficulty arises, prime.
9. When finished, flush out pump with fresh water.

Emergency repairs

Almost anything can be stuffed into a hole in the hull to help stop the inflow of water—cushions, pillows, bedding, spare sails—all of these will have some beneficial effect.

Material used to stop a leak will be more effective if it can be applied from the outside where water pressure will aid in holding it in place. This will, of course, require that the boat be stopped while the temporary patch or plug is positioned and secured. If a hole must be plugged from the inside, the pillow, bedding etc., can sometimes be held in place by nailing a batten or bed slat across it. If no better solution can be found, a member of the crew can be assigned to hold the plug in place. In any event, station a crewman or passenger to watch the patched hole and give immediate alarm if the patch or plug fails to hold.

ASSISTANCE

In any form of emergency, it is well to alert possible sources of assistance without delay. Use your radio with an

*18 in. = 46 cm.   45 in. = 1.14 m.   72 in. = 1.83 m.

urgent ("Pan-Pan") call to advise the Coast Guard and others of your problem. Don't put out a "Mayday" distress call unless you are in obvious danger of sinking, have an uncontrollable fire on board, etc. Don't panic and make a distress call under conditions that do not warrant such action, but also don't fail to alert others to your possible need for assistance soon.

FIG. 928 A radio is probably the primary means of summoning assistance. Do not put out a "Mayday" call unless you are in distress. If you need help, but are not in danger, use the urgent signal "Pan" on VHF Channel 16 (156.8 MHz) or 2182 kHz.

Summoning assistance

A boat's radio is probably the primary means of obtaining assistance, although it is far from being the only method. Use VHF Channel 16 (or 2182 kHz single-side-band) and follow the procedures of Chapter 25.

Other distress signals are described on pages 87 and 88. The Coast Guard requirements for carrying certain visual distress signals are discussed on page 59. Additionally, however, any device or procedure that attracts attention and brings help is a satisfactory distress signal.

Don't overlook the possible use of a small signal mirror equipped with sighting hole and cross-line target. The reflected mirror signals can be seen as flashes of light for many miles and may be just the device that could attract the attention of aircraft.

There are several recently recognized distress signals for small boats on waters of the United States. A simple orange-red flag may be waved from side to side. Even better is a 72-inch by 45-inch fluorescent orange-red panel cloth bearing an 18-inch black square and an 18-inch black circle, 18-inches apart on the major axis of the flag.* This could be tied across a hatch or cabin top as a signal to aircraft. A signal may also be made by slowly and repeatedly raising and lowering arms outstretched to each side. This is a distinctive signal, not likely to be mistaken for a greeting. To be as effective as possible, this signal should be given from the highest vantage point on the boat with consideration given to color contrasts.

Helicopter rescue

In more and more instances, Coast Guard assistance is being provided by helicopters rather than patrol craft. This new technique requires new knowledge on the part of the boat skipper and is most effective with advance preparations.

Prior to arrival of helicopter

1. Listen continuously on 2182 kHz, VHF Channel 16, or other specified frequency if possible.
2. Select, and clear most suitable hoist area. For boats, sail and power, it probably will be necessary to tow a dingy or raft due to lack of clear deck space.
3. If hoist is at night, light pick-up areas as well as possible. Be sure you do not shine any lights on the helicopter and blind the pilot. If there are obstructions in the vicinity, put a light on them so the pilot will be aware of their positions.
4. Advise location of pick-up area before the helicopter arrives so that he may adjust for and make his approach as required.
5. Remember that there will be a high noise level under the helicopter, so conversation between the deck crew will be almost impossible. Arrange a set of hand signals between those who will be assisting.

Rescue by hoist

1. Change course so as to permit the craft to ride as easily as possible with the wind on the bow, preferably on the port bow.
2. Reduce speed if necessary to ease the boat's motion, but maintain steerageway.
3. If you do not have radio contact with the helicopter, signal a "Come on" when you are in all respects ready for the hoist; use a flashlight at night.
4. Allow basket or stretcher to touch down on the deck prior to handling to avoid static shock.
5. If a trail line is dropped by the helicopter, guide the basket or stretcher to the deck with the line; line will not cause shock.
6. Place person in basket sitting with hands clear of sides, or strap person in the stretcher. Place a life

FIG. 929 The Coast Guard is making increased use of helicopters for rescue and assistance work. The gas-turbine powered HH-52A shown can land on the water if necessary. Note the hoisting winch above the door. Skippers should know how to cooperate with helicopter crews.   (U.S. Coast Guard photo)

jacket on the person if possible. Signal the helicopter hoist operator when ready for hoist. Person in basket or stretcher nods his head if he is able. Deck personnel give "thumbs up."

7. If necessary to take litter away from hoist point, unhook hoist cable and keep free for helicopter to haul in. *Do not secure cable to vessel or attempt to move stretcher without unhooking.*
8. When person is strapped in stretcher, signal helicopter to lower cable, hook up, and signal hoist operator when ready to hoist. Steady stretcher from swinging or turning.
9. If a trail line is attached to basket or stretcher, use to steady. Keep feet clear of line.

ABANDONING SHIP

Many boats involved in casualties have continued to float indefinitely. If it becomes necessary to abandon your boat due to fire, danger of sinking, or other emergency, don't leave the area. Generally a damaged boat can be sighted more readily than a person, and it may help to keep you afloat.

Keep in mind that distance over water is deceptive. Usually the estimated distance is much shorter than the actual distance. Keep your head and restrain your initial impulse to swim ashore. Calmly weigh the facts of the situation such as: injuries to passengers, the proximity of shore, and your swimming abilities, before deciding upon your course of action.

Before abandoning your craft, put on your life preserver and give distress signals. Don't foolishly waste signaling devices where small likelihood of assistance exists. Wait until you sight someone or something. If your vessel is equipped with a radio telephone, a distress message should be sent.

Maintenance

The condition of a boatman's craft can be an indication of his overall seamanship knowledge and abilities. Using a boat is only part of its ownership—maintenance, keeping her shipshape and Bristol Fashion, is the other part.

For most recreational boat owner-skippers, his craft represents a considerable investment of family funds. She must be properly and continuously maintained to keep up the value of this investment. The secret of getting the fullest measure of pleasure from your boat is to make the necessary maintenance effort enjoyable, even fun, and not a grudging chore. The key to this happy situation is proper planning and a low but continuous level of effort.

Don't let your boat get run down; it will not only look worse, but will require more total maintenance than if it had been properly cared for. Deferred maintenance is always more of a burden and more expensive. Maintain the value of your boat—and your pride in her—by continuous attention to maintenance, perhaps peaking in the spring of each year, but not neglected at any time.

USE AND CARE OF EQUIPMENT

A planned maintenance program can start with the use and care of the boat and its equipment. Let us first consider equipment and supplies. To have one's craft in true shipshape condition means a place for everything and every-

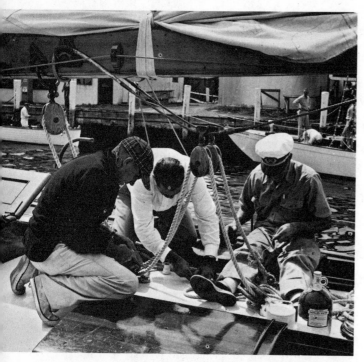

FIG. 930 The key to proper and adequate maintenance, without its becoming a burdensome chore, is a low but continuous level of effort. Do small jobs when they need it—don't put them off. Have a regular schedule for preventive maintenance. (Peter Stackpole photo)

thing in its place; and, too, everything in good working condition.

Lines and sails

While synthetic cordage and sail cloth are not subject to rot, mildew can form from deposited spores of fungus unless these items are clean and dry when stowed. Manila will rot if stowed wet. The unseamanlike practice of stowing wet ropes and sails below decks will inevitably result in damp, uncomfortable conditions.

The same reasoning applies to foul weather gear and any other materials of that sort.

Clean, dry, well-ventilated compartments contribute to the soundness of vessel and gear and to the crew's pleasure.

Stowage of supplies

Every item of equipment should be well marked and kept in its specific place. Any article with labels should have the contents painted on the bottle or can proper; it is a good idea even to remove any paper labels, as they may come off in any dampness and cause problems. Some skippers use adhesive tape on the articles and print the contents on the tape; others merely place a letter on each different item (A means potatoes, B means beans, C means sunburn ointment) and keep a key list on board. The only trouble with the latter method is if you lose the key list you're in trouble.

The new felt-tip marking pens are excellent for labeling cans and other containers. Experiment with different ones until you find the most moisture-resistant type.

Use a checklist

If all equipment is clearly marked and always in its proper place it eases the skipper's mind, to say nothing of adding to his safety. Not only is he sure of having every-

thing, but he doesn't worry for the first day trying to remember what he has forgotten. In order to carry this thought out successfully, it is necessary and good seamanship to have and use a sailing checklist. A sailing checklist is a list of all items that a competent skipper will provide for the boat, her equipment, supplies, stores, and condition prior to shoving off from the mooring. If this list is kept aboard, and if the skipper checks off each item before he shoves off, there will never be any need to worry about being without the necessary equipment.

THE HULL

In order to preserve a wooden hull, it must be kept well painted. Every year the old coat of paint should be sanded down before new is applied, and every so often, depending on how thick the old coats of paint are, all paint should be removed, the hull sanded, and seams and scars filled before a new coat of paint is applied.

The number of different types of paint has expanded remarkably in recent years. If you don't feel qualified to make a selection, ask the professionals at your boatyard and talk to other skippers about their experiences with various hull finishes.

No matter which paint you select, proper surface preparation and application of the paint are *absolutely essential* if the desired results are to be obtained. Follow the manufacturer's directions explicitly from start to finish. Select the proper weather conditions for your work—wait until the morning dew has evaporated, and stop well before sundown.

"Between wind and water," that part of the vessel at or near the waterline, is the most difficult part of the hull to keep protected. This is because it is always getting wet and drying off and also that the water causes a lot of friction at this location. A special quick-drying paint called boottopping is used here, the principal ingredients of which are varnish and dryer.

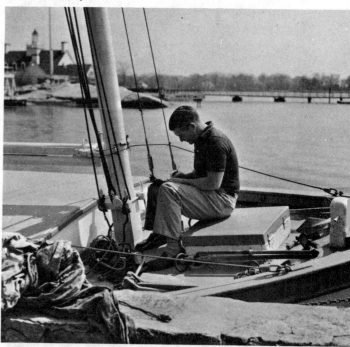

FIG. 931 Prepare a checklist to be sure all necessary supplies and equipment are on board before setting out on a cruise. Use it every time, modifying and updating from experience.

SAILBAG Spinnaker Wraps and Unwraps

The Spinnaker is surely one of the most unseamanlike sails the mind of man has devised, but it is fun to sail with one. They are enormous sails, frequently equalling in area all of the working sails combined, are made of lightweight nylon and are set flying, being attached at three points and supported at only two of those. See fig. 141.

Should the crew or helmsman be inattentive or un-skilled the spinnaker can collapse completely which can happen suddenly with very little warning. When that happens, it may wrap itself around the headstay. In strong breezes, the light, billowing fabric can wrap itself around the stay in many turns so tightly that the only way to free it is to take a knife to the cloth.

So when the spinnaker starts to wrap, it is impor-tant to unwrap it quickly before it tightens. Frequently, this can be accomplished simply by jibing the main-sail and sailing downwind so the spinnaker is blanketed in the wind shadow of the main. The wind eddying forward around the mast spins in the opposite direction from that which caused the wrap in the first place. Often this will unwrap the spinnaker in short order.

If the wrap is intransigent and the weather not too severe, a man must be sent aloft in the bosun's chair. Sometimes he can free the sail by releasing it from the halyard, creating enough slack to allow the cloth to slide down the headstay to the deck.

Some sailors seek insurance against a wrap by hoist-ing a *spinnaker net* made of line or shock cord. One end is hoisted to the masthead and the other secured to the deck so it blocks off the passage between the mast and headstay like a spider web. Occasionally, a wrap develops despite the net, which then adds to the prob-lem, especially when shock cord is used.

Fiberglass hulls

Fiberglass hulls need less maintenance, but some is still required.

A fiberglass hull should be cleaned as required to keep it free of dirt and oily scum; more cleaning will be needed near the waterline than higher on the topsides. Try to get the job done using only a detergent without an abrasive powder that can dull a high-gloss finish. If you must use a scouring powder to remove marks and greasy streaks, use a mild one and use it with caution.

Liquid cleaner wax is excellent for fiberglass hulls, par-ticularly for mid-season continuing maintenance. Once a year, usually at spring fitting-out, do a more thorough two-step job with a paste cleaner followed by a paste wax. This is also the time to patch up any hair-line cracks that have appeared in the gel (surface) coat of the fiberglass.

After a few years of use, a fiberglass hull may require painting to restore it to top appearance. Many paints are available for this purpose, most of which are two-part products to be mixed just prior to application. Advances in chemical and plastics technology are now resulting in one-part paints for fiberglass surfaces that are easier to use and will give satisfactory results. The problem is to get proper adhesion to the fiberglass plus a high-gloss finish. As with painting a wooden hull, the best procedure is to

FIG. 932 Two secrets to success in painting are proper prepara-tion of the surface and application of the paint in strict conformity with manufacturer's instructions.

ask a professional and talk with people who have used various products to get their opinions, and preparation is all-important.

BOTTOM MAINTENANCE

Special attention must be given to the maintenance of the bottom of the boat; this is a most important item as it is usually available for inspection only once or twice a year.

Except for small boats that are taken out of the water after each period of use, the bottom must be kept covered with anti-fouling paint. This type of paint, usually with a copper base, has properties that tend to keep worms out of the bottom as well as to discourage marine growth that attaches itself to the bottom.

Coming into wider use are bottom paints employing other metals and chemicals toxic to marine life. With these, bottom paints are now available in a wide range of colors.

FIG. 933 In most locations, antifouling paint must be applied to a boat's underwater surfaces to protect against worms and marine growth. Bottom finishes are available in many colors as well as the old familiar "copper" paint. (Wm. H. Koelbel photo)

Launching wet or dry

There are two theories about applying bottom paint. Some say that the boat should be put into the water as soon as the paint has been applied, that is, while it is still fairly wet, while others state that the paint should be dry before launching. Follow the manufacturer's directions on the can for the best results.

BRIGHTWORK

Brightwork, natural wood surfaces finished with varnish or similar products, requires special care. Horizontal areas of brightwork should be wiped clear of morning dew each day to prolong their life. All brightwork will require a good sanding at least yearly followed by a fresh coat of varnish. Those parts of the brightwork that receive a lot of wear or spray will need to be given more than one coat each season. Unless varnished areas are kept well covered, moisture will get into the wood and the result will be that

FIG. 934 Varnished surfaces, called "brightwork," require more care than painted or natural wood or fiberglass areas, but to many boat owners their added beauty is worth the effort. Often, care of brightwork can be turned over to the "first mate." (Rosenfeld photo)

it will turn dark, in extreme cases, black.

Wooding down

To keep brightwork looking well is a lot of work, but the beauty of it can make it worthwhile. No matter how much care is taken, it will turn just a little darker each year. Many modern varnishes and synthetic equivalents now include a "filter" to screen out ultraviolet rays of the sun that are most damaging to brightwork. The additive slows down the aging process. Even with this added protection, however, it will be necessary every few years to remove all of the varnish with varnish remover, sand the bare wood, and then bleach and restain as required before starting with the first of four to six coats of fresh varnish.

Reduction of brightwork

In recent years more and more boats have appeared with almost no brightwork at all. The cabins and spars are painted and in fact the only parts left natural may be the handrails, toerails, and trim around hatches.

This move toward little or no brightwork has even invaded interiors. A few years ago this would have been looked upon as sacrilege. No matter how much oldtimers view this trend with alarm, it does have this advantage—it does not reduce the protective qualities which are the main reasons for keeping surfaces covered, and it does make less work. In many cases, natural, unfinished teak is being substituted for mahogany that must be kept varnished.

DECK CARE

Canvas decks present a special problem. They must be kept covered with a good deck paint for protection, but the less paint you put on the better. If you get too much paint on the decks, not only will it crack but they will become smooth. This is not good especially on a small boat, as a smooth deck makes for precarious footing in wet weather. This has been overcome on some boats by sprinkling fine sand on the decks while the paint is still wet. Also, some paint manufacturers are putting out a special paint with a non-skid surface.

Fiberglass decks

Decks of fiberglass require little care other than rinsing off dirt and salt spray. On most boats, anti-slip protection is built in by the manufacturer. In some cases, however, additional non-skid strips or specially painted areas will be required for safety. If it becomes necessary to paint a fiberglass deck, don't fail to provide for continued anti-skid protection where needed.

Teak decks

Decks on large power and sail craft are often made of unfinished teak. Such decks are attractive, quite non-skid, and require little maintenance. They may be allowed to assume a natural, weathered appearance, or they can be periodically bleached to a lighter color, as the individual skipper prefers.

Teak decks should be washed down to keep them free of dirt that might get ground in when walked upon. Salt sea water is excellent for washing down teak decks. A periodic scrubbing with a special teak cleaner is not a difficult chore and will improve overall appearance, but it should not be done too often.

FIG. 935 Teak is an excellent material for decks. The wood can be left unfinished or given a light treatment with special preservatives. It weathers well and provides a non-skid surface. (Rosenfeld photo)

Decks of teak wood are subject to staining from oily liquids or solids—particularly from some types of food such as bits of potato chips or mayonnaise drippings from sandwiches—but special paste or spray cleaners will efficiently remove these spots.

PAINTING METAL SURFACES

If any metal is to be painted, be sure to use a priming coat of anti-corrosive paint against the metal first. Popular types of such paint include the familiar red lead, zinc chromate, and aluminum. Paints for this purpose will be so labeled on the container; don't use a paint for anti-corrosion protection unless it is so designated.

If your boat has a metal bottom it is specially important that anti-corrosive paint be used before the anti-fouling paint. Ingredients of most bottom paint are oxides of mercury and copper, and if these come in contact with steel, corrosion will result. The anti-fouling paints offer no protection to the hull against sea-water corrosion, but the anti-corrosion paints have no anti-fouling properties, so both must be used.

Painting aluminum

Boats having aluminum hulls may be painted for protection against corrosive attack although this is not generally required with modern alloys properly selected. Underwater anti-fouling paint will be needed for aluminum bottoms under the same conditions as for wood or fiberglass boats.

Aluminum will hold paint very well *provided* that the metal surface has been properly prepared and a suitable primer has been used. Greater care must be taken with this metal than with others commonly used. The aluminum must be *absolutely clean,* free of all oil, scale, dirt, etc., even free of fingerprints. Sand-blasting or wire brushing will be needed to etch the surface slightly in order to make the paint adhere. Zinc chromate is a suitable primer; two

coats should be used to insulate the aluminum hull from any lead-pigmented paint or copper-bearing bottom coating so as to prevent galvanic action between the dissimilar metals.

When patching up the paint job on any area of an aluminum hull, always be sure to prepare the metal surface thoroughly and use a primer coat next to the aluminum.

GENERAL RULES FOR PAINTING

There are a few simple rules for painting. If observed, they will make such work simpler and more satisfactory. These are:

1. Never paint over a wet, dirty, or greasy surface.
2. Never paint during wet weather.
3. Never paint before cleaning and sanding.
4. Do not continuously apply new over old coats.
5. Never apply paint heavily.
6. Paint with reasonable frequency.
7. Use surfacing putty (trowel or brushing cement) to fill nicks and gouges after the prime coat of paint, unless manufacturer's instructions indicate otherwise.
8. Never use a blow torch immediately after applying paint remover.
9. Never scrape or sand near fresh paint.

Sequence for painting

There is a generally preferred order for painting the various parts of a boat as follows:

1. All interiors, including bilge (if painted) and engines.
2. Spars.
3. All deck gear, cockpits, ventilators, hatches, etc.
4. Cabin exterior and decks.
5. Hull topsides.
6. Bottom.
7. Boot-topping.

FIG. 935(a) For boatmen, a power sander can be a real energy-saver. These come in many styles, both as a separate tool as above, and as an attachment for an electric drill.

a   b

FIG. 936 Whenever your boat is hauled, inspect underwater areas. Zinc blocks and collars, as shown in (a), are used to control galvanic corrosion and must be regularly checked and replaced when needed. Failure to do this may have the results pictured in (b).

INSPECTION NECESSARY

Besides keeping all appropriate surfaces well covered with paint or varnish, there are many other parts that must be inspected regularly. For example, on some boats you must be constantly on the lookout for galvanic corrosion. This chemical reaction is caused when different metals such as brass or bronze and iron come together or in close proximity to each other in salt or impure water. This is often noticeable on boats between an iron rudder and a bronze propeller. Cases have been known where the rudder is just eaten up. This can be checked by placing a zinc plate nearby so that the zinc, in contact with the part to be protected, will be affected instead of the iron. However, if this is done, care must be taken to watch the zinc plate and replace it whenever necessary. Systems may be installed in which a reverse flow of current is used to equalize and offset any destructive current.

Make regular checks

Regular checks of shaft logs, stuffing boxes, bearings, underwater fittings, and the propeller are essential. Your steering system and cables should be gone over often. If your steering system goes wrong in a tight place, you will not only damage your own vessel but may also injure some person or damage another boat.

Keep your boat clean

All equipment as well as the hull itself must be kept clean at all times. This also includes the bilges. Dirty bilges can result in stopped-up inlets to bilge pumps, and this is sure to happen just when the pump is most needed. There is nothing that gets dirty easier than a boat. Not only is it uncomfortable to try to live on, but it is injurious to the hull and the equipment. Regular cleaning makes for little work to keep your boat spick-and-span; if you let it go, it is a hard job to clean up.

Inspection checklist

It is desirable that every boat have its pre-departure checklist to be used before getting underway. In order to assist the skipper in preventing breakdowns, every boat should have an *inspection checklist* on board and in use. An inspection checklist is a list of all items that the skipper will regularly inspect, and the scheduled periods for such inspections, with a place for the skipper to write in the date of each inspection in order to keep his boat well found.

ENGINE CARE

In a motor boat the engine is the only means of propulsion, and in an auxiliary it is the means of getting in and out of tight places. Therefore, the engine is something that should be in the best of shape at all times and should always start at once. All of us are not good mechanics, but all of us should be able to (1) obtain, read, and follow the manufacturer's instruction book; (2) know enough not to fool with something we are not sure of; and (3) get instruction on simple trouble diagnosis and emergency repairs. The next time a mechanic works on your engine, stay with him and watch—you can learn much that way.

Routine care

There are, however, a number of things that any skipper can do not only to keep his engine running well for whenever it is needed, but also to keep down the cost of repair bills. All should be done at intervals and in the manner prescribed by the maker's operating manual.

FIG. 937 Regular cleaning makes for little work to keep a boat spick-and-span.
(Rosenfeld photo)

FIG. 938 The average powerboat skipper is not expected to be a mechanic, but he must have an idea of how to maintain his engines. The manufacturer's instruction book should be aboard and its preventive maintenance procedures carried out. (Charles Anderson photo)

For more dependable engine operation:

1. Frequently check oil level; change oil regularly.
2. Check cooling systems, including intake, regularly.
3. Keep batteries filled and fully charged.
4. Oil starter, generator, and distributor regularly.
5. Replace ignition system components regularly.
6. Keep engines clean, especially all filters.
7. Keep fuel lines tight; check for vibration.
8. Check all electric wiring periodically.
9. Do not race a cold motor.
10. Cool down engine before stopping it.
11. Engage clutch only at moderate speeds.
12. Carry spare parts and know how to install them.
13. Carry proper tools.

CARE OF SAILS

Modern sailboats use nearly all synthetic sailcloth—dacron and nylon. These materials have greatly improved characteristics over canvas, but they do require proper use and maintenance.

Care in use

Protect sails from chafing—use wooden or rubber protectors over turnbuckles and at the tips of spreaders. Don't let sails slat needlessly; it wears the stitching and tears batten pockets. Use properly fitted battens and remove them when the sail is furled.

Care in stowage

The greatest enemy of synthetic sailcloth is the sun. Excessive sunlight ultimately causes the material to break down and lose its strength. If sails are left on, they should be furled *and covered.* Water and moisture will not harm dacron and nylon and so such sails can be stored damp if necessary. It is, however, advisable to dry them if you can in order to avoid mildew and the general carrying of mois-

ture below decks.

Wash sails once or twice a season with pure water and soap—no detergents; and never use a washing machine. Hose off, spread to dry, and inspect before folding. Try to keep them as free from salt as possible.

When storing for the winter, wash, clean, and dry. In folding, lay out on the floor, fold lengthwise accordion fashion. When you have a bundle 2 to 3 feet (60 to 90 cm) square, fold head to foot, tie up, and store safely or hang to protect from vermin.

Sail maintenance

Although any major repairs should be left to a professional sailmaker, every sailor should be familiar with four basic emergency repairs: the round stitch, the herringbone stitch, the patch, and sail repair tape.

Round Stitch. The round or overhand stitch is used particularly for light sails and in repairing minor tears of from one to four inches. Gather the two sides of the rip, starting about an inch above it. Secure the thread *not* by knotting, but by passing it under the first few stitches; then

FIG. 939 Sails of modern craft are almost entirely synthetic—dacron, nylon, and others. While more resistant to damage from misuse, they still require proper care and maintenance for good service and long life. (Rosenfeld photo)

187

FIG. 940 When sails are furled on the boom, they should be protected by a cover. Sunshine, more than use, rain, or salt spray, is the greatest enemy of synthetic sails.   (Schwarm, Sheldon photo)

sew over it and continue round and round, ending about an inch below the tear. Finish your job in the same turn-under way.

Herringbone Stitch. This is used for more serious repairs. Before placing the two sides of the rip together, fold under a narrow margin on each and "iron" it like a pair of pants by gently scraping the edge of the sailcloth with your knife. Then make alternate long and short stitches to avoid an even line, starting about a quarter-inch from the end of the tear, and finish a quarter-inch below it. Tuck the end of the twine under the final few stitches as in the round job, and cut it. This is a stitch that is best learned from someone who knows how.

FIG. 941 A sailboat skipper should be able to make minor repairs, but all major maintenance and alteration work should be referred to a professional sailmaker. The herringbone stitch, above, is used for tears too extensive to permit use of the simpler round stitch. Start ¼-inch from the tear and finish below it.   (Frank Rohr photo)

Patch. Cut your patch, if possible, from the same weight and type of material as the damaged sail. Allow about one and one-half inches of margin on either side of the tear and turn the patch under a half-inch all the way round, "ironing" folds with knife treatment to keep them manageable, especially with heavier weight cloths. Try to get the weave of the patching cloth to run identically with the sail being repaired. Measuring the approximate area and marking the patch material with pencil before cutting will help.

Miter corners of the patch and, pinning it to sail with extra needles, use the round or overhand stitch to sew your patch to the sail. Pound it into submission with a knife handle; turn the whole lot over; miter the corners of the torn sail itself; sew it to the back of the patch, and hoist away.

Tape. Spinnaker and white rigging tape can be pressed into service swiftly and efficiently to help you finish—even win—a race, or perhaps withstand the wind in some cruising crisis till you reach port.

In making the repair, separate the sticky part from its guard which comes as part of the roll; then, as you unroll the ready tape, press with your fingers on both sides of the rip or seam. It should hold till you can get to it with needle and thread, or bring it ashore to the sailmaker.

Sail repair kit

Various sailmakers can supply emergency repair kits suitable for the sails used on your boat. These include sewing twine, needles, beeswax, a sewing palm, and other useful items, including a booklet of instructions on the care and repair of sails.

WINTER LAY-UP

Perhaps the greatest damage is done to a boat during the long winter months when she is laid up. In the north boats are usually pulled out during the winter, while in the south they are usually left in the water. Of course these call for slightly different techniques.

Storage on land

In general, these are the things to do when laying up for the winter hauled out on shore:

1. Thoroughly clean the bottom, decks, cockpit, bilge, all compartments, and lockers.
2. Apply a coat of good anti-fouling paint to the bottom, and sand down and prime all other marred surfaces.
3. Drain fuel lines, pumps, and carburetor; drain tank, or fill completely and add stabilizer.
4. Drain and flush out all water systems and tanks; drain the toilets.
5. Winterize the engine in accordance with the manufacturer's instruction manual. This will normally include draining and flushing the cooling system; draining and refilling the crankcase; applying oil to inside of each cylinder through the sparkplug holes; and other preservative actions. Thoroughly clean the exterior of the engine; sand and touch up with paint any scarred areas to prevent rusting.
6. Remove the batteries from the boat; store in an area not subject to freezing temperatures; test periodically with hydrometer and charge if necessary.
7. Place a light coating of grease over all chromeplated

metal surfaces.

8. Leave all floorboards up, doors ajar, ports and sky-lights open, hatches partly open, drawers and lockers open.

9. Carefully fit a well-made winter cover, provided with ventilation ports, if boat is to be stored outdoors.

Storage afloat

When making plans for your boat's winter lay-up, don't fail to give consideration to "wet storage." New ice-protection techniques are coming into wider usage, and more owners are leaving their craft in the water for the winter months—it has many advantages.

The cost is often less, but the real gains are in the better storage conditions for the boat. Water temperatures do not fluctuate so widely or rapidly as do those of the air, and so there is less "sweating" inside the hull. Properly protected with antifreeze, the engine can be periodically started and run, which is better for it than standing idle for several months.

Another advantage of wet storage is that there is less danger of the hull's warping or becoming distorted. A boat's structure is designed to be uniformly supported by water; resting on a few blocks, or even in its own special cradle, is distinctly "unnatural" for it. If protected against ice, covered, in-water storage is the best way for your boat to sit out the winter months until the next boating season.

FIG. 943 More and more boats are being kept in the water over the winter season even where ice normally is a problem. Air pumped through pipes on the bottom brings warmer water to the surface and prevents formation of ice near the hull. (Chicago Sun-Times photo)

FIG. 944 An electric drill is a virtually indispensable tool in boat maintenance. Many models feature variable speed operation and some can be reversed in rotation.

Winterizing procedures afloat

The actions to be taken for a winter lay-up afloat will, of course, be somewhat different from those in the list above for when the boat is to be hauled out. The engine should be winterized, but the details, as in connection with the cooling system, will vary. Fuel tanks may be filled, to reduce condensation, rather than being drained. Excess gear should be removed from the boat, and all lockers, drawers, etc., should be left open to promote ventilation.

Getting a head start on fitting out

Some annual maintenance chores may be suitable for accomplishment in the fall at the time of laying-up. Any that can be done at this time will reduce the effort required the following spring and so expedite your next boating season.

KEEP YOUR BOAT WELL MAINTAINED

Once a boat is "Shipshape and Bristol Fashion" it doesn't take much work to keep her so. It is only when she is allowed to run down that the work is heavy.

FIG. 942 In northern waters, boats are normally hauled out for dry storage during the winter. Proper blocking and shoring are necessary so that the hull is adequately supported and will not distort in shape. Canvas cover should provide protection and ventilation.

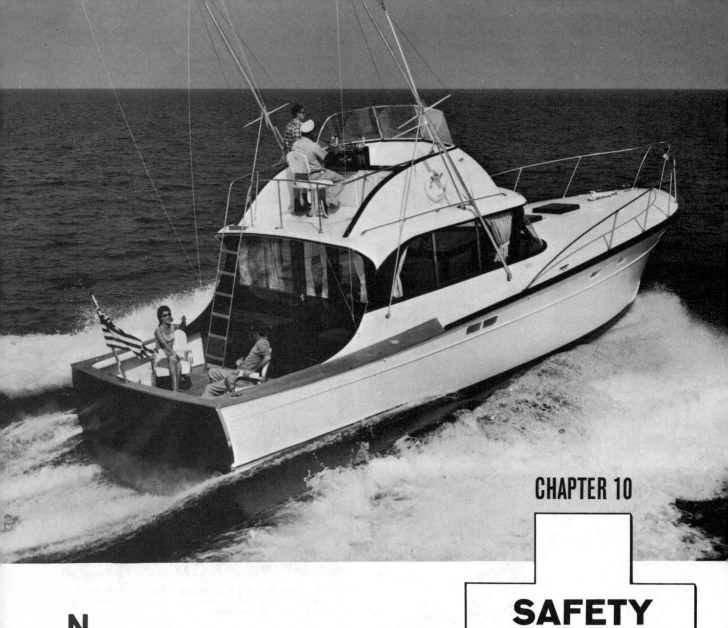

CHAPTER 10

SAFETY AFLOAT

No one should ever be deterred from enjoying the wholesome pleasures of boating by hazards that *might* be encountered; neither should he take safety for granted. No one—skipper, first mate, crew, nor guests—need fear the water and recreational boating if it is approached in a sensible manner.

While not allowing it to detract from the enjoyment of boating, the wise skipper practices safety at *all* times while afloat and studies it frequently ashore. He recognizes its importance, and safety is always in the back of his mind, never forgotten nor ignored. He views safety not as an arbitrary set of rules, but rather as the practical application of knowledge, as commonsense requirements and practices that should be thoroughly understood and followed. If "hazards" of any nature are recognized and respected, they largely cease to be hazards.

It is an established fact that most boating accidents and difficulties arise from ignorance, and could have been avoided. A man does not knowingly put his life, and the lives of others, and the safety of valuable property in jeopardy, but he may do so through lack of knowledge. Serious study and thought toward safety can significantly reduce the problems encountered while on the water.

Photograph by Schwarm and Sheldon, Inc.

Safety afloat is a broad topic encompassing essentially all aspects of boating. It is involved in the construction of boats, their equipment, operation, and maintenance. Safety matters are touched on in other chapters of this book in their relationship to government regulations, Rules of the Road, boat handling, seamanship, and other major topics. Here, safety afloat will be the *principal* consideration, with appropriate cross-references to other sections.

SAFETY ORGANIZATIONS

There are a number of public and private organizations devoted to the promotion of safety in boating. Several of these approach safety as an educational matter; others are concerned with the material and operational aspects of boats and boating. Each plays an important part in enhancing the safety of small craft, their crews and passengers.

Educational organizations

The **United States Power Squadrons** is a volunteer organization of more than 63,000 members organized into over 452 local Squadrons. These units, located throughout the United States and in some overseas areas, offer educational programs of basic safety and piloting to the public, and more advanced courses to their members.

It is a nonprofit, self-sustaining, private membership organization dedicated to the teaching of better and safer boating. Despite the word "Power" in its name, the USPS today includes many sailboat skippers in its ranks. The boats of members can usually be identified by the USPS Ensign with its blue and white vertical stripes; see color page R.

More than 34,000 boatmen and members of their families received free instruction in the USPS Boat Course every year. Information on local classes is published often in *Motor Boating & Sailing* magazine or an inquiry can be addressed to USPS Headquarters, P.O. Box 30423, Raleigh, NC 27612.

Additional information on the USPS will be found in Chapter 31.

In Canada, the Canadian Power Squadrons are organized in a manner generally similar to the USPS, with modifications to fit that country's laws and customs. Power Squadron ideals and programs are spreading also to other nations and parallel organizations may be seen developing throughout the world in future years.

The **United States Coast Guard Auxiliary** is a voluntary civilian organization of owners of boats, private airplanes, and shore radio stations; it is a non-military group although administered by the U.S. Coast Guard. It promotes safety in the operation of small craft through education, boat examinations, and operational activities.

Although uniformed and organized along military lines, and closely affiliated with the regular Coast Guard, the Auxiliary is strictly civilian in nature; it has no law enforcement powers. See color pages T and U for illustrations of USCG Aux flags and uniform insignia.

The Auxiliary carries on a program of free public instruction and members take specialty courses to increase their knowledge and abilities.

Courtesy Marine Examinations are a well-known program of the Coast Guard Auxiliary. Specially trained members conduct annual checks on boats, but only with the consent of the owner. Boats that meet a strict set of

FIG. 1001 The United States Power Squadrons is an organization of volunteers dedicated to making boating safer through education. Craft skippered by USPS members are usually identified by the distinctive flag, with blue and white vertical stripes, shown here at the starboard yardarm. The flag at the masthead identifies the owner as an officer of the USPS; in this case, the blue trident on a white field signifies Rear Commander.

requirements are awarded a distinguishing decal, fig. 1002. No report is made to the authorities of craft that fail to qualify; the owner is urged to remedy the defect and request a reexamination.

Operationally, the Auxiliary promotes safety afloat by assisting the Coast Guard in patrolling marine regattas and racing events. In many areas, the Auxiliary also participates in search and rescue for craft that are disabled, in distress, or have been reported overdue.

Information on public classes of the Auxiliary or membership in the organization may be obtained from the Flotilla in your vicinity or by writing to the appropriate Coast Guard District Headquarters; see fig. 1502, page 301.

More information on the USCG Aux will be found in Chapter 32.

The **American National Red Cross** offers programs of water safety education through its more than 3,000 local chapters in all areas of the country. The swimming and water safety skills taught by the Red Cross range from beginning through advanced swimmer, survival swimming, and life saving. (Many schools, YMCAs, and other organizations also teach these subjects by Red Cross methods and to its standards.) The small craft safety instructional programs include courses in canoeing, rowboating, outboard boating, and sailing.

Red Cross first aid training is also available to the public

FIG. 1002 The Coast Guard Aux-iliary makes Courtesy Marine Ex-aminations, but only with the consent of the craft's owner. Boats meeting all legal require-ments and certain additional safe-ty standards of the Auxiliary are awarded the "Seal of Safety" sticker for the current year.

FIG. 1003 Local chapters of the American National Red Cross teach swimming, lifesaving, and other water safety subjects to per-sons of all ages. Every boatman should set a personal goal of be-ing a competent swimmer and having enough lifesaving knowledge to help others in trouble in the water.

through local chapters. A wise skipper would do well to learn the proper action to be taken in cases of bleeding, fractures, stoppage of breathing, shock, burns, and other common emergencies.

Textbooks used in Red Cross training programs may be purchased from larger bookstores or through local chap-ters; all of these are valuable reference publications. Texts which are available include *Swimming and Water Safety, Lifesaving and Water Safety, First Aid, Basic Canoeing, Canoeing, Basic Rowing, Basic Outboarding*, and *Basic Sailing*; all are very reasonably priced.

The Red Cross publishes a variety of safety pamphlets and posters, and produces a number of informational and instructional films; these are made available to interested groups free of charge. Full information on classes, publi-cations, films, and other safety activities can be obtained from local chapters.

Equipment organizations

In addition to the national volunteer organizations working toward greater safety afloat through education, there are nonprofit groups within and related to the boat-ing industry that promote safety through higher standards for equipment, including its installation and use.

The **American Boat & Yacht Council, Inc.** is a nonprofit, public service organization founded for the purpose of "improving and promoting the design, construction, equipage, and maintenance of small craft with reference to their safety." Membership in the Council is open to anyone interested in furtherance of its objectives. Regular Mem-bers may serve in administrative offices and on administra-

FIG. 1004 The American Boat & Yacht Council, Inc. is a non-profit, public service organization founded to increase safety in the design, construction, equipment, and maintenance of small craft. It periodi-cally publishes a compilation of its "Safety Standards"—worthwhile reading for all skippers.

tive committees, but only Technical Members (highly qualified individuals) may serve on the Council's Technical Board and technical committees.

The American Boat & Yacht Council publishes "Safety Standards." These recommended specifications and practices are intended as good guidance toward making small craft as free from dangerous defect or deficiency as practicable in the interest of minimizing loss of life, injury, and loss of property. Standards are stated largely in terms of desired performance and are not intended to preclude attainment of the desired safety level by other means.

Safety Standards are prepared by Project Technical Committees formed as broadly based groups of recognized authorities with the objective of obtaining a maximum of agreement and acceptance. All technical reports and safety standards are advisory only; the Council has no powers of enforcement.

The AB&YC does not "approve" boats, equipment, materials, or services. Compliance with appropriate standards may be indicated by listings of nationally recognized testing laboratories whose findings may be used as a guide to approval. All standards are reviewed at intervals of three years, or more frequently if necessary because of comments received or advances in technology.

The American Boat & Yacht Council publishes its "Adopted" and "Proposed" standards as they complete a careful review and approval process. The standards are sent out as supplements to the complete compilation published in loose-leaf form. Included are standards for such diverse matters as "good visibility from the helm position," "life saving equipment," "engine exhaust systems," "electrical grounding of DC systems," "lightning protection," "sewerage treatment systems," and "distress signals." The full set of recommended practices is published as "Safety Standards for Small Craft," available for $35 from the Council at P.O. Box 806, 190 Ketcham Ave., Amityville, N.Y. 11701. The serious skipper can well devote some spare time to reading this volume; it is a good book to have on hand for reference.

The **Marine Department of Underwriters Laboratories, Inc.,** is the successor organization to the Yacht Safety Bureau. Underwriters Labs, well-known for its "UL" label, is a not-for-profit corporation that dates from 1894. This is neither a government agency nor a commercial enterprise. The Marine Department has its testing facilities at Tampa, Florida. It serves industry and the boating public by conducting safety investigations and tests of marine products, by developing Marine Safety Standards, and by preparing special Marine Supplements to UL Electrical Safety Standards. An important activity is the translation of written standards into properly engineered testing procedures.

The principal activity of the Marine Department is the testing of boating equipment for safety. This process be-

gins with the voluntary submittal by manufacturers of product samples. These are then tested for compliance with appropriate safety requirements and evaluated for overall design and construction in relation to the device's ultimate use. After a product has successfully completed a Marine Department evaluation, and complied with all of the UL requirements, a follow-up investigation is conducted at the factory to audit and counter-check the manufacturer's continuing production controls for compliance with UL requirements.

A device that passes all its tests is "Listed" by Underwriters Labs and may carry on both products and their advertising the UL "Listing Mark" consisting of the Laboratories name or symbol (see Fig. 1005), the product name, a control number, and the word "Listed." The name of the device is included, with the name of the manufacturer, in the annual UL Marine Product Directory. UL does not approve or disapprove anything. Listing is an expression of UL's good-faith opinion, based on tests, that the item meets minimum applicable safety standards. It is not a warranty of quality or performance, nor are all listed products of the same class necessarily equivalent in quality, performance, or merit.

The presence of a UL or UL Marine label on any device means that a production sample has been successfully evaluated to related safety requirements, and nothing else. The label may, however, be the basis on which "authorities having jurisdiction" grant approval. Such authorities include individuals making judgments for their own purposes, industry people making judgments for components or original equipment installations, marine surveyors for insurance purposes, and administrators of regulations making judgments required by law.

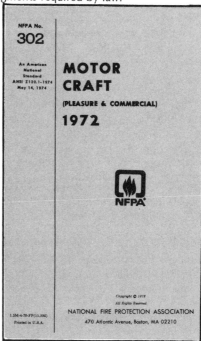

FIG. 1006 Fire Protection Standards for Motor Craft, No. 302, is a small yet valuable safety bulletin issued by the National Fire Protection Association. A copy should be studied by every boat owner and carried aboard as a useful reference document. See text for how a copy may be obtained.

FIG. 1005 Boating products that have passed a safety evaluation by the Marine Department of Underwriters Laboratories are "Listed." The UL Marine label can be used in advertising the items and may be found on them in form of a sticker, tag, etc. Periodic re-testing ensures the continued safety of all listed products.

Only products commercially available are eligible for listing. New products may be submitted in their model stage for evaluation, but no final listing action is taken until production units are submitted.

The **National Fire Protection Association** is an organization whose activities extend far beyond boating and marine interests to include all aspects of the science and methods of fire protection. NFPA issues codes, standards, and recommended practices for minimizing losses of life and property by fire.

NFPA does not approve, inspect, or certify any installations, procedures, equipment, or materials, nor does it approve or evaluate testing laboratories. It does prepare, by coordinated action of committees of experts, codes and standards for the guidance of all persons in the matter of fire protection. Frequently, NFPA codes and standards are written into law or regulations by various governmental units.

Of interest to boatmen is NFPA Fire Protection Standard No. 302 for Motor Craft (Pleasure and Commercial).

Originally isued in 1925, it has been amended and revised many times. This small booklet, available from the National Fire Protection Association, 470 Atlantic Ave., Boston, MA 02110, is a useful guide to any boat owner.

Construction for Safety

In one respect, safety afloat may be considered to start with the design and construction of the craft itself. The average skipper is not likely to build his own boat, but he should be able to recognize proper design features and sound construction characteristics. He should be at least broadly familiar with safe and unsafe aspects of boat construction—the points that should be checked in determining whether or not a particular craft, new or used, should be bought. There is little the average yachtsman can do directly to influence the design and construction of boats, but he can, through knowledge and careful inspection, avoid those that fail to measure up to desirable standards.

A boatman contemplating purchase of a used boat should seriously consider use of the services of a qualified marine surveyor. He is an expert in determining the condition of the hull, engine, and equipment. He may well discover hidden defects that the would-be buyer overlooked in his enthusiasm. An impartial survey is sound protection for a purchaser; the modest cost involved will be well-justified. Such a survey is often required to obtain insurance, particularly on older boats.

HULL CONSTRUCTION

Modern boats, built by reputable manufacturers, are basically seaworthy because they are honestly constructed to proven designs. This points out the proper course in the selection of a good, sound boat. There is no necessity of trying some freak of questionable worth. If you have no experience in selecting a boat, it is easy enough to avail yourself of the advice and guidance of others who are better qualified; be sure to talk to several persons to avoid personal biases.

Construction materials

For seaworthiness and safety, suitable materials for boatbuilding and highgrade construction are equally essential. Use of fire-retardant materials wherever practicable is suggested. Boats may be built equally well of wood, fiberglass, steel, or aluminum. Combinations of materials may also be used, such as a fiberglass superstructure on a wooden hull. It should be noted, too, that boats can also be built poorly in any of these materials. Many arguments can be made for and against each hull material, but basically the decision is one for the individual owner, considering the use of the boat, cost factors, maintenance, and not least, his personal preferences.

Water-tight bulkheads (or as tight as practicable) are recommended to isolate bilges of fuel and machinery spaces from those of living quarters. Where feasible, two means of exit should be provided from compartments where persons may congregate or sleep. Thus, in a small craft having only one cabin and cockpit, a forward hatch is a desirable feature.

FIG. 1007 Anti-slip protection on deck walkways and at boarding areas is a must for safety. This can be obtained from the natural qualities of the deck, ingredients added to the deck paint, or by applying special strips of material having a non-slip surface and an adhesive backing.

FIG. 1008 A well-made lifeline stanchion. The heavy flange has provision for four good-sized through bolts. The bails welded on fore and aft stiffen the structure and provide convenient tie points for ship's gear. The heavy-walled stanchion tube is drilled for both lower (shown) and upper lifelines and fitted with grommets to reduce chafe. The wire line is plastic covered.

FIG. 1009 Lifelines are important on all boats, but are an absolute must on offshore cruising and racing sailboats. The lines must have adequate strength and the stanchions must be securely through-bolted. Note how lines merge into metal pulpit rails at bow and stern.
(Photograph by Romaine-Skelton)

 Lifelines

Just because a boat is equipped with lifelines, do not assume they are ones you can rely on.

The stanchions should be well-made (fig. 1008A) and through-bolted. On lightly-framed wooden boats this poses something of a dilemma. You do not want the boat to come apart when a heavy crewman falls against the stanchion, but you don't want the stanchion to carry away, either. Don't rely simply on a backing-block up under the covering board in such cases, but make the stanchion bolts long enough to reach below the clamp into backing plates located there. On fiberglass boats you must rely on the quality of the deck construction, but check to be sure that each stanchion base bolts through into a generous backing block on the deck's undersurface.

The top lifeline should be high enough from the deck so it doesn't catch you behind the knees and assist you overboard.

Even if your lines and stanchions pass muster, don't necessarily conclude they are the best point of attachment for the snap of your safety harness in bad weather. Take a look at fig. 1009, above. In bad weather, a dock line stretched between the mooring cleat on the foredeck and the cleat on the stern would have a number of advantages as a point of attachment, primarily because it would allow you to move relatively freely about the deck without ever having to stop, unsnap and snap on again as you will have to do at each stanchion if you rely on the lifelines.

If you want to remain on good terms with the watch sleeping below, you will, for sure, have to hold your snap up off of the deck as you move about because if it drags along the deck, it makes a teeth-jarring racket below. Even so, that is a small price to pay for the added freedom and security.

Safety on deck

Weather decks, to be safe, must be wide enough for secure footing, must have a non-skid surface, must be provided with adequate handholds, and should be equipped with lifelines (see discussion at left).

Owners of offshore cruising sailboats would be wise to meet the requirements set by the United States Yacht Racing Union: Fixed bow and stern pulpits (unless lifelines are arranged to adequately substitute for a stern pulpit); pulpits and stanchions through-bolted or welded to the deck; taut, double life lines with wire upper line secured to pulpits and stanchions; pulpits and upper life line at least 24" (61 cm) above deck at any point; and stanchions not over 7' (2.1 m) apart except in the way of shrouds when the lifelines are permanently attached to the shrouds. The lifelines need not be affixed to the bow pulpit if they terminate at, or pass through, 24" high stanchions set inside of and overlapping the bow pulpit. These requirements are compatible with those of the American Boat & Yacht Council for lifelines and rails on both power and sail boats. There are also nine other AB&YC safety standards relating to hulls of small craft, all of which will make interesting reading to those seriously concerned with safety afloat.

Superstructure and stability

The mistaken notion that a boat can carry weight anywhere as long as she appears to trim right in the water must be corrected. Addition of more superstructure, such as a flying bridge, is particularly bad, as is the shifting of heavy weights such as motors, ballast, tanks, machinery, etc. Where stability is concerned, no shifts of major weights or changes in design should be considered without the advice of a qualified naval architect. Amateur boatbuilders sometimes ruin boats and reduce their safety factors by deviating from architect's plans in which the proportioning of weights has been given the most painstaking attention.

Through-hull fittings

Fittings which pass through the hull near or below the water line should have sea-cocks installed internally close to the planking to permit positive closing. It is desirable that solid, seagoing metal pipe extend from the sea-cock to a level above the water line, from which point flexible hoses may be run to the pump or other accessory. Where hose is placed over pipe nipples for connections, hose clamps should be used.

There are now available through-hull fittings and sea-cocks that have been safety evaluated by the Yacht Safety Bureau and "listed" by that organization. AB&YC Safety Standard A-2 furnishes additional information on these.

FIG. 1010 Seacocks are important items of safety equipment on boats of all sizes. Every through-hull fitting should have one for cutting off the entry of water in case of hose leakage or for working on equipment. Seacocks should be tested for easy shut-off action at least twice each year; adjust or replace without delay any seacock stuck in the open position.

Engines and Fuel Systems

Probably the first thought that comes to mind in connection with safety afloat is that of preventing fire and explosion. Fire is usually traceable to the engine room or galley where improper equipment, faulty installation, or careless operation is the direct cause. All of these are under the owner's control.

ENGINE INSTALLATION

Engines should be suited to the hulls they power. Extremes of underpowering and overpowering are both bad. Original installations and subsequent changes require the advice of a naval architect or one thoroughly familiar with this phase of boat design.

Conversions of automobile engines for marine duty by amateur mechanics are invariably a source of trouble because of basic differences between the two types. Lubrication and cooling are the chief problems. Selection of an accepted type of marine engine or a commercially-produced conversion is advisable.

Pans, preferably made of copper, are recommended for installation under the engine to catch any oil and grease drippings and prevent these from getting into the bilge. Accumulations should be removed promptly for fire safety.

FUEL SYSTEMS

The primary aspect of fuel system safety is the prevention of fires and explosion. Not to be forgotten, however, are the reliability aspects of the system that will ensure a continuous flow of clean fuel to the engine.

The discussion that follows will be principally concerned with boats using gasoline engines; exceptions and special requirements relating to diesel fuel systems will be covered separately.

Fire prevention

It is of primary importance that the entire fuel system be liquid- and vapor-tight with respect to the hull interior. Gasoline fumes, mixed with air, form an explosive combination. These fumes, several times heavier than air, settle to the bottom of the bilge. A concentration of gasoline in air as low as $1\frac{1}{4}\%$ can be exploded by a slight spark with tremendous effect—a half-teacup of gasoline can create

enough explosive vapor to totally destroy a large motorboat.

The obvious answer for safety is *prevention*—make it impossible for gasoline, either in liquid or gaseous form, to get into the bilge in the first place. Then keep the bilge clean and ventilate the engine compartment thoroughly, and there will be nothing that can be ignited.

Leakage of liquid gasoline into the bilge can be prevented by proper installation, using strongly built gasoline tanks, copper tubing for fuel lines, leakproof connections, tight fittings, and lengths of flexible metallic fuel hose to take care of vibration. Gasoline vapors created when the tanks are filled must be prevented from finding their way down through open hatches and companionways. Finally, avoidable sparks and flames should not be permitted in the engine room.

Carburetors

Carburetors must be equipped with flame arresters for protection against backfire; see fig. 1011. If not of the downdraft type, they should also have a pan covered with a fine mesh screen attached under the carburetor to collect any drip. Leakage will be sucked back into the engine if a copper tube is run from the bottom of the pan to the intake manifold. Flame arresters should be kept clean both for safety and best engine operation.

Air intakes to the engine compartment should be directed so that any backfires will not tend to blow into the bilges.

Fuel tanks

Fuel tanks should be permanently installed in such a manner as to be secure against moving about in a seaway. The use of portable tanks below decks is not good practice.

Fuel tanks must be constructed of a metal that is compatible with both the fuel and a normal marine environment. Copper, copper alloys of certain specific compositions, hot-dipped galvanized sheet steel, and terneplate steel are all used for gasoline tanks. In each case, construction, installation, and inspections should be in accordance with standards of the American Boat & Yacht Council. The AB&YC also provides specifications for fiberglass reinforced plastic tanks, but notes that "Compliance with these requirements does not necessarily guarantee acceptance by the authority having jurisdiction."

Gasoline tanks must not be integral with the hull. The shape of the tank should be such that there are no exterior pockets that would trap moisture after the tank is in its installed position. Tank bottoms must not have sumps or pockets in which water could accumulate.

Internal stiffeners and baffle plates will normally be used to provide necessary rigidity and resistance to surging of liquid in the tanks. Baffles must meet certain specified design criteria to prevent formation of liquid pockets in the bottom of tanks and vapor pockets in the tops.

There should be no drains or outlets for drawing off fuel from the tank, nor outlets or fittings of any type in the bottom, sides, or ends of tanks. Fuel lines to the engine should enter the tank at its top and internally extend nearly, but not quite all the way, to the bottom.

Fuel filler pipes and vents

One of the most essential requirements in the proper installation of a fuel system is that there be a completely tight connection between the gasoline tank and the filling plate on deck. The fuel fill must be located so any spillage will go overboard, not inside the hull, and tight pipe connections between deck plate and tank will prevent leakage or spillage below. Fill pipes, at least 1½" (3.8 cm) inside diameter, should run down inside the tank nearly to the bottom to lessen the production of vapors.

A suitable vent pipe for each tank should lead *outside the hull;* vents should *never* terminate in closed spaces such as the engine compartment or under the deck. Minimum inside diameter of vent pipes should be 9/16" (1.4 cm). Where a vent ends on the hull, the outlet should be fitted with a removable flame screen to protect against flash-backs from outside sources of ignition. In boats that normally heel, such as auxiliary sailboats, it may be necessary to have dual vents with the port tank vent led to the starboard side and vice versa.

Non-metallic hose may be used as a coupling between

FIG. 1011 Carburetors on marine engines (other than outboards) must be equipped with a flame arrester. Out of sight beneath the updraft carburetor shown above is a drip pan for further safety. Downdraft carburetors do not need such a pan.

sections of metallic piping. The hose must be reinforced or of sufficient thickness to prevent collapse. A grounding jumper wire must be installed across the non-conducting section so as to provide a complete electrical path from the deck fitting to the fuel tank, which in turn is grounded.

A fuel level indicator, if used, should be of an approved type. If the fuel supply for an auxiliary electric plant is not drawn from the main tank, the separate tank should be installed with fillers and vents similar to those of the main tank.

Fuel lines

Fuel lines should be of seamless copper tubing, run so as to be in sight as much as possible for ease of inspection, protected from possible damage, and secured against vibration by soft non-ferrous metal clips with rounded edges. A short length of flexible tubing with suitable fittings should be used between that part of the fuel line that is secured to the hull and that part which is secured to the engine itself; this will prevent leakage or breakage as a result of vibration.

Reinforced non-metallic hose in the fuel line should be limited to the short flexible section described above, but may be used for the full distance from the tank shutoff valve to the engine if the line is fully visible and accessible for its entire length. Wherever used, non-metallic hose must be dated by the manufacturer and not be used for a period longer than that recommended by the maker.

Tube fittings should be of non-ferrous drawn or forged metal of the flared type, and tubing should be properly flared by tools designed for the purpose, preferably annealing the tube end before flaring.

A shut-off valve should be installed in the fuel line directly at the tank connection. Arrangements should be provided for ready access and operation of this valve from outside the compartment in which tanks are located, preferably from above deck. Where engine and fuel tank are separated by a distance exceeding 12 feet, an approved-type manual stop-valve should be installed at the engine end of the fuel line to stop fuel flow when servicing accessories.

Valves should be of non-ferrous metal with ground seats installed to close against the flow. Types which depend on packing to prevent leakage at the stem should not be used. For fuel, gas, and oil lines a type of diaphragm packless valve is available which is pressure-tight in any position. A YSB-listed electric fuel valve shuts off the flow of gasoline whenever the ignition switch is turned off; it can also be independently turned off in an emergency.

Fuel pumps and filters

Electric fuel pumps, where used, should be located at the engine end of fuel lines. They must be so connected as to operate only when the ignition switch is on and the engine is turning over.

A filter should be installed in the fuel line inside the engine compartment, properly supported so that its weight is not carried by the tubing. Closure of the filter must be so designed that its opening for cleaning will minimize fuel spillage. It should also be designed so that the unit can be disassembled and reassembled in dim light without undue opportunity for crossing threads, displacing gaskets

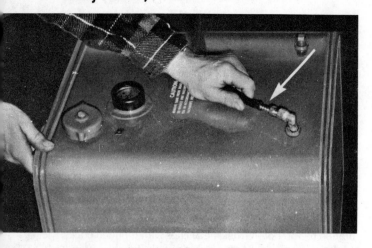

FIG. 1012 Portable gasoline tanks used with outboard motors may have a quick-disconnect fitting on the fuel line. This fitting must be designed so as to minimize leakage of gasoline when it is detached.

or seals, or assembly of parts in an improper order, resulting in seepage of fuel after reassembly. Fuel filter bowls should be highly resistant to shattering due to mechanical impact and resistant to failure from thermal shock.

Fuel systems for outboards

Fuel tanks and systems permanently installed in the hull of outboard-powered boats should be designed, constructed, and installed in accordance with the above principles. No pressurized tanks should be built into or permanently attached to hulls. A quick-disconnect coupling may be used between motor and fuel line but, when disconnected, it must automatically shut off fuel flow from the tank. Arrangements should be provided so that the operation of making and breaking the connection can be accomplished with a minimum of spillage.

Extreme caution must be exercised in the use of plastic containers for storing gasoline. These can accumulate a static electricity charge that is not drained off by grounding connections. A static electricity-generated spark could ignite vapors in the container.

Plastic containers, if used, should meet fire retardance and compatibility with fuel requirements of the AB&YC. Such containers will carry the approval of a national listing agency or a major city fire department. Do not use any other plastic container for gasoline or other flammable liquid. Any portable fuel container must be stowed on the boat in a well-ventilated place, protected from both physical damage and exposure to direct sunlight. Any leakage or vapors must drain overboard.

Every possible precaution must be taken to ensure that not even a single drop of gasoline can find its way into the bilge. Bilge ventilation is most important. It is a strict legal requirement and it is a vital safety measure; see pages 607 to 610.

Fuel systems of diesel-powered boats

Fuel systems of diesel-powered boats will generally conform to safety standards for gasoline-fueled craft, with a few exceptions as required or permitted by the nature of the fuel and characteristics of diesel engines.

Tanks for diesel fuel may be made of iron or steel as well as nickel-copper. Tanks may be painted if not galvanized externally; iron tanks must not be galvanized internally. Diesel tanks may have a sump or pocket in the bottom for collection of water but, if so, must have a positive means for removal of any accumulations from above deck. Tanks for diesel fuel may be integral with the hull.

Fuel lines for diesel oil may be of iron or steel pipe or tubing in addition to the metals approved for gasoline. A return line to carry excess fuel from the engine back to the tank will be needed.

Additional information

Many additional technical details on gasoline and diesel fuel systems for boats will be found in AB&YC Safety Standard P-2.

Underwriters Laboratories Marine Division has evaluated and accepted for listing a number of tanks, filters, valves, and related equipment by various manufacturers.

EXHAUST SYSTEMS

Exhaust lines and pipes should be installed so that they cannot scorch or ignite woodwork. Where necessary, gratings can be used to prevent gear from touching the line. Exhaust systems must be gas-tight, constructed and installed so that they can be inspected and repaired readily along their entire length. Any leaks must be rectified at once to prevent escape of exhaust gases into various compartments. *Carbon monoxide is a deadly gas.*

A "wet" exhaust system requires a continuous flow of cooling water (from the heat exchanger or the engine block) discharged through the exhaust line, entering as near the manifold as practicable. Exhaust systems of the "dry" type (no cooling water) operate at considerably higher temperatures and their use is relatively rare except on larger yachts.

An exhaust system should be run with a minimum number of bends. Where turns are necessary, long-sweep elbows or 45° ells are recommended. The exhaust system must not result in back pressure at the exhaust manifold greater than that specified by the engine manufacturer. A small pipe tap, located not more than 6" (15.2 cm) from the exhaust manifold outlet, should be provided for measuring back pressure.

The exhaust system should be designed to prevent undue stress on the exhaust manifold, particularly where an engine is shock-mounted. All supports, hangers, brackets, and other fittings in contact with the exhaust should be noncombustible and so constructed that high temperatures will not be transmitted to wood or other combustible materials to which fittings are secured.

The exhaust piping or tubing should have a continuous downward pitch of at least ½" per foot (1 cm per 24 cm) when measured with the vessel at rest. It must be so designed and installed as to eliminate any possibility of having cooling water or sea water return to the engine manifold through the exhaust system.

Exhaust systems for sailboat engines

Exhaust systems for auxiliary sailing craft should be carefully designed to prevent sea or cooling water from running back into the engines because such engines are usually installed close to or below the water line. A riser must

TYPICAL SAILBOAT EXHAUST SYSTEM

WATER JACKETED
EXHAUST RISER

WATER DISCHARGED INTO
EXHAUST AT THIS POINT

EXHAUST MANIFOLD

WATER LINE

FIG. 1013 The AB&YC Safety Standard for small-craft exhaust systems has special provisions for auxiliary-powered sailboats. Unusual precautions must be taken in such installations as the engine is often below the waterline and a normally-sloping exhaust line cannot be installed.

reach sufficiently high above the water line to allow a steep drop-off of at least 12″ (30.4 cm); the remaining piping should have a downward pitch to the outlet of at least ½″ per foot (1 cm in 24). The high point should be a goose neck, with cooling water injected aft of this point; see fig. 1013. The vertical dry section must be either adequately insulated and provided with a metallic bellows flexible section or water-jacketed. As an alternate arrangement, a water-trap silencer is recommended.

Flexible exhaust lines

Steam hose or other non-metallic material may be used for exhaust lines where greater flexibility is desired. Every flexible line of this type must be secured with adequate clamps of corrosion-resistant metal at each end. Hose used for this purpose must have a wall thickness and rigidity sufficient to prevent panting (internal separation of plies) or collapse. Full-length nonmetallic exhaust tubing may be used in wet exhaust systems providing it is water-cooled throughout its length and is not subjected to temperature above 280°F (138°C). Tubing used for exhaust service should be specifically constructed for that purpose and so labeled by the manufacturer. Tubing should be installed in a manner that will not stress or crimp the inner or outer plies, or permit any local impingement of exhaust gases or cooling water.

Additional information

The AB&YC Safety Standard P-1 provides much additional information on "wet" and "dry" exhaust installations. It should be studied by persons building or rebuilding any boat equipped with an inboard engine.

ELECTRICAL SYSTEMS

The entire electrical installation should comply rigidly with the best and most modern safety practices. Requirements of marine installations are more exacting than other applications where salt- and moisture-laden atmospheres are not prevalent. Wiring and other electrical equipment should be installed correctly in the beginning and kept safe by frequent inspection.

Information on electrical systems will also be found in chapter 25 on pages 487 and 488.

The sources of electrical power for engine starting, lights, pumps, electronic gear, and other electrical accessories are usually lead-acid storage batteries kept charged by a generator or alternator integral with the main engine. Larger craft equipped with electrical cooking and air-conditioning will have a separate engine-driven generator producing AC electrical power similar to shore current. The discussion in this section will be directed to the more-common 12- and 32-volt DC electrical systems found on all boats, even though also equipped with AC power.

All direct-current electrical systems should be of the two-wire type with feed and return wires parallel throughout the system. Conductors should be twisted together where their magnetic field would affect compasses or automatic pilots. Where one side of a DC system is grounded, connections between that side and ground should be used only to maintain that side at ground potential and should not normally carry current.

Wiring diagrams

All boats should be provided with a complete wiring diagram of the electrical system as originally installed. It is recommended that the diagram be enclosed in a suitable plastic envelope and secured to an accessible panel door, preferably near the main switchboard. Diagrams should include an indication of the identification provided for each conductor.

Additions to and/or changes in electrical circuits should be drawn in on the wiring diagram without delay so that it is correct at all times.

Batteries

Storage batteries should be so located that gas generated during charging will be quickly dissipated by natural or mechanical ventilation. They should be located as high as practicable, where they are not exposed to excessive heat, extreme cold, spray, or other conditions which could impair performance or accelerate deterioration. Caution should be taken to avoid locating batteries in areas subject to accumulation of gasoline fumes and also in proximity to any electrical or electronic devices. Engine starting batteries should be located as close to the engine as practicable.

Batteries must be secure against shifting. Care also should be taken to secure a battery against vertical motion which would allow it to pound against the surface on which it is resting while cruising in rough water. Batteries should be chocked on all sides and supported at the bottom by non-absorbent insulating supports of a material that will not be affected by contact with electrolyte. These supports should allow air circulation all around. Where the hull or compartment material in the immediate vicinity of the battery is aluminum, steel, or other material readily attacked by the acid, a tray of lead, fiberglass, or other suitable material resistant to the deteriorating action of electrolyte should be provided.

Batteries should be arranged to permit ready access for inspection, testing, watering, and cleaning. A minimum of 10″ clear space above the filling openings should be available.

A non-conductive, ventilated cover or other suitable means should be provided to prevent accidental shorting

FIG. 1014 Storage batteries should have a cover to protect terminals from being shorted by an accidentally dropped tool or other metal object. Such covers must be ventilated to prevent accumulation of gases during charging.

of the battery's terminals; fig. 1014.

An emergency switch capable of carrying the maximum current of the system (including starter circuits) should be provided in each ungrounded conductor as close to the battery terminal connection as practicable. This switch should be readily accessible; a switch with a remote operating handle that can be opened or closed from the bridge or other location outside the compartment containing the batteries is highly desirable.

Generators and motors

Generators, alternators, and electric motors intended for use in machinery spaces or other areas which might contain flammable or explosive vapors must be designed and constructed so as to prevent such devices from becoming a source of ignition of these vapors. These units must be of a type approved for marine service.

Generators, alternators, and electric motors must be located in accessible, adequately ventilated areas as high above the bilge as possible. They must not be located in low or pocketed positions.

Ground connections from battery to starter should be made as close to the starter as possible. It is recommended that all other ground connections to the engine be made at this same point. By making all ground connections at one point, damaging stray-current flow through the metal of the engine will be minimized.

Distribution panels and switches

Switchboards and distribution panels should be located in accessible, adequately ventilated locations, preferably outside of engine and fuel-tank compartments. They should be protected from rain and spray; where necessary, panels should be provided with a drip shield to prevent wetting of terminals or electrical components from overhead dripping.

Totally enclosed switchboards and distribution panels of the dead-front type are recommended. Metal enclosures are desirable, but wood may be used if all terminal strips,

fuse blocks, switches, etc., are mounted on non-absorbent, non-combustible, high-dielectric insulating material. It is recommended that the interior of enclosures be lined with asbestos sheet or other fire-resistant material.

All switches should have suitable electrical ratings for the particular circuits on which they are used; distribution panels should have several spare switches to take care of additional equipment that may be added later.

Switches used in fuel-tank and machinery spaces, or other hazardous locations, must be designed so as to prevent ignition of flammable or explosive vapors. Such switches must be of a type approved for marine use.

Wiring

Conductors used for general wiring throughout the boat should be approved for marine use to indicate adequate mechanical strength, moisture resistance, dielectric strength, insulation, and current-carrying capacity for the intended marine service.

The table of wire gauges on page 488, fig. 2504, is for an allowable voltage drop of 3% on a 12-volt system. For lighting and other non-critical purposes, the wire size shown there may be reduced to the gauges shown in fig. 1015 (wire gauge number varies *inversely* with conductor size). The "length" for these tables is the distance from the source to the load, one way, measured along the route followed by the wires; this is much greater than the direct distance—don't estimate; measure.

Current in Amps.	Length of Wire, in feet					
	10	15	20	30	40	50
5	16	16	16	14	14	12
10	16	14	14	12	10	10
15	14	14	12	10	8	8
20	14	12	10	8	6	6
25	10	10	10	8	6	6

Fig. 1015 Table above, extracted from AB&YC Safety Standard E-9, 1975, specified the wire gauge to be used versus conductor length for a voltage drop of not more than 10% in a 12-volt system. This drop is satisfactory for all but the most critical electronic equipment. For such critical applications, see Fig. 2504 which provides for a drop not exceeding 3%. (1 foot = 0.305 m).

All wiring must be routed as high above the bilge as possible with consideration given to protection of wire and connections from physical damage. Wiring should be secured throughout its length, at intervals not exceeding 14 inches, in a manner that will not crush or cut insulation around the conductor. Non-metallic clamps are excellent; if metallic clamps are used, they must be lined with a suitable insulating material. All non-metallic material must be resistant to the effects of oil, gasoline, and water.

Unless absolutely necessary, wire splices should not be made in any circuit vital to the operation of the boat nor in the navigation light circuit. Splices, where made, should be taped to relieve all strain from the joint. If solder is used, it should be a low-temperature resin-core radio solder. Acid-core solder must *not* be used.

Terminal connections

Terminal connections should be designed and installed so as to insure a good mechanical and electrical joint without damage to conductors. Metals used for terminal studs, nuts, and washers should be corrosion-resistant and galvanically compatible with the wire and terminal lug.

Terminals should be of solderless type, preferably with ring-type ends. Solderless terminals should be attached with crimping tools specified by the manufacturer of the terminal. The holes in ring-type terminals should be of a size that will properly fit the terminal stud. Formed and soldered wire terminal connections should not be used. It is recommended that terminal lugs include a means of clamping the wire insulation for mechanical support. A short length of insulated sleeving over the wire at each terminal connection is desirable.

No more than four conductors should be secured to any one terminal stud. Where additional connections are necessary, two or more terminal studs should be used and connected together with copper jumpers or straps.

Wires terminating at switchboards, in junction boxes or fixtures, etc., should be arranged to provide a surplus length of wire sufficient to relieve all tension, allow for repairs, and permit multiple wires to be fanned at terminal studs, etc.

Electrical shock hazards

Voltage is only one factor in determining whether a shock will be fatal or only startling. Many people have received shocks from spark-plugs, where the voltage is 10,000 or more, with no more harm than a few bruised knuckles. The actual factors that determine the extent of harm are: (1) the amount of current that flows through the body, the amperage; (2) the path of the current through the body; and (3) the length of time that the current flows.

The effects of different levels of current are not exact and will vary with the individual victim and the path of current through his body. Unfortunately, there is no way of predicting in advance how much current will flow in any given situation—play safe, work only on de-energized circuits.

Additional information

Further guidance and recommendations for DC electrical systems for boats will be found in Safety Standards E-1, E-3, E-5, E-6, E-9, and E-10 issued by the American Boat & Yacht Council.

AC electrical systems

More and more boats are being wired for 115-volt AC electrical systems so that larger, home-type appliances and equipment may be used afloat. Power may be obtained from dockside connections only or from such sources plus an engine-driven generator for use while under way. From a safety viewpoint, it is important to recognize the increased hazards from this higher-voltage wiring and devices.

All component parts of a 115-volt AC system must be designed, constructed, and installed so as to perform with safety under environmental conditions of continuous exposure to vibration, mechanical shock, corrosive salt atmosphere, and high humidity. The system must provide maximum protection against electrical shock for persons on the boat, in the water in contact with the boat, or in contact with the boat and a grounded object on shore.

Appliances and fixed AC electrical equipment used on boats must be designed so that current-carrying parts of the device are effectively insulated from all exposed metal parts by a dielectric material suitable for use in damp and/or wet locations as determined by location of the item and its intended use.

Further technical specifications for AC electrical systems on boats will be found in AB&YC Safety Standard E-8. Portions of standards E-3, E-5, and E-6 are also applicable.

LIGHTNING PROTECTION

One seldom hears of a boat, power or sail, being struck by lightning, yet cases have been reported. A skipper can add to both his physical safety and his peace of mind by obtaining some basic information and taking a few precautionary actions.

FIG. 1016 Under *certain* conditions, a grounded radio antenna can provide a "cone of protection" from lightning strikes for a boat and its occupants. See text for details.   (from A.B. & Y.C. Safety Standards)

Protective principles

A grounded conductor, or lightning protective mast, will generally divert to itself direct lightning strokes which might otherwise fall within a cone-shaped space, the apex of which is the top of the conductor or mast and the base a circle at the water's surface having a radius approximately twice the conductor's height. Probability of protection is considered to be 99.0% within this 60° angle as shown in fig. 1016. Probability of protection can be increased to 99.9% if mast height is raised so that the cone apex angle is reduced to 45°.

To provide an adequately grounded conductor or protective mast, the entire circuit from the masthead to the ground (water) connection should have a conductivity equivalent to a #8 gauge wire. The path to ground followed by the conductor should be essentially straight, with no sharp bends.

If there are metal objects of considerable size within a few feet of the grounding conductor, there will be a strong tendency for sparks or side flashes to jump from the grounding conductor to the metal object at the nearest point. To prevent such possibly damaging flashes, an interconnecting conductor should be provided at all likely places.

Large metallic objects within the hull or superstructure of a boat should be interconnected with the lightning protective system to prevent a dangerous rise of voltage due to a lightning flash.

Protective measures

For power boats, a radio antenna may serve as a lightning or protective mast provided it is equipped with a transmitting-type lightning arrester or means for grounding during electrical storms, and that the antenna height is sufficient to provide an adequate cone of protection for the length of the craft. Antennas with loading coils are considered to end at a point immediately *below the coil* unless the coil has a suitable gap for bypassing lightning current. This protection can be obtained *only* with an antenna of metal rod or tubing. Fiberglass whip antennas with an internal wire conductor—almost universally used for VHF, CB, or SSB—will *not* provide lightning protection.

Sailboats with metallic standing rigging will be adequately protected provided that all rigging is bonded together and connected to ground. A wooden mast must have a heavy metal conductor running down the mast from a short, sharp-pointed "lightning rod" at the masthead; this conductor is tied into the grounding system.

Metal objects situated wholly on a boat's exterior should be connected to the grounding conductor at their upper or nearest end. Metal objects within the boat may be connected to the lightning protective system directly or through the bonding system for underwater metal parts.

Metal objects that project through cabin tops, decks, etc., should be bonded to the nearest lightning conductor at the point where the object emerges from the boat and again at its lowest extreme end within the boat. Spotlights and other objects projecting through cabin tops should be solidly grounded regardless of the cone of protection.

A ground connection for lightning protection may consist of any metal surface, normally submerged, which has an area of at least one square foot. Propellers and metallic rudder surfaces may be used for this purpose; the radio ground plate is more than adequate. A steel hull itself constitutes a good ground connection to the water.

Protection for personnel

As the basic purpose of lightning protection is safety of personnel, the following precautions should be taken by the crew and guests.

Individuals should remain inside a closed boat as much as practicable during an electrical storm.

Persons should avoid making contact with any items connected to a lightning protective conductor, and especially in such a way as to bridge between two parts of the grounding system. For example, it is undesirable to touch either the reverse lever or spotlight control, particularly in contact with both at the same time.

No one should be in the water during a lightning storm.

Equipment for Safety

Some items of safety equipment are required by laws and Coast Guard regulations. These are generally written, however, in such broad language that additional knowledge and guidance are required for the greatest degree of safety afloat.

Additional items of equipment above legal minimums are required to receive the approval decal of the Coast Guard Auxiliary Courtesy Marine Examination.

Still further pieces of equipment are desirable for safety, or convenience, or both. Many of these are discussed in Chapter 3 and other chapters. This chapter will supplement rather than duplicate equipment considerations covered elsewhere in the book.

LIFESAVING EQUIPMENT

As noted in Chapter 3, each boat must, by law, have a personal flotation device (PFD) for each person on board, and water skiers towed behind are counted as being "on board." A wise skipper does not skimp on the quality or quantity of his PFDs, making sure that he has enough even if a few unexpected guests show up.

Recreational boats less than 16 feet in length (and canoes and kayaks of any length) must have one approved PFD of Type I, II, III, or IV for each person on board. (See pages 53-54 for discussion of the various "Types.")

Recreational boats 16 feet or more in length (except canoes and kayaks) must have at least one approved PFD of Type I, II, or III for each person on board. Boats of this length category must *additionally* have at least one Type IV "throwable" PFD. (Buoyant cushions may be used to meet the requirement for the "throwable" device, but are not acceptable toward the basic "one per person on board" requirement.)

Where the type of PFD that is carried comes in sizes, such as adult and children's life preservers, and the three sizes of buoyant vests, the PFD used to meet the requirements of the regulations must be of an "appropriate" size for the person for whom it is intended.

Although the regulations allow a choice from three or four categories of PFDs, the truly safety-conscious skipper will choose Type I. This type provides the maximum buoyancy and will hold a person's face clear of the water so that he can breathe even though unconscious.

PUMPS AND BAILERS

Oddly enough, there are no federal legal requirements for a boat (if used exclusively for pleasure) to be equipped with a device of any type for removing water that leaks in or comes aboard as spray. Essentially all boats are, of course, equipped with some form of pump or bailer, but too many skippers place their *full* dependence on electrical bilge pumps, and perhaps on only one of those. Once water rises in the bilge to a level sufficient to short out the battery, there is no way to combat the further rise of water. (Incidentally, on most boats the batteries are placed low in the bilge—excellent for stability, but not for safety if the craft starts taking on water.)

FIG. 1017 Life jackets of the type shown provide a greater measure of safety than other lifesaving devices that may be acceptable on small craft. Properly worn, they will not only provide buoyancy but will float an individual in the best position for breathing. As these are strapped to the person, he cannot lose his grasp as he could with a buoyant cushion. Two children's sizes are also available.
(Courtesy Atlantic-Pacific Mfg. Corp.)

Only the smallest boats should depend on a hand bailer or bucket. Other boats should be equipped with a hand-operated pump of generous capacity. Such an item can be either a fixed installation or a portable pump stowed where it can be quickly and easily reached when needed.

DISTRESS SIGNALING EQUIPMENT

A boat's radiotelephone is probably the most often used means of summoning assistance in an emergency. Use of the radio for this purpose is covered on pages 500–503. Visual distress signal requirements are on page 59.

Without special equipment a distress signal can be made to other craft in sight by standing where one is clearly visible and slowly raising and lowering one's arms. Another visual distress signal is a fluorescent red-orange rectangular panel displayed where most visible to boats and/or aircraft. This item of safety equipment is described more fully on page 87.

Signal flares may be projected several hundred feet into the air by a special type of pistol, or to a lesser height from a pocket "tear gas" gun that resembles an old-fashioned fountain pen. The laws of several states regulate possession of these and similar explosive projectile devices; check carefully before putting one aboard, but if permissible, these are effective and desirable items of safety equipment.

There are also hand-held flares of the single- and double-ended types, the latter producing a bright flame at one end for night use and a dense smoke at the other end for day distress situations. Before using any flare, read all instructions carefully so as to avoid personal injury or aggravation of the emergency. Read carefully *before* any emergency arises, you won't have time then!

MISCELLANEOUS ITEMS OF SAFETY EQUIPMENT

There are many small items of equipment that serve to increase safety and convenience.

Every boat should be equipped with several **flashlights** and at least one battery-powered **electric lantern,** fig. 1019. If provided with an adjustable head, the beam can be directed where needed. Flashlights should be distributed so as to be quickly available in an emergency. One should be within reach of the skipper's bunk and the first mate's, too. There should also be a flashlight in the guest cabin, if any, and another on the bridge. The electric lantern should be kept in an accessible place. Batteries in all units should be checked at least monthly to be sure that they have sufficient power. All should be completely waterproof.

An installed searchlight of adequate intensity is desirable on medium-sized and large boats operated at night. It is useful both in routine navigation and docking, and in emergencies such as man-overboard situations or assisting another boat in distress. On smaller boats, the electric lantern can serve as a hand-held searchlight.

FIG. 1018 A night distress signal will be seen at much greater distances if projected to a height of several hundred feet. Flare pistols and related devices will do this, but in some states these items of boating safety equipment are subject to firearms laws and regulations.
(Courtesy Abercrombie & Fitch)

FIG. 1019 An electric lantern should be aboard every boat. If provided with adjustable head, it projects a stronger beam of light than most flashlights and has the added advantage of being able to be set down with the light directed where needed, thus making both hands available for working.

FIG. 1020 Every boat should have aboard some emergency drinking water and food. The quantity and type of these supplies will vary, of course, with the number of persons aboard and the cruising area. Prepared kits of long shelf-life food and water can be purchased, or the boat owner can assemble his own supplies. (Courtesy Winslow Company Marine Products)

Boats of medium or large size should have on board a small **hand axe** to be used in cutting lines in an emergency. The axe should be stowed on deck, where it might be needed in a hurry.

Tools and **spare parts** for the engine and major accessories can be considered parts of a boat's essential safety equipment. Personal experience and conversation with seasoned skippers will offer the best guidance to just what tools and parts should be carried aboard any particular craft. Insofar as practicable, tools should be of rust-proof metal; tools susceptible to rust or corrosion, and all spare parts, should be properly protected from adverse effects of a marine environment.

All but the smallest craft should be equipped with **emergency drinking water** and **food** supplies. The amount will vary with the number of persons normally on board. The type of food is not important—anything will do when you get hungry enough! Non-perishability over a long period is important, but it might be wise once each year to consume your emergency supplies (a shipwreck party?) *after* they have been replaced with a fresh stock. Such items can usually be purchased from marine supply stores or from Army-Navy surplus stores; food should be simple and compact, but sustaining and energy-producing.

First aid kits are essential safety items; they will be considered in more detail later in this chapter.

Navigation equipment, charts, and **ground tackle** are all items of safety equipment, but each is considered in detail elsewhere in this book, see index.

SAFETY ASPECTS OF OTHER EQUIPMENT

Several items generally found on boats are not "safety equipment" per se, but have definite aspects of safety about their design, installation, or operation that must be considered by boat owners.

Galley stoves

All boatmen seem to love to eat, especially when out on the water. Cabin boats will normally have a galley, the degree of size and elaborateness varying with the design and use of the craft.

Galley stoves should be designed, manufactured, and approved for marine use. Types of fuel that are ordinarily used include alcohol, electricity, and liquified petroleum gas (LPG—normally propane or butane). Stoves fueled with kerosene, coal, wood, or canned heat (solidified alcohol) are only rarely seen now. Gasoline is *not* a safe stove fuel and should *never* be used on a boat.

Electricity is probably the safest source of heat for cooking, but an auxiliary generating plant is required to produce the large amounts of AC power required. Because of the inexpensive and simple nature of the equipment, alcohol stoves are widely used on boats despite their rather high fuel costs; with moderate and reasonable precautions, such installations can be quite safe. Plain water will extinguish alcohol fires.

LPG stoves are excellent for cooking, but can present a serious safety hazard unless installed and operated in accordance with strict rules—their use is prohibited on certain classes of commercial vessels.

FIG. 1021 This galley stove installation shows the use of insulating board behind, beside, and below the stove to protect woodwork from unsafe high temperatures. The stove also has a drip pan beneath it, another safety feature.

Stoves should be permanently and securely fastened in place when in operation. Portable stoves are not recommended; if one must be used, it should be secured temporarily while in use. Adequate ventilation should be provided to prevent any excess rise in temperature of an area in which a stove is operated for extended periods of time (for the sake of safety as well as the cook's comfort!). All woodwork or other combustible material directly above or immediately surrounding a stove, including smoke stacks, must be effectively protected with non-combustible sheathing; see fig. 1021. A recommended means is the use of ⅛" (3.1 mm) asbestos board covered by sheet metal.

Fuel for alcohol and kerosene stoves may be supplied to the burners either by gravity or pressure systems provided fuel tanks cannot be filled while the burners are in operation except where the supply tank is remote from burners and the filling operation will not introduce a fire hazard. A removable or accessible liquid-tight metal drip pan at least ¾" (1.9 cm) deep should be provided under all burners. Pressure tanks should have suitable gauges and/or relief valves.

Refrigeration

Ice is used on many boats as a means of keeping food fresh and for cooling beverages. It offers no safety hazards, but water from melting ice should be piped overboard rather than into the bilge. Fresh-water drip tends to promote dry rot. A collection sump, with pump, may be used if desired.

Mechanical refrigeration will normally be of the electric-motor-driven compressor type similar to units found in the home. Occasionally, a compressor will be belt-driven from a main engine, but this is rare.

Safety aspects of mechanical refrigeration include use of a non-toxic and non-flammable refrigerant, non-sparking motors, safety valves on high-pressure portions of the system, and general construction adequate to survive rigors of marine service.

Kerosene and bottled-gas refrigerators have a constant small open flame. This can produce an explosion hazard, and the use of such absorption-type units is presently excluded from the AB&YC Safety Standard A-6.

Heaters

Cabin heaters are sometimes used on boats in northern waters to extend the boating season or to ward off the chill of a sudden cold snap. Gasoline should never be used as a fuel and portable kerosene or alcohol heaters are not recommended. Built-in electrical heaters are safe; portable electrical heaters should be used only if secured in place while in operation.

Any heater discharging combustion products must be vented through a stovepipe and a charley noble set in a water-cooled deck plate or other fire-preventive fitting. Many sailors favor coal or charcoal-burning heaters, despite the mess they create and the problems of storing fuel, because of the even, dry heat they deliver, which can keep a cabin warm, dry and cheerful despite rain and fog outside.

Gas-burning heaters should be equipped with an automatic device to shut off the fuel supply if the flame is extinguished. Pilot lights should not be used. Coast Guard regulations prohibit use of LPG fuel for any purpose on certain commercial craft.

Many models of air-conditioning equipment used on boats are of the "reverse cycle" or "heat pump" type and can supply warmth rather than cooling when the former is needed. This is a thoroughly safe method of heating.

Safety in Operations

Safety should be a part of every aspect of the operation of small craft. Boat handling has been covered in Chapter 8. Safety in such operations as stranding and towing was considered in Chapter 9. Navigation and piloting—essential for safety—are discussed in Chapter 21 and other chapters. The aspects of operational safety afloat to be considered here are those that do not fall under other major headings.

FUELING PRECAUTIONS

Certain precautions must be carefully and completely observed *every* time a boat is fueled with gasoline. Step by step, these are:

Before fueling

1. Make sure that the boat is securely tied to the fueling pier. Fuel before darkness, if possible.

2. Stop engines, motors, fans, and other devices capable of producing a spark. Open the master switch if the electrical system has one. Put out all galley fires and open flames.

3. Close all ports, windows, doors, and hatches so that fumes cannot blow aboard and below.

4. Disembark all passengers and any crew members not needed for the fueling operation.

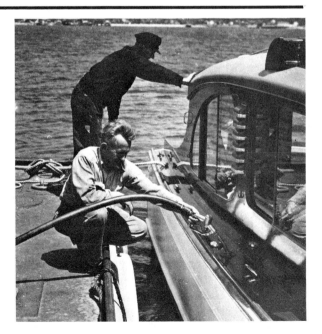

FIG. 1022 Fueling must be accomplished in a safe manner to reduce hazards of gasoline explosion and fire. Refer to the text for a 16-point checklist of actions before, during, and after fueling.

5. Prohibit all smoking on board and in the vicinity.

6. Have a filled fire extinguisher close at hand.

7. Measure the fuel in the tanks and do not order more than the tank will hold; allow for expansion.

While fueling

8. Keep nozzle or can spout in contact with the fill opening to guard against static sparks.

9. Do not spill gasoline.

10. Do not overfill. The practice of filling until fuel flows from the vents is highly dangerous.

11. For outboards, remove portable tanks from boat and fill on shore.

After fueling

12. Close fill openings.

13. Wipe up any spilled gasoline; dispose of wipe-up rags on shore.

14. Open all ports, windows, doors, and hatches; turn on bilge power exhaust blower. Ventilate boat this way at *least* five minutes—time it, don't guess.

15. Sniff low down in tank and engine compartments. *If any odor of gasoline is present, do not start engine;* continue ventilation actions until odor can no longer be detected.

16. Be prepared to cast off lines as soon as engine starts; get clear of pier quickly.

SAFETY IN LOADING

Overloading is probably the greatest cause of accidents in smaller boats and dinghies, and is even a significant factor in medium-size boats such as those of Class 2. Overloading is particularly hazardous as it is not so feared as are fires and explosions. Many a skipper, cautious in his handling of gasoline, will unknowingly load his craft far beyond safe limits. The number of seats in a boat is *not* an indication of the number of persons it can carry safely.

Determining capacity

"Loading" and "capacity" are terms primarily related to the weight of persons, fuel, gear, etc., that can be safely carried. The safe load of a boat in persons depends on many of its characteristics, such as the hull volume and dimensions; the material of which it is built, if it is an outboard hull, whether there is an effective engine well inboard of the transom notch where the engine is mounted; how heavy the engine is; and other factors.

BIA capacity plates. Many small boats manufactured before 31 October 1972 *may* carry a "capacity plate" in accordance with standards of the Boating Industry Association. These show the recommended maximum loading in terms of number of persons and in total weight (pounds) for gear, fuel, persons, and outboard motors.

USCG capacity plates. Boats under 20 feet in length—inboard, outboard, inboard-outboard, and unpowered, other than sailboats and certain special types—manufactured after 31 October 1972 *must* carry a capacity plate specified by Coast Guard regulations issued under the Federal Boat Safety Act of 1971. These capacities are computed from rather complex formulas. Plates on outboard craft show both maximum weight for persons (and, since 1980, maximum number of persons) and the total maximum weight for motor, fuel, gear, *and persons*. Plates for in-

---

```
┌─────────────────────────────────────┐
│         U. S. COAST GUARD           │
│     MAXIMUM CAPACITIES              │
│─────────────────────────────────────│
│  XX PERSONS OR XXX LBS              │
│  X X X LBS PERSONS, MOTORS, GEAR    │
│  X X X H.P. MOTOR                   │
└─────────────────────────────────────┘
```

FIG. 1023 A Coast Guard required capacity plate for outboard boats. The horsepower limit may be stated as separate figures for with or without remote steering. For inboards and I-Os, the horsepower limit is omitted, as is the motor weight from the last line of the plate. Compliance with safety standards may be certified on this plate, or on a separate plate.

board, inboard-outboard, and unpowered craft show only the maximum weight for fuel, gear, and persons. A capacity plate must be displayed where it is visible to the operator when he is getting the craft underway.

If there is no capacity plate on a boat, the skipper can make a rough determination for himself by applying the formulas for safe capacity in persons and weight-carrying capacity which are given on page 551.

Capacities from plates or self-determination are based on good weather conditions and should be reduced in rough waters. The presence of a capacity plate does not relieve the boatman of the responsibility for exercising sound judgment. This includes knowledge of probable future weather conditions as well as those prevailing at the start of a period of use of the boat.

Safe loading

It must always be remembered that people represent a "live" load (no pun intended); they move about and affect a boat quite differently than a "dead" or static load such as the engine or fuel tank. If the capacity of the boat is fully utilized, or the weather gets rough, distribute the load evenly, keep it low, and don't make abrupt changes in its distribution. Any shifting of human or other weights should be done only after stopping or slowing the boat so that the change can be made safely.

Horsepower capacity

A second aspect of the capacity of an outboard boat is the maximum horsepower motor that can be *safely* put on it. This is exceeded perhaps as often as the weight-carrying capacity. The safe maximum horsepower will also be included on both the older BIA and the newer USCG regulation capacity plates. If a boat does not have such a plate, the maximum horsepower can be determined from the tables and graphs on pages 554 and 555.

The maximum horsepower that is safe need not be used; most boats will give satisfactory, and more economical, service with motors of less horsepower. A larger engine does not always mean more speed. If the horsepower of the engine is doubled, it does not mean that boat speed will be doubled. It does mean, however, that because of the increased weight of the engine, fuel and accessories it will require, the number of persons that can be safely carried will be significantly reduced.

Boarding a boat

There is a safe way to step aboard a small boat—outboard or dinghy—and an unsafe way. In boarding from a pier, step into the boat as near to the center as possible, keeping body weight low. If you're boarding from a beach, come in over the bow. Keep lines tight or have someone steady the boat.

Never jump into a boat or step on the gunwale (edge of the hull). If you have a motor or other gear to take aboard, pile it on the pier so that you can easily reach it from the center of the boat. Better still, have someone hand it to you after you're aboard.

SAFETY IN THE WATER

Anyone who goes boating regularly should know how to care for himself in the water. Fortunately, most boatmen and their families do know "how to swim," but this is often limited to taking a few strokes in a calm, relatively warm pool, with safety and rest only a few feet away. More attention should be given to staying afloat under adverse conditions of water temperature, waves, etc. Seldom is it necessary, or even desirable, to "swim" any distance; the problem is that of remaining afloat until help arrives. The skipper and crew should all have instructions in "drownproofing."

Safety *in* the water can well start with swimming and/or lifesaving class at the local "Y" or community recreation center. Local chapters of the American Red Cross also give instruction in these subjects.

Lifesaving devices

A person in the water following a boating accident should, of course, have a life jacket or buoyant cushion. It is of extreme importance that these devices be worn or used properly. Buoyant cushions are far from the best flotation device, but are widely used because of their convenience and low cost. Buoyant cushions are *not* intended to be worn. The straps on a buoyant cushion are put there primarily for holding-on purposes and also to aid in throwing the device. Because they must be grasped, cushions are

not suitable for small children or injured persons, and are not desirable for non-swimmers. Cushions should never be worn on a person's back since this tends to force his face down in the water.

As mentioned earlier in this chapter, the lifesaving device providing the greatest safety is the canvas jacket with flotation material in sealed plastic pouches. But the real potential of this most important safety item will be realized *only* if several conditions are met. Life preservers should be stored in several locations about the boat so that fire or other disaster cannot cut you off from all of them, and they must be stowed so as to be easily and quickly accessible. Everyone on board, including guests who may be aboard for only a few hours, *must* know where the life preservers are stowed. The skipper and regular crew must have tried them on and must be able to get into them quickly even in the dark (practice wearing a blindfold). Most importantly, the skipper must not delay in ordering everyone into life preservers in advance of their need if the emergency is of the type that builds up rather than striking suddenly without warning. It is far better to put them on, as bulky and uncomfortable as they may be, when trouble first threatens than it is to wait until near-panic develops. At night, anyone on deck should routinely wear a life jacket; non-swimmers, young children, and persons physically handicapped should wear one at all times—a person with a cast on an arm or leg goes down like a rock without added buoyancy.

The wise skipper never carries non-approved, damaged, or condemned lifesaving devices as "extra"—someone might grab one of them in an emergency.

Swimming tips

Even with the best of lifesaving equipment aboard, a boatman may find himself in the water without the aid of a buoyant device. If the boat remains afloat or awash, *stay with it*. Search vessels and aircraft can spot a boat or its

FIG. 1024 Swimming is a fine sport and an excellent capability to have for anyone who goes boating. Every skipper and his crew should know how to stay afloat and swim moderate distances. Take lessons at your local "Y" or Red Cross if you do not have this most desirable ability.

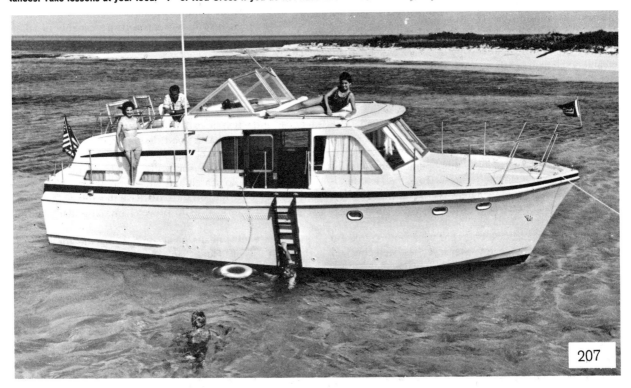

wreckage far easier than an individual whose head only is above water.

A swimmer may find temporary relief from fatigue by floating or by varying his style of swimming. Cold or tired muscles are susceptible to cramps. A leg cramp can often be overcome by moving your knees up toward your chest so that you can massage the affected area. Save your breath as much as possible; call for help only when there is someone definitely close enough to hear you.

PRE-DEPARTURE SAFETY

A worthwhile degree of increased safety afloat can be achieved if certain actions are taken routinely before departing on a short cruise. If it is to be an extended cruise of days or weeks, most of these items should be repeated each day.

Final weather check

Few, if any, boats are of such size for the waters on which they are operated that no heed need be given to possible worsening of weather conditions before return to the home berth or reaching the next port. The wise skipper makes a final weather check just as close as possible to his departure time so as to have the latest weather report of current conditions and most up-to-date forecast. He learns the time of best weather broadcasts, radio and TV, in his home area (such broadcasts vary widely in their scope and suitability for boating); he knows the telephone numbers of agencies that he can call for last-minute information. When away from his home area, he finds on arrival at each overnight stop how he can get early morning forecasts before his departure.

The Coastal Warning Facilities Charts published each year in early summer by the Weather Bureau (see pages 264 and 265) provide information on major radio and TV weather broadcasts as well as the location of day and night storm warning displays. The Weather Bureau also is steadily expanding the number of VHF-FM radio transmitters that broadcast continuous weather information on 162.55 MHz or 162.40 MHz.

Pre-departure check list

Each skipper should prepare his own pre-departure checklist *and use it.* The following items are of general applicability; all may not be needed, and others certainly will have to be added for your own boating.

1. All safety equipment is aboard, accessible, and in good working condition, including one Coast Guard-approved life-saving device for each person embarked.

2. The bilge has been checked for fuel fumes and water. Ventilate or pump out as necessary.

3. Horn and all navigation lights operate satisfactorily.

4. All loose gear is stowed securely. Dock lines and fenders should be stowed immediately after getting under way.

5. All guests aboard have been properly instructed in safety and operational matters, both do's and don'ts.

6. Engine oil levels have been checked, both crankcase and reverse/reduction gears; water level has been checked in closed cooling systems. After starting engines, check overboard flow of cooling water.

7. Fuel tanks have been checked for quantity of gasoline or diesel fuel. Know your tank capacity and fuel consumption at various RPMs, thus knowing your cruising radius.

FIG. 1025 Although boating is generally a leisure-time activity, a skipper often leaves his pier or mooring in a hurry. A "pre-departure checklist" will ensure that no essential preparatory step has been left undone. This is especially important for safety when running single-handed and the skipper cannot leave the helm once underway.

FIG. 1026 A "Float Plan" is a handy means of leaving behind on shore essential information when you go out fishing or for a cruise. Should you become overdue and a search must be made, much valuable time may be saved. Be sure, however, to report in when you return so as to avoid needless concern and wasted action.

Make sure there is enough fuel aboard for your anticipated cruising, plus an adequate reserve if you must change your plans for weather or other reasons.

8. There is a second person on board capable of taking over from the skipper should he become disabled or excessively fatigued.

Float plan

Before departing on a cruise, the skipper should advise a responsible relative or friend as to where he intends to cruise and when he expects to make port again; make sure that this person has a good description of the boat. Keep him advised of any changes in your cruise plans. By doing these things, this person will be able to tell the Coast Guard where to search and what type of boat to look for if you are overdue. Be sure to advise this relative or friend when you return so as to prevent any false alarms about your safety.

An excellent means of accomplishing the foregoing is through use of "Float Plan" forms made available by the Marine Office of America, a leading insurer of boats. These forms, fig. 1026, provide a simple and convenient way of filing the necessary information. A pad of forms may be obtained by writing to 123 William Street, New York, N. Y. 10038, or from a local agent of the company.

SAFETY IN WATER SKIING

Water skiing has become an ever more popular sport and its spread brings with it new problems in safety afloat. The following guides should do much to reduce hazards.

1. Allow no one who is not qualified as a basic swimmer to engage in water skiing. A ski belt or vest is intended to keep a stunned or unconscious skier afloat.

2. Water ski *only* in safe areas, out of channels and away from other craft. Some bodies of water will have areas designated for this sport with skiing prohibited elsewhere.

3. Install a wide-angle rear-view mirror or take along a second person to act as lookout. This will permit watching the skier *and* the waters ahead. Some state laws require this mirror or a second person in the boat to assist the operator, or both; check before starting to ski.

4. Make sure that the skier is wearing a proper lifesaving device.

5. If the skier falls, approach him from the lee side; stop your motor before starting to take him aboard.

6. In taking the skier on board, be careful not to swamp the boat. For smaller craft, it is usually safer to take a person aboard at the stern.

Skiing signals

The following set of signals is recommended by the American Water Ski Association; see fig. 1027. Make sure that the skier, boat operator, and safety observer all know and understand the signals.

Faster—palm of one hand pointing upward.

Slower—palm pointing downward.

Speed O.K.—arm upraised with thumb and finger joined to form a circle.

Right Turn—arm outstretched pointing to the right.

Left Turn—arm outstretched pointing to the left.

Return to Drop-off Area—arm at 45° from body pointing down to water and swinging.

Cut Motor—finger drawn across throat.

Stop—hand up, palm forward—policeman style.

Skier O.K. After Fall—hands clenched together overhead.

Pick Me Up or **Fallen Skier, Watch Out**—one ski extended vertically out of water.

FIG. 1027 This simple set of hand signals will allow adequate communication from the skier to the operator or observer on the towing craft. They must all be thoroughly familiar with the full set of signals if maximum safety is to be achieved.

(from the USCG Recreational Boating Guide)

Maintenance for Safety

Safety afloat is achieved, as we have seen in this chapter, by good design, sound construction, proper equipment, and sensible operating practices. The remaining element is continued maintenance for safety. Continual attention is needed for some of the material aspects of safety; for others, periodic checks at weekly, monthly, or annual intervals is sufficient. The important thing is that these checks of safety equipment be made *regularly* when needed.

Keep your boat clean

Cleanliness aboard a boat is an important aspect of safety. Accumulations of dirt, sawdust, wood chips, and trash in the bilge will soak up oil and fuel drippings and become a fire hazard. Such accumulations may also stop up limber holes and clog bilge pumps. Keep your bilge absolutely free of dirt and trash; check frequently and clean out as often as needed.

LIFESAVING EQUIPMENT

Lifesaving equipment usually requires no maintenance, but such items should be carefully inspected at the beginning of each boating season and again near its mid-point. These devices are not permanent; they do slowly wear out. Check for cut or torn fabric, broken stitches, and other signs of deterioration. **Do not delay in replacing below-par lifesaving devices;** attempt repairs *only* where *full* effectiveness can be restored. In case of doubt, ask the Coast Guard.

FIRE EXTINGUISHERS

Portable fire extinguishers and installed systems should be checked at least annually; the best time is at the beginning of the year's activities afloat and again at mid-season if required.

Dry chemical extinguishers

Pressurized dry chemical extinguishers are widely used on boats. These will have a gauge that should be checked every six months for an indication of adequate pressure—needle in center or green area of scale. Do not, however, merely read the gauge; tap it lightly to make sure that it is not stuck at a safe indication. If it drops to a lower reading, take the extinguisher to a service shop for recharging. Even if the gauge reads O.K., take the unit out of its bracket and shake it a bit to loosen the dry chemical inside to keep it from settling and hardening. Any areas on the exterior of the cylinder showing rust should be cleaned and repainted.

CO2 extinguishers

Carbon dioxide extinguishers must be checked annually by weight. Any seals on the valve trigger must be unbroken. Portable units and built-in systems have a weight stamped at the valve. If the *total* weight is down by 10% or more of the *net* weight of the contents, the cylinder must be recharged. Weighing is normally the only check for CO_2 fire extinguishers, but it must be done accurately. Portable units can be checked by the skipper if he has suitable scales. Built-in systems are best checked by a professional serviceman with his special knowledge and equipment.

CO2 cylinders should also have verified the date on which the cylinder was last hydrostatically pressure-tested. This should be done every 12 years if the cylinder is not discharged. If the extinguisher is used, it must be pressure-tested if this has not been done within the preceding five years. If a used CO2 extinguisher is purchased, it should be discharged, hydrostatically tested, and recharged before it is installed aboard. Remember that the pressure confined in these cylinders is tremendous, and if the cylinder has been damaged (through rust or corrosion), it is just like having a time bomb aboard, not knowing when it is set to go off!

Carbon dioxide extinguishers should not be installed where bilge or rain water will collect and cause rust. Any exposed metal should be painted at each annual inspection. If a cylinder becomes pitted from rust, have it hydrostatically tested for safety. Replace any damaged hoses or horns on this type of extinguisher.

Halon-type extinguishers

Automatic systems using Halon-1301 must be checked by weighing the cylinder and comparing actual weight with that stamped on it. Check every six months; a loss of only several ounces is significant. Use accurate scales; bathroom scales are not precise enough.

Periodic discharges

It is a good policy to discharge a fire extinguisher periodically even though it is not needed for fighting a fire. An effective way of doing this would be to discharge one of the portable units each year on a regular rotation basis. This should be done in the presence of the whole crew and preferably in the form of a drill, putting out an actual small fire—off the boat, of course—in a metal pan or tub. Probably 99% or more of all persons who go boating have never discharged a fire extinguisher, let alone used one to put out an actual fire! There is no time to read the instructions carefully and practice after a real fire has started on the boat.

A word of warning with respect to CO2 extinguishers—*never* unscrew the hose from the cylinder and then discharge it openly. This would have the same effect as trying to hang onto a rocket. A strong, heavy man would have trouble in hanging onto the cylinder, and if it were to get loose, it could cause a great deal of trouble.

Make sure that when fire extinguishers are removed for testing or practice discharge they are serviced by a competent shop and reinstalled *as soon as possible*. Sitting empty in the basement or garage at home or in the trunk of your car, an extinguisher cannot protect your boat. It is also wise not to denude your boat of fire protection by removing all extinguishers at the same time for servicing; do a half or a third at a time.

Log entries

An entry should be made in the boat's log of all inspections, tests, and servicing of fire extinguishers. This will help keep these essential checks from being overlooked and may prove valuable in the event of insurance surveys or claims.

ENGINE AND FUEL SYSTEM

Frequent safety checks should be made of the engine and fuel system for cleanliness and leaks. Any drippings of oil or grease should be kept wiped up and stopped as soon as possible. Immediate action must be taken in the case of any gasoline leaks—do not use the boat and disconnect the leads from the battery (with all loads turned off so that no spark will jump) in order that the engine cannot be started.

Annually, the entire fuel system should be checked inch by inch, including fuel lines in areas not normally visible. Look for any evidence of weepage of fuel or external corrosion of the lines. If any suspicious joints or lengths of tubing are found, it would be well to call in a qualified mechanic without delay.

ELECTRICAL SYSTEMS

A thorough annual inspection should be made of a boat's electrical system, including all wiring in areas not normally visible. This should be done by a person qualified to evaluate what he finds—the skipper if he has the necessary knowledge and experience, or an outside expert if needed. A search should be made for any cut or chafed insulation, corrosion at connections, excessive sag or strain on conductors, and other visible signs of deterioration. A leakage test should be made by opening each circuit at the main distribution panel and measuring current flow when all loads are turned off. Ideally there should be no current flow; current of more than a few milliamperes indicates electrical "leakage" that should be traced down and corrected without delay.

Bonding systems

If all through-hull fittings, struts, shafts, etc., are electrically connected by an internal bonding system, this wiring should be checked annually. Especially careful checks should be made where connections are made to the fitting or other metal part; connections in the bilge are subject to corrosion and development of poor contacts with high electrical resistance.

The skipper can make a visual check of the bonding system, but an electrical expert with specialized equipment is needed for a thorough evaluation. Should any signs of corrosion at points of connection of bonding wires to through-hull fittings be noted, a complete electrical test is recommended.

With respect to possible electrolysis damage, a bonding system with one or more poor connections is worse than no system at all. Electrolysis can and does cause weakening of through-hull fittings, bolts on struts and rudder posts, etc., that could result in serious safety hazards.

HULL SAFETY MAINTENANCE

Boats that are kept in the water will be hauled out periodically for bottom cleaning and repainting. This occasion should not be overlooked as an opportunity for a *safety* inspection of hull and fittings below the waterline.

Hull planking should be carefully checked for physical damage from having struck floating or fixed objects, and for any general deterioration from age. In general, it is best to call upon the services of an expert if any suspicious areas are found.

Through-hull fittings

An inspection should be made each time the boat is hauled to see that through-hull fittings and their seacocks are in good condition. This check should include fastenings susceptible to damage from electrolytic action.

Underwater components

Underwater fittings should get an annual inspection. This includes such parts as shafts, propellers, rudders, struts, stuffing boxes, and metal skegs. Stuffing boxes should be repacked as often as necessary to keep them from leaking excessively, shafting checked for alignment and excessive wear at strut bearings, and propellers examined to see if they need truing up.

FOLLOW-UP OF INSPECTIONS

Nothing is gained if prompt and thorough follow-up actions are not taken on findings of periodic safety inspections. *Maintenance related to the safety of the craft and those aboard must not be delayed.* **Do not operate a boat that has a known safety defect.**

First Aid Afloat

No one who is not educated and properly qualified to practice medicine should attempt to act as a doctor. There are, however, many instances where availability of a first aid kit, some knowledge on the part of the boatman, and a ready reference book have materially eased pain or even saved the life of a sick or injured person on a boat. All skippers should prepare themselves and their craft to render emergency first aid, doing no more than is absolutely necessary while getting the victim to a doctor or hospital as rapidly as possible.

FIRST AID KITS

There are many published guides to the proper contents of a first aid kit. Probably each of these has merit, and the list that follows can, and should, be modified for the size of boat, the number of persons aboard, the length of an average cruise, the area to be cruised, and the hazards likely to be encountered.

The first aid kit must be accessible and each person aboard should be made aware of its location.

Basic first aid materials

There are certain basic first aid materials that should be carried aboard all classes of boats. Bandages should be ready for instant use—each dressing individually wrapped, a complete dressing in itself. Each should be sterilized and designed to provide protection against infection and contamination.

Antiseptic liquids are preferably packaged so that the solution stays at its original strength until used. This type of packaging is available as a swab that contains a sealed ampoule in a sleeve of multi-layered cardboard; when the ampoule is broken there is no chance for the user to be

FIG. 1028 All boats should have on board adequate first aid equipment, supplies, and instructions. Kits may be either home-assembled or bought ready-made. See text for recommended items to be included. Skippers should also consider taking a standard first-aid course of instruction.

cut by glass. A close-packed cotton tip saturates instantly and then is applied to the wound area. There is no wasteage, spillage, or deterioration.

Basic first aid materials should also contain burn treatment compounds to take care of sunburn or burns caused by other hazards. Scissors have multiple uses. Forceps, to remove splinters, should be blunt-end, to preclude possi-

Artificial Respiration

Every boatman should have a working knowledge of the principles of artificial respiration. When the need for it arises, there is no time to search for instructions nor to study each step while, at the same time, attempting to apply the treatment. A boatman who has familiarized himself in advance with one of the accepted methods is more likely to work with calm assurance, saving precious minutes that could mean the difference between success and failure.

Through the courtesy of The American National Red Cross, we reproduce below the simplified illustrated methods they advocate. In recent years the mouth-to-mouth method, illustrated in steps 1 to 5, has come into widespread use. Recognizing, however, that some rescuers cannot or will not apply this method, the Red Cross includes instructions for the older manual chest pressure—arm lift (Silvester) and back pressure—arm lift (Holger Nielsen) methods. Study carefully the additional instructions at the bottom of the page applicable to all methods.

If victim is not breathing, begin some form of artificial respiration at once. Wipe out quickly any foreign matter visible in the mouth, using your fingers or a cloth wrapped around your fingers.

MOUTH-TO-MOUTH (MOUTH-TO-NOSE) METHOD

Tilt victim's head back. (Fig. 1). Pull or push the jaw into a jutting-out position. (Fig. 2).

If victim is a small child, place your mouth tightly over his mouth and nose and blow gently into his lungs about 20 times a minute. If victim is an adult (see Fig. 3), cover the mouth with your mouth, pinch his nostrils shut, and blow vigorously about 12 times a minute.

If unable to get air into lungs of victim, and if head and jaw positions are correct, suspect foreign matter in throat. To remove it, suspend a small child momentarily by the ankles or place child in position shown in Fig. 4, and slap sharply between shoulder blades.

If the victim is adult, place in position shown in Fig. 5, and use same procedure.

MANUAL METHODS OF ARTIFICIAL RESPIRATION

Rescuers who cannot, or will not, use mouth-to-mouth or mouth-to-nose technique should use a manual method.

THE CHEST PRESSURE-ARM LIFT (SILVESTER) METHOD

Place the victim in a face-up position and put something under his shoulders to raise them and allow the head to drop backward.

Kneel at the victim's head, grasp his wrists, cross them, and press them over the lower chest (Fig. 6). This should cause air to flow out.

Immediately release this pressure and pull the arms outward and upward over his head and backward as far as possible (Fig. 7). This should cause air to rush in.

Repeat this cycle about 12 times per minute, checking the mouth frequently for obstructions.

If a second rescuer is available, have him hold the victim's head so that the jaw is jutting out (Fig. 8). The helper should be alert to detect the presence of any stomach contents in the mouth and keep the mouth as clean as possible at all times.

THE BACK PRESSURE-ARM LIFT (HOLGER NIELSEN) METHOD

Place the victim face-down, bend his elbows and place his hands one upon the other, turn his head slightly to one side and extend it as far as possible, making sure that the chin is jutting out. Kneel at the head of the victim. Place your hands on the flat of the victim's back so that the palms lie just below an imaginary line running between the armpits (Fig. 9).

Rock forward until the arms are approximately vertical and allow the weight of the upper part of your body to exert steady, even pressure downward upon the hands (Fig. 10).

Immediately draw his arms upward and toward you, applying enough lift to feel resistance and tension at his shoulders (Fig. 11). Then lower the arms to the ground. Repeat this cycle about 12 times per minute, checking the mouth frequently for obstruction.

If a second rescuer is available, have him hold the victim's head so that the jaw continues to jut out (Fig. 12). The helper should be alert to detect any stomach contents in the mouth and keep the mouth as clean as possible at all times.

RELATED INFORMATION FOR ALL METHODS

If vomiting occurs, quickly turn the victim on his side, wipe out the mouth, and then reposition him.

When a victim is revived, keep him as quiet as possible until he is breathing regularly. Keep him from becoming chilled and otherwise treat him for shock. Continue artificial respiration until the victim begins to breathe for himself or a physician pronounces him dead or he appears to be dead beyond any doubt.

Because respiratory and other disturbances may develop as an aftermath, a doctor's care is necessary during the recovery period.

bility of doing further injury by probing, which is *not a* first aid measure.

Pre-packed first aid kits, available at most drug stores and marine supply stores, are generally acceptable, but their contents should be checked against recommendations that follow. Consideration should be given to separate purchase of any significant shortages; such items should be stored in or near the kit.

The container

The container for a first aid kit for a boat should not be made of a metal that could rust, nor of cardboard that could soak up moisture. A plastic box such as is often used to hold fishing tackle or tools is a good choice. It should close securely and be moisture-tight. It should *never* be locked, although it may be sealed with tape. Keep it on a high shelf out of the reach of small children. The kit may be lightly secured in place for safety in rough weather, but it must be portable and capable of being quickly unfastened and taken to the scene of an emergency.

Contents (instruments)

First aid kits should contain both simple instruments and consumable supplies. In the first category, the following are recommended:

Scissors—small and sharp; if there is room for two pairs, one should be of the blunt-end surgical type. Also a packet of single-edge razor blades.

Tweezers—small, pointed; tips must meet exactly to pick up small objects.

Safety pins—assorted sizes.

Thermometer—inexpensive oral-rectal type, in case.

Tourniquet—use only for *major* bleeding that cannot be controlled by compresses; follow instructions *exactly*.

Eye-washing cup—small, metal.

Cross Venti-breather—resuscitation device for drowned or asphyxiated person; aids in mouth-to-mouth resuscitation; follow directions on box.

Hot-water bottle and **ice bag**—these items, or a single unit that will serve both purposes, can do much to ease pain. Use with caution, following instructions in the first aid manual or medical advice book; improper use can aggravate conditions, sometimes seriously.

Contents (supplies)

The first aid kit should contain approximately the following types, sizes, and quantities of consumable supplies. Within reasonable limits, substitutions can be made to reflect local availabilities, personal preferences, etc.

Bandages—1", 2", and 4" sterile gauze squares, individually wrapped. Bandage rolls, 1" and 2". Band-aids (or equivalents) in assorted sizes, plus "butterfly closures." A minimum of one unit of each item, more on larger craft with greater number of persons aboard.

Triangular bandage—40" for use as sling or major compress.

Elastic bandage—3" width for sprains or splints.

Adhesive tape—Waterproof, 1" and 2" by 5 or 10 yards.

Absorbent cotton—standard size roll, for cleaning wounds, padding, etc.

Applicators—cotton-tipped individual swabs (Q-tips or equivalent) for applying antiseptics, removing foreign objects from cuts, eyes, ears.

Note: 1 inch = 2.54 cm. 1 ounce (liquid) = 29.56 ml. 1 pint = 0.473 l.

Antiseptic liquid—Tincture of iodine of merthiolate; or zephiran chloride, aqueous solution, 1:1,000. Antiseptic may be in bottle, but preferably in form of individual crushable ampoule applicators. Also a 4 oz. or larger bottle of antiseptic (70% alcohol) solution, or Phisophex solution.

White petroleum jelly—small jar, or preferably tube; plain, not carbolated; for small burns, dressings. An antiseptic burn cream may be substituted. This may be supplemented by a tube or bottle of sunburn remedy and a package of sterile petroleum-jelly-saturated gauze squares.

Antiseptic ointment—1 oz. tube of Bacitracin or Polysporin, or as recommended by your physician (prescription required); for general cuts, abrasions, and infections of the skin.

Nupercainal ointment—1 oz. tube; for local anesthetic purposes—apply to raw surface before cleaning or if painful. Calamine lotion is good for relief from itching.

Pain killer—Aspirin or related compound for ordinary pain. Also Darvon Compound, Codeine, or Demerol tablets or capsules for more severe pain (prescription required).

Sleeping pills—Seconal or equivalent as prescribed by your physician; use with caution as directed. If sleeplessness is related to pain, also give aspirin or Darvon Compound.

Antibiotics—Use *only* if there will be a delay in reaching a doctor and infection appears serious. Use Achroymcin, Eryothromycin, or similar drug as prescribed by your doctor.

Ophthalmic (eye) ointment—small tube of butyn sulphate with metaphen. If necessary to flush out eye, use sterile solution of 1 teaspoon of salt in 1 pint of water; do *not* use sea water.

Antihistamine—Pyrabenzamine tablets or as prescribed by your physician; use for allergies and allergic reactions to stings and insect bites. Also an antihistamine ointment.

Ammonia inhalants—crushable ampoules; for relief of symptoms of faintness or dizziness.

Seasickness remedy—Dramamine, Marezine, Bonamine, or Bonine tablets; may also be obtained in suppository form. Prescription required for all except Bonine. These should be taken before embarking; usually not effective after vomiting starts.

Anti-acid preparation—liquid or tablet, or both, for heartburn and indigestion.

Laxative—one or two forms for variations in personal preferences; Milk of Magnesia is excellent. Also Fleets disposable enemas are desirable items to have an board.

Anti-diarrhea drug—3 oz. bottle of Paregoric (prescription required) or 8 oz. bottle of Kaopectate.

First aid manual

A compact first aid manual should be packed in the top of the first aid kit. A larger medical-adviser and first aid book may be carried in a book shelf, but there should always be a small booklet of instructions in or immediately adjacent to the container of instruments and supplies.

First aid manuals can be obtained from the American Red Cross and other safety agencies. Books relating specifically to medical problems afloat and their management can be obtained through book stores and at many marine supply stores.

Replenishment

A first aid kit missing some items does not provide a full measure of safety afloat. As supplies are used, they should be replenished promptly. Further, some drugs do not last indefinitely. They may lose their strength, become unstable and toxic, or evaporate to increased concentrations that could be harmful. Ask your physician about the safe shelf-life of drugs prescribed by him and other supplies carried in your first aid kit. Replace questionably-old supplies whether used or not.

If instruments, or the first aid manual, become lost or damaged, they, too, should be replaced at the earliest opportunity.

Medicine cabinet

Most cruisers have medicine cabinets in the head where additional first-aid supplies may be found. A word of caution should be sounded here—this cabinet should supplement rather than replace the first-aid kits as outlined above because its contents are not portable to the scene of the emergency. It should contain the items which normally are stocked in a medicine cabinet at home such as aspirin, upset stomach remedies, etc.

ADMINISTERING FIRST AID

It would be highly impractical to attempt the instruction of first aid in the few paragraphs that can be devoted to that topic in this book. It is the skipper's responsibility to his passengers and crew to acquaint himself with the proper first-aid procedures. This can be done through classes given by each Chapter of the American Red Cross in a standard first-aid course. It should be remembered that when you are aboard your boat and at sea, you are out of immediate touch with professional medical attention and thus advance preparedness is necessary.

Rule one. Always take first aid to the victim, not the victim to the first aid. You may well aggravate an injury by attempting to move an accident victim. You will add to a sick person's discomfort by requiring him to move about. Limit movement of the affected individual to that absolutely necessary to get him clear of a hazardous area.

Rule two. When giving first aid, take your time. Usually there is more damage done by the well-meaning amateur than was ever caused by the actual injury. Remember, there are only three instances when speed in giving first aid is required: (1) when the victim has stopped breathing; (2) when there is arterial bleeding; and (3) when the victim has been bitten by a poisonous snake. The measures required in these instances are taught in the standard Red Cross first aid course available locally; get a group of your fellow boatmen together and attend one soon.

It should be noted that we have eliminated splints from the first-aid kit. The average first-aider is not qualified to set a broken limb; it is much safer to place the limb in pillows or blankets, tying them securely around the fractured member so that no further damage will be done. And always remember that first-aid should stop at first aid . . . which is administering aid and comfort to avert further complications until professional medical attention can be obtained.

Radio advice

In many emergency situations, a call to the Coast Guard can bring medical advice for treatment of serious injuries or illness. If within VHF range, initial contact should be made on Channel 16, followed by a shift to Channel 22. If farther offshore, initial calls should be made on 2182 kHz, then shifting to 2670 kHz; or on a 4, 6, or 8, MHz Coast Guard frequency using single sideband.

Basic Guides to Boating Safety

1. Carry proper equipment—know how to use it.
2. Maintain boat and equipment in top condition.
3. Know and obey the Rules of the Road afloat.
4. Operate with care, courtesy, and common sense.
5. Always keep your boat under complete control.
6. Watch posted speeds; slow down in anchorages.
7. Under no circumstances, overload your boat.
8. See that life-saving equipment is accessible.
9. Check local weather reports before departure.
10. Inspect hull, engine, and all gear frequently.
11. Keep bilges clean, electrical contacts tight.
12. Guard rigidly against any fuel system leakage.
13. Have fire extinguishers instantly available.
14. Take maximum precautions when taking on fuel.
15. Be sure to allow adequate scope when anchoring.
16. Request a USCG Auxiliary courtesy examination.
17. Enroll in a US Power Squadrons piloting class.

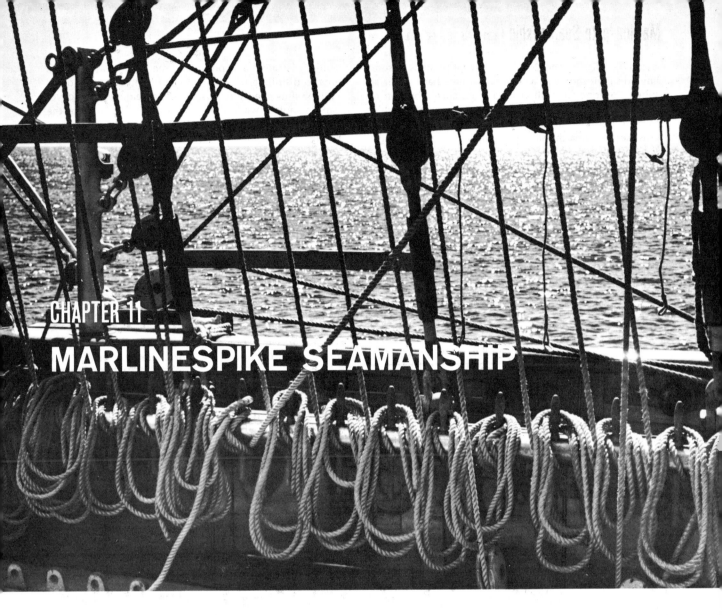

CHAPTER 11
MARLINESPIKE SEAMANSHIP

The Selection and Care of Rope—

Knots, Bends,

Hitches and Splices—

Blocks and Tackles—

The Bosun's Locker—

FIG. 1101 Running rigging on a windjammer. Sails are power on wind-ships; their rigging is as important as the engines of motorboats.

Cordage

Earlier editions of Piloting, Seamanship and Small Boat Handling, before the coming of many types of synthetic cordage, were much concerned with the prevention of rot, which is one of the two worst enemies of natural or vegetable fiber rope. The other is abuse. Abuse, rather than any other factor, is today probably the cause of most cordage failures.

In Table 11-1 you will note the variation in weight and strength—size being equal—between ropes made of different fibers or fiber combinations. Manufacturers compare rope of different fibers, or different constructions of the same fiber, by calculating "breaking length." This means the length of rope that would break from its own weight if it were hung on a sky hook. For instance, the "breaking length" of nylon is approximately 100,000 vs. manila at approximately 32,000. The strength of the fiber, the unit weight of the fiber and the rope construction all enter into breaking strength and breaking length.

It would appear that ropes could be substituted on the

basis of strength alone. NOT SO!, except perhaps in some limited applications. A *working* line must have other attributes beyond strength alone. For instance, abrasion resistance; a small line presents less surface area over which to distribute the surface wear. Notice the proportion of cross section area the same size cut or nick makes in two lines of different diameters which might be of the same strength. (Fig. 1102)

FIG. 1102 Relative effect on strength of cuts or nicks in rope of different diameter.

Perhaps as important in size selection, even for large hawsers for ships and tugs, is handling convenience. On a small sailboat a *Dacron 3/16" diameter sheet might be strong enough but it would not be easy to hold or grasp. Therefore, a ³/₈" main sheet and 5/16" jib sheets are about the smallest that can be handled except in very light wind.

Another factor in the surface area is that twisted rope has "crowns" which reduce this area and abrade more rapidly; as contrasted to double braided rope which essentially is round and presents some 30% greater surface area to distribute the wear. Double braid also provides a visible safety check, because severe abraiding of the cover can be spotted while there is still more than 50% of the strength left in the line from the inner core.

SELECTION OF SIZE

Now, to select the size synthetic to substitute for manila or cotton lines, and referring to Table 11-1 of weights and strengths, the following method has worked out in practice:

There are two ways to approach selection. The first is a straight synthetic substitute for manila or cotton line. The other is to select a different type and fiber combination such as 2-in-1 double braid, depending on the use. For sheets and halyards, where low stretch is required, you can use Dacron, or a double braid that combines a polyester cover with a polypropylene core that has 25% less stretch than Dacron alone. For mooring, anchor, and tie-up lines, you can select nylon twisted, or double braided nylon for a better stretch and strength combination. For example, a ³/₄" diameter, 2¼" (2.25") circ. manila rope (@ 16.3 lbs. per 100; 5400 lb. strength) could well be replaced by ⁹/₁₆" dia. (1³/₄" circ.) or ⁵/₈" dia. (2" circ.) twisted nylon or Dacron; or by a ⁷/₁₆" dia. 2-in-1 double nylon braided line. Added strength and less weight and

---

FIBER CORDAGE — TYPICAL WEIGHTS AND MINIMUM BREAKING STRENGTHS (POUNDS)

NOMINAL SIZE (inches)		MANILA Fed. Spec. TR 605			NYLON (High Tenacity—H.T.)			DU PONT DACRON or H.T. POLYESTER			POLYOLEFINS (H.T.) (Polypropylene and/or Polyethylene)			DOUBLE NYLON BRAID			POLYESTER/POLYOLEFIN DOUBLE BRAID		
Dia.	Circ.	Net Wt. 100'	Ft. per lb.	Breaking Strength	Net Wt. 100'	Ft. per lb.	Breaking Strength	Net Wt. 100'	Ft. per lb.	Breaking Strength	Net Wt. 100'	Ft. per lb.	Breaking Strength	Net Wt. 100'	Ft. per lb.	Breaking Strength	Net Wt. 100'	Ft. per lb.	Breaking Strength
³/₁₆	⁵/₈	1.47	68	450	1	100	1,000	1.3	77	1,000	.73	137	750	NA	NA	NA	.75	133	900
¼	¾	1.96	51	600	1.5	66.6	1,700	2.1	47.5	1,700	1.24	80	1,250	1.66	60.3	2,100	1.7	60.2	1,700
⁵/₁₆	1	2.84	35	1,000	2.5	40	2,650	3.3	30	2,550	1.88	53	1,850	2.78	36	3,500	2.6	38.4	2,600
³/₈	1⅛	4.02	25	1,350	3.6	28	3,650	4.7	21.3	3,500	2.9	34.5	2,600	3.33	30	4,200	3.5	28.5	3,500
⁷/₁₆	1¼	5.15	19.4	1,750	5	20	5,100	6.3	15.9	4,800	3.9	25.5	3,400	5.0	20	6,000	5.1	20	5,100
½	1½	7.35	13.6	2,650	6.6	15	6,650	8.2	12.2	6,100	4.9	20.4	4,150	6.67	14.9	7,500	6.8	15	6,800
⁹/₁₆	1¾	10.2	9.8	3,450	8.4	11.9	8,500	10.2	9.8	7,700	6.2	16	4,900	8.33	12	9,500	NA	NA	NA
⁵/₈	2	13.1	7.6	4,400	10.5	9.5	10,300	13.2	7.6	9,500	7.8	12.8	5,900	11.1	9	12,000	11	9	11,000
¾	2¼	16.3	6.1	5,400	14.5	6.9	14,600	17.9	5.6	13,200	11.1	9	7,900	15.0	6.7	17,000	15	6.7	15,000
⅞	2¾	22	4.55	7,700	20	5	19,600	24.9	4	17,500	15.4	6.5	11,000	20.8	4.8	23,700	20	5	20,000
1	3	26.5	3.77	9,000	26	3.84	25,000	30.4	3.3	22,000	18.6	5.4	13,000	25.0	4	28,500	28	3.6	28,000
1⅛	3½	35.2	2.84	12,000	34	2.94	33,250	40.5	2.5	26,500	24.2	4.1	17,500	35.0	2.8	39,000	35	2.8	35,000
1¼	3¾	40.8	2.45	13,500	39	2.56	37,800	46.2	2.16	30,500	27.5	3.6	20,000	40.0	2.5	44,000	40	2.5	40,000
1⁵/₁₆	4	46.9	2.13	15,000	45	2.22	44,500	53.4	1.87	34,500	31.3	3.2	23,000	45.0	2.2	49,500	45	2.2	45,000
1½	4½	58.8	1.7	18,500	55	1.8	55,000	67	1.5	43,000	39.5	2.5	29,000	60.0	1.6	65,000	60	1.6	60,000

1 inch = 2.54 cm.   1 foot = 0.3048 m.   1 pound = 0.4536 kg.

Table 11-1

NOTE:—The figures on synthetics, above, are an average of those available from four large cordage manufacturers. Those for the rope you buy should be availabe at your dealers. Check them carefully. Also check the rope. In general a soft, sleazy rope may be somewhat stronger and easier to splice but it will not wear as well and is more apt to hockle or unlay than a firm, well "locked-up" rope. Blended ropes, part polyolefins and part other fibers, may be found. Multifilament (fine filament) polypropylene looks like nylon—don't expect it to be as strong or do the job of nylon. (It floats, nylon doesn't.) Spun, or stapled, nylon and Dacron are not as strong as ropes made from continuous filaments but are less slippery and easier to grasp. Sometimes used for sheets on sailing craft.

*Du Pont registered Seadmark.

storage room, in addition to long life and other advantages, would be gained.

By similar method, use 80 to 85% factor to find the polyolefin size to use. (2" circ. ⅝" dia. indicated by previous example). The polys are not as strong and have lower melting points, thus are not as abrasion-resistant. They are, however, the lightest weight and they float which are advantages for "female hands" for tie-up lines and towing, such as dinghies and passing a tow line.

Table 11-3 gives the preferred ropes for different uses. Others may be used if care is taken in the selection, and the limitations are taken into account.

CARE AND PROTECTION OF ROPE

The anchor and mooring lines, standing and running rigging, and similar gear that constitute one of the most important parts of a yachtsman's equipment may be used with intelligent care—to which it will respond with years of useful service—or it may be abused by ignorance and neglect, ruining it in short order.

NINE RULES TO LENGTHEN ROPE LIFE

These nine commandments for the care of rope may not be all-inclusive, but it is safe to say that if they are observed a boatman may very well, in many cases, be able to double the useful life of his rope.

1. Look Out for Kinks

One sure way to destroy the value of a piece of line is to allow it to get a kink in it and then put it under strain. For example, you decide to play the Good Samaritan and break out your new spare line to haul a stranded boat off a bar. The new line is unruly and doesn't handle like the well-used anchor line, so there are a dozen kinks between your quarter bitt and his samson post when you ease the clutch in and open the throttle. In thirty seconds, you'll take more out of that line than you would in thirty weeks of normal service—if you don't shake those kinks out first.

What happens is this: The fibers are overstressed at the sharp bend, weakening fibers of the strands. Rapid wear follows and later the line may part at that spot, right at a critical time—through no fault of its own.

The time to start watching for kinks is in the very beginning when the rope is first taken from the coil or reel. There are right and wrong ways of doing this. The right way is to lay the coil on deck with the inside end down according to direction on the tag attached to the coil. Now reach down into the coil and pull this inner end up through the center, unwinding counter-clockwise. (See fig. 1120.) If it uncoils in the wrong direction, turn the coil over and pull the end out from the other side.

Synthetic rope should be shipped on reels and should be pulled or rolled off, disturbing the lay as little as possible. If it becomes unruly when coiling, try "faking down" in a figure 8. Do not "loop" off over the end of the reel —let it roll.

In natural fiber ropes kinks are most troublesome in wet weather; yachtsmen therefore have more to watch than those who use their rope ashore. Wet manila rope shrinks in length and swells in diameter and the lay shortens, making it more difficult to handle.

Knots have the same effect as a sharp kink. Some knots

Table 11-2

ROPE AND FIBER COMPARISON CHART				
	MANILA	**NYLON**	**DACRON**	**POLY-OLEFINS**
Relative Strength	1	4	3	2
Relative Weight	3	2	4	1
Elongation	1	4	2	3
Relative Resistance to Impact or Shock Loads	1	4	2	3
Mildew and Rot Resistance	Poor	Excellent	Excellent	Excellent
Acid Resistance	Poor	Fair	Fair	Excellent
Alkali Resistance	Poor	Excellent	Excellent	Excellent
Sunlight Resistance	Fair	Fair	Good	Fair
Organic Solvent Resistance	Good	Good	Good	Fair
Melting Point	380° (Burns)	410°F.	410°F.	about 300°F.
Floatability	Only when new	None	None	Indefinite
*Relative Abrasion Resistance (*Depends on many factors— whether wet or dry, etc.)	2	3	4	1
KEY TO RATINGS: 1 Lowest—4 Highest				

$$(°F - 32) \times 0.56 = °C$$

may take 40 to 50 per cent out of a rope's efficiency. (See table 11-4.) A good splice, on the other hand, will allow a rope to retain 85 to 95 per cent of its original strength. Therefore, if a splice is indicated, don't use a knot.

2. Keep Your Rope Clean

Simple cleanliness in taking care of rope pays big dividends. In the course of use it is bound to pick up mud and sand. When this occurs, the rope should be draped in loose loops over a rail and hosed down gently, with fresh water if available. Don't use a high pressure stream with the intent of doing a more thorough job, as this will only force dirt and grit deeper into the rope. After washing, allow it to dry and then rap or shake it thoroughly to get out any remaining particles of dirt. Grit cuts the fibers.

3. Stow Carefully

Natural fiber rope will rot so it must be dried and carefully stowed in a place with adequate ventilation. This applies to manila, sisal, cotton and, to a lesser extent, linen and flax. Many a yachtman has been embarrassed or worse because of rot. Dry lines on deck before stowing. Hang up light lines. Loosely coil heavier ones on gratings so air can circulate. Don't subject them to intense heat.

Synthetic rope *may* be stowed wet but introduces unpleasant dampness below. Iron rust from rusty chain and thimbles is not good for nylon.

Keep lines away from exhaust pipes and batteries.

4. Guard Against Chafe and Abrasion

Chafe and abrasion are among rope's worst enemies. Heavy coils are sometimes dragged along the ground instead of being carried on the shoulder. Dragging over a rough surface causes the outside fibers to be cut or rubbed off while grit works inside the strands and is equally destructive in cutting inside fibers.

Rope should never be allowed to rub on sharp edges, or one rope chafe against another. Surface wear is accelerated and fraying often starts as a result of it. If it is necessary to have a rope pass over a sharp edge like a rail on the deck edge or a badly designed chock, rig a canvas

RECOMMENDED ROPE FOR VARIOUS USES								
	Tie-Up or Mooring Lines	Anchor Ropes or Mooring Pennants	Sheets and Halyards	Flag Halyards	Seizing and Whipping	Bolt Rope Synthetic Sails	Towing	Water Skiing
MANILA	✓	✓	✓	✓			✓	
NYLON	✓	✓		✓				
DACRON	✓		✓	✓		✓		
POLYOLEFIN	✓						✓	✓
BRAIDED DACRON			✓	✓				
BRAIDED NYLON	✓	✓		✓	✓		✓	
WIRE (Stainless)		Pennants	✓					
BRAIDED COTTON				✓	✓			
NYLON SEINE TWINE					✓			
LINEN or FLAX			✓	✓	✓			

pad to prevent excessive wear from damaging the fibers.

When riding to an anchor for considerable periods, it is always well to "freshen the nip" by paying out a little line to bring the chafe of chocks in another place.

Chafing gear of canvas will protect the line from this source of trouble; it is particularly desirable on mooring lines where chafing always comes in one spot. Some boatmen carry a split length of rubber hose which can be readily clapped on the line where required. Specially molded rubber and plastic chafing gear is available.

Another trick to lengthen the life of a line like an anchor line or halyard, where most of the wear comes on one end, is to turn the line end-for-end occasionally. Any rope ends that do not terminate in a splice should be whipped to prevent fraying.

When making fast at a dock, select smooth round piles of good diameter to make fast to, and shun square or rectangular timbers with sharp corners. If there is no alternative, pad the sharp edges.

5. Prevent Slipping

When using rope on the drums of winches or hoists it is bad practice to let the rope slip on the drum as it revolves. This not only increases wear on the rope, but the sudden jerks as the rope is snubbed, strain the fibers badly.

Similarly the rope should not be allowed to lie against the revolving drum of a hoist or winch. In addition to objectionable chafe, there is the element of heat from friction to be considered; this may be enough to burn or melt the fibers.

Synthetic ropes that are highly strained and/or repeatedly stretched while around a cleat or winch may melt and grab so they will not run or pay out smoothly.

6. Avoid Small Blocks

There are two sources of trouble when rope is expected to run over too small a block. On the one hand there is excessive internal friction. Wear from such friction is always present when rope runs over the sheaves of blocks and the smaller the sheave diameter, the greater the friction. On the other hand, there is the external wear as the rope chafes against the inside of sheave holes providing insufficient clearance. Faulty alignment of blocks which causes the rope to rub against the sides, or cheeks, of the blocks is also bad. A combination of this internal friction and external chafe breaks down fibers much faster than would be expected in normal use.

One place where trouble of this kind shows up quickly if installation is faulty is in the use of small sheaves in the steering lines or cables. These get a great deal of hard usage and their life can be extended by the use of sheaves of generous diameter.

In tackles, when matching blocks to rope, use a block with a shell length of at least 3 inches for $3/8$-inch (diameter) rope; 4 inches for $1/2$; 5 inches for $5/8$; 6 inches for $3/4$; 8 inches for $7/8$; 9 inches for 1 inch; and 12 inches for $1 1/4$-inch rope. (1 inch = 2.54 cm) (See Table 11-5.)

Care should be exercised to see that sheaves are never allowed to become rough or rusty. See to it that they are well lubricated to reduce friction and to prevent their seizing. A sheave frozen by rust or corrosion on its pin would work havoc on a piece of rope.

7. Don't Lubricate

For natural fiber, the manufacturer has already treated the rope with an oil or solution which preserves it and lubricates internal fibers. This may account for roughly 10 per cent of the rope's weight. Even some synthetics have special fiber treatments.

Users are cautioned not to attempt to improve upon the manufacturer's work by using additional lubricant of any kind upon it. The treatment given the rope originally when manufactured prolongs its life and retains its strength.

8. Beware of Chemicals

Both acids and alkalis attack vegetable fiber rope and some synthetics. See fiber comparison table 11-2. Consequently it should never be stowed any place where it might be brought into accidental contact with chemicals or even be subject to exposure to the fumes. In testing storage batteries with a hydrometer, for example, acid dropped on a rope will burn it badly. Even paint and drying oils, like linseed, should not be allowed to get in contact with it.

Alkalis and acids burn the fibers and kill the life of rope by rendering the fibers brittle. Wet rope is more susceptible to chemical fumes than if it were dry. Rust, too, is bad for rope. If a line must be used around chemicals, it is essential to check it frequently. Spots of discoloration are a danger sign showing when fibers have broken down.

In the case of double braided rope, excessive wear will show up on the cover (or outside braid) by a parting of the strands. The inner core is rarely, if ever, affected by abrasion and provides 50% strength retention as a safety factor.

9. Never Overload

Many tables have already been published giving suitable sizes of anchor and mooring lines for motor and sailing craft of all sizes. See Tables 6-2 and 6-3, pages 98-99.

Table 11-1 will serve as a guide in this respect. It shows the minimum breaking strain carried by standard brands of manila, and typical synthetic ropes. It should be understood these strengths are for new cordage.

The factor of safety to be allowed in determining the working load on a rope is commonly taken as 5. That is, if a rope must lift 200 kg, a rope with tensile strength of 1,000 kg should be selected. With synthetic ropes, the same factor of 5, or sometimes 4 (800 kg in the example above) may be used. The condition of the rope must be considered when making a selection. If the load ever exceeds 75% of the rope's breaking strength, the chances are good that it will have been permanently damaged; in that case, it may fail unexpectedly, without warning.

SAILBAG Going Aloft

Maintaining rig and sails are problems the new sailboat skipper must learn to deal with. Sooner or later, for example, a small child, while helpfully setting the club burgee at the main truck, will lose the bitter end of the signal halyard, and the whole length of it will come tumbling down on the deck. Someone must go aloft and re-reeve it.

Experienced sailors dislike being hauled to the masthead by crewmen cranking on winch handles in circumstances where, should some accident occur at the winch, the man aloft will plummet to the deck. Furthermore, there isn't always a crewman at hand when someone has to go to the masthead in a hurry.

The problem is easily solved if you carry a spare rode for the lunch hook that is at least five times the distance from deck to truck in length, and two double blocks through which the line can be reeved as a two-fold purchase. (see p. 227). Shackle one end of the purchase to the bosun's chair and the other to the main halyard, so arranged that the hauling part will lead down from the masthead. Two-block the main halyard and stopper it off so that it can't be dislodged accidentally. A man seated in the bosun's chair can easily haul himself to the masthead in an emergency, and if the crew is at hand he can be hauled to the truck in ease and comfort. A short length of line should be left attached to the bosun's chair so that, when he is at the proper height, he can take a rolling hitch around the hauling part of the tackle with it and have both hands free.

	HOW KNOTS AND SPLICES REDUCE THE STRENGTH OF ROPE	% EFF.
	Normal rope	**100%**
KNOTS	Anchor or Fisherman's bend	76
	Timber hitch	70-65
	Round turn	70-65
	Two half-hitches	70-65
	Bowline	60
	Clove hitch	60
	Sheet bend or Weaver's knot	55
	Square or Reef knot	45
SPLICES	Eye splice (over thimble)	95-90
	Long splice	87
	Short splice	85

Based on a normal rope strength of 100% (without knots) the figures above show what percentage of strength is left in a straight rope after a knot has been tied in it. Under differing conditions of test and stress, results vary. Therefore the percentages of efficiency tabulated are necessarily approximate, but they do serve as a base for general calculations.

HOW TO INSPECT YOUR ROPE

In an external examination of the rope, watch out for abrasion, cuts and broken fibers, variations in size and shape of the strands, and uniformity of the lay. Excessive wear on the outside is revealed when fibers appear to be about half worn out and yarns $\frac{1}{2}$ or $\frac{2}{3}$ worn through. Then, depending on the rope size and percentage of good yarns remaining, it may be time to down-grade to lighter work loads or time to renew the rope. Acid stains, frayed strands and broken yarns should all be revealed in such an examination, which should include the entire length of the rope.

Now twist the strands so as to open the rope up, revealing the condition of interior fibers. Evidence of powdered or melted or fused fiber is a danger signal warning of excessive internal bending, tension and wear. Repeat this test in several places. If yarns (the twisted fibers inside) appear to be clean, bright and free from spots of discoloration or melting (harsh and brittle) the chances are that the rope is still in good condition—assuming the exterior is also OK.

Signs of damage due to overloading are also found in the interior yarns of the strands. A rope in which these inner yarns have been broken or partly broken or melted by excessive or repeat loading can never be trusted.

A good rope will be free from splinters of fiber— just another earmark of quality in good rope. A rough and ready breaking test that the owner can apply is to unlay about a foot of one yarn and break it, or fibers taken from it, with the hands. If this single yarn breaks easily, or fibers have little strength, the rope undoubtedly has lost strength from old age or perhaps has rotted.

The real problem in advising the boatman as to the knots he should learn to tie and use is to select the few that are of real utility on the average cruiser and exclude the numerous knots which, although serving a special purpose excellently, are of little practical use to the average boatman.

The short list of knots described below and illustrated in the accompanying sketches will meet all ordinary situations. Better know these knots—practice until they can be tied with certainty in the dark or blindfolded—than to have a superficial knowledge of a greater number of knots, including many that are of little practical value.

A knot or splice is never as strong as the rope itself. See table 11-4. Splices are preferred for heavy loads. It may be of some interest to recall that the strength of a rope is derived largely from the friction that exists between the individual fibers, yarn and strands, of which the rope is made. The twisting of these fibers into yarn, then into strands, hawsers and finally cables is always carried out in such a manner as to increase the amount and effectiveness of the friction between the rope elements. In the tying of knots this principle of making use of friction is also applicable, for in this manner, much more can be accomplished by the use of a simple knot, so tied that the strain on the rope adds to the knot's holding power, than will ever develop from a conglomeration of hitches, many of which serve no useful purpose, and which, moreover, make it more practicable in the end to cut the rope than to untie the knots. From the examples which follow it will be evident that wherever possible the most effective use is made of friction between two or more portions of a knot in order to increase its holding power.

Knots, Bends and Hitches

FIG. 1103a Overhand

The simple overhand knot is used to keep the end of a rope from unlaying. This knot jams and may become impossible to untie. A better knot for the purpose is shown below.

FIG. 1103b Figure Eight

The figure eight knot. This does not jam.

FIG. 1103c Square or Reef Knot

The square or reef knot is perhaps the most useful and common knot The rope manipulated by the right hand (this is the rope leading from the left side of the sketch and terminating in the arrow in A) is turned over the other rope in tying both the first and second half of the knot. Learn to always turn this rope over the other and the knot can be tied with certainty in the dark. If the rope manipulated by the right hand is first turned over and then under the other rope the treacherous granny knot will result.

Do not use the square knot to tie together lines of different sizes, as it will slip. The reef or square knot is used for tying light lines together (not for tying heavy hawsers), for tying awning stops, reef points, cord on packages, and in fact is put to such numerous uses by sailors that many landsmen call it the sailor's knot. The knot has one serious fault. It jams and is difficult to untie after being heavily stressed.

FIG. 1103d Sheet or Becket Bend

The sheet or becket bend has been known to landsmen as the weaver's knot, and it is used for tying two lines together. It will not slip even if there is great difference in the sizes of the lines. To make the knot secure for connecting hawsers for towing, the free ends of the lines should be stopped down with twine in the manner illustrated in fig. 1103j, the reeving line bend.

FIG. 1103e Bowline

The bowline is considered a knot second in usefulness only to the square knot. The bowline will not slip, does not pinch or kink the rope as much as some other knots, and does not jam and become difficult to untie. By tying a bowline with a small loop and passing the line through the loop the running bowline is obtained. This is an excellent form of running noose.

Bowlines are used wherever a secure loop or noose is needed in the end of a line, such as a line which is to be secured to a bollard in making a boat fast to a pier or wharf. They may also be used in securing lines to anchors where there is no time to make a splice. Hawsers are sometimes connected by two bowlines, the loop of one knot being passed through the loop of the other.

FIG. 1103f Clove Hitch

The clove hitch is used for making a line fast temporarily to a pile or a bollard.

FIG. 1103g   Two Half Hitches

Two half hitches are used for making a line fast to a bollard, pile, timber, or stanchion. Note that the knot consists of a turn around the fixed object and a clove hitch around the standing part of the line.

FIG. 1103h   Correct Method of Making Fast to a Cleat

Correct method for making fast to a cleat is shown. The half hitch which completes the fastening is taken with the free part of the line. The line can then be freed without taking up slack in the standing part.

FIG. 1103i   Incorrect Method of Making Fast to a Cleat

Common incorrect method of making fast to a cleat is shown. The half hitch is taken with the standing part of the line and the line consequently can not be freed without taking up slack in the standing part. Accidents have been caused by the use of this type of fastening on lines which must be freed quickly.

FIG. 1103j   Reeving Line Bend Free ends must be stopped down with twine

The reeving line bend is so called because it is used to connect lines which must pass through a small opening, such as a hawsepipe.

FIG. 1103k   Fisherman's Bend

The fisherman's bend, also called the anchor bend, is handy for making fast to a buoy or spar or the ring of an anchor. In some localities it is preferred to the thimble and eye splice for attaching the anchor line to the ring. As is evident from the illustration, it is made by taking two round turns around the ring, then passing the end under both turns to form a half hitch around the standing part of the line. For further security, a second half hitch is taken around the standing part only, or in place of the last half hitch, the end may be stopped down or sized back to the line with twine.

FIG. 1103l   Two Methods of Whipping a Rope End

All butt-ended ropes should of course be whipped to prevent raveling of the strands. Two common methods for doing this are illustrated above. While these figures are not strictly to scale this has been done purposely to avoid difficulty in following the several steps involved in either of the two methods.

FIG. 1103m   Sheepshank

The sheepshank is used to shorten a line. Lay the bight in three parts and take a half hitch around each doubled part.

FIG. 1103n   Cat's Paw

The cat's paw is used to secure a line to a hook. Make a double loop by twisting two bights of the line as shown,

FIG. 1103o   Rolling Hitch

The rolling hitch is used to bend a line to a spar or rope. Close turns up tight and take the strain on the arrow-tipped end.

FIG. 1103p   Timber Hitch

The timber hitch is used to temporarily secure a line to a spar or timber, as in towing. The half hitch shown is sometimes omitted. If used, it should be taken first. In both hitches, strain should be kept on the line to make it hold.

FIG. 1103q   Blackwall Hitch

The Blackwall Hitch is easy to make and practical to use when *temporarily* securing a rope to a hook. It will carry a heavy load, *provided* the tension is constant.

The Art of Splicing

EYE SPLICE OR SIDE SPLICE

Start the splice by unlaying the strands, about six inches to a foot or more, or 6 to 10 turns of lay, depending on the size of rope you are splicing. Now whip the end of each strand to prevent its unlaying while being handled. If working with synthetic rope, it is sometimes helpful to use masking or friction tape wrapped around the unlaid strands every 4 to 6 inches to help hold the "turn" in the strand. The ends may be fused with a flame or whipped.

Next form a loop in the rope by laying the end back along the standing part. Hold the standing part away from you in the left hand, loop toward you. The stranded end can be worked with the right hand.

The size of loop is determined by the point X (fig. 1104) where the opened strands are first tucked under the standing part of the rope. If the splice is being made around a thimble, the rope is laid snugly in the thimble groove and point X will be at the tapered end of the thimble. The thimble may be temporarily taped or tied in place until the job is finished.

Now lay the three opened strands across the standing part as shown in fig. 1104 so that the center strand B lies over and directly along the standing part. Left-hand strand A leads off to the left; right-hand strand C to the right of the standing part.

Tucking of strand ends A, B and C under the strands of the standing part is the next step. Get this right and the rest is easy. See fig. 1105.

Start with the center strand B. Select the topmost strand (2) of the standing part near point X and tuck B under it. Haul it up snug but not so tight as to distort the natural lay of all strands. Note that the tuck is made from right to left, against the lay of the standing part.

Now take left-hand strand A and tuck under strand (1), which lies to the left of strand (2). Similarly take strand C and tuck under strand (3), which lies to the right of strand (2). Be sure to tuck from right to left in every case.

The greatest risk of starting wrong is in the first tuck of strand C. It should go under (3), from right to left. Of course, strands (1), (2), and (3) are arranged symmetrically around the rope.

It may help to visualize this by referring to fig. 1106, a cross-section through the rope at X, seen from below.

If the first tuck of each of strands A, B and C is correctly made, the splice at this point will look as shown in fig. 1107.

The splice is completed by making at least two additional tucks in manila rope or 4 full tucks in synthetic rope with each of strands A, B and C. As each added tuck is made be sure it passes over one strand of the standing part, then under the strand next above it, and so on, the tucked strand running against the lay of the strands of the standing part. This is clearly shown in fig. 1108, the completed splice. Note C, C¹ and C², the same strand as it appears after successive tucks.

Suggestions: The splice can be made neater by tapering. This is done by cutting out part of the yarns from the tucking strands, before the finishing tucks. In any case, the first

3 tucks in manila or 4 tucks in synthetics, are made with the full strands. (Synthetics are slippery and stretchy and thus require at least one extra tuck.) After that, some prefer to cut out one-third of the yarns, make a tuck, then cut out another third of the yarns, and make the last tuck. This produces an even taper. After the splice is finished, roll it on deck under foot to smooth it up. Then put a strain on it and finally cut off the projecting ends of the strands. Do not cut off the "tails" of synthetic rope too short. If possible seat the splice in use or whip down the ends before cutting. The loose fibers may be fused with a match or candle to finish off, but be careful not to melt the rope.

FIG. 1108 How the eye splice should look when completed. A thimble, if spliced in, would fit as shown by the dotted lines.

From the earliest days of rope, marlinspike seamanship had concerned itself with the splicing of 3-strand or twisted rope. With the increasing use of 2-in-1 double braided rope, however, a new method of splicing has

Fig. 1108a Tightly tape end with one layer of tape. Mark a big dot one fid length from end of line. From the dot, form a loop the size of the eye you want, and mark with an X as shown.

Fig. 1108b Bend line sharply at X, and spread strands apart firmly to make opening so center can be pried out. Mark one big line on center where it comes out (this is Mark #1), and use your fingers to pull all the center out of the cover from X to the end. Pull on paper tape inside center until it breaks back at slip knot; you need to get rid of it so you can splice. Put a single layer of tape on end of center.

Fig. 1108c Pull out more of the center. From Mark #1 measure a distance equal to the short section of the fid, and mark two heavy lines (this is Mark #2). Mark three heavy lines at a distance of one fid length plus one short section of fid from Mark #2. This is Mark #3.

Fig. 1108d Insert fid into center at Mark #2, and slide it lengthwise through "tunnel" until point sticks out at Mark #3.

Fig. 1108e Cut across taped end of cover to form a point, and re-tape tightly with one layer of tape. Jam this point into open end of the fid. Jam pusher into fid behind the tape. Hold center gently at Mark #3, and push both fid and cover through the center until dot almost disappears at Mark #2.

Fig. 1108f Note how center tail must travel through cover. It must go in close to dot, and come out through opening at X. On large eyes several passes may be necessary for fid to reach X. When this occurs simply reinsert fid at exact place it comes out and continue to X. To start, insert fid in cover at dot and slide it through tunnel to X. Form tapered point on center tail, jam it into open end of fid, and push fid and center through the cover. After fid comes out at X, pull all center tail through cover until tight, then pull cover tail tight.

Fig. 1108g Unravel cover tail braid all the way to Mark #3, and cut off groups of strands at staggered intervals to form a tapered end. Hold loop at crossover in one hand, and firmly smooth both sides of loop away from crossover. Do this until the tapered tail section completely disappears inside Mark #3.

Fig. 1108h Hold rope at slipknot, and gently begin to "milk" or slide the cover slack toward the loop. You'll see the center begin to disappear into the cover. Go back to the knot, and continue sliding cover more and more firmly until all center and the crossover are buried inside the cover.

come into being. The splicing of braided rope is best done by following an 8-step procedure that, in an over-simplified way, starts by extracting the core from inside the cover, then inserting the cover into the core in one direction, inserting the core back into the cover in the opposite direction, and then "milking" a slack section of cover over the core. A fid and pusher are used in the process. The holding power is related to the old Chinese finger trick, and the result is a sure and good looking splice. A thimble can be inserted during the splicing process. The 8 steps for a basic eye splice are shown in the sketches

HOW TO MAKE A SHORT SPLICE

A short splice is used where two ropes are to be permanently joined, provided they do not have to pass through the sheave hole, swallow or throat, of a block. The splice will be much stronger than any knot.

The short splice enlarges the rope's diameter at the splice, so in cases where the spliced rope must pass through a sheave hole, a long splice should be used.

To start the short splice, unlay the strands of both rope ends for a short distance as described for the eye splice. Whip the six strand ends, or fuse or tape them, to prevent unlaying. A seizing should also be made around each of the ropes to prevent strands from unlaying too far. These seizings can be cut as the splice is completed.

Next "marry" the ends so that the strands of each rope lie alternately between strands of the other as shown in fig. 1109. Now tie all three strands of one rope temporarily to the other. See fig. 1110. (Some omit this step; it is not absolutely essential.)

Working with the three free strands, remove temporary seizing from around other rope and splice them into the other rope by tucking strands exactly as described for the eye splice, working over and under successive strands from right to left against the lay of the rope. When first tucks have been made, snug down all three strands. Then tuck two or three more times on that side.

Next cut the temporary seizing of the other strands and the rope and repeat, splicing these three remaining strands into the opposite rope.

Just as in the eye splice, the short splice can be tapered as desired by cutting out yarns from the strands after the full tucks are made. Figure 1111 shows how the short splice would appear if not tapered, after finally trimming off the ends of strands. Never cut strand ends off too close. Otherwise when a heavy strain is put on the rope, the last tuck tends to work out, especially with synthetics.

Another method which some find easier, is to start as in fig. 1109 and tie pairs of strands from opposite ends in an overhand knot. See fig. 1112. This, in effect, makes the first tuck.

FIG. 1109 FIG. 1111

FIG. 1110 FIG. 1112

HOW TO MAKE A LONG SPLICE

The long splice (fig. 1113) is used where the spliced ropes are to reeve through blocks or sheaves. There are several methods of making this splice. Some splicers unlay both ends, marry as in the short splice and work from the center both ways. But by starting as in fig. 1113 you do not lose any of the lay of strands. For a long splice in a 3-inch circumference line allow not less than 6 feet, or about 2 feet for each inch of *circumference,* as the farther apart the three splices are staggered, the stronger will be the completed splice. In the illustration 2-inch circumference rope was used, but the illustration does not show proper spacing of tucks. After seizing or taping the ends of each strand, to start this splice, unlay one strand of one rope for about 6 feet and cut off, leaving about one foot as in Illustration 1, strand C. Then unlay one strand from other rope and lay in space formerly occupied by strand C, allowing a foot for splicing as in Illustration 1 at A.

When laying the first strand A (1), plan the spacing of splices so that B will be about central in the finished long splice. Next unlay a strand from right hand rope and a strand from left hand rope and lay the left hand strand in the respective space formerly filled by the strand from right hand rope as in Illustration 2. Continue strand C until all three strands are about equal distance as in Illustration 3.

Then with all pairs of strands (for example Illustration 4A) tie an overhand knot with all yarns flat and even. Next take spike and tuck strands over one and under one as in 4B, unlaying or untwisting strands sufficient to allow yarns to lay flat when tucked. The overhand knot at 4A and, after tucking as at 4B, should be as near as possible to an original strand in size and volume of fiber by reducing twist in the tucked strand. Make another full tuck with all strands.

You now have an overhand knot and two full tucks. Halve each strand and tuck as in 4C, again halve the re-

maining yarns and tuck as in 4E. Roll tucks under foot and stretch before cutting off ends. Here, again, do not cut off too short. Much better a little fuzz or whiskers than tucks starting to pull out.

To make a long splice in fishing line, make the same as above, using a sail needle to tuck the strands. The small sail needle, used in fine work, takes the place of the larger fid.

SPLICING WIRE ROPE

In general, wire rope is spliced in a similar way except that tucks are made with the lay rather than against the lay. Splicing vises are used to hold the rope and metal tools and hammers are usually needed.

Splices of wire-to-fiber rope should be left to professional riggers. They can usually be found at sail lofts where wire halyards with rope tails can be made to specification. With the right tools and a lot of practice, you can work out a method yourself.

A FEW TIPS

Practice these knots and splices with a couple of short lengths of line and put them to practical use. Always keep lines dry and clean. Keep ends of lines neatly served or whipped with twine to prevent unlaying. Serving or whipping is preferable to the crown knots or splices sometimes used to prevent unlaying as these knots and splices prevent reeving the line through the openings of a block which would otherwise take the line nicely.

The knots, hitches, bends and splices just described are sufficient for all practical purposes aboard the average pleasure boat. To make them with facility in a seamanlike manner, have some experienced yachtsman, sailor or fisherman show you how he'd do it, especially the bowline, clove hitch and splice.

LONG SPLICE

FIG. 1113 While the short splice is excellent for strength and neatness, as compared to a knot, there are times when the spliced line must reeve through a block. In such cases, the long splice should be used. Illustrated above are steps in the making of a long splice.

Blocks and Tackles

The use of blocks and tackle (pronounced tay-kle) or, to use a higher sounding name, mechanical appliances, on board a small cruising type boat is very limited. The competent seaman, however, should have a basic knowledge of them, as their use enables one man to do the work of many.

Blocks and tackle on small boats are almost entirely confined to sailboats where the hoisting of heavy sails, as well as setting them, requires some means for one or two men to match the strength of many. No matter how small the sailboat, the sheets usually run through one or more blocks, which means we have a mechanical appliance.

To see how this aids, go for a sail in a 20-foot boat, in a moderate breeze, and bend a line to the boom. While under way attempt to trim in the sail with your improvised sheet. It will come in but it will be a struggle, so try it with the regular system of blocks and tackle and you will see with what ease the sail comes in. About the most common use on a motorboat is in hoisting your dinghy.

A *block* consists of a frame of wood or metal inside of which is fitted one or more *sheaves* (pulleys—the word is pronounced shiv), and is designated according to the number of sheaves it contains, such as single, double, or triple. The size of the block to be used is, of course, de-termined by the size of the rope to be reeved. If a fiber rope is being used, the size of the block should be *about* three times the *circumference* of the rope and the sheave diameter about twice the circumference. Therefore, if 2-inch rope, $5/8''$ diameter, is being used the block could be 6 inches (three times the circumference) and the sheave diameter 4 inches (twice the circumference). This is an approximation. See Table 11-5, block sizes and rope diameter, for recommended sizes.

Wire rope is also used but usually only as halyards on sailboats. Some larger sailing craft use wire sheets and guys. This should be stainless steel and sheaves should be as large as possible for long rope life. Make sure the rope cannot squeeze between the sheave and the cheeks of the block or a "panic party" may ensue.

The term *tackle* is used for an assemblage of *falls* (ropes) and *blocks*. When you pass ropes through the blocks, you *reeve* them and the part of the fall made fast to one of the blocks, or the weight, as the case may be, is known as the *standing part,* while the end upon which the force is to be applied is called the *hauling part*. To *overhaul the falls* is to separate the blocks; to *round in* is to bring them together; and *chock-a-block* or *two blocks* means they they are tight together.

FIG. 1114 PARTS OF A BLOCK

1. Hook
2. Inner Strap
3. Outer Strap
4. Pin
5. Swallows
6. Cheeks
7. Sheaves — either plain, roller, or self-lubricating
8. Breech
9. Becket
10. Thimble
11. Shell

DEFINITIONS:

Block
A frame of wood or metal within which are fitted sheaves or pulleys over which a rope runs. Blocks may be single, double, treble, etc. They are designated by the number of sheaves they contain. The lifting power is multiplied in ratio to the number of sheaves used.

Tackle
A combination of blocks, ropes and hooks for raising, lowering or moving heavy objects. A "tackle" increases lifting power but reduces lifting speed.

Fall Rope
That part of the tackle to which lifting power is applied.

Fall Block or Running Block
The block attached to the object to be moved.

Fled Block or Standing Block
Is fixed to a permanent support.

Standing End
The end of the fall fixed to the tackle.

Running End
The end opposite the standing end.

Return
Each part of the fall between the two blocks or between either end and the block.

Lifting Force
Is in ratio with the number of times the rope passes to and from the fall block.

To Overhaul
Is to separate the blocks.

To Round In
Is to bring the blocks closer together.

Two Blocks
Means the blocks of the fall are in contact.

Shell or Frame
Part which holds sheave or wheel.

(From Columbia Rope Co. rigger's booklet)

KINDS OF TACKLE

Tackles (fig. 1116) are named according to the number of sheaves in the blocks that are used (single, two-fold, three-fold purchases), according to the purpose for which the tackle is used (yard-tackles, stay-tackles, etc.), or from names handed down from the past (luff-tackles, watch-tackles, gun-tackles, Spanish-burtons, etc.). The tackles that may be found aboard cruising boats, and should be known are:

1. Single Whip—A single fixed block and fall—no increase in power. Gain only in height of lift or change in direction of pull.

2. Gun Tackle—Two single blocks. If lower block is movable, double force is gained. If upper block is movable, triple force is gained.

3. Luff Tackle—A double hook-block and single hook-block. Force gained three if single block is movable, four if double block is movable.

4. Two-Fold or Double Tackle—Two double sheave hook-blocks. Force gained four or five, depending upon application.

CALCULATING POWER OF A TACKLE

The force gained as given in all of these tackle combinations is theoretical only, as the friction of the blocks has been ignored. The method of calculating the actual force gained and compensating for this friction is to add

A — Hauling part
B — Standing part
C — Fixed block
D — Movable block
W — Weight

RATIO — 1:3   RATIO — 1:4

FIG. 1115 The number of falls leading to and from the movable block determines the ratio of force to weight necessary for lifting. In the right-hand sketch, the hauling part, A, "counts" in figuring the ratio because the pull on it is upward, unusual but possible.

10% to the weight W, for each sheave in the tackle before dividing by the number of falls. Thus, in Illustration 4 (fig. 1116) if W is 500 kg: 10% is 50 kg; 4 sheaves x 50 = 200 kg; total theoretical W then is 500 plus 200 = 700 kg. With 4 falls, the force needed on A to lift W would be 700 ÷ 4 or 175 kg, rather than an apparent 125 kg if friction were disregarded. This will vary with the type of bearings and pins, lubrication of the blocks, and sheave diameter.

There are, of course, a number of other purchases, the heaviest commonly used aboard ship being a three-fold purchase, which consists of two triple blocks. It must be remembered the hauling part reeved through a triple block should be led through the center sheave. If not, the block will cant causing it to bind and, in extreme cases, to break the block. This is especially true with a three-fold purchase.

TO OBTAIN GREATEST EFFICIENCY

To get the greatest mechanical efficiency, the hauling part should lead from the block with the most sheaves, and if both blocks have the same number it is best for the hauling part to lead from the movable block. It is also best to have the block with the greatest number of sheaves the movable block, as the number of falls leading to and from the movable block determines the ratio of force-to-weight necessary for lifting.

In the illustration (fig. 1116) showing two arrangements of luff tackles, in one there are three falls leading from the movable block and ratio of force-to-weight would be 1:3. Now change the blocks—the single block fixed and the double block made movable with the weight attached and the hauling part leading from it. Notice that, counting the hauling part, there are four falls leading to or from the now movable block, and the ratio becomes 1:4, which is quite an increase.

FIG. 1117 The size of line should be matched to the block it reeves through; see Table 11-5. Chafing at blocks can cause serious damage. The second and fourth blocks from the left in the photograph below are swivel blocks.

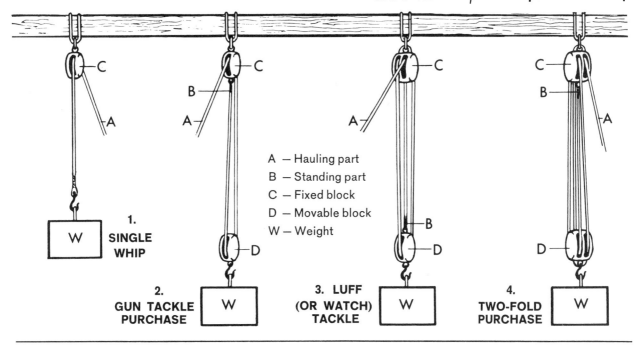

A — Hauling part
B — Standing part
C — Fixed block
D — Movable block
W — Weight

**1.
SINGLE
WHIP**

**2.
GUN TACKLE
PURCHASE**

**3. LUFF
(OR WATCH)
TACKLE**

**4.
TWO-FOLD
PURCHASE**

FIG. 1116 Some of the common tackles that are found aboard cruising boats.

Table 11-5

BLOCK AND ROPE SIZES *			
Size of Block (Length of Shell)	Diameter of Rope	Size of Block (Length of Shell)	Diameter of Rope
3	⅜ "	8	⅞ " – 1 "
4	½ "	10	1⅛ "
5	⁹⁄₁₆ "–⅝ "	12	1¼ "
6	¾ "	14	1⅜ "–1½ "
7	¹³⁄₁₆ "	16	1⅝ "

*NOTE—Some heavy blocks can accommodate larger rope sizes but the use of smaller blocks for larger rope than recommended reduces rope life. Too small diameter sheaves cause extra strain on outer rope fibers and increases internal friction. (1 inch = 2.54 cm)

FIG. 1118 Main sheet tackle rigged with a double block (movable) on the boom, and single block (fixed, with becket) on deck. The extra single block (foreground) does not increase power but serves as a fairlead. Note eye splice around thimble.

FIG. 1117A, left shows a snatchblock equipped with a swivel snap shackle. It is light, being made of phenolic resin, and very strong, being strapped with stainless steel. Snatchblocks open from the side, so that the bight of the line can be dropped onto the sheave, rather than reeved in from its end. Such blocks are indispensable in modern sailboats to allow rapid adjustment of sheet leads and quick rigging of emergency tackle. FIG. 1117B, right, shows the same block shackled to a car that can be fixed, by means of the knurled handle, in any of the holes in the track along which it slides.

THE BOSUN'S LOCKER

There is nothing that distinguishes a seaman from a lubber as much as his proficiency in marlinespike seamanship. There is nothing more pitiful than seeing someone make fast with a multitude of turns around a pile finished off with many fancy loops only to see a puff of wind cause the boat to tug and the entire conglomeration fall apart and the boat begin to drift. Again, it is impossible to keep a boat shipshape and Bristol fashion, if the ends of your lines have "cow's tails" (frayed or untidy ends of rope).

TERMINOLOGY

First let us all make sure that we understand certain terms. Marlinespike seamanship deals with rope and the methods of working it. *Rope* is cordage of all types and sizes: fiber, wire, small cordage. *Small stuff* is small cordage, usually made of tarred hemp, such as spun-yarn, seine twine, either cotton, linen or synthetic, marlin, ratline, houseline, roundline, frequently used as seizing for whipping, worming and serving line. *Line* is a general term applied on board ship to a piece of rope in use.

There are few ropes on shipboard. Here is a good question to ask boating friends or to send to a quiz program: "How many ropes are there aboard ship? Name them." There are but nine principal ropes on board ship. These are bell ropes, man ropes, top ropes, foot ropes, bolt

ropes, back ropes, yard ropes, bucket ropes, and tiller ropes. There may be one or two more, of less importance. The main thing to remember is that you don't make fast with a rope, you use a line; you don't trim in a sail with a rope or a sheet-rope, but with a sheet.

KINDS OF FIBER ROPE

There are various types of fiber rope, mainly manila, nylon, polyesters such as Du Pont Dacron or the English Terrylene, and polyolefins such as polyethylene and polypropylene. In addition you may find linen or flax, cotton, sisal, ropes made of two or more fibers in many combinations, and other fibers. New ones seem to come out every year.

Because the synthetics have proved themselves, both as to ultimate cost and ease of handling, they have replaced much of the natural fiber rope for yacht use.

Usually the rope is made from three strands but sometimes four-strand rope is made. A cable is made by twisting three ropes together. To keep rope from unlaying easily, each successive step is twisted in the opposite direction. This is done as follows: yarn—right-handed; strands—left-handed; rope—right-handed; and cable—left-handed. It is possible, however, to get left-handed rope and in this case the procedure is reversed. Left-laid genoa jib sheets and others that are winched hard run more freely (without kinks) when spun off the winch and released for tacking.

The newest kind of fiber rope is referred to as 2-in-1 double braid. This consists of an inner braided core of nylon or polypropylene and a braided cover of nylon or polyester. The double braid construction has gained wide acceptance for sheets and anchor rodes because its fiber combinations provide very low stretch, and because it is

FIG. 1119 Anchor line neatly coiled, clockwise, on deck. Note the grating below it to aid in drying.

FIG. 1120 Taking line from a new coil of natural fiber rope, reach down inside and take the inner fag end from the bottom. Coil clockwise if the rope is right-handed, as most is.

non-rotational so it will always run free (not kink). The double braid has greater bearing surface, so it holds better on winches and in the hand. It also retains flexibility, whether wet or dry, over extensive periods of use.

HOW ROPE IS MEASURED AND SOLD

The size of rope is measured in different ways. Marine fiber rope is measured by its circumference, although most yachtsmen have always designated it by its diameter. On the other hand wire rope is designated by its diameter. Therefore, two-inch wire rope is much thicker than two-inch (5.1 cm) fiber rope (⅝ inch or 1.6 cm diameter).

"Prepacked" lines made of double-braided rope are sold in many sizes, as pre-spliced dock lines ready for use.

FIG. 1122   Line is flemished down for neatness by laying it down in close concentric coils, one against the other, in the form of a flat mat, free end at the center. If left long in one spot it may discolor the deck. It does not dry as well as a loose coil. Sunlight may damage nylon and poly ropes.

FIG. 1121   Line faked down ready to run out rapidly. Coils, in practice, would lie closer together.

SAILBAG   **The Riding Turn Revisited**

The accompanying photograph shows a simple way to release the riding turn shown in Fig. 133B, provided a free winch is available on the lee side. A spare line (in this case the tail of the jammed sheet is being used for illustration) is clapped onto the sheet ahead of the turning block by means of a rolling hitch, and a strain taken on it which relieves the tension that binds the jammed winch drum—you can see the sheet hanging slack in the picture as it leads to the fouled winch.

If no other winch is available, the weather sheet winch, which is idle at this time, must be used to take the strain, and the relieving line must be led to it by snatchblock.

The rolling hitch, because of its unique property to hold under strain, yet slide freely when not under load, is one of the most useful knots aboard a sailboat.

Rope of natural fiber will deteriorate rapidly from continued dampness and therefore should always be dry before stowed. To dry, it is best to coil down loosely and place where the sun can get at the rope and the air can pass freely all about it. Of course, such rope should never be stowed in a locker that is not well ventilated and dry; for if not, there is not much use in drying the rope as it will rot in the locker.

One thing not generally understood about synthetic ropes is *cold flow.* Due to the nature of the fiber, a long sustained load may cause the fibers to stretch or elongate permanently with a consequent reduction in rope diameter and ultimate strength. Some synthetics are worse than others in this respect. Temperature affects the flow. In a surging load such as anchoring in moderate weather, the anchor line can recover. But in a hurricane or a long passage at sea the load might be continuous and cold flow could become a hazard.

USE AND CARE OF WIRE ROPE

Wire rope or strand is generally used on board cruising boats as standing rigging. On a number of sailboats, however, it is also used as running rigging. Steel is used almost exclusively in making wire rope. To preserve it from corrosion it is sometimes galvanized. Stainless steel is fine, but expensive. Some wire rope has a hemp core. This greatly increases flexibility and also acts as a cushion against sudden stress or heavy pull.

Great care must be taken of wire rope also. It should always be kept on a reel when not in use and must be reeled off and not slipped off over the ends of the reel. If kept in a coil it should be rolled off at all times. If a kink ever gets into a wire rope it is a disaster, as this practically ruins it. As with fiber rope, sharp bends will cause an excessive strain and greatly impair the efficiency.

It is important to note that whenever you see broken wires, "meat hooks" that surely cut up the hands, or when the diameter of the outside wires is worn to one-half the original diameter, it is time to condemn the rope as it is no longer safe.

COILING, FAKING AND FLEMISHING

When line is left on deck, or put in a locker, it should never be thrown down in a heap. Not only would this give a lubberly appearance, but if you needed to use the line, especially in a hurry, it might kink or tangle. For safety and good seamanship we always either coil, fake, or flemish down a line.

When it must be kept ready for emergency use, clear for running, a line is generally coiled down (figures 1119-1120) always with the lay (clockwise for right lay rope). To make a straight coil, a circular bight of the secured end is laid and successive bights are placed on top. When all the line has been used, the entire coil is capsized to leave it clear for running.

When the entire length of a line must be run out rapidly it is usually faked down (fig. 1121). To do this a short length of the free end is laid out in a straight line and then turned back to form a flat coil. Successive flat coils are then formed, laying the end of each coil on top of the preceding coils, rather like figure 8s.

When great neatness is desired a line is flemished down (fig. 1122). Successive circles of the line are wrapped about each other with the free end at the center. When it is finished it looks like a mat and with an old piece of line can be used as one.

A disadvantage of coiling down is that you must watch out for kinks. With a flemished-down line care must be taken to prevent coils from falling back and fouling the preceding coil. If a line is flemished down and left on deck

for some time it will mark the deck and remain wet on the under side. On small boats lines are usually either coiled down or flemished down.

KNOTS THE SEAMAN KNOWS

Before a person dares to take a boat out he should be able to make a bowline, two half hitches, clove hitch, square knot and sheet bend. (See figures 1103 c-g.) This is not all he should know, but they are the minimum. The following are those that every competent seaman should know:

A.—Knots in the end of a rope:

1. Overhand	6. Sheepshank
2. Bowline	7. Blackwall hitch
3. Running bowline	8. Figure 8
4. Bowline on a bight	9. Cat's-paw
5. French bowline	

B.—Knots for bending two ropes, or two ends of the same rope, together:

1. Square or reef	4. Single and double
2. Two bowlines	carrick bend
3. Single and double	5. Reeving line bend
sheet or becket bend	

C.—Knots for securing a line to ring or spar:

1. Fisherman's bend	6. Rolling hitch
2. Timber hitch	7. Clove hitch
3. Timber and half hitch	8. Studding sail tack bend
4. Two half hitches	9. Studding sail halyard
5. Round turn and two	bend
half hitches	

D.—Knots worked in the end of a rope:

1. Wall knot	3. Single Matthew Walker
2. Wall and crown	4. Lanyard knot

Rope end dip. A new, effective way to treat rope ends is to dip them into a red vinyl liquid called Whip-End Dip. It seals all rope ends in seconds, setting into a tough, flexible permanent finish that eliminates whipping.

SERVING MALLET · PARCELLING · WORMING · SERVING

FIG. 1123 Worming, parcelling and serving guards against severe chafe. The rule is: Worm and parcel with the lay; turn and serve the other way.

OTHER ARTS OF THE SAILOR

Besides the general classes of knots and the splices shown earlier, there are other types of work that all seamen should be able to do.

Back Splice: To put an enlarged, finished end on a line.
Stopper on a rope: A length of rope secured at one end used in securing or checking a running line.
Strap on a rope: Turns taken around a standing part with the tackle hooked through the bights.
Mouse a hook: A method of closing the open part of a hook with small stuff to assist in preventing the object to which it is hooked from jumping out.
Grommet strap: A grommet or continuous loop of rope, used to attach a hook to a block permanently.
Seizing: The lashing together of two ends of rope by continuous turns of small stuff. Word sometimes used to mean whipping.

As said before there is nothing more unseamanlike than cow's tails on the end of a line. There are many ways to prevent this such as a back splice, wall knot, etc., but perhaps the best method is by whipping. See fig. 1103-l. Another method, sewed whipping, is preferred as it is easier to get taut and much harder to pull off. Plastic whips that are shrunk on with heat are available but good "fancy" work is preferred over substitutes like friction tape. The advantage of whipping over the other methods of eliminating cow's tails is that it does not increase the size of the rope. This can work as a disadvantage: for example, a sheet can run through all the blocks, making it necessary to re-reeve. Another type, such as a wall and crown, will not allow the end to run through a block.

HOW TO PREVENT CHAFE

There is nothing that wears rope so fast as chafing. In order to prevent this, it is necessary to rig *chafing gear*. When the chafe is of only temporary nature the rope can be protected by wrapping a piece of canvas around it. However, when the chafe will be more or less permanent

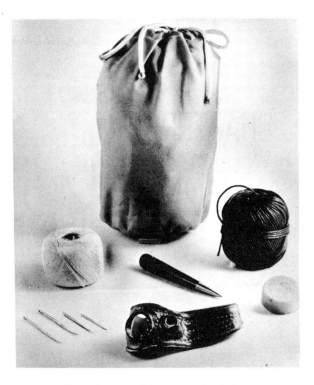

FIG. 1125 This ditty bag contains all the essentials for splicing and sail and canvas repair. Included are palm, assorted needles, marline, sail twine, and 6-inch heavy-duty steel spike.

or severe, the line should be wormed, parceled, and served or molded rubber gear, leather or rawhide, permanently attached.

Worming: consists of following the lay of the rope, between the strands, with small stuff, to keep the moisture out and for filling out the round of the rope.
Parceling: consists of wrapping the rope spirally with long overlapping strips of canvas, following the lay of the rope.
Serving: consists of wrapping small stuff over the parceling opposite to the lay of the rope to form a taut, protective cover. Should be hard-laid marline or seine twine for the best wear.

REPAIRS TO CANVAS

All seamen should be able to work with canvas and a needle. You should provide yourself with a sewing kit consisting of a small canvas kit bag, two or three short and long needles, some beeswax, and some small stuff. The long needle, usually triangular, straight, or curved, is generally used for sewing canvas, while the short needle, usually broad, straight or curved, is generally used for rope work.

There are four main types of stitches used in sewing canvas. Flat is used for seams in sails, tarpaulins, etc.; round is for making duffel bags; baseball, where a snug edge-to-edge fit in canvas is desired; and herringbone is for very stiff or painted canvas.

Have the right cordage for the job and take care of it well—then it will take care of you if you use it correctly.

FIG. 1124 This sail repair kit, created by Ratsey & Lapthorn, contains a sailmaker's palm, bench hook, thread, seven needles, awl, knife, wax, rule, pencil and booklet on sail care and handling.

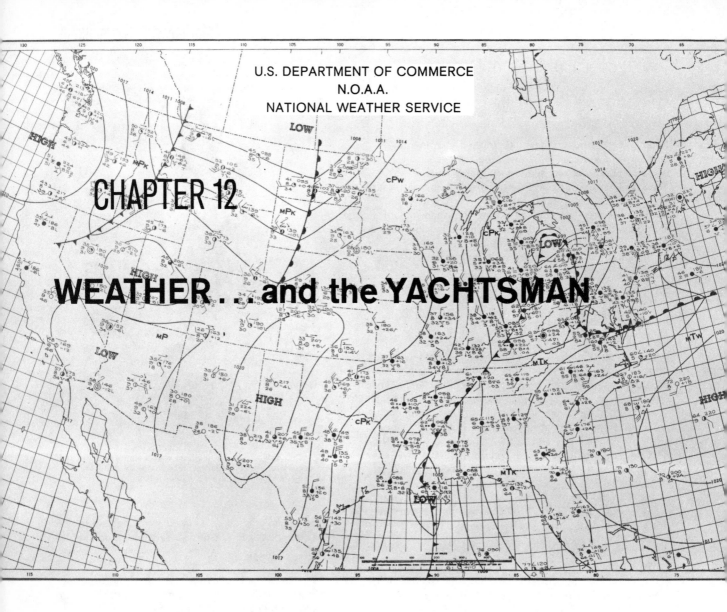

CHAPTER 12

WEATHER . . . and the YACHTSMAN

How to Read a Weather Map

THE WEATHER MAP provides a bird's-eye view of the weather over a large area. With its many figures, symbols and lines, the map at first appears to be puzzling. But with a little study of these markings and an understanding of their meaning, the map becomes a picture of the weather giving you a good idea of what's in store.

Some boatmen may receive the weekly compilations of daily weather maps mailed to subscribers by the National Weather Service, NOAA. Most skippers, however, depend upon newspaper maps for their information. These are drawn from Weather Service master weather charts. Four times each day, the Weather Service in Washington prepares and analyzes surface and upper air weather charts for the entire Northern Hemisphere.

On surface charts, weather data are plotted as received every six hours from more than 750 reporting stations in North America, more than 200 ships at sea, and 1500 stations in other countries. Each station reports the amount of sky covered by cloud, direction and speed of wind,

visibility distance in miles, present weather, weather during the last three hours, sea level barometric pressure, air temperature, kinds of low, middle and high clouds, dewpoint temperature, character and amount of pressure change in the last three hours, and the character, duration and amount of rainfall in the last six hours. Many of these stations also furnish twelve-hour reports of pressure, temperature, moisture and wind conditions for several levels of upper air. Thus, the central weatherman with his daily surface and several upper air charts has a detailed picture of the weather occurring at the same time over the entire Northern Hemisphere. These charts are used in issuing the daily weather forecasts and warnings of approaching storms.

Over 150 *symbols* are used in entering data on weather maps. Although you may never need know what all the symbols mean, nor have occasion to plot them on a weather map, a knowledge of those most often used will help you to understand and interpret the daily maps appearing in newspapers. See fig. 1201.

THE STATION MODEL

Fig. 1202 shows the *"station model,"* a system weathermen the world over developed for entering data on weather maps. It presents a "model" or picture of the weather at a station, using symbols and numbers, which can be understood in any language. Not only the symbols and numbers but their positions around the station circle tell what each item means. Fig. 1202 represents a typical arrangement.

Study these for a few moments. By referring to fig. 1201 and reading the parenthetical explanations in fig. 1202, you can interpret the weather at this particular station.

For example, starting with the "station circle" itself (the black dot in the middle)—the fact that this circle is solid black indicates that the sky is completely covered with clouds here.

Let's go counterclockwise around the station circle to examine and understand what's shown. Take the wind first. The symbol indicates a pretty windy day, the wind being from the northwest at 21 to 25 mph. The wind

arrows always "fly" with the wind (1 mph = 1.6 km/h).

Next is temperature in degrees Fahrenheit. As you can see, it was relatively cold, the thermometer registering only 31°. [(°F−32) x 0.56 = °C)]

Since we know the sky was completely overcast, the next two markings—Visibility and Present Weather—begin to give us a picture of conditions at the station. It was a nasty day with a stiff, cold wind blowing light snow all over the place.

PRECIPITATION SYMBOLS

A word about precipitation symbols is in order here. Fig. 1201 shows the symbols used to indicate different forms of precipitation—drizzle, rain, snow, etc. Increasing precipitation is indicated by more than one symbol being plotted, the range being from one to four identical symbols.

In fig. 1202 the use of the two stars (or asterisks) tells you that it is snowing continuously but lightly at this station. If there had been three stars the snow would have

SYMBOLS

SKY COVER				WEATHER Present and Past		WIND Miles per Hour		
0	○	5	◓	≡ FOGGY		○ Calm	○ 21-25	○ 50-54
1	◔	6	◕	, DRIZZLING		○ 1-4	○ 26-31	○ 55-60
2	◔	7	◑	• RAINING		○ 5-8	○ 32-37	○ 61-66
3	◒	8	●	✳ SNOWING		○ 9-14	○ 38-43	○ 67-71
4	◑	9	⊗	▽ SHOWERS		○ 15-20	○ 44-49	○ 72-77
				℞ THUNDERSTORMS				

FIG. 1201

FIG. 1202   Illustrating how symbols in fig. 1201 are used by weathermen to show weather conditions at a station.

FIG. 1203 A section of the Atlantic coast from a National Weather Service Surface Chart with data for several stations.

been moderate to heavy. Now, if the *shower* symbol (a triangle) had been shown instead of the star it would have carried a star symbol above it to indicate that the showers were *snow* showers. If the showers were *rain* the shower symbol would have carried a dot (the rain symbol) above it.

Hail is indicated by a small triangle (inverted shower symbol) above the thunderstorm symbol. Fog is represented by three horizontal lines.

Other symbols around the station circle in fig. 1202 are interesting and important to weathermen and anyone wishing to use the information. They are worth studying but since most of them do not appear on the abbreviated maps appearing in newspapers we won't go into a detailed description here. Fig. 1202 does provide a brief explanation of each.

Fig. 1203 shows a small portion of a Weather Service surface chart with data plotted for several stations. By re-

Cold Front ▼▼▼   Occluded Front ▲▲▲   Stationary Front ▲▼▲▼

FIG. 1205 Section of a weather map with fronts, isobars, HIGHS, LOWS, and direction of fronts plotted on it.

Inches	Millibars	Inches	Millibars
28.44	963	29.77	1008
28.53	966	29.86	1011
28.62	969	29.94	1014
28.70	972	30.03	1017
28.79	975	30.12	1020
28.88	978	30.21	1023
28.97	981	30.30	1026
29.06	984	30.39	1029
29.15	987	30.48	1032
29.24	990	30.56	1035
29.32	993	30.65	1038
29.41	996	30.74	1041
29.50	999	30.83	1044
29.59	1002	30.92	1047
29.68	1005	31.01	1050

FIG. 1204 Conversion table for a weather map's millibars.

ferring to figs. 1201 and 1202 you can tell what the weather conditions at any given station are. Let's take Raleigh, N. C. as a case in point:

You can see that the sky is completely overcast, the wind is south, at 9 to 14 mph, the temperature is 69°F., the dew point is 68°, the numeral 2 indicates the clouds were low, the letter T says that precipitation in the past 6 hours was very slight, T standing for "Trace," the barometer has fallen 1.0 millibar during the past 3 hours, there were thunderstorms at the station during the past 6 hours, and

FIG. 1206 Typical abridged weather map commonly appearing in newspapers.

the pressure is 1018.5 millibars or 30.08 inches of mercury.

Fig. 1204 provides a conversion table for changing millibars to inches and vice versa.

ISOBARS AND FRONTS

When data from all stations are entered on the map, the weatherman draws black lines, called *isobars*. These are lines drawn through points having the same ("iso-" means equal) barometric pressure. For example, a 1020 millibar (30.12 inches) isobar is a line drawn through all points having a barometric pressure of 1020 millibars. Ad-

FIG. 1207 Diagrams indicate action of cold and warm fronts and show how their interaction forms occluded fronts.

ditional isobars are drawn for every four millibar intervals. The purpose of the isobars is to position the centers of low and high pressure—the familiar "LOWS" and "HIGHS" which govern our weather. The centers of high pressures are marked "H" or "High" and the low pressures are marked "L" or "Low." It is the movement of these HIGHS and LOWS which enables the weatherman to forecast weather, taking into consideration, of course, the various data supplied by the weather stations.

The heavier lines in fig. 1205 are drawn to indicate "*fronts*"—the boundaries between different air streams. Triangles and half circles are attached to these heavier lines pointing in the direction in which the fronts are mov-

ing. The triangle indicates a "*cold front*," the half circle a "*warm front*." (See also fig. 1207.)

A front which is not moving, one which is "*stationary*," is shown by attaching triangles on one side of the line and half circles on the opposite side. An "*occluded front*" is indicated by attaching both triangles and half circles to one side of the line. Fronts and their significance will be explained later.

WEATHER OFFICES

If you visit a Weather Service office you can see the latest surface and upper air weather maps. Maps prepared at the Weather Service Headquarters are sent to various stations over a picture (facsimile) transmission circuit. Maps prepared by local stations appear much the same as the Washington maps with a few exceptions. The cold fronts, for instance, will be drawn on the map in blue pencil, warm fronts in red, occluded fronts in purple, while the stationary front will be shown by a line of alternating red and blue dashes.

NEWSPAPER WEATHER MAP

Because of their reduced size, it is impossible to include on newspaper maps all of the data usually entered on a map prepared at a Weather Bureau office. To permit easier reading, only sky covered by cloud or other forms of present weather, wind direction and speed, and air temperature are plotted for each station. Barometric pressure at each station is omitted because it can be estimated for any place from the nearest isobar (remember—isobars represent lines of equal barometric pressure). Incidentally, on some weather maps, isobars may be drawn for 3 millibar intervals; for example, 996, 999, 1002, etc., rather than the 4 millibar intervals. Some maps show isobars marked at one end with the millibar pressure and at the other end in inches. Symbols used for entry of all this information, including those for types of fronts, are usually shown in the margin of newspaper maps. See fig. 1206.

Morning newspapers usually contain the weather map prepared from data collected the evening before, while afternoon editions publish the early morning chart. The time is noted on the newspaper chart.

Analysis of the Weather Map

We don't need to know how to draw the isobars and fronts on a weather map in order to be able to read one, but we can review to advantage the method used by the professional weatherman. First, the meteorologist enters on the chart the observations at all stations from which he has received reports. The entries, which include both instrumental and visual observations, are recorded partly in numerical and partly in symbolic form, as illustrated in fig. 1202. Second, he delineates any fronts that may exist, using preceding maps, in addition to present information, as a guide to their locations.

Let's take an actual case as analyzed by the late Dr. B. C. Haynes, Senior Meteorologist with the U.S. Weather Bureau, and published by the Bureau in its booklet "An-

alysis of a Series of Surface Weather Maps." Fig. 1208 is the finished map for 1930 EST Wednesday, 17 April, in the year the analysis was made. Given the observations at each station, how was analysis of the data accomplished?

LOCATING THE FRONTS

Consider first the location of the fronts. A *front* is the boundary between two contiguous bodies, or masses, of air which have come from different geographical regions and traveled along different routes (see fig. 1209) and which, therefore, have different physical properties. The *position of a front* is marked principally by the difference in the temperatures of the two air masses, the difference

U. S. DEPARTMENT OF COMMERCE
NATIONAL WEATHER SERVICE

FIG. 1208 The finished weather map for 1930 EST Wednesday, 17 April.

in dew points (the temperature at which the air is saturated with moisture), differences in barometric pressure and pressure tendency, and differences in wind direction and velocity.

To make a start, we examine the plotted data and find that the lowest barometric pressure (998.0 millibars for this map) is at a station in western Indiana. Note that the general wind pattern over Kentucky, Tennessee and the southwestern states is from south to southwest. Over Illinois, Missouri, Kansas and the central plains states the general wind pattern is northwest to north. Different air masses must be over each of these regions and these air masses must be separated by a front. Beginning at our station in western Indiana we will draw this front.

To confirm our finding that a front exists, we look at the next station due west of our starting point; it is located in central Illinois. Here are the salient data at the two stations:

	Western Indiana	Central Illinois
Air temperature	65°	37°
Dew point	60°	36°
Pressure	998.0 mb	1,004.4 mb
Pressure tendency	−2.2 mb	+2.4 mb
Wind direction	SW	N

The differences are sharp; we are on the right track.

We continue southwestward across Illinois, southeastern Missouri, central Arkansas, the northwestern tip of Louisiana, eastern Texas, and into Mexico, all the time comparing the observations at different stations and placing the front between those showing critical contrasts.

Kinds of Fronts

We have drawn a front on our map, but what kind of front is it? To the west and northwest of this front, the observations show relatively colder air moving from the north or northwest; to the east and southeast they show relatively warmer air moving from the south. The colder air is moving toward the front. As it is colder and heavier, it pushes the warmer, lighter air eastward before it, at the same time driving under this warmer air and lifting it off the ground. Cold air is displacing warm; we have a *cold front*.

Are there any more fronts to be found? Starting again at our station in western Indiana, suppose we work eastward this time. Through southern Michigan and northern Ohio we again find differences in wind direction and velocity, in air temperature and dew point. These differences remain quite sharp all the way to western Pennsylvania. We have located another front, a *warm front* this time as the somewhat colder air north of our line is retreating to the northeast and warmer air south of the line is following and replacing the colder.

As we continue eastward from western Pennsylvania, the front becomes more obscure; the differences between the air masses become less pronounced. On the other hand, reports of rain, overcast skies and fog continue. The winds are lighter. We draw in a *stationary front* (neither air mass moving appreciably against the other), all the way across West Virginia, Virginia, and North Carolina to the sea.

Warm fronts and cold fronts are *active* weather factories; a stationary front is a *potential* weather factory. The latter may gradually dissipate or it may resolve itself into an active front.

Taking a final glance at the map, we notice another wind shift and temperature difference in eastern Montana. Applying the same technique, we locate another, a short, warm front in this region. We now have our frontal analysis complete.

FIG. 1209 North American Air Masses. Source regions and directions of movement of air masses influencing North American weather are shown. Air remaining in contact with earth's surface gradually acquires properties characteristic of the surface beneath it. Then, as this air mass subsequently moves over the earth, its properties, and its conflicts with other air masses that it may encounter en route, cause changes in weather of the area invaded.
(Reproduced by courtesy of Aviation Training Division, U.S. Navy)

ANALYSIS OF PRESSURE INDICATIONS

Our next action is to analyze the map for pressure indications; we need to know the pattern of the *isobars*, where high and low pressure centers exist, *the nature of the pressure field*. Because of the earth's rotation, the wind blows, not directly from high to low pressure, but nearly parallel to the isobars and only slightly across them toward low pressure. The more closely spaced the isobars, the stronger the winds in that area. The closely spaced isobars mean that a greater pressure difference exists, hence the winds are stronger, but the earth's rotation still makes them blow almost along the isobars. Observe the wind direction arrow at each station, then note the direction of adjacent isobars. Compare the velocity of the wind, as indicated by the number of feathers on the arrow, with the spacing of the isobars.

To get back to the map for 17 April, we have a low-pressure center in western Indiana. We find a high-pressure center in northeastern Nevada and another off the coast of Maine. There is a high over the central plains states, another over central Canada, and others off the South Atlantic and Pacific coasts. In addition to our western Indiana low, there are lows in the southwest, off the east coast of Texas, and over western Canada.

As we approach our long cold front, the isobars become more closely spaced; the pressure differences are greater and the winds are stronger. It is not too promising a time for a comfortable cruise along the east coast, the Gulf, Mississippi or Great Lakes.

FIG. 1210 Cumulonimbus cloud, indicative of very unstable air. Strong updrafts and severe turbulence are found in and around center of the cloud. Note heavy rain shower falling out of it.

FIG. 1211 A layer of stratus cloud, typical of moist, stable air. In this picture the stratus is very low; shreds of cloud trailing downward from base of the layer are visible against dark hillside.

LABELING THE AIR MASSES

The fourth step is to determine the *kinds of air masses* on either side of each front. A given air mass has its own individual properties; these properties tell us much about the kind of weather we can expect. Having located our fronts and completed the pressure analysis, we can label these air masses. Look at fig. 1208 again.

In the southeastern United States, the winds and pressure gradient indicate that a broad current of air is flowing from over the warm waters of the Gulf northward across the southeastern states. The high temperatures and high dew points in this area tell us that this air is warm and moist. As this is a late afternoon (1930 EST) map, the air has been further heated for many hours by re-radiation of the sun's heat by the earth, which means that the air probably is unstable. The thunderstorms and showers, cumulus and towering cumulonimbus clouds (see fig. 1210) reported at various stations confirm the diagnosis. We label this air with the symbol mTk, meaning that it is *unstable, tropical maritime air,* air that can result in foul weather.

Looking north of the front along the Atlantic Coast, we note that the winds and pressure gradient indicate an onshore movement of air from over the Atlantic Ocean. Temperatures and dew points are fairly low; fog and low clouds (see fig. 1211) are shown at many stations. These are signs of *maritime, stable polar air* so we label it mPw, the w indicating that it is relatively warmer than the land over which it is moving and hence not given to heating from below. It will lose heat to the earth; more low clouds, fog and light rains are probable.

To the west of our main cold front, we observe northerly winds, low temperatures and low dew points. Many stations report stratocumulus clouds (see fig. 1212) and a few report cumulus clouds. The temperatures recorded tell us that this air mass is being warmed as it moves southward. Again we have unstable air. As it came, however, from northward over Canada and not from over an ocean, it is

unstable, continental, polar air. We label it cPk.

Studying our map further, we find *stable continental polar air* over the Dakotas (cPw) and *unstable moist (maritime) polar air* (mPk) over the northwestern states.

ESTIMATING EXPECTED CHANGES

We can now make a rough estimate of the changes that will take place during the next 12 hours. The cold front extending from western Indiana to eastern Texas should move eastward in response to the push of the relatively cold northwesterly winds over Illinois, Missouri, Arkansas, Oklahoma and Texas. The warm front across northern Ohio and western Pennsylvania should advance across Lake Erie as the relatively cool air situated to the northeast of the warm front gives way to the moist tropical air flowing from the south. The low-pressure center over western Indiana should be displaced northeastward along the advancing warm front. We should expect this center to move toward the area where the largest negative pressure tendencies are observed, namely, southern Michigan.

A feature of the 1930 EST 17 April map which should not pass unnoticed is the small low-pressure center spotted in the Gulf of Mexico just southeast of the southern tip of Texas. This center appears to be unconnected with the cold front, and its future behavior is hard to judge.

Now let's look at the map for 0730 EST 18 April (fig. 1213). We find that the low-pressure center which was over western Indiana twelve hours earlier has moved in a general northeasterly direction and is situated somewhere between Lake Huron and Lake Ontario. The actual center may be spotted about 100 miles east of the station in eastern Michigan that reports a pressure of 1000.3 millibars, temperature 35°, dew point 35°, and a northwest wind. (Incidentally, twelve hours earlier this same station reported a due north wind, an indication that the cold air there was holding its ground against the advancing warm front. This fact explains why the low-pressure center

PHOTOGRAPH CREDITS: Figure 1212, W. Humphreys. Figures 1210, 1211, 1218, 1223, 1224, 1228, and 1239, Frank A. Montgomery.

U. S. DEPARTMENT OF COMMERCE
NATIONAL WEATHER SERVICE

C-1

FIG. 1212 Stratocumulus clouds in the rear of a LOW.

0730 E. S. T., THURSDAY, APRIL 18

FIG. 1213

moved in a slightly more easterly direction than we had expected from our consideration of the pressure tendencies reported at 1930 EST 17 April.)

From the point of lowest pressure north of Lake Erie we can start our diagnosis of the location of the cold front. The front quite clearly runs southwestward through Ohio and Kentucky, between the stations reporting northwest winds and the stations reporting southerly winds. To the east of the front, temperatures are quite uniformly in the low sixties and dew points in the upper fifties. To the west of it both temperatures and dew points decrease rapidly westward, being in the thirties at a distance of 200 miles (320 km) from the wind shift line.

In Tennessee the east-to-west contrasts of temperature and dew point become less sharp, but pronounced differences in wind direction still exist, with winds from the south over eastern Tennessee, Alabama and eastern Mississippi, in contrast to winds generally from the north over western Tennessee, northwestern Mississippi and central and western Louisiana.

If we look at the pressure reports from the region near the Gulf Coast we find a barometric reading at New Orleans of 1004.1 millibars (fig. 1213). This indicates the presence of another low-pressure center, which is almost certainly the same one that we noticed southeast of Texas twelve hours earlier. It has now made connections with the original cold front, and is affecting the movement of this front, as we shall now determine.

In drawing the 1008 millibar isobar northward from the Gulf Coast we find that it no longer can be traced with practically no change in direction all the way to western Pennsylvania, as it could on the preceding map (fig. 1208). It intersects the front in northeastern Mississippi and thence must make a sharp turn to the left, with the result that it returns to the Gulf via western Louisiana. It has become separated from the 1008 millibar isobar to the north, which crosses the front in southwestern Ohio and closes around the northern low-pressure center.

Changes in Wind Pattern

This splitting of the isobaric pattern means that changes in the wind pattern have taken place from Tennessee southward. In eastern Louisiana especially, it can be seen that the winds in the moist tropical air have backed to southeast, while on the other side of the front the winds in the cold air have, in general, veered to a straight northerly, or even north-northeasterly direction. Hence, the winds in the cold air have become more nearly parallel to the front. The result is that the eastward advance of the front has been abruptly stopped; the front has become stationary or is even beginning to reverse its course and to move slowly to the west. Therefore, from the point in Tennessee to just west of New Orleans the front may now be marked a warm front. Southwest of the low-pressure center near New Orleans we assume that the cold air is advancing eastward across the Gulf of Mexico and so we indicate there that the front is acting as a cold front.

RELOCATING THE WARM FRONT

Let us now see how to locate the warm front that extended eastward across northern Indiana, northern Ohio, and thence southeastward to the Middle Atlantic Coast at 1930 EST of 17 April (see fig. 1208). The determination of the position of this front has to be based largely on temperature differences and dew-point differences, since the contrast of wind directions on either side of it are nowhere near as marked as in the case of the cold front.

Beginning at the center of low pressure just east of Lake Huron (fig. 1213), the warm front runs southeastward and may be found in western New York lying between the station that reports a south-southwest wind, pressure 1001.0 millibars, temperature 60°, dew point 58°, and the station in central New York with a southeast wind, pressure 1006.1 millibars, temperature 52°, dew point 45°.

From this point the front extends southward through western Pennsylvania. We determine that it lies between the station in extreme southwestern Pennsylvania (Pittsburgh) which reports a south-southwest wind, temperature 61°, dew point 58°, and the station in central Pennsylvania reporting a southeast wind, continuous light rain, temperature 54°, dew point 47°. (The temperature-dew point combination of 61°/58° observed at Pittsburgh is characteristic, for that latitude, of the moist tropical air that has come from the Gulf of Mexico.)

Beyond this point the position of the front does not show up clearly, owing to the lack of reports from stations in Maryland and northeastern Virginia. We are on safe ground, however, if we draw it between stations reporting south to southwest winds and places where the winds range from northeast to southeast. On this basis we determine that the front intersects the coastline at about latitude 38°. From there we project it eastward out to sea.

We shall not take time to analyze the weather features over the western part of the United States at 0730 EST of 18 April, since little of interest is occurring there. And so we conclude our brief study of the weather map.

SUBSEQUENT DEVELOPMENTS— IN RETROSPECT

The reader, however, may be interested to hear what happened to the principal frontal system and its two associated low-pressure centers during the next four days. During the interval between 0730 EST of 18 April and 0730 EST of 19 April the northern low-pressure area continued its northeastward movement and reached a position just north of the St. Lawrence River. But, meanwhile it weakened considerably, its lowest pressure on 19 April being not less than about 1005 millibars. The northern part of the cold front which extended southwestward from it pushed across Pennsylvania, New York and New England, all the way to the Atlantic. Further south, however, the advance of cold air was slowed by the developing low-pressure center which we noted near New Orleans at 0730 EST of 18 April. During the next 24 hours this center moved north-northeastward to Tennessee, all the while strengthening; by 0730 EST of 19 April it had become more prominent than the northern center.

Subsequently it continued to intensify, as it changed course to a more easterly direction, and eventually it developed into a severe storm. At 0730 EST of 22 April it was located about 250 miles (400 km) east of Nantucket; the pressure at its center has fallen to about 972 millibars (28.70″). It caused exceptionally strong gales off the New England coast during 21 April.

Note: (°F. − 32) × 0.56 = °C.

Types of Storms

EXTRA-TROPICAL CYCLONES

The principal source of rain, winds and generally foul weather in the United States is the *extra-tropical cyclone.* There are other storms—the hurricane, the thunderstorm and the tornado—that are usually more destructive but it is a fact that the extra-tropical cyclone is the ultimate cause of most of our weather troubles. Fog is another enemy not to be taken lightly, as we shall see, but let's concentrate on storms right now. If we would take proper and timely precautions for them, we should know something of their characteristics.

A definition of an extra-tropical cyclone in the Northern Hemisphere is: a traveling system of winds rotating counterclockwise around a center of low barometric pressure and containing a warm front and a cold front.

How extra-tropical cyclones develop

We saw what one looked like on the daily weather map. Fig. 1214 is a diagram (plan view) of the birth, development and death of an extra-tropical cyclone. Our thanks are due Captain Charles G. Halpine, USN, for permission to reproduce this diagram from his book "A Pilot's Meteorology," published by D. van Nostrand Company.

In part (a) of fig. 1214, we have a warm air mass, typically moist tropical air, flowing northeastward and a cold air mass, typically polar continental, flowing southwestward. They are separated by a heavy line representing the boundary or front between them. The next stage is shown in part (b). The cold air from behind pushes under the warm air; the warm air rushes up over the cold air ahead of it. A cold front is born on the left, a warm front on the right. Where they are connected, the barometric pressure is lowered and the air starts circulating counterclockwise around this LOW. At the rear of the cold front, a high-pressure area

develops. At the same time, the whole system keeps moving in a general easterly direction. The crosshatched area represents rain. When warm, moist air is lifted, as it is when a cold air mass pushes under it or when it rushes up over cold air ahead, it cools by expansion. After its temperature has fallen to the dew point, excess water vapor condenses to form first clouds and then rain.

In parts (c) and (d) of fig. 1214, the storm matures, the low-pressure area intensifying more and more, the clouds and rain increasing and the winds becoming stronger. In part (e), the cold front begins to catch up with the warm front; an occluded front is formed. The storm is now at its height. It will do about one-half of its mischief while in occlusion. In part (f), it has begun to weaken; after a while, the weather should clear, as the high-pressure area reaches us.

Extra-tropical cyclones often occur in families of two, three or four storms. It takes about one day (24 hours) for this disturbance to reach maturity with three or possibly four days more required for complete dissipation. In winter, these storms occur on the average of twice a week in the USA; in summer they occur somewhat less frequently and are less severe. Their movement is eastward to north of east at a speed in winter of about 700 miles (1125 km) per day and in summer perhaps 500 miles (805 km). Finally, this storm usually covers a large area; it can affect a given locality for two days or more.

Parts of the extra-tropical cyclone

The component parts of an extra-tropical cyclone are:
1. A warm front, with its two conflicting air masses and its weather.
2. A cold front, with its two conflicting air masses, one of which (the warmer) is situated between the cold front and the warm front.

FIG. 1214 Diagram of development of extra-tropical cyclone.
(Reproduced by courtesy of Captain C. G. Halpine, U.S.N., and D. van Nostrand Co., Inc.)

(A)

(B)

(C)

(D)

(E)

(F)

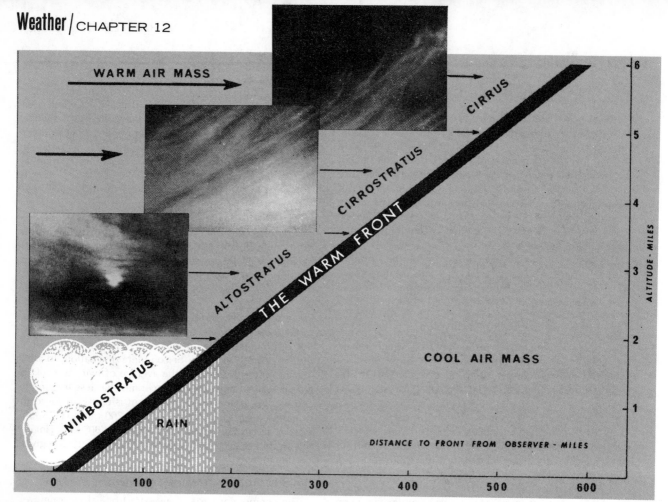

WARM AIR MASS

CIRRUS

CIRROSTRATUS

ALTOSTRATUS

THE WARM FRONT

COOL AIR MASS

NIMBOSTRATUS

RAIN

DISTANCE TO FRONT FROM OBSERVER - MILES

ALTITUDE - MILES

FIG. 1215

3. A center of low barometric pressure with its wind system, at the junction of the fronts.

4. A high pressure area behind the cold front.

A typical cruising experience

In early May a few years ago we were cruising down the Mississippi. We noticed on the weather map that there was an extra-tropical cyclone far to the WSW, its center moving NE along a path that would leave us SSE of it. The warm front, the warm sector between the fronts, and the cold front would pass over us if we continued our cruise. Being stubborn, we kept on but watched carefully for the approaching trouble.

The first day the weather was fine with gentle winds and light fluffy cumulus clouds. The next morning we observed cirrus (Ci) clouds (fig. 1215) to the westward and noted that the barometer was falling. As these slowly thickened, we knew that the warm front was perhaps 500 miles, about one day, away. As the day wore on, the barometer fell more rapidly, the wind blew increasingly strong from the southeast, and the clouds thickened to the cirrostratus (Cs) of fig. 1215. A halo appeared around the sun.

Altostratus (As) clouds (fig. 1215) next were seen approaching from westward. Knowing that these clouds precede a warm front by about 300 miles and that rain can be expected about 200 miles ahead of the front, it required no magician to tell us that we had better begin securing

Note: 100 statute miles = 161 km.

ship and breaking out the oilskins. We observed that the spread between the air temperature and dew-point temperature was growing less and less; it looked as though we could also expect fog. We decided to anchor until the warm front had passed over.

Next came the low nimbostratus (Ns) clouds and the rain, the barometer continuing to fall and the temperature slowly to rise. The visibility grew worse and worse. The ship's bell began its clamor and we spent a not too comfortable night. By morning, however, the wind had veered to SSW, the clouds had begun to break, the barometer had stopped falling, the rain had ceased. Knowing that it might be 6 to 12 hours before the cold front struck us, we got under way, keeping our eyes peeled for altocumulus (Ac) clouds to the westward. The watch below was set to airing the cabins and our duffle as we ran through the warm sector.

About 1400 the lookout spotted the altocumulus clouds (fig. 1216); the cold front was perhaps 100 miles away. As the day was hot and quite humid, we thought that thunderstorms were probable and that they might be severe. We decided to anchor early, about 1500, and prepare for the worst. The barometer was again falling, the wind was SW and increasing. Nimbostratus (Ns) clouds with cumulonimbus (Cb) (fig. 1216) towering out of them appeared to the west. Rain set in and the wind rose sharply. We had a busy few hours—and were mighty glad that we had known enough to recognize and time the warning signs. By the

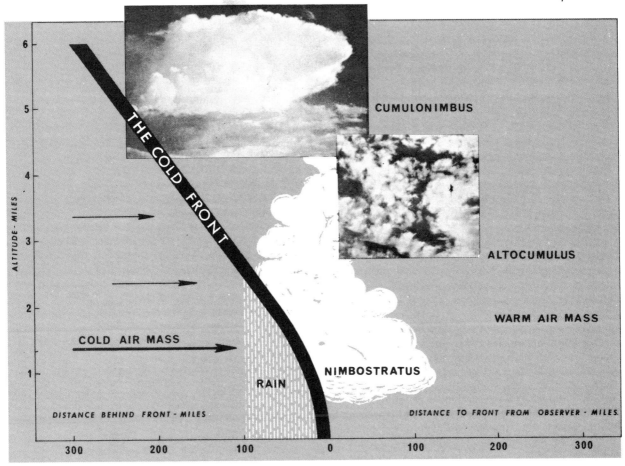

CUMULONIMBUS

ALTOCUMULUS

WARM AIR MASS

NIMBOSTRATUS

COLD AIR MASS

RAIN

DISTANCE BEHIND FRONT - MILES

DISTANCE TO FRONT FROM OBSERVER - MILES

FIG. 1216

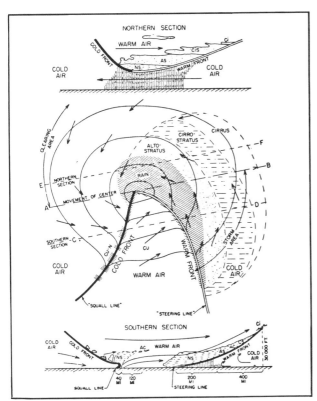

FIG. 1217 Cross-sections of extra-tropical cyclone. (Reproduced by courtesy of Captain C. G. Halpine, U.S.N., and D. van Nostrand Co., Inc.)

next morning the storm was over and we continued our cruise with a blue sky and fair winds.

Thus, we passed through an extra-tropical cyclone. Fig. 1217 is a picture of it, again with acknowledgement to Captain Halpine. The central portion is a plan view of the storm; the lower portion is a vertical cross-section along the line CD, our "course" through the storm. The cloud sequences and the rain are clearly shown (Cb symbol omitted). Had we passed north, instead of south, of the center, the upper diagram would represent the clouds and weather.

HURRICANES

Another type of cyclone which is of concern principally to those of us cruising the Gulf of Mexico and the southeast Atlantic coast is the *tropical cyclone*, which in its most violent (and best known) form is called a *hurricane*. Unlike the extra-tropical cyclone, it does not contain warm and cold fronts, and its occurrence (over waters adjacent to the United States) is restricted to summer and autumn.

The hurricane as a storm type is too well known among sailors to require any description here of the various premonitory signs, the violence of the wind and rain accompanying such a storm and the steps to be taken to minimize the dangers of encounter. These are fully detailed in standard nautical works, such as Bowditch's "American Practical Navigator."

FIG. 1218 Wall cloud around eye of a hurricane, as seen from an aircraft within the eye. Upper edge of wall cloud is at an altitude of nearly 40,000 feet. Note clear space in right foreground.

Over the years much statistical information on the frequency of hurricanes in various regions of the world has accumulated. In the Far East hurricanes (or *typhoons*, as they are called in the western Pacific) may occur in any month, although late summer and early autumn are the preferred seasons. In North American waters, however, the period from early December through May is hurricane-free. August, September and October are the months of greatest frequency; in these months hurricanes form over the tropical Atlantic, mostly between latitudes 8°N and 20°N. The infrequent hurricanes of June and November almost always originate in the southwestern part of the Caribbean Sea.

Development of a hurricane

The birthplace of a hurricane typically lies within a diffuse and fairly large area of relatively low pressure situated somewhere in the latitude belt just mentioned. The winds around the low-pressure area are not particularly strong, and, although cumulonimbus clouds and showers are more numerous than is usual in these latitudes, there is no clearly organized "weather system." This poorly-defined condition may persist for several days before hurricane development commences.

When development starts, however, it takes place suddenly. Within an interval of 12 hours or less the barometric pressure drops 15 millibars or more over a small, almost circular area. Winds of hurricane force spring up and form a ring around the area; the width of this ring is at first only 20 to 40 miles. The clouds and showers become well-organized and show a spiral structure. At this stage the growing cyclone acquires an eye. This is the inner area enclosed by the ring of hurricane-force winds, which, by the time the cyclone reaches maturity, has expanded to a width of 100 miles or more. Within the eye we find the lowest barometric reading.

Hurricane eyes average about 15 miles in diameter but may be as large as 25 miles. The wind velocities in the eye of a hurricane are seldom greater than 15 knots and often are less. Cloud conditions vary over a wide range. At times

Note: 1 statute mile = 1.61 km. 1 nautical mile = 1.85 km.

FIG. 1219 Path of the hurricane, showing positions of the center at 0700 EST, 18-22 September 1938.

244

there are only scattered clouds, but usually there is more than 50% cloud cover. Through the openings the sky is visible overhead and at a distance the dense towering clouds of the hurricane ring can be seen extending to great heights (fig. 1218). This feature has been given the name *wall cloud*.

Hurricane tracks

The usual track of an Atlantic hurricane describes a parabola around the semipermanent Azores-Bermuda high-pressure area. Thus, after forming, a hurricane will move westward on the southern side of the Azores-Bermuda HIGH, at the same time tending to work away from the equator. When the hurricane reaches the western side of this HIGH, it begins to follow a more northerly track, and its direction of advance changes progressively toward the right. Thus, the usual movement of Atlantic hurricanes at first is roughly westward, then northwestward, northward, and finally northeastward. The position where the westward movement changes to an eastward movement is known as the *point of recurvature*.

Occasionally when a hurricane is in a position near the

FIG. 1220 Constancy of anticyclonic flow, as shown by unchanged orientation of sea-level isobars from September 19 to September 20. Upper figure of each pair of numbers is barometric reading on September 19, lower figure that on September 20. Although a general fall of pressure took place during the interval, flow pattern remained the same.

southeast Atlantic coast, the Azores-Bermuda HIGH happens to have an abnormal northward extension. In this type of situation the hurricane will fail to execute a complete recurvature in the vicinity of Cape Hatteras. It will skirt the western side of the HIGH and follow a path almost due north along the Atlantic coast, as occurred in the case of the famous New England hurricane of September 1938 (see figs. 1219 and 1220).

The rate of movement of tropical cyclones while they are still in low latitudes and heading westward is about 15 knots, which is considerably slower than the usual rate of travel of extra-tropical cyclones. After recurving they begin to move faster and usually attain a forward speed of at least 25 knots, sometimes 50 to 60 knots, as in the case of the September 1938 hurricane. A small proportion of hurricanes, however, do not recurve at all, and a few of these follow highly irregular tracks which may include a complete loop.

Hurricanes gradually decrease in intensity after they reach middle and high latitudes and move over colder water. Many lose their identity by absorption into the wind circulation around the larger extra-tropical cyclones of the North Atlantic.

THUNDERSTORMS

We stated at the beginning of this section that the extra-tropical cyclone was the ultimate cause of most of our foul weather. We said this advisedly, because in addition to the strong winds and generally wet weather which it generates, smaller-scale storms, such as *thunderstorms* and *tornadoes,* usually are created by the contrasting air masses and conflicting winds within the large-scale, over-all air circulation of the extra-tropical cyclone. Thus, thunderstorms are commonly linked to the cold front of the cyclone. But if the air comprising the warm sector is sufficiently unstable, which is often the case in summer, thunderstorms together with general rain will occur during the approach of a warm front as the warm-sector air ascends over the cold air ahead. They also develop on their own in the middle of an air mass, unaided by frontal activity.

We know a thunderstorm as a storm of short duration, arising only in a cumulonimbus cloud, attended by thunder and lightning, and marked by abrupt fluctuations of temperature, pressure and wind. A *line squall,* now usually referred to in meteorological parlance as a *squall line,* is a lengthy row of thunderstorms stretching for 100 miles (160 km) or more.

Incidentally, a *shower* (as opposed to gentle, steady rain) is a smaller brother, though the rainfall and wind in it may be of considerable intensity. It characteristically is the product of relatively large cumulus, or small cumulonimbus, clouds separated from one another by blue sky. It is not accompanied by thunder and lightning.

Features of the thunderstorm cloud

In all cases the prime danger signal is a cumulus cloud growing larger. Every thunderstorm cloud has four distinctive features, although we may not always be able to see all four as other clouds may intervene in our line of sight. Fig. 1221 shows these four features; the anvil top is better illustrated in fig. 1222. These three photographs of an anvil were taken from the same position over a period of one-half hour!

FIG. 1221 Diagram of thunder-storm cloud.
(Courtesy of Aviation Training Division, U.S. Navy)

Key to Diagram of Cumulonimbus Cloud

A – Anvil Top		**U** – Up Drafts	
B – Dark Area		**R** – Primary Rain Area	
C – Roll Cloud		**R'** – Secondary Area	
C$_u$ – Advance Cumulus Clouds		**W** – Wind Direction	
D – Down Drafts			

Fig. 1221 is a drawing, by courtesy of the Navy Bureau of Aeronautics from their booklet "Thunderstorms" (Aerology Series Two), of a cumulonimbus cloud; it shows these four features diagrammatically. Starting at the top, we notice the layer of cirrus clouds, shaped like an anvil and consequently called "anvil top," leaning in the direction toward which the upper wind is blowing. This tells us the direction in which the storm is moving.

The next feature is the main body of the cloud; it is a large cumulus of great height with cauliflower sides. It must be of great height, as it must extend far above the freezing level if the cirrus anvil top is to form. Cirrus clouds are composed of ice crystals, not water droplets. The third feature is the roll cloud formed by violent air currents along the leading edge of the base of the cumulus cloud. The fourth and final feature is the dark area within the storm and extending from the base of the cloud to the earth; at the center this is rain, at the edges hail and rain.

Requirements for thunderstorm formation

There are three requirements for the formation of thunderstorms. One, there must be strong upward air currents such as are caused by a cold front burrowing under and lifting warm air or by heating of the air in contact with the surface of the earth on a summer day. Warm, humid air blowing up a mountain slope also can produce a thunderstorm. Two, the air parcels forming the storm must be buoyant relative to their neighbors outside the storm and willing, therefore, to keep on ascending higher and higher until they pass the freezing level. Third, the air must have a large concentration of water vapor. The most promising thunderstorm air is of tropical maritime origin; whenever it appears in our cruising area, especially when a cold front is approaching, we need to be suspicious.

Frequency of thunderstorms

Thunderstorms occur most frequently and with the greatest intensity in the summer over all parts of the USA. While they may strike at any hour, they prefer the late afternoon and early evening over inland and coastal waters. The surrounding land has been a good "stove" for many hours, heating the air to produce strong upward currents. Over the ocean, well away from shore, thunderstorms more commonly occur between midnight and sunrise. Finally, thunderstorms are most frequent and most violent in tropical latitudes; they are less common and less intense in the higher latitudes. The southeastern states experience as many as four thunderstorms per week in summer.

Ahead of a thunderstorm the wind may be either steady or variable, but as the *roll cloud* (fig. 1221) draws near, the wind weakens and becomes unsteady. As the roll cloud passes overhead, violent shifting winds, accompanied by strong downdrafts, may be expected. The wind velocity may reach 60 knots. Heavy rain and sometimes hail begins to fall just abaft the roll cloud. However, the weather quickly clears after the passage of the storm, which brings cooler temperatures and lower humidity.

If the cumulonimbus cloud is fully developed and towers to normal thunderstorm altitudes, 35,000 feet (10.7 km) or more in summer, the storm will be violent. If the anvil top is low, only 20,000 feet (6.1 km) or so, as is usual in spring and autumn, the storm will be less severe. If the cumulonimbus cloud is not fully developed, particularly if it lacks the anvil top, and the roll cloud is missing, only a shower may be expected.

We can time the approach of a thunderstorm, once the cumulonimbus cloud is visible, by a series of bearings. If we wish, we can estimate its distance off by another

FIG. 1222 Growth of the anvil of thunderstorm cloud. Top photograph was taken at 1200, the middle at 1220, the lower at 1230 from same position as storm developed.
(Courtesy National Weather Service)

method. The thunder and lightning occur simultaneously at the point of lightning discharge, but we see the lightning discharge much sooner than we hear the thunder. Consequently, time this interval, in seconds. Multiply the number of seconds by 0.2; the result will be approximate distance off in statute miles (multiply by 0.34, or divide by 3, to get distance off in kilometers.

TORNADOES

When numerous thunderstorms are associated with a cold front, the storms are apt to be organized in a long, narrow band. The forward edge of this band is usually marked by a *squall line,* along which the cold downdrafts from a series of thunderstorms meet the warm air (see fig. 1221). Here the wind direction changes suddenly in vicious gusts, and a sharp drop in temperature occurs. The importance of squall lines is that they often spawn a most destructive type of storm, the deadly *tornado.* We should keep firmly in mind the fact that tornadoes have wrecked boats on the Mississippi and elsewhere in the southern part of the USA.

Tornadoes formed at squall lines often occur in families and move with the wind that prevails in the warm sector ahead of the cold front. This wind direction is usually from the southwest. The warm air typically consists of two layers, a very moist one (source: Gulf of Mexico) near the

FIG. 1223 The terrifying "funnel" of a tornado is actually a cloud of water droplets mixed with dust and debris. Close to the ground, dust and debris are plentiful, because greatly reduced atmospheric pressure inside funnel (a lowering of pressure of the order of 50 millibars) causes air to whirl violently inward and upward.

FIG. 1224 Waterspout over St. Louis Bay, off Henderson Point, Mississippi. Note cloud of spray just above sea surface.

ground and a relatively dry layer above. The temperature decreases with altitude relatively rapidly in each layer. When this combination of air layers is lifted along a squall line or cold front, excessive instability develops and violent updrafts are created.

A tornado is essentially an air whirlpool of small horizontal extent which extends downward from a cumulonimbus cloud and has a funnel-like appearance (see fig. 1223). The average diameter of the visible funnel cloud is about 250 yards (230 m) but destructive effects of the system of whirling winds may extend outward from the tornado center as much as ¼ mile (0.4 km) on each side. The wind speed near the core can only be estimated, but it undoubtedly is as high as 200 knots. This means almost certain death of the occupants of a boat which might have the misfortune to be in the path of a tornado.

Fortunately, the tornado belt in the USA is in the interior section of the country, but still there are boating areas which can be affected. So, if you live in the Midwest or the southern tier of states, keep your radio tuned to your local station, if weather conditions look threatening. The National Weather Service has a highly refined and reliable system for forecasting the likelihood of tornadoes.

Waterspouts

The marine counterpart of the tornado is the *waterspout*. The conditions favoring the formation of waterspouts at sea are similar to those conducive to the formation of tornadoes over land. Waterspouts are much more frequent in the tropics than in middle latitudes. Although they are less violent than tornadoes, nevertheless they are a real danger to small craft.

A waterspout, like a tornado, forms under a cumulonimbus cloud. A funnel-shaped protuberance first appears at the base of the cumulonimbus and grows downward toward the sea. Beneath it the water becomes agitated and a cloud of spray forms. The funnel-shaped cloud descends until it merges with the spray; it then assumes the shape of a tube that stretches from the sea surface to the base of the cloud (see fig. 1224).

The diameter of a waterspout may vary from 20 to 200 feet (6 to 60 m) or more. Its length from the sea to the base of the cloud is usually between 1000 and 2000 feet (300 to 600 m). It may last from 10 minutes to half an hour. Its upper part often travels at a different speed and in a different direction from its base, so that it becomes bent and stretched-out. Finally, the tube breaks at a point about one-third of the way up to the cloud base, and the "spout" at the sea surface quickly subsides.

The existence of considerably reduced air pressure at the center of a waterspout can be inferred from visible variations of the water level. A mound of water, a foot or so high, sometimes appears at the core, because the atmospheric pressure on the water surrounding the spout is perhaps 30 to 40 millibars greater than that on the sea surface inside the funnel. This difference causes the rise of water at the center.

Like the tornado, the visible part of a waterspout is composed, on the whole, of tiny water droplets formed by the condensation of water vapor in the air. Considerable quantities of salt spray, however, picked up by the strong winds at the base of the spout, are sometimes carried far aloft. This has been verified by observations of the fall of salty rain following the passage of a waterspout.

FOG

How, Why, Where and When It Forms — Its Distribution in the United States

The essential part is not always to know things; it is to know how to reason about them. This truism applies to fog. The basic causes of fog are few in number and easy to understand. What we want is a working knowledge of these causes; then we can judge if and when fog is likely to upset our plans.

Fog is merely a cloud whose base rests upon the earth, be the latter land or water. It consists of water droplets, suspended in the air, each droplet so small that it cannot be distinguished individually, yet present in such tremendous numbers that objects close at hand are obscured.

If we are to have innumerable water droplets suspended in the air, there must be plenty of water vapor originally in that air. If droplets are to form from this vapor, the air must be cooled by some means so that the vapor will condense. If the droplets are to condense in the air next to the earth, the cooling must take place at the surface of the earth. If the fog is to have any depth, successively higher

layers of air must be cooled sufficiently to cause condensation in them. Fog forms from the ground up. Thus, the land or water must be colder than the air next to it; the lower layers of air progressively must be colder than the layers above them.

If water vapor is to condense out of the air, then the temperature of the air must be lowered to or below the *dew-point temperature,* that is, the temperature at which the air is saturated with water vapor and below which condensation of water vapor will occur.

Air is said to be *saturated* with water vapor when its water-vapor content would remain unchanged if it were placed above a level surface of pure water at its own temperature. The amount of water vapor which is required to saturate a given volume of air depends on the temperature of the air, and increases as the temperature increases. The higher the temperature the more water vapor can the air hold before it becomes saturated, and the lower the temperature the less water vapor can the air hold before it becomes saturated.

If a mass of air is originally in an unsaturated state, it can be saturated by cooling it down to a temperature at which its content of water vapor is the maximum containable amount, that is to say, to the dew-point temperature. Or we can saturate it by causing more water to evaporate into it, thereby raising the dew-point temperature to a value equal to the air temperature. In regard to the latter process, unsaturated air, as it passes over rivers and lakes, over the oceans or over wet ground, picks up water vapor and has its dew point raised. Also, rain falling from higher clouds will increase the amount of water vapor in unsaturated air near the earth.

JUDGING THE LIKELIHOOD OF FOG

In order to judge the likelihood of fog formation, we should periodically measure the air temperature and dew-point temperature and see if the spread (difference) between them is getting smaller and smaller. The Navy, in its Aviation Training booklet "Fog" (Aerology Series 3) has provided us with a diagram of the change in spread; it is reproduced here as fig. 1225.

Fig. 1226 is a graph of a series of air and dew-point temperatures. By recording these temperatures and plotting their spread over a period of several hours, as is indicated by that part of the curve drawn as a solid line, we have a basis for forecasting the time at which we are likely to be fog-bound. The dot-dash portion of the curve represents actual data but it could just as easily have been drawn by extending the solid portion. If an error were made in this extrapolation, it would probably indicate that the fog would form at an earlier hour. This is on the safe side; we would be secure in our anchorage some time before the fifty-ninth minute of the eleventh hour!

Note that the curve is not a straight line. While the average decrease in spread is about one and one-half degrees (Fahrenheit) per hour, the decrease is at a much greater rate in the earlier hours. So long as we do not make unreasonable allowances for a slowing up in the rate of change of the spread, this also will help to keep us on the safe side.

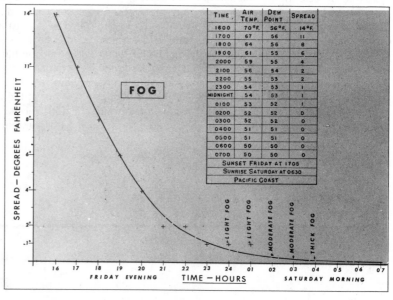

FIG. 1226 Graph of a series of air and dew-point temperatures.

FIG. 1225 Why fog forms.
(Reproduced by courtesy of Aviation Training Division, U.S. Navy)

DETERMINING THE DEW POINT

How do we determine the dew point? By means of a simple-to-operate, inexpensive little gadget known as a *sling psychrometer* (fig. 1227). A sling psychrometer is merely two thermometers, mounted in a single holder with a handle that permits it to be whirled overhead. One thermometer, know as the *dry bulb,* has its bulb of mercury exposed directly to the air. This thermometer shows the actual temperature of the air. The other thermometer, known as the *wet bulb,* has its bulb covered with a piece of gauze. We soak this gauze in water so that the bulb is moistened. If the air is not saturated with water vapor, evaporation then takes place from the wet-bulb thermometer, and the wet bulb is cooled, since the process of evaporation requires the expenditure of heat. The reduced temperature shown by the wet-bulb thermometer, the so-called "wet-bulb temperature," represents the lowest temperature to which the air can be cooled by evaporating water into it.

FIG. 1227 A pocket-type sling psychrometer, having two 5" etched tubes, 20° to 120° in 1° divisions.
(Courtesy Taylor Instrument Companies)

When we whirl the psychrometer we create a draft around the instrument. The ventilation so produced increases the efficiency of the evaporation process and makes the wet-bulb reading more reliable than it would be if there were little or no air movement past the wet bulb. This is the reason why the psychrometer is designed for whirling.

From the wet-bulb temperature and dry-bulb temperature, the dew point may be determined by referring to a suitable table. As we are far more interested, however, in knowing the *spread, or difference, between the air temperature and dew point,* we will save ourselves some work by using another table (Table 12-1), its use being explained in the next two paragraphs.

If the air is already actually saturated with water vapor, then no water can evaporate from the gauze and both thermometers must show the same value. The dew point then has this same numerical value and so the spread between air temperature and dew point must be zero. But, as explained above, if the air is not already saturated with water vapor, the wet-bulb thermometer will give a lower reading than the dry-bulb thermometer. We subtract the wet-bulb temperature from the dry-bulb temperature. With this difference and the dry-bulb (the air) temperature, we consult Table 12-1 and find directly the corresponding spread between the air temperature and the dew-point temperature. This is the figure we want.

If, in the late afternoon or early evening, the spread between the air temperature and dew point is less than approximately 6°F, and the air temperature is falling, fog or greatly restricted visibility will probably be experienced in a few hours. These critical values are emphasized by the heavy line above which they lie in Table 12-1. Incidentally, should we ever want to know the dew-point temperature itself, all we need do is to subtract the spread figure given in the table from the temperature shown by the dry-bulb thermometer. Thus, when the dry-bulb thermometer indicates an air temperature of 70°F and the difference between the dry-bulb and wet-bulb temperatures is 11°F, the spread is 19°F and the dew point is 51°F.

FOUR TYPES OF FOG

We can distinguish four types of fog: (a) *radiation fog,* formed in near-calm conditions by the cooling of the ground on a clear night as a result of radiation of heat from the ground to the clear sky; (b) *advection fog,* formed by the flow of warm air over cold sea or lake; (c) *steam fog,* or "sea smoke," formed when cold air blows over much warmer water; and (d) *precipitation fog,* formed when rain coming out of warm air aloft falls through a shallow layer of cold air at the earth's surface.

Radiation fog

There are four requirements for the formation of *radiation fog* (sometimes called "ground fog"). First, the air must be stable, that is, the air next to the earth must be colder than the air a short distance aloft. Second, the air must be relatively moist. Third, the sky must be clear, so that the earth readily can lose heat by radiation to outer space. This enables the ground to become colder than the overlying air, which subsequently is cooled below its dew point both by contact with the ground (conduction of heat) and by radiative loss of heat to the ground.

The fourth requirement is that the wind must be light to calm. If there is a dead calm, the lowest strata of air will not mix with the ones above, and fog will form only to a height of two to four feet. If there is a slight motion of the air (say a wind of three to five knots) and, hence, some turbulent mixing, the cooling is spread through a layer which may extend to a height of several hundred feet above the ground. With strong winds, the cooling effect is distributed through so deep a layer that the temperature nowhere falls to the dew point and fog does not form.

Radiation fog is most prevalent in the middle and high latitudes. It is local in character and occurs most frequently in valleys and lowlands, especially near lakes and rivers where we may be cruising. The cooled air drains into these terrain depressions; the lake or river aids the process of fog formation by contributing water vapor, which raises the dew point.

This type of fog, which may be patchy or uniformly dense, forms only at night. Shortly after sunrise, it will start

TABLE 12-1	AIR TEMPERATURE —— DEWPOINT SPREAD											
(All figures are in degrees Fahrenheit at 30" pressure)												

Difference Dry-Bulb Minus Wet-Bulb	Air Temperature Shown By Dry-Bulb Thermometer												
	35	40	45	50	55	60	65	70	75	80	85	90	95
1	2	2	2	2	2	2	2	1	1	1	1	1	1
2	5	5	4	4	4	3	3	3	3	3	3	3	2
3	7	7	7	6	5	5	5	4	4	4	4	4	4
4	10	10	9	8	7	7	6	6	6	6	5	5	5
5	14	12	11	10	10	9	8	8	7	7	7	7	6
6	18	15	14	13	12	11	10	9	9	8	8	8	8
7	22	19	17	16	14	13	12	11	11	10	10	9	9
8	28	22	20	18	17	15	14	13	12	12	11	11	10
9	35	27	23	21	19	17	16	15	14	13	13	12	12
10	–	33	27	24	22	20	18	17	16	15	14	14	13
11	–	40	32	28	25	22	20	19	18	17	16	15	15
12	–	–	38	32	28	25	23	21	20	18	17	17	16
13	–	–	45	37	31	28	25	23	21	20	19	18	17
14	–	–	–	42	35	31	28	26	24	22	21	20	19
15	–	–	–	50	40	35	31	28	26	24	23	21	21

Opposite — Difference Dry-Bulb Minus Wet-Bulb and
Under   — Air Temperature Shown By Dry-Bulb Thermometer
Read   — Value of Spread: Air Temperature minus Dewpoint Temperature

Based on U.S. Weather Bureau Psychrometric Tables

(°F. — 32) × 0.56 = °C.

FIG. 1228 Fog bank over Lake Huron. This is basically an advection-type fog which has formed over an area of relatively cold water. When the wind is very light and unsteady, as in this case, fog tends to concentrate in patches, even after it has drifted away from its source.

FIG. 1229 Sea smoke in Great Harbor, Woods Hole, Massachusetts, 0915 EST, 31 December 1962. Water temperature 31.6°F; air temperature (30 feet above sea level) +5°F. Wind NW 20 knots. Height of steaming approximately 15 feet. Rigging of vessel encountering this type of condition will become coated with rime ice. Note frosty deposit on beach grass in lower right corner of photograph.
(Courtesy of P. M. Saunders, Woods Hole Oceanographic Institution)

to evaporate ("burn off") over the land, the lower layers being the first to go. It is slow to clear over water, since the temperature of the water does not vary nearly as much from day to night as does the temperature of the land.

Advection fog

Radiation fog bothers us chiefly in the late summer and early autumn; *advection fog* can be an annoyance at any season. (Advection means transport by horizontal motion.) Winds carrying warm, moist air over a colder surface produce advection fog. The dew point of the air must be higher than the temperature of the surface over which the air is moving. Thus, the air can be cooled below its dew point by conduction and by radiation of heat to the colder surface. Other requirements for the formation of advection fog are as follows: (a) the air at a height of 100 feet or so must be warmer than the air just above the surface; (b) the temperature of the surface—be it land or water— must become progressively colder in the direction toward which the air is moving. Fig. 1230, again by courtesy of the U.S. Navy from its "Flying the Weather," illustrates the formation of advection fog along the coast and fig. 1231

its formation at sea. Advection fog may form day or night, winter or summer, over the sea.

Coastal Fog. For yachtsmen the most bothersome variety is *coastal fog* (fig. 1230). When steady winds blow landward and carry warm oceanic air across cold coastal water, the resulting fog may blanket a great length of coastline and, especially at night, may extend many miles inland up bays and rivers. For example, let's go to the Pacific coast, where the water close to the land is often colder than the water to westward. The prevailing winds in summer are onshore and the air, since it frequently has come from mid-Pacific, usually is nearly saturated with water vapor. Fig. 1230 illustrates the result; the same thing happens when southerly winds carry air across the Gulf Stream and thence northward across the colder Atlantic coastal waters. Advection fog also may form over the larger inland lakes whenever relatively warm and moist air is carried over their colder surfaces.

Advection fog is generally much harder to dissipate than is radiation fog. A wind shift or a marked increase in wind velocity usually is required. Sunshine has no effect on it over the water.

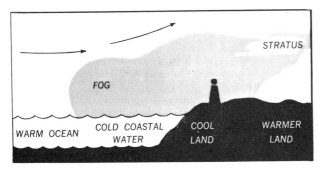

FIG. 1230 Coastal fogs are common along the West Coast—warm ocean, cool coastal water, frequent winds from the sea. (Courtesy Aviation Training Division, U.S. Navy)

FIG. 1231 Most persistent sea fog is an advection fog that forms when air blows from warm sea to cold sea.

FIG. 1233 Formation of precipitation fog.

American coastal waters are concerned, this variety of steam fog occurs most frequently off the coasts of Maine and Nova Scotia, and in the Gulf of St. Lawrence, where it can be a serious navigational hazard. However, its occurrence is not restricted to the higher latitudes. Off the east coast of the United States it has been observed as far south as Florida and it occurs occasionally over the coastal waters of the Gulf of Mexico.

Steam fog

On the Mississippi and Ohio rivers, a special type of fog, known as *steam fog* is a particular hazard to late evening or early morning cruising in the autumn. When cold air passes over much warmer water, the lowest layer of air is rapidly supplied with heat and water vapor. Mixing of this lowest layer with unmodified cold air above can, under certain conditions, produce a supersaturated (i.e., foggy) mixture. Owing to the fact that the water is much warmer than the air, vertical air currents are created, and we observe the phenomenon of steaming. Hence, this type of fog is called "steam fog"; it forms in just the same way as steam over a hot bath.

Sea Smoke. When, in winter, very cold air (having a temperature less than about 10°F) blows off the land and across the adjacent coastal waters, steam fog may be widespread and very dense. It is then known as "*sea smoke*" (sometimes called "*Arctic sea smoke*"). As far as North

Precipitation fog

As mentioned earlier, we can distinguish a fourth type of fog, which we may call "*precipitation fog,*" or "*rain fog.*" When rain, after descending through a layer of warm air aloft, falls into a shallow layer of relatively cold air at the earth's surface, there will be evaporation from the warm raindrops into the colder air (see fig. 1233). Under certain conditions, this process will raise the water-vapor content of the cold air above the saturation point and fog will form. Its mode of formation is similar to that of the fog produced in the bathroom when one takes a hot shower.

It may be noted that both steam fog and rain fog are basically the result of evaporation from relatively warm water, a process which increases the dew point. These fogs can be placed in the single category of "*warm-sur-face*" fogs. Likewise, radiation fog and advection fog come under the single heading of "*cold-surface*" fogs.

FIG. 1232 Steam fog forming, then dissipating upwards, over pond near Mount Kisco, N.Y., 0700 EST, 12 October 1964. Air temperature approximately 25°F; water temperature not known, but probably 50°F or higher. Wind less than 1 knot.
(Photograph by Caroline S. Emmons)

FIG. 1234 Map showing distribution of fog in the United States. Isopleths show mean annual number of days with "dense fog, i.e., fogs obscuring visibility to 1000 feet or less." In order to bring out more detail in the large portion of the country where fogginess is less than 20 days, an interval of 5 days was selected. For regions with more than 20 days of fog a 10-day interval is used.

DISTRIBUTION OF FOG IN THE UNITED STATES

Turning our attention now to the distribution of fog (all types included) in the United States, we find that the coastal sections most frequently beset by fog are (1) the area from the Strait of Juan de Fuca to Point Arguello (Calif.), on the Pacific Coast, and (2) the area from the Bay of Fundy to Montauk Point (N.Y.), on the Atlantic Coast. In these waters the average annual number of hours of fog occurrence exceeds 900, that is, more than 10% of the entire year. In the foggiest parts of these areas, namely, off the coast of Northern California and the coast of Maine, fog is present about 20% of the year.

As we go southward along both the Atlantic and Pacific Coasts the frequency of fog decreases, but it does so much more rapidly on the Atlantic Coast than on the Pacific. Hence, we find that the average annual fog frequency over the waters adjacent to Los Angeles and San Diego is about three times that in the same latitude along the Atlantic Coast.

SEASONAL FREQUENCIES

The *time of maximum occurrence* of fog off the Pacific Coast varies somewhat with the various localities and, of course, with the individual year. In general, however, over the stretch from Cape Flattery (Wash.) to Point Arguello the season of most frequent fog comprises the months of July, August, September and October, with more than 50% of the annual number of foggy days occurring during this period. However, along the lower coast of California, that is, from Los Angeles southward, the foggiest months are those from September through February, and the least foggy from May through July.

On the Atlantic side: Off the coast of New England the foggiest months are usually June, July and August, with a maximum of fog generally occurring during July, in which month fog normally is encountered from one-third to one-half of the time. Off the Middle Atlantic Coast, however, fog occurs mostly in the winter and spring months, with a distinct tendency toward minimum frequency in summer and autumn. Along the South Atlantic Coast (from Cape Hatteras to the tip of Florida) and in the Gulf of Mexico fog rarely creates a problem for the yachtsman. It is virtually non-existent during the summer, and even in the winter and early spring season (December through March), when it has maximum frequency, the number of days with fog hardly anywhere exceeds 20, on the average, during this four-month period.

The *fog regime of the Great Lakes* is essentially like that of the oceanic coastal waters in middle latitudes; the Great Lakes as a whole tend to have more fog in the warmer season. The explanation of this circumstance is to be found in the comparison of the lake temperatures with the air temperatures over the surrounding land. From March or April to the beginning of September the lakes are, on the average, colder than the air. Hence, whenever the dew-point temperature is sufficiently high, conditions are favorable for the formation of advection fog over the water.

The greatest fogginess occurs when and where the lakes are coldest in relation to the air blowing off the surrounding land. On Lake Superior, north-central Lake Michigan, and northwestern Lake Huron the *time* of maximum frequency is late May and June; elsewhere it is late April and May. As to the *location* of maximum fogginess, since the lake temperatures become colder from south to north and from the shores outward, the occurrence of fog increases northward and towards the central parts of each lake.

Observations Afloat—Weather signs

We have already discussed fog and how we can use a sling psychrometer to help us in forecasting its occurrence. There are a few other weather instruments which are practical on shipboard and which provide us with helpful information.

WIND OBSERVATIONS

Every sailor is familiar with the *wind direction indicators* that may be mounted at the masthead. Because a boat, at anchor or under way, can head in any direction all around the compass, a few mental calculations are necessary before we can use this indicator or an owner's flag or club burgee to determine the true direction of the wind. At anchor, the fly will give us the bearing of the wind relative to the boat's head; this must be converted to the true bearing of the wind itself. We can use our compass to obtain these values, provided we know its deviation on our heading and know the variation for our anchorage. Also, we need to remember that wind direction is always stated as the true direction *from* which, not toward which, the wind is blowing.

FIG. 1235 Danforth/White's anemometer with flush-mounted wind velocity indicator supplies accurate readings on two scales (0-25 and 0-120 knots). Two-wire conductor leads from indicator to masthead or spreader. Wind direction indicator is a matching unit.

The anemometer

For measuring *wind velocity* we need something else. This is an *anemometer;* the principal parts of the instrument are illustrated in fig. 1235. The anemometer is essentially a speedometer. It consists of a rotor with conical cups attached to the ends of spokes and is designed for mounting at the masthead, where the wind is caught by the cups, causing them to turn at a speed proportional to the speed of the wind. Indications of the rotor's speed are transmitted to an indicator which may be mounted in the cabin.

In the type of instrument illustrated in fig. 1235, the indicator is direct-reading, in two scales from 0 to 25 and 0 to 120 knots for velocity, gusts and variations. Battery drain (.09 amp.) is insignificant. A 60-foot (18 m) cable is supplied to connect the rotor aloft with the illuminated indicator below. At anchor, the reading is the actual or true wind velocity at masthead height.

True and apparent wind

So far we have been considering the determination of the direction and speed of the wind while at anchor. Under way, the determination is more difficult, but the Oceanographic Office of the Navy has worked out the problem, so we may as well use their results. Table 12-2 is based on wind tables formerly published in Bowditch. Using our true course and speed, we can determine from this table the approximate *true* wind direction and velocity, provided we know the *apparent* direction and velocity. Our wind indicator or owner's flag will give us the apparent direction and our anemometer will give us the apparent velocity.

The Beaufort Scale

Another method is to estimate the strength of the wind in terms of the *Beaufort Scale* of Wind Force. Visually we can observe the sea condition and note the Beaufort number to which it corresponds (see Table 12-3). The range of wind velocity represented by each force number on the Beaufort scale is shown in the extreme left-hand column of Table 12-3.

Wind direction can be judged by observing the direction from which the smallest ripples are coming, since these ripples always run with the wind, responding instantly to changes in wind direction.

We don't need to determine wind direction and velocity with great precision, but reasonable estimates are helpful in preparing our own local forecasts. Estimating direction to two points is sufficient; within one Beaufort number is enough for velocity. By observing wind direction and velocity regularly and making a record of them we can obtain clues concerning potential weather developments as the wind shifts direction and changes its velocity.

TABLE 12-2

TRUE FORCE AND DIRECTION OF THE WIND FROM ITS APPARENT FORCE AND DIRECTION ON A BOAT UNDER WAY

APPARENT WIND VELOCITY (Knots)	SPEED OF BOAT							
	5 Knots		10 Knots		15 Knots		20 Knots	
	TRUE WIND		TRUE WIND		TRUE WIND		TRUE WIND	
	Points off Bow	Velocity Knots	Points off Bow	Velocity Knots	Points off Bow	Velocity Knots	Points off Bow	Velocity Knots
I. APPARENT WIND DIRECTION IS DEAD AHEAD								
Calm	D. As.	5 K.	D. As.	10 K.	D. As.	15 K.	D. As.	20 K.
4 K.	D. As.	1 K.	D. As.	6 K.	D. As.	11 K.	D. As.	16 K.
8 K.	D. Ah.	3 K.	D. As.	2 K.	D. As.	7 K.	D. As.	12 K.
12 K.	D. Ah.	7 K.	D. Ah.	2 K.	D. As.	3 K.	D. As.	8 K.
16 K.	D. Ah.	11 K.	D. Ah.	6 K.	D. Ah.	1 K.	D. As.	4 K.
22 K.	D. Ah.	17 K.	D. Ah.	12 K.	D. Ah.	7 K.	D. Ah.	2 K.
30 K.	D. Ah.	25 K.	D. Ah.	20 K.	D. Ah.	15 K.	D. Ah.	10 K.
42 K.	D. Ah.	37 K.	D. Ah.	32 K.	D. Ah.	27 K.	D. Ah.	22 K.
60 K.	D. Ah.	55 K.	D. Ah.	50 K.	D. Ah.	45 K.	D. Ah.	40 K.
II. APPARENT WIND DIRECTION IS 4 POINTS (BROAD) OFF THE BOW								
4 K.	11 pts.	4 K.	14 pts.	8 K.	15 pts.	12 K.	15 pts.	17 K.
8 K.	7 pts.	6 K.	11 pts.	7 K.	13 pts.	11 K.	14 pts.	15 K.
12 K.	6 pts.	9 K.	9 pts.	9 K.	11 pts.	11 K.	13 pts.	14 K.
16 K.	5 pts.	13 K.	7 pts.	11 K.	10 pts.	12 K.	11 pts.	14 K.
22 K.	5 pts.	19 K.	6 pts.	16 K.	8 pts.	15 K.	9 pts.	16 K.
30 K.	5 pts.	27 K.	6 pts.	24 K.	7 pts.	22 K.	8 pts.	21 K.
42 K.	4 pts.	39 K.	5 pts.	36 K.	6 pts.	33 K.	6 pts.	31 K.
60 K.	4 pts.	57 K.	5 pts.	53 K.	5 pts.	51 K.	6 pts.	48 K.
III. APPARENT WIND DIRECTION IS 8 POINTS OFF THE BOW (ABEAM)								
4 K.	13 pts.	6 K.	14 pts.	11 K.	15 pts.	16 K.	15 pts.	20 K.
8 K.	11 pts.	9 K.	13 pts.	13 K.	14 pts.	17 K.	14 pts.	22 K.
12 K.	10 pts.	13 K.	12 pts.	16 K.	13 pts.	19 K.	13 pts.	23 K.
16 K.	10 pts.	17 K.	11 pts.	19 K.	12 pts.	22 K.	13 pts.	26 K.
22 K.	9 pts.	23 K.	10 pts.	24 K.	11 pts.	27 K.	12 pts.	30 K.
30 K.	9 pts.	30 K.	10 pts.	32 K.	10 pts.	34 K.	11 pts.	36 K.
42 K.	9 pts.	42 K.	9 pts.	43 K.	10 pts.	45 K.	10 pts.	47 K.
60 K.	8 pts.	60 K.	9 pts.	61 K.	9 pts.	62 K.	10 pts.	63 K.
IV. APPARENT WIND DIRECTION IS 12 POINTS OFF THE BOW (BROAD ON THE QUARTER)								
4 K.	14 pts.	8 K.	15 pts.	13 K.	15 pts.	18 K.	15 pts.	23 K.
8 K.	14 pts.	12 K.	14 pts.	17 K.	15 pts.	21 K.	15 pts.	26 K.
12 K.	13 pts.	16 K.	14 pts.	20 K.	14 pts.	25 K.	15 pts.	30 K.
16 K.	13 pts.	20 K.	14 pts.	24 K.	14 pts.	29 K.	14 pts.	33 K.
22 K.	13 pts.	26 K.	13 pts.	30 K.	14 pts.	34 K.	14 pts.	39 K.
30 K.	13 pts.	34 K.	13 pts.	38 K.	13 pts.	42 K.	14 pts.	46 K.
42 K.	12 pts.	46 K.	13 pts.	50 K.	13 pts.	54 K.	13 pts.	58 K.
60 K.	12 pts.	64 K.	13 pts.	67 K.	13 pts.	71 K.	13 pts.	75 K.

CONVERSION OF POINTS OFF BOW TO TRUE DIRECTION OF WIND

POINTS OFF BOW	BOAT'S HEADING—TRUE							
	000°	045°	090°	135°	180°	225°	270°	315°
I. WHEN WIND DIRECTION OBTAINED FROM TABLE ABOVE IS OFF STARBOARD BOW								
Dead Ahead	N	NE	E	SE	S	SW	W	NW
4 points	NE	E	SE	S	SW	W	NW	N
8 points	E	SE	S	SW	W	NW	N	NE
12 points	SE	S	SW	W	NW	N	NE	E
Dead Astern	S	SW	W	NW	N	NE	E	SE
II. WHEN WIND DIRECTION OBTAINED FROM TABLE ABOVE IS OFF PORT BOW								
Dead Ahead	N	NE	E	SE	S	SW	W	NW
4 points	NW	N	NE	E	SE	S	SW	W
8 points	W	NW	N	NE	E	SE	S	SW
12 points	SW	W	NW	N	NE	E	SE	S
Dead Astern	S	SW	W	NW	N	NE	E	SE

Abreviations: D. As. = Dead Astern. D. Ah. = Dead Ahead. K. = Knots. pts. = Points off bow.

TO USE THIS TABLE

1. **With Wind Direction Indicator:** Determine Apparent Wind Direction off the Bow.
2. **With Anemometer:** Determine Apparent Wind Velocity, in Knots.
3. **Enter Upper Part of Table:** Use portion for nearest Apparent Wind Direction Opposite Apparent Wind Velocity and under nearest Speed of Boat, read Wind Direction in Points off Bow and True Wind Velocity in Knots. Note whether True Wind Direction is off Starboard or Port Bow.
4. **Enter Lower Part of Table:** Use portion for proper Bow: Starboard or Port. Opposite Points off Bow and under nearest Boat's True Heading, read True Wind Direction.
5. **Log:** Record True Wind Direction as obtained from Lower Part of Table and True Wind Velocity as obtained from Upper Part of Table in Boat's Weather Log.

			Wind force (Beaufort)	Probable wave height (in ft.)
TABLE 12-3				
DETERMINATION OF WIND SPEED BY SEA CONDITION				
Knots	Descriptive	Sea Conditions		
0-1	Calm	Sea smooth and mirror-like.	0	—
1-3	Light air	Scale-like ripples without foam crests.	1	¼
4-6	Light breeze	Small, short wavelets; crests have a glassy appearance and do not break.	2	½
7-10	Gentle breeze	Large wavelets; some crests begin to break; foam of glassy appearance. Occasional white foam crests.	3	2
11-16	Moderate breeze	Small waves, becoming longer; fairly frequent white foam crests.	4	4
17-21	Fresh breeze	Moderate waves, taking a more pronounced long form; many white foam crests; there may be some spray.	5	6
22-27	Strong breeze	Large waves begin to form; white foam crests are more extensive everywhere; there may be some spray.	6	10
28-33	Near gale	Sea heaps up and white foam from breaking waves begins to be blown in streaks along the direction of the wind; spindrift begins.	7	14
34-40	Gale	Moderately high waves of greater length; edges of crests break into spindrift; foam is blown in well-marked streaks along the direction of the wind.	8	18
41-47	Strong gale	High waves; dense streaks of foam along the direction of the wind; crests of waves begin to topple, tumble, and roll over; spray may reduce visibility.	9	23
48-55	Storm	Very high waves with long overhanging crests. The resulting foam in great patches is blown in dense white streaks along the direction of the wind. On the whole, the surface of the sea is white in appearance. The tumbling of the sea becomes heavy and shock-like. Visibility is reduced.	10	29
56-63	Violent Storm	Exceptionally high waves that may obscure small and medium-sized ships. The sea is completely covered with long white patches of foam lying along the direction of the wind. Everywhere the edges of the wave crests are blown into froth. Visibility reduced.	11	37
64-71	Hurricane	The air is filled with foam and spray. Sea completely white with driving spray; visibility very much reduced.	12	45

(Courtesy National Weather Service)

THE BAROMETER

Another weather instrument with which we are all familiar is the *aneroid barometer*. The one illustrated (fig. 1236) has several interesting features.

First, there are two *pressure scales*. Not a few of us are accustomed to thinking of barometric pressure in terms of *inches of mercury*, so the outer scale is graduated in these units. Weather maps are now printed with the pressures shown in *millibars* and many radio weather reports specify this value. Consequently, the inner scale is graduated in millibars, and so we don't have to worry about conversions between units.

Second, it is a rugged instrument, a feature not to be despised on board a 40-footer. It has a high order of accuracy.

Third, it has the usual reference hand, so we can keep track of changes in pressure.

The words "Fair—Change—Rain," in themselves, when they appear on the face of an aneroid barometer, are meaningless. It is not the actual barometric pressure that is so important in forecasting; it is the *direction* and *rate of change of pressure*. The words may be misleading if this fact is not clearly understood.

FIG. 1236 A modern aneroid barometer, graduated in both millibars (inner scale) and inches of mercury (outer scale). Pointer indicates reading at last setting.
(Courtesy Airguide Instrument Company)

How it is used

Now, a good barometer is a helpful instrument, *provided* a few things: provided we read it at regular intervals and keep a record of the readings; provided we remember that there is much more to weather than just barometric pressure.

An individual reading of the barometer tells us only the pressure being exerted by the atmosphere on the earth's surface at the particular point of observation. But, suppose we have logged the pressure readings at fairly regular intervals, as follows:

Time	Pressure	Change
0700	30.02 inches	—
0800	30.00	−0.02
0900	29.97	−0.03
1000	29.93	−0.04
1100	29.88	−0.05
1200	29.82	−0.06

The pressure is falling, at an increasing rate. Trouble is brewing. A fall of 0.02 inch per hour is a low rate of fall; consequently, this figure would not be particularly disturbing. But a fall of 0.05 inch per hour is a pretty high rate.

Next, there is a normal *daily change in pressure*. The pressure is usually at its maximum value about 1000 and 2200 each day, at its minimum value about 0400 and 1600. The variation between minimum and maximum may be as much as 0.05 inch change in these six-hour intervals (about 0.01 inch change per hour). Thus, when the pressure normally would increase about 0.03 inch (0700 to 1000) our pressure fell 0.09 inch.

Suppose, now, around 1200 we also observed that the wind was blowing from the NE with increasing force and that the barometer continued to fall at a high rate. A rocky lee shore close aboard would not be pleasant to contemplate as a severe northeast gale is on its way. On the other hand, given the same barometer reading of about 29.80, rising rapidly with the wind going to west, we could expect improving weather. Quite a difference.

Barometer rules

A few general rules are often helpful. First, *foul* weather is usually forecast by a *falling* barometer with winds from the *east* quadrants; *clearing* and *fair* weather is usually forecast by winds shifting to *west* quadrants with a *rising* barometer. Second, there are the rules formerly printed on every Weather Bureau daily surface weather map:

"When the wind sets in from points between south and southeast and the barometer falls steadily, a storm is approaching from the west or northwest, and its center will pass near or north of the observer within 12 to 24 hours, with the wind shifting to northwest by way of south and southwest.

"When the wind sets in from points between east and northeast and the barometer falls steadily, a storm is approaching from the south or southwest, and its center will pass near or to the south of the observer within 12 to 24 hours, with the wind shifting to northwest by way of north.

"The rapidity of the storm's approach and its intensity will be indicated by the rate and amount of fall in the barometer."

There are some other generally useful barometer rules.

With our sling psychrometer we can determine the air temperature, so: a falling barometer and a rising thermometer often forecast rain; barometer and thermometer rising together often forecast fine weather. A slowly rising barometer forecasts settled weather; a steady, slow fall of pressure unsettled or wet weather.

Barometric changes and wind velocity

We shall now give some rules relating barometric changes to changes in wind velocity. First, it is generally true that a *rapidly falling barometer* forecasts the development of strong winds. This is so because a falling barometer indicates the approach or development of a LOW, and the pressure gradient is usually steep in the neighborhood of a low-pressure center. On the other hand, a *rising barometer* is associated with the prospect of lighter winds to come. This is true because a rising barometer indicates the approach or development of a HIGH, and the pressure gradient is characteristically small in the neighborhood of a high-pressure center.

The barometer does not necessarily fall before or during a strong breeze. The wind often blows hard without any appreciable accompanying change in the barometer. This means that a steep pressure gradient exists (isobars close together, as seen on the weather map) but that the well-developed HIGH or LOW associated with the steep pressure gradient is practically stationary. In this case the wind may be expected to blow hard for some time; any slackening or change will take place gradually.

It not infrequently happens that the barometer falls quite rapidly, yet the wind remains comparatively light. If we remember the relation between wind velocity and pressure gradient, we conclude that the gradient must be comparatively small (isobars relatively far apart). The rapid fall of the barometer must be accounted for, then, in either one or both of two ways. Either a LOW with a weak pressure gradient on its forward side is approaching rapidly, or there is a rapid decrease of pressure taking place over the surrounding area, or both. In such a situation the pressure gradient at the rear of the LOW is often steep, and in that case strong winds will set in as soon as the barometer commences to rise. (It will rise rapidly under these circumstances.) The fact, however, that the barometer is now rising indicates that decreasing winds may soon be expected.

The barometer and wind shifts

Nearly all extra-tropical cyclones display an unsymmetrical distribution of pressure. The pressure gradients are seldom the same in the front and rear of an extra-tropical cyclone. During the approach of a LOW the barometer alone gives no clue as to how many points the wind will shift and what velocity it will have after the passage of the low-pressure system. This is particularly applicable to situations in which the wind blows from a southerly direction while the barometer is falling. The cessation of the fall of the barometer will coincide with a *veering* (gradual or sudden) shift of the wind to a more westerly direction. Unfortunately, an observer having no information other than that supplied by his barometer cannot foretell the exact features of the change.

In using barometric indications for local forecasting it is most important to remember that weather changes are

FIG. 1237 Forecast—Severe Storm. Squall line clouds mark an advancing cold front; storm will be severe, with sharp, violent shift in wind, rain and probably lightning and thunder. (Courtesy U.S. Weather Bureau)

influenced by the characteristics of the earth's surface in our locality. All rules should be checked against experience in our own cruising waters before we can place full confidence in their validity.

VISUAL WEATHER SIGNS

In addition to our instrumental weather observations there are certain *visual signs* that we can record. First, we should note the *visibility*. Haze, dust and smoke are nearly as important as fog. Many of the tiny particles which are suspended in the air and which reduce the visibility serve as nuclei on which water vapor can condense. Unless the water vapor in the air does condense, we can have no fog nor clouds. If haze thickens to a degree where it restricts the visibility to 3 miles (4.8 km), this indicates that condensation has begun on the more active condensation nuclei, a warning the fog may soon develop.

Next, we should note the *clouds*. First, we ask ourselves: "What form (or forms) of cloud is (or are) present?" In order to answer this question we need to know the international system of cloud classification. This system resembles the method of classification used in the biological sciences. The different cloud types are given descriptive names which depend mainly upon appearance, but also sometimes upon the processes of formation as seen by an observer on the ground or at sea. Despite an almost infinite variety of shapes and forms, it is still possible to define 10 basic types.

High clouds (above 18,000–20,000 feet)

1. Cirrus (Ci)—Detached clouds in the form of white, delicate filaments, or white or mostly white patches or narrow bands. These clouds have a fibrous (hair-like) appearance, or a silky sheen, or both.

2. Cirrocumulus (Cc)—Thin, white patch, sheet or layer of cloud without shading, composed of very small elements in the form of grains, ripples, etc., merged or separate, and more or less regularly arranged; most of the elements have an apparent width of less than one degree.

H. T. Floreen

FIG. 1238 Cumulus clouds of fair weather, illustrating situation in which atmosphere is stable a short distance above bases of clouds which, therefore, cannot grow vertically. Appearance of sky indicates fine weather will continue for at least another 6 hours.

Middle clouds (from about 7,000 feet up to 18–20,000)

3. Cirrostratus (Cs)—Transparent, whitish cloud veil of fibrous (hair-like) or smooth appearance, totally or partly covering the sky, and generally producing halo phenomena.

4. Altocumulus (Ac)—White or gray, or both white and gray, patch, sheet or layer of cloud, generally with shading, composed of laminae, rounded masses, rolls, etc., which are sometimes partly fibrous or diffuse, and which may or may not be merged; most of the regularly arranged small elements usually have an apparent width between one and five degrees.

5. Altostratus (As)—Grayish or bluish cloud sheet or layer of striated, fibrous or uniform appearance, totally or partly covering the sky, and having parts thin enough to reveal the sun at least vaguely, as through ground glass. Altostratus does not show halo phenomena.

Low clouds (from near ground up to about 7,000 feet)

6. Nimbostratus (Ns)—Gray cloud layer, often dark, the appearance of which is rendered diffuse by more or less continuously falling rain or snow, which in most cases reaches the ground. It is thick enough throughout to blot out the sun. Low, ragged clouds frequently occur below the layer, with which they may or may not merge.

7. Stratocumulus (Sc)—Gray or whitish, or both gray and whitish, patch, sheet or layer of cloud which almost always has dark parts, composed of tessellations, rounded masses, rolls, etc., which are non-fibrous (except for virga) and which may or may not be merged; most of the regularly arranged small elements have an apparent width of more than five degrees.

8. Stratus (St)—Generally gray cloud layer with a fairly uniform base, which may give drizzle, ice prisms or snow grains. When the sun is visible through the cloud, its outline is clearly discernible. Stratus does not produce halo phenomena except, possibly, at very low temperatures. Sometimes stratus appears in the form of ragged patches.

9. Cumulus (Cu)—Detached clouds, generally dense and with sharp outlines, developing vertically in the form of rising mounds, domes or towers, of which the bulging upper part often resembles a cauliflower. The sunlit parts of these clouds are mostly brilliant white; their bases are relatively dark and nearly horizontal. Sometimes cumulus is ragged.

10. Cumulonimbus (Cb)—Heavy and dense cloud, with a considerable vertical extent, in the form of a mountain or huge towers. At least part of its upper portion is usually smooth, or fibrous or striated, and nearly always flattened; this part often spreads out in the shape of an anvil or vast plume. Under the base of this cloud, which is often very dark, there are frequently low ragged clouds either merged

FIG. 1239 Semi-transparent altocumulus clouds. Clouds in this picture clearly show signs of evaporation; edges of individual elements are frayed and indistinct. This indicates continuing fair weather.

FIG. 1240 Altostratus clouds, together with some altocumulus, over Mt. Kisco, New York, 1655 EST, 11 February 1965. (Note aircraft condensation trail in lower left portion of photograph.) At this time a LOW was centered over southeastern Missouri, moving northeastward. Rain began to fall about 7 hours after picture was taken. (Photograph by Caroline S. Emmons)

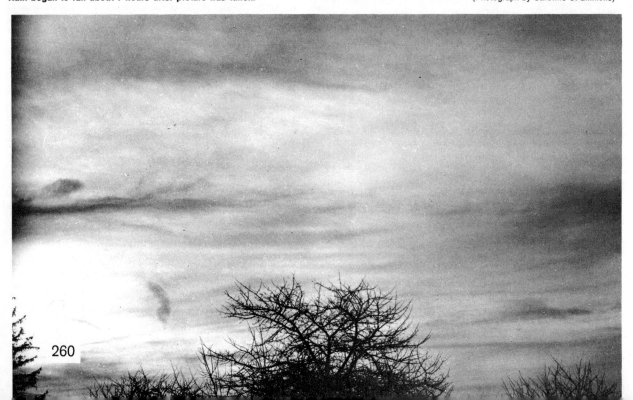

with it or not, and precipitation, sometimes in the form of virga (precipitation trails).*

Significance of changing cloud forms

Having identified the cloud form (or forms) present in the sky, we should next note whether the clouds are *increasing* or *decreasing* in amount, and whether they are *lowering* or *lifting*. In general, thickening and lowering of a cloud layer, be it a layer of cirrostratus, altocumulus or altostratus, is a sign of approaching wet weather. On the other hand, when a layer of clouds shows signs of evaporation, that is, when holes or openings begin to appear in a layer of altostratus, or the elements of an altocumulus layer are frayed and indistinct at the edges, we have an indication of improving weather or, at least, delay of the development of foul weather.

Finally, we should note the *sequence of cloud forms* during the past few hours. Cirrus clouds are frequently the advance agents of an approaching extra-tropical cyclone, especially if they are followed by a layer of cirrostratus. In this case the problem is to forecast the track the low-pressure center will take to one side or the other, the nearness of approach of the center and the intensity of the low.

As the clouds thicken steadily from Ci to Cs and from Cs to As, we naturally expect further development to Ns with its rain or snow. There are usually contrary indications if such is not to be the case, or if the precipitation will arrive late, amount to little and end soon, or will come in two brief periods separated by several hours of mild, more or less sunny, weather.

If the northern horizon remains clear until a layer of altostratus clouds overspreads most of the sky, the low-pressure center will probably be passing to the south without bringing precipitation. If the northern horizon is slow in clouding up but becomes covered by the time the cloud sheet is principally As, there will probably be some precipitation but not much. If the cloud sheet, after increasing to As, breaks up into Ac and the sky above is seen to have lost most of its covering of Cs, the low-pressure area is either weakening or passing on to the north.

The approach of a squall line accompanied by thunderstorms may be detected an hour or more in advance by observing the thin white arch of the cirrus border to the anvil top of the approaching cumulonimbus cloud. The atmosphere ahead of a squall line is often so hazy that only this whitish arch will reveal the presence of a moderately distant Cb, for the shadowed air under the dense anvil will be invisible behind the sunlit hazy blue air near the observer. Thus this part of the sky will appear to be clear and will resemble the blue sky above the cirrus arch.

THE WEATHER LOG

Although the latest Weather Service forecasts are readily available to us via the medium of radio, it is often helpful to keep a record of our own observations of clouds and weather as they develop. This procedure will enable us to check the reliability of the latest prediction. Occasionally the professional forecaster misjudges the future rate of travel of the weather pattern, which may move faster or

TABLE 12-4A Boat Weather Log.

```
                    BOAT WEATHER LOG


Yacht_____At/Passage_____to_____
Day____Date_____Time Zone_____Skipper_____
1.  Latest Weather Map: Date____Time_____Summary of forecast and
    of principal regional weather features:_____
    _____
    _____
    _____
    _____

2.  Radio Weather Reports Received (state source and time):_____
    _____
    _____
    _____
    _____

3.  Local Weather Observations (see over for record)

4.  Remarks and Local Forecast for Next____Hours (state time fore-
    cast effective):_____
    _____
    _____
    _____
    _____
    _____
```

TABLE 12-4B Local Weather Observations.

```
              LOCAL WEATHER OBSERVATIONS


Time -- ZT, Navy Style       :   :   :   :   :   :
Latitude - degrees, minutes  :   :   :   :   :   :
Longitude -   "      "       :   :   :   :   :   :
Course - degrees psc         :   :   :   :   :   :
       -   "    true         :   :   :   :   :   :
Speed - Knots                :   :   :   :   :   :
Barometer - in. or mb.       :   :   :   :   :   :
        - tendency           :   :   :   :   :   :
Clouds - form                :   :   :   :   :   :
       - moving from         :   :   :   :   :   :
       - amount              :   :   :   :   :   :
       - changing to         :   :   :   :   :   :
Sea - condition              :   :   :   :   :   :
    - swells                 :   :   :   :   :   :
    - moving from            :   :   :   :   :   :
Temperatures - air, dry bulb :   :   :   :   :   :
            - dewpoint       :   :   :   :   :   :
            - water          :   :   :   :   :   :
Visibility                   :   :   :   :   :   :
Wind - direction, true       :   :   :   :   :   :
     - shifting to           :   :   :   :   :   :
     - velocity, true        :   :   :   :   :   :
     - force (Beaufort)      :   :   :   :   :   :
Weather - present            :   :   :   :   :   :
```

*Note: Altitude groupings are not absolute. Portions of cumulus and cumulonimbus become middle clouds; at times altostratus and the tops of cumulonimbus may be in the high cloud category.

more slowly than anticipated. (This is known as an error of timing.) Or there may occur a new, unforeseen development in the pattern.

Table 12-4 shows a form of *Weather Log* which is similar to that used in the Weather Course of the United States Power Squadrons. Table 12-4 A is the face sheet, Table 12-4 B the reverse side. The first weather items recorded are based on a perusal of the latest weather map (if available to us) and a summary of radio reports received. Then we use the reverse side to jot down our local observations. Sufficient columns are available to permit the entry of these data six times during one 24-hour day, or at four-hour intervals. Entries may be made using the standard weather code symbols or any other way we choose, provided we use the same system consistently.

From these records we can estimate in what way and to what extent the actual weather during the next few hours is likely to differ from the official forecast.

FIG. 1241 Semi-transparent layer of altostratus clouds over Mt. Kisco, New York, 1445 EST, 14 February 1965, looking south-southwestward. Sun is dimly visible. Later in the afternoon, altostratus layer thickened and lowered. Light snow began to fall about 6 hours after picture was taken. (Photograph by Caroline S. Emmons)

FIG. 1241-A Squall line approaching Mt. Kisco, N.Y., late afternoon of 27 July 1965. View at left looking toward WNW, center and right toward NW. Time interval between pictures approximately three minutes. Thunderstorm overhead one hour later. (Photographs by Caroline S. Emmons.)

Appendix

The National Weather Service has an ascending series of alerting messages—advisories and warnings—for mariners, including boatmen. These are keyed to increasingly hazardous weather and sea conditions.

Each advisory or warning condition has both a day and a night signal. These are displayed at prominent locations ashore, such as Coast Guard stations and lighthouses, marinas, yacht clubs, etc.; at some but not all such locations, check locally to know where to watch for them. Some of the locations will display only the day signal, others both the day and night signals. Day signals only are flown from Coast Guard lightships while on station, in some areas the small craft advisory red pennant will be shown on local law enforcement patrol craft.

The Weather Service emphasizes that these visual storm warnings displayed along the coast are supplementary to —and not a replacement for—the written advisories and warnings given prompt and wide distribution by press, radio, and television. In most cases, important details of the forecasts and warnings in regard to the time, intensity, duration, and direction of storms cannot be given satisfactorily through visual signals alone.

Following is a detailed explanation of the signals:

Small Craft Advisory: One red pennant displayed by day and a red light above a white light at night to indicate winds up to 38 mph (33 knots) and/or sea conditions dangerous to small craft operations are forecast for the area.

Gale Warning: Two red pennants displayed by day and a white light above a red light at night to indicate winds ranging from 39 to 54 mph (34 to 47 knots) are forecast.

Storm Warning: A single square red flag with black center displayed by day and two red lights at night to indicate winds 48 knots (55 mph) and above *(no matter how high the velocity)* are forecast for the area. NOTE—If winds are associated with a tropical cyclone (hurricane) the *storm*

DISSEMINATION OF STORM WARNINGS AND ROUTINE WEATHER INFORMATION

warning display indicates forecast winds of 48 to 63 knots (55 to 73 mph). The *hurricane warning* is displayed only in connection with a tropical cyclone (hurricane).

Hurricane Warning: Two square red flags with black centers displayed by day and a white light between two red lights at night to indicate that winds 74 mph (64 knots) and above are forecast for the area.

The term *Small Craft Advisory* needs some explanation. In the first place, small craft, as defined by the Weather Service, consist of "small boats, yachts, tugs, barges with little freeboard, or any other low-powered craft." In the second place, a small-craft advisory does not distinguish between the expectation of a general, widespread, all-day blow of 25 knots or more and, for example, a forecast of the occurrence of isolated, late-afternoon thunder-squalls in which winds dangerous to small craft will be localized and of short duration. It is up to the individual skipper to deduce from his own observations, supplemented by any information he can obtain from radio broadcasts about the current over-all weather picture, to which type of situation the advisory applies and to plan his day's cruise accordingly.

Storm warnings and advisories issued by the National Weather Service are broadcast by designated United States Naval and Coast Guard radio stations. A large number of commercial radio stations also broadcast storm warnings, although at somewhat irregular intervals.

VHF-FM BROADcasts: At many places, the National Weather Service has *continuous* broadcasts of conditions and forecasts with emphasis on marine use. New tapes are prepared every few hours. Frequencies used (in order of preference) are: 162.550, 162.400, and 162.475 MHz.

These can be received on regular VHF sets, on inexpensive transistor receivers, and on some newer AM-FM receivers and MF-band radiotelephones. The broadcasts are of excellent quality and are most useful to boatmen.

FIG. 124 2 **SMALL CRAFT, GALE, STORM AND HURRICANE WARNINGS**

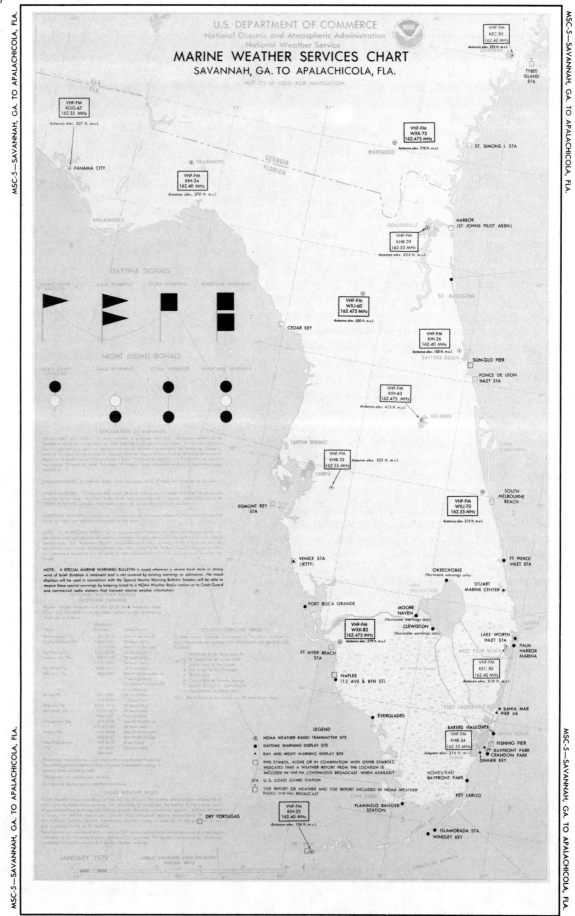

Fig. 1243 Marine Services Weather Chart. See text, page 265.

MARINE WEATHER SERVICES CHARTS

Coast Guard vessels now display storm warning signals. Headquarters of the Coast Guard are supplied with weather information by the Weather Service and Coast Guard vessels receive instructions to fly the proper signals when bad weather is approaching.

The shore stations where storm warning signals are displayed are prominently marked on the *Marine Weather Services Charts*, a series which is published annually by the Weather Service. These charts, of which fig. 1243 is an example, also contain detailed information concerning the times of weather broadcasts from commercial stations, the radio frequencies of marine broadcast stations, the specific type of storm warnings issued and the visual display signals (already described and illustrated in the text above) which are used in connection with the warnings. This series consists of fifteen charts, twelve of which cover coastal waters of the United States and the Great Lakes. The other three charts are for (a) Hawaiian Islands, (b) Puerto Rico and Virgin Islands, and (c) Alaskan waters. These can be purchased from Superintendent of Documents, Government Printing Office, Washington, DC 20402.

Yachtsmen will find much interesting weather information on the various Pilot Charts of the North Atlantic and North Pacific Oceans issued by the DMA Hydrographic/ Topographic Center. The Pilot Charts show average monthly wind and weather conditions over the oceans and in addition contain a vast amount of supplemental data on subjects closely allied to weather.

Weather Maps at Sea

Just because you are offshore and not receiving your daily newspaper, or are out of range of a TV station, you need not be without a reliable and up-to-date weather map. These have significant advantages over voice announcements as you have a specific "hard-copy" picture of current or forecast conditions to study in detail. There are methods by which you can receive either the map itself or information from which you can plot your own pattern of highs and lows, warm and cold fronts. One is inexpensive but more work; the other requires costly equipment but you receive an official weather map.

Facsimile radio transmissions are received by a high-frequency receiver and processed in a unit that prints a weather map line by line. These transmissions, often called *radiofax*, are broadcast on regular schedules by a number of shore stations. The receiver can be your regular communications set, or it can be built into the printer; the latter is more convenient to use, but more costly, by several thousands of dollars. A number of different charts are transmitted: surface analysis, prognosis (forecasts for 12, 24, 36, or 48 hours) wave analysis, sea water temperature, satellite photographs, and others.

But expensive equipment is not needed. Information is broadcast in Morse Code from which you can sketch in your own weather map on standard blank chart forms that are available at no charge from Port Meteorological Officers at major ports. And you don't even have to know the code! All data are the figures zero through nine and these fit a simple pattern of five dots or dashes that is easily learned. Instructions on how to use the

data are given in the publication *Worldwide Marine Weather Broadcasts* (see page 610) which also contains information on station frequencies and schedules. The speed of transmission is not great, but accuracy in copying the figures, which are in groups of five, can be improved by using a tape recorder and replaying one or more times for double-checking or to fill in any gaps. It is even better to have a two-speed recorder, recording at the higher speed and then playing back at the lower speed to record the figures.

WIND FORCE—AND ITS EFFECT ON THE SEA

Boatmen, like mariners at sea, frequently use the Beaufort Scale to log wind speed and the condition of the sea. Too often the description of sea conditions relies solely upon a verbal statement like "moderate waves, large waves, moderately high waves" (column 3, Table 12-3) which leaves the boatman pretty much "at sea" in trying to visualize exactly what these relative terms imply.

England's Meteorological Office has solved this problem by issuing a State of Sea card (M.O. 688A) with photographs to accompany each of the descriptions of thirteen wind forces of the Beaufort Scale. Thus the observer has a guide in estimating wind strength (*in knots*) when making weather reports or in logging sea conditions. Fetch, depth of water, swell, heavy rain, tide and the lag effect between the wind getting up and the sea increasing, may also affect the appearance of the sea. Range of wind speed and the mean wind speed are given for each force. By special permission, we are privileged to reproduce (figure 1244, page 266) seven of these photographs (Forces 1, 3, 5, 6, 8, 10, 12). Forces 0, 2, 4, 7, 9, and 11, though not illustrated, may be estimated in relation to those above and below them in the scale.

TABLE 12-5
WIND PRESSURE AT VARIOUS WIND VELOCITIES
(Air temperature 50°F, barometric pressure 1000 mbs.)

WIND VELOCITY (Knots)	WIND PRESSURE (Lbs. Per Square Foot)
0	0.0
5	0.1
10	0.3
15	0.8
20	1.3
25	2.1
30	3.1
35	4.2
40	5.5
45	6.9
50	8.5
55	10.3
60	12.3

This table gives the wind pressure exerted on the windward side of a flat surface oriented at right angles to the wind. The values in the table have been computed for air temperature equal to 50°F and barometric pressure equal to 1000 millibars. At greater barometric pressures and lower air temperature the wind pressure corresponding to a given wind velocity will be somewhat greater; at higher air temperatures and lower barometric pressures, somewhat less.

FORCE 1—Wind speed 1-3 kt.; mean 2 kt.

FORCE 8—Wind speed 34-40 kt.; mean 37 kt.

FORCE 3—Wind speed 7-10 kt.; mean 9 kt.

FORCE 10—Wind speed 48-55 kt.; mean 52 kt.

FIG. 1244 — HOW THE SEA LOOKS IN WINDS OF VARYING FORCE

Wind forces used in these illustrations are based on the Beaufort Scale. See column 3, table 12-3, for verbal description of the state of the sea for Forces 0-12.

(All photographs Crown Copyright, by R. R. Baxter, except Force 10, J. Hodkinson, and Force 12, G.P.O. Reproduced by permission of the Controller of Her Brittanic Majesty's Stationery Office.)

FORCE 5—Wind speed 17-21 kt.; mean 18 kt.

FORCE 12—Wind speed 64-71 kt.; mean 68 kt.

FORCE 6—Wind speed 22-27 kt.; mean 24 kt.

CHAPTER 13

FIG. 1301 A magnetic compass as used on boats.

*Planning a voyage,
or when under way,
the navigator or the
small boat pilot is always
concerned with direction
and distance.
Methods of determining
and recording distance
are thoroughly
covered elsewhere in
this book. This chapter
is about direction
and, more particularly,
about the most commonly
used direction
indicator afloat,
the mariner's compass.*

THE MARINER'S COMPASS

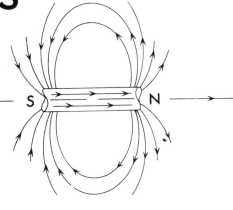

FIG. 1302 The external effect of a magnet exists within its field which is represented by "lines of force." Each magnet has two poles of opposite nature; these are named North and South.

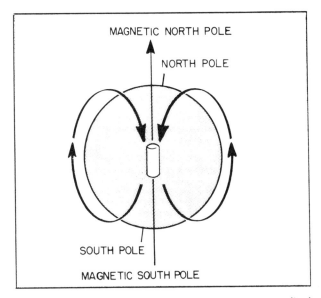

FIG. 1303 · The magnetic properties of the earth can be visualized as a powerful bar magnet at the earth's center but not aligned with the geographic axis.

Why It Works

Magnetism is a phenomenon of nature that cannot be seen, heard, smelled, tasted, or directly felt; its existence can only be known from its effects. It is a basic natural force and one which is essential to a vast number of devices, from incredibly complex electronic equipment to our simple ship's (or boat's) magnetic compass.

Magnetism appears as a physical force between two objects of metal, usually iron or an alloy of iron and other metals, at least one of which has been previously magnetized and has become a *magnet*. The area around a magnet in which its effect can be detected is called a *magnetic field*. This is commonly pictured as innumerable *lines of force* but these are purely a convention for illustration and actual lines as such do not exist; fig. 1302 is a typical illus-

FIG. 1304 This cross-section of a mariner's compass shows four parallel permanent magnets mounted beneath the card, both of which are attached to a light frame which is supported on a bearing by a pivot. The lubber's line is on the bowl near the mark on the card for South. An expansion bellows for the liquid in the compass is at the bottom of the bowl.

tration of a *bar magnet* with some of the lines of force shown. (An electric current flowing in a wire also creates a magnetic field, more on this later.)

Basic Law of Magnetism

Each magnet, regardless of size, has two *poles* where the magnetic action may be thought of as being concentrated. These poles have opposite characteristics and are termed *North* and *South*; see fig. 1302. The basic law of magnetism is very simple—"Opposites attract; likes repel." Thus an N pole is attracted to an S pole, but repels another N.

The Earth

The earth as a whole has magnetic properties and can be thought of as having a powerful bar magnet near its center, fig. 1303. The magnetic properties of the earth are not uniformly distributed, and as a consequence its magnetic poles are *not* at the locations of the geographic poles. The magnetic pole in the northern hemisphere is named the *North magnetic pole* because of its location; actually it has "southerly" magnetic properties. Conversely, the *South magnetic pole* is the one located several hundred miles from the South geographic pole.

The basic compass

The basic principle of a magnetic compass is very simple —a small bar magnet freely suspended in the magnetic field of the earth will align itself parallel to the lines of force of that field and thus will establish a *direction*. The end of a magnet that points generally north is termed its *North* pole although it is actually the "north-seeking" pole; the other end is its *South* pole. As will be discussed later in more detail, this direction will not normally be the same as geographic north, nor even the correct direction to the north magnetic pole. It is, however, a reliable and consistent direction, and for the purposes of navigation, it can be considered as being relatively constant over a period of several years.

The navigator usually has at hand information and rapid means for converting the reading of his compass to true geographic directions. He knows that if any local influences from iron or steel objects and electrical wires can be neutralized (or measured and recorded), his compass

will be a dependable magnetic direction finder, needing neither mechanical nor electrical power, and virtually immune to wear.

Construction

A typical compass has more than one bar magnet from which to derive its force to align with the earth's magnetic field. Usually, several long, thin permanent magnets, each enclosed in a non-magnetic tube, are attached, parallel to each other, to a light non-magnetic wire frame; like poles of the magnets are adjacent. A light, round, non-magnetic disc is mounted on the frame; this is the card of the compass and is marked around its circumference with graduations from which the direction can be read. Fig. 1304 shows a cross-section of a card with the magnets below.

Centrally placed under the frame is a bearing which rides on a hard, sharp point called the *pivot;* this in turn is supported from the outer case which is the *bowl* of the compass. A cover of transparent material, either flat or hemispherical, is rigidly fastened to the top of the bowl with a leak-proof seal. Through a pluggable opening, the bowl is filled with a non-freezing liquid, formerly alcohol, but now usually a special oil. An *expansion bellows* in the lower part of the bowl allows the fluid to expand and contract with temperature changes without bubbles being formed.

Usually a *float* is attached under the frame to partially suspend the card and magnets, and thus reduce friction and wear on the bearing and pivot. The compass liquid also serves to dampen out any rapid oscillations or overswings of the card when direction is changed or rough weather is encountered. *Gimbals* are provided, either internally or externally, so that the compass card can remain essentially level despite any rolling or pitching of the vessel; these are two sets of rings, one pivoted on a fore-and-aft axis and the other on an athwartship axis; see fig. 1305.

FIG. 1305 This compass has a full spherical bowl with two sets of internal gimbals. The lubber's line is attached to one set of gimbals and there are three other smaller index marks at 90° intervals around the same gimballed frame.

Courtesy DANFORTH

FIG. 1306 Compass cards are graduated in various manners. Those on most boats have graduations every 5° with the 10° marks being heavier for ease of reading. Numbers usually appear at 30° intervals with the cardinal headings being identified by letters in lieu of numbers.

FIG. 1307 Compasses for larger vessels will have cards of larger diameter, often with graduations down to 1° intervals.

COMPASS CARDS

The card of a modern compass is divided into *degrees*, 360° to a full circle; the degrees increase clockwise around the card. North is 0° and the scale continues on around through 90° (East), 180° (South), and 270° (West) back to North which is 360° or 0°. The spacing between graduations on the card will vary with the size of the compass, but 5° spacings are normal for most small-craft compasses, see fig. 1306, with some larger boats having 2° cards. Ships will normally have compasses with cards having 1° divisions, see fig. 1307. Numbers may be shown every ten degrees from 10° to 350°; every fifteen degrees from 15° to 345°; or every thirty degrees from 30° to 330°.

Just outside the card is the index mark against which the graduations are read. This is the *lubber's line*; it may be a mark on the inside of the bowl or it may be a part of the internal gimbals system. See figs. 1304 and 1305.

Front-reading compasses

Some smaller compasses are designed for mounting with direct reading from the front rather than from above or

FIG. 1308 When the compass is designed for front viewing, rather than from an angle above, the lubber's line is on the near side to the helmsman. In this case, the readings increase to the left and a skipper used to more conventional compasses must exercise care to avoid confusion when reading values between numbered marks.

nearly so. Here the lubber's line is nearer the skipper rather than on the far side of the card. The card is still graduated clockwise, but the greater readings are to the left of the index line rather than to the right. This fact can be confusing to a skipper used to a more conventional compass and must always be kept in mind when determining an exact value between the numbered marks on the card; see fig. 1308.

The "point" system

In olden days, compass cards were subdivided into "points"—32 points to a complete circle, one point equals 11¼°. These were named, not numbered, and a seaman early learned to "box the compass" by naming all the points—forward, and backwards, too! There were also half and quarter-points when a smaller subdivision was needed.

The *cardinal* points, North, East, South, and West—and the *intercardinal* points, Northeast, Southeast, Southwest, and Northwest—are still in common use as rough directions and as descriptions of wind direction. The *combination*

CONVERSION TABLE—POINTS TO DEGREES

	Angular Measure	
	°	′
NORTH TO EAST		
North	0	00
N by E	11	15
NNE	22	30
NE by N	33	45
NE	45	00
NE by E	56	15
ENE	67	30
E by N	78	45
EAST TO SOUTH		
East	90	00
E by S	101	15
ESE	112	30
SE by E	123	45
SE	135	00
SE by S	146	15
SSE	157	30
S by E	168	45
SOUTH TO WEST		
South	180	00
S by W	191	15
SSW	202	30
SW by S	213	45
SW	225	00
SW by W	236	15
WSW	247	30
W by S	258	45
WEST TO NORTH		
West	270	00
W by N	281	15
WNW	292	30
NW by W	303	45
NW	315	00
NW by N	326	15
NNW	337	30
N by W	348	45
North	360	00

FIG. 1309 Conversion table between the point and degree systems.

FIG. 1310 The cards of some larger compasses will be marked for the intercardinal directions as well as the cardinal points.

FIG. 1311 Some compass cards show the point system for all points. A few, as above, will have subdivisions as fine as the quarter-points.

points, such as NNE, ENE, and so on, are sometimes used for general directions, but the *by-points*, NxE, NNExN, NNExE, and their like, seem almost lost except to occasionally embellish (often erroneously) some movie or television drama.

The point system is now otherwise obsolete except that the unit is still used in the measurement of angles for navigation lights and right-of-way rules. For those who do not wish to forget the past, and for some sailors who learn points for ease in steering their wind-driven craft, there is included here a table of conversions between the point and degree systems, fig. 1309.

Some modern compass cards label the intercardinal points as well as the cardinal headings, fig. 1310, and a few go further to mark all points and even quarter-points, fig. 1311. The examples and problems that follow in this and other chapters will, however, all be in terms of degrees.

SPHERICAL COMPASSES

When the top over a compass card is hemispherical, the dome serves to magnify and make the card appear much larger than it actually is. This aids in reading it closely, making it possible to steer a better course or take a better bearing. On some compasses with a hemispherical cover, the card itself is concave or dish-shaped rather than flat. This feature, combined with the shape of the dome, makes it possible to read the compass from a lower angle and at considerably greater distances. A compass with such a card of five-inch (12.7 cm) "apparent diameter" (actually somewhat smaller) can be read from 10 feet (3m) or more away.

If the compass as a whole is spherical, bowl as well as dome, there is a considerable gain in stability of the card. The effect of a whole sphere is to permit the fluid inside to remain relatively undisturbed by roll, pitch, or yaw; the result is superior performance in rough seas.

BINNACLES

Compasses are sometimes mounted directly on a

horizontal surface. More often, however, the compass is mounted in an outer supporting case called a *binnacle*. This can be a simple case, sometimes with a light-shielding hood, which is then fastened down, fig. 1312. Or it can be a complete pedestal stand as might be used on larger sailboats, fig. 1313.

The outside of the compass case or binnacle, or a mounting bracket, should be black, preferably with a dull finish. There should be no shiny chromed metal parts that could reflect sunlight into the eyes of the helmsman.

Lighting

When compasses are lighted for night use, the lighting system is often a part of the binnacle. The light should be red in color and its intensity at a suitable level. If the light

FIG. 1312 Compasses should have light-shielding hoods to cut off excessive sunlight to aid in reading the instrument. Many hoods can be completely closed when the compass is not in use to cut off all light and help protect the unit.

is not red, or is too bright, there is risk of loss of the "night vision" of the helmsman; this will make it more difficult, or even impossible, for him to see other vessels, aids to navigation, etc. On the other hand, a too-dimly lit compass can be a source of eye-strain and a detriment to good steering; if the compass cannot be properly read, the tendency is to steer by instinct, and that doesn't always get you where you want to go!

Internal compensators

As we will note in more detail later in this chapter, it is usually *not* possible to have a situation where there are no magnetic effects from iron and steel objects on the boat. The compass must then be "adjusted" or "compensated" with small additional bar magnets so located and polarized as to counter-balance the unwanted but unavoidable magnetic influences on the boat. Such "compensators" may be external to the compass and binnacle, but are more likely to be internal, usually a part of the latter unit; see fig. 1314.

Selection

Although a compass is a relatively simple mechanism in terms of its construction and operation, it is probably the most important navigational tool on any boat. Considerable thought should be given to the selection of a compass; this is not the place for a hasty decision or for money-saving by the purchase of a small, cheap unit. In fog or night, or any other form of reduced visibility, your compass will be the basic instrument to tell you in what direction to go—*it has to be right!*

Quality

Almost any new compass looks fine in the store, or aboard a boat in the quiet motion of a marina slip or at a mooring. But its behavior underway, when the sea makes up and the craft pitches, rolls, and yaws, is of supreme importance. Will the card stick at some angle of heel? Will its apparent motion be jerky, or smooth and easy? Are the card graduations legible and are different headings easily distinguished? Is the compass going to be subjected to large temperature changes? What if a bubble appears under its glass which might distract the helmsman? The answers

FIG. 1313 **Compasses on sailboats are often mounted in a pedestal-type binnacle in the cockpit just forward of the wheel.**

to these questions will depend upon the quality of the compass.

No aviator will knowingly accept a cheap parachute; no seaman seeks a bargain in personal flotation devices or fire extinguishers. No skipper should settle for a compass of inferior quality. Select one fully adequate for your expected needs, and if a choice must be made, err on the side of quality. Examine a number of them before buying. Pick them up; tilt and turn them, simulating motions to which they would be subject in actual use afloat. The card should have a smooth and stable reaction, coming to rest without oscillating about the lubber's line. Reasonable tilting, comparable to the rolling and pitching of your boat, should not appreciably affect the reading. In fairness to the compass, however, if it has internal correctors, they must be zeroed-in (to be covered later under installation) before making these tests.

Size

All too often, a small compass will be selected and installed on a small boat for the simple reason that the boat is just that, small. This is *not* the correct approach! Because the boat is small, it will be subjected to greater movement, both in normal operation and in rough waters. A small, cheap compass will have less stability and may even be completely unusable in severe conditions, perhaps just when it is most needed.

A compass for a boat should be as large as the physical limitations of mounting space allow—and the quality should be just as high as the owner's budget will allow!

Card selection

In selecting a compass for your boat, pay particular attention to the design of the card. Its graduations should be suited to the intended use. That a large craft may be held on course more easily and precisely than a small one is a readily understandable situation. Thus the larger the vessel, the greater the number of divisions normally found around the outer edge of the card. Skippers of large ocean-going craft seem to prefer cards that can be read directly to two degrees, or even to single degrees. Studies have shown, however, that subdivisions smaller than five degrees may not be desirable. Cards with finer subdivisions may produce more eye-strain, require a higher intensity of illumina-

FIG. 1314 **Most modern boat compasses have two sets of internal compensating magnets. These are often mounted in the base of the binnacle with the adjusting screw-heads accessible at the outer edge.**

tion, and may result in greater steering action although no better course is made good. The experiences and preferences of the individual must govern here.

Testing

Although not always absolutely true, price is generally a fair indicator of quality. There are, however, simple tests that you can make yourself to aid in judging between different units. When making any of these tests, make sure that any other compasses are at least three or four feet (0.9-1.2 m) distant.

Test for minimum pivot friction (it should be zero) by turning the compass as a whole until a card graduation mark is exactly aligned with the lubber's line, then bring a small magnet in your hand just close enough to the compass to cause the card to deflect two to five degrees to either side. Next, take the magnet well away from the compass quickly, watching the card as you do so. The card should return to its former position exactly. This test is completed by drawing the card off to the other side— by reversing the small magnet end-for-end, or by moving it to the other side of the compass. Again the card should return to its initial position when the influence of the external magnet is removed. (Make sure that the small magnet is moved far enough away each time for a fair test; turn it end-for-end, the card should not be affected.) Sticky pivots are rare, but they do occur and the test is too simple and easy to make to omit doing it. Do not purchase a compass that does not pass this test.

Repeat the above procedure, but this time draw the card off to each side about 20° to 30°. Release the external influence abruptly and observe the amount of over-swing as the card returns back to, and past, its original position. A compass with proper dampening will have a minimum over-swing and will return to its proper position with a minimum of oscillation about that position.

These tests are relative; there are no absolute values to use as a standard. Thus they should be made on a comparative basis between several different compasses of the same model and between different models. Be fair, be careful— try to see that comparable tests are made on each compass.

SUMMARY OF SELECTION CRITERIA

1. The card should be easily read and graduated to your preference.

2. The card should remain level and not stick through reasonable angles of pitch and roll.

3. The card should move but slightly during any course change simulated by slowly and smoothly rotating the compass through 90° or more. (Some small motion due to the inertia of the card is permissible, but the card should be dead-beat, swinging but once to a steady position, not oscillating about the lubber's line.)

4. The compass or its binnacle should have built-in correcting magnets.

5. The compass or binnacle should include provision for night lighting. (A means of adjusting the intensity of the light desirable, but not mandatory.)

6. The dome should be hemispherically shaped, rather than flat.

7. The compass should have an internally gimballed card and lubber's line.

8. The compass should have an expansion bellows in the assembly to prevent bubbles forming in the liquid due to temperature changes.

9. The compass or binnacle should be waterproof and have some form of light-controlling hood.

10. Buy a quality instrument and pay the price. This is no place to cut corners; you will get what you pay for.

Final selection

When you make your final selection, don't be miserly! Buy an instrument made by a reputable manufacturer and pay the price. Hidden in the construction of a compass are things that make for accuracy and life long. Among these are: precise positioning of the magnetic element, the magnets under the card, so that the 000°–180° axis indicates exactly the direction of the magnetic meridian; the permanency of the markings on the card, of the expansion bellows, and of the case seals; the life of the pivot bearing, its resistance to wear or to warping or distension from being on one heading for the greater part of the time, as is the case with craft made fast in the same manner in the same berth whenever not in use. Here quality will pay off—in the long run, the best is usually the least expensive.

Installation

The installation of a compass, from initial site selection through the actual mounting of the unit, can be of critical importance to the performance of this most essential navigation tool. If any step is omitted or is not done carefully, it may never be possible to get the compass properly adjusted for precise navigation. Follow each step in detail and don't rush the work.

LOCATING THE COMPASS

The first step in installing any compass is selection of the location in which it is to be mounted. There are a number of factors to be considered, and some limitations that must be faced up to. Actually, consideration of the placement of the unit should have been made before the compass was selected and purchased, but if this has not been done, site consideration and selection must be accomplished before any physical work can be started.

On larger craft

Look critically at the possible locations. Ideally, the compass should be directly in front of the helmsman, placed so that he may read it without bodily stress as he sits or stands in a posture of relaxed alertness. Give some thought to his comfort in rough weather, and in conditions of poor visibility, day or night. His position is fairly well determined by the wheel or tiller he handles. The compass has to be brought into what might be called his "zone of comfort." Too far away, he bends forward to watch it; too close, he bends backwards for better vision. Much of the time he may be not only the helmsman but the forward and after lookout as well. So put the compass where he can bring his eyes to it for reading with a minimum of body movement. For the average person, a distance of 22 to 30 inches (56-76 cm) from his eyes with the head tilted forward not more than 20° is about right; see figs. 1317 and 1320.

On smaller boats

Locating a compass on a small boat can be something of a problem. This matter is one that seems universally overlooked by designers and manufacturers; much ingenuity may be required for a solution. The compass must, of course, be located where it can be easily seen by the skip-

FIG. 1315 This view of a Navy-type 7½-inch compass shows the magnet tubes and float visible through the open center of the card. Note the external gimbals and flat top as well as the lubber's line index mark on the side of the bowl. This design of compass is relatively undesirable as compared with modern spherical compasses having internal gimbals.

per, preferably directly before him. Such a location may not be physically possible, or it may be subject to undesirable magnetic influences which will cause *deviations* in the compass readings (see next paragraph). It may be necessary to locate the compass to one side of the helm position—on the centerline of the craft is common for smaller boats. If so, check carefully for *parallax error,* the change in *apparent* reading when the compass is viewed from one side as compared with directly behind. A slight difference in reading, perhaps up to 5°, may be accepted, but more than that, which can easily occur, will result in defective and perhaps dangerous navigation. If you have this mounting problem, check several models of compasses as some designs will have less parallax error than others.

Check for magnetic influences

With the best location selected from the viewpoint of visibility and use, now check that site for undesirable magnetic influences. The site should be at least two feet (0.6 m) from engine instruments, radios, bilge vapor detectors, electric gauges and instruments and any iron or steel. (Stainless steel is nearly always non-magnetic, but there are many different alloys and such metal should be checked.) Six or more feet (1.8 m) would be better than two, but almost always there must be compromises on boats. When one of these magnetic influences is too close, either it or the compass must be relocated. Vertical magnetic influence is to be especially avoided.

If, from this visual inspection, a location seems satisfactory, test it. There may be magnetic materials or other magnetic influences concealed from ready view. Make your tests with the compass itself. If the compass has built-in correctors, be sure before testing that they have been zeroed-in (see below). If this has not been done, motion of the case can make the card move, nullifying the test procedures.

Move the compass slowly and smoothly all around the

Choosing a Sailboat Compass Card

The helmsman of a sailboat is usually in an unprotected cockpit exposed to the weather. Spray and rain on the glass cover of the binnacle may obscure or distort the markings on the compass card. The smaller and more uniform the markings on the card, the easier it is for the helmsman to confuse one marking for another, lose his place on the card, and wander off course. This is especially true at night or offshore when he has no landmarks to warn him that he has been steering, for example, 55° instead of his intended course of 65°. And when he discovers his error, he may not know how *long* he has been off course.

If the pattern on the card shows a large and prominent patch of contrasting color at the cardinal points and an even larger one at "North," even an inexperienced helmsman can steer with surprising accuracy by relying on the general position of this distinctive pattern as his guide, vague and blurry though it may be.

proposed location without changing its orientation with the boat's centerline. Watch the card; one thing only will make it turn, a magnetic influence—find this with the compass. If such cannot be moved away or replaced with non-magnetic material, test to determine whether it is merely magnetic metal, a random piece of iron or steel, or it is a magnetized object. Successively bring the North and South poles of the compass near it. Both poles will be attracted if it is unmagnetized. If it attracts one pole and repels the other, the object is magnetized. Demagnetization may be attempted (see page 290).

Metal objects that move in normal operation should be moved. Turn the steering wheel; work the throttle, move the gear shift; open and close the windshield if it is near the compass. Try to duplicate all the changes that can occur in normal operation of the boat.

Checking for electrical influences

Electrical currents flowing in wires near the proposed location can also exert undesired influences on the compass. Hold or tape down the compass at the proposed location—test every electrical circuit that might affect the compass. Switch on and off *all* the electrical loads, radio, bilge pump, depth sounder, lights, windshield wipers, etc.; don't overlook anything controlled by a switch on the panel or located near the proposed compass site. Start the engine so that the electrical instruments will be operating. If there is an auxiliary light plant, start it.

Make a complete check

In summary, check everything, one at a time, that might influence the compass at the intended location, carefully watching the card as items are switched on and off, moved

FIG. 1317 The magnetic environment must be given careful attention when selecting the location for a boat's compass, but consideration must also be given to the ease with which it can be read underway.

back and forth, or started and stopped. When on any of these tests, the card moves, the compass has been affected. Ideally, the compass should be relocated or the cause of the influence removed or demagnetized. In actual practice, however, you may have to settle for two separate states of magnetic environment; for example, say, with and without the windshield wipers working.

Vibration

Vibration can make a compass completely unusable at an otherwise desirable location. It can actually make a card slowly but continuously spin—this may seem unbelievable, but it does happen! Even if vibration did not cause the card to spin, it could result in excessive pivot wear. Mount the compass temporarily but firmly in the planned location and watch for vibration at all ranges of engine rpm and boat speed; vibration is unpredictable and may occur only at certain engine speeds.

ZEROING-IN

A modern compass having internal compensators should be *zeroed-in* before being mounted on a boat. (If there is any doubt that a compass already mounted has been zeroed-in, it may be demounted and taken ashore for this purpose.) Zeroing-in is nothing more than adjusting the built-in compensators so that they have no effect on the compass. A compass that is subject only to the earth's field has no need for compensation; there are no deviations to remove. Thus before being installed any deviation caused by the improper position of the compensators themselves must be removed so that the unit can go aboard ready for whatever magnetic influences the boat may have. Setting the compensators by aligning screw slots with marks on the case or housing may not be sufficient for accurate navigation. Zeroing-in by trial-and-error is simple and effec-

FIG. 1318 Smaller boats nearly always present problems in locating a compass. It is difficult to find adequate space for a compass large enough to be really useful, and the magnet environment is usually poor. Ingenuity and patience will be required for a successful solution.

FIG. 1319 A board with parallel edges and a large book are all that is needed to accomplish the zeroing-in process. A non-magnetic screwdriver, or a thin coin, must be used to adjust the screws controlling the compensating magnets.

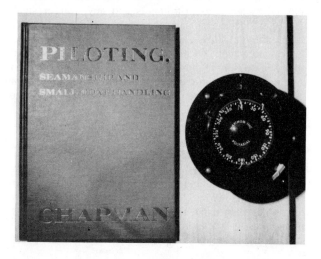

tive; it does not require any knowledge of the direction of magnetic North.

How to do it

Zeroing-in must be done off the boat and in an area well away from any known magnetic influence such as iron or steel pipes and girders, radios, electric motors, refrigerators, etc. Don't work wearing a steel belt buckle or watchband; keep all tools well away from the work area.

Using non-magnetic screws or tacks (check them with a small magnet to be sure) mount the compass temporarily on a small board with two exactly parallel edges. Line up the lubber's line with these parallel edges as closely as possible, but precise alignment is not mandatory. On a level, flat surface—a plank will do fine, but not a table which may have screws or braces of magnetic material—place a large book and the compass on its small board. Move the board in to close contact with the side of the book; see fig. 1319. Turn the book and board as a unit until the compass reads North exactly. Hold the book steady in this position; it serves as a fixed direction reference. Remove the compass and board, turn it end for end, and bring the opposite side of the board snugly against the book; the lubber's line has now been exactly reversed. If the compass now reads South exactly, the N—S internal compensator is already zeroed-in and requires no adjustment.

If, however, the reading is not exactly South, an adjustment is needed; read the difference from 180° and record it. With a non-magnetic screwdriver (a thin coin, such as a dime, will do for most compasses) slowly turn the N—S screw until half this difference is removed. If the difference increases when you first turn the screw, then turn it in the opposite direction until the desired result is obtained. Now slightly realign the book and compass board combination as a unit until the compass reads South exactly. Hold the book firmly and reverse the board.

The compass should now read North. If it does not, the difference will be much smaller than the initial difference at South. If there is a difference, again halve it by turning the N—S adjusting screw. Realign the book and compass, always keeping the board snugly against the book, until the reading is North exactly. Once again reverse the board and check to see that the compass reads South. If it does not read South exactly, again halve the difference. Continue this procedure until the reversal yields zero difference, or as nearly zero as possible. When this process has been completed, the North—South axis of the compass coincides with the magnetic meridian.

Next adjust the East—West compensators in the same way. Line up on either an East or West heading, reverse, and if the resultant heading is not exactly the opposite, then remove half the difference by turning the E—W screw in the correct direction as determined by trial-and-error. Continue working on East and West headings just as on North and South until the desired results are obtained.

If exact reversals are not attainable, move the zeroing-in operations to a different location; some unseen magnetic influence may be present. If the compass manufacturer provided instruction for zeroing-in, they should be followed.

Do not discard the temporary mounting board. It may be useful in testing a possible permanent site on the boat.

FIG. 1320 Although the preferred position for a compass is on the vessel's centerline, off-center location of the wheel may require other mounting so that the instrument is directly forward of the helmsman.

MOUNTING

Once the compass has been zeroed-in and the prospective location checked for undesirable magnetic influences, the boat owner can then proceed to the actual mounting of the compass. Certain basic requirements must be met.

1. The compass must be securely fastened to the boat.

2. A line from the center of the card through the lubber's line must be exactly parallel to the keel, the center line of the boat, fig. 1321. (Ideally, the compass would be directly over the centerline, but this is not mandatory if it is kept exactly parallel.)

3. The compass must be level; this is often at least partially accomplished by mounting brackets; if the compass has a cylindrical case, the bottom must be shimmed so that the unit is level; see fig. 1320 right.

4. Magnetic material in the vicinity of the compass should be minimal. Wires near it, carrying direct current, should be twisted.

Fastening the compass down

Establish the fore-and-aft centerline of the craft with stout cord or string. Carefully transfer this direction to the compass site. Drill one mounting hole only. If during compensation later, the compass must be slightly turned to correct any misalignment of the lubber's line, more than one hole could present problems. When compensation has been accomplished, the remaining hole(s) can be drilled and the fastening job completed; a partial check of the compensation should be repeated after this is done.

If Your Boat Already Has A Compass

If you have a boat and it already has a compass installed, or if you are buying a boat that comes equipped with a compass, you can still benefit from the above information.

If you did not make the installation of the compass on the boat in accordance with the guidance given above, you should first check that it is properly aligned with the craft's centerline; any error here will affect every reading of the instrument.

The compass can be easily removed from the boat and a check made that the zeroing-in process has been done. (This assumes that a satisfactory deviation table does not

FIG. 1322 On some compasses, the width of the lubber's line is equal to 1° on the card. The center sketch shows how this could be used to read 1° either side of a main graduation. A reading slightly more or less than half-way between marks would indicate 2° more or less than the nearest mark.

FIG. 1321 If the compass is not mounted directly over the keel line of the boat, great care must be taken to make sure that a line through the center of the card and the lubber's line is directly parallel to the craft's centerline.

exist.) While the compass is off the boat, make the tests described above for the selection of a new compass; consider replacing the unit if it doesn't pass all tests.

When the internal compensators have been zeroed-in, put the compass back in place and make a thorough check for disturbing influences from nearby objects and electrical wiring. Fasten it down securely and check for undesirable vibrations.

Using A Compass

A compass is read by observing the graduation of the card that is opposite the lubber's line. The card of a typical boat compass has major graduations every 10° with lighter marks at intermediate 5° intervals; see fig. 1306. On some models the width of the lubber's line is just about 1°. Thus it is possible to use this width to rather accurately estimate a reading of one degree more or less than each card marking. A reading slightly less or more than midway between the card markings gives the other individual degree values; see fig. 1322.

Always remember, when a boat turns, it is the boat, and the lubber's line, that turns—the compass card maintains the same direction.

Using an uncalibrated compass

Although a compass that has not been calibrated—compensated to remove or reduce deviations, or else had a deviation table prepared—cannot be used to navigate with a chart, there are simple, but practical, uses to which it can be put.

An uncalibrated compass may not measure direction correctly related to magnetic North, but it does indicate directions in a stable, repeatable way if local conditions on the boat are unchanged. You can proceed from one point to another—for example, from one channel marker to the next—read the compass when you are right on course, and record that value. If you make the same run on another day, the reading will be the same, *provided* that you haven't added, removed, or altered any magnetic influences near the compass. Thus if the day comes when it is foggy, or night catches you still out on the water, you can follow the compass heading that you recorded in good visibility. The figures may not have any absolute meaning, but they will get you where you want to go!

A skipper should record his compass headings on all the runs that he regularly makes. If during periods of reduced visibility he would take a less direct route of more but shorter legs, then this route should be run in good visibility and the compass headings recorded. One word of caution, however, the reverse course *must* be *run* for each heading; you *cannot* add or subtract 180° from the forward run to get a reading for the return.

Keep your compass course records handy and check the various headings frequently. If there is a change, look for the reason and eliminate it.

Protection when not in use

The worst enemy of a compass is direct sunlight; the next worse is prolonged sitting on the same heading. While there is little that can be done about the latter when a boat sits day in and day out in a marina slip, something can, and should be done about excess sunlight.

When a compass is not in use, it should be thoroughly shielded from the sun. This will prevent discoloration of the liquid, and perhaps of the card. Sometimes a binnacle will have a light-shielding hood; if so, keep it closed at all times when the compass is not in use. If such a shield is not a part of a compass, one must be improvised. Use something that is completely lightproof; do not use cloth, not even the heaviest and darkest kind is fully adequate.

Any bubbles that form under the cover, usually from temperature changes, can be removed by adding liquid. This must be of the same type that is already in the compass to avoid further problems. This is a job that is best done by a professional compass repairman in his shop.

CHAPTER 14

THE MARINER'S COMPASS

**VARIATION,
DEVIATION,
COMPENSATION,
and
ADVANCED
COMPASS TOPICS**

A VESSEL'S SAFETY may depend upon her compass. Cruising under conditions of poor visibility, the small craft pilot may have no other means of keeping to his desired track and, crossing a body of open water, no other means of making a good landfall. Running out the time on a given course in thick weather and neither seeing nor hearing the expected aid to navigation is not conducive to peace of mind. There is little comfort in a chain of soundings that does not match what the chart shows in the expected vicinity. Stranding because of unexpected contact with rock, shoal or any bottom is unnerving.

The preceding chapter covered the basic principles of compasses and their selection, installation, and use without adjustment. Here we will consider compass errors—variation and deviation—and conversions between true, magnetic, and compass directions, as well as compass compensation.

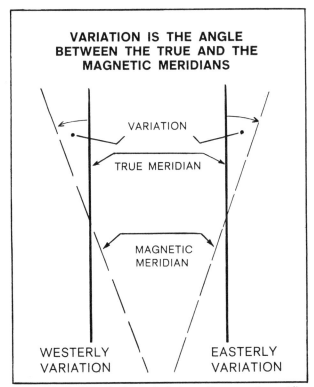

VARIATION IS THE ANGLE BETWEEN THE TRUE AND THE MAGNETIC MERIDIANS

VARIATION

TRUE MERIDIAN

MAGNETIC MERIDIAN

WESTERLY VARIATION

EASTERLY VARIATION

FIG. 1401 Variation is the angle between the magnetic meridian and the true meridian. It can be either easterly or westerly as shown above. Variation depends upon geographic location and is the same for all vessels in that vicinity.

Compass Errors

Before a compass can be used to truly navigate, consideration must be given to *compass errors*, the differences between compass readings and true directions measured from geographic North. In his normal day's work, the navigator of a ship or the skipper of a small boat, working with his charts, has need to know true directions. His courses and bearings are normally recorded and plotted with respect to true North. (Some boatmen work in terms of magnetic directions, but this should only be done by an experienced skipper.)

VARIATION

The first, and most basic, compass error is *variation* (*V* or *Var*). This is, for any given location on land or sea, the angle between the magnetic meridian and the geographic meridian; see fig. 1401. It is the angle between true North and the direction indicated by a compass which is free from any nearby influences. Variation is designated as *East* or *West* in accordance with the way in which the compass needle is deflected. Any statement of variation, except zero, must have one of these labels; it is meaningless otherwise.

Variation is a compass error about which a navigator can do nothing but recognize its existence and make allowances for it. Variation is the compass error that would exist on a completely non-magnetic ship or boat that was entirely free from any on-board magnetic materials or other internal magnetic influences.

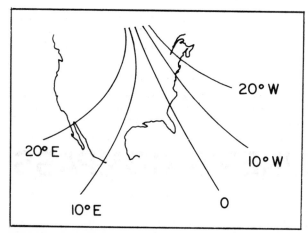

FIG. 1402 Magnetic variation is different for different geographic locations. It is generally westerly on the U.S. Atlantic coast, and easterly on the Gulf and Pacific Coasts.

FIG. 1403 The change in variation with change in location must not be overlooked. Here the true and magnetic courses from X to Y are both 039° initially, but the magnetic soon changes while the true remains constant. An aviator would end up 150 miles NW of his goal, but a skipper would have run aground on the Rhode Island coast—neither got to his Nova Scotia destination.

General variation

The earth is not a homogeneous mass, and thus its magnetic field is by no means uniform. As a result of this non-uniformity of the earth's field, and the displacement of the magnetic poles from the geographic poles (see page 268), *variation changes with location*; see fig. 1402. An awareness of this basic fact is part of the duty of every navigator and pilot. If he neglects it, he will be in trouble, big trouble! Fig. 1403 illustrates the results of failure to apply different variation as a vessel moves from one location to another.

At any given place, the amount of variation is essentially constant. (There is usually a small annual change, but if the navigator is using the latest chart, or one not more than two or three years old, this quite small amount of change in variation can be neglected.) Information on the amount of variation, and its annual rate of change, will be found on the chart that is being used for navigation.

On nearly all types of charts published by the National Ocean Survey, including those of the Lake Survey Center, there will be found several *compass roses* suitably placed for convenient plotting. These are circular figures several inches (perhaps 5 to 10 cm) in diameter with three concentric circular scales; see fig. 1404. The outer one is graduated in degrees and is oriented so that its zero point, indicated by a star symbol, points to true (geographic) north. The inner pair of scales is graduated in degrees and in the point system down to quarter-points. The zero point of these scales, identified by an arrow symbol, shows the direction of the northern half of the magnetic meridian at that point.

The angle at the center of a compass rose between the star and arrow symbols is the variation *in that* vicinity for the year stated. This information is printed at the center of the rose to the nearest 15'; for example, "Var 14° 45'W (1976)." There is also a notation as to the annual rate of change, to the nearest 1', and whether the variation is increasing or decreasing; for example, "Annual Increase 2'" or "Annual Decrease 6'" or "No Annual Change"; see fig. 1404.

As we have seen above, magnetic variation changes with location. Thus, except for charts of a limited area such as a single harbor and its approaches, variation will most likely be different in various areas of a typical chart. For this reason, the variation graphically indicated by the several compass roses on any particular chart will be different. It is important to *always* refer to the compass rose *nearest your position* on the chart to read variation or to plot from its scales.

Local Attraction

In addition to the overall magnetic variation encountered generally, the navigator must also reckon with the possibility of *local attraction*. (In this case, "local" means in a limited geographic vicinity, as opposed to the other use of the term for magnetic influences on board the ship or boat.) In some localities, fortunately few, the compass is subject to irregular magnetic disturbances in the earth's field over relatively small areas. A striking example is found in Kingston Harbor, Ontario, Canada, where a variation may vary as much as 45° in a distance of a mile and a half (2.4 km).

FIG. 1404 Each chart has several compass roses which show the variation graphically and descriptively. These are located so as to be convenient for plotting. On any chart, but especially on small-scale charts of large areas, always use the compass rose nearest the vicinity concerned.

Charts of areas subject to such local attraction situations will bear warnings to this effect. Other means of navigation will be needed when within range of such disturbances.

DEVIATION

A compass on a boat rarely exists in an environment that is completely free of nearby magnetic materials or influences from electrical currents. Normally the mariner's compass is subject to magnetic forces in addition to those of the earth's field. Material already magnetized, or even not previously magnetized but capable of being magnetized by the magnets of the compass, will cause the compass to deviate from its ideal position along the magnetic meridian. Currents flowing in improperly installed electrical wiring can have the same effect.

The deflection of the compass from its magnetic north orientation is called *deviation (D or Dev)*. It is the angle between the magnetic meridian and a line from the pivot through the north point of the compass card. Theoretically, its amount can range from 0° to 180°, but in practice large values cannot be tolerated. Just as for variation, deviation can be *East* or *West* as determined whether the compass north lies to the east or west of the north branch of the compass meridian; it *must* carry one of these labels, unless it is zero. See fig. 1405.

It will be recalled that variation changes with geographic location. *Deviation changes with the craft's heading*; it does not change noticeably in any given geographic area. (Causes for this effect will be explained

FIG. 1405 Deviation is the difference between the north direction indicated by the compass and the magnetic meridian. As for variation, it can be easterly or westerly. Deviation depends upon the magnetic conditions on a vessel and changes with different headings. It is not affected by the vessel's geographic location and is not the same for different craft in the same area.

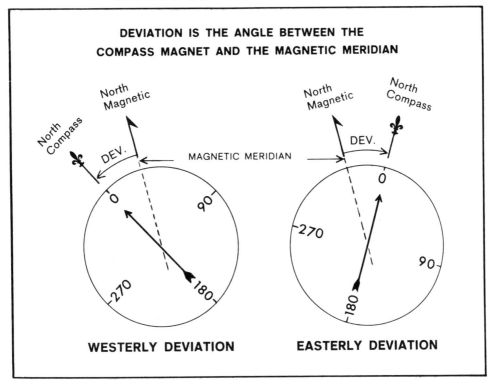

DEVIATION IS THE ANGLE BETWEEN THE
COMPASS MAGNET AND THE MAGNETIC MERIDIAN

WESTERLY DEVIATION   EASTERLY DEVIATION

Ship's Head Compass	Range bears Compass	Range bears Magnetic	Deviation
000°	082°	087°	5°E
015°	086°	087°	1°E
030°	091°	087°	4°W
045°	096°	087°	9°W
060°	100°	087°	13°W
075°	104°	087°	17°W
090°	106°	087°	19°W
105°	106°	087°	19°W
120°	104°	087°	17°W
135°	101°	087°	14°W
150°	097°	087°	10°W
165°	093°	087°	6°W
180°	089°	087°	2°W
195°	085°	087°	2°E
210°	082°	087°	5°E
225°	079°	087°	8°E
240°	076°	087°	11°E
255°	073°	087°	14°E
270°	070°	087°	17°E
285°	069°	087°	18°E
300°	070°	087°	17°E
315°	072°	087°	15°E
330°	075°	087°	12°E
345°	078°	087°	9°E

FIG. 1406a The navigator takes a bearing on a range for each 15° of heading of his craft. By comparison with the known magnetic direction, he determines the deviation of his compass for each compass heading. (The values in this table are larger than would be tolerated for actual navigation, but could represent an uncompensated compass.)

Ship's Head Magnetic	Deviation
000°	7°E
015°	1°E
030°	6°W
045°	12°W
060°	17°W
075°	19°W
090°	18°W
105°	17°W
120°	14°W
135°	11°W
150°	8°W
165°	5°W
180°	2°W
195°	2°E
210°	4°E
225°	6°E
240°	9°E
255°	11°E
270°	14°E
285°	16°E
300°	17°E
315°	17°E
330°	15°E
345°	11°E

FIG. 1406b Deviation in terms of magnetic headings, rather than compass headings, is needed to determine compass course to be steered. Here the values have been calculated and tabulated for each 15° of magnetic heading of the craft.

later; see page 291.) To cope with these changes, a vessel will carry a *deviation table*, a compilation of the respective deviations, usually for every 15° of heading by the compass; fig. 1406a. For added convenience, a deviation table can also be prepared in terms of magnetic headings, fig. 1406b. (Note: In these examples, the values of deviation are large for purposes of illustration. They are typical of an uncompensated compass; they would be considerably reduced for practical navigation.)

Using deviation tables

For ordinary navigation of boats, it is normally sufficient to use the value of deviation from the line of the table that is nearest to the actual heading of the craft; either compass or magnetic. This is particularly true for compensated compasses where the deviations will rarely exceed a few degrees. (Typically, a small craft cannot be held on course closer than two or three degrees at best in moderate or rough waters.)

For more precise navigation, such as in contests and perhaps some races, it will be necessary to *interpolate* between tabular entries to get a more precise value of deviation; see page 293 for interpolation procedures.

Compass adjustment

The objective of reducing deviation to a minimum has brought into existence professional compass adjusters. A boat owner may avail himself of their expert services, but with common sense and an understanding of the causes of deviation, he may do a reasonable job of *compensating* his compass himself. Note that a compass is not "corrected"; its deviations are reduced, and the process is tremed "*compensating*" or "*adjusting*." Seldom is even a compensated compass entirely free of deviation on all headings. As will be seen later, there usually will be residual deviations of small, but practical, significance.

Changes in deviation

It must be thoroughly understood by all who navigate or pilot a boat that any deviation table is valid *only* on the boat for which it was prepared, and *only* for the magnetic conditions which prevailed at the time the table was prepared. If magnetic materials within the radius of effect, some three to five feet (0.9–1.2 m) are added, taken away, or relocated, a new deviation table must be prepared, or as a minimum, sufficient checks must be made of the old table to ensure that its values are still correct. If any electrical or electronic equipment is installed, removed, or relocated, the same possibility of changes in deviation exists and checks must be made which may show the need for the preparation of a new table.

Compass Calculations

A heading or course is merely an angle. It is the angle which the centerline of the boat, or a line on a chart, makes with some other line of reference. Three lines of reference have been established: the direction of true North

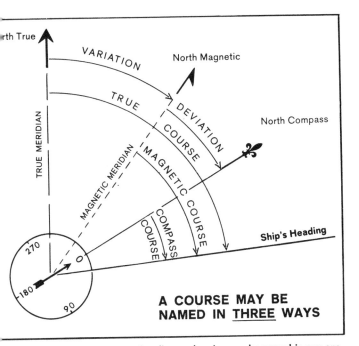

A COURSE MAY BE NAMED IN THREE WAYS

FIG. 1407 A course, heading, or bearing can be named in any one of three systems based on the reference direction used. It is, of course, the same line any way it is named.

FIG. 1408 "Correcting" a magnetic course with easterly variation to a true course—"Correcting Add East."

WHAT IS THE TRUE COURSE?

MAGNETIC COURSE	061°
VARIATION	11°E
DEVIATION	0

RULE: CORRECT ADD EAST

TRUE COURSE 072°

MAGNETIC COURSE 061°

VAR. 11°E

072° True — Ship's Heading

CC 061°

270 — 061 — 90 — 180

Deviation: 0°
Mag. & Compass Courses Coincide

TRUE COURSE 072°

---

or the true meridian; the direction of the magnetic meridian; and the direction of the north point of the compass. Thus *there are three ways to name a course or heading:* true, magnetic, or compass. Always remember—no matter how the course (heading) is named among these three ways, it applies to the same direction. Fig. 1407 illustrates the three reference lines and the three measurements of direction for one heading. (The amount of variation and deviation in this figure is somewhat exaggerated for greater clarity.) The above remarks are, of course, equally applicable to the measurement of directions for bearings.

THE APPLICATION OF VARIATION AND DEVIATION

To be able to fully use his boat's compass, a skipper must develop an ability to quickly and accurately *convert* directions between true, magnetic, and compass. These directions include headings, courses, and bearings. He will need compass courses to use in steering his boat; he will get compass bearings when he takes a reading across his compass to a distant aid to navigation or landmark. He will normally use true directions to plot on his chart and record in his log. In between compass and true, will be found magnetic directions, necessary intermediate steps in going from one to the other, and sometimes directly useful in themselves. Hence, there is need for continual interconversion between the three systems of naming direction.

Like learning to read or tell time by a clock, ease and accuracy in making these conversions come with practice. At first a boatman reasons out each step. Later, reasoning is dropped as the process becomes one of habit.

Single-step calculations

Although most compass calculations involve the double conversion from true to magnetic to compass, and vice versa, it is convenient to first consider single-step computations.

The terms "correct" and "correcting" are not really valid as relating to the various types of directions. They do, however, make possible simple and easily remembered phrases for the rules for determining whether to add or subtract deviation and variation. Let us then consider true directions as being more "correct" than magnetic, and magnetic as being more "correct" than compass directions. [This can be rationalized and easily remembered by observing that true has no "errors," magnetic has one error (variation), and compass includes two errors (variation and deviation).] We can then see that going from magnetic to true—or compass to magnetic— can be termed "correcting." Conversely, the term used is "uncorrecting" when going from true to magnetic, or from magnetic to compass. The purist may object to these terms, and in a literal sense he may be right, but they do serve their purpose.

The basic rule is: *"When correcting, add easterly errors"* which can be shortened to *"Correcting add east"* and memorized as *"C-A-E."*

Example 1. The magnetic course is 061°; the variation is 11°E.

Required: The true course, TC.

The conversion is one of *"correcting"* and the variation

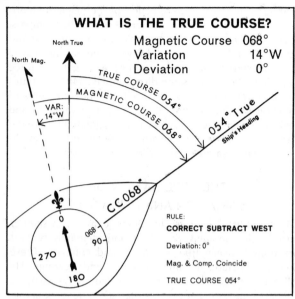

WHAT IS THE TRUE COURSE?

Magnetic Course	068°
Variation	14°W
Deviation	0°

RULE:
CORRECT SUBTRACT WEST

Deviation: 0°

Mag. & Comp. Coincide

TRUE COURSE 054°

FIG. 1409 "Correcting" a magnetic course with westerly variation to a true course—"Uncorrecting Subtract West."

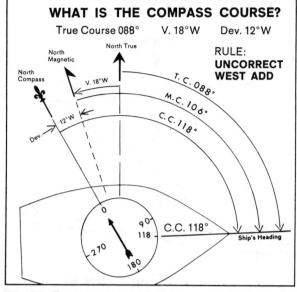

WHAT IS THE COMPASS COURSE?

True Course 088° V. 18°W Dev. 12°W

RULE:
UNCORRECT WEST ADD

FIG. 1410 Two-step conversion, both "uncorrecting"—a true course, with variation and deviation both westerly, to a compass course—"Uncorrecting Add West."

is easterly, so the basic rule is used, "Correcting add east."

$$061° + 11° = 072°$$

Answer: TC 072°; see fig. 1408.

The basic rule is easily altered for application to the three other operations of conversion. Remember to *always change two, but only two words* in the phrase for any application; see the following examples.

Example 2. The magnetic course is 068°; the variation is 14° West.

Required: The true course, TC.

The conversion is "correcting" and the variation is westerly. In the basic rule, "east" has been changed to "west"; one word has been changed, another must be. Since it is "correcting," the other word must be changed to meet the rule of "always two changes, but only two" and so "add" becomes "subtract." The rule to be applied here is thus: "Correcting subtract west."

$$068° - 14° = 054°$$

Answer: TC 054°; see fig. 1409.

Example 3. The course of the boat by its compass is 212°; the deviation for that heading is 5°E.

Required: The magnetic course, MC.

The conversion is "correcting" and the deviation is easterly; the applicable rule is "Correcting add east."

$$212° + 5° = 217°$$

Answer: MC 217°.

Consider now the reverse process of conversion that is "uncorrecting." We again change two, but only two, words to the basic rule and we get: "Uncorrecting add west" and "Uncorrecting subtract east." (Don't worry about remembering all four of the rules. It's easier and surer to remember the basic rule of "C-A-E" and how to change it to fit the other situations.)

Example 4. The true course is 351° and the variation is 12°W.

Required: The magnetic course, MC.

The conversion is "uncorrecting" and the variation is westerly. The applicable rule is "Uncorrecting add west."

$$351° + 12° = 363° = 003°$$

Answer: MC 003°.

Example 5. The magnetic course is 172° and the deviation for that heading is 7°E.

Required: The compass course, CC.

The conversion is uncorrecting and the deviation is easterly. The applicable rule is "Uncorrecting subtract east."

$$172° - 7° = 165°$$

Answer: CC 165°.

Two-step conversions

The same rules as above apply when two-step conversions are made from true to compass, or from compass to true. It is important to remember that the proper rule must be used for *each step separately.* It will always be "correcting" or "uncorrecting" for both steps, *but* the addition or subtraction may not be the same as this is determined individually by the east or west nature of the variation and deviation.

Example 6. The true course is 088°; the variation is 18°W and the deviation is 12°W.

Required: The compass course, CC.

Both conversions are "uncorrecting" and both errors are westerly. The rule for both calculations is "Uncorrecting add west."

$$088° + 18° + 12° = 118°$$

Answer: CC 118°; see fig. 1410.

Example 7. The compass bearing is 107°; the variation is 6°E and the deviation for the heading that the boat is on is 2°W.

Required: The true bearing, TB.

Both conversions are "correcting"; the variation is easterly but the deviation is westerly, so two rules are re-

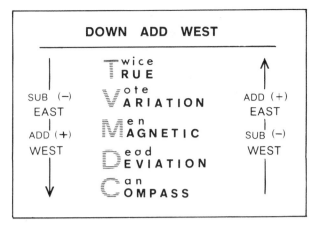

DOWN ADD WEST

Twice
TRUE
SUB (−)   Vote   ADD (+)
EAST   VARIATION   EAST
ADD (+)   Men   SUB (−)
WEST   MAGNETIC   WEST
          Dead
          DEVIATION
          Can
          COMPASS

FIG. 1411 The rules for interconverting between true, magnetic, and compass can also be remembered from a pictorial diagram— T V M D C. The basic rule is "Down Add West"; the other rules can be derived from this by changing two, but only two, of these three words.

quired: "Correcting add east, subtract west."

$$107° + 6° − 2° = 111°$$

Answer: TB 111°.

Other examples could be shown for two-step conversions, consisting of same name or opposite name for the two errors. It will always be "correcting" or "uncorrecting" for both steps, but there could be two additions or two subtractions, or one of each. Remember to consider each step separately when selecting the proper rule to apply.

Other "rules"

The basic rule of "Correcting add east" and its variations are only one set of memory-aids for compass calculations: there are many more. Only one need be known; each skipper should study several and pick the one that is easiest for him to remember and apply.

Another that is easily memorized and used is "Compass least, error east; Compass best, error west." This can be used for conversions such as those shown in the examples above, but it is of particular value when the difference between compass and magnetic is known numerically and it must be decided whether the deviation is east or west. For example: if the magnetic course is known to be 192° but the compass reads 190°, what is the deviation? The numerical difference is 2° and the compass is "least"— 190° is less than 192°—so the error is east; deviation is 2°E. If on the same course, the compass had read 195°, the compass would then have been "best"—195° being more (better) than 192°—and the deviation would be 3°W.

When considering variation as the difference between true and magnetic, apply the same phrase but with "magnetic" substituted for "compass"—the rhyme is not as good, but the principle is the same. For example: if a true bearing is 310° and the variation is 4° west, then the magnetic bearing will be "best" (more than the true value) or 314°. If the variation had been easterly, then magnetic would have been "least" or 4° less for 306°.

Visual aids

Many boatmen find a pictorial device a better memory-aid than a phrase or sentence. Letters are arranged vertically representing the three ways of naming a direction—

true, magnetic, and compass—with the respective differences—variation and deviation—properly placed between them. The arrangement can be memorized in several ways, such as "True Virgins Make Dull Company" or in the reverse direction as "Can Dead Men Vote Twice."

On each side of the letters, an arrow is drawn to indicate the direction of conversion; on the left, down for true to compass, and on the right, up for compass to true. Also on each side, the appropriate arithmetic process is indicated for use with easterly or westerly errors. See fig. 1411. The right side indicates what has been termed above as "correcting"; the left side illustrates "uncorrecting." If one memorizes "D-A-W" for "Down add West," then the correct signs can always be added to the letters and arrows. (The three other actions follow the same pattern as above—always change two, but only two, words. Thus it would be Down subtract east, Up add east, and Up subtract west.)

Example 8(a). From the chart, the true course is 107° and the variation in the locality is 5°E.

Required: The magnetic course, MC.

The conversion is "down" the diagram; use the left side. The variation is easterly so it is to be subtracted.

$$107° − 5° = 102°$$

Answer: MC 102°. See below.

	DOWN	T	107°
	SUBTRACT	V (−)	5°E
	EAST	M	102°

Example 8(b). For this magnetic heading, the deviation aboard this boat is 4°W.

Required: The compass course, CC.

The conversion is still downward on the diagram; continue to use the left side. The deviation is westerly so it must be added.

$$102° + 4° = 106°$$

Answer: CC 106°. See below.

DOWN	M	102°
ADD	D (+)	4°W
WEST	C	106°

Conversions such as this could be done in a single two-step operation.

Example 9. A boat is on compass course (CC) 193°. The deviation for this craft on this heading is 6°E; the variation for the vicinity is 9°W.

Required: The true course, TC.

The conversion is "up" the diagram; use the right side. Easterly deviation is to be added; westerly variation is to be subtracted.

T	190°	
V	(−) 9°W	ADD
M	199°	EAST
D	(+) 6°E	SUBTRACT
C	193°	WEST

Answer: TC 190°.

ALWAYS TRUST YOUR COMPASS

A skipper should learn to always trust his compass; failure to do this may be disastrous! If you are dependent upon your compass for navigation, make a quick check for any objects near it that could cause additional, unmeasured deviations; typical objects that get placed too close to a compass include knives, beer and soft drink cans, small radios, cameras and light meters, and tools. If your magnetic situation has been checked and is "all clear," then trust your compass to direct you to safety or your desired destination—it is better than your instincts! For years a compass will faithfully indicate directions, if properly guarded. No watch is without some rate of error, which must be allowed for; not so for a well-treated compass.

The importance of accuracy

It is well for a skipper to keep in mind the results of not running an accurate course. If his compass, or his compass calculations, should be in error by only 5°, he will be a full mile off course for every 11½ miles run (1 km for every 11½ km). This could well be hazardous when making a landfall or a coastal run at night or in poor visibility. Also dangerous with an inaccurate compass would be running a narrow channel in fog or heavy rain. Note the following table:

Error in Course	Number of feet off course after sailing one nautical mile	Miles sailed to be one mile off course
1°	106	57.3
2°	212	28.6
3°	318	19.1
4°	424	14.3
5°	530	11.5
6°	635	9.6
7°	740	8.2
8°	846	7.2
9°	950	6.4
10°	1055	5.7

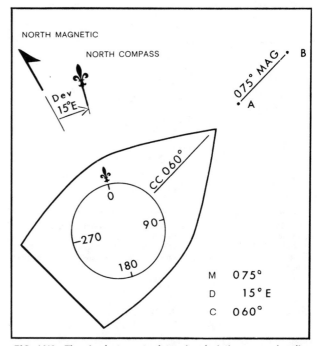

M	075°
D	15° E
C	060°

FIG. 1412   The simplest way to determine deviation on any heading is to locate two objects to use as a range whose magnetic direction can be established from the chart. Then head the boat toward this range and read the compass; the difference, if any, is the deviation on that heading.

FIG. 1413   Carefully run courses between two charted positions can be used to determine deviation on a number of headings. The deviation will not be the same for reciprocal courses and each must be run individually.

OTHER COMPASSES

No mention has been made of dry compasses. At one time, mariner's compasses were dry. The needles were affixed to a card, and the assembly, extremely light in weight, supported on a pivot as in wet compasses. The installation of reciprocating engines in vessels caused vibrations which affected the instruments' accuracy. The wet compass, literally damping these vibrations, then came into general use.

Do not attempt to use the above rules for conversion with a compass having a free needle supported above a card. In this type of compass, the card and magnet do not move as a unit. Such a compass has no lubber's line and is useful only for estimating directions from its center.

DETERMINING DEVIATION

Deviation is the angle between the compass card axis and the magnetic meridian, fig. 1405.

Aboard any craft the direction of compass north is easily learned by a quick glance at the compass card. Not so the direction of the magnetic meridian, or, as it is loosely termed, magnetic north. Thus it is not possible to compare visually the angle between these two reference directions, the deviation on that heading. But the difference between an observed compass bearing and the known correct magnetic value for that bearing yields that same angle.

Deviation by bow bearings

The bearing is sighted over the compass with the boat headed directly toward the object or range. The magnetic direction is taken from the chart. The distant target can be a range of two objects, or it can be a single object if the location of the boat can be fixed precisely, such as close aboard an aid to navigation with the object far enough away that the slight offset of the boat is immaterial.

The range technique is the more accurate and is done as follows: Two visible objects, preferably ashore or fixed to the bottom and both accurately charted, are selected. From the chart, the magnetic direction from the nearer to the farther mark is measured and recorded. (The very best range is one that is an aid to navigation; its true direction is given precisely in the Light List, just apply variation to get magnetic.) See fig. 1412; A and B are two visible objects with B visible behind A. The magnetic bearing of this range is 075°. The boat is run straight toward A on the range, keeping A and B visibly in line. While steady on this heading, the compass is read and recorded. In this example, it reads 060°; the amount of the difference is the deviation, 15°. Reference to any of the conversion rules makes it clear that the deviation is East. Other ranges can be set up and the deviation on such headings found by repeating the bow bearing procedure as above. The side of a long object such as a pier or large building ashore can also be used as a range if the direction can be determined from the chart.

A buoy and a fixed object, or even two buoys, may be used if a range of fixed objects is unavailable. The charted position of a buoy is that of its anchor; wind or current, or both, may swing a buoy around its charted position. Large ships and tugs have been known to move buoys off-station inadvertently by collision in thick weather. Hence the use of a buoy or two gives less accurate results

and this fact must be kept in mind when using a deviation table prepared by such references; it should be replaced as soon as practicable with a table made under better conditions.

Deviation by courses

Steering a visible course from one aid to navigation to another and noting the heading by compass will, if the observation is made at the start of each leg, give reasonably good results when compared with the charted magnetic directions, fig. 1413.

Deviation table by "swinging ship"

A precise technique for developing a deviation table is to "swing the ship" about its compass by running different headings across a range, recording the compass bearing of the range on each crossing. For example, two prominent charted objects are on a range with a magnetic bearing measuring 087°. On a calm day, the boat WATER WITCH sails across this range on compass headings successively 15° apart. Using sight vanes, and an azimuth cricle mounted on the compass (see fig. 1913) the compass bearing of the range is taken for each crossing. The results are recorded and tabulated.

The skipper averages the various compass bearings and get 086.9°. He notes that this is very close to the magnetic bearing of the range and decides that he has a good set of data.

The first and last columns of this table now constitute a deviation table for WATER WITCH provided no changes are made in the magnetic environment of the compass; see fig. 1406a. It should be noted that while the above figures do constitute a valid deviation table, they are much larger than would normally be tolerated in actual navigation or piloting. With deviations this large, action would be promptly taken to adjust (compensate) the compass so as to reduce these deviations to zero, or nearly so.

It is important also to note that the deviations of the above table are in terms of compass headings. These are not, of course, the same as magnetic headings; when on a heading 045° magnetic the boat's bow points in a direction quite different than it does when she heads 045° by compass. This leads to a problem. The skipper determines from the chart his magnetic course; he then wants to know what deviation to apply to get the compass course he should steer. Use of the above table for that purpose requires tedious, repetitive, and time-consuming trial-and-error steps. To avoid this, he makes a second table listing the deviations in terms of magnetic headings; see fig. 1406b. This can be done by the trial-and-error method (but will only have to be done once to make the table, rather than each time such deviation is desired) or the desired information can be taken from a Napier diagram (see page 294).

Compensation

It can be assumed that a boat's compass will have deviation errors. The area available for a control station on most craft, especially motorboats, is so limited that it is impossible to have engine instruments, controls, and other "magnetically undesirable" objects at a safe distance from the compass. It is possible to "live with" known values

FIG. 1414 Nearly all modern boat compasses have a pair (or two pairs) of internal compensating magnets built into the compass base or binnacle. When adjusted properly, these will eliminate, or greatly reduce, deviation.

Two methods

Two basic techniques are used to adjust the compasses of small craft. Both use a pair of small compensating magnets; in one instance they are internal to the compass case or binnacle, in the other they are external and are mounted near the compass location. The objective of both methods is the same, to provide weak magnetic fields in opposition to the disturbing influences so as to have a zero net effect on the compass card. Compensation consists of adjusting the effect of each of the magnets so as to achieve the counterbalancing of their fields with the fields of the disturbing influences.

USING INTERNAL CORRECTORS

Most modern boat compasses now have internal compensating magnets and this technique of compensation will be considered first. The two magnets are installed at right angles to each other. Usually there will be two slotted screw heads at the edge of the compass; one will be marked "E—W", and the other "N—S"; see fig. 1414.

Preliminary steps

The internal compensators must have been "zeroed-in" before the compensation procedures are begun. This should have been done off the boat before the compass was installed, but if there is any doubt about this step having been taken, the instrument can be removed and the procedures of pages 274–276 followed.

It is well also to take a few minutes to check that the line from the center of the compass through the lubber's line is *exactly* parallel to the centerline of the craft. If the compass is not properly aligned, a satisfactory adjustment cannot be achieved. This check can be made by close measurements on board, but it is perhaps more easily accomplished by sighting on a distant object, both over the compass and down the centerline of the boat, while the craft is held absolutely motionless. [If the compass is mounted to one side of the boat's centerline, the distant target object must be far enough away, a half-mile (0.9 km) or more, that the small offset spacing will not affect the test. If a shorter distance must be used, aim at two separate points exactly separated by the offset spacing.]

of deviation provided that they are not too large—deviations much in excess of about 6° can cause trouble in rough waters. It is, however, much better if the compass is adjusted (also termed *compensated)* so that the deviation is reduced to zero, or nearly so, on as many headings as possible. This procedure is within the capabilities of an average skipper who will study the instructions carefully and take the time to do a good job. No special skills are required, just patience and attention to detail.

FIG. 1415 With a little practice, a skipper can learn to make smooth turns of 180° and come back directly over the spot where the turn was started. Swing out far enough initially on the opposite side to the main turn so that the reciprocal course can be picked up without overshooting it.

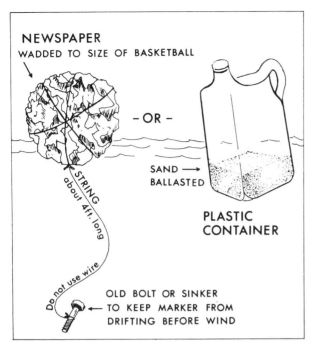

NEWSPAPER
WADDED TO SIZE OF BASKETBALL

– OR –

STRING
about 4ft. long

Do not use wire

SAND →
BALLASTED

PLASTIC
CONTAINER

OLD BOLT OR SINKER
← TO KEEP MARKER FROM
DRIFTING BEFORE WIND

FIG. 1416 The spot where the turn was started becomes the near mark of a temporary range with the initial departure point as the distant mark. Identify this spot with a disposable buoy dropped off the stern just before starting the 180° turn.

Running reciprocal courses

The process of adjusting a compass by running reciprocal courses will be seen to be much like that of zeroing-in. In that procedure, the book and board served to make certain that the lubber's line was turned exactly 180° at each reversal of the compass. It was as if the compass had been aboard a vessel which, on each reversal, sailed an exactly reciprocal magnetic course.

Zeroing-in ashore began by using an unknown magnetic direction or course, identified only as North (000°) by the compass. Zeroing-in was successful because this, or any other unknown magnetic heading, could be accurately reversed. Afloat, compensation can be started in the same way. Afloat, the heart of the problem is achieving accurate reversal, putting and holding the craft on a course over the bottom which is exactly the reciprocal of the original unknown magnetic heading. This, as will be shown, is not as difficult as might be expected.

Setting the courses

Between any two visible marks, or on a range, reversing the magnetic heading is obviously easy. In the procedures of compensation, however, there is need to run at least the four cardinal *magnetic* directions, North and South, East and West. Seldom does a skipper find in his local waters natural marks or aids to navigation on these exact magnetic headings. If you are fortunate, you may find in your anchorage or harbor area special ranges on these headings which have been established for compass adjustment purposes. More likely, though, a skipper will not be so fortunate, and he will then have a "do-it-yourself" project; he must make his own temporary basic courses.

Departing from a fixed mark (a buoy will do, but a day-

beacon or light is better), he sails on a steady compass heading until ready to reverse his course. He then drops a disposable buoy (see below) creating the desired range. Next he executes a "buttonhook" turn (known technically as a Williamson turn), lines up the disposable buoy with the object marking the original departure point, steadies on this range visually, and, *ignoring the compass,* heads for the departure point, runs down the disposable buoy, and continues back toward the departure point; see fig. 1415. The turn is made as tightly as possible, keeping the buoy in sight, so as to complete it before the buoy has had time to drift from the spot on which it was dropped. The skipper, knowing the characteristics of his craft, will choose a right or left turn, whichever can be made tightest if there is any difference; he will swing enough to the *opposite* side before making the main turn that when the main turn is completed, he can pick up the desired reciprocal course smoothly without overshooting and having to again apply opposite rudder. This maneuver is not difficult to learn; all that is required are a few trials and then some practice. It has other uses, too; for example, it is the quickest and most accurate procedure to return to the spot where a person or object has been lost overboard.

This maneuver has put the boat accurately on a reciprocal course, providing that the buoy remained where it was dropped and that no wind or current set the boat to either side of her heading on the *outward* run from the starting point. Compensation will be inaccurate if the craft has moved crabwise, headed one way but actually going another. It is necessary, therefore, for the various courses of compass compensation procedures to be run when wind and water conditions produce no leeway.

The skipper who hesitates to run directly over the disposable buoy should take it very close alongside, touching it if possible. On a range of ½ nautical mile (0.9 km), when the buoy is 10 feet (3 m) to one side of the craft's centerline, the course error will be only 11′, less than 1/5th of a degree.

Disposable buoys

Excellent disposable buoys can be made of cardboard milk cartons or plastic bleach bottles ballasted down with some sand or dirt, fig. 1416. Newspapers wadded into a ball about the size of a basketball and tied with string can be used if they are weighted with a small heavy object such as a large bolt or old spark plug at the end of three or four feet (0.6–0.9 m) of string; wire or rope should not be used for such a buoy.

Other preparations

A *non-magnetic screwdriver must be used* to adjust the screws of the compensating magnets. Often a thin coin, such as a dime, can be used; otherwise make a simple non-magnetic screwdriver from a piece of heavy sheet copper or brass, or from a brass machine screw by filing it down to a flat point.

Every magnetic article of the boat's gear should be stowed in its regular place, the windshield wiper blades in their normal position of rest, no magnetic material near the compass, either obviously or hidden in the clothes of the helmsman or others. It must be recognized that steel eyeglass frames, steel partial dentures, or the steel grom-

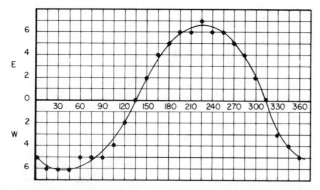

FIG. 1417 Before a deviation table is accepted as final, make a simple plot of the values so as to quickly see one or more that is not consistent with the others. Don't expect to get all points exactly on a smooth curve, but they shouldn't be off more than a fraction of a degree.

met in a yachting cap if brought within a few inches of the compass might cause deviation; someone may be working that close to the compass during adjustment.

COMPENSATION ON CARDINAL HEADINGS

As noted above, compensation must be accomplished under wind and current conditions such that there will not be leeway to either side of the intended course; the winds and seas must also be such that accurate steering is possible. First, steer 000° by compass from the chosen departure mark, holding rigorously to this course by the compass for at least a half-mile, a mile would be better. Next have someone drop a disposable buoy over the stern, execute the turn described above, and run the reciprocal course, fig. 1415. This course is *not* run by the compass, but by heading for the original departure point. The compass is now read and the figures recorded.

If the compass reading is 180°, there is no deviation on north or south headings and compensation is not needed; the athwartship internal compensator (marked N–S) should not be touched.

If the compass reading is not 180°, compensation is required. Exactly as in the process of zeroing-in, *half* the difference between 180° and the observed reading is to be removed. Halving the difference is based on the assumption that the deviation on reciprocal courses is equal and opposite. This may not be exactly so, but it serves as a good initial approach.

Assume, for example, that the compass reading was 200° then one-half of the 20° difference, or 10°, is to be removed while the reciprocal course is carefully run. Turn the N–S adjusting screw, and watch the compass closely. If the compass reading increases rather than decreases, the screw has been turned in the wrong direction (there is no way to tell in advance which is the correct direction); turn the screw in the opposite direction. Move the screw slowly until the compass reading is 190° while the boat is exactly on the reciprocal course.

Return to the starting mark and make another N–S run. Head out again on a compass course of 000° (the track through the water will *not* be the same as for the first run), drop a new disposable buoy, turn and line up for the reciprocal course back to the point of departure. If the compass reading is not now 180°—it should be close—

again remove half the difference by turning the screw of the compensating magnets (by now you should know which way increases the compass reading, and which decreases it).

Repeat these north–south runs until the deviation is eliminated on these headings. Do not touch the N–S adjusting screws again.

If the available water area and object for a starting point require it, the initial run can be made on a compass heading of 180° with the return reciprocal course to the north.

East-west adjustments

A similar method is used on east-west headings. Run from a buoy or other mark to the eastward on 090° by compass (or to the westward on 270°), drop a disposable buoy, make the turn, and head back visually toward the departure point. Remove half of the error by adjusting the fore-and-aft compensating magnets with the screw marked "E–W." Repeat such runs as necessary just as was done for the north-south compensation.

When the east-west compensation has been completed, make a quick check for any north-south deviation; it should not have changed, but it doesn't hurt to be sure. The deviation on all cardinal headings should now be zero, or as near zero as is attainable in this boat.

RESIDUALS ON INTERCARDINAL HEADINGS

Any deviations remaining on the intercardinal headings —NE, SE, SW, and NW—may be determined by any of the methods discussed earlier in this chapter; alternatively, they may be estimated by making reciprocal runs on these headings. In this latter method, the deviation will be half the difference between the outward course steered by compass and the reading of the compass when the turn has been made and the craft pointed back to the starting point. Proper attention must be paid to the direction of the deviation, East or West. *Do not touch the N-S or E-W adjustment screws.*

FAILURE TO ACHIEVE COMPENSATION

When compensation cannot be satisfactorily achieved, there undoubtedly is an undetected magnetic field. If care was used to remove or relocate the more obvious sources of trouble, look for the existence of a magnet nearby. Prime suspects are the tachometer cable(s) and the steering mechanism. Test them with a thin piece of steel; a machinist's thickness gauge for a few thousands of an inch (0.05 to 0.10 mm) is ideal. Make sure that this thin piece of steel is not itself magnetic; bring it close to a compass; one end should exert a slight attraction on *both* N and S marks on the card, turning the gauge end-for-end at either N or S should not show a reversal of effect on the compass.

Touch one end of this thin piece of steel to the part being tested for magnetism and gently pull it away. If it tends to stick to the part, the latter is magnetized. Test all around thoroughly. Open the wheel housing or look under the instrument panel; test all metal parts found.

If a magnet is located, demagnetization will be required. Professional advice and assistance may be needed, but a skipper can try his hand at the job first, using the procedures of page 290.

THE FINAL DEVIATION TABLE

When the compass has been adjusted to the greatest practicable degree, it is necessary to make a complete deviation check and prepare a table for any deviations found; any of the methods described earlier can be used. It is advisable to check under all of the conditions under which the compass might be used. For example, check with the navigation lights on and off (they may be distant from the compass but wires running to their switch will be nearby), with the windshield wipers operating and not operating, and with the electronic depthsounder, radio direction finder, and radio each on and off. Look also for other electrical equipment whose operation could affect the boat's compass. Remember to check on two cardinal headings 90° apart. Most of this equipment will not disturb the compass, *but some could,* and you must be aware of it. If it is anticipated that such items would have to be on any time that the compass was in use, it may be necessary to have more than one deviation table; it may be necessary sometimes to turn on certain equipment, whether needed or not, in order to recreate the same magnetic environment that existed when the deviation table was prepared. A sailboat may need different deviation tables for port and starboard tacks because of different heeling errors. If two or more deviation tables are necessary, it is a good idea to use different color paper for each so that they may be more readily identified.

Before preparing the final deviation table, it is useful to plot a simple graph of the values to be used. Lay out a horizontal base line for compass headings from 0° to 360°; plot easterly deviation vertically above the base line and westerly deviations below that line at a suitable scale. When all values of deviation have been plotted, draw a *smooth* curve through the points, but don't expect all values to be exactly on that line since the deviations have been measured only to the nearest whole degree; see fig. 1417. It should be possible to get a smooth curve through or near all of the points; if any value lies significantly off the curve, it is probably in error and should be rechecked. If a smooth curve is obtained, but its center axis does not coincide with the horizontal base line for 0° deviation, it is possible that the alignment of the lubber's line is not correct; recheck carefully.

The final deviation table can be prepared as a direct-reading table of critical values; see page 293. It can be used with confidence if care is taken to see that the magnetic environment is not altered. An annual check is advisable even though you think that no changes have been made that would upset the deviation table.

ADVANCED COMPASS TOPICS

The following sections on various topics on magnetism and compasses are generally beyond the "need-to-know" of the average skipper. Some, however, will be of value to those with special problems, and many others will be of interest to those boatmen who want to have a bit more than the minimum knowledge.

Magnetism

Contrary to some popular ideas, the location of the earth's *magnetic poles* is of little interest to the navigator or pilot. (Should he ever get to their vicinity, he would then have to rely for directional information on some other instrument than his magnetic compass.)

Variation is *not* the angle between the direction to the true and magnetic poles. This concept, a fictitious visualization useful in helping students to realize that true and magnetic North are usually different directions, has been accepted by many as truth. This, most certainly, is not so; it must be recognized as merely a learning aid, not a factual representation. The magnetic pole does not control the compass. The controlling force, as previously stated, is the earth's magnetic field. The compass magnet does not necessarily point in the precise direction of the magnetic pole.

Actually, two specific points on the earth's surface that are the magnetic poles do not exist. There are north and south *magnetic polar areas* containing many apparent

FIG. 1418 Charts of large areas show magnetic variation by a series of lines for each degree of variation. Each such isogonic line is labeled with its variation.

magnetic poles, places where a dip needle would stand vertically. If this seems strange, consider the problem of pinpointing the precise pole in the end of a bar magnet that is the pole.

For scientific purposes, rough approximate positions of the theoretical north and south magnetic poles have been computed from a large number of continuing observations made over the world for many years. They are not diametrically opposite each other as are the geographic poles. The magnetic poles do not stay in the same place; they wander about with both short-term and long-term cycles. They are relatively distant from the geographic poles. Very roughly, the north magnetic pole is at 76°N., 100°W. with the south magnetic pole at 66°S., 139°E. A magnetic compass at 80°N., 100°W. would show north in a direction actually southward of the compass.

A magnetic meridian is generally not a segment of a great circle passing through the magnetic poles, since only one great circle can pass through any two surface points not at the ends of a diameter. Not so obvious, but just as true, the magnetic meridian is generally not part of a great circle from a given point to the adjacent magnetic pole.

ISOGONIC LINES

On smaller scale charts covering larger areas, variation is shown by *isogonic* lines; every point on such a line has the same variation. Each line is labeled with the amount and direction of variation, the date, and the annual rate of change. The line joining all points having zero variation is called the *agonic* line.

INDUCED MAGNETISM

Masses of iron or related metals that do not show any

magnetic properties under usual conditions will acquire *induced magnetism* when brought near a magnet and into its field. The polarity of an induced pole is *opposite* to that of the nearest pole of the magnet that caused it. When the inducing field is removed, any magnetism that remains is termed *residual*. If the object retains magnetism for a long period of time without appreciable reduction in strength, this is permanent magnetism.

MAGNETISM FROM ELECTRICAL WIRES

Although the copper of electrical wires is a non-magnetic material, currents flowing in them produce magnetic fields. It is this effect that makes possible electrical motors, generators, relays, electromagnets, etc. A direct current in a wire results in a field that can affect a vessel's compass. (Alternating current electricity also produces magnetic fields, but not of the type to disturb a compass.) The polarity of a field around a wire carrying DC is related to the direction of the current; this fact can be used to advantage. The two wires carrying power to any load have currents in the opposite directions, thus producing opposing fields. If these wires are twisted together, the field around one wire will essentially cancel out the field produced by the other, and the net effect on the compass will be zero, or nearly so. Always use two wires, don't use a common ground for return current, and always twist pairs of wires that pass near a compass. Don't fail, however, to also make an actual check by observing the compass closely as the electrical circuit is switched on and off; make this test on two cardinal headings 90° apart.

Demagnetization

If tests with a thin strip of steel (see page 273) have

FIG. 1419 If there are no magnetic influences aboard the craft to disturb the compass, there is no deviation on any heading.

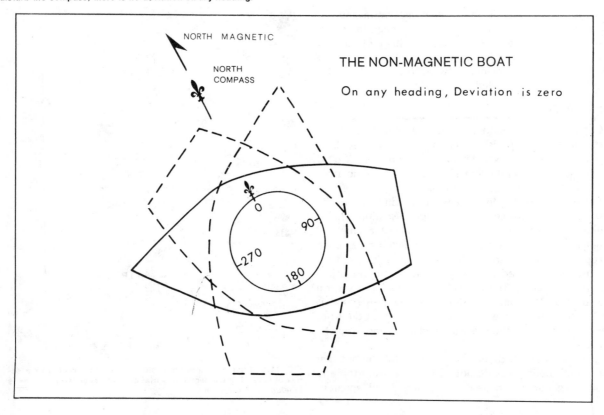

NORTH MAGNETIC

NORTH COMPASS

THE NON-MAGNETIC BOAT

On any heading, Deviation is zero

0
90
270
180

shown that some metal object at the control station is magnetized, it *may* be possible to *demagnetize* it with a device used by electronic repair shops such as a degaussing coil for TV sets or a magnetic tape bulk eraser. If the magnetized object cannot be removed from the boat for this effort, it is mandatory that the compass be taken off lest the effectiveness of its magnets be destroyed.

The demagnetizing device is operated from 115-volt shore power; it uses alternating currents to produce magnetic fields that reverse at the 60 Hz. frequency. Hold the device about a foot (0.3 m) from the target object and turn on the power; do not turn off the device until the full process has been carried out. Advance the device slowly toward the object until it touches; move it around slowly over all the accessible surfaces of the object. Then remove the device slowly away until it is at least the starting distance away and then turn it off. (If power to the demagnetizing device was interrupted at any time during the process, repeat all steps.) Take care not to demagnetize anything that is properly magnetic, such as electrical instruments or radio speakers.

Now test the disturbing object again with the thin strip of steel. If it has been possible to reach all of the object, it should be demagnetized. Often, however, complete access is not possible, and the object may have to be disassembled and/or removed from the boat for complete demagnetization.

After the demagnetization process is completed, remount the compass if it was removed, and in *all* cases make an entirely new deviation table.

WHY DEVIATION DEPENDS ON THE BOAT'S HEADING

Aboard a boat, the compass is subject to two magnetic forces, that of the earth and that of objects on the craft. If the boat were absolutely free of magnetism—no permanent magnets, no magnetic material subject to acquiring induced magnetism, and no fields from electrical currents—there would be no deviation on any heading, fig. 1419. The earth's force depends upon geographic location; the compasses of all vessels in the same harbor are subject to the same variation. The deviations aboard these ships and boats will be unlike because of the differences in the magnetic characteristics of each vessel. Thus if all of them were put in identical magnetic headings, their compasses would differ, except in the remote circumstance that each compass was completely compensated.

Deviation, it will be remembered, *varies with the craft's heading* because of the magnetic material on board. A few examples may make this clearer. Refer again to fig. 1419, the non-magnetic boat. No heading of this craft affects its compass card; its north point always lies in the magnetic meridian; the compass has no deviation. As the boat changes heading, the lubber's line, turning with the bow, indicates the magnetic heading on the card.

Now put aboard the craft, in the vicinity of the compass, items such as radios, electronic depth sounders, and electrical gauges and other instruments. Also on the boat, but usually farther from the compass, are metallic masses such as anchors, chain, fuel and water tanks, and other magnetic items, including the engine (the engine is by far the largest mass of magnetizable material but

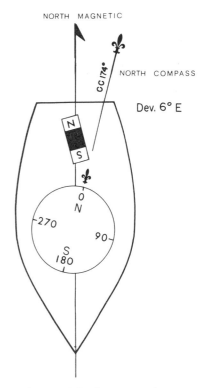

FIG. 1420 On a north magnetic heading, the S pole of the compass (180° on the card) is repelled by the S pole of the imaginary magnet; the card is deflected counterclockwise; there is westerley deviation.

FIG. 1421 On a south magnetic heading, the N pole of the compass (000°) is nearest the S pole of the imaginary magnet and is attracted to it. The card is deflected clockwise and there is easterly deviation.

it is relatively distant from the compass). The boat has now acquired a magnetic character of its own; in addition to any permanent magnetism of some objects, there are now masses of unmagnetized material that can affect the compass by acquiring induced magnetism. The effects on the compass of permanent magnetism and induced magnetism are quite different and must be considered separately.

Effect of permanent magnetism

On typical boats of wood or fiberglass, the effect of permanent magnetism is by far the greater. To visualize this, let us assume that the same net effect would be exerted by a single permanent magnet located aft of the compass and slightly askew of the boat's centerline. This representation by an imaginary magnet is quite applicable; it well simulates conditions found on most boats other than those with a steel hull. (The exact position of the imaginary magnet, its polarity, strength, and angle of skew are not important in this illustration of principles.)

Two forces, that of the field of the earth and that of the field of the imaginary magnet, now affect the compass; its poles will be attracted or repelled in accordance with the basic law of magnetism. Without the influence of the imaginary magnet, the compass magnets and card will line up with the magnet meridian. The 0° mark of the card is an N (north-seeking) pole, and the 180° mark is at an S pole. Now, in addition to the effect of the earth's magnet poles on them, the N and S poles of the compass magnets will be attracted or repelled by the S pole of the imaginary magnet (the pole nearer the compass in these examples). The result is easterly deviation on some headings, westerly on others, and zero on those where the sign of the deviation changes from east to west, or from west to east.

Consider a typical boat, MORNING STAR, headed north (000°) *magnetic*, fig. 1420. The S pole of the compass, 180° on the card, is repelled by the S pole of the imaginary magnet. The result is that the card is rotated counterclockwise; the compass reading is increased, 006° in this instance, and there is westerly deviation.

On a south *magnetic* heading, fig. 1421, the N pole of the compass magnet, 000° on the card, is nearer the S pole of the imaginary magnet and is attracted by it. The card is deflected clockwise and the compass reading decreases, 174° in this example; the deviation is easterly.

If the magnetic heading of MORNING STAR is to the east, fig. 1422, the N pole of the compass magnet is the nearer pole to the S pole of the imaginary magnet and it is attracted. This results in a counter-clockwise rotation of the compass card giving westerly deviation. On a west magnetic heading, the deflection of the card is clockwise for easterly deviation. (It is a good exercise for the reader to diagram this situation for himself.)

In the above examples, the deviation is westerly on an east magnetic heading, but easterly on a south·magnetic heading. Thus there must be some intermediate heading where the deviation passes through zero as the sign changes from west to east. Fig. 1423 approximates this situation. There is still attraction of the N pole of the compass by the S pole of the imaginary magnet, but on this heading the compass card has its N pole as close to the S pole of the magnet as it can get. Thus there is no

FIG. 1422 When the boat heads east (magnetic), the N pole of the compass is again the nearer pole to the imaginary magnet and is attracted. The deflection is counterclockwise and the deviation is westerly.

FIG. 1423 On this heading, roughly 165°, the N pole of the compass is attracted by the S pole of the imaginary magnet. Here, however, the compass N pole is already as close as it can get; hence there is no deflection and thus no deviation.

deflection of the card in either direction, no deviation.

As has been illustrated above, deviation resulting from permanent magnetism will normally swing through one cycle of west to east and back to west in 360°, with two headings having zero deviation.

Do not assume that the location, polarity, and angle of skew of the imaginary magnet would be same on any other boat as in the above examples which are for the sole purpose of illustrating principles. A change of one or more of these factors would result in an entirely different set of deviations.

Effect of induced magnetism

The effect of induced magnetism on a compass can be visualized in a series of examples much like the above with an imaginary mass of magnetizable material. In this case, the disturbing pole would be the one induced in that mass and its sign would change as determined by the changing sign of the nearer pole of the inducing magnet. The sign of the deviation would change four times in 360°, with four headings having zero deviation.

If the effects of permanent and induced magnetism are combined, a complex situation results; fortunately, this is unlikely for most small craft.

Effect of geographic position

Deviation can change with changes in *magnetic latitude* of a vessel. The strengths of most magnetic influences on a boat are unchanged at different geographic positions, but the horizontal component of the earth's field lessens in higher latitudes. Hence the interaction of these two forces, the cause of deviation, changes with varying magnetic latitude.

FIG. 1424 **The two factors of Variation and Deviation are sometimes combined algebraically into a single value, termed "Compass Error (CE)" These sketches show the four possible combination of East and West, Variation and Deviation.**

Compass Calculations

Compass Error (CE) is sometimes used in compass calculations as a specific term. It is the algebraic sum of the variation and deviation. Because variation depends on geographic location, and deviation upon the craft's heading, there are various possible combinations of these two quantities, fig. 1424. Similarly to variation and deviation, it is expressed in degrees and direction; for example, 5°E or 7° west; in boating, it is given to the nearest whole degree.

This is a term used for convenience. The compass is *not* actually "in error"; it is operating according to the forces that control its behavior. Compass error is merely another angle, the one between the direction of true north and the direction of north as indicated by the compass.

INTERPOLATION

The process of determining intermediate values between tabular entries is called *interpolation*. It is most easily explained by several examples. Let us consider the following extract from a deviation table:

Compass Heading	Deviation
090°	7°E
105°	4°E

Assume that we need the deviation for a compass heading of 100°. The interval between tabular entries is 15°; the difference between deviation values is 3°. Since 100° is 10/15ths of the way between 090° and 105°, we multiply the value difference by that fraction: 3° x 10/15 = 2°. Since the deviation is decreasing, this is subtracted: 7°E − 2° = 5°E, the deviation for 100°.

If the values are not so even as above, an answer with a fraction will result. If we had desired the deviation for 098°, the fraction would have been 8/15, and the result 3° x 8/15 = 1.6°; then 7°E − 1.6 = 5.4°E; but for boat use deviation is not used more precisely than the nearest whole degree and thus the deviation for 098° would be recorded and used as 5°E.

Caution must be used when the two values of deviation are of *opposite* name. The value difference between 3°W and 1°E is *four* degrees, not two.

CRITICAL VALUES TABLES

A skipper will need deviation values in terms of both compass headings (for "correcting" calculations) and magnetic headings (for "uncorrecting"). A simple way to combine both of these, and have a more easily used table as well, is to prepare a direct-reading table of *critical values*. Such a table is prepared in basic terms of deviations rather than headings. There is a line in the table for each whole degree of deviation; opposite this is listed on one side the range of compass headings for which that value of deviation is applicable; on the other side is the range of magnetic headings which have that value of deviation. See the below-example.

VARIATION, DEVIATION and COMPASS ERROR

VAR: W
DEV: W

VAR: E
DEV: E

VAR: W
DEV: E

VAR: E
DEV: W

Magnetic	Deviation	Compass
133°-144°	0°	133°-145°
145°-153°	1°E	146°-153°
154°-163°	2°E	154°-162°
164°-176°	3°E	163°-174°
177°-187°	4°E	175°-185°

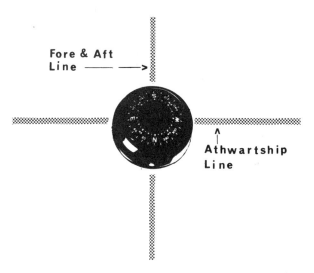

FIG. 1425 Before installing external compensating magnets, it is necessary to chalk in two lines, as shown, through the center of the compass. The magnets must always be placed so that their centers are on one of these lines.

FIG. 1426 Magnets are placed forward or aft of the compass and on one side as shown above. See text for detailed instructions for their placement. They must be fastened down with non-magnetic tacks or screws.

NAPIER DIAGRAMS

A *Napier diagram* (named after the man who developed it more than a century ago) is a graphic plot of deviation values which permits rapid and accurate determination of intermediate values as well as changes back and forth between compass and magnetic headings. It consists of a vertical base line marked from 000° to 360° with dots every degree, every fifth dot being slightly heavier for ease of reading. Usually the base line is printed in two sections of 180°, sometimes with extensions of a few degrees at either end to facilitate use in these areas. There are two series of cross lines making angles of 60° with the base line and with each other; the lines appear at intervals of 15° along the base line and those sloping downward to the left are solid. Deviations for compass headings are plotted along the dotted cross lines, easterly to the right of the base line and westerly to its left. A curve is drawn through the various plotted points; see page 294.

To convert a magnetic heading to a compass heading, find the value of the magnetic heading on the center line, move along or parallel to a *solid* cross line until the curve is reached, then return to the center line by moving parallel to a *dotted* line. The compass heading is the value on the center line at the point of return. The reverse process is used to convert a compass heading to a magnetic heading.

A Napier diagram is of particular value when the deviations are large and changing rapidly. If the deviations have been reduced to relatively small values by successful compensation, a Napier diagram is not needed, except perhaps briefly for the construction of a critical values table which will then become the practical source of deviation information for use in piloting.

Special Compensation Situations

The procedures of compensation described earlier in this chapter will fit most, but not all, recreational boats and their compasses. Special situations will be discussed below.

USING EXTERNAL MAGNETS

If the boat's compass does not have internal compensating magnets, it still can be adjusted to near zero deviation if there is space to place external magnets where they are needed.

Two compensating magnets will be needed. Each is an encased permanent magnet having two holes for screw fastening. The ends of the magnets will either be marked N and S or be colored red on the north end and blue on the south. Adhesive tape is good for temporary fastening; be sure that the screws used for final fastening are non-magnetic. Carefully mark the longitudinal center of each magnet. In the areas where the external magnets will be placed, carefully mark out in chalk two lines through the compass center, one fore-and-aft and one athwartship; see fig. 1425.

General procedures

The compensation process will consist of making outward runs on cardinal headings by compass, dropping a disposable buoy, turning, and heading back toward the point of departure. All this is done in the same manner as was done for internal compensators. Keep all external magnets far from the compass until each one is to be used.

Adjustment on N—S headings

If compensation is shown to be needed—for example, the compass reads 200° on the reciprocal of a 000° outward run—the correction is made by *centering* an external magnet athwartship on the chalked fore-and-aft line. If there is space, place a compensator forward of the compass in the position D, A, or C of fig. 1426. Should the compass reading become more than 200°, the compensator is increasing the deviation and must be turned end-for-end. The card will then move in the desired direction.

FIG. 1427 Vessels, including boats, with steel hulls present special cases for compass compensation. It will normally be necessary to mount two quadrential spheres of soft iron on the binnacle and then adjust them very carefully.

Should the card stop moving before 190° (the reading for removal of half the error), the compensator, in a position such as at D, is too far from the compass. On the other hand, if the card moves past 190°, the compensator is too close to the compass, as at C, and must be moved farther away. Move the external magnet aft or forward as necessary until the desired reading is attained. Now tape the compensator down; no screws yet. If there is no room for the magnet in front of the compass, place it aft of the instrument in the vicinity shown as A'. *Do not let it get off the centerline as at E.* As with internal compensators, a second N—S run is made, perhaps more, until zero deviation is achieved.

E—W compensation

After the turn back on an east or west run, one-half of any deviation is adjusted out by placing a compensator in a fore-and-aft position *centered* on the athwartship chalk line, such as at B or B' in fig. 1426. When after sufficient runs, the deviation is zero, or as nearly so as can be gotten, screw down the magnets (non-magnetic screws) with care that their position is not shifted.

HEELING MAGNETS

Sailing craft, heeling out of a horizontal trim, frequently require *heeling magnets* below the compass to reduce their deviations. The proper adjustment of this compensating magnet is a matter for a professional compass adjuster, or a quite experienced skipper; it is beyond the scope of this book.

COMPENSATION ON STEEL BOATS

Steel hulls may present problems whose solution may require the installation of soft iron quadrantial spheres (fig. 1427), the use of Flinders bars, and possibly heeling magnets. All this is for the professional, or for the exceptional skipper who, by study and practice in methods not discussed in this book, has achieved professional competence.

Iron and steel craft are subject to changes in deviation upon large changes in latitude. This must be considered when cruising in such craft.

COMPENSATION BY SHADOW PIN

A method of sailing reciprocal courses without setting up temporary ranges with disposable buoys uses a vertical

FIG. 1428 All magnets and magnetic materials must be kept well away from a compass. Note here how the photographic light meter moves the compass card by roughly 30°.

shadow pin in the center of a horizontal disc graduated similar to a compass card; the disc should be gimbal-mounted.

As the boat heads north by the compass, the disc is rotated by hand so that the shadow of the sun falls on the zero mark. The turn is made and the craft is steadied on such a heading that the shadow falls on the opposite side of the disc, exactly on the 180° mark. If the compass now reads 180°, there is no deviation on N—S headings. If not 180°, the previously-described procedures are followed for compensation. A similar technique is used for E—W headings.

This procedure has advantages. The boat need not run far on any heading. No departure mark or disposable buoy is required. Neither wind nor current will affect the result. But, and a big but, there is one complicating factor—the sun and its shadow do not stand still! Regardless of how steady the boat is being held on a heading, the shadow is moving. Time becomes a factor in the execution of the procedure; compensators must be gotten into the proper position and fastened down before the shadow moves enough to upset the process, taking the boat off a true reciprocal heading. An experienced navigator knows how to make the proper allowances. An inexperienced skipper would best plan to use this method only near the time of

FIG. 1429 A hand bearing compass is a compass with a handle so that it can be held in front of a skipper's eye for the taking of bearings that cannot be sighted directly across the boat's compass. Be careful of local deviation from nearby magnets or magnetic material.

winter or summer solstice (roughly 21 December or 21 June) when the rate of change of the shadow position is less than 1° in approximately ten minutes of time, depending upon latitude.

Maintenance

In addition to simple protection from direct sunlight when not in use, as covered in Chapter 13, compass maintenance has two aspects. The first is the preservation of

Other Instruments

Several other direction instruments will be of general interest to boatmen although few skippers will have more than one or two of them, if any.

HAND BEARING COMPASSES

A small compass equipped with a handle so that it can be easily held in front of one's face is termed a *hand bearing compass*, see fig. 1429. This instrument is normally used for taking bearings, especially those that cannot be conveniently sighted across the steering compass, but in an emergency it could be pressed into use for steering the boat.

Pelorus

A *pelorus* (see pages 378-379) is an instrument having sight vanes and a compass-like card, either of which can be clamped in a fixed position. Sometimes referred to as a "dumb compass," it is used to take bearings when it is not possible to do so across the steering compass. The pelorus is placed in a location suitable for observation; its zero point is adjusted to either compass north or the boat's current heading, depending upon whether compass or relative bearings are desired.

Gyro-compass

Details on *gyro-compasses* are beyond the scope of this book. Interested readers are referred to Publication No. 9 —"Bowditch"—of the Defense Mapping Agency Hydrographic Center, or *Dutton's Navigation and Piloting* published by the U.S. Naval Institute. The gyro-compass is an expensive, complex instrument designed to maintain a

the magnetic environment surrounding the instrument. Except for occasional testing, no piece of iron or steel should be brought or installed near it. An ashtray, a beverage can, a portable radio, a camera or lightmeter, steel tools, and many other items must be kept well away from a compass at all times. Such will cause unknown deviations; see fig. 1428.

The second aspect of maintenance consists mainly of getting to know your compass. Watch how it swings. Check that its readings are consistent on frequently-run courses. Note if it appears to become sluggish and above all if it becomes erratic—these conditions warn you of undetected disturbances or a damaged pivot bearing.

Test for a damaged bearing or undue pivot friction by deflecting the card two or three degrees with a small magnet or piece of iron. There is need for shop tests and probably repair if the card does not return to its former position.

A bubble can be removed by adding some liquid, but this liquid must be the same as that with which the compass is filled. This is an action best left to a compass repair shop.

Lightning and electric welding aboard may change the craft's own magnetic field. After exposure to either of these, a check of deviations should be made.

Do read and follow the manufacturer's instructions for winter storage if the boat is taken out of regular service. They may add years to the compass' useful life.

fixed direction in space. Contrary to the usual belief, it is not without "errors." Aboard ship, allowances have to be made of changes in latitude and for rapid changes in the speed of the vessel. Its great advantage, however, is the absence of magnetic effects, variation and deviation; Gyro-compasses are also suitable for integrating into complex navigation systems using computers. Gyro error is termed east or west and is applied exactly as is compass error.

Sun compass

A *sun compass* is not a true compass; it is an instrument for taking bearings of the sun. The observer looks, not at the sun, but at a shadow cast by a small pin in the center of a card. The card is graduated clockwise through 360° starting with zero at South. The shadow thus marks the sun's bearing. If the instrument is properly oriented with the vessel's heading, the shadow will show the ship's true course. The difference between its reading and the ship's compass is the compass error, CE. Applying variation yields the deviation of the ship's compass on that heading.

Accuracy depends upon knowledge of the sun's true bearing. Since latitude, date, and time affect this, and since the rate of change of the sun's true bearing is not constant, the procedure is complex and requires experience for satisfactory results. Some spherical compasses have a shadow pin mounted on the card directly above the pivot. A knowledgeable skipper can use this in checking deviation by azimuths of the sun. (This pin is also very useful when bearings are taken directly over the compass.)

COMPASS BRIEFS

→ The heart of the compass is a magnetic element so mounted that on any heading of the ship, it lies in a constant direction in a horizontal plane. A card is rigidly attached to the magnetic element. To the helmsman the card may appear to move, but this is not so. The compass bowl, carrying the lubber's line, the hand,' moves around the card, the 'dial,' to mark the course. Except for movements caused by deviation, *the card is stationary*. The ship rotates about the card.

Card graduations are in degrees or points, or in various combinations of the two. Scales read from 000° at North clockwise through 360° or in points logically named by their positions relative to the cardinal or intercardinal points. There are eight points to a quadrant, thus a point is 11¼° and a quarter-point approximately 2¾°.

→ Buy the best compass you can afford, or one a little better. A large card makes for easy steering. By virtue of its optical magnification, so does a spherical compass. Card graduations should suit your needs. Many craft sail on only short coastwise, lake or river voyages. On most of these, 'open' cards graduated every 5°, are adequate. Skippers of larger boats or of small ones making blue-water passages prefer graduations in single degrees and points. Some wind sailors still use quarter-points.

→ Mount the compass as far as possible from any known shipboard magnetic influences and yet where the helmsman may watch it without strain. There may have to be compromise here. Be sure that a line through the pivot and the lubber's line is parallel to the keel's fore-and-aft direction. See that the instrument is level at cruising speed and *particularly not canted* to port or starboard.

Once mounted, preserve the compass's magnetic environment, except for the adjustments made during compensation.

→ Keep the bowl filled with liquid. Should additions be made, check the tightness of the seals and top-off with nothing foreign to the original contents lest the card, bellows, seals and even the pivot and bearings be damaged. Watch the compass in operation. If it becomes sluggish, test for pivot friction. Should it oscillate in a seaway, look for and consider removing vertical iron aboard.

→ A course may be named in three ways: true (TC), magnetic (MC) and compass (CC). A course (or a bearing) is a fixed direction. The scale zero, the line of reference for the angle, may be in one of three directions: the true meridian, the magnetic meridian or the direction of the north point of the compass. Hence courses have to be converted, that is, expressed with respect to the three different reference lines.

Converting courses expressed in degrees is simple.

True	↑	Conversion from true through
Variation		magnetic to compass is in
Magnetic		the rule: *Down Add West* or
Deviation	↓	*DAW*, which should be memorized.
Compass		The changes in the rule are obvious:

Down Subtract East, Up Subtract West, Up Add East.

→ When courses are expressed in points and quarter-points "add" and "subtract" can be confusing instructions. (Try

adding ½ pt E to E ¾ N and you will be 1 point in error!) The direction in which the deviation or variation is to be applied is substituted. For 'add' use 'clockwise' and for 'subtract' use counterclockwise. Call conversion from compass to magnetic to true 'correcting' and the reverse conversion 'uncorrecting.' Then a basic rule emerges, Correct Easterly Errors Clockwise, shortenable to *Correct Easterly Clockwise, CEC*. With this in memory, remember further that in any change of this basic, *only two and always two* of the terms are changed. Thus there are UWC, UECC and CWCC. UWC is immediately recognizable as the DAW of the degree system.

→ Deviation changes with the heading because the ship rotates about the compass card. Hence magnetic material aboard located in the compass's first quadrant while the vessel heads North, will be moved into the compass's fourth quadrant when she heads West. Similarly all the other magnetic material aboard shifts its position relative to the compass on this 90° course change. The compass card, subject to two influences, that of the earth and that of the moved field of the ship, may deviate from its original direction on CC north. Thus it should be seen that any change in heading may change the deviation.

→ Among the methods of determining deviation are running ranges or sailing across one range on different headings. Recording the deviations so observed yields a deviation table for compass headings. Plotting these on a Napier diagram and taking therefrom the deviations for magnetic headings gives a table of deviations on magnetic headings.

Thence for everyday use, deviation cards of various types, pictorial or tabular, are constructible, as the user desires.

→ A word of warning. *Never enter a deviation table with a bearing.* The deviation to be applied to a bearing is that of the ship's *head* at the time of bearing. For convenience in plotting bearings the proper deviation and the variation are algebraically combined to give one quantity, the so-called compass error (CE). CE = Var + Dev. When the two are in the same direction they are added, when opposite in direction the smaller is subtracted from the larger and the remainder takes the name of the larger.

→ Compensating, often called adjusting, a compass is the act of neutralizing, by small magnets near the compass, the effect on the compass of the ship's own magnetic field. Many compasses are equipped with two small magnets, whose position is adjustable, built into their cases. Adjust-

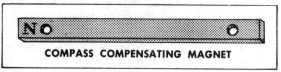

COMPASS COMPENSATING MAGNET

ment or compensation consists of positioning these compensators so that they negate the action of the ship's field. A compass not so equipped is compensated by fastening one or two small magnets near the compass. The proper position of these magnets is most important. Each must be centered on a line passing through the compass pivot. The athwartship magnet is centered on such a line running truly fore-and-aft; the fore-and-aft one on such a line running truly athwartship.

→ A table of deviations may be analyzed to ascertain

approximately its components or coefficients and so determine, again approximately, the position of the compensators. This is usually unnecessary in small craft.

→ Compensation in small craft is not difficult. Run from a fixed mark on compass course North, establishing a range with a disposable buoy. Reverse course by sailing the range, ignoring the compass. Now observe the course the compass shows. The difference between 180° and the compass-indicated course is approximately twice the deviation. Remove half of this by adjusting the N-S internal compensator or temporarily taping down an athwartship external compensator on the fore-and-aft line through the compass pivot. Repeat this operation on N-S and S-N headings until the deviations reach a minimum. Then do the same on the E-W compass headings, adjusting the E-W internal compensator or taping down, on the athwartship line through the pivot, a fore-and-aft external compensator. Permanently fasten the external compensators or leave the internal ones in the optimum positions found.

With a thin piece of steel (.001") locate any strong magnetic influence which prevents reasonable compensation. Demagnetize it or remove it from the boat and recompensate. *Caution. Do not subject the compass to demagnetization.* Before turning on any demagnetizer unship the compass, take it ashore, well away from the influence of this powerful equipment.

Swing the ship for residuals and make a working deviation table or tables as desired.

Reasonable compensation is obtainable by this method. There may be residuals near the intercardinal points which merit some explanation here.

→ Windshield wipers in operation may cause significant deviations. Test for these. When existent, make a deviation table for use only when they are turned on. In reduced visibility, fog, rain or snow, comes greater need for trying to be sure that the course steered is the one desired to be made good.

→ Preserve the compass's magnetic environment. When it is altered by the installation of a new motor or other equipment, or by electric welding aboard, check the deviations.

→ Know your compass. Know its deviations. Above all, trust it. Not without good reason has it been dubbed the mariner's best friend. * * *

The Sailboat Compass and Heeling Error

When choosing a sailboat compass and selecting a place to mount it, buy a true spherical compass with a card having a tall pin at its center, like the compasses shown in Figs. 1305 and 1312, and locate it in the cockpit where it is exposed to sunlight whenever the sun is out.

A good hood on the binnacle will give the compass all the protection it needs from sunlight when it is not in use. The importance of the location is to permit easy determination at any time of compass error by comparison of the tall pin's shadow, as read on the scale at the edge of the compass card, with the sun's azimuth. This configuration of the compass makes unnecessary the use of a solar pelorus.

A power boat sails on an even keel in calm water.

In a seaway it rolls, but so quickly that its short-term average position is still upright. A sailboat, on the other hand, often sails for many hours at a steady angle of heel. This difference makes heeling error, which is of little concern to the powerboat skipper, a serious concern to the sailboat skipper. Furthermore, the change in deviation resulting from heeling error will vary with the direction and amount of heel as well as with the vessel's heading, so it is impractical to deal with it by means of a simple deviation card.

Professional compass adjusters seldom mention heeling error unless the owner brings up the subject, as its measurement and compensation can be very time consuming, and its effects are often found, after measurement, to be small.

Use of the pin shadow to measure compass error requires knowledge of the vessel's approximate position, the time to about the nearest minute, an almanac and a set of azimuth tables, such as may be found in Reed's Nautical Almanac. The almanac and tables are entered with the ship's approximate position and the approximate time, and the sun's azimuth is calculated. The reciprocal of this is the true bearing of the pin shadow. The numerical value of the division mark lying under the shadow on the rim of the compass card differs from the true shadow bearing by the algebraic sum of local variation and compass error.

If you plan to check your compass thoroughly on a particular morning, precompute the sun's azimuth for several consecutive whole hours (local time), such as 0800, 0900 and 1000, plot a graph of these values and put a smooth curve through the computed points. Accuracy of a degree or two will be entirely satisfactory. Your graph will give you, at a glance, the solar azimuth for any time in the two-hour span. Comparing results when the vessel is heeled under sail with those when she is upright on the same heading will give you a good feel for the amount of heeling error present. If it is negligible, that is one uncertainty laid to rest. If it is substantial and gives consistent values, take your data back to your compass adjuster and he can compensate for it to some degree, as described, for example, in Bowditch.

You will learn a good deal from this exercise and will automatically adopt a good habit in consequence, that of noting in the deck log the time and the card graduation lying under the shadow of the compass pin whenever, in the early morning or late afternoon, you are at the helm and notice that the shadow is long enough to reach the edge of the compass card. You need not compute the error, merely note the data that are necessary for its determination. Then, if ever a question of compass accuracy should arise, you will have some data to test the matter, whether the sun happens to be shining at the moment or not.

Another "free" check of compass error is available whenever a solar sight is reduced, provided the navigator, as he notes down the data from his sight, thinks to ask the helmsman to read the compass graduation that the pin shadow, suitably prolonged, intersects.

In many sailboats heeling error is negligible, but the prudent skipper will not assume this to be the case when he steps aboard a strange boat.

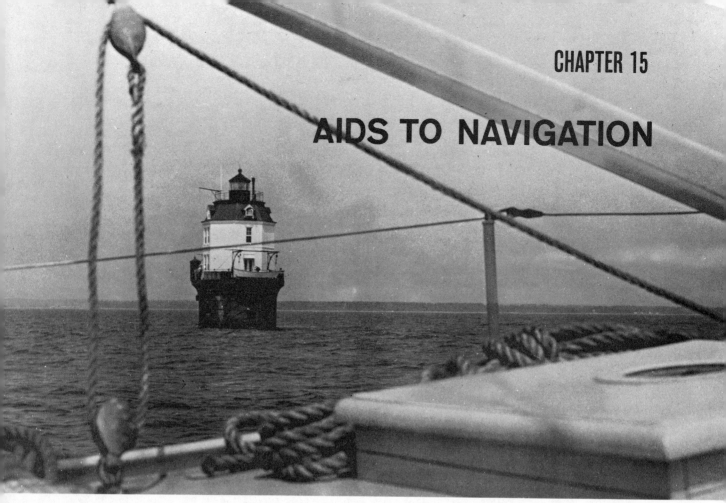

AIDS TO NAVIGATION

FIG. 1501 The skipper of a boat of any size is highly dependent on aids to navigation to warn him of unseen underwater hazards. He must be able to recognize such aids and know their significance.

Buoyage Systems

Although few mariners or boatmen may be aware of it, directing the movements of a vessel of any size in near-shore waters is closely akin to "flying blind" in an aircraft. It is not the few visible obstacles that are dangerous, but rather the more numerous shoals and rocks that lie unseen beneath the surface.

Natural landmarks may be used as reference points for navigation, but these are often few and far between, and may not be located to best advantage. It is to protect the mariner from these unseen dangers, and to allow him to safely direct his course, that government agencies and private individuals establish and maintain *aids to navigation*.

Figures 1502-1510, 1512, 1514, 1516 and 1517 reproduced from official U.S. COAST GUARD photographs.

The term *aid to navigation* may be applied to any man-made object prepared and located so as to indicate to a mariner the location of his vessel or the safe and proper course on which to proceed. The term includes buoys, day-beacons, lights, lighthouses, lightships, radiobeacons, fog signals, and loran, consolan, and other electronic systems. It covers unlighted objects, floating and non-floating; and visible, audible, and electronic signals and their supporting structures.

The term "aid to navigation" should always be stated thus, and not as "navigational aid". The latter term has been more broadly defined as also including "charts, instruments, devices, methods, etc., intended to assist in the navigation of a craft."

PURPOSE OF AIDS TO NAVIGATION

Aids to navigation are placed at various points along the coasts and navigable waterways as markers and guides to enable mariners to determine their position with respect to the shore and to hidden dangers. They assist mariners in making landfalls when approaching from the high seas, mark isolated dangers, make it possible for pilots to follow natural and improved channels, and provide a continuous chain of charted marks for coast piloting.

Establishment and maintenance of any aid must have economic justification. Aids established by the Federal government must, by law, be needed for the safety of a reasonable amount of water traffic, not just the occasional craft or the coming and going of a few local boats.

Within the bounds of actual necessity and reasonable cost, every aid to navigation is designed to be seen or heard over the greatest practicable area. As all aids serve the same broad purposes, such structural differences as those between an unlighted buoy or beacon, a minor light, or a major lighthouse with radiobeacon, are solely for the purpose of meeting requirements and conditions of the particular location at which the aid is established.

OPERATING AGENCIES

The United States Coast Guard, since 1967 a part of the Department of Transportation, is the agency responsible for maintenance of the system of aids to navigation on waters of the United States subject to Federal jurisdiction. Federal "navigable waters" are legally defined as coastal waters; rivers, bays, sounds, lakes, etc. navigable from the sea; and rivers, canals, and lakes *not* lying wholly within the boundaries of a single state. Such areas include the Atlantic, Gulf, and Pacific coasts of the continental United States, the Great Lakes, the Mississippi River and its tributaries, Puerto Rico, the Hawaiian Islands, and Alaskan waters. Aids to navigation may also be maintained by the Coast Guard at other places where required to serve the needs of our armed forces.

The senior officer of the Coast Guard is its Commandant, with headquarters in Washington, D.C. Functions of planning, procurement, establishment, operation, and maintenance of aids to navigation are carried on under his direction. Because of the wide geographic distribution of such aids on our coasts and inland waters, actual field work is executed by district organization.

There are 12 Coast Guard Districts. They maintain the system of aids to navigation and carry out other Coast Guard functions. The ten continental Districts are numbered from 1 to 13, omitting 4, 6, and 10; see fig. 1502. Hawaii is in the 14th Coast Guard District, Alaska in the 17th. Each District has its Commander, assisted by a suitable engineering and administrative force. Each District has the necessary supply and buoy depots, and specially designed and equipped vessels for the maintenance of aids to navigation. See fig. 1503.

"Private" aids to navigation

Aids to navigation may, with prior approval, be established in waters subject to Federal jurisdiction by agencies other than the Coast Guard. Information on procedures for obtaining such permission may be obtained from any Coast Guard District office. These aids must be patterned after Federal aids, and if a fixed structure is to be erected in navigable water, a permit must also be obtained from the Army Corps of Engineers.

All such aids to navigation—whether established by an individual, a corporation, a state or local government, or even a Federal agency other than the Coast Guard, such as the Navy—are termed "private" aids. These will have the same appearance as Coast Guard-maintained aids, but will be specially designated in the Light Lists.

State-maintained aids

On bodies of water wholly within the boundaries of a single state, and not navigable to the sea, the state government has the responsibility for the establishment and maintenance of aids to navigation.

Although each state retains authority over its waters, agreement has been reached on a uniform system of aids

FIG. 1502 Maintenance of aids to navigation is a district responsibility in the Coast Guard organization. There are ten districts covering the continental 48 states. District boundaries and headquarters are shown. Note that there are no districts numbered 4, 6, or 10.

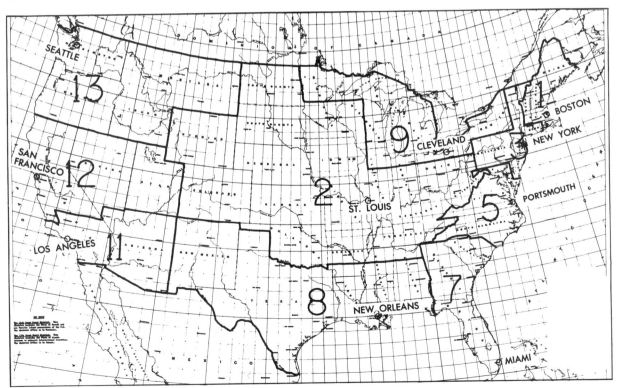

to navigation and regulatory markers. These will be described and discussed in detail on pages 314–316.

PROTECTION BY LAW

Whether established by the Coast Guard or by another agency, all aids to navigation are protected by law. It is not only a violation of common sense, but also a criminal offense, to cause any damage or hindrance to the proper operation of any aid. Do not deface, alter, move, or destroy any aid to navigation. Never tie your boat to a buoy, daybeacon, or light structure. Avoid anchoring so close to a buoy that you obscure the aid from the sight of other passing craft.

If you should unintentionally or unavoidably collide with or damage an aid to navigation, this fact must be reported to the nearest Officer in Charge, Marine Inspection, U.S. Coast Guard in full detail and without delay.

For your own safety and that of others, cooperate with the Coast Guard and other agencies by promptly reporting any missing or malfunctioning aid. This will normally be done immediately after returning to port; if the safety of navigation is threatened seriously, the report should be made by radio without delay.

Types of Aids to Navigation

The term "aid to navigation" encompasses a wide range of fixed and floating objects from a single pile with a pointer or a small sixth-class buoy to manned lightships and lighthouses with an array of visible, audible, and electronic signals. Conspicuous shapes and objects on shore, such as mountain tops, radio antennas, smoke stacks, etc., may be charted and used to assist in piloting, but these are generally grouped under the term *landmark* and are excluded from the definition of an aid to navigation. This latter term is applied to objects that have been *primarily* established to assist in navigation. Also excluded are such informal aids as bush stakes placed in many side creeks by

local watermen to mark minor natural channels or hazards. These do indeed help the skipper to pilot his boat safely, but they are not a part of the organized system of aids to navigation.

MAJOR TYPES

Buoys are floating objects moored or anchored to the bottom as aids to navigation; lightships fit this overall definition, but they are excluded as they form a separate category of aids. Buoys will have a distinctive shape and color as determined by their location and purpose. They may be equipped with visual, audible, and/or electronic signals.

Daybeacons are unlighted fixed structures established to aid navigation. They may be a single pile or a multiple-pile structure. Clusters of piles are called dolphins. Daybeacons are equipped with one or more signboards ("daymarks") of a distinctive shape and color as determined by the information that they indicate; see color pages I–K. (Pointers were used in some areas but are now being phased out.)

Lights are aids to navigation that have active visual signals. These are fixed aids (lighted floating aids are designated as lighted buoys or lightships). Lights are classified by the Coast Guard and other authorities as *primary seacoast lights, secondary lights,* or *minor lights,* as determined by their location, importance, and physical characteristics; the intensity of the light and its visible range will vary with the classification. The shape and color of the structure supporting the light source may be distinctive for purposes of identification, but will not convey information as, for example, in the case of buoys. The unofficial term "lighthouse" is often applied to primary seacoast lights and to some secondary lights.

Fog signals are audible signals transmitted to assist mariners during periods of low visibility, primarily fog. Occasionally they may be separate aids, as when located on the end of a jetty, but more often they will be part of a buoy, light, or larger aid to navigation.

Ranges are pairs of unlighted or lighted fixed aids so

FIG. 1503 The Coast Guard is the principal agency maintaining aids to navigation in U.S. waters. Specially designed and equipped vessels do this work. The USCGC Red Wood is the first of a class of 157-foot coastal buoy tenders.

FIG. 1504 "Large Navigation Buoys" are now used at some locations. The one shown, built of high-strength low alloy steel plate, is 40 feet in diameter with a 5,000 candlepower light 33 feet above the water. It replaces the old Scotland Lightship in the approaches to New York Harbor.

located that when observed in line the pilot is on the centerline of a channel. The individual structures may, in some cases, also serve as separate aids to navigation marking a turn in a channel.

Lightships are specially equipped vessels moored or anchored at specific locations to serve as aids to navigation. They are of distinctive shape and color, and will have lights and sound signals, and radiobeacons.

Radiobeacons are transmitters broadcasting a characteristic signal specifically to aid navigation at night, in fog, or at distances exceeding normal visibility. These, too, are usually at another aid, but may at times be located separately.

Electronic navigation systems are radio transmitters, usually in groups, which emit special signals that may be used for assistance in navigation when in fog or otherwise out of sight of land or offshore aids. Such systems include *Loran-C* and *Omega* operated by the Coast Guard, aeronautical radiobeacons and "Omni" stations run by the Federal Aviation Administration, and other systems operated by government or private interests. In general, only USCG and FAA systems will be of use to boatmen.

Buoys

Buoys are floating objects, other than lightships, anchored or moored to the bottom at specific locations so as to serve as aids to navigation. They are shown on charts by special symbols and lettering that will indicate their shape, color, and visual and/or sound signals. They will vary in size from sixth-class buoys projecting only a few feet above the surface to the "super buoys" that are some 40 feet (12.2 m) in diameter with a superstructure rising to 30 feet (9.1 m) or more in height; see fig. 1504.

The buoyage system adopted for waters of the United States consists of several different types of buoys, each kind designed to serve under definite conditions. Broadly speaking, all buoys serve as daytime aids; those having lights are also available to aid navigation at night, and

those having sound signals are especially useful in time of fog as well as at night.

The shape, color, and light characteristic, if any, will convey to a pilot information as to his location and the proper guidance of his vessel to remain in safe waters. The size of a buoy does *not* indicate such information and is usually determined by the importance of the waterway and size of vessels using it. The size of a buoy need not be taken into consideration by a skipper, except when estimating distances.

Buoys are normally anchored to the bottom using chain to heavy concrete sinkers weighing up to six or more tons, fig. 1505. The length of chain will vary with the location, but will generally be two to three times the depth of water.

FIG. 1505 Buoys are anchored with cast concrete blocks called "sinkers." These range in weight from 500 pounds to more than six tons; a one-ton sinker is seen above. Normally, only a single sinker of appropriate size is used for any buoy.

BUOY CHARACTERISTICS

Buoys may be subdivided into types as lighted or unlighted, sound buoys, or combination buoys. This latter type is comprised of buoys that have both an audible and a visual signal.

The Coast Guard maintains about 21,000 unlighted and 3,700 lighted and combination buoys in waters under its jurisdiction. Many others are maintained by state and private agencies in non-federal waters.

Buoy shapes

Unlighted buoys may be further classified by their shape.

Can buoys are objects made up of steel plates so that the above-water appearance is cylindrical, like a can or drum floating with its axis vertical and flat end upward; see fig. 1506. Two lifting lugs may project slightly above the flat top of a can buoy, but these will not significantly alter its appearance.

Nun buoys are objects made up of steel plates so that the above-water appearance is that of a cylinder topped

FIG. 1506 Can buoys have a cylindrical shape with a flat top. An older-type, still used, is shown on the left. Newer can buoys have integral radar reflectors as shown in (b) above.

FIG. 1507 Nun buoys have a conical shape coming to a near-point at the upper end. This is a modern nun buoy with radar reflector plates in its upper section.

with a cone, pointed end up, fig. 1507. The cone may come to a point or the tip may be slightly rounded. Smaller nun buoys will have a single lifting ring at the top; larger buoys will have several lugs around the sides.

Unlighted buoys come in standardized sizes. These are designated in classes—first through sixth—and as standard or nonstandard. Knowledge of the various sizes is not important to the boatman, although it may be of general interest to note that the above-water visible portion of a nun buoy may vary from 2'-6" for a sixth-class standard to 14'-0" for a first-class tall. Can buoys are somewhat shorter, ranging from 1'-4" to 9'-9" above the waterline. The smaller buoys are, of course, lesser in diameter also, with a range of 1½ to 5 feet. Pilots should remember that a considerable portion of a buoy is under water, and that they are really much larger and heavier objects than they would appear to be from a casual observation.

The Coast Guard has now eliminated the use of *spar* buoys, but they may be found in some private or foreign systems of aids. These are usually large logs, trimmed, shaped, and appropriately painted; they are anchored from one end with a suitable length of chain.

Special shapes will sometimes be found in use as markers, but these are not regular aids to navigation. Spherical buoys are the most generally used of the special shape category.

Lighted, sound, and combination buoys are described by their visual and/or audible signals rather than by their shape.

Sound buoys

Buoys are often equipped with a characteristic sound signal to aid in their location during periods of reduced visibility, chiefly fog. Several different sound signals are available and are used to distinguish between different aids to navigation that may be within audible range of each other.

Bell buoys are steel floats surmounted by short skeleton towers in which a bell is mounted, fig. 1512. They serve

Note: 1 inch = 2.54 cm. 1 foot = 30.5 cm or 0.305 m.

with considerable effectiveness both by day and night, and especially in fog; they are much used because of their moderate maintenance costs. Most bell buoys are operated by the motion of the sea—four tappers, loosely hung externally around the bell, are readily set in motion. When the buoy rolls as a result of waves, ground swells, or the wake of passing vessels, a single note is heard at irregular intervals. Since bell buoys require some motion of the sea to operate, they are not normally used in sheltered waters; a horn buoy, see page 305, is established here if a fog signal is needed.

Gong buoys are similar in construction to bell buoys, except that a set of gongs is substituted for the bell, fig. 1512. Gong buoys are used to give a distinctive character-

FIG. 1508 Buoys equipped with both a light and a sound signal are called combination buoys. Shown above in (a) is a lighted buoy with a whistle below the radar reflector. In (b) at the right, the lighted buoy has an electric horn fog signal.

AIDS TO NAVIGATION ON NAVIGABLE WATERS
except Western Rivers and Intracoastal Waterway

LATERAL SYSTEM AS SEEN ENTERING FROM SEAWARD

PORT SIDE
ODD NUMBERED AIDS
◼ GREEN OR ☐ WHITE LIGHTS

FIXED
FLASHING
OCCULTING
QUICK FLASHING
EQ INT

LIGHTED BUOY "9"

CAN "7"

SG

DAYMARKS 1

G "1"

MID CHANNEL
NO NUMBERS—MAY BE LETTERED
☐ WHITE LIGHT ONLY

MORSE CODE

T CAN BW C "T"

N LIGHTED BW MoA "N"

B NUN BW N "B"

A MB "A" BW DAYMARK

JUNCTION
MARK JUNCTIONS AND OBSTRUCTIONS
NO NUMBERS—MAY BE LETTERED
INTERRUPTED QUICK FLASHING

☐ WHITE OR ◼ GREEN   ☐ WHITE OR ◼ RED

M "M" RB "D" Ra ref LIGHTED D

PREFERRED CHANNEL TO STARBOARD
TOPMOST BAND BLACK
N CAN RB C "N"

PREFERRED CHANNEL TO PORT
TOPMOST BAND RED
L NUN RB N "L"

A △

JR B △

STARBOARD SIDE
EVEN NUMBERED AIDS
◼ RED OR ☐ WHITE LIGHTS

FIXED
FLASHING
OCCULTING
QUICK FLASHING
EQ INT
GROUP FLASHING (2)

LIGHTED BUOY 8 R "8"

NUN 6 R N "6"

TR

DAYMARK 2 R "4"

BUOYS HAVING NO LATERAL SIGNIFICANCE—ALL WATERS

SHAPE HAS NO SIGNIFICANCE
NO NUMBERS—MAY BE LETTERED
MAY BE LIGHTED
ANY COLOR LIGHT EXCEPT
RED OR GREEN

FIXED
FLASHING
OCCULTING

SPECIAL PURPOSE WOr C

N ANCHORAGE W C "N"

FISH NET AREA BW C

DREDGING GW C

UNLIGHTED

DANGER

EXCLUSION AREA

DAYMARKS HAVING NO LATERAL SIGNIFICANCE
MAY BE LETTERED

NW SUBMERGED DANGER JETTY △

NR A △

A △

NB M △

Note: Square black (SB) and square white (SW) daymarks are being gradually phased out by replacement with square green (SG) daymarks with green reflective borders as shown above.

AIDS TO NAVIGATION ON THE INTRACOASTAL WATERWAY

AS SEEN ENTERING FROM NORTH AND EAST—PROCEEDING TO SOUTH AND WEST

PORT SIDE
ODD NUMBERED AIDS
■ GREEN OR □ WHITE LIGHTS

FIXED ▬▬▬ OCCULTING ▬ ▬ ▬
FLASHING ▬ ■■ ▬ ■■ QUICK FLASHING ■■■■■■■
EQ INT ▬ ■ ▬ ■

LIGHTED BUOY
"3"
Fl G 4sec
Ra Ref

CAN
C "9"
Ra ref

SG-I
G "1"

DAYMARKS

JUNCTION
MARK JUNCTIONS AND OBSTRUCTIONS
NO NUMBERS—MAY BE LETTERED
INTERRUPTED QUICK FLASHING

□ WHITE OR ■ GREEN LIGHTS   □ WHITE OR ■ RED LIGHTS

BR "J"
I Qk Fl G
Ra Ref

RB "N"
I Qk Fl R
Ra Ref

PREFERRED CHANNEL
TO STARBOARD   TO PORT
TOPMOST BAND   TOPMOST BAND
BLACK   RED

BR C "A" Ra ref   RB N "S"

CAN   NUN

GR "A"   RG "B"
                JR-I

MID CHANNEL MORSE CODE   NO NUMBERS-MAY BE LETTERED
□ WHITE LIGHT ONLY

MB-I   BW "B"   C "T"   BW Mo(A) "N"   BW N"B"
DAYMARK   Ra Ref   Ra Ref   Ra Ref
        CAN LIGHTED NUN

STARBOARD SIDE
EVEN NUMBERED AIDS
■ RED OR □ WHITE LIGHTS

FIXED ▬▬▬ OCCULTING ▬ ▬ ▬
FLASHING ▬ ■ ▬ ■ QUICK FLASHING ■■■■■■■
EQ INT ▬ ■ ▬ ■
GROUP FLASHING (2) ▬ ■ ■ ▬ ■ ■

LIGHTED BUOY
R "8"
Fl R 4sec
Ra Ref

NUN
R N "6"
Ra ref

TR
R "2"
DAYMARK

ILLUSTRATION—DUAL PURPOSE MARKING
WHERE ICW AND OTHER WATERWAYS COINCIDE

When following the ICW from New Jersey through Texas, a △ should
be kept to your starboard hand and a □ should be kept to your port hand,
regardless of the color of the aid on which they appear.

SG-SY
G "5"
DUAL PURPOSE DAYMARKS
C "5" Ra Ref
DUAL PURPOSE BUOYS

TR-SY
R "6"
R N "6" Ra Ref

JG-SY
RG "A"
JR-SY
RG "B"

TR-TY
R "6"
DUAL PURPOSE DAYMARKS
R N "6"
DUAL PURPOSE BUOYS

SG-TY
G "5"
C "5"

JG-TY
RG "C"
JR-TY
RG "B"

AIDS TO NAVIGATION ON WESTERN RIVERS

AS SEEN ENTERING FROM SEAWARD

PORT SIDE	JUNCTION	STARBOARD SIDE

PORT SIDE

■ GREEN OR □ WHITE LIGHTS
FLASHING

LIGHTED BUOY

CAN

SG

PASSING DAYMARK

CG

CROSSING DAYMARK

176.9

MILE BOARD

JUNCTION

MARK JUNCTIONS AND OBSTRUCTIONS
INTERRUPTED QUICK FLASHING

PREFERRED CHANNEL TO STARBOARD
TOPMOST BAND BLACK

PREFERRED CHANNEL TO PORT
TOPMOST BAND RED

□ WHITE OR ■ GREEN LIGHTS

□ WHITE OR ■ RED LIGHTS

LIGHTED

CAN

NUN

JG

JR

STARBOARD SIDE

■ RED OR □ WHITE LIGHTS
GROUP FLASHING (2)

LIGHTED BUOY

NUN

TR

PASSING DAYMARK

CR

CROSSING DAYMARK

123.5

MILE BOARD

RANGE DAYMARKS AS FOUND ON

NAVIGABLE WATERS EXCEPT — ICW — MAY BE LETTERED

KWB KWR KRW KRB KBW KBR KGB KBG KGR KRG

INTRACOASTAL WATERWAY — MAY BE LETTERED

KWB-I KWR-I KRW-I KRB-I KBW-I KBR-I KGB-I KBG-I KGR-I KRG-I

K

UNIFORM STATE WATERWAY MARKING SYSTEM

AIDS TO NAVIGATION

PORT (left) SIDE

COLOR — Black
NUMBERS — Odd
LIGHTS — Flashing green
REFLECTORS — Green

THE LATERAL SYSTEM—In well-defined channels and narrow waterways, USWMS aids to navigation normally are solid-colored buoys. Though a can and a nun are illustrated here, SHAPES may vary. COLOR is the significant feature. When proceeding UPSTREAM or toward the head of navigation, BLACK BUOYS ← mark the *left* side of the channel and must be kept on the left (port) hand. RED BUOYS → mark the *right* side of the channel and must be kept on the right (starboard) side. This conforms with practice on other federal waterways. On waters having no well-defined inlet or outlet, arbitrary assumptions may be made. Inquire in the locality for further information and charts when available.

STARBOARD (right) SIDE

COLOR — Red
NUMBERS — Even
LIGHTS — Flashing red
REFLECTORS — Red

Note: In some areas red buoys may be of "can" shape.

THE CARDINAL SYSTEM—Used where there is no well-defined channel or where an obstruction may be approached from more than one direction.

BLACK-TOPPED WHITE BUOY indicates boat should pass to NORTH or EAST of it. Reflector or light, if used, is white, the light quick-flashing.

RED-TOPPED WHITE BUOY indicates boat should pass to SOUTH or WEST of it. Reflector or light, if used, is white, the light quick-flashing.

RED-AND-WHITE VERTICALLY STRIPED BUOY indicates boat should not pass between buoy and nearest shore. Used when reef or obstruction requires boat to go *outside* buoy (away from shore). White stripes are twice the width of red stripes. Reflector or light, if used, is white, the light quick-flashing.

MOORING BUOY—White with horizontal blue band. If lighted, shows slow-flashing light unless it constitutes an obstruction at night, when light would be quick-flashing.

NOTE—The use of lights, reflectors, numbers and letters on USWMS aids is discretionary.

LIGHTS—On solid-colored (red or black) buoys, lights when used are flashing, occulting, or equal interval. For ordinary purposes, *slow-flashing* (not more than 30 per minute). *Quick-flashing* (not less than 60 per minute) used at turns, constrictions, or obstructions to indicate *caution*.

REFLECTORS—On lateral-type buoys, *red* reflectors or retro-reflective materials are used on solid-red buoys, *green* reflectors on solid-black buoys, *white* on all others including regulatory markers (except that *orange* may be used on orange portions of markers).

NUMBERS—*White* on red or black backgrounds. *Black* on white backgrounds. Numbers increase in an upstream direction.

LETTERS—When used on regulatory and white-and-red striped obstruction markers, letters are in alphabetical sequence in an upstream direction. (Letters I and O omitted.)

UNIFORM STATE REGULATORY MARKERS

Diamond shape warns of DANGER! Suggested wording for specific dangers: ROCK (illustrated), DAM, SNAG, DREDGE, WING-DAM, FERRY CABLE, MARINE CONSTRUCTION, etc.

Circle marks CONTROLLED AREA "as illustrated." Suggested wording to control or prohibit boating activities: 5 MPH (illustrated), NO FISHING, NO SKI, NO SWIM, NO SCUBA, NO PROP BOATS, SKI ONLY, FISHING ONLY, SKIN DIVERS ONLY, etc.

SWIM AREA

Diamond shape with cross means BOATS KEEP OUT! Explanatory reasons may be indicated outside the crossed diamond shape, for example SWIM AREA (illustrated), DAM, WATERFALL, RAPIDS, DOMESTIC WATER, etc.

Square or rectangle gives INFORMATION, names, activities. May give place names, distances, arrows indicating directions, availability of gas, oil, groceries, marine repairs, etc.

REGULATORY MARKERS are *white* with *international orange* geometric shapes. Buoys may be used as regulatory markers. Such buoys are *white* with two horizontal bands of *international orange*—one at the top, another just above the waterline. Geometric shapes, colored *international orange*, are placed on the white body of the buoy between the orange bands. When square or rectangular *signs* are displayed on structures as regulatory markers, they are *white* with *international orange* borders. Diamond and circular shapes, when used, are centered on the signboard.

L

FIG. 1509 This is a late design of lighted buoy without sound signal. Note the straight sides of the tower-like superstructure; older designs had towers that first tapered in and then out near the top.

FIG. 1510 The Coast Guard is experimenting with an atomic power source for a buoy. This buoy is lighted from a strontium-90 thermoelectric system. It is hoped that the use of atomic power will increase the reliability of remote buoys and decrease the number of servicing visits required.

istic when there are several sound buoys in one vicinity. In these buoys, four gongs of different tones are mounted, with one tapper for each gong. As the sea rocks the buoy, the tappers strike against their respective gongs, sounding four different notes in an irregular sequence. If a channel is marked with both types, the preferred system is gongs to port and bells to starboard.

Whistle buoys provide yet another distinctive audible signal useful at night or in fog. The whistle is sounded by compressed air produced by the motion of the buoy in the sea. For this reason, such buoys are used principally

FIG. 1512 Shown here are models, all to the same scale, of four typical buoys. Note the range of sizes and large mass of the lighted buoys that is below the waterline. The smaller lighted buoy has a bell and the larger one four gongs; both have external "tappers" to strike and sound the fog signal. These are all of the so-called "1962" design, many of which are in use.

in open and exposed locations where a ground swell normally exists, fig. 1508.

Horn buoys are rather infrequently used, but boatmen should be aware of their existence and know how to recognize them. They differ from whistle buoys in that they are electrically powered rather than depending upon the motion of the sea.

Lighted buoys

Buoys may be equipped with lights of various colors, intensities, and flashing characteristics (called "phase characteristics"). The color and characteristics of the light are used to convey information to the mariner. Intensity of the light will be determined by the distance at which the aid must be detected, influenced by such factors as background lighting, normal atmospheric clarity, etc.

Lighted buoys are constructed as metal floats with a short skeleton tower at the top of which the light is placed; see fig. 1509. The light is powered by electric batteries placed inside the lower body of the buoy below the waterline. Lighted buoys are designed to operate for many months without servicing.

Lighted buoys are now generally equipped with "daylight controls" that automatically turn the light on and off as darkness falls and lifts. Buoys equipped with such electric eye controls may be specially marked with a symbol in white paint consisting of a circular spot with a horizontal bar running through its center. This symbol was used for some years when the automatic daylight controls were being introduced, but are now being discontinued as conversion has essentially been completed.

Lights on buoys, as on other lighted aids, are either red, green, or white. The colors red and green have specific applications as will be discussed later in this chapter. White lights are prescribed for certain specific functions, and may also be substituted for red or green where a greater range of visibility is desired.

305

Color of buoys

Buoys used for navigation may be painted red, black, red-and-black, or black-and-white. Buoys for special purposes will use these colors and also yellow, green, orange, and blue. The specific meanings of the various colors will be discussed later in this chapter when buoyage systems are considered.

Optical reflectors

Almost all unlighted buoys are fitted with areas of reflective material. These greatly facilitate the detection of such buoys at night when using a searchlight. The reflectors may be white, red, or green, and have the same significance as lights of these colors.

Reflective sheeting is used extensively by the Coast Guard for marking buoys. This flexible plastic film is easily attached to any reasonably smooth surface and has improved reflective characteristics over conventional glass reflectors. The reflective material may be in the form of square "patches" or as bands around the buoy.

Although primarily intended to make unlighted buoys more visible at night, reflective material is also placed on the numbers or letters of buoys to aid in their nighttime identification. Reflective numbers and/or letters will be found on both lighted and unlighted buoys of all types.

Radar reflectors

Many buoys are equipped with radar reflectors, vertical metal plates set at right angles to each other in such a manner as to greatly increase the echo returned to a radar receiver on a ship or boat. The plates are shaped and mounted so as to preserve the overall characteristic shape of an unlighted buoy or the general appearance of a lighted buoy. See fig. 1512.

LIGHT PHASE CHARACTERISTICS

The lights on lighted buoys will generally flash in one of several specific patterns. The flashing-light type of operation serves a number of useful purposes:

(1) It conserves the energy source within the buoy by having the light on only a small portion of the total time. Fixed lights, continuously lit with no variation of color or intensity, are not used on Coast Guard buoys, and only occasionally on buoys maintained by other agencies.

(2) Flashing assists in the detection of the lighted aid against a background of other lights.

(3) Flashing allows the signaling during hours of darkness of a limited amount of information, such as the need to exercise special caution at a certain point in a channel.

(4) The flashing characteristic of the light can be selected from a number of available patterns so as to be able to distinguish between several buoys of the same general function that may be within visible range of each other.

Lights are classed as *flashing* when the light comes on for a single brief flash at regular intervals; the period of light is always *less* than the period of darkness. Coast Guard-maintained buoys designated as of the flashing type will flash their light not more than 30 times per minute. This is the more-generally used characteristic for buoys. It is sometimes termed "slow flashing," but the official and correct description is simply "flashing."

Flashing (Fl)

Quick Flashing (Qk Fl)

Interrupted Quick Flashing (I Qk Fl)

Morse Code "A" (Mo A)

FIG. 1513 Buoys show various light phase characteristics which help in conveying information and assist in distinguishing between buoys of the same type located near each other.

Quick flashing lights will flash not less than 60 times each minute. These buoys are used for special situations where they will be more quickly spotted and where particular attention to piloting is required.

Interrupted quick flashing lights show a group of six quick flashes followed by a dark interval of five seconds, repeated every ten seconds. These are used in special situation as will be described later.

Morse code "A" flashing lights have a cycle consisting of a short flash, a brief dark interval, a longer flash, and a longer dark interval, repeated every eight seconds. This is the "dot-dash" of the letter "A" in Morse Code; the characteristic was formerly known as "short-long flashing." The color of the light is always white.

The above light phase characteristics are shown diagramatically in fig. 1513. The *period* of a light is the time required for the completion of one full cycle of flash and dark interval, or flashes and dark intervals. A light de-

FIG. 1514 Buoys should be used with caution because of natural hazards to which they are exposed. A Coast Guardsman is seen here removing ice from a large lighted buoy; such ice may have interferred with the buoy's normal operation.

scribed as "Flashing 4 seconds" has a period of four seconds. One flash and one dark interval lasts just that long before the cycle is repeated.

Standardized flashing rates

As noted earlier, "flashing" lights may have various repetition rates for individual buoy identification, provided that there are not more than 30 flashes each minute. Over the years, the Coast Guard has used various characteristics involving different flash lengths and intervals. Buoys have been operated in the past that flashed at intervals of 2, 2½, 3, 4, 5, and 6 seconds; individual flashes have varied in length from 0.05 to 1.0 second. Standardization has now been introduced into the system of lighted buoys to reduce the number of different light phase characteristics.

Three standard characteristics will be used—flashing at intervals of 2.5, 4, and 6 seconds. These correspond to 24, 15, and 10 flashes per minute. These three light phase characteristics will provide sufficient differences for individual buoy identification and will provide economic battery service periods.

Another part of the Coast Guard's continuing effort to improve the reliability of its aids to navigation is the replacement of motorized mechanical flashers with solid-state (transistorized) electronic equipment having no moving parts. The use of precision moulded acrylic plastic lenses on buoys and minor lights has made possible substantial increases in the candlepower of such aids.

CAUTIONS IN USING BUOYS

A pilot should not rely on floating aids to navigation to always maintain their charted positions, or to constantly and unerringly display their specified characteristics. Obstacles to perfect performance are of such magnitude that complete reliability is manifestly impossible. The Coast Guard makes a continuous effort to keep aids working properly, but cannot be completely successful with all of the many thousands to be checked and maintained.

Buoys are heavily anchored, but they may shift in location, be carried away, capsized, or sunk as a result of violent storms or of having been struck by passing ships. A pilot must be prepared for the possible absence of a buoy he planned to use in his navigation, or its displacement off-station.

Buoys that have been placed to mark shifting shoals may not always be properly located in relation to the hazards they are meant to mark. This is particularly true during and immediately after heavy storms when shoals are liable to shift their positions relative to the buoys.

Lighted buoys may become extinguished, or their control apparatus become broken or deranged causing them to show improper light characteristics. Essentially all audible signals on buoys are operated by action of the sea, and may consequently be silent during periods of calm water. They may fail to sound, regardless of wave activity, due to mechanical defects in their sound-producing mechanism. Even if functioning properly, a sound buoy may not be heard at relatively close range due to erratic transmission of sound in air.

Buoys do not maintain their position directly over their anchors as they must be provided with some scope on their anchor chains; they swing in small circles around the anchor, which is the charted location. (See Chapter 18 for how buoys are charted.) For this reason, buoys are inferior

to fixed aids to navigation when precise bearings are desired.

Moored as they are, buoys have a tendency to yaw about under the influence of wind and current. This action is unpredictable, and a vessel attempting to pass close aboard risks collision with a yawing buoy. In extremely strong currents, buoys may even be pulled beneath the surface.

Buoys are sometimes removed to make way for dredging operations, or for other reasons. In northern waters, buoys may be discontinued for the winter, or smaller unlighted buoys substituted for lighted and combination buoys to prevent damage or loss from ice floes. The dates shown in the Light Lists for seasonal buoys, or seasonal changes in buoys, are only approximate and may vary slightly due to weather or other conditions.

Temporary or permanent changes in buoys may be made between editions of charts. A wise skipper keeps informed of existing conditions through reading Notices to Mariners or Local Notices to Mariners—see Chapter 17.

All buoys (especially those located in exposed positions) should, therefore, be regarded as warnings or guides, and not as infallible navigation marks. Whenever possible, a boat should be navigated by bearings or angles on fixed objects on shore (see Chapter 21), and by soundings, rather than by total reliance on buoys.

FIG. 1515 The simplest daybeacon is a single pile with one or two "daymarks" either square (green, black, or white) or triangular (red). Reflective borders of green or red, and reflective numbers of the same color, show up brilliantly in a searchlight. Other shapes are used for special purposes; see color pages I, J, and K.

Daybeacons

Daybeacons are unlighted structures established as an aid to navigation; they are "fixed" rather than "floating" aids. Daybeacons may be located either on shore or in waters up to perhaps 12 to 15 feet deep.

Daybeacons vary greatly in design and construction, depending upon their location and the distance at which they must be seen. A continuing effort is now being made by the Coast Guard to standardize daybeacon structures and markings for easier identification as aids to navigation.

FIG. 1516 Buoys must be periodically hauled out for servicing. A new buoy is placed on station, and the old one is taken in to a depot for scraping and repainting.

CHARACTERISTICS

The simplest daybeacon is a single pile with a number sign, called a "daymark," located at or near the top, fig. 1515. The pile may be wood, concrete, or metal.

A larger, more visible, and more sturdy daybeacon is the "three-pile dolphin" type. Here the single pile is replaced by three piles separated a few feet at their lower ends, but coming together at their tops where they are strongly held together with wire cables. Such structures are equipped with a daymark at the top, or more likely two daymarks facing in opposite directions. (Some dolphins may be made of five piles, four around one central pile.)

Daymarks and pointers

The daybeacon must be properly identified if it is to serve its purpose as an aid to navigation. Thus a daymark usually bears a number, occasionally a letter or letters.

Daymarks are normally either square or triangular in shape, corresponding to can and nun buoys; see page 304. Square daymarks will now be green with green reflective border (some older ones may be black or white). Triangular daymarks are red with red reflective border. The number or letters will be of the same color reflective material as the border. These reflective areas show up brilliantly at night in a boat's searchlight and aid in both the location and identification of the daybeacon. In some special applications, a daymark may be octagonal (eight-sided) or diamond-shaped carrying a brief warning or notice.

In some areas, pointers have been used in lieu of square or triangular daymarks. These are now being phased out, but some may remain for years to come.

FIG. 1517 A minor light may consist of a single-pile structure with the light itself at the top and number identification on the daymark below. The light shown here is receiving periodic maintenance from a Coast Guard crew.

THE USES OF DAYBEACONS

For obvious reasons, the use of daybeacons is restricted to relatively shallow waters. Within this limitation, however, a daybeacon is often more desirable than a buoy. From a navigator's point of view, it is a superior aid to navigation — firmly fixed in position, and more readily seen and identified. From the Coast Guard's viewpoint, a daybeacon is more desirable too—once established, it is in position and requires but little maintenance (buoys must be regularly hauled out for scraping and repainting, fig. 1516).

Daybeacons are used primarily for channel marking and serve in the same manner as buoys in the buoyage systems to be described later in this chapter.

Minor Lights

Just as daybeacons are sometimes substituted for unlighted buoys, so may lighted buoys be replaced with *minor lights*. These are fixed structures of the same overall physical features as daybeacons, but equipped with a light generally similar in characteristics to those found on buoys. Most minor lights are part of a series marking a channel, river or harbor; also included, however, are some isolated single lights if they are of the same general size and characteristics. The term "minor light" does not include the more important lights marking harbors, peninsulas, major shoals, etc.; these have lights of greater intensity and/or special characteristics — these are designated as "secondary" or "primary seacoast" lights and are discussed in detail in Chapter 16.

CHARACTERISTICS

Minor lights are placed on single piles, fig. 1517, on multiple-pile dolphins, fig. 1518, or on other structures in the water or on shore. Daymarks are placed on the structures for their identification, and reflective material is added for nighttime safety should the light be extin-

FIG. 1518 Structures for daybeacons or minor lights may also consist of three or more piles driven in a few feet apart and then bound together at their top. (Morris Rosenfeld photograph)

guished. In general, the description of daybeacons is applicable plus the addition of the light mechanism.

Light characteristics

A minor light will normally have the same color and flash with the same phase characteristics that a lighted buoy would have if the aid were of floating rather than fixed type. Intensity of the light will generally be of the same order as that of a lighted buoy, occasionally somewhat greater, but visibility may be increased by its greater height above water and its more stable platform.

Flashing characteristics of minor lights have been standardized with flashes at intervals of 2.5, 4 and 6 seconds. This is part of the same light modernization program as previously described for lighted buoys.

Sound signals

Minor lights may, in some locations, have an audible fog signal. These cannot, of course, be of a type operated by wave action, as in the case of bell and gong buoys. A bell, horn, or siren will be electrically operated on the structure, in some cases continuously for months during which fog may be expected.

Buoyage Systems

The primary function of buoys is to warn the mariner of some danger, obstruction, or change in the contours of the bottom, and to delineate channels leading to various points, so that he may avoid hazards and continue on his course safely. The greatest advantage is obtained from buoys used to mark specifically defined spots, for if a pilot knows his precise position at the moment and is properly equipped with charts, he can plot a safe course. Such features as shape, coloring, and signaling characteristics of buoys are but means to these ends of warning, guiding, and orienting the navigator.

Most maritime nations use either the *lateral system of buoyage* or the *cardinal system,* or both. In the lateral system, the buoys indicate the direction to a danger relative to the course that should be followed. In the cardinal system, characteristics of buoys indicate location of the danger relative to the buoy itself. The term "cardinal" relates to cardinal points of the compass, see Chapter 13, pages 269–270.

The Lateral System of Buoyage

In the United States, the lateral system of buoyage is uniformly used in all Federal-jurisdiction areas and on many other bodies of water where it can be applied. In this system, the shape, coloring, numbering, and light characteristics of buoys are determined by their position with respect to the navigable channel, natural or dredged, as such channels are entered and followed from seaward toward the head of navigation. The lateral system is described in detail in the subsequent sections covering each of the basic characteristics.

THE BASIC U. S. SYSTEM

The lateral system of buoyage employs a simple arrangement of shapes, colors, numbers, and light characteristics to indicate the side on which a buoy should be passed when proceeding in a given direction. The system is easily learned and should be known in detail by all boatmen.

As all channels do not lead from seaward, certain arbitrary assumptions must be made in order that the lateral system may be consistently applied. In coloring and numbering offshore buoys along the coasts, the following system has been adopted: proceeding in a southerly direction along the Atlantic Coast, in a northerly and westerly direction along the Gulf Coast, and in a northerly direction along the Pacific Coast will be considered the same as coming in from seaward. This can be remembered as proceeding around the coastline of the United States in a clockwise direction.

On the Great Lakes, offshore buoys are colored and

numbered as proceeding from the outlet end of each lake toward its upper end. This will be generally westerly and northward on the Lakes, except on Lake Michigan where it will be southward. Buoys marking channels into harbors are colored and numbered just as for channels leading into coastal ports from seaward.

On the Mississippi and Ohio Rivers and their tributaries, characteristics of aids to navigation are determined as proceeding from seaward toward the head of navigation,

although local terminology describes "left bank" and "right bank" as proceeding with the flow of the river.

Coloring

All buoys are painted distinctive colors to indicate the side on which they should be passed, or their special purpose. In the lateral system, the significance of colors is as shown below.

TABLE 15-1				LATERAL SYSTEM IN U.S. AND CANADIAN WATERS		
Returning from sea*	**Color**	**Number**	**Unlighted Buoy Shape**	**Lights or Lighted Buoys**		**Daymark Shape**
				Light Color	**Light Phase Characteristic**	
Right side of channel	Red	Even	Nun	Red or White	Flashing or Quick Flashing	Triangular
Left side of channel	Black	Odd	Can	Green or White	Flashing or Quick Flashing	Square
Channel Junction or Obstruction	Red-and-black horizontally banded**	Not Numbered; May be Lettered	Nun or Can**	Red, Green or White**	Interrupted Quick Flashing	Triangular or Square**
Midchannel or Fairway	Black-and-white vertically striped	May be lettered	Nun or Can	White	Morse Code "A"	Octagonal

*or entering a harbor from a larger body of water, such as a lake.
**Preferred channel is indicated by color of uppermost band (shape of unlighted buoy), color of light, if any.

Black buoys mark the left (port) side of a channel when entering from seaward, or the location of a wreck or other obstruction that must be passed by keeping the buoy on the left hand.

Red buoys mark the right (starboard) side of a channel, or the location of a hazard to navigation that must be passed by keeping the buoy to starboard. It is from this color designation that the often-used phrase "Red — Right — Returning" is derived, meaning that *red* buoys should be kept on the *right* side of the boat when *returning* to harbor from the sea or other large body of water.

Red-and-black horizontally banded buoys mark junctions in a channel, or wrecks or obstructions that may be passed on *either* side. If the topmost band is black, the preferred channel will be followed by keeping the buoy on the left (port) hand. If the topmost band is red, the preferred channel is followed by keeping the buoy on the right (starboard) side of the vessel. (Note: When proceeding *toward* the sea, it may *not* be possible to pass such buoys safely on either side. This is particularly true in situations where you are following one channel downstream and another channel joins in from the side, see fig. 1519; always consult the chart for the area.)

Black-and-white vertically striped buoys mark the fairway or midchannel. They are also used to divide the "in" and "out" channels of a Traffic Separation Scheme.

It should be noted that when the areas of color run horizontally, they are "bands"; when they are arranged

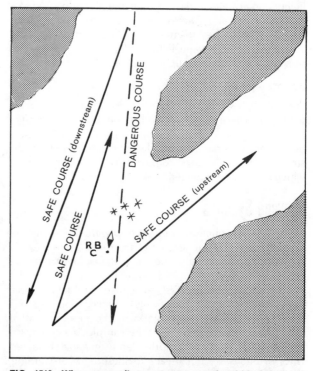

FIG. 1519 When proceeding upstream, a red-and-black horizontally-banded junction buoy may be safely passed on either side. This is not true, however, when going downstream, as examination of the above situation will quickly show.

vertically, they are "stripes." These terms are used in other color combinations in the case of special-purpose buoys.

Shapes of buoys

In the lateral system of buoyage, definite shape characteristics are given to the unlighted buoys to indicate which side of the channel they mark. The use of shapes is particularly valuable when a buoy is first sighted in line with the sun and only its silhouette rather than its color can be distinguished.

Can buoys, painted black, mark the left (port) side of the channel when returning from seaward, or the location of a wreck or shoal that must be passed by keeping the buoy on the left hand.

Nun buoys, painted red, mark the right (starboard) side of channels, or hazards that must be passed by keeping the buoy to starboard.

Channel junction and obstruction buoys may be of *either* can or nun shape. If the uppermost band is *black,* the buoy will be a *can;* if the uppermost band is *red,* it will be a *nun.*

Black-and-white vertically striped midchannel buoys may be either nuns or cans, and in this situation the shape has no significance.

No special significance is to be attached to the shape of spar buoys, bell buoys, gong buoys, whistle buoys, lighted buoys, or combination buoys. The purpose of these is indicated by their coloring, number or the characteristic of the light.

Numbering

Most buoys are given "numbers" that actually may be numbers, letters, or a combination of numbers and letters. These markings facilitate identification and location of buoys on charts.

In the lateral system, numbers serve as yet another indication of which side the buoy should be passed. The system is as follows:

Odd numbered buoys mark the left hand side of a channel leading in from seaward. In accordance with the rules stated above, these will be black buoys, cans if they are unlighted.

Even numbered buoys mark the right (starboard) side of a channel; these will be red (nun) buoys.

Numbers increase from seaward and are kept in approximate sequence on the two sides of a channel by omitting numbers as appropriate if buoys are not uniformly placed in pairs. Occasionally, several numbers will be omitted on longer stretches without buoys in order to allow for possible later additions.

Numbers followed by letters, such as 24A, 24B, 24C, etc., indicate buoys that have been added to a channel with the series not being immediately renumbered.

A buoy marking a wreck will often be designated with a number derived from the number of the buoy next downstream from it, preceded by the letters "WR". Thus, a buoy marking a wreck on the left-hand side of a channel between buoys 17 and 19 would be numbered "WR17A". A wreck buoy not related to a channel may be designated by one or two letters relating to the name of the wrecked vessel or a geographic location.

Letters, without numbers, are applied in some cases to black-and-white vertically striped buoys marking fairways, and to red-and-black horizontally banded buoys marking channel junctions or obstructions.

Numbers followed by letters may be used on some buoys marking offshore dangers. An example of this usage is the buoy marked "2TL" where the number has the usual sequential significance and the letters "TL" indicate the place as a shoal known as "Turner's Lump." This form of marking buoys is now more traditional than necessary.

Color of lights

For all buoys in the lateral system that have lights, the following system of colors is used.

Green lights on buoys are used only on those marking the left-hand side of a channel returning from seaward (black, odd-numbered buoys) or on red-and-black horizontally banded buoys that have the topmost band painted black.

Red lights on buoys are used only on those marking the right-hand side of a channel when entering from sea (red, even-numbered buoys) or on red-and-black horizontally banded buoys having a red topmost band.

White lights on buoys may be used on either side of channels in lieu of red or green. White lights are frequently employed where a greater visible range is desired, such as at a change in the direction of the channel. No special significance is derived from a white light, the purpose of the buoy being indicated by its color, number, or its light phase characteristic.

Light phase characteristics

Flashing lights (flashing at a rate of not more than 30 flashes per minute) are placed only on black or red buoys, or on special purpose buoys.

Quick flashing lights (not less than 60 flashes each minute) are placed only on channel-edge-marking black and red buoys; these are used at points where it is desired to indicate that *special caution* in piloting is required, as at sharp turns or changes in the width of the waterway, or where used to mark wrecks or dangerous obstructions that must be passed only on one side.

Interrupted quick flashing lights are used only on buoys painted with red-and-black horizontal bands. These are the buoys at channel junctions and obstructions that can be passed on either side.

Morse code "A" flashing lights (short-long flashing) are placed only on black-and-white vertically striped buoys that mark a fairway or midchannel; these are passed close to, on either side. The lights are always white.

On the Mississippi and other Western Rivers, the light characteristics are somewhat different; see page 532.

WRECK BUOYS

Buoys established by the Coast Guard to mark dangerous wrecks are generally placed on the seaward or channel side of the obstruction and as near to it as conditions permit. Lighted buoys are normally used. Buoys are solid red or black if they can be safely passed on only one side; horizontally banded if passed on either side. Wreck buoys are numbered in regular sequence, preceded by "WR."

Caution must be exercised when navigating in the vicinity of buoys marking wrecks because, due to sea action, the wreck may shift in location between the time that the buoy is established and when it is later checked or serviced.

STATION BUOYS

Important buoys, usually large combination buoys, with both light and sound signals, are sometimes accompanied by *station buoys*. These are smaller, unlighted buoys, see fig. 1520, placed in the vicinity of the main buoy on the side away from marine traffic. They are colored and numbered the same as the main buoy. Station buoys are not charted; their existence is noted, however, in the Light Lists in the remarks column for the major aid to which they are related.

The purpose of the station buoy is to mark the location should the main buoy be sunk or carried away for any reason, such as being struck by a passing ship. The station buoy serves as a temporary substitute and aids in the replacement of the main buoy on the correct location.

DAYBEACONS AND MINOR LIGHTS

Although the lateral system of buoyage has been described in terms of unlighted and lighted buoys, the use of comparable daybeacons and minor lights is fully applicable.

Daybeacons with red triangular daymarks may be substituted for nun buoys, or ones with green (black) square daymarks may replace can buoys, where the water is shallow enough to make such installations practicable. Minor lights may be used in place of lighted or combination buoys. Structures subject to being repeatedly struck by vessels may be set back from the channel edge; if this is done, it will be noted in the applicable Light List.

Occasionally, daybeacons will be used to indicate a channel junction or obstruction. In such a case, the daymark will be red-and-black horizontally banded with the color of the uppermost band indicating the main or preferred channel. The shape of the daymark will be either square or triangular as determined by the color or the top band, similar to the use of a can or nun buoy for this purpose.

Daybeacons used to mark fairways or the middle of a channel will have an octagonal-shaped daymark, painted white and black, divided vertically down the middle.

A diamond-shaped daymark has *no* significance in the lateral system. A typical application might be to increase the daytime detectability of a minor light which is not a part of a channel or waterway series.

INTRACOASTAL WATERWAY AIDS

The Coast Guard maintains the system of aids to navigation along the Atlantic and Gulf Intracoastal Waterway (ICW). The coloring and numbering of buoys and daybeacons, and the color of lights on buoys and light structures, is in conformity with the lateral system of buoyage as described above. The system is applied by considering passage from north to south along the Atlantic coast, and from south to north and east to west along the Gulf coast, as corresponding to returning from sea in an entrance channel. Thus, red buoys and fixed aids are on the right side of the channel when proceeding from New Jersey toward Florida and then on to Texas; black aids are on the left hand side of the Waterway when proceeding in the same direction. This rule is applied in a uniform manner from one end of the Intracoastal Waterway to the other, regardless of widely varying compass headings on

FIG. 1520 Station buoys are occasionally used in conjunction with major combination buoys. These are placed near the main buoy on the side away from ship traffic. Such buoys are not separately charted, but they are mentioned in the Light Lists. The older tapered "wasp-waist" design of buoy superstructure is giving way to a newer straight-sided design.

many stretches, and the fact that rivers and other waterways marked by the seacoast system are occasionally followed.

The aids to navigation do differ in one respect, however, in that they carry on additional distinctive marking to identify the ICW route. This special marking is applied to the so-called "inside route" and to those portions of all connecting waterways that must be crossed or followed to make a continuous passage.

Distinctive ICW markings

All buoys, daymarks on daybeacons and lights, marking the Intracoastal Waterway have some portion painted *yellow*. This is the distinctive coloring adopted for the ICW. Buoys will be marked with a band of yellow at the top; daymarks will have a yellow border or a yellow stripe immediately below the numeral or letter. For examples of these markings, see the color illustrations on page J.

The numbering of Intracoastal Waterway aids follows the same basic rule as for entrance channels, with numbers increasing in the direction from New Jersey toward Florida and Texas: Aids are numbered in groups, usually not exceeding 99, beginning again with "1" or "2" at specified natural dividing points.

Lights on buoys follow the standard system of red or white lights on red buoys, and green or white lights on black buoys. The color of lights on fixed structures follows the same general system. Range lights, not being a part of the lateral system, may be any of the three standard colors.

Dual marking

In order that vessels may readily follow the Intracoastal Waterway where it coincides with another route such as an important river marked on the seacoast system, special *dual markings* are employed. These are applied to the buoys or other aids that mark the river channel for other traffic. Special marks consist of a yellow square or a yellow triangle painted on a conspicuous part of the dual-purpose aid. The yellow square, in outline similar to a can buoy, indicates that the aid on which it is placed should be kept on the left-hand side when following the ICW in the direction from New Jersey to Texas. The yellow triangle, in outline similar to a nun buoy, indicates that the aid should be kept on the right hand side when traveling in the same direction.

The yellow squares may appear on *either* a black can or a red nun of the river channel marks (or comparable daybeacons and light structures). Similarly, the yellow triangle dual markings may appear on any type of lateral aid. These similarly contradictory markings result from the fact that in some situations a southbound ICW route (red nuns on the right side) will be *up* a river channel from seaward (red nuns on the right side); and in other situations, the same ICW route will be down a river toward the sea where black cans will be on the skipper's right side. In both of these situations, however, the yellow triangle will be kept to the right. See page J.

Where the yellow squares and triangles are added to regular river or harbor aids to navigation, the ICW yellow band or border is omitted.

Where dual marking is employed, the boatman following the ICW disregards the shape and coloring of the aid on which the yellow square or triangle is placed and pilots his craft solely by the shape of the yellow markings. The numbers on the aids will be those of the river's lateral system, and in some instances where the southward ICW proceeds down a river, the numbers will be temporarily decreasing rather than increasing. See page J.

By this system of dual marking, the mariner approaching a body of water such as the Cape Fear River, and realizing that he must follow it for some distance before again entering a dredged land cut of the Intracoastal Waterway, knows that his course lies along such buoys or other aids as are specially marked in yellow. He determines the side of his craft on which these aids should be passed by the shape of the yellow marks, keeping always in mind the basic direction of his ICW travel.

Special Purpose Buoys

In addition to the lateral system of buoyage maintained by the Coast Guard in Federal-jurisdiction waters, several special-purpose buoy characteristics, having no lateral significance, are used to mark dredging areas, anchorages, quarantine areas, fish net areas, race courses, experiments or tests, etc.

The meaning of special-purpose buoys is indicated by their colors as follows:

White buoys mark *anchorage* areas.

Note carefully the difference between an *anchorage* buoy and a *mooring* buoy — an anchorage buoy is an aid to navigation marking the boundary of an area in which vessels may be anchored in accordance with prescribed regulations. A mooring buoy is a strong, heavily anchored buoy to which vessels can be made fast in lieu of anchoring; they are charted and, while not properly aids to navigation, they can help in piloting.

White buoys with green tops are used in connection with *dredging* and *survey* operations.

White-and-black horizontally banded buoys mark fish

net areas. Particularly, but not exclusively, in the Chesapeake Bay area, such buoys are used to mark the boundaries of areas in which fish nets and traps may be placed; such areas and buoys are indicated on charts. (See fig. 1521.) These buoys may be cans or nuns, the shape has no significance; they carry identification numbers and letters.

White-and-international-orange buoys, with either horizontal bands or vertical stripes, are used for special purposes to which neither the lateral-system colors nor the other special-purpose colors are applicable. (See fig. 1522.)

Special-purpose buoys are illustrated in color at the bottom of page L.

Yellow-and-black vertically striped buoys mark seaplane operating areas and have no marine significance other than to indicate the need for caution and a sharp lookout for aircraft.

FIG. 1521 A black-and-white horizontally banded buoy is charted here at the intersection of lines (long and short dash) indicating outer limits of a fish trap area.

FIG. 1522 Positions of white-and-orange horizontally banded special purpose buoys marking a measured half-mile are indicated on this chart. These are lettered for identification and it is indicated that they are privately maintained.

313

Special-purpose buoys may be lighted or unlighted, and some may have a fog signal. These buoys may be of any shape if unlighted—can, nun, or spherical.

SPECIAL—TYPE BUOYS

Special-type buoys may be encountered in all waters. Typical of these in inland waters are the buoys used in current surveys. The shape, size, color, lights (if any), markings, etc., vary too widely to be described here, but will be completely listed in the public notices that are always published before such buoys are placed in navigable waters.

Offshore boatmen may occasionally encounter large sea buoys used for gathering meteorological or oceanographic data, or those employed in naval defense operations.

Uniform State Buoyage System

Each state has authority over control of navigation on waters that lie wholly within its boundaries. This includes the responsibility for the establishment and maintenance of aids to navigation. Each state is free to mark its waters according to any system that it desires. Initially, the result of this freedom was a considerable variance in the ways that inland waters not subject to Federal jurisdiction were marked. More recently, however, although the states still retain their authority, they have agreed to adopt a single consistent system of markers. With trailer-borne craft traveling freely over the highways from state to state, the gain for boatmen from the uniform system is too obvious to discuss in detail. The rambling skipper no longer has to try to decipher the significance of what had been intended to serve him as an "aid to navigation."

By Act of Congress, the Uniform State Waterway Marking System (USWMS) may be extended to cover waters subject to Federal jurisdiction, but which have not been marked with aids by the Coast Guard. Agreements may be entered into between a Coast Guard District Commander and state officials for the designation of "state waters for private aids to navigation." In such waters, state or local governments may establish and maintain aids to navigation which comply with the standards of the USWMS.

MAJOR FEATURES OF THE USWMS

The Uniform State Waterway Marking System has been developed to provide a means to convey to the small craft operator, in particular, adequate guidance to indicate safe boating channels by indicating the presence of either natural or artificial obstructions or hazards. The USWMS also provides means for marking restricted or controlled areas and for providing directions. The system is suited for use in all water areas and designed to satisfy the needs of all types of small vessels. It supplements and is generally compatible with the lateral system of aids to navigation maintained by the Coast Guard.

The USWMS consists of two categories of aids to navigation:

(1) A system of regulatory markers to indicate to the pilot the existence of dangerous areas as well as those which are restricted or controlled, such as speed zones and areas set aside for a particular use, or to provide general information and directions.

(2) A system of aids to navigation to supplement the Federal lateral system of buoyage.

Regulatory markers

On Federal waters, the boatman can turn to his charts, Light Lists, Coast Pilots, and other publications for information on natural hazards, zoned areas, directions, distances, etc., to supplement the knowledge that he gets from buoys, daybeacons, and other aids. On state waters, he now has a uniform system of water signs or markers that, in themselves, convey their message without reference to any publication — an obvious advantage, especially for inexperienced boatmen.

Just as Intracoastal Waterway markers are distinguished by their special yellow borders or other yellow marks, state regulatory markers are identified by international-orange-and-white colors. On buoys, an orange band will be seen near the top and bottom; on the white area between these bands, a geometric shape, also in orange, will be noted. An open diamond shape indicates danger. A diamond with a cross inside indicates a prohibited area; vessels are excluded from the area marked by such buoys. A circle signifies zoning or control; vessels operating in such areas are subject to certain operating restrictions. A square or rectangular shape signals the conveying of information, the details of which are spelled out within the shape. (See fig. 1523 and color page L.)

Where the regulatory marker consists of a square or

FIG. 1523 Uniform state regulatory markers convey their meaning to the boatman without need for reference to charts or other publications.

DANGER! Warns of rocks, reefs, dams, snags, or other hazards.

BOATS KEEP OUT! Marks waterfalls, swim areas, rapids, and other restricted areas.

RESTRICTION! Type of control is indicated within the circle such as No ski, speed zone, No anchoring.

INFORMATION! Tells distances, locations, other official information.

FIG. 1524 Running upstream, in state waters, a boat passes between black buoys (on port side) and red buoys (to starboard), outside of (away from shore) a red-and-white striped obstruction buoy, south (or west) of a white buoy with red top, and north (or east) of a white buoy with black top.

How buoys might be placed in a typical waterway under state jurisdiction

(UPSTREAM)

| Black | White | Red | Blue |

rectangular shaped sign displayed from a structure, the sign is white with an international orange border. If a diamond or circular shape is associated with the meaning of the marker, it will be centered on the signboard.

The geometric shape displayed on a regulatory marker is intended to convey the basic idea of danger, or control, etc., so that the boatman can tell at a distance whether he should stay away or may safely approach for more information. To convey a specific meaning, spelled-out words or recognized abbreviations appear within the shape. The sole exception to this is the cross within the diamond shape that is used to absolutely prohibit boats from entering an area, because of danger to the boat, swimmers in a protected area, or for any other reason sufficient to warrant exclusion by law.

To minimize the risk of misinterpretation, initials, symbols, and silhouettes have not been used. In some cases, words may be needed outside the geometric shape to give the reason, authority, or some clarification of the specific meaning.

Aids to navigation

The second category of marker in the USWMS is the aid to navigation having lateral or cardinal meaning. In selecting types of buoys for use on waters not marked by the Coast Guard, the principal objective was to make the state system compatible with the Federal.

On a well-defined channel, including a river or other relatively narrow natural or improved waterway, an aid to navigation of the USWMS is normally a solid-colored buoy. A buoy that marks the left side of a channel viewed *looking upstream* or toward the head of navigation is colored *solid black*. A buoy that marks the *right* side, looking in the same direction, is colored *solid red*. (This, it will be noted, is the same as the Coast Guard lateral system.) On a well-defined channel, solid-colored buoys will be found

in pairs, one for each side of the channel that they mark, and opposite each other, leaving no doubt that the channel lies between the red and the black buoys, and that the skipper should pilot his boat between them.

On irregularly defined channels, solid-colored buoys may be used singly in staggered fashion on alternate sides provided that they are spaced at sufficiently close intervals to clearly inform the skipper that the channel lies between the buoys and that he should pass between them.

Where there is no well-defined channel, or when a body of water is obstructed by objects whose nature or location is such that the hazard might be approached from more than one direction, a *cardinal* system is used. The use of cardinal system aids to navigation is strictly limited to waters wholly subject to state jurisdiction or waters covered by a Coast Guard-state agreement. This restriction is necessary as the Coast Guard's lateral system makes no provision for markers of the cardinal system.

A white buoy with red top indicates that a boat must pass to the *south or west* of the buoy.

A white buoy with black top indicates that the safe water is to the *north or east* of the buoy.

A buoy with alternate red and white vertical stripes indicates that an obstruction extends from the nearest shore to the buoy, and that the boat must not pass between the buoy and that shore. The number of red and white stripes may vary, but the width of the white stripes will always be twice that of the red ones. See fig. 1524.

Characteristics of markers and aids

The size, shape, material, and construction of all markers, fixed or floating, is discretionary with the state authorities. They must, however, be such as to be observable under normal conditions of visibility at a distance such that the significance of the marker or aid will be recognizable before a craft stands into danger.

Numbers.

State aids to navigation and regulatory markers may carry numbers, letters, or words. These must be placed in a manner so as to be clearly visible to approaching and passing boats, with characters in block style, well proportioned and as large as the available space permits. Numbers and letters on red or black backgrounds will be in white; on white backgrounds, they will be black. The use of numbers on buoys is optional, but if used will conform to the following system:

Odd numbers will be used on *solid black* buoys and on *black-topped* buoys.

Even numbers will be used on *solid red* buoys and on *red-topped* buoys.

All numbers will *increase* in an *upstream* direction or toward the head of navigation.

Letters only may be used to identify regulatory markers and red-and-white vertically striped obstruction buoys. If used, letters will follow an alphabetical sequence in the upstream direction; the letters "I" and "O" will not be used to prevent possible confusion with numbers.

Reflectors

The use of reflectors or reflective tape is discretionary with the local authorities maintaining the markers and aids. If used, red reflectors or reflective material will be used on solid red buoys, and green on solid black buoys.

All other buoys will have white reflectors or reflective material, as will regulatory markers, except that orange reflectors may be placed on the orange portions of such markers.

Lights

Lights may be used on USWMS regulatory markers and aids to navigation if desired by the state authorities. When used, lights on solid colored buoys will be regularly flashing, regularly occulting, or equal interval. (An "occulting" light is one that is on more than it is off.) For ordinary purposes, the rate of flashing will not be more than 30 times per minute.

When lights have a distinct cautionary significance, such as at sharp bends in a channel, the light may be quick flashing, not less than 60 flashes each minute.

When a light is placed on a cardinal system buoy or a red-and-white vertically striped buoy, it will always be quick flashing.

Red lights are used only on solid red buoys, green lights only on solid black buoys. White lights will be used on all other buoys and on regulatory markers.

Ownership markings

The use and placement of ownership identification is discretionary. If used, such markings must be worded and placed in such a manner that they will not detract from the meaning being conveyed as a regulatory marker or aid to navigation.

Mooring buoys

Mooring buoys in waters covered by the Uniform State Waterway Marking System will be white with a horizontal blue band around them midway between the waterline and the top of the buoy.

A lighted mooring buoy will normally show a slow flashing white light. If, however, its location is such that it is an obstruction to craft operating during hours of darkness, the light will be quick flashing white.

A mooring buoy may carry ownership identification provided that such markings do not detract from the meaning intended to be conveyed by the color scheme and identification letter, if assigned.

Illustration of the USWMS
The Uniform State Waterway Marking System is illustrated in color on page L.

Other Buoyage Systems

Buoyage on the "Western Rivers of the United States" (the Mississippi and its tributaries, and certain other designated rivers) conforms to the lateral system, but includes some additional shapes and daymarks not found in other areas. See the color illustration on page K.

On these rivers, unlighted buoys are not numbered, while the numbers on lighted buoys have no lateral significance, rather indicating the number of miles upstream from a designated reference point.

Additional details on the buoyage of the Western Rivers will be found in Chapter 27.

Foreign waters

Boatmen who carry their cruising into foreign waters should, prior to departure, fully acquaint themselves with the buoyage systems to be encountered. Significant differences from the U. S. lateral system may be found, and there will be variations between the systems used in different countries.

In Canadian waters, the lateral system of buoyage is essentially the same as in the United States. Minor differences in the physical appearance of buoys may be noted, but these should not be great enough to result in any confusion. Chart symbols, likewise, may be slightly different from those standardized for use on U. S. charts.

The nations of northwestern Europe—England and France, west to Ireland, north to Norway and Sweden, east to Poland and Russia—are establishing a new uniform buoyage system known as "System A—The Combined Cardinal and Lateral System (red to port)." Implementation will start in 1977 and extend to 1981 and beyond.

The new buoyage system will use five types of "marks" —those of lateral and cardinal systems, plus three different marks for isolated dangers and safe waters, and for special indications. Not all types will be used in all waters, but those that are used will conform to System A with respect to shapes, colors, topmarks, and light color and "rhythm."

Skipper's responsibility

A skipper must be familiar with the system of buoyage he will encounter before entering foreign coastal waters. He must consult the appropriate official publications or cruising guides for the necessary information.

CHAPTER 16

AIDS TO NAVIGATION —
Lighthouses and Other Aids

The preceding chapter covered the many thousands of aids to navigation that mark rivers and channels for watercraft of all sizes. These constitute the majority in the system of aids in U.S. waters, but there are other, major aids to serve the mariner. These other aids and systems provide guidance to the navigator making a landfall after a sea voyage or piloting his vessel along a coast. Electronic systems serve to help the navigator fix his position when he is out of sight of land because of darkness, fog, or distance. Primary and secondary lights, lightships and offshore tower light stations, fog signals, and ranges and directional lights will be considered in this chapter to complete the topic of aids to navigation. Electronic navigation systems are covered in Chapter 25.

Primary Seacoast and Secondary Lights

Primary seacoast and *secondary lights* are so designated because of their greater importance as aids to navigation. In general, they differ from the minor lights considered in Chapter 15 by their physical size, intensity of light, and complexity of light characteristics. These lights are more individual in nature than minor lights and buoys; only broad, general statements can be made about them as a group.

Primary seacoast lights are maintained to warn the high-seas navigator of the proximity of land. They are the first aids to navigation to be seen when making a landfall (except where there may be a lightship, light tower, or large navigational buoy). A coastwise pilot can use these lights to keep farther offshore at night than by using other visual aids. These are the most powerful and distinctive lights in the U.S. system of aids to navigation.

Primary seacoast lights may be located on the mainland or offshore on islands and shoals. When located offshore, they may mark a specific hazard or they may serve merely as a marker for ships approaching a major harbor.

Many primary seacoast lights are so classified from the importance of their location, the intensity of the light, and the prominence of the structure. Other aids will be classed as *secondary lights* because of their lesser qualities in one or more of these characteristics. The dividing line, however, is not clear cut, and lights that may seem to be more properly in one category may be classified in the other group in the Light Lists (see page 331). The difference in classification is of no real significance to boatmen and it can be ignored in practical piloting situations.

STRUCTURES

The physical structure of a primary seacoast light and many secondary lights is generally termed a *lighthouse,* although this is not an official designation used in the Light Lists. The principal purpose is to support a light source and

Figures 1606-1609

from official U. S. COAST GUARD

photographs

lens at a considerable height above water. The same structure may also house a fog signal, radiobeacon, equipment, and quarters for the operating personnel. In many instances, however, the auxiliary equipment and personnel are housed in separate buildings nearby; such a group of buildings is called a *light station.*

Lighthouses vary greatly in their outward appearance, determined in part by their location, whether in the water or on shore, the importance of the light, the kind of soil on which it is constructed, and the prevalence of violent storms; see fig. 1601.

Lighthouses also vary in appearance with the distance at which their lights must be seen. Where the need is for a relatively great range, a tall tower with a light of high candlepower is erected. Conversely, at points intermediate to the principal lights, where ship traffic is light, and where long range is not so necessary, a less expensive structure of more modest dimensions is constructed.

The terms, "secondary light" and "minor light," indicate in a general way a wide variety of lights, one class shading imperceptibly into the other. These lights may be displayed from towers resembling the most important seacoast lights, or from a relatively inexpensive structure. The essential features of a light structure where operating personnel are not in residence are: best possible location as determined by the physical characteristics of the site, sufficient height for the requirements of the light, a rugged support for the light itself, and proper shelter for the power source. Many

(Text continued on page 320)

MILE ROCKS LIGHT, at the entrance to San Francisco harbor, was built in 1906. In 1966, its tower superstructure was cut off to provide a landing platform for helicopters. No longer manned, operation is automatic. A horn fog signal is remotely controlled from Pt. Bonita Light.

During periods of low visibility, CHARLESTON LIGHT on south side of Sullivans Island (S.C.) shows a 28,000,000 candlepower flash visible 26 miles (48 km) seaward. Built in 1962, this modern 140-foot (42.7 m) elevator-equipped structure is one of the world's tallest lights.

New and old lights at CAPE ▲ HENRY, Va., at the entrance to Chesapeake Bay. The old tower, no longer lighted, was the first built by the Federal Government.

On the lower coast of Maine, CAPE NEDDICK LIGHT is situated on a small rock islet called The Nubble, separated by a narrow channel from Cape Neddick, a headland which juts out a mile into the Atlantic.

AMERICAN LIGHTS –

▲ PEMAQUID POINT LIGHT (Maine) is a secondary light of 10,000 candlepower, visible 14 miles (25.9 km) from a white pyramidal tower, 79 feet (24 m) above water. Originally established in 1827, the rebuilt structure dates to 1857.

◄ SPLIT ROCK LIGHT, on a rocky cliff in Minnesota on Lake Superior, is one of the most frequently visited. Standing 178 feet (54.3 m) above water, its 1,000,000 candlepower beam is visible 23 miles (42.6 km).

318

▲ **EASTERN POINT LIGHT** (Mass.) has guided Gloucestermen for more than a century. Its white brick tower, built in 1890, replaces one built in 1832.

▲ **PORTLAND HEAD LIGHT,** at Cape Elizabeth, Me., guards the entrance to Portland harbor with a 200,000 candlepower beam. The original station dates back to 1791.

◄ Isolated **CAPE SPENCER LIGHT,** 150 miles (278 km) from a town, marks the northern entrance from the Pacific into the Inside Passage of southeastern Alaska. It is a primary light, fog signal, and radio-beacon station.

▶

FOWEY ROCKS LIGHT, a skeleton iron structure, is typical of those used on the Florida Reefs at Carysfort Reef, Alligator Reef, Sombrero Key, American Shoal and Sand Key.

—Safeguards of Coastal Navigation

PHOTO CREDITS—Cape Henry, Sullivan's Island, Fowey Rocks, Dry Tortugas, Galveston, and Mile Rocks Official U.S. Coast Guard photos. Portland Head, Cape Neddick and Pemaquid from Kodachromes by Wm. H. Koelbel.

GALVESTON (Texas) **SOUTH JETTY LIGHT** flashes an Equal Interval Green light which has a period of 6 seconds—3 seconds on, 3 seconds off. A horn fog signal operates seasonally from 1 November to 1 May.
▼

◄ **DRY TORTUGAS LIGHT** on Loggerhead Key in the Gulf of Mexico was established in 1826, rebuilt in 1858. The conical black and white tower is 157 feet (47.9 m) high; the light is visible 19 miles (35.2 km).

forms of structures meet these requirements—small houses topped with a short skeleton tower, a cluster of piles supporting a battery box and light, and countless others.

Many lights originally tended by resident keepers are now operated automatically because of the availability of commercial electric power and reliable equipment. There are also a great many automatic lights on inexpensive structures, cared for by periodic visits of Coast Guard cutters or by attendants who are in charge of a group of such aids.

The recent introduction of much new automatic equipment means that the relative importance of lights can no longer be judged on the basis of whether or not they have resident personnel. A number of major lights are now operated without continuous attention; humans have been replaced by automatic failure indicators and telemetry.

Coloring of structures

Lighthouses and other light structures are marked with various colors for the purpose of making them readily distinguishable from the backgrounds against which they are seen, and to make possible the identification of individual lights among others that are in the same general area. Solid colors, bands of color, stripes, and various other patterns are used, fig. 1602.

LIGHT CHARACTERISTICS

Primary seacoast and secondary lights are assigned distinctive light characteristics so that one may be distinguished from another. These characteristics are achieved by using lights of different colors, and by having some that show continuously while others go on and off in regular patterns of great variety. Actually, in these days of modern electronic navigation there is much less need for special distinctive characteristics of major lights—those were necessary when a navigator making a landfall might have been in doubt as to whether he was approaching the coast of Maryland or Virginia, or even farther to the north or south.

The three standard colors used for the lights of major aids to navigation are white, red, and green.

Light phase characteristics

By varying the length of the intervals of light and darkness, a considerable number of individual *light phase characteristics* may be obtained.

The term "flashing" has already been defined in Chapter 15 as a light that is on less than it is off in a regular sequence of single flashes occurring less than 30 times each minute. Some primary seacoast and secondary lights will "flash" in accordance with such a definition although their characteristics will have no relation to the flashes of buoys and minor lights. In general, a flashing major light will have a longer period (time of one complete cycle of the characteristic) and may have a longer flash; for example, Cape Hatteras Light flashes once every 15 seconds with a 3-second flash. On the other hand, some of the newer aids are equipped with xenon-discharge-tube lights that give a very brilliant, but very brief, flash. The intensity of these lights can be varied for periods of good or bad visibility. A few major lights may be "fixed"—a continuous light without change of intensity or color.

Typically, however, the light phase characteristic of a primary seacoast or secondary light will be more complex. These are described below aids and are illustrated in fig. 1603.

MASONRY STRUCTURE   CYLINDRICAL TOWER SQUARE HOUSE ON CYLINDRICAL BASE   SKELETON IRON STRUCTURE

TYPICAL LIGHT STRUCTURES

FIG. 1601. Primary seacoast and secondary lights are mounted on a wide variety of structures. The location of the light, whether on shore or rising from the water; the degree of exposure to violent storms; the need for great height; and many other factors determine the type of structure. Physical characteristics of the structures are described in the Light Lists.

Group flashing (Gp. Fl.)—the cycle of the light characteristic consists of two or more flashes separated by brief intervals and followed by a longer interval of darkness.

Alternating flashing (Alt. Fl.)—flashes of alternating color, usually white and red, or white and green.

Occulting (Occ.)—the light is on more than it is off. The interval of time that the light is *lighted* is greater than the time that it is *eclipsed*.

Equal interval (E. Int.)—the periods of light and darkness are equal; the light will be described in the Light List or on charts in terms of the period, the lighted and eclipsed portions each being just half of that time interval.

Group Occulting (Gp. Occ.)—intervals of light regularly broken by a series of two or more eclipses. This characteristic may have all eclipses of equal length or one may be greater than the others.

Fixed and Flashing (F. and Fl.)—a fixed light varied at regular intervals by a flash of greater intensity. The flash may be of the same color as the fixed light (usually white) or of another color. This characteristic may also appear as *fixed and group.flashing (F. and Gp. Fl.)*.

Complex characteristics

The above light phase characteristics may be combined. Examples might include "Group flashing white, alternating flashing red" (Gp. Fl. W. Alt. Fl. R.)—Gay Head Light—with three white and one red flash in each 40-second period; or "Gp. Fl. W., (1 4 3)"—Minots Ledge Light where 1½-second flashes occur at 1½-second intervals in groups of one, four, and three separated by 5-second intervals and followed by a 15½-second longer interval to indicate the proper starting point of the 45-second period; or others of a generally similar nature.

Perhaps one of the most complex characteristics was that of Halfway Rock Light off the Maine Coast where the description was "alternating fixed white, red, and flashing red" (Alt. F. W., R., and Fl. R.)—in a 90-second, period, the light showed fixed white for 59 seconds, fixed red for 14 seconds, a high-intensity red flash for 3 seconds, and fixed red again for the final 14 seconds—this was certainly a distinctive enough characteristic to avoid any confusion.

BOSTON, MASS.　　ST. AUGUSTINE, FLA.　　CAPE HENRY, VA.　　TYBEE, GA.

FIG. 1602. The physical structure supporting a primary seacoast light, usually referred to as a lighthouse, may be painted in a number of different patterns for better daytime identification. The colors are usually black and white. Details are given in the Light Lists.

COLORING OF TYPICAL LIGHTHOUSES

Sectors

Many lights will have *sectors,* portions of their all-around arc of visibility in which the normally white light is seen as red. These mark shoals or other hazards, or warn mariners of nearby land.

Lights so equipped show one color from most directions, but a different color or colors over definite arcs of the horizon as indicated on charts and in the Light Lists. A sector changes the color of a light when viewed from certain directions, but *not* the flashing or occulting characteristic. For example, a flashing white light having a red sector, when viewed from within the sector, will appear as flashing red, fig. 1604.

Sectors may be a few degrees in width, as when marking a shoal or rock, or of such width as to extend from the di-

FIG. 1604. Many lights that are basically white in color have one or more **red sectors** to mark areas of shoal water or other hazards. The light will have the same phase characteristics in both the white and red sectors. Red sectors will be indicated on charts and described in the Light Lists.

rection of deep water to the shore. Bearings referring to sectors are expressed in degrees *as observed from a vessel toward the light.*

In the vast majority of situations, water areas covered by red sectors should be avoided, but in all cases the extent of the hazard should be determined from an examination of the chart for the vicinity. A few lights are basically red (for danger) with one or more white sectors marking the direction of safe passage through the hazards. A narrow white sector may also be used to mark a turning point in a channel.

Lights may also have sectors in which the light is *obscured* and cannot be seen. These will be shown graphically on charts, see fig. 1605, and described in words and figures in the Lights Lists.

THE VISIBILITY OF LIGHTS

The theoretical visibility of a light in clear weather depends upon two factors, its intensity and its height above water. The intensity of the light fixes its *nominal range* which is defined in Coast Guard Light Lists as "the maximum distance at which the light may be seen in clear weather (meteor-

Illustration	Symbols and meaning		
	Lights which do not change color	Lights which show color variations	Phase description
	F. = Fixed . . .	Alt. = Alternating.	A continuous steady light.
	F. Fl. = Fixed and flashing	Alt. F. Fl. = Alternating fixed and flashing.	A fixed light varied at regular intervals by a flash of greater brilliance.
	F. Gp. Fl. = Fixed and group flashing.	Alt. F. Gp. Fl. = Alternating fixed and group flashing.	A fixed light varied at regular intervals by groups of 2 or more flashes of greater brilliance.
	Fl. = Flashing	Alt. Fl. = Alternating flashing.	Showing a single flash at regular intervals, the duration of light always being less than the duration of darkness.
	Gp. Fl. = Group flashing.	Alt. Gp. Fl. = Alternating group flashing.	Showing at regular intervals groups of 2 or more flashes.
	Gp. Fl. (1+2) = Composite group flashing.	——	Light flashes are combined in alternate groups of different numbers.
	E. Int. = Equal interval.	——	Light with all durations of light and darkness equal.
	Occ. = Occulting.	Alt. Occ. = Alternating occulting.	A light totally eclipsed at regular intervals, the duration of light always greater than the duration of darkness.
	Gp. Occ. = Group Occulting.	——	A light with a group of 2 or more eclipses at regular intervals.
	Gp. Occ. (2+3) = Composite group occulting.	——	A light in which the occultations are combined in alternate groups of different numbers.

FIG. 1603. Primary seacoast and secondary lights flash with specific **light phase characteristics.** These permit rapid and positive identification at night. The time for a light to go through one full cycle of changes is called its **period.**

ological visibility of 10 nautical miles)." Height is, of course, important because of the curvature of the earth. It determines what is known as the *geographic range* which is not affected by the intensity (provided that the light is bright enough to be seen out to the full distance of the geographic range).

As a rule, the nominal range of major lights is greater than the geographic, and the distance from which such aids can be seen is limited only by the earth's curvature. Such lights are often termed "strong"; conversely, a light limited by its luminous range can be called a "weak light."

Often, the glare, or *loom,* of strong lights may be seen far beyond the stated geographic range. Occasionally, under rare atmospheric conditions, the light itself may be visible at unusual distances. On the other hand, and unfortunately more frequently, the range of visibility may be lessened by rain, fog, snow, haze, or smoke.

FIG. 1605. Some lights — particularly those on shore—will have sectors in which they cannot be seen at all. The light is said to be "obscured" in these sectors which are indicated on the chart and described in the Light Lists.

Light Lists show the nominal range when such is 5 miles (9.26 km) or more. Rules are given for a conversion of nominal range to *luminous* range, the maximum distance at which a light may be seen in *existing* visibility. Both nominal and luminous ranges take no account of elevation, observer's height of eye, or the curvature of the earth. For lights of complex characteristics, nominal ranges are given for each color and/or intensity.

The geographic range of lights is no longer given in the Light Lists, but may be calculated from information in the front pages of each Light List volume or from Table II, page 603. Boatmen should know their height of eye when at the controls of their craft and be aware of the greater range obtainable from a greater height above water.

Lights on inland waters, where their radius of usefulness is not great, are frequently "weak" lights of insufficient intensity to reach the full limit of their geographic range.

IDENTIFICATION OF LIGHTS

Charts can only briefly describe the characteristics of a primary seacoast or secondary light by means of abbreviations and a notation of the total period of the light cycle. It will often be necessary to consult the Light List for the details of the characteristic that may be needed for positive identification.

When a light is first observed, its color should be noted, and, by means of a watch or clock with a second hand, a check made of the time required for the light to go through its full cycle of changes. If color, period, and number of flashes per cycle agree with the information in the Light

List, correct identification has been accomplished. As a further check, however, the charts and Light List should be examined to see if any other light in the vicinity might have such similar characteristics that there could be a case of mistaken identity. If there is any doubt, a careful timing of the length of all flashes and dark intervals should be made and compared with the Light List entries; this will normally be conclusive.

CAUTIONS IN USING LIGHTS

Complex lights with several luminous ranges may appear differently at extreme distances where, for example, a white fixed (or flashing) light could be seen but a red flash of the same light was not yet within luminous range. Examination of a Light List will show that usually the nominal range of a red or green light is 15% to 30% *less* than that of the white light from the same aid. Caution must be used in light identification under such circumstances.

The effect of fog, rain, snow, haze, etc., on the visibility of lights is obvious. Colored lights are more quickly lost to sight than are white lights under weather conditions that tend to reduce visibility. On the other hand, refraction may cause a light to be seen at a greater distance than would normally be expected.

Caution must also be applied when using light sectors. The actual boundaries between the colors are not so sharp and distinct as indicated on the chart; the lights shade gradually from one color into the other. Allow an adequate margin for safety when piloting by colored light sectors.

The increasing use of brilliant shore lights for advertising, illuminating bridges, and other purposes may cause marine navigational lights, particularly those in densely populated areas, to be outshone and difficult to distinguish from the background lighting.

There is always the possibility of a light's being extinguished. In the case of unattended lights, this condition may not be immediately detected and corrected. If lights are not sighted within a reasonable time after prediction from the course and speed of the boat, a dangerous situation may exist requiring prompt action to ensure the safety of the craft and its crew.

Do not rely on any *one* light, except perhaps for making a landfall. Use several lights *together* as a system, checking each against the others.

High intensity lights

At some locations, there is a "high intensity light" which has a greater intensity than the "main light" normally operated from that location. This is operated only under conditions of reduced visibility.

Emergency lights

Emergency lights of reduced nominal range are displayed from many light stations when the main light is inoperative. These standby lights may or may not have the same characteristics as the main light. The existence of the standby light (if any) and its characteristics (if different) may be noted in the Light List.

Fog Signals

Any sound-producing instrument operated in time of fog from a definite point shown on a chart serves as a useful fog signal. To be effective as an aid to navigation, a pilot must be able to identify it and know from what location it is sounded.

The simpler fog signals used on buoys and at minor lights have been covered in Chapter 15. There it was noted that such signals operated by the action of the sea cannot be entirely depended upon and identification might be difficult. At all lighthouses and lightships equipped with fog signals, these devices are operated by mechanical or electrical means and are sounded on definite time schedules during periods of low visibility to provide the desirable feature of positive identification.

SIGNAL CHARACTERISTICS

Fog signal characteristics are described in terms of the length of a total cycle consisting of one or more *blasts* of specific length and one or more *silent intervals,* also of definite lengths. These times are shown in the Light Lists to aid in identification. (Normally, only type of fog signal, without further details, is indicated on charts.) Where counting the number of blasts and the total time for the signal to complete a cycle is necessary for identification, reference must be made to details in Light List.

Fog signal equipment

The various types of fog signals differ in tone, and this also aids in identification. The type of fog signal for each station is shown in the Light Lists and on charts.

Diaphones produce sound by means of a slotted reciprocating piston actuated by compressed air. Blasts may consist of two tones of different pitch, in which case the first part of the blast is higher pitch and the latter is lower. These alternate-pitch signals are termed "two-tone."

Diaphragm horns produce sound by means of a disc diaphragm vibrated by compressed air or electricity. Duplex or triplex horn units of different pitch are sometimes combined to produce a more musical signal.

Sirens produce sound by means of either a disc or cup-shaped rotor actuated by compressed air, steam, or electricity. These should not be confused with what might be called "police sirens"; these may produce a sound of constant pitch much like a diaphragm horn or a whistle.

Whistles produce sound by compressed air, emitted through a circumferential slot into a cylindrical bell chamber.

Bells are sounded by means of a hammer actuated by an electric solenoid.

Operation of signals

Fog signals at stations where a continuous watch is maintained are placed in operation whenever the visibility decreases below a limit set for that location; typically, this might be five miles. Fog signals at such stations are also sounded whenever the fog signal of a passing vessel is heard.

Fog signals at locations where no continuous watch is maintained may not always be sounded promptly when fog conditions occur, or may operate erratically due to mechanical difficulties.

Where fog signals are operated continuously on a seasonal basis or throughout the year, this information will be found in the Light Lists.

Fog signals on buoys are usually operated by sea motion and may be heard in any condition of visibility.

FIG. 1606. Light structures rising out of the water are often protected by piles of rocks known as "rip-rap." Skippers should keep well clear as obstructions below the surface may extend far out. This is the light shown in the chart extract of fig. 1604—note there how the rip-rap is indicated around the light.

CAUTIONS IN USING FOG SIGNALS

Fog signals depend upon the transmission of sound through air. As aids to navigation, they have certain inherent limitations that *must* be considered. Sound travels through air in a variable and unpredictable manner. It has been established as fact that:

(a) Fog signals can be heard at greatly varying distances, and the distance at which such an aid can be heard may at any given instant vary with the bearing of the signal, and may be different on different occasions.

(b) Under certain conditions of the atmosphere, when a fog signal has a combination of high and low tones, it is not unusual for one of them to be heard but not the other. In the case of sirens which produce a varying tone, portions of the blast may not be heard.

(c) There are occasionally areas close to the signal in which it will not be heard. This is particularly true when the fog signal is screened by intervening land masses or other obstructions, or when the signal is on a high cliff.

(d) The apparent loudness of a fog signal may be greater at a distance than in the immediate vicinity.

(e) A patch of fog may exist at a short distance from a manned station but not be seen from it. Thus the signal may not be placed in operation.

(f) Some fog signals require a start-up interval.

(g) A fog signal may not be detected when the vessel's engines are in operation, but may be heard when they are stopped, or from a quieter location on deck.

Based on the above established facts, a mariner must *not* assume:

(1) That he is out of ordinary hearing distance from a fog signal because he fails to hear it.

(2) That because he hears a fog signal faintly, he is at a greater distance from it.

(3) That he is near to it because he hears it loudly.

(4) That the fog signal is not sounding because he does not hear it, even when in close proximity.

(5) That the detection distance and sound intensity under any one set of conditions is an infallible guide for any future occasion.

In summary, fog signals are valuable as warnings, but the boatman should not place implicit reliance upon them in navigating his vessel. They should be considered solely as warning devices.

Standby fog signals

Standby fog signals are sounded at some of the more important stations when the main signal is inoperative.

The standby signals may be of a different type and characteristic than the main signal. If different, details are given in the Light Lists.

Lightships and Offshore Towers

Lightships are vessels of distinctive design and markings, equipped with lights, fog signals, and radiobeacons. They are anchored or moored at specific, charted locations to serve as aids to navigation; see fig. 1607.

Purpose

Lightships mark the entrances to important harbors, warn of dangerous shoals lying in much-frequented waters, and serve as departure marks for both ocean and coastwise traffic.

Lightships serve the same essential purposes as lighthouses. They take the form of vessels only because they are at locations where it is (or has been until recently) impracticable to build lighthouses. As will be noted later, modern construction technology has now made possible the replacement in U.S. waters of all but one lightship with more efficient fixed structures or large buoys.

LIGHTSHIPS

The hulls of lightships in United States waters are always painted red with the name of the station in large white letters on each side. All the signals—the light, fog signal, and radiobeacon—have distinctive characteristics so that the lightship may be identified under all conditions. As with lighthouses, details regarding these signals are shown briefly on charts and more completely in the Light Lists. A riding light on the forestay indicates the direction that the ship is heading, and since lightships ride to a single bow anchor, this also indicates the direction from which the current is flowing, whenever the current is stronger than the wind.

Identification

A lightship underway to or from its station will fly the International Code flags "LO" which signify "I am not in my correct position," fig. 1608. She will not show or sound any of the signals of a lightship, but will display the lights prescribed by the International or Inland Rules for a vessel of her class.

FIG. 1607 Lightships are used to mark both offshore hazards and the entrance to major harbors. Nantucket Shoals have been marked since 1854. The lightship shown below is anchored in 192 feet of water. Her light is 55 feet above the water and has a nominal range of 23 miles. The lightship has a two-tone diaphone fog signal which sounds one blast every 30 seconds. This is the last lightship in active service in U.S. waters.

When on station at night, a lightship shows only the aid to navigation and riding lights. By day, lightships will display the International Code signal of the station whenever a vessel is in the vicinity and there are any indications that her crew fails to recognize the station, or whenever a vessel asks for information. The International Code signal for each lightship station is stated in the Light Lists.

Relief lightships

Whenever the regular lightship must be withdrawn from her station for maintenance, she is temporarily replaced with a *relief lightship*. These are painted the same colors as regular lightships, but have the word "RELIEF" on each side in lieu of a station name.

Relief lightships usually have lights and sound signals with the regular characteristics of the station; they may differ in minor details of appearance. (There are no more "RELIEF" lightships in U.S. waters; both vessels used at Nantucket are marked as shown in Fig. 1607.)

Station buoys

Station buoys, also referred to as "watch buoys," are used to mark the position of lightship stations. These buoys are located from several hundred yards to as much as a mile from the station as shown on the chart; the distance and direction are given in the Light Lists. They are *not* separately charted.

Station buoys serve as a substitute if the lightship is forced to seek shelter in extreme weather, and they aid in later returning the lightship to its correct position. They are always of an unlighted type and are marked with "LS" and the initials of the lightship station.

Cautions in using lightships

A skipper should set his course so as to pass a lightship with sufficient clearance to avoid the possibility of collision from any cause. It should be borne in mind that most lightships are anchored by a very long scope of chain and as a result the radius of their swinging circle is considerable. The charted position is the location of the anchor.

It must also be remembered that during extremely heavy weather lightships may be carried off station despite the best efforts of their crews, and perhaps without their knowledge. A navigator should not, therefore, implicitly rely on the position of a lightship during and immediately after severe storms. A lightship known to be off station will secure her light, fog signal, and radiobeacon, and will fly the International Code signal "LO."

A craft steering toward a radiobeacon on a lightship, "homing" on it, should exercise particular care to avoid collision. Sole reliance should *never* be placed on sighting the lightship or hearing her fog signal in time to prevent hitting her. The risk of collision will be lessened by ensuring that the radio bearing does not remain constant.

Skippers must also use care in passing lightships so as to not collide with the station buoy, remembering that it is unlighted and may be at a considerable distance from the lightship. Particular caution must be exercised in fog and at night.

OFFSHORE LIGHT TOWERS

Along the Atlantic Coast, lightships are being partially replaced with offshore light structures, fig. 1609. The first

FIG. 1608 A lightship flies the International Code flags "LO" when she is not on her station. These are seen above flying from the foremast. The vessel shown here is used as a temporary substitute for other lightships when those must return to port for maintenance, hence the name "RELIEF" on the side rather than the name of the specific station. (These are no longer used in U.S. waters.)

of these was placed in operation in 1961 and others have been added subsequently. Towers and large navigational buoys (see fig. 1504) have replaced all lightships on the Pacific Coast and all but one on the Atlantic Coast.

Characteristics

A typical tower deckhouse is 60 feet (18.3 m) above water, 80 feet (24.4 m) square, supported by steel lag pilings driven nearly 300 feet (91.4 m) into the ocean bottom. It accommodates living space, radiobeacon, communications, and oceanographic equipment. The deckhouse top serves as a landing platform that will take the largest helicopters flown by the Coast Guard. On one corner of the deckhouse is a 32-foot radio tower supporting the radiobeacon antenna and a 3½-million candlepower light. At an elevation of 130 feet (39.6 m) above the water, it is visible for 18 miles (33.3 km). The construction details of other towers will vary slightly.

Advantages

Fixed offshore light stations have five major advantages over lightships:

(1) Lower operating costs. The annual operating, personnel, and maintenance expenses of a tower light station are only about one-third of those of a lightship.

(2) Greater light range. Greater luminous range is made possible by more efficient optics, and greater geographic range results from the increased height of the light above the water—some 50 to 70 feet (15-21 m) higher than one on a lightship.

(3) Better fog signal projection. By eliminating the swinging to which a lightship is subject, fog signals may be projected specifically in the most useful directions under all circumstances.

(4) More accurate guidance for ships. The location of a tower light is fixed; it does not swing about the charted position and cannot be blown off station in violent storms.

(5) Longer life. Towers are expected to last 75 years, as compared with the average 50-year lifespan of lightships.

Cautions in using offshore towers and buoys

Much the same cautions are needed when navigating by offshore light towers and large buoys as was previously discussed for lightships. These buoys are also on chain of long scope and swing about their charted position. Both buoys and fixed towers require caution when "homing" on their radiobeacons (see page 324).

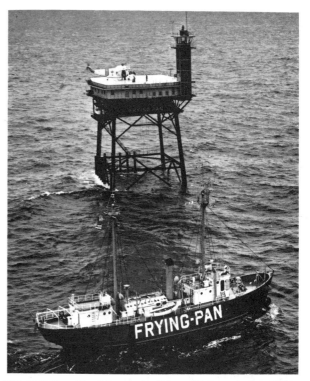

FIG. 1609. The old and the new in offshore aids to navigation. Lightships have been used since 1820, but in 1961 the Coast Guard started their replacement along the Atlantic Coast with tower structures. The fixed towers offer many advantages over lightships and will be constructed wherever hydrographic conditions permit. Frying Pan Shoals Light off the coast of North Carolina stands in 46 feet (14 meters) of water.

Unmanned offshore aids

In addition to the manned offshore light stations, there are several unmanned light towers, such as the one at Brenton Reef, and an increasing number of "large navigational buoys" as replacements for lightships.

Ranges and Directional Lights

Ranges and directional lights serve to indicate the centerline of a channel and thus aid in the safe piloting of a vessel. Although they are frequently used in connection with channels and other restricted waterways, they are not a part of the lateral system of buoyage and so were not covered in Chapter 15.

RANGES

A *range* consists of two fixed aids to navigation so positioned with respect to each other that when seen in line they indicate that the observer's craft *may* be in safe waters, fig. 1610. The aids may be lighted or unlighted as determined by the importance of the range, and may take a wide variety of physical appearances.

The conditional phrase "may be in safe waters" is used in the definition above since observation of the two markers in line is *not* an absolute determination of safety. A range is "safe" only within specific limits of distance from the front marker; a vessel too close or too far away may be in a dangerous area. The aids that comprise the range do not in themselves indicate the usable portion of the range; reference *must* be made to a chart of the

FIG. 1610. The principle of range markers. A boat B follows a safe mid-channel course between shoals S and S' by aligning the front marker directly below the rear marker. If the range opens and the rear marker shows to the **left** of the front marker, the boat is off course, displaced toward B'. If the rear marker shows to the **right** of the front marker, she is displaced toward B". Ranges may be lighted or unlighted.

area and to other aids.

Ranges are described in the Light Lists by first giving the position of the front marker, usually in terms of geographic coordinates—latitude and longitude; and then stating the location of the rear marker in terms of direction and distance from the front marker. This direction, given in degrees and minutes, true, need not be used in ordinary navigation, but is useful in making checks of compass deviation. The rear daymark (and light, if used) is always higher than the one on the front aid.

Because of their fixed nature, and the accuracy with which a vessel can be positioned by using them, ranges are among the best aids to navigation. Preference should always be given to using a range when one is available; buoys should be referred to only in order to determine the beginning and end of the usable portion of the range.

Unlighted ranges

Although any two objects may be used as a range, the term is properly applied only to those pairs of structures built specifically for that purpose. Special shapes and markings will be used for the front and rear markers of a range for easier identification and more accurate alignment. Many different designs have been used in the past, but to make ranges more easily identifiable, and easier to use, the Coast Guard now has standardized on the use of rectangular daymarks, longer dimension vertical, painted in vertical stripes of contrasting colors, see color page I. The design of specific range daymarks will normally be found in the Light Lists.

Lighted ranges

Because of their importance and high accuracy in piloting, most range markers are equipped with lights to extend their usefulness through the hours of darkness. Entrance channels are frequently marked with range lights; the Delaware River on the Atlantic Coast and the Columbia River on the Pacific Coast are examples of this.

Range lights may be of any color used with aids to navigation—white, red, or green—and may show any of several characteristics. The principal requirement is that they be easily distinguished from shore backgrounds and from other lights. Front and rear lights will, however, often be of the same color (white is frequently used because of its greater visibility range), with different phase characteristics. Since both lights must be observed together for the proper steering of the craft, range lights will generally have

a greater "on" interval than will other lights. Range rear lights will normally be on more than their front counterparts. Many ranges now show an equal interval rear light and a quick-flashing front light.

Many range lights will be fitted with special lenses that result in a much greater intensity being shown on the range center line than off of it; the lights rapidly decrease in brilliance when observed from only a few degrees to either side. In some cases, the light will be visible only from on or very near to the range line; in other cases, a light of lesser intensity may be seen all around the horizon—this can be either from the main light source or from a small auxiliary "passing" light. Light is shown around the horizon when the front aid also serves to mark the side of a channel at a turn of direction.

Often range lights will be of such high intensity that they can be seen and used for piloting in the daytime, being of more value than the painted daymarks.

FIG. 1611 Lighted ranges provide excellent guidance both day and night to keep craft in a channel through shoal areas. Here a single front light is common to two ranges. The quick flashing characteristic of the forward light and equal interval for the rear light are standard for most ranges. The Light List will give the height of each light and the colors of the daymarks.

DIRECTIONAL LIGHTS

The establishment of a range requires suitable locations for two aids, separated adequately both horizontally and vertically. In some areas, this may not be possible and a single light of special characteristics will be employed.

A *directional light* is a single light source fitted with a special lens so as to show a white light in a narrow beam along a desired direction, with red and green showing to either side. Width of the sectors will depend upon the local situation, but red will be seen if the pilot is to the right of the center line as he approaches the aid from seaward, and green if he is to the left of the desired track. A typical directional light, at Deer Island, Massachusetts, shows white for a sector of 2.4° with red and green showing for 8.5° to either side. Another directional light in Delaware Bay has a white beam width of 1° 50' with red and green sectors of 6.5° to either side.

Directional lights will normally have an occulting or equal interval characteristic, so that they are easily followed.

Caution regarding direction lights

A pilot should not place too great reliance on the various colors of a direction light for safe positional information. As noted for light sectors, the boundaries between colors are not sharp and clear; the light shades imperceptibly from one color to the other along the stated direction lines.

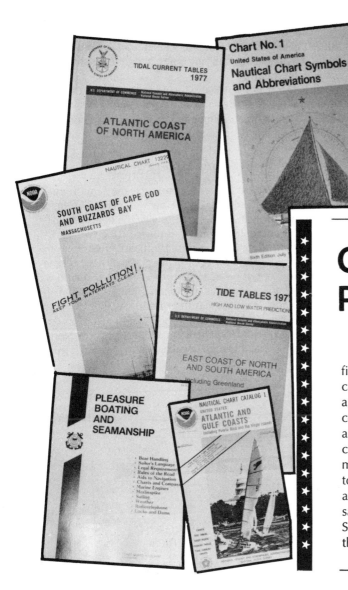

GOVERNMENT PUBLICATIONS

The typical boatman undoubtedly thinks first of charts when considering the publications that are issued by governmental agencies to aid his safe boating. This is certainly a valid thought—so much so that another chapter is devoted entirely to charts—but he should not overlook the many other publications that are available to make his boating safer and more enjoyable. Generally, these are issued by the same governmental agencies as are charts. Such publications will be considered in this chapter.

PUBLISHING AGENCIES

Agencies of the Federal Government that issue publications valuable to the boatman include:

National Ocean Survey (formerly the Coast & Geodetic Survey, and now including the Lake Survey Center), National Oceanic and Atmospheric Administration, Department of Commerce.

United States Coast Guard, a part of the Department of Transportation.

The U.S. Naval Observatory.

The Defense Mapping Agency Hydrographic/Topographic Center (DMAHTC).

U.S. Army Corps of Engineers (District Offices).

National Weather Service (formerly the U.S. Weather Bureau), also a part of NOAA.

Government Printing Office

The Government Printing Office, an independent agency, does much of the actual printing of the publications prepared by the agencies listed above. The Superintendent of

Documents is responsible for the sale of most of these publications, but not all of them. Unfortunately, there seems to be no rule for the determination of whether a publication is sold by GPO or by the government agency that prepared it.

Publications that are sold by the GPO can be purchased by mail. The address is Superintendent of Documents, Government Printing Office, Washington, D.C. 20402. There is also a retail bookstore in the GPO building at North Capital and H Streets in Washington where over-the-counter purchases can be made. There are now GPO Bookstores in a number of major cities that can handle mail and in-person orders. Personal checks for the purchase of publications are acceptable; they should be made payable to the "Superintendent of Documents."

State agencies

Publications of interest to boatmen are also prepared by many State agencies, so many that it is not possible to list them all in this book. Boatmen should check with local authorities in their own state and write ahead to other states when they expect to cruise into new waters. Information may be obtained that will add to safety and convenience, possibly avoiding legal embarrassment as well. "Ignorance is no excuse" applies both afloat and ashore!

The name of the state agency to be addressed will vary widely from state to state. Consult page 640 for the name and address of an office to which inquiries may be sent. Requests for information and literature should be as specific as possible.

SALES AGENTS

Various boating supply stores, marinas, and similar activities have been designated by governmental agencies as official *sales agents* for their publications. These agents accept responsibility for maintenance of adequate stocks of the various charts and documents of interest to mariners and boatmen in their respective areas.

Authorized sales agents may carry stocks of publications of the National Ocean Survey, the Defense Mapping Agency Hydrographic/Topographic Center, or Coast Guard, or combinations of two or three of these. It does *not* hold true that because an activity is an agent for one source of publications it will have any of the others.

Other information

Additional information on where to obtain certain specific government publications will be found on pages 608–610.

National Ocean Survey Publications _____

The National Ocean Survey (N.O.S.) is charged with the survey of the coast, harbors and tidal estuaries of the United States and its insular possessions. It issues the following publications relating to these waters as guides to navigation: Charts, Coast Pilots, Tide Tables, Tidal Current Tables, Tidal Current Charts, and chart catalogs.

In 1970, the National Ocean Survey was created from the former Coast & Geodetic Survey and the Army Engineers' Lake Survey District. This agency is part of the National Oceanic and Atmospheric Administration in the Department of Commerce.

TIDE TABLES

Tide Tables, fig. 1701, are of great value in determining the predicted height of the water at almost any place at any given time. These tables are calculated in advance and are published annually in four volumes, one of which covers the East Coast of North and South America and another the West Coast of these continents.

The Tide Tables give the predicted times and heights of high and low waters for each day of the year at a number of important points known as *reference stations*. The East Coast Tide Tables include 48 sets of detailed listings for such points as Portland, Boston, Sandy Hook, Baltimore, Miami, Pensacola, and Galveston. Additional

data are tabulated showing the differences in times and heights between these reference stations and thousands of other points, termed *subordinate stations*. From these tables, the tide at virtually any point along the coast can be easily computed.

The N.O.S. Tide Tables also include other useful data including tables of sunrise and sunset, reduction of local mean time to standard zone time, and moonrise and moonset.

The Tide Tables and their use in piloting are discussed at length in Chapter 20, pages 397–402.

TIDAL CURRENT TABLES

The Tidal Current Tables are in much the same format as the Tide Tables, see fig. 1702. However, instead of times of high and low waters, these tables give the times of maximum flood and ebb currents and times of the two slacks when current direction reverses. The times of slack water do *not* correspond to times of high and low tides, and the Tide Tables *cannot* be used to predict current situations. Velocity of the current at maximum strength is given in terms of knots (nautical miles per hour).

Tidal Current Tables are published in two volumes—Atlantic Coast of North America and Pacific Coast of North America and Asia. Included in each volume are tables from

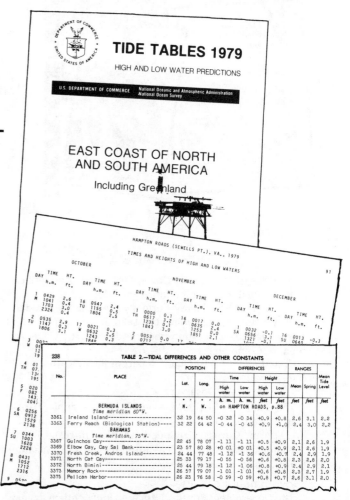

FIG. 1701 Tide Tables published by the National Ocean Survey provide necessary data for predicting height of tide at thousands of coastal points for any desired day and hour. Separate volumes are issued for the Atlantic-Gulf and Pacific Coasts.

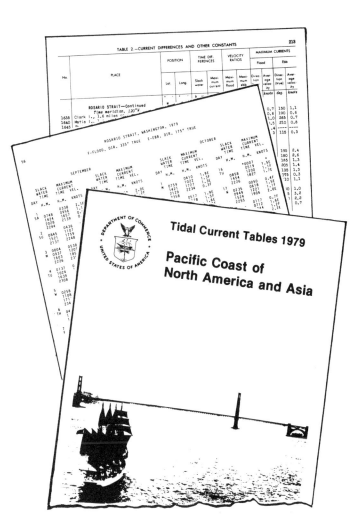

FIG. 1702 Tidal Current Tables are prepared in much the same format as the Tide Tables. A system of a limited number of reference points together with thousands of subordinate stations permits calculation of current strengths and slacks at virtually any location of navigational interest.

which may be calculated current velocity at any intermediate time and the duration of slack water or weak currents.

Tidal Current Tables and their use in piloting are covered in detail in Chapter 20, pages 406-409.

TIDAL CURRENT CHARTS

Tidal Current Charts are now available for 13 bodies of water—Boston Harbor, Narragansett Bay to Nantucket Sound (two sets), Long Island and Block Island Sounds, New York Harbor, Delaware Bay and River, Upper Chesapeake Bay, Charleston Harbor, Tampa Bay, San Francisco Bay, and Puget Sound (two sets). Each "chart" consists of a series of 12 reproductions of the chart of the locality, each of which indicates graphically the direction and velocity of tidal currents for a specific hour with respect to the state of the tide or current prediction for a major reference station. Currents in the various passages are indicated with red arrows and velocities are noted at numerous points; see fig. 1703. By following through the sequence of charts, hourly changes in velocity and direction are easily seen. These charts make it possible to visualize how tidal currents act at various points throughout every part of the entire twelve-hour-plus cycle.

Where currents run at considerable velocity, and espe-

cially where tidal currents are complex, often flowing in opposite directions at the same stage of tide, a real advantage can be gained in consulting one of these charts. A few minutes' study may well be the means of carrying a favorable current through the entire passage, instead of needlessly bucking an opposing flow for much or all of the time. As is the case for all current predictions, it must be remembered that these charts indicate normal conditions; a strong wind from certain directions may have a decided influence on both the strength of currents and the times that maximums are reached.

The Narragansett Bay and New York Harbor Tidal Current Charts are used in conjunction with annual tide tables. All other Tidal Current Charts are used with the annual tidal current tabels for their respective areas. See also pages 409-410.

TIDAL CURRENT DIAGRAMS

The Tidal Current Diagrams are a series of 12 monthly diagrams to be used with the Tidal Current Charts for Boston Harbor, and for Block Island Sound and Eastern Long Island Sound to give the navigator a convenient method of determining current flow on a particular day. These are republished for each year; the proper edition must be used.

FIG. 1703 Tidal Current Charts are available for a number of major bodies of water where such flows are of significance in piloting. A series of twelve charts, for hourly intervals in the cycle of ebb and flood, comprise each Tidal Current Chart.

COAST PILOTS

The amount of information that can be printed on nautical charts is limited by available space and the system

United States Coast Pilot 4

Atlantic Coast: Cape Henry to Key West

Sixteenth Edition
July 1978

U.S. DEPARTMENT OF COMMERCE
National Oceanic and Atmospheric Administration
National Ocean Survey

FIG. 1704 The Coast Pilot is published in nine volumes for various sections of the coastline and for the Great Lakes. Each includes sailing directions, courses and distances between ports; information on hazards and aids to navigation, data on facilities for supplies and repairs; and much other useful information that cannot be conveniently shown on nautical charts.

7. CHARLESTON HARBOR TO SAVANNAH RIVER

Charts 11480, 11521, 11513.–This chapter describes the coastline from Charleston Harbor to Savannah River. The coast, low and timbered, trends in a southwesterly direction for 65 miles and is broken by St. Helena, Port Royal, and Calibogue Sounds, and by numerous inlets from which there is access to the interior by way of the rivers emptying into them. Shoal water extends 3 to 8 miles offshore.

Numerous fish havens, some marked by private buoys, are from 5 to 12 miles off the coasts of South Carolina and Georgia.

This section of the coast, due to its low relief, presents no good radar targets except for the structure of Savannah Light.

Included in this chapter are the deepwater ports of Savannah and Port Royal; the fishing and smallcraft port of Beaufort, S.C.; Stono, and North Edisto Rivers; the tributary waters of the various sounds of which South Edisto, Coosaw, Beaufort, Broad, and Savannah Rivers are the more important; and several small towns along these waterways.

The section of the Intracoastal Waterway from Charleston to Savannah is described in chapter 12.

Caution.–The areas generally to the east and southeast of Charleston Harbor are used extensive-

trance buoys are not charted, because they are frequently shifted in position to mark the best water. Local fishermen use the inlet.

An offshore **drill minefield**, about 4.5 miles square and marked by buoys, is about 7 miles southeastward of Stono Inlet and about 10 miles southwestward of the Charleston Harbor entrance buoy. An unmarked fish haven, covered 15 feet, is in about 32°29.0'N., 80°00.3'W., about 5.6 miles southwestward of the drill minefield.

Stono River, which joins Stono Inlet from northward, is of little commercial importance except in its upper reach above **Elliott Cut**, where it forms part of the Intracoastal Waterway. In May 1975, the reported controlling depth from inside the inlet bar for about 12 miles to the highway bridge was 11 feet, thence 7 feet to a junction with the Intracoastal Waterway at Elliott Cut. Vessels usually enter the river by way of the waterway from Charleston. In the summer, numerous pleasure craft use Stono River and Folly River to reach Folly Beach. The highway bridge about a mile below Elliott Cut has a swing span with a clearance of 8 feet. (See 117.240, chapter 2, for drawbridge regulations and opening signals.)

Folly River flows into Stono Inlet from the northeast and **Kiawah River** from the west. Both

of symbols that is used. Additional information is often needed for safe and convenient navigation. The National Ocean Survey publishes such information in the *Coast Pilots*. These are printed in book form, covering the coastline and the Great Lakes in nine separate volumes.

Each Coast Pilot, see fig. 1704, contains sailing directions between ports in its respective area, including recommended courses and distances. Channels, with their controlling depths, and all dangers and obstructions are fully described. Harbors and anchorages are listed, with information on those points at which facilities are available for boat supplies and marine repairs. Information regarding canals, bridges, docks, etc., which cannot be adequately expressed on charts due to limitations of space, is provided in full in the Coast Pilots. Information on the Intracoastal Waterways is contained in the various applicable volumes.

The Coast Pilot volumes cover the following areas:

Atlantic Coast
- No. 1 Eastport to Cape Cod
- No. 2 Cape Cod to Sandy Hook
- No. 3 Sandy Hook to Cape Henry
- No. 4 Cape Henry to Key West
- No. 5 Gulf of Mexico, Puerto Rico, and Virgin Islands

Great Lakes
- No. 6 Great Lakes and connecting waterways

Pacific Coast
- No. 7 California, Oregon, Washington and Hawaii

Alaska
- No. 8 Dixon Entrance to Cape Spencer
- No. 9 Cape Spencer to Beaufort Sea

All Coast Pilots, except Coast Pilot 6 (Great Lakes), have been converted to an automatic (magnetic tape) typesetting process; all are published annually, except Coast Pilots 8 and 9 (Alaska) which are issued every two years. Coast Pilots are corrected through the dates of Notices to Mariners shown on the title page and should not be used without reference to Notices to Mariners issued subsequent to those dates. Changes to Coast Pilots that affect the safety of navigation and have been reported to N.O.S. in the interim period between new editions are published in the weekly and Local Notices to Mariners, except those for Coast Pilot 6 which are published only in Local Notices to Mariners.

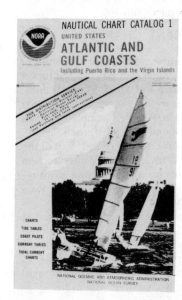

FIG. 1705 The National Ocean Survey issues catalogs of their nautical charts; these also include listings of other useful publications of the N.O.S. and other agencies. These catalogs show the area covered by each chart, the scale, price, etc. They are updated at intervals of 6 to 12 months.

CHART CATALOGS

The National Ocean Survey publishes four free Chart Catalogs, fig. 1705. There is a volume for the Atlantic and Gulf Coasts, including Puerto Rico and the Virgin Islands; one for the Pacific Coast, including Hawaii and the other U.S. Pacific islands; and one for Alaska, including the Aleutian Islands. A fourth volume covers the Great Lakes and adjacent waterways, fig. 1711.

These are actually small-scale outline charts with diagrams delineating the area covered by each nautical chart published by the N.O.S. These catalogs are also sources of much additional information regarding charts and publications of other agencies; they also contain a listing, by states, of the names and addresses of local sales agents for charts and other publications.

A somewhat different catalog is N.O.S. Map and Chart Catalog 5—Bathymetric Maps and Special Purpose Charts. This publication indexes such items as Tidal Current Charts, Marine Weather Service Charts, and Storm Evacuation Maps. The index charts show Fishery Conservation Zone boundaries 200 miles offshore, Continental Shelf limits (200-meter depth curve), and the outer edge of the Continental Shelf (2500-meter depth curve).

N.O.S. OFFICES

Nautical charts, Tide and Tidal Current Tables, Tidal Current Diagrams, Coast Pilots, and other publications of

---

Distribution Division (C44)
National Ocean Survey
6501 Lafayette Avenue
Riverdale, MD 20840

FIG. 1706 If not available at local sales agents, publications and charts of the National Ocean Survey can be purchased by mail from the office listed above. A check or money order for the total price should accompany the order; the material will be sent postpaid.

The National Ocean Survey can be purchased over-the-counter at the Distribution Office near Washington, D.C.; the address is shown in fig. 1706. Publications can also be purchased by mail if payment is sent with the order.

Other offices

Information regarding N.O.S. charts, publications, and activities can be obtained by addressing the National Ocean Survey, Rockville, Maryland 20852. Regional Marine Centers are located at Norfolk, Virginia; Seattle, Washington; and Anchorage, Alaska.

Coast Guard Publications

The United States Coast Guard prepares a major navigational publication and a number of minor ones. All of these are worthy of a boatman's serious consideration.

LIGHT LISTS

The Coast Guard has a series of annual publications for the coastal and inland waters known as the *Light Lists*. These books provide more complete information concern-

ing aids to navigation than can be conveniently shown on charts, see fig. 1707. They are *not* intended to be used in navigation in place of charts and Coast Pilots, and should not be so used. Charts should be consulted for the location of all aids to navigation. It may be dangerous to use aids to navigation without reference to charts.

The Light Lists describe, for the use of mariners, the lightships, lighthouses, lesser lights, buoys, and daybeacons maintained in all navigable waters of the United States by the Coast Guard and various private agencies. (In this

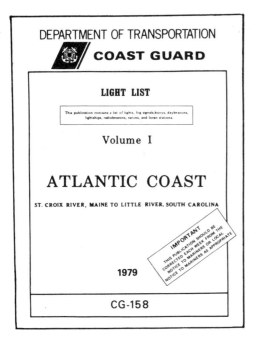

FIG. 1707 Light Lists, published by the U.S. Coast Guard, provide more detailed information on aids to navigation than can be shown on charts. Five volumes cover all coasts, the Great Lakes, and the Mississippi River system. Light Lists are to be used with, not as a substitute for, nautical charts. Information in column 6 regarding daymarks is now being converted to abbreviations, such as "SG" for a green square daymark, "TR" for a red triangular daymark, etc.; see introductory pages of new volumes of the Light Lists.

usage, the Navy and all other non-USCG governmental organizations are considered to be "private agencies.") The data shown in the Lists includes the official name of the aid, the characteristics of its light, sound, and radio signals, its structural appearance, position, and other significant factors.

Light Lists are published in five volumes as follows:

Volume   I—Atlantic Coast from St. Croix River, Maine to Little River, S.C.

Volume II—Atlantic and Gulf Coasts from Little River, S.C. to Rio Grande, Texas

Volume III—Pacific Coast and Pacific Islands

Volume IV—Great Lakes

Volume V—Mississippi River System

Within each volume, aids to navigation are listed by Coast Guard Districts in the following order: seacoast, major channels, Intracoastal Waterway, minor channel, and miscellaneous. Lighted and unlighted aids appear together in their geographic order, with amplifying data on the same page.

Seacoast aids are listed in sequence from north to south along the Atlantic Coast, from south to north and east to west along the Gulf Coast, and from south to north along the Pacific Coast. On the Atlantic and Gulf Coasts, aids along the Intracoastal Waterway are listed in the same sequence. For rivers and estuaries, the aids to navigation are shown from seaward to the head of navigation. Where an aid serves both a channel leading in from sea and the ICW, it will be listed separately in both sequences.

All volumes of the USCG Light Lists are for sale by the Superintendent of Documents, Government Printing Office; the volume for the local area concerned is sold by many of the authorized chart and publication sales agents.

RULES OF THE ROAD

The Coast Guard has published an excellent booklet on the two sets of rules of the road. This is the 1981 edition of CG-169, Navigation Rules, International-Inland. (The 1977 edition remains useful only for its coverage of the 1972 International Rules of the Road.)

This booklet presents the various rules and annexes side-by-side—international on the left, inland on the right. Illustrations for specific rules are located adjacent to the applicable text; there are now illustrations for the steering and sailing rules, as well as lights and shapes. The rule number and title are in large type at the top of each page to facilitate the location of desired subjects.

The demarcation lines that separate waters subject to the U.S. Inland Rules from those governed by the International Rules are described in detail. Other items of useful information include penalties for violations of rules or regulations; rules and procedures for bridge-to-

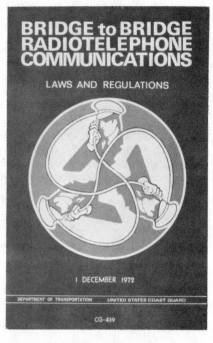

FIG. 1709 Bridge-to-bridge communications between vessels is covered in CG-439. Boatmen on busy waterways will find it useful to get a copy and listen on VHF-FM Channel 13.

bridge radio communications (VHF-FM Channel 13); excerpts from the Federal Boat Safety Act of 1971; regulations relating to regattas and marine parades; and information on Vessel Traffic Services (traffic separation schemes at many major ports and harbor entrances).

Although earlier editions of CG-169 were distributed by the Coast Guard without charge, budgetary limitations now require that it be sold. Copies may be ordered by mail from the Superintendent of Documents, Government Printing Office, Washington, DC 20402; they may also be obtainable from local sales agents for charts and other nautical publications.

OTHER USCG PUBLICATIONS

The Coast Guard issues a number of publications relating to the safety of navigation and covering such topics as aids to navigation, applicable rules and regulations, general safety matters, etc. See page 609 for a more complete listing and information on where they may be obtained. Some of these are free, others are available for a nominal charge.

CG-290 is a small pamphlet covering federal requirements for recreational boats. Topics include laws and regulations, numbering and documentation, reporting accidents, approved equipment, etc. It, and CG-151 below, can be obtained from USCG Headquarters (G-BA), Washington, D.C. 20593.

Another free USCG pamphlet is "Emergency Repairs Afloat" (CG-151). The Coast Guard reasons that if you can help yourself, they will have fewer emergency calls!

FIG.   1708 Waters subject to the International Rules of the Road and those governed by the U.S. Inland Rules are separated by "demarcation lines." These are described in detail in the 1981 edition of CG-169.

DMA Hydrographic/Topographic Center

The Defense Mapping Agency Hydrographic/Topographic Center was created in 1978 as a combination of two prior activities. DMAHTC has several publications of interest to boatmen. Charts, publications, and other products of DMAHTC are identified with a prefix to the individual chart or publication number as follows:

The identification of nautical charts has been changed to a system using a number of one to five digits, without prefix, as determined by the scale and assigned on a basis of regions and subregions. Publications and some other items will continue to have an "H.O." prefix until reprinted with a DMAHTC number.

Oceanographic products, primarily publications, related to the dynamic nature of the oceans or the scientific aspects of oceanography will continue to be printed by the Naval Oceanographic Office and will carry numbers with prefixes such as "NOP," "RP," "SP," or "TR."

BOWDITCH (PUB. NO. 9)

The *American Practical Navigator*, originally written by Nathaniel Bowditch in 1799, and generally referred to simply as "Bowditch," is an extensive treatise on piloting, celestial navigation and other nautical matters. It is Publication No. 9 of DMAHTC; the 1958 edition, reprinted in 1962 and 1966, is now replaced by a 1975/77 edition.

"Bowditch" has long been accepted as an authority on questions of piloting and other forms of navigation. The new edition consists of two volumes. The 1975 Volume II contains tables, data, equations, and instructions needed to perform navigational calculations. The 1977 Volume I contains basic reference material.

OTHER DMAHTC PUBLICATIONS

Other Hydrographic/Topographic Center publications that may be found useful to a boatman include Pubs. 117 A-B, *Radio Navigational Aids*; and Pub. 102, *International Code of Signals* (see Chapter 26).

The Hydrographic/Topographic Center publishes a series of *Sailing Directions* which provide supplementary information for foreign coasts and ports in a manner generally similar to the Coast Pilot for U.S. waters.

The *Lists of Lights* published by this agency likewise cover foreign waters and so are not duplicatory of the Coast Guard Light Lists. These are Pubs. No. 111A and 111B, and 112 through 116.

The DMAHTC catalog of charts is Publication 1-N. There are nine Regional Sections which may be purchased separately (25¢ each); Regions 1 and 2 would be of interest to U.S. boatmen, see fig. 1710a. There is also a numerical listing of charts (Pub. 1-N-L) and a catalog of miscellaneous charts and sheets (Pub. 1-N-A).

DMAHTC publications include a number of tables for the reduction of celestial observations, and tables and charts for plotting lines of position from Loran-A and Loran-C measurements. These are of interest only to those yachtsmen making extensive voyages on the high seas.

Additional DMAHTC publications are listed on page 610.

FIG. 1710 "Bowditch" is the name by which this popular and highly useful government publication is usually known. It contains a wealth of material on piloting, electronic and celestial navigation, and related topics. The 1975/77 edition is published in two volumes.

FIG. 1710a Charts formerly published by the Naval Oceanographic Office, and now by the Defense Mapping Agency Hydrographic Center, are numbered according to regions and subregions. The new system is a considerable improvement over the random numbering formerly employed.

Obtaining DMAHTC publications

Charts and other publications of the Defense Mapping Agency Hydrographic/Topographic Center are available through many local sales agents and all purchases should be made from these sources whenever possible. A complete listing of agents for DMAHTC products is contained in Pub. No. 1-N-L which is available without charge. [Some agents for N.O.S. charts also sell DMAHTC charts and publications; these are so indicated in the four volumes of the N.O.S. Nautical Chart Catalog.]

If DMAHTC charts and other publications cannot be obtained from local sales agents, they may be ordered by mail from DMA Office of Distribution Services (DDCP), 6500 Brookes Lane, Washington, DC 20315.

Mail orders for charts and publications must be accompanied by a check or money order made payable to the "Defense Mapping Agency" for the amount of the purchase. Such materials will be mailed at government expense in regular printed-matter postal service. The added cost of requests for any special handling, such as air mail, special delivery, etc., must be borne by the purchaser.

Naval Observatory Publications

The Naval Observatory publishes the *Nautical Almanac* in annual editions and the *Air Almanac* for six-month periods also the *Almanac for Computers,* useful with programmable calculators. These books contain astronomical data needed for celestial navigation; they are not required by boatmen using only piloting.

The Naval Observatory also participates in and assists the publication of other navigational documents such as the Tide Tables and celestial sight reduction tables, but it is not the agency directly responsible for them.

Army Engineers Publications

The Corps of Engineers of the U.S. Army has the responsibility for navigational and informational publications on major inland (non-tidal) rivers such as the Tennessee, Ohio, and Mississippi, and many lakes and reservoirs behind the large dams.

INTRACOASTAL WATERWAY BOOKLETS

The Army Engineers has prepared two paperbound booklets on the Intracoastal Waterway, which comes under its jurisdiction. These booklets contain descriptive material, photographs, small-scale charts, and tabulated data. Caution must be exercised, however, when using the distance tables as considerable differences exist between these publications and the N.O.S. charts of the Atlantic ICW. The Army Engineers use statute (not nautical) miles, and their zero point is at Trenton, N.J. rather than Norfolk, Va. Mileage differences will also be noted along the Gulf Intracoastal Waterway.

Unfortunately, these publications are *not* periodically updated, and they are of far less value than the corresponding volumes of the N.O.S. Coast Pilots with their annual supplements.

Bulletins on the Intracoastal Waterways are issued periodically by the Engineers District Offices. Addresses of these offices are given on page 608.

RIVERS AND LAKES INFORMATION

Regulations relating to the use of many rivers and lakes (reservoirs), *Navigational Bulletins,* and *Notices to Navigation Interests* are issued by various offices of the Corps of Engineers, U.S. Army, as listed on page 608. Other government publications relating to inland river and lake boating are also listed on that page, together with information as to where they may be obtained.

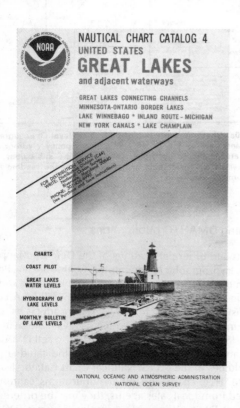

FIG. 1711 N.O.S. Chart Catalog 4 covers not only the Great Lakes, but also its outflow rivers, Lake Champlain, N.Y. State Barge Canal system, and the Minnesota-Ontario border lakes.

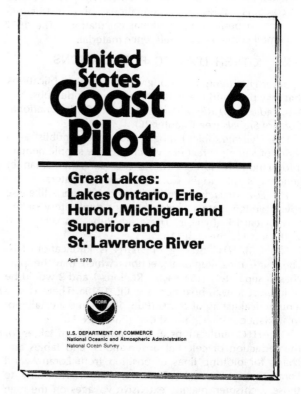

FIG. 1712 Coast Pilot 6 is a comprehensive volume prepared to supplement information given on charts of the Great Lakes published by the National Ocean Survey.

National Weather Service Publications ———

The National Weather Service, a part of NOAA, Department of Commerce, prepares weather maps that appear in many newspapers, but boatmen generally make use greater of radio and television broadcasts of current weather and sea conditions and predictions.

To assist mariners and boatmen in knowing when and where to listen for radio and TV weather broadcasts, the Weather Service publishes a series of *Marine Weather Services Charts* in annual editions. These are discussed in more detail in pages 264-265 and 498.

Keeping Publications Up to Date ———

It is essential that certain navigational publications, as well as charts, be kept corrected and fully up to date with respect to the information contained in them. Incorrect, outdated information can be considerably more harmful than no information at all; a false sense of knowledge and confidence can easily lead to a dangerous situation.

Coast Pilots and Light Lists are the primary publications that need continual correction. Fortunately, the government has provided a convenient means for executing this most necessary function. The time and effort required are not great, provided a skipper keeps at it regularly and does not permit the work to build up a backlog.

NOTICE TO MARINERS

The Defense Mapping Agency Hydrographic/Topographic Center publishes a weekly *Notice to Mariners* which is prepared jointly with the National Ocean Survey and the Coast Guard; see fig. 1713. These pamphlets advise mariners of important matters affecting navigational safety, including new hydrographic discoveries, changes in channels and navigation aids, etc. Besides keeping mariners informed generally, the Notice to Mariners also provides information specifically useful for updating the latest editions of nautical charts and publications.

Each issue contains instructions on how it is to be used to correct charts and other publications. Certain supplementary information is published as Notice No. 1 of each year; lists of charts affected are included quarterly.

A "Summary of Corrections" is published semiannually covering charts, Coast Pilots, and Sailing Directions.

LOCAL NOTICES TO MARINERS

The Commander of each Coast Guard District issues *Local Notices to Mariners*, fig. 1714. These are reproduced and mailed from the respective District offices, bringing information to users several weeks in advance of the weekly Notices that are printed in Washington, D.C. and mailed from there.

Local Notices are of particular interest to small-craft skippers, as the weekly Notices no longer carry information regarding inland and other waters not used by large ocean-going vessels.

Report all useful information

All boatmen are urged to cooperate with governmental agencies in keeping the buoyage system up to its highest

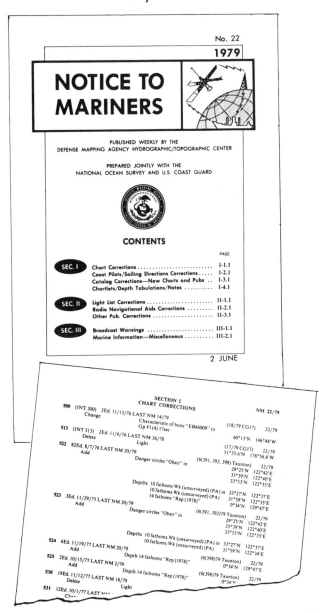

FIG. 1713. Notice to Mariners is a free weekly publication used to correct charts and other navigational publications. A single volume covers the major navigable waters of the world. Information appears in the form of descriptive paragraphs, inserts for pasting on charts, and cut-outs for insertion in volumes such as Light Lists. Information is limited to waters used by ocean-going vessels; for inland waters, Local Notices to Mariners must be used.

efficiency and helpfulness by reporting any facts that may come to their attention concerning damage to aids, malfunctioning of lights, shifting of shoals and channels, new hazards, etc. Defects in navigational aids and new hazards should be reported to the nearest Coast Guard activity by the fastest means available, including radio if the situation is of sufficient urgency. Suggestions for the improvement of aids to navigation should be sent to the Commandant, U.S. Coast Guard, Washington, D.C. 20590.

Data concerning dangers to navigation, changes in shoals and channels, and similar information affecting charts or publications of the N.O.S. should be sent to the Director, National Ocean Survey, NOAA, Rockville, Maryland 20852.

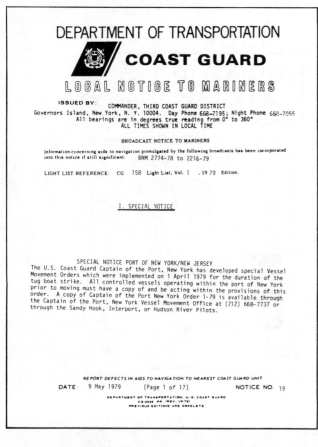

DEPARTMENT OF TRANSPORTATION

COAST GUARD

LOCAL NOTICE TO MARINERS

ISSUED BY: COMMANDER, THIRD COAST GUARD DISTRICT
Governors Island, New York, N. Y. 10004. Day Phone 668-7195; Night Phone 668-7055
All bearings are in degrees true reading from 0° to 360°
ALL TIMES SHOWN IN LOCAL TIME

BROADCAST NOTICE TO MARINERS

Information concerning aids to navigation promulgated by the following broadcasts has been incorporated
into this notice if still significant: BNM 2774-78 to 2216-79

LIGHT LIST REFERENCE: CG 158 Light List, Vol. 1 , 1979 Edition.

1. SPECIAL NOTICE

SPECIAL NOTICE PORT OF NEW YORK/NEW JERSEY
The U.S. Coast Guard Captain of the Port, New York has developed special Vessel
Movement Orders which were implemented on 1 April 1979 for the duration of the
tug boat strike. All controlled vessels operating within the port of New York
prior to moving must have a copy of and be acting within the provisions of this
order. A copy of Captain of the Port New York Order 1-79 is available through
the Captain of the Port, New York Vessel Movement Office at (212) 668-7737 or
through the Sandy Hook, Interport, or Hudson River Pilots.

REPORT DEFECTS IN AIDS TO NAVIGATION TO NEAREST COAST GUARD UNIT
DATE: 9 May 1979 (Page 1 of 17) NOTICE NO. 19
DEPARTMENT OF TRANSPORTATION, U.S. COAST GUARD
CG-3925 PP (REV. 10-73)
PREVIOUS EDITIONS ARE OBSOLETE

**FIG. 1714 Local Notices to Mariners are published by each Coast
Guard District on a "when required" basis, often several times per
week. Information in Local Notices often reaches boatmen several
weeks before it appears in weekly Notices from Washington. Check
your local yacht club or marina for its file of Local Notices.**

Quasi-Governmental Publications ────────

In addition to the governmental agencies and their publications noted above, there are several activities that can
be best described as "quasi-governmental." Publications
issued by them are of considerable interest to boatmen.

RADIO TECHNICAL COMMISSION FOR MARINE SERVICES

This organization with the long name is for obvious reasons better known by its initials, RTCM. It includes representatives of governmental agencies such as the FCC, the
Coast Guard, NOAA, Maritime Administration, and others;
user organizations, such as ocean steamship operating
groups, Great Lakes shipping interests, and the United
States Power Squadrons; equipment manufacturers; labor
organizations; and communications companies such as the
Bell System. The RTCM does not have authority to make
binding decisions, but it wields considerable influence
through its function as a meeting place for the presentation
and resolution of conflicting views and interests.

The RTCM publishes *How to Use Your Marine Radiotelephone,* an authoritative handbook on the FCC Rules
and Regulations which also has much useful information
on the selection, installation, and proper use of radios on
boats. The 1977 edition is completely updated for VHF-
FM and single sideband communications; see fig. 2524.

This useful booklet can be ordered from the Radio
Technical Commission for Marine Services, c/o FCC,
P.O. Box 19087, Washington, DC 20036. The single
copy price is $3.00, with discounts for quantity purchases.

NAVAL INSTITUTE PUBLICATIONS

The United States Naval Institute is not a governmental
agency; rather it is a private association "for the advancement of professional, literary, and scientific knowledge in
the Navy." One of its principal activities is the publication
of books on naval and maritime matters.

The Naval Institute publishes a large number of books,
but none will be more familiar to boatmen than *Dutton's
Navigation and Piloting.* Like Bowditch, this volume has
come to be an accepted authority on matters of piloting
and navigation. Again like Bowditch, the current volume is
an outgrowth of many years of development from an early
work; the book was initially known as "Navigation and
Nautical Astronomy" by Benjamin Dutton. This useful book
—now in its 13th edition—can be purchased in boating
supply and book stores, or directly by mail from the U.S.
Naval Institute, Annapolis, MD 21402.

★ ★ ★ ★ ★ ★ ★ ★ ★ ★ ★ ★ ★ ★ ★ ★ ★ ★ ★ ★

CHAPTER 18

THE NAUTICAL CHART

...Indispensable Aid to Safe Piloting

IN ORDER to travel anywhere safely in his boat, a skipper must have knowledge of the depths of the water, the shoals, and the channels. He must also know the location of aids to navigation and landmarks, and where ports and harbors can be found. At any given position, he can generally measure the depth, and he sees some landmarks; but for true safety he has to know the depth ahead, the actual location of those aids to navigation which he can presently see, and where more aids are located relative to the course he plans to follow. For the best route to his destination, he must know where it lies with respect to his present position, and the dangers to navigation which may be along the way.

All of this information can only be determined from charts, one of the most essential and important items of equipment for piloting a boat. It would take a skillful boatman indeed to cruise any distance into strange waters without the necessary charts, even if he were equipped with all the other needed devices—and it would be foolhardy of him to attempt it. The skipper must not only have the required charts; he must know how to use them.

FIG. 1801   You are at Buoy "4" and the water is measured to be 18 feet deep, but what is the course to your destination, and how deep is the water along the way? Only a chart can give you this information —be sure that you have the right charts on board, and that you know how to use them.

FIG. 1802   A nautical chart is a representation in miniature of a portion of the earth's surface with emphasis on natural and man-made features of particular interest to the navigator of a ship or boat.

CHARTS VS. MAPS

A *nautical chart,* fig. 1802, is a representation in miniature, on a plane surface, of a portion of the earth's surface emphasizing natural and man-made features of particular interest to a navigator. A map, fig. 1803, is a similar miniature representation for use on land in which the emphasis is on roads, cities, political boundaries, etc. For a boatman to refer to a chart as a "map" is to reveal his lack of nautical knowledge and experience.

A chart covers an area which is primarily water and includes such information as the depth of water, obstructions and other dangers to navigation, and the location and type of aids to navigation. Adjacent land areas are portrayed only in such detail as will aid a navigator—the shoreline, harbor facilities, prominent natural or man-made features, etc. Charts are printed on heavy-weight, durable paper so that they may be used as worksheets on which courses may be plotted and positions determined.

A basic requirement of a nautical chart is to provide the navigator with the proper information to enable him to make the *right* decision *in time to avoid danger.* Charts are prepared by various agencies of the Government to furnish the pilot or navigator with absolutely accurate representations of navigable bodies of water showing the depths, aids to navigation, shorelines, and other essential features. They differ from road maps both in the great amount of detailed information that they contain and in the precision with which they are constructed. The need for this accuracy can be appreciated when it is realized that an error of only a small amount in charting the position of a submerged obstruction could constitute a serious menace to navigation.

Several major oil companies used to produce a series of "cruising guides" which cover important boating areas, fig. 1804. These are useful in planning a nautical trip, but lack the detail, accuracy, and provision for revisions between printings (by means of Notices to Mari-

ners) required for actual navigational use. Do *not* try to substitute them for official government charts.

GEOGRAPHIC COORDINATES

Charts will also show a grid of intersecting lines to aid in the description of a position on the water. These lines are the charted representations of a system of *geographic coordinates* which exist on the earth's surface, although in an unseen, imaginary sense like state boundaries.

The earth is nearly spherical in shape—it is slightly flattened along the polar axis, but the distortion is slight and

© General Drafting Co., Inc.

FIG. 1803 A map differs from a nautical chart in that the emphasis is on towns, roads, political boundaries, etc. It is designed primarily for motorists and should never be used for navigation.

FIG. 1804 At one time, several major oil companies issued "cruising guides." These could be useful in planning a cruise, but should never be depended upon for the actual navigation of a boat.

need be of concern only to scientists, not boatmen. A *great circle,* fig. 1805a, is the line traced out on the surface of a sphere by a plane cutting through the sphere at its center. This is the largest circle that can be drawn on the surface of a sphere. A *small circle,* fig. 1805b, is one marked on the surface of a sphere by a plane that does not pass through its center.

Meridians and parallels

Geographic coordinates are defined by two sets of great and small circles. One is a set of great circles each of which passes through the north and south geographic poles — these are the *meridians of longitude,* fig. 1806. The other set is a series of circles each established by a plane cutting through the earth perpendicular to the polar axis. The

For greater precision in position definition, degrees may be subdivided into *minutes* (60 minutes = 1 degree) and *seconds* (60 seconds = 1 minute).

From figures 1808b and 1809, it will be seen that the meridians of longitude get closer together as one moves away from the equator in either direction, and eventually converge at the poles. Thus the distance on the earth's surface between adjacent meridians is not a fixed quantity but varies with latitude. On the other hand, the parallels of latitude are essentially equally spaced and the distance between successive parallels is nearly the same. One degree of latitude is, for all practical purposes, 60 nautical miles: and *one minute of latitude may be taken as one nautical mile,* a relationship which we will later see is quite useful.

FIG. 1805 a   A GREAT CIRCLE is the line traced out on the surface of a sphere by a plane cutting through the center point of the sphere. (From Dutton)

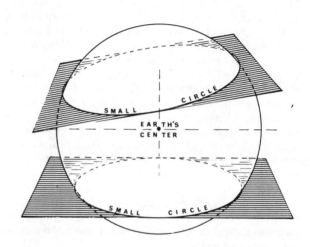

FIG. 1805 b   A SMALL CIRCLE is the line traced on the surface of a sphere by a plane which cuts through the sphere but does NOT pass through the center point of the sphere.

largest of these is midway between the poles and thus passes through the center of the earth, becoming a great circle; this is the *equator,* fig. 1807a. Other parallel planes form small circles which are known as the *parallels of latitude,* fig. 1807b.

Geographic coordinates are measured in terms of degrees (one degree is 1/360th of a complete circle). The meridian that passes through Greenwich, England is the reference for all measurements of longitude and is designated as the *prime meridian,* or 0°. The longitude of any position on earth is described as —° East or West of Greenwich, to a maximum in either direction of 180°. The measurement can be thought of as either the angle at the north and south poles between the meridian of the place being described and the prime meridian, or as the arc along the equator between these meridians, fig. 1808a. The designation of "E" or "W" is an essential part of any statement of longitude, abbreviated as "Long." or "Lo" or as "λ" (the Greek letter *lambda*).

Parallels of latitude are measured in degrees North or South from the equator, from 0° at the equator to 90° at each pole. The designation of latitude (abbreviated as "Lat." or "L") as "N" or "S" is necessary for a complete position; see fig. 1808b.

FIG. 1806   MERIDIANS of LONGITUDE are formed on the earth's surface by great circles which pass through the North and South Poles. (From Bowditch)

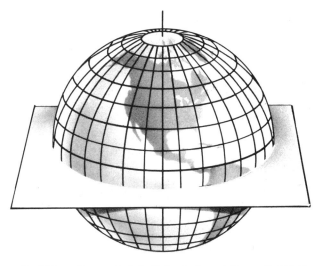

FIG. 1807 a The great circle that cuts through the earth perpendicular to the polar axis traces out the EQUATOR at the earth's surface.

FIG. 1807 b PARALLELS of LATITUDE are the small circles formed at the earth's surface by planes perpendicular to the polar axis but not passing through the center of the earth. They are parallel to the plane of the Equator.

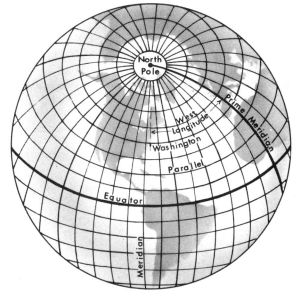

FIG. 1808 a Longitude is measured in degrees from the Prime Meridian (0°), which passes through Greenwich, England, East or West to a maximum of 180°. The designation of "E" or "W" is an essential part of any statement of longitude.

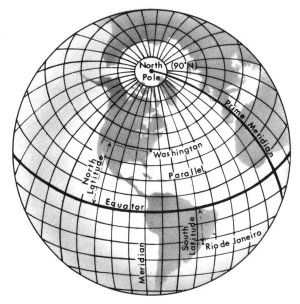

FIG. 1808 b Latitude is measured in either direction, North or South, from the Equator (0°) to the Poles (90°). Statements of latitude, abbreviated "L", must be labeled either "N" or "S" to be complete. (From Bowditch)

CHART CONSTRUCTION

The construction of a chart for a portion of the earth's surface immediately produces the problem of representation of a spherical, three-dimensional surface on a plane, two-dimensional sheet of paper. Actually, it is impossible to accomplish this exactly. A certain amount of distortion is inevitable, but various methods, called *projections*, have been developed which provide practical and sufficiently accurate results.

The transfer of information from the sphere to the flat surface of the chart should be accomplished with as little distortion as possible in the shape and size of land and water areas, the angular relation of positions, the distance between points, and other more technical properties. Each of the different projections is superior to others in one or more of these qualities; none is superior in all characteristics. In all projections, as the area covered by the chart is decreased, the distortion diminishes, and the difference between various types of projections lessens.

Of the many techniques of projection that might be used, two are of primary interest to boatmen. The *Mercator projection* is an example of the most common; it is used for charts of ocean and coastal areas. The *polyconic projection* is employed for charts of the Great Lakes and inland rivers. The average skipper can quite safely navigate his boat using either type of chart without a deep knowledge of the techniques of projection. (For those who would know more of the various projection methods, see pages 359-363.

FIG. 1809 Meridians of longitude converge toward each other as one moves away from the Equator in the direction of either pole. All meridians meet at the North and South Poles.

DIRECTION

Direction is defined as the angle between a line connecting one point with another point and a base, or reference, line extending from the origin point toward the true or magnetic north pole; the angle is measured in degrees clockwise from the reference line. Thus direction on charts may be described as so many degrees "True" (T) or so many degrees "Magnetic" (M). The difference between these directions is "variation" and must be allowed for as described in Chapter 14. The principal difference in the use of charts on the Mercator projection from those on the polyconic projection lies in the techniques for measuring direction; this will be covered in Chapter 19 when the use of piloting instruments is considered.

Measurement of direction

To facilitate the measurement of direction, as in plotting bearings and laying out courses, most charts will have compass roses printed on them. A *compass rose*, fig. 1810, consists of two or three concentric circles, several inches in diameter and accurately subdivided. The outer circle has its zero at *true* north; this is emphasized with a star. The inner circle or circles are oriented to magnetic north. The middle circle, if there are three, is *magnetic* direction expressed in degrees, with an arrow printed over the zero point to indicate magnetic north. The innermost circle is also magnetic direction, but in terms of "points," and halves and quarters thereof; its use by modern boatmen will be limited. (One point = 11¼ degrees.) The use of points with the rules of the road is covered in Chapter 4 and with the mariner's compass in Chapter 13.

The difference between the orientation of the two sets of circles is, of course, the magnetic variation at the loca-

tion of the compass rose. The amount of the variation and its direction (Easterly or Westerly) is given in words and figures in the center of the rose, together with a statement of the year that such variation existed and the annual rate of change. When using a chart in a year later than the date shown on the compass rose, it *may* be necessary to modify the variation shown by applying the annual rate of change. Such cases are, however, relatively rare as rates are quite small and differences of a small fraction of a degree may be ignored from a practical standpoint.

Each chart will have several compass roses printed on it at convenient locations where they will not conflict with navigational information. Roses printed on land areas may cause the elimination of topographical features in these regions.

Until a skipper has thoroughly mastered the handling of compass "errors," he should use only true directions and the true (outer) compass rose. Later, the magnetic rose may be used directly, thus simplifying computations.

Several cautions are necessary when measuring directions on charts. When large areas are covered, it is possible for the magnetic variation to differ for various portions of the chart. Check each chart when you first start to use it, and, to be sure, always use the compass rose nearest the area for which you are plotting. Depending upon the type and scale of the chart, graduations on the compass rose circles may be for intervals of 1°, 2°, or 5°. On some charts, the outer circle (true) is subdivided into units of 1° while the inner (magnetic) circle, being smaller, is subdivided into steps of 2°. Always check carefully to determine the interval between adjacent marks on each compass rose scale.

FIG. 1810 A compass rose graphically illustrates true and magnetic directions. The outer circle is in degrees with zero at true north. The inner circles are in degrees and "points" with their zero oriented to the magnetic north. Several will be found on each chart conveniently located for plotting courses and bearings. Some charts of the small-craft series may omit the innermost circle that uses the "point" system of subdivision.

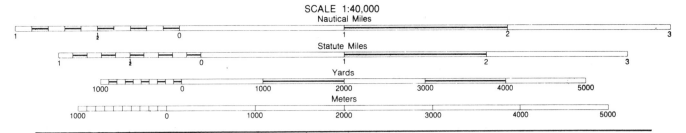

SCALE 1:40,000
Nautical Miles
Statute Miles
Yards
Meters

FIG. 1811   N.O.S. charts at scales of 1:80,000 or larger will have two sets of graphic scales. Each set consists of a scale of nautical miles and a scale of yards. On Intercoastal Waterway Charts, a scale of statute miles will also be shown. With the growing conversion to the metric system, future chart editions will additionally carry a scale of kilometers.

DISTANCE

Distances on charts may be measured in statute or in nautical miles. Use of the *statute (land) mile* of 5280 feet is limited to the Great Lakes, inland rivers, and the Atlantic and Gulf Intracoastal Waterways. The *nautical mile* of 6076.1 feet is used on ocean and coastal waters. The use of *kilometers* may increase in the future.

It is sometimes necessary to convert from one unit to the other. This is not difficult—*1 nautical mile = 1.15 statute miles*, or roughly 7 nautical miles = 8 statute miles. One kilometer = 0.62 statute = 0.54 nautical mile.

In navigation, distances of up to a mile or so usually are expressed in *yards,* a unit that is the same no matter which "mile" is used on the chart.

SCALE

As a chart is a representation in miniature of an area of navigable water, actual distances must be "scaled down" to much shorter dimensions on paper. This reduction is termed the *scale* of the chart. The basic way of describing the scale of a chart is its so-called *natural scale,* an expression of the relationship between a given distance on the chart to the actual distance that it represents on the earth. This may be expressed as a ratio, 1:80,000 meaning that 1 unit on the chart represents 80,000 units on the actual land or water surface, or as a fraction $\frac{1}{80,000}$ with the same meaning.

The ratio of chart to actual distance can also be expressed as a *numerical* or *equivalent scale.* This is such a statement as "1 inch = 1.1 miles," another way of expressing a 1:80,000 scale. Equivalent scales are not as commonly used on nautical charts as on maps, but they may be encountered from time to time on such publications as cruising guides.

It is important that at all times the pilot have clearly fixed in his mind the scale of the chart then being used—in order that he will not misjudge the distance to aids to navigation, dangers, etc. Quite often in a day's cruise, a skipper will use charts of different scales, changing back and forth between small-scale coastal charts and larger-scale harbor charts. Unless he is keenly aware of the scale

of the chart being used at the moment, a pilot may find himself unexpectedly in a dangerous position.

Large-scale and small-scale

When chart scales are expressed fractionally, confusion sometimes results from the use of the terms "large-scale" and "small-scale." Since the number that is varied to change the scale is in the *denominator* of the fraction, as it gets larger, the fraction, and hence the scale, gets smaller. For example, $\frac{1}{80,000}$ is a smaller fraction than $\frac{1}{40,000}$, and thus a chart to the former scale is termed a smaller-scale chart. The terms "large-scale" and "small-scale" are relative and have no limiting definitions. Scales may be as large as 1:5,000 for detailed harbor charts, or as small as 1 to several million for charts of large areas of the world.

Charts at a scale of 1:80,000 or larger will normally carry, in addition to a statement of scale, two sets of *graphic scales,* fig. 1811, each subdivided into conveniently and commonly used units. Note that one basic unit is placed to the *left* of the scale's zero point and is subdivided more finely than is the main part of the scale. The use of these graphic scales will be covered in Chapter 19.

When using Mercator charts, the navigator can take advantage of the fact that one minute of the *latitude* scale on each *side* of the chart is essentially equal to one nautical mile. On charts of a scale smaller than 1:80,000, the latitude scale will be the only means of measuring distance.

A *logarithmic speed scale,* fig. 1812, is printed on all charts of 1:40,000 or larger scale. Its use is explained in Chapter 19.

SOURCES OF CHARTS

Who issues charts

Charts are prepared and issued by several agencies of the Federal Government. This is not duplication, however, as different areas and types of charts are the responsibility of each office. The majority of boatmen will use charts prepared by the National Ocean Survey of the National

LOGARITHMIC SPEED SCALE

To find SPEED, place one point of dividers on distance run (in any unit) and the other on minutes run. Without changing divider spread, place right point on 60 and left point will then indicate speed in units per hour. Example: with 4.0 nautical miles run in 15 minutes, the speed is 16.0 knots

FIG. 1812 N.O.S. charts of 1:40,000 or larger scale will have a LOGARITHMIC SPEED SCALE from which a graphic calculation of speed may be made if the time of run is measured between two known points. See Chapter 19 for a detailed discussion of its use.

Oceanic & Atmospheric Administration, Department of Commerce. N.O.S. charts cover the coastal waters of the United States, including harbors and rivers extending inland to the head of tidal action.

On 1 July 1972, the Defense Mapping Agency was created by combining the mapping, charting, and geodetic activities of the Military Departments. The Naval Oceanographic Office became the Defense Mapping Agency Hydrographic/Topographic Center. DMAHTC publishes charts of the high seas and foreign waters based on its own and other nations' surveys. Boatmen will use DMAHTC charts, for example, when cruising in the Bahamas. (The "N.O." prefix, which replaced the old "H.O." when charts were renumbered, has now been dropped and no prefix is used.) Canadian waters, however, are charted by that country's Hydrographic Service.

Charts of major inland rivers such as the Mississippi and Ohio are issued by the U.S. Army Corps of Engineers. Also available are charts and "Navigational maps" of many inland lakes and canal systems.

Where to buy them

Charts may be purchased directly from the headquarters or field offices of the issuing agencies, or from retail sales agents. The government offices may be addressed as shown in fig. 1813. Sales agents are widely located in boating and shipping centers. The names and addresses of local sales agents for N.O.S. charts and publications are listed in the various N.O.S. Chart Catalogs. These lists are footnoted to indicate agents also stocking DMAHTC charts and publications and USCG publications. DMAHTC Pubs. No. 1-N-A and 1-N-L also list sales agents including those in foreign countries.

The cost of charts is amazingly little for the vast amount of information furnished to the navigator. The prices charged for charts include only a small part of the cost to the government for their production. Traditionally, it has been the duty of a country to aid safe navigation by publishing low-cost charts and nautical guides. Recent increases in chart prices have reflected only the general rise in costs, not a change in pricing policy.

N.O.S. and DMAHTC charts are sold by government offices and sales agents located in most boating areas; a discount is allowed to each dealer for his quantity purchases. A boat or yacht club, or other boating organization, also may purchase charts in quantity for a discount; get the details from the issuing agency.

CHART ISSUING AGENCIES

⚓ National Ocean Survey, NOAA
Rockville, Maryland 20852

⚓ Defense Mapping Agency Hydrographic/Topographic Center, Washington, DC 20315

FIG. 1813 Information on nautical charts can be obtained by writing to the appropriate headquarters at the address shown above. Regional and District Offices may also be able to provide answers to questions on charts.

The prudent skipper carries on his boat a full set of charts covering the waters that he cruises, and he regularly replaces worn-out or outdated charts with new ones. Charts are among his best boating bargains!

Chart catalogs

Catalogs are available from issuing agencies which indicate the area covered by each chart, the scale used, and the price. These will be found useful when planning a cruise into unfamiliar boating waters.

The National Ocean Survey publishes four Chart catalogs that are available to boatmen without charge.* Catalog No. 1 covers the waters of the Atlantic and Gulf Coasts, including Puerto Rico and the Virgin Islands. Catalog No. 2 is for the Pacific Coast, including Hawaii and Pacific islands such as Guam and Samoa. Catalog 3 covers Alaskan waters, including the Aleutian Islands. Catalog No. 4 is for the Great Lakes, including connecting and adjacent waterways.

Each catalog contains several small-scale outline charts with lines showing the limits of each nautical chart in that region. These catalogs are also excellent sources of information on other N.O.S. publications as well as charts and publications of other agencies. The names and addresses of local sales agents for charts and other publications are listed in each catalog. These lists are updated with each edition of the four catalogs.

DMAHTC chart catalog, publication number 1-N, is issued in "Regions" at a price of 25¢ each. Region "1" covers U.S. coastal waters; Region "2" includes the Bahamian and West Indian cruising areas as well as the waters bordering Central and South America.

What Charts Show

Charts include a great amount of information and a boatman should carefully study each chart soon after he purchases it, certainly well before he must use it to safely navigate his craft.

BASIC INFORMATION

Located at some convenient place on the chart, where space is available, will be found the *general information block,* fig. 1814. Here is the chart title which is descriptive of the waters covered (the chart number will not appear

here, but rather in several places around the margins), a statement of the type of projection used and the scale, the unit of measurement of depth (feet or fathoms—one fathom equals six feet—or meters), and the datum plane for such soundings.

Elsewhere on the chart where there is space available (normally in land areas), other information will be found, such as the meaning of abbreviations used on this chart, special notes of caution regarding dangers, the units of measurement of heights and the reference plane from

*N.O.S. Chart Catalog 5 lists bathymetric maps and special purpose charts; it is of lesser interest to boatmen.

FIG. 1814 The title block shows the official name of the chart, the type of projection, scale, and datum and unit of measurement for depths. Printed nearby will be much valuable information—be sure to read all notes and data before using any chart.

which measured, tidal information, references to anchorage areas, and many other useful bits of data. *All* notes on charts should be read carefully and fully, as they may cover important information that cannot be graphically presented, such as information applying to an extended length of a river or channel; see fig. 1815.

Editions and revisions

The edition number and date appear in the margin at the lower left-hand corner; immediately following these figures will be the date of the latest revised printing, if any; see figs. 1816a and b. Most nautical charts are printed to supply a normal demand for one or two years, from four to twelve years in areas where few changes occur; quantities are so limited to provide for updating as required. (Certain less-frequently printed charts of remote areas have a note as follows: "For this chart, a listing of Notice to Mariners corrections subsequent to the print date is available from the Director, National Ocean Survey, Rockville, Maryland 20852, Attn: C32")

Charts may be reprinted as-is when the stock runs low, but a *revised print* is more likely. Revisions include all changes that have been printed in Notices to Mariners since the last revision. When major changes in hydrography occur, such as significant differences between charted depths and actual conditions revealed by new surveys, a *new edition* will be published. This will also include all other changes which have been made in aids to navigation, etc.

Special charts, for which there is an urgent need, are printed directly from smooth drafting without engraving; these are designated as "Provisional Charts" and are so labeled in the title block. A chart constructed from unverified information will be marked as a "Preliminary Chart."

It is of the utmost importance that only the latest edition of a chart be used. All new editions supersede older issues, which should be discarded. New editions contain information published in Notices to Mariners, *plus* all other corrections from extensive application of hydrographic and topographic surveys considered essential for safe navigation but not published in the Notices. Skippers are cautioned against using superceded charts that may not con-

tain all information essential to safe navigation.

Between editions, charts should be corrected from information published in Notices to Mariners (see page 335). Charts are no longer kept corrected by the National Ocean Survey while in stock awaiting sale. The purchaser of a chart should make every effort to check all Notices subsequent to the printed edition date and enter all applicable corrections. The safest chart is the one that is fully corrected up to date.

LATITUDE AND LONGITUDE SCALES

Nautical charts of the conventional type with the geographical north direction toward the top of the sheet will have latitude scales in each side border and longitude scales in the top and bottom borders. The meridians and parallels will be drawn across the chart as fine black lines at intervals of 2', 5', or 10' as determined by the scale of the particular chart.

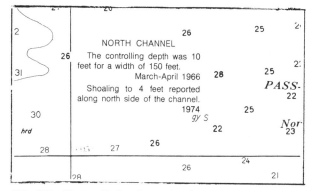

FIG. 1815 Charts will often have printed notes with information of considerable importance. These may concern navigation regulations, hazardous conditions at inlets, information on controlling depths that cannot be conveniently printed alongside the channel (as above), or other matters. Check each chart that you buy for such notes and read them carefully.

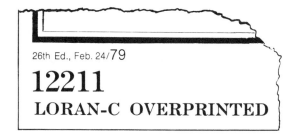

FIG. 1816 a The edition number and date are printed in the margin of each N.O.S. chart in the lower-left corner. Also shown here is the chart number.

FIG. 1816 b Between editions, revised printings are made of charts to include all changes that have been published in Notices to Mariners. Be safe—do not use obsolete charts!

On N.O.S. charts having a scale larger than 1:49,000, such as on harbor charts, the subdivisions in the border scales are in terms of minutes and seconds of latitude and longitude, fig. 1818a.

On smaller-scale charts, the subdivisions are in minutes and fractions of minutes—charts at a scale of 1:80,000, such as 1210Tr, use minutes and tenths of minutes, fig. 1818b. Still smaller scale charts will use fifths or halves of minutes.

Where skewed projections are used, and north is not toward the top of the sheet, as on Intracoastal Waterway charts, the subdivisions of latitude and longitude are indicated along parallels and meridians at several convenient places, or near the graphic scales.

USE OF COLOR

Most charts use color to emphasize various features and so facilitate reading and interpretation. The number of colors will vary with the agency publishing the chart and its intended use. The N.O.S. color system uses five multipurpose colors. By using screening techniques, the intensity of the full-strength colors can be reduced to provide many shades of black, purple, gold, blue, and green.

Land areas are colored in a light screened gold;* water areas are white, the color of the paper, except for the shallower regions which are shown in blue. Areas that may be submerged at some tidal stages, but which un-

cover at others, are represented in green. Sand bars, mud flats, coral reefs, and marshes are typical of such green areas on charts. On some charts, water areas that have been swept with wire drags to ensure the absence of isolated rocks or coral heads may be shown in a greenish half-tone with the depth of the sweep indicated.

Nautical purple ink is used for many purposes on charts; it was selected for its good visibility under red light which is used on many vessels for reading charts during darkness because it does not destroy night vision as white light would. Red buoys are printed in this color, as are red day-beacon symbols. Lighted buoys of any color have a purple disc over the dot or small circle portion of the symbol to assist in its identification as a lighted aid to navigation. A purple flare symbol extending from the position dot is used with lights, lighted ranges, etc. Caution and danger symbols and notes are printed in nautical purple; also compass roses are recommended courses where shown. Black is used for most symbols and printed information.

The new N.O.S. gold and blue colors give many features better definition under both daylight and red-light viewing conditions. The yellow land color used previously became invisible under red light, and there was no contrast between the old blue and low-water green. The new land and water colors, and green for low-water areas, become separate and distinct shades when viewed by red light. The low-water green produces the darkest

FIG. 1817 N.O.S. and Defense Mapping Agency Hydrographic/Topographic Center (DMAHTC charts, and light Lists and Coast Pilots, are corrected by Notices to Mariners. Most changes can be made by hand, but more extensive ones will require use of a small area paste-on chartlet. These are bound in the Notice with directions for their use given in the regular listing of changes to be made. Shown here are the directions and actual extract for change to Chart 12234.

*On DMAHTC charts, land areas are in gray tint.

346

FIG. 1818(b) On charts with relatively small scales, the latitude and longitude border markings will be in minutes and fractions of minutes. On this 1:80,000 chart, meridians are drawn in every 10 minutes and the subdivisions are in minutes and tenths of minutes. On yet smaller scale charts, the smallest subdivision might be fifths, halves, or whole minutes of latitude and longitude.

shade, providing a safety characteristic for such critical areas.

LETTERING STYLES

In order to convey to the chart reader as much information as possible in the clearest form, a system has been adopted whereby certain classes of information are printed in one style of lettering and other classes in another style. By knowing what type of lettering is used for which class of information, one can more easily and quickly grasp the data being presented.

VERTICAL lettering is used for features which are dry at high water and are not affected by movement of the water, except for the height of the feature above the water, which may be changed by tidal action. See the use of vertical lettering for the power line towers and the bell fog signal in fig. 1819.

LEANING, or slanting letters (*such as these*) are used for water, underwater, and floating features, except depth figures. Note the use in fig. 1819 of leaning lettering for "*hrd S*" meaning a hard sand bottom at that point*

On smaller-scale charts, a small reef (covering and uncovering with tidal action) often cannot be distinguished by symbol from a small islet (always above water); the proper name for either might be "—— Rock." Following the standard of lettering, the feature in doubt is an islet if the name is in vertical letters, but is a reef if lettered in leaning characters.

Similarly, a piling visible above water at all tidal stages will be charted as "Pile," but one beneath the surface will be noted as "*subm pile*."

Periods after abbreviations are omitted in water and in land areas, but the lower-case *i* and *j* are dotted. Periods are used only where needed for clarity, as, for example, in certain notes.

WATER FEATURES

The information shown on charts is a combination of the natural features of the water and land areas and various selected man-made objects and features. Each item shown will have been carefully chosen for its value to those navigating vessels of all sizes.

Depths

The principal feature of concern to boatmen and mariners regarding water areas is the *depth*. For any system of

* Minor changes in the use of vertical and slant lettering are being introduced on metric nautical charts in order to better conform to international standards.

FIG. 1818a On charts with scales of 1:49,000 or larger, the longitude and latitude scales in the borders are subdivided into minutes and seconds. On this extract from a 1:40,000 harbor chart, meridians are drawn at 5-minute intervals, tick marks are placed every minute, and one 1-minute interval is subdivided into units of 5 seconds each. Scales in the 1:30,000 to 1:40,000 category south of 49°N will include a 10-second subdivision. Usually on charts with skewed projections, breakdowns of one minute of latitude and longitude are shown in the vicinity of the graphic scales.

FIG. 1819 This chart excerpt illustrates the use of vertical lettering for features above water—"TOWER"—and leaning letters for under water features—"hrd" and "Grs" for hard and grassy bottom at two places. Note also the designation of a CABLE AREA.

depth information, there must be a reference plane, or *datum*. This is obvious in coastal areas where depths may change hourly as a result of tidal action; it is likewise true in inland areas where lake or river levels may also change, though more slowly on a seasonal basis. Each chart will have printed on it a statement of the datum from which all depths, also called *soundings,* are measured. The choice of the reference plane is based on many factors, most of them technical, but the primary consideration is that of selecting a datum near to normal low-water levels.

Planes of reference

On Pacific Coast charts the datum for the depths has long been *mean lower low water*, each tidal day having two low tides of different heights; see page 395. In late 1980, the National Ocean Survey changed the tital datum for the Atlantic and Gulf Coasts from mean low water to mean lower low water to make all U.S. charts consistent; this change is of no practical effect and does not change any charted depths. Lake and river charts will generally use a datum which is based on past records of variations in level over many years. When entering strange waters always be sure to check the chart for the statement of the datum used for depths.

By definition, "mean lower low water" is an *average* of all lowest water levels for tidal days over a period of time (usually 19 years). Thus on some days the lower low tide will be *below* the datum. This will result in actual depths being shallower than the charted figures. However, these variations are not often great enough to affect navigation. Many charts will have a small box with a tabulation of the extreme variations from charted depths that may be expected for various points, fig. 1820. Prolonged winds from certain directions, or persistent extremes of barometric pressure, may cause temporary local differences

TIDAL INFORMATION			
	Height referred to datum of soundings (MLW)		
Place	Mean High Water	Mean Tide Level	Mean Low Water	Extreme Low Water
	feet	feet	feet	feet
Wilmington, Del.	5.3	2.9	0.0	−4.0
Chester, Pa.	5.4	2.9	0.0	−4.0
Billingsport, N.J.	5.5	3.0	0.0	−4.5
Phila. Pier 9N., Pa.	5.8	3.1	0.0	−5.0

FIG. 1820 Coast and Harbor Charts will usually have information on the normal range of tides and the extreme variations from charted depths that may be expected. Check all newly-purchased charts for this important information.

FIG. 1821 The side limits of "improved" (dredged) channels are marked by dashed lines. Information on the depth (and date of measurement) will often be printed between or alongside the dashed lines. In some cases, information on the width of the channel will also be shown.

from charted depths. *It must always be remembered that exceptional conditions may occur at which time the water may be much shallower than indicated on the chart.*

How depths are shown

Depth information is shown on the chart by many small printed figures. These indicate the depth at that point measured in feet or fathoms. A few charts may mix these units, using feet in shallower areas and fathoms offshore in deeper waters; such charts are relatively rare. Some newer charts have depths measured in meters and decimeters (tenths of a meter); 1 fathom is 1.83 meters. The depth figures are only a small part of the many soundings taken by the survey team. Only the more significant and representative are selected for use on the final chart.

The boatman can form some opinion of the characteristics of the bottom by noting the density of the depth information. Where depth figures are rather widely spaced, he can be assured of a reasonably flat or uniformly sloping bottom. Wherever the depths vary irregularly or abruptly, the figures will be more frequent and more closely spaced.

Fathom curves

Most charts will have *contour lines,* sometimes called *fathom curves,* connecting points of equal depth. Such lines will appear at certain depths as determined by the scale of the chart and the relative range of the depths. Typically, fathom curves are shown for 1, 2, 3 5, 10, and multiples of ten fathoms. Continuous solid lines or various combinations of dots and dashes are used to code the depth along each line, but it is often easier to learn a line's significance by inspection of the depth figures on either side of it.

On many charts, a blue tint is shown in water areas out to the curve that is considered to be the danger curve for that particular chart. In general, the 6-foot curve is considered the danger curve for small-craft and Intracoastal Waterway charts, the 12- or 18-foot curve for harbor charts, and the 30-foot curve for coast and general charts. (These types of charts are discussed in more detail on pages 356-358.) In some instances, the area between the 3-fathom and the 5- or 6-fathom curves may be tinted in a lighter shade of blue than the shallower areas. Thus it can be seen that while blue tint means shallow water, this symbolism does not have the same exact meaning on all charts. Check each chart that you use to determine at just what depth the coloring changes.

Charts on which no fathom curves are marked for water areas must be regarded with some suspicion and used with caution as this may indicate that soundings are too scarce to allow the lines to be drawn with accuracy.

Isolated soundings, shoaler than surrounding depths, should always be avoided, particularly if ringed around, as it is doubtful how closely the spot may have been examined and whether the least depth has been found.

Dredged channels

Dredged channels are shown on a chart by two dashed lines to represent the side limits of the improvement. The depth of the channel and the date on which such data were obtained will be shown within the lines or close alongside, see fig. 1821. A dredged basin will be similarly outlined with printed information on depths and date.

The depth shown, such as "6 feet 1980," is the controlling depth through the channel on the date shown but does not mean this depth exists over the full width of the channel.

Channels are sometimes described on charts in terms of specific width as well as depth; for example, "8 feet for width of 100 feet." The printing of such depth information does not insure that it may not have subsequently changed due to either shoaling or further dredging. Such changes do occur, and therefore if your craft's draft is close to the depth shown for the channel, local information on existing conditions should be obtained if possible before entering.

Detailed information for many dredged channels is shown in tabular form on the applicable charts, with revisions of the data published in Notices to Mariners as changes occur.

Nature of the bottom

The nature of the bottom, such as sand, rocky, mud, grass, etc., or a more general description such as "hard" or "soft," will be indicated for many areas by means of abbreviations. This information is of value when anchoring, and advantage should be taken of it wherever it appears. The meanings of these and other abbreviations are usually given on the face of the chart near the basic identification block; many are self-evident, the more frequently encountered ones should be memorized.

The shoreline

The shoreline shown on charts is the mean high-water line (high-water line in lakes and non-tidal areas) except in marsh or mangrove areas where the outer edge of vegetation is used. Natural shoreline is represented by a slightly heavier line than man-made shoreline. Unsurveyed shoreline, or shoreline connecting two surveys that do not join satisfactorily, is shown by a dashed solid line. The low-water line is marked by a single row of dots. The outer limits of marsh are indicated by a fine solid line.

The region between the high- and low-water lines will be tinted green, and may be labeled "Grass," "Mud," "Sand," etc.

FEATURES OF LAND AREAS

Features and characteristics of land areas are shown on nautical charts in only such detail as will be of assistance to a navigator. Details are usually confined to those near the shoreline or of such a prominent nature as to be clearly seen for some distance offshore.

How topography is shown

The general topography of land areas will be indicated by contours, form lines, or hachures. *Contours* are lines connecting points of equal elevation. The specific height, usually measured in feet, of such contour lines may be shown by figures placed at suitable points along the lines. The interval of height between adjacent contours is uniform over any one chart.

Form lines, or *sketch contours,* are shown by broken lines and are approximations of contours intended to give an indication of terrain formations without exact information on height. They are used in areas where accurate data are not available in sufficient quantity to permit the exact location of contours. The interval between form lines is not necessarily uniform and no height figures are given.

Hachures are short lines, or groups of lines, indicating approximately the location of steep slopes. The lines follow generally the direction of the slope, the length of the lines indicating the height of the slope.

Cliffs, vegetation and the shore

Cliffs are represented by bands of irregular hachures. The symbol is not an exact "plan view," but rather somewhat of a "side elevation"; its extent is roughly proportional to the height of the cliff. For example, a perpendicular cliff of 100 feet height will be shown by a hachured band wider than one representing a cliff of 15 feet with

FIG. 1822 Information on the elevation of hills or mountain summits, or the tops of conspicuous landmarks, is often printed on a nautical chart. Heights are usually measured from Mean High Water in feet, but meters and decimeters (tenths of a meter) are now being used on some charts.

FIG. 1823 a On relatively large-scale charts, detailed information may be shown of the streets and buildings of a city or town, particularly near the waterfront. Some street names may be given, also the location of public buildings such as a customhouse and post office.

slope. According to the principles of "plan" drawing (viewing from directly above), a perpendicular cliff would be shown by one line only and could not be distinguished from an ordinary shoreline.

Spot elevations are normally given on nautical charts only for summits or the tops of conspicuous landmarks, fig. 1822. Heights are measured from mean high water.

The type of vegetation on land will sometimes be indicated by symbols or wording where such information may be of use to the mariner.

The nature of the shore is indicated by various symbols—rows of fine dots denote a sandy beach, small circles indicate gravel, irregular shapes mean boulders, etc.

MAN-MADE FEATURES

Man-made features on land will be shown in detail where they relate directly to water-borne traffic. Examples of these are piers, bridges, overhead power cables, and breakwaters. Other man-made features on land, such as built-up areas, roads, streets, etc., will be shown in some detail or will be generalized as determined by their usefulness to navigation and the scale of the chart. On large-scale charts the actual network of streets will at times be depicted, with public buildings such as the post office and customs house individually identified, fig. 1823a. On less detailed charts, the town or city may be represented by a halftone shaded area for the approximate limits of the built-up area with major streets and roads shown by single heavy lines, see fig. 1823b. Prominent isolated objects, tanks, stacks, spires, etc., will be shown accurately

FIG. 1823 b On smaller-scale charts, cities, towns, and other built-up areas are generalized by "screening," a shading process that shows up as a darker, but not black, area. Only principal roads and streets are shown, these by a single, heavy solid line.

located in order that they may be used for taking bearings.

Specific descriptive names have been given to certain types of landmark objects for the purpose of standardizing terminology. Among the more often used are the following:

Building or **House**—the appropriate one of these terms is used when the entire structure is the landmark, rather than any individual feature of it.

Spire — a slender, pointed structure extending above a building. It is seldom less than two-thirds of the entire height of the structure, and its lines are rarely broken by intermediate structures. Spires are typically found on churches.

Dome — a large, rounded, hemispherical structure rising above a building; for example, the dome of the United States Capitol in Washington.

Cupola — a dome-shaped tower or turret rising from a building, generally small in comparison with the size of the building.

Chimney — a relatively small projection for conveying smoke from a building to the atmosphere. This term is used when the building is more prominent than the chimney, but a better bearing can be taken on the smaller feature.

Stack — a tall smokestack or chimney. This term is used when the stack is more prominent as a landmark than the accompanying buildings.

Flagpole — a single staff from which flags are displayed. This term is used when the pole is not attached to a building.

Flagstaff—a flagpole arising from a building.

Radio Tower—a tall pole or structure for elevating radio antennas.

Radio Mast—a relatively short pole or slender structure for elevating radio antennas; usually found in groups.

Tower—any structure with its base on the ground and high in proportion to its base, or that part of a structure higher than the rest, but having essentially vertical sides for the greater part of its height.

Lookout Station or **Watch Tower**—a tower surmounted by a small house from which a watch is regularly kept.

Tank—a water tank elevated high above ground by a tall skeleton framework. *Gas Tank* and *Oil Tank* are terms used for distinctive structures of specialized design.

Standpipe—a tall cylindrical structure whose height is several times its diameter.

Tree—an isolated, conspicuous tree useful as a navigational landmark.

When two similar objects are so located that separate landmark symbols cannot be used, the word "TWIN" is added to the identifying name or abbreviation. When only one of a group of similar objects is charted, a descriptive legend is added in parentheses; for example, ("TALLEST OF FOUR)" or "(NORTHEAST OF THREE)".

Radio broadcasting station (AM) antennas are shown on charts where they may be used for taking visual or radio bearings. The call letters and frequency are often shown adjacent to the symbol marking the location of the towers.

Symbols and Abbreviations

The vast amount of information to be shown on a chart, and the closeness with which many items appear, necessitate the extensive use of symbols and abbreviations. It is essential that a boatman have a high degree of familiarity with the symbols and abbreviations encountered on the charts that he uses. A skipper must be able to read and interpret his charts quickly and accurately; the safety of his boat may depend on this ability. Knowledge will come with use, but dependence upon a build-up from experience alone may be costly—specific study is recommended.

INTERNATIONAL STANDARDS

Symbols are conventional shapes and designs which indicate the presence of a certain feature or object at the location shown on the chart. No attempt is made at an accurate or detailed representation of the object, but the correct location is shown. Symbols and abbreviations used on charts of the National Ocean Survey and the Defense Mapping Agency Hydrographic/Topographic Center have been standardized. These are published in a small pamphlet as Chart No. 1, available for $1.50. Generally similar information is printed on the reverse side of Training

Chart 1210 Tr, but these have not been corrected for recent changes. The symbols and abbreviations are in general conformance with world-wide usage as adopted by the International Hydrographic Organization.

The standardized symbols and abbreviations are shown in figures 1844 a-o; they are grouped into *classifications* and are *numbered* in accordance with Chart No. 1. In these designations, vertical figures indicate that the symbol or abbreviation is in conformity with the standards of the International Hydrographic Organization. Slanting figures mean that the symbol or abbreviation shown either differs from that of the IHO or that it does not appear in the IHO standards; those items that differ from the IHO standard are underlined. Where letter designations are in parentheses, the symbol or abbreviation is in addition to those on the international list.

These standardized abbreviations will be used on all new charts or new editions of existing charts by the National Ocean Survey and the Defense Mapping Agency Hydrographic/Topographic Center. Older charts may continue to show other symbols and abbreviations until they are next revised and brought into conformity.

Charts / CHAPTER 18

Classification

In Chart No. 1, the standardized symbols and abbreviations are grouped into classifications as follows:

A—The Coast Line
B—Coast Features
C—The Land
D—Control Points
E—Units
F—Adjectives
G—Harbors
H—Topography
I—Buildings
J—Miscellaneous Stations

K—Lights
L—Buoys and Beacons
M—Radio Stations
N—Fog Signals
O—Dangers
P—Various Limits
Q—Soundings
R—Depth Contours
S—Quality of the Bottom
T—Tides and Currents
U—The Compass

Chart No. 1 also includes a table for the conversion of meters, fathoms, and feet.

BASIC SYMBOLS & ABBREVIATIONS

Simple inspection of many symbols will reveal a pattern or system to the way that they are formed. Knowledge of the general principles of chart symbols will facilitate learning of the details.

Buoys

Buoys, except mooring buoys, are shown by a diamond-shaped symbol and a dot or small open circle indicating the position. (The circle is replacing the dot as it better indicates the approximate position of the buoy's anchor; the dot implies a too precise location.) To avoid interference with other features on the chart, it is often necessary to show the diamond shape at various angles to the dot or circle; in some instances, the symbol might even appear "upside down."

A *black buoy* is shown as a solid black symbol without further identification of color. On charts using the normal number of colors, *red buoys* are in nautical purple; the

FIG. 1824 Ranges are excellent aids to navigation. They are charted by showing the front and rear markers with a line denoting the center of the range. This line is solid over the portion that is to be navigated, and dashed elsewhere.

FIG. 1825 This is a section from a "sailing chart." These charts, at scales of 1:600,000 or less, are the smallest scale series and cover long stretches of coastline. They are used by vessels approaching the coast from the high seas or when voyaging between distant coast ports.

letter "R" may also be shown adjacent to the symbol. Other buoys are shown by open outline symbols with the color indicated by an appropriate abbreviation, such as "Y" for yellow, "W Or" for white and orange, etc. On charts without colors, red buoys are printed as open symbols with the identifying abbreviation "R."

A buoy symbol with a line across its shorter axis indicates a *horizontally banded buoy*. For a junction buoy, if colors are used, the upper half (away from the dot) will be red and the lower half black. This is true whether in actuality the uppermost band is red (as on a nun buoy) or black (as on a can buoy).* The letters "RB" will appear near the symbol. Other kinds of horizontally banded buoys, such as white-and-orange *special purpose buoys,* will be shown by an open symbol with appropriate letters for the colors.

A buoy symbol with a line across its longer axis represents a *vertically striped buoy.* No colors will be used on this symbol; the colors of such a buoy will be indicated by abbreviations, usually "BW" for black and white.

The type and shape of *unlighted buoys* is often indicated by an abbreviation such as "C" for can, "N" for nun, or "S" for spar.

Lighted buoys are indicated by a small nautical purple disc over the dot or small circle that marks the buoy's position. The color and characteristics of the light are indicated by abbreviations near the symbol. Buoys are now so increasingly being equipped with radar reflectors that the use of "Ra ref" or a "crown" symbol is being phased out and replaced with a brief note on the chart.

Daybeacons

The symbol for *daybeacons,* unlighted aids to navigation, is a small triangle.* In general, the same scheme for indicating color is used as for buoys except that two colors are not combined in a single symbol. A red-and-black horizontally-banded daybeacon is printed as an open symbol with the description of colors abbreviated "RB."

Lights and Lighthouses

On older charts, lights and lighthouses are shown as black dots with a small magenta disc as for lighted buoys. On newer charts, the symbol will be a black dot with a purple "flare" giving much the appearance of a large exclamation mark (!). In addition to color and characteristics, there may be information on the height of the light and its nominal range (no allowance is made for curvature of the earth or observer's height of eye).

Fog Signals

The type of *fog signal* on buoys, lights, and lighthouses so equipped will be indicated by a descriptive word or abbreviation adjacent to the chart symbol.

Identification by number

Buoys and lights are usually *numbered* (or less-frequently, designated with letters or combinations of letters and numbers). This identification is placed on the chart near the symbol and is enclosed in quotation marks to distinguish the figures from depth data or other numbers. Lighthouses and some major lights are named; the words

FIG. 1826 A small portion of Chart 12300. This is at a larger scale than Fig. 1825, but still lacks many details. "General charts" should be used only for offshore navigation. Only major aids to navigation are shown. For comparison purposes, Figs. 1825 through 1828 show portions of the same area at progressively larger scales.

*In mid-1978 N.O.S. adopted new symbols that will appear on charts as new editions are printed. Daybeacons with green square daymarks will be shown as *square green symbols with the letter "G" nearby. The symbol for a horizontally-banded buoy will have its upper half red or black as the buoy is marked; the letters will be "RB" or "BR" as appropriate.

FIG. 1827 A portion of Chart 12326. "Coast charts," usually at a scale of 1:80,000, are used for closein coastwise navigation, entering and leaving harbors, and for cruising on some large inland bodies of water. The scale of this series is such that many more buoys and other aids to navigation can be shown. The depth of water is given in greater detail, the soundings being given in feet.

or abbreviations will be printed near the symbol where space permits.

Ranges

Ranges are indicated by the two symbols of the front and rear markers (lights or daybeacons), plus a line joining them and extending beyond. This line is solid over the distance for which the range is to be used for navigation; it continues on as a dashed line to the front marker and on to the rear marker, see fig. 1824.

Radiobeacons

Radiobeacons are indicated by a magenta circle around the basic symbol for the aid to navigation at which the beacon is located plus the abbreviation "R Bn." Aeronautical radiobeacons are shown only if they are useful for marine navigation; the same symbol is used and the iden-

tification "AERO" is added. The frequency, in KiloHertz, is given, as is the identifying signal in dots and dashes of the Morse code. Aeronautical radio ranges use the same symbol as beacons plus "AERO R Rge."

Dangers to navigation

Symbols are also used for many types of *dangers to navigation*. Differentiation is made between rocks that are awash at times and those which remain below the surface at all tides, between visible wrecks and submerged ones, and between hazards which have been definitely located and those whose position is doubtful. There are a number of symbols and abbreviations for objects and areas dangerous to navigation. The prudent skipper will spend adequate time studying them, with the greatest emphasis being placed on those types commonly found in his home waters.

Chart Numbering System

On 1 July 1974, all N.O.S. and Lake Survey charts were renumbered into a new system; a smaller number of DMAHTC charts were renumbered at that time. The new system uses a logical sequence of numbers and eliminates the duplication of numbers for different charts prepared by different agencies, such as the old C&GS 234 and L.S. 234. Each U.S. chart will now have its own unique number.*

The new system is based on the region/subregion concept adopted in 1971 for all former H.O. charts. Boatmen digit numbers. Such charts have a scale of 1:2,000,000 or larger. The first digit refers to the region of the world, the second to a subregion, and the final three, assigned

systematically within the subregion, denote the specific chart area.

Region 1 includes the waters in and around the United States and Canada. Region 2 covers Central and South America, including both coasts of Mexico, the Bahamas, and the West Indies. There are a total of nine regions.

Region 1 has nine subregions designated counter-clockwise around North America from Subregion 11 for the Gulf of Mexico and the Atlantic Coast up to Cape Hatteras. Subregion 12 extends from there to the eastern tip of Long Island, and 13 goes on to the Canadian border. Subregion 14 covers the Great Lakes; 18 is the U.S. Pacific Coast.

The final three digits of a five-digit number are as-

*N.O.S. has available a free booklet, "Nautical Chart Number Conversion Table," for both old to new and new to old conversions.

FIG. 1828 Portion of Chart 12327. This extract shows some of the same areas as the preceding three figures but at a greater scale and with more detail. "Harbor charts" at a scale of 1:40,000 or larger include all hazards and aids to navigation, some of which may have been omitted from smaller scale charts. More details of features on land are also shown.

signed counter-clockwise around the subregion or along the coast. Many numbers are left unassigned so that future charts can be fitted into the system.

A few examples of the new system may make it clearer. Old chart 141-SC, Miami to Marathon, Florida, is now numbered 11451—Region 1, Subregion 11, plus three new digits. Chart 848, Miami to Elliott Key, covering part of the same area at a larger scale, becomes 11465. Miami's harbor chart, 547, becomes 11468. All numbers are closely related. It is thus possible to use a new chart number to roughly identify the area covered by that chart.

Of lesser interest to boatmen is the balance of the new system. Charts with one-digit numbers have no scale and are not for navigation; an example is Chart No. 1, the booklet of chart symbols and abbreviations. Two digits indicate a chart on a 1:9,000,000 or smaller scale. Three-digit numbers indicate a scale of 1:2,000,000 to 1:9,000,000; there are only a few of these. Charts with two and three digits are numbered on an "ocean basin" concept rather than by regions. Four-digit numbers are used for special purpose and miscellaneous charts only. Training edition charts will continue to carry their old numbers.

Chart "Series"

FOUR N.O.S. SERIES

As previously mentioned, charts are published in a wide range of scales. For general convenience of reference, the issuing agencies have classified charts into "series" as follows:

1. Sailing Charts—the smallest scale charts covering long stretches of coastline; for example, Cape Sable, Newfoundland to Cape Hatteras, N. C.; or the Gulf of Mexico; or San Francisco to Cape Flattery, Washington; see fig. 1825. The charts of this series are published at scales of 1:600,000 and smaller. Sailing charts are prepared for the use of the navigator in fixing his position as he approaches the coast from the open ocean, or when sailing between distant coast ports. They show the offshore soundings, the principal lights and outer buoys, and landmarks visible at

great distances. Other than for ocean cruising races, the average boatman will have little use for charts in this series, except perhaps to plot the path of hurricanes and other tropical disturbances.

2. General Charts—the second series comprises charts with scales in the range of 1:150,000 to 1:600,000. These cover more limited areas, such as Cape May, N.J. to Cape Hatteras; or Mississippi River to Galveston Bay; or San Francisco to Point Arena, Calif. General charts are intended for coastwise navigation outside of offshore reefs and shoals when the vessel's course is mostly within sight of land and her position can be fixed by landmarks, lights, buoys, and soundings. Fig. 1826 is a portion of a general chart.

3. Coast Charts—this next larger scale series consists of charts for close-in coastwise navigation, for entering and

FIG. 1829 The above diagram shows the various subregions of Regions 1 and 2 of the new chart numbering system. The number of the subregion forms the first two digits of a five-digit chart number. The world-wide system of nine regions is shown in Fig. 1710a.

leaving harbors, and for navigating large inland bodies of water. The scales used range from 1:50,000 to 1:150,000 with most at 1:80,000. See fig. 1827. Typical examples of coast charts are the widely-used training chart No. 1210Tr, and such navigational charts as the series of five which cover Chesapeake Bay or 18746 which takes the California boatman from Long Beach or Newport to Santa Catalina Island and back. The average boatman will use several charts from this series.

4. Harbor Charts — this is the largest-scale and most-detailed series, see fig. 1828. Scales will range from 1:40,000 to 1:5,000, with an occasional insert of even larger scale. The scale used for any specific chart is determined by the need for showing detail and by the desired area to be covered by a single sheet. Skippers of small craft will find this the most generally useful type of chart.

Stowage and use

N.O.S. charts in the four series above are printed by accurate techniques on highly durable paper. Individual charts will range in size from approximately 19 x 26 to 36x54 inches. As they are among the most important tools of the navigator, they should be given careful handling and proper stowage. If circumstances permit, they should be stowed flat or rolled, and in a dry place. Charts should never be folded if this can be avoided.

It is advisable that permanent corrections be made in ink so that they will not be inadvertently erased; all other lines and notations should be made lightly in pencil so that they may be erased when no longer applicable without removing permanent information or otherwise damaging the chart.

Lake Chart series

Charts of the Great Lakes are also grouped into series. *General charts* include one of all the Lakes plus one for each lake. *Coast charts* are at a scale of 1:80,000 or 1:120,000. *Harbor charts* have larger scales.

SELECTING THE PROPER CHART

From a consideration of the four categories of charts discussed above, it will be noted that most boating areas will appear on two charts of different series, and that some will be covered by three or four charts of different scales. Such charts will vary widely in the extent of the area covered and the amount of detail shown. The selection of the proper chart to use is important.

The chart catalogs (fig. 1830 is an example of one published by the National Ocean Survey) indicate graphically the area covered by each chart. Also included is a listing giving the name, scale, and price of each chart. These catalogs provide a starting point for the selection of the proper charts for your cruise. In general, the closer you will be to shoal water and dangers to navigation, the larger you will want the scale of the chart that you are using.

What coast charts show

Coast charts show only the *major* hazards and aids to navigation, and give generalized information on depths. Some charts in this series will omit entirely any details on portions thereof which are covered by larger scale charts. For example, Narragansett Bay appears on Chart 13218, but no details at all are given, merely a small note "(Chart 13221)." Other 1200 series coast charts include in their area coverage portions of the Atlantic Intracoastal Waterway, but the navigator is referred to the ICW route charts for all information on the inland route. Many coast charts include a small diagram outlining the areas covered by each larger scale chart—on No. 13218, this amounts to all or portions of 13 more-detailed charts.

What harbor charts show

Harbor charts will show more numerous soundings and *all* aids to navigation, and will permit the most accurate fixing of position from plotted bearings. The question may arise as to why ever select any but the largest-scale chart. The answer lies in the fact that as the scale is increased, the area that can be covered on a given size sheet of paper is proportionately reduced. Thus, for a cruise, many more charts of the harbor series would be required than from the coast series. Further, in some areas, continuous coverage from port to port is not possible from harbor charts alone. Another problem is that the increased number of larger-scale charts complicates the task of laying out a long run between ports.

The selection of the proper charts will usually result in a mixture of coast charts for the longer runs and harbor charts for entering ports and exploring up rivers and creeks. For some areas, one or more general charts, in addition to the coast and harbor charts, may be found useful. For example, the best route down Chesapeake Bay is more easily plotted on 12260 and 12220 than on the series of coast charts 12273 to 12221. When you have a variety of charts on board, duplication of area coverage may result but the right chart is available for the various specific requirements.

In the margin of many charts, you will find helpful information regarding the next chart to use when you are going in a particular direction. This note will take the form of a statement such as "(Joins Chart 13233)" or "(Continued on Chart 13236)."

"SMALL-CRAFT" CHARTS

The charts in the four series just discussed are referred to as "conventional" charts and are intended for flat or rolled stowage. There is another category, a fifth series, which is of special interest to boatmen—these are the *Small-craft Charts* of the National Ocean Survey, designed for more convenient use in the limited space available on boats, and for folded stowage, fig. 1831. (see also color plate, page N.) Originally, the letters "SC" following the number identified charts in the small-craft series, but this practice ceased with the new five-digit numbering system, and "SC" charts are now assigned an appropriate new-style number.

The first chart in this series was 101-SC of the Potomac River. It was introduced in 1957 and immediately was popular beyond all expectations. Requests were soon received from hundreds of boatmen throughout the United States for similar coverage of their waters. The years since 1959 have seen a steadily increasing number of "SC" charts published, as well as revised editions for those already out. As of January, 1979, there were 86 small-craft editions printed, with more in the planning stage.

FIG. 1830 Chart Catalogs published by the various issuing agencies show the area coverage of each chart and greatly aid the skipper in the selection of the proper charts to be used in cruising unfamiliar waters. The title, scale, and prices are listed in tabular form. Shown here is one of the three volumes issued by the National Ocean Survey; all are available free upon request.

FIG. 1831 "Small-craft" Charts are a special series designed for the boatman. They are easier to use and stow, and contain added information of particular interest to the operators of power and sail boats. Included are data on boating facilities, tides and currents, weather broadcasts, etc.

printed front and back, accordion folded, and slipped into a suitable jacket.*

Small-craft area charts, usually consisting of a conventional chart printed on lighter-weight paper with additional data for the small boat skipper. Half of the chart is printed on each side of the paper with a slight area of overlap in printed detail. The chart is accordion folded and issued in a protective jacket.*

Facilities data

A unique feature of these most-modern charts is the variety of data printed on the chart and its protective jacket, fig. 1832. No longer is it necessary to use other sources to locate repair yards and marinas; their locations are clearly marked on the chart, and the available services and supplies are tabulated on the jacket. A tide table for the year, current and marine weather information, rules of the road, signals, and warning notes are included for ready reference.

Small-craft charts make frequent use of "insets" to show such features as small creeks and harbors in greater detail. Fig. 1833 shows an inset from Chart 12285 of the Potomac River.

Courses indicated

Many of the folio and route types of Small-craft charts will indicate a recommended track to be followed. The longer stretches of these tracks will be marked as to true course (some older charts showed magnetic courses; check each chart used) and the distance in miles and tenths. Route charts of the Atlantic Intracoastal Waterway also have tick marks every five statute miles indicating the accumulated distance southward from Norfolk, Virginia to Florida; see fig. 1834. Facilities along the Atlantic ICW are designated in accordance with a numbering system that starts fresh with "1" on each chart of the series.

Types of small-craft charts

Small-craft charts are printed in three general formats termed folio, route, and area as follows:

Small-craft folio charts, consisting of three or four sheets printed front and back, accordion folded, and bound in a suitable cover.

Small-craft route charts, consisting of a single sheet

*Small-craft charts are being redesigned into a 5-inch by 10-inch "pocket-fold" format without a cover jacket. All information previously shown on the separate covers is now included on the chart itself. The elimination of the jacket allows a lower price.

Revised annually

Small-craft charts are revised and reissued annually, usually to coincide with the start of the boating season in each locality. SC charts are *not* hand corrected by the N.O.S. after they are printed and placed in stock. The skipper should keep his chart up-to-date between yearly editions by applying all critical changes as published in the local and weekly editions of Notices to Mariners—this is not a great chore, *if* you keep up with the changes and don't get behind!

Canoe charts covering the Minnesota-Ontario Border Lakes are designed to meet the needs of operators of small, shallow-draft craft. They do not show hydrography.

DMAHTC CHARTS

Charts from the Defense Mapping Agency Hydrographic/Topographic Center will be used by boatmen making long ocean voyages or visiting foreign waters (except Canada). The depicting of information will not differ much from the more familiar N.O.S. charts, and few difficulties will be encountered. Symbols and abbreviations will be familiar to the coastal boatman, but land areas will be found to be tinted gray rather than buff. Symbols will be different for lighted buoys and those with radar reflectors. Some charts will show depths and heights in meters and fractions, rather than in feet or fathoms.

The DMAHTC often issues special editions for some of the major ocean sailing races. These are regular editions of the applicable charts overprinted with additional information for the yachtsman, including the direct rhumb line, typical sailing tracks for seasonal winds, additional current data, and other useful items. The publication of these special charts is well-publicized in Notices to Mariners and boating periodicals.

It must be remembered that many such charts are based on foreign surveys, fig. 1835. The authority for the charted information will always be given at will the date of the surveys. Check for this information, and apply appropriate judgment and caution when using charts of foreign waters; their accuracy and completeness will almost invariably be poor in comparison with N.O.S. charts of U.S. waters.

GREAT LAKES CHARTS

Polyconic projection is used for most maps of the Army Engineers and charts formerly from the Lake Survey; other small variations between these and coastal charts may be noted. Often courses and distances (in statute miles) will be shown for runs between important points.

On the Great Lakes and connecting waters, special editions of charts for small craft are called "Recreational Craft Charts" and are issued in a bound volume of large-

FIG. 1832 Small-craft Charts are printed on lighter weight paper than those in the conventional series. These "SC" charts are then folded and placed in protective jackets. Some are bound-in (13229 on the right) and others are merely slipped into their jackets (11553 on the left).

scale individual charts of special interest to boatmen.

On the Great Lakes and connecting waters, special editions of charts for small craft are called "Recreational Craft Charts" and are issued in a bound volume of large-scale individual charts of special interest to boatmen.

INLAND RIVER CHARTS

Boatmen on inland rivers will use charts that are different in many respects from those used in coastal waters. Often these will be called "navigational maps" and be issued in book form with several pages covering successive stretches of a river.

Probably the most obvious difference is the usual lack of depth figures. In lieu of these, there will generally be a broken line designating the route to be followed. In order to make the best use of the paper sheet, each page may be oriented differently; north will seldom be toward the top, its actual direction being shown by an arrow. Some symbols may vary slightly in appearance from those on "salt water" charts, and additional ones may be used as required by local conditions. Distances are often designated in terms of statute miles upriver from a specified origin point.

More detailed information on river charts will be found in Chapter 27; see pages 532-534, 544, and 547. A complete listing of where river charts and related publications can be obtained is presented on page 608.

FIG. 1833 Insets are used liberally on Small-craft Charts to show local cruising areas in greater detail. This inset, No. 1 from Chart 12285, for the Little Wicomico River, is typical. Depths under six feet are tinted blue. Channel marks (black triangles in this reproduction) are in red and black on the original.

FIG. 1834 Charts of the Atlantic Intracoastal Waterway show a fine magenta line indicating the route to be followed. Tick marks are placed at five-mile intervals along this course line and are labeled with the accumulated mileage southward from Norfolk, Virginia. Since 1969, distances have been measured in statute miles. Passages over large bodies of water may show information on true course and distance. The "D-D" line on the chart extract above is a matching indicator to facilitate shifting from one chart to another.

CAUTIONS REGARDING USE

The production of charts is a major undertaking for the vast coastline and contiguous waterways of the United States. Our Atlantic coastline exceeds 24,500 nautical miles, the Gulf Coast 15,000 miles, the Pacific Coast 7,000 miles, and the Alaskan and Hawaiian shorelines total more than 30,000 nautical miles. The National Ocean Survey publishes almost 1000 charts covering over two million square miles, and both of these figures continue to increase each year. In meeting its global responsibilities, the DMA Hydrographic/Topographic Center put out charts numbered in the thousands, and there are, in addition, the many Army Engineer charts, or "navigational maps".

It can easily be seen that the task of keeping so many charts up-to-date is literally staggering. Surveys are constantly being made in new areas and must be rechecked in old areas. An extensive program of cooperative reporting by boatmen is used by the National Ocean Survey to supplement the information-gathering capability of the Government.

Every effort is made by the charting agencies to keep their products accurate and up-to-date with changing editions. Major disturbances of nature such as hurricanes along the Atlantic coast and earthquakes in the Pacific Northwest cause sudden and extensive changes in hydrography, and destroy aids to navigation. The everyday forces of wind and wave cause slower and less obvious changes in channels and shoals.

All boatmen must be alert to the possibility of changes in conditions and inaccuracies in charted information. Most charts will cite the authorities for the information presented and frequently the date of the information will be given. Use additional caution when the surveys date back many years.

FIG. 1835 Many charts issued by the DMA Hydrographic/Topographic Center are based on foreign surveys. This fact will be noted in the title block. Such charts should be used with caution, particularly if the surveys date back many years, as is often the case.

Chart Projections

The small craft skipper can safely navigate his boat without extensive knowledge of the various types of projection used in the preparation of charts. It is adequate to know that the projection of a spherical surface onto a plane surface inevitably results in some distortions; for small areas, these can be safely neglected.

As in almost any field, however, greater knowledge of the "how" and "why" will assist in understanding and using nautical charts. Hence the following paragraphs will provide additional detailed information on chart projections for those who would extend their knowledge in that direction.

The Mercator projection used in ocean and coastal waters and the polyconic projection used in inland lakes and rivers have been mentioned earlier in this chapter. These, plus the gnomonic projection used in polar regions, will now be presented in more detail. There are many other systems of projection, but each has limited application and need not be considered here.

MERCATOR PROJECTION

The Mercator projection is often illustrated as a projection onto a cylinder. Actually, the chart is developed mathematically to allow for the known shape of the earth, which is not quite a true sphere. The meridians appear as straight, vertical lines, fig. 1836a. Here we have our first example of distortion, and it is quite obvious—the meridians no longer converge, but are now shown as being

FIG. 1836a A Mercator projection can be visualized as the placement of a cylinder around the earth parallel to the polar axis and touching the earth at the equator. The meridians are projected out onto the cylinder and appear as a series of straight lines when the cylinder is unrolled into a flat plane.

FIG. 1836 b Parallels of latitude are projected onto the enveloping cylinder. They appear as parallel straight lines intersecting the meridians at right angles. The actual spacing of the meridians and parallels is adjusted to account for the true shape of the earth which is not an exact sphere. See text.

parallel to each other. This changes the representation of the shape of objects by stretching out their dimensions in an East-West direction.

To minimize the distortion of shape, one of the qualities that must be preserved as much as possible, there must be a stretching-out of dimensions in a North-South direction. The parallels of latitude appear as straight lines intersecting the meridians at right angles. Their spacing increases northward from the Equator, fig. 1836b, in accordance with a mathematical formula that recognizes the slightly oblate shape of the earth. This increase in spacing is not obvious in the case of charts of relatively small areas, such as in the harbor and coastal series, but it is quite apparent in Mercator projections of the world, fig. 1837, or of a large area such as covered by a sailing chart.

The Mercator projection is said to be "conformal," which means that angles are correctly represented and the scale is the same in all directions from any point.

By the Mercator technique of distortion, then counter-distortion, the shape of areas in high latitudes is correctly shown, but their size appears greater than that of similar areas in lower latitudes. An island, for example, in 60° latitude (Alaska) would appear considerably larger than an island of the same size located 25° above the equator (Florida). Its shape, however, would still be true to actual proportions.

Advantages and disadvantages

The great value of the Mercator chart is that the meridians of longitude appear as straight lines all intersecting the parallels of latitude, also straight lines, at right angles to form an easily-used rectangular grid. Directions can be measured with reference to any meridian or any compass rose. The geographic coordinates of a position can easily be measured from the scales along the four borders of the chart. *We can draw upon a Mercator chart a straight line between two points and actually sail that course* by determining the compass direction between them; the heading is the same all along the line. Such a line is called a *rhumb line*. However, a great circle, the shortest distance between two points on the earth's surface, is a curved line on a Mercator chart; this is more difficult to calculate and plot. For moderate runs, the added distance of a rhumb line is insignificant, and this is the track that is used. Radio waves follow great circle paths and radio bearings on stations more than about 200 miles distant will require correction before being plotted on a Mercator chart.

The scale of a Mercator chart will vary with the distance away from the equator as a result of the N-S expansion. The change is unimportant on charts of small areas such as harbor and coastal charts, and the graphic scale may be used. The change in scale with latitude does become signi-

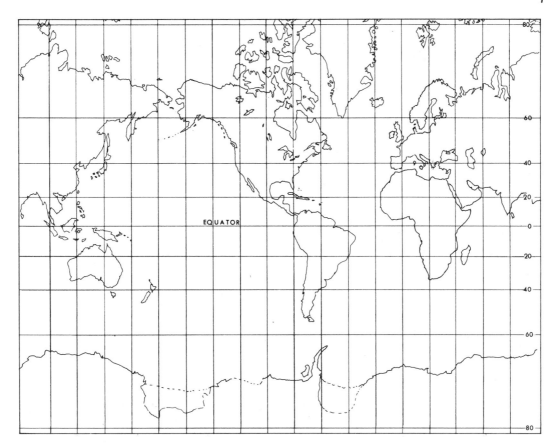

FIG. 1837   This Mercator projection of the world shows the considerable distortion in near-polar latitudes. Note that the spacing between parallels is not uniform, but increases as the distance from the Equator increases.

FIG. 1838   Polyconic projections are developed onto a series of cones, each cone tangent to a different parallel of latitude. This perspective drawing shows three cones tangent at 40, 50 and 60 degrees north latitude. For clarity, the central projection of the earth's surface onto the cones is not shown.

ficant, however, in charts covering greater areas, as on general and sailing charts. On such charts, it is necessary to measure distances using the latitude scale on either side margin, remembering that 1' of latitude is essentially 1 nautical mile. *Take care that distance is measured at a point on the latitude scale directly opposite the region of the chart being used. Never use the longitude scale at the top and bottom of the chart for measuring distance.*

POLYCONIC PROJECTION

Another form of chart construction is the *polyconic* projection. This method is based on the development of the earth's surface upon a series of cones, a different one being used for each parallel of latitude, fig. 1838. The vertex of the cone is at the point where a tangent to the earth at the specified latitude intersects the earth's axis extended. At the edges of the chart, the area between parallels is expanded to eliminate gaps.

The polyconic projection yields little distortion in shape, and relative sizes are more correctly preserved than in the Mercator projection. The scale is correct along any parallel and along the central meridian of the projection. Along other meridians, the scale increases with increased difference in longitude from the central meridian.

Parallels appear as nonconcentric arcs of circles and meridians as curved lines converging toward the pole, concave toward the central meridian, see fig. 1839. These characteristics contrast with the straight-line parallels and meridians of Mercator charts, and are the reasons why this

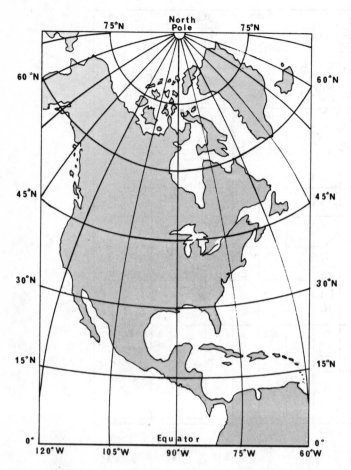

FIG. 1839 This polyconic projection of a large area emphasizes the curved characteristics of the parallels and meridians on this type of chart. Such curvatures exist on smaller area charts but are not so noticeable.

FIG. 1840 A Gnomonic projection is made by placing a plane surface tangent to the earth. Points on the earth's surface are then projected onto this plane. The point of tangency may be at any location.

projection is not so widely used in marine navigation. Directions from any point should be measured relative to the meridian passing through that point; in actual practice, the nearest compass rose is used. Great Lakes polyconic charts have a graphic "plotting interpolator" for close measurements of latitude and longitude.

GNOMONIC PROJECTION

A *gnomonic* chart results when the meridians and parallels of latitude are projected onto a plane surface tangent to the earth at one point, fig. 1840. For the oblique case, meridians appear as straight lines converging toward the nearer pole; the parallels, except for the equator, appear as curves, fig. 1841.

Distortion is great, but this projection is used in special cases because of its unique advantage—*great circles appear as straight lines,* which of course is not so with the other two projections discussed above. Probably the easiest way to obtain a great circle track on a Mercator or polyconic chart is to draw it as a straight line on a gnomonic chart and then transfer points along the line to the other chart using the geographic coordinates for each point. The points so transferred are then connected with short rhumb lines and the result will approximate, closely enough, the great circle path, fig. 1842a and b.

A special case of gnomonic chart projection occurs when a geographic pole is selected as the point of tangency. Now all meridians will appear as straight lines, and the parallels as concentric circles. The result is a chart easily used for polar regions where ordinary Mercator charts cannot be used.

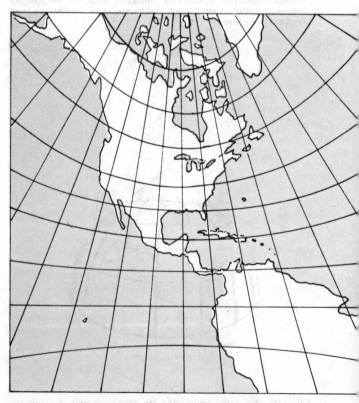

FIG. 1841 A chart made on the Gnomonic projection shows meridians as straight lines converging toward the nearer pole. The parallels, other than the Equator, appear as curves.

FIG. 1842 a A great circle provides the shortest distance between two points on the earth's surface, but is difficult to plot directly on a Mercator chart. An easier procedure is to draw it as a straight line on a Gnomonic chart, noting the latitude of each intersection of the track with a meridian.

FIG. 1842 b Using the geographic coordinates of each point previously marked on the track, it is reconstructed on the Mercator chart by joining the points with short straight (rhumb) lines. This approximation can then be steered without great difficulty.

THE LAMBERT CONFORMAL PROJECTION

A projection can be made onto a single cone tangent to the earth at a single specified parallel of latitude; this is termed a *simple conic projection*. It is generally a poor projection as the scale is not correct except along the standard parallel. Areas not projected equally and correct angular relationships are not preserved.

The polyconic projection, previously considered, avoids some of these distortions, but only at the cost of the complexity of using a series of cones. Another technique to minimize the distortions of the simple conic projection is to have the cone *intersect* the earth's surface at two parallels. This general type is called a *conic projection with two standard parallels*.

If the spacing of the parallels is altered so that the distortion is the same along them as along the meridians, the projection becomes conformal, that is, the angular relationships are correctly represented, a highly desirable chart quality. This is known as the *Lambert conformal projection*. It is the most widely used conic projection,

although its use is more common among aviators than navigators. Its appearance is very much the same as the simple conic or polyconic projections. If the chart is not carried far beyond the standard parallels, and these are not a great distance apart, the distortion over the entire chart is small.

A straight line on this projection so nearly approximates a great circle that the two can be considered identical for most purposes of navigation. Radio bearings, from signals which are considered to travel great circle paths, can be plotted on a Lambert conformal chart without the correction needed when using a Mercator chart. This feature, gained without sacrificing conformality, has made this projection popular for aeronautical charts, since aircraft make much use of radio aids to navigation. It has made little headway in replacing the Mercator projection for marine navigation, except in high latitudes. In a slightly modified form, the Lambert conformal projection is sometimes used for polar charts.

PILOT CHARTS

No discussion of nautical charts would be complete without at least brief mention of a unique but valuable chart issued quarterly by the DMA Hydrographic/Topographic Center. These *Pilot Charts* present in graphic form information on ocean currents and weather probabilities for each month, plus other data of interest to a navigator. Timely articles are printed on the reverse side of each chart. They are issued in two editions—

Chart No. 16, North Atlantic Ocean
Chart No. 55, North Pacific Ocean

ORTHOPHOTO CHARTS

The National Ocean Survey is now publishing some of its charts in an "orthophoto" process. Land areas are shown as reproductions of aerial photographs, providing greater details of natural and man-made features. This increased level of detail will assist all boatmen in determining their position on the water.

Regular hydrographic details for nautical charts—such as water depths, channel limits, and aids to navigation—are shown as before.

⚓

FIG. 1843 Portion of the North Atlantic Pilot Chart for the month of November, 1979. The three arrows leading from the titles of the explanatory notes have been added for clarity. The small numbered arrows visible at the lower right corner (green on the original) give set and drift of current. The long-short dash line gives mean maximum iceberg limit, and dated triangles indicate sightings of unusual icebergs. Normal shipping tracks for various classes of vessels between selected ports are shown. Inset charts, not shown, give data on temperatures, visibility and weather. The charts for three months, plus additional data, are printed on both sides of a single sheet, 30″ × 40″ square (75 × 100 cm.)

STANDARDIZED CHART SYMBOLS AND ABBREVIATIONS

The nautical chart can convey much or little to its user, depending upon the extent of his understanding of all those many small, odd shapes, marks, and lines. A great amount of information must be shown on a chart for safe navigation and, in many areas, there is little room for it. Thus, extensive use is made of *symbols* and *abbreviations*. To make chart reading easier, quicker, and surer, the various U.S. agencies that produce nautical charts have adopted a standardized system of abbreviations and symbols.

It is essential that a boatman have the ability to read and understand his charts rapidly and accurately. Knowledge of symbols and abbreviations is a "must" for this ability.

The standardized symbols and abbreviations are broadly grouped into classifications as follows:

A—The Coast Line
B—Coast Features
C—The Land
D—Control Points
E—Units
F—Adjectives
G—Harbors
H—Topography
I—Buildings
J—Miscellaneous Stations
K—Lights
L—Buoys and Beacons
M—Radio Stations
N—Fog Signals
O—Dangers
P—Various Limits
Q—Soundings
R—Depth Countours
S—Quality of the Bottom
T—Tides and Currents
U—The Compass

Most of the symbols used on nautical charts published by the National Ocean Survey and DMA Hydrographic/Topographic Center conform to standards of the International Hydrographic Organization (IHO), but a few do not. In numbering all symbols and abbreviations in figs. 1844 a to 1844 o on this and the following pages, vertical figures indicate that the designated symbol or abbreviation is in conformity with the IHO standards. Slanting figures

mean that it either differs from the standard or does not appear in the international list. Where the figures are enclosed in *parentheses*, the symbols or abbreviations are in addition to those included in the IHO standards. The symbols shown are from the 1975 edition of Chart No. 1; changes from the 1972 edition are indicated by a dagger (†) symbol before the number.

The symbols and abbreviations shown in fig. 1844 will be used on NOS and DMAHTC charts issued in the future. Cases may occur where older symbols still appear on charts that have not yet been reissued in the new editions.

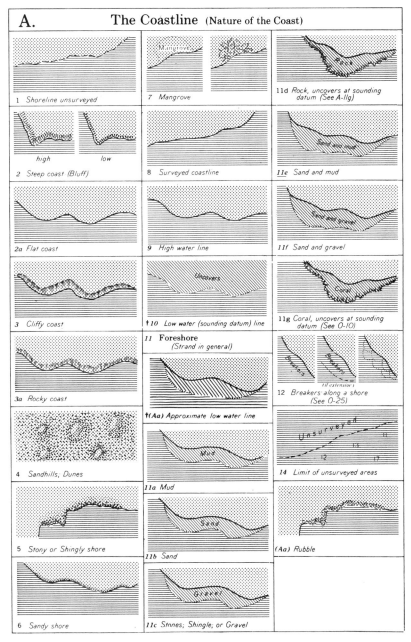

A. The Coastline (Nature of the Coast)

1 *Shoreline unsurveyed*
2 *Steep coast (Bluff)* — high — low
2a *Flat coast*
3 *Cliffy coast*
3a *Rocky coast*
4 *Sandhills; Dunes*
5 *Stony or Shingly shore*
6 *Sandy shore*
7 *Mangrove*
8 *Surveyed coastline*
9 *High water line*
†10 *Low water (sounding datum) line*
11 *Foreshore (Strand in general)*
†(Aa) *Approximate low water line*
11a *Mud*
11b *Sand*
11c *Stones; Shingle; or Gravel*
11d *Rock, uncovers at sounding datum (See A-11g)*
11e *Sand and mud*
11f *Sand and gravel*
11g *Coral, uncovers at sounding datum (See O-10)*
12 *Breakers along a shore (See O-25)* (if extensive)
14 *Limit of unsurveyed areas*
(Aa) *Rubble*

FIG. 1844 a   SYMBOLS—The coastline

COLOR KEY:

Blue
Green
Yellow
Naut. Purple

F. Adjectives, Adverbs, Nouns, and Other Words

No.	Abbr.	Term
1	gt	Great
2	lit	Little
3	Lrg	Large
4	sml	Small
5		Outer
6		Inner
7	mid	Middle
8		Old
9	anc	Ancient
10		New
11	St	Saint
12	conspic	Conspicuous
13		Remarkable
14	D. Destr	Destroyed
15		Projected
16	dist	Distant
17	abt	About
18		See chart
18a		See plan
19		Lighted, Luminous
20	sub	Submarine
21		Eventual
22	AERO	Aeronautical
23		Higher
23a		Lower
24	exper	Experimental
25	discontd	Discontinued
26	prohib	Prohibited
27	explos	Explosive
28	estab	Established
29	elec	Electric
30	priv	Private, Privately
31	prom	Prominent
32	std	Standard
33	subm	Submerged
34	approx	Approximate
35		Maritime
36	maintd	Maintained
37	aband	Abandoned
38	temp	Temporary
39	occas	Occasional
40	extr	Extreme
41		Navigable
42	N M	Notice to Mariners
(Fa)	L N M	Local Notice to Mariners
43		Sailing Directions
44		List of Lights
(Fb)	unverd	Unverified
(Fc)	AUTH	Authorized
(Fd)	CL	Clearance
(Fe)	concr	Concrete
(Ff)	cor	Corner
(Fg)	fl	Flood
(Fh)	mod	Moderate
(Fi)	bet	Between
(Fj)	1st	First
(Fk)	2nd, 2d	Second
(Fl)	3rd, 3d	Third
(Fm)	4th	Fourth
(Fn)	DD	Deep Draft
(Fo)	min	Minimum
(Fp)	max	Maximum
(Fq)	N'ly	Northerly
(Fr)	S'ly	Southerly
(Fs)	E'ly	Easterly
(Ft)	W'ly	Westerly
(Fu)	Sk	Stroke
(Fv)	Restr	Restricted

D. Control Points

No.	Symbol	Description
1	△	Triangulation point (station)
1a		Astronomic station
2	⊙ (See In)	Fixed point (landmark, position accurate)
(Da)	o (See Io)	Fixed point (landmark, position approx.)
3	• 256	Summit of height (Peak) (when not a landmark)
(Db)	⊚256	Peak, accentuated by contours
(Dc)	256	Peak, accentuated by hachures
(Dd)	256	Peak, elevation not determined
(De)	⊙256	Peak, when a landmark
4	⊕ Obs Spot	Observation spot
*5	BM	Bench mark
6	View X	View point
7		Datum point for grid of a plan
8		Graphical triangulation point
9	Astro	Astronomical
10	Tri	Triangulation
(Df)	C of E	Corps of Engineers
12		Great trigonometrical survey station
13		Traverse station
14	Bdy Mon	Boundary monument
(Dg)	◇	International boundary monument

E. Units

No.	Abbr.	Term
†1	hr, h	Hour
†2	m, min	Minute (of time)
†3	sec, s	Second (of time)
4	m	Meter
4a	dm	Decimeter
4b	cm	Centimeter
4c	mm	Millimeter
4d	m^2	Square meter
4e	m^3	Cubic meter
5	km	Kilometer
6	in	Inch
7	ft	Foot
8	yd	Yard
9	fm	Fathom
10	cbl	Cable length
11	M, Mi, NMi	Nautical mile
12	kn	Knot
12a	t	Tonne (metric ton = 2,204.6 lbs.)
12b	cd	Candela (new candle)
13	lat	Latitude
14	long	Longitude
14a		Greenwich
15	pub	Publication
16	Ed	Edition
17	corr	Correction
18	alt	Altitude
19	ht; elev	Height; Elevation
20	°	Degree
21	'	Minute (of arc)
22	"	Second (of arc)
23	No	Number
(Ea)	St M, St Mi	Statute mile
(Eb)	μsec, μs	Microsecond
(Ec)	Hz	Hertz (cps)
(Ed)	kHz	Kilohertz (kc)
(Ee)	MHz	Megahertz (Mc)
(Ef)	cps, c/s	Cycles/second (Hz)
(Eg)	kc	Kilocycle (kHz)
(Eh)	Mc	Megacycle (MHz)
(Ei)	T	Ton (U.S. short ton = 2,000 lbs.)

FIG. 1844 c   Control points, units, adjectives, adverbs

FIG. 1844 b   Features of the coast and natural features of the land

C. The Land (Natural Features)

No.	Description
1	Contour lines (Contours)
1a	Contour lines, approximate (Contours)
2	Hachures
2a	Form lines, no definite interval
2b	Shading
3	Glacier
4	Saltpans
5	Isolated trees
5a	Deciduous or of unknown or unspecified type
5b	Coniferous
5c	Palm tree
5d	Nipa palm
5e	Filao
5f	Casuarina
5g	Evergreen tree (other than coniferous)
5	Cultivated
6	Cultivated fields
6a	Grass; Grass fields
7	Rice; Paddy (rice) fields
7a	Park; Garden
8	Bushes
8a	Tree plantation in general
9	Deciduous woodland
10	Coniferous woodland
10a	Woods in general
11	Tree top height (above shoreline datum)
12	Lava flow
13	River; Stream
14	Intermittent stream
15	Lake; Pond
16	Lagoon (Lag)
17	Marsh; Swamp
18	Slough (Slu.)
19	Rapids
20	Waterfalls
21	Spring

B. Coast Features

No.	Abbr.	Term
1	G	Gulf
2	B	Bay
(Ba)	B	Bayou
3	Fd	Fjord
4	L	Loch, Lough; Lake
5	Cr	Creek
5a	C	Cove
6	In	Inlet
7	Str	Strait
8	Sd	Sound
9	Pass / Thoro	Passage; Pass / Thorofare
10	Chan	Channel
10a		Narrows
11	Entr	Entrance
12	Est	Estuary
12a		Delta
13	Mth	Mouth
14	Rd	Road; Roadstead
15	Anch	Anchorage
16	Hbr	Harbor
16a	Hn	Haven
17	P	Port
(Bb)	P	Pond
18	I	Island
19	It	Islet
20	Arch	Archipelago
21	Pen	Peninsula
22	C	Cape
23	Prom	Promontory
24	Hd	Head; Headland
25	Pt	Point
26	Mt	Mountain; Mount
27	Rge	Range
27a		Valley
28		Summit
29	Pk	Peak
30	Vol	Volcano
31		Hill
32	Bld	Boulder
33	Ldg	Landing
34		Table-land (Plateau)
35	Rk	Rock
(Bc)		Isolated rock
36	Str	Stream
(Bd)	R	River
(Be)	Slu	Slough
(Bf)	Lag	Lagoon
(Bg)	Apprs	Approaches
(Bh)	Rky	Rocky
(Bi)	Is	Islands
(Bj)	Ma	Marsh
(Bk)	Mg	Mangrove
(Bl)	Sw	Swamp

H. Topography (Artificial Features)

1 Road (Rd) or Highway (Hy)
(Hu) Highway markers
   Small-scale chart
2 Track, Footpath, or Trail
3 Railway (Ry) (single or double track), Railroad (RR)
   Sunk grade / Ry above / Ry below / M & LS RR
3a Tramway
3b Railway station
3c Tunnel (railroad or road)
3d Embankment, Levee
3e Cutting
3f Causeway — OVERHEAD POWER CABLE AUTHORIZED CL 140 FT / TOWER TOWER
4 Overhead power cable (OVHD PWR CAB)
5 Power transmission line
5a Power transmission mast
6 Prominent telegraph or telephone line — Tel
7 Aqueduct, Water pipe
8 Viaduct
8a Pipeline
9 Pile, Piling, Post (above MHW) (See L-59, O-30) — °Pile **Piling **Post
9a Mast — MAST °Mast
10 Highway (See H-1)
11 Sewer — Sewer or Outfall
12 Culvert

Canal / Lock / Ditch / Sluice (Tidegate Floodgate) / Sluice (point upstream)
   Small scale chart
13 Canal, Ditch, Lock, Sluice (point upstream)
Bridge (BR) in general
14
14a Stone, concrete bridge (Same as H-14)
14b Wooden bridge (Same as H-14)
14c Iron bridge (Same as H-14)
14d Suspension bridge (Same as H-14)
15 Drawbridge (in general)
16 Swing bridge (Same as H-15)
16a Lift bridge
16b Weighbridge or Bascule bridge
17 Pontoon bridge
17a Footbridge
18 Transporter bridge (Same as H-14)
18a Bridge clearance, vertical — VERT CL 6 FT
18b Bridge clearance, horizontal — HOR CL 28 FT
   On small-scale chart
19 Ferry (Fy) — Ferry
(Hb) Cable ferry
20 Ford
21 Dam
22 Fence
23 Training wall
+24 Log boom

1844 e **Artificial features of topography**

FIG. 1844 d Ports and harbors

G. Ports and Harbors

1 Anch Anchorage (large vessels)
2 Anch Anchorage (small vessels)
3 Hbr Harbor
4 Hn Haven
5 P Port
6 Bkw Breakwater
6a
7 Dike
8 Mole
8a Jetty (partly below MHW)
(Ga) Submerged jetty
9 Pier Jetty (small scale)
10 Pier
11 Spit
12 Groin (partly below MHW)
12 ANCH PROHIB Anchorage prohibited (See P-251)(Screen Opt)
12a QUAR ANCH Anchorage reserved
12b QUARANTINE ANCHORAGE Quarantine anchorage
13 Spoil Area Spoil ground
(Gb) Dumping Ground Dumping ground
(Gc) 80 / 85 Disposal Area / Depths from survey / 90 / 98 JUNE 1968 Disposal area
+(Gd) Pump-out facilities
14 Fsh stks Fisheries; Fishing stakes
14a Fish trap, Fish weirs (actual shape charted)
14b Duck blind
15 Tunny nets (See G-14a)
15a Oys Oyster bed
16 Ldg Landing place
17 Watering place
18 Whf Wharf
19 Quay

20 Berth
20a Anchoring berth
20b 3 Berth number
21 Dol Dolphin
22 Bollard
23 Mooring ring
24 Crane
25 Landing stage
25a Landing stairs
26 Quar Quarantine
27 Lazaret
*28 Harbor Master Harbor master's office
29 Cus Ho Customhouse
30 Fishing harbor
31 Winter harbor
32 Refuge harbor
33 B Hbr Boat harbor
34 Stranding harbor (uncovers at LW)
35 Dock
36 Dry dock (actual shape on large-scale charts)
37 Floating dock (actual shape on large-scale charts)
38 Gridiron, Careening grid
39 Patent slip, Slipway; Marine railway
39a Ramp Ramp
40 Lock (point upstream) (See H-13)
41 Wet dock
42 Shipyard
43 Lumber yard
44 Health Office Health officer's office
45 Hk Hulk (actual shape on lrg scale charts)(See O-1)
46 PROHIB AREA Prohibited area
46a Calling-in point for vessel traffic control
47 Anchorage for seaplanes
48 Seaplane landing area
49 Work in progress
50 Under construction
51 Work projected
((e)) Submerged ruins

I. Buildings and Structures (continued)

No.	Abbr.	Name
61	Inst	Institute
62		Establishment
63		Bathing establishment
64	Ct Ho	Courthouse
65	Sch	School
(1g)	HS	High school
(1h)	Univ	University
66	Bldg	Building
67	Pav	Pavilion
68		Hut
69		Stadium
70	T	Telephone
71		Gas tank, Gasometer
72	GAB	Gable
73		Wall
74		Pyramid
75		Pillar
76		Oil derrick
(1i)	Ltd	Limited
(1j)	Apt	Apartment
(1k)	Cap	Capitol
(1l)	Co	Company
(1m)	Corp	Corporation
(1n)		Landmark (position accurate) (See D 2)
(1o)		Landmark (position approximate) (See Da)

J. Miscellaneous Stations

No.	Abbr.	Name
1	Sta	Any kind of station
2	Sta	Station
3	C.G	Coast Guard station (Similar to LS. S.)
(1a)	C.G WALLIS SANDS	Coast Guard station (when landmark)
4	LOOK.TR	Lookout station; Watch tower
5		Lifeboat station
6	L.S.S	Lifesaving station (See J-3)
7	Rkt. Sta	Rocket station
8	PIL. STA	Pilot station
9	Sig Sta	Signal station
10	Sem	Semaphore
11	S. Sig Sta	Storm signal station
12		Weather signal station
†(1b)	NWS SIG STA	Nat. Weather Service signal sta
13		Tide signal station
14		Stream signal station
15		Ice signal station
16		Time signal station
16a		Manned oceanographic station
16b		Unmanned oceanographic station
17		Time ball
18	FS	Signal mast
19	FP	Flagstaff, Flagpole
19a	F. TR	Flag tower
20		Signal
21	Obsy	Observatory
22	Off	Office
(1c)	BELL	Bell (on land)
(1d)	HECP	Harbor entrance control post

FIG. 1844 g   Other buildings and structures, and miscellaneous stations

FIG. 1844 f   Buildings and structures

I. Buildings and Structures (see General Remarks)

No.	Abbr.	Name
1		City or Town (large scale)
(1a)		City or Town (small scale)
2		Suburb
3	Vil	Village
3a		Buildings in general
4	Cas	Castle
5		House
6		Villa
7		Farm
8	Ch	Church
8a	Cath	Cathedral
8b	Spire	Spire; Steeple
9		Roman Catholic Church
10		Temple
11		Chapel
12		Mosque
12a		Minaret
(1b)		Moslem Shrine
13		Marabout
14	Pag	Pagoda
15		Buddhist Temple, Joss-House
15a		Shinto Shrine
16		Monastery; Convent
17		Calvary; Cross
17a		Cemetery, Non-Christian
18	Cem	Cemetery, Christian
18a		Tomb
19		Fort (actual shape charted)
20		Battery
21		Barracks
22		Powder magazine
23	Airport	Airplane landing field
24		Airport, large scale (See P-13)
(1c)		Airport, military (small scale)
(1d)		Airport, civil (small scale)
25		Mooring mast
26	King St / St	Street
26a	Locust Ave / Ave	Avenue
26b	Grand Blvd / Blvd	Boulevard
27	Tel	Telegraph
28	Tel Off	Telegraph office
29	P O	Post office
30	Govt. Ho	Government house
31		Town hall
32	Hosp	Hospital
33		Slaughterhouse
34	Magz	Magazine
34a		Warehouse; Storehouse
35	MON / Mon	Monument
36	CUP / Cup	Cupola
37	ELEV / Elev	Elevator; Lift
(1e)	Elev	Elevation; Elevated
38		Shed
39		Zinc roof
40	Ruins / Ru	Ruins
41	TR / Tr	Tower
(1f)	ABAND LT HO	Abandoned lighthouse
42	WINDMILL	Windmill
43		Watermill
43a	WINDMOTOR	Windmotor
44	CHY / Chy	Chimney; Stack
45	S'PIPE / S'pipe	Water tower; Standpipe
†46		Oil tank
47	Facty	Factory
48		Saw mill
49		Brick kiln
50		Mine; Quarry
51	Well	Well
52		Cistern
†53	TANK / Tk	Tank
54		Noria
55		Fountain

K. Lights (continued)

No.	Abbr.	Description
69		Unwatched light
70	Occas	Occasional light
71	Irreg	Irregular light
72	Prov	Provisional light
73	Temp	Temporary light
(Ke)	D Destr	Destroyed
74	Exting	Extinguished light
75		Faint light
76		Upper light
77		Lower light
78		Rear light
79		Front light
80	Vert	Vertical lights
81	Hor	Horizontal lights
(Kf)	VB	Vertical beam
(Kg)	RGE	Range
(Kh)	Exper	Experimental light
(Ki)	TRLB	Temporarily replaced by lighted buoy showing the same characteristics
(Kj)	TRUB	Temporarily replaced by unlighted buoy
(Kk)	TLB	Temporary lighted buoy
(Kl)	TUB	Temporary unlighted buoy

L. Buoys and Beacons (see General Remarks)

† new standard symbols

No.	Abbr.	Description
†		Approximate position of buoy
†2		Light buoy
†3	BELL	Bell buoy
†3a	GONG	Gong buoy
†4	WHIS	Whistle buoy
†5	C	Can or Cylindrical buoy
†6	N	Nun or Conical buoy
†7	SP	Spherical buoy
†8	S	Spar buoy
†8a	P	Pillar or Spindle buoy
†9		Buoy with topmark (ball) (see L-70)
†10		Barrel or Ton buoy
†(La)		Color unknown
†(Lb)	FLOAT	Float
†12	FLOAT	Lightfloat
13		Outer or Landfall buoy
†14	BW	Fairway buoy (BWVS)
†14a	BW	Midchannel buoy (BWVS)
†15	R "2"	Starboard-hand buoy (entering from seaward)
†16	"1"	Port-hand buoy (entering from seaward)
†17	RB	Bifurcation buoy (RBHB)
†18	RB	Junction buoy (RBHB)
†19	RB	Isolated danger buoy (RBHB)
†20	G	Wreck buoy (RBHB or G)
†20a	G	Obstruction buoy (RBHB or G)
†21		Telegraph-cable buoy
22	Tel	Mooring buoy (colors of mooring buoys never carried)
22a		Mooring
22b	Tel	Mooring buoy with telegraphic communications
22c	T	Mooring buoy with telephonic communications
†23		Warping buoy
†24		Quarantine buoy
24a		Practice area buoy
†25	Explos Anch	Explosive anchorage buoy
†25a	AERO	Aeronautical anchorage buoy
†26	Deviation	Compass adjustment buoy
†27	BW	Fish trap (area) buoy (BWHB)
†27a		Spoil ground buoy
†28	W	Anchorage buoy (marks limits)
†29	Priv maintd	Private aid to navigation (buoy) (maintained by private interests, use with caution)

FIG. 1844 i   Other lights, buoys and beacons

FIG. 1844 h   Lights

K. Lights

No.	Abbr.	Description
1		Position of light
2	Lt	Light
(Ka)		Riprap surrounding light
3	Lt Ho	Lighthouse
4	AERO	Aeronautical light (See F-22)
4a		Marine and air navigation light
5	Bn	Light beacon
6		Light vessel; Lightship
8		Lantern
9		Street lamp
10	REF	Reflector
11	Ldg Lt	Leading light
12		Sector light
13		Directional light
14		Harbor light
15		Fishing light
16		Tidal light
17	Priv maintd	Private light (maintained by private interests, to be used with caution)
21	F	Fixed light
22	Occ	Occulting light
23	Fl	Flashing light
23a	Iso E Int	Isophase light (equal interval)
24	Qk Fl	Quick flashing (scintillating) light
25	Int Qk Fl / I Qk Fl	Interrupted quick flashing light
25a	S Fl	Short flashing light
26	Alt	Alternating light
27	Gp Occ	Group occulting light
28	Gp Fl	Group flashing light
28a	S-L Fl	Short-long flashing light
28b		Group short flashing light
29	F Fl	Fixed and flashing light
30	F Gp Fl	Fixed and group flashing light
30a	Mo	Morse code light
31	Rot	Revolving or Rotating light
41		Period
42		Every
43		With
44		Visible (range)
†(Kb)	M, Mi, N.M.	Nautical mile (See E-11)
(Kc)	m, min	Minutes (See E-2)
†(Kd)	s, sec	Seconds (See E-3)
45	Fl	Flash
46	Occ	Occultation
46a		Eclipse
47	Gp	Group
48	Occ	Intermittent light
49	SEC	Sector
50		Color of sector
51	Aux	Auxiliary light
52		Varied
61	Vi	Violet
62		Purple
63	B	Blue
64	G	Green
65	Or	Orange
66	R	Red
67	W	White
67a	Am	Amber
67b	Y	Yellow
68	OBSC	Obscured light
68a	Fog Det Lt	Fog detector light (See Nb)

M. Radio and Radar Stations

No.	Symbol	Description
1	°R Sta	Radio telegraph station
2	°RT	Radio telephone station
3	⊙R Bn	Radiobeacon
4	⊙R Bn	Circular radiobeacon
5	⊙RD	Directional radiobeacon; Radio range
6	⊙	Rotating loop radiobeacon
7	⊙RDF	Radio direction finding station
†(Ma)	ANTENNA (TELEM) TELEM ANT	Telemetry antenna
(Mb)	⊙R RELAY MAST	Radio relay mast
(Mc)	⊙MICRO TR	Microwave tower
9	⊙R MAST / ⊙R TR	Radio mast / Radio tower
9a	⊙TV TR	Television mast; Television tower
10	⊙R TR (WBAL) 1090 KHz	Radio broadcasting station (commercial)
10a	⊙R Sta	QTG radio station
11	⊙Ra	Radar station
12	⊙Racon	Radar responder beacon
13	Ra Ref	Radar reflector (See L-Lf)
14	Ra (conspic)	Radar conspicuous object
14a		Ramark
15	° D F S	Distance finding station (synchronized signals)
16	⊙AERO R Bn 302 ⋮⋮⋮	Aeronautical radiobeacon
17	° Decca Sta	Decca station
18	° Loran Sta Venice	Loran station (name)
19	⊙CONSOL Bn 190 kHz	Consol (Consolan) station
(Md)	⊙MMF ⋮⋮⋮ AERO R Rge 342 ⋮⋮⋮	Aeronautical radio range
(Me)	⊙Ra Ref Calibration Bn	Radar calibration beacon
(Mf)	°LORAN TR SPRING ISLAND	Loran tower (name)
(Mg)	°R TR F R Lt	Obstruction light
†(Mh)	⊙RA DOME °Ra Dome / ◉DOME (RADAR) °Dome (Radar)	Radar dome
†(Mi)	uhf	Ultrahigh frequency
†(Mj)	vhf	Very high frequency

N. Fog Signals

No.	Symbol	Description
1	Fog Sig	Fog-signal station
2		Radio fog-signal station
3	GUN	Explosive fog signal
4		Submarine fog signal
5	SUB-BELL	Submarine fog bell (action of waves)
6	SUB-BELL	Submarine fog bell (mechanical)
7	SUB-OSC	Submarine oscillator
8	NAUTO	Nautophone
9	DIA	Diaphone
10	GUN	Fog gun
11	SIREN	Fog siren
12	HORN	Fog trumpet
13	HORN	Foghorn
13a	HORN	Electric foghorn
14	BELL	Fog bell
15	WHIS	Fog whistle
16	HORN	Reed horn
17	GONG	Fog gong
18	°	Submarine sound signal not connected to the shore (See N 5,6,7)
18a		Submarine sound signal connected to the shore (See N 5,6,7)
(Na)	HORN	Typhon
(Nh)	Fog Det Lt	Fog detector light (See K 68a)

FIG. 1844 k   Radio and radar stations, fog signals

FIG. 1844 j   Buoys and beacons (continued)

L. Buoys and Beacons (continued)

No.	Symbol	Description
29 (cont.)	R	Starboard-hand buoy (entering from seaward)
30	B	Port-hand buoy
30a		Temporary buoy (See Ki, j, k, l)
†31		Winter buoy
†32	HB	Horizontal stripes or bands
†33	VS	Vertical stripes
†33a	Chec	Checkered
	Diag	Diagonal bands
41	W	White
42	B	Black
43	R	Red
44	Y	Yellow
45	G	Green
46	Br	Brown
47	Gy	Gray
48	Bu	Blue
48a	Am	Amber
48b	Or	Orange
†51		Floating beacon
52	△RW Bn △W Bn ▲R Bn / ▲Bn / △Bn	Fixed beacon (unlighted or daybeacon) / Black beacon
		Color unknown
(Lc)	°Marker	Private aid to navigation
53	Bn	Beacon, in general (See L 52)
54		Tower beacon
55		Cardinal marking system
56	△ Deviation Bn	Compass adjustment beacon
57		Topmarks (See L 9, 70)
58		Telegraph-cable (landing) beacon
59	Piles	Piles (See O 30; H 9, 9a)
		Stakes
	Stumps	Stumps (See O 30)
		Perches
61	○CAIRN °Cairn	Cairn
62		Painted patches
63	○TR °Tr	Landmark (position accurate) (See D 2)
(Ld)		Landmark (position approximate)
64	REF	Reflector
65	○MARKER ⊘w Or ⊘w Or ⊘w Or	Range targets, markers
†(Le)		Special-purpose buoys
66		Oil installation buoy
67		Drilling platform (See Of, Og)
70	Note:	TOPMARKS on buoys and beacons may be shown on charts of foreign waters. The abbreviation for black is not shown adjacent to buoys or beacons.
(Lf)	Ra Ref	Radar reflector (See M 13)

Note: A new page 10a was added to Chart No. 1 by Notices to Mariners No. 42/1976 and 11/1977; it adds to Section L new buoy symbols used on charts of northern European waters.

*In mid-1978 N.O.S. adopted new symbols that will appear on charts as new editions are printed. Day-beacons with green square daymarks will be shown as square green symbols. The symbol for a horizontally-banded buoy will have its upper half red or black as the buoy is marked.

P. Various Limits, etc.

1	Leading line, Range Line
2	Transit
3	In line with
4	Limit of sector
5 (Pa)	Channel, Course, Track recommended (marked by buoys or beacons) (See P 21)
	Alternate course
6	Radar-guided track
7	Submarine cable (power, telephone, etc.)
7a	Submarine cable area
7b	Abandoned submarine cable (includes disused cable)
8	Submarine pipeline
8a	Submarine pipeline area
†8b	Abandoned submarine pipeline
9	Marine limit in general
(Pb) 10	Limit of restricted area (fish trap areas)
(Pc) 10	U.S. Harbor Line
11	Limit of dumping ground, spoil ground (See I 23, 24)
12	Anchorage limit
13	Limit of airport (See I 23, 24)
13a	Limit of military practice areas
14	Limit of sovereignty (Territorial waters)
15	Customs boundary
16	International boundary (also State boundary)
17	Stream limit
18	Ice limit
19	Limit of tide
20	Limit of navigation
21	Course of recommended (not marked by buoys or beacons) (See P 5)
	District or province limit
23	Reservation line (Options)
24	Measured distance
25	Prohibited area (See G 12, 46) (Screen optional)
(Pd)	Shipping safety fairway
(Pe)	Directed traffic lanes

Q. Soundings

No.	Description
1	SD — Doubtful sounding
2	No bottom found
3	Out of position
4	Least depth in narrow channels (with controlling depth indicated)
5	Dredged channel
6	Dredged area
7	Swept channel (See Q 9)
†8	Drying (or uncovering) heights above chart sounding datum
9	Swept area, not adequately sounded (shown by green tint)
9a	Swept area adequately sounded (swept by wire drag to depth indicated)
10	Hairline depth figures
10a	Figures for ordinary soundings
11	Soundings taken from foreign charts
12	Soundings taken from older surveys (or smaller scale chts)
13	Echo soundings
14	Sloping figures (See Q 2)
15	Upright figures (See Q 10a)
16	Bracketed figures (See O 1, 2)
17	Underlined soundings figures (See Q 8)
18	Soundings expressed in fathoms and feet
22 (Qa)	Unsounded area / Stream

FIG. 1844 m   Various limits, and soundings

FIG. 1844-I   Dangers

O. Dangers

No.	Description
1	Rock which does not cover (height above MHW) (See General Remarks)
†2	Rock which covers and uncovers, with height above chart sounding datum
3	Rock awash at (near) level of chart sounding datum
	Dotted line emphasizes danger to navigation
(Ou)	Rock awash (height unknown)
	Dotted line emphasizes danger to navigation
4	Submerged rock (depth unknown)
5	Shoal sounding on isolated rock
6	Submerged rock not dangerous to surface navigation (See O 4)
6a	Sunken danger with depth cleared by wire drag (in feet or fathoms)
7	Reef of unknown extent
8	Submarine volcano / Sub Vol
9	Discolored water / Discol water
10	Coral reef, detached (uncovers at sounding datum) (See A 11d, 11g) / Coral or Rocky reef, covered at sounding datum (See A 11d, 11g)
11	Wreck showing any portion of hull or superstructure (above sounding datum)
12	Wreck with only masts visible (above sounding datum) / Masts
13	Old symbols for wrecks
†13a	Wreck always partially submerged
14	Sunken wreck dangerous to surface navigation (less than 11 fathoms over wreck) (See O 6a)
15	Wreck over which depth is known
15a	Wreck with depth cleared by wire drag
†15b	Unsurveyed wreck over which the exact depth is unknown, but is considered to have a safe clearance to the depth shown
16	Sunken wreck, not dangerous to surface navigation
†17	Foul ground, Foul bottom (fb)
18	Tide Rips / Overfalls or Tide rips
19	Eddies
20	Kelp, Seaweed / Kelp
21	Bk Bank
22	Shl Shoal
23	Rf Reef (See A 11d, 11g; O 10)
23a	Ridge
24	Le Ledge
25	Breakers (See A 12)
26	Submerged rock (See O 4)
27	Obstruction
(Ox) 28	Fish haven (artificial fishing reef) / Obstruction (Fish haven)
29	Wreckage
29a	Wreck remains (dangerous only for anchoring)
†30	Submerged piling / Subm piles Subm piling
31	Snags; Submerged stumps (See H-9, 9a; L 59) / Stumps
31a	Lesser depth possible
32	Uncov Dries (See A 10, O 2, 10)
33	Cov Covers (See O 2, 10)
34	Uncov Uncovers (See A 10, O 2, 10)
35	Rep (1958) Reported (with date) / Eagle Rk (rep 1958) Reported (with name and date)
36	Discol Discolored (See O 9)
37	Isolated danger
38	Limiting danger line
39	Limit of rocky area
41	PA Position approximate
42	PD Position doubtful
43	ED Existence doubtful
44	P Pos Position
45	D Doubtful
46	Unexamined
(Od)	LD Least Depth
(Oe)	Subm Crib Crib (above water)
(Of)	Platform (lighted) HORN
(Og)	Offshore platform (unnamed)
(Oh)	Obstr Subm well Subm well (buoyed) / Hazel (lighted) HORN
(Oi)	Offshore platform (named)

U. Compass

Compass Rose

The outer circle is in degrees with zero at true north. The inner circles are in points and degrees with the arrow indicating magnetic north.

1	N	North
2	E	East
3	S	South
4	W	West
5	NE	Northeast
6	SE	Southeast
7	SW	Southwest
8	NW	Northwest
9	N	Northern
10	E	Eastern
11	S	Southern
12	W	Western
21	brg	Bearing
22	T	True
23	mag	Magnetic
24	var	Variation
25		Annual change
25a		Annual change nil
26		Abnormal variation, Magnetic attraction
27	deg	Degrees (See E-20)
28	dev	Deviation

T. Tides and Currents

1	HW	High water
1a	HHW	Higher high water
2	LW	Low water
(Ta)	LWD	Low water datum
2a	LLW	Lower low water
3	MTL	Mean tide level
4	MSL	Mean sea level
4a		Elevation of mean sea level above chart (sounding) datum
5		Chart datum (datum for sounding reduction)
6	Sp	Spring tide
7	Np	Neap tide
7a	MHW	Mean high water
8	MHWS	Mean high water springs
8a	MHWN	Mean high water neaps
8b	MHHW	Mean higher high water
8c	MLW	Mean low water
9	MLWS	Mean low water springs
9a	MLWN	Mean low water neaps
9b	MLLW	Mean lower low water
10	ISLW	Indian spring low water
11		High water full and change (vulgar establishment of the port)
12		Low water full and change
13		Mean establishment of the port
13a		Establishment of the port
14		Unit of height
15		Equinoctial
16		Quarter; Quadrature
17	Str.	Stream
18		Current, general, with rate
19		Flood stream (current) with rate
20		Ebb stream (current) with rate
21		Tide gauge; Tidepole, Automatic tide gauge
23	vel.	Velocity, Rate
24	kn.	Knots
25	ht.	Height
26		Tide
27		New moon
28		Full moon
29		Ordinary
30		Syzygy
31	fl.	Flood
32		Ebb
33		Tidal stream diagram
34		Place for which tabulated tidal stream data are given
35		Range (of tide)
36		Phase lag
(Tb)		Current diagram, with explanatory note

FIG. 1844 o   Tides and currents, the compass

FIG. 1844 n   Depth contours and tints, quality of the bottom

R. †Depth Contours and Tints (see General Remarks)

	Fms/Meters
0	0
6	1
12	2
18	3
24	4
30	5
36	6
60	10
120	20
180	30
240	40

Feet	Fms/Meters
300	50
600	100
1,200	200
1,800	300
2,400	400
3,000	500
6,000	1,000
12,000	2,000
18,000	3,000

Or continuous lines, with values

5 ——— 100 (blue or black) ——— (blue or black)

S. Quality of the Bottom

1	Grd	Ground		24	Oys	Oysters		50	spk	Speckled
2	S	Sand		25	Ms	Mussels		51	gty	Gritty
3	M	Mud; Muddy		26	Spg	Sponge		52	dec	Decayed
4	Oz	Ooze		27	K	Kelp		53	fly	Flinty
5	Ml	Marl		28	Wd	Sea-weed		54	glac	Glacial
6	Cl	Clay		28	Grs	Grass		55	ten	Tenacious
7	G	Gravel		29	Stg	Sea-tangle		56	wh	White
8	Sn	Shingle		31	Spi	Spicules		57	bk	Black
9	P	Pebbles		32	Fr	Foraminifera		58	vi	Violet
10	St	Stones		33	Gl	Globigerina		59	bu	Blue
11	Rk; rky	Rock, Rocky		34	Di	Diatoms		60	gn	Green
11a	Blds	Boulders		35	Rd	Radiolaria		61	yl	Yellow
12	Ck	Chalk		36	Pt	Pteropods		62	or	Orange
12a	Ca	Calcareous		37	Po	Polyzoa		63	rd	Red
13	Qz	Quartz		38	Cir	Cirripeda		64	br	Brown
13a	Sch	Schist		38a	Fu	Fucus		65	ch	Chocolate
14	Co	Coral		38b	Ma	Mattes		66	gy	Gray
(Sa)	Co Hd	Coral head		39	fne	Fine		67	lt	Light
15	Mds	Madrepores		40	crs	Coarse		68	dk	Dark
16	Vol	Volcanic		41	sft	Soft				
(Sb)	Vol Ash	Volcanic ash		42	hrd	Hard		70	vard	Varied
17	La	Lava		43	stf	Stiff		71	unev	Uneven
18	Pm	Pumice		44	sml	Small		(Sc)	S/M	Surface layer and Under layer
19	T	Tufa		45	lrg	Large				
20	Sc	Scoriae		46	stk	Sticky				
21	Cn	Cinders		47	brk	Broken		76		Fresh water springs in sea-bed
21a	Ash	Ash		47a	grd	Ground (Shells)				
22	Mn	Manganese		48	rt	Rotten				
23	Sh	Shells		49	str	Streaky				

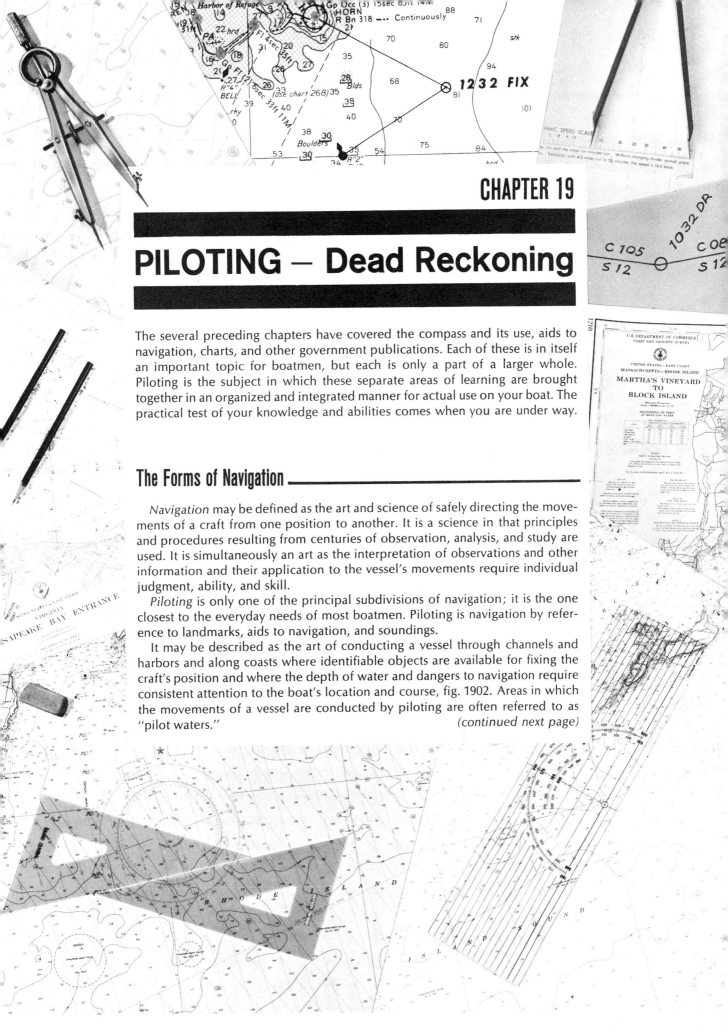

PILOTING — Dead Reckoning

The several preceding chapters have covered the compass and its use, aids to navigation, charts, and other government publications. Each of these is in itself an important topic for boatmen, but each is only a part of a larger whole. Piloting is the subject in which these separate areas of learning are brought together in an organized and integrated manner for actual use on your boat. The practical test of your knowledge and abilities comes when you are under way.

The Forms of Navigation

Navigation may be defined as the art and science of safely directing the movements of a craft from one position to another. It is a science in that principles and procedures resulting from centuries of observation, analysis, and study are used. It is simultaneously an art as the interpretation of observations and other information and their application to the vessel's movements require individual judgment, ability, and skill.

Piloting is only one of the principal subdivisions of navigation; it is the one closest to the everyday needs of most boatmen. Piloting is navigation by reference to landmarks, aids to navigation, and soundings.

It may be described as the art of conducting a vessel through channels and harbors and along coasts where identifiable objects are available for fixing the craft's position and where the depth of water and dangers to navigation require consistent attention to the boat's location and course, fig. 1902. Areas in which the movements of a vessel are conducted by piloting are often referred to as "pilot waters." *(continued next page)*

Dead Reckoning / CHAPTER 19

Along with piloting, the boatman will often use another form of navigation, *dead reckoning,* a procedure by which the craft's approximate location at any time is deduced from its movements since the last accurate determination of position.

Other subdivisions of navigation are *electronic,* which will be touched on briefly in the following chapters insofar as specific systems are applicable to small craft, and *celestial,* which will be left to more advanced students and texts.

The importance of piloting

Piloting is a most important part of navigation, and perhaps the form requiring the least study but the most experience and best judgment. It is used by boatmen in

FIG. 1902 Piloting, by reference to landmarks and aids to navigation, is most often done in waters restricted by shoals and other dangers and which are relatively heavily traveled by other boats.

FIG. 1901 Piloting is the principal form of navigation used by boatmen. It requires study and practice, but it often becomes one of the major sources of enjoyment in boating. M. Rosenfeld.

rivers, bays, lakes, and close alongshore when on the open oceans. In such waters, the hazards to safe navigation may be quite frequent and the density of traffic quite high. The navigator of a craft of any size in pilot waters must have adequate training and knowledge; he must give his task close attention and constant alertness. Frequent determinations of position are usually essential, and changes in course or speed may be necessary at relatively short intervals.

The high seas vs. pilot waters

On the high seas, or well offshore in such large bodies of water as the Great Lakes, navigation can be more leisurely and relaxed. An error or uncertainty of position of a few miles will present no immediate hazard to the safety of the boat and its crew. But when one approaches the shore line, or the water shoals, a greater degree of accuracy is required. An error of only a few yards can result in running aground with certain embarrassment, and possibly much more serious consequences. The proximity of other craft requires constant knowledge of where the dangers lie and where one's own boat can be safely steered.

The enjoyment of piloting

Piloting can be "fun" for a boatman, but it will be most enjoyable when done without tension or anxiety; this happy state can be achieved only with a sound background of study and practice. The wise skipper "overnavigates" in times of fair weather so as to acquire the skill that will let him navigate his boat safely through fog or rain or night without fear or nervous strain.

The Dimensions of Piloting

The basic "dimensions" of piloting are direction, distance, and time. Other quantities which must be measured, calculated, or used, include speed, position, and depths and heights. A qualified pilot must have a ready understanding of how each of these dimensions is measured, expressed in units, used in calculations, and plotted on charts.

DIRECTION

Direction is the position of one point relative to another point without reference to the distance between them. As discussed earlier in the chapters on compasses and charts, modern navigation uses the system of angular measurement in which a complete circle is divided into 360 units called "degrees." Although each degree can in turn be subdivided into 60 minutes, the more common practice

in angular measurement in piloting is to use ordinary fractions such as $1/2$ and $1/4$, or decimal fractions in tenths.

True, magnetic, or compass

Directions are normally referred to a base line running from the origin point toward the geographic North Pole. Such directions can be measured on a chart with reference to the meridians of longitude and are called "true" directions. Measurements made with respect to the direction of the earth's magnetic field at that point are termed "magnetic" directions, and those referred to local magnetic conditions as measured by the craft's compass are designated "compass" directions, see fig. 1903. *It is of the utmost importance to always designate the reference used for directional measurement, true (T), magnetic (M), or compass (C).*

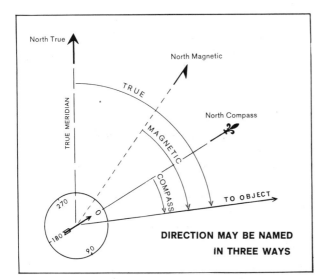

FIG. 1903 Direction is one of the basic "dimensions" of piloting. It can be measured with respect to True, Magnetic, or Compass North. Always be sure to designate the reference used.

Directions and angles

The basic system of measurement uses the reference direction as 0° (North) and measures clockwise through 90° (East), 180° (South), and 270° (West) around to 360° which is North again. Directions are expressed in three-digit form such as 005°, 030°, 150°, etc. Note that zeros are added before the figures denoting direction if necessary to make a three-digit number, for example, 005° or 030°, fig. 1904a. *Angles* which are *not* directions are expressed in one, two, or three digits as appropriate, 5°, 30°, 150°, etc., fig. 1904b.

Occasionally, directions will be expressed as so many degrees east or west of North or South, such as N30°E (030°), S20°E (160°), S40°W (220°), or N15°W (345°), fig. 1905. This form of expression, "direction in quadrant," is useful for some types of computations, but it is not employed for general navigational purposes.

Directions in the "point" system

The "point" system of angular measurement, so widely used in the days of sailing ships, has now fallen almost completely from practical use in navigation. It divided a complete circle into 32 points of 11¼ degrees each which could then be further subdivided fractionally. It is cumbersome to use and complicates calculations; with respect to the piloting of modern small craft, it is now of historical interest only.

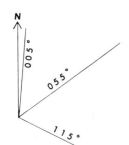

FIG. 1904a Directions are always designated by a *three-digit* number. Add zeros before a single or double-digit number as shown here.

FIG. 1904b An angle between two directions, as distinguished from the directions themselves, is *not* expressed as a three-digit number. An angle such as BAC above is shown as simply 50°, not as 050°.

FIG. 1905 Directions may be described "in quadrant," but this technique is rarely used in modern boating. In this obsolete procedure, angles are measured in either direction from North or South to a maximum of 90°.

FIG. 1906a   FIG. 1906b

The *reciprocal* of a direction is simply the opposite direction, shown here as a broken line. To find a reciprocal, add 180° to the given direction. If the total exceeds 360°, subtract that amount. Alternatively, subtract 180° from the given direction if it is greater than that amount.

Reciprocals

For any given direction, there is its *reciprocal*. This latter direction is the direct opposite, differing by 180°. Thus the reciprocal of 030° is 210°, and the reciprocal of 300° is 120°. To find the reciprocal of any direction, simply add 180° if the given direction is less than the amount; or subtract 180°, if it exceeds that figure, as shown in fig. 1906.

DISTANCE

This is the second of the basic dimensions of piloting. *Distance* is defined as the spacial separation between two points without regard to the direction of one from the other. It is commonly thought of as the length of the shortest line that can be drawn between the two points.

The basic unit of distance in piloting is the *mile,* but, as noted in Chapter 18, there are two types of miles that a boatman may encounter. The *statute mile* is used on inland bodies of water such as the Mississippi River and its tributaries, the Great Lakes, etc. (also the Atlantic and Gulf Intracoastal Waterways since 1969). It is 5280 feet in length, the same mile commonly used on land.

On the high seas and connecting tidal waters, the unit of measurement is the *nautical mile* of 6076.1 feet. This "salt-water" mile is essentially equal to one minute of latitude, and this relationship is often used in navigation. Nautical miles are slightly longer than statute miles, and the comparison is usually taken as 7 nautical miles equals 8 statute miles. More precisely, the conversion between nautical and statute miles uses the factor of 1.15.

It is quite possible to cruise from an area using one kind of mile into waters where the other kind is used. Care must be exercised at such times to determine which type of mile is being used and so specify in calculations.

For shorter distances, a few miles or less, the unit of measurement may be the *yard;* feet are seldom used as a unit of horizontal distance in boating.

With the coming of the metric system, boatmen must be prepared for greater use of meters (m) and *kilometers* (km); they must be familiar with these units and conversion to and from English units. Factors are: 1 foot = 0.3048 meter; 1 yard = 0.9144 meter; 1 statute mile = 1.609 kilometers; 1 nautical mile = 1.852 kilometers.

TIME

The third basic dimension of piloting is *time*. Although the pilot does not need so accurate a knowledge of the exact time of day as does a celestial navigator, ability to determine the passage of time and to perform calculations with such *elapsed time* is essential. A boat should have aboard a clock or watch of reasonable time-keeping accuracy; a second one in reserve is desirable. For many practical problems in piloting, a stop watch will be found useful.

Units of time

The units of time used in boating are the everyday ones of *hours* of 60 *minutes* each. In piloting, measurements will not often be carried to the preciseness of *seconds* of time although decimal fractions of minutes may occassionally occur in calculations. Seconds and fractions of minutes may be used in competitive events such as races and predicted log contests, but seldom otherwise.

The 24-hour clock system

In navigation, including piloting, the time of day is expressed in a 24-hour system that eliminates the necessity for using the designations of "am" and "pm." Time is written in four-digit figures; the first two are the hour and the second pair represents the minutes. The day starts at 0000 or midnight; the next minute is 0001, 12:01 am in the old system; 0100 would be 1 am, and so on to 1200 at noon. The second half of the day continues in the same pattern with 1300 being 1 pm, 1832 being 6:32 pm, etc., to 2400 for midnight. Time is spoken as "zero seven hundred" or "fifteen forty." The phrase "hours" should *not* be used. The times of 1000 and 2000 are correctly spoken as "ten hundred" and "twenty hundred," *not* as "one thousand" or "two thousand."

When performing arithmetic computations with time caution must always be exercised to remember that when "borrowing" or "carrying" there are *60* minutes in an hour, and not 100. As obvious and simple a matter as this may be, the mistake occurs all too often.

Time zones

A navigator in pilot waters must also be alert to *time zones.* Even in coastal or inland waters, it is possible to cruise from one zone to another resulting in the necessity for changing clocks, the plot on the chart, and the log; plus one's arrival time at the next port.

A further complication in time is the prevalence of "daylight time" in many boating areas during the summer months. Government publications are in standard time; local sources of information such as newspapers and radio broadcasts will undoubtedly use daylight time if it is in effect. Daylight time is one hour *later* than standard time. When going from standard time to daylight, *add* one hour; from daylight to standard, *subtract* one hour.

SPEED

No matter how fast or slow one's craft may be, speed is an essential dimension of piloting. *Speed* is defined as the number of units of distance that would be traveled in a specified unit of time.

The basic unit of speed is *miles per hour*, whether these be nautical or statute miles, as determined by location. A special name, *knot,* has been given to the nautical mile per hour. Note well that the word "knot" includes the element of time—to say "knots per hour" is not only incorrect, it is a mark of ignorance.

Conversion of knots and MPH

The conversion factors between statute miles per hour (MPH) and knots are the same as for the corresponding units of distance—1 knot = 1.15 MPH, or 7 knots roughly equals 8 MPH. (1 knot = 1.852 km/h)

The unit "knot" may be abbreviated either as "kn." or "kt."; the former has a somewhat greater usage.

POSITION

The ability to describe accurately the position of his craft is an essential requirement for a pilot, and one that marks him as well qualified. To realize the importance and the difficulties of this seemingly simple task, one has only to listen to his radio on VHF Channel 16 or 22 on a weekend afternoon during the boating season. The hesitant, inadequate, and inaccurate attempts to simply say where they are must surely irritate the Coast Guard and embarrass all competent boatmen.

Relative and geographic coordinates

Position may be described in relative terms or by geographic coordinates. When defined as a *relative position,* the location of the craft is described as being a certain distance and direction from a specified identifiable point such as a landmark or aid to navigation. A boat's position may be described with varying degrees of preciseness as determined by the accuracy of the data on which it is based. A skipper might say that he was "about two miles southwest of Brenton Reef Light"; or if he had the capability of being more precise, he could say, "I'm 2.2 miles, 230°. True from Brenton Reef Light." In relative positioning, the distance may, of course, be essentially zero, as would be the case with a position report such as "I am at Lighted Whistle Buoy 2." See fig. 1907.

FIG. 1907 A boat's position may be described in "relative" terms. It is stated to be at a certain distance and direction from an identifiable object such as an aid to navigation. In this example, it would be "1.8 miles, 120 degrees True from Point Judith Light."

FIG. 1908 The position of a boat can be described in terms of "geographic coordinates." Using the subdivisions of the chart's borders, the latitude and longitude of the plotted position are measured and recorded. (from DUTTON'S NAVIGATION AND PILOTING)

FIG. 1909 Depth is a "dimension" of piloting that is often of the greatest importance to the safety of a boat and its crew. Be sure that you know whether the charted depths on the chart you are using are shown in feet or fathoms (or meters and decimeters).

The preceding examples of position description have all used visible identifiable objects. It is also possible to state one's *geographic position* in terms of *latitude* and *longitude* using those nice straight, uniformly-spaced lines on charts which so unfortunately do not appear on the surface of the water. Using this procedure, the position is measured from the markings on either side and the top or bottom of the chart.

The units of measurement for geographic coordinates are *degrees* and *minutes,* but this degree is not quite the same unit as used in the measurement of direction, nor is this minute the same as the unit of time. Care must be used to avoid confusion between these units of position and other units with similar names. For precise position definition, one may use either *seconds* or *tenths of minutes* as determined by the chart being used. Typically, the smallest unit on the marginal scales of N.O.S. coast charts will be tenths of minutes, but for harbor charts it will be seconds; see pages 345–346 and figs. 1818a and 1818b.

In a statement of geographic position, latitude is given first, before longitude, and the figures must be followed by "North" or "South" as appropriate. In U.S. waters, the latitude is, of course, always "North," even for the most unreconstructed "rebel." Similarly, longitude must be designated "East" or "West" to be complete; all U.S. waters are in West longitude, fig. 1908.

DEPTHS

The *depth* of the water is important both for the safety of a boat in preventing grounding and for navigational purposes. Thus, this vertical measurement from the surface of the water to the bottom is an essential dimension of piloting. Measurements may be made continuously or only occasionally as appropriate, but you can be sure that at some time or another on almost any cruise, knowledge of the depth will become critically important.

In pilot waters, depths will normally be measured in *feet.* In open ocean waters, the small craft operator may find himself on charts indicating depths in *fathoms* of six feet each. Some charts of foreign waters may use meters and decimeters. It is important to check each chart when purchased and again when used to note the unit of measurement of depth; see fig. 1909.

In many areas, depths will fluctuate somewhat from the printed figures on charts due to tidal changes. Charts will indicate the *datum* used, the reference plane from which measurements were made. They will also indicate the normal range of tidal variations and the extreme low-water condition that must be considered.

HEIGHTS

The height, or elevation, of certain objects will be of concern to the pilot. The height of some landmarks and lighted aids to navigation may determine their range of visibility. Of more critical importance, however, are such vertical measurements as the clearance under a bridge, fig. 1910. *Heights,* or vertical dimensions upward from the surface of the water, are measured in *feet* (or meters). It should be noted that in tidal areas, the datum, or plane of reference, for heights is *not* the same as for depths. Examine each chart carefully and note the datum from which heights are measured.

The usual datum for the measurement of heights is *mean high water.* This will be an imaginary plane surface above the mean low-water datum for depths by an amount equal to the *mean tide range;* the height of mean high water will usually be shown on a chart; see fig. 1820.

FIG. 1910 Charts will show the heights of bridges or other structures that will affect navigation. Heights are measured vertically in feet, usually from mean high water (MHW).

377

The Instruments of Piloting

The practice of piloting in coastal and inland waters requires the use of a few simple tools or instruments, fig. 1911. These are not particularly expensive items, but they should be of good quality, well cared for, and used with the proper respect. A skilled man in any profession or trade is known by his tools, when that term is used in its broadest sense. A navigator may well be judged by his instruments and how he uses them.*

FIG. 1911 Only a few simple instruments are needed for piloting, but these should be of good quality, used with respect, and properly maintained.

DIRECTION

Many instruments are used in the measurement of direction. Some are concerned with such measurement directly, and others with its measurement on a chart. Still other instruments are used to both measure direction from a chart and to plot directions from observations.

Determining Direction

The basic instrument on a boat for the determination of direction is a *compass*. With rare exceptions, this will be a *magnetic* compass as shown in fig. 1912 and described in Chapter 13. Directions obtained from this instrument will be "compass" directions and will require correction for deviation and variation as covered in Chapter 14.

A *gyro* compass is a complex device capable of indicating the true north direction without regard to magnetic conditions. However, its size, weight, electrical power requirements, and particularly its high cost, limit its use to the largest and most luxurious yachts. The average boatman must make do with a magnetic compass, but, properly used, this traditional piloting instrument will serve him well.

The compass is used primarily to determine the direction in which the craft is headed. Depending upon its loca-

* For electronic calculators, see pages 441–447.

tion, and how it is mounted, the steering compass may also be used for determining the direction of other objects from the boat. Rough readings may be taken by sighting across the compass itself and estimating the reading of the compass card. More exact readings can be taken if a pair of *sight vanes* can be mounted on the compass as illustrated in fig. 1913. Sights taken with a steering compass are satisfactory as to accuracy, but are generally limited by physical considerations to objects forward of the beam.

Pelorus. A more flexible instrument for measuring the direction of objects from the boat is the *pelorus*, fig. 1914. This simple device consists of a set of sighting vanes mounted over a circular scale calibrated in degrees like a compass card. A means must be provided for mounting or temporarily locating the pelorus so that it may be properly oriented to the fore-and-aft center line of the boat. Peloruses may be purchased or made in the home workshop; see fig. 1915.

The circular scale of a pelorus is usually made so that it may be rotated to a desired position and there clamped in place. With the scale so set that 000° is dead ahead, over or parallel to the center line of the boat, the directions that are then measured are termed *relative bearings*.

FIG. 1912 A magnetic compass is the basic instrument for measuring direction on a boat. See Chapters 13 and 14 for detailed coverage of the compass.

FIG. 1913 The compass can be used to determine the direction from the boat to an object such as an aid to navigation. Greater accuracy will be obtained if *sight vanes* are used as shown here.

FIG. 1914 A *pelorus* **is used to take bearings on objects from a boat. It consists of a set of sights mounted over an angular scale calibrated like a compass card.**

The sight vanes placed on a compass, or those of a pelorus, may be replaced with a small telescope having cross-hairs. Greater accuracy will be achieved, but the telescope must be of low power in order to have a wide enough field of view to pick up and hold objects at a distance despite the movements of the boat.

Even greater flexibility of use can be obtained with one of several patented instruments now on the market. Each of these consists of a small magnetic compass conveniently mounted for holding in front of one's eyes, plus a set of sights and a prismatic optical system for simultaneously observing a distant object through the sights and reading the compass card. Internal lighting for night use is usually provided. Typical of these instruments is the hand-bearing compass (fig. 1916) with open sights. Fig. 1917 illustrates how some small compasses may be unshipped from their mounting and held at eye level to take a bearing.

Plotting directions

Once direction has been determined by compass, pelorus, or other device, it must be plotted on the chart. For this action, there are a number of instruments available. These same tools will be used when the problem is the determination of direction from the chart itself.

These may be converted to compass directions or compass bearings, by numerically adding the heading of the boat as read from the steering compass at the instant of observation (subtract 360° from this sum if it exceeds that amount). A steady hand at the wheel is required, and the observer should call "Mark" at the time that he reads the pelorus so that the helmsman may simultaneously read the boat's compass. Alternatively, the helmsman may call a series of "marks" as he is on the prescribed heading, remaining silent if the boat falls off to either side. When using this technique, the observer takes his reading only when the helmsman is indicating that he is directly on the correct heading.

A second method of using a pelorus is to set the scale so that it matches the compass for the heading being steered. Readings then taken with the pelorus are directly compass bearings without further conversion. Two cautions must be observed — the craft must be directly on course at the time of observation; and, when correcting for *deviation,* the value used is that for the *heading* of the boat, *not* that for the observed direction. Because of these possible errors, particularly the latter one, this technique should be avoided, or used only with much practice and great care.

Course plotters. These are pieces of clear plastic, usually rectangular in shape, with one or more semi-circular angular scales marked thereon, see fig. 1918. The center of these scales is at or near the center of one of the longer sides of the plotter and is usually emphasized with a small circle or "bull's-eye." There are normally two main scales, one from 000° to 180° and the other from 180° to 360°; each is calibrated in degrees. There may also be smaller auxiliary scales offset 90° from the main scales. Lines are marked on the plotter parallel to the longer sides. Some instruments have distance marks along the edges corresponding to the more commonly-used chart scales.

Course plotters are used in the following manner:

1. *To determine the direction of a course or bearing from a given point,* place the plotter on the chart so that one of its longer sides is along the course or bearing line and slide the plotter until the bull's-eye is over a *meridian.* The true direction is then read on the scale where it is intersected by the meridian. Easterly courses are read on the scale that reads from 000° to 180°, and westerly courses are read on the other main scale, see fig. 1919.

FIG. 1915 A pelorus may be purchased or it is easily made in a home workshop. A compass rose or card diagram such as Fig. 1310 or 1335 is cut out and mounted on a wooden or metallic base. A set of rotatable sighting vanes completes the pelorus.

FIG. 1916 A hand bearing compass has the advantage that it may easily be used from almost any place on a boat. Be careful, however, of using it near large masses of magnetic material that will introduce deviation errors.

FIG. 1917 Some compasses, like this Corsair, are so mounted (particularly on small boats) that they can be easily unshipped and held at eye-level for taking bearings. The same precautions regarding deviation must be observed as for a hand bearing compass.

If it is more convenient, the course or bearing may be lined up with one of the marked parallel lines rather than the edge of the course plotter. In measuring courses and bearings, it is not absolutely necessary to actually draw in the line connecting the two points, the plotter can be aligned using only the two points concerned. Usually, however, it will be found easier and safer to draw in the connecting line.

When the direction to be measured is within 20° or so of due North or South, it may be difficult to reach a meridian by sliding the course plotter across the chart. The small inner auxiliary scales have been included on the plotter for just such cases. Slide the plotter until the bull's-eye intersects a *parallel of latitude* line. The intersection of this line with the appropriate *auxiliary* scale indicates the direction of the course or bearing, see fig. 1920.

2. *To plot a specified direction (course or bearing) from a given point,* put a pencil on the origin point, keep one of the longer edges of the course plotter snug against the pencil, and slide the plotter around until the center bull's-

FIG. 1918 A *course plotter* is a single rectangular piece of transparent plastic ruled with circular scales and a set of lines parallel to its longer sides. Shown here is the model used by the U.S. Power Squadrons.

FIG. 1919 The course plotter is lined up with the course line along one of the longer sides, and then is moved until a meridian cuts through the "bull's eye." Direction can then be read from the appropriate main scale.

eye and the desired mark on the appropriate main scale both lie along the same meridian. With the plotter thus positioned, draw in the specified direction from the given point.

Alternatively, the plotter may first be positioned using the bull's-eye and scale markings without regard to the specified origin point. The plotter is then carefully slid up or down the meridian until one of the longer edges is over the origin point and then the direction line is drawn in.

For directions nearly North or South, one of the small auxiliary scales can be used in conjunction with a parallel of latitude.

3. *To extend a line* which must be longer than·the length of the course plotter, place a pair of dividers, opened to three or four inches, tightly against the edge of the plotter and then slide the plotter along using the divider points as guides. Draw in the extension of the course or bearing line after the plotter has been advanced.

4. In piloting, it is sometimes necessary *to draw a new line parallel to an existing course or bearing line*. For such situations, the parallel lines marked on the course plotter may be used as guides.

Course protractors. Many pilots use a *course protractor,* fig. 1921, as their primary plotting tool. This instrument, with its moving parts, is not as easily used as the course plotter described above; but, when it is employed with care, it gives as satisfactory results.

In using the course protractor *to measure the direction of a course or bearing,* its center should be placed on the chart exactly over the specified origin point, such as the boat's position or an aid to navigation. The arm of the protractor is then swung around to the nearest compass rose on the chart, making the upper edge of the arm (which is in line with the center of the compass part of the course protractor) pass directly over the center of the compass rose.

Holding the course protractor arm firmly in this position, the compass part of the protractor is then turned around until the upper edge of the arm cuts across the same degree marking of the protractor compass as it does at the compass rose. The compass and the rose are now parallel. Holding the protractor compass firmly against the chart, the protractor arm is then moved around until its edge cuts across the second point involved in the course

FIG. 1920 If a meridian cannot be easily reached, as may be the case with courses within a few degrees of North or South, use the *auxiliary* inner scales and a *parallel* of latitude as shown here.

Main Scale

Auxiliary Scale

or bearing. The direction in degrees can then be read directly from the protractor compass scale.

To lay off a line in a specified direction from the given point, the protractor rose is first lined up with the compass rose on the chart as in the preceding instructions. Then the arm is rotated until the desired direction is indicated on the compass scale, and the line is drawn in; this line will have to be extended back to the origin point after the course protractor has been lifted off the chart.

Parallel rulers. A traditional instrument for measuring and plotting directions on charts is a set of *parallel rulers.* Their use on boats has declined somewhat in recent years, but they are still capable of giving good results if the navigator is careful to avoid slippage. Parallel rulers may be

FIG. 1922 *Parallel rulers* are a traditional charting instrument. The two straightedges are kept in parallel alignment by the connecting links. Directions are transferred from one place to another by "walking" the rulers across the chart.

FIG. 1921 Some skippers prefer to use a *course protractor* as their primary plotting tool. It consists of two pieces of plastic movable with respect to each other.

FIG. 1923 A pair of ordinary drawing triangles can be used for transferring a direction from one part of a chart to another, but not for great distances. See text for method of their use.

made of black (as shown in fig. 1922) or clear transparent plastic material. The two rulers are connected by metal linkages so that the edges always remain parallel. To measure the direction of a line, one ruler is lined up with the desired objects on the chart and then the pair is "walked" across the chart to the nearest compass rose by alternately holding one ruler and moving the other. To plot a line of stated direction, the process is essentially reversed; the procedure is started at the compass rose and worked to the desired origin point.

Drawing triangles. A pair of ordinary plastic *drawing triangles* can also be used for transferring a direction from one part of a chart to another, although not for very great distances. The two triangles need not be similar in size or shape. The two hypotenuses (longest sides) are placed together and one of the other sides of one triangle is lined up with the course or bearing line, or with the desired direction at the compass rose, fig. 1923. The other triangle is held firmly in place as a base, and the first one is slid along in contact with it, carrying the specified line to a new position while maintaining its direction. If necessary, the triangles may be alternately held and slid for moving somewhat greater distances.

Courser. One rather unique direction instrument, particularly useful in outboards or other situations of limited space, is a "Courser," a patented device consisting of a sheet of flexible plastic upon which are ruled a series of parallel lines, fig. 1924. One line is placed over the course or bearing to be measured and another will fall across or near the center of a compass rose on the chart. By slight adjustments to the Courser, directions can be read off the

FIG. 1924 A "Courser" is a sheet of soft flexible transparent plastic on which parallel lines have been ruled. It is simple and convenient to use in smaller boats, and the accuracy obtained with it is adequate for such applications.

rose with sufficient accuracy for practical use in a small boat.

An ordinary *drawing protractor* may find some use aboard a boat for measuring angles, but it is not a highly useful instrument and can be omitted. A chart compass rose can always be used for angle measurement if this becomes necessary.

FIG. 1925 A *radar set* on a boat can measure the direction and distance to other boats, aids to navigation, prominent structures and terrain features, etc. The use of radar is covered more fully in Chapter 25.

FIG. 1926 A *patent log*, used for determining distance run and speed. A log line connects the rotator to a registering device near the stern of the boat. The log line must be long enough to clear the wake as it is towed astern. In use, the rotator revolves as it is towed through the water, and the line transmits this rotary motion to the registering device which is calibrated so that the distance can be read directly from the dial.

FIG. 1927 A more modern patent log consists of a much smaller impeller mounted on the bottom of the boat connected to a dialed instrument for measuring speed and distance run through the water.

DISTANCE

Distance to an object can be measured directly by *radar*, fig. 1925; and distance traveled can be measured directly by a *summing log,* figs. 1926 and 1927. However, few boats are equipped with either of these items of equipment. Distance is usually measured in piloting by taking it from a chart.

Chart measurements for distance

Dividers. Distance is measured on a chart with a pair of *dividers*, fig. 1928a. The two arms of this small drafting instrument can be opened as desired, and the friction at the pivot is sufficient to hold them in place with the same separation between the points. Most dividers have some means for adjusting this friction; it should be enough to hold the arms in place, but not so much as to make opening or closing difficult. A special type of dividers has a center cross-piece (like the horizontal part of the capital letter "A") which can be rotated by a knurled knob to set and maintain the opening between the arms, fig. 1928b; thus the distance between the points cannot accidentally change. This type of dividers is particularly useful if kept set to some standard distance, such as one mile to the scale of the chart being used.

The dividers are first opened to the distance between two points on the chart, then they are transferred without change to the chart's graphic scale (see fig. 1929). Note that the zero point on this scale is not at the left-hand end, but rather is one basic unit up the scale. This unit to the left of zero is more finely divided than are the remaining basic units. For the measurement of any distance, the right-hand point of the dividers is set on the basic unit mark that will result in the left-hand point falling somewhere on the more-finely-divided unit to the left of the zero. The distance measured is the sum of the basic units counted off to the right from the scale's zero point plus the fractional unit to the left from zero. In fig. 1929, the distance is 1.4 nautical miles.

If the distance on the chart cannot be spanned with the dividers opened widely (about 60° is the maximum practical opening), set them at a convenient opening for a whole number of units on the graphic scale or latitude subdivisions, step this off the necessary number of times, then measure the odd remainder. The total distance is then the simple sum of the parts stepped off and measured separately, fig. 1930.

To mark off on the chart a desired distance, set the right point of the dividers on the nearest lower whole number of units, and the left point on the remaining fractional part of a unit measured leftward from zero on the scale. The dividers are now properly set for the specified distance at the scale of the chart being used and can be applied to the chart. If the distance is too great for one setting of the dividers, it may be stepped off in several increments.

Charts at a scale smaller than 1:80,000 will not have a graphic scale. In lieu thereof, distances are measured on the latitude scales at either side of the chart. Care should be taken to measure on these scales near the same latitude as the portion of the chart being used; in other words, move directly horizontally across the chart to either of its sides to use the scales.

FIG. 1928 Dividers are used to measure distances on a chart. A—Friction at the pivot holds the arms to the desired opening. B—In this type of dividers, an adjustable center cross-arm maintains the separation between points and avoids accidental changes. C—Long-legged dividers enable the pilot to step off long runs on a chart, without "walking" them.

FIG. 1929 After the dividers have been set for the distance on the chart between the points concerned, they are moved to the graphic scale or latitude subdivisions at the edge of the chart. Distance is measured on these scales as described in the text.

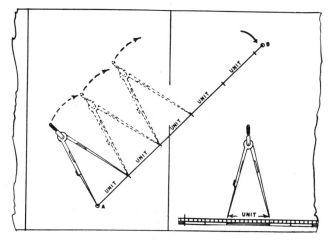

FIG. 1930 When a chart distance is too great to be measured with a single setting of the dividers, open the points to a convenient whole number of units. Step these along the chart for the required number of times and then measure any small left-over distance (arrow) in the usual manner. (Figs. 1908 and 1930 are based on DUTTON'S NAVIGATION AND PILOTING, copyright © 1957 and 1958 by U. S. Naval Institute, Annapolis, Maryland.)

With a little experience, dividers can be set and used with one hand. Making sure that the friction at the pivot is properly adjusted, practice this technique until it can be used with ease; such ability will add convenience and speed to your piloting work.

An instrument that looks much like a pair of dividers, except that a pencil lead or pen is substituted for one point, is called a *compass* (or *drawing compass* to distinguish it from a magnetic compass). This is used primarily for drawing arcs or circles.

Distance can also be measured across a chart with reduced, but generally acceptable, accuracy by using a *chart measurer*, fig. 1931. This device has a small wheel that is rolled along the chart; the wheel is internally geared to an indicating dial. Chart measurers will read distances directly in miles at various typical chart scales; separate models are available for charts using statute and nautical miles. They are particularly useful in measuring distances up rivers with many bends and changes of direction.

TIME

Every pilot, no matter how small his craft, should have a dependable and reasonably accurate timepiece. This can be a clock, wrist watch, or pocket watch. Long-term accuracy is of secondary importance in piloting, but short-term errors, those accumulated over the length of a day or half-day, should be small. A knowledge of the time of day within a few minutes will usually be sufficient. A clock, if used, should be mounted where it is clearly visible from the helm-seat or plotting table. If two clocks are used, be sure that they show the same time.

Elapsed time is usually of greater interest than *absolute* time. A stop watch will often be handy although it cannot be classed as a necessary instrument of piloting. Most stop watches have a second hand that makes one revolution for each minute, but there are some that sweep completely around in 30 seconds, and even a few that have a 10-second period. Know for sure the type of stop watch that you are using.

FIG. 1931 If a *chart measurer* is rolled across a chart, between two points, an indicating dial will show the distance directly for typical chart scales. It is especially useful in measuring distances on waterways with many bends and curves.

FIG. 1933 Many small boats are fitted with a simple device that measures speed by the pressure built up in a probe as a result of the movement of the boat through the water. Accuracy is quite good, but it must be remembered that it is speed through the water that is measured, and not speed made good over the bottom.

SPEED

Speed is a dimension that can be measured directly or calculated from knowledge of distance and time. Direct reading instruments are convenient, but they give only the relative speed through the water, and not the speed made good between two geographic points.

In years gone by, speed through the water was measured by use of a *chip log*, fig. 1932. More modern marine speedometers use the static pressure built up in a small tube by motion of the boat, fig. 1933, an impeller turned by the passing water, or a finger-like strut projecting below the bottom of the boat, fig. 1934. Many different models are available in a wide variety of speed ranges from those for sailboats to models reading high enough for fast speedboats.

Speed can be calculated from a knowledge of the distance covered and the elapsed time, to be discussed later in this chapter, or by the use of special calculating devices. These calculators are specialized adaptations of slide rules used for general mathematical calculations; they may be either linear or circular in form, figs. 1935a and b.

DEPTH

This most important dimension of piloting can be measured manually or electronically. A hand *lead line*, fig. 1936, is simple, accurate, and not subject to breakdowns. It does have the disadvantages, however, of being awkward to use, inconvenient in bad weather, and capable of giving only one or two readings per minute; a lead line can be used only at quite slow speeds.

Many small craft today are equipped with an *electronic depth sounder*. These devices can clearly, accurately, and most conveniently provide measurements of the depth of water beneath the boat. Moreover, soundings are indicated many times each second, so frequently that they appear to be a smooth, continuous measurement of depth. For more information on these relatively inexpensive but most useful piloting aids, see Chapter 25, pages 499 to 501.

FIG. 1934 This speedometer, designed primarily for sailboats, is actuated by a strut or finger which projects below the bottom of the boat. A modern solid-state electronic instrument, it measures speed variations to 1/100 knot. An optional feature measures distance up to 999.9 nautical miles.

FIG. 1932 The old chip log, consisting of the log-chip, log-line, and log-glass. The log-chip is a thin piece of wood, weighted so that it will float vertically. The chip is thrown from the stern and the log-line is allowed to flow freely over the rail. The line is marked at intervals of 47 feet 3 inches (14.40 m), called "knots," and the number of knots that pass over the rail in the time that it takes the glass to empty is a direct measure of the speed.

FIG. 1934 a Unipas-300, a versatile 12-volt solid-state navigational instrument, measures depth on 25- or 100-foot scales; speed, on various scales from 0-2.5 or 0-25 knots, with sensitivity as fine as .01 knot; and distance logged, in steps of .001 mile. Plug-in modules provide for twin-engine synchronization, wind-speed measurement, detection of gasoline vapors, and a battery check. At anchor, it will even measure current velocity.

FIG. 1935a   Speed need not be measured directly; it may be calculated from a knowledge of distance and time. A circular calculator as shown here will make all speed-time-distance computations quickly and accurately.

FIG. 1935b   This calculator enables the pilot to solve 18 different types of navigational problems—speed-time-distance, conversions and measurement, and includes special aids for the sailboatman, even a plotting board on the reverse side.

FIG. 1936   Depth can be measured manually with a marked weighted line—a lead line. Markings can be of the traditional type with strips of leather and rags, or with modern direct-reading plastic tags.

MISCELLANEOUS PILOTING TOOLS

Among the most important of all piloting tools are the ordinary *pencils* and *erasers*. Pencils should be neither too hard nor too soft. If too hard, there will be a tendency to score into the chart paper; if too soft, smudging may result. A medium, or No. 2, pencil will often be found to be satisfactory, but personal preferences may cause some variation. Pencils should be kept well sharpened, and several should be handy to the piloting table.

FIG. 1937   A good pair of binoculars is almost a necessity on a boat. The size most often recommended is designated "7 x 50." The eyepieces may be individually or centrally focused.

A soft eraser of the "Pink Pearl" type will be satisfactory for most erasures; an art gum eraser can be used for general chart cleaning.

Binoculars. A good pair of *binoculars* will be found essential for most piloting situations, fig. 1937. In selecting a pair of binoculars, it should be remembered that higher powers will result in greater magnification, bringing distant objects closer, but only at the cost of a more limited field of view. An adequate field of view is essential on small boats with their rapid and sometimes violent motion. Binoculars are designated by two figures, such as "6x30" or "10x50." The first figure indicates the power of magnification, the second is the diameter of the front lens in millimeters. This latter characteristic is important in night use. Most authorities recommend a 7x50 set of binoculars as best suited for marine use.

The binoculars may be individually focused (IF) for each eye, or centrally focused (CF) for both eyes, with a minor adjustment on one eyepiece to balance any difference between a person's two eyes. The choice between IF and CF glasses is a matter of personal preference.

Binoculars should be kept in their case when use is not imminent. When taken out, they should be carefully placed where they cannot be thrown from a table or ledge to the deck and damaged; protect your binoculars from any rough usage.

A boat should be equipped with several *flashlights* for emergency use. One of these should have a red lens or filter in order that it may be used to read charts and other printed matter at night without undue loss of night vision by a person who must both check the chart and act as helmsman or lookout.

MEASUREMENTS

In considering the measurement of various quantities in piloting, and the calculations in which they are used, some attention must first be given to standards of accuracy and precision. Statements of distance as 32 miles or 32.0 miles are not quite the same thing. The former merely says that to the best of observation and measurement the distance is not 31 nor 33 miles; the latter says that it is not 31.9 nor 32.1 miles. Note the difference in the degree of preciseness of these two statements of the same distance. Never write 32.0 for 32 unless your measurements are sufficiently precise to warrant such action.

STANDARD LIMITS OF PRECISION

The navigation of various sizes of vessels naturally involves different standards of precision or accuracy as befitting the different conditions encountered. The piloting of small craft does not permit so high a degree of accuracy as on large ships that offer a more stable platform.

Direction

Direction is measured in small-craft navigation to the nearest whole degree. It is not reasonable to measure or calculate directions to a finer degree of precision when a boat is seldom steered with a precision closer than 2° or 3°.

Distance

Distances are normally expressed to the nearest tenth of a mile. This degree of precision, roughly 200 yards, is reasonable in consideration of the size of the craft and other measurement standards.

Time

Time is measured and calculated to the nearest minute. Fractions of a minute are rarely of any significance in routine piloting. In contests, however, time will be calculated to decimal fractions and used in terms of seconds.

Speed

Speed is calculated to the nearest tenth of a knot or mile-per-hour. It is seldom measurable to such fine units, but a calculation to the nearest tenth is not inconsistent with the expressed standards of precision of distance and time. This same degree of precision is used in calculations of current velocity.

Position

Geographic coordinates will be expressed to the nearest tenth of a minute of latitude and longitude, or to the nearest second, as determined by the scale of the chart. As explained in Chapter 18, latitude and longitude markings will be subdivided into minutes and seconds on the larger-scale charts (1:49,000 and larger) and in fractions of minutes on smaller-scale charts (1:50,000 and smaller).

Depths and heights of tide

Tidal variations in the depth of water are normally tabulated to the nearest tenth of a foot (or meter); calculations are carried out to the same degree of precision. It must be recognized, however, that modifications to tidal action from winds and atmospheric pressure variations make such a degree of precision hardly warranted.

ABERDEEN, WASHINGTON, 1977

TIMES AND HEIGHTS OF HIGH AND LOW WATERS

	JANUARY					FEBRUARY				
DAY	TIME h.m.	HT. ft.	DAY	TIME h.m.	HT. ft.	DAY	TIME h.m.	HT. ft.	DAY	TIME h.m.	HT ft.
1 SA	0402 0958 1655 2318	4.3 10.9 1.5 8.6	16 SU	0404 1001 1700 2320	4.1 11.9 0.1 9.2	1 TU	0518 1059 1800	4.2 10.8 0.7	16 W	0003 0548 1145 1824	9. 3. 11. -0.
2 SU	0454 1044 1743	4.3 11.1 0.9	17 M	0506 1057 1755	3.8 12.1 -0.5	2 W	0019 0608 1145 1843	9.1 3.8 11.0 0.3	17 TH	0049 0640 1235 1907	10.1 2.4 11. -0.
3 M	0004 0547 1129 1827	8.9 4.2 11.2 0.5	18 TU	0019 0603 1153 1844	9.7 3.5 12.2 -0.8	3 TH	0059 0654 1230 1925	9.5 3.4 11.1 0.1	18 F	0128 0726 1322 1950	10.
4 TU	0049 0622	9.2	19								

FIG. 1938 Heights of tides are tabulated in the tables of daily predictions to the nearest tenth of a foot. However, local conditions of wind and barometric pressure will often cause variations of greater magnitude.

Arithmetic Calculations and Rounding of Numbers

Any mathematical expression of a quantity will have a certain number of "significant figures." These can perhaps be better explained through the use of examples rather than by a complicated definition. The quantity "4" has one significant figure; 4.0 or 14 has two significant figures; 5.12, 43.8, or 609 each has three significant figures, etc.

A quantity ending in one or more zeros may have a varying number of significant figures as determined by the degree of precision with which it was measured. The number 150 may have either two or three significant figures; 2000 may have one, two, three, or four significant figures.

Consideration must be given to the number of significant figures occurring in the result of mathematical calculations, especially multiplication and division. Results should not have an excessive and unwarranted number of significant figures. For example, if 83 is multiplied by 64, the result is 5312. But note that this quantity has four significant figures whereas each of the input quantities had only two significant figures. A more meaningful statement of the result would be 5310 or even 5300.

The process of reducing the number of significant figures is called "rounding." In order to have uniform results, rules have been established for the rounding of numbers.

1. If the digit to be rounded off is "4" or less, it is dropped or changed to a zero.

8.23 can be rounded to 8.2
432 can be rounded to 430

2. If the digit to be rounded off is "6" or larger, the preceding digit is raised to the next higher value and the rounded digit is dropped or changed to a zero.

8.27 can be rounded to 8.3
439 can be rounded to 440

3. If the digit to be rounded off is a "5," the rounding is to the nearest *even* value.

8.25 is rounded to 8.2
435 is rounded to 440

This rule may seem somewhat arbitrary, but it is followed

for consistency in results; it has the advantage that when two such rounded figures are added together and divided by two for an average, the result will not present a new need for rounding.

4. Rounding can be applied to more than one final digit; but all such rounding must be done in *one* step. For example: 6148 is rounded to 6100 in a single action; do not round 6148 to 6150, and then round 6150 to 6200.

In many of the statements of precision requirements in the preceding section, the phrase "to the nearest _____" has been used. Rounding is used to reduce various quantities to such limitations. For example: if you calculated the distance traveled in 5 minutes at 13 knots, you would get 1.08 miles. However, distance is normally stated to the nearest tenth of a mile, and so the proper expression for distance run would be 1.1 mile.

FIG. 1939 A Dead Reckoning plot should always be maintained when a boat is off-shore or cruising in large, open bodies of water.
M. Rosenfeld.

Dead Reckoning

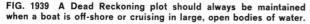

When operating his boat offshore in large bodies of water, a pilot should have at all times at least a rough knowledge of his position on the chart. Basic to such knowledge is a technique of navigation known as *dead reckoning,* usually abbreviated to *DR.* This is the advancement of the boat's position on the chart from its last accurately determined location, using the course (or courses) steered and the speed (or speeds) through the water. No allowance is made for the effects of wind, waves, current, or steering errors.

Terms used in dead reckoning

At this point, we will deal with only those terms related to *dead reckoning.* Later, when the influence of current is being considered, additional terms will be introduced and defined.

The *DR track* (or *DR track line)* is the path that the boat is expected to follow (no current) represented on the chart by a line drawn from the last known position using courses and speeds through the water. The path the boat actually travels may be different due to one or more offsetting influences, to be considered later.

Course is the direction in which a boat is to be steered, or is being steered; the direction of travel through the water. Courses are normally plotted as true directions labeled with three-digit figures with zeros added as necessary—8° becomes 008, 42° becomes 042. Some skippers may label courses as magnetic or compass directions.

Heading, the direction in which a boat is pointed at any given time, is often given in terms of magnetic or compass directions; these values are not part of a plot.

Speed, abbreviated "S," is the rate of travel through the water. This is the DR track speed; it is used, together with elapsed time, to determine *DR positions* along the track line.

The Basic Principles of Dead Reckoning

It is important that the pilot adhere to certain basic principles of dead reckoning.

1. A DR track is always started from a known position.

2. Only true courses steered are used for determining a DR track.

3. Only the speed through the water is used for determining distance traveled and a DR position along the track.

Although it may appear unusual to ignore the effects of a current that is known to exist, this is always done for reasons that will be established later.

The importance of dead reckoning

A DR track should always be plotted when navigating in large, open bodies of water. It is the primary representation of the path of the boat, the base to which other factors, such as the effect of current, are applied. Dead reckoning can be considered to be the basic method of navigation to which corrections and adjustments from other sources of information are applied.

At the same time, it must be remembered that this DR track is rarely a representation of the boat's actual progress. If there were no steering errors, speed errors, or external influences, the DR track could be used as a means of determining the craft's position at any time desired, as well as the ETA (Estimated Time of Arrival) at a stated destination. Despite the fact that this will rarely, if ever, be the case, a DR plot is highly desirable at all times as a safety measure in the event of unexpected variations in current, and it is most useful in the event of a sudden fog or other loss of visibility.

PLOTTING

Fundamental to the use of dead reckoning is the use of charts and plots of the craft's intended and actual positions.

387

FIG. 1940a The course is labeled above the line as shown here. The direction is indicated as a three-digit number (zeroes added as necessary) preceded by "C" for Course and followed by "T," "M," or "C" (for True, Magnetic, or Compass) as appropriate spaced about the width of one character. Omit the degree symbol.

FIG. 1940b Speed is labeled below the course line. Write in the letter "S", a space, and the speed in knots or MPH as appropriate. Distance may be shown along a course segment using "D" and the number of statute or nautical miles below the course line.

Basic requirements

The basic requirements of plotting are *accuracy, neatness,* and *completeness.* All measurements taken from the chart must be made carefully, all direct observations must be made as accurately as conditions on a small craft will permit, and all calculations should be made in full and in writing. If time permits, each of these actions should be repeated as a check; errors can be costly!

Neatness in plotting is essential to avoid confusion of information on the chart. The drawing in on charts of excess or overly-long lines, or the scribbling of extraneous notes, may obscure small bits of vital information.

In addition to being neat, information on a chart must be complete. Often a pilot will have need to refer back to information that he placed on the chart hours, or even days, ago. It could be dangerous if he should have to rely on memory to supply part of the details. In some cases, the piloting duties may be shared among several persons; here it is obvious that all plotted information must be fully identified.

The use of standardized procedures for identifying information on charts will ensure neatness, completeness, and understandability to any person who uses it.

Labeling

Lines on charts should be drawn lightly and no longer than necessary. Be alert to the fact that a straightedge must be placed a slight distance off the desired position of the line to be drawn to allow for the thickness of the pencil point, no matter how finely it is sharpened.

The requirements of neatness and completeness combine to establish a need for *labeling.* To meet these requirements, certain rules and procedures have been established. The proper labeling of any plot is essential.

Immediately after any line is drawn on a chart, or any point is plotted, it should be labeled. The basic rules for labeling are:

1. The label for any *line* is placed *along* that line.

2. The label for any *point* should *not* be along any line; it should make such an angle with any line that its nature as the label of a point will be unmistakably clear.

The above basic rules are applied in the labeling of DR plots in the following manner:

1. The direction label is placed *above* the track line as a three digit number, preceded by "C" for Course and followed by "T," "M," or "C" to indicate True, Magnetic, or Compass. Note that the degree symbol "°" is omitted.

2. The speed along the track is indicated by numerals

placed *under* the track line, usually directly beneath the direction, fig. 1940b. Units, knots or MPH, are omitted.

3. A known position at the start of a DR track, a *Fix* (see Chapter 21), is shown as a circle across the line. It is labeled with time placed horizontally; the word "Fix" is understood and is not shown; see fig. 1941.

4. A DR position, calculated as a distance along the track at the set speed through the water, is shown as a half-circle along the track line; it is labeled with the time placed at an angle to the horizontal; see fig. 1942.

5. When planning and pre-plotting a run, speed, which is often affected by sea conditions, may not be known in advance. In this case, distance, D, may be labeled below the course line; as before, units are not shown.

Further applications of the basic rules of labeling will be given as additional piloting procedures and situations are introduced in subsequent chapters.

All lines on a chart should be erased when no longer needed to keep the chart clear. Erasures should be made as lightly as possible to avoid damage to the surface of the chart and its printed information.

FIG. 1941 A known position of a boat, a Fix, is plotted as a dot with a small circle around it (a dot is not needed at the intersection of two lines). It is labeled with time in the 24-hour system placed horizontally. The word "Fix" is understood and is not shown.

FIG. 1942 A dead reckoning position along a track is plotted as a half-circle on the line plus the time at an angle to the horizontal. The letters "DR" are not needed as this symbol is not used for any other purpose.

D, T, AND S CALCULATIONS

As mentioned earlier, calculations involving distance (D), time (T), and speed (S) are often done by means of a small calculator. The use of such a device is perfectly acceptable, but the good pilot can accurately and quickly make his calculations without one, using only a simple set of equations and ordinary arithmetic. An ability to make arithmetical computations is necessary as a calculating device may not always be available.

The three basic equations are:

$$D = ST \qquad S = \frac{D}{T} \qquad T = \frac{D}{S}$$

Where D is distance in miles, T is time in *hours,* and S is speed in knots or miles per hour as determined by the type of mile being used. Note carefully that T is in hours in these basic equations. To use time in *minutes,* as is more normally the case, the equations are modified to read:

$$D = \frac{ST}{60} \qquad S = \frac{60D}{T} \qquad T = \frac{60D}{S}$$

Examples of the use of these practical equations may serve to make them clearer:

1. You are cruising at 14 knots; how far will you travel in 40 minutes?

$$D = \frac{ST}{60} \qquad D = \frac{14 \times 40}{60} = 9.3 \text{ miles}$$

Note that the calculated answer of 9.33 is rounded to

FIG. 1943a On some charts, a logarithmic speed scale may be used to graphically determine speed. First, set one point of your dividers on the scale division indicating the miles traveled, and the other on the number corresponding to the time in minutes.

FIG. 1943b With the dividers maintaining the same spread, transfer them so that the right point is on the "60" of the scale (right end). The left point will indicate the speed in knots or MPH, as determined by the type of mile used.

the nearest tenth according to the rule for the degree of accuracy to be used in stating distance.

2. On one of the Great Lakes, it took you 40 minutes to travel 11 miles; what is your speed?

$$S = \frac{60D}{T} \qquad S = \frac{60 \times 11}{40} \qquad = 16.5 \text{ MPH}$$

3. You have $9\frac{1}{2}$ miles to go to reach your destination, your cruising speed is 11 knots; how long will it take you to get there?

$$T = \frac{60D}{S} \qquad T = \frac{60 \times 9.5}{11} \qquad = 52 \text{ minutes}$$

Note again the rounding of results; the calculated answer of 51.8 minutes would be used as 52 minutes, except in contests where it would probably be used as 51 minutes 48 seconds.

The equations are also usable with kilometers and km/h.

The three equations for distance, speed, and time should be carefully memorized. Practice using them until you become thoroughly familiar with them and can obtain answers to typical problems quickly and accurately.

Use of logarithmic scale on charts

Charts of the National Ocean Survey at scales of 1:40,000 and larger will have printed on them a logarithmic speed scale. To find speed, place one point of your dividers on the mark on the scale indicating the distance in nautical miles, and the other point on the number corresponding to the time in minutes, fig. 1943a. Without changing the spread between the divider arms, place the right point on the "60" at the right end of the scale; the left point will then indicate on the scale the speed in knots, see fig. 1943b.

This same logarithmic scale can also be used *to determine the time* required to cover a given distance at a specified speed (for situations not exceeding one hour). Set the two divider points on the scale marks representing speed in knots and distance in miles. Move the dividers, without changing the spread, until the right point is at "60" on the scale; the other point will indicate the time in minutes.

Likewise, *distance can be determined* from this logarithmic scale using knowledge of time and speed. Set the right point of the dividers on "60" and the left point at the mark on the scale corresponding to the speed in knots. Then, without changing the spread, move the right point to the mark on the scale representing the time in minutes; the left point will now indicate the distance in nautical miles.

N.O.S. charts will have instructions for determining speed printed beneath the logarithmic scale, but not the procedures for determining distance or time. In all cases, you must know two of the three quantities in order to determine the other.

Use of S-D-T calculators

It is not possible here to give detailed instructions for the operation of all models of speed-distance-time calculators. In general, such devices will have two or more scales, each logarithmically subdivided. The calculator will be set using two of the factors and the answer, the third factor, will be read off at an index mark.

If you have a calculator for S-D-T problems, read the instructions carefully and practice with it sufficiently, using simple, self-evident problems, to be sure of obtaining reliable results, even under the stress of difficult situations or emergencies.

SPEED CURVES

Although some boats may be equipped with marine speedometers, the more-often used method of determination of speed is through the use of engine speed as measured by the *tachometer* in revolutions per minute (RPM). A *speed curve* is prepared as a plot on cross-section (graph) paper of the boat's speed in knots or MPH or km/h for various engine speeds in RPM.

Factors affecting speed curves

The speed that a boat will achieve for a specified engine setting may be affected by several factors. The extent of each effect will vary with the size of the boat, type of hull, and other characteristics.

Load is a primary factor influencing a boat's speed. The number of persons aboard, the amount of fuel and water in the tanks, and the amount and location of other weights on board will affect the depth to which the hull sinks in the water and the angular trim. Both displacement and trim may be expected to have an effect on speed.

Another major factor affecting speed is the *underwater hull condition*. Fouling growth, such as barnacles or moss, increases the drag, the resistance to movement through the water, and slows the speed of the boat at any given engine RPM.

Whenever preparing speed data on a boat, the loading and underwater hull conditions at the time of the trials should be noted with the figures for RPM and speed. If a speed curve is made at the start of a boating season when the bottom is clean, it should be checked later on in the season if the boat is used in waters where fouling is a problem. A new speed curve may be required, or it may be possible to determine what small corrections can be applied to get a more accurate measure of speed. A good skipper also knows what speed differences he may expect from full tanks to half to nearly empty; the differences can be surprising in many boats.

Obtaining speed curves

Speed curves are obtained by making repeated runs over a known distance using different throttle settings and timing each run very accurately. Any reasonable distance can be used. Ordinarily, it should not be less than a half-mile in order that small timing errors will not excessively influence the results; it need not be more than a mile, to avoid excessive time and fuel requirements for the trials.

The run need not be an even half-mile or mile if the distance is accurately known. Do not depend upon floating aids to navigation — they may be slightly off-station, and, in any event, they have some scope on their anchor chains and will swing about under the effects of wind and current. Many areas will have *measured miles* (or half-miles), fig. 1944. These are accurately surveyed distances with each end marked by ranges. Use these courses whenever possible; they can be depended upon for accuracy and calculations are made easier by the even-mile distance. But do not let the absence of such a measured mile in your local waters keep you from having a speed curve for your boat. Use accurately charted wharves, fixed aids to navigation, points of land, etc.

In most speed trials, it will be necessary to run the known distance twice, once in each direction, in order to allow for the effects of current. Even in waters not affected by currents, it is advisable to make round-trip runs for each throttle setting to allow for wind effects.

For each *one-way* run, measure the time required; steer the boat carefully so that the most direct, the shortest run is made. Compute the speed for each run by the equations previously used. If a measured mile is used for the speed trials, speeds can be found easily by use of the table on page 603. If the measured distance is an exact half-mile, the tabulated speeds must be divided by two. Then average the *speeds* of each run of a pair at a given RPM to determine the true speed of the boat through the water. The strength of the current is one-half the difference between the speed in the two directions of any pair of runs. *Caution:* do *not* average together the *times* of a pair of runs to get a single time for use in the calculations; this will *not* give the correct value for speed through the water.

If time is measured with a regular clock or watch, be

RPM	N-S		S-N		Average Speed	Current
	Time	Speed	Time	Speed		
900	7m 54s	7.60	11m 25s	5.26	6.43	1.17
1100	6 53	8.72	9 14.2	6.50	7.61	1.11
1300	6 08.8	9.76	7 36.8	7.88	8.82	.94
1500	5 35.8	10.72	6 40.4	9.00	9.86	.86
1700	5 10.8	11.59	5 54.2	10.17	10.88	.71
1900	4 38.0	12.96	5 06.4	11.76	12.36	.60
2150	3 48.6	15.75	4 05.6	14.73	15.24	.51

FIG. 1945 Tabulated results of speed trials made for "Trident." Note that runs were made in each direction to account for the effect of current. Entries were made in the log as to fuel and water loads aboard and condition of the bottom of the hull.

careful in making the subtractions to get elapsed time. Remember that there are 60 seconds in each minute, not 100, and likewise 60 minutes in one hour. Most people are so used to decimal calculations that foolish errors are sometimes made when "borrowing" in the subtraction of clock times.

If one is willing to use a slightly more complex equation, the boat's speed through the water (or the strength of the current) can be found from a single calculation using the times of the two runs of each pair.

$$S = \frac{60D(Tu + Td)}{2TuTd} \qquad C = \frac{60D(Tu - Td)}{2TuTd}$$

Where S is speed through the water in knots or MPH
C is current in knots or MPH
Tu is time upstream, in minutes
Td is time downstream, in minutes
D is distance, in nautical or statute miles

In the preparation of a speed curve for a boat, sufficient pairs of runs should be made to provide points for a plot of speed versus RPM; some six or eight points will usually be enough for a satisfactory curve. With some types of hulls, there will be a break in the curve at a critical speed when the hull changes from displacement action to semi-planing action. At this portion of the curve, additional, more closely-spaced measurements may be required. For this reason, it is often a good idea to calculate speeds during runs and make a rough plot as you go along.

FIG. 1944 Many boating areas have *measured mile* courses established for making accurate speed trials. These will be shown on the chart of the area.

FIG. 1946 The speed curve for "Trident" plotted from the data of fig. 1945. This curve is truly accurate only for load and underwater hull conditions similar to those on the day of the trials.

It may also be found desirable to calculate the strength of the current for each pair of runs. It will probably be noted that the current values will vary during the speed trials, but such variations should be small and in a consistent direction, either steadily increasing or decreasing, or going through a slack period. The best results will normally be obtained if the trials are run at a time of minimum current.

Example of a Speed Curve

A set of speed trials was run for the motor yacht "Trident" over the measured mile off Kent Island in Chesapeake Bay, fig. 1944. This is an excellent course as it is marked both by buoys offshore and by ranges on land. The presence of the buoys aids in steering a straight run from one end of the course to the other; the ranges are used for greater accuracy in timing.

On this particular day, it was not convenient to wait for slack water, but a time was selected that would result in something less than maximum ebbing current. A table was set up in the log, and runs were made in each direction at speeds of normal interest from 900 RPM to 2150 RPM which was maximum for the 6-71 diesels.

The results of the runs are shown in fig. 1945. An entry was also made in the log that these trials were made with fuel tanks 0.35 full, the water tanks approximately 1/3 full, and a clean bottom. The column of the table marked "Current" is not necessary, but it serves as a "flag" to quickly expose any inconsistent data. Note that on these trials the current is decreasing at a reasonably consistent rate.

After the runs had been completed, a plot was made on cross-section paper of the boat's speed as a function of engine RPM. This resulted in the speed curve shown as fig. 1946.

DEAD RECKONING PLOTS

With knowledge of dead reckoning terms and principles, the rules for labeling points and lines, and the procedures for making calculations involving distance, time, and speed, it is possible to consider now the use of DR plots.

There are several specific rules for making and using DR plots.

1. A DR plot should be made when leaving a known position, fig. 1947.

2. A DR position should be shown whenever a change is made in course, fig. 1948a, or in speed, fig. 1948b.

3. A DR position should be plotted each hour on the hour, fig. 1949.

4. A new DR track should be started each time the boat's position is fixed. The old DR position for the same time as the fix should also be shown at the end of the old DR track, see fig. 1950.

FIG. 1948b If a variation in speed is made without a change in direction, a DR position is plotted on the track and new labels of course and speed are entered following it.

FIG. 1949 A DR position should be plotted each hour on the hour along the track even though there is no change in course or speed. These plots will keep the pilot informed of his progress and are useful in sudden emergencies.

FIG. 1947 A dead reckoning plot is started when leaving a known position. The time of that position is plotted as a Fix (full circle symbol); course and speed are labeled along the DR track.

FIG. 1950 Whenever the boat's position is fixed, such as by passage close by a buoy as shown here, a DR position is plotted for that time, calculated from speed and distance information. The fix is also plotted and a new DR track is started. The difference between the DR position and the Fix for the same time indicates the effect of offsetting influences such as current.

FIG. 1948a Whenever a change in course is made a DR position (half-circle symbol) is plotted for that time; the new course and speed are labeled along the new track.

Tides and currents are of much interest and concern to the skipper who does his boating on coastal waters. Time invested in mastering their theory and practice will pay dividends in the form of increased safety, convenience, and economy. And too, there is the satisfaction of developing an ability to deal with natural phenomena that you can't change, but which can often be used to your advantage.

CHAPTER 20

PILOTING
—Tides
and
Currents

FIG. 2001 Boatmen in coastal regions must learn to cope with tidal conditions. The range from high water to low may be only inches, or it may be many feet.

Dead Reckoning and Currents

In the preceding chapter, it was noted that a dead reckoning plot is based upon the course steered and the boat's speed through the water. Even though offsetting factors were known to exist, they were *not* included in a DR plot. Thus, it can readily be seen that while a DR plot is a basic representation of a boat's motion, it fails to account for all existing circumstances.

Offsetting influences that will make the boat's actual path diverge from the DR track include current, leeway from wind and waves, and steering errors. Of these, the one that can be most easily and accurately handled is current. The extent of its effect will vary widely with the relative values of current strength and boat speed through the water, but often the influence of current can be a major factor in piloting.

Tides vs. Current

Perhaps at this point we should pause to make clear the proper meaning and use of several terms that are often loosely and incorrectly used. *Tide* is the rise and fall of the ocean level as a result of changes in the gravitational attraction between the earth, moon, and sun. It is a *vertical* motion only. *Current* is a *horizontal* motion of water from any cause. *Tidal current* is the flow of water from one point to another that results from a difference in tidal heights at those points. How often have you heard others say (or perhaps even said it yourself) that "The tide is certainly running strongly today!" This is not correct, for tides may be high or low, but they do not "run." Obviously, the correct expression would have been "The (tidal) current is certainly strong today." Remember—tide is vertical change; current is horizontal flow.

Tides

As tidal action is a primary cause of currents, let us consider it first, and save our consideration of currents for later. Actually, tides in themselves are important factors in the safe navigation of watercraft as will be discussed in the following pages.

Tides originate in the open oceans and seas, but are only noticeable and significant close to shore. The effect of tides will be observed along coastal beaches, in bays and sounds, and up rivers generally as far as the first rapids,

waterfall, or dam. Curiously, the effect of tides may be more noticeable a hundred miles up a river than it is at the river's mouth. Coastal regions in which the water levels are subject to tidal action are often referred to as "tide-water" areas.

Definition of Terms

In addition to the basic definition of tide as given above, certain other terms used in connection with tidal action must be defined. The *height of tide* at any specified time is the vertical measurement between the surface of the water and the *tidal datum* or reference plane. Do not confuse "height of tide" with "depth of water." The latter is the total distance from the surface to the bottom. The tidal datum for an area is selected so that the heights of tide are normally positive values, but the height can at times be a small negative number when the water level falls below the datum.

High water, or *high tide,* is the highest level reached by an ascending tide. Correspondingly, *low water,* or *low tide,* is the lowest level reached by a descending tide, fig. 2003. The difference between high and low waters is termed the *range* of the tide.

The change in tidal level does not occur at a uniform rate; starting from, say, low water, the level builds up slowly, then at an increasing rate which in turn tapers off as high water is reached. The decrease in tidal stage from high water to low follows a corresponding pattern of a slow buildup to a maximum rate roughly midway between stages followed by a decreasing rate. At both high and low tides, there will be periods of relatively no change in level; these are termed *stand.* *Mean sea level* is the average level of the open ocean and corresponds closely to mid-tide levels offshore.

TIDAL THEORY

Tidal action can be studied both from a theoretical view and in terms of actual conditions. It is perhaps best approached from an initial consideration of basic principles, with practical departures from theory being noted afterwards. Tidal theory involves the interaction of gravitational and centrifugal forces—the inward attraction of the earth on one hand and the sun and the moon on the other, balanced by the outward forces resulting from the revolution of the earth in its orbit. The gravitational and centrifugal forces are in balance as a whole—otherwise the bodies would fly apart from each other or else

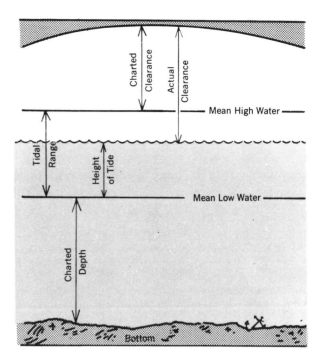

FIG. 2003 This diagram illustrates the relationship between some of the terms used to describe tidal conditions. Terms are defined in the text. Mean lower low water may be substituted for mean low water in some areas.

crash together—but they are not quite in balance at most points on the earth's surface, and is what causes the tides. In order to simplify the presentation, the effects of the sun and moon will be described separately, although, of course, in actuality they both act simultaneously.

Earth-Sun Effects

Each year the earth and the sun revolve around a common point located close to the center of the sun; for all

FIG. 2002 The rise and fall of ocean tidal levels will cause a flow first into and then out of inland bodies of water such as bays, sounds, and the lower reaches of rivers. These tidal currents may have important effects on the piloting of boats in such waters.　　(from Kodachrome by Wm. H. Koelbel)

Tides and Currents / CHAPTER 20

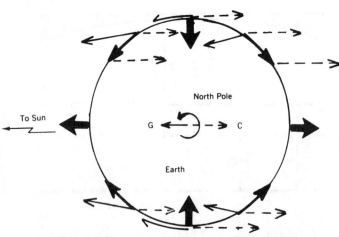

FIG. 2004 Centrifugal forces (broken arrows) are everywhere equal and parallel; gravitational forces (solid arrows) are not equal or parallel; see text. These effects combine to form the resultant force that acts generally along the surface of the earth. (For clarity and emphasis, all forces are shown exaggerated in strength and direction.)

FIG. 2005 The resultant forces from the imbalance of gravitational and centrifugal effects cause water to flow toward areas of the earth's surface that are both nearest and farthest from the sun (or moon). This forms the theoretical "tidal bulge" on opposite sides of the earth with high tides there are low tides midway between.

practical considerations, the earth can be thought of as revolving around the sun. Just as a stone tied to the end of a string tends to sail off when a young boy whirls it about his head, so the earth tends to fly off into space. This is known as centrifugal force; it is designated as C in fig. 2004. (Remember that we are talking about the centrifugal force related to the sun-earth system, and not that of the day-night spinning of the earth on its axis.)

The earth is kept from flying off into space by the gravitational attraction of the sun, designated G in fig. 2004. These forces are in overall balance.

This balance is not exact at all points. The centrifugal force is everywhere the same, and parallel to a line from the center of the earth to the center of the sun. Gravitational forces are *not* everywhere equal and parallel; from each point on the earth's surface, they extend toward the center of the sun, greater on the nearer side as a result of the lesser distance. Figure 2004 shows these forces at representative points, and the resultant force from their combination.

Continuing our theoretical analysis, we can think of the earth as being a smooth sphere uniformly covered with water (no land areas). Figure 2005 shows how the resultant forces cause the water to flow toward the areas of the earth's surface that are *both nearest and farthest* from the sun; here there will be "high tides." As this water flows, the areas from which it comes will have less, and hence "low tides." (The tides on the side of the earth nearer the sun are slightly greater than those on the far side, but the difference is not great, only about 5%.)

As the earth rotates on its axis, once every 24 hours, the line of direction to the sun constantly changes. Thus each point of the earth's surface will have two high and two low tides each day. As a result of the tilt of the earth's axis, the pairs of highs, and those of the lows, will not normally be of the same level.

Earth-Moon Effects

The moon is commonly thought of as revolving about the earth; actually, the two bodies revolve around a common point on a monthly cycle. This point is located about

2900 miles (4667 km) from the center of the earth toward the moon (about 1100 miles or 1770 km deep inside the earth). By the same logic as applied to the earth-sun system, a second set of tidal forces occurs. In explaining tidal forces in the earth-moon system, however, one must always remember to think of both the earth and the moon as revolving around a common point, rather than the moon merely going around the earth. It is only by the former concept that we can get the necessary centrifugal forces for tides on the earth.

Spring and Neap Tides

Now combine the earth-sun and earth-moon systems. Since the moon is much closer to the earth (about 238,860 miles, 384,400 km, away), its tidal forces are roughly 2¼ times greater than those of the sun (about 92,900,000 miles or 149,500,000 km away). The result is that the observed tide usually "follows the moon," but the action is somewhat modified by the sun's relative position. The two high and two low waters each day occur about 50 minutes later

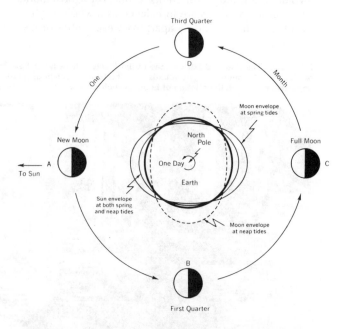

FIG. 2006 At new and full moon, combined gravitational "pull" of sun and moon acts to produce maximum effect; at these times, tidal ranges are greatest. At first and third quarters of the moon, the two gravitational forces partially offset each other and the net effect is at a minimum; tidal ranges are then least.

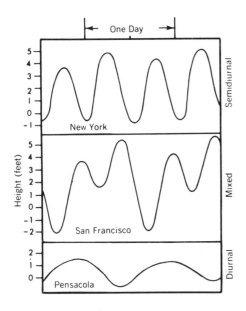

FIG. 2007 Characteristics of the daily cycle of tides vary widely at different places. Shown here are three basic types—from the top, semi-diurnal, mixed, and diurnal.

than the corresponding tides of the previous day.

In the course of any one month, the three bodies line up sun-moon-earth (position A in fig. 2006) and sun-earth-moon (position C). These are the times of the new and full moon, respectively. In both cases, the sun's effect (or "envelope") lines up with and reinforces the moon's effect, tending to result in greater-than-average tidal ranges (about 20%), called *spring tides;* note carefully that this name has nothing to do with the season of the year.

At positions B and D in fig. 2006, when the moon is at its first and third quarters, the tidal "bulge" due to the sun is at right angles to that caused by the moon (they are said to be "in *quadrature*"). The two tidal effects are in conflict and partially cancel each other, resulting in smaller-than-average ranges (again about 20%); these are *neap tides.*

It should also be noted that the tidal range of any given point varies from month to month, and from year to year. The monthly variation is due to the fact that the earth is not at the center of the moon's orbit. When the moon is closest to the earth (at perigee), the lunar influence is maximum and tides will have the greatest ranges. Conversely, when the moon is farthest from the earth (at apogee), its effect and tidal ranges are least.

In a similar manner, the yearly variations in the daily ranges of the tides are caused by the changing gravitational effects of the sun as that body's distance from the earth becomes greater or less.

ACTUAL TIDES

We have been considering the tidal forces and their envelope rather than the actual tide as we observe it in the sea. Why do they differ? The following are the main reasons:

1. Great masses of land, the continents, irregularly shaped and irregularly placed, act to interrupt, restrict, and reflect tidal movements.

2. Water, although generally appearing to flow freely, is actually a somewhat viscous substance and therefore lags in its response to tidal forces.

3. Friction is present as the ocean waters "rub" against the ocean bottom.

4. The depth to the bottom of the sea, varying widely, influences the speed of the tidal motion horizontally.

5. The depths of the ocean areas and the restrictions of the continents often result in "basins" which have their own way of responding to tidal forces.

Although these reasons account for great differences between theoretical tidal forces and actual observed tides, there nevertheless remain definite, constant relationships between the two at any particular location. By observing the tide, and relating these observations with the movements of the sun, moon, and earth, these constant relationships can be determined. With this information, tides can be predicted for any future date at a given place.

Types of Tides

A tide which each day has two high waters approximately equal in height, and two low waters also about equal, is known as a *semidiurnal* type. This is the most common tide, and, in the United States, occurs along the east coast (fig. 2007, New York).

In a monthly cycle, the moon moves north and south of the Equator. Fig. 2008 illustrates the importance of this action to tides. Point A is under a bulge in the envelope. One half-day later, at point B, it is again under the bulge but the height is not as large as at A. This situation, combined with coastal characteristics, tends to give rise to a "twice daily" tide with unequal high and/or low waters in some areas. This is known as the *mixed* type of tide; see fig. 2007, San Francisco. The term "low water" may be modified to indicate the more pronounced of the two lows. This tidal stage is termed *lower low water* and is averaged to determine the *mean lower low water* (MLLW); this is used as the tidal datum in many areas subject to mixed tides. Likewise, the more significant of the higher tides is termed *higher high water.*

Now consider point C in fig. 2008. At this place, it is still under the bulge of the envelope. One half-day later, at point D, however, it is above the low part. Hence, the tidal forces tend to cause only one high and one low water each day (actually each 24 hours and 50 minutes approximately). This is the *diurnal* type, typified by Pensacola in fig. 2007.

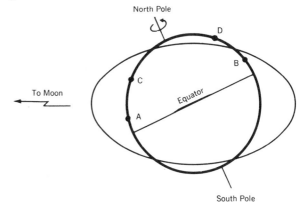

FIG. 2008 The moon travels north and south of the earth's equatorial plane. This change results in variations in the daily tidal cycle at any given location. Similar, but lesser, effects result from changes in the sun's position with respect to the earth.

FIG. 2009 Watch out for falling tides! A prudent skipper knows not only the depth of water when he anchors, but also how it is going to change over the next 12 hours or so. In this river in Nova Scotia, the river bed will be exposed for about five hours; in the sixth hour the flood will rush in as a "bore" and rise 20 feet.
(from Kodachrome by Wm. H. Koelbel)

Whenever the moon is farthest north (as in fig. 2008) or south, there will be a tendency to have the diurnal or mixed type. When the moon lies over the Equator, we tend to have the semidiurnal type. These are *Equatorial tides* and the tendency toward producing inequality is then at a minimum.

The above theoretical considerations are, however, modified by many practical factors such as the general configuration of the coastline.

Special Tidal Situations

Peculiarities in the tide can be found almost everywhere, but none compare with those in the Bay of Fundy. Twice each day, the waters surge in and out of the Bay, producing, at Burntcoat Head, the highest tidal range in the world a typical rise and fall of nearly 44 feet (13.4 meters). At normal spring tides, it rises 51½ feet (15.7 m) and on perigee springs, as much as 53 feet or 16.2 meters.

This great range is often attributed to the funnel-like shape of the Bay, but this is not the main cause. Just as the water in a wash basin will slosh when you move your hand back and forth in just the right period of time, depending upon the depth of water and the shape of the basin, so the tide will attempt to oscillate water in bays in cycles of 12 hours and 25 minutes. It would be a coincidence indeed if a bay were of such a shape and depth as to have a complete oscillation with a period of exactly 12 hours and 25 minutes. A bay, however, can easily have a part of such an oscillation; such is the case in the Bay of Fundy.

A further factor in creating the large tidal ranges in the Bay of Fundy is the circumstance that they are controlled by the Gulf of Maine tides which, in turn, are controlled by the open ocean tides. The relationships between these tides are such as to exaggerate their ranges.

THE IMPORTANCE OF TIDES

A good knowledge of tidal action is essential for safe navigation. The skipper of a boat of any size will be faced many times with the need for knowledge of the time of high water and low water, and their probable heights. He may be faced with the desirability or necessity of crossing some shoal area, passable at certain tidal stages but not at others. He may be about to anchor, and the scope to pay out will be affected by the tide's range. He may be going to make fast to a pier or wharf in a strange harbor and will have need of tidal information if he is to adjust his lines properly for overnight.

Tidal effects on vertical clearances

The rise and fall of the tide will change the vertical clearance under fixed structures such as bridges or overhead power cables. These clearances are stated on charts and in Coast Pilots as heights measured from a datum which is *not* the same plane as used for depths and tidal predictions. The datum for heights is normally mean high water (MHW), the average of all high water levels. The use of this datum ensures that clearances and heights are normally greater than charted or Coast Pilot values.

It will thus be necessary to determine the height of MHW above the tidal datum. In any area where the tidal datum is mean lower low water (MLLW), the plane of mean high water is above MLLW by an amount equal to the sum of the "mean tide level" plus one-half of the "mean range"; both of these values are listed in Table 2 of the Tide Tables for all stations.

If the tidal datum for any given location is mean low water (MLW), mean high water level is above MLW by the "mean tide range."

If the tide level at any given moment is below MHW, the vertical clearance under a bridge or other fixed structure is then greater than the figures shown on the chart; but if the tide height is *above* the level of MHW, then the clearance is *less*. Calculate the vertical clearance in advance if you anticipate a tight situation, but *also* observe the clearance gauges usually found at bridges. Clearances will normally be greater than the charted MHW values, but will occasionally be less.

SOURCES OF TIDAL INFORMATION

The basic source of information on the time of high and low water, and their heights above (or below) the datum, is the *Tide Tables* published by the National

Ocean Survey, fig. 2010. Any predictions appearing in newspapers, or broadcast over radio and TV stations, will have been extracted from these tables. The cover jackets of charts in the small-craft series sometimes include excerpts from the Tide Tables as applicable to the area covered by the chart, fig. 2011.

Not to be overlooked is the possibility of "local knowledge." Never be hesitant to ask experienced local watermen when you are in unfamiliar waters and need information of any kind. The best of tables prepared by electronic computers sometimes cannot compare with a knowledge of what to expect that is based on years of local experience.

TIDE TABLES

The National Ocean Survey Tide Tables are of great value in determining the height of water at any place at a given time. These are calculated in advance and published annually. There are four volumes, one of which covers the East Coast of North and South America, and another the West Coast of these continents.

These Tables can usually be bought at any authorized sales agent for N.O.S. charts. The price for each volume is $3.75.

The Tide Tables give the predicted times and heights of high and low water for each day of the year at a number of important points known as *reference stations*. Portland, Boston, Newport, and Sandy Hook are examples of points for which detailed information is given in the East Coast Tables. Reference stations in the West Coast Tables include

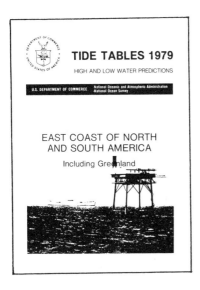

FIG. 2010 The National Ocean Survey uses modern electronic computing equipment to prepare advanced predictions of tidal levels at many points. These are published in the annual Tide Tables.

San Diego, the Golden Gate at San Francisco, and Aberdeen, Washington.

Additional data are tabulated showing the difference in times and heights between these reference stations and thousands of other points termed *subordinate stations*. From these tables, the tide at virtually any point of significance along the coasts can easily be computed. The West Coast Tide Tables contain predictions for reference sta-

tions and differences for about 1100 subordinate stations in North and South America.

Heights given in the Tide Tables must be reckoned from some specific datum; the one used is the same as on charts of that area. The datum long used on the Pacific Coast, where mixed tides widely prevail, is *mean lower low water* (MLLW), the average of the lower of the two low water heights of each tidal day. The datum on the Atlantic Coast has long been *mean low water* (MLW), the average of *all* low waters. The *Gulf Coast Low Water Datum* is essentially the same as MLW. Now, however, N.O.S. is in the process of changing Atlantic and Gulf Coast charts and Tide Tables to mean lower low water; this technical change will have no practical significance for navigation.

taken into account in tide predictions, but in the use of the tables, it must be remembered that certain other factors which have a pronounced influence on the height of tides, cannot be forecast months or years in advance. Such influences include barometric pressure and wind. In many areas, the effect of a prolonged gale of wind from a certain quarter is sometimes sufficient to offset all other factors. Tidal rivers may be affected by changes in the volume of water flowing down from the watershed. Normal seasonal variations of flow are allowed for in the predictions, but unexpected prolonged wet or dry spells may result in significant changes to the predictions of tidal heights. Intense rainfall upriver may result in changes to both the heights and times of tides; these effects may not appear downstream for several days.

Caution should therefore be exercised whenever using the Tide Tables, especially since low waters may at times go considerably lower than the level predicted.

Explanation of the Tables

Table 1 of the Tide Tables, fig. 2012, gives the predicted times and heights of high and low water at the main reference stations and is practically self-explanatory. Where no sign is given before the predicted height, the quantity is positive and is to be added to the depths as given on the chart. When the value is preceded by a minus (−) sign, the "heights" are to be *subtracted* from charted depths.

Time is given in the four-digit system from 0001 to 2400 (see page 376). In many areas, caution must be exercised regarding *daylight time*. The Tide Tables are published in terms of local *standard* time, and a correction must be applied if you are in a DT locality.

While there are normally two high and two low tides each date, they are, on an average, nearly an hour later each succeeding day. Consequently, there will be instances when a high or low tide may skip a calendar day, as indicated by a blank space in the Tide Tables, fig. 2013. If it is a high tide, for example, that has been skipped, it will be noted that the previous corresponding high occurred late in the foregoing day, and the next one early in the following day; see the sequence for the late evening high tides of 1, 2, and 3 February in fig. 2013.

It may also be noted from a review of the Tide Tables that at some places there will be only one high and one low tide on some days, with the usual four tides on other days. This is not a diurnal tide situation, where a single high and low would occur every day. The condition considered here arises when the configuration of the land and the periods between successive tides are such that one tide is reflected back from the shore and alters the effect of the succeeding tide.

Sometimes the diurnal inequality (the difference in the height of the two high or two low waters of a day) is so increased as to cause only one low water each day. These tides are not unusual in the tropics and consequently are called *tropic tides*.

Table 2, Tidal Differences and Constants, fig. 2014, gives the information necessary to find the time and height of tide for thousands of subordinate stations by the application of simple corrections to the data given for the main reference stations. The name of the applicable reference station in each case is given in bold-face type at the head of the particular section in which the subordinate station

is listed. The following information is given in separate columns of Table 2:

    a. Latitude and longitude of the subordinate station.

    b. Differences in time and height of high (and low) waters at the subordinate station and its designated reference station.

    c. Mean and spring (or diurnal) tidal ranges.

    d. Mean tide level.

Note carefully that the existence of a "minus tide" means that the actual depths of water will be *less* than the figures on the chart.

To determine the time of high or low water at any station in Table 2, use the column marked Differences, Time. This gives the hours and minutes to be added to (+) or subtracted from (−) the time of the respective high or low water at the reference station shown in bold-face type next *above* the listing of the subordinate station. Be careful in making calculations near midnight. The application of the time difference may result in crossing the line from one day to another. Simply add or subtract 24 hours as necessary.

The height of the tide at a station in Table 2 is determined by applying the height difference or ratio. A plus sign (+) indicates that the difference, in feet and tenths, is to be added to the height at the designated reference station for the same time; a minus sign (−) indicates that it should be subtracted.

Where height differences would give unsatisfactory predictions, *ratios* may be substituted for heights. Ratios are identified by an asterisk. These are given as a decimal fraction by which the height at the reference station is to be multiplied to determine the height at the subordinate station.

In the columns headed Ranges, the *mean range* is the difference in height between mean high water and mean low water. This figure is useful in many areas where it may

FIG. 2011 Small-craft charts give annual tidal predictions for reference stations covered by that chart. Information tabulated for marinas and other boating facilities includes tidal ranges at such locations and time differences from a reference station.

FIG. 2012 Table 1 of the Tide Tables lists daily predictions of the time and height of high and low tides at selected reference stations.

Note: Beginning in 1981 heights in metric units have been added to the Tide Tables.

FIG. 2013 An extract from Table 1 showing how a high tide may occasionally be omitted near midnight; see text for explanation. Similarly, a low tide near midnight may be skipped about once each two weeks.

Table 2.—TIDAL DIFFERENCES AND OTHER CONSTANTS 169

No.	PLACE	POSITION Lat.	POSITION Long.	DIFFERENCES Time High water	DIFFERENCES Time Low water	DIFFERENCES Height High water	DIFFERENCES Height Low water	RANGES Mean	RANGES Di-urnal	Mean Tide Level
	WASHINGTON—Continued	° '	° '							
	Admiralty Inlet—Continued	N.	W.	on PORT TOWNSEND, p.88						
	Time meridian, 120°W.			h. m.	h. m.	feet	feet	feet	feet	feet
897	Port Townsend (Point Hudson)	48 07	122 45	−0 04	−0 04	+0.3	+0.1	5.3	8.6	5.2
899	Marrowstone Point	48 06	122 41	+0 09	+0 07	+0.5	0.0	5.6	8.8	5.3
900	Mystery Bay, Marrowstone Island	48 03	122 41	+0 20	+0*50	−0.1	0.0	5.0	8.2	5.0
901	Bush Point	48 02	122 36	+0 39	+1 13	+0.5	0.0	5.6	8.8	5.3
902	Oak Bay	48 01	122 43	+0 15	+0 29	+1.0	+0.1	6.0	9.4	5.6
	Hood Canal			on SEATTLE, p.92						
903	Port Ludlow	47 55	122 41	−0 27	−0 18	*0.88	*0.88	6.4	9.9	5.9
905	Port Gamble	47 52	122 35	−0 16	−0 08	*0.91	*0.91	6.7	10.4	6.1
907	Bangor Wharf	47 45	122 44	−0 20	+0 04	−0.3	0.0	7.3	10.9	6.4
908	Zelatched Point, Dabob Bay	47 43	122 49	−0 09	−0 05	+0.1	+0.1	7.6	11.5	6.7
909	Seabeck	47 38	122 50	−0 03	+0 03	+0.1	+0.1	7.8	11.6	6.8
910	Pleasant Harbor	47 40	122 55	−0 14	+0 01	+0.2	+0.1	7.8	11.6	6.8
911	Union	47 21	123 06	−0 04	+0 10	+0.4	+0.1	7.9	11.8	6.9
	Puget Sound									
912	Hansville	47 55	122 33	−0 07	+0 04	−1.0	−0.1	6.7	10.3	6.1
913	Point No Point	47 55	122 32	−0 16	−0 16	*0.92	*0.92	6.7	10.4	6.1
914	Edmonds	47 49	122 23	−0 05	+0 02	−0.4	0.0	7.2	10.9	6.4
915	Port Madison	47 42	122 32	−0 08	−0 08	−0.1	0.0	7.7	11.4	6.6
917	Poulsbo, Liberty Bay	47 44	122 39	+0 02	+0 08	+0.6	+0.1	8.1	11.9	6.9
919	Brownsville, Port Orchard	47 39	122 37	+0 02	+0 08	+0.4	0.0	8.0	11.7	6.8
921	SEATTLE (Madison St.), Elliott Bay	47 36	122 20	Daily predictions				7.6	11.3	6.6
923	Eighth Ave. S., Duwamish Waterway	47 32	122 19	+0 05	+0 07	−0.1	0.0	7.5	11.1	6.5
925	Port Blakely	47 36	122 30	+0 08	+0 03	+0.2	0.0	7.8	11.5	6.7
927	Pleasant Beach, Rich Passage	47 36	122 32	+0 01	+0 07	+0.2	0.0	7.8	11.5	6.8
929	Bremerton, Port Orchard	47 33	122 38	+0 07	+0 12	+0.4	0.0	8.0	11.7	6.8
931	Tracyton, Dyes Inlet	47 37	122 40	+0 30	+0 56	+1.0	0.0	8.2	12.3	7.1
933	South Colby, Yukon Harbor	47 31	122 32	+0 01	+0 07	+0.3	0.0	7.9	11.6	6.7
935	Des Moines	47 24	122 20	+0 03	+0 09	−0.4	0.0	8.0	11.7	6.8
937	Burton, Quartermaster Harbor	47 23	122 28	+0 07	+0 13	+0.6	0.0	8.2	11.9	6.9
939	Gig Harbor	47 20	122 35	+0 06	+0 14	+0.6	0.0	8.2	11.8	6.9
941	Tacoma, Commencement Bay	47 17	122 25	+0 07	+0 06	+0.5	0.0	8.1	11.8	6.8
943	Arletta, Hale Passage	47 17	122 39	+0 23	+0 36	+1.7	0.0	9.3	13.7	7.4
945	Home, Von Geldern Cove, Carr Inlet	47 16	122 45	+0 27	+0 39	+2.3	+0.1	9.7	13.6	7.8
947	Wauna, Carr Inlet	47 23	122 38	+0 20	+0 34	+1.8	0.0	9.4	13.1	7.5
949	Steilacoom	47 10	122 36	+0 22	+0 35	+1.8	0.0	9.4	13.1	7.5
951	Hyde Point, McNeil Island	47 12	122 39	+0 23	+0 41	+2.1	+0.2	9.5	13.4	7.7
953	Sequallitchew Creek, Nisqually Reach	47 07	122 40	+0 24	+0 42	+2.1	+0.1	9.6	13.4	7.7
955	Longbranch, Filucy Bay	47 13	122 45	+0 26	+0 39	+2.2	+0.1	9.7	13.5	7.7
957	Henderson Inlet	47 09	122 50	+0 27	+0 45	+2.6	+0.1	10.0	14.0	8.0
959	Vaughn, Case Inlet	47 20	122 46	+0 35	+0 47	+2.8	+0.2	10.2	14.1	8.1
961	Allyn, Case Inlet	47 23	122 49	+0 27	+0 46	+2.8	+0.2	10.2	14.1	8.1
963	Walkers Landing, Pickering Passage	47 17	122 56	+0 35	+0 47	+2.9	+0.2	10.3	14.3	8.1
965	Arcadia, Pickering Passage	47 12	122 56	+0 35	+0 54	+3.0	+0.2	10.4	14.4	8.2
967	Shelton, Oakland Bay	47 13	123 05	+1 12	+1 54	+2.8	−0.2	10.6	14.2	7.9
969	Burns Point, Totten Inlet	47 07	123 03	+0 36	+0 54	+3.6	+0.2	11.0	14.7	8.5
971	Rocky Point, Eld Inlet	47 04	123 01	+0 36	+0 52	+3.3	+0.1	10.6	14.7	8.4
973	Dofflemyer Point, Budd Inlet	47 08	122 54	+0 29	+0 47	+3.1	+0.2	10.5	14.4	8.2
975	Olympia, Budd Inlet	47 03	122 54	+0 31	+0 46	+3.1	+0.2	10.5	14.4	8.2
	Possession Sound and Port Susan									
977	Mukilteo	47 57	122 18	−0 08	−0 12	−0.3	−0.1	7.4	11.0	6.4
979	Everett	47 59	122 13	−0 09	−0 11	−0.2	0.0	7.4	11.1	6.5
981	Tulalip	48 04	122 17	+0 02¹	−0 02	0.0	+0.1	7.6	11.2	6.6
982	Kayak Point	48 08	122 22	−0 04¹	−0 01	−0.4	−0.1	7.3	10.9	6.3
983	Stanwood,¹ Stillaguamish River	48 14	122 22	+0 18	+2 10	*0.63	*0.29	5.7	7.4	3.6

*Ratio.
¹The low water seldom falls below the chart datum.

FIG. 2014 Table 2—Tidal Differences and Other Constants. Data are given for hundreds of subordinate stations so that predictions can be made for almost any point of significance to navigation.

	TIME FROM THE NEAREST HIGH WATER OR LOW WATER															
h. m.	h. m.	h. m.	h. m.	h. m.	h. m.	h. m.	h. m.	h. m.	h. m.	h. m.	h. m.	h. m.	h. m.	h. m.	h. m.	h. m.
4 00	0 08	0 16	0 24	0 32	0 40	0 48	0 56	1 04	1 12	1 20	1 28	1 36	1 44	1 52	2 00
4 20	0 09	0 17	0 26	0 35	0 43	0 52	1 01	1 09	1 18	1 27	1 35	1 44	1 53	2 01	2 10
4 40	0 09	0 19	0 28	0 37	0 47	0 56	1 05	1 15	1 24	1 33	1 43	1 52	2 01	2 11	2 20
5 00	0 10	0 20	0 30	0 40	0 50	1 00	1 10	1 20	1 30	1 40	1 50	2 00	2 10	2 20	2 30
5 20	0 11	0 21	0 32	0 43	0 53	1 04	1 15	1 25	1 36	1 47	1 57	2 08	2 19	2 29	2 40
5 40	0 11	0 23	0 34	0 45	0 57	1 08	1 19	1 31	1 42	1 53	2 05	2 16	2 27	2 39	2 50
6 00	0 12	0 24	0 36	0 48	1 00	1 12	1 24	1 36	1 48	2 00	2 12	2 24	2 36	2 48	3 00
6 20	0 13	0 25	0 38	0 51	1 03	1 16	1 29	1 41	1 54	2 07	2 19	2 32	2 45	2 57	3 10
6 40	0 13	0 27	0 40	0 53	1 07	1 20	1 33	1 47	2 00	2 13	2 27	2 41	2 54	3 07	3 20
7 00	0 14	0 28	0 42	0 55	1 10	1 24	1 38	1 52	2 06	2 20	2 34	2 48	3 02	3 16	3 30
7 20	0 15	0 29	0 44	0 59	1 13	1 28	1 43	1 57	2 12	2 27	2 41	2 56	3 11	3 25	3 40
7 40	0 15	0 31	0 46	1 01	1 17	1 32	1 47	2 03	2 18	2 33	2 49	3 04	3 19	3 35	3 50
8 00	0 16	0 32	0 48	1 04	1 20	1 36	1 52	2 08	2 24	2 40	2 56	3 12	3 28	3 44	4 00
8 20	0 17	0 33	0 50	1 07	1 23	1 40	1 57	2 13	2 30	2 47	3 03	3 20	3 37	3 53	4 10
8 40	0 17	0 35	0 52	1 09	1 27	1 44	2 01	2 19	2 36	2 53	3 11	3 28	3 45	4 03	4 20
9 00	0 18	0 36	0 54	1 12	1 30	1 48	2 06	2 24	2 42	3 00	3 18	3 36	3 54	4 12	4 30
9 20	0 19	0 37	0 56	1 15	1 33	1 52	2 11	2 29	2 48	3 07	3 25	3 44	4 03	4 21	4 40
9 40	0 19	0 39	0 58	1 17	1 37	1 56	2 15	2 35	2 54	3 13	3 33	3 52	4 11	4 31	4 50
10 00	0 20	0 40	1 00	1 20	1 40	2 00	2 20	2 40	3 00	3 20	3 40	4 00	4 20	4 40	5 00
10 20	0 21	0 41	1 02	1 23	1 43	2 04	2 25	2 45	3 06	3 27	3 47	4 08	4 29	4 49	5 10
10 40	0 21	0 43	1 04	1 25	1 47	2 08	2 29	2 51	3 12	3 33	3 55	4 16	4 37	4 59	5 20

	CORRECTION TO HEIGHT								
Ft.	Ft.	Ft.	Ft.	Ft.	Ft.	Ft.	Ft.	Ft.	Ft.
0.5	0.0	0.0	0.0	0.0	0.0	0.1	0.1	0.1	0.1
1.0	0.0	0.0	0.0	0.0	0.1	0.1	0.2	0.2	0.3
1.5	0.0	0.0	0.0	0.1	0.1	0.2	0.3	0.4	0.4
2.0	0.0	0.0	0.1	0.1	0.2	0.3	0.4	0.5	0.6
2.5	0.0	0.0	0.1	0.2	0.3	0.4	0.5	0.6	0.7
3.0	0.0	0.1	0.1	0.2	0.3	0.4	0.5	0.6	0.8
3.5	0.0	0.1	0.1	0.2	0.3	0.4	0.6	0.7	0.9
4.0	0.0	0.1	0.1	0.2	0.3	0.5	0.7	0.9	1.1
4.5	0.0	0.1	0.1	0.2	0.3	0.5	0.7	0.9	1.1
5.0	0.0	0.1	0.1	0.2	0.3	0.5	0.7	0.8	1.0
6.5	0.0	0.1	0.1	0.2	0.4	0.5	0.7	0.9	1.1

FIG. 2015 Table 3—Height of Tide at Any Time. This table is used in determining tide level at intermediate times between low and high waters.

be added to mean low water to get mean high water (MHW), the datum commonly used for the measurement of vertical heights above water, bridge and other vertical clearances, etc. The *spring range* is the average semidiurnal range occurring twice monthly when the moon is new or full. It is larger than the mean range where the type of tide is either semidiurnal or mixed, and is of no practical significance where the tide is of the diurnal type. Where this is the situation, the table gives the *diurnal range,* which is the difference in height between mean higher high water and mean lower low water.

Table 3, fig. 2015, is provided in order that detailed calculations can be made for the height of the tide at any desired moment between the times of high and low waters. It is equally usable for either reference stations in Table 1 or the subordinate stations of Table 2. Note that Table 3 is not a complete set of variations from one low to one high. Since the rise and fall are assumed to be symmetrical, only a half-table need be printed. Calculations are made from a high or low water, whichever is nearer to the specified time. In using Table 3, the nearest tabular values are used; interpolation is not necessary.

If the degree of precision of Table 3 is not required (it seldom is in practical piloting situations), a much simpler and quicker estimation can be made by using the following one-two-three rule of thumb. The tide may be assumed to rise or fall 1/12 of the full range during the first and sixth hours after high and low water stands, 2/12 during the second and fifth hours, and 3/12 during the third and fourth hours. The results obtained by this rule will suffice for essentially all situations and locations, but should be compared with Table 3 calculations as a check when entering new areas.

The table shown at the bottom of page 440 has been prepared from the above rule of thumb to supply multiplying factors for half-hour intervals of a rising or falling tide.

The Tide Tables also include four other minor tables which, although not directly related to tidal calculations, are often useful. Table 4 provides sunrise and sunset data at five-day intervals for various latitudes. Table 5 lists corrections to convert the local mean times of Table 4 to standard zone time. Table 6 tabulates times of moonrise and moonset for certain selected locations. The inside back cover lists other useful data such as the phases of the moon, solar equinoxes and solstices, etc.

Each Table is preceded by informative material which should be read carefully prior to its use.

EXAMPLES OF TIDAL CALCULATIONS

The instructions in the Tide Tables should be fully adequate for the solution of any problem. However, examples will be worked out here for various situations as guides to the use of the various individual tables. Comments and cautions relating to the solution of practical problems involving the Tide Tables will also be given.

Example 1. Determination of the time and height of a high or low tide at a reference station.

Problem: What is the time and height of the evening low tide at Seattle on Sunday, 9 October 1977?

Solution: Using Table 1, fig. 2012, it will be seen directly that the evening low water occurs at 2046 Pacific Standard Time on this date and that the height is 3.3 feet above the tidal datum of mean lower low water.

Notes: a. observe that if the date had been 12 November, the tide level at low water stand would have been a *minus* figure, —2.7 feet. At this time, the water level is predicted to be *below* the datum and actual depths will be *less* than those printed on the charts of this area.

b. Observe that if the date had been 13 November, there would have been no solution as the normal progression of the tides on a cycle of roughly 24 hours and 50 minutes has moved the normal evening low tide past midnight and into the next day. Thus Sunday, 13 November has only three tides rather than the usual four.

c. It should be further noted that the reference stations are also listed in Table 2 and additional information is shown there. This table, fig. 2014, indicates, for reference stations as well as subordinate stations, the specific location for which predictions are given, the mean and spring (or diurnal) tidal ranges, and the mean tide level.

d. Remember to add one hour if you are in an area using daylight saving time.

Example 2. Determination of the time and height of a high or low tide at a subordinate station.

Problem: What is the time and height of the morning low water at Shelton on Oakland Bay, Puget Sound on Tuesday, 13 December 1977?

Solution: From the Index to Table 2 in the back of the Tide Tables, Shelton is found to be Subordinate Station No. 967. It is then located in Table 2 (fig. 2014). First, note that the Reference Station shown next *above* this place is "Seattle." Then note the time and height differences for Shelton for *low* waters; be sure to use the correct columns.

Th differences are then applied as follows:

Time		Height
00 01	At Seattle	—2.7 feet
1:54	Differences	—0.2
01 55	At Shelton	—2.9 feet

Thus, at Shelton on 13 December 1977, the predicted morning low water will occur at 0155 PST with a height of —2.9 feet (2.9 feet *below* the tidal datum).

Notes: a. If the date had been 14 October, the morning low water at Seattle for that date is at 1132. Adding the time difference of 1h 54m would have resulted in a time prediction at Shelton of 1326, which is *not a morning* tide at the subordinate station. In this case it would be necessary to use the low water at the reference station that occurs before midnight on the *preceding* day. At Seattle on 13 October, there is a low water at 2312; adding the time difference gives a morning low tide at Shelton of 0106 on 14 October.

b. Observe that if the subordinate station had been Port Gamble on Hood Canal, the height would be determined by multiplying the height at the reference station by the *ratio* of 0.91 rather than adding or subtracting a difference in feet. (Ratios may be either greater or less than 1.) Note also that here the time differences are *negative;* the high and low waters at the subordinate station occur *earlier* than at the reference station of Table 1.

c. The use of minus time differences with predictions of

FIG. 2016 Table 4—Local Mean Time of Sunrise and Sunset. Times are tabulated for various dates and latitudes, usually at intervals of 5 days and 2°; interpolation is used for exact dates and locations.

Date	30° N. Rise	30° N. Set	32° N. Rise	32° N. Set	34° N. Rise	34° N. Set	36° N. Rise	36° N. Set	38° N. Rise	38° N. Set	40° N. Rise	40° N. Set
	h. m.	h. m.	h. m.	h. m.	h. m.	h. m.	h. m.	h. m.	h. m.	h. m.	h. m.	h. m.
Jan. 1	6 56	17 11	7 01	17 07	7 06	17 02	7 11	16 57	7 16	16 51	7 22	16 45
6	6 57	17 15	7 02	17 11	7 06	17 06	7 11	17 01	7 17	16 56	7 22	16 50
11	6 57	17 19	7 02	17 15	7 06	17 10	7 11	17 05	7 16	17 00	7 22	16 55
16	6 57	17 23	7 01	17 19	7 05	17 15	7 10	17 05	7 15	17 05	7 20	17 00
21	6 55	17 28	6 59	17 24	7 04	17 20	7 08	17 15	7 12	17 11	7 17	17 06
26	6 54	17 32	6 57	17 28	7 01	17 25	7 05	17 21	7 09	17 16	7 14	17 12
31	6 51	17 36	6 55	17 33	6 58	17 29	7 02	17 26	7 06	17 22	7 10	17 18
Feb. 5	6 48	17 41	6 51	17 37	6 54	17 34	6 58	17 31	7 01	17 27	7 05	17 24
10	6 44	17 45	6 47	17 42	6 50	17 39	6 53	17 36	6 56	17 33	6 59	17 30
15	6 40	17 49	6 43	17 46	6 45	17 44	6 48	17 41	6 50	17 39	6 53	17 36
20	6 36	17 53	6 38	17 50	6 40	17 48	6 42	17 46	6 44	17 44	6 47	
25	6 31	17 56	6 32	17 55	6 34	17 53	6 36	17 51	6 38	17 49		16 47
Mar. 2	6 25	18 00	6 27	17 58	6 28	17 57	6 29	17		16 47	6 47	16 42
7	6 20	18 03	6 22	18 02	6 22	18 01			48	16 44	6 53	16 39
12	6 14	18 06	6 14	18				16 47	6 53	16 42	6 58	16 37
17	6 08	18 10				16 55	6 48	16 51	6 53	16 46	6 58	16 41	7 03	16 35
22	6 02				16 55	6 48	16 51	6 53	16 46	6 58	16 41	7 03	16 35
27		00	17 01	6 51	16 56	6 56	16 52	7 01	16 46	7 07	16 41	7 12	16 35
	6 49	17 03	6 54	16 58	7 05	17 04	16 48	7 10	16 42	7 16	16 36
22	6 52	17 05	6 56	17 00	7 01	16 55	7 07	16 49	7 12	16 44	7 18	16 38
27	6 54	17 08	6 59	17 03	7 04	16 58	7 09	16 53	7 15	16 47	7 21	16 41
Jan. 1	6 56	17 11	7 01	17 07	7 06	17 02	7 11	16 57	7 16	16 51	.7 22	16 45

Local mean time. To obtain standard time of rise or set, see table 5.

FIG. 2017 Table 5—Reduction of Local Mean Time to Standard Time. A correction, obtained from this table, is applied to the time of sunrise or sunset computed from Table 4 to get the time of the event in standard zone time. A further correction of one hour is needed for Daylight Saving Time.

Difference of longitude between local and standard meridian	Correction to local mean time to obtain standard time	Difference of longitude between local and standard meridian	Correction to local mean time to obtain standard time	Difference of longitude between local and standard meridian	Correction to local mean time to obtain standard time
° ' ° '	*Minutes*	° ' ° '	*Minutes*	°	*Hours*
0 00 to 0 07	0	7 23 to 7 37	30	15	1
0 08 to 0 22	1	7 38 to 7 52	31	30	2
0 23 to 0 37	2	7 53 to 8 07	32	45	3
0 38 to 0 52	3	8 08 to 8 22	33	60	4
0 53 to 1 07	4	8 23 to 8 37	34	75	5
1 08 to 1 22	5	8 38 to 8 52	35	90	6
1 23 to 1 37	6	8 53 to 9 07	36	105	7
1 38 to 1 52	7	9 08 to 9 22	37	120	8
1 53 to 2 07	8	9 23 to 9 37	38	135	9
2 08 to 2 22	9	9 38 to 9 52	39	150	10
2 23 to 2 37	10	9 53 to 10 07	40	165	11
2 38 to 2 52	11	10 08 to 10 22	41	180	12
2 53 to 3 07	12	10 23 to 10 37	42		
3 08 to 3 22	13	10 38 to 10 52	43		
3 23 to 3 37	14	10 53 to 11 07	44		
3 38 to 3 52	15	11 08 to 11 32	55		
3 53 to 4 07	16	13 53 to 14 07	56		
4 08 to 4 22					
6 38 to 6 52	27	14 08 to 14 22	57		
6 53 to 7 07	28	14 23 to 14 37	58		
7 08 to 7 22	29	14 38 to 14 52	59		

If local meridian is east of standard meridian, subtract the correction from local time.

If local meridian is west of standard meridian, add the correction to local time.

tides to occur shortly after midnight at the reference station may result in a change of date backward into the preceding day. Always be careful in making calculations close to 2400.

Example 3. Determination of the level of the tide at a reference station at a given time between high and low waters.

Problem: What is the height of the tide at Seattle at 1740 on Saturday, 10 December 1977?

Solution: From Table 1, we first note that the given time of 1740 falls between a high tide at 1517 and a low tide at 2229. We compute the time difference and range as follows:

Time	Height
15 17	12.1 feet
22 29	−3.0
7:12 time difference	15.1 feet range

Thus our desired tide level is on a falling tide whose range is 15.1 feet (since the low water height is a negative value, we are substracting a minus number which is arithmetically equivalent to adding the numerical values).

The desired time is nearer to the time of the high water, so calculations will be made in Table 3; fig. 2015, using this starting point.

17 40	Desired time
15 17	Time of nearest high or low water
2:23	Difference

The given time is $2^h 23^m$ after the nearest high water. Table 3 is used to the nearest tabulated value; do not interpolate. Entering the *upper* part of the Table on the line for Duration of rise or fall of $7^h 20^m$ (nearest value to $7^h 12^m$) read across to the entry nearest $2^h 23^m$; this is $2^h 27^m$ in the tenth column from the left. Follow *down* this column into the *lower* part of Table 3 to the line for Range of Tide of 15.0 feet (nearest value to actual range of 15.1 feet). At the intersection of this line and column is found the correction to the height of the tide; in this case, 3.8 feet.

Since we have noted that in this example the tide is falling, and we are calculating from high water, the correction is subtracted from the height of high water: 12.1 − 3.8 = 8.3.

The predicted height of the tide at Seattle at 1740 PST on 10 December 1977 is 8.3 feet above the tidal datum.

Notes: a. Be sure that calculations are made for the right pair of high and low tides; be sure that the calculations are made for the *nearest* high or low water.

b. Be careful to apply the final correction to the nearest high or low water as used in its computation; do not apply it to the range; apply it in the right direction, down from a high, or up from a low.

Example 4. Determination of the height of tide at a subordinate station at a given time.

Problem: What is the height of the tide at Port Ludlow at 0830 on Saturday, 10 December, 1977?

Solution: First, the times of the high and low waters on either side of the stated time must be calculated for the subordinate station using tables 1 and 2. This is done as follows:

High water	05 00	At Seattle	12.3 feet
	−:27	difference/ratio	0.88
	04 33	At Point Ludlow	10.8 feet
Low water	10 12	At Seattle	6.7 feet
	−:13	difference/ratio	0.88
	09 54	At Point Ludlow	5.9 feet

Next, we calculate the time difference and range:

09 54	10.8
04 33	5.9
5:21 time difference	4.9 feet range

The time from the nearest high or low is calculated

09 54
08 30
1:24 time from nearest low

With the data from the above calculations, enter Table 3 for a Duration of rise or fall of $5^h 21^m$ (use $5^h 20^m$), a time from nearest high or low of $1^h 24^m$ (use $1^h 25^m$), and a range of 4.9 feet. From these data, we find a correction to height of tide of 0.8 feet. We know that the tide is falling and that the nearest time of stand was the low water at 0954. From these facts, we can see that the correction is to be added to the low water height; 5.9 + 0.8 = 6.7.

The height of the tide at Port Ludlow at 0830 PST on 10 December 1977 is predicted to be 6.7 feet above the datum.

Note: Be sure to use the high and low tides occurring *at the subordinate station* on either side of the given time. It may be that in some instances with large time differences, a correction of times from the reference station to the subordinate station will show that you have selected the incorrect pair of tides; in this case select another high or low tide so that the pair used at the subordinate station will bracket the given time.

Example 5. Determination of the time of the tide reaching a given height at a reference station.

Problem: At what time on the afternoon of 13 October 1977 will the height of the rising tide reach 10 feet at Seattle?

Solution: This is essentially Example 3 in reverse. First, determine the range and duration of rise (or fall).

16 29	High water	11.5 feet
10 47	Low water	3.7
5:42	Duration	7.8 feet range

It is noted that the desired difference in height of tide is 11.5 − 10.0 = 1.5 feet. Enter the *lower* part of Table 3 on the line for a range of 8.0 feet (nearest value to 7.8) and find the column in which the correction nearest 1.5 feet is tabulated; in this case, the nearest value (1.6) is found in the ninth column from the left. Proceed *up* this column to the line in the upper part of the Table for a Duration of 5h 40m (nearest value to 5h 42m). The time from nearest high or low found on this line is 1h 42m. Since our desired level is nearer to high water than low, this time difference is subtracted from the time of high water; 1629 − 1:42 = 1447.

Thus the desired tidal height of 10 feet above datum is predicted to occur at 1447 PST on 13 October.

Note: A similar calculation can be made for a subordinate station by first determining the applicable high and low water times and heights at that station.

Example 6. Determination of vertical clearance.

Problem: What will be the vertical clearance under the fixed west span of the bridge across the Hood Canal near Port Gamble, Washington, at the time of morning high tide on 16 December 1977?

Solution: Chart 18445 (185-SC) states the clearance to be 35 feet. The datum for heights is mean high water; the tidal datum in mean lower low water.

From Tables 1 and 2, we determine the predicted height of the tide at the specified time:

At Seattle	12.7 feet
ratio	0.91
At Port Gamble	11.6 feet

From Table 2, we calculate the height of mean high water for Port Gamble:

Mean tide level	6.1 feet
½ mean range	3.4
Mean high water	9.5 feet above tidal datum.

The difference between predicted high water at the specified time and MHW is 11.6 − 9.5 = 2.1 feet. The tide is above MHW and the bridge clearance is reduced, 35 − 2.1 = 33 feet, to nearest whole foot.

On the morning of 2 December 1967, the clearance at high tide under the fixed west span of the bridge across Hood Canal near Port Gamble is predicted to be 33 feet; this is *less* than the clearance printed on the chart.

ASTRONOMICAL DATA FROM THE TIDE TABLES

Table 4 gives sunrise and sunset information for various latitudes at five-day intervals. If more precise times are needed, interpolation can be used. Times are *local* meridian and must be corrected to standard zone time.

Example 7. Determination of the time of sunrise at a specified location.

Problem: What is the time of sunrise at Catalina Harbor, Santa Catalina Island on 12 February 1977?

Solution: From Table 2, we note that the latitude and longitude of the given point are 33° 26′N, 118° 30′W.

Fig. 2016 is an extract from Table 4; the applicable entries are set up as follows:

	32°N	34°N
Feb 10	0647	0650
Feb 15	0643	0645

Then we interpolate to the nearest minute vertically for the desired date:

	32°N	34°N
Feb 10	0647	0650
Feb 12	**0645**	**0648**
Feb 15	0643	0645

Next, interpolation is done horizontally for the latitude of the given point:

	32°N	**33° 26′N**	34°N
Feb 12	0645	**0647**	0648

This time of 0647 is local meridian time and must be corrected to zone time by Table 5, fig. 2017. The meridian of Pacific Standard Time is 120° W (from Table 1, bottom of any page).

120° 00′
118° 30′
1° 30′ Longitude difference

From Table 5, the time correction for 1°30′ is 6 minutes. Since Catalina Harbor is *east* of the zone meridian, the correction is *subtracted*; 0647 − 6ᵐ = 0641.

On the morning of 12 February 1977, the time of sunrise at Catalina Harbor is 0641 PST.

Notes: a. Interpolation can be done first horizontally for the latitude difference and then vertically for the desired date. The results may vary slightly due to rounding to the nearest minute, but the difference should not exceed one minute.

b. Calculations for the time of sunset are made in exactly the same manner.

c. Latitude and longitude data may be taken from a chart or any other source.

d. Times must be corrected for daylight time, if in effect.

Times of moonrise and moonset

Table 6 gives daily times for moonrise and moonset for selected points. Correction or interpolation for other points is *not* possible.

Currents

Current is the horizontal motion of water. This motion may be the result of any one of several factors, or of a combination of two or three. Although certain of these causes are of greater importance to a boatman than are others, he should have a general understanding of all.

TIDAL CURRENTS

Boatmen in coastal areas will be most affected by *tidal currents*. The rise and fall of tidal levels is a result of the flow of water to and from a given locality. This flow results in tidal current effects.

The normal type of tidal current, in bays and rivers, is the *reversing* current that flows alternately in one direction and then the opposite. Off-shore, tidal currents may be of the *rotary* type, flowing with little change in strength, but slowly and steadily changing direction; these are more common on the Pacific Coast than on the Atlantic.

A special form of tidal current is the *hydraulic* type such as flows in a waterway connecting two bodies of water. Differences in the time and height of the high and low waters of the two bays, sounds, etc., cause a flow from one to the other and back again. A typical example of hydraulic current is the flow through the Cape Cod Canal between Massachusetts Bay and Buzzards Bay.

Remember to use the terms correctly—tide is the *vertical* rise and fall of water levels; current is the *horizontal* flow of water.

FIG. 2018 The major ocean currents of interest to boatmen are the Gulf Stream off the East Coast and the California Current along the Pacific Coast.

OTHER TYPES OF CURRENT

Although most piloting situations involving current are concerned with tidal currents, there will be times when river, ocean, and wind-driven currents must be considered.

River currents

Boatmen on rivers above the head of tidal action must take into account *river currents*. (Where tidal influences are felt, river currents are merged into tidal currents and are not considered separately.) River currents will vary widely with the width and depth of the stream, the season of the year, recent rainfall in the river basin, etc.

Ocean currents

Off-shore piloting will frequently require knowledge and consideration of *ocean currents*. These result from regions of relatively constant winds such as the often-mentioned "trade winds" and "prevailing westerlies." The rotation of the earth and variations in water density are also factors in the patterns of ocean currents.

The ocean currents of greatest interest to boatmen are the Gulf Stream and the California Current, fig. 2018. The *Gulf Stream* is a northerly and easterly flow of warm water along the Atlantic Coast of the United States. It is quite close to shore along the southern part of Florida, but moves progressively further to sea as it flows northward, where it both broadens and slows.

The *California Current* flows generally southward and a bit eastward along the Pacific Coast of Canada and the United States, turning sharply westward off Baja California (Mexico). It is a flow of colder water and, in general, is slower and less sharply defined than the Gulf Stream.

Wind-driven currents

In addition to the consistent ocean currents caused by sustained wind patterns, local *wind-driven currents* may be established by temporary conditions. The effect of wind blowing across the sea is to cause the surface water to move. The extent of the effect varies with many factors, but generally a steady wind for 12 hours or longer will result in a discernible current.

For a rough rule-of-thumb, the strength of a wind-driven current can be taken as 2% of the wind's velocity. The direction of the current will *not* be the same as that of the wind, a result of the earth's rotation. In the Northern Hemisphere, the current will be deflected to the right to a degree determined by the latitude and the depth of the water. The deflection may be as small as $15°$ in shallow coastal areas, or as great as $45°$ on the high seas; it is greater in the higher latitudes.

DEFINITIONS OF CURRENT TERMS

Currents have both strength and direction. The proper terms should be used in describing each of these characteristics.

The *set* of a current is the direction *toward* which it is flowing. A current that flows from North to South is termed a southerly current and has a set of $180°$. (Note carefully the difference here from the manner in which wind direction is described—it is exactly the opposite: a wind from North to South is called a northerly wind with a direction of $000°$.)

FIG. 2019 In some narrow passages, tidal currents are so strong that a lightly powered boat could not make headway against them, and must wait for slack water. Here, an auxiliary races through Cobscook Falls in Maine, propelled by a 10-knot "down-hill" current.

(Photograph courtesy Donald W. Gardner)

Tides and Currents / CHAPTER 20

FIG. 2020 Table 1 of the Tidal Current Tables. Daily predictions are listed for the times and strengths of maximum flood and ebb currents, and the time of slack water, at major reference stations.

62

CHESAPEAKE BAY ENTRANCE, VA., 1977
F-FLOOD, DIR. 305° TRUE   E-EBB, DIR. 125° TRUE

SEPTEMBER

DAY	SLACK WATER TIME H.M.	MAXIMUM CURRENT TIME H.M.	VEL. KNOTS	DAY	SLACK WATER TIME H.M.	MAXIMUM CURRENT TIME H.M.	VEL. KNOTS
1 TH	0127	0506	1.5E	16 F	0051	0430	1.7E
	0822	1100	1.0F		0749	1033	1.4F
	1353	1729	1.4E		1331	1702	1.6E
	2051	2316	0.9F		2024	2253	1.1F
2 F	0158	0545	1.4E	17 SA	0131	0515	1.7E
	0906	1141	0.9F		0838	1122	1.3F
	1436	1816	1.3E		1425	1755	1.5E
	2137	2356	0.7F		2118	2344	0.9F
3 SA	0231	0629	1.3E	18 SU	0215	0607	1.6E
	0953	1225	0.8F		0932	1219	1.3F
	1522	1904	1.1E		1524	1856	1.4E
	2229				2218		
4 SU	0306	0039	0.6F	19 M	0306	0037	0.8F
	1046	0717	1.2E		1034	0706	1.6E
	1613	1315	0.7F		1631	1321	1.2F
	2327	2000	1.0E		2326	2003	1.3E
5 M	0347	0130	0.4F	20 TU	0406	0140	0.7F
	1143	0811	1.1E		1142	0815	1.5E
	1713	1412	0.6F		1744	1431	1.1F
		2102	0.9E			2116	1.2E
6 TU	0031	0229	0.4F	21 W	0039	0252	0.6F
	0439	0912	1.1E		0517	0927	1.5E
	1244	1516	0.6F		1254	1544	1.0F
	1819	2205	0.9E		1858	2227	1.3E
7 W	0135	0330	0.3F	22 TH	0149	0406	0.6F
	0541	1014	1.1E		0636	1039	1.5E
	1343	1619	0.6F		1403	1654	1.1F
	1924	2306	1.0E		2004	2329	1.4E
8 TH	0232	0436	0.4F	23 F	0250	0517	0.7F
	0649	1110	1.2E		0752	1142	1.6E
	1437	1716	0.7F		1506	1757	1.1F
	2021	2357	1.1E		2101		

OCTOBER

DAY	SLACK WATER TIME H.M.	MAXIMUM CURRENT TIME H.M.	VEL. KNOTS	DAY	SLACK WATER TIME H.M.	MAXIMUM CURRENT TIME H.M.	VEL. KNOTS
1 SA	0111	0506	1.4E	16 SU	0107	0456	1.8E
	0827	1105	1.0F		0818	1108	1.5F
	1406	1744	1.2E		1419	1745	1.6E
	2106	2317	0.6F		2105	2325	0.9F
2 SU	0142	0544	1.3E	17 M	0156	0548	1.7E
	0911	1147	0.9F		0914	1205	1.4F
	1447	1829	1.1E		1517	1845	1.4E
	2155				2207		
3 M	0216	0000	0.5F	18 TU	0251	0024	0.8F
	1000	0629	1.2E		1017	0649	1.6E
	1533	1236	0.8F		1621	1308	1.2F
	2250	1921	1.0E		2315	1950	1.3E
4 TU	0257	0049	0.4F	19 W	0355	0130	0.7F
	1056	0724	1.1E		1125	0802	1.5E
	1626	1327	0.7F		1729	1415	1.1F
	2352	2018	0.9E			2100	1.3E
5 W	0349	0144	0.3F	20 TH	0026	0241	0.6F
	1156	0825	1.0E		0511	0913	1.4E
	1728	1428	0.6F		1237	1526	1.0F
		2124	0.9E		1836	2207	1.3E
6 TH	0054	0248	0.3F	21 F	0133	0357	0.7F
	0455	0927	1.1E		0632	1024	1.4E
	1258	1531	0.6F		1347	1635	1.0F
	1831	2222	1.0E		1938	2308	1.4E
7 F	0150	0353	0.4F	22 SA	0232	0505	0.8F
	0609	1029	1.1E		0747	1130	1.5E
	1356	1628	0.7F		1451	1736	1.0F
	1929	2315	1.1E		2032	2359	1.5E
8 SA	0237	0451	0.5F	23 SU	0323	0604	0.9F
	0719	1124	1.3E		0852	1225	1.6E
	1447	1724	0.8F		1547	1828	1.0F
	2019				2119		

The *drift* of a current is its velocity, normally in knots (except for river currents which will be in MPH). As noted in the preceding chapter, current drift is stated to the nearest tenth of a knot.

A tidal current is said to *flood* when it flows in from the sea and results in higher tidal stages. Conversely, a tidal current *ebbs* when the flow is seaward and water levels fall.

Slack vs. Stand

As these currents reverse, there are brief periods of no discernible flow, called *slack,* or *slack water.* The time of occurrence of slack is *not* the same as the time of *stand,* when the vertical rise or fall of tide has stopped. Tidal currents do *not* automatically slack and reverse direction when tide levels stand at high or low water.

High water at a given point simply means that the level there will not get any higher. Further up the bay or river, the tide will not have reached its maximum height and water must therefore continue to flow in so that it can continue to rise. The current can still be flooding after stand has been passed at our given point and the level has started to fall.

For example, let us consider the tides and currents on Chesapeake Bay. High tide occurs at Baltimore some 7 hours after it does at Smith Point, roughly half way up the 140 miles from Cape Henry at the entrance to Baltimore. On a certain day, high water occurs at 1126 at Smith Point, but slack water does not occur until 1304. The flooding current has thus continued for 1ʰ 38ᵐ after high water was reached.

Corresponding time intervals occur in the case of low water stand and the slack between ebb and flood currents.

In many places, the time lag between a low or high water stand and slack water is not a matter of minutes but hours. At The Narrows in New York Harbor, flood current continues for about 2 hours after high water is reached and the tide begins to fall, ebb for 2¹/₂ hours after low water stand. After slack, the current increases until mid-flood or mid-ebb, then gradually decreases. Where ebb and flood last for about six hours—as along the Atlantic seaboard—current will be strongest about three hours after

Note: 1 knot = 1.15 MPH = 1.85 km/h.

slack. Thus, the skipper who figures his passage out through The Narrows from the time of high water, rather than slack, will start about two and a half hours too soon and will run into a current at nearly its maximum strength.

NEED FOR KNOWLEDGE

Currents, primarily of the tidal type, will affect many boating situations. Currents will be a definite factor in piloting in tidal rivers, bays, and sounds. Coastal currents, resulting from waves striking the beaches at an angle, will often influence coastal piloting problems.

Effect on course and speed made good

A current directly in line with a boat's motion through the water will have a maximum effect on the speed made good, but with no off-course influence. The effect can be of real significance in figuring your ETA at your destination. It can even affect the safety of your craft and its crew if you have figured your fuel too closely and run into a bow-on current.

A current that is nearly at a right angle to your course through the water will have a maximum effect on the course made good and a minor effect on the distance you must travel to reach your destination. The off-course effect can be of great importance if there are shoals or other hazards near your desired track.

Knowledge of current set and drift can be applied to assist your cruising. Departure times can be selected to take advantage of favorable currents, or at least to minimize adverse effects. A 12-knot boat speed and a 2-knot current, reasonably typical situations, can combine to result in either a 10-knot or a 14-knot speed made good—the 40%

gain of a favorable current over an opposing one is significant both in terms of time en route and fuel consumed.

Even lesser currents have some significance. A half-knot current would hinder a swimmer and make rowing a boat noticeably more difficult. A one-knot current can seriously affect a sailboat in light breezes.

Difficult locations

In many boating areas, there will be locations where current conditions can be critical.

Numerous ocean inlets are difficult, or even dangerous, in certain combinations of current and onshore surf. In general, difficult surf conditions will be made more hazardous by an outward-flowing (ebbing) current. The topic of inlet seamanship is covered in more detail on page 164.

There are a number of narrow bodies of water where the maximum current velocity is such as to make passage impossible at times for boats of limited power, and to seriously slow boats of greater engine power, fig. 2019. Such narrow passages are particularly characteristic of Pacific Northwest boating areas, but do occur elsewhere. Currents in New York City's East River reach a maximum of 4.6 knots, and at the Golden Gate of San Francisco velocities greater than 5 knots occur. Velocities of 3½ to 4 knots are common in much-traveled passages like Woods Hole, Mass., and Plum Gut, at the eastern end of Long Island, N. Y.

FIG. 2021 Table 2— Current Differences and Other Constants. Data are given for hundreds of subordinate stations so that predictions for current may be made for many points of navigational significance.*

No.	PLACE	POSITION Lat.	POSITION Long.	TIME DIFFERENCES Slack water	TIME DIFFERENCES Maximum current	VELOCITY RATIOS Maximum flood	VELOCITY RATIOS Maximum ebb	Flood Direction (true)	Flood Average velocity	Ebb Direction (true)	Ebb Average velocity
		° ′ N.	° ′ W.	h. m.	h. m.			deg.	knots	deg.	knots
	DELAWARE BAY and RIVER—Continued				on DELAWARE BAY ENTRANCE, p.52						
	Time meridian, 75°W.										
3055	Fisher Point	39 59	75 04	+5 45	+5 25	0.8	0.9	040	1.4	225	1.7
3060	Torresdale, west of channel	40 02	74 59	(¹)	+5 50	0.5	0.8	045	0.9	225	1.6
3065	Rancocas Creek, off Delanco	40 03	74 58	+6 15	+6 15	0.6	0.5	090	1.0	270	0.9
3070	Bristol, south of	40 05	74 52	(²)	(²)	0.7	0.8	025	1.3	200	1.6
3075	Burlington Island, channel east of	40 06	74 50	(³)	(³)	0.5	0.9	020	0.9	205	1.8
3080	Whitehill	40 08	74 44	----	⁴+7 00	----	0.7	----	----	235	1.4
	DEL., MD. and VA. COAST										
3085	Indian River Inlet (bridge)	38 37	75 04	+0 10	+0 10	1.0	1.1	265	1.8	085	2.1
3090	Fenwick Shoal Lighted Whistle Buoy 2	38 25	74 46	See table 5.							
3095	Winter-Quarter Shoal Buoy 6WQS⁵	37 55	74 56	See table 5.							
				on CHESAPEAKE BAY ENTRANCE, p.58							
3100	Cape Charles, 70 miles east of	37 05	74 51	See table 5.							
3105	Smith Island Shoal, southeast of	37 05	75 43	-2 10	-2 10	0.3	0.3	300	0.3	070	0.4
3110	Chesapeake Light, 4.4 miles NE. of	36 59	75 42	*Current too weak and variable to be predicted*							
3115	Cape Henry Light, 2.2 miles SE. of	36 54	75 59	-1 15	-1 30	1.0	0.6	345	1.0	165	0.9
	CHESAPEAKE BAY										
3120	Cape Henry Light, 1 mile north of	36 56	76 00	0 00	-0 25	1.1	1.3	280	1.1	090	2.0
3125	Cape Henry Light, 1.8 miles north of	36 57	76 00	-0 05	-0 15	1.2	1.0	290	1.2	100	1.5
3130	CHESAPEAKE BAY ENTRANCE	36 59	76 00	Daily predictions				305	1.0	125	1.5
3135	Cape Henry Light, 4.6 miles north of	37 00	75 59	-0 35	-0 50	1.3	0.9	295	1.3	105	1.3
3140	Cape Charles Light, 9.5 mi. WSW. of	37 04	76 05	+0 10	0 00	1.5	0.9	320	1.5	125	1.4
3145	Cape Henry Light, 8.3 mi. NW. of	37 02	76 07	-0 05	-0 10	1.0	0.7	330	1.0	135	1.1
3150	Lynnhaven Roads	36 55	76 05	-0 35	-0 40	0.8	0.6	280	0.8	070	0.9
3155	Lynnhaven Inlet bridge	36 54	76 06	-2 05	-2 35	0.6	0.9	180	0.6	000	1.4
	Chesapeake Bay Bridge Tunnel										
3160	Chesapeake Beach, 1.5 miles N. of	36 57	76 07	-0 15	-0 20	0.8	0.6	305	0.8	100	0.9
3165	Thimble Shoal Channel	36 58	76 07	-0 40	-0 40	1.4	0.9	310	1.4	095	1.3
3170	Tail of the Horseshoe	37 00	76 06	-0 25	-0 40	0.9	0.7	300	0.9	110	1.0
3175	Middle Ground, channel west of	37 03	76 05	-0 25	-0 10	1.6	0.9	335	1.6	150	1.3
3180	Chesapeake Channel	37 02	76 04	-0 15	-0 15	1.8	1.0	335	1.8	145	1.5
3185	Fisherman I., 3.2 miles WSW. of	37 04	76 02	-0 55	-1 05	1.2	1.1	330	1.2	135	1.6
3190	Fisherman I., 1.4 miles WSW. of	37 05	76 00	(⁶)	-1 15	1.8	0.7	330	1.8	140	1.1
3195	Fisherman I., 1.8 miles south of	37 04	75 59	-0 45	-1 10	1.6	0.9	320	1.6	120	1.4
3200	Fisherman I., 0.4 mile west of	37 06	75 59	-0 45	-1 10	2.0	1.3	005	2.0	175	2.0
3205	Fisherman I., 1.1 miles NW. of	37 06	76 00	(⁷)	-0 40	1.8	1.1	355	1.8	165	1.6
3210	Cape Charles, off Wise Point	37 07	75 58	(⁸)	(⁸)	0.7	0.1	305	0.7	075	0.2
	Little Creek										
3215	North of east jetty	36 56	76 11	-1 50	-2 00	0.9	0.7	280	0.9	075	1.0
3220	0.5 mile north of west jetty	36 56	76 11	-1 10	-1 15	0.9	0.6	275	0.9	110	0.9
3225	Old Plantation Flats Light, west of	37 14	76 04	+1 10	+0 50	1.2	0.9	005	1.2	175	1.3
3230	York Spit Channel	37 13	76 09	+0 55	+0 55	0.8	0.7	010	0.8	195	1.1
3235	Wolf Trap Light, 0.5 mile west of	37 23	76 12	+1 05	+1 05	1.0	0.8	015	1.0	190	1.2
3240	Wolf Trap Light, 5.8 miles east of	37 23	76 04	+1 45	+1 45	0.9	0.9	015	0.9	175	1.3
3245	Stingray Point, 5.5 miles east of	37 35	76 10	+1 50	+2 20	1.0	0.6	345	1.0	180	0.9
3250	Stingray Point, 12.5 miles east of	37 34	76 02	+1 40	+2 05	1.0	0.5	030	1.0	175	0.8

¹ Flood begins, +6ʰ 55ᵐ; ebb begins, +5ʰ 00ᵐ.
² Flood begins, +6ʰ 55ᵐ; maximum flood, +5ʰ 30ᵐ; ebb begins, +4ʰ 55ᵐ; maximum ebb, +6ʰ 10ᵐ.
³ Flood begins, +7ʰ 30ᵐ; maximum flood, +5ʰ 45ᵐ; ebb begins, +4ʰ 15ᵐ; maximum ebb, +6ʰ 45ᵐ.
⁴ Data for ebb only. Flood is usually weak and of short duration. A weak ebb or flood current occurs about 6 hours after maximum flood at Delaware Bay Entrance.
⁵ Tidal current is weak and rotary, averaging less than 0.1 knot.
⁶ Flood begins, -1ʰ 45ᵐ; ebb begins, -0ʰ 40ᵐ.
⁷ Flood begins, -1ʰ 15ᵐ; ebb begins, -0ʰ 05ᵐ.
⁸ Flood begins, -0ʰ 30ᵐ; maximum flood, -0ʰ 20ᵐ; ebb begins, +0ʰ 25ᵐ; maximum ebb, +0ʰ 50ᵐ.

* Beginning with the Tidal Current Tables for 1981, the format of Table 2 has been changed to provide additional and more precise information.

TIDAL CURRENT PREDICTIONS

Without experience or official information, local current prediction is always risky. East of Badgers Island in Portsmouth, Maine, for example, the average ebb current flows at a maximum velocity of less than a half-knot. Yet, southwest of the same island, it averages 3.7 knots.

One rule is fairly safe for most locations—the ebb is stronger and lasts longer than the flood. Eighty percent of all reference stations on the Atlantic, Gulf, and Pacific coasts of the U.S. report currents stronger at the ebb. This is normal because river flow adds to the ebb, but hinders the flood.

On the Atlantic coast, expect to find two approximately equal flood currents and two similar ebb currents in a cycle of roughly 25 hours. On the Pacific coast, however, two floods and ebbs will differ markedly. On the Gulf coast, there may be just one flood and one ebb in 25 hours. In each case, these patterns are, of course, generally similar to tidal action in the respective areas.

Don't try to predict current velocity from the time that it takes a high tide to reach a given point from the sea's entrance. Dividing the distance from Cape Henry to Baltimore by the time that it takes high water to work its way up Chesapeake Bay gives a speed of 13 knots. True maximum flood current strength is only about one knot.

Another useful truism about tidal currents is that tidal currents at different places *cannot* be forecast from their tidal ranges. You would expect strong currents at Eastport, Maine, where the difference between successive high and low waters reaches as much as 20 feet. And you would be right; there are three-knot currents there. But Galveston, Texas, with only a two-foot range of tides has currents up to more than two knots. So has Miami with a three-foot range, and Charleston, S. C. with a six-foot range—these are stronger currents than Boston where the range is often more than 10 feet and as strong as at Anchorage, Alaska where it's as much as 35 feet from some highs to the next low.

A good forecasting rule for all oceans: expect strong tidal currents where two bays meet. The reason: tidal ranges and high water times in the two bodies of water are likely to be different.

For the coasting skipper, here is another tidal current fact that may be useful: near the beach, flood and ebb don't usually set to and from the land, but rather parallel with the coast. This is as true off New Jersey and Florida as it is off California and Oregon. A few miles offshore, however, and in some very large bays, the current behaves quite differently—the rotary current mentioned previously in this chapter.

TIDAL CURRENT TABLES

At any given place, current strength varies with the phases of the moon and its distance from the earth. It will be strongest when tidal ranges are greatest—near new and

FIG. 2022 Table 3—Velocity of Current at Any Time. Using the appropriate part, A or B, of this table, the velocity of current at intermediate times between maximum strength and slack may be calculated for either a reference or a subordinate station. Table B is for use at Cape Cod Canal, Hell Gate, or Chesapeake and Delaware Canal <u>only</u>; use Table A for all other locations.

DURATION OF WEAK CURRENT NEAR TIME OF SLACK WATER

Table A

Maximum current	Period with a velocity not more than—				
	0.1 knot	0.2 knot	0.3 knot	0.4 knot	0.5 knot
Knots	Minutes	Minutes	Minutes	Minutes	Minutes
1.0	23	46	70	94	120
1.5	15	31	46	62	78
2.0	11	23	35	46	58
3.0	8	15	23	31	38
4.0	6	11	17	23	29
5.0	5	9	14	18	23
6.0	4	8	11	15	19
7.0	3	7	10	13	16
8.0	3	6	9	11	14
9.0	3	5	8	10	13
10.0	2	5	7	9	11

Table B

Maximum current	Period with a velocity not more than—				
	0.1 knot	0.2 knot	0.3 knot	0.4 knot	0.5 knot
Knots	Minutes	Minutes	Minutes	Minutes	Minutes
1.0	13	28	46	66	89
1.5	8	18	28	39	52
2.0	6	13	20	28	36
3.0	4	8	13	18	22
4.0	3	6	9	13	17
5.0	3	5	8	10	13

FIG. 2023 Table 4—Duration of Slack. Although actual slack water is only a momentary event, current velocity is quite small for a significant period while the direction is reversing. Part A or B of this table is used in the same situations as for Table 3.

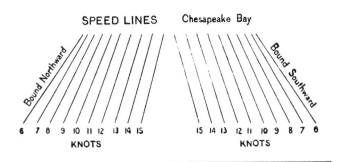

SPEED LINES   Chesapeake Bay

Bound Northward   Bound Southward

6 7 8 9 10 11 12 13 14 15   15 14 13 12 11 10 9 8 7 6
KNOTS   KNOTS

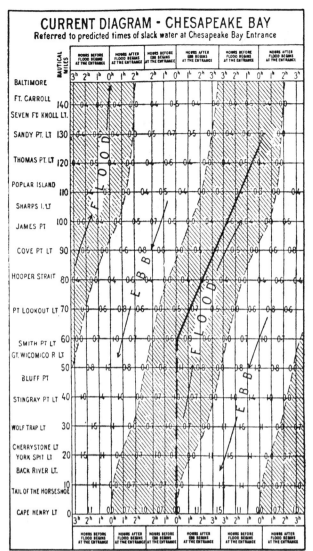

CURRENT DIAGRAM · CHESAPEAKE BAY
Referred to predicted times of slack water at Chesapeake Bay Entrance

FIG. 2024 Current Diagrams from the Tidal Current Tables (East Coast volume only) provide a quick and simple way of determining the best speed and time of departure for a run up or down several of the major waterways subject to tidal currents.

full moon—and weakest when tidal ranges are least—near first and last quarters. Current velocity may vary as much as 40 percent above and below its average value.

The relationship between currents and tides makes possible the prediction of tidal currents. The National Ocean Survey publishes two volumes of predictions annually; one covers the Atlantic Coast of North America and the other the Pacific Coast of North America and Asia.

Each volume includes for its area, predictions of tidal currents in bays, sounds, and rivers, plus ocean currents such as the Gulf Stream. General information on wind-driven currents is also included although these, of course, result from temporary, local conditions and so cannot be predicted a year or more ahead. Your own past experience and "local knowledge," the advice of experienced watermen of the area, will be the best source of information regarding the effect of storm winds on local waters and their currents.

Tidal Current Tables are available at authorized sales agents for N.O.S. charts. Each volume is $3.75.

Description of the Tables

The format and layout of the *Tidal Current Tables* is much the same as for the *Tide Tables* discussed earlier in this chapter. A system of reference stations, plus constants and differences for subordinate stations, is used to calculate the predictions for many points.

Table 1. There are 20 *reference stations* in the Atlantic Coast volume and 10 for the Pacific Coast. The Gulf of Mexico is included in the Atlantic Coast volume. For each station, there are tabulated the predicted times and strengths of maximum flood and ebb currents, plus the times of slack water. The direction of the flood and ebb currents is also listed, see fig. 2020.

Table 2. Time differences and velocity ratios are listed for hundreds of *subordinate stations*, fig. 2021. The location of these stations is described in terms of place names or position relative to identifiable points; the latitude and longitude are also given as an aid to their precise location. The direction and strength of typical maximum currents for each station are also tabulated. A number of subordinate stations will have only the footnoted entry "Current too weak and variable to be predicted." This information, even though negative in nature, is useful in planning a cruise.

Table 3. This table, fig. 2022, provides a convenient means for determination of the strength of the current at times intermediate between slack and maximum velocity. Use nearest tabulated values without interpolation.

Table 4. Although slack water is only a momentary event, there is a period of time on either side of slack during which the current is so weak as to be negligible for practical piloting purposes. This period, naturally, varies with the maximum strength of the current, being longer for weak currents. Two sub-tables, fig. 2023, predict the duration of currents from 0.1 to 0.5 knot by tenths for normal reversing currents and for the hydraulic currents found at certain specified locations.

Table 5. For the Atlantic Coast only, information is given on rotary tidal currents at various offshore points of navigational interest. These points are described in terms of general location and specific geographic coordinates. Predictions of velocity and direction are referred to times after maximum flood at designated reference stations.

The inside back cover of the Tidal Current Tables has the same astronomical data as is found in the Tide Tables; see page 399.

Current Diagrams

For a number of major tidal waterways of the United States, a *current diagram,* such as fig. 2024, is provided in the Tidal Current Tables. These give a graphic means of quickly and easily selecting a favorable time for traveling in either direction along these routes.

Time

The Tidal Current Tables list all predictions in *local standard time*. Be sure to make a conversion to daylight time if you are piloting in an area using such "fast" time; this is done by adding one hour to the tabulated times.

Cautions

As with tidal predictions, the data in the Tidal Current Tables may often be upset by sustained abnormal local conditions such as winds or rainfall. Use the current predictions with caution during and immediately after such weather abnormalities.

It should also be noted carefully that tidal current predictions are generally for a *spot location only;* the set and drift may be quite different only a mile or less away. This is at variance from predictions of high and low tides which can usually be used over fairly wide areas in the vicinity of the reference or secondary station.

EXAMPLES OF TIDAL CURRENT CALCULATIONS

The Tidal Current Tables contain all the information needed for the determination of such conditions as the time of maximum current and its strength, the time of slack water, the duration of slack (actually, the duration of the very weak current conditions), etc. Examples will be given of typical problems and their solution, plus comments and cautions to be used in connection with such situations.

Example 1. Determination of the time and strength of maximum current, and the time of slack, at a reference station.

Problem: What is the time and strength of the maximum ebb current at Chesapeake Bay Entrance during the afternoon of 16 October 1977?

Solution: As with the Tide Tables, the answer is available for a reference station by direct inspection. Fig. 2020 is a typical page from the Tidal Current Tables; we can see that the maximum ebb current on the specified afternoon is 1.6 knots setting 125° True; it is predicted to occur at 1745 EST.

Problem: What is the time of the first slack before ebb at this station on 21 October 1977?

Solution: Table 1 does not directly identify the slacks as being "slack before ebb" or "slack before flood"; this must be determined by comparison of the slack time with the nature of the next occurring maximum current.

From fig. 2020, we can see that the earliest slack that will be followed by an ebbing current at Chesapeake Bay Entrance on 21 October is predicted for 0632 EST.

Notes: a. Times obtained from the Tidal Current Tables are *standard*; add one hour for daylight time if in effect.

b. The set of the current for a reference station is found at the *top* of the page in Table 1; it is also given in Table 2 where further information, such as the geographic coordinates of the station, and the average velocity of maximum flood and ebb currents, is listed.

c. The normal day at Chesapeake Bay Entrance, where the tide is of the semi-diurnal type, will have four slacks

and four maximums. The tidal cycle of 24^h and 50^m will result in the occasional omission of a slack or maximum.

Example 2. Determination of the time and strength of maximum current, and the time of slack, at a subordinate station.

Problem: What is the time and strength of the morning flood current in Lynnhaven Inlet at the bridge on 17 September 1977?

Solution: Table 2, fig. 2021, gives time differences and velocity ratios to be applied to the predictions at the appropriate reference station. There is an Index to Table 2 in the rear of the Tidal Current Tables if it is needed to locate the given subordinate station.

In this problem, the time difference and velocity ratio are applied as follows:

11 22	at Chesapeake Bay Entrance	1.3 knot
−2:35	Difference/ratio	0.6
08 47	at Lynnhaven Inlet	0.8 knot

The set (direction) of the current is also noted from the appropriate column of Table 2; in this case, it is 180° True.

Thus the predictions are for a maximum current of 0.8 knot setting 180° True at Lynnhaven Inlet bridge at 0847 EST on 17 September 1977.

Problem: What is the time of the first afternoon slack water at Lynnhaven Inlet bridge on 6 September 1977?

Solution: From Table 2, the time difference is found to be −2:05. This is applied to the time of slack at the reference station:

18 19	at Chesapeake Bay Entrance
−2:05	difference
16 14	at Lynnhaven Inlet bridge

The time of the first afternoon slack water at Lynnhaven Inlet bridge on 6 September 1977 is 1614 EST.

Notes: a. Observe that often there may be two separate time differences, one for slack and the other for maximum current, either flood or ebb. More complex situations with varied time differences will be shown by special footnotes to Table 2 where required. Note also that the velocity ratios may differ between ebb and flood.

b. Note that the direction of the current at a subordinate station must be taken from Table 2. It will nearly always differ from that at the reference station. No statement of current is complete without giving direction as well as strength.

c. The locations in Table 2 are usually a point some distance and direction from a landmark or aid to navigation. There may be several subordinate stations referred to the same base point (see subordinate stations 3120-3145 and 3185-3205 in fig. 2021); be sure to use the correct subordinate station.

Example 3. Determination of the current at an intermediate time at a reference station.

Problem: What is the velocity and set of the current at Chesapeake Bay entrance at 1620 EST on 1 October 1977?

Solution: The time of slack and maximum current (ebb or flood) which bracket the desired time are found from Table 1. The interval between these times is determined, as is the interval between the desired time and the slack.

```
17 44
14 06
 3:38  interval, slack—maximum  current

16 20
14 06
 2:14   interval, slack—desired time
```

With these time intervals, Table 3A is used to determine the ratio of the velocity of the current at the desired time to its maximum velocity. The nearest tabulated values are used, no interpolation. In this example, the ratio at the intersection of the line for $2^h 20^m$ and the column for $3^h 40^m$ is found to be 0.8. Multiply the maximum current by this decimal factor, $1.2 \times 0.8 = 1.0$.

From the times used, we note that the current is ebbing. From the top of Table 1, we determine that the direction is 125° True.

Thus at 1620 EST on 1 October 1977, the current at Chesapeake Bay Entrance is predicted to have a velocity of 1.0 knots and be setting 125° True.

Notes: a. Except as specially indicated, use Table 3A, the upper portion of Table 3. The lower, B, portion is for use in designated waterways only.

b. Be sure that the interval is calculated between the desired time and the time of *slack,* whether or not this time is nearer to the given time than the time of maximum current.

c. Note that calculations of current velocity are rounded to the nearest tenth of a knot.

Example 4.   Determination of the current at an intermediate time at a subordinate station.

Problem: What is the velocity and set of the current at a point 5½ miles east of Stingray Point at 0535 EDT on 16 October 1977?

Solution: First, the predictions for slack and maximum current must be found for the subordinate station after converting 0535 EDT to 0435 EST for entering the Tables.

Slack		Maximum	
01 07	at Chesapeake Bay		
	Entrance	04 56	1.8 knots, Ebb
+1:50	difference/ratio	+2:20	0.6
02 57	at subordinate station	07 16	1.1

With the information developed above, and the desired time, further calculations are made as follows:

```
07 16
02 57
 4:19   interval, slack—maximum current
04 35   (EST)
02 57
 1:38   interval, slack—desired time.
```

Using Table 3A, fig. 2022, the velocity ratio is found to be 0.6; then $1.1 \times 0.6 = 0.7$. From Table 2, the direction is seen to be 180° True.

The current at 0535 EDT at a point 5½ miles east of Stingray Point on 16 October 1977 is predicted to be 0.7 knot setting 180° True

Note: Calculations for the strength at an intermediate time of a hydraulic current, such as in the Cape Cod Canal or at Hell Gate in East River, New York City, are handled exactly as above, except that the lower, B, part of Table 3 is used.

Example 5.   Determination of the duration of slack (weak current) at a designated point.

Problem: For how long will the current be less than 0.4 knots around the time of slack before ebb on the evening of 22 October 1977 at Chesapeake Bay Entrance?

Solution: From Table 1 (fig. 2020), for this date, the maximum currents on either side of this slack (at 2032) are 1.0 knots flood at 1736 and 1.5 knots ebb at 2359.

Using Table 4A (fig. 2023), the duration of current less than 0.4 knot is determined for each maximum. One-half of each such duration is used for the period from 0.4 to 0 knots and then 0 to 0.4 knots.

The value for the ending flood current is one-half of 94, or 47 minutes; for the beginning ebb current, it is one-half of 62, or 31 minutes.

On 22 October 1977 at Chesapeake Bay Entrance, the predicted duration of a current less than 0.4 knots is $47 + 31 = 78$ minutes; from $2032 - 47 = 1945$ until $2032 + 31 = 2103$. Notes: a. If maximum strengths of the ebb and flood currents are essentially the same, only one figure need be taken from Table 4. Interpolate as necessary.

b. Use the A or B portion of Table 4 in the same manner as for Table 3.

Example 6.   Use of a Current Diagram

Problem: For an afternoon run up Chesapeake Bay from Smith Point to Sandy Point Light at 10 knots on 16 October 1977, what time should you depart from Smith Point for the most favorable current conditions?

Solution: We use the current diagram for Chesapeake Bay and a graphic solution, fig. 2024. Draw a line on the diagram parallel to the 10-knot northbound speed line so that it fits generally in the center of the shaded area marked "Flood." Project downward from the intersection of this line with the horizontal line marked Smith Point Light to the scale at the bottom of the diagram. The mark here will be seen to be "0^h after ebb begins at the entrance."

Referring to Table 1, it will be seen that on the given date, the afternoon slack before ebb occurs at 1419.

For a run up Chesapeake Bay to Sandy Point Light at 10 knots on the afternoon of 16 October 1977, it is predicted that the most favorable current conditions will be obtained if you leave Smith Point Light at about 1419 EST or 1519 EDT.

Notes: a. Similar solutions can be worked out for southbound trips, but it is likely that on longer runs you will be faced with both favorable and unfavorable current conditions. Selection of starting time may be made, however, to minimize adverse conditions.

b. Conditions shown on Tidal Current Diagrams are averages and for typical conditions; small variations should be expected in specific situations.

TIDAL CURRENT CHARTS

The National Ocean Survey also publishes a series of *Tidal Current Charts.* These are available for 13 bodies of water, from Boston Harbor around to Puget Sound (see complete listing on page 329).

THREE HOURS AFTER "SLACK, FLOOD BEGINS" AT THE RACE

FIG. 2025 Tidal Current Charts are published for certain major bodies of water. Each is a set of 12 small-scale chartlets showing currents existing at hourly intervals throughout a complete cycle of flood and ebb.

Tidal Current Charts are made up in the form of a series of 12 reproductions of a small-scale chart of the area. Each of the charts depicts the direction and velocity of the current for a specific time in terms of hours after the predicted time of the beginning of flood or the beginning of ebb at the appropriate reference station.* See fig. 2025. The currents in various passages and portions of the body of water are indicated by arrows and numbers. By following through the sequence of the charts, the hourly changes in strength and direction are easily seen.

These charts must be used with caution as tidal current strengths may vary widely between points separated by only a short distance.

Tidal Current Charts are updated when required by new surveys; only the latest edition should be used.

TIDAL CURRENT DIAGRAMS

A development of the "computer age," *Tidal Current Diagrams* are a series of 12 monthly graphs to be used with Tidal Current Charts instead of the Tidal Current Tables. The diagram method is more convenient as the graphs indicate directly, from the date and time, the chart to be used

and the speed correction factor to be applied.

Tidal Current Diagrams are available only for use with the Tidal Current Charts of Boston Harbor and of Block Island Sound and Eastern Long Island Sound. A new set of diagrams is required each year; the price is $4.

RIVER CURRENTS

River currents, above tidal action, will consistently flow in one direction, but the velocity may vary widely. For further information on river currents and river piloting, see Chapter 27.

SUPPLEMENTARY SOURCES OF INFORMATION

The ultimate source of current information is your own eyesight and past experience, fig. 2026. These are most helpful even where there are predictions from the N.O.S. tables. As noted before, the tabular data are to be expected under "normal" conditions, and may be easily upset by unusual circumstances. Strong winds will, for example, drive water into or out of bays and modify tidal levels and currents.

* Tidal Current Charts for Narragansett Bay and New York Harbor are used with Tide Tables rather than Tidal Current Tables.

0.3 KNOT

1.0 KNOT

These photographs by Larry Riordan show clearly how buoys can be a helpful aid in estimating the direction and strength of current. Even though some data are available in Current Tables, predictions may be in error because of wind. Turbulence and eddies around a buoy increase with current velocity. In very strong currents, buoys may tow completely under. Note (top left) how at 0.3 knot a wake is evident and the buoy inclines slightly. Doubling the velocity (0.6 knot, at left) increases the disturbance on both sides of the buoy. At 1.0 knot (top right) it leans over and a whirlpool-like eddy has developed. Finally, at 2.2 knots (bottom right), the wake has whitened. Buoy shapes affect the pattern and inclination. (1 knot = 1.85 km/h)

0.6 KNOT

2.2 KNOTS

FIG. 2026 Tidal current predictions are often upset by temporary local conditions of wind or rainfall. There is no substitute for an ability to interpret currents from visual observations. This excellent set of photographs shows visible indications on a buoy of currents of various strengths. Be careful; do not overestimate current velocity.

Currents and Piloting

One of the most interesting problems in small-craft piloting is the matter of currents, their effect upon boat speed, the determination of courses which must be steered to make good a desired path, and the time required to reach a destination. This is often know as *current sailing.*

Contrary to popular belief, the solution of current problems is really comparatively simple and does not require the use of higher mathematics to obtain results of practical accuracy. Indeed, when the fundamental principles have been mastered, the working out of current problems can be fun.

As a boat is propelled through the water, by oars, sails, or motor, and as it is steered, it moves with respect to the water. At the same time, the water may be moving with respect to the bottom and the shore as a result of current. The resultant motion of the boat is the net effect of these two motions combined, with regard to both velocity and direction. The actual track made good over the bottom will not be the same as the DR track, neither in terms of course nor speed.

The importance of tidal currents should not be underestimated. Unexpected current is always a threat to the skipper because it can carry his craft off course, possibly into dangerous waters. The risk is greater with slower boat speeds and under conditions of reduced visibility. A prediction of current effect can be added to a plot of a DR

track to obtain an *estimated position (EP)* plotted as a small square with a dot in the center, fig. 2027.

Leeway

Before proceeding further with current effects, let us here introduce, and then dispense with, the term *leeway.* By definition, leeway is the leeward (away from the wind)

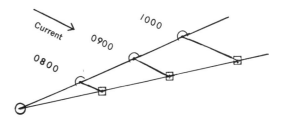

FIG. 2027 If the current is known, or can be estimated, a DR plot (half-circles) can be modified to show a series of Estimated Positions (squares) showing the effect of current.

motion of a vessel due to the wind. The term is most applicable to sailing craft, but it can be appreciable on larger motorboats and yachts. Its effect, however, need not be considered separately from current; the two may be lumped together, plus such factors as wave action on the boat, and the total offsetting influence termed "current."

411

Sailing Directions emphasize the necessity of taking such influences into account. A typical caution might read: "The directions 'steer' or 'make good' a course mean, without exception, to proceed from a point of origin along a track having the identical meridional angle as the designated course. Vessels following the directives must allow for every influence tending to cause deviation (not to be confused with compass deviation—Ed) from such track, and navigate so that the designated course is continuously being made good."

DEFINITION OF CURRENT SAILING TERMS

The terms "Course" and "Speed" were used in DR plots for the motion of the boat through the water without regard to current. Now this most important influence will be studied and additional terms must be introduced.

The *intended track* is the expected path of the boat, as plotted on a chart, after consideration has been given to the effect of current.

Track, abbreviated as TR, is the direction (true) of the intended track line.

Speed of advance, SOA, is the intended rate of travel along the intended track line.

It must be recognized that the intended track will not always be the actual track, and so two more terms are needed.

Course over the ground, COG, is the direction of the *actual* path of the boat, the track made good.

Speed over the ground, SOG, is the actual rate of travel along this track; sometimes termed "Speed made good."

CURRENT SITUATIONS

A study of the effects of current resolves itself into two basic situations, as follows:

1. When the direction of the current, its *set,* is in the same direction as the boat's motion, or is in exactly the opposite direction.

2. When the direction of the current is at an angle to the boat's course, either a right or an oblique angle.

The first situation is, of course, the simplest and most easily solved. The velocity of the current, the *drift,* is added to, or subtracted from, the speed through the water to obtain the speed over the ground. The course over the ground (or intended track) is the same as the DR course—COG equals C, as does TR.

CURRENT DIAGRAMS

When the boat's motion and the set of the current form an angle with each other, the solution for the resultant course and speed is more complex, but still not difficult. Several methods may be used, but a graphic solution using a *current diagram* will usually be found to be the easiest to understand.

Basically, a current diagram represents the two component motions separately, as if they occurred independently and sequentially, which, of course, they do not. These diagrams can be drawn in terms of velocities or distances. The former is easier and is usually used; current diagrams in this book will be drawn in terms of velocities and labeled as shown in fig. 2028. If distances are plotted, be sure to use the same period of time for each component motion—one hour is commonly used since the units of distance will then be the same numerically as the units of speed.

Accuracy of current diagrams

The accuracy with which the resultant course and speed can be determined depends largely on the accuracy with which the current has been determined. Values of the current usually must be taken from tidal current tables or charts, or estimated by the skipper from visual observations; see fig. 2026.

Current diagrams may also be called "vector triangles of velocity," a profound title for a simple graphic procedure. The term "vector" in mathematics means a quantity that has both magnitude and direction. Directed quantities are important things. In current sailing, the directed quantities are the motions of the boat and the water (the current).

Vectors

A vector may be represented graphically by an arrow, a segment of a straight line with an arrowhead indicating the direction, and the length of the line scaled to the velocity, fig. 2029. If we specify that a certain unit of length is equal to a certain unit of speed—e.g., that 1 inch equals 1 knot—then two such vectors can represent graphically two different velocities. Any speed scale may be used, the larger the better for accuracy. The size of the available paper and working space will normally control the scale.

Current diagrams may be drawn on a chart either as part of the plot or separately. They may also be drawn on plain paper; in this case, it is wise to draw in a north line as the

FIG. 2028 The component lines of a current diagram must always be correctly and completely labeled. Direction is shown above the line; velocity is noted below the line. Typical labels are shown above.

FIG. 2029 A vector is a line representing a *directed quantity*. It has direction (shown by the arrowhead) and magnitude (length). Any convenient scale may be selected to indicate magnitude.

reference for measuring directions.

Since boats are subject to two distinct motions—the boat through the water, and the water with respect to the bottom—we will now consider how the resultant motion, or vector sum, is obtained by current diagrams.

Vector triangles

When the two motions are not in line with each other, they form two sides of a triangle, fig. 2030. Completing the triangle gives the third side which will be a vector representing the resultant motion or velocity. Thus, when any two velocity vectors are drawn to the same scale and form the sides of a velocity triangle, the third side will be the resultant velocity vector (the vector sum of the other two), and its direction and magnitude may be measured from the diagram.

It may be an aid to the visualization of the component motions if a time period of one hour is used and the points that are the corners of the triangle are considered as positions of the boat before and after certain motions, as follows:

O—the origin.

DR—the DR position of the boat as a result solely of its motion through the water.

W—the position of the boat solely as a result of the motion of the water.

P—the position (intended or actual) of the boat as a result of the combined action of the component motions.

(It should be noted that, in some cases, two of the above letters are applicable to a position; it is customary to use only one.)

"Tail-to-head" relationship. Note very carefully how the vectors for boat motion through the water and the current are drawn. These vectors are always drawn "tail-to-head," *not* so that both are directed out from the same source. (This rule applies only when one of the vectors is current; not when they both represent boat's motion.)

If both boat motion through the water and current are known, either may be drawn first from the origin; fig. 2031b will give the same resultant motion as fig. 2031a.

The four "Cases" of current problems

There are four typical current problems, different combinations of known and unknown factors. For convenience, we will call them Case 1, 2, etc.

CASE 1—Known: Boat's course (C) and speed (S) through the water; current set and drift.
    To be determined: The course and speed over the ground (COG and SOG).
    This is the determination of the effect of a known current if no allowance is made for its effect.

CASE 2—Known: Boat's course (C) and speed (S) through **the water; the course (COG) and speed over the ground (SOG).**
    To be determined: The set and drift of the current.
    This is the determination of the nature of an unknown current from observation of its effect.

CASE 3—Known: Boat's speed through the water (S), the set and drift of the current, and the intended track (TR).
    To be determined: The course to be steered (C) and the speed of advance (SOA) along the intended track.
    This is the determination of corrected course to be steered, but without regard for the effect on speed or ETA.

CASE 4—Known: The set and drift of the current, the intended track (TR), and the speed of advance desired (SOA).
    To be determined: The course to be steered (C) and speed to be run through the water (S).
    This is the "rendezvous" or "contest" case where the destination and the time of arrival are specified.

(a)

(b)

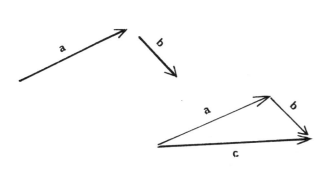

FIG. 2030 Vectors may be combined graphically to determine the vector sum. Typically, vectors *a* and *b* above, representing component motions, are combined as vector *c*, the resultant motion of the two components.

FIG. 2031 The two vector triangles shown above appear to be different because in one vector *a* was drawn before vector *b*, and in the other, *b* was drawn before *a*. The resultant vector, *c*, however, is exactly the same for either procedure.

FIG. 2032 If a boat is traveling through the water on a course of 070°, and the current is setting in the direction 130°, it is obvious that the craft will be set off course to starboard. The question of how much, and the effect on speed over the bottom, is what must be determined. A current diagram will provide the answers.

Illustrative examples

Let us first consider **Case 1**—the effect of current on a boat's course and speed. If the set of the current is as shown in fig. 2032, then the boat will be set off to the right of the direction in which it is being steered. We will use a current diagram to determine the exact extent of this effect, the path the boat can be expected to follow and its speed (the intended track and speed of advance).

We first draw in a north line as a reference for measuring directions, fig. 2033a, and then the vector for the boat's speed through the water, O-DR, a line drawn from the origin in the direction 070° for a length of 10 units, fig. 2033b. Next we add the vector for current, DR-W, three units in the direction 130°, fig. 2033c. Note that we have remembered to observe the "tail-to-head" relationship rule. (Either of these two vectors could have been drawn first; the triangle would appear differently, but the result will be the same.) Because these vectors form two sides of a triangle of velocities, the third side O-W, fig. 2033d, is the resultant velocity at which the boat moves with respect to the bottom under the combined influences of its propulsion and the current. The point W can now be relabeled "P." The intended (or expected) track (TR) and the speed of advance (SOA) can be measured from the O-P line. In this example, it turns out that the boat can be expected to sail a course over the ground of 083° and to have a speed of advance of 11.8 knots. Note that the directions of these vectors are always plotted as *true* directions.

Summarizing briefly, we have drawn vectors to indicate independently the motion of the boat from two different influences, its own propulsion and the current. Actually, of course, the boat will *not* go first from O to DR and then on to P. All the time, it will travel directly along the intended track O-P. The boat is steered on course C, the direction of O-DR, but, due to the effect of current, it is expected to travel along the intended track O-P. This is the route that must be considered for shoals and other hazards to navigation.

Cruising men can never afford to ignore the effect of current. Down East, for example, in Maine waters big tidal ranges often cause baffling current conditions, compounded by unusual influences of headlands and river currents. Fog in such areas places a special premium on piloting skill.

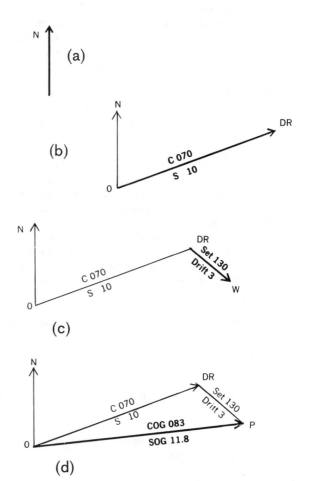

FIG. 2033 Current Diagram — CASE 1. These diagrams illustrate the step-by-step graphical solution: (a) the reference North line; (b) the vector for boat's motion through the water; (c) the vector for current, the motion of the water with respect to the bottom; and finally (d) the vector for the resultant motion of the boat with respect to the bottom.

FIG. 2034 Current Diagram — CASE 2. The prevailing current (actually the net effect of all offsetting influences) can be found graphically from a vector triangle of velocities.

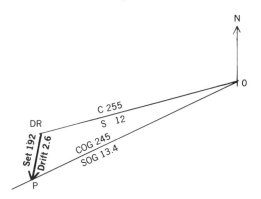

Now for a **Case 2** situation in which you know the course you have steered and the speed through the water from either the speed curve of your boat or a marine speedometer. It is also obvious to you that you did not arrive at your DR position. From your chart plot, you have been able to determine the course and speed over the ground. Current has acted to set you off your course—you desire to know its set and drift.

After again drawing a north reference line, plot vectors for your motion through the water—C 255°, S 12 knots; and your motion with respect to the bottom—COG 245°, SOG 13.4 knots. See fig. 2034. These vectors are both drawn outward from the origin, O, to points DR and P respectively. The "tail-to-head" rule is not applicable as neither of these vectors represents current. The action of the current has been to offset your boat from DR to P (which is also point W in this case), thus the set is the direction *from* DR *toward* P, and the drift is the length of this line in scale units.

In fig. 2034, the current is found to be setting 192° with a drift of 2.6 knots. This is the *average* current for the time period and location of the run from O to P for which the calculations were made; it is not the current at P. For the next leg of your cruise, these current values can be used as is, or modified as required by the passage of time and/or the continuing change in position of the boat.

Case 3 is a typical cruising situation—here, you know the track you desire to make good (TR 080°), you have decided to run at your normal cruising speed through the water (S 10 knots), and you have calculated (or estimated) the current's set (140°) and drift (4 knots). What you desire to know is the course to be steered (C) and the speed of advance (SOA) which can be used to figure your estimated time of arrival (ETA).

Draw in a north line and measure directions from it, fig. 2035a. Plot the current vector, O-W, at the specified direction and length, and a line (not a vector yet) in the direction of the intended track—this line should be of indefinite length at this time. From point W, swing an arc, with dividers or drawing compass, equal in length to the speed through the water in scale units. The point at which this arc intersects the intended track line is point P and the vector triangle has been completed. The direction of W-P is the course to be steered (C 060°); the length of the vector O-P is the speed over the ground (SOG 11.4) and from this the ETA can be calculated.

Let us look at the reasoning behind this graphic solution of Case 3. Again considering the component motions separately for the sake of simplicity, the boat is moved by current from O to W. It is to move from W at the specified speed through the water, but must get back on the intended track line; the problem is to find the point P on the track which is "S" units from point W. The solution is found by swinging an arc as described above.

Remember that all vectors are plotted as *true* directions, including C, the course to be steered in the preceding solution. This must be changed to a compass direction (course) for actual use at the helm.

In accordance with the principles of dead reckoning, it is desirable to plot the DR track even though a current is known to exist. This line, drawn from point O in the direction C and with a length of S scale units, forms a basis for consideration of possible hazards if the current is not as calculated or estimated, fig. 2035b.

FIG. 2035 Current Diagram — CASE 3. If you know your desired track, and have decided upon your speed through the water, a graphical solution (a) can be used to determine the course to be steered and the speed of advance. For safety's sake, a DR plot from the origin should be added as in (b).

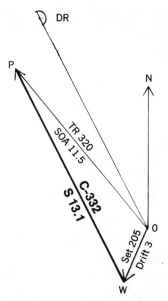

FIG. 2036 Current Diagram—CASE 4. This problem concerns the course to be steered and the speed at which to run in order to arrive at a specified destination at a predetermined time. This could be useful in a predicted log contest or in rendezvousing with another boat.

A **Case 4** situation is an interesting variation of Case 3—you desire to arrive at a specified point at a given time. It may be that you are competing in a predicted log contest, or merely that you have agreed to meet friends at that time and place. In addition to the data on current that you have, you have decided upon your track and your speed of advance. For fig. 2036, let us assume that the current sets 205° at 3 knots. You need to make good a track of 320°, and a quick distance-time-speed calculation sets your required speed of advance at 11.5 knots.

From the north reference line, draw the current vector O-W and the intended track vector O-P. Complete the triangle with the vector W-P which will give you the course to be steered (C 332 True) and the speed to run through the water (S 13.1) to arrive at the destination at the desired time. Line O-DR should be drawn in from the origin as a dead reckoning track for the sake of safety.

Solutions of Cases 1, 2, 3, and 4 by use of a calculator, rather than graphic plots, are shown on pages 441–447.

These tables should not be used without a clear understanding of the fundamentals of current sailing, the component motions and their relationships to each other. These fundamentals, and the terms and symbols used, should be learned from simple graphic solutions as presented above.

FIG. 2037 Ability to estimate the set and drift of currents on a proposed course is of paramount importance to contestants in a predicted log race, where accuracy of the highest order is required to win.

CHAPTER 21
PILOTING—Position Determination

The art of piloting reaches its climax in *position determination*. Underway on a body of water of any size, where the safety of your boat and its crew is at stake, it's not "where you ought to be," or "where you think you are," but your knowledge of "where you are for sure" that counts. The development of an ability to determine your position quickly and accurately under a wide range of conditions should be one of your primary goals as a skipper.

The need for position determination

In three of the current sailing situations covered in the preceding chapter, the set and drift of the current were taken as known values. In everyday cruising, it is more than likely that the strength and direction of the actual current will be somewhat different from that calculated or estimated. Local wind conditions or abnormal rainfall will frequently upset tabular predictions; estimates based on visual observations of current will often be inaccurate unless the boatman has had considerable experience. Because of these uncertainties, current sailing solutions can be considered only as *estimates* of present positions and of future motions and positions.

Buoy positions are usually reliable; the Coast Guard expends much effort in keeping them on station and operating properly. They are, however, not infallible, and the position of a boat should be determined by other means as often as practicable.

Accurate position determination whenever the opportunity presents itself is essential in order that the safety of the craft can be verified, or corrective action taken promptly. By so doing, the true effects of the current may also become known. Further, such fixing of position makes possible the start of a new DR plot, fresher and more accurate than the old one.

Frequent position determination is an essential safety precaution. No matter how safe your boat is, no matter how experienced you are in boating, no matter how good the weather nor how calm the seas, emergencies can arise, and suddenly, too. Knowledge of where you are, extended from a *recent* position determination, can be of the greatest value when you must call for help. Or, if it is another boat that has trouble, you can set the most direct course to render assistance if you are sure of where you are.

THE SKIPPER'S RESPONSIBILITIES

It is the duty of a skipper to fix the position of his craft with such degree of precision and at such frequent intervals as is required by the proximity to hazards to safe navigation. This is an absolute requirement of the person in charge of the vessel, whether he is personally doing the piloting or this is being done by another person. He can assign the function, but he cannot delegate his responsibility.

The actual procedures in position determination will vary widely in practice. Proceeding down a narrow channel, positioning will be informal and a chart plot will not be maintained. But this does not mean that position de-

St. Petersburg Times Photo by Dan Hightower

FIG. 2101 The skipper of any boat is responsible for the safety of it and of all persons on board. He must be able to determine his position accurately, and do so as often as required by prevailing conditions.

termination is being omitted; indeed, it is being done essentially continuously by visual reference to the aids to navigation. On the other hand, during an open ocean passage, a plot will be maintained, but positions will be determined, other than by DR calculations, perhaps only three or four times each day.

Between the extremes cited above, there will be found the normal cruising situations in pilot waters. Cruising just offshore, or in the larger inland bodies of water, a skipper will usually maintain a plot of his track with periodic checks on its accuracy, perhaps every 15 or 20 minutes, perhaps at hourly intervals.

The ability to determine the position of his craft to an acceptable degree of accuracy under any condition of visibility is essential to safe boating. The absence of this ability, or any limitation on it, should restrict the extent of a person's boating activities, setting the boundaries of the water areas and weather conditions into which he will enter.

DEFINITION OF TERMS

A *line of position* (LOP) is a line, in actuality or drawn on a chart, at some point along which an observer is presumed to be located, fig. 2102. A LOP may result from observation or measurement; from visual, electronic, or celestial sources. It may be straight or curved; a circular LOP is sometimes referred to as a *circle of position*, fig.

2103. A line of position may be *advanced* (moved forward) or *retired* (moved backward) in time according to the movement of the vessel during the time interval involved. In piloting, the more usual situation will be the advancement of a previously taken LOP to the time of another LOP just taken.

A *bearing* is the direction of an object from the observer, expressed in degrees as a three-digit number—005°

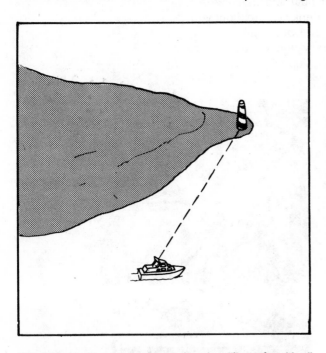

FIG. 2102 Position determination is based on "lines of position." These are lines, in actuality or on a chart, along which the observer is presumed to be located. A single line will not determine position, but it does tell the observer where he is *not* located, and such information is often useful.

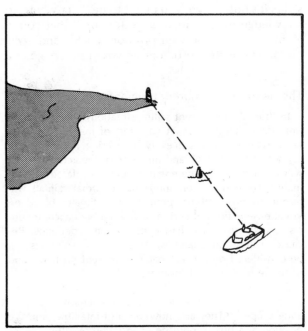

FIG. 2104 When two objects can be observed in line, an excellent line of position is established. Such "ranges" may have been set up with specific aids to navigation, or they may be any two identifiable objects such as ordinary navigational aids, landmarks, or natural or man-made features.

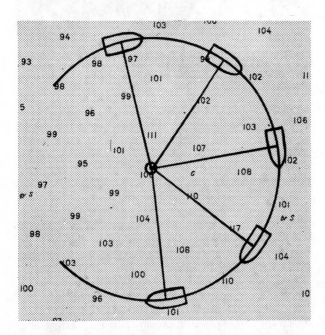

FIG. 2103 Lines of position may be curved as well as straight. A measurement of distance from an identified object yields a circular LOP. It may be plotted as a complete circle or as only a partial arc.

FIG. 2105 A "fix" is an accurately determined position for the observer and his craft. It is not based on any prior position, but is determined from currently observed lines of position or other data.

062°, 157°, etc. A *true bearing* is a bearing measured with reference to the true north direction as 000°. *Magnetic* and *compass bearings* are, respectively, observations with reference to the local magnetic north direction or to the craft's steering compass as it is affected by deviation at that moment. A *relative bearing* is a bearing measured with reference to the ship's heading—it is measured clockwise from the fore-and-aft line with 000° being dead ahead,

090° broad on the starboard beam, 180° dead astern, etc. (An older method of measuring relative bearings 180° to port or starboard is seldom used any more; it made calculations more complicated than necessary.)

A *range* consists of two objects that can be observed in line with each other and the observer, fig. 2104.

A *fix* is an accurately located position determined without reference to any prior position, fig. 2105. A *running fix* is a position that has been determined from LOPs at least one of which has been taken at a different time and advanced or retarded to the time of the other observation.

An *estimated position (EP)* is the best position obtainable short of a fix or good-quality running fix. It is the most probable position, determined from incomplete data, or from data of questionable accuracy.

FIG. 2106 The correct labeling of lines of position is most important; unlabeled lines on a chart can only be a source of confusion. The time is always shown above the line (in 24-hour clock system) and direction below the line as a three-digit number without the "o" symbol.

Lines of Position

Lines of position are the basic elements of position determination. By definition, the observer, and his craft, are located somewhere along a LOP. If two LOPs intersect, the only position at which the vessel can be, and be on both lines, is their intersection. Thus, the usual fix is determined by the crossing of two lines of position.

Labeling

Since LOPs are also lines that are drawn on a chart, it is essential that they be labeled immediately, and that such labels conform to a standardized system. A label should contain all information necessary for identification, but nothing further that might cause confusion or clutter up the chart. The information to be recorded for each line of position is the time that it was observed or measured and its basic dimension, such as direction toward, or distance from, the object used.

A bearing is a LOP that has time and direction. Fig. 2106 shows several examples of correctly labeled bearings. Time is always shown *above* the line of the bearing, and direction *below* the line. Time is given as a four-digit figure in the 24-hour system. Directions may be True ("T") or Magnetic ("M") and are written as a three-digit group with zeros prefixed as necessary.

A circle of position has dimensions of time and distance; it may be plotted as a complete circle, fig. 2107a, or merely as a partial circle, an arc, as in fig. 2107b. Time is labeled above the curved line and distance, with units, is shown below the line.

A range is a line of position whose direction is self-evident from the two points which define it. In this case, only time need be shown; it is placed above the line as for other LOPs; see fig. 2108.

Do not draw the line completely through the chart symbols for the two objects used as the range; this will avoid the necessity for subsequent erasure across the symbols. Draw the line neatly and no longer than necessary; it need not extend all the way to the front range marker or other object if the two features used to form the range are clearly evident.

A line of position that has been advanced (or retired) in time is labeled with *both* times above the line, the time of original observation or measurement and the time to which it has been advanced (or retired). The time of the original LOP is written first, followed by a dash and then

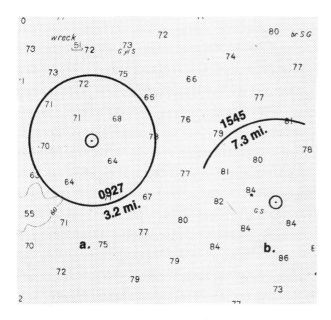

FIG. 2107 Circles of position are labeled in the same general manner as straight lines of position. The time is placed above the line and the distance below, as it would normally be viewed and read. Thus, the time may be "inside" or "outside" the circle as determined by the curvature of the arc.

FIG. 2108 Since a range is based on the relationship between the two sighted objects, it is often used without a measurement of its actual direction. Ranges need be labeled only with the time of the observation.

FIG. 2110 A simple, but excellent, determination of position occurs when a boat passes close alongside an aid to navigation or other identifiable point. A good pilot always notes the time of such an event on his chart.

the second time, fig. 2109.

Always label lines of position as soon as they are drawn. Unmarked lines on a chart can easily be a source of confusion. If labeling is put off until a later time, mistakes may be made.

FIXES

As previously defined, a fix is an accurately located position for a vessel. On many occasions in small-craft piloting, position will be established by passing close by an

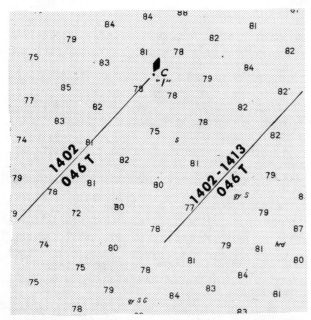

FIG. 2109 A line of position may be "advanced," that is, used at a later time than when it was observed if it is replotted to account for the movement of the boat since the time of observation. An advanced LOP is labeled with the original time and the time for which it is replotted. The direction, of course, remains the same.

identifiable object, usually an aid to navigation. This is, of course, a fix of the highest possible accuracy, and a skipper should always note the time of such an event on his chart plot, fig. 2110.

Fix from two LOPs

The typical fix obtained from lines of position will be the intersection of two such lines. It is important to consider the effect of the angle of intersection between the two LOPs on the accuracy of the position determination. Let us look first at the situation where the two lines cross at right angles, 90°, fig. 2111a. If there should be an error of, say, 2° in one LOP, the resulting fix from this mistake would be off only a short distance.

Consider now fig. 2111b in which the intersection angle is only 30°. An error of 2° in one LOP would result in a considerably greater change in the location of the intersection.

Two lines of position should intersect as nearly as possible at right angles; the angle of intersection should never be less than 60° nor more than 120° if this can be avoided.

Where there is no alternative, a fix from two lines of position intersecting at angles of 30° to 60° (120° to 150°) can be used, but only with caution. A position from two LOPs intersecting at less than 30° (more than 150°) is of too dubious accuracy for safe navigation.

Areas of uncertainty. Lines of position will normally be stated as having a specific direction, such as 072°, 147°, etc. In actuality, there may be an uncertainty in each line of two or three, or even more, degrees. This condition can be shown graphically on the chart by additional lines drawn lightly on either side of the basic LOP; this should always be done if such uncertainty could mean the difference between a safe position and a hazardous one.

Lines of position from various sources and techniques will have different degrees of uncertainty. Only experience will give the pilot the ability to judge various methods and assign relative values of probable accuracy.

If two LOPs, each with its graphic representation of uncertainty, are drawn, the result is an *area of uncertainty* about the intersection of the lines of position; there is an element of doubt about the location of the fix. Figs. 2112a and b show how the angle of intersection alters this area of uncertainty and why it is desirable to have the LOPs cross as nearly as possible at 90°. Based on the mathematics of statistics and probability, the area of uncertainty is elliptical (circular if the LOPs cross at 90°) rather than the quadrilateral formed by the outside limiting lines for each bearing. In actual piloting, this distinction is more theoretical than practical. A detailed discussion of this topic, including the additional complexities that arise if one line of position can be considered to be more accu-

rate than the other, is beyond the scope of this book, but may be found in Bowditch.

More than two LOPs

Since most lines of position obtained in small-craft piloting (except possibly ranges) are reasonably, but certainly not exactly, accurate, it is highly desirable to use more than two LOPs to reduce the uncertainty of position. There is no theoretical upper limit to the number of lines of position that can be used, but practical considerations with a boat underway will normally limit the pilot to three LOPs.

Ideally, since the observer is presumed to be on all three lines of position, they will intersect in a common point, fig. 2113a. The much more likely result is that when the observations are plotted, the lines will form a triangle, fig. 2113b.

The use of three LOPs results in a modification of the previously stated rule about the desirable intersection angle of the lines. For optimum results, the three lines should each differ in direction as closely as possible to 60° (or 120°), fig. 2114. In this configuration, an inaccuracy in any of the LOPs will result in the minimum net error of position.

An alternative technique to the above is to obtain two

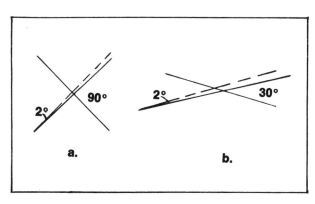

FIG. 2111 Lines of position taken from a small craft are seldom precisely accurate. Selection of an optimum angle of intersection between LOPs reduces the uncertainty of position. Shown here is the difference that a change of 2° in one LOP makes in the intersection point when the lines cross at 90° or at 30°.

FIG. 2112 When each of two LOPs may have an inaccuracy of several degrees, there is an *area of uncertainty* around the intersection point. This is least, a circle, when the angle of intersection is 90°. Angles of 60° to 90° are satisfactory; those of 30° to 60° may be used with caution.

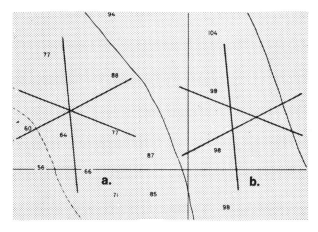

FIG. 2113 The use of more than two LOPs will enhance confidence in the resulting fix. Ideally, three lines of position will intersect at a common point, as in *a* above. More often in actual piloting, a triangle will be formed as shown in *b*. If the triangle is unreasonably large for the prevailing conditions, the observations should be checked or discarded.

FIG. 2114 For an optimum set of three observations, the lines of position should cross at 60° to each other. This will seldom be exactly possible in actual piloting situations, but should be kept in mind as fundamentally desirable.

lines of position at nearly 90° to each other, and then a third LOP making an angle of approximately 45° with those of the original pair, figs. 2115a and b. This procedure has the advantage of providing an optimum two-LOP plot in the event that a change of visibility or other circumstance should suddenly prevent the third observation.

Triangles of position

As noted above, three lines of position will usually form a *triangle of position*. If this triangle is quite large, it is probable that there is a significant error in one or more of the LOPs, and a check should be made of the observations, calculations, and plotting.

If, however, the triangle is relatively small (and "relatively" will have to be defined in each situation as determined by the techniques used, the experience of the observer, the size of the boat, sea state, and other conditions), it can be assumed that no more than normal inaccuracies and uncertainties exist. In the everyday practice of piloting on boats, it is customary to use the center of the triangle of position, as estimated by eye, for the fix.

Labeling fixes

A fix is plotted on a chart as a small circle (with a dot in its center, if required); it is labeled with time placed horizontally; see fig. 2116a. A running fix is labeled similarly, with "R Fix" added; see fig. 2116b.

If there are three lines that do not meet in one point a dot is placed in the triangle and then circled. If the fix is obtained by passing close to a buoy or other aid to navigation, the dot or center of the symbol may be used for the plot. The usual distance off, 50 to 100 yards (45-90 m) or so, is not significant at typical chart scales; greater distances are estimated and the fix is plotted in the correct direction at a scaled distance.

THE VALUE OF A SINGLE LOP

The preceding discussion has centered on the use of two or more lines of position for obtaining a fix. While admittedly this is the most desirable situation, the value of a single LOP should not be overlooked.

Basically, a single line of position cannot tell a pilot where he is at the moment, but it can, within the limitations of its accuracy, tell him where he is *not*. If he is presumed to be somewhere along the LOP, then he cannot be at a position appreciably distant from the line. This information, although lacking in detail and negative in sense, may often be of value to a navigator concerned with the safety of his vessel.

A single line of position can frequently be combined with a DR position to obtain an "estimated position." This EP is the point along the LOP that is closest to the DR position for the same time. A line is drawn from the DR position perpendicular to the LOP until it intersects that line. An estimated position is marked by a dot within a square; the line can go through the square. As a square is used only for estimated positions, it is not necessary to add "EP"; time may be omitted as it appears on the LOP.

It is also possible to obtain an "estimated position with current" from a single LOP if the set and drift of the current have been determined from predictions or from its effect on the boat's course and speed made good. From

FIG. 2115 An alternative procedure for taking three observations is to select the first two objects so that their LOPs will cross at as near 90° as possible, *a* **above. Then the third sight is taken so that its plotted LOP will cross the other two at approximately 45°, as in** *b* **above. If circumstances prevent the pilot from getting the third sight, he will still have a near-optimum two-LOP fix.**

FIG. 2116 A *fix* **is labeled with the time followed by "FIX" not written parallel to any line. A** *running fix* **is labeled with the time and "R FIX".**

the DR position for the specified time, a line is drawn to scale to represent the effect of the current since the DR track was started from the last fix. This line is drawn in the direction of the set of the current and for a length equal to the "total drift," the distance found by multiplying the drift by the elapsed time since the last fix. This total drift line is labeled and from its end another line is drawn perpendicular to the LOP until it intersects that line; see fig. 2117c. The intersection is the *EP with current;* it is labeled in the same manner as before (the fact that current has been included is obvious from the plot).

In using an EP, make generous allowances for the uncertainty of the position; always err on the side of safety.

In some piloting situations, a single bearing on an object can be advanced and crossed with a later LOP on the same object. This will result in a running fix, not as desirable as a fix from two independent lines of position, but far better than a DR position or the pilot's "best guess."

Running fixes, and the use of a single LOP with depth measurements, will be discussed later in this chapter.

FIG. 2117 An *estimated position* can be obtained from a single line of position. It is the point on the LOP closest to the DR position for that time, see *a* above. If a beam bearing is used, the EP will fall along the DR track, as in *b* above.

FIG. 2117c If information about the current is available, an improved "estimated position with current" can be plotted. The off-setting effect of the current since the start of the DR track is calculated and plotted; the nearest point on the LOP from this current-influenced point is the EP.

FIG. 2118 A very simple, yet fully accurate method of taking bearings is to "aim" the boat directly at the sighted object and read the compass. Brief off-course swings for this purpose will not materially affect the DR plot but be sure that there are no hazards close alongside your course. Correct such compass bearings to true directions before plotting them.

Visual Observations

For the pilot of a typical motorboat or sailboat, the primary source of lines of position will be visual observations. These will include direct and relative bearings, ranges, and horizontal and vertical angle measurements. Correct identification of the sighted object is essential. Other methods and equipment may lead to LOPs such as those from radio direction finding, radar, and depth measurements, but these will normally be secondary to visual observations.

SIMPLE VISUAL BEARINGS

It will amaze the novice pilot (and perhaps some of the more experienced ones, too) how much navigational information can be obtained from the most simple of visual bearings, those directly ahead or broad on the beam.

Bearings dead ahead

Bearings taken directly ahead require no auxiliary equipment; the boat's steering compass will suffice. Only insignificant effects will be made on the DR track of a boat if the bow is momentarily swung off course and pointed toward an object on which it is desired to take a bearing. The craft should be held on this new heading long enough for the helmsman to properly line up on the object and for the compass to settle down and be read. This is normally a matter of less than a minute, perhaps only 20 or 30 seconds.

To use this technique, the pilot must be sure enough of his general location that the off-course swing can be made safely. But if such is the situation, he should not hesitate to use this quick and simple way of getting a line of position. The accuracy of bearings obtained by this method will normally be considerably greater than those of the more complex techniques to be discussed later.

The procedure of taking bearings dead ahead by "aiming" the boat at the object sighted upon has an additional advantage in that it can be accomplished by the helmsman alone, without the assistance of another person. Other methods will generally require the services of a second individual as the bearing-taker while the helmsman continues his normal duties, plus reading the steering compass at the time of the observation.

Beam bearings

If the observed aid to navigation or landmark is well around on either beam, it may not be feasible to make so great a deviation from the normal heading being steered in order to take a dead-ahead bearing. Or perhaps the limited width of the available deep water does not permit so large an excursion from the DR track. In this case, the other simple bearing technique may be used.

Determine some portion of the boat that is at a right angle to the fore-and-aft axis of the craft. Among the possibilities are bulkheads, seat backs, deck seams, etc. Sights taken along these features will determine when the observed object is directly abeam—a relative bearing of 090° or 270°.

The boat may be held on course and the passage of time awaited until sighting along the pre-selected portion of the boat indicates that the aid to navigation or other object is exactly broad on the beam. Its direction then is, of course, 90° greater or less than the direction read from the boat's compass at that moment.

If waiting until the object comes abeam in the normal course of events is not feasible or desirable, then the heading of the craft can sometimes be temporarily altered slightly as needed to bring the sighted object directly on the beam more quickly. Should such a temporary change of heading be made, the pilot must be sure that the 90° is added to, or subtracted from, the compass reading at the exact moment that the sighted object is abeam; do not use the normal base course.

Correction of compass bearings

The pilot should always remember that in either of these types of observations the bearings that are taken are *compass bearings*. It will be necessary to correct them for deviation and variation (see Chapter 14) and then plot them as *true* bearings. Any of the plotting instruments and techniques described in Chapter 19 may be used.

Beam bearings are obtained by adding 90° to or subtracting 90° from the boat's *true* heading. Be sure to correct the boat's compass heading for deviation and variation *first,* and *then* add the 90° if the observation was to starboard or subtract the 90° if the sighting was on the port beam. Do not use the direction of the bearing for entering the craft's deviation table; use the heading.

Plotting bearings

The direction measured by the visual observation is *from the boat toward the object.* When plotting is being done, the position of the boat is not known, but it is still possible to draw the line so that it will have the correct direction and lead toward, to, or through the chart symbol for the sighted object. The particular plotting instrument used will determine the exact procedures used.

It is also possible to plot a line of position outward from the sighted object by using the *reciprocal* of the corrected observed bearing. (In fact, this is the formally correct procedure, but it is usually by-passed in favor of the more direct technique mentioned in the paragraph above.) Here, caution must be taken to *first* correct the observed compass (or relative) bearing to a true direction, and then add or subtract 180° to obtain the reciprocal; do not reverse this sequence.

MORE SOPHISTICATED BEARINGS

The procedures just described above for bearings dead ahead and broad on the beam will suffice in many situations, but not in all. It may be neither safe nor convenient to alter the boat's heading for the purpose of taking a bearing.

Greater flexibility of navigation is obtained if bearings can be taken in any direction without a change in the normal heading of the craft. Such bearings will involve the use of the boat's compass, a pelorus or hand bearing compass, or some combination of these instruments.

Using the boat's compass

On many boats, it will be possible to take bearings directly over the steering compass, at least through a limited angle on either side of the bow. As determined by the construction of the compass, it may be feasible to sight directly over the card and get bearings of acceptable accuracy. On other models, a set of sighting vanes may be placed on the compass for greater precision in direction measurement. The directions in which bearings may be taken using the boat's steering compass will normally be limited by the nearby superstructure of the boat. Bearings taken using the boat's compass must be corrected for the deviation on the heading of the boat, *not* that for the bearing direction, and for the variation of the locality.

Using a hand-held compass

Direct visual bearings can also be taken using a hand-bearing compass, or even with the boat's compass if it is a model that has been designed for quick and easy dismounting with accurate remounting. It is normally not feasible to prepare a deviation table for such hand compass use because of the many different positions and circumstances connected with this procedure. Careful tests should be made to determine the locations about the boat, if any, at which a hand-held device can be used without deviation errors. These tests are best made from known positions by taking bearings on objects whose actual direction can be established from the chart. If deviation-free locations can be found on board, then correction will be required for magnetic variation only, to obtain true bearings for plotting.

Using a pelorus

Alternatively, a pelorus may be used to measure directions, usually as relative bearings. This instrument is, of course, not affected by magnetic disturbances on the boat and may be used at any location from which the desired object can be seen. The caution to be observed in this case is that the pelorus must be accurately aligned with the fore-and-aft axis, the keel-line, of the vessel. The correct positioning of the pelorus should be worked out for several locations on the boat so that sights may be taken on an object regardless of its relative position with respect to the boat.

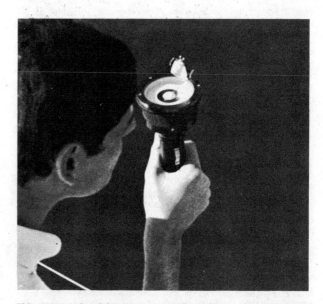

FIG. 2119 A hand bearing compass can be used to take direct readings on objects that cannot be sighted over the boat's steering compass. Before using such an instrument on your boat, however, make checks to find locations at which it will not be affected by local magnetic influences.

The scale of the pelorus can be aligned to the boat's heading and observations made directly in terms of compass bearings, but this procedure is generally less desirable than the technique of relative bearings to be described below. In all cases, the compass bearings must be converted to true bearings before plotting.

An exception to the above statement can be made in the case of an *experienced* pilot. It is possible to omit the step of correction from magnetic to true direction and plot in terms of magnetic bearings. This procedure, while appearing to be a handy short cut, has two pitfalls. First, it requires the use of the magnetic directions circle of the compass roses printed on the chart plus the use of a plotting instrument that determines direction from these compass roses rather than from the meridians and parallels; this rules out use of the convenient and accurate course plotter. Secondly, this technique requires the use of magnetic directions for all purposes, such as courses, ranges, set of current, etc., or else a confusing mixture of directions. Because of these two serious disadvantages, the possibility of plotting bearings as magnetic directions will be noted here, but will be discarded immediately in favor of the "old reliable" procedure of using only true directions on the chart.

RELATIVE BEARINGS

Relative bearings are those taken with respect to the vessel alone, without reference to geographic directions. Relative bearings offer some advantages, but also have some built-in problems.

The instrument for taking relative bearings is the pelorus. As noted before, it has the advantage of being usable anywhere on the boat if properly oriented. Its disadvantage is that close coordination is required between two persons, the bearing-taker and the helmsman. The heading of the boat at the instant of observation must be known, and direct communication between these two individuals is required.

To take a relative bearing, the scale of the pelorus is set with 000° dead ahead. The helmsman is alerted to the fact that a bearing is about to be taken; he concentrates on steady steering and continuously reads the compass. When the observation is made, the bearing-taker calls out "Mark," and reads the scale of the pelorus. (It is very helpful if the bearing-taker calls out "Stand by" a few seconds before his "Mark.") At the word "Mark," the helmsman notes the reading of the steering compass and calls it off to the observer or other person who will compute the bearing. If the compass should be swinging at the moment, so that an accurate reading cannot be taken, the helmsman calls out that information and the pelorus reading is discarded; another attempt is then made to take the bearing.

As noted in Chapter 19, an alternative technique is to have the helmsman call a series of "Marks" when, but only when, he has the boat directly on course. The bearing-taker makes his observation only when it is so indicated that the boat is on the specified heading.

When the relative bearing has been taken by either of the above techniques, it must be converted to a true bearing for plotting. This is done by adding the numerical values of the relative bearing and the *true* heading of the boat at the instant of observation. If the sum so obtained is more than 360°, that amount is subtracted. The true bearing can then be plotted and labeled.

If the true heading is not known for any reason, such as the boat's being momentarily off-course when the bearing was taken, it is, of course, necessary that it be determined before the addition of the preceding paragraph can be accomplished. *Always be sure to use the deviation value for the heading of the boat, and not for the bearing angle.* This is an often-made error, and one that must be continually guarded against.

In fig. 2121a, an observer on a boat heading 047° takes a relative bearing on a buoy of 062°. To determine the true bearing of this aid to navigation, these two numbers are added, 047° + 062° = 109°.

FIG. 2120 A pelorus eliminates the magnetic difficulties that may be experienced with a hand-held compass. It can be used at any point from which the target object can be seen. A pelorus must, however, be properly oriented to the fore-and-aft axis of the boat.

FIG. 2121 Relative bearings must be converted to true bearings before they are plotted. To do this, the relative bearing is added to the true heading of the craft at the moment of observation. If the sum exceeds 360°, that amount is subtracted.

In fig. 2121b, the boat is heading 306° by its compass when a relative bearing of 321° is measured. The variation is 6°W and the deviation (for the compass heading of 306°) is 2°E. The true heading of the boat is thus 306° − 6° + 2° = 302°. The sum of the relative bearing, 321° and the true heading 302° is 623°; therefore 360° is subtracted and a value of 263° is found to be the true bearing of the object.

If the pilot is so fortunate as to have multiple objects on which to take bearings, he should select the nearer ones (provided, of course, that desirable angles of intersection between the LOPs will result). An angular error of 1° will result in a lateral error of about 100 feet at a distance of one mile—at two miles, the *same* angular error will cause a lateral displacement of 200 feet; at three miles, 300 feet, etc. (17 m at 1 km, 35 m at 2 km, etc.).

RANGES

Lines of position from ranges are of exceptional value in position determination. They are free from all of the magnetic effects that might cause errors in bearings taken with a compass or a pelorus. Such LOPs are also easily obtained, much more so than those from bearings. Ranges can be absolutely accurate, as accurate as the charted positions of the two objects lined up in the observation. No matter how small the boat, how rough the water, or how poor the visibility, if you can see the objects come into line, you can plot a good line of position on your chart and so have half of an accurate fix.

Ranges can be classified into two groups. First, there are those that consist of two aids to navigation constructed specifically to serve as a range and are charted with a special symbol, see fig. 1824, page 352. The true direction of such ranges can be determined from the information in the Light List for the rear marker. Ranges are particularly useful in determining compass deviation because of their high accuracy.

It is not necessary, however, to have an especially constructed pair of aids to navigation in order to have a range. Any two objects that can be identified by sight and on the chart form a natural range and can be used in the same manner as one consisting of two formally established navigational aids. Among such objects are ordinary aids to navigation of all types; spires, radio towers, flagpoles, stacks, etc.; identifiable portions of bridges, such as center spans; and other prominent, isolated features; see fig. 2122. Caution should be exercised in using points of land as either a front or rear range mark; errors may be made in attempting to sight on the exact end of the point, particularly if it is of low elevation.

The taking of a LOP from a range requires no more than the observation of the time that the two objects came into line. The LOP is plotted on the chart by lining up the symbols for the two objects with a straightedge and drawing a light solid line over such portion of the chart where the LOP has significance. The line will normally not be drawn all the way back to the two objects that established the range. Its actual direction will not ordinarily need to be determined. The line should be labeled as soon as it is drawn on the chart.

This line of position can be crossed for a fix with another range, or with any other form of LOP. If such is not available at the time, the LOP from the range may often be advanced later and used as part of a running fix.

FIG. 2122 Pilots are not limited to those ranges that have been established as such by the Coast Guard or other authorities. Any two identifiable objects can be used. Here a skipper northbound along the New Jersey coast uses a tower and a tank to get a line of position to check his progress. Always be sure to have positive identification of the objects; the direction of the range will normally do this.

FIG. 2123 Ranges are excellent means of keeping your position centered in a channel, but caution must be exercised not to follow them beyond their proper limits. One or two buoys may be used to mark the beginning or end of a range-marked channel, the point at which to make a change of course.

Never pass up an opportunity to obtain a line of position from a range; there are none better. And there is no better fix than one obtained from the intersection of two ranges.

Ranges are often established by the Coast Guard or other authority to mark the center of important waterways, usually dredged channels or natural channels with hazards close on either side. When so established, the range center line will be printed on the chart, see fig. 1827, page 354. Such ranges will normally be used for direct steering rather than as a line of position, but there is no reason that they should not be used for the latter purpose if desired.

Two cautions should be observed in steering up or down a channel marked by a range. A vessel traveling in the opposite direction on the range will be on a collision course, or will pass too close aboard for comfort. Secondly, the beginning and end of the range, the ends of the solid portion of the line on the chart, must be noted carefully—a range can be followed for too great a distance on either end. Buoys will often be used to mark the spot at which to turn onto or off of the range line, fig. 2123. Always study your chart carefully when using a range.

HORIZONTAL ANGLES

A fix may also be obtained by measuring the two horizontal angles between the lines of sight to three identifiable objects, without a measurement of the relative or geographic direction to any of them. This procedure avoids the inaccuracies involved in relative or compass bearings. Such horizontal angles can be measured to a high degree of accuracy (as close as $1/2°$) with a sextant.

For plotting these horizontal angles, a *three-arm protractor*, fig. 2124, is the preferred instrument. Each side arm is set for the angle measured to its side of the line of sight to the center object. Then the instrument is moved about on the chart until the arms line up with the symbols for the

objects sighted upon in measuring the angles. There is a small hole in the center of the protractor through which a pencil point can be placed to mark the fix on the chart.

The same general technique can be used without a special instrument by drawing lines with the proper angles between them on a piece of transparent paper, fig. 2125. This is then moved about as before until the lines and points are properly related.

FIG. 2125 If a three-arm protractor is not available, the angles can be drawn on a sheet of transparent paper. This is then moved about on the chart until correctly positioned.

Some caution must be exercised in selecting the objects between which the angles are to be measured. Three points, not in a straight line, will all lie on the circumference of a specific circle, such as points *X*, *Y*, and *Z* in fig. 2126a. An angle measured between *X* and *Y*, or *Y* and *Z*, will be the same measured at *A* or *B*, or at any point on the circular arc from *X* around through *A* and *B* to *Z*. Thus,

FIG. 2124 A three-arm protractor is a specialized plotting instrument used with the two-horizontal-angles technique of position determination. When the angles have been set, the arms are lined up with the appropriate chart symbols; then the position is marked with a pencil point through a hole in the center of the device.

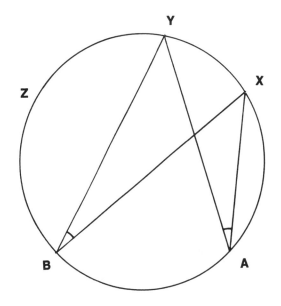

FIG. 2126a In using the two-horizontal-angles method of positioning, the center of the three objects, Y in this illustration, should *not* be farther away from the observer than the other two. If this caution is neglected, the result may be an indeterminate solution called a "revolver," as shown above, where the boat may be at any point on a circle containing the three objects.

427

if the observer should be on the circle, his position will be indeterminate. This situation, known as a "revolver," can occur if the center object sighted upon is farther away from the observer than the other two. By selecting three objects so that they are essentially in line, or that the center one is closer to the observer, an indeterminate situation is avoided. (If the center object is closer, a circle still exists, but it curves away from the observer, and he could not possibly be on it.) See fig. 2126b.

A "revolver" should be avoided; but if one does develop, it can be made determinate by the addition of another LOP, such as a single bearing on one of the three objects, or on any other point.

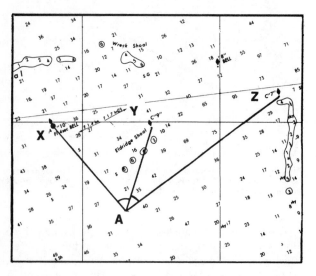

FIG. 2126b If the center object is on line with the other two, or is nearer to the observer, as Y is above, an indeterminate solution is avoided and a fix is found.

LOPS FROM HORIZONTAL ANGLES

A fix can also be determined from lines of position derived from two horizontal angles that may or may not share a common point as discussed above. Each angle can be used to establish an LOP, circular in this case. The circle contains both of the objects sighted upon and the position of the observer. The radius of the circle is the distance between the two objects divided by twice the sine of the measured angle; after the distance is measured from the chart, this is an easy computation with an electronic calculator or a slide rule. Set a pair of dividers—or better yet, a drafting compass—for the computed radius, scribe an arc from each observed point, and where the two intersect is the center of the circle. Using this center, draw in as much of the circular LOP as you need. Do this for two angles and the intersection of the circles fixes your position. (There will be two intersections, but common sense, or a single rough bearing, will suffice to eliminate the ambiguity.)

This procedure is useful on any boat, but it can be especially valuable on sailboats in rough weather or when racing. Under such conditions, the taking of accurate direct bearings across the steering compass, or with a hand-bearing compass, may be very difficult. A simple plastic sextant is not expensive and is all that is required. This procedure is also a good introduction to the use of a sextant in more advanced navigation techniques.

VERTICAL ANGLES

A circular line of position represents points at a constant distance from a specific object. Such distances are often found by the measurement of vertical angles with a marine sextant, or with a specialized device for such purposes alone.

The height of many natural and man-made features is

FIG. 2128 A marine sextant, most commonly used for celestial navigation sights, may also be used in piloting for the measurement of vertical or horizontal angles.

FIG. 2129 If a vertical or horizontal dimension of a distant object is known, this simple optical rangefinder can make an accurate measurement of the distance to it.

shown on charts. Such objects include lighthouses, bridges, radio towers, and generally similar features. Caution must be exercised to determine if the height shown is that above the structure's base on land or the vertical distance above the chart's datum for heights, usually mean high water. Frequently, a correction may be required for the tidal level at the time of observation, its difference from MHW, see Chapter 20. On such features as lighthouses, the height usually given is that of the *light,* not that of the top of the structure.

Using a sextant, the vertical angle is measured between the base and the top or other part of the structure, fig. 2128. This angle (A) and the known height (h) can be used to determine the distance (d) from the observer to the object by a simple trigonometric equation: d = h ÷ tan A. Use trig tables or a hand-held electronic calculator.

Special range finder instruments are now being marketed which use the principle of matching images much like the focusing mechanism of many cameras. It is still necessary, however, to know the height (or a horizontal dimension) of the object on which the observation is made. Fig. 2129 shows one such instrument.

DANGER BEARINGS AND ANGLES

The safety of navigation can often be insured without the establishment of a complete fix. As noted earlier, a single line of position has value—if it is of reasonable accuracy, it can assure you that you are somewhere along it and not elsewhere. A line of position can be chosen, in many piloting situations, that will keep a boat in safe water without precisely defining its position.

Danger bearings

A bearing line can be established so that positions on one side will assure the craft's being in safe waters, while a position on the other side may signify a hazardous situation; such a *danger bearing* is shown in fig. 2130. Here, a shoal, unmarked by any aid to navigation, lies offshore; the problem is to pass it safely. A lighthouse is observed on shore just beyond the shoal, and is identified on the chart. The danger bearing is a line from the lighthouse just tangent to the shoal on the safe side. This line is drawn on the chart and its direction is measured. The line is labeled with the direction preceded by the letters "NMT" (not more than) or "NLT" (not less than). No time is shown as it is not an actual observation. For emphasis, hachures can be added on the side toward the danger, and use of a red pencil is desirable to make it stand out from other lines on the chart.

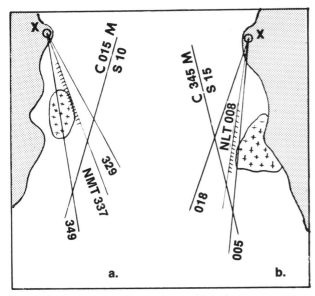

FIG. 2130 A *danger bearing* can be established so as to avoid an unmarked hazardous area. In *a* above, any bearing on object *X* that is more than 337° indicates a potentially hazardous position for the boat. In *b*, the reverse is true, bearing less than 008° are indications of possible danger if the craft continues on the same course.

As the boat approaches the hazardous area, a series of observations are made on the selected object. In the example shown in fig. 2130a, any bearing on the lighthouse *less* numerically than the danger bearing indicates a *safe* position; any bearing *greater* than the danger bearing indicates that the boat is in or approaching the shoal area if it continues on the same course. Should the danger area lie to starboard, rather than to port as in fig. 2130b, the "greater" and "less" factors above would be reversed.

Danger bearings cannot always be established for the safe passage of hazardous areas, but their use should be considered whenever conditions permit. It is necessary to have a prominent object, although it need not be an aid to navigation, that can be seen from the boat and positively identified on the chart. This object should lie beyond the danger area in the same general direction as the course of the boat as it approaches and passes the area to be avoided.

HORIZONTAL DANGER ANGLES

A horizontal angle measured between two identifiable fixed objects defines a circle of position. In fig. 2131, an observer at *X* or *Y* would measure the same angle between *A* and *B;* he would also measure the same angle at any point along that semi-circular arc. If the observer were on the other side of the center of the circle, at *X'* or *Y'*, or

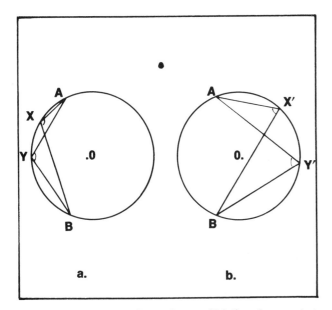

FIG. 2131a and b The various points at which there is a constant angle between the lines of sight to two objects form a circle. The angle between the lines to A and B is the same at X or Y. At points X' and Y', the angle is likewise the same.

other point on that arc, a constant angle also would be observed. This angle, however, is not the same as that measured across the circle at X and Y. Note that the angle will be greater than 90° if the sighted objects are on the same side of the circle as the observer, as in fig. 2131a, and less than 90° if they are on the opposite side as in fig. 2131b.

Such a circle may be established to indicate the boundary between positions of safety and those of possible danger. When such a LOP is set up, the angle defined by the circle is termed the *horizontal danger angle*.

Fig. 2132 illustrates the use of a single horizontal danger angle to avoid an unmarked shoal area. The problem is to

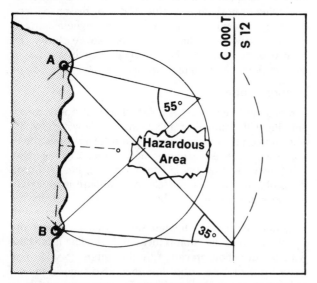

FIG. 2132 Horizontal angles between *A* and *B* are measured as the boat approaches the hazardous area. Any angle *less* than the *horizontal danger angle* of 55° indicates that the boat is in safe waters.

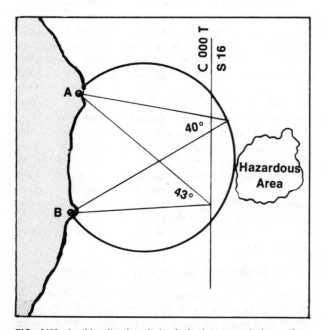

FIG. 2133 In this situation, it is desired to pass inshore of an unmarked hazardous area. The horizontal danger angle is established as before, but now the safe angular measurements are those greater than the horizontal danger angle.

stay sufficiently offshore to miss the hazard. The horizontal danger angle is found by drawing a circle that includes two prominent identifiable objects ashore, *A* and *B* in fig. 2132, and the shoal area. The circle is established by drawing a line between the sighted objects, and then drawing a second line at right angles to the first line at its midpoint. The center of the circle is found by trial-and-error along this second line so that the arc includes the desired points.

Lines are then drawn to *A* and *B* from any point on the circle near the shoal area and the angle between them is measured; in this example, it is 55°.

If the angle between the objects, measured from the boat as it approaches the area, is *less* than the horizontal danger angle, then the radius of the circle on which the boat is located is larger, and the boat is farther offshore in *safe* waters. On the other hand, if the measured horizontal angle is greater than the danger angle, the boat is closer in and may be in or approaching a hazardous area. The angle is preferably measured with a sextant, but it can be calculated from the difference between two compass or relative bearings.

Should the piloting situation require passage inshore of a shoal area, fig. 2133, a single horizontal danger angle can again be used. In this case, *safe* waters are indicated by angles *greater* than the danger angle.

Double horizontal danger angles

The two situations described above can be combined into *double horizontal danger angles* where the requirement is for a safe passage between two offshore hazardous areas. Fig. 2134 is essentially a combination of the two preceding illustrations. The principles are the same; here the safe horizontal angles are those *between* upper and lower danger limits.

Vertical danger angles

A circle of position, obtained from a vertical angle measurement, can also be used to mark the boundary between safe and hazardous waters. With a selected prominent object identified visually and on the chart, a circle is drawn using that object as the center and having a radius that will just include all of the hazardous area. The radius is measured from the chart and converted to a vertical angle by geometric formula or Table 9 in Bowditch. The danger circle is then labeled with the *vertical danger angle*. Fig. 2135 shows such a circular LOP outlining a shoal area.

As the boat approaches the dangerous area, a series of vertical angle measurements are taken on the selected object. Measurement of a vertical angle *less* than that specified as the vertical danger angle indicates that the observer is farther offshore, and consequently he is in *safe* waters.

Measurements of distance directly from an optical range finder can be substituted for vertical angles if such a device is on board.

Corresponding situations would prevail for safe passage inshore of a hazardous area, or between two danger areas, as was shown for horizontal danger angles.

Positioning Procedures

As mentioned earlier, the "basic" fix is obtained by crossing two lines of position. A third LOP is desirable, but this can be obtained in only a limited number of situations. It is assumed for the fix that the observations or measurements for these LOPs are made simultaneously, and this may often be the procedure on a naval ship or other large vessel. On small craft, however, the normal situation will be that of a single bearing-taker and one piece of equipment. Of necessity, therefore, observations will be taken sequentially rather than concurrently. If the observations are taken quickly, the distance traveled between them will be negligible, and adherence to the procedures to be described here will minimize the error from sequential observations.

As a result of the movement of the boat along its course, the observed bearing angles will be changing. Consider the relative *rate of change* of the bearing to each object to be sighted upon; those on the beam will be changing at a more rapid rate than those nearly dead ahead or astern; those on nearer objects will be changing more rapidly than those at greater distances.

For the most accurate determination of a fix from two lines of position, first take a sight on the object with the *least* rate of change, then on the other object, and finally a repeat on the first object. Use the second observation and the average of the first and third bearings (which are, of course, on the same object). If circumstances permit only one observation on each object, it is usually preferable to take the more rapidly changing bearing last and then make an immediate chart plot of both bearings.

If you are able to take observations on three objects, take them in descending order of rate of change of bearing and consider taking a repeat of the first bearing, if possible, for averaging as before.

The time of the fix should be that of the approximate middle of the series of observations. At typical boat cruising speeds and chart scales, a difference of a minute or two will not be significant. At 12 knots, a boat will travel 1/5 mile in one minute; on a 1:80,000 scale chart, this distance of approximately 400 yards is less than 3/16 inch.*

Positioning standards of precision

As set forth in Chapter 19, there are generally accepted standards of precision in describing position of a vessel. If geographic coordinates are used, latitude and longitude, in that sequence, are stated to the nearest tenth of a minute on charts with scales of 1:50,000 or smaller, and to the nearest second on charts of larger scale.

If the position is stated with respect to some aid to navigation or landmark, direction from that point is given to the nearest degree (true) and distance is given to the nearest tenth of a mile.

THE RUNNING FIX

The lack of a second object on which to make an observation may at times prevent the immediate determination of the boat's position by a normal fix, even though one good line of position has been established. In such situations, a somewhat less accurate determination of position may be made by a *running fix (R Fix)*. In this technique there is one line of position at the time of the running fix and another from a different time, usually earlier. This latter LOP must be replotted from its position at the time of its measurement to account for the movement of the boat during the intervening time. The act of advancing the first LOP brings it to a common time with the second obser-

vation so that their intersection may be considered as a determination of position. It should be noted that this line so advanced (or retired) may have resulted from an observation on the *same* object as that used for the second sighting at the time of the running fix, or on a different object.

Advancing a line of position

A line of position is advanced as follows:

(1) A point is selected on the original LOP. This can be

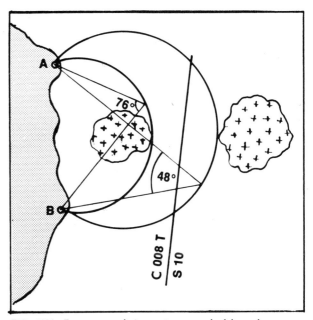

FIG. 2134 For passage between two unmarked hazardous areas, *double horizontal danger angles* **may be used. This technique is essentially the combination of the two preceding situations; a safe passage is indicated by measurement of horizontal angles between specified upper and lower limits.**

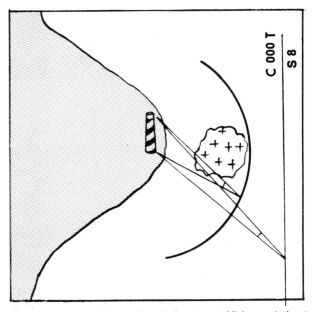

FIG. 2135 A measurement of vertical angle establishes a circle of position at a specific distance from a point. Such an angle can be calculated for an object of known height so as to insure that a boat does not get too close. Safe vertical angles are those *less* **than the** *vertical danger angle.*

*In metric units, the speed would be 22¼ km/h and the boat would travel about 370 meters, but the chart distance would be the same, less than ½ cm.

431

the intersection of the line with the DR track, *X* in fig. 2136, or any point on the LOP, such as *X'*.

(2) The selected point is moved in an amount equal in distance and direction to the boat's motion during the time interval involved. This is most easily measured from the DR position at the time of observation to the DR position for the advanced time.

(3) The new LOP is drawn in through the advanced point parallel to the original LOP.

(4) The advanced LOP is labeled as soon as it is drawn: both times are shown above the line and the direction beneath it.

FIG. 2136 A line of position is *advanced* by moving forward any point on it an amount equal to the boat's motion during the time interval and re-drawing the line through the advanced point. The intersection of this LOP and another LOP for this time is a running fix.

FIG. 2137 A circle of position, or circular LOP, is advanced by merely moving the center point an amount equal in direction and distance to the motion of the boat during the time interval, and redrawing the circle on the new center. In the illustration above, *C = C'* is equal to the spacing between the two DR positions.

Advancing a circular LOP

If the LOP to be advanced is circular, as would be the case with a distance measurement by vertical angle or range finder, the center of the circle is the point advanced by the procedure described above, fig. 2137. The circle or arc is redrawn using the new center, and is then labeled as for any other advanced LOP.

Advancing a LOP with course and/or speed changes

The advancement of the selected point on the initial LOP must take into account all changes in course and/or speed of the boat during the time interval. It is frequently a convenient procedure to calculate and plot the DR positions for the time of the initial observation and for the advanced time. The movement of the selected point on the initial LOP should parallel and equal a line drawn between these two DR positions. This technique is particularly useful if there has been more than one change in course and/or speed, fig. 2138.

Advancing a LOP with current

The advancement of a line of position may take into account current effects if they are adequately known or can be estimated. The selected point on the initial LOP is first advanced for DR speeds and courses, and then for the set and drift of the current, both calculations using the elapsed time interval between the two observations; see fig. 2139.

The accuracy of advanced LOPs

The accuracy of an advanced line of position can be only as good as the accuracy of the initial observation *decreased* by any errors or uncertainties in the navigator's data for the boat's course and speed (and current data, if used). Obviously, the longer the time interval over which

FIG. 2138 The advancement of a LOP must take into consideration all changes of course and/or speed during the time interval. The net effect can be determined by drawing a light line between the DR positions for the two times concerned. The selected point on the original LOP is advanced in the same direction and distance as this net effect line.

the sight is advanced, the greater the uncertainties become. The interval should, therefore, be the minimum possible, and, in piloting, should rarely exceed 30 minutes. (In navigation on the high seas, celestial lines of position are often advanced several hours, but the accuracy of positioning is less critical in these circumstances.)

The same criteria for the angle of intersection of lines of position apply to running fixes as were discussed previously for normal fixes. Running fixes involving three lines of positions (two of them advanced) are possible but are unusual in actual piloting practice.

Lines of position may be retired, moved back to an earlier time, in a similar manner. Such retrograde movement is, however, quite rare in piloting situations.

Running fixes and DR plots

The DR plot may be interrupted and restarted from a running fix if it is considered of reasonable accuracy. In all cases, however, a fix obtained from two or more essentially simultaneous observations or measurements is to be preferred over a running fix.

OBSERVATIONS ON A SINGLE OBJECT

In addition to the technique of the running fix using advanced lines of position, position information can be obtained from successive observations on a single object by means of several other more specialized procedures. These include: bow-and-beam bearings, doubling the angle on the bow, two bearings and run between, and two relative bearings.

In each case, it is important to note that the angles and distance run be measured with respect to the course being made good over the bottom; corrections to the DR track and all relative bearings must be made for current or other offsetting influences if such information is known or can be estimated.

Bow-and-beam bearings

Position determination is easily accomplished by the technique of taking two particular successive bearings on an object to one side or the other of the craft's course. The first bearing is taken when the object sighted upon bears either 45° to starboard (RB 045°) or to port (RB 315°). The second bearing is taken when the same object is broad on the respective beam (RB 090° or 270°), fig. 2140. The time of each bearing having been noted, the time interval is found, and then the distance traveled between the two sightings is calculated using the boat's speed. Because of the nature of the triangle established by the two bearings and the course line, the boat is away from the sighted object at the time of the second (beam) bearing at the same distance as that traveled during the time interval. Since there is an LOP (the beam bearing) and a distance, the position of the boat has been fixed.

The principal advantage of this procedure is the ease with which it can be accomplished. Beam bearings are easily taken, and 45° relative bearings can be quickly set up using crude sights oriented with an ordinary plastic drafting triangle. On some boats, it may be possible to make the 45° sight over the steering compass. The bow-and-beam technique often can be done by the helmsman without assistance.

Doubling the angle on the bow

This is a more generalized application of the same principles as those involved in bow-and-beam bearings, in which a 45° angle was doubled to 90°. Geometric principles establish that whenever an angle on the bow is doubled, the distance from the position at which the second bearing is taken to the object sighted upon is equal to the distance traveled (over the bottom) during the time

FIG. 2139 If the LOP is to be advanced with allowance for current, the same procedure as before is followed, except that a further movement is made from the second DR position to account for the current during the time interval and obtain an estimated position.

FIG. 2140 If a bearing is taken when an object bears 45° on either bow (RB = 045° or 315°), and again when the same object is broad on the beam (RB = 090° or 270°), the distance to the object at the time of the second bearing will be equal to the distance run (over the bottom) between the bearings; B-L = A-B.

interval between the two observations, fig. 2141. The angle referred to above is the relative bearing to starboard or to port. A relative bearing of, say 340° measured in the conventional manner, must be converted to an angle of 20° to port for the purpose of "doubling"; in this case, the doubled angle would be RB 320° (40° to port).

The doubling-of-the-bow-angle technique has the advantage of determining the boat's position *before* the sighted object is abeam. With information as to the boat's position at such an earlier moment, the course can be projected ahead on the chart. Should the craft be traveling too close to shore for passing a headland, a more adequate warning of the dangerous course will thus be in hand, and corrective action can be taken sooner.

This technique does, however, have a disadvantage in that it requires the possession and use of a pelorus or other instrument for measuring relative bearings with reasonable accuracy. Another disadvantage is that a second person is needed as a bearing-taker.

Two-bearings-and-run-between

With only a single object upon which sights can be taken, another method, known as "two-bearings-and-run-between" for lack of a better name, may be used. In this procedure, a bearing is taken on the object, the boat proceeds along her course, and a second bearing is taken after the angle has changed by at least 30°. This second bearing may be taken before or after the sighted object is passed abeam. From the times of each bearing, the time interval is calculated, and from this, the distance run is determined.

Both bearings are plotted, as is the course of the boat, fig. 2142. A pair of dividers is opened to the distance run between the two bearings and is then moved parallel to the course line until the points fall on the bearing lines.

FIG. 2142 If two bearings are taken on a single object as the boat passes it, and are plotted on the chart, then only one point can be found on each LOP so that the course and distance made good will fit between these LOPs.

The divider points now indicate the positions of the boat at the times of the first and second bearings.

As before, the distance run must be that *over the bottom;* suitable corrections must be made for any current. The accuracy of this technique depends upon many factors: the accuracy of each of the two bearings, the accuracy of the calculation of the distance run over the bottom, and the accuracy with which the boat was steered during the interval between the two sightings. The net effect of this compounding of accuracies is to make the positions so determined somewhat less certain than the other techniques described above.

Two relative bearings

A more generalized solution from two relative bearings can be used if a copy of "Bowditch" is on board. Table 7 of that book uses two items of information—the angle between the course and the first bearing (the first relative bearing) and the difference between the course and the second bearing (the second relative bearing). Columns of the Table are in terms of the first item and lines are in terms of the second item above; the interval between tabular entries is two degrees in both cases.

For any combination of the two relative bearings within the limits of Table 7, two factors will be found. The first

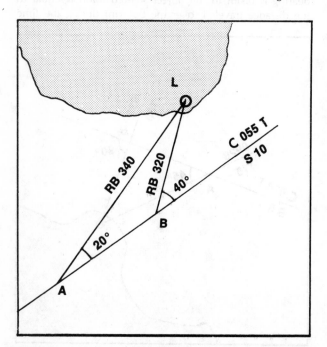

FIG. 2141 If two observations are made so that the second relative bearing is twice that of the first (as measured from the bow to either starboard or port), then the distance to the sighted object at the time of the second bearing is the same as the distance made good between the sightings; again, **L·B = A·B.**

number is a factor by which the distance run between the bearings is multiplied to obtain the distance away from the sighted object at the time of the second bearing. The second factor of the same entry in Table 7 is the multiplier to be used to determine the distance off when the object is abeam, assuming, of course, that the same course and speed are maintained. See fig. 2143.

Electronic Piloting

Although electronic navigation is essentially a topic in itself, and outside of the scope of piloting, brief mention will be made here of two techniques which have direct comparability and applicability to visual piloting.

RADIO BEARINGS AND FIXES

With relatively simple equipment, observations can be made of the direction to radio stations, even though such "objects" lie far beyond visual range, either as a result of night, fog, or simply great distance. See fig. 2144. Bearings can be taken on radiobeacons operated by the Coast Guard as aids to navigation; some aeronautical ranges and beacons operated by the FAA; on standard AM radio broadcast stations; and on stations in the 2-3 MHz marine band (but SSB signals are poor for RDF use). In general, the desirability for use in radio direction finding is in descending order as listed above. Radio bearings can be taken under any condition of visibility, and on stations at ranges as great as hundreds of miles; accuracies will, of course, be more favorable with nearer stations.

Radio bearings are taken with a *radio direction finder,* usually referred to as an RDF if it is manually operated, or as an ADF if the bearings are taken and displayed automatically. These items of electronic equipment are discussed more fully in Chapter 26.

Using radio bearings

Radio bearings are plotted in essentially the same manner as visual bearings. They are not as sharp as visual observations, however; an accuracy of 2° to 3° is the best that can be expected, and this precision will be achieved only with experience. Accordingly, it is advisable to obtain three radio LOPs, and even so, the position so determined should not be considered as precise as one from visual bearings.

Accurate identification of the station being received is essential, and the exact location of the transmitting antenna must be plotted on the nautical chart if it is not already shown there. Radiobeacons, both marine and aeronautical, are normally plotted on nautical charts, although sometimes additional aeronautical beacons can be found on aviation charts and transcribed to nautical charts. The antenna location of a few standard AM broadcasting radio stations will be found on charts identified by call letters and frequency, but often others can be added. Antenna locations in latitude and longitude for many stations are tabulated on the reverse side of Marine Weather Services Charts, see page 265.

Radio bearings taken on a station more than approximately 200 miles (370 km) distant must be corrected before being plotted on a Mercator chart. (Distance will vary with latitude and the relative position of the vessel and the radio station.) This correction is required because

TABLE 7
Distance of an Object by Two Bearings

Difference between the course and second bearing	Difference between the course and first bearing													
	34°		36°		38°		40°		42°		44°		46°	
°														
44	3.22	2.24												
46	2.69	1.93	3.39	2.43										
48	2.31	1.72	2.83	2.10	3.55	2.63								
50	2.03	1.55	2.43	1.86	2.96	2.27	3.70	2.84						
52	1.81	1.43	2.13	1.68	2.54	2.01	3.09	2.44	3.85	3.04				
54	1.63	1.32	1.90	1.54	2.23	1.81	2.66	2.15	3.22	2.60	4.00	3.24		
56	1.49	1.24	1.72	1.42	1.99	1.65	2.33	1.93	2.77	2.29	3.34	2.77	4.14	3.43
58	1.37	1.17	1.57	1.33	1.80	1.53	2.08	1.76	2.43	2.06	2.87	2.44	3.46	2.93
60	1.28	1.10	1.45	1.25	1.64	1.42	1.88	1.63	2.17	1.88	2.52	2.18	2.97	2.57
62	1.19	1.05	1.34	1.18	1.51	1.34	1.72	1.52	1.96	1.73	2.25	1.98	2.61	2.30
64	1.12	1.01	1.25	1.13	1.40	1.26	1.58	1.42	1.79	1.61	2.03	1.83	2.33	2.09
66	1.06	0.96	1.18	1.07	1.31	1.20	1.47	1.34	1.65	1.51	1.85	1.69	2.10	1.92
68	1.00	0.93	1.11	1.03	1.23	1.14	1.37	1.27	1.53	1.42	1.71	1.58	1.92	1.78
70	0.95	0.89	1.05	0.98	1.16	1.09	1.28	1.21	1.43	1.34	1.58	1.49	1.77	1.66
72	0.91	0.86	1.00	0.95	1.10	1.05	1.21	1.15	1.34	1.27	1.48	1.41	1.64	1.56
74	0.87	0.84	0.95	0.92	1.05	1.01	1.15	1.10	1.26	1.21	1.39	1.34	1.53	1.47
76	0.84	0.81	0.91	0.89	1.00	0.97	1.09	1.06	1.20	1.16	1.31	1.27	1.44	1.40
78	0.80	0.79	0.88	0.86	0.96	0.94	1.04	1.02	1.14	1.11	1.24	1.22	1.36	1.33
80	0.78	0.77	0.85	0.83	0.92	0.91	1.00	0.98	1.09	1.07	1.18	1.16	1.28	1.27

FIG. 2143 Distance off at time of second bearing, *L-B,* and distance off when abeam, *L-C,* can be found by applying multiplying factors to the distance run, *A-B.* These factors for various pairs of angles will be found in Table 7 of Bowditch.

FIG. 2144 Radio direction finders (RDFs) can be used to take bearings on transmitters located a fraction of a mile, or several hundreds of miles, distant. Lines of position can be found at night, in fog, or when visibility is good but the station is too far away to be seen.

FIG. 2145a Because the accuracy of a fix derived from radio bearings is usually less than that of one obtained from visual observations, it should be labeled "RDF".

FIG.2145b If a combination of LOPs includes one from an RDF measurement, it may be well to add the letters "RDF" above the line where applicable.

radio waves travel via the most direct route, a great circle path, and this does not plot as a straight line on a Mercator chart; see page 363. Table 1 in Bowditch provides the correction factor and instructions on how it should be applied. No correction is needed for nearer stations, or on stations at any distance if the plotting is done on a gnomonic chart.

A sequence, or "round," of several radio bearings on different radiobeacons or other stations can normally be taken quickly enough so that any movement of the boat during this time can be ignored and the lines of position can be plotted as of the mid-time of the sequence. If any appreciable time delays are encountered, however, an RDF line of position can be advanced or retarded in the same manner as a visual LOP.

To assist in plotting RDF bearings, special charts are available for some areas. These are commercial adaptations of government charts with compass roses entered on each radiobeacon or other usable station. Alternatively, a skipper may apply adhesive, transparent plastic compass roses to regular nautical charts at the location of sources of signals upon which radio bearings can be taken.

In considering the accuracy of radio bearings, it must be kept in mind that these are referenced to the boat's heading as determined by its magnetic compass. Any compass deviation must be known and taken into consideration before bearings can be plotted. Any sloppy steering or yawing off-course as a result of rough water will directly affect the RDF bearings.

Labeling RDF bearings and fixes

In view of the lesser accuracy of RDF bearings as compared to visual sighting, and particularly those radio bearings taken on distant stations, it is desirable that the fix obtained from such lines of position be so identified. A

FIG. 2146 Marine radiobeacons are included in Coast Guard Light Lists with the related visual or audible aid to navigation. If the transmitting antenna is not at the principal aid, its distance and direction from it will be given. Frequencies, characteristic signal, ranges, and schedules of operation are tabulated in the front pages of each Light List volume.

	SEACOAST		MASSACHUSETTS				FIRST DISTRICT		
(1)	(2) Name	(3) Location		(4) Nominal Range	(5) Ht. above	(6) Structure	(7)		
No.	Characteristic	Lat. N.	Long. W.		water	Ht. above ground	Daymark	Remarks	Year
29 J 280	**Eastern Point Light** .... Fl. W., 5ˢ	On east side of entrance to harbor. 42 34.8	70 39.9	20	57	White conical tower, covered way to dwelling. 36		RBN: 314 kHz (• ■ • ■)V. Antenna 150 feet 009½° from light tower. HORN: 2 blasts ev 20ˢ (2ˢbl-2ˢsi-2ˢbl-14ˢsi). See p. XIX for special Direction Finder Calibration Service. Storm warning signals displayed day and night.	1832–1890
30	*Eastern Point Lighted Whistle Buoy 2.* **Fl. R.,** 4 ˢ	In 99 feet 42 34.2	70 39.9	4	....	Red		Ra ref.	
30.50	*Raytheon Lighted Instrument Buoy C.* **Fl. W.,** 4ˢ	In 125 feet 42 32.0	70 43.0	....	....	Orange and white horizontal bands.		Private aid.	

(For Gloucester Harbor, see No. 400)

circle symbol, with a dot in the center if necessary, is used—just as for a visual fix—but it is clearly identified as a radio direction finder position by "RDF" after the time; see fig. 2145a.

If RDF bearings must be used to establish a position in possibly hazardous waters, it is advisable to plot additional lines two or three degrees (or more if conditions make for a reduction of normal accuracy) on either side of the basic LOP. These will clearly show the possible *area*, rather than specific position, in which the RDF-equipped boat is located; see fig. 2112.

Although it is of much lesser accuracy, an RDF Running Fix is better than no position information beyond dead reckoning if only one radiobeacon or other station can be used. Just as with visual techniques, an initial radio bearing is taken and plotted. Then after sufficient movement of the boat to ensure an adequate change in direction, a second radio bearing is taken on the same signal source and is plotted. One or the other of these LOPs can be advanced or retired to a common time and thus an RDF Running Fix is established.

Combined lines of position

It is often possible, or necessary, to combine an RDF line of position with a visual bearing or range; this might occur only when one visual LOP could be obtained and it was necessary to cross it with another LOP from any source to get a fix. If radio lines of position are mixed with visual bearings or ranges, the former should be identified by adding the letters "RDF" below the line following the direction figures; see fig. 2145b.

Radio direction finding may also help the skipper whose craft is *not* equipped with an RDF. By establishing communications on the 2-3 MHz marine band, an RDF-equipped boat or Coast Guard unit can take bearings on his signals as he gives a "long count" and then advise him of his position or home in on him to render assistance. There are, however, some limitations on this procedure. The newer single-sideband signals are not as good for direction finding purposes as the older double-sideband signals, and as yet RDFs for the VHF-FM band are not widely available.

RADAR BEARINGS AND DISTANCES

Radar is another item of electronic equipment that is covered in greater detail in Chapter 25, but which will be considered here in connection with piloting situations. Radar has unique advantages in that a single instrument can measure both direction and distance (range), and that these measurements can be accomplished under visibility conditions that would preclude visual observations.

Radar observations

Measurements of direction by radar are *not* as accurate as those by visual sightings, but radar will penetrate darkness; light and moderate rain without difficulty, and heavy rain with some reduction in effectiveness; fog; and other restrictions that would prohibit visual bearings or range measurements.

On the other hand, measurements of distance by radar can be quite accurate, much more so than such observations taken by vertical sextant angles or with simple optical range finders.

Use of radar information

Radar data are used in the same manner as information from visual observations. Lines of position are combined to obtain fixes—typical combinations include two bearings, a bearing with a distance measurement to the same or another object, or two distance measurements. A fix obtained by radar bearings and/or distance measurements is labeled with time and "RADAR"; see fig. 2147.

FIG. 2147 A fix obtained from radar lines of position is plotted on the chart with a circle and labeled with time and "RADAR"; in the example above, a fix has been obtained on a single object by measurement of both bearing and distance.

When visibility conditions permit, a frequent combination, and an excellent one, is that of a visual bearing on an object and a radar measurement of distance to that same point.

Radar distance measurements also may be used in the same manner as distance determinations by vertical sextant angle to avoid a shoal area delineated by a circular LOP from a prominent object identifiable on the radarscope.

Radar observations on isolated objects such as buoys, offshore lighthouses, etc., usually are made without difficulty in identification of the object on the radarscope. When the radar target is on shore, however, some problems may be encountered in picking out the exact object on which the bearing and range information is to be obtained. Navigate with caution when using radar information from such objects. Even more so than other types of piloting, radar requires practice and the building up of experience. If you have a radar, use it often in non-critical times so that you can employ it and have the advantage of its unique capabilities when its use is essential. You must be capable of using it with competence and confidence when it is needed.

Depth Information in Piloting_____

Information on the depth of water under a vessel is usually considered to be merely a safety matter for the prevention of running aground. In actuality, such data can be of considerable value in piloting. The essential characteristic of depth information is the fact that although it cannot tell the pilot where he is, it can tell him *positively* where he is *not.* If an accurate measurement of depth gives a reading of 26 feet, you may be at any number of places where such is the depth, but you certainly are not at a position where the depth is significantly greater or less.

HOW DEPTH INFORMATION IS OBTAINED

Data on the depth of the water beneath a craft can be obtained manually or electronically. A hand lead line, see page 384, is a time-honored instrument of piloting, and every boat should have one of a length suitable for the waters usually sailed. It is accurate and dependable in use, although far from efficient or convenient. The modern-day trend is toward electronic depth sounders that can provide information at a much faster rate and with the convenience of reading a simple dial. They can also measure great depths that would be impracticable with a lead line. Electronic sounders are discussed in detail in Chapter 26.

USE OF DEPTH INFORMATION

In using depth information, regardless of how obtained, a correction for the height of tide may be required. The use of Tide Tables and the necessary calculations with their data are covered in Chapter 20.

Depth data can be combined with a line or lines of position obtained from other means to yield positional information. Under some circumstances, depth information alone may be of value in position determination.

Depth information and a single LOP

If the bottom of the body of water being navigated has some slope, and this slope is reasonably uniform, it may be possible to get positional information from a single LOP, typically a beam bearing, and a depth reading. The bearing line is plotted and then examined for a spot where the depth figure on the chart agrees with the measured depth as corrected for the tidal stage; be sure that there aren't several such depths along the LOP, fig. 2148. Such a location should be considered as an Estimated Position (EP) rather than a Fix.

Matching measured depths to the chart

In some instances, a rough estimate of the position of a boat can be obtained by matching a series of depth readings, appropriately corrected for the prevailing height of the tide, with depths printed on the chart. Depth readings are taken and recorded at regular time intervals, such as those corresponding to intervals of distance of one-tenth to one-half mile, as determined by the scale of the chart concerned, the density of printed depth figures, etc. (Electronic depth sounders can provide far more depth measurements than can be used.) These depths are marked on a piece of transparent paper at intervals determined by the scale of the chart, fig. 2149a. This piece of paper is then moved about on the chart, keeping the line of sound-

depth sounder reading 23 ft. corrected to MLW

FIG. 2148 Depth information can often be used with a single LOP, such as a simple beam bearing, to determine an estimated position.

ings parallel to a line representing the course steered while they were being taken. A maximum degree of match is sought between the observed depths and the charted depths; exact concurrence should not be expected.

In the example shown here, the 60-foot depth as measured is aligned with the 10-fathom curve on the chart, and a search for a match is started. If the line of soundings is moved north of the position shown in fig. 2149b, the depths at the outer end would still be in general agreement, but the mismatch at the inshore end would generally show that the line was incorrectly placed. If the line were moved down the chart, keeping it parallel to the course sailed, then the 37-foot measurement near the inshore end would mismatch with the actual 48-foot depth. The matching found by the location shown in fig. 2149b is as close as may be expected, and this position of the line can be considered to fairly well indicate the track of the craft as the soundings were made.

Position determination by the use of depth data is not well suited to shorelines that are foul with offshore rocks, or areas that have varying, irregular depths. Nor can this technique be used where the depth is quite uniform with few or no variations. There are, however, many situations where it can, and should, be used.

Position checking by depth data

If an EP has been determined by some other method or combination of methods, consideration should be given to checking it by a depth measurement. Remember that confirmation cannot be positive, but that denial can be quite

FIG. 2149a Position by a line (or chain) of soundings. The soundings are taken at regular intervals and plotted on transparent paper as shown.

FIG. 2149b The paper is then moved about on the chart until measured depths correspond with the charted depths.

certain if there is a significant difference between the depth at the boat's actual location and that charted for the estimated position. If such should be the case, a further verification of the estimated position is a necessity, perhaps even an urgent necessity!

Fathom curve sailing

When cruising along a coast that has a fairly uniformly sloping bottom offshore, piloting can often be simplified by an examination of the chart for a fathom curve that will keep the craft in safe waters generally and will avoid any specific hazards. The boat is then steered so as to keep the

reading of the electronic depth sounder within a few feet of the selected depth. If readings increase, the boat is gently steered toward shore; if they decrease, the wheel is put over a bit to edge farther offshore.

For the sake of safety, the chart should be checked for the *full* distance that this technique is to be used to be sure that there are no sudden changes in depth, or bends in the depth curve, that might result in an unexpectedly hazardous situation. For added safety, this examination of the chart should be carried beyond the intended end of fathom-curve sailing to prevent unexpected hazards from arising should your speed over the bottom be greater than anticipated.

FIG. 2150 As a general rule, it is better practice to lay two short courses between buoys than one long one. This is especially true in thick weather.

Practice — and More Practice

Position determination is the part of piloting that truly cannot be learned "from the book." Study is important, it is essential, but the skipper must put into actual practice the various procedures and techniques. He must know the rules and principles involved, but he must also be able to *apply* them. Make a habit of "over-navigating" during daylight and good weather conditions so that you will be experienced and capable at night or in foul weather.

TABLE FOR FINDING HEIGHT OF TIDE ABOVE LOW WATER AT ANY HOUR OF THE EBB OR FLOOD		
FALLING TIDE Hours after high water	RISING TIDE Hours after low water	CONSTANT Rising or Falling
0	6	1.0
½	5½	0.98
1	5	0.92
1½	4½	0.84
2	4	0.75
2½	3½	0.63
3	3	0.50
3½	2½	0.38
4	2	0.26
4½	1½	0.16
5	1	0.08
5½	½	0.025

1. Find rise of tide for given day in Tide Tables (difference between heights of nearest high and low tides)
2. Enter column 1 or 2 on line corresponding to time for which height of tide is to be calculated
3. In column 3, find constant given for that time
4. Multiply constant obtained in (3) by total rise of tide (1)

FIG. 2151

Preceding pages in this chapter have provided all of the basic information required for the safe navigation of a boat in pilot waters —the dimensions and instruments of piloting, the procedures of dead reckoning, calculations involving tides and currents, and position determination. The material to be presented in this supplementary section extends beyond these fundamentals. These are techniques that will be useful in specialized situations, or which may provide a quicker or easier solution to a piloting problem. The material of this section might be considered as "graduate study" in small-craft piloting. These techniques should not be approached without a thorough understanding of Chapters 19 and 20, and the basic methods already discussed in Chapter 21. FIG. 2151 (left): Current problems, for example, may be solved more easily and quickly with the use of an electronic calculator—but first understand the principles.

PILOTING—Specialized Techniques

Piloting by Calculator

The development of *transistors* vastly changed the nature of electronic equipment used by boatmen, providing them radios, depth sounders, direction finders, radars, and many other devices of much lower power drain and higher reliability than vacuum tube-equipped units. The combination of transistors with printed-circuit boards was subsequently further developed into *integrated circuits*. These "ICs" have been miniaturized to a degree almost beyond comprehension. In 1960 a typical circuit density was 4 transistors per square inch of open printed-circut board. By 1977, the density is a near-unbelievable 400,000 components per square inch in a sealed unit with all internal cross-connections made as part of the IC and only a few external leads to be connected into the overall circuit of the device.

The Personal Calculator

The availability of integrated circuit "chips" with steadily expanding capabilities, at lower and lower costs, has made possible the small *electronic calculator* variously termed "hand," "pocket," or "personal." This small device of considerable versatility has done much to remove the dislike and fear of figures held by many persons, and generally make them "mathematically-minded." They will now think nothing of multiplying 12.56 by the cosine of 34° by pushing a few buttons and seeing the answer in a direct-reading digital display. Previously it was necessary to use trigonometric tables and long-hand multiplication, or logarithim tables and addition, or a slide-rule—all fairly complicated procedures. An entire new area of *mathematical piloting* has been opened to *all* persons.

The versatility of calculators

Calculators can be applied by boatmen to a wide variety of problems to obtain answers more easily, more quickly, and with greater accuracy than ever before. And there has seldom been an item of "boating equipment" which has such additional onshore capabilities; the boat's calculator is just as readily used for the skipper's business activities, the first mate's shopping trips, or the children's school problems—just don't fight over who gets to use it next!

Personal electronic calculators are available in a range of physical size and computational capability. All contain several integrated circuit chips plus a small number of other components. The answers are normally shown by small figures produced by light-emitting diodes (LED) although some instruments use liquid crystal displays (LCD) or vacuum fluorecsent displays which are more visible in bright light, but which have off-setting disadvantages, such as shorter battery life, which limit their desirability. These calculators are powered by internal batteries, usually of the rechargeable type using an external 115-volt AC charger-adapter. Some calculators are smaller than a pack of cigarettes, but more typical models measure roughly 5 to 6½ inches (130–165 mm) by 2½ to 3½ inches (64–89 mm) and are about 1½ inches (38 mm) thick; units with a capability to print out answers on a paper tape are, of course, larger and no longer can be termed "hand" or "pocket."

Types of Calculators

In computational capability, personal calculators are often subdivided into various "classes" or "types" although the dividing lines are not in all cases sharply defined. The simplest calculators, which we can call type or class "A," can perform the *four mathematical functions* of addition and subtraction, multiplication and division. Such models may also include a *memory* register to serve as a "scratch-pad" for recording an intermediate result in the solution of a problem or series of problems with recall whenever later desired. This capability is extended on some calculators to *memory arithmetic* whereby the

441

FIG. 2152 This moderately-priced calculator is typical of "slide-rule" or "scientific" models; it can solve many problems for a boatman. The SR-40 is capable of all arithmetic operations, plus powers, roots, and reciprocals. It can also perform trigonometric and inverse trig functions, and store intermediate results in a memory register. The SR-40 operates from an internal battery that can be recharged from a 115 V-AC or a 12 V-DC source, or it can be operated directly from either of these sources through the adapter/charger unit.

FIG. 2153 The HP-25C has a full "scientific" capability and also can store a "program," a series of steps used to solve a problem such as current sailing. This feature facilitates the successive running of similar problems. This calculator has eight "addressable" memories for the storage of constants or intermediate results in a long problem. The HP-25C is unique in that the information stored in the data program memories is *not* lost when the calculator is turned off to conserve battery power.

results of a calculation as shown by the display may be added to, or subtracted from, a quantity previously stored in the memory. The upper limit of category "A" calculators is reached with models that have special keys for the direct calculation of squares and square roots, and perhaps reciprocals, of numbers punched in on the keyboard. There may also be a key for "changing sign" to permit the direct entry of negative numbers, and a key for percentage calculations.

Scientific or slide-rule calculators

The next level of hand or pocket calculators, the "B" category, has all the features of the "A" design plus additional capabilities. These models, often described as *slide rule* or *scientific* calculators, can provide direct trigonometric functions, and their inverses, by the touch of a key; all necessary information is stored within the unit. These units can also raise numbers or take roots to any value of exponent, and have a key for π, that "pi" value used in computing the area or volume of circular and cylindrical shapes. Even the simplest of the "B" calculators will have a memory with memory arithmetic. More expensive units in this category will have a number of *addressable memories* into which quantities can be stored and later added to or multiplied by the value shown in the display (which can be a number keyed in or the result of a calculation); stored quantities can be selectively recalled as they are later desired.

The number of various functions performed by these calculations has now reached a point where it is necessary to assign two functions to all or most of the keys on the keyboard. This is done by inclusion of a "second function" or "shift" key much the same as on a typewriter for capital letters (except that it need not be held down when the next key is punched).

Programmable and printing calculators

Beyond the scientific or slide-rule models are the *programmable* models of category "C." These offer all the capabilities of the "B" units, plus a few more, and the special feature that the steps of a mathematical process can be "programmed" into an internal memory for repeated use with different input data. With one exception, however, the program which has been keyed in punch-by-punch on the keyboard is lost when the calculator is turned off between uses to conserve battery power. The exception is the HP-25C which will retain information for an extended period of time. At the top of the line of general-purpose personal calculators are the category "D" *card programmable* models. With these units, after a program has been keyed into the calculator, a small magnetic card is passed through the machine, and the program is "written" onto the card much as music or voice is recorded on a tape cassette. Although the program stored in the memory registers of the calculator is lost when the unit is turned off, it is easily put back into the calculator by passing the magnetic card through the machine again, this time in the "read" mode. In addition to recording your own programs, it is possible to purchase magnetic cards for many applications from the manufacturer, or to exchange cards with other owners of similar calculators.

Calculators with a *paper-tape print-out* offer the convenience of a "hard copy" of the results (and the intermediate calculations also, if desired). The disadvantage, particularly for boating, is a bulkier machine and a greater use of battery power.

APPLICATIONS FOR PILOTING

The first, and most important, point to note about the use of calculators in piloting is that the problem to be

FIG. 2154 A small personal calculator can be used aboard almost any boat for solving a wide variety of problems. It will give highly accurate results more easily and quickly than manual computation.

solved is not changed. The calculator only makes your efforts easier, quicker, and more accurate—*you* must still solve the problem, the calculator does not do it for you. In essence, this means that you must have the same knowledge of input data and procedures to be used as if you were getting the answer by paper and pencil.

Distance-Time-Speed

Even the simplest class "A" calculator will be sufficient for problems of distance, time, and speed. The usual equations are:

$$D = S \times T$$
$$\text{where T is in hours} \tag{1}$$

$$D = \frac{S \times T}{60}$$
$$\text{where T is in minutes} \tag{2}$$

These equations can, of course, be algebraically transposed in calculating S or T when the other factors are known; see page 388.

The caution to be observed here is that when subtracting two clock or watch times to get elapsed time for a run there are 60 minutes in an hour and not 100 as in ordinary mathematics—hours and minutes of 24-hour time cannot be subtracted decimally. Time may be calculated in minutes for use in equation (2) by multiplying the hours by 60 and then adding the minutes. Alternatively, equation (1) can be used by dividing minutes by 60 to obtain a decimal fraction which is appended to the whole number of hours, if any, of the elapsed time.

Calculations Involving Tides and Currents

A personal calculator that has the trigonometric functions—sine, cosine, and tangent—and their inverse functions arc sin or sin⁻¹, etc.—can greatly ease the solution of problems involving tides and currents.

Height of tide

Calculation of the height of tide at an intermediate time between high water and low water can be done by use of Table 3 of the Tide Tables—*If* you happen to have a copy handy. If you don't, you can use your calculator and the times of high and low water from the local newspaper or the data now included on small-craft editions of charts.

The equation used is based on the variation of the height of tide from low to high or high to low following a cosine curve. This is the procedure used by the National Ocean Survey in the preparation of Table 3, but it must be remembered that actual conditions of time and height will not always match predictions, due to short-term local conditions.

The predicted height of tide at any desired time is the low water predicted height plus a correction.

$$Ht_D = Ht_{LW} + Corr$$

The correction is equal to the product of a factor (F), which varies with time, and the range of the tide.

$$Corr = F\,(HT_{HW} - Ht_{LW})$$

The correction factor is determined by use of a *haversine* relationship:

$$F = \frac{1 - \cos\left(\dfrac{T_{LW} \sim T_D}{T_{HW} \sim T_{LW}} \times 180°\right)}{2}$$

where T_{LW} is the time of low water,
T_{HW} is the time of high water,
T_D is desired time.

The symbol $\sim$ means absolute difference, the lesser quantity from the larger; it is used to avoid negative numbers.

Caution: Times may be in terms of hours and minutes for subtraction, but must be expressed decimally for division.

Thus the equation for the height of tide at a **desired** time is

$$Ht_D = Ht_{LW} + (Ht_{HW} - Ht_{LW})\left[\frac{1 - \cos\left(\dfrac{T_{LW} \sim T_D}{T_{HW} \sim T_{LW}} \times 180°\right)}{2}\right]$$

While the mathematics may appear formidable, in actual practice it is merely the punching of a few buttons and the instantaneous appearance of the answer! This answer may vary a small amount from that obtained by normal use of Table 3, but it is actually more correct as that table is used to nearest values without interpolation.

Calculations may be similarly made for a subordinate station after applying time differences and height differences or ratios.

Example (same as Example 3, page 401):

$Ht_D =$

$$-3.0 + [12.1 - (-3.0)] \left[\frac{1 - \cos\left(\frac{2229 - 1740}{2229 - 1517} \times 180° \right)}{2} \right]$$

$$-3.0 + 15.1 \left[\frac{1 - \cos\left(\frac{4.82}{7.20} \times 180° \right)}{2} \right]$$

$$-3.0 + 15.1 \left[\frac{1 - \cos\ (-120.5°)}{2} \right]$$

$$-3.0 + 15.1 \left[\frac{1 - (-.506)}{2} \right]$$

$$-3.0 + (15.1 \times .753) = -3.0 + 11.37 = 8.37$$
$$= 8.4 \text{ feet}$$

Strength of current

A generally similar method is used for determining the strength of current at a desired time. In this instance, however, the time interval is between a maximum current and slack water, rather than between one maximum and the opposite maximum. The equation used is:

$$S_D = S_M \times \cos\left[90° - \left(\frac{T_D \sim T_S}{T_M \sim T_S} \times 90° \right) \right]$$

where T_D is the desired time
T_S is the time of slack water
T_M is time of maximum current, ebb or flood
S_M is strength of maximum current, ebb or flood
S_D is strength of current at the desired time

The direction of the current will be the same as the maximum used, ebb or flood; ignore any negative signs appearing in the answer. This equation is not to be used with "hydraulic currents"; see page 402.

Example (same as Example 3, page 408).

$$S_D = 1.2 \cos\left[90° - \left(\frac{1620 - 1406}{1744 - 1406} \times 90° \right) \right]$$

$$= 1.2 \cos\left[90° - \left(\frac{2.23}{3.63} \times 90° \right) \right]$$

$$= 1.2 \cos (90 - 55.32°)$$

$$= 1.2 \cos 34.68° = 1.2 \times .82 = .987$$

$$= 1.0 \text{ knots}$$

Current sailing

A personal electronic calculator is very useful in solving problems of current sailing. Rather than using the graphic techniques of pages 412–416, addition and subtraction of the vectors can be accomplished by pushing a few buttons, and a more accurate result obtained. The general procedure is the resolution of two vectors into their North-South and East-West components, the addition (or subtraction) of these components, and the establishment of the third vector from these net values.

For comparison purposes, the illustrative examples shown below will be the same as those solved graphically on pages 412–416.

FIG. 2157 Current Sailing—Case 1: The light lines represent the known data: boat course and speed through the water, plus current set and drift. The heavy lines indicate the course and speed over the ground as determined by use of a hand calculator.

Case 1 (fig. 2157): This is a situation of adding two vectors:

$$\overrightarrow{\text{Path over ground}} = \overrightarrow{\text{path thru water}} + \overrightarrow{\text{Current}}$$

$$COG = \tan^{-1}\left(\frac{S \sin C + \text{Drift} \sin \text{Set}}{S \cos C + \text{Drift} \cos \text{Set}} \right)$$

$$= \tan^{-1}\left(\frac{10 \sin 70° + 3 \sin 130°}{10 \cos 70° + 3 \cos 130°} \right)$$

$$= \tan^{-1}\left(\frac{9.40 + 2.30}{3.42\ (-1.93)} \right)$$

$$= \tan^{-1}\left(\frac{11.70}{1.49} \right) = 82.74°$$

$$= 083°$$

$$SOG = \frac{S \sin C + \text{Dft} \sin \text{Set}}{\sin COG}$$

$$= \frac{9.40 + 2.30}{0.99} = 11.82$$

$$= 11.8 \text{ knots}$$

In the above and all other computations by electronic calculators, do not be misled by the long detailed readings of the machine. The value for sin 70° may be shown as 0.9396926208, and this will be used in internal operations of the machine. The result may be computed to be 11.78982612 knots, but if the speed boat were measured only to the nearest tenth of a knot, and current estimated only to the nearest whole knot, it is meaningless to state Speed over Ground to a higher order of precision than 17.8 knots and a more "honest" answer might be simply 18 knots.

These equations will work when the times involved straddle a midnight and fall into two days, but caution must be used. The simplest method is to add 24 hours to the times of the second day so that they are numerically larger than those of the first day. For example, a low water time of 2254 and a desired time of 0115 the following day is best handled as 2515 − 2254 = 2:21 (It is desirable to actually write down the later time with 24 hours added rather than trying to accomplish the addition then subtraction mentally.)

Some calculators will have a key for changing angles in degrees, minutes, and seconds (D.MS) to degrees and decimal fractions (DD.d). This will function equally well for converting hours, minutes, and seconds (H.MS) to hours and decimal fractions (HH.h). The conversion

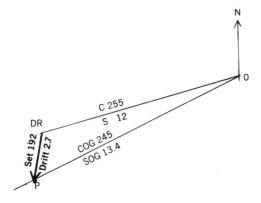

FIG. 2158 Current Sailing—Case 2: The known values are boat course and speed through the water, plus the course and speed made good over the bottom. The heavy lines indicate the calculator solution of the set and drift of the "current"—actually the sum of current, leeway, and other offsetting influences.

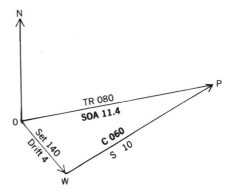

FIG. 2159 Current Sailing—Case 3: Here the known values are the set and drift of the current, the boat's speed through the water, and the direction of the track along which it is desired to run. The calculator easily and quickly solves the vector triangle for course to be steered and the speed of advance along the intended track.

process is usable in either direction and is very helpful in equations such as those used here where times must be both subtracted and divided.

Case 2 (fig. 2158): Again, two vectors are known, subtraction will yield the other.

$$\overrightarrow{\text{Current}} = \overrightarrow{\text{Path over ground}} - \overrightarrow{\text{Path thru water}}$$

$$\text{Set} = \tan^{-1} \left(\frac{\text{SOG sin COG} - \text{S sin C}}{\text{SOG cos COG} - \text{S cos C}} \right)$$

$$= \tan^{-1} \left(\frac{13.4 \sin 245° - 12.0 \sin 255°}{13.4 \cos 245° - 12.0 \cos 255°} \right)$$

$$= \tan^{-1} \left(\frac{-0.55}{-2.56} \right)$$

$$= \tan^{-1} 0.216 = 12°$$

$$= 192°$$

$$\text{Dft} = \left(\frac{\text{SOG sin COG} - \text{S sin C}}{\sin \text{Set}} \right)$$

$$= \left(\frac{13.4 \sin 245° - 12 \sin 255°}{\sin 192°} \right)$$

$$= 2.617 = 2.6 \text{ knots}$$

As the calculator result will be an angle between 0° and 90°, this answer is "angle in quadrant." From inspection of a rough sketch or the vectors, it will be seen that the set is 180° + 12°, or 192°.

Case 3 (fig. 2157): In this instance, one vector is known plus one item for each of the other two; a different type of solution is required here.

$$C = TR - \sin^{-1} \left[\left(\frac{\text{Drift}}{\text{S}} \right) \sin (\text{Set} - TR) \right]$$

$$= 080° - \sin^{-1} \left[\left(\frac{4}{10} \right) \sin (140 - 80°) \right]$$

$$= 080° - \sin^{-1} (.346)$$

$$= 080° - 20.3° = 59.7 = 060°$$

$$\text{SOA} = [\text{S cos} (C - TR)] + [\text{Drift cos} (\text{Set} - TR)]$$

$$= [10 \cos (060 - 080)] + [4 \cos (140 - 080)]$$

$$= (10 \cos - 20°) + (4 \cos 60°)$$

$$= (9.40) + (2.00)$$

$$= 11.4 \text{ knots}$$

Case 4 (fig. 2160): This is again the subtraction of one known vector from another to obtain the third, unknown vector.

$$\overrightarrow{\text{Path thru water}} = \overrightarrow{\text{Path over ground}} - \overrightarrow{\text{Current}}$$

$$C = \tan^{-1} \left[\frac{\text{SOA sin TR} - \text{Drift sin Set}}{\text{SOA cos TR} - \text{Drift cos Set}} \right]$$

$$= \tan^{-1} \left[\frac{11.5 \sin 320° - 3 \sin 205°}{11.5 \cos 320° - 3 \cos 205°} \right]$$

FIG. 2160 Current Sailing—Case 4: The personal calculator here solves the vector triangle for course to be steered and speed to be run through the water in order to reach a specified destination at a predetermined time. This problem is typical of predicted log contests, and might also be useful when a rendezvous with another boat has been set.

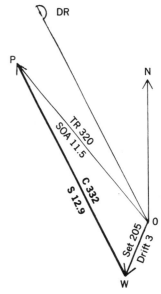

$$= \tan^{-1} \left[\frac{-7.39 - (-1.27)}{8.81 - (-2.72)} \right]$$

$$= \tan^{-1} \left[\frac{-6.12}{11.53} \right] = 28.0°$$

Again this is an angle in quadrant, and C = 360° − 28.0° = 332°.

$$S = \frac{SOA \sin TR - Drift \sin Set}{\sin C}$$

$$= \frac{-6.12}{\sin 332°} = 13.05$$

$$= 13.0 \text{ knots}$$

Some more elaborate category "B" calculators as well as "C" and "D" units will have a key for conversion from rectangular coordinates to polar coordinates. This use of an internally stored program makes short and simple the task of resolving a vector into its N–S and EW components which are then added to or subtracted from the components of another vector. After the net components are determined, the inverse procedure is used to obtain the resultant vector.

Bearings and Distances

Information on a vessel's position can be obtained from two successive bearings on a single object. In some instances, these can be handled quite simply as cases of "doubling the angle on the bow," or bow and beam bearings as discussed on pages 433–435, or as special pairs of angles as considered on pages 447–448. More often, however, it is impracticable or inconvenient to wait until two particular angles can be measured—a more general solution is desirable or necessary. If a copy of Bowditch Table 7 is on board, a solution can be made for bearings at 2° intervals. The most generalized solution accepts any value for either bearing and gives an accurate solution quite quickly—it uses a personal calculator.

In the following calculations, an input element that critically affects the accuracy of the solution is the distance traveled during the interval between bearings. In computing this, the boat's course and speed must be combined with estimated current to obtain Course over Ground (COG) and Speed over Ground (SOG); this latter figure is combined with time to obtain distance traveled —all of these computations can be made by calculators as explained above.

In fig. 2143, the first bearing is the angle as A, the second bearing is the angle at B, the distance traveled is AB, and the distance off when abeam is LC.

Although the distance LA could be calculated, this cannot be done until the boat has reached B where the second bearing is taken—hence, it is of little interest and the position at B is the one normally determined. Quite often, the point of nearest approach to L is of interest, the distance off when abeam L. It, too, can be easily calculated, and *in advance* of reaching point C.

$$LB = \frac{D \sin B_1}{\sin (B_2 - B_1)}$$

$$LC = LB \sin B_2$$

= where D is distance run between the two bearings

= B_1 is first bearing (at A)

= B_2 is second bearing (at B)

Note carefully that B_1 and B_2 are angles to the Course over Ground (COG); relative bearings must be corrected for any difference between COG and C, the course being steered.

Example: (fig. 2143): First bearing 37°, second bearing 61°, distance run between bearings 2.3 miles.

$$LB = \frac{2.3 \sin 37°}{\sin (61 - 37°)}$$

$$= \frac{2.3 \times 0.602}{0.407} = 3.40$$

$$= 3.4 \text{ miles}$$

$$LC = 3.40 \times \sin 61° = 3.40 \times 0.874$$

$$= 2.9 \text{ miles}$$

Distance to horizon

The distance to the horizon for a given height of eye can be determined easily on any calculator having a square root capability.

$$D = 1.144 \sqrt{h}$$

where D is in nautical miles, and h is in feet, or

$$D = 2.072 \sqrt{h}$$

where D is in nautical miles and h is in meters.

If the distance is required in statute miles, multiply D by 1.15; if required in kilometers, multiply D by 1.852.

Traverse Sailing

When a boat is running a course with a number of "legs" of different direction and length, the net change of position can be calculated by means of a traverse table. This situation arises in some navigational contests or when a boat is trolling for fish out of sight of land or aids to navigation. Again, solution is possible from Bowditch, Table 3 in this instance—if a Bowditch is available. With or without a copy of Bowditch, the problem is easily solved by calculator and the simplest of trigonometric equations.

The various legs are broken down into North-South and East-West components, the components summed taking care that southerly and westerly components are given a negative sign, and the resultant single course and direction determined from the net N-S and E-W components. This is simply vector addition of as many legs as have been run.

OTHER NAVIGATIONAL APPLICATIONS

Small electronic calculators, particularly programmable models, have extensive application to navigational problems that are generally beyond the scope of this book. These include: plane sailing, mid-latitude sailing, Mercator sailing, and great-circle sailing; plus all the aspects of celestial navigation.

Many specialized applications can be developed by a skipper to meet his own piloting needs once he has gained some experience and developed a moderate level of skill with his personal calculator. Typical of these uses are: position determination by two non-simultaneous bearings with run between them (on separate objects rather than on a single object as described above), determining course over ground from three bearings on a single object (without knowledge of distance run between times of each bearing), compass deviation table preparation, true and apparent wind, and many others limited only by the skipper's needs, imagination, and abilities with his calculator.

GENERAL ARITHMETIC USE

A category "A" (or more complex) calculator can also be put to good use in boating for general arithmetic problems. These include speed over a measured distance, fuel consumption and cost, and the height of tide at intermediate times using the multiplication factors of page 440. A calculator is also useful for many problems of simple subtraction or addition, such as checking on that yard repair bill that just couldn't total up to so much money!

Calculators can be helpful in converting between various units such as feet, yards, and miles; they are particularly convenient in making conversions in both directions between customary and metric units.

CALCULATORS ABOARD BOATS

The small size and light weight of personal calculators make them suitable for any type of boat and boating; the many applications discussed above make one a desirable "tool" for navigation. They are, however, complex electronic devices and should be protected from the harsher aspects of a marine environment.

A possible problem is the matter of electric power. Only the simplest calculators operate from replaceable dry-cell batteries; many of these can be, and usually are, converted to rechargeable batteries. Most calculators are used with an adapter-charger for direct operation from a 115V, AC, source plus concurrent recharging of an internal battery.

As "shore-type" AC power is not normally available underway, the question is usually the operating life of the internal rechargeable battery. The life in operating hours of fully-charged battery will differ with the calculator model and with the on-off time ratio, but can be expected to be from roughly six hours for simpler units to perhaps three hours for larger models. Much of the power is used for display digits; battery drain can be much reduced by immediately "clearing" to display to a single "0" as soon as the results of a calculation have been noted. The greatest saving of battery power is achieved by turning the calculator off between periods of use. With the exception of one model, however, any data in a calculator's memory registers, and the program in category "C" and "D" units, is lost when power is turned off and must be re-entered when the calculator is next used. (The exception is the HP-25C which will retain information in both data and program memories for an extended period of time.)

For short-term use on boats, a spare battery can be carried and installed when needed. For longer-term cruising with most calculators, it is possible to purchase, or make, a charger-adapter which will permit operation from the boats 12V, DC, electrical system. The drain is negligible, on the order of ¼ ampere.

Specialized Positioning Procedures

In addition to the generally used procedures for position determination previously described in this chapter, there are other, more specialized, techniques. These should not be scorned as "short cuts"; they will provide valid position information and fixes under the particular circumstances that permit their use.

COMBINATIONS OF RELATIVE BEARINGS

The bow-and-beam-bearings technique has already been described, fig. 2140. This was a particular set of two relative bearings, 045° and 090° (or 315° and 270°). It was included there because of its basic simplicity and the ease with which such a pair of bearings could be obtained. There are other combinations of relative bearings, not so easily obtained, but quite easily used.

Special pairs of bearings

The following sets of bearings have such a relationship to each other that the run between the first bearing and the second will nearly equal the distance away from the sighted object when it is passed abeam:

20°-30°	21°-32°	22°-34°
23°-36°	24°-39°	25°-41°
27°-46°	29°-51°	30°-54°
31°-56°	32°-59°	34°-64°
35°-67°	36°-69°	37°-71°
38°-74°	39°-77°	40°-79°
41°-81°	43°-86°	44°-88°

There are also additional pairs of angles that could theoretically be used, but these involve half-degrees and have been omitted here as such precision is not usually obtainable on small craft.

It should be noted that these are pairs of relative bearings to port as well as to starboard. In the table above, "20°-30°" can be either relative bearings 020° and 030°, or 340° and 330°; "31°-56°" can be either RB 031° and 056°, or RB 329° and 304°; etc.

The 7/8th rule

If observations are made when the relative bearings are 30° and 60° on either bow, simple calculations will give *two* useful items of information. The distance run between the two bearings is equal to the distance to the object at the time of the second bearing (doubling the angle on the bow). Also, this same distance, fig. 2168, multiplied by $7/8$ is the distance that the craft will be off from the sighted object when it is broad on the beam, provided that course and speed are not changed.

The 7/10th rule

A situation comparable to the preceding rule is that which exists when the two relative bearings are $22^1/2°$ and $45°$ to port or starboard (assuming that bearings can be taken to a half-degree). In this case, as before, the distance away from the sighted object at the time of the second bearing is equal to the distance run between bearings, but the multiplier is 7/10 to determine the distance off the sighted object when it is abeam.

THREE BEARINGS AND RUN BETWEEN

The technique of using *two* bearings and the run between them was illustrated in fig. 2142. The positional information derived from this procedure was dependent upon the assumption that the course and speed made good with respect to the bottom during the run between bearings was accurately known. Along strange coasts, without current predictions or means of estimating current effects, this assumption is often of doubtful validity.

By taking a *third* bearing and timing a second run (between the second and third bearings), enough additional known factors are entered into the problem so that no assumption need be made about the course made good nor the actual speed over the bottom. All that is required for this technique is a prominent object or mark on shore, plus the means for taking bearings and measuring time intervals.

As soon as you spot the object, "X" in fig. 2169, take a bearing on it and note the exact time; record both items of information. Plot the bearing line on your chart, line XA in fig. 2169(a). Next, when the object is exactly broad on the beam, note the time. Plot this line of position on the chart. Later, when the bearing to X has changed enough to give a good angle of intersection, take a third bearing and again note the time carefully. Plot this line, XC. Be sure that throughout this procedure you are maintaining a steady course and speed through the water.

Since you have recorded the time of each bearing, you can determine the two elapsed times, and compute the *ratio* between these intervals.

For example, if you ran for $32^1/2$ minutes between the first and second (beam) bearings, and then for $22^1/2$ minutes more to the third bearing, the ratio would be $32^1/2 / 22^1/2$, which can be reduced to 6.5/4.5.

Through a convenient point, B, on the beam bearing line, draw a light "construction" line in the direction of your course (C) as steered. Using point "B" as the reference or zero point, measure off to each side, along the construction line, distances proportional to the ratio of the time intervals using any convenient scale, fig. 2169(b).

Erect perpendiculars to the construction line at the spots determined by these proportionate distances. These lines, drawn at $90°$ angles to the construction line, intersect the bearing lines XA and XC at points A' and C' respectively, fig. 2169(c).

Connect points A' and C' with a line and you have your answer. Line A'-C' is the course you are making good and

FIG. 2168 If observations are made when the relative bearings of a fixed object are 30° and 60°, and the distance made good between these observations is calculated, the pilot can determine his distance from the object both at the time of the second bearing and when it is abeam by the "$7/8$th Rule."

includes the effects of currents, wind, and errors in steering. Its direction may be taken from the chart and compared with the intended course. It should be noted that this is *not the actual track*—the selection of the scale to represent the two time intervals would determine the location of points A' and C', and hence the line's location, although not its direction.

It is because *ratios* are used, and not actual speeds, that an accurate speed over the bottom is not needed here as it was in the case of the technique of *two* bearings and run between. Although it does not allow the navigator to determine his position nor his speed over the bottom, this technique does show plainly whether he is making good his intended course, or is being set onto or off the shore; it helps determine whether the actual track parallels the beach or not.

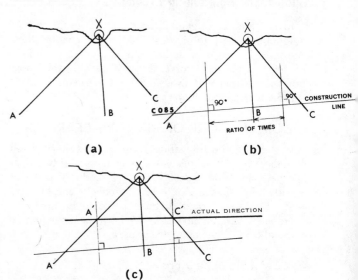

FIG. 2169 The course of a boat under unknown conditions of current can be determined by taking three bearings on a single object. See text for details of this technique.

Relative Motion

The easiest way to acquire what is often called a "sailor's eye" is to learn the simple, but basic, principles of *relative motion*. The term "relative motion" scares some people, but it is really quite a simple subject to master. It is also one of the most useful skills that a boatman can acquire as it gives quick and accurate answers to problems involving moving vessels.

For example, you find that your motorboat is converging on another boat that has the right of way. If you hold your present course and speed, will you clear her? Or your sailboat is beating to windward on a port tack, and you find a boat coming in on the starboard tack. Will you cross safely ahead, or must you pass astern? Or you have laid a course for a buoy, making allowance for the current. Have you made the right allowance? Relative motion will give you the answers to all such questions.

When a boat is under way, its movement across the water is termed *actual motion*. If it is anchored, the movements of another craft appear in their actual relationship to the earth's surface; you are observing that boat's actual motion. But if you get under way, the movement of the other boat appears to be different because you are now observing *relative motion*. Some objects, especially moving ones, seem to be doing things that are not actually happening; elements of what may be almost an optical illusion can exist.

Let us suppose that you are under way and proceeding north at 5 knots up a marked channel. You sight another boat coming directly toward you; this other craft is also making 5 knots. The two boats are converging at a *relative speed* of 10 knots which is simply the sum of your speed and his. Both craft are passing the stationary channel markers at the same actual speed, but the distance between them is lessening at a rate which is the sum of the individual speeds.

As the other boat approaches, you recognize the skipper as a friend and turn around to join him on his southerly course. As soon as the boats are alongside each other on the same course and at the same speed, *relative motion* ceases to exist because the other boat stays in the same place relative to your boat. Only *actual motion* remains—that of your boat past the buoys and over the bottom. If the other craft develops engine trouble and slows down, there is again relative motion between the two vessels. He will appear to be moving aft because of his reduced speed. Thus, the rule may be stated as follows: *relative motion is present only when the actual movements of two or more objects are not the same.*

Relative bearings

The bearing of an object is usually taken as a relative bearing; these were discussed in pages 352a, b. See fig. 2170. With practice, the relative bearing of an object can be estimated within five or ten degrees. It must be remembered that a change in course of your own boat will change the relative bearings of all objects around it. Thus, if you are on a course of 050° True and sight an object bearing 090° relative, the true bearing of that object will be 140°, fig. 2171a. Come left to a course of 020°, and although the true bearing will remain unchanged at 140°, the rela-

FIG. 2170 In determining relative motion in small-craft piloting, much use is made of relative bearings measured clockwise from 000° dead ahead.

tive bearing will now become 120°, fig. 2171b.

In small craft piloting, approximations will usually suffice in relative motion problems and special instruments are not needed. A steady hand at the wheel or tiller, a clear eye, and a rough mental diagram are all that are needed. A pelorus can be used, but seldom is, in actual practice.

TO CROSS OR NOT TO CROSS

When determining the relative motion of another boat, it is necessary either to convert relative bearings to compass (or true) bearings, or to maintain a steady course. In practice, it is easier to maintain a steady course, with the result that any change in relative bearing will be the result of a change in the positions of the boats relative to each other, rather than the result of the changing course of your craft. Since the desired information is the changing positions of the boats relative to each other, the actual value of the relative bearing is of far less importance than the direction and rate of change, if any.

Collision bearings

What we want to know in any crossing or converging situation is: will we cross ahead of, or astern of, the other boat, or will we hit her? Because the two boats are considered relative to each other, it is convenient to think of one's own boat as stationary—relative to the other boat. Thus, we have three basic situations:

1. The relative bearing of the other boat moves ahead (toward the bow), or
2. The relative bearing of the other boat moves aft, or
3. The relative bearing of the other boat remains constant.

Fig. 2172a illustrates the first situation, that of a boat passing ahead. This illustration indicates the actual successive positions of the two boats. Fig. 2172b represents

FIG. 2171 If a boat's heading changes, the relative bearing of an object is changed by the same amount. From the situation in *a* below to that in *b*, the true heading of the boat has changed from 050° to 020°; the relative bearing has changed by the same amount, from 090° to 120°. (Note that the sum of the heading and the relative bearing remains constant.)

FIG. 2172 The positions of two boats are shown for three intervals of time separated by five minutes each. In *a*, the actual positions of each craft are shown. In *b*, the motion of the other boat is shown *relative* to our craft. In both cases, the relative bearings move forward on our boat and the other craft will cross ahead of us. The distance *x* is the separation at the *point of closest approach*.

the same situation shown in terms of motion relative to our own boat as stationary. The bearing change is then more clearly seen.

The line connecting the positions of the other boat in fig. 2172b is the *line of relative movement,* the relative course and relative distance traveled by the other boat in relationship to our boat. Provided both boats maintain course and speed, it is a straight line. In this situation, when the line of relative motion is extended, it passes the bow of our "stationary" boat; therefore, the other boat following that line relative to us will cross ahead. The distance "x" fig. 2172b is the distance apart that the two boats will be at the *closest point of approach* (CPA).

The second case, in which the relative bearing moves aft, is the opposite of the first situation. The relative mo-

FIG. 2173 In this crossing situation, the relative bearings move aft, and the other boat will pass astern of us (we will pass ahead of her). The actual successive positions of each craft are shown in *a*, and relative motion is shown in *b*.

tion line passes astern, and so will the other boat. Figs. 2173a and b illustrate this situation.

If the relative bearing does not change, the line of relative motion will pass through our boat's position, the distance "x" is zero, and the two boats will collide unless one or both changes course or speed. See figs. 2174a and b.

It is important to note that figs. 2172-2174 are intended to illustrate situations rather than actual chart plots on a boat. The position of the other craft could not be plotted unless distance as well as bearing information was available, and this is unlikely unless your boat has radar. The significance here is that *bearing information only,* which is available to any pilot, will by its change, if any, tell him whether he will pass ahead, astern, or "through" the other craft. The closest point of approach can be determined only if an actual plot based on distances is made, but lack of this information is not significant.

Rules for crossing situations

The foregoing discussion, formulated into rules, results in the following procedures for a crossing situation:

1. Maintain a reasonably steady course and speed.
2. Observe the relative bearing of the other boat only when you are on your specified compass course. You must be on the *same* course each time you take a relative bearing.
3. Watch the other boat for changes in course or speed which would obviously upset the relative motion conditions.
4. (a) If the relative bearing moves ahead, the other boat will pass ahead.
   (b) If the relative bearing moves aft, the other craft will pass astern.
   (c) If the relative bearing is steady, there is a dangerous possibility of collision.

FIG. 2174 Here is a crossing situation in which the relative bearing does *not* change! A collision will result if both craft maintain course and speed. Note that in *b* the line of relative movement passes *through* our boat and the value of *x* is reduced to zero.

Offsetting effects of current or wind

There is another useful application of relative motion in the case of allowances for offsetting the effects of current and/or wind.

In fig. 2175, the boat has been put on a course that her skipper believes will put her close aboard the buoy marking the shoal. At the time of the first bearing, "0" minutes, the buoy bears 340° relative. Five minutes later, the relative bearing has changed to 350°. It is clear from this change that the boat is being set down more than expected and that the relative movement line of the buoy will pass ahead of the boat, i.e., the boat will pass on the shoal side of the buoy. If the bearings on the buoy remained steady, the boat would pass close to it; and if the bearings shifted gradually away from the bow, the skipper would know that he would clear the shoal safely.

In fig. 2175a, the problem is shown in terms of the boat moving relative to the buoy. In fig. 2175b, the boat is considered to be stationary and the relative movement line is that of the buoy. Note that the relative movement lines in the two representations are parallel, equal, and opposite.

FIG. 2175 Relative motion considerations are also applicable when the other "craft" is stationary, such as a buoy. The change, if any, of the relative bearings on the object can be used to determine on which side of it you will pass. In *a* and *b* below, the motion is considered relative to the buoy and to your boat, respectively.

The Maneuvering Board

The Defense Mapping Agency Hydrographic Center now publishes a plotting sheet known as the *Maneuvering Board* (in pads of 50 sheets; No. 5090, or 5091 in larger size). These forms are used by ships at sea for the solution of relative motion problems. Complicated movements of large task forces, as well as the tracking of a single ship, are plotted on maneuvering boards to facilitate the solution of problems of interception and the determination of the course and speed of radar contacts.

Use on boats

Here we will consider a few of the simpler, though useful, applications of the maneuvering board, using only the plotting sheet, parallel rulers or equivalent, and a pair of dividers. For the fortunate yachtsman who has radar aboard, however, the applications are increased ten-fold.

Description of the sheet

To observe the physical appearance of a maneuvering board, examine fig. 2176 which shows one reduced about 40% from its original size of approximately 12 inches square. On it is printed, in green, a large circle with bearing lines radiating outward from the center every 10 degrees, and 10 concentric circles ½ inch apart to indicate speed or distance. At the right and left sides are lines of scale with numbered marks spaced equal to the distance between the concentric circles. Thus, a speed line drawn out to the fifth circle could indicate 5, 10, 15, 20, or 25 knots as determined by your choice of scale.

At the bottom of the sheet are three lines divided into logarithmic scales for use in solving time, distance, and speed problems. If two of these quantities are known, the third may be found by drawing a line between the known values on the appropriate scales, and finding the answer at the intersection of this line with the third scale.

In fig. 2177, observe the solution to three problems: (1) if you run 6 miles in 30 minutes, your speed is 12 knots; (2) to run 6 miles at 12 knots will require 30 minutes; or (3) running at 12 knots for 30 minutes, you will cover 6 miles. Distance, time, speed—knowing two, you can quickly, easily, and accurately solve for the third. This alone makes the maneuvering board a handy device, but it is only a small sample of its usefulness.

FIG. 2176 The Defense Mapping Agency Hydrographic Center publishes a useful plotting sheet known as a maneuvering board. These sheets, which come in pads of 50 sheets of either of two sizes, are particularly handy when plotting situations of relative motion.

FIG. 2177 Extract from a maneuvering board showing the logarithmic distance-time-speed scales. The problem illustrated by the line drawn across the scales is discussed in the text.

451

The bearing lines and circles of distance facilitate the plotting of positions of other craft or objects relative to the boat on which the maneuvering board is being used. These radial lines and concentric circles can also be used for vector diagrams with lines drawn to represent actual and relative motion. Each vector, according to its length and direction, depicts a statement of fact in the problem. For example: a vector line to indicate a course of 040° and a speed of 5 knots would be drawn outward along the 40° bearing line to a length of 5 units, i.e., to the fifth circle. If the speed is greater than 10 units (knots or MPH), use is made of the 2:1, 3:1, 4:1, or 5:1 scales at the sides of the chart.

A vector line indicates graphically the direction and velocity of an element of the problem, such as the course and speed of your boat, another boat, the wind, or the current. In some instances, the vector will not be drawn from the center of the sheet, but its direction is always measured with reference to the center point and the outer circular scale.

Points on diagrams of positions are labeled with upper-case (capital) letters; points on vector diagrams are labeled with lower-case letters.

Maneuvering boards come in pads of 50 sheets. Each sheet is printed on both sides, and the paper is sufficiently heavy that both sides may be used. The cover sheets of both the 5090 and 5091 pads include instructions for their use in various situations and problems. On this cover sheet, there is also a sample problem, but unfortunately it is in terms of a formation of naval ships and as such is not of much value to boatmen.

USE OF THE MANEUVERING BOARD

The 5090 or 5091 sheets may be used for plots of the relative motion of two vessels in a crossing situation as shown in figs. 2172-2174. These sheets are particularly useful on board radar-equipped craft where distance as well as bearing can be measured. Fig. 2178, for example, is a re-plot of fig. 2173b on a maneuvering board sheet.

FIG. 2178 This is a re-plot of the situation of fig. 2173b on a Maneuvering Board sheet. Note that the plot has been rotated so that the direction of one's own boat is toward the top of the sheet (RB 000° dead ahead). The direction of relative motion (DRM) can be readily taken from the sheet, and the point of closest approach (CPA) and "miss distance" easily determined.

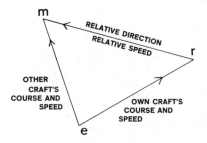

FIG. 2179 A vector triangle of relative motion. The course and speed of your own craft is plotted as *e - r* and the apparent (relative) motion of the other craft as *r - m*. The triangle can be closed with the line *e - m* which is the *actual* course and speed of the other craft.

From a plot such as fig. 2178, with successive relative positions of the other craft plotted at recorded times, the direction of relative movement (DRM) and speed of relative movement (SRM) can be found. SRM is determined from the logarithmic scales at the bottom of the sheet using distance and time as the known factors. Knowing these relative motion quantities, and the course and speed of your own boat, a *vector triangle* can be used to determine the *actual* course and speed of the other craft. The relationships between these quantities are shown in fig. 2179. Point e, always at the center of the maneuvering board, represents earth, the reference for actual motion. Point r is the outer end of the speed vector, *e-r*, for the *reference* craft (your boat). The vector *r-m* represents the relative motion of the *maneuvering* (other) craft. By completing the triangle with the vector *e-m*, always outward from the point e at the center, the actual course and speed of the other boat are found. When such a vector triangle is drawn on a maneuvering board sheet, as in fig. 2180, the actual course can be read directly from the outer circular scale, and the actual speed can be read from the convenient concentric circles of the sheet, remembering to apply the same scale factor as used in plotting the speed of your own boat.

True wind problem

Fig. 2181 illustrates what is called a *true wind problem.*

Situation: Your sailboat is close-hauled on true course 080°, speed 5 knots. The apparent (relative) wind is coming over the starboard side from 125° true with a velocity of 15 knots.

Problem: You want to sail your boat as close to the wind as possible, say at an angle of 45° off the true wind. You wish to know the direction and velocity of the *actual* wind so as to be able to determine whether you can lay the mark on the next tack, and the best course that you will be able to make to windward.

Solution: Draw your course and speed vector, *e-r*, along the bearing line for 080° outward from the center for 2½ circles (5 knots at a scale of 2:1). From point r, draw a line for the relative wind in the direction *toward* which the wind is traveling; use parallel rulers or another plotting instrument to transfer this direction from the bearing line out to the point r. With dividers, measure off the length for 15 knots along the 2:1 scale at the left side of the chart; lay off this distance along the relative wind line and so obtain the vector for that element of the problem. Where this vector ends is point w.

Next, draw a line from point e at the center to point w;

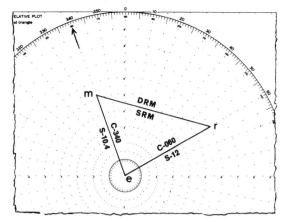

FIG. 2180 This is a re-plot of the preceding illustration on a Maneuvering Board sheet. The actual course of the other craft can be read directly from the outer scale of figures and the speed from the concentric rings; note that in this example the speed ratio is 2:1, each circle represents 2 knots or MPH.

this vector, e-w, represents the direction and velocity of the *true wind*. Since wind direction is never expressed in terms of where it is going (blowing toward), we look directly across the board and see that it is blowing *from* 142°. The velocity of 12 knots is read directly from the circles, the sixth circle at a scale of 2:1. Now it can be seen that the motion of your boat through the water has caused the apparent wind to come from a direction 17° counterclockwise from its true direction. (The actual wind velocity is seen to be less than the apparent velocity, but this information is not pertinent to this particular problem.)

To determine our course for sailing at an angle of 45° to the actual wind on the next, port, tack, it is merely a matter of adding 45° to the true wind direction of 142° to get 187°

Current sailing problems

One problem common to both sail boats and motor boats is that of choosing the correct course in traversing an area where the current will set the craft off her intended track if allowances are not made. In fig. 2182 we have the graphic solution of two questions. What is the current doing? What course do we take to correct for it?

Assume that your boat is on course 320° at a speed of 6 knots to pass close aboard a light vessel that now, at 0800, is dead ahead, 9 miles distant. As you progress through the water on your specified course, you notice that the light vessel appears to be moving to your left. This indicates that a current is at work on your port side.

To learn the set and drift of the current, and the course needed to correct for it: Plot the 0800 position of the light vessel from you—320°, 9 miles. Fix your present position and determine from the chart the new relative position of the light vessel. In fig. 2182 this is 310° and 7 miles; label this position with the time, 0829.

Now, draw in your boat's course and speed vector, e-r, of 320° and 6 knots, using a 2:1 scale ratio and the third circle. Note that the same scale ratio does not have to be used for both distance and speeds; it must, however, be constant within either category.

With parallel rulers or other plotting instrument, transfer the direction of the line of relative movement between the two plots of the light vessel's position to point r and draw in a line to some convenient length. After measuring the distance "traveled" by the light vessel, solve for its relative speed using the distance-time-speed logarithmic

scales. In this case, 2.4 miles in 29 minutes gives 5.2 knots.

Using the speed scale factor of 2:1, the speed of 5.2 knots is laid off along the line drawn from r. The point so found is labeled m and a line drawn *from m* to e at the center represents the set and drift of the current. This is found to be 080° and 3 knots.

With this information, we can now determine a new course to correct for the effect of the current. Remembering that our vessel *never* leaves the center of the maneuvering board, we must make the light vessel "come to us." A line drawn from the 0829 position of the light vessel, the broken line in fig. 2182, is the line that we wish the light vessel to follow on its way to us.

Parallel a line to this, starting at a convenient distance out, beyond the third circle (6 knots at our 2:1 speed scale), and draw toward point m in the same direction as the intended track of the light vessel; this is line a-m in the illustration. Where this relative movement line crosses the third circle is the course to steer for a speed of 6 knots —287°. It should be noted that there are many possible

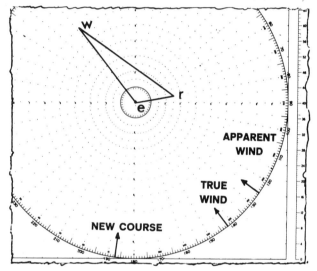

FIG. 2181 The maneuvering board can be used to determine the velocity and direction of the true wind to aid in setting a new course on the next tack. See the text for details of this technique.

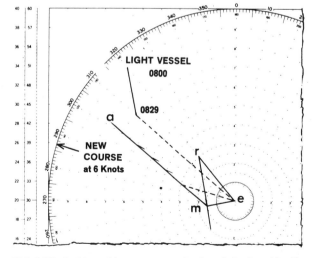

FIG. 2182 In this problem, a maneuvering board sheet enables the pilot to determine the current setting the boat off the desired track. It is also possible to graphically determine the necessary new course to be steered for any given speed.

combinations of courses and speeds available along this line, and that any increase in speed would bring a lesser course change, and vice versa. For example: looking out along the line *a-m,* we would find that for 8 knots, the course would be 293°; for 10 knots, 297°; for 12 knots, 299°.

Other uses for the maneuvering board

The examples above have barely touched on the many uses of the maneuvering board sheets. There are many more applications—all interesting, but of lesser direct use in small-craft boating. Those interested in this topic in more detail can satisfy their curiosity in the many pages of *Bowditch* and *Dutton* devoted to the maneuvering board and its uses.

A pad of maneuvering board sheets, either 5090 or 5091, may be obtained almost anywhere charts and publications of the Defense Mapping Agency Hydrographic Center are sold. The cost is only a few cents for each sheet, a small price to pay for safety and interesting, easy piloting.

Longshore Piloting

There are a number of specialized techniques that might well be a part of every skipper's piloting skills. Their practicability has been thoroughly tested.

DELIBERATE OFFSET OF COURSE

One of these specialized piloting techniques is used in making a landfall. The essence of it is this—lay your course, *not* for your objective, but decidedly to one side to allow for possible inaccuracies in the offsetting effect of the current, or to account for possible uncertainties of position. The advantage of this procedure lies in the fact that should you not arrive at your destination at the scheduled time, you have a near-certainty, rather than considerable doubt, as to which way you should turn to reach your objective.

The technique is best explained by use of an example.

Situation

Let us assume that you have been fishing somewhere in the area between Block Island and Martha's Vineyard. After several hours of trolling, drifting, and just circling around, your position is quite problematical. Just as you decide that your fishing luck has run out for the day and it is time to head for Block Island Harbor, fog sets in to make the situation more interesting.

Your best "guesstimate," in the absence of any positional information, is that you are somewhere to the east of bell buoy "1", marked as point *B* in fig. 2183; you believe that you are somewhere in the vicinity of point *A* on the chart.

Solution with deliberate offset of course

It's a good plan to lay your course for the off-lying bell buoy—as a matter of fact, that's what they are there for— but even if there were no such buoy, there can be merit in laying the course decidedly off to one side of the ultimate objective, Block Island Harbor.

Suppose you lay your course AB to the bell buoy and miss it by ⅛ mile to the north. When you pick up the 3-fathom (18-foot) curve, at *C,* you know you are north of

Note: ⅛ mile = 0.20 km; ¼ mile = 0.40 km; ⅜ mile = 0.60 km.

FIG. 2183 If you are caught in a fog somewhere offshore in the vicinity of point *A*, the inclination might be to head directly for the harbor entrance at *E*. It is much safer, however, to deliberately head for a point more to the north on a course that will take you past the bell buoy at *B*. The text explains why.

the harbor—a fact confirmed by the realization that you would have picked it up much sooner if you were south of the harbor entrance.

Had you missed it by ⅛ mile to the south, and picked up the 3-fathom curve at *D,* you could still follow the curve southeastward to buoy C "3". Even if your position were ¼ mile south of *A* when you laid your course westward, you would still pick up the 3-fathom curve at the harbor entrance.

You find added assurance of your general position above the harbor entrance when you find depths holding generally at 3 fathoms on your course southeastward. If your calculations were completely wrong and you ran southeastward from any point below the harbor entrance, depths would increase.

Solution without deliberate offset of course

Consider, however, what could happen if you missed your objective E by ¼ mile to the south if the course had been laid direct to buoy C "3". Picking up the 3-fathom curve at F, you could not be sure whether you were north or south of the entrance.

Your first conclusion might be that, since you have run a few minutes overtime before reaching the 3-fathom curve, you are north of the harbor. But don't forget that you didn't accurately know your starting point. Suppose you had been several minutes eastward of where you thought you were when the fog set in. In this event, the additional few minutes running time before reaching 18-foot depths is reasonable.

On the assumption that you are indeed somewhat to the north of the harbor, you turn south, proceeding slowly and carefully. A few minutes pass, but still no buoy or harbor entrance. How far to continue? That buoy may be just ahead, obscured by the fog. On the other hand, doubt creeps in. You couldn't have been that far off in your reckoning—or could you? So there you are, in a fog—literally and figuratively.

General procedures

In the first example above (where we laid a course for the bell) the intended track was laid about ⅜ mile to the north of the objective (the harbor entrance). How much deliberate offset of course is made in any given case varies within limits determined by what you feel would be a maximum error under the circumstances. On a long run in from offshore, making a landfall on a beach that trends in a straight line for miles in either direction with few marks of identification even if visibility is good, you may prefer to make an allowance of a mile or more. It adds little to the total run, but eliminates much uncertainty. But don't use this technique blindly, without regard to possible dangers that may line the beach. Study the chart carefully and adapt the procedure to the situation at hand.

Crossing the Gulf Stream

This same procedure may be used in crossing the Gulf Stream. Rather than attempting to make an exact allowance for the distance you will be set northward, a somewhat overly-generous allowance is made, with the knowledge that if you don't pick up your target landmark after the allotted passage time, you have only to turn northward. It can be comforting to know the proper direction in which to turn, rather than to have to make a choice with perhaps a 50-50 chance of being wrong.

The same technique can be used in recrossing the Gulf Stream on your westward passage back to Florida. Again, over-allow for the northward offsetting influence of the Stream and plan to turn northward as you approach the coast if you see no identifiable landmarks.

NIGHT PILOTING BY TIMETABLE

Another specialized piloting technique that will go far toward increasing the pleasure of nighttime piloting is the establishment of a "timetable" for your particular cruise.

Preparing the timetable

When you anticipate a night run, don't wait until you are on your way before studying out courses, distances, running times, etc. Go over the entire trip in advance and acquaint yourself thoroughly with the separate legs of the cruise, the aids to navigation that you will pass, the characteristics of the lights, and other items of piloting interest.

Then set up a timetable, assuming that you will leave your point of departure at exactly 0000, and note in orderly fashion the predicted time of arrival abeam of every light and buoy on both sides of your intended track. Alongside each entry, show the characteristics of the navigational aid and the compass course at the time. You can also enter into your timetable the approximate times that major lights can be expected to become visible.

Using the timetable

Invest in an alarm clock or watch with a luminous dial and set it for 12 o'clock when you start your run from the point of departure on which your predetermined timetable is based. Then as the flashing, occulting, or other lights successively wink over the horizon, you won't have to dash below to puzzle out characteristics and identify each in turn. The elapsed time from your start will clue you as to the identity of the aid to navigation.

The timetable will aid you in knowing where you are at any time, what light you just passed, what the characteristics will be of the next light to appear, and when that should happen. The use of elapsed time, rather than actual clock time, allows flexibility in the starting time; it is not necessary to revise your entire timetable if you take your departure earlier or later than originally planned. If any discrepancy creeps in consistently between when events should happen and when they actually do, the hands of the clock or watch can be shifted as needed.

NIGHT COASTWISE PILOTING BY SHORE LIGHTS

For night piloting alongshore, the lights of towns and settlements along the beach can be used to estimate distances offshore. An experienced boatman reports that he has been able to maintain a course approximately 5½ miles (10.2 km) offshore going down the Jersey coast simply by keeping in sight of the reflected glow in the sky above lights in towns along the shore.

The appearance of direct rays of light would be a signal indicating that the distance offshore was decreasing to 5 miles (9.3 km) or less, whereupon it would be advisable to haul off until the reflected glow was visible once more. The objective of keeping so far offshore was to avoid the extensive areas of fish net stakes, and yet not lose contact with land.

The distance that the direct rays will be seen will be determined by the height of the observer's eye, and should be determined by the individual skipper for his own boat. The principles involved, however, remain the same for all craft.

FOLLOWING THE BEACH

Elsewhere, we have considered how a boat may be piloted along a coast by following a constant depth, or fathom curve. It is possible, however, that the sounder might be inoperative or not available for some other reason. It is well to have another means of following the shoreline approximately when visibility conditions permit the observation of objects on the beach.

Let's say that you wish to parallel the Jersey or Long Island beach (or any average coast where there are no hills or mountains ashore to stand out prominently at long range). Fig. 2184 shows such a coastline. From the deck of a typical small boat at sea, you will be unable to see the beach if you are more than about 4½ miles (8.3 km) offshore, due to the earth's curvature. If you can just see the beach, you are roughly 4 miles (7.4 km) out. This, of course, will not hold true if there is fog or haze.

FIG. 2184 With just a little effort, you can determine for your height of eye on your boat the distances off shore at which you can see the beach and certain features of the buildings. Your distances shouldn't vary much from those shown here for a typical boat.

Specialized Piloting Techniques / CHAPTER 21

Distance off by visibility of details

Now as you follow the coast, you will probably trend in closer without realizing that you are off your intended track. Buildings appear, and you find that you can distinguish detail enough to make out individual windows of houses. This means that you are within roughly 2 miles (3.7 km) of the beach.

Thus you have established two limits—by keeping within sight of the beach, but far enough off that you cannot count windows, you are averaging 2-4 miles (3.7-7.4 km) off shore. Meticulous pilots may object that this is too loose, but there are many cruises that do not require any higher degree of precision.

Check for your height-of-eye

The 2-mile (3.7-km) distance at which windows can be counted will not vary with the observer's height of eye. This is a matter of distance and detail. The 4- to 4½-mile (7.4- to 8.3-km) limits of visibility for the beach, however, are subject to variation from one boat to another. These are average figures; establish more exact distances for your own craft by using the bow-and-beam technique or any other positioning procedure.

USING A POSITION FINDER

Earlier in this chapter, we considered a positioning technique using two horizontal angles between the lines of sight to three identifiable objects. See figs. 2124-2126. Although this is a standard method, it has not been widely used on small boats because a sextant is normally required to measure the angles and a three-arm protractor to plot them accurately. As a sextant would be a relatively large investment for this use only, those who do not venture onto the high seas and use celestial navigation do not normally have one aboard.

The Weems Position-Finder is a combination instrument that can be used both to measure the angles and do the chart plotting. It eliminates the need for a sextant for making observations, and the attendant steps of reading angles from the sextant scale and setting these values on the protractor. This results in a saving of time, effort, and risk of error. As the observations are taken, the arms of this instrument are locked in position, and the device becomes, in effect, a three-arm protractor with the angles already set. The actual values of the angles need never be known. The solution is entirely independent of the compass or other instruments. The optical principle employed is shown in fig. 2185.

FIG. 2187 The position-finder in place on a chart. The arms are set directly as the observations are made, and no angles need be read in order to determine the fix. The three arms are aligned with the chart symbols for the objects sighted upon; the observer's position is at the center of the instrument.

The observing portion of the device, fig. 2186, consists of a fixed horizon mirror, *A*, in which the reflected image of one object is seen immediately below the true image of the center object viewed over the top of the mirror. This is called a horizon mirror because it has the same function as the horizon mirror of a marine sextant.

The rotatable index mirror, *B*, is moved by the index arm, *C*, to reflect the image of the right or left object into the fixed mirror. By viewing through the slot in the center of this mirror, it is possible to use this one mirror for both the right and left angles. This is not possible with a sextant, where the index mirror is offset and can be used for only one horizontal angle at a time.

The plotting portion of the position-finder consists of three arms, pivoted at one center point, at which a pencil mark can be made through a hole onto the chart. The center arm is permanently located with an etched centerline at 90° to the plane of the horizontal mirror. The two movable arms can be locked in position during the observations, avoiding the need for any reading of scales and subsequent setting of the arms before plotting. The inside edges of the movable arms are used for plotting.

Using the position-finder

Three objects are selected that can be identified visually and on the chart. The procedure is to measure the angle between the line of sight to the center object and those to the right-hand and left-hand objects. The two angles cannot be measured simultaneously. If it is apparent that one angle is changing at a more rapid rate than the other, the angle changing more slowly should be measured first and the angle changing more rapidly last; otherwise, it is not important which angle is measured first.

Each angle is measured in accordance with the detailed instructions furnished with the instrument. As the angles are measured, the movable arms are locked into place. The instrument is then transferred to the chart and used as a conventional three-arm protractor, lining up each arm with the respective chart symbol and marking the position with a pencil through the hole in the center of the device. Fig. 2187 shows the Position-Finder in place on a chart.

FIG. 2185 Optical principle of Position Finder. Angle *a* is angle between two objects on shore being observed. Angle *b* is amount index arm, and therefore index mirror, is turned. This is always one-half of angle *a*. Angle *c* is angle of light rays coming from right hand object to index mirror and reflected to horizon mirror. Always the same as angle *a*.

FIG. 2186 The observing portion of the position finder. A, fixed horizon mirror. B, rotatable index mirror. C, index arm. See text for a description of the use of this instrument.

ECHO PILOTING

An approximate method of determining distance, in passages or other bodies of water where there are sheer cliffs that will produce echoes, is to sound a short blast of the whistle or horn, and time, preferably with a stop watch, the interval before the echo is received.

Divide this interval in seconds by two (because the sound has to travel to the shore and return as the echo), and multiply that figure by 1100, a rough value for the speed of sound in air in feet per second. (Actually, at 32°F, the speed is 1088 feet per second and at 72°F. it is 1132 fps, but the figure of 1100 is close enough for the accuracy of the timing method used.*

For example, you sound a short blast on your horn and time the interval until the return of the echo as five seconds. Half of this time is 2½ seconds; multiply by 1100, and you have 2650 feet or a distance off of slightly less than one-half nautical mile.

This is sometimes called "dog-bark navigation" and is used to a limited extent in the inside passage to Alaska on the British Columbia coast. If an echo can be received from both shores, a vessel can be kept in the approximate middle of the passage by holding such a course that an echo will be received simultaneously from both sides.

THE RULE-OF-SIXTY

Another useful specialized piloting technique is the *Rule-of-Sixty*. It provides a simple, practical way of changing course to clear an off-lying danger area without a lot of chart work. Again, the technique is best explained with an example.

Let's assume in this case that you have come out of Portsmouth Harbor and are running a southerly course down the coast to Cape Ann. See fig. 2188. Somewhere out off Newburyport you pick up dead ahead the light on Straitsmouth Island, marked *C* in the figure. Your course made good along the line *AC* has been 164° True. A bell buoy has been placed a mile and a half eastward of the light to mark a number of rocks and ledges that must be cleared. It is obvious that you must make a change of course for safety. The problem is how much?

Instead of getting out the chart and plotting a position and a new course to clear the bell buoy, you can apply the Rule-of-Sixty and get a new course with a simple mental calculation. You know from the chart or Light List that the light on Straitsmouth Island is visible for 8 miles, assuming good visibility. (With less than perfect visibility, you will have to establish your distance from the light by other means. But on this night, the visibility is good and you can accept the distance as 8 miles when the light appears on the horizon.)

The procedure is to divide 60 (the rule) by 8 (the distance); the result is 7.5. Since you want to clear the light by a mile and a half, you multiply 7.5 by 1.5 and get 11.25. This is rounded to 11, and is the number of degrees that you must change your course. Thus, your new course is 164° − 11° = 153° True. Long before you need to be concerned about the rocks and ledges, you will pick up the bell buoy north of Flat Ground and then the light on the bell buoy at *D*.

Although this technique is quite valid and acceptable as a specialized procedure, it should not be considered a full

*Multiply by 340 for distance in meters.

FIG. 2188 The Rule of Sixty can guide you in determining how much to change course to clear an obstacle seen ahead at a known distance. The rule can be applied without making a chart plot of the situation.

FIG. 2189 The length of the several straight courses required to pass around a point of land can be added graphically and measured all at one time, rather than measuring them separately and adding the distances numerically.

substitute for the basic and conventional procedure of accurately determining your position and plotting a revised course. There may be circumstances where the Rule-of-Sixty will be useful, such as on a single-handed passage or under conditions too rough for accurate plotting, but consider it a "secondary" method rather than a first-choice method.

DETERMINING THE DISTANCE AROUND A HEADLAND

A pilot may be confronted with the problem of determining the total distance to be covered when rounding a headland or point of land in a series of short, straight courses. There is a graphic method that will give a quick and accurate solution.

In fig. 2189, the boat is at *A*. You want to know the total run to *F* on the other side of the point if you proceed to *B*, then *C*, *D*, and *E* in turn.

In the figure, lines are drawn from point to point, but after you become familiar with the technique, you can merely swing the legs of your dividers from point to point so as to ensure that the invisible line determined by the points will be far enough offshore to be safe.

Step-by-step procedures

The starting point is *A*; use a pair of dividers and measure the distance to *B*. Keep the dividers' leg point that is at *B* on that point, and swing the other leg around from *A* to the right until it touches the broken line extended backwards from *C* to *B* at A^1. Hold this dividers' point on A^1, and extend the other leg from *B* to *C*.

Now hold the point at *C* fast and swing the other point around from A^1 until it touches the broken line extended backward from *D* to *C* at A^2. Hold this point fast at A^2 and open the dividers further, as before, until the point at *C* reaches to *D*.

This same step-by-step procedure is repeated to find A^3 and A^4. When the dividers have been finally extended from A^4 to *F*, they are set to measure the total distance around the headland using the chart's graphic scale or latitude markings.

This technique saves much time and is more accurate than the usual procedure of measuring each leg separately and adding the distance together to get the total run.

Fig. 2201

Mastless motorboat. At the stern, US, Yacht, or USPS Ensign. At the bow, club burgee, Squadron pennant, private signal, officer's flag, or USCG Aux. Ensign (but only one of these at a time).

Note: The Ensigns of the U.S. Power Squadrons and the U.S. Coast Guard Auxiliary may be flown *only* by members of those organizations in good standing.

Fig. 2202 (above)

Typical outboard cruiser or open boat with radio antenna. A USPS officer's flag or past officer's signal may be flown from the antenna at the same height as if on a signal mast. A USCG Auxiliary Ensign may be flown from the same location, but only one flag at a time.

Fig. 2203 (left)

Small cruiser having signal mast without spreader. Same flags as Fig. 2202.

Chapter 22

FLAG ETIQUETTE

How to fly your flags afloat—

Where and when to fly them—

Flag, pennant or burgee, which?—

Origin of the national and yacht ensigns—

Flags for masts ashore—

Etiquette in foreign waters

Fig. 2204
Cruiser with bow and stern staffs, with signal mast and spreader. At bow, Squadron pennant or club burgee. Aft, US, Yacht, or USPS Ensign. At masthead, officer's flag, private signal, or USCG Aux. Ensign. At starboard spreader, USPS Ensign (if not flown aft), absent flag, or guest flag.

Fig. 2205
Typical mastless outboard boat. Same flags as Fig. 2201.

Fig. 2206
Cruiser with signal mast, gaff and spreader. Same flags as Fig. 2205 except, when under way, ensigns should be flown at gaff (at the stern, when at anchor).

Fig. 2207
Two-masted documented motor boat, at anchor, with jack staff and 2 spreaders. Union jack at jack staff* (when at anchor, only). Club burgee, Squadron pennant, or USCG Aux. Ensign at forward masthead. Private signal or officer's flag at after masthead. US or Yacht Ensign at stern staff. USPS Ensign at after starboard spreader (if member). Crew's meal pennant at forward port spreader.

Fig. 2208
Single-masted sailing vessel, under way. Club burgee, Squadron pennant, private signal or officer's flag at masthead. Ensign at the leech of the main approximately ⅔ the length of the leech above the clew (or on a stern staff as below if not racing).

Fig. 2209
Single-masted sailing vessel, at anchor. Same flags at masthead as Fig. 2208. US or Yacht Ensign from stern staff. USPS Ensign from starboard spreader (if member and not flown from stern staff).

*Note: Although "jack staff" has a traditional definition, in typical practice the union jack is flown from the normal bow staff.

Fig. 2210

Two-masted sailing vessel under way. Ensign at leech of main. Club burgee or Squadron pennant at the fore masthead. Officer's flag or private signal at the main masthead.

Fig. 2211

Dress-ship. Flags of the International Code arranged as shown. Union jack at jack staff.* Club burgee or Squadron pennant at fore masthead. Officer's flag or private signal at main masthead. Guest flag at starboard main spreader. Crew's meal pennant at port fore spreader. Ensign at stern staff. (Dress-ship only at anchor.) See text, page 467, for order of displaying code flags.

Fig. 2212

Yawls and ketches. Club burgee or Squadron pennant at the main masthead. Private signal or officer's flag at the mizzen masthead. Ensign at the leech of the mizzen (may be flown from a stern staff while not racing if boom does not overhang). At anchor or in port, US or Yacht Ensign is flown from stern staff; USPS Ensign at starboard main spreader, if member.

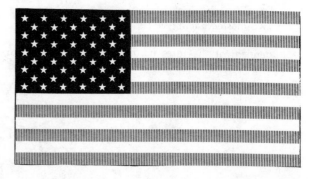

U.S. ENSIGN

U.S. ENSIGN, the one and only U.S. National flag, proper for all yachts, without reservation. Old Glory, the flag with 50 stars and 13 stripes. Flown, when at anchor, at the stern staff. When under way in inland waters, and when meeting or passing other vessels on the high seas, weather and rig permitting, by: motor yachts at the stern staff; by motor yachts with mast and gaff at the gaff.

U.S. POWER SQUADRON ENSIGN

U.S. YACHT ENSIGN

U.S. COAST GUARD AUXILIARY ENSIGN

Marconi-rigged sloops and cutters, when under sail, fly the ensign at the leech of the mainsail approximately ⅔ the length of the leech above the clew. When Marconi-rigs have more than one mast, the ensign is flown from the leech of the aftermost sail.

Gaff-rigged sloops and cutters, when under sail, fly the ensign at the peak of the mainsail gaff. When gaff-rigs have more than one mast, the ensign is flown from the peak of the aftermost gaff.

A sailboat of any rig, when under sail but not racing, may, in lieu of the above, fly its ensign from a stern staff if desired and the aftermost boom does not so overhang as to prevent the mounting of a stern staff.

Under power alone, or when at anchor or made fast, the ensign should be flown from the stern staff of all sailboats. If an overhanging boom requires that the staff be off-center, it should be on the starboard side.

U.S. POWER SQUADRONS ENSIGN is flown as an outward and visible signal to other craft that the boat is commanded by a member of USPS in good standing. USPS is a nation-wide fraternity of boatmen dedicated to better and safer boating through education and civic service.

The preferred location for flying the USPS Ensign is the starboard yardarm or spreader, underway and at anchor, and made fast to the shore, on motor and sailing craft. It may be flown from a stern staff in lieu of the US or Yacht Ensign, but this is usually done only on smaller boats lacking a mast. On sailboats underway, it may be flown from the aftermost peak or leech in place of other ensigns, but this is rarely seen.

U.S. YACHT ENSIGN, by custom and by rulings of governing authorities, may be flown on recreational boats of all sizes in lieu of the U.S. Ensign. Originally, the flying of the Yacht Ensign was restricted to documented vessels

of a special classification, but all such restrictions have now been removed. Many yacht clubs now provide in their by-laws that the Yacht Ensign be flown regardless of size or documentation status.

Strictly speaking, the Yacht Ensign is *not* the American flag. Thus, it is proper that a 50-star U.S. Ensign be substituted for the Yacht Ensign whenever the craft is taken into international or foreign waters.

U.S. COAST GUARD AUXILIARY ENSIGN, known as the "Blue Ensign," is flown *day and night* on a boat that has been approved as a facility for the current year. Here's how:

- [ ] On a vessel without a mast—at the bow staff.
- [ ] On a vessel with one mast—at the truck.
- [ ] On a vessel with two or more masts—at the main truck.
- [ ] NEVER in place of the national ensign.

The USPS Ensign may be flown at its proper location on boats displaying the USCG Aux. Ensign to indicate that the owner is a member of both organizations.

YACHT CLUB BURGEE, generally triangular in shape, sometimes swallow-tail; may be flown by day only or day and night as set by the rules of the Yacht Club concerned.

Flown from the bow staff of mastless and single-masted vessels (foremost truck of vessels with two or more masts); at the main truck of yawls and ketches.

Burgee may be flown under way and at anchor. It is, however, permissible to substitute the private signal for the burgee on single-masted yachts without bow staff when under way.

SQUADRON PENNANT. A distinguishing Squadron pennant which has been authorized by the Governing Board of USPS may be flown in lieu of a club burgee and from the same positions. This pennant may be flown by day only or both day and night.

YACHT CLUB BURGEE*

SQUADRON PENNANT*

OWNER'S PRIVATE SIGNAL*

USPS OFFICER'S FLAG*

COLOR KEY

RED

BLUE

WHITE

OPTIONAL

UNION JACK

OWNER'S ABSENT FLAG

GUEST FLAG
DIVER (Red)

U.S.C.G. AUXILIARY OFFICER'S PENNANT

OWNER'S MEAL FLAG

CREW'S MEAL PENNANT

OWNER'S PRIVATE SIGNAL, generally swallow tail in shape, sometimes rectangular or pennant, flown from masthead of single-masted motor and sailing craft, or from the aftermost masthead of motor or sailing craft with two or more masts; may be flown by day only or day and night.

Mastless motorboats may fly this signal from the bow staff in lieu of a club burgee; see fig. 2201 and 2204.

OFFICER'S FLAG, rectangular in shape, blue (with white design) for senior officer(s); red for next lower in rank; white (with blue design) for lower rank. Other officer's flag (except fleet captain) may be swallow tail or triangular in shape, as provided in the regulations of those organizations making provisions for such flags. Flown in place of private signal on all rigs of motor and sailing vessels except on single-masted sailing vessels, when it is flown in place of burgee at masthead.

UNION JACK, a rectangular blue flag with 50 white stars. The Union Jack may be displayed *only* at the jackstaff on sailing yachts and at the jackstaff on motor yachts with more than one mast, between morning and evening colors, and only while at anchor on Sundays or holidays, or when dressing ship. On modern craft, the normal bow staff is used as the "jackstaff".

ABSENT FLAG, rectangular blue flag, flown during owner's absence in daylight hours. Flown from starboard yardarm, starboard main spreader or equivalent, provided USPS Ensign is not flown at this hoist. (Replaced at night, at anchor, by blue light.)

GUEST FLAG, a rectangular blue flag, crossed diagonally by a white stripe, flown during daylight, when owner is absent but guests are on board. Flown from the starboard yardarm, starboard main spreader or equivalent, provided USPS Ensign is not being flown from this hoist.

*Typical design; there are many others in this category.

U.S.C.G. AUXILIARY OFFICER'S PENNANT, or a past officer's burgee (same design except swallow-tail shape), flies day and night when officer is on board. On a vessel without a mast, flown at the bow staff in lieu of the Auxiliary flag. On a vessel with a mast, at starboard spreader.

Only *one* officer's pennant or burgee may be flown at one time; an incumbent may elect to fly burgee of highest past office held. When the Auxiliary Ensign is up, it is improper to hoist a guest, cocktail, or novelty flag.

OWNER'S MEAL FLAG, a white rectangular flag, flown at anchor, during daylight meal hours of owners, from the main starboard spreader or yardarm, if the USPS Ensign is not at this hoist. (Replaced by white light at night.)

CREW'S MEAL PENNANT, red, flown during daylight, at anchor, during meal hours of the crew at the fore port yardarm or spreader. Seldom seen now.

RAISING AND LOWERING FLAGS. On a typical cruiser, fig. 2204, "colors are made" each morning at 0800. The ensign at the stern is hoisted (or its staff set in place). This is followed by the USPS Ensign at the starboard yardarm if the skipper is a member of USPS. Then, if not already flying on a day-and-night basis, comes the club burgee or Squadron pennant at the bow and private signal at the masthead. (An officer's flag, if flown in lieu of a private signal, would be flown continuously.)

If the craft bears a valid USCG Aux. Facility decal, it would be flying, day and night, the Auxiliary Ensign at the masthead. A USCG Aux. officer's pennant or burgee may be flown, day and night, at the starboard yardarm.

At sunset, colors not properly flown on a day-and-night basis should be lowered in reverse sequence, the ensign at the stern always being the last to be secured. If you are leaving your boat before sunset and will not be aboard at that time, colors should be secured before departing.

FLYING FLAGS AT YACHT CLUBS

These diagrams illustrate how flags can be displayed for a variety of situations and on different types of yacht club masts and poles.

NOTES: The flag of the Senior Club Officer present on the club grounds or aboard his boat in the club anchorage, or Storm Signal flags can be substituted for the International Code Flags shown in the diagrams, except in the case illustrated at bottom left. The diagrams show hoists as if you were standing ashore facing seaward.

If only a Yacht Club single pole with no yard or gaff, only the U.S. Flag should be flown, at the truck.

If a pole with yardarm only, the U.S. Flag should be flown at truck, Club burgee at starboard yardarm, USPS Ensign or other organizational flag may be flown at port yardarm during activities ashore of such organization.

On national holidays and on days of special yachting significance, it is permissible to fly the flags of the International Code.

The code for "flying flags ashore at Yacht Clubs" may be followed for flags flown ashore at the homes of yachtsmen.

Signal flags, such as storm and weather flags, etc. should be flown from a conspicuous hoist.

Flags of yachting organizations should not be flown from commercial establishments, except by special permission.

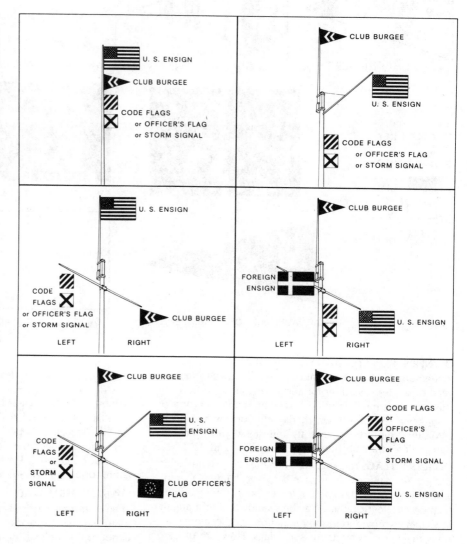

About Pennants

Pennant or Burgee. Adrift in a foggy sea of semantics, a sea lawyer could easily founder, groping for the right terms to describe those bits of bunting he flies from the truck and bow staff. Basically, there are four shapes his signals may take—rectangular, triangular, rectangular swallow-tailed, and triangular swallow-tailed. What to call them? Pennants or burgees?

We can't go far wrong if we think of a *pennant* as a flag smaller at the fly than at the hoist which is (1) commonly pointed, triangular (2) often truncated, as in some Navy signals (3) sometimes swallow-tailed (4) occasionally a long thin streamer.

The *burgee* we might regard as a swallow-tailed flag which is (1) often rectangular (2) may be pennant-shaped (3) by popular usage, the identifying signal of a yacht club, regardless of shape.

Coast Guard Auxiliary Pennant. The boat of a member of the USCG Auxiliary is termed a "Facility." Such a craft that meets a higher standard of equipment and availability for use in assistance and other missions under Coast Guard orders is designated an "Operational Facility."

All Coast Guard Auxiliary Facilities are authorized to fly the Auxiliary Ensign; those that are Operational Facilities can additionally fly the *Auxiliary Operational Pennant*, blue and white diagonal stripes, above the Auxiliary Ensign at a distance twice the width of the pennant; see color page T.

Racing Pennant. A distinctive pennant has been designed by the Sea Cliff (N.Y.) Yacht Club as an identifying signal for racing boats. The field is blue, with white fluorescent strip in the middle, and red anchor superimposed. Cruising yachts carry it at the starboard spreader; smaller boats fly it from the leech of the mainsail. It aids race committees in distinguishing contesting boats; other boats, hopefully, will give them a wide berth. It is suggested that other clubs follow Sea Cliff's lead, standardizing on the design illustrated below.

U.S. GOVERNMENT AND YACHTING FLAGS

PRESIDENT OF THE UNITED STATES

NATIONAL
ENSIGN AND MERCHANT FLAG

VICE PRESIDENT

COAST GUARD ENSIGN

UNION JACK

U. S. CUSTOMS

YACHT ENSIGN

U.S. POWER SQUADRONS
ENSIGN

UNITED STATES COAST GUARD
AUXILIARY ENSIGN

YACHT CLUB
BURGEE°

YACHT CLUB
COMMODORE

YACHT CLUB
VICE COMMODORE

YACHT CLUB
REAR COMMODORE

YACHT CLUB
FLEET CAPTAIN

YACHT CLUB
PAST COMMODORE

YACHT
PRIVATE SIGNAL°

YACHT
OWNER ABSENT

YACHT
OWNERS' MEAL

YACHT
GUEST FLAG

YACHT PROTEST

TRANSPORTATION

QUARANTINE
INTERNATIONAL Q

DIVER
INTERNATIONAL A

DIVER

°Typical design; there are many others in this category.

O

UNITED STATES POWER SQUADRONS FLAGS and INSIGNIA

USPS ENSIGN

The Ensign of United States Power Squadrons may be displayed only by enrolled members of USPS. It is an outward and visible sign that the vessel displaying it is under the charge of a person who has made a study of piloting and small boat handling, and will recognize the rights of others and the traditions of the sea. The Squadrons' Ensign also marks a craft as being under the command of a man who has met certain minimum requirements and is so honored for meeting them. This honor may not be bought, sold, rented, loaned or given away. The USPS Ensign is displayed, during the hours from 0800 to sundown, from the starboard staff or from the starboard yardarm of a power vessel. On craft under sail, it is flown from the leach or peak of the mainsail or aftermost sail.

USPS OBJECTIVES

Shall be to establish a high standard of skill in handling and navigation of yachts, to encourage the study of the science of navigation, and small boat handling, to cooperate with the agencies of the United States Government charged with the enforcement of the laws and regulations relating to navigation and to stimulate interest in activities which will tend to the upbuilding of our Army, Navy, Coast Guard and Merchant Marine.

NATIONAL OFFICERS

OFFICE	INSIGNIA	FLAG	SLEEVE
CHIEF COMMANDER			
VICE COMMANDERS			
REAR COMMANDERS			
STAFF COMMANDERS			
USPS FLAG LIEUTENANT			
AIDES TO C/C CHAPLAIN			

DISTRICT OFFICERS

OFFICE	INSIGNIA	FLAG	SLEEVE
DISTRICT COMMANDER			
DISTRICT LIEUTENANT COMMANDERS			
DISTRICT 1st LIEUTENANTS			
DISTRICT LIEUTENANTS			
DISTRICT FLAG LIEUTENANT			
DISTRICT AIDES CHAPLAIN			

EDUCATIONAL INSIGNIA

NATIONAL COMMITTEES

MEMBERS	RULES
ADVANCED GRADES	PILOTING
INSTRUCTOR QUALIFICATION	ELECTIVE COURSES
GOVERNING BOARD GENERAL MEMBERS	

LOCAL BOARDS

MEMBERS	CHAIRMAN
ADVANCED GRADES	PILOTING
INSTRUCTOR QUALIFICATION	ELECTIVE COURSES

OIC PENNANT

A blue pennant, six inches on the hoist and 36 inches on the fly, tapering to a point from the hoist, may be flown above the officer's flag by the designated officer in charge of a USPS, District or Squadron activity afloat.

SQUADRON OFFICERS

OFFICE	INSIGNIA	FLAG	SLEEVE
SQUADRON COMMANDER			
SQUADRON LIEUTENANT COMMANDERS			
SQUADRON 1st LIEUTENANTS			
SQUADRON LIEUTENANTS, CHAPLAIN			
SQUADRON FLAG LIEUTENANT			

PAST OFFICERS' SIGNALS

| PAST CHIEF COMMANDERS | PAST VICE COMMANDERS | PAST REAR COMMANDERS |
| PAST STAFF COMMANDERS | PAST DISTRICT COMMANDERS | PAST SQUADRON COMMANDERS |

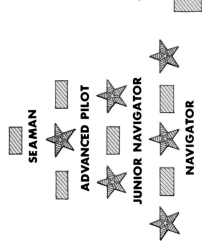

CAP DEVICE

SENIOR MEMBER

MERIT MARKS

WORN ON LEFT SLEEVE ONLY

SEAMAN	
ADVANCED PILOT	JUNIOR NAVIGATOR
	NAVIGATOR

Note: A Senior Member who has completed all courses may wear a gold border around the Navigator and Senior Member insignia.

Q

U.S. COAST GUARD AUXILIARY
FLAGS AND INSIGNIA

COAST GUARD AUXILIARY
ENSIGN

NATIONAL COMMODORE

OPERATIONAL FACILITY PENNANT

NATIONAL VICE COMMODORE

NATIONAL REAR COMMODORE

DISTRICT COMMODORE

DIVISION CAPTAIN

FLOTILLA COMMANDER

DISTRICT VICE COMMODORE
(White field, blue markings, Dist. Rear Commodore)

DIVISION VICE CAPTAIN

FLOTILLA VICE COMMANDER

CHIEF OF DEPARTMENT
3 Bars—Division Chief
2 Bars—Branch Chief and
Aide to National Commodore
1 Bar—Branch Assistant

DISTRICT STAFF OFFICER
1½ Bars—Assistant DSO

DIVISION STAFF OFFICER

FLOTILLA STAFF OFFICER
(Also Aide to District Commodore)

CAP DEVICE	SHIELD Elected Officer and Member	SHIELD Staff Officer	SHIELD Past Officer	AUXOP DEVICE	AUXILIARY AVIATOR

METAL COLLAR INSIGNIA[1]	SHOULDER BOARDS[2]	METAL COLLAR INSIGNIA[1]	SHOULDER BOARDS[2]
 National Commodore		 Division Captain With Red "A": Branch Chief; Dist. Staff Officer; Aide to NACO	
 National Vice Commodore National Rear Commodore		 Division Vice Captain; Flotilla Commander With Red "A": Branch Asst.; Asst. Dist. Staff Officer	
 District Commodore		 Flotilla Vice Commander With Red "A": Division Staff Officer	
 District Vice Commodore With Red "A": Department Chief		 Flotilla Staff Officer Aide to DCO	
 District Rear Commodore With Red "A": Division Chief		 Member	

[1] Large metal shoulder insignia is worn on blue raincoats; the same insignia in smaller size is worn on khaki, blue flannel, and khaki tropical shirts.
[2] Shoulder Marks are worn on Khaki coats, blue overcoats, and white tropical shirts.

R

WHEN AND WHERE TO FLY FLAGS ON BOATS

FLAG	WHEN FLOWN	Powerboat with Bow and Stern Staffs Only	Powerboat with Bow and Stern Staffs and Signal Mast	Single-Masted Sailboat	Powerboat or Sailboat With Two Masts	FOOTNOTES:
U.S. ENSIGN[1] OR U.S. YACHT ENSIGN	0800 to Sundown[5]	Stern Staff[3]	Stern Staff[3]	At anchor or underway: from stern staff[3](except when racing). (Optional: from peak if gaff-rigged, or from leech of mainsail if Marconi-rigged[4])	At anchor or underway: from stern staff[3](except when racing). (Optional: from peak if gaff-rigged, or from leech if Marconi-rigged[4])	[1] A USPS member has the option of flying the U.S. Ensign, the U.S. Yacht Ensign, or the USPS Ensign. In foreign waters, U.S. Ensign preferred with foreign flag at bow staff or starboard spreader.
USPS ENSIGN[1]	0800 to Sundown[5]	Stern Staff[3]	Stern Staff or Starboard Spreader[2,3]	As Above or from Starboard Spreader[2]	As Above or from Starboard Spreader[2] of Mainmast	[2] If the USPS Ensign is flown from the spreader (starboard in U.S. waters — port spreader in foreign waters), the U.S. Ensign or the U.S. Yacht Ensign should be flown from the stern staff.
SQUADRON PENNANT OR YACHT CLUB BURGEE	0800 to Sundown[5] or Day and Night While Boat Is In Commission	Bow Staff	Bow Staff	At Bow Staff If Yacht So Equipped; Otherwise At Masthead When At Anchor Or Underway	Foremost Masthead	[3] On boats with outboard motors and on sailboats with overhanging booms, the stern staff should be located to starboard of motor or boom.
ELECTED (FLAG) OFFICER'S (RECTANGULAR) OR APPOINTED OFFICER'S (SWALLOWTAIL)	0800 to Sundown[5] or Day and Night While Boat Is In Commission	Not Flown[6]	At Masthead Instead of Private Signal	At Masthead (Instead of Squadron Pennant, Yacht Club Burgee, USPS Past Officer's Signal or Private Signal)	Aftermost Masthead Instead of Private Signal	[4] Approximately two-thirds of the length of the leech above the clew.
USPS PAST OFFICER'S SIGNAL OR PRIVATE SIGNAL	0800 to Sundown[5] or Day and Night While Boat Is In Commission	Not Flown[6]	At Masthead	At Masthead (Instead of Squadron Pennant or Yacht Club Burgee)	Aftermost Masthead	[5] Yachts that will be unmanned at color time shall make evening colors beforehand.
UNION JACK	0800 to Sundown, At Anchor Only, On Sundays and Holidays or When Dressing Ship[5]	Not Flown	Not Flown	Not Flown	Jack Staff	[6] On mastless boats with a radio antenna, it may be flown from the antenna at a height equivalent to where it would be if there were a mast. (Note: the USPS Ensign shall never be flown from antenna.)
GUEST FLAG	0800 to Sundown When Owner is Absent, But Guests are on Board[5]	Not Flown	Starboard Spreader	Starboard Spreader	Starboard Main Spreader	[7] NOTICE: The flying of two flags or signals from the same hoist is Not Authorized except for International Code Flags and the Officer-in-Charge pennant which is flown above the Officer's Flag.
OFFICER-IN-CHARGE (OIC) PENNANT	Day and Night During Activity for which Authorized	Not Flown[6]	At Masthead[7]	At Masthead[7]	Aftermost Masthead[7]	Where the same hoist is indicated for more than one flag or signal, the choice is optional.

NOTE—When a motor yacht with mast and gaff is underway, the Ensign (U.S., U.S. Yacht, or USPS) should be flown at the gaff instead of the stern staff. A mastless boat may display, on a staff erected on the superstructure, the flag designated by this code to be flown from masthead of single-masted boats.

UNITED STATES COAST GUARD AUXILIARY FLAG CODE FOR POWER VESSELS

FLAG	NATIONAL ENSIGN	COAST GUARD ENSIGN	AUX. ENSIGN	AUX. OFFICER PENNANT OR BURGEE	YACHT ENSIGN	USPS ENSIGN	USPS OFFICER FLAG	YACHT CLUB PENNANT OR UNIT	YACHT CLUB OFFICER FLAG	HOUSE FLAG	GAG FLAGS — MEAL, ETC.
FACILITY NORMAL CONDITION — FLOWN CAT 1	STERN STAFF OR GAFF (Note #1)	NO	TRUCK — BOW STAFF (Note #2) (Note #14)	STB'D. YARD — BOW STAFF (Note #3) (Note #6)	DOCUMENTED YACHT ONLY (Note #4)	STB'D. YARD ONLY (Note #5)	(Note #6)	BOW STAFF (Note #10)	STB'D. YARD (Note #6)	NO (Note #7)	NO (Note #8)
UNDER ORDERS — FLOWN CAT 2 & 3	STERN STAFF OR GAFF (Note #1)	NO	TRUCK — BOW STAFF (Note #2) (Note #14)	STBD. YARD — BOW STAFF (Note #3) (Note #15)	NO (Note #15)	NO (Note #15)	NO (Note #15)	NO (Note #15)	NO (Note #15)	NO (Note #7)	NO (Note #8)
UNDER ORDERS USCG OFFICER ABOARD — FLOWN CAT 2 & 3	STERN STAFF OR GAFF (Note #1)	TRUCK (Note #16)	NO (Note #16)	NO (Note #16)	NO (Note #16)	NO (Note #16)	NO (Note #16)	NO (Note #16)	NO (Note #16)	NO (Note #7)	NO (Note #8)
HOURS FLOWN	0800 TO SUNSET (Note #18)	DAY AND NIGHT UNDER ORDERS (Note #13)	DAY AND NIGHT (Note #9)	OFFICER ABOARD DAY AND NIGHT (Note #4)	0800 TO SUNSET (Note #4)	0800 TO SUNSET Note #5	DAY AND NIGHT (Note #6)	0800 TO SUNSET (Note #11)	DAY AND NIGHT (Note #12)	(Note #7)	NO

NOTES

#1 **The National Ensign** shall be flown from the stern staff on a power boat except when the vessel is equipped with a gaff, in which case the ensign is flown from the stern staff at anchor, and the gaff when underway.

#2 **Auxiliary Ensign**
  (a) Shall be flown from the main truck when the vessel is equipped with a mast(s).
  (b) Without a mast, from the bow staff. (See Configuration (A)).

#3 **Auxiliary Officer**—Pennant or burgee shall be flown from the starboard yardarm when the vessel is equipped with a signal mast. (See Configuration (D)). If the vessel has no mast, it may be flown in lieu of the Auxiliary Ensign from the bow staff. (See Configuration (A)).

#4 **The Yacht Ensign**
  (a) Authorized by law to be flown by yachts documented by the U.S. Coast Guard. However, the flying of this flag on a Documented Yacht is not mandatory.
  (b) A documented yacht operating under official orders, becomes a Government vessel, and Government vessels *may not* fly the "Yacht ensign."
  (c) All facilities *not documented* shall fly the U.S. ensign, whenever the Auxiliary ensign is flown.

#5 **USPS Ensign**—This is the only "service" organization recognized by this code. The USPS ensign may be flown only from the starboard yardarm of a signal mast, *never* from the stern staff or gaff. On facilities flying the Auxiliary ensign, this position of honor is *reserved* for the national ensign.

#6 **Officer Flags**—Auxiliary, USPS, yacht or boat club, either pennants or burgees, are flown from the starboard yardarm, except as noted in #3. Only *one* of these flags may be flown at a time.

#7 **House Flag**—The owner's private signal known as a house flag is correctly flown at the truck between morning and evening colors; therefore, it *cannot* be flown at the same time as the Auxiliary ensign.

#8 **Gag Flags**—Because of the quasi-official status of an Auxiliary facility, cocktail flags, ball-and-chain, or other humorous flags *shall not* be flown when the Auxiliary ensign is flown. Other flags, such as crew's pennant, owner's meal flag, guest flag, absent flag, also shall not be flown with the Auxiliary ensign.

#9 **The Auxiliary Ensign**—may be flown *day* and *night* on currently inspected facilities displaying decal, while in commission.

#10 **The Yacht Club Pennant**—can be flown from the Bow Staff. See Configuration (B), (C), or (D), except when under orders.

#11 **The Yacht Club Pennant, Flotilla, or Division, Unit Flags**—shall be flown from 0800 to sunset.

#12 **Yacht Club Officer Flags**—shall be displayed day and night.

#13 **The Coast Guard Ensign**—shall be flown day and night while the facility is under orders with a Coast Guard officer aboard.

#14 **No Signal Mast**—When a boat is equipped with a bow and stern staff, and does not have a signal mast, but has a radio antenna, the Auxiliary ensign may be properly displayed by substituting the antenna for a signal mast. The height of the uppermost portion of the hoist of the Auxiliary ensign should be affixed at a point approximately 2/3 the height of the antenna. *No additional* antennas or outriggers may be utilized.

#15 **A Facility Under Official Orders** (STATUS 2) shall be permitted to fly the Auxiliary officer's pennant or burgee, in addition to the U.S. and Auxiliary ensigns. All other flags—yacht ensign, USPS ensign, yacht club pennants, officer flags, flotilla, division, etc. *shall not* be flown.

#16 **Coast Guard Officer Aboard Facilities Under Orders** (STATUS 3) the Coast Guard Ensign substitutes for the Auxiliary ensign; *all* other flags except the national ensign shall be taken down. This includes Auxiliary officer pennants or burgees, yacht ensign, unit flags, USPS ensign, yacht or boat club flags, etc.—only *two flags* shall be permitted—the national ensign and the Coast Guard ensign.

#17 **Operational Facility Pennant**—Auxiliary Operational Facilities may fly the Operational Facility Pennant whenever the auxiliary Ensign is flown. It is flown above the Auxiliary Ensign at a distance equal to twice the width of the pennant. This may be accomplished by an extended bow staff, securing to a radio antenna above the Ensign, or flying above the Ensign at the mast truck in accordance with the Flag Code configurations on page 601. The size of the pennant to be flown will be the numerical size equivalent to the Auxiliary Ensign being flown, i.e., size 3 pennant with a size 3 Ensign.

#18 **The National Ensign**—shall be flown night and day while the facility is under orders.

INTERNATIONAL FLAGS AND PENNANTS

ALPHABET FLAGS			NUMERAL PENNANTS
Alfa — Diver Down; Keep Clear	**K**ilo — Desire to Communicate	**U**niform — Standing into Danger	1
Bravo — Dangerous Cargo	**L**ima — Stop Instantly	**V**ictor — Require Assistance	2
Charlie — Yes	**M**ike — I Am Stopped	**W**his-key — Require Medical Assistance	3
Delta — Keep Clear	**N**ovem-ber — No	**X**ray — Stop Your Intention	4
Echo — Altering Course to Starboard	**O**scar — Man Overboard	**Y**ankee — Am Dragging Anchor	5
Foxtrot — Disabled	**P**apa — About to Sail	**Z**ulu — Require a Tug	6
Golf — Want a Pilot	**Q**uebec — Request Pratique	**REPEATERS** — 1st Repeat	7
Hotel — Pilot on Board	**R**omeo	2nd Repeat	8
India — Altering Course to Port	**S**ierra — Engines Going Astern	3rd Repeat	9
Juliett — On Fire; Keep Clear	**T**ango — Keep Clear of Me	CODE — Code and Answering Pennant (Decimal Point)	0

U

How International Code Flags are Used in Signaling

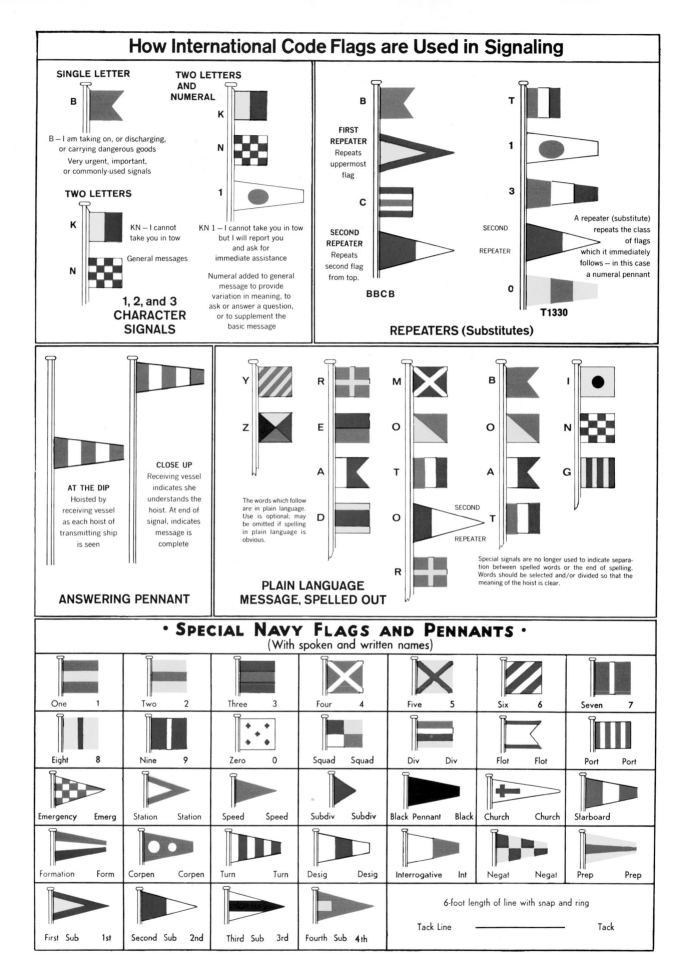

SINGLE LETTER

B

B — I am taking on, or discharging, or carrying dangerous goods

Very urgent, important, or commonly-used signals

TWO LETTERS

K
N

KN — I cannot take you in tow

General messages

TWO LETTERS AND NUMERAL

K
N
1

KN 1 — I cannot take you in tow but I will report you and ask for immediate assistance

Numeral added to general message to provide variation in meaning, to ask or answer a question, or to supplement the basic message

1, 2, and 3 CHARACTER SIGNALS

B

FIRST REPEATER
Repeats uppermost flag

C

SECOND REPEATER
Repeats second flag from top.

BBCB

T
1
3

SECOND REPEATER

0

T1330

A repeater (substitute) repeats the class of flags which it immediately follows — in this case a numeral pennant

REPEATERS (Substitutes)

AT THE DIP
Hoisted by receiving vessel as each hoist of transmitting ship is seen

CLOSE UP
Receiving vessel indicates she understands the hoist. At end of signal, indicates message is complete

ANSWERING PENNANT

Y
Z
A
D

R
E
A
D

M
O
T
O
R

B
O
A
T

SECOND REPEATER

I
N
G

The words which follow are in plain language. Use is optional; may be omitted if spelling in plain language is obvious.

Special signals are no longer used to indicate separation between spelled words or the end of spelling. Words should be selected and/or divided so that the meaning of the hoist is clear.

PLAIN LANGUAGE MESSAGE, SPELLED OUT

• SPECIAL NAVY FLAGS AND PENNANTS •
(With spoken and written names)

One 1	Two 2	Three 3	Four 4	Five 5	Six 6	Seven 7
Eight 8	Nine 9	Zero 0	Squad Squad	Div Div	Flot Flot	Port Port
Emergency Emerg	Station Station	Speed Speed	Subdiv Subdiv	Black Pennant Black	Church Church	Starboard
Formation Form	Corpen Corpen	Turn Turn	Desig Desig	Interrogative Int	Negat Negat	Prep Prep
First Sub 1st	Second Sub 2nd	Third Sub 3rd	Fourth Sub 4th			

6-foot length of line with snap and ring

Tack Line ——————— Tack

V

"And yet, though silent, it speaks to us—speaks to us of the past, of the men and women who went before us, and of the records they wrote upon it." —PRESIDENT WILSON

The Flag of Your Country

THE FLYING of flags and colors on motor craft, sailing and other yachts is governed largely by custom. Few, if any, laws or government regulations have ever been enacted on this subject. Mention has seldom if ever been made by Congress in all of its years, of any requirements for the flying of any flag on numbered, undocumented, or unlicensed vessels or yachts. Documented yachts are expected to fly the yacht ensign but the enforcement of even this regulation is questionable.

A review or a brief history of the United States National Flag should permit one to better understand some of the fundamentals on which many of the customs of flags and colors are based, especially their evolution for use on the water.

The origin and early history of the use of national flags is very indefinite. This is especially true of the national ensign of the United States. Early Colonial and American history makes very little mention of our flag or flags. Our Navy seems to have begun the use of the Stars and Stripes immediately after the Continental Congress had passed an Act in June, 1777, establishing the Stars and Stripes as the flag of this country. However, it was not until 1895 or some 30 years after the close of the Civil War, that the United States cavalry was given the right to carry the Stars and Stripes as the national standard. It was in 1841 that the infantry first used the national colors. Not until 1876 did the Marines carry the Stars and Stripes.

As the Navy made use of the national flag from the beginning and the other branches of the U.S. government were slow in adopting it, it emphasizes that the Stars and Stripes as the national ensign is a flag of the sea and its right to be flown from yachts is clearly established.

On the subject of the origin and development of the flag from which the Stars and Stripes has been evolved, accounts are too conflicting to warrant placing much credence in them. Prince Edward, afterwards Edward I of England, about the middle of the last half of the 13th century, adopted the Red Cross of St. George, on a white field, as the national flag of England. After James VI of Scotland ascended the throne of England in 1603, as James I, he was much annoyed by the wrangling between the masters of English and Scotch ships when they met at sea as to which one should dip its colors to the other. Therefore, in 1606, he stopped this annoyance and to help unite the two kingdoms into one country, combined the two crosses into a new flag, which subsequently became known as the Union

Jack. This he required all vessels of both countries to carry at their mainmast. A century later when the two countries agreed upon their union, a national agreement required the union of the crosses to be used on flags, banners, standards, and ensigns both at sea and on land.

Near the beginning of the revolution, General Washington assigned to the various officers as a distinction of rank, ribbons varying in color and these were worn by them until something more formal was designed. There were practically no flags or colors although some of the individual companies of the Colonial Army are supposed to have brought with them those which they had previously used. Later General Washington urged the various Colonels to provide for their regiments colors of such design as might appeal to them. This was frequently done and in many instances, some designs of 13 units were used to represent the 13 colonies.

Some of the colonies adopted flags of their own. Massachusetts adopted the Pine Tree, with the motto An Appeal to Heaven. Rhode Island selected one having an anchor and the word Hope and within the canton a union of 13 white stars on a blue field, said to be the first flag on which the 13 colonies were represented by 13 stars.

South Carolina's flag has an interesting history. In September 1775, the Committee of Safety of Charleston instructed Colonel William Moultrie to take possession of Fort Johnson on James Island, which he did. The uniforms of their troops were blue with a silver increscent in the cap. Soon realizing that a flag was needed, he improvised one having a blue field with a white increscent in the canton. This was the flag which sergeant Jasper so gallantly rescued on June 28, 1776, when the fort of palmetto logs on Sullivans Island was attacked by the British Fleet under Admiral Sir Peter Parker. It was under this flag that the Declaration of Independence was read to the people of Charleston on August 8, 1776. When the state came to officially adopt a flag, it took the one which Colonel Moultrie had designed and in recognition of the good services of the palmetto logs, placed upon it a palmetto tree.

While our first flag act was adopted June 14, 1777, by resolution of the Continental Congress and reading as follows: "Resolved, That the flag of the United States be thirteen stripes, alternate red and white; that the union be thirteen stars, white in a blue field, representing a new constellation" yet there is nothing to show that the Revolutionary Army ever carried any flags furnished by the American Congress. Those which were carried were purely personal, each made by or for some officer, company or regiment, and represented the sentiments of the makers. However, the United States Navy began to use the flag immediately after it was authorized by the Continental Congress.

History records only one Stars and Stripes that was carried by the American Army during the Revolutionary War. It was carried by the North Carolina Militia at the Battle of Guilford Courthouse, March 15, 1781, but the stripes were blue and red and the union had a white field with 13 eight-pointed stars. There is also another flag hanging in the State House at Annapolis, which it is claimed was carried by the Third Maryland Regiment in 1781. It has 13 five-pointed stars, one in the center, and 12 arranged in the form of a circle around it. In both of these cases, the flags were purely personal, not official.

The Stars and Stripes preserved in the State House of Boston is claimed to have flown over Fort Independence during the American Revolution but was not carried by the Army. In 1863 each battery of artillery and each company of cavalry was allowed to carry a small flag consisting of Stars and Stripes but that privilege was revoked at the end of the Civil War. The U.S. Marines did not carry the Stars and Stripes as national colors until 1876, yet those which they carried as such in the Mexican and Civil Wars had an eagle in the union.

In none of the three acts adopting the United States national flag is there any mention as to how the stars should be arranged or how many points they should have. In one of the first flags, the stars were sometimes arranged in a circle or with one star in the center and the remaining 12 either in the form of a circle or hollow square, or three horizontal rows of 4, 5 and 4 stars respectively. In a later flag, they were also arranged in several different orders, three horizontal rows of five each or three vertical rows of five each; sometimes in the quincunx order as was the flag that floated over Fort McHenry when Key wrote the Star Spangled Banner.

Apparently about 1841, when the United States Infantry was first given the right to carry the Stars and Stripes, there was a desire on the part of some to preserve their old national colors in the union of the new flag. One of these had an eagle with a bunch of arrows in one claw and the Indian pipe of peace in the other with 13 stars above and a like number below. During the Mexican War, the Fourth Indiana Volunteers carried a flag having in the union an eagle standing on a segment of the globe with a bunch of arrows in one claw, as though intending to conquer the earth.

Near the beginning of the 20th Century, the different departments of our National Government appointed representatives to confer and see if they could not bring order out of chaos. The proportions of Naval flags and Army colors were quite different, the former being much longer in proportion to its height, the latter being much shorter to avoid interfering with the color or standard bearer. It was decided to leave the Army colors alone but to fly the Naval flag from flagstaffs and from Government buildings.

Accordingly, following the recommendations of this committee, President Taft, in 1912, issued an executive order defining minutely the proportions and other details of the Stars and Stripes, at the same time approving a cus-

tom which had existed in the Navy of placing on their small boats flags having only 13 stars instead of the full complement. The use of only 13 stars on our small or boat flags was discontinued by an executive order of President Wilson, dated May 29, 1916, and now all flags, colors, etc., used by the United States Government are required to have their full complement of 50 stars. In all of the discussion by the conference it does not appear that there was any mention whatsoever of the yacht ensign or the rights or duties of yachts or any other vessels to fly any particular flag.

From the foregoing it will be seen that the United States has only one flag. The use of the yacht ensign is misleading. England has, by law, created a flag for its navy, another for its merchant service, another for yachts and another for its land forces; each is a national flag and entitled to the position and courtesy due the colors of a nation. But, in the United States, wherever, whenever and for whatever purpose the national colors are flown, there is but one flag to fly.

The place of honor for the national colors on land and sea is as follows: on land on a straight mast, at the head; on a mast with a gaff, at the gaff. At sea and at anchor on a steam or motor vessel, at the flag staff aft; on vessels under sail, at the peak; and on vessels with a gaff, at this gaff when under way.

There has never been passed a law compelling boats to fly the national flag or none at all from the place of honor. It has probably never been contemplated that a loyal citizen would ever do otherwise. Yet, we are free to do as we

The American flag is properly flying here from the gaff at a yacht club ashore. Although the club burgee may be higher than the national flag, it is not "above" it, a practice prohibited by custom and law.

M. Rosenfeld.

like and in the use of this freedom there has grown the custom of flying the yacht ensign at the point of honor at shore stations and aboard yachts. There are today ardent yachtsmen in high places who believe this custom aboard yachts should be continued.

The yacht ensign had its beginning on August 7, 1848, when the Congress passed "an act to authorize the Secretary of the Treasury to license yachts and for other purposes" providing for the enrollment and licensing of yachts and exempting them from entering and clearing at Customhouses. The third paragraph of the act provided "that all such licensed yachts shall *use a signal* of the form, size and colors prescribed by the Secretary of the Navy." (This paragraph has been subsequently reenacted as Sec. 4215 Revised Statutes of the United States.) The Secretary of the Navy acted promptly, and on August 26, 1848, he requested the New York Yacht Club to submit a design for this signal. The design they submitted on January 9, 1849, was the then adopted American ensign, which carried thirteen stars in a circle in the blue field and the thirteen red and white stripes (the Betsy Ross flag), in which they placed a fouled anchor in the center of the circle of stars. The Secretary of the Navy accepted the suggestion of the New York Yacht Club and authorized the adoption of the design.

It is the design of the yacht "signal" that has resulted in the present confusion because its similarity in appearance to the national ensign promptly led yachtsmen to fly the "signal" now known as the yacht ensign in place of the national ensign and the custom has grown until at present nearly all pleasure craft, from outboard speedsters up, are flying the "signal" as an ensign. The yacht ensign was created only as a signal for yachts enrolled and licensed (documented) and exempted them from entering and clearing at Custom-houses. Presumably it was to be flown in addition to the national ensign on documented yachts. To fly it from a club mast ashore signifies nothing.

Under present law it is the general rule that "the ownership of a vessel determines its national character." Several cases bear upon this and explain also how else a vessel's nationality may be proved.

In one called the Merritt (17 Wall 582, 21 L.Ed. 682) Mr. Justice Hunt, writing for the U.S. Supreme Court in October 1873, observed that "The documents a vessel carries furnish the only evidence of her nationality."

In the 1880's, U.S. v. Seagrist (27 F. Cas. No. 16,245) held that the register of a vessel, while proper evidence of nationality, is not indispensable, and the flag and ownership of the vessel may be proved by *any* competent evidence.

In 1894 in St. Clair v. United States (154 U.S. 134) the Supreme Court ruled not only that the "certificate of the vessel's registry, and its carrying the American flag, was admissible in evidence," but that "such evidence made, at least, a *prima facie* case . . . of the nationality of the vessel. . . ." This means that such evidence is sufficient to prove the points for which it is introduced unless it is contradicted by other evidence.

Conclusion: Generally the nationality of a vessel is determined by the nationality of her owner. Her papers or her flag may indicate otherwise, however, but neither is conclusive on the issue. Both elements are entitled to prima facie weight—that is, they will stand unless overcome by other evidence. Obviously there are no exclusive ways

Never fly the American flag from the masthead of a mast equipped with a gaff, as illustrated here. Just as on a ship, the gaff, even though lower in height, is the place of honor.

to prove this matter in a court of law; all material and relevant evidence on the issue will be allowed.

DRESSING SHIP

On national holidays, at regattas, and on other special occasions, yachts often dress ship with International Code signal flags. Flag officers' flags, club burgees, and national flags are not used. The ship is dressed at 8:00 A.M. and remains so dressed from morning to evening colors. (While at anchor only.) See fig. 2211, page 461.

In dressing ship, the yacht ensign is hoisted at the peak or staff aft, and the jack at the jackstaff. Then a rainbow of flags of the International Code is arranged, reaching from the waterline forward to the waterline aft, by way of the bowsprit end to the foretop masthead, then across to the main topmast, and down to the main boom end, allowing several flags to touch the water line from both the bowsprit end and the main boom end. To keep the flags in position, a weight should be attached to the end of each line. Where there is no bowsprit, flags will start at the stemhead. Flags and pennants should be bent on alternately, rather than in any indiscriminate manner. Since there are twice as many letter flags as numeral pennants, it is good practice, as in the Navy, to follow a sequence of two flags, one pennant, etc., etc., throughout. In order to effect a degree of uniformity in yacht procedure, the following arrangement has been proposed:

Starting from forward, AB2, UJ1, KE3, GH6, IV5, FL4, DM7, PO Third Repeater, RN First Repeater, STo (zero), CX9, WQ8, ZY Second Repeater.

The arrangement here proposed is designed to effect a harmonious color pattern throughout.

The Evolution of the United States Flag

GRAND UNION:
Before the American Revolution, the Colonies used a flag with a British ensign as the canton, plus 13 alternate red and white stripes signifying the original Colonies.

GADSDEN FLAG:
Even before 1776, there were those who resented anything in our flag resembling the British ensign. The Gadsden flag was developed about this time with a coiled rattlesnake on a yellow field with the words "Don't Tread On Me." Other flags used by some of the Colonies carried such slogans as "Liberty or Death."

BUNKER HILL FLAG:
In the New England area, the pine tree of Maine was the popular-flag emblem. This appeared on the banner hoisted by the Colonies at Bunker Hill. It showed a red background with the pine tree in the canton. Another was the British blue ensign with a pine tree in the canton.

FIRST "STARS AND STRIPES":
Congress passed the first flag resolution on June 14 (now flag day), 1777. The battle of Bennington in August of the same year is believed to mark the first display of Old Glory with 13 stars and 13 stripes, with 11 stars arranged in a semi-circle and one in each corner. The 76 denotes the year of Independence.

COWPENS FLAG:
This flag, consisting of 12 white stars in a circle with one in the center, with 13 alternate red and white stripes, was first carried in the battle of Cowpens, January 1781.

BETSY ROSS FLAG:
The legend has it that Betsy Ross of Philadelphia was asked in 1776 to design a national flag suggested by General Washington. She is credited with making the stars 5-pointed and arranging them in a circle on the national flag.

FLAG OF 1795:
This flag had 15 stripes and 15 stars indicating the 15 States at that time. Five new stars were added during the five years this flag flew, but no additional stripes. This flag is credited with being the first official flag to fly over the Capitol in Washington.

FLAG OF THE CONFEDERACY:
Of the four Confederate flags, the one shown was most popular and best known; it consisted of a blue cross arranged diagonally across a red field. On the cross were 13 stars.

FLAG OF 1912:
Two stars were added to the flag when this design became offical, representing the new States of Arizona and New Mexico. The stars were arranged in six rows of 8 stars each and remained unchanged for 47 years.

OLD GLORY OF TODAY:
With the admission of the 49th and 50th States, Alaska and Hawaii, 2 more stars were added to the flag, making a total of 50, arranged in 5 rows of 6 stars each and 4 rows of 5 stars each. The flag became official on July 4, 1960.

The United States ensign proudly flies from the tallest single-masted, unguyed flagpole in the world (172 ft.) at the United States Merchant Marine Academy, Kings Point, N. Y.

Suggested Flag Ceremonies and Etiquette at Yacht Club and Squadron Meetings

FLAG CEREMONIES AT SQUADRON MEETINGS

It is better to place the flags with ceremony than to consider them merely a part of the decorations and equipment.

The route of march in advancing the colors will depend upon the size and layout of the meeting place, width of aisles, etc. In the following it is assumed that the flag of the United States and the USPS flag are to used, mounted on staffs, and with stands properly located in advance.

In small or congested rooms the following is recommended.

The bearer of the flag of the United States stands at the right side of the room as viewed from the audience, with the bearer of the USPS flag on the opposite side of the room, in the open space between the front rows of seats and the platform or table at the front of the room for the presiding officer.

The Commander raps his gavel for order, and as soon as obtained announces "We will now have the presentation of the colors. All please rise and stand at attention."

As soon as this is accomplished the Commander orders, "Color Guard—Present the colors." The Color Guard, on the order, marches in opposite directions across the room in front of the speaker's platform. At the center point and just before passing, each comes to a distinct stop facing each other. The bearer of the USPS flag dips his flag slightly and as soon as his flag is back up in carrying position both bearers continue their march and place the flags in their respective stands.

As soon as each flag is placed both bearers step back and come to the position of breast salute, facing the flag of the United States.

Referring back in the above, as soon as the bearers start their march across the room, the Commander orders all present "Breast Salute."

As soon as the bearers have come to the position of breast salute as above, the Commander orders "Two." (Second count of the salute routine.) On this order all present return to the position of attention and the color bearers retire.

The Commander then raps his gavel and orders all present "Be seated" or calls for the Invocation, after which he seats the audience.

If a larger hall is used or more formal ceremonies are desired, the flags may be marched up the center aisle or right aisle. If in single file, with the United States flag in the lead, if abreast with the U.S. flag on the right of marchers.

If marching up the center aisle, at the point where the cleared space between the front seats and the table is reached, both flag bearers halt. After a momentary pause, the bearer of the U.S. flag proceeds and seats the staff of that flag in its stand. Then the bearer of the USPS flag does the same for his flag. The Commander uses the same orders as for the first method above.

The above procedures can be readily adapted for other organizations, substituting that unit's flag, or a state flag, for the USPS Ensign.

COLOR RETIRING CEREMONIES

Color retiring ceremonies may properly and easily be followed at all formal business meetings, where there is a definite moment of official closing. It is not recommended at social gatherings.

Color retiring ceremonies are as follows:

Just before declaring the meeting adjourned the Commander gives the order "Color Guard, stand by to retire the colors." On receiving this order, the Color Guard advances and stands directly in front of their respective colors. When both are in position the Commander orders "Attention" and all present rise and stand at attention. When this is accomplished the Commander orders "Color Guard, secure the colors."

Each color bearer at this command removes his flag from the stand and together do an about-face to face the audience, and then hoist the flags to carry position.

As soon as this is accomplished the Commander orders "Breast salute" and all present except the color bearers comply. As soon as the position of breast salute is accomplished, the color bearers step off together to retrace their presentation march. If the first method described for presenting colors is used, the dipping ceremony is repeated just before they cross in the center of the room. In this method, as soon as the colors reach the side of the room, or if the aisle method is used, as soon as the colors pass from sight or reach the back of the room, the Commander orders "Two" and all present return to the position of attention.

The Commander may now order the meeting adjourned, or may seat the audience first if there are to be informal activities following.

On a shore mast equipped with gaff, at yacht clubs and similar marine installations such as marinas, USPS and USCG Auxiliary shore headquarters, etc., the U.S. Ensign should be flown from the gaff, the position of honor. The illustration above, made from a poster issued by the U.S. Government, shows Old Glory flying from the gaff. Even though there may be positions at a greater height above the ground, yet the flying of the ensign from the gaff is not a violation of the statutes that "no flag should be displayed 'above' the U.S. Ensign."

DISPLAY OF FLAGS AT YACHT CLUB AND SQUADRON MEETINGS

1. The flag of the United States should be displayed either from a staff, or flat against the wall above and behind the speaker's table.

2. The flag of the United States should never be draped or laid over anything except a casket, at which time special rules apply.

3. When displayed flat against a wall it should be fastened along the upper edge only, with the union to the flag's right, to the left as viewed by the audience. This applies whether the flag is hung with stripes vertical or horizontal. The horizontal position of the stripes is preferable.

4. When displayed on a staff indoors, the U.S. ensign is stood at the right of the speaker regardless of whether there is or is not a platform or stage at the front of the room. (This is a 1976 change from the previous custom whereby the position of the flag was determined by the presence or absence of a stage or platform.) The USPS ensign, USCG Auxiliary ensign, or other organizational or state flag, if also displayed, is stood at the speaker's left; see fig. F on page 601. If the Canadian ensign is also displayed, it should be at the right, just inboard of the U.S. ensign; similarly, the CPS ensign would be at the left, just inboard of the USPS ensign.

5. If the flag of the United States, and another, are displayed with crossed staffs, as at the head of a room, the flag of the United States should be at the flag's right, to left as viewed by the audience, and with its staff in front of the other.

6. If the flag of the United States is displayed with other flags in a group, from staffs, it should be in the center and slightly higher or in front of the other flags.

7. If the USPS flag is to be displayed flat against a wall, it is hung as prescribed for the Flag of the United States, as in paragraph 3 above, but on the opposite wall.

DISPLAY OF STATE FLAGS

Any citizen of any state, according to William B. Matthews, Jr., former Boating Administrator for the State of Maryland, may fly the flag of that state unless it is specifically prohibited by law.

On a *vessel with one or more masts,* the State flag is flown at the main masthead in place of the private signal, officer's flag, or Coast Guard Auxiliary Ensign.

On a *mastless boat,* the State flag would be flown at the bow staff in place of a club burgee.

It should be understood that, when a State flag displaces a Coast Guard Auxiliary Ensign at the masthead, an Auxiliary officer cannot fly his officer's pennant from the starboard yardarm. When the State flag at the masthead displaces the flag of an officer of a yacht club or the USPS, he cannot fly his officer's flag at any hoist.

The flying of a State flag at the stern of a boat is *not* proper; nor is it proper to fly from this place of honor any Confederate, "pirate," or other "gag" flag.

Honoring Other National Flags_____

Just as a certain code of etiquette has been adopted to govern the display of flags by American yachts on the waterways of our own nation, so too there is a certain accepted procedure to which pleasure boats should properly adhere when they cross international boundaries into the waters of another nation.

There are only a limited number of positions from which flags may be properly displayed on motor boats and consequently when a foreign flag is to be flown, it must displace one of the flags commonly flown in home waters.

Unfortunately, the customs observed in various foreign waters differ from each other; in case of doubt, inquire locally or observe other U.S. craft.

It is preferable for U.S. vessels while in international or foreign waters to fly the U.S. Ensign (50-star flag) at the stern rather than the Yacht or USPS Ensign.

It would be normal while in foreign waters *not* to fly at all the flags of purely U.S. organizations such as the USPS and USCG Auxiliary. An exception might be made for cruising groups from these organizations.*

MOTOR BOATS

For the purposes of this flag code, motor boats may be divided into three general groups: (1) mastless vessels, having bow and stern staffs only; (2) single-masted motor vessels, with spreader; and (3) vessels with two masts.

Mastless vessels. A motor boat having only bow and stern staffs, if in home waters, would fly the yacht club burgee forward and her own ensign aft. In foreign waters, she must obviously keep her own ensign at the place of

---

*When the starboard spreader is being used for the "courtesy ensign" of the foreign country, the USPS Ensign may be flown from the port spreader.

MASTLESS VESSEL

On the Great Lakes, St. Lawrence River, and adjacent waters, the foreign national flag (often called a "courtesy ensign") is flown from the bow staff. This displaces the club burgee which then may be flown from the starboard spreader. See illustrations on this page and page 472.

On other waters such as the Pacific Northwest, the Bahamas, and the Mexican Pacific Coast, a different procedure is followed. Here, it is expected that the U.S. boats will fly the local national flag from the starboard spreader, retaining the club burgee at the bow. See illustrations this page and page 472.

Motor vessels with two masts. Some of the larger motor craft have two masts. Assuming that the mainmast has no gaff, then the practice is as follows. Her own ensign is at

honor aft. Therefore she has no alternative but to display the national flag of the foreign country which she is visiting at the bow staff in place of her own club burgee. Under no circumstances should she try to fly both flags from one staff at the same time. That principle holds consistently true throughout all flag etiquette.

NOTE:—

Ashore, it is common practice among U. S. yacht clubs on the border to fly the Canadian flag at the masthead, with the U.S. flag at the gaff, when they have Canadian entries in races or Canadian flag officers officially in the club house.

MOTOR VESSEL WITH TWO MASTS

Motor vessels with one mast. Consider next the motor vessel with one mast and spreader—possibly the most common of all arrangements aboard cruising motor boats—her own ensign remains at the stern staff and her private signal or officer's flag at the masthead.

the stern staff as usual, and her private signal or officer's flag stays at the main masthead. The club pennant goes to the bow staff, making way for the foreign national flag at the fore masthead. This is correct practice whether the vessel is under way or laying at anchor, or at a dock.

The only variation of this procedure for two-masted vessels is found when the mainmast is equipped with a gaff. In such cases, the craft's own national ensign is flown at the gaff when underway, just as in home waters.

MOTOR VESSEL WITH ONE MAST:
GREAT LAKES, EASTERN CANADA

MOTOR VESSEL WITH ONE MAST

SAILING VESSELS

Where foreign flag flies to starboard

In the majority of foreign waters, where the courtesy ensign is flown from the starboard spreader on masted motorboats, a similar procedure is followed for sailing vessels.

YAWLS, KETCHES, SCHOONERS, GREAT LAKES

SLOOPS & CUTTERS

SLOOPS & CUTTERS, GREAT LAKES

YAWLS, KETCHES, SCHOONERS

The foreign national flag is flown, at anchor and underway, from the starboard spreader (foremost starboard spreader if there is more than one mast). See illustrations on this page.

Where foreign flag flies forward

In those waters where it is the custom for motorboats to fly the courtesy ensign from the bow staff, problems arise when applying this procedure to sailing vessels. These craft do not normally have bow staffs and a place for the foreign national flag must be found that best approximates that location.

On sailing vessels of all rigs *at anchor* in these waters, the foreign national flag is flown from the forestay at a height so as to be easily seen and clear any personnel on deck, yet not so high as to be inconsistent with the concept that this is in lieu of flying from a bow staff. This is usually about ⅓ of the mast height. (If a large multi-masted sailing vessel should have a bow staff, it is, of course, used, instead of the more general procedure described above.)

Sailboats underway under sail may optionally fly their own national ensign from a stern staff as shown above.

As this location is not practical when *underway under sail,* another location must be found for the courtesy ensign. On sloops and cutters, it is flown from the starboard shroud, again at a height above deck of about ⅓ of the mast height. On ketches and yawls, this is the starboard shroud of the mainmast. Schooners fly the foreign national flag from the foremost starboard shroud, or from the foremost masthead (where it would displace the flags normally flown there).

Sailing vessels *underway under power* may fly the courtesy ensign from either the forestay or starboard shroud.

In all foreign waters

The US Ensign, club burgee, officer's flag, and private signal are flown in a similar manner as in home waters (except for schooners underway in certain areas as noted above).

Many boatmen spend their time afloat with little or no thought to the customs and etiquette of yachting. This is regrettable, for their activities can be more enjoyable both to themselves and to others with some knowledge and practice of doing things "the proper way."

A *custom* is defined in one dictionary as "the habitual practice; the usual way of doing a thing in given circumstances." Such long-standing practices and procedures have usually developed out of trial and error over many years into the "best," or "safest," or "most appropriate" method. By adhering to yachting customs, a boatman is benefiting from long years of others' experience — to defy custom is really to miss a fine opportunity. A love of boats and the water should be accompanied by respect for the traditions and long-established customs of the sea.

Etiquette has been described as "a prescribed or accepted code of usage as established for any occasion." Since recreational boating is a purely voluntary activity, let us drop the "prescribed" aspect of that description and emphasize the "accepted" qualities of the usages. If etiquette were regarded as no more than blind adherence to certain set conventionalities and amenities of social life, there might be sound reasons why one could question the need for, or desirability of, conforming to relatively rigid rules of conduct.

Just as soon, however, as one realizes that these principles of etiquette are not mere arbitrary laws demanding conformity on the part of all individuals—that they are basically the natural expressions of those who instinctively conduct themselves in a sincerely considerate manner toward all others, regardless of rank or race—it becomes quite obvious why anyone should seek to follow the practices that distinguish the true gentleman and yachtsman.

YACHTING CUSTOMS and ETIQUETTE

CHAPTER 23

Customs in general

In the varied relationships of people in many walks of life, a natural body of customs and accepted procedures inevitably develops to govern such relationships. Nowhere is this better exemplified than in the various branches of government service. In the departments that are concerned with diplomacy and statesmanship, observance of the correct form is inextricably woven into the act itself. In the military services, it is safe to say that efficient functioning could not be achieved without the many established customs and procedures.

Customs in Boating

The direct application of all naval customs and forms of etiquette to boating activities would be quite inappropriate and quickly rejected by most boatmen. There are, however, many customs and items of service etiquette that can be used as-is or modified for the circumstances of non-military small craft. Other boating customs derive directly from the ways of the sea and seafaring men.

The Skipper

By custom and by law, the skipper of a craft has the sole ultimate responsibility and authority aboard, especially in emergencies. These are spelled out in some detail in Chapter 7; here it is enough to note that these duties and powers have developed over the years, first as desirable and necessary practices, then as customs, and finally, in many cases, into legal requirements.

Leadership

Even on non-military and non-commercial small craft leadership is an important requirement. Getting things done by a willing and happy crew is a large step forward in putting the "pleasure" into pleasure boating. Proper attention to customs and etiquette provides a basis for effective leadership.

Leadership is said to be largely a matter of intelligent and just administration of authority. Knowledge along technical lines and of practical matters does not automatically provide the capability for leadership. This involves a study and cultivation of such qualities as self-control, judgment, courage, earnestness, sympathy, and loyalty, to name just a few of the many necessary attributes. One of the best methods of acquiring these qualities is to consciously take stock of one's own shortcomings with a view toward eliminating deficiencies and developing the desired characteristics—do this rather than demand in one's crew a degree of perfection that one has not himself attained.

Discipline

Leadership and discipline, including self-discipline, are logically considered in conjunction with each other—they are inseparable. Given a group of individuals in which all have the qualities of leadership developed to a greater or lesser degree, discipline will give each person an appreciation of the authority and responsibilities of their appointed or elected leader. Consequently, they will each work at assigned tasks in mutual cooperation, and will not waste time or mental effort in envy of their superior's position. The leader, in turn, will have the ability to inspire his subordinates to self-development and the voluntary

acceptance of higher responsibilities. It is an error for any leader to believe that he can grow no more; the effective leader grows as well as the men he leads.

It should be quickly apparent that the principles above have great applicability to the world of boating. The yacht club, Power Squadron, or unit of the Coast Guard Auxiliary that reflects an understanding of these ideas will flourish. Of all places, there is none where the demand for capable leadership and discipline is more vital than aboard a vessel, whether it be a large yacht, an ocean-racing sailboat, or a motorboat of any size. The skipper has, and must have, the final authority; he must be equal to that responsibility. If he is worthy of his trust as a "leader," he will get the cooperation of his crew by "leading" and not by driving.

PERSONAL SALUTES

Hand salutes are not often given by civilian boatmen, although they may be used in some formal ceremonies. In a way, this lack of personal saluting is unfortunate, for what better way is there to say "thank you" to a cooperative bridge tender or to the skipper of a boat that slowed down in passing you than to give him a snappy—but not exaggerated—hand salute. Its meaning will never be misunderstood and it will often be much appreciated. It is more of a show of appreciation than merely a wave of the hand in greeting.

Origins

The practice of hand salutes is believed to have had its origins at least as far back as the days of the Romans, when the raising of one's hand, palm forward, was a gesture to show that no dagger was concealed in it. The native American Indians used much the same gesture to indicate a lack of harmful intent. Today, happily, we have other motives when showing respect for superiors.

Uncovering the head also dates back to ancient days. Certain types of headgear, however, were not easily removed, and so the present day salute evolved as a gesture in which the hand is raised to the visor of the cap in much the same manner as if the visor of a helmet were going to be lifted.

Exchanging salutes

Etiquette prescribes that in ceremonies a person junior in rank or seniority should salute first. It is emphasized that this deference to superiors does not imply an admission of inferiority, no more than one could logically be accused of cowardice when displaying a wholesome respect for laws. Those who might take the attitude that a salute is undemocratic should recognize that such an act is merely an extension of the courtesies of everyday life. The salute, thus understood, becomes an opportunity to respect the authority an official represents with no thought of personal inferiority.

BOARDING AND LEAVING
GOVERNMENT SHIPS

It is not inappropriate for a civilian boatman in an organizational uniform, or even in informal clothing but wearing a uniform or visored cap, to observe the proper naval etiquette when boarding and leaving a ship of the Navy, Coast Guard, NOAA, Corps of Engineer, or other gov-

FIG. 2301 By law as well as long-established custom, the skipper of a boat has the sole ultimate responsibility and authority for the actions of the craft and the safety of all those aboard.

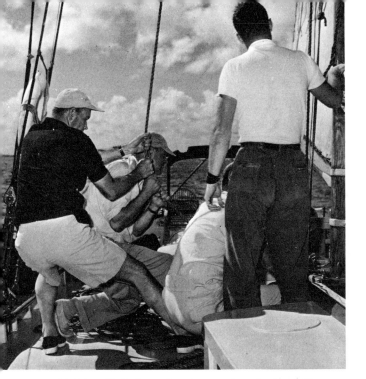

FIG. 2302 Of all places, there is none where the demand for capable leadership and discipline is more vital than aboard an ocean-racing sailboat. The skipper must have final authority.

ernmental agency. He can be assured that his actions will be promptly and properly responded to by the personnel of the watch.

Procedures

When reaching the upper platform of the gangway or accommodation ladder, the person about to board, and before stepping aboard, should stop, then turn toward the stern of the vessel and salute the national ensign. He then turns back to the Officer of the Deck (O.O.D.), salutes, and says: "Request permission to come aboard, sir." The O.O.D. returns both salutes as they are given and with the second one says "Permission granted."

When leaving the vessel, the individual first salutes the Officer of the Deck and says: Request permission to leave ship, sir." The O.O.D. returns the salute and grants permission. At the top of the gangway or other platform, the departing person stops, faces aft, and salutes the U.S. Flag; the O.O.D. returns this salute also, but says nothing.

If the individual is *not* wearing a cap, the *salutes* are *omitted,* but the request for permission to board or depart is made as noted above.

DAILY COLOR CEREMONIES

If a boatman is at a yacht club, or a military or naval base, where formal morning and evening color ceremonies are held, he should follow the actions of local personnel who are not in formation. If he is outdoors when the flag is raised or lowered, and he is wearing a uniform or visored cap, he should face the flag and give a hand salute, holding it until the ceremony is completed. If he is wearing a civilian hat, this should be removed and held over the left breast. If no headgear is worn, the right hand should be placed over the left breast. This is the "breast salute." Women not in uniform stand at attention and give the

breast salute. Automobiles are stopped and personnel remain inside.

The above rules do not, of course, apply if the boatman is engaged in hoisting or lowering his own colors. He should complete his actions and then, if the official ceremonies have not ended, he should stand at attention, and salute if appropriate.

On official occasions, the same salutes as above are given for the playing of the Star Spangled Banner or national anthem of another country.

Yachting Etiquette

Etiquette in yachting takes many forms, but all are essentially the act of showing consideration and courtesy to others. The range of correct etiquette extends from simple everyday actions to formal daily routines and official ceremonies.

Boarding another boat

The etiquette to be observed when coming on board another person's boat is derived from that explained above for boarding a naval vessel. Salutes are seldom exchanged, but a simple request for permission to come aboard is always in good taste. An occasion for saluting might be if the individual boarding were wearing a uniform cap and the craft were that of the commodore of the yacht club or the commander of a Power Squadron.

When leaving another's boat, the naval form of requesting permission is not used. A simple statement of thanks for the hospitality or best wishes for a pleasant cruise is sufficient.

SALUTES BETWEEN VESSELS

In formal ceremonies such as a rendezvous of a yacht club or Power Squadron, the fleet of boats present may pass in review before the flagship of the commodore or USPS commander. In such cases, each craft will salute as it passes. In other isolated instances, joining a club cruise or passing a ship with a high public official embarked, salutes may be exchanged between vessels.

Dipping the ensign in salute

Federal law prohibits dipping the Flag of the United States (the 50-star flag) to any person or thing, and only government vessels are permitted to dip the national ensign in reply to a dip.

The law does, however, permit organizational or institutional flags to be dipped. Thus the U.S. Power Squadrons Ensign, when flown from stern or gaff, may be dipped to salute another craft, or dipped in reply to a dip.

The status of the Yacht Ensign (13 stars in a circle around an anchor on a blue field) is not spelled out clearly, but since the law specifically covers only the Flag of the United States, the assumption has been made that the Yacht Ensign may be dipped.

In a fleet review of a unit of the Power Squadrons, the USPS Ensign should be flown from the stern staff or gaff if a suitable size flag is available. In this way, the flag dipped would be that of the organization holding the review.

All vessels in any review, flying either the USPS or Yacht Ensign at the stern or gaff, should dip that flag when their

FIG. 2303 "Dressing ship" is an old custom applicable to yachts as well as to naval and merchant vessels. This is done only on special occasions and the proper procedures must be followed to be correct.

bow comes abreast of the stern of the flagship and return it to full height when their stern clears the bow of the flagship.

On this occasion, the Flag of the United States should *not* be flown, but if it is, *do not dip it* and use only the hand salute described below. Do not dip any flag other than the flag being flown at the stern staff or the gaff (including the equivalent position on a Marconi sail).

Hand saluting

When a vessel is officially reviewing a parade of other vessels, the senior officer present stands on the deck of the reviewing ship with his staff in formation behind him. Only he gives the hand salute in return to salutes rendered him.

On a boat passing in review, if the skipper has his crew and guests in formation behind him, only he gives the hand salute. If the crew and guests are in uniform and standing at attention at the rail facing the reviewing boat as they pass, they all give the hand salute. The criterion is whether or not the other persons aboard are in formation. If in formation, only the skipper salutes; but if not in formation, all salute.

For both situations, the hand salute is given as the flag is dipped and is held until it is raised again.

Gun salutes

Guns should not be used in salutes between yachts unless ordered by a national authority or by the senior officer present.

YACHT ROUTINES

The following regulations, particularly applicable to a consideration of yachting etiquette, are taken from that portion of the New York Yacht Club code entitled *Yacht Routine*. These deal with salutes, boats (meaning tenders and dinghies), and general courtesies. Other sections, not given here, relate primarily to the display of flags, signaling, and lights.

The routines of other yacht clubs may be considerably less formal and detailed than that which follows, but whatever routines are used they are likely to have been derived from the procedures of the New York Yacht Club.

Salutes

All salutes shall be made by dipping the ensign once, lowering the ensign to the dip and hoisting it when the salute is returned. All salutes shall be returned.

Whistles shall never be used in saluting.

Guns may be used to call attention to signals, but their use otherwise shall be avoided as much as possible.

Vessels of the United States and foreign navies shall be saluted.

When a flag officer of the Club comes to anchor, he shall be saluted by all yachts present, except where there is a senior flag officer present.

When a yacht comes to anchor where a flag officer is present, such officer shall be saluted. A junior flag officer anchoring in the presence of a senior shall salute.

Yachts passing shall salute, the junior saluting first.

All salutes shall be answered in kind.

A yacht acting as Race Committee boat should neither salute nor be saluted while displaying the Committee flag.

Boats

Upon entering and leaving boats, deference is shown seniors by juniors entering first and leaving last.

When in boats, flag officers display their flags, captains (owners) their private signals, and members (non-owners) the club burgee. When on duty, the fleet captain and race committee display their distinctive flags. The flag of the senior officer embarked takes precedence. A flag officer embarked in a boat not displaying his distinctive flag should be considered as present in an unofficial capacity.

When two boats are approaching the same gangway or landing stage, flag officers shall have the right of way in order of seniority.

Whenever possible, boat booms shall be rigged in at night. Otherwise, a white light shall be shown at the end. All boats made fast to the stern of a yacht at anchor shall show a white light at night.

Courtesies

When a flag officer makes an official visit, his flag, if senior to that of the yacht visited, shall be displayed in place of the burgee while he is on board.

A yacht may display the personal flag of a national, state, or local official when such individual is on board, or the national ensign of a distinguished foreign visitor. This flag should be displayed in place of the private signal or officer's flag for the President of the United States, and in place of the burgee for all other officials and visitors.

On Independence Day, and when ordered on other occasions, a yacht shall, when at anchor and the weather

FIG. 2304 Cruising will usually take a boatman well away from familiar home waters. He should be alert to the peculiarities of local customs and should conform to the way in which things are done at the club or harbor he is visiting.

permits, *dress ship* from morning to evening colors. See pages 461 and 467.

After joining the Squadron during the Annual Cruise, a yacht shall request permission before leaving.

Cruising

When cruising away from home waters, the wise skipper keeps a sharp eye out for local customs. It is a mark of courtesy to conform to local procedures and practices.

While visiting at a yacht club of which you are not a member, observe the actions and routines of the local owner-members, and particularly the club officers. This is especially important with respect to evening colors. Not all clubs strictly calculate the daily time of sunset, and some may be earlier than you would normally expect.

If you will be off your boat at the time of evening colors —in the clubhouse for dinner, for example—be sure to take down your flags before you leave your craft.

Be a good neighbor

Consideration of the other skipper is an important element of yachting etiquette. Don't anchor too close to another boat so as to give cause for concern for the safety of both craft; consider the state of the tide and the effect of its range on the radius about which you will swing. Use a guest mooring only with permission; tie up to a fuel pier only briefly.

In the evening hours at an anchorage, don't disturb your neighbors on other boats. Sound travels exceptionally well across water and many cruising boatmen turn in early for dawn departures. Keep voices down and play radios only at low levels. If you should be one of the early departees, leave with an absolute minimum of noise.

Be a good neighbor in other ways, too. Don't throw

trash and garbage overboard. Secure flapping halyards; they can be a most annoying source of noise for some distance. When coming into or leaving an anchorage area, do so at a dead slow speed to keep your wake and wash at an absolute minimum.

Passing other boats

A faster boat overtaking and passing a slower one in a narrow channel should slow down *sufficiently* to cause no damage or discomfort. Often overlooked is the fact that it may be necessary for the *slower* boat itself to reduce speed. If that boat is making, say, 8 knots, the faster boat can only slow down to about 10 knots in order to have enough speed differential left to get past. At this speed, the passing boat may unavoidably make a wake that is uncomfortable to the other craft. In such cases, the overtaken boat should slow to 4 or 5 knots to allow herself to be passed at 6 or 7 knots with little wake.

If adequate depths of water extend outward on one or both sides of the course, it is the courteous thing for the passing boat to swing well out to a safe side to minimize the discomfort of the overtaken boat.

Proper etiquette calls for power boats to pass sailing craft astern or well to leeward.

GUESTS ABOARD

If you are invited to go cruising for a day, a weekend, or a more extended period, there are many things to be considered—clothes, promptness, gifts, aids, noise, smoking, privacy, and time.

FIG. 2305 Whenever circumstances such as the depth of water permit, power boats should observe the proper etiquette of passing sailboats on their lee side or crossing under their stern. Consideration of the other skipper is a mark of a good yachtsman. The wake must always be kept down to a reasonable level.

Take a minimum of *clothes,* packed in collapsible containers, or at least in suitcases that will nest inside each other when empty—storage space is severely limited aboard boats. Bring one outfit of "city clothes" for use at those places ashore requiring such dress. Bring two bathing suits if you plan to do much swimming—at times, things dry slowly around a boat. For additional comments on boating clothing and shoes, see Chapter 24.

For the *stowage of clothing* you bring aboard, the skipper may assign a special locker which he has cleared for your convenience. Don't scatter gear and clothing all over the boat. Use the locker provided, keep it orderly, and thus help the skipper keep things shipshape.

When a *sailing time* is given, be there ahead of time. The skipper generally chooses a time with a purpose in mind—the tides and currents, normal weather patterns, the length of the planned run, etc.

Meal times are set for the convenience of the galley hand. It is inconsiderate for a tardy guest to delay meals. In any event, it is bad manners to be late for a meal.

Rising and *bedtimes* are a matter of convenience to everyone aboard because of the generally limited washing and toilet facilities. Get up promptly when the skipper or paid hands are heard moving about. Use the head as expeditiously as possible, make up your bunk, stow any loose gear about the cabin, and appear on deck. When the skipper suggests that it is time to retire for the evening, take the hint and bed down.

Noise on a boat seems to amplify, so walk and speak softly and your shipmates will be glad you're aboard.

Smoking is stopped, of course, when gasoline is to be taken aboard, but care is the order of the day even when smoking is permissible. A carelessly flicked cigarette ash or butt has started many a fire in a chair, awning, or compartment. Cigars leave a particularly unpleasant after-odor and should be enjoyed only in the open air.

Many small particles—pipe tobacco and ashes, peanut shells, bits of potato chips, crumbs, etc.—have a way of getting into cracks, crevices and corners, and there defying the ordinary cleaning facilities found on a boat. Use care with all of these things.

Privacy becomes valuable on a protracted cruise. Part of every day should be set aside for getting away from everyone else aboard. Your cruisemates will be more glad of your company if it is not constant.

Should occasions arise where you board the boat from a *dinghy,* or have an opportunity to use the skipper's dinghy (with his permission, of course) use care in coming alongside. Unship oarlocks which could scar the boat's planking, and stow oars in the boat; never leave them in the oarlocks.

Gifts are certainly not expected, but are always acceptable. Be sure, however, that they are appropriate for boating—if in doubt, make it liquid and consumable. When invited on board for a day or a week, ask what you can bring. If the owner wants to provide all of the food and drink, the guest might take the cruising party ashore for a good dinner at the first port of call. Buying part of the fuel, or bringing food and/or liquid refreshments by pre-arrangement, is viewed by the Coast Guard as a partial charter and commerical operation; see page 45.

Assistance on board a boat can be useful, or it can do more harm than good. If you don't know what to do, sit down out of the way and be quiet. Always keep out of the line of vision of the helmsman and be particularly quiet and unobtrusive when the craft is being docked or undocked.

If being on board is not a new experience, or you wish to learn to be more useful, you may ask what you can do to help. Ask, however, when things are calm and uneventful; don't ask in the midst of getting under way or coming alongside a pier.

Above all, if you are assigned to do something, do exactly that. If you think that the instructions were wrong, say so, but don't go off on your own when the skipper thinks that you are doing what he asked.

FIG. 2306 Having guests aboard for a day's cruise or longer period can add to a boat owner's enjoyment of his recreation by sharing his enjoyment with others. Guests can do their part by "fitting in" with the routine of the craft.

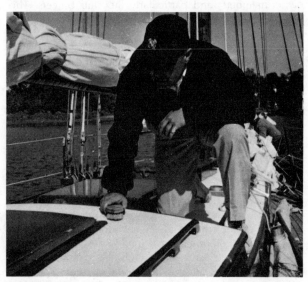

FIG. 2307 Guests aboard for a cruise may offer their assistance in the operation of the craft or in the daily chores. They should not, however, tackle work without the skipper's knowledge and should work under proper supervision.

CHAPTER 24

BOATING CLOTHING and UNIFORMS

FIG. 2401 Many boatmen find an informal visored cloth cap the most practical form of headgear afloat. It is comfortable, provides good shade for the eyes, and stays on well in a breeze. Club emblems, but no insignia of rank, may be worn on such caps.

(Photograph by Frank Rohr)

The subject of "clothing and uniforms" encompasses both the matter of wearing or not wearing a uniform and that of safe, sensible apparel for today's boating. In each of these areas rather strong differences of opinion will be found to exist.

When it comes to clothing, most boatmen have rather strong convictions as to whether or not they should, or must, abide by any arbitrary set of regulations. The spokesmen of one faction argue that they go afloat for pleasure and relaxation, and propose to dress as they please—for comfort and practicability. The other group advocates strict adherence to all the proprieties, frowning on those who do not conform to the dictates of etiquette, whether it be in dress, the display of flags, or other areas.

Who is right? Actually neither, in the sense that the other would be wrong. There is room for differences of opinion, and no logical reason why each group and individual should not be entitled to his own position and actions.

Good taste

Few boatmen would deliberately violate the principles of good taste in regard to dress aboard their craft. In some cases, it is merely a matter of not realizing that such principles exist. Errors are often made in the use of various devices and insignia worn on uniforms, and in the choice of articles of uniforms themselves. Generally these practices would be corrected if the wearer knew that he was in error.

One thing is certain. The clothing that might be appropriate and acceptable in one situation may be decidedly in bad taste in another. It would be hard to say who would be more uncomfortable—the outboarder in shorts at a yacht club dinner party or the commodore in spotless whites tinkering with a balky engine under a blazing sun.

Origins of present-day clothing

The clothing that is worn while boating today has developed over the years from the quite stiff and formal uniforms of the late 1800's and early years of this century. The steady trend toward smaller, owner-operated craft has taken its toll on the rigid customs of yachting circles—the "dressing for dinner" routine. The establishment of many small, much less formal yacht clubs and boating clubs has likewise supported the gradual change to a more informal mode of attire. A third factor is the general trend of modern life to an easier, more casual mood.

These developments all combine to make a full yachting uniform something of a rarity aboard present-day craft or at typical yacht clubs.

479

Yacht Club Uniforms

Essentially all yacht clubs provide in their by-laws for uniforms and insignia of rank. In actual practice, however, there will be found a wide variance in the degree to which such apparel is worn. In a very few clubs, the officers, many members who are boat owners, and even some non-owner members have uniforms and will wear them on formal occasions. Hardly ever will full uniforms be worn while cruising or at every-day activities around the clubhouse. It should be noted, though, that members are not required to have uniforms; their purchase and use are purely optional.

Uniforms in typical clubs

In most yacht and boating clubs, the officers will own uniforms, but few members will have them. Rare indeed in these clubs would be a uniform on a member who did not own a boat.

In the smaller and even less formal clubs, the uniforms of officers and members may be limited by general agreement and custom to the wearing of a uniform cap only, worn with any boating clothes of good taste. This is not "wrong" although it may be viewed with disfavor by older, more tradition-minded yachtsmen. It is well in tune with the informality of modern life and family-style boating, particularly outboarding.

When uniforms are worn

Yacht and boating club uniforms are typically worn only on special occasions, although it is quite reasonable to wear a uniform cap with regular clothing while engaged in ordinary activities while afloat or at the club piers. Formal occasions for uniform wearing might include the ceremonies at the beginning of a new season, the installation of officers, holiday regattas, and the like. The best guidance at any club regarding the wearing or non-wearing of the full uniform or cap only is the policy adhered to by the majority of the officers and members.

On board and under way, the cap will probably be the only item of uniform worn on owner-operated boats. On larger craft where there are paid hands to take care of the operation of the yacht, a uniform for the owner would seem to be in far better taste, as well as more sensible, than on a small boat where the owner-captain must break out his own anchor, swab his own deck, and attend to numerous other chores both clean and dirty.

Derivation of the uniform

On one point, at least, there can be little argument. For the occasions where a uniform is appropriate, it should certainly follow the style prescribed by yacht clubs as correct. For authority, no better source can be found than the code to which the New York Yacht Club has adhered for many years. While there may be minor deviations in the practices of other clubs, the N.Y.Y.C. rules are the basic form on which the others are patterned.

Basic uniforms

The service dress uniform prescribed for yacht club officers and members is normally a double-breasted sack coat of navy blue or white cloth, serge or flannel, with trousers of the same material or of white drill. The cap is of navy blue cloth and has a patent leather visor, black chin strap, and black buttons. The white cap is of the same style with a fixed or removable cover. White shirts with black or dark ties are appropriate; some clubs have ties of their own design. White or black shoes are worn to match the trousers; boating shoes are not worn with a uniform except under limited circumstances afloat when advisable for safety.

Cap emblems

There are a number of styles of yachting caps offered by the manufacturers of uniforms. In every case, an emblem or device will be found on the front of the band over the visor. This identifies the club to which the individual belongs and indicates his status in the club. See figures 2402(a), (b), (c), (d). The central part of the device will be an enameled metal or silk embroidered disc showing the distinctive emblem of the club, basically its burgee. This is placed at the intersection of two crossed fouled anchors in gold embroidery.

Insignia of rank

If the yachtsman holds the office of commodore, there will be three gold stars around the anchors, one at the top and one at each side. See fig. 2402(a).

COMMODORE ★ ★ ★

Trefoil with 4 additional black stripes; 3 gold stars within loops.

VICE COMMODORE ★ ★

Trefoil with 3 additional black stripes; 2 gold stars within side loops.

REAR COMMODORE ★

Trefoil with 2 additional black stripes; 1 gold star in center loop.

FIG. 2402(a) Yacht club officers are distinguished by insignia on sleeve and cap. Stars of current officers are gold, those of past officers, when used, are silver.
(All insignia illustrations courtesy Commodore Uniform Company, Inc.)

The vice-commodore of the club, next lower in rank, has the same device except that he is entitled to two stars, one on each side of the anchors.

The third-ranking officer, the rear commodore, rates one star, placed above the device the same as the top star of the commodore.

Members and staff officers

The N.Y.Y.C. code prescribes that captains (owners of boats) and ex-flag officers rate only the two gold fouled anchors without the gold stars of incumbent officers. In some clubs, however, this practice is modified to authorize past officers to wear silver stars of the same number and in the same locations.

In most yacht clubs, a member who is not a boat owner uses a cap device with a *single* fouled anchor placed vertically, fig. 2402(c). Some clubs, however, omit this separate insignia and allow the wearing of two crossed fouled anchors for all members not holding office.

Other officers of a club (often referred to as "staff officers") are distinguished by certain symbols in gold placed above the regular cap emblem, fig. 2402(b). A fleet captain, for example, is identified by a horizontally placed anchor. The secretary is entitled to a maple leaf; the treasurer, an acorn; the measurer, a short bar; and a member of the race committee, a half-inch anchor placed vertically. A fleet surgeon is identified by a red cross.

Variations exist in some clubs—the letter M for the measurer; the letters RC for race committeemen.

Sleeve insignia

Rank and status are also indicated by stripes on each sleeve of the uniform coat, fig. 2402(a). On blue uniforms, the stripes are black; on white coats, they are white.

A commodore wears five stripes of mohair braid, the upper one taking the shape of what is known as a trefoil— this might be described as a triple loop, one part vertical and the others horizontal. In each loop of the trefoil, the commodore wears a gilt star. Regulations, of course, prescribe the width of the braid, how far from the cuff the

lower stripe is and how far apart the others are, the size of the stars, etc.

The vice-commodore wears four stripes, the upper one being a trefoil, and there are two stars, one in each horizontal loop.

The rear-commodore has three stripes with one star in the upper loop of the trefoil formed by the top stripe.

Boat owners and staff officers are entitled to two stripes, the upper one having the trefoil; they, of course, have no stars. Members not owning boats wear a single stripe which has the trefoil.

Ex-flag officers continue to wear the stripes designating their former rank, but omit the stars that they were entitled to while holding office.

No gold braid

Note particularly that in all of the uniform descriptions above there is *no* mention of *gold braid* for the yachtsman, whether member, owner, or officer. The only gold permissible is the gold fouled anchors of the cap device, the stars on cap and sleeve, and the insignia of the staff officers.

The yachtsman does *not* wear a gold chin strap on his cap, nor is there any sanction for the wearing of gold embroidery on the cap visor as is worn by senior Navy and Coast Guard officers—the so-called "scrambled eggs." This has been seen in some boating circles in recent years, but is entirely incorrect and improper for a boatman.

Formal dress

In some of the older clubs, the uniform regulations prescribe a mess jacket for the most formal occasions. This might be compared with a tuxedo or dinner jacket of civilian dress. The yacht club mess jacket is single-breasted, of blue undress worsted, with rolling collar made with a long roll, and pointed lapels. It is trimmed with black silk braid and appropriate collar and sleeve ornaments.

In most clubs, however, the more formal uniform will consist of the regular service dress coat with a bow tie substituted for the usual four-in-hand tie.

STAFF OFFICERS' INSIGNIA

RACE COMMITTEE **FLEET CAPTAIN** **FLEET SURGEON**

SECRETARY **TREASURER** **MEASURER**

FIG. 2402(b) Cap insignia worn by staff officers are illustrated at the right. Sleeve insignia is shown above—trefoil with one additional black stripe, and insignia of officer in the center loop (in this case the gold anchor of the Race Committee).

Blazers

A relatively recent development in boating clothing is the wearing of a blazer jacket with matching or contrasting slacks. This is a comfortable and attractive alternative to the full club uniform except on formal occasions. It has been widely adopted and its use continues to spread.

Blazers are dark blue, two- or three-button style, single-breasted with a left upper and two lower patch pockets. Either black or gilt buttons may be prescribed by the club's rules for the front and sleeves of the jacket.

A patch of the club burgee on crossed fouled anchors, or other design derived from the club insignia, is worn on the upper left pocket. The blazer is not, however, an item of uniform and thus no insignia of rank is worn on the sleeve or elsewhere on the blazer. The club uniform cap should be worn with the blazer only if authorized by the club's rules.

UNIFORMS OF PAID CREW

The uniform regulations of the New York Yacht Club, from whence most other clubs' procedures are derived, include a complete set of descriptions of uniforms for various *paid* crew members. Crews, in general, are much smaller today than they were in the days of very large sail and steam yachts when the regulations were originally drafted, but logical adaptations to current conditions can easily be made.

Rare indeed will be the yacht paid captain—"sailing master" in NYYC terminology—in blue uniform with four gold sleeve stripes, or chief engineer with three red stripes, overseeing a crew of mates, assistant engineers, boatswains, oilers, coxswains, and launchmen. If blue crew uniforms are seen, it will be noted that the trefoil device of club members is not worn by professionals.

The typical work and cruising uniform of paid crew is khaki. Blue coats and trousers may be worn in port or for more formal occasions. White uniforms may be worn in warm or hot climates.

Caps for paid crew

The cap is the distinguishing device of the professional. See fig. 2402(d). The use of gold for the chin strap is as proper for the paid crewmen as it is improper for the owner. Further, the insignia above the gold strap is always quite different. There is no single accepted design for the cap ornament for the professional. Many owners have adopted an embroidered design consisting of their club burgee and their personal flag crossed and partially surrounded by a gold wreath. Others use a more simple design of crossed clear anchors (*not* the fouled anchors of the owner's emblem) within a plain gold circle. Engineering personnel would wear a three-bladed propeller in lieu of the anchors.

Skippers and mates of charter fishing boats may be seen using the last design described above with or without the word "captain" or "mate" embroidered in gold above the circle.

CLUB UNIFORMS IN GENERAL

Having read all of the above, one might reach the conclusion that most boatmen own a wardrobe full of uniforms and never relax in anything less formal. That, how-ever, is not at all true. While the formal occasions mentioned contribute in large measure to the general good fellowship and enjoyment found in yachting circles, if the sport were ever to lose its basic character as a freedom from shore-based conventions, it would very rapidly lose some of its virtues, and most likely many of its followers.

OWNER - CLUB MEMBER

MEMBER (non-owner)

FIG. 2402(c) While practice varies among yacht clubs, the cap and sleeve insignia illustrated here satisfy the dictates of etiquette. Above—the boat-owning yacht club member has a trefoil with one additional black stripe on the sleeve; the member who owns no boat has the trefoil without additional stripes.

OWNER (non-member)

CAP INSIGNIA FOR YACHTING PROFESSIONALS

FIG. 2402(d) Traditionally correct devices for paid hands aboard yachts. Crossed flags in gold wreath may be used, at the yacht owner's discretion, by professional officers and crewmen. Crossed anchors in gold wreath often designate the paid captain. Crossed anchors (in circle) are worn by deck officers, propeller in circle by engineer officers. Lettering in gold wreath (below) is self-explanatory.

CAPTAIN

DOCK MASTER

FIG. 2403 Officers and members of the U.S. Power Squadrons may wear a variety of uniforms for different climates and occasions. Uniform "C" shown here with long-sleeve white shirt, black tie, and long white trousers is typical of those worn at outdoor summer ceremonies such as flag-raisings. The Sea Explorer Scouts forming the color guard are not a part of the USPS, but many Squadrons do sponsor such units.
(Photograph by Frank P. Beauchamp)

USPS Uniforms

Although the United States Power Squadrons is not a military organization, it has a rather full set of uniforms, winter and summer, formal and informal. These are not required to be worn by all members, and many do not, but they are authorized and specified if desired. Most officers will wear uniforms for meetings, rendezvous ceremonies, and other special occasions. Uniforms are not generally worn to various USPS educational classes.

Uniform combinations

The USPS uniforms range from informal white Bermuda shorts worn with open-neck, short-sleeve shirt to regular dark blue coat and trousers that can be worn with four-in-hand tie during the day or with bow tie for evening events. In between are uniforms consisting of the short-sleeve shirt and long white trousers, or a long-sleeve white shirt and black tie worn with the same trousers. See fig. 2403. The blue uniform coat may also be combined with white trousers for more formal affairs in warm climates. Although not a part of the uniform series, there is a USPS blazer that may be worn for many occasions.

Insignia of rank

Officer's rank in the United States Power Squadrons is indicated on the uniform coat by sleeve braid and embroidered insignia. A varying number of black stripes, up to four, is used as on yacht club uniforms, but in addition there are three different widths of braid used in combination. The long-sleeved white shirt also carries the sleeve insignia but not the braid.

Uniform cap

As with yacht clubs, there is a uniform cap that is worn both with the various uniforms and by itself with informal boating clothes. The rank of various local, District, and National officers is also indicated on the cap. A USPS cap ornament may be worn on non-uniform boating caps, but in such cases no insignia of rank is shown.

Further information

Details of the USPS uniforms and insignia of rank are spelled out in the by-laws of that organization and are illustrated in the officers' manual. A table of information on officers' sleeve braid and insignia, cap insignia, and flags will be found on pages R and S.

Coast Guard Auxiliary Uniforms

The uniforms worn by officers and members of the Coast Guard Auxiliary have evolved through several distinct phases over recent years. The uniforms are now more "military" than "yachting" although the organization remains basically civilian in nature. Its supervision and administration by the regular Coast Guard does not change the Auxiliary's non-military status. The title of "Commodore" in various combinations remains in use also as a carry-over from earlier days.

Various uniforms

The uniforms of the USCGAUX include Coast Guard Blue Dinner Dress, Service Dress, and Working uniforms; tropical blue and tropical white; and Dinner Dress, White Jacket or Dinner Dress, Navy Blue Jacket. Members of the Auxiliary do not, of course, need all of these uniforms, only those appropriate to their area and normal duties. There are also uniform jackets and raincoats. Uniforms are required for certain activities, such as official patrols and when doing Courtesy Marine Examinations; instructors will normally wear uniforms.

Insignia of rank

The rank of various officers is now indicated by sleeve braid, shoulder boards, and pin-on insignia, all patterned after those worn by regular Coast Guard officers, but with differences designed to distinguish the Auxiliarist.

Braid on sleeves and shoulder boards is of silver rather than gold and is worn in stripes, half-stripes, and broad stripes in a series comparable to those worn by Ensigns to Vice Admirals in the Coast Guard and Navy. The Auxiliary, however, does not use rank titles like those of the regular and reserve services. Braid is prescribed for the office held rather than for rank titles.

Shoulder boards, worn with most uniforms, such as Service Dress, carry the same number of stripes as those worn on the sleeves of certain other uniforms. Shoulder boards of the most senior Auxiliary officers are of solid silver braid with one, two, or three stars as appropriate to the office that they hold.

The Auxiliary shield is worn above the stripes of both shoulder boards and sleeve rings.

Collar insignia, worn with Working uniforms, consists of the same series of designs used for officers of the U.S. Armed Forces, but with a letter "A" in blue or red super-

FIG. 2404 Eyeglasses, if accidentally dropped overboard, are likely to be lost. To prevent this, "keeper" cords or holders are available. Light flotation devices may also be attached to the frames.
(Courtesy Commodore Uniform Company, Inc.)

imposed. Similar insignia, in a larger size, is worn on uniform jackets (windbreakers) and raincoats.

Rank insignia of the Coast Guard Auxiliary are illustrated on page V.

Uniform caps

Officers and members of the Auxiliary wear frame caps similar to those used by regular officers; white covers are used—the blue cover is no longer used by the Coast Guard and Navy.

Chin straps of members' frame caps are black or Coast Guard Blue; those of officers are silver. Visor ornamentation in silver is worn on the caps of senior officers.

A "working cap" of boating style is authorized in Coast Guard Blue. The fore-and-aft "garrison cap" has been reduced to an optional item only.

INFORMAL CLOTHING

Informal boating clothing varies widely with the individual, the area, and the activities engaged in. Essentially the only degree of uniformity exists at the two extremes—

top and bottom, cap and shoes. In between, the individual is "on his own," guided only by good sense and good taste. "Gag" or extreme uniforms and clothing do not meet the latter criterion and should be avoided.

Caps

The yachtsman who is particular to wear the correct style of yachting cap on formal occasions may often go hatless in the summer time. The sun is strong around the water, however, and protection of some kind for head and eyes is usually necessary, which probably gives rise to the custom of wearing the yachting cap even when other parts of the uniform are omitted. See fig. 2401.

When informal boating caps of the visored style, often referred to as "flat-top" or "flight deck" type, are worn, the careful skipper adds no organizational or rank insignia except as prescribed by the organization concerned.

Especially among the sailing enthusiasts a white cloth hat with wide brim all around, frequently with green underneath or with a green transparent visor, is popular.

Sun glasses

Sun glasses are widely used afloat to prevent eye strain from sun glare. Glasses with Polaroid lenses are among the best as they are particularly efficient in glare reduction.

Those individuals who must wear glasses with prescription lenses for distant vision will find it highly desirable to have a pair made with the prescription in tinted glass. The tint must be dark enough to cope adequately with the extreme degrees of brightness found on and near the water. Persons using bifocals for both near and distant vision correction will also find the use of tinted glass most desirable while afloat.

Regular eyeglasses or sun glasses must be protected from accidental loss overboard. See fig. 2404. A keeper chain or cord can be worn around the back of the person's neck, or a light flotation device can be attached to the frames to keep them from sinking if dropped into the water.

Foot-gear

Shoes that cannot be relied upon to give you a sure, slip-proof footing on a wet or slippery deck are highly dangerous on a boat. Coupled with this is the necessity of using a type of sole and heel that will not scratch fine decks.

For all-around use afloat, the best informal footwear available is a sneaker type of shoe with cloth uppers and soles of special material and designs that can be depended upon to give a grip on a wet, heeling deck. Slits in the soles of Sperry Topsiders, Randy Boatshus, and others provide an effective "squeegee" action. For more dressy occasions, shoes with leather uppers, but the same non-slip soles, are available.

Cork soles and special designs are available that will not pick up grit and sand when worn ashore, to be tracked back on deck when returning to the boat. Ordinary sneakers or tennis shoes may be worn provided they do not have a smooth sole that would permit slipping on a wet deck. Crepe-soled shoes, though comfortable, are doubtful items on a boat.

Women may wear much the same footgear as men. High heels, obviously, have no place on a boat.

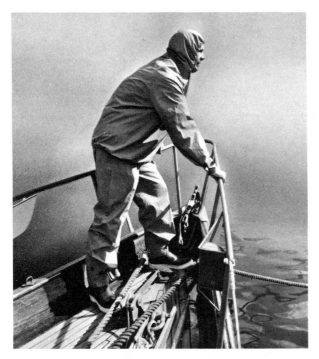

FIG. 2405 Foul weather gear is essential for most boatmen, especially those on sailing craft. It should provide full protection from wind-driven rain and spray. The type shown above is of international orange color to provide the greatest visibility should the wearer fall overboard. Matching boots with non-slip soles complete the outfit.

Foul-weather gear

Wet weather clothing is essential afloat. You may have a closed-in deckhouse for protection while under way, but there will be occasions when you must go on deck regardless of rain to make fast to a pier, handle an anchor, or pick up a mooring.

Oilskin slickers and sou'westers were the traditional heavy-weather garments, but now foul-weather gear is made of more modern materials and in a variety of styles. See fig. 2405. Articles are available that are light-weight and comfortable to wear. Check your boating store or mail order catalog for the protective clothing best suited to your boating activities.

The secret of greater comfort is to put on foul-weather gear *before* you get wet. It is equally effective in keeping moisture *in* as well as out if you delay in donning it until after you are partially or thoroughly wet.

Clothing for warmth

Boating activities are often extended into months of chilly weather. Special parka-style coats with hood attached are made for yachtsmen, where warmth and light weight, together with wind- and water-resistant qualities, are prime requisites. These are made of soft waterproof canvas or synthetic material, backed up with a lining for warmth.

A recent development is the flotation jacket which will not only provide warmth on deck but also a considerable measure of buoyancy should the wearer fall overboard. See fig. 2406.

BAGGAGE

Closely related to clothing for boatmen is the luggage that they and their guests use to bring aboard such apparel and related personal items. Storage space always seems to be at a premium on boats, and baggage should be soft and collapsible if possible. Canvas duffel bags are probably the most practical luggage, but other types that will fold and stow flat can be used.

IN SUMMARY

Summing up on the question of what to wear while boating, it would seem reasonable to say that if the occasion requires the use of a uniform, then the uniform should be correct in detail according to the regulations and customs of the organization concerned. If, on the other hand, the clothing is being chosen for informal wear, comfort and utility would seem to be the major considerations.

FIG. 2406 A flotation jacket is comfortable, light weight and functional, serving not only as a practical garment but providing buoyancy like a life preserver if the wearer should fall overboard.
(Courtesy Commodore Uniform Company, Inc.)

Don't mix uniforms

Since the insignia and devices used by yacht clubs differ from those prescribed for the USPS, it is evident that breaches of etiquette would result from wearing, at the same time, articles associated with two different organizations. This might be compared with wearing two socks that were not mates, or a brown shoe and a black one. For example, fouled anchors belong on the cap of an amateur yachtsman, the member of a yacht club. In the center of these anchors belong the yacht club insignia, not the USPS emblem. Again, the sleeve braid with trefoil identifies the member of a yacht club; USPS insignia of rank or merit marks would definitely be improper in combination with such braid.

Similarly, items of the USCGAux uniform, or rank insignia of that organization, should never be mixed with USPS or yacht club apparel or insignia.

The key to correct practice, of course, is to wear the insignia of only one organization at any one time. And, naturally, to avoid the use of any uniform item or insignia to which you are not entitled.

CHAPTER 25

ELECTRONIC EQUIPMENT AND ITS USE

FIG. 2501 Electronic equipment now makes boating safer and more pleasurable — radiotelephones, direction finders, depth sounders, radar sets, loran receivers, fuel vapor detectors, and many others.

THE EVER-INCREASING variety of electronic equipment that is available for small craft places on all boatmen the burden of knowing more about this subject. "Electricity" and "electronics" are generally mysterious topics to the average person on the water; you can't see or feel them, but you know that they exist from their effects. The typical boatman shrinks from technical details on electricity and electronics, yet if he fails to put them to work for him on his boat, he is seriously neglecting valuable assistance easily available to him.

The owner of a boat of any size should know four things about electronic equipment—(1) what items are available for his craft, see fig. 2501, (2) how, in very general terms, such equipment operates, (3) how it should be used for greatest effectiveness, and (4) what he should and should not do regarding its maintenance. Such knowledge and understanding will mean not only greater safety on the water, but also increased convenience and pleasure. There is no intention or expectation of making an electronics technician out of Mr. Average Boatman, but he will be surprised how much can be understood and how much better his equipment will serve his requirements when used with greater knowledge of its capabilities and limitations. Technical language will be kept at a minimum in this chapter; only enough details will be included as are needed to make the necessary explanations.

"Electrical" and "electronic" are terms often used in an overlapping manner. In this chapter, *electronic* will be the term applied to equipment primarily employing tubes and transistors. *Electrical* equipment will be considered to include such things as motors, generators, lights, etc. The items of electronic equipment to be covered here are radiotelephones, direction finders, depth sounders, radar, loran, Omega, automatic steering devices, and several minor items.

Electrical Systems

Electrical power must be considered briefly before electronic equipment for this is the life-blood of such devices as radios, direction finders, and the like. Although a few transistorized items may operate from self-contained batteries, the bulk of electronic equipment is powered from the boat's electrical system. With many of today's outboard motors having generators or alternators, there is almost no lower limit to the size of boat which can have one or more electronic devices, but the total load must not exceed the electrical system's capacity.

Voltages

Electronic equipment is available for input voltages of 6, 12, 32, or 115, the first three being for direct current (DC) systems, and the last for alternating current (AC) operation. By far the most popular voltage is 12; its primary advantages are the widest selection of items and generally the lowest cost.

Six-volt systems are regarded today as obsolete; the lower voltage requires higher currents for the same power, and this results in heavier wiring or excessive voltage drops

FIG. 2502 Basic source of electrical power for operation of electronic equipment is a generator or alternator (arrow) driven by main engine. Most electrical systems are 12-volts DC; larger craft may use 32-volt DC systems.

between the battery and the load. The use of 32-volt equipment has the advantage of requiring even smaller currents for a given load than do 12-volt systems, but many items such as low and medium power radios, depth sounders, etc., are largely unavailable in this voltage rating. A 32-volt electrical system also has the disadvantage of requiring a larger and more expensive battery.

The current popularity of 12-volt systems in automobiles makes economical the use of such alternators, batteries, and regulators on boats. Equipment powered by 115 volts AC can be used, but the primary power must be continuously generated as AC cannot be stored in batteries as can DC. Thus, except where specifically mentioned as being different, it will be assumed throughout this chapter that items of electronic equipment being discussed are powered from a 12-volt DC electrical system.

Generators and Alternators

On essentially all boats, the basic source of electrical power will be a generator or an alternator driven by a main engine. See fig. 2502. The difference between these electrical devices is technical and the boat owner need not concern himself with them, except to know that the alternator is the more modern of the two and has the advantage of a greater output at low engine rpm. The external result is the same with both devices: a DC voltage somewhat greater than that of the battery (about 14 volts for a 12-volt system) so that energy can be put into the battery against its natural tendency to discharge into a completed circuit.

The flow of electricity from the generator or alternator into the battery will be through a *voltage regulator*. This device prevents an alternator from charging at a rate in excess of its capacity, prevents the battery from being overcharged, and cuts out a generator from the circuit when the engine is not running in order to prevent the generator from acting as a load on the battery and running it down. For more on the operation of such generators and alternators, see books and pamphlets on engine electrical systems.

For boats that are in port with people aboard for a considerable portion of the time, it may be necessary to install a *charger*. This electrical device takes 115-volt AC shore power, *transforms* it to a lower voltage, and then *rectifies* it to DC. Thus as energy is taken from the boat's battery, it is replaced from shore power and the battery is completely or partially protected from becoming discharged.

Storage Batteries

Fortunately, DC electrical energy can be stored in batteries, and electronic equipment can be used without the operation of the main engine. See fig. 2503. There are several types of storage batteries that might be used in a boat but cost, that most practical of considerations, eliminates all but the lead-acid type used in automobiles.

FIG. 2503 Direct current (DC) electrical energy can be stored in a battery. Boats commonly use automobile-type lead-acid batteries. (Protective cover, which should be over all batteries, has been removed for this photograph.)

In connection with electronic equipment, the basic question may be stated as "Is there enough storage capacity in the boat's electrical system for me to add this new equipment?" Capacity is measured in *ampere-hours*—the product of current drain in amperes multiplied by time in hours. This must be computed for all electrical loads, lights, motors, pumps, etc., as well as for electronic equipment. And there must be enough left over to start the main engine if only one set of batteries is installed! If the estimate of demand exceeds capacity (or if this has been found out the hard way!), a larger battery is needed. The installation of a larger battery may or may not require a larger alternator and new regulator. The ratio of running time to idle time will determine this. Batteries must be properly installed in any boat; see pages 199-200.

Wiring

If the generator and battery are the heart of a boat's electrical system, then the wires supplying the power to the electronic equipment are the veins and arteries. The wires must be heavy enough, of sufficient cross-sectional area, to carry the current of the loads connected to that

Fig. 2504 RECOMMENDED WIRE GAUGE SIZES 12-Volt Systems Length of wire in feet*—Source to Load						
Current in Amps	10 or less	15	20	30	40	50
5	14	12	12	10	8	8
10	12	10	8	6	6	4
15	10	8	6	4	4	3
20	8	6	6	4	2	2
25	8	6	4	2	2	1

FIG. 2504 The table above, extracted from ABYC Safety Standard E-9, 1975, specifies the wire gauge to be used versus conductor length for a voltage drop of not more than 3% in a 12-volt system. If a larger drop can be tolerated by a less critical item of equipment, smaller wire can be used. See Fig. 1015 for wire gauges allowing a drop of not more than 10%. Length is measured, one way, along path followed by wiring. Note: 1-foot = 0.3048 m.

circuit. Adequate size is determined by two factors: heating effect and voltage drop. The passage of current through a wire increases its temperature; obviously it must not become so hot that it is a fire hazard. As a general rule of thumb, a wire should not become appreciably warm to the touch when carrying its full load.

The voltage drop problem is the more common one. The heating losses just mentioned result in a lower voltage being delivered to the load than is put into the wire at the generator/battery end. The voltage drop increases with a greater load, being directly proportional to the current in the wire. If the conductors are not of adequate size, the voltage delivered may be too low to operate the electronic device or other load efficiently.

Most, but not all, boats are delivered with wiring adequate for the then-installed equipment. A problem may arise as further accessories are installed. The solution requires either the replacement of existing wires with

larger conductors, or the installation of additional main circuits back to the battery (assuming, always, that the various load combinations have been calculated and the battery capacity is adequate).

The gauge number of wire runs opposite to its size; the larger the wire, the smaller the gauge number. Wires of smaller diameter than 18 gauge should not be used for any purpose in a boat's electrical system; most circuits should have heavier wire. The voltage drop is proportional to the length of the circuit between source and load. The longer the circuit, the larger the wire must be to prevent an excessive drop. Figures 2504 and 1015 provide information as to the minimum size of wire to be used for various loads and lengths in a 12-volt system. For a 6-volt system, subtract 2 from the gauge numbers in either table. For a 32-volt system, 4 may be added, but never use wire smaller than #18.

The insulation of wiring used on boats should be suitable for the damp conditions which will be found below decks; thermoplastic insulation is best. Stranded wire should be used rather than solid; all wiring should be well secured and protected from abrasion and chafing.

Switches, Fuses, Circuit Breakers

Of the utmost importance in the electrical system providing power to the boat's electronic equipment are the various protective devices, including *switches, fuses,* and *circuit breakers.* Every marine electrical system should have a *main distribution center* where there are switches and overload protective devices. In addition to the switches on the individual pieces of electronic gear which are used to turn them on and off in regular operation, the various loads should be connected together into several *branch circuits,* each with a protective element and a means of shutting off power. This is necessary in order that a short-circuit or other failure on one branch circuit will not require turning off all electrical power.

The combining of loads into branch circuits should be carefully considered, as should the selection of the existing circuit to which a new accessory is to be connected. Loads which are likely to be used at the same time should be connected to different branch circuits; likewise, the loads that are most vital to the boat's safety should be connected to different branch circuits.

Further, there should be a *master switch* by means of which all electrical power can be cut off in case of fire, for working on the electrical system, or when the boat is to be left unattended. An excellent type of master switch is an enclosed, explosion-proof, heavy-duty switch which can be mounted directly at the battery and operated remotely from the instrument panel by means of a cable such as is used on engine chokes and throttles.

Overload protection may be by means of either fuses or circuit breakers. Fuses are less expensive initially, but are a one-time-use device. The cartridge type which fits into clips is preferred over the screw-in plug type often found on shore. The cartridge type is less subject to loosening under vibration, with resulting poor contact. On circuits with motors, be sure to use a "slow-blow" type of fuse in order to withstand the initial starting current surge without going to an overly large capacity fuse for the wiring to be protected. Circuit breakers are a greater initial expense, but there are no spares to be bought and carried aboard as there are with fuses. Many types of circuit breakers can be tripped manually and thus can additionally serve as switches.

Coast Guard Safety Standards

The Coast Guard has established safety standards for electrical systems of boats powered with gasoline engines (except outboard engines). These are designed to prevent fires and explosions; they are not primarily focused on the proper and efficient operation of electrical and electronic devices installed on board the craft. The standards are not retroactive, applying only to new boats manufactured after the several effective dates of the various sections of the regulations.

With respect to electronic equipment, and associated wiring and overload protection equipment, the Coast Guard standards will provide a most desirable level of safety, but wire sizes may not be as large as recommended in fig. 2505 to ensure adequate operating voltage at the device. Even on new boats built to the Coast Guard standard, it is desirable to measure the voltage at each item of electronic equipment with an accurate voltmeter when the unit is operating at maximum current drain (a radio while transmitting, for example).

Courtesy of Marinetics Corp.

FIG. 2505 Each item of electronic equipment should be on its own separate fuse or circuit breaker so that trouble in one unit, or the line to it, will not put other devices out of operation.

Radiotelephones

When the subject of electronic equipment for boats arises, the first thought probably will be "radio." See fig. 2506. The principal purpose of a radio on any recreational boat is *safety*. Certain other uses are authorized, but by law these are secondary to safety communications.

Safety Communications

A boat's radio may be used to summon assistance in a wide variety of situations. A leak may have started, involving risk of sinking; the motor may have failed in the face of worsening weather; or there may have been illness or injury to some person aboard. The possibilities of radio's adding to the safety of a boat and its crew are virtually unlimited.

There are many stations listening on the distress frequency—Coast Guard shore facilities, lighthouses, and craft of all sizes, plus many commercial stations on shore. In addition, the regulations of the Federal Communications Commission (FCC) require that a listening watch be maintained when the radio equipment of a boat is turned on but is not actively being used to communicate with another station. Thus there is a high degree of likelihood—a near certainty—that someone (probably many) will hear your distress call and either come to your assistance or get help for you.

Operational Communications

In addition to its safety value, a radio on a boat may be used for contacts with other boats for "operational" communications. The large number of marine band stations, and the few radio channels available, have made it necessary for the government to impose severe restrictions on the use of radios. As defined by the FCC, operational communications are limited to matters relating to "navigation, movement, and management." *Navigation* includes the actual piloting of a vessel, while *movement* relates to

future moves of the boat such as might occur during a club cruise. Radio messages of the *management* category pertain to the obtaining of fuel, dockage, repairs, etc., and are limited to matters too urgent to permit handling by slower means of communication.

Business Communications

A third type of operational radio traffic is called "business communications," but this is limited to commercial and government craft, and so need not be considered here. Note that for talking between recreational boats, the *only* permitted kinds of radio transmission are *safety* and *operational* communications as narrowly defined by the FCC. Social and personal conversations between boats—any "superfluous" communications—are strictly prohibited.

Ship-to-shore Communications

In most areas of the United States, a radio on a boat also makes possible contact with various commercial shore sta-

FIG. 2506 A radiotelephone, properly selected, installed, and used, can provide safety and operational communications to other boats, the Coast Guard, and to shore stations.

tions on channels designated for that purpose. Through these stations, the boat becomes part of the nationwide telephone system; calls may be placed to, or received from, any home or business telephone. The restrictions placed on boat-to-boat contacts do not apply on these channels; calls placed through a "Marine Operator" may be of a personal or social nature. The charges for ship-to-shore calls are quite reasonable.

It is possible for two boats, out of range of each other, to communicate via a shore based marine operator; this is not often done, but the possibility of such a means should not be overlooked. This can even involve two marine operators in different ports with a land-line connection between them, each using radio to the boat in her service area.

EQUIPMENT

Without going too deeply into technicalities, certain characteristics of radio equipment must be considered to understand the proper selection, licensing, and use of radiotelephones. These characteristics include frequency bands, types of modulation, power, antennas, and operating range.

Frequency bands

Radio frequencies are measured in kiloHertz (kHz) and MegaHertz (MHz); one MHz = 1,000 kHz; the older terms of "kilocycle" and "megacycle" are now being phased out.

The total radiofrequency spectrum is divided into various *bands*—from very low frequency (VLF) to extremely high frequency (EHF); see fig. 2507. Various communications and navigation systems work in one or more of these bands.

Radio communications for boats are in the medium frequency (MF), high frequency (HF), and very high frequency (VHF) bands. The characteristics of each band are rather different and the use to which a band is put is determined by its characteristics, principally operating range.

VHF. The very high frequency portion of the spectrum extends from 30 to 300 MHz, but the portion of interest to boatmen lies between 156 and 163 MHz (this happens to lie in the gap between TV channels 6 and 7). VHF radio signals are often described as "line of sight" but actually

the range is somewhat greater due to a slight degree of bending over the horizon. While visual distance to the horizon is 1.144 $\sqrt{H}$ (where H is height above the surface in feet and distance is in nautical miles), a formula often used for VHF radio range calculations is 1.4 $\sqrt{H}$, or about 22% greater. (The formula would be 2.5 $\sqrt{H}$ where height is in meters with distance still in nautical miles.) These formulas do not yield an exact or precise determination and variations are to be expected. However, it can be seen that height of antenna is a primary factor in determining communications range at very high frequencies; the amount of power used has some effect but it is quite slight. Signals may, however, sometimes be heard at distances of 200 miles (370 km) or more under "freak" conditions. This usually occurs during temperature inversions where a "duct" is formed between the earth and air layers at several thousand feet that are warmer, rather than colder, than conditions at the surface. VHF transmission ranges are normally the same day or night.

MF and HF. Medium frequencies (MF) lie between 300 and 3,000 kHz, and high frequencies (HF) between 3 and 30 MHz. Of interest to boatmen is a section of MF between 2 and 3 MHz and small slices of HF near 4, 6, 8, 12, 16, and 22 MHz. The transmission characteristics of these frequency bands vary from one to another, from day to night, and, in some cases, from summer to winter. Propagation is both by *ground waves*, whereby the signal follows around the surface of the earth gradually diminishing in strength, and by *sky waves*, where the signal is radiated straight outward at an angle to the horizon, encounters an *ionized* layer in the upper atmosphere, and is reflected back to the earth. These ionized layers (there are more than one) are at heights varying from 30 to 215 miles (55-440 km) as determined by daylight/darkness conditions, season of the year, and the status of the 11-year cycle of sunspots (radiation from the sun causes the ionization). Communications may be established over distances up to a few hundred miles by use of the ground waves, or out to thousands of miles using sky-waves. There will normally be a "skip zone" between where the ground wave fades out and the nearest range of reception of sky waves; see fig. 2508.

The selection of a frequency band for communications with a distant ship or shore station is a complex matter affected by the distance, time of day, and season of the year. Specific instructions will be found in the operation manuals of radios used for high-seas HF communications, and experience gained by use of such equipment will be of great assistance in selecting the optimum frequencies. In

FIG. 2507 The radio frequency spectrum is divided into broad "bands"—from very low frequency (VLF) to extremely high frequency (EHF). The boatman may use equipment in all bands from VLF (Omega navigation system) to SHF (radar) as shown above. Radio communications will be in the MF, HF, and VHF bands, each of which has different operating characteristics.

FIG. 2508 Signals are transmitted both by groundwaves extending out along the earth for a few hundred miles, and by sky waves that are reflected by the ionosphere and return to earth farther out. Between the reception zones for ground waves and sky waves is an area of no signals called the "skip zone."

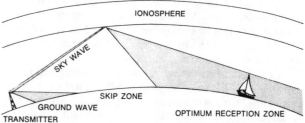

general terms, the following guidance can be offered.

1. The 2 MHz band is usable for shorter distances of 20 to 100 miles (37-185 km) day or night, with somewhat greater distances being reached at night. (Remember, use VHF for short distances where it will reach.)

2. The 4 MHz band is a short to medium distance, 20 to 250 miles (37-460 km), band during the day but can open out to longer distances at night, 300 to 700 miles (550-1,300 km).

3. The 8 MHz band is a medium distance, 200 to 1,000 miles (370-1,850 km) band during the day and a long distance 300 to 2,000 miles (550-3,700 km), band at night.

4. The highest frequency band that can be used is normally the best choice as signals will be stronger and atmospheric noise least.

An excellent way to determine which frequency band to use is to listen; if you can hear the distant station with whom you wish to communicate, it is likely that he can hear you when you call after the channel has been cleared. If you don't hear him on a specific frequency, try channels on higher and lower frequency bands.

Types of modulation

The radio signal transmitted must be *modulated* to carry the information to the other end (except for Morse code, with which a boatman is not concerned). The voice or other information can be transmitted by either amplitude modulation (AM) or frequency modulation (FM).

AM. *Amplitude modulation* is the technique used by conventional standard broadcast stations between 550 and 1600 kHz. In this procedure, the signal is varied in strength (amplitude) at voice frequency rates. The result of amplitude modulations is a complex signal consisting of a *carrier* wave, and two *sidebands*, one on either side. The simplest form of transmitter sends out the entire signal, carrier plus both upper and lower sidebands; this is *double sideband* (DSB) transmission, designated as "A3" in the rules and regulation of the Federal Communications Commission (FCC). This full signal is not needed for communications and can be reduced to a single sideband, with little or no carrier; this is sideband transmission (SSB), designated as A3J for fully suppressed carrier, as A3A for reduced carrier (a "pilot" carrier is used for some specialized applications), or A3H for full carrier (for use by receivers designed for DSB signals). A3H is sometimes referred to as "AME" for AM equivalent, or as "compatible AM." In marine communications, the upper sideband is the only one used.

The advantages of SSB transmissions are "narrower" signals that take up less space in a crowded spectrum and so allow more channels to be used within a given band, plus more "talk power," a greater portion of the transmitted power carries useful intelligence. (The carrier wave bears no intelligence, and a second sideband is redundant.) The disadvantage of SSB is that it requires a more complex transmitter and receiver which are more expensive and a bit more difficult to operate.

A technically incorrect practice has, unfortunately, become well-established. It has been common to refer to marine radios as "AM" sets (meaning DSB) or "SSB" sets. This is not consistent as both DSB and SSB are forms of amplitude modulation. This book will use the terms DSB and SSB correctly; you should be aware that persons referring to "AM" radio are most likely speaking only of DSB equipment or transmissions.

FIG. 2509 All VHF transmitters must have a switch (arrow) to reduce output power to 1 watt or less. Low power should be used wherever it is sufficient, especially for very short distances; it must be used on Channel 13.

FM. With *frequency modulated* signals the strength of the radio waves is constant (no carrier, no sidebands) but its frequency is varied at an audio rate by the information (voice or music) being transmitted; within limits, the extent to which it is varied is a measure of the "loudness" of the audio signal. Frequency modulation, too, has its advantages and disadvantages. On the plus side, the signal is relatively immune to atmosphere noise ("static") and man-made electrical noise such as ignition interference. FM signals are normally of excellent intelligibility and clarity with properly functioning transmitters and receivers. (FM also allows higher-fidelity sound but this is of no interest in voice communications.) On the negative side, FM signals are much broader than AM signals and take up more spectrum space. For this reason, FM is used only at VHF and higher frequencies where adequate space is available.

An unusual feature of frequency modulation is the "capture effect." When two signals are on the same AM channel, they interfere with each other, often rendering both unreadable. With FM, the stronger signal "captures" the receiver and is received well, to the exclusion of the other —too bad for the weaker signal, but at least one gets through!

Power

The power of a radio transmitter can be measured and stated in a number of ways: input power to the final amplifier, output power, carrier power, peak envelope power (PEP), power to the antenna, radiated power, and even "effective radiated power."

VHF/FM transmitters are rated in carrier power. This is the output power from the set at the point to which the antenna feedline is connected; it is normally one-half of the input power to the final amplifier. VHF sets on boats are limited to 25 watts carrier power and must have a front-panel control for readily reducing output to 1 watt or less; see fig. 2509. (Operating rules of the FCC require that the lower power be used for short-range communications where such is sufficient; the use of low-power for contact with nearby boats may provide more readable signals.)

Single sideband radiotelephones are measured as to their peak envelope power (PEP), the average power output "during one radio frequency cycle at the highest crest of

FIG. 2510 Higher gain antennas achieve greater range by "squeezing down" the radiation pattern, increasing signals at lower, desirable angles and decreasing the power that is wasted in unproductive upward directions.

FIG. 2511 An antenna with too much gain—too flat a radiation pattern—may be disadvantageous in rough water. As the boat rolls and pitches, the radiated signal may go above the receiving boat, or down into the water—either will cause fading and intermittent reception.

the modulation under conditions of normal operation." SSB transmitters on boats are subject to power limits between 150 and 1,000 watts, PEP, as determined by the geographic area concerned, the frequency used, and the type of communications involved. For practical purposes, however, few small craft will have need for more than 150 watts and many can operate effectively with sets rated at 50 to 100 watts.

Antennas

The best transmitter-receiver combination is severely handicapped, or even worthless, if it is not connected to an efficient antenna by an efficient feedline. The outgoing signal must be effectively radiated and the incoming signal adequately picked up; the transmitting requirement is normally much more severe.

MF and HF. The antenna requirement for SSB transmitters is a difficult one to meet on small craft, especially motorboats. Except for sailing craft, the antenna is normally a self-supporting vertical pole of fiberglass with a wire conductor inside. This is electrically one-quarter of a wavelength long; "electrically" because an actual physical quarter wavelength would be a structural impossibility, at 2 MHz about 117 feet (35.6 m) high! In actual practice, a *loading coil* is built into the antenna near the midpoint so that it appears to the radio waves to be a quarter wave length while physically being much smaller. On sailboats, it is common to install an insulator near the upper and lower ends of a backstay and use the intervening length of metal wire as an antenna. On larger sailing craft, this makes a quite efficient antenna after loading and tuning adjustments have been made.

Most SSB radio installations on boats present difficult problems of antennas and grounding (a proper ground connection is a vital part of a quarter-wavelength antenna). The problem is not in the type of modulation but in the fact that SSB sets normally cover a very wide range of frequencies, 2 MHz to 12 or 16 MHz, all with the same antenna. (A few installations may use two different antennas for more efficient operations.) This requires the use of an *antenna coupler* and often considerable effort by a highly skilled technician. The results obtained are worth every bit of effort expended in obtaining as good a MF-HF antenna installation as is possible.

VHF. A half-wavelength antenna fed by coaxial cable is used on boats; no ground connection is needed for such an antenna. At 156-163 MHz, this is only about 36 inches (0.9 m). Antennas for VHF sets, therefore are simple from a physical viewpoint and can be expanded for greater *gain*, greater effective radiated power, while still remaining small enough for practical use on boats. The "gain" of an antenna, its ability to increase effective radiated power, is measured in decibels (dB). This is a logarithmic ratio in

which 3 dB is equivalent to doubling power; another 3, making 6 dB, doubles again, quadrupling the original power; and 9 dB is power multiplied by a factor of eight.

Advertisements for VHF antennas customarily make claims for gains in terms that are rarely supportable by factual engineering data. In general, antennas are described as having 3 dB more gain than is strictly true. To avoid confusion, however, the generally-accepted, although somewhat inflated, terms will be used in the discussion below.

The basic VHF antenna, often called a "sailboat" antenna because of its primary use at a masthead, is a short fiberglass "whip" (with a wire inside) roughly 3½ to 4½ feet (1.1-1.4 m) in length. This antenna is usually described as a "3 dB" model although it is the smallest marine antenna used, the basic design to which others are compared, and thus actually should be termed 0 dB. This same basic antenna is sometimes used on smaller power boats, but more often the antenna is 8 to 9 feet (2.4-2.7 m) in length, a "6 dB" model. The largest antenna normally used on boats is 16 to 20 feet (4.9-6.1 m) in length and termed an "8" or "9 dB" design.

The use of a gain antenna is desirable, provided it is not overdone. The gain of a VHF communications antenna is achieved by "squeezing down" the radiation pattern so that power is, in effect, "pushed out" in a useful direction rather than being radiated upward and thus wasted; see fig. 2510. The disadvantage of higher gain antennas is that the sharpened beam becomes somewhat like a searchlight beam and in rough water (which often exists in emergency situations when the radio is needed most) it may move off the other station from time to time causing fading and intermittent reception; see fig. 2511.

A VHF antenna should be as high as physically practicable and provide as much gain as can be obtained without possible detrimental effects. For sailboats, the amount of heel and masthead motion limits antennas to the small, simple types, but the masttop height provides the desirable range. For power boats up to perhaps 35 feet (11m) or so in length, the antenna used will be 8-foot, "6dB" model. Larger boats could physically mount a "9dB" 18-foot antenna but probably would do better with an 8-foot antenna mounted at the upper end of a 10-foot "extender" tube—thus height is gained while keeping to a reasonable amount of gain and directivity. (Sailboats using a masthead antenna should carry a simple secondary antenna for mounting on deck if dismasted; this may be when communication is most needed, and the masthead antenna is down with the mast.)

The antenna feedline is important in VHF radio. There is a loss of power that is proportioned to length; co-ax cables are rated as so many "dB per foot." For short runs, up to 20 feet (6 m), typical of power craft, the smaller RG-58 cable is satisfactory; for the greater distances up to sailboat mastheads, the use of larger RG-8 will conserve an appreciable amount of power for radiation by the antenna.

Modes of operation

One of two different modes of operation is used. In *simplex* operation, both stations transmit and receive on the same frequency. For *semi-duplex* operation, two frequencies are used, each station transmitting on one and receiving on the other alternately. *(Full-duplex* allows a station to transmit and receive simultaneously, as with a conventional telephone on land; this is not possible with boat radio equipment.)

THE MARINE RADIO SYSTEM

For recreational boats, the maritime communications system is divided into two parts—short range, and medium and long range. Each of these portions involves different equipment—VHF/FM for short range, and MF-HF/SSB for greater distances. By regulations of the FCC, a boat must first be fitted with VHF before SSB equipment can be installed and licensed; for the vast majority of privately-owned small craft, VHF is all that will be needed.

The VHF/FM radio service

Frequencies between 156 and 163 MHz have been allocated to maritime use by international agreements. Within this band, *channels* have been established at 25 kHz spacing. Some channels will be assigned a single frequency for simplex operation, others will have two frequencies for semi-duplex operation. A standardized system of channel numbering has been adopted, and a boatman will rarely need to concern himself with specific frequencies in megahertz; see fig. 2512.

The great advantage of the very high frequency portion of the radio spectrum is the availability of adequate space for many channels. VHF/FM radio operations are much facilitated by having enough channels to assign separate ones for the different types of communications and even for various types of vessels. *A primary advantage of VHF/FM radio communication is lost to a skipper if his set is not equipped to operate on an adequate number of channels.*

The primary VHF channel is 16; this is the distress, safety, and calling frequency required by law to be on every vessel. The other mandatory channel is 6 (sometimes called 06), limited to intership *safety* communications; this frequency is *not* to be used for ordinary operational or navigational exchanges, and certainly not for personal communications.

A feature of the VHF service is the assignment of different channels to commercial and non-commercial vessels for operational communications. No more will recreational boatmen suffer interference from commercial fishermen, shrimpers, etc., and vice versa. Communications are further enhanced by the availability of a considerable number of channels (provided *your* set can operate on them), plus the limited range of VHF which excludes interference from stations 30 to 50 miles (56-93 km) or more away. Non-commercial craft are assigned seven channels for intership, only one of which is shared with commercial vessels (who have 12 other channels of their own). The most used intership non-commercial channels are 68 and 70. Channel 9 (or 09) is the only frequency common to both non-commercial and commercial vessels; it is the only channel

PRIORITY LIST OF VHF-FM CHANNELS FOR RECREATIONAL BOATS

Channel Number	Frequency (MHz) Transmit	Receive	Communications Purpose
16	156.800	156.800	DISTRESS SAFETY and CALLING (mandatory)
06	156.300	156.300	Intership safety communications (mandatory)
22	157.100	157.100	Primary liaison with USCG vessels and USCG shore stations, and for Coast Guard marine information broadcasts
68	156.425	156.425	Non-commercial intership and ship to coast (marinas, yacht clubs, etc.)
.09	156.450	156.450	Commercial and non-commercial intership and ship to coast (commercial docks, marinas, & some clubs)
26	157.300	161.900	Public telephone, first priority
28	157.400	162.000	**Public telephone, first priority**
25	157.250	161.850	**Public telephone (Also 24, 84, 85, 86, 87, 88)**
27	157.350	161.950	**Public telephone**
13	156.650	156.650	Navigational—Bridge to Bridge (1 watt only). Mandatory for ocean vessels, dredges in channels, and large tugs while towing. Army installing for communications with boats in their locks. Will be found, also, on Army operated bridges
14	156.700	156.700	Port Operations channel for communications with bridge and lock tenders. Some Coast Guard shore stations have this channel for working
70	156.525	156.525	Non-commercial only, intership
12	156.600	156.600	Port Operations—traffic advisory—still being used as channel to work USCG shore stations.
72	156.625	156.625	Non-commercial intership (2nd priority)
WX-1		162.550	Weather broadcasts
WX-2		162.400	Weather broadcasts
WX-3		162.475	Weather broadcasts
69	156.475	156.475	Non-commercial intership and ship to coast
71	156.575	156.575	Non-commercial intership and ship to coast
78	156.925	156.925	Non-commercial intership and ship to coast

FIG. 2512 This table lists the required and recommended VHF channels for recreational boats. Not all radios can be set up for all these channels, nor will all skippers wish to buy a full set of crystals, hence the priority sequence. Four public telephone channels are listed; there are also other, less-used channels. Select the one or ones needed for your cruising area. Consider use of a separate receiver for the second weather frequency; some areas use a third weather frequency. Coast Guard Auxiliary boats may use Channel 83 (157.175 MHz) for drills, patrols, and similar official activities.*

available for any necessary intercommunication between these two types of vessels and its use should be limited to that function.

Ship-shore communications to "marine operators" are possible on a number of channels. Certain ones, such as 26 and 28, are assigned in preference to others so as to limit the number of different frequencies on which a boat must be capable of operating. Ship-shore radio contacts are also possible on VHF with yacht clubs, marinas, and similar "limited shore stations" as they are designated in the FCC Rules; these use other channels such as 69 or 71.

Channel 22 is basically a U.S. government frequency, but non-government vessels, including recreational boats, are allowed to use it for non-distress communications with the Coast Guard. *Every boat should be fitted with this channel.*

Channel 13 is restricted to "Bridge-to-Bridge" communications. (The "Bridge" here refers to the control station of a vessel, not to a structure carrying traffic across a waterway.) Large vessels, tugs, and dredges in channels must guard this in addition to Channel 16. It is used with abbreviated operating procedures to ensure navigational safety while maneuvering in close quarters. It must not be used for any other purpose, and power is limited to 1 watt. It is not required for recreational craft but may often be of use.

Other channels will be used in specified areas solely for such purposes as vessel traffic control, and bridge and lock operations.

A word of caution here—certain channels used interna-

*Under limited conditions, aircraft are authorized to use Channels 6 and 16; 9, 68, 70, and 72; and 8, 18, and 67 for communications with ships and boats.

tionally for two-frequency semi-duplex operation have been converted by the United States to one-frequency simplex operation (using the lower of the two frequencies). In this case, the letter "A" is sometimes, but not always, appended to the channel number. Typical of this is Channel 22 which properly should be called 22A. In this book, however, the simpler designation without the "A" will be used.

MF-HF single sideband operation

If a boat is fitted with a VHF/FM radio, and the owner can show that his cruising will take him farther off shore than that short-range set will provide service, single sideband equipment for the medium and high frequencies may be installed. Communication services are generally of the same nature as on VHF. Specific frequencies are allocated in various "bands" generally near 2, 4, 6, 8, 12, 16, and 22 MHz. The type of SSB modulation—A3J, A3H, or A3A—will vary with the frequency and the use being made of it.

The MF distress, safety, and calling frequency is 2182 kHz; this must be installed in every set. Modulation is A3J for U.S. vessels in U.S. waters; A3H modulation is allowed for contacts with foreign ships and shore stations if needed. (Full DSB modulation is permitted on an interim basis for distress and safety only; this is the only authorized use of "old-fashioned" DSB on U.S. vessels.)

The frequency 2670 kHz, using A3J or A3A modulation, is used for communications with the U.S. Coast Guard. For such contacts at greater ranges, there are Coast Guard frequencies in the 4, 6, 8, 12, and 16 MHz bands. (When calling on the HF channels, response may be briefly delayed if the Coast Guard station is busy on another frequency.)

Various frequencies in the 2 MHz band are authorized for intership contacts, normally using SSB in its most efficient mode, A3J. Frequencies may be limited to certain geographic areas, types of vessels, or non-interference to other services. The frequencies 2082.5 and 2638 kHz have no limitations and are widely used. Other ship-to-ship channels will be found in the 4, 6, 8, 12, and 16 MHz bands, two or three in each band.

Ship-shore communications to marine operators are divided into two "services." The Coastal Service operates in the 2 and 4 MHz bands with stations in 20 to 30 major U.S. port cities, plus, of course, many foreign ports. Ranges are up to roughly 200 miles on 2 MHz and several times that distance on 4 MHz at night. The "High Seas" telephone service uses frequencies in the 4, 8, 12, and 16 MHz bands.

Because of the long distances covered, there are U.S. shore stations only at limited points—New York, Miami (Ft. Lauderdale), Mobile, San Francisco, and Honolulu. On both services, semi-duplex mode is used with A3A modulation. Care will have to be taken with respect to the frequency selected for calling a marine operator, considering time of day, distance, and, to a lesser degree, the direction of the shore station from the boat.

EQUIPMENT SELECTION

The selection of a specific VHF/FM radiotelephone for a recreational boat basically involves power, channel capacity, and cost; the factors involved in the selection of an antenna, all that is needed to complete the installation, have been discussed above.

Power. The maximum power for VHF is 25 watts *output* (which equates roughly to 50 watts input for comparison with other methods of measuring transmitter power). Power is not a major factor in operating range, but can make the difference in the "capture effect" of VHF/FM communications that essentially prevents interference between the signals being received at the same time. Although there are a few sets on the market rated at less than 25 watts, there are even fewer reasons to purchase one.

All sets will have a "low power" switch to reduce output to 1 watt or less as this is required by FCC regulations.

Channel capacity. A fully adequate number of channels is necessary to obtain the best use of a VHF set. Although the FCC requires only three channels, the wise skipper will equip his craft with a set having at least 12-channel capacity. Even though he may not initially have crystals installed for all channels, it is likely that after a period of use he will find that he needs to be able to communicate on additional channels. (It should be noted, however, that the installation of crystals is normally much less expensive if done at time of purchase of set.)

Figure 2512 is a listing of channels by number and frequency with a brief statement of their use. This list is in general order of priority for installation, but consideration must be given to local conditions on such matters as commonly-used intership channels, local channels used by marine operators, and any need for Channels 12, 13, or 14. A boat that cruises widely will need a greater number of channels than one that remains in one local area, particularly channels for ship-shore communications.* Such a craft will also probably need both Weather 1 and 2 frequencies.

VHF radios are available with an "all-channel" capability at prices that are only slightly more than that of a 12-channel set with all crystals installed. Consideration should be given to such a set as it will provide the greatest flexibility of use of VHF communications—no more being unable to shift to a working frequency requested by another station. (These sets use a "synthesizer" that includes one or more crystals, but not a pair for each channel.) The more-expensive models of such radios may have additional desirable features. These include, but are not limited to: dual receivers to permit simultaneous monitoring of Channel 16 (required by law) plus a working channel (desirable when cruising with a group, or expecting a telephone call from on shore); push buttons for quick selection of the more-often-used channels; or crystal control for a few of the

FIG. 2513 An "all-channel" VHF radio offers the maximum of flexibility of operation. Care must be exercised to not use an unauthorized channel. The set shown here has a dual receiving capability so that both Channel 16 and any other desired frequency can be simultaneously monitored.

*Some channel uses will be different in foreign waters. In Canada, for example, recreational boats cannot use 70 and 72 for intership communications but can use 8; Canadian weather broadcasts are on 161.65 MHz.

FIG. 2514 A scanning receiver is a most useful accessory to a VHF radio station on a boat. It will rapidly sample a number of channels, stopping if there is activity or passing on to the next if no signals are received. A variable squelch control sets the sensitivity level and the unit can be locked on any desired single frequency.

FIG. 2515 A hand-held VHF set is useful when off in the dinghy. It can now be licensed as an "associated portable unit" of a regular boat radio station. Power is limited to 1 watt and it must not be used on shore.

more important channels as back up for the main frequency control component in the set (a failure in the synthesizer could put the radio out of operation on *all* channels).

Accessory equipment. On some craft it will be necessary to have a remote-control unit so that the radio can be operated from either of two steering positions. FCC regulations now require that a remote control unit have the capability of channel selection so as to avoid the temptation not to switch to a working channel after Channel 16 has been used to establish contact.

As most VHF radios for boats do not have dual receivers, it is often useful to install a "scanner" as a second receiver. This compact unit can scan across additional channels, from 1 to as many as 12 in some models, stopping to receive on that frequency if there are communications in progress, or going on rapidly to the next if that channel is quiet (or when transmissions cease on a channel at which it has stopped). The scan rate is adjustable on many models; switches can be set to bypass any channel, or to stop scanning action and operate on a selected frequency. Channels can be controlled by crystal or synthesizer.

The FCC Rules now provide for an "associated portable ship unit" with a regular boat radio station. This is a small, hand-held, two-way VHF set that can be taken into a dinghy; see fig. 2515. Strict limitations have been placed on these units: it must have Channel 16 and at least one intership channel; it can be used *only* to communicate with the "mother" vessel; it can *not* be used on or from the shore. The call sign is that of the mother craft plus an appropriate unit designator. Power is limited to *one watt* which *excludes* many hand-held units previously marketed with two to five watts power.

A multi-test meter can be installed in the feedline between a VHF set and its antenna. This will give a positive indication of power from the transmitter (the front-panel lights that glow when the microphone switch is pressed are generally meaningless as to actual transmission). This meter can also indicate antenna condition and power output in watts; a short piece of wire from the unit will pick up enough signal so that it can function as a field strength meter. There is negligible insertion loss and the tester can be left in the line as a constant monitor; this will give continuing assurance of proper operation and eliminate the need for on-the-air "radio checks."

SSB equipment

The first thing that will be noticed about single sideband equipment is the price tag! These modern sets are quite complicated as compared with the MF/DSB radios that were used for many years. Modulation circuitry is more complex and the frequency stability requirement is ten times more rigid. SSB sets can easily cost three to five times the price of a DSB radio.

SSB sets will have the same 150 watts power limit as with DSB equipment, but the more modern modulation technique provides greater "talk" power, and this should result in greater range—not to mention the better communications resulting from lessened interference. Often a set of 50 or 100 watts PEP will provide fully adequate service for a recreational boatman.

Major considerations in the selection of SSB equipment are frequency range and number of channels. In general, all sets will cover the MF band and the lower HF bands, typically up through the 8 MHz frequencies. More expensive sets will also have the higher—12, 16, and 22 MHz—bands. The requirement for various bands will primarily be determined by the intended operating area of the craft,

FIG. 2516 A single sideband (SSB) radio transmitter and receiver are required for communications beyond VHF range. Frequencies are available for various distances and day or night operation in various bands from 2 to 22 MHZ.

the distances to stations with whom contact is desired, and any need for full 24-hour capability (higher frequencies will be needed for daytime distant contacts). Quite often a set of 75 to 100 watts power, limited to the 2, 4, 6, and 8 MHz bands will provide adequate communications for the skipper who is going not too far beyond VHF range, and at a considerable savings in cost.

The number of channels is obviously related to the number of bands used, with fewer being required on a four-band SSB radio than with a set covering six or seven bands. It is important, however, to have *enough* channels to meet one's needs for communications with the Coast Guard, other boats and ships, and with marine operators, keeping in mind that different bands must be used at different times of day and at different distances. With a four-band set, ten channels would probably be a minimum.

Installation and maintenance

VHF radios can be installed by the boat owner or other person even though they are not a licensed technician, provided that the crystals had been put in the set by the manufacturer and the frequencies checked at that time. The later addition of crystals for other channels may only be done by a holder of an FCC first or second class license. The installation of a SSB set will require certain on-board tests made by a licensed technician. Radio installations on gasoline-powered boats may require some form of engine noise suppression; this is a job for a technician. With regard to maintenance, an unlicensed person is limited to matters which will not affect the quality of the signal on the air. For example, he can replace bad fuses, tubes, etc., but cannot change crystals, or adjust antenna loading.

The crystals used to control the frequency of a radio—VHF (including synthesizer sets) or MF-HF—are subject to "aging" with a resultant gradual shift in frequency. The licensee of a station is responsible for any off-frequency operation that could result in a citation from the FCC. No exact guide can be stated as to how often a frequency check should be made—this requires a licensed technician and sophisticated equipment—but every two years would be a maximum interval, plus after reports on the air of weak or "fuzzy" signals.

RADIO LICENSES

With over 300,000 marine radio stations on the air, the need for licensing and regulations can easily be seen. The FCC issues its Rules and Regulations in various "Parts," of which "Part 83—Stations on Shipboard in the Maritime Service" is applicable to recreational boats.

To control the use of radio stations, holding down interference and making possible emergency and essential communications, a system of licenses is used. Recognizing that harmful interference could result from either malfunctioning equipment or from misuse of a properly operating set, licenses are required for both the station (see fig. 2617) and the person operating it. Although it is termed a station license, the FCC authorization is essentially concerned with the transmitting component only. The set owner need not concern himself with the many technical requirements for equipment provided that he has a set that is "type accepted."

The Station License

A station license may be issued to a U.S. citizen or an alien individual, but not a foreign government or its representative (if a corporation, see section 82.23 of the FCC Rules.) Application is made on Form 506 which should be mailed to the FCC, P.O. Box 1040, Gettysburg, PA 17325. The fee for a station license is $4 for a five-year term.* The issuance of the license may take as long as 60 days; if immediate use of the radio is desired, Form 506–A for "temporary operating authority" can be completed and retained by the applicant. This allows legal use of the set and provides for a temporary call sign based on the boat's documentation or state registration number.

Radio station licenses are issued in the name of the *owner* and the *vessel*. A station license is not automatically transferred to another person upon sale of the boat, nor may a license be moved with the radio set to a new craft owned by the same person. A simple change in the name of the boat or licensee (but not a change in ownership), or his address does *not* require license modification. Just send a letter to the FCC advising them of the change; a copy of this letter must be posted with the license.

The regulations require that a station license be conspicuously posted aboard the vessel. At the end of its five-year term, it must be renewed if continued operation of the station is desired. Form 405-B is used for renewal; it should be sent to Gettysburg with a $4 renewal fee before the expiration of the license.* If, but only if, timely application for renewal has been made, operation may continue even should the renewed license not be received before the expiration date. If the use of the radio station is permanently discontinued at any time, the license must be returned to the FCC in Washington for cancellation.

The Operator's Permit

A personal license is required for the operation of any marine band radio station. The average boatman will obtain either a *Restricted Radiotelephone Operator Permit* or a *Marine Radio Operator* (formerly Third Class) *Permit*. Higher class licenses are available for those persons with technical training and experience, but they are needed

*On 1 January 1977 the FCC suspended the collection of all fees for licenses and permits until further notice.

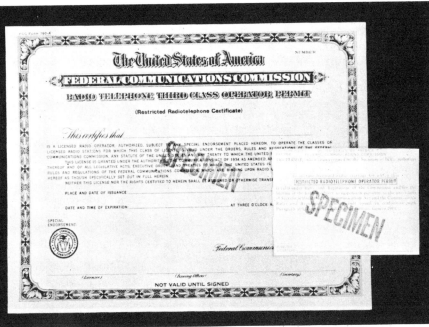

FIG. 2517 Transmitter on boat must have radio station license issued by Federal Communications Commission (FCC). No license required for receiver, radio direction finder, or depth-sounder.

FIG. 2518 In addition to station license, person in charge of set must have an operator permit. A Restricted Radiotelephone Operator Permit suffices for recreational boats, but some skippers get the higher-grade Marine Radio Operator (formerly Third Class) Permit.

only for making tuning adjustments and repairs. An unlicensed person may talk into the microphone of a radio, but a licensed operator must be present and responsible for the use of the station.

An applicant for any grade of license may be either a U.S. citizen or an alien. A Restricted Permit is obtained by submitting an application on FCC Form 753, which is mailed to the FCC, P.O. Box 1050, Gettysburg, PA 17325. There is no need to appear in person at any FCC office. The permit is issued, without test or examination, by "declaration." The applicant must be at least 14 years old and "certify" that he (1) can receive and transmit spoken messages in the English language; (2) can keep a rough log in English, or in a foreign language translatable into English; (3) is familiar with the applicable laws, treaty provisions, rules, and regulations; and (4) understands his responsibility to keep currently informed of the regulations, etc. The Restricted Permit fee, $4, is valid for the lifetime of the person to whom issued, unless, of course, it is suspended or revoked.*

For the Marine Radio Operator Permit, there is no age limit, but an examination is required. This test is non-technical, covering only operating rules and procedures; questions are all of the multiple-choice type. You will find the examination not at all difficult if you prepare yourself for it properly. A free Study Guide is available from FCC offices. For skippers of recreational boats the privileges of this higher class license are no greater than those of a Restricted Permit, but it is a matter of pride for many to qualify and post it on their craft. Boats that carry more than six passengers for hire, however, are "compulsorily equipped" and must have a crewman with at least a Third Class Permit, or the newer Marine Radio Operator Permit. Upon expiration, existing Third Class Permits will be renewed as Marine Radio Operator Permits.

If your radio operator permit is lost, or becomes so mutilated that it is illegible, you should immediately apply for a duplicate. The fee is $2 and the same form as for an original is used.* State the circumstances fully, and, if the license has been lost, you must certify that a reasonable search has been made. Continued operation is authorized if a signed copy of the application for a duplicate is posted. Should a lost license be found later, either it or the duplicate must be sent at once to the FCC for cancellation.

FIG. 2519 The FCC Rules require that a radio transmitter be secure against use by unauthorized persons. A set in an exposed location, as above, can be fitted with a key-operated switch for its electrical power. Physical security may also be used, such as a lock for the panel door in Fig. 2520.

*On 1 January 1977 the FCC suspended the collection of all fees for licenses and permits until further notice.

RADIO OPERATING RULES

Hand in hand with licensing, radio operating rules have been established to bring order out of chaos on the air and reduce the interference that would inevitably result from the overcrowded conditions on the few frequencies available. Actually, the legally required procedures are only a bare minimum and must be supplemented with voluntary procedures for the most efficient communications.

As stated before, radio communications (other than ship-shore telephone calls) must be necessary and of a "safety" or "operational" nature. Even within these limitations, a system of priorities has been established to make sure that the more important messages get through. First, of course, are *distress* calls and related follow-up messages; these are identified by the signal "Mayday" and receive "absolute priority" over other communications. Second are *urgent* messages; these are defined as relating to the safety of a ship, aircraft, or other vessel, or of some person on board or in sight. Urgent communications are identified by "Pan-Pan." In third place on the priority list are *safety* messages, those concerning the safety of navigation or giving important weather warnings; these transmissions are identified by the safety signal, "Security."

The system of priorities has been established to ensure that the message that *has* to get through does so without delay. No station or operator has any exclusive rights to any frequency; the nature of his traffic determines whether he should transmit or keep silent. One of the most important FCC regulations requires that an operator *listen before transmitting* to ensure that he will not interfere with the communications of others, and particularly not with distress or other priority traffic.

Frequencies for Calling and Distress

The most important channel on the VHF band is Channel 16—156.80 MHz—the distress, safety, and calling frequency.

FIG. 2520 Radio station license must be posted near equipment. On voluntarily-equipped boats, an Operator Permit may be posted. Alternately, a Restricted Permit may be carried in one's personal possession.

In order to keep one channel relatively clear of traffic so that even a weak distress call can be heard, the use of this frequency is limited to distress traffic and the initial contact between vessels. This latter use as a "Calling Frequency" is permitted to ensure that when a station is not working on another channel, it is listening on Channel 16 for calls. Thus many stations are constantly monitoring the distress frequency and a call for help is much more likely to be heard.

Listening on Channel 16 is not only a logical procedure, it is legally required. A "voluntarily equipped" boat need not have its radio turned on, but if it is, it must be tuned to the distress and calling frequency when not being actively used on another channel.

On the MF band, 2182 kHz is used in a similar manner for distress, safety, and calling; there are no such channels on the HF bands. It should be carefully noted that if the distance is relatively short, contact on VHF *must* be attempted first before a MF or HF channel is used.

Ship-to-ship communications

After making their initial contact on Channel 16, boats using the VHF band *must* shift from the calling channel to a "working" channel to communicate with each other. *No conversation, no matter how brief, is authorized on Channel 16.*

For recreational craft, the working channels are 68, 70, 72, 69, 71, and 78. Any of these may be used; they are listed above in sequence of probable availability on boats. (Here the advantage of an "all-channel" VHF set becomes apparent; two boats so equipped can talk on a channel that is not usually installed on most 12-channel radios.)

Channel 9 must be used if communications are with a commercial vessel. Channel 22 will be used if with a Coast Guard boat or cutter.

Ship-to-shore communications

VHF communications with marine operators are normally begun directly on the working channel without an initial contact on Channel 16. Even if the call is originating from a shore station and the operator makes a call on "16," the boat should respond only on the working channel, such as 26, 28, 27, 25, etc., as the marine operator will not be listening on 16. It will be necessary to consult local boatmen, cruising guides, or other publications to determine the channels (there may be more than one) used by the marine operator in any specific area.

VHF stations are authorized for yacht clubs, marinas, and the like. These activities will have sets much like those on boats and initial calls on Channel 16 should be followed by a shift to channels 69, 71, or 78. (Channels 68 and 9 are authorized for this use but are normally busy with other traffic.)

The working frequency to Coast Guard shore stations is Channel 22.

Special communications

It will be seldom necessary for a recreational boat to use Channel 13, the Bridge-to-Bridge frequency. This channel may be monitored but is best left for use by ships and tugs. In some instances, however, it is of value, as when passing a dredge or a tug and tow in restricted waters. In this situation, use only the lower power (1 watt or less) output; call directly on 13, not 16; use vessels' names only, without call signs.

*In some areas commercial vessels guarding bridge-to-bridge and vessel movement control channels do not have to maintain a watch on Channel 16 and may not do so.

Communications with drawbridges and canal locks may involve special procedures that are best learned locally.

Legal Requirements

Legal operation of a radio station aboard a boat requires four things. First, a license for the station, properly posted. Second, an operator's license. This may be posted, or a Restricted Permit or a Verification Card for a Third Class Permit may be carried on one's person. Third, a station log. Fourth, on board or in a secure place on shore, an up-to-date copy of the FCC Rules and Regulations relating to marine radios. This may be *either* the full "Part 83" of the Rules or the new Subpart CC of Part 83, the basic rules in a highly simplified, question-and-answer style.

Part 83 is in Volume IV of the Rules which can be purchased from the Government Printing Office for $24 which includes a subscription for changes as they are issued. The Simplified Rules cost only $3.00, but no changes are issued.

The Radio Log

Log keeping for a radio station on a voluntarily equipped boat has been made much easier than it used to be, but don't let this simplification stop you from meeting the present minimum requirements of the FCC. See fig. 2521. Each page of the log must show the name of the vessel and radio call sign; each entry must be signed by the person making it. Entries are required for all distress calls heard or transmitted, for all urgent and safety communications transmitted, and any information related to maritime safety. The log must also show the time of starting and ending of a listening watch on Channel 16 (or 2182 kHz), but remember that the keeping of such a watch is not mandatory on recreational boats.

All installation, service, and maintenance work performed on the radio equipment must be logged. It is *not* necessary to make entries for ordinary communications to other boats, the Coast Guard, or shore stations. Logs must be retained for one year following the last entry, except for unusual circumstances described in the Rules. Logs must be made available for inspection upon request from any authorized FCC representative. Inspection of the station by such an official must be permitted at any reasonable hour, and at such frequent intervals as may be determined necessary in the discretion of the FCC.

Rules Governing Transmissions

Transmissions on the calling channel must be limited to the securing of an agreement as to the working frequency to be used, and this may not take longer than two minutes. Any one calling transmission must not take longer than 30 seconds and, if no reply is heard, you must wait two minutes before calling again. Another two minutes must separate a second and a third attempt to make contact and, if these fail, a delay of 15 minutes is required before a new calling cycle can be started (the 15 minutes may be reduced to 3 if other stations will not receive interference from the calls.) These restrictions do not apply to an emergency involving safety.

Once contact is made on a working frequency, the exchange of transmissions between boats must (1) be for a legally permissible nature, and (2) be of the *minimum length possible.* (On MF working frequencies, the ex-

FIG. 2521 Every radio station on a boat must have a radio log. Requirements are simple, but don't neglect them.

change must not exceed 3 minutes in duration, and must not be resumed until another 10 minutes shall have elapsed; this does not apply to communications relating to safety of life or property.) Use no more than the minimum power that will get through—1 watt on VHF.

The Communications Act of 1934, together with the FCC Rules, strictly prohibit the use on the air of any language which is "obscene, indecent, or profane." This is watched as closely as possible by various government monitoring stations and violators have been taken into court a number of times. Special, more severe, penalties are specifically provided for this offense.

Procedure for Station Identification

The FCC has established certain procedures to be followed in identifying your station on the air. Such identification must be given in the English language by stating the official call sign. Phonetic words for the letters may be used, but are not legally required and should not be used unless they are necessary as they will lengthen the transmission; any understandable word may be used, but the international aviation and military alphabet is probably the best; see figure 2522.

Radio stations must be identified, as a minimum, at the beginning and end of an exchange of transmissions with another station, but identification of each transmission is *not* required. If both Channel 16 (or 2182 kHz) and a working frequency are used, identification by call sign need be given only at the beginning of the calling frequency and at the end on the working frequency. Identification must be made of each transmission for any other purpose, such as a test. If transmissions continue for more than 15 minutes, the station must be identified at intervals of 15 minutes or less, except that on a ship-shore telephone call this may be deferred until the end of such call.

Secrecy Requirements

The Communications Act of 1934 and the Rules of the FCC protect the *secrecy* of communications. No person may divulge to another person, except the addressee or his authorized agent, any knowledge gained from receiving or intercepting radio transmissions not addressed to himself, *nor shall he use such knowledge for his own benefit.* This basic point of law should be carefully noted by all who operate radios on boats. It does not apply to distress communications nor to broadcasts for the general use of

Standard Phonetic Spelling Alphabet

A	ALFA	**N**	NOVEMBER
B	BRAVO	**O**	OSCAR
C	CHARLIE	**P**	PAPA
D	DELTA	**Q**	QUEBEC
E	ECHO	**R**	ROMEO
F	FOXTROT	**S**	SIERRA
G	GOLF	**T**	TANGO
H	HOTEL	**U**	UNIFORM
I	INDIA	**V**	VICTOR
J	JULIETT	**W**	WHISKEY
K	KILO	**X**	X-RAY
L	LIMA	**Y**	YANKEE
M	MIKE	**Z**	ZULU

FIG. 2522 When receiving conditions are poor, use phonetic equivalents for individual letters in spelling such difficult words such as name of boat or person. Do not, however, overuse phonetics—when not necessary they just add to transmission length and possible interference.

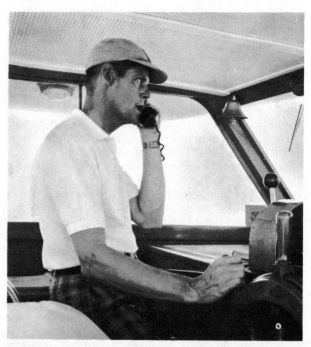

FIG. 2523 To minimize interference, FCC has established strict rules. Listen before transmitting and do not interfere with communications in progress. Keep contacts short and observe the time limitations.

the public, but it does apply to *all* other conversations heard on the air. It could even be construed to apply to the fellow who listened to find out where the fish were biting and then moved in on the good spots.

OPERATING PROCEDURES

The FCC Rules contain only a few instances of specific operating procedures, chiefly in connection with emergency communications. The various examples of operating procedures given below are in conformance with the regulations, but go further than the legal requirements; they are offered as examples of good practices on the air. See fig. 2524.

How to Make a Call

Listen carefully to make sure that the channel you want to use is not busy. If it is busy, you will hear voices, or from most public shore stations, an intermittent busy tone. Except in a safety emergency, don't interrupt.

When the conversation is to take place on a ship-to-ship frequency—unless you have reached an agreement in advance as to the time and frequency, establish contact on Channel 16 (or 2182 kHz) and then shift to an agreed-upon intership channel.

When the conversation is to take place through a commercial shore station—make your initial contact on a working frequency of that station

Both of these practices are designed to relieve the load on Channel 16 and 2182 kHz so that their availability for safety purposes will not be jeopardized.

Steps to Follow in Making a Call (other than a Distress, Urgency, or Safety Call)

Boat-to-boat calls. Listen to working channels to find one not being used. Listen to Channel 16 (or 2182 kHz) to make sure that it is not in use. If it is free, put your transmitter on the air and say—

"(Name of boat called) This is (Name of your boat and call sign), Over." To avoid confusion, always observe the proper sequence of call signs—state the name or call sign of the other station *first*, then give your own identification after saying "This is"—don't reverse the sequence. (If necessary, the identification of the station called may be given two or three times, but not more; it is rarely necessary to give your own boat name and call sign more than once.) The entire calling transmission must not take longer than 30 seconds.

FIG. 2524 The booklet "How to Use Your Marine Radiotelephone" explains the FCC Rules in simple language, and has much other valuable information on radio selection, installation, and proper use. Available from RTCM, P.O. Box 19087, Washington, DC 20036.

Listen for a reply. If no contact is made, repeat the above *after an interval of at least two minutes.*

Ship-to-ship contacts on HF working channels will have to be by prior arrangement as there are no specified calling frequencies on the 4 MHz and higher bands.

After establishing contact on Channels 16 (or 2182 kHz), switch to the agreed intership working channel. After the conversation is completed, say—"This is (Name of your boat and call sign), Out."

If the two stations have been in recent communications, or the distance is short, the other skipper is expecting the call, or similar circumstances, the operating procedures can be considerably abbreviated from what was described above. For example, the calling station can propose the working channel in his first transmission, and the called station merely says "Roger" or repeats the working channel number to agree to the shift, and gives his call sign. The procedure word "Over" indicating that you are ending your transmission and are awaiting a response can usually be omitted when using VHF with "solid" contact between stations; its omission does no harm and speeds up communications.

Ship-to-shore Service

Listen to make sure the working channel you wish to use is not busy. See fig. 2523. If it is clear, put your transmitter on the air and say—

"(Location) Marine Operator This is (Name of your boat and call sign), Over."

Listen for a reply. If no contact is made, repeat after an interval of at least two minutes.

When the Marine Operator answers, say—

"This is (Name of your boat and call sign) calling (telephone number desired), Over."

After the telephone conversation is completed, say—

"This is (Name and call sign of your boat), Out."

How to Receive a Call

Your boat can be reached only when your receiver is turned on and tuned to the frequency over which you expect to receive calls. Some, but not all, marine operators will make an announcement on Channel 16 that they have traffic for a specific vessel; such calls should be answered on that operator's working frequency, *not* on 16.

The receiver you use to maintain watch on Channel 16 will ensure that you get calls addressed to you by other boats; it *may* give you information that a marine operator has a call for you. When, however, you are using your set on a working channel you will miss any marine operator calls. It is thus advisable, if you are expecting a telephone call from shore, to periodically call the operator on her working channel to "check for traffic"—some shore stations will have regular schedules to announce the names of vessels for which calls are being held.

Steps in Receiving a Call

Boat-to-boat calls—When you hear your boat called, put your transmitter on the air and say—

"(Name of boat that called) This is (Name of your boat and call sign), Over."

Switch to the agreed upon intership channel. After the conversation is completed, say—

"This is (Name of your boat and call sign), Out."

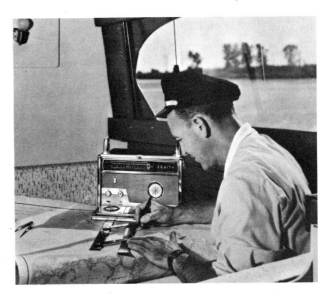

FIG. 2525 Prudent skipper tunes in latest weather bulletin before plotting day's course, especially when considering long runs offshore. Continuous weather broadcasts can be received on VHF communications sets, or on portable receivers as shown above.

Shore-to-ship calls—When you hear the name of your boat called, put your transmitter on the air and say—

"(Name of station that called) This is (Name of your boat and call sign), Over."

After the conversation is completed, say—

"This is (Name of your boat and call sign), Out."

Again, good contact between stations can result in abbreviated procedures including the elimination of "Over." (Except perhaps in ship-shore calls patched to a shore station where the other person is not familiar with marine semi-duplex operation and will need to be told to wait for each "over" as a cue to when to start talking.)

Distress, Urgency, Safety

In an emergency, as part of the marine safety and communications system, you have help on Channel 16 (or 2182 kHz) at your fingertips wherever you may be. (On the high seas far offshore, a call on a Coast Guard 4 or 6 MHz or other HF channel using pure SSB, A3J, may be more effective than a call on 2182 kHz using DSB or compatible SSB, A3H.)

Only when grave and imminent danger threatens your boat and immediate help is required, use the distress procedure—radiotelephone alarm signal (if available) and MAYDAY. Transmitted on Channel 16, it should be heard by many boats, as well as by the Coast Guard and other shore stations within range.

The *Radiotelephone Alarm Signal* consists of two audio tones of different pitch, 1300 and 2200 Hz, transmitted alternately ¼ second of each tone. The purpose of this signal is to attract the attention of persons on watch, and at some stations, to actuate automatic devices giving an alarm. It must be used *only* to announce that a distress call or message is about to follow. (Exception: it may be used with the urgency signal in two specified instances; see FCC Rules.) Some Coast Guard shore stations are now equipped with devices to generate this signal, and you should know what it means if you hear it.

The Distress Procedure—"Mayday"

Distress communications include the following actions:

1. The RADIOTELEPHONE ALARM SIGNAL (whenever possible for at least 30 but not more than 60 seconds) followed by—
2. The DISTRESS SIGNAL "MAYDAY."
3. The DISTRESS MESSAGE.
4. Acknowledgment of Receipt of Distress Message.
5. Further Distress Messages and other communications.
6. Transmission of the Distress Procedure by a boat or shore station not itself in distress.
7. Termination of Distress Situation.

The DISTRESS CALL consists of:

—the Distress Signal MAYDAY, spoken once;
—the words THIS IS
—the identification (name and call sign) of the craft in distress, spoken three times.

The DISTRESS MESSAGE follows immediately and con-sists of:

—the Distress Signal MAYDAY, spoken three times;
—the identification of the craft;
—particulars of its position (latitude and longitude, or true bearing and distance in miles from a known geo-graphical position);
—the nature of the distress and the kind of assistance desired;
—any other information that might facilitate the rescue; especially a description of the boat: length, color, type, etc.; and the number of persons aboard; OVER.

Example of Distress Procedure

"(Alarm Signal, if available, for one minute). Mayday, Mayday, Mayday. This is yacht Blue Duck, yacht Blue Duck, yacht Blue Duck, WZ 1234:

Mayday, Yacht Blue Duck, WZ 1234, 133 degrees true, 12 miles from Montauk Point. Struck submerged object, taking on water fast, engine disabled, estimate cannot stay afloat more than one hour. Four persons on board. Blue Duck is a 26-foot cabin cruiser, white hull. Maintaining watch on Channel 16. This is yacht Blue Duck, WZ 1234, Over."

General Rules for Distress

With your life at stake, you have a far better chance by following the correct procedure, but the provisions of the International Radio Regulations authorize a vessel in dis-tress to use *any means* at its disposal to attract attention, make known its position, and obtain help.

Stay on Channel 16 (or 2182 kHz), repeating the call several times if no answer is immediately received. If, how-ever, no response is then received, repeat the distress call on any other available frequency on which attention might be attracted.

Speak slowly and distinctly. Use phonetic words for let-ters when necessary, especially when giving the letters of your call sign.

You may be requested to transmit a "long count" or other suitable signals to permit direction finding stations to determine your position; always end your transmission with the name and call sign of your boat.

If you have to abandon ship, the radio transmitter should be locked on the air, if considered necessary and condi-tions permit. The purpose of this is to locate you by radio direction finding bearings. If you have already been visu-ally located, do not lock your transmitter on the air as the signal would interfere with rescue operations.

All vessels having knowledge of distress traffic, and which cannot themselves assist, are *forbidden* to transmit on the frequency of the distress traffic; but they should listen and follow the situation until it is evident that as-sistance is being provided. Always listen before transmit-ting. It is *unlawful* for any radio operator to *willfully* or *maliciously interfere with* or cause interference to *any radio communication* or *signal*. No person shall knowingly transmit, or cause to be transmitted, any *false* or *fraudulent signal of distress* or *communication* relating thereto.

Radio Silence

The signal "Seelonce Mayday" has been adopted inter-nationally to control transmissions on the distress fre-quency, telling all other stations to leave the air and main-tain radio silence. This signal is to be used *only* by the unit in distress and the station controlling the distress traffic. Any other station which considers it necessary to advise one or more other stations of the need to keep off the air should use the signal "Seelonce Distress" followed by its identification.

The signal to indicate the end of radio silence and per-mission to resume normal operation is "Seelonce Feenee."

The oddly spelled words above are phonetic equivalents from the French as adopted for international use.

If You Hear a MAYDAY Call

If you are not in distress, but hear a "Mayday" call, this is what you should do:

1. *Listen—Do Not Transmit.*
2. Try to determine if you are the craft in the best posi-tion to take action, or if some other vessel is better located or better equipped.
3. *If* yours is the logical boat to render assistance, reply with a call to the distressed vessel. When he has acknowl-edged your call, continue with your offer of assistance as follows—

"(Name of craft in distress) This is (Name of your boat and call sign), Received Mayday (your position, your course and speed toward the scene of the distress, and your esti-mated time of arrival), Over."

4. If yours is not the logical boat to take action, main-tain radio silence, but continue to monitor the frequency closely for any further developments—make an entry in your radio log of the Mayday call and your actions.

When another station retransmits a distress message, the words "Mayday Relay" must be spoken three times before station identification.

Use "Mayday" sparingly

The distress signal "Mayday" should be used *only* when the vessel is "threatened with *grave* and *immediate danger* and requests *immediate assistance.*" It should *not* be used for situations such as being out of fuel, running aground, or engine failure under conditions of no immediate dan-ger. Reserve "Mayday" for true emergencies of real hazard to life and property; don't "cry wolf" when it is not a desperate situation. Make an ordinary call for assistance, or if appropriate, use the urgency signal "Pan-Pan"—pronounced "Pahn-Pahn"—three times before the call.

The safety signal "Security"—pronounced "Saycuritay"—is spoken three times before transmissions such as those relating to defects in aids to navigation and weather warnings; it is used mainly by shore stations.

Test Transmissions

Always remember, when making tests, to take every precaution not to cause interference to others. Listen before testing, to make sure that the frequency is not busy. You must obtain the consent of any station affected before proceeding. If the air appears clear, put your transmitter on the air and say—

"This is (name of your boat and call sign) Test."

If you hear no station tell you to "Wait," you may proceed, saying "Testing" followed by a number count or other phraseology that will not confuse listeners.

At the end of the test, announce the name and call sign of your boat,

Calls for a routine "radio check" should be made to a specific vessel, not "any boat." Calls may be initiated on Channel 16 but the exchange of reports must be made on a working channel. (If you hear other stations on a working channel, there is no need to use Channel 16 at all and it should be avoided.) A report of reception should be short and specific—there's nothing better than "loud and clear" if such is the case.

Information broadcasts

Marine weather is broadcast by NOAA stations continuously from many stations; see page 263. In areas not so served, weather broadcasts are transmitted by commercial broadcast stations and marine operators; see page 264.

Coast Guard stations on VHF and on MF/HF bands broadcast marine information on regular schedules. VHF transmissions are on Channel 22 following an alerting announcement on Channel 16; special broadcasts may be made at any time for safety purposes. Coast Guard broadcasts may include weather summaries and forecasts.

VIOLATIONS AND PENALTIES

Hopefully, you will never be in violation of the FCC Rules and will have no need for knowledge of the procedures and penalties involved. Yet things do not always work out that way, so it is just as well to be informed.

If you receive a citation of violation from the FCC, you must reply in duplicate within 10 days, to the office that issued the citation of violation. If a complete reply cannot be given in that time, an interim reply must be sent and supplemented as soon as possible. If for reasons beyond your control, you cannot reply at all within 10 days, do so at the earliest date practicable, and fully support your reasons for the delay. Each letter to the FCC must be complete and contain all the facts without cross-reference to other correspondence. The answer must contain a full explanation of the incident and describe the actions taken to prevent a recurrence of it. If personnel errors are involved, your reply must state the name and license number of the operator concerned.

You may be lucky, however, and receive a "warning

notice" rather than a citation. In this instance, no reply is required. The FCC form that you receive will indicate whether or not an answer is necessary. If one is required, don't get yourself into further trouble by failing to answer *within 10 days.*

Revocation and Suspension of License

A station license may be revoked for any one of a number of specified violations of the Communications Act or the FCC Rules. Operator licenses and permits normally are not revoked but are suspended for varying periods of time.

FIG. 2526 If you receive citation for violation of FCC Rules and Regulations, submit written reply within ten days. No reply is required if you receive "warning," rather than citation.

Notice of suspension must be given in writing and is not effective until 15 days after receipt. Within this period, you can apply for a hearing, and this automatically defers the suspension until after the hearing has been held and the FCC has ruled.

Fines Imposed

In addition to the revocation or suspension of licenses, the FCC can prosecute violators in the Federal District Courts. Any violation of the Communications Act may be punished by a fine of not more than $10,000, or imprisonment for not more than one year, or both. A second offense, not necessarily a repeat of the first, increases the maximum limit on the prison term to two years. For a violation of any FCC rule, regulation restriction, or condition, or of any treaty provision, a court may additionally impose a fine of not more than $500 for *each and every day* during which the violation occurred.

Administrative Forfeitures

To avoid the delays, costs, and general cumbersomeness of formal court prosecutions, the FCC has the authority to levy its own "administrative forfeitures," actually small fines, for 12 specified violations. These fines are in addition to any other penalties that may be imposed by law.

Among these twelve, the violations of principal concern to the operators of radio stations of boats are.

—Transmission of any unauthorized communications on a distress or calling frequency.

—Failure to identify the station at the times and in the manner prescribed by the Rules.

—Interference with a distress call or distress communications.

—Operation of a station without a valid permit or license of the proper grade.

—Transmission of any false call contrary to the Rules.

—Failure to respond to official communications from the FCC.

The maximum forfeiture for a single violation, or a series of violations all falling within a single category as listed above, is $100. If, however, more than one category is involved, the maximum liability is raised to $500 for a station licensee, or $400 for an individual operator. It should be noted that the term "operator" may be applied to any person using the equipment, whether or not licensed by the FCC. In some cases, if two different persons are involved, forfeitures may be assessed against both the station licensee and the person who was operating the station.

The procedures for the imposition of these administrative fines have been kept simple, yet ample protection is afforded to the rights of individuals. Upon receipt of a "notice of apparent liability for forfeiture," the addressed person has open to him three courses of action. He can pay the fine and so close the incident; or he may, within 30 days, submit a written statement to the FCC giving reasons why he should be allowed to pay a lesser fine, or none at all; or he may request an interview with an FCC official. These last two courses of action can be combined, submitting both an explanation and a request for an interview. If either or both of these actions are taken, the FCC will review all of the information relative to the case, and make a final determination.

There is no judicial appeal from the FCC's ruling, and you had best pay up as there are established procedures for turning over cases of non-payment to a District Attorney for prosecution.

Citizens Band Radio

Citizens Band (CB) radio operations must be considered separately from those on the VHF and MF-HF bands as they come under an entirely different set of FCC Rules. The CB sets are relatively inexpensive, easy to install, and simple to operate. See fig. 2527.

The Citizens Band Radio Service is unique; it is not intended to duplicate any other radio service. It is *not* a substitute for the safety features of regular marine radio service in the VHF band, nor for the ship-to-shore connections into the public telephone system. Likewise, it is *not* a new type of hobby or amateur service for casual contacts at great distances. The CB Service has its own particular functions and these do not overlap or conflict with other established services.

Citizens Band communications can relate to either the business or personal activities of the licensee. CB stations may not, of course, be used to further any illegal activity.

CB LICENSES

Licenses for stations in the Citizens Band have been made as easy as possible to obtain, and operator permits are not required at all. There are only a minimum of legal restrictions on the applicant and the equipment. To get a station license, a person may be either a U.S. citizen or an alien individual, but must be at least 18 years of age. A license also can be issued to a corporation, but not to any foreign government or a representative thereof. Licenses may not be transferred to another person; prompt report by letter is required for a change in address (but not for a change in approved equipment). Licenses are good for 5 years; renewal requires the same form and fee.*

Application for a CB station license is made on Form 505

*On 1 January 1977 the FCC suspended the collection of all fees for licenses and permits until further notice.

FIG. 2527   A Citizens Band radio can be very useful on a boat for personal communications of a nature not proper for the VHF band. CB units can also be installed in cars, homes, offices, etc., to keep in contact with boats.

available from an FCC office, but mailed to Gettysburg, PA 17326 when completed. A CB station may be used only when licensed and its call sign has been assigned, but provisions exist for a "temporary permit" which will allow operation immediately after purchase of equipment while waiting for a regular station license (this includes the use of a temporary call sign). A check or money order for $4 must accompany an application for a station license, which may, at no additional cost, include any number of sets owned by the same individual or organization.* No person can hold more than one CB station license, thus the same call sign will be used at his home, automobile, boat, etc.

AUTHORIZED CHANNELS

The Citizens Band consists of 40 channels between the limits of 26.965 and 27.405 MHz. Although specific frequencies are listed in the FCC Rules, these are commonly referred to by channel number, 1 to 40. Any channel may be used for either double or single sideband modulation. Any of them may be used for communications between units of the same station or different stations, subject to the limitations placed on Channel 9 as described below. No channel is assigned to any particular user or group of users; all must be shared.

Channel 9 is reserved for "emergency communications involving the immediate safety of life or the immediate

FIG. 2528   As useful as it is on a boat, a CB radio is not a substitute for the marine distress and safety VHF Channel 16. CB channel 9 is designated for emergency communications, but it is not monitored by the Coast Guard.

FIG. 2529 CB radios must be properly operated and station identification must be given by the official call sign of letters and numbers. Boat names, CB "handles," and other designations may also be used, but they are not a substitute for the required station identification.

protection of property." It is also available for "traveler assistance"; this term is not defined in FCC Rules, but presumably it could be applied to a boatman needing help but not in an emergency situation. (Other channels can be used for emergency communications, but will probably be subjected to much more interference.) Some Coast Guard stations now guard CB Channel 9 on a secondary basis, but this is *not* a substitute for the regular marine distress frequencies of VHF Channel 16 and 2182 kHz.*

Citizen Band stations are limited to 4 watts carrier (output) power on AM and 12 watts peak power of single sideband; external power amplifiers are specifically and strictly prohibited. On boats, a "marine-type" antenna must be used, an antenna as used on automobiles will not work.

The usual reliable range is on the order of 5 miles (8 km), but may extend to 15 miles (24 km) or more. These are groundwave ranges; skywave transmission will often occur and CB signals will be heard at distances of several thousand miles. The FCC Rules prohibit exchanges between stations more than 250 km (155.3 miles) apart.

Communication between an unlicensed unit and a licensed station is prohibited. All low-powered (100 milliwatts) "handi-talkies" used with a CB station must have been included in the CB license application. If so licensed, they must be properly identified on the air.

A CB set must be "type accepted" by the FCC and internal modifications are not permitted; external power amplifiers are specifically prohibited. Repairs must be done by a holder of a commercial license.

OPERATING PROCEDURES

Operation of a Citizens Band station is quite simple. No specific operating procedures need be learned and used; no log is required. However, there are regulations which must be known and obeyed.

The FCC Rules require that *all* communications be restricted to the *minimum practicable transmission time*, but no time limits are placed on intercommunications between

units of the same station. Between different stations, however, an exchange must be limited to a maximum of 5 minutes; after its completion, both stations must remain off the air for an additional 1 minute.

Station identification *must* be given at the *end* of each exchange of communications; it may be given at the beginning or during communications, but this is not required. The FCC-assigned call sign must be clearly given in the English language; a phonetic alphabet *may* be used as an aid to identification. A CB "handle" may be used in addition to the call sign, but not instead of it.

Communications may be in any language, but identification must be in English. A CB station is for personal and business communications, and emergencies. It may not be used for any illegal activity, to transmit music, to advertise goods, or to intentionally interfere with another CB station. Profane, obscene, or indecent language is prohibited. Although an operator permit is not required, CB stations may be operated only by the licensee, members of his immediate family, his employees, and certain other individuals specifically authorized in the regulations. CB stations may *not* be operated by a person who has had his own license revoked or has surrendered it for cancellation as the result of rule violations. The licensee must remember that he retains full responsibility for all use of all units of his station. The same system of administrative forfeitures (small fines) that applies to marine band radio operations is also applicable to CB.

The FCC requires that a CB Licensee have a current copy of the applicable Rules and Regulations; this is Subpart D of Part 95, Personal Radio Services. A copy of Part 95 can be purchased from the Superintendent of Documents, Government Printing Office, Washington, DC 20402; the price is $1.25. Changes are no longer issued separately, but a new, revised edition is published annually. Various commercial publications are also available that contain the CB regulations.

Amateur Radio

Amateur ("ham") radio is another form of communications available to the boatman. It is most useful to those who cruise to places distant from their home port, but it can be used for personal communications under many circumstances. Ham radio does *not* provide a specific distress channel, but there are many recorded instances where the amateur bands were used in emergency situations on the high seas. No service is provided to marine operators, but friendly hams ashore are usually glad to pass along personal messages. There are no restrictions on boat-to-boat ham communications (except in the waters of some foreign countries).

The amateur radio service has many kinds of frequencies from 1.8 to 24,000 MHz. In this extremely wide spread, there are suitable frequencies for communications at any distance desired. Radiotelegraph (Morse code), radio-telephone (AM or FM), radio teletype, and television signals may be sent in specified sub-bands; some hams even communicate by "moon-bounce" signals! Equipment may be purchased or home-made; installation and maintenance can be by the owner-operator as the required licenses cover appropriate technical knowledge.

*Older 23-channel CB radios are fully compatible on Channels 1-23 with the newer 40-channel sets.

Electronics / CHAPTER 25

Licenses

Amateur radio operation requires both a station license and an operator license; these are separate from any commercial or CB license or permit. Ham radio operator licenses are issued in various grades—Novice, Technician, General, Advanced, and Extra. A knowledge of Morse code is required even though all planned operation will be by voice. Five words per minute sending and receiving speed will get you started as a Novice with limited radio-telegraph privileges but you need not go through this stage. A General Class license will be needed for voice communications, and this requires a 13 words/minute code speed, plus a written exam on regulations and radio fundamentals.

A ham license is not easily obtained, but neither is it impossible for anyone who seriously desires it and will devote some time to study and code practice.

Other Communications

There is often need for communications at very short distances, a few yards to perhaps a quarter- or half-mile from the boat, or on board the craft itself. Two systems are available to meet this requirement.

Hailers

For voice communications from boat-to-boat or boat-to-shore over distances up to several hundred yards or more, a *loud hailer* is most useful. This may be either an installed item of equipment or a portable *power megaphone*; the installed unit will have the most power and greatest range, but a hand-held model will be more convenient on smaller motorboats and on sailboats.

Various models of installed hailers offer additional useful features such as auxiliary use as a fog horn, perhaps sounding automatically at selected intervals; or a listening capability whereby the loudspeaker can also act as a microphone to pick up distant sounds, aiding in *two-way* voice communications. In selecting equipment, it is necessary to get a unit with adequate power; 25 to as much as 75 watts is desirable. (The "P.A." output from many CB sets is only 2 to 4 watts and is not enough for boats except for on-board use.)

Proper installation is essential for satisfactory performance. This requires adequate primary power wiring (a powerful hailer will draw 10 amps or more, check voltage at the unit), adequate wiring from the amplifier to the speaker (remember the many watts being carried), and proper location and mounting of the speaker (to disperse the sound in the desired direction and prevent feedback into the microphone). An excellent feature of some installations is the mounting of the speaker either on the searchlight or on a separate mount that can be both elevated and

FIG. 2531 If an installed hailer is not feasible because of the size of your boat, a power megaphone can serve very well. Power is less, but it can be used very flexibly boat-to-boat and boat-to-shore.

trained in direction in the same manner as a searchlight. This permits the most efficient use of the hailer to craft off to one side or to a bridge tender high above the boat. The combination of a hailer that can pick up and amplify distant sounds with a directional speaker on a trainable mount will permit "audio direction finding" on fog signals to a surprising degree of precision—a real help in zero-visibility piloting situations.

Intercom systems

While most people think of a boat as being too small and compact to have internal communications problems,

FIG. 2532 Small intercom system permits easy communication between all areas aboard cruisers and yachts. Master unit shown above controls five substations, including one on foredeck, useful when anchoring or docking.

FIG. 2530 An installed loud hailer is excellent for direct voice communications over distances from a few yards to a half-mile or more. Some models will pick up and amplify incoming sounds and thus make two-way communications possible. Some hailers will also serve as fog horns, with automatic timing of blasts.

there are numerous possible applications for simple intercom systems. See fig. 2534. The interior of many larger cruisers, particularly those of the double-cabin type, are so divided that voices do not carry well from one compartment to another. A simple three-station intercom system connecting the bridge, forward cabin, and after cabin will make possible easy conversation between these locations and save many steps. On a boat with a small crew, such as a couple living aboard by themselves, a quick and easy means of internal communications is truly a safety item as the helmsman need not leave the controls or divert his attention to carry on a conversation or summon assistance.

On a larger boat, the intercom system can be extended to include a unit in a weather-proof box on the foredeck. Then you can have constant contact between the person at the boat's controls and the person raising or lowering the anchor, or handling the docking lines. Just try to get up a badly fouled anchor without communicating with the helmsman, and you will quickly appreciate this small electronic device.

★ ★ ★ ★ ★ ★ ★ ★ ★ ★ ★ ★ ★ ★ ★ ★ ★ ★ ★

ELECTRONIC EQUIPMENT
Navigation and Other Uses

While the greater part of attention to electronic equipment for boats is normally focused on radios, there are many other devices ranging from those that are highly desirable, even necessary, to units that may be classed as merely useful for conveniences or comfort. This chapter will examine a number of these items, in roughly that sequence, as used for navigation, safety, and other purposes.

Depth Sounders

Depth sounders (fig. 2601) closely rival radiotelephones as the most popular item of electronic equipment for boats; they have a wide range of use—lakes, rivers, bays, and off-shore. Your sounder can be one of the most interesting and useful devices on your boat.

Depth sounders are a modern replacement for the hand-held lead line used for uncounted centuries to determine the depth of water beneath a ship. This electronic device furnishes a vastly greater amount of information, and does it with much greater ease, especially in nasty weather. It provides safety as well as convenience in boating, and so is doubly advantageous to have on board.

How Depth is Measured

Depth is determined by measuring the round-trip time for a pulse of ultrasonic energy to travel from the boat to the bottom of the water and be reflected back to the point of origin. See fig. 2602. The frequency of the audio pulses generally lies between 50,000 and 200,000 cycles per second, too high to be heard by human ears. Their average velocity through the water is approximately 4800 feet per second; slight variations in speed will occur between salt and fresh water and with different temperatures. The resulting small errors, however, can be safely ignored for the relatively shallow depths of interest to the operators of recreational boats.

Probably the greatest advantage of the electronic device over the hand-held lead line is the essentially continuous nature of the information furnished. Depth sounders vary widely in the rate at which readings are taken, but in all cases many more soundings are taken than could be accomplished by hand. Current equipment takes readings at rates between 1 and 30 per second, with an accuracy of about ± 5%; fully sufficient for normal navigation.

Components of a Depth Sounder

The major components of a depth sounder are a source of energy (transmitter), a means of sending out the pulses

FIG. 2601 Electronic depth sounders are useful navigation tools on all waters and on boats of most sizes and types. The digital model shown here gives a clear, unmistakeable indication of depth.

and picking up the echoes (transducer), a receiver to amplify the weak echoes, and a visual presentation of the information. See fig. 2601. The transducer usually takes the form of a round block of hard ceramic material several inches in diameter and an inch or so thick. In many cases, it is given an oblong, streamline shape to reduce drag.

The visual presentation of information on the depth of the water is accomplished by either an "indicator" or a "recorder." The indicator provides a non-permanent indication of the depth by one of three methods—flashing light, electrical meter, or direct-reading digital display. The flashing light is mounted on the end of an arm which rotates around a scale much like the second hand of a clock, only much faster. The zero of the scale is usually at the top of the dial and a flash of light occurs there when the outgoing pulse leaves the transducer on the boat's bottom. A second flash occurs when the pulse is received back at the transducer, having been reflected back from the bottom of the water. The deeper the water, the longer it will take for the echo to return to the boat; the longer this takes, the farther the arm will have rotated around the dial. (Fig. 2603.) Thus the scale of depths increases clockwise around the face of the indicator.

The electrical meter indicator reads on a scale directly calibrated in units of depth. A digital display is probably the simplest to use, but may be difficult to read in conditions of bright light such as in an open boat or on a flying

FIG. 2602 An electronic depth sounder measures depth by sending pulses of high frequency sound waves, reflected back from the bottom. Distance is measured by time taken by pulses for round trip.

Principle of the Depth Sounder Illustrated

An example may make this clearer. If the sounder has a depth range of 240 feet, at full scale the sound pulses will have traveled a round-trip distance of 480 feet. Taking the speed of sound in water at 4800 feet per second, the round-trip will have taken 1/10 second. Therefore the arm carrying the flashing light must make one full rotation in 1/10 second; this is 10 rps or 600 rpm.

If the depth is only, say, 80 feet, the echo will cause the light to flash when the arm has made only 1/3 of a full revolution, and the flash will occur at a position corresponding to four o'clock on a clock dial. In many models, it is possible to detect greater than full-scale depths by turning up the sensitivity control until a flash is seen on the "second trip around" of the rotating arm. Using the same sounder as in the preceding example, if the water was known to be quite deep, and a weak reading of 60 feet was seen with the sensitivity control well advanced, it could mean an actual depth of 300 feet (full scale plus 60 feet). Some models are now calibrated with two sets of numbers around the dial for first and second revolutions of the flashing light. Caution is essential to avoid reading the depth as much greater than is actually the case.

With the recording type of sounder, a permanent record is made of the depths, and notations as to the boat's position can be made directly on the paper tape. See fig. 2605. The paper moves horizontally from a supply roll to a take-up spool at the rate of one inch in several minutes. A dry method of chemically marking the paper is normally used to avoid the messiness of ink. A recording type of depth sounder has some advantages, but this type is more expensive. Some models are now available with both flashing light indicator and a permanent paper tape record. Sounds are available that show depths in meters.

Correction to "Zero" Depth

If you have a sounder on your boat, you must know its "zero" depth. In most instances, the transducer is mounted on the hull several feet below the water surface and, as depths are measured from the transducer, the indications will be neither the depth of water from the surface nor the depth beneath the keel of the boat. On some models, the

bridge; a light-shield (hood) may be desirable. Any type of lighted display that is bright enough for exposed daytime use should have a dimming control for night operation.

Many depth sounders are designed to read on two or more scales; with corresponding maximum depths. One model with meter-type indications reads 0-12 and 0-120 feet; this provides detailed measurement for safety in shallow water, plus a greater range for navigation in deeper waters. Some flashing-light models use the same scale markings for either feet or fathoms, thus providing two ranges with a 1:6 ratio; digital readouts are particularly suitable for multiple ranges. Models are now available with depth measurements in meters and fractions to match a growing use of the metric system on charts.

FIG. 2603 On this sounder, indicator shows flash of light at "0" on scale and another opposite depth.

FIG. 2604 Typical depth sounder consists of transducer, not shown, and electronics package with indicator which is mounted near helmsman. Model shown has calibrated meter with two ranges.

FIG. 2605 With recording type of sounder, depth is measured many times each second and presented as a series of dots on scaled tape.

FIG. 2606 Navigator notes when the tank ashore is abeam, but can get no other line of position. The depth sounder reading, corrected for the state of the tide, can be plotted along the one LOP for an Estimated Position at 2137.

zero flash can be offset on the dial to its depth below the surface, then the indicated depths are correspondingly increased to show directly the full distance between the water surface and the bottom without need for adding a correction. This is advantageous when the sounder is used for navigation.

The nature of the bottom of the body of water will have an effect on the appearance of the flash which indicates the depth. Learn how to determine roughly the nature of the bottom by the characteristics of the flashing light; a surprising amount of information can be obtained. Sharp, clear indications mean a hard bottom. Conversely, broad and fuzzy flashes indicate a soft, muddy bottom. Multiple flashes, each fairly sharp, can result from rocky bottoms; the ultrasonic pulses are reflected more or less horizontally to adjacent rocks before being returned upward. The added time delays for these sideward bounces make them show up as if they were at greater depths. Additional flashes at multiples of the least depth indicated may result, in shallow water with a hard bottom, from pulses being reflected downward again by the craft's hull following the first round-trip. Two or even three round-trips may occur; the cure for this is to turn back the sensitivity control until only the first indication is seen. In *all* cases of multiple flashes, play it safe and assume that the minimum reading is the true depth! As the depth indication flash will always have some width, be sure to read the "trailing" edge, or least indicated depth. This is the correct value.

Application in Piloting

The primary application of an electronic depth sounder is to assist in the safe navigation of the boat in unfamiliar waters. It can provide much useful information, but must be used with care as *it makes no predictions ahead.* (There are larger, much more expensive *scanning* sonar devices that look ahead and to each side, presenting a radar-like view of underwater conditions, but these are rarely found on recreational boats.)

Information on the depth of water is reassuring in itself; furthermore, it can be used to assist in determining the boat's position. It can be used to make rough position data somewhat more exact. For example, if only a single line of position (LOP) is available, an estimated position (EP) can often be obtained from the additional knowledge of the depth of the water. See fig. 2606. This requires a fairly uniform sloping bottom and some knowledge of the state of the tide. Many times, a rough EP can be obtained from indications of an abrupt change in depth.

A line of soundings can sometimes be matched with chart figures to locate the boat's track. See page 439. This is most easily done on depth recorders, but is also possible on indicating types by logging depths at regular time intervals. Depths are plotted on a strip of paper with their distance apart matched to the scale of the chart and the speed of the boat. The paper strip is moved about on the chart parallel to the boat's course until the depths match. This technique is not possible in all locations and should be used with caution lest an erroneous conclusion as to the boat's position lead to danger. Often in conditions of low visibility, a boat can be navigated to a desired destination by using the depth sounder to follow along a path of roughly constant depths. This is the technique of "following a fathom curve."

A depth sounder may also be used navigationally in a negative sense. If your depth indication agrees with the charted depth for your estimated position, you may, *or may not*, be there; the same depth figures occur in many places on any chart. If, however, your sounder shows a considerably different value than that charted for your DR (dead reckoning) position, it is an almost sure indication that your DR is *not* correct. Thus, while a depth sounder cannot positively confirm a DR plot, it can surely call it wrong.

Depth alarms

Many models of electronic depth sounders have audible alarm signals that are activated whenever the depth de-

FIG. 2607 When visibility is poor, RDF can help fix position, or navigator may "home in" on transmitter near his destination.

creases to a predetermined value. On some units, this is one or more fixed depths; on others, the alarm can be set for any desired depth.

Fish finding

The location of fish with a depth sounder is possible, but you may be disappointed with your initial results. Experience is required and you will improve with practice. Detection will generally be limited to schools of fish or quite large single fish. The echoes are quite weak and the sensitivity control will have to be advanced.

Radio Direction Finders

On the seacoasts of the United States, and on the Great Lakes and other large inland bodies of water, a *radio direction finder* (RDF) is an important piece of electronic equipment. See fig. 2607. Primarily installed as a safety item, it can also be a great convenience to the boat operator. It is the primary radio aid to navigation for small craft.

A complete radio direction finding system consists of four components:

1. One or more radio transmitters at known locations.
2. An RDF set on the boat.
3. Charts covering both the location of the transmitters and the area of operation of the boat.
4. A person who knows the operation of the system.

To be fully effective, the RDF system must be used with competence and confidence — an incorrect radio bearing can lead to disaster; a correct bearing that is ignored because of mistrust can be equally disastrous.

Special RDF Features

Basically, an RDF is a radio receiver with two additional features. First and vitally important is the directional an-

tenna. Usually, this antenna is rotatable so that the set may be secured firmly in a convenient location. The directional antenna employed with an RDF set is an improved version of the simple loop used on portable receivers, the directional characteristics of which are familiar to most boatmen. This antenna may take the form of a loop a foot or so in diameter or it may appear as a plastic bar measuring about an inch square by some six inches in length. Both types will be mounted on top of the set; either will do the job.

As the antenna is rotated through 360°, these directional antennas show two positions of maximum signal strength and two positions of minimum sensitivity called "nulls." With properly balanced construction and no local interfering objects, the two maximum signal positions will be separated by 180°, as will be the nulls which are found 90° in either direction from the maximums. It is characteristic of these antennas that the maximum signal points are broad and poorly defined, while the nulls are marked and precise. For this reason, the nulls are used for direction finding. On some models, the antenna is rotated by turning a front-panel knob; this is desirable as there is a possibility of the null being affected if the user's hand is placed on the antenna. If the loop must be handled, it should be touched only at the outer edge of its base.

The second special feature of RDFs is a visual null indicator. While the operator can judge by ear the position of the antenna at minimum signal with fair accuracy, a more precise bearing can be obtained by observing a visual indicator. This is normally a small electric meter, read for either a maximum or minimum deflection of its needle in accordance with the instructions for the particular set being used.

RDF Frequency Bands

Radio direction finders normally cover three frequency bands: a low frequency (LF) beacon band, the standard AM radio broadcast band, and the 2-3 MHz MF communications band. The LF beacon band is of primary interest for the marine radiobeacons operated by the Coast Guard on frequencies between 285 and 325 kHz at locations along or just off our coastlines and the Great Lakes. See fig. 2608. Aeronautical beacons, somewhat lower and higher in frequency, are also within the tuning range of these sets and can be used for direction finding. (These aero beacons, or "ranges" as they are called, are an excellent source of weather information at 15 and 45 minutes past each hour.)

Coverage of the standard AM radio broadcast band is desirable because of the large number of stations on which bearings can be taken. It should be noted, however, that the accuracy of bearings on this band will not be quite as good as it will be on the LF beacon band. Use of the 2-3 MHz marine communications band has been greatly lessened with the change to single sideband operation. A few models of RDFs are designed to adequately receive such signals, but the lack of a carrier component of the signal makes direction finding much less effective; this band is generally used only for "homing" on another vessel, such as in distress situation, since the accuracy of bearings is quite low.

Direction finders are now available for the VHF band, see page 515. (A few LF-MF direction finders can receive VHF signals; some can pick up only weather frequencies,

FIG. 2608 Radiobeacon charts are published in Light Lists to assist in identifying the beacons. Frequencies, schedules of operation and identification signals are shown on the charts.

others can be tuned to any channel. These RDFs can be used for monitoring a second channel, but they do *not* have any direction finding capability in this mode.)

Another type of radio direction finder is the hand-held unit. These are popular because they can be moved about the boat to any location where radio deviation (see page 512) is absent or at a minimum. Hand-held RDFs are powered by internal dry-cells, cover the beacon band only, and have an integral small magnetic compass. Some have a null meter, others depend on an audible indication of the null.

In direction finding the location of the transmitting antenna must be known. The location of beacons operated by the Coast Guard is shown on standard charts and in the Light List. The *Marine Weather Services Charts* (Fig. 1243) give latitude and longitude of many broadcast band transmitters, as well as the location of many aeronautical radio ranges and beacons.

Marine Radiobeacons

Radiobeacons are rated in terms of "service range" from 200 miles (370 km) to as little as 10 miles (18 km) for

FIG. 2609 The location of the antenna of a radiobeacon is shown in the Light List under the listing of the basic aid to navigation with which it is associated.

SEACOAST		NORTH CAROLINA					FIFTH DISTRICT	
(1)	(2)	(3)	(4)	(5)		(6)	(7)	
	Name	Location	Nominal	Ht.		Structure		
			Range	above	Ht. above			
No.	Characteristic	Lat. N. Long. W.		water	ground	Daymark	Remarks	Year
	(Chart 11536)							
184	OAK ISLAND LIGHT	On southeast point of		24	169	Cylindrical tower, top third	RBN: 298 kHz	
	Gp. Fl. W., 10ˢ	Oak Island.				black, middle third white,	OA(■■■ ●■) II.	
	0.1ˢfl., 0.9ˢec.	33 53.6 78 02.1				lower third gray.	Antenna 33 yards 102°	
	0.1ˢfl., 0.9ˢec.					155	from light tower.	
	0.1ˢfl., 0.9ˢec.						Shows reduced intensity	
	0.1ˢfl., 6.9ˢec.						between 190° and 250°.	
	4 flashes.						Emergency light.	
								1958

FIG. 2610 For accurate RDF bearings, you must have a table of radio deviation corrections. RDF shown here has built-in sighting vanes for visual bearings, or separate pelorus may be used.

Courtesy of Ray Jefferson

FIG. 2611 To ensure accuracy always use portable RDF from the same position. Do NOT, however, place it too close to compass. Speaker magnet may affect it; three feet is safe minimum separation.

"marker" beacons such as those at harbor entrances.

Many, but not all, radiobeacons operate continuously. The others are "sequenced," up to six beacons operating in turn on the same frequency, each being on the air for one minute and then off while the others take their turn. The sequence of operation can be determined from the charts or by reference to the Light List. It is indicated by a Roman numeral immediately following the frequency; if no Roman numeral is shown, the beacon operates continuously.

Radio Deviation

All RDFs are subject to local deviation errors caused by the reflection of the radio signals by nearby wires and other metallic objects. This is generally similar to the effect of masses of iron on a magnetic compass. One important difference, however, is that the radio bearing errors vary with respect to the *relative* bearing angle; the heading of the boat is not the deciding factor as it is with compass deviation. A table, or curve, must be prepared to show the corrections for RDF error on various relative bearings. Separate tables will generally be required for each of the frequency bands.

Determining RDF Deviation Error

RDF deviation errors are determined by comparison of observed radio bearings with known correct bearings. Either of two methods may be used. The simplest is to take radio bearings on a radiobeacon or other type of transmitting antenna within sight, at the same time having another person take direct visual bearings. See fig. 2610. The difference between these readings is the radio deviation error. If no radio station is within sight, take radio bearings from a known location and compare them with correct bearings as taken from a chart. Avoid doing this while made fast to the club pier; erroneous readings may result from reflections caused by adjacent boats. In both cases, the deviation corrections have the same numerical value as the errors, but with the opposite sign.

Calibration readings should be taken of a strong local station which is received clearly without interference. A complete deviation correction table, preferably in steps of not more than 15°, should be prepared for the low frequency band. Then spot checks can be made to determine if the same corrections will apply on higher frequency bands or if separate tables must be made for each band. Correction tables should be checked at least annually, and additionally if the direction finder is relocated on the boat or major changes are made in the electrical wiring, rigging, etc.

Direct and Reciprocal Bearings

Due to the technical characteristics of a loop antenna, two nulls can be found 180° apart. In most situations, the navigator's general knowledge of his approximate position will suffice to eliminate the reverse reading. If this is not possible, or to be absolutely sure, special measures can be taken. Nearly all direction finders have either an integral auxiliary "sense" antenna or a connection terminal for an external antenna. By operating a switch, this antenna is connected into the circuit to change the directional characteristics to a single null and single maximum pattern. Simple procedures will then indicate which of the previous nulls is the direct bearing and which is the reciprocal reading. (The sense antenna is not left in the circuit all the time as more precise readings are obtained from the loop alone.)

Always use a portable RDF set from the same position on the boat; a change in location may require a completely new deviation table. As an RDF contains strong magnets in the speaker and meter, be sure to keep it at least several feet away from the boat's compass, both while in and out of use.

How to Take a Radio Bearing

To take a radio bearing, follow these steps:

1. Set the scale built into the set, usually around the base of the antenna, so that 000° is dead ahead.

2. Rotate the directional antenna (fig. 2610) until a null point is precisely located, read the angle from the scale; this is the uncorrected relative radio bearing. Caution: the boat must be directly on course at the moment that the

FIG. 2612 Boat shown here could determine position by bearings on any two radiobeacons at "1", "2" and "3". Better fix would be obtained by using all three beacons.

bearing is taken as any error in heading will be reflected in the resultant radio bearing.

3. If there is any doubt as to whether the reading just taken is the direct or reciprocal bearing, use the sense antenna to identify it. If the reading is the reciprocal, do *not* add or subtract 180°, take a new bearing.

4. Having determined the direct bearing angle, apply the proper deviation correction; the sum is the corrected relative radio bearing.

5. Add the boat's *true* heading, subtracting 360° if the sum exceeds that amount; this is now the true radio bearing from the boat, plot in the same manner as a visual bearing.

The above steps outline in basic terms the correct procedures to be followed in taking a radio bearing. In the use of any particular RDF set, however, the manufacturer's manual should be studied and the instructions followed closely.

Some specialized RDF models combine the radio direction finder with an integral compass. The entire unit is made with a "pistol grip" handle and is held to the eye and "aimed" at the source of radio signals. Direct radio bearings are read in terms of compass direction, but care must be taken for both radio and compass deviation.

Plotting the Radio Bearing

If the transmitting station is more than 200 miles (370 km) away, and the plotting is to be done on a Mercator chart, a further correction is required because the great circle path along which radio waves travel does not plot as a straight line on this type of chart. The amount of correction, and the procedure for applying it, can be found in Table 1 of Bowditch, or in any Coast Pilot.

Radio bearings are plotted in the same manner as visual bearings, and the use of an RDF requires the same degree of piloting knowledge and plotting skill. Radio bearings do not have as high a degree of precision as visual bearings, and for this reason a three-bearing fix is desirable. See fig. 2612. The best probable accuracy for radio bearings is on the order of plus or minus 2°, and some experience and practice are required to reach this precision. In situations

involving close proximity to dangerous waters, a careful navigator will draw additional lines 2° to either side of the corrected bearing; these will indicate graphically the probable limits of his position. See fig. 2613.

Position-finding by Radio Bearings

Radio bearings can also be used in any of the other forms of position plotting—bow and beam bearings, doubling the angle, danger angles, etc. If only a single radio bearing can be obtained, it is possible to combine this with a visual bearing, an astronomical line of position, or a depth reading to determine an estimated position. Remember that this EP will be no better than the accuracy of the poorest method used, and navigate accordingly.

In order to ensure the most accurate position from radio bearings:

1. Take bearings from as strong signals as possible.

2. Use the low frequency band in preference to higher frequencies.

3. Avoid taking bearings on radio stations located inland, particularly those behind coastal hills or mountains.

4. Take three or more bearings on different stations if possible; make sure that you identify the station correctly and know the location of the transmitting antenna.

5. Take bearings so that the intersection angle is at least 30°, preferably 90° for two-station fixes or 60° for three-station fixes.

More on position finding with RDF bearings will be found in Chapter 21.

Factors Affecting Accuracy

There are two circumstances which tend to degrade the accuracy of radio bearings. "Night effect" is the term applied to the fact that all radio bearings taken at night, but particularly those made near sunset and sunrise, show a broader and sometimes shifting null. This makes less precise any bearing taken at these times, and efforts should be made to take bearings under these conditions only on stations less than 30 to 40 miles (50 to 70 km) distant. If this is not possible, the next best procedure is to take a series of readings on each station and average them for a mean reading—but still consider the accuracy to be less than that of a reading taken in the daytime.

The second special circumstance of lessened accuracy comes into effect when the radio waves travel approximately parallel to a coastline for any appreciable portion of the distance from the transmitting station to the RDF. There is a bending effect on the signals which can be as much as 10°, pulling the waves in toward the land. Fortunately, the effect is to make the boat appear closer to land than it actually is.

Homing with an RDF

In addition to determination of the position of a boat, an RDF can be used in several other interesting ways. When the directional antenna is set on 000° relative, the craft may be directed toward a radio station by steering so as to keep the signal strength at the deepest point of the null. One RDF model has a direct-reading meter which shows the helmsman whether he is to the right or left of his course. This homing procedure provides a simple navigational technique for getting into port when visibility conditions are bad or other navigational aids are not avail-

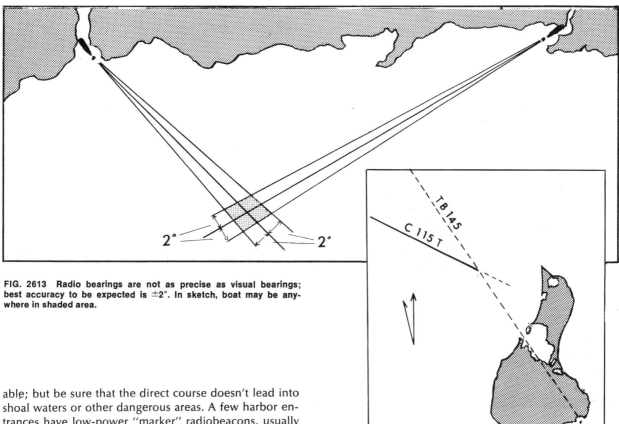

FIG. 2613 Radio bearings are not as precise as visual bearings; best accuracy to be expected is ±2°. In sketch, boat may be anywhere in shaded area.

able; but be sure that the direct course doesn't lead into shoal waters or other dangerous areas. A few harbor entrances have low-power "marker" radiobeacons, usually at the outer end of a jetty if one exists.

Homing also makes possible the steering of a boat on the most direct course to the scene of a distress situation. Such an application normally makes use of signals in the 2-3 MHz marine communications band. Here the accuracy of radio bearings is less than on lower frequency bands, but the homing process works satisfactorily because the signal strength gets stronger as the source is approached. Caution must be exercised not to run directly into the source of the signals (this may seem like rather obvious advice, but it has happened!).

Use and Care of an RDF

Throughout any consideration of the purchase, installation, and use of a radio direction finder, it must be remembered that such an item of electronic equipment is first of all a safety device. Any other planned use, such as an auxiliary receiver, is a bonus feature only, and must not be allowed to detract from readiness for its primary use when needed. Most portable RDFs are powered by small drycell ("flashlight") batteries; many models have a switch position for the null meter so that battery strength may be checked at any time. It is advisable to carry a set of spare batteries on cruises to guard against the possibility of loss of RDF capability should the unit be accidentally left on for an extended period of time. Batteries should be replaced annually, whether indicated or not, to ensure freshness and adequate life when needed.

An RDF should be used often in periods of good visibility so as to gain familiarity with its operation under circumstances permitting visual checks on the radio bearings which are obtained. Frequent practice reduces the personal error component of the total error in radio bearings,

FIG. 2614 From his chart, a skipper notes that a bearing of 145° on Southeast Pt., Block Island, will bring him safely to Great Salt Pond. He holds his 115° heading, taking frequent radio bearings. When they increase to 145°, he changes course and homes on signal to entrance buoy.

thus improving the overall accuracy. If these procedures are followed, there is every reason for a boat owner to trust his RDF to bring him safely into port under any conditions of visibility.

Automatic Radio Direction Finders

An automatic radio direction finder (ADF) indicates on a dial the direction to a transmitter once it has been tuned in—no swinging of a loop, no 180° ambiguity.

ADFs cover the same frequency bands as manual RDFs and use the same types of transmitting stations. They are, of course, more complex in circuitry and thus more expensive. The antenna is continuously rotated, either mechanically or electronically, whenever the set is turned on. Often such equipment is a fixed installation with a remote antenna, but portable models are available.

The advantages of ADFs lie in their ease and speed of operation. They are, however, subject to the same radio deviation as manual RDFs and a correction table must be prepared.

VHF radio direction finding

Direction finders for VHF are all of the automatic (ADF) type. Most models are self-contained, complete units, but

Courtesy of Ray Jefferson

FIG. 2615 Direction finders for VHF signals are of the automatic type. They require a special antenna and yield about the same accuracies as those used on lower frequencies.

a few are designed to function with a VHF radio used for communications. All VHF direction finders require a separate special antenna, and all are several times more expensive than LF-MF models. Most units hold crystals for 8 to 12 channels and some can be additionally used as scanners.

The indication of direction may be by a pointer rotating around a dial (as used by many ADFs for the LF and MF bands), by a pattern on a cathode-ray tube, or by a direct-reading digital display; one simplified model can only be used for homing and gives a left-right indication by the needle on a meter. The accuracy of VHF radio bearings is approximately the same as on the lower frequencies.

The Coast Guard does not operate any radiobeacons on the VHF band, but the continuous transmissions of the NOAA weather stations provide a good signal for determination of a line of position; the range would be the same as in regular reception of weather information. This will normally provide only one LOP, but in limited areas it may be possible to receive two weather stations and thus get a fix. The usual applications, however, of a VHF direction finder will be for homing or for taking bearings on ship or shore stations transmitting by request for DF-ing.

Radar

Radar is an excellent means of marine navigation and it is used on vessels of all sizes down to boats of about 30 feet (9.1 m) length. Although space and cost limit its use on recreational boats, its capabilities and limitations should be known to all boatmen for their own safety when cruising on waters navigated by radar-equipped vessels.

Radar Principles

A radar set sends out brief pulses of super-high frequency radio waves that are reflected by objects at a distance. The time that it takes for the pulse to go out and the echo to return is a measure of the distance to the reflecting object. See fig. 2616. In broad principles, this is the same technique as previously described for depth sounders, except that transmission is through air rather than water, and radio waves have been substituted for ultrasonic pulses. A refinement has been made in that the radar

pulses are sent out in a very narrow beam which can be pointed in any direction around the horizon and used to determine direction as well as distance.

Components of a Radar Set

The major components of a radar set are:

1. The *transmitter* which generates the radio waves; it includes the *modulator* which causes the energy to be sent out in brief pulses.

2. The *antenna* which radiates the pulses and collects the returning echoes. The antenna is highly directional in its horizontal characteristics, but 8 to 10 times wider vertically. The beam pattern can be thought of as being like a fan turned up on edge. The beam's narrow horizontal directivity gives it a fairly good angle-measuring capability, while its broadness in the vertical plane helps keep the

FIG. 2616 A marine radar set operates by sending brief pulses of super high frequency radio waves, reflected back by other ships, navigational aids and land masses. Sketch shows pulse traveling outward and echo returning. Speed is so great echoes are received before next pulse is transmitted.

FIG. 2617 Most radars have two major sections. Shown are the antenna and upper electronics unit, and the receiver. Antenna must be mounted high to have a clear "look" in all directions.

FIG. 2618 Marine radars present information on ships, buoys, shorelines, etc., as patches of light on face of PPI scope. Radar-equipped boat is at center of scope.

beam on an object despite any rolling or pitching of the vessel. The antenna may be exposed as shown in fig. 2617 or covered by a plastic *radome* which is transparent to radar waves; never paint a radome except in accordance with the manufacturer's instructions. An exposed antenna is generally somewhat larger than one in a radome with a resultant narrower beam and slightly better resolution in bearings. A radar antenna on a boat should be located so that no person is in line with the radiated energy and close to the antenna, so as to avoid any possible health hazard.

3. The *receiver* which detects the returned reflections and amplifies them to a usable strength.

4. The *indicator* which provides a visual display of objects sending back reflections.

Radars operate at frequencies far above the usual radio communications bands. At such super-high frequencies, radar pulses act much like light waves in that they travel in essentially straight lines. They travel at the speed of light, 186,000 miles per second. For each nautical mile of distance to the target, only a fraction more than 12 microseconds are required for the round-trip of the outgoing pulse and the returned echo.* Pulses, each of which lasts for only a fraction of a microsecond, (one millionth of a second) are sent out at a rate of from 600 to 4000 each second depending upon the design of the equipment. The directional antenna rotates at a rate of one revolution in about 2 to 4 seconds. The round-trip time for a pulse is so short that the antenna has not appreciably moved before the reflection is returned.

The Plan Position Indicator (PPI)

Marine navigational radars use a Plan Position Indicator (PPI) type of display. A circular cathode ray tube of a spe-

cial type from 5 to 20 inches (12.77 to 50.8 cm) in diameter is used, see figure 2618; smaller scopes may have a magnifying lens added. The center of the face represents the position of the radar-equipped vessel and the presentation is roughly like a navigational chart.

A bright radial line on the face of the tube represents the radar beam; it rotates in synchronism with the antenna. Reflections show up as points or patches of light depending upon the size of the echo-producing object. The persistence of the screen is such that the points and patches of light do not completely fade out before the antenna has made another rotation and they are restored to brilliance. Thus the picture on the radarscope is repainted every few seconds.

Radar Range Scales

The relative bearing of an object is indicated directly on the screen; a position corresponding to the "12" on a clock face is directly ahead. The distance to the object is proportional to the distance from the center of the screen to the point of light which is the echo. On most radars, concentric circles of light are used as range markers to make the estimation of distances both easier and more accurate. All radar sets have multiple range scales which may be selected to suit the purpose for which the radar is being used. Longer range scales provide coverage of greater areas, but at a cost of less detail and poorer definition. Typical ranges for a small-craft radar might be ½, 1, 2, 4, 8, and 16 miles.

Radar sets have both a maximum and a minimum range, each of which is of importance in the operation of the equipment. The maximum range is determined by the transmitter power and the receiver sensitivity, provided, of course, that the antenna is at a sufficient height above

*In metric terms, the speed of light is 300,000 km/s. and the roundtrip time for a pulse is 7.46 microseconds/km.

FIG. 2619 Maximum range of radar set on small craft is more likely to be limited by antenna height than by transmitter power. Radar waves bend slightly but distance to radar horizon is only 7% greater than to optical horizon.

FIG. 2620a

FIG. 2620b

FIG. 2620a Radar fix may be obtained from single object, using both distance and bearing measurements. Navigator must be sure he has correctly identified object both on radar scope and chart.

FIG. 2620b Getting navigational fix by plotting distance to two identifiable objects as measured by radar. Radar measurement of distance provide more accurate fix than do radar bearings. Ranges to more than two objects are desirable.

FIG. 2621 For greatest benefit, radar information must be plotted. Here two successive measurements of bearing and range of a fixed point on shore provide data to plot track and speed made good by radar-equipped boat. Track can be projected ahead to give estimated time of arrival (ETA) at any point. Effect of currents may be determined by comparison of heading and slack-water speed with track and speed made good.

water that the range is not limited by the distance to the horizon. See fig. 2619 (The radar pulses normally travel with just a slight amount of bending; thus the radar horizon is about 7% farther away than the visual horizon.)

Because a radar pulse has a definite duration, and therefore occupies a definite length in space as it moves outward from the antenna, there is a minimum range within which objects cannot be detected. This minimum range, usually between 20 and 50 yards (18 to 46 m), is important when maneuvering in close quarters, as when passing buoys at the side of a narrow channel.

Radar sets are rated in terms of peak pulse power; for boats, sets will generally be 3-10 kw. The average power consumption from the craft's electrical system is, of course, much less, 50-250 watts.

Units for Small Craft

Radar sets for small craft usually consist of two units. Modern design of the components makes it possible to combine the antenna, transmitter, and a portion of the receiver into a single unit installed on a mast or on the pilothouse. This unit, usually 35 to 100 pounds (15.9 to

45.4 kg) should be located as high as practicable. Not too much is gained by increasing the height of a boat's radar antenna by just a few feet, and attention must be given to any stability problems that may arise. Radar "targets" that will be of interest at distances approaching the horizon will be large ships or land masses, both of which will be considerably above the line-of-sight horizon. The antenna should have an unobstructed "look" in all directions. The remainder of the receiver and the indicator are located near the helmsman's position. Some indicator units are so small that they may be fitted into a pilot-house in any number of positions.

Because radar sets radiate radio frequency energy, they must be licensed by the FCC, but this is not difficult to do for commercially produced equipment. No license is required to operate a radar, but for its installation and maintenance, the technician must have a second- or first-class radio operator's license with a special "ship radar" endorsement. The owner and station licensee of a marine radar installation is responsible that only a properly licensed individual does all of the technical work on the equipment.

Principal Applications

Radars have two principal applications aboard ships and small craft. They are often thought of primarily as anticollision devices, but are even more often used to assist in the piloting of the vessel.

Radar was originally conceived for the detection and tracking of ships and aircraft. It offers an excellent means of extending the coverage of a visual lookout, especially at night and under conditions of reduced visibility. This greater range of detection affords more time for a ship to maneuver to avoid another vessel or an obstacle. With a radar plot, an early determination can be made of the other vessel's course and speed.

Radar also provides valuable assistance in the piloting of a vessel making a landfall when returning from offshore; running down a coast, picking up landmarks for fixes; or traveling in confined waters, entering an inlet, and the like. Radar has real advantages even in the daytime, and, of course, becomes particularly helpful at night or in fog, or other circumstances of reduced visibility.

Fixes by Radar

The daytime advantages of radar stem from its ability to measure distance. Often a landmark or navigation aid can be seen and a visual bearing easily obtained. If, however, only one such object can be seen, only a single line of position is obtained and a fix is not possible. With a measurement of distance by radar, a fix becomes possible. See fig. 2620a. The bearing could have been made by radar simultaneously with the range measurement, but a visual bearing is more precise and should be used if possible. The capability of getting a fix from a single object is often of great importance to the navigator.

Fixes may also be obtained in low visibility situations—from a single radar bearing and range measurement, from crossed bearings (but this is not too accurate due to the finite width of the radar beam), and preferably from distance measurements to two or more points that can be identified on both the radar screen and the chart, fig. 2620b. More than two ranges or bearings should be taken and plotted to prevent the possibility of a false fix which might occur if one of the echoes on the scope were incorrectly identified. In all cases, the use of radar lines of position and fixes is the same as for visual plotting, giving due consideration to the lesser accuracy of bearing information.

Coastline Pictures on the PPI

The use of radar to determine a vessel's approximate position from observation of the presentation of a coastline on a radarscope is not a safe procedure. The image seen on the PPI will often vary appreciably from the appearance of a chart. This is true despite some widely publicized photographs of radar screens showing such distinctive patterns as New York harbor appearing nearly identical with the actual scene. Because the radar beam, as narrow (1° to 4°) as it is, does have a finite width, and because the pulse, as brief (0.1 to 0.5 microsecond) as it is, does have a definite length in space, the picture on a radar PPI scope is not an exact replica of the land area or other object returning the echoes. Normally, radar echoes will be returned from buildings, hills, etc., some distance inland from the shorelines shown on charts.

Passive Radar Reflectors

A boat owner who does not have radar can still increase his safety—he can equip his craft with a *passive radar reflector*; see fig. 2622. This simple, inexpensive item consists of thin metal sheets or fine-mesh screening arranged in mutually perpendicular planes. These may fold for storage, but must be flat and rigid with respect to each other when open for use. A reflector with each surface only about two feet (60 cm) square can provide a strong return signal if properly used. The echo from a wooden or fiberglass boat is so weak as to be easily overlooked if no reflector is used. For maximum effectiveness, it should be hoisted from three corners so that one of the eight "pockets" is straight down; this is sometimes termed the "rain catching" position. With a reflector hoisted as high as possible, a skipper can be more sure that his craft will be detected on the radars of passing

FIG. 2622 In waters frequented by radar-equipped ships, every boatman should use a passive radar reflector. It makes the boat's echo many times brighter on scope of ship using only radar as its "eyes."

ships. Coast Guard vessels, and often other rescue craft, searching for a boat in distress are radar-equipped; the proper use of a passive radar reflector will greatly increase the chances of being quickly spotted.

Radionavigation Systems

There are a number of radionavigation systems that are available to skippers of offshore cruising and fishing boats as well as to navigators of larger ships. These vary in degree of complexity and cost of receiving equipment. Many boatmen will probably never use any of them personally, but it is desirable to have a general familiarity with their method of operation, and their advantages and disadvantages.

The radionavigation system most widely used by boatmen in U.S. waters is *Loran-C.* Another system is *Omega*, now operational with nearly global coverage.

Decca is a short-range, high-frequency radionavigation system that is available only in limited areas; it is more widely used in Europe than North America. Decca is unique in that in the United States it is commercially operated, rather than by a government agency.

VHF Omnirange (VOR for short), a VHF aeronautical navigation system that is useful to high-altitude aircraft at a range of hundreds of miles from the transmitting antenna, is a line-of-sight system. It is sometimes used by boats, but at sea level its useful range is limited to a few tens of miles from the transmitting antenna.

Satellite navigation is becoming more widely used by ocean-cruising boats as the cost of receivers steadily declines. The NavSat, or Transit, system has been operational for many years. The more advanced NavStar, or GPS, system is still under development and test, with a scheduled availability date of the later 1980s.

LORAN

Loran—the name is derived from LOng RAnge Navigation—is an electronic system using shore-based radio transmitters and shipboard receivers to allow mariners to determine their position at sea. Loran works in all kinds of weather, 24 hours a day.

The original form of this electronic navigation system, *Loran-A*, was developed during World War II for military applications. At the conclusion of that war the Coast Guard was operating 70 transmitting stations; by 1971 the number had grown to 83. By the early 1970s, however, advances in electronic technology had made possible an improved system. The Loran-A transmitters were beginning to "show their age" and a decision was made to change to the newer *Loran-C*. The Loran-A system has now been phased out in U.S. waters, although operation continues in the northwest Pacific Ocean in the general area of Japan.

Loran-C

The transmitters of Loran-C all operate on 100 kHz in *chains* of a *master station* (M) plus two to four *secondary* stations designated as W, X, Y, and Z. Each station transmits groups of pulses on the same frequency; signals from secondaries follow those from the master station at very precise time intervals. Chains are identified by their individual pulse group repetition intervals (GRI). All Loran-C transmitters are frequency and time stabilized by atomic standards; if, however, the signals of a pair should get out of tolerance, the chain will "blink" in a code that indicates the nature of the trouble.

The *difference* in the time of arrival at the receiver of pulse groups from the master and each secondary is measured very precisely by electronic circuitry, and this information is used to determine a line of position. The use of two, or more, master-secondary pairs of signals yields the same number of LOPs and thus a Loran-C fix.

Loran-C has a groundwave (most reliable) range of up to 1200 miles (2200 km), with skywave reception out to as far as 3000 miles (5600 km). The accuracy of Loran-C positions from groundwave signals varies from 0.1 to 0.25 miles (0.2 to 0.5 km) depending upon where the receiver is in the coverage area; positional errors on skywave signals may be as much as eight times greater. A significant feature of Loran-C is the "repeatability" of positions obtained with this system. Groundwave signals are very stable and a boat should be able to return to a prior position within 50 to 200 feet (15–60m).

As of mid-1981, there were 41 Loran-C stations operating in 13 chains. Basic groundwave coverage exists for the U.S. and Canadian Atlantic and Pacific Coasts, the upper North Atlantic Ocean, the Mediterranean Sea, and small areas in the North Pacific west of Hawaii and south of Japan. Reception of skywave signals extends these coverage areas, but at lessened positioning accuracy.

Loran-C receivers

Essentially all Loran-C receivers now marketed automatically acquire and track the signals from the chain to which the set is tuned. The system is complex, but such complexity is handled internally by advanced solid-state circuits—all the operator has to do is turn the set on and tune to the proper GRI. (The coverage of a single chain is quite great and many boats will never need to change the GRI setting.) The Loran-C receiver will take several minutes to "settle down" and give steady readings; then the operator has merely to read out the measured time differences and use this information to plot his position on a chart that has been overprinted with Loran-C lines of position.

Loran-C charts are at a scale of 1:80,000 or smaller—charts in the coastal and sailing series (see Chapter 18). Loran-C lines are not placed on harbor charts—scales of 1:40,000 and larger—as the accuracy of this system is

FIG. 2623 Portion of N.O.S. chart 11424 showing sets of Loran-C lines of position —in different colors for each set. Although position can be determined from Loran tables, direct plotting on a chart is the simplest and quickest way of getting a fix. Generally similar charts showing Omega lines of position are published by the Defense Mapping Agency Hydrographic/Topographic Center.

FIG. 2625 Some Loran-C receivers feature automatic signal aquisition and tracking with cycle matching. The model shown here can provide up to four lines of position, displaying the readngs sequentially on a digital readout.

not sufficient for navigation down a channel or in close proximity to hazards. A prudent skipper, however, can, and should, record Loran-C readings at points of specific interest on harbor charts and take full advantage of the excellent capability of repeatability. A series of such points could describe the desired track from harbor entrance to home berth, and would be very valuable under conditions of reduced visibility.

When charts were first overprinted with Loran-C lines, the positioning of such lines was based on theoretical radio propagation conditions. It was soon found, however, that often these lines were not accurately placed, although as a whole they were correctly drawn with respect to each other. As field experience is gained, subsequent chart editions are published with the pattern of lines shifted so as to reflect the actual time delays encountered. (Positions can be plotted on charts without Loran-C lines by use of "lattice tables" but this cumbersome process is seldom used.) Commercial fishermen often use Loran readings only for positions without the use of latitude and longitude, or even charts at all!

The simplest Loran-C receivers have only a single display of time differences; readings of various station-pairs are shown sequentially at about two-second intervals. Many sets, however, have two displays allowing for a simultaneous readout of the two time differences required for a fix; at least one manufacturer has a model with three displays. Often a receiver will make measurements on three or four station-pairs with these additional readings being displayed sequentially.

More expensive Loran-C receivers include a microprocessor that provides a direct readout in latitude and longitude, plus direction and distance to a pre-set destination; also speed along the track, cross-track error, time to go, and even a destination arrival signal when almost there. Some caution must be used with Loran-C sets that give position in latitude and longitude as their computations are based on theoretic propagation conditions and actual conditions may often be different.

Loran-C receivers are subject to interference from other signals on nearby frequencies. Such unwanted noise can seriously degrade the receiver's performance, or even make time difference measurements impossible. This interference is eliminated by "notch filters" sharply tuned to the unwanted signals. Loran-C receivers will have from two to four such filters; these may be factory-tuned or operator-tunable, or a combination of both. The number and type of such filters needed will depend upon the interference conditions in the area(s) in which the receiver is used. In general, a combination of two preset (internally tuned) and two front-panel, operator adjustable filters will provide excellent interference protection and adequate flexibility even if cruising from one area to another.

The latest development in Loran navigation is an "interface unit" that permits positional information from a Loran-C receiver, converted in most cases to cross-track error, to be fed to the craft's autopilot with the result that she is brought back onto the intended track. The nearly continuous flow of these corrective signals causes the boat to automatically "crab into" any offsetting current. For a number of decades, autopilots have taken the tedium out of manual steering in fair weather and foul, but the problem has always been that these automatic units were *not* truly "piloting" the craft, only maintaining a heading calculated and inserted into it by the skipper. If the boat was set off-course due to any reason, no corrective action was taken until the human pilot detected the error, recalculated the course, and changed the setting of the autopilot. Now electronic wizardry has made possible the elimination of these manual steps with a flow of data from a Loran-C receiver into the craft's autopilot. Cross-track errors of only a few hundred feet, or less, can be sensed and corrective instructions generated. One model of Loran/autopilot interfac operates in a slightly different manner—here the "electronic brain" senses any difference in the direction to the preset destination from the craft's actual position and from where she would be if on-course at that time.) Interface units include delay times to "smooth" the flow of data and make course changes more gradual.

Also available are Loran-C *plotters*. These draw a trace on a chart using data from the receiver—you can see your course and speed made good as you go along.

OMEGA

The *Omega* electronic navigation system uses very low frequency (VLF) radio waves; four different frequencies from 10.2 to 13.6 kHz are used. Such VLF signals have considerable range and stability over day and night paths. An advantage of the system is that complete global coverage can be obtained by the use of only six transmitters properly situated. Ideally, stations would be located at the North and South Poles and 90° apart on the Equator; such a requirement must, of course, be modified to meet practical considerations. In actual practice, the Omega network will have eight transmitting sites to allow for possible equipment failures and off-air time for routine maintenance. The transmitters are located approximately 6,000 miles apart and at any point signals from at least four stations wil be usable. As the global network of stations is established, transmitters will be operated by the U.S. (by USCG personnel) and by foreign nations.

The Omega system

The Omega system was originally developed by the U.S. Navy for its submarines, surfaced or submerged (VLF signals can be received while under water), as well as for surface vessels and aircraft. Receiving equipment is now available, however, for civilian ships and aircraft, including fishing and recreational boats. Omega equipment is now quite expensive, but advancing technology and increased production can be expected to bring price reductions.

Omega fixes

Omega stations transmit continuous-wave signals, rather than pulses, for approximately one second out of every ten seconds on each frequency used. Signals from a single pair of stations on a single frequency can furnish a hyperbolic line of position, but rough position knowledge is required to within about four miles to identify the set of lines, called a "lane," within which the receiver is located. Use of a second frequency reduces the need for position knowledge to 12 miles, and use of a third frequency extends this to 36 miles, and the fourth to 144 miles.

Two or more lines of position are combined in the normal manner to obtain an Omega fix. Station pairs should be selected so as to get lines crossing at large angles, as near 90° as possible for two lines, or 60° for three lines. As with Loran, special charts are used with over-printed Omega lines of position. Receivers have "lane counters" to keep a record of the number of lanes crossed since the counter was re-set after a fix was established, and so lessen the problem of lane identification. More expensive models of receivers can internally compute and display position directly in latitude and longitude.

Omega signals are affected by sky-wave propagation conditions and it is necessary to refer to published correction tables in the use of this system. The nominal all-

FIG. 2626 The VLH signals of the Omega navigation system now cover almost the entire world, providing fixes of good accuracy for vessels on the high seas. Receiver outputs show either lines of position or direct readouts in latitude and longitude.

weather accuracy is one mile in the daytime and two miles at night. Special techniques are available within local areas for increased degree of precision in position fixing, this is known as *Differential Omega*, and is useful for high-accuracy work such as surveys.

The signals from Omega transmitters are controlled by atomic frequency standards and can be used for adjusting or calibrating less accurate frequency standards; these signals can also be used for highly accurate time data.

The Omega Navigation System has become operational in stages. In January 1981 seven of the eight stations were transmitting at 10 kilowatts on all four navigational frequencies plus each on its own unique frequency. The final station, Australia, is due on the air in mid-1981; this will provide improved coverage for the North and South Pacific and Indian Oceans.

Automatic Steering Devices

Automatic steering devices are electrical or electro-hydraulic equipment used to hold a boat on a predetermined heading. They are often, but erroneously, referred to as "automatic pilots"; they do no part of the piloting of a boat.

In lieu of the direct application of human muscle power to the steering mechanism of a boat, electric or hydraulic motors may be used to move the rudder to the desired angle and to hold it there. See fig. 2627. The control of these motors may be made automatic by the addition of a direction-sensing element and suitable electronic amplifiers. Either magnetic or gyroscopic compasses can be used to sense heading changes, but the former is nearly always used because of its lower cost.

Most automatic steering devices have controls which allow temporary manual over-riding of the automatic controls with the boat returning to the preset heading when the over-ride switch is released. This permits brief course changes to avoid obstructions or other boats without having to reset the desired heading. Local control boxes on long cords make possible the maneuvering of the boat while away from the normal helm position. This control of

FIG. 2627 Automatic steering mechanism can do better job than human helmsman! Components are shown—magnetic compass with sensing attachments, electronic amplifier, steering motor, and control boxes.

the craft, however, does not include throttle changes or forward-reverse shifting.

The latest designs of automatic pilots are described as

"nonhunting proportional rate." Corrections are applied immediately whenever the boat strays off the set heading, but small errors are corrected gently and large errors are corrected vigorously. The correction of errors in proportion to the speed and amount of error results in smooth steering action, eliminating overcorrection or "overshooting" across the correct heading to an opposite error.

The use of automatic steering devices is simple. They do much to relieve boredom and fatigue on long, straight stretches. The device can, under most circumstances, steer a straighter course than a human helmsman. The disadvantage in this equipment lies in its misuse, excessive reliance on the device and failure to keep a person at the helm as a lookout ready to take over immediately if a dangerous situation should develop. It must also be remembered that the sensing element is usually no more "intelligent" than a magnetic compass; it is subject to all of the same outside corrupting influences such as tools, portable radios, beer cans, etc., if they are placed too close.

Miscellaneous Electronic Equipment

There are many small items of electronic equipment that can be installed on a boat for the greater safety and convenience of the owner and his guests. The boatman should consider each for possible installation on his craft, not forgetting that each item will usually add a bit to the load on the battery and electrical wiring.

EMERGENCY POSITION INDICATING RADIOBEACONS (EPIRB)

Every boat that goes offshore beyond reliable VHF radio range, roughly 20 miles, should carry a Class A or Class B *Emergency Position Indicating Radiobeacon* (EPIRB). This small device transmits a distinctive tone signal on two *aircraft* frequencies—121.5 MHz, the emergency channel of civil aviation, and 243.0 MHz, the "guard" channel for military aircraft. This signal serves first to alert passing aircraft that an emergency exists and later to guide searchers to the scene of distress. The transmitter is not powerful—a fraction of one watt—but its signals can usually be heard out to as far as 200 miles by high-flying aircraft. Coast Guard planes are equipped with automatic direction finders for the EPIRB frequencies.

EPIRBs are battery-powered and must operate continuously with rated power for at least 48 hours (many will operate for as long as a week); the battery must be dated as to when it was manufactured and when it must be replaced (50% of life remaining). The transmitter must be completely transistorized and suitable for storage in a marine environment over a long period of time.

Class A EPIRBS are for certain types of vessels on which they must, by law, be carried. The less-expensive Class B model is for voluntary carriage by other craft, such as all recreational boats. The simpler design need not be capable of floating by itself, but a floatation collar is usually added if the unit is not buoyant; this type of EPIRB can be activated either manually or automatically upon floating in the water. A Class A EPIRB must be capable of floating free from a sinking vessel and activating automatically, including extending its antenna from the stored position.

EPIRBs have a test switch so that readiness for use can be ascertained. This must be done only under certain conditions and at specified times. Every effort must be made to avoid "false alarms."

EPIRBs for recreational boats are available for less than $200; they are an essential safety item for any boat going offshore. There is no guarantee that the signal will be picked up and the authorities notified; many aircraft monitor 121.5 or 243.0 MHz, but this is not required by law or regulation. Many actual cases, however, have occurred where an EPIRB was the direct and only means of getting assistance to the survivors of a sunken boat. As these devices send out radio waves, they must be licensed; this is easily done by modification of the radio station license (if no other radio is licensed on the boat, a separate EPIRB license must be obtained).

FIG. 2628 An Emergency Position Indicating Radiobeacon (EPIRB) transmits a continuous signal on two aircraft emergency frequencies. For boats offshore beyond VHF communications range, it can be essential for alerting authorities to a distress situation and for guiding search and rescue efforts.

FIG. 2629 Fuel vapor detector, properly installed and used, will warn of explosive vapors in bilge. Models are available with audible alarm and visual indicator.

FIG. 2631 Inverters can change DC electrical power of boat's batteries to 115-volts AC for operation of shore-type electrical equipment, up to a few hundred watts. For heavier loads, install auxiliary electric plant driven by its own gasoline or diesel engine. (Diagram from Technical Bulletin T-021, Installation of Onan Marine Generating Plants.)

FIG. 2630 Boat batteries are normally charged by generator or alternator-driven by main engine. At dockside, marine converter keeps batteries up by converting shoreside AC power to DC at proper voltage for boat's electrical system.

Class C EPIRBs

A new and different type of Emergency Position Indicating Radiobeacon was authorized in 1979 and became available in 1981. These are the Class "C" units, operating on different frequencies and intended for use in *coastal* waters out to roughly 20 miles from shore—this is the area covered by Coast Guard and other VHF shore stations.

A Class C EPIRB operates on VHF Channels 16 and 15, transmitting the radiotelephone alarm signal (see page 501). A very brief alerting transmission is made on Channel 16—on this channel because it is the one monitored by the Coast Guard and by ship and shore stations, brief so as to not interfere with essential communications on this frequency. The alarm signal is then transmitted at greater length on Channel 15 for verification and possible use for direction finding. A complex cycle of transmissions on these two channels, plus periods of no signal, continues automatically for 24 hours after which the EPIRB goes silent unless the activation switch is again manually operated.

Class C EPIRBs are generally similar in appearance and design to the previously-authorized Class A and B units described above with respect to size, weight, solid-state circuitry, power source, floatability, antenna, etc. It is intended by the FCC and Coast Guard that Class C EPIRBs be available at a low-enough cost that they will be carried by many smaller boats not equipped with two-way VHF radios. (If carried on a radio-equipped boat that set must first be used in an attempt to get assistance *before* the EPIRB is activated.) The Class C units do not duplicate the operational use of Class A and B EPIRBs, and it would not be redundant to carry both. If the boat has no radio station license, one must be obtained as the Class C EPIRB is an active radio transmitter.

FUEL VAPOR DETECTORS

A *fuel vapor detector* is considered by many boatmen to be an essential piece of safety equipment aboard any craft using gasoline as fuel. See fig. 2629. These devices provide a visual warning of the build-up of any dangerous concentration of fuel vapors in the bilges. Frequently, such a device also provides an audible alarm in addition to the visual warning. It should be remembered, however, that these units are *not an absolutely positive* means of warning of a hazardous condition, they are not as infallible as the human nose. In case of doubt, open the hatches and use your nose, it is the best "bilge sniffer" of them all.

Fuel vapor detectors are available in several designs, each with their good points and their disadvantages. These include the hot wire, cold sensors, and semiconductor types of detector units. Price is not a factor between these types, and a choice should be made on the general features and suitability for your particular installation.

The installation of a fuel vapor detector is not difficult electrically or mechanically, but it is essential that it be done correctly. The location of the detector unit is important if the maximum safety benefit is to be obtained. Have your installation checked by a surveyor or safety inspector from your insurance company. Even the best fuel vapor detector is no substitute for electric bilge blowers, forced ventilation fans that pull air and fumes out of the lower parts of your boat's interior.

MARINE CONVERTERS

The growing use of electrical equipment on boats has resulted in a steadily increasing demand for power from the craft's batteries. The generator or alternator on the boat's engine will suffice to keep the batteries charged if the engine is operated a large enough percentage of the time that the electrical equipment is in use. There is no way to state a general figure as to what proportion of the time is required as individual conditions will vary too widely.

If you are one of the boat owners who finds that all too often his battery is down so far that it won't start the engine, then you are a candidate for a *marine converter*. See fig. 2630. This relatively simple electrical device converts the 115-volt AC dockside electricity into the 6, 12, or 32 volts DC required for the boat's electrical system. It is essentially a continuous-duty battery-charger with control circuits to permit it to operate safely left unattended.

INVERTERS

It may seem a bit contradictory to immediately discuss a means of getting 115-volt AC electrical power from the boat's low voltage DC system just after having considered the reverse process, but there is a reason. There is no way to store AC in a battery, and if AC is needed when away from the shore, the only means of getting it (without installing an auxiliary generating plant) is to "invert" the DC power from the batteries into AC.

Alternating current aboard a boat of any size is useful for the powering of television or hi-fi sets, tape recorders, electric razors, electric mixers or other small household appliances. Small transistorized inverters are available that can quietly and efficienctly supply small or moderate amounts of "shore-type" electrical power. These DC to AC inverters are *not* suitable for use with those electrical devices whose function is to produce heat, such as toasters and irons; the power required for such items is beyond the capacity of inverters.

AUXILIARY GENERATING PLANTS

Solid-state inverters are usually limited to continuous output power ratings of 500 to 1000 watts, with briefly higher loads possible for starting electrical motors; at these outputs a considerable drain is placed on a boat's 12- or 32-volt batteries. If greater amounts of 115-volt AC power are required for cooking, heating, air conditioning, etc., the installation of a small auxiliary generating plant should be considered. See fig. 2631. These units are available in sizes from 500 watts to 10 kilowatts or more, with either gasoline or diesel engines to match the type of fuel used in the main engines.

Calculation of the size of generator you will need is not difficult as nearly all items of electrical equipment are

FIG. 2632 Rudder position indicators are always found on large ships and tugs, infrequently on small craft. They deserve wider use. Knowledge of rudder angle helps when docking, undocking, entering canal locks, etc.

plainly rated in watts of power consumed. Be careful, however, about loads that are not constant. For example, an electric refrigerator unit may consume only about 100 watts *average* power since it does not run continuously, but while it is running it may require 400 watts, and the starting load may be higher still.

RUDDER POSITION INDICATORS

A simple and inexpensive, but very useful, item is a *rudder position indicator*. See fig. 2632. These are standard equipment of large vessels and tugboats, but are seldom found on recreational boats. This small degree of use probably results from a lack of knowledge of the availability of the device and how it works. A small unit is installed at the rudder post and wires are run forward to a meter located within easy view of the helmsman. This meter is calibrated in degrees of right or left rudder. A quick glance will instantly tell the exact position of the rudder at that moment; such information is of considerable value when getting under way or docking with little steerageway. Once you have and use one of these electronic items, you will never be without it.

★ ★

FIG. 2633

Although for many years radio has been the dominant means of communications between ships, and from ships to the shore, it is by no means the only method of transmitting and receiving information over these paths. For a number of reasons, it is often desirable to supplement radio communications with other methods. Among such reasons are incompatibility of language, lack of a common radio frequency or other technical factor, or an emergency situation involving failure of the radio equipment. Various supplementary means of communication will be considered under the overall term of *signaling*. Merchant ships are often seen flying a single flag from the International Code of Signals. The ship in FIG. 2633 (left) has the "H" flag hoisted to signify that there is a pilot aboard. The "G" flag would indicate a request for a pilot. All of the alphabet flags have a special meaning when flown singly as well as when hoisted in groups of two or more, or combined with numeral pennants.

SIGNALING

Visual signaling should not be a new or strange concept to a boatman, although he may lack the detailed knowledge to read such signals. Crossing a busy harbor, he will certainly see many ships flying signal flags, and should it be a naval anchorage, such as Hampton Roads or San Diego, he will undoubtedly also see flashing signal lights, and perhaps sailors sending semaphore.

The value of visual signaling

The time taken to acquire a rudimentary knowledge of visual signaling can be of value to a boatman in at least two ways. Not the least of these is the pleasure and satisfaction of knowing what is going on and being able to explain it to the other crew members and guests aboard his boat. Merchant ships, fig. 2633, will be flying signal flags indicating the presence of a pilot aboard, the handling of dangerous cargoes, or an imminent sailing. Navy and Coast Guard vessels will probably be flying many more flags. Knowing the meaning of at least a portion of these signals will give a boatman a greater sense of "belonging" to the maritime world around him.

The greater value, however, in a knowledge of signaling lies in the added margin of safety that it can provide. So much dependence is placed today on the boat's radiotelephone that one often overlooks the possibility of its not being available when needed. It need not be an electronic failure that precludes your communicating with another craft; it could be merely a lack of a common frequency or type of modulation. Radio will undoubtedly remain your primary means of boat-to-boat and boat-to-shore communications, but don't overlook the added possibilities of signaling.

The International Code of Signals

The International Code of Signals is printed as DMAHTC Publication No. 102. It can be bought from local sales agents, or it can be ordered by mail, see page 333.

Pub. 102 includes both general procedures applicable to all forms of communication and specific rules for flag signaling, flashing light signaling, sound signaling, radiotelegraphy, radiotelephony, and signaling by hand flags, using either semaphore or the Morse code.

The signals used consist of: (1) single-letter signals allocated to meanings which are very urgent, important, or of very common use; (2) two-letter signals for general messages; and (3) three-letter signals (all beginning with "M") for medical messages.

In certain cases, *complements* are used—an added numeral following the basic two-letter signal. Complements express: (1) variations in the meaning of a basic signal; (2) questions and answers related to the meaning of the basic signal; and (3) supplementary, specific, or more detailed meanings.

Typical code-signals from Pub. 102

The simple single-letter signal codes are shown beneath the flags on page W. Typical two-letter groups are listed in fig. 2634.

Special procedures

When names must be sent, or other words for which there are no signal groups in the International Code, they must be spelled out. The signal group YZ *may* be used to indicate that the groups that follow are plain language words rather than code signals; it can, however, be omitted if the spelling is obvious.

The International Code provides special procedures for many purposes such as signaling time, courses and bearings, geographical coordinates, etc.; see Pub. No. 102.

The problem of compiling a code from which expressions in any one of nine languages might be taken was a difficult one, and certain priciples must be followed in its use. These are outlined in Pub. No. 102 and should be read carefully before attempting to use the code itself. Otherwise, because of the form used, erroneous interpretations might be placed on a message sent in code.

AE	I must abandon my vessel.
CJ	Do you require assistance?
CN	I am unable to give assistance.
JI	Are you aground?
JL	You are running the risk of going aground.
JW	I have sprung a leak.
KN	I cannot take you in tow.
LN	Light (name follows) has been extinguished.
LO	I am not in my correct position. (To be used by a lightship.)
LR	Bar is not dangerous.
LS	Bar is dangerous.
MF	Course to reach me is . . .
MG	You should steer course . . .
NF	You are running into danger.
NG	You are in a dangerous position.

FIG. 2634 Typical two-letter signals from the International Code of Signals, Pub. No. 102. These may be made by flag-hoist, sound, flashing light, or other means.

Flag-hoist Signaling

The set of international code flags prescribed for flag-hoist signaling consists of 26 alphabetical flags, 10 numeral pennants, three substitutes, and the answering pennant. The names "substitute" and "repeater" are used interchangeably in publications on flag-hoist signaling. In either case, they are pennants that are employed as replacements for flags (or pennants) already used once in a hoist, since there is only one of each letter or number in a set.

Five standardized colors are used for signal flags—red, white, blue, yellow, and black. Most of the flags are of two colors, selected and arranged for maximum contrast. Two flags are of a single solid color, several use three colors, and one uses four colors. Each flag and pennant has a piece of line sewn into its hoist edge, extending slightly above the cloth to a metal ring, and for several inches below the cloth ending in a snap hook. This "tail line" provides the spacing between the flags of a hoist; the combination of snaps and rings permits the rapid joining together of the individual flags and their connection onto a signal halyard.

The flags and pennants of the International Code are shown in full color on page W. Also indicated here are the meanings of the flags when flown singly. Of these,

probably the most often seen will be the "B" flag, displayed while a ship is carrying or handling an explosive cargo, and the "H" flag flown when a pilot is on board.

Signal flags are flown singly and in combinations of two or more; see page X. Flags and pennants may be mixed as required. In the procedures of the International Code, substitutes repeat the same *class* of flag that precedes them; following alphabet flags, they repeat them, but if used with numeral pennants, they repeat such pennants. The answering pennant is used as a decimal point.

General yachting uses of signal flags

Most boats will not carry a full set of signal flags and pennants, fig. 2635, but may carry one or more for special use under certain conditions.

The flying of the single flag "Q" when returning from a foreign port is correct and desirable in accordance with its International Code meaning "My vessel is healthy and I request free pratique." *Pratique* is the formal term for permission to use a port.

The code flag "T" is often seen flying on boats at yacht club moorings. Its meaning at such times is a request for "transportation"—a call for the club launch to come alongside and pick up passengers for shore. This is not in accordance with the International Code of Signals, but has general acceptance and understanding through wide usage.

Another single code-flag signal is the flying of the letter "M" to signify "Doctor on board"; this differs from the revised International Code meaning. Not yet in general use, its value is gradually being recognized and the practice is spreading. While most, if not all, doctors look to their boating hours as a time "to get away from it all," knowledge that a boat has a doctor on board is of great importance should an accident happen within sight; it is to be hoped that the practice of flying the "M" flag will be adopted by more and more physicians and surgeons.

Flashing Light Signaling

Signaling by short and long flashes of light is widely used by naval forces. It is much faster than hoists of code flags and has a greater range than semaphore signaling.

FIG. 2635 On boats equipped with a full set of signal flags and pennants, a flag chest or locker may be built in, with letter or name plates to identify code flags in their individual pigeonholes.

A	• —	J • — — —	R • — •
B	— • • •	K — • —	S • • •
C	— • — •	L • — • •	T —
D	— • •	M — —	U • • —
E	•	N — •	V • • • —
F	• • — •	O — — —	W • — —
G	— — •	P • — — •	X — • • —
H	• • • •	Q — — • —	Y — • — —
I	• •		Z — — • •

1 • — — — —	2 • • — — —	3 • • • — —
4 • • • • —	5 • • • • •	6 — • • • •
7 — — • • •	8 — — — • •	9 — — — — •
		0 — — — — —

Period • — • — • —
Comma — — • • — —
Interrogative • — • — — • — (RQ)
Distress Call • • • — — — • • • ($\overline{SOS}$)
From — • • (DE)
Invitation to transmit (go ahead) — • — (K)
Wait • — • • • ($\overline{AS}$)
Error • • • • • • • • ($\overline{EEEE}$ etc.)
Received • — • (R)
End of each message • — • — • ($\overline{AR}$)

NOTE:
A dash is equal to three dots.
The space between parts of the same letter is equal to one dot.
The space between two letters is equal to three dots.
The space between two words is equal to five dots.

FIG. 2636 The International Morse Code, with certain simple procedure signals.

FLASHING LIGHT SIGNALING BY BOATS

Although the average boatman may have little regular use for flashing light signaling, this means of communications may prove of great value in emergencies. Take, for example, the situation in which a boat is aground at night. It may be unsafe for another boat to approach close enough for shouting back and forth across the gap between them—there may be uncertainty as to where the shoal water lies, or the other craft may draw considerably more water and thus have to stand off at a distance.

Flashing light signaling has the advantage of needing little or no special equipment; an ordinary flashlight is usually used as the signaling light. There is, however, the disadvantage that a knowledge of the Morse Code is required.

THE INTERNATIONAL MORSE CODE

As noted above, the International Morse Code of *dots* and *dashes* is used for flashing light signaling. The flashes and the spaces between them are defined in terms of *units* —a *dot* is *one* unit long; a *dash* is *three* units; the space between the dots and dashes of a single character (letter or number) is one unit long, between characters it is three units, and between words or groups it is five units in length. The length of a "unit" is roughly set by the skill of the operator and the speed at which he can transmit accurately; it is always well to transmit somewhat more slowly than one's maximum capability to minimize errors and, in case of doubt, it is better to exaggerate slightly the lengths of dashes and spaces than it is to shorten them.

The letters of the alphabet, numbers, and punctuation marks are signaled in Morse code by combinations of dots and dashes. Letters have from one to four components, numbers have five, and punctuation symbols have six. The basic Morse code is shown in fig. 2636.

Time is required to memorize the Morse code characters for the letters, numbers, and simple punctuation marks; but it *can* be done by anyone, and it is well worth the effort required. Once learned, and occasionally used, it will not be forgotten and may prove extremely valuable some day in an emergency.

Semaphore Signaling

Semaphore signaling is normally done with a pair of hand flags for greater visibility. Such flags can be omitted for signaling over short distances, although the use of handkerchiefs, rags, etc. will aid in the reading of the signals. Semaphore signaling is very satisfactory for day use, but it requires the learning of a new code and regular practice to develop any degree of competence.

Even though a boatman does not develop a full qualification in semaphore signaling, a knowledge of the letter "R" is often useful. "R" has wide recognition (as "Roger" on radiotelephone circuits) as meaning "received and understood." The semaphore "R"—both arms stretched straight out to the sides—is a simple, but highly effective, way of signaling to another person that you "got the message." Clearly and distinctly given, it is a much more satisfactory means of acknowledging information or instructions than a careless wave of one hand.

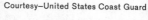
Courtesy—United States Coast Guard

FIG. 2737 The semaphore signaling code is based on the position of the sender's two hands (flags).

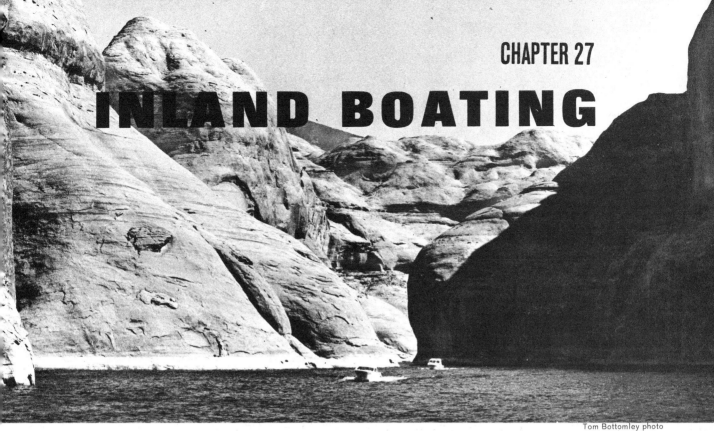

INLAND BOATING

Tom Bottomley photo

*Boating on inland lakes, rivers, and canals is different in some respects from that on
coastal rivers, bays and sounds, and along our salt-water shores.
Or perhaps to keep peace among all hands, we might say that coastal boating
is different from that on inland waters! The differences are not total; many aspects
of safe and enjoyable recreational boating are the same on all waters,
but differences do exist and must be carefully considered for full safety.*

The pleasures of inland boating

For the cruising boatman who has never laid his course inland, there are many surprises in store. He is likely to have regarded the interior waterways as little better than glorified "canals" to be used only as links between large bodies of salt water. Cruising them for their own sake might never occur to him, and canalling, in his mind, would be synonymous with "ditch-crawling."

As a matter of fact, some of the finest cruising this country affords can be found on the vast network of interconnected rivers and lakes which give access to areas far removed from tidal waters. Throughout the United States there are more than 30,000 miles (48,000 km) of improved inland waterways. The Mississippi River system alone has more than 12,000 miles (19,000 km) of waterways navigable by small craft. Using the Mississippi, the Great Lakes, the N.Y. State Barge Canal, and other waterways linking these with the Atlantic and Gulf Intracoastal Waterways, a boatman can circumnavigate the entire eastern portion of the United States, a cruise of more than 5,000 miles (8,000 km). Only a small portion of this would be in the open sea, although the Great Lakes are, of course, sizeable bodies of water, comparable to the ocean insofar as small craft cruising is concerned.

To these vast networks of interconnected waterways must be added the many isolated rivers and the hundreds, if not thousands, of lakes large enough for recreational boating. Many of these lakes have been formed behind dams in regions far removed from what is normally thought of as "boating areas." Today, there is virtually no place in our nation where one should be surprised to see a sign reading "marina" or "boating supplies"; truly, "inland boating" has no geographical boundaries.

Limitations

All cruising areas have their disadvantages and limitations. On rivers and lakes, shoals and rocks may be a factor. On other rivers, you may have problems of overhead clearance; there may be streams where a fixed bridge will arbitrarily determine your "head of navigation."

On some of our principal inland waterways, the overhead clearance is severely limited—on the New York State Canal System in some areas it is only 15½ feet (4.7 m). Masts on sailboats and auxiliaries must be unstepped and secured on deck for the transit; on motorboats, all signal masts, radio antennas, and outriggers must be folded down or otherwise kept low and out of the way.

Fixed overhead power cables are usually high enough to cause no problems to masted vessels, and this clearance is noted on charts. High water stages on rivers naturally reduce overhead clearances under bridges and similar structures by the amount of the rise above normal levels. Chart books for the Ohio River give examples of how to calculate existing clearances at open river stages from the vertical clearances charted for normal pool stages and at 1936 high water stage, shown on charts.

FIG. 2701 Many inland waterways have been constructed to link major bodies of water to make possible through navigation. Seen above is the Illinois Waterway which interconnects the Great Lakes with the Mississippi River System for both commercial and recreational vessels.

River Piloting

While rivers seldom offer great open expanses similar to coastal waters where the usual techniques of navigation are needed, they do demand unique piloting skills. Here, local lore often outweighs some of the fundamental piloting principles which are the coastal skipper's law. Ever-changing conditions on rivers put a premium on local knowledge and elevate river navigation to the status of more an art than a science.

The fundamental difference is, of course, the closeness of the shore, usually with easily identifiable landmarks or aids to navigation. Knowledge of one's position, therefore, is *not* a problem. The skill of piloting here lies in the careful direction of the craft so as to avoid hazards, and on many rivers, this is not a simple or easy matter.

FIG. 2702 The eastern part of the United States has an extensive network of inland waterways, natural and man-made or man-improved. Additions have been made in recent years, and further extensions are either authorized or are in the planning stage.

LEGEND
IMPROVED INTRACOASTAL WATERWAY
OPEN BAY WATER
AUTHORIZED FOR IMPROVEMENT
PRINCIPAL IMPROVED CONNECTING WATERWAYS

Water Level Changes

Because inland waters may be termed "non-tidal," it does *not* follow that there are no fluctuations in level. On the coast, there are daily changes in height, normally two highs and two lows each day. Inland, the variations are more apt to be of a seasonal nature as spring freshets, loaded with debris, flood down from the headwaters, overflow banks, and course on down to the sea at considerable velocities. The annual changes in level can be astounding; at St. Louis, the seasonal fluctuation in river level from flood conditions in late winter and early spring to normal levels in late summer and fall may range to as much as 40 to 50 feet (12-15 m). In some smaller navigable streams, sudden hard rains may raise the water level several feet (a meter or two) in a matter of hours.

FIG. 2705 The upper Mississippi River is no longer a free-flowing stream, but a series of permanent pools regulated by navigation dams. Many craft of all types spend pleasant hours and days on these waters; the houseboat shown here is anchored out of the channel below Dam No. 4.

AIDS TO NAVIGATION

The larger inland rivers, those that are navigable from the sea, have aids to navigation maintained by the U.S. Coast Guard. Many of the lights, buoys, and daybeacons are similar in appearance and significance to those discussed in Chapters 15 and 16, but a few are of special design for their particular "inland" purpose. Many rivers under state jurisdiction will have aids to navigation conforming to the Uniform State Waterway Marking System; see pages 314-316 and color page L.

The "right" and "left" banks of a river

Designation of the banks of a river may at first be confusing. Left and right banks are named relative to a craft's course *downstream*. The left bank, in river terminology, is the one on your left hand as you face in the direction that the river flows; the right bank is that one on your right when you face downstream.

On the New York State Canal System, however, when regulations refer to the "starboard" side of the canal, they mean the right side when entering from Waterford. Thus the starboard side of the Champlain Canal is the east side; but on the Barge (Erie) Canal westward, the north side becomes the starboard side.

Mileage markers

Aids to navigation along the banks of many major rivers are conspicuously marked with mileages which correspond

FIG. 2703 River piloting differs from that in coastal waters in that the skipper usually can tell at all times where he is quite precisely. Here, the navigational problems consist mainly of avoiding underwater hazards such as shoals, sand bars, and snags.

FIG. 2704 The U.S. Coast Guard is responsible for the maintenance of aids to navigation on inland rivers under Federal jurisdiction.

FIG. 2706 The banks of a river are designated as "right" and "left" as one stands looking downstream.   Corps of Engineers, U.S. Army

FIG. 2707 The daymark for this lighted aid to navigation consists of two white boards in the form of an "X"; there is also a mileage sign.

to the distance from a designated zero reference point. It is always an easy matter, therefore, to get a "fix." All you need to do is read the mileage as posted on one of the daybeacons or light structures and compare with the mileage figures given on the chart. The mileage figures take the place of the arbitrary odd and even numbers that are used on coastal waters. They are a great convenience in computing distance travelled and speeds being made good.

Lights

Most lights on major rivers, such as the Mississippi, show through 360°—visible, that is, all around the horizon. In some cases, however, light is projected in one direction only. Some of these directional aids supplement the power of an all-around light by a lens which increases its intensity in one direction only. The width of the beam will vary with the location, a narrower beam for a more critical channel. Flashing lights on the port (proceding upstream) side of the river show a single green or white flash; those on the starboard side show double red or white flashes.

Generally speaking, lights on the Western Rivers are placed strategically at the upper and lower ends of "crossing" (see page 536) as marks to steer by, with additional lights between as required by conditions. Where there are no crossings, lights are used along the banks as passing lights. Reference to the chart of the locality will reveal how a specific light is to be used.

Daymarks

On the Mississippi River, two types of daymarks are to be found. "Passing" daymarks on the port side are square green with green reflective borders; on the starboard side they are red triangles with red reflective borders. "Crossing" daymarks are diamond-shaped, green or red as before, with small reflectors of the same color in each corner. See color page K.

Daymarks on some rivers may consist of two white boards placed on trees on shore in the form of a large "X"; see fig. 2707.

Buoys

The skipper who is familiar with the basic U.S. system of buoyage will have no difficulty whatever with buoyage on rivers. They will generally follow the same basic principles whereby black can-type buoys will be on the left and red nun-type buoys will be on the right when proceeding from seaward, which, of course, is upstream.

On the Mississippi and its tributaries, buoys will be unnumbered and will have white tops for improved visibility against shore backgrounds.

Buoys on the Mississippi River carry reflectors similar to those used on shore aids—red on the left (when descending) side of the channel and white or green on those on the right (descending) side. Lighted buoys show a white or red light if on the left side of a channel, a white or green light if on the right side. Buoys marking wrecks show a quick flashing light of an appropriate color. Buoys marking channel junctions or obstructions are red and black horizontally banded and if lighted show an interrupted quick-flashing characteristic.

Color illustrations

Buoys and daymarks used on the "Western Rivers" (see definition on page 38) are illustrated in color on page K. For those used on other waters, see pages I and J.

Caution required

In all cases, buoys should be followed with reference to whatever charts or navigational maps may be available, as deviations from conventional systems may be found on some rivers. On the New York State Canals, for example, buoys are alike in shape on both sides of the channel, although the color of the buoy and light will differ; red buoys and red lights on the "starboard" side (as defined above) and white buoys and white lights on the port side.

The chart will invariably prevent confusion and misunderstanding in following any system of buoyage. The symbols for buoys on charts of the Ohio River, for exam-

FIG. 2708 Portion of Chart 14852 for the Saint Clair River, scale 1:40,000 on polyconic projection, in which distortion is small and relative sizes are correctly preserved. Depths are referred to the sloping surface of the river at specified lake levels above mean tide at New York. Note the International Boundary in midstream, and the separate channels for traffic up- and down-stream.

ple, are unique to that waterway and may cause initial confusion to strangers until carefully studied.

Ranges

On some rivers, such as the Hudson and the Connecticut, where channels through flats in the river are stabilized and maintained through dredging, ranges with conspicuous markers on shore are of great aid to the skipper in staying within the limits of a narrow channel. Aligning the front and rear markers, he can hold his course safely in mid-channel despite any off-setting forces of current or wind.

CHARTS

River charts are commonly in the form of books of "navigational maps," each page covering successive short stretches of the river in strip form. A typical example is the bound volume published annually by the Mississippi River Commission, Vicksburg, Miss., to cover that river from Cairo, Illinois to Gulf of Mexico. The scale is 1:62,500 (roughly 1 inch = 1 mile, or 1.6 cm = 1 km). All of the depth information (with a few exceptions) and detailed positions of rocks, reefs, shoals, and ledges so familiar on coastal charts are omitted. In their place, the course of the river is traced in blue tint between heavy black lines delineating the banks. A broken red line is used to indicate the channel line. Navigation lights are shown by a star with a white dot in the center together with a number which indicated its distance upstream from a fixed reference point—in this case, A.H.P., "Above the Head of Passes." The Head of Passes is the point not far above the mouth of the river where the river splits into separate channels leading through the delta into the Gulf. Mileages are given every five miles (statute), with red circles at one mile intervals. Mileages above and below the Head of Passes are printed in red. A detailed table is given in the book listing in alphabetical order all towns, cities, bridges, mouths of tributary rivers, and other important features adjacent to the main channel, with distances (AHP) in miles and the numbers of the map on which each feature appears.

River charts are usually on a polyconic projection (see

FIG. 2709 On charts of Pools 25 and 26 (Mississippi River and Illinois Waterway) hazards are shown in bright red. Distances are in statute miles above a specified reference point.

pages 361-362), and elevations normally refer to a specified mean water level.

Variations in river charts

Not all river charts use the same symbol and coloring scheme. Before using any such chart, a skipper should make a careful study of its *legend*. This will give the symbols used for aids to navigation together with the associated abbreviations, information on topographic and hydrographic features that are shown, and probably illustrations of any characteristics that are peculiar to that chart. A few minutes study of an unfamiliar chart will prove very valuable before venturing out on strange waters.

Some charts of the Middle and Upper Mississippi Rivers are done only in black and white with no color to help distinguish significant features.

In the book of charts for the Illinois Waterway, the main channel is shown in white with shoal areas tinted blue.

FIG. 2710 Ohio River chart. Arrow (top) indicates true north, seldom at top of chart. Arrow at left indicates direction of river flow. Note symbols for cans and nuns (see legend, right). Location of bulletin board showing river gages is shown on chart.

Right, legend of symbols used on navigation charts of the Ohio River. Some of these are illustrated on the chart extract shown.

A small booklet of charts for Navigation Pools 25 and 26 of the Mississippi River is distinguished primarily by the fact that it shows hazard areas (under 6-foot, 1.8 meter, depths) in bright red shading, harbors or anchorage areas with an anchor symbol, and the availability of fuel, water, marine railways, launching ramps, and repair and docking facilities at specified location.

The charts in the book for the New York State Canals, published by the National Ocean Survey, are much like the charts of all coastal areas described in Chapter 18. Land areas are tinted buff, channels of 12 feet (3.7 m) or more are white, lesser depths are light blue with depth contour lines for 6 and 12 feet (1.8 and 3.7m), and distinct black lines delineate the banks. Buoy symbols have magenta discs if they are lighted. Aids to navigation are numbered and scattered depth figures give the skipper a good idea as to whether he dare venture out of the channel to seek an anchorage or for any other reason. Rocks and wrecks are indicated with standard symbols from Chart No. 1 (see page 371). Arrows indicating current flow direction, used on many other inland charts, do not appear on those of New York inland waterways.

Missing from the river chart or navigational map is the compass rose of coastal and off-shore charts which enables the navigator to lay a compass course and determine true and magnetic course and bearings. River charts generally show instead a simple arrow to indicate true north; on strip charts, north may not necessarily be at the top of the sheet. On charts of the Lower Mississippi, parallels of latitude and meridians of longitude are printed, but most river charts omit such information.

PUBLICATIONS

Charts can convey to the river skipper a great amount of information, and he should always use the most detailed and latest editions obtainable, but they cannot show all that he needs to know. The limitations of space and the necessary use of symbols and abbreviations require that additional data be published in the form of books and pamphlets.

Engineer publications

The Army Engineers at Vicksburg, Miss., publish an informational pamphlet, "Mississippi River Navigation" which contains not only a great deal of interesting background information on navigation of that river, but also a few pages with explicit instructions "For Part-Time Pilots," the recreational boatmen who use the great river in such large numbers.

Since conditions on the Mississippi, Ohio, and other major rivers are in a constant state of change, with channels shifting and water levels fluctuating, the river boatman must keep posted on the latest information at all times. The various Army Engineer District and Division offices issue a number of publications to provide data on current conditions. These are variously termed *Divisional Bulletins, Navigational Bulletins, Navigation Notices, Notices to Navigational Interests* (weekly), and *Special Notices to Navigation Interests* (as required). These show river conditions such as channel depths, and widths, estimated current velocities, controlling bridge clearances for specified stretches of rivers, construction projects and other hazards, and facilities such as marine railways and lifts.

FIG. 2711 Section of a typical Mississippi River chart. On the original, the shaded areas appear in blue tint. Channel lines, lights and mileages are printed in red. River stages, or heights, are given on the bulletin boards, locations of which are indicated on the chart in red. Small circles are 1 statute mile apart. Parallels of latitude and meridians of longitude appear, but no compass rose, as used on coastal charts.

Coast Guard Notices

The 2nd Coast Guard District, with Headquarters at St. Louis, issues *Local Notices to Mariners* with information on changes in aids to navigation, hazards to navigation, and other matters within Coast Guard cognizance. The USCG also publishes "Channel Reports" periodically with the least depth found by Coast Guard Cutters and Buoy Tenders on their patrols of various sections of the major rivers.

Light List

One of the most helpful documents to the river skipper is the Light List, Volume V, published by the Coast Guard and covering all of the Mississippi River System. In it all lights, buoys, and other aids to navigation are tabulated, together with the river mileage (in statute miles) from the specified reference point. Aids are described in much more detail than can be shown by symbols and abbreviations on charts.

NAVIGATION "TOOLS"

The compass is but little use on river boats and binoculars become the primary piloting tool to aid the skipper in sighting from one navigational aid to the next. In fog, this means that recreational boat traffic comes pretty much to a standstill, although large commercial craft normally carry on using their radar for "eyes." This should not be taken to mean that a compass can be dispensed with on all inland rivers; some are wide enough that navigation can be continued on in fog using a compass, speed curve, watch or clock, *and due caution.*

LOCAL KNOWLEDGE

Not even the best of charts and publications can "tell all" about a particular body of water. Many rivers are particularly prone to seasonal or irregular changes of condition, and a skipper new to a specific stretch of river should take advantage of every opportunity to ask experienced and responsible local people about special hazards or recent changes in conditions.

ILLINOIS WATERWAY - Illinois River					
Name of aid Character and period of light	Number of miles from Grafton	Bank or side of channel	Daymark		Remarks
			Up	Down	
DFORD, ILL.	48.5	Right ...	...	...	
t Peak Bend Light	47.8	Left....	TR	TR	Visible 360° with higher intens
Gp. Fl. W., 5 sec., 2 flashes.					
CKHORN ISLAND DAYMARK	46.1	Right ...	SG	SW	
Geson Island Light	44.9	Left....	TR	TR	
Gp. Fl. W., 5 sec., 2 flashes.					
nd Pass Bridge Upper Light	44.1	Right ...	SW	CW	Visible 360° with higher int
Fl. W., 4 sec.					

FIG. 2712 Charts show much of the information needed for safe navigation of the rivers, but they cannot "tell all." The USCG Light List, Volume V, furnishes many details on aids to navigation that are not shown on charts by symbols and abbreviations.

RIVER CURRENTS

Broadly speaking, river currents, although they may fluctuate in velocity, will trend always in one direction—from the headwaters to the mouth. Despite this, tidal rivers connecting with the sea may feel the effect of tidal conditions occurring at the mouth, backing the water up so that a skipper can take advantage of a favorable current going *upstream* when tidal conditions are right. On the Hudson, for example, an economy-minded skipper electing to run at 9 to 10 knots, and properly selecting his starting time, can carry a favorable current all the way from New York City to Albany, 150 miles (241 km) inland. Tides at this latter city, even so far from the sea, may range in excess of 6 feet (1.8 m), although at other points far *downstream* the range will be only *half* that amount.

Current velocities

The strength of river currents varies widely from river to river, and from season to season for any particular river. Velocities on the Mississippi will range between 1 and 6 mph under average conditions, depending upon the particular section of that river concerned. At extreme high water stages, current strengths may be much greater, 9 mph or more in narrow and constricted areas.

River currents sometimes attain such speeds that navigation upstream is not feasible, although capably handled craft can safely be taken down. Such is the case in the Galop Rapids of the St. Lawrence where the velocity may run as much as 12 to 13 mph. Some river boats have power enough to ascent certain rapids, but, as a general rule, it is best to avoid them by using the canals and locks that bypass them, unless the skipper has local knowledge or engages the service of a local pilot.

"Selecting" your current

River currents have been the subject of extensive studies and their characteristics are of the utmost importance to the masters of deep-draft commercial vessels. The surface current acting on a small craft may, in fact, be actually contrary to that which grips the keel of a large ship near the river bottom. Even with respect to surface currents alone, there is a variation from bank to mid-stream. Friction of the bank and bottom retards velocity. The skipper of the commercial vessel—where fuel costs and time of run are of considerable importance—knows this difference. He uses the strength of the mid-stream current to aid his run downstream. Returning upstream, he runs as close to the bank as he safely can, even turning into small coves behind points of land to take advantage of any counter-current that flows opposite to the main stream.

Perhaps the economic factors that the professional pilot weighs so carefully are of less significance to the recreational boatman. Even so, the small craft skipper can profitably heed the same principles and cut his running time and fuel costs by running courses that make the river's current work for him, or at least minimize its adverse effect. It is only simple arithmetic to note that a 12-mph boat in a 4 mph current is making good either 8 or 16 mph, a significant effect! Even for a faster 20-mph craft, the difference between 16 and 24 mph speeds is 50%. Steer your course so that you can "select" your current; take advantage of your relatively shallow draft, but don't run aground!

CHANNELS AT RIVER BENDS

River channels have a basic tendency for the flow of water to carry across the stream on the outside of the bend, scouring out a natural channel at the outside while depositing a bar extending out from the point around which it is turning. Exceptions to the above may occur where there are unusual bottom contours or man-made structures exist.

Study a river chart which gives the depths (those prepared by the Nation Ocean Survey do) and note this characteristic. Then when you are on a river where the "navigational maps" give no data as to the depths (such as those for the Mississippi and Ohio), you will have a better feeling for where the deeper water will be found. Try to visualize the picture as if you were in an aircraft above and looking down on the river and your boat. This understanding of the natural channels at bends will make you less likely to run straight courses from marker to marker, cutting corners and running the risk of hanging up on a bar.

The proper course at each bend is, of course, a curved line conforming roughly to the trend of the river as a whole. If there are no aids to navigation to guide you, a general rule is to keep about one-quarter of the river's width off the outside bank.

On some river charts even the markings showing the

FIG. 2713 Typical crossing channel, as illustrated in chart book, Cairo to Gulf of Mexico. Note how channel sweeps toward outside of bend. Channel line, lights and mileages in red on original.

Note: 1 knot = 1.85 km/h. 1 mph = 1.61 km/h

FIG. 2714   The most often encountered hazards in river cruising are shoals and sandbars. In some waters, caution must be exercised for underwater rocks.

topography ashore supply clues as to what may be expected in the river itself. Contour lines crowded close together on land at the water's edge indicate a cliff rising steeply from the bank, with good chances of deep water close under the bluff. The cliff or hill may at the same time provide a prominent landmark to steer by.

Channel "crossing"

Where there is an "S" curve—a curve in one direction followed by a curve in the opposite direction—the straight section between the curves is termed a "crossing." On major rivers, these are usually marked by ranges or directional lights. In some instances, such as at low later stages, buoys may be added to mark the route of best water; these buoys may be found in pairs or singly; see fig. 2713.

"EYEBALL" PILOTING

Much of a good river pilot's success depends on his acquired skill in interpreting what he sees. Experience is the true teacher, but some fundamentals can be discussed in a book.

No flat statement can be made as to the relative depth of water indicated by certain sets of surface conditions. On one hand, where there is a chop in the channel, there may be areas of relatively smooth slicks over the bars, especially if there is any weed growth present. As against this, there will be combinations of wind-current conditions where the channel will be comparatively smooth with ripples revealing the bars.

In some narrow river channels, with wind against the current, a small sea builds up in which the larger waves disclose the deeper water, growing progressively smaller until there are no seas at the channel's edge. But under any given set of conditions, the boatman with an eye peeled for natural signs will, with the aid of his chart and the buoys, quickly learn to read the signs that the river has for those eager to understand its secrets.

Watch your wake

If you will glance astern while in unfamiliar waters, your wake can provide a clue to the safety of your course. When the natural sequence of waves in your wake is broken, there must be something to have disturbed it. As it rolls off into shallow water, the smooth undulations will give way to a sharper formation, even cresting on the flats in miniature "breakers." When they encounter a shoal or a flooded area where submerged stumps lie close to the surface, the wake will show the difference. When any short, peaked unnatural wake closes up toward your stern, sheer

off, and fast, away from the side on which this telltale signal appears.

Shoals

Shoaling is a serious problem in most rivers. Spring floods build up current velocities, stir up silt in river bottoms, wash away portions of river banks, and carry this total load of dirt in suspension to be deposited in the form of mud flats and sand bars where the strength of the current lessens; these become hazards to safe navigation. The Connecticut River is a good example of this, where considerable expenditures are required annually to keep channels dredged to authorized depths. In the Mississippi River, a jellied mass of muck, called flocculation, is deposited as a sediment on the river bottom to a depth of 10 to 15 feet (3.0-4.6 m). Deep-draft vessels will plow through it, and high water stages of the river flush it out into the Gulf, so the Army Engineers do not bother to dredge it at low water stages. Over the centuries, this is how the river's delta has been built up.

On a smaller scale, a bar or shoal is often formed at the mouth of a river where the current slows to a degree where the silt is no longer held in suspension. On bars of this kind, bad seas may build up in strong outflowing currents opposed by an on-shore wind. This may even occur inland at the confluence of some rivers, with disturbed surface conditions where smooth water would normally be expected.

Practice makes perfect

Gradually developing a sense of river piloting, you'll become more acutely conscious of the actual track you should make good over the bottom relative to nearby shoals and the side limits of channels. Where currents do occasionally flow diagonally across your course, you will allow for them instinctively and look astern frequently to help maintain that sense of position.

River Seamanship

Boatmen on inland rivers are subject to many of the requirements for safety and good seamanship covered in earlier chapters. A skipper must also be prepared for certain conditions specifically related to those waters on which he is boating.

Boat handling at piers and on entering or leaving slips may be made more complicated by swift river currents. Grounding hard on river shoals may be more troublesome than it is on tidewater, where the next rising tide will often free a craft without any other assistance.

RIVER CRUISING

One of the greatest of all the many pleasures in boating is "cruising," or in other words, going somewhere in your craft. This can be most enjoyable on inland rivers, but requires adequate planning and careful execution.

Problems of where to make fast (tie up) or anchor for the night are a part of cruising in any waters. On coastal waters, the problem may be essentially a matter of finding a sheltered cove or basin to avoid the risk of a rough night in an exposed anchorage. As a rule on the rivers, shelter from blows is closer at hand, yet there are areas great enough in expanse to work up a sizeable chop or even

FIG. 2715 Many groups of outboard skippers get to-gether for cruises along America's scenic rivers; others cruise such waters singly for a day, week, or longer. Campsites can often be found along banks.

seas, especially when the wind opposes the current. Then, too, there is the matter of having protection in narrow waterways from passing river traffic and the wake and wash resulting therefrom. Finally, there is always the question of personal preference as to whether one seeks the seclusion of quiet anchorages off the beaten track, or prefers the activity usually associated with towns and cities.

The development in recent years of many new marinas on some of the inland waterways—the Tennessee River network, for example—has been a great boon to river cruising. Not only do these provide a place to make fast for the night, but fuel, supplies, and other necessities are generally available at the marina or close at hand.

Safety harbors and landings

On the Tennessee River, and others, safety harbors and landings have been provided for use in case of bad weather, mechanical difficulties, or other emergencies. Their locations are shown on charts. Safety harbors are usually coves off the navigable channel. Direction boards on shore indicate the entrance and cross boards mark the upper limits.

Safety landings are areas where the banks have been cleared of stumps, boulders, snags, or other underwater hazards so that craft may safely come to shore. Upper and lower limits are marked by direction boards. These signs

FIG. 2716 Guntersville (Ala.) Yacht Club on TVA's Guntersville Lake. In many areas, the piers must be floating to accommodate quite large changes in water levels at various times of the year.

are color-coded on the Tennessee, white if a 9-foot (2.7 m) depth is available at all water level stages, orange if this depth is not available at lower levels.

The New York State Barge Canal provides terminals at intervals along the route; these are used intermittently by commercial craft, but are available to recreational boats at other times. Of concrete with rather rough faces, these require adequate fendering when used by small craft.

In order to allow for the seasonal range in water levels, or stages, on Western Rivers, most marinas and yacht clubs are afloat on strings of barges, necessitating a long climb up the river bank at low-water stages to get to town.

Anchoring

Frequently study of the chart or navigational map will reveal a likely place to anchor for the night. A widening of the river may offer an opportunity to get out of the reach of traffic, or a small tributary or slough may invite exploration (entering with caution, checking depths as you go), or the natural configuration of river banks and bars may provide a natural "harbor" with complete protection. Islands occurring in mid-river often leave a secondary channel for small-craft on the opposite side from that used by large, deep-draft commercial vessels. When a river cuts a channel behind a section of bank, a "towhead" is formed. Sometimes these are filled in or dammed across at the upper end by river deposits, forming a nautral protected harbor which can be entered from the lower end.

At times, a skipper can get his craft behind a pile dike, a type of structure used on rivers to protect banks from washing away. The dike juts out into the river and, by making fast to one of the piles just inside the outer end, on the downstream side, the boat will have protection not only from passing traffic but from floating debris as well.

Use caution outside channels

When entering sloughs between islands or an island and the bank in search of an anchorage, beware of submerged wing dams at the upstream end. To be safe, always enter and leave from the downstream end.

When anchoring on the larger rivers near a sandbar or island—or when beaching a small boat to go ashore at such a place—a good rule to follow is to pick the downstream rather than the upper end. If an anchor drags, or if for any other reason you get aground on the upstream end, the current will be pushing you harder ashore, complicating the task of getting free. Water at the downstream end is likely to be quieter and the eddies which normally exist

FIG. 2717 At Mile 715.0 on the Lower Mississippi River, just a few miles below Memphis, pleasure craft anchor on the back side of a bar in slack water with complete protection from the wake of passing towboats. There are many such bars along the Mississippi from Baton Rouge on north. The river boatman will find them a snug haven for anchorage at night or during severe weather. J. D. Tennison, Jr. Photo

there may help to free a grounded craft.

Sandy bars that are exposed during periods of low water may be quite unstable. Caution, therefore, should be exercised in using them for camping or swimming.

Check characteristics of the bottom

The character of the bottom varies widely on inland waterways. Particularly in their lower reaches, river bottoms are often soft mud, pointing to the desirability of carrying at least one anchor with broad flukes of a design that will dig down until it reaches good holding strength. In such spots, an anchor with spidery arms and flukes will cut through and provide no holding power at all; yet on a hard bottom, such an anchor might be highly efficient and needed rather than the other type described above.

When anchoring over rocky bottoms or in areas infested with snags and roots, it is highly desirable to rig a "trip line," a light line from the anchor's crown long enough to reach the surface where that end is buoyed. If the anchor snags and will not come free in a normal fashion, pick up the buoy and raise the anchor by the trip line, crown first. Some anchors are provided with slip rings, shear pins, or other devices to make them snag proof; see Chapter 6 for additional information.

An anchor light should be left burning all night if there is danger of being run down by other vessels; in case of doubt as to the necessity for an anchor light, be on the safe side and have one showing.

FIG. 2718 A typical Mississippi river bank riprapped with cement to protect banks against erosion. Boatmen must use care near such banks due to risk of damage to the boat's bottom. J. D. Tennison, Jr.

Making fast to the bank

In many areas, cruising boatmen make fast (tie up) to the river's bank for a lunchtime break in the day's journey, or even overnight. In so doing, caution is essential. The first necessity is that there be adequate depths and the area is free of underwater obstacles; approach slowly. It is advisable to avoid vertical banks that may be in a stage of active caving; exposed tree roots in the bank should be viewed with suspicion as possible evidence of recent erosion. Rock riprap along the banks can be rough on a boat's bottom; see fig. 2718.

One trick used on Western Rivers is the so-called "river hitch." To make fast to the bank, the boat's bow is held up to the bank with power while a line is run to a nearby tree. Then a sapling is cut, some 15-20 feet (4.6-6.1 m) long, and lashed from bank to stern to hold the stern *off*, while another line to shore is used to hold the stern *in*.

Allowance for water level changes

As a general rule, when making fast for the night on inland rivers, lines need not be put out with allowance for the tidal changes common on the coasts, except, of course, on tidal rivers (a 6-foot, 1.8-meter, range at Albany on the Hudson, for example). On non-tidal waterways, however, there is always the chance of a change in level with hard thunderstorms or otherwise heavy rainfalls. It is advisable to observe the practices of local craft, and be guided accordingly.

Making fast to a barge or float which will itself rise or fall with a change in levels is advantageous. Here, it is only necessary to leave enough slack in lines as may be required for comfort and safety if a passing vessel throws a disturbing wake.

River cruising problems

Boatmen cruising the rivers bring back widely conflicting reports of hazards encountered, or the absence of them. Perhaps this may be attributed to the fact that one made his cruise in the early spring, encountering high water, flood conditions, racing currents, and much floating debris. Another, no doubt, has made his trip under ideal conditions in September or October with water levels at a low stage and currents at reasonable velocities so that few, if any, obstacles were encountered. There is that much difference in seasonal conditions. River navigation at extreme flood conditions, is not as a rule to be recommended without the services of an experienced pilot.

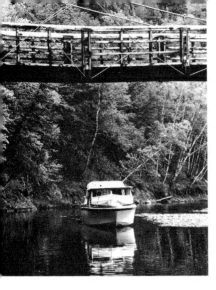

FIG. 2719 The moderate current flow in many smaller inland rivers can increase considerably—rapidly and without warning—as a result of heavy rainfall upstream. Caution must be exercised during times of summer thunderstorms.

Gary Miller photo

Eddies and "whirlpools"

A typical example of this conflict in reports of conditions encountered or observed is the story of "sand boils" in the Mississippi caused by sand piling up on the river bed. One skipper reports that these whirlpool-like disturbances were so violent that they almost threw his boat out of control. Another might say, in more favorable months, they were no worse than surface eddies, felt, but certainly of no danger to the boat.

Problems from silt

Some river boatmen have reported underwater bearings ruined, engine jackets filled with silt, and water pump impellers worn out at the end of one river run. Others have observed no difficulties of these types. As a general rule, as in all places where the water is heavily laden with silt, the logical course is to provide, in advance, whatever protection is possible in the form of effective raw water strainers, fresh water cooling systems, cutless-type underwater bearings, and pump impellers of a type that will handle mud and sand better than bronze gears.

Debris

Floating and partially submerged debris, such as tree trunks and branches, constitute a navigational hazard for small craft and a sharp lookout should be maintained in waters where such have been seen or reported. Floating debris is usually at its worst in the spring months when flood or near-flood water levels have swept away downed trees and other items that litter the banks of waterways just above the normal water line.

Towed-under buoys

River currents sometimes flow so fast that buoys are towed under, leaving only a V-shaped eddy on the surface to reveal their location. Sometimes the top of the buoy will

FIG. 2720 River flow increases markedly during times of spring thaws and run-off, and decreases during the "dry season." Buoys are sometimes aground, as seen above, during times of low water level.

be visible to a boat bound upstream, or the wake of a passing vessel will expose it momentarily.

The V-shaped surface eddy of a towed-under buoy always points upstream as its "wake" divides downstream around it. Any surface disturbance such as this is to be avoided, as a submerged obstacle is likely lurking beneath. This, however, is not to be confused with the condition where two currents meet at the downstream end of a middle bar with converging eddies that may also show as a V-shape, but in this case pointing downstream.

Misplaced buoys

Another hazard of river piloting at spring-time high water levels is the shifting of buoys from their charted positions when they are dragged by large floating trees or logs.

Hazards generally

Some rivers present special hazards. The Army Engineers caution against regarding the Mississippi with insufficient respect. The lower river is very large, with low-water widths of ½-mile (0.8 km) and bank-full widths up to 9,000 feet (2.7 km). The bank-full stages generally occur between December and July, most frequently in March or April. Low-water stages occur in the fall months.

Lake Pepin typifies the kind of exposed area that may be encountered, even on the upper river. This "lake," actually a broadening of the river proper, is 21 miles (33.8 km) long and up to 2½ miles (4 km) in width; sizeable seas can build up in such a body of water.

Many kinds of equipment are found at work along rivers, especially the larger ones. Hydraulic pipeline dredges may have long lengths of floating pipeline which must be avoided. Bank protection equipment carried on barges may extend several hundred feet from shore into the stream, frequently in the swiftest part of the current. Small craft should keep *well* clear of such equipment because of the hazard of being swept under it. In general, boats should exercise both caution and consideration when passing any form of construction or maintenance work, slowing down to avoid doing any damage with their wake. Regulations exist governing lights and day shapes for dredges and other "floating plant" working on river projects, and for the passing of such equipment by other vessels; see "Army Engineer Navigation Regulations" on page 83.

Signals

Whistle signals for passing other vessels, fog or otherwise restricted visibility, and other situations are prescribed by the Rules of the Road and Pilot Rules for the waters concerned, either Inland or Western Rivers. Details will be found in Chapter 5.

Signals for the opening of drawbridges are not uniform in all waters; it will be necessary to consult local regulations, or ask local watermen. For the major rivers, information will be available from Army Engineer District and Division Offices; see page 608.

PASSING COMMERCIAL TRAFFIC

Most of our inland waterways handle considerable commercial traffic. Whether cruising on a river, or just out for a day on the water, the recreational skipper must know how to handle a situation involving his craft and a large commercial vessel. In a channel of narrow width, a big tug

FIG. 2721 Among the longest "vessels" in the world, along with the big ocean liners and the supertankers, are the tows on Western Rivers made up of barges pushed by a towboat at the stern. Length often exceeds 1000 feet (305 meters). Always pass tows with great care, avoid passing at bends. U.S. Army Corps of Engineers photo

or tanker requires the better part of the available water. As she approaches, you'll see a sizeable bow wave built up ahead of her, and the water drawn away by suction to lower the level at her sides amidships. Give such vessels as wide a berth as you possibly can, and be alert for violent motions of your boat as she passes.

Tugs with tows astern in narrow waterways present a real problem to approaching small craft. Fortunately, most of the "towing" today is done by pushing scows and barges ahead of the tug. This keeps the whole tow under better control as a single unit. Passing at a bend is more dangerous than on a straightaway, and in many instances should be avoided entirely. The tug and its barges cannot help but make a wide swing; where there is ample room to pass at the beginning of the turn, there may be none at all later. If small craft *must* pass at a bend, it is usually wiser for them to take the *inside* of the curve regardless of how this affects the normal side for passing.

Jumbo tows on the Mississippi

Big rafts of barges bunched together on the Mississippi River in one vast tow may cover many acres in extent. The prudent recreational craft skipper will appreciate the problems of handling such colossal floats and will never jeopardize their activities, regardless of any considerations of right-of-way. Integrated tows are often made up of a bow-piece, a group of square-ended barges, and a towboat (at the stern) all lashed together in one streamlined unit 1000 feet (305 m) or more in length. At night, to the skipper of a small boat, the towboat's lights may be more conspicuous than the side lights on the tow far out ahead. To make them more visible, the rules now require that barges towed alongside or pushed ahead must show a quick-flashing *amber* light all the way forward on the centerline.

Thus it can be seen that special caution is needed when running rivers at night, even though the river itself be so well lighted as to make this feasible. When commercial traffic is using powerful searchlights, their blinding beams may make it impossible for the boatman to see anything at all. Shore lights may add to the difficulty because of their reflections in the water. Then, too, in some rivers, especially in flood, there's the hazard of floating trees and other partially submerged debris that could not be seen in time, if at all, in the darkness.

Give all tows a wide berth

On all rivers, recreational craft should give tows a wide berth. In particular, they should *stay away from in front of tows* when underway. If the small craft should happen to lose power in such a spot, it might be impossible for the tow to stop or steer clear. With the way she carries, a commercial tow may at times travel a half-mile or more before she can come to a full stop.

Boats equipped with VHF/FM radiotelephones should call the tug and coordinate the passing before it is started.

WATCH YOUR WAKE

Much inland boating is done on rivers that are relatively narrow. Skippers should so regulate the speed of their craft that no *destructive* wake is caused. The banks of the river may be close to the boat's course, and excessive wake can cause damage to shoreside installations. Some wake is almost inevitable from motorboats, but it must not be "destructive"; keep your speed, and your wake, at a minimum when passing boats, and piers and other shoreline facilities.

Canal Boating

Before the days of dams and locks, many of our rivers were unnavigable. Water coursing down valleys at the land's natural gradient, dropping perhaps hundreds of feet in tens of miles, runs too fast and encounters too many natural obstacles for safe navigation. To overcome them, engineers dam natural waterways at strategic spots, creating a series of "pools" or levels that may be likened to a stairway. Good examples of how closely these can resemble an actual flight of stairs will be found at places like Waterford, N.Y., and the Rideau Waterway at Ottawa where vessels descend or ascent a series of locks in immediate succession. This section will cover boating on both completely man-made waterways, which might be termed "pure canals," and on "canalized" natural rivers.

Water levels

To a river pilot, the term "pool stage" indicates the height of water in a pool at any given time with reference to the datum for that pool. On many rivers, pool stages are posted on conspicuous bulletin boards along river banks so as to be easily read from passing vessels. Locations of these bulletin boards are given on charts.

On the Ohio, gauge readings are displayed at the powerhouses of the dams. These indicate depths of the pool impounded by the dam *next below*. A depth of 9 feet (2.7 m) is uniformly taken to indicate the pool at normal elevation. A reading of 7.9 feet (2.4 m) would indicate that the *lower* pool at this dam is 1.1 feet (0.3 m) below normal elevation. These readings are preceded by the letters NP (normal Pool) in white on a green background.

LOCKS AND DAMS

Dams on our inland waterways, without locks, would restrict river cruising to the individual pools and would prevent through navigation except for small craft which were light enough to be portaged around the dams. Locks, in conjunction with the dams, provide the means for watercraft to move from level to level. Locks vary in size,

FIG. 2722 Locks and dams make rivers navigable by changing levels in successive stages. On some waterways, locking through on a Sunday is somewhat reminiscent of highway motoring. Note the need for many fenders on each craft.

but since they almost invariably handle commercial traffic, their limiting dimensions offer no restriction to the movement of recreational boats. On the New York State Barge Canal, a tanker will almost fill a lock, with very little room to spare; in fact, the tanker or barge was designed to fit the canal lock, and not vice versa!

Principles of locks and locking

Locks are watertight (or almost so) chambers with gates at each end. Valves are provided to admit water as required. When a vessel needs to be locked upstream to a higher level, the upstream gates are first closed, valves are opened to let the water run out to the lower level, and then the downstream gates are opened. The vessel enters the lock through the opened lower gates; these are then closed and water is allowed to flow in from above through another set of valves until the chamber is full to the upper pool level. Next the upstream gates are opened and the vessel is free to resume her course upstream. Locking a vessel down is the reverse of this process.

Water is not pumped at locks; the natural flow is utilized and this is why some canals must impose restrictions limiting the number of lockings each day during droughts or annual dry seasons.

Variations in lock design

There are various kinds of locks, all of which accomplish the same end result of effecting a change of level. Gates may swing to the side or roll back; sometimes they lift vertically permitting water traffic to pass under them.

At some smaller locks where the water level change is not great, valves are omitted and water flows into or out of the chamber by opening the gates just a crack at first, then gradually widening the opening as the levels begin to equalize inside and outside the gates.

On the Trent Waterway in Canada, a hydraulic elevator lifts the boat in a water-filled chamber, and at another location a marine railway actually hauls the boat out to get her up and over a hill. Through passage on a waterway like the Trent is obviously limited to craft within the capacity of the railway to haul it, both as to length and weight.

Whistle signals

Signals are prescribed for vessels approaching a lock and these are answered by the lockmaster. These vary in different areas; the river boatman should familiarize himself with the special signals applicable to the particular waterway he is using. At many locks, VHF/FM radios are used for direct communications between vessels and the lockmaster.

The Army Engineers at Pittsburgh publish an informative illustrative leaflet entitled "Locking Through," which sets forth, very concisely, the main essentials as they apply to the Ohio River. Several other Army Engineer offices publish generally similar pamphlets for the waters under their control.

FIG. 2733 Locks at dams provide the means for boats to go "uphill" and "downhill" to and from lakes and "pools" of different elevations. Without locks, such navigation would be impossible. Here the lift is 80 feet (24 m) at Fort Loudon Dam on the Tennessee.

FIG. 2724 Locks are massive chambers of concrete and steel which may be flooded and emptied through valves and gates. On many waterways, commercial craft are designed to fit the lock chambers with only inches to spare.

FIG. 2725 On some heavily traveled waterways, locks have been built in pairs. This is a view of the upstream side of Alton Lock and Dam No. 24 on the Mississippi above St. Louis. The landward lock is considerably larger than the riverward lock; signals indicate which to use.

FIG. 2726 The locks shown here at Lockport on the New York State Barge Canal have a double set of gates. Variations from the basic design of a chamber with one set of gates at each end may be found on many waterways.

FIG. 2727 Signal lights and air horn signals used on the Western Rivers to control traffic at locks. (From "Locking Through," prepared by Army Engineers.)

FIG. 2728 Skippers of recreational boats must be prepared for rough and dirty walls in lock chambers. Fenders that are adequate in design and number are essential—and they must be in position before entering the lock.

Sound signals

On the Ohio River, vessels sound a long and short blast on the whistle from a distance of not more than one mile from the lock. When approaching a lock, boats must wait for the lockmaster's signal before entering. When bound downstream, they must stay clear at least 400 feet (122 m) upstream from the end of the guidewall along the bank bank into the lock. Approach must be made through the buoyed channel directly to the lock, keeping clear of the spillway sections of the dam. Boats must take care not to obstruct the movement of any large commercial vessel that may be leaving the lock. When bound upstream, small craft must keep clear of the turbulent water that is invariably found beneath a dam.

Where locks are in pairs (designated as landward and riverward), the lockmaster on the Ohio may also use an air horn to give directions as follows: one long, enter landward lock; two longs, enter riverward lock; one short, leave landward lock; two shorts, leave riverward lock.

On the New York State Canal System, a skipper signals his request for lockage by sounding three distinct blasts.

Manual signals

On the Mississippi, signs are placed on the river face of the guidewall warning small craft not to pass a certain point until signalled by the lock tender. Near this sign, a signal cord is placed. Small craft with horns not loud enough to attract the attention of the lock attendant may use this to alert him that passage is desired. Generally similar arrangements are found on the Okeechobee Waterway crossing Florida and elsewhere.

Signal lights

Traffic signal lights at the Ohio locks resemble those you find on city streets—red, amber or yellow, and green, vertically arranged. Flashing red warns: do not enter, stand clear. Flashing amber cautions: approach, but under full control. Flashing green is the go-ahead: all clear to enter.

On New York State Canals, a fixed green is the signal to enter; a fixed red required the vessel to wait.

Precedence at locks

The Secretary of the Army has established an order of priority for the users of locks controlled by the Engineer Corps. The precedence in the handling of traffic is as follows: (1) U.S. Military craft; (2) mail boats; (3) commercial passenger craft; (4) commercial tows; (5) commercial fishermen; (6) non-commercial craft. In the descending order ot precedence, the lockmaster also takes into account whether vessels of the same priority are arriving at landward or riverward locks (if locks are paired), and whether they are bound upstream or downstream.

Recreational boats *may*, at the discretion of the lockmaster, be locked through with commercial vessels if a safe distance can be maintained between them and the commercial vessels are *not* carrying petroleum products or other hazardous substances.

LOCKING PROCEDURES

The concrete walls of locks are usually rough and dirty. Some of the older locks have been metal-sheathed on the inside surfaces, but most are hard on small craft. Consequently, a boat will need adequate fender protection. Ordinary cylindrical fenders will pick up dirt and roll on the wall to smear the topsides. Fender boards consisting of a plank (generally 2 by 6 inches, several feet long) suspended horizontally outside the usual fenders hung vertically, will normally work well amidships or where sides are reasonably straight.

Bags of hay have the same objection as cylindrical fenders, except on heavily flared bows at the edge of the deck where they flatten down and work fairly well. Auto tires wrapped in burlap would be ideal except that their use is illegal in most canals (if they came adrift they would sink and probably foul the lock's valves).

As you can't be sure which side of the next lock you will be using, it's wise to have duplicate fender systems, one for each side.

Have enough line

Another essential in locking is adequate line. How heavy it must be depends on the size of the boat; how long it must be, on the depth of the locks. Lines can be slightly smaller in diameter than one's normal mooring lines; ½-inch manila is often used for boats in the 35 to 50 foot size range, ⅜-inch for smaller craft. (Manila is suggested in preference to synthetic material because of its lower cost; locking lines will soon get too dirty for further use and must be discarded.)

In general, each line (bow and stern) will have to be at least twice the depth of the deepest lock that is expected to be encountered. The reason for this is to permit running the bight of the line around a bollard on the top of the lock wall, using it doubled. Then at the lower level when you are ready to cast off after locking down, you can turn loose one end and haul in on the other without assistance

FIG. 2729 The easiest locking through is accomplished where the mooring posts are recessed into the chamber walls and float up and down with changes in water level. Here, lines do not have to be adjusted during the locking process.

from above (which you are not likely to get anyway); see fig. 2728.

Use of ladders and other methods

Ladders are often recessed into lock walls for safety reasons should someone be unlucky enough to fall in. On some canals, small craft may follow a ladder up or down, rung by rung, holding on with boathooks or short lengths of line. On other canals, this is not permitted by the rules and the ladders must be kept clear for emergency use.

In addition to large bollards at the top, some locks have other posts recessed in the walls at intervals in a vertical line. Locking up, lines can be cleared successively from lower posts and transferred to higher ones within reach. Locking down would use the reverse procedure.

In some of the newer locks, floating mooring posts are built into the side walls, moving up or down with changes in the water level in the lock. This makes for the simplest and easiest of all locking through as relatively short lines

FIG. 2730 Larger boats should use two separate mooring lines leading from bow and stern to separate mooring posts on the lock wall. This will require a person at each end of the boat to pay out or take in mooring lines as the water level changes.

From "Locking Through" U.S. Army Engineers

Note: 1 inch = 2.54 cm. 1 foot = 0.305 m

FIG. 2731 Small boats, and larger craft with only one person aboard, may use one long line securely fastened at one end of the boat with the bight of the line around the mooring post on the lock wall and the free end of the line around a cleat at the other end of the boat. This will allow the person at the free end of the line to pay out or take in mooring as the water level changes.

FIG. 2732 Recreational craft may sometimes be locked through with commercial vessels. Skippers must beware of considerable turbulence behind these from their large propellors and powerful engines; be especially wary of tugs.

can be used to make fast, and they need not be adjusted as the boat moves up or down.

Tend your lines carefully

Rising or falling, stand by your lock lines at all times and tend them carefully. This requires a crewman forward and another aft; with only two persons aboard, it is usually possible for the helmsman to move to and tend the aft line. One of the most dangerous practices is to make fast to a bollard above and then secure the line to a bitt or cleat on the boat. If the level drops unexpectedly, the boat can be "hung," with risk of serious damage.

In some locks, coming up, special caution is required at the top of the lift. The boat may have been adequately fendered to keep her off the lock wall, but if the water rises to nearly completely fill the lock chamber, the boat's gunwale will be above the top of the wall and the topsides below would then be unprotected from the lip of the chamber, particularly at a bow with flare.

Entering and leaving

It is always imperative to enter locks, and leave them, at a slow speed with the craft under full control. This is especially true when locking through with other boats. Sometimes, especially on fleet cruises, it will be necessary to make fast two abreast at each lock wall. This is entirely practicable if all boats are intelligently handled.

Occasionally one hears cautions concerning the possibility of a boat being tossed about as water boils into the lock from open valves. This is a possibility, and one for which a skipper must be on the alert, but in almost all instances the lock tenders on our inland waterways are careful to control the rate of inflow to minimize any turbulence in the lock chamber, and there is no real need to fear the locking process for this reason. With a light craft, however, some thought should be given to extra caution when locking through in company with large commercial vessels. A boat directly astern of a tug ("tow boat"), for example, can be subjected to quite a bit of being tossed around when the big propellor of the tug starts to kick out its wash astern on leaving the lock.

Approaching a lock from upstream

Caution is especially necessary when approaching a lock from the upstream side; the marked channel must be followed closely. Some years ago, a cruiser bound down the Hudson River missed the lock at Troy, which lies far toward the east bank, and went over the dam. By rare good fortune, she was able to continue her journey to New York under her own power. Looking down the river from above many dams, it is virtually impossible to see any break in the water's surface, yet there is no excuse for

FIG. 2733 Extract from one of the Illinois Waterway charts. With wicket-type dams which can be lowered at high-water stages, traffic uses the navigable pass through the dam, indicated by "high water sailing line." System of lights, explained on chart, shows whether lock or navigable pass is to be used. Lights and nun buoys in red on original.

FIG. 2734 A view of the wickets at one of the Ohio River movable dams. Wickets are held in an upright position during low water stages of the river. At high water, they can be lowered, creating a navigable pass which river boats use without locking.   J. M. Wallace photo

such an occurrence if the skipper pays attention to the buoys as indicated on the chart, or to the general configuration of the dam and locks if there are no buoys.

Actually, there are times and places where it is proper to go *over* a dam, strange as that may sound. On the Ohio River, a moveable type of dam is used which has a lock chamber on one side and "bear traps" on the other. In the middle, between them, there are moveable wickets that can be held in an upright position during low water stages and lowered at times of high water. When the wickets are up, water traffic necessarily uses the lock. With the wickets down, at high water, boats run through the navigable pass, over the dam without locking. By day, it is important to watch the bulletin boards at the locks to know whether the lock or the navigable pass is to be used. At night, distinguishing lights are shown at the guide walls. When the navigable pass is being used, the gauge reading on the power house bulletin board shows the depth of water over the pass sill at the dam. The reading is in white on a red background, and is preceded by the word "Pass."

FIG. 2735 Often canals consist of entirely artificial "land cuts." West of Rochester, the New York State Barge Canal passes through such a section. Speed limit is 6 statute miles per hour.

SAFETY FIRST

Recreational boatmen *must* keep clear of the spillway area below dams. The fishing in such areas may be particularly good, but the hazards are great—a good catch is not worth your life! These water areas are subject to sudden changes as gates and valves in the dam are opened and closed; placid waters may become very turbulent with no warning at all, a heavy stream of water may unexpectedly boil up from beneath the surface. Spillway areas can be extremely dangerous for small craft; heed the warning signs and stay out.

ARTIFICIAL LAND CUTS

Not all waterways are merely improved versions of natural rivers and lakes. Artificial land cuts are often needed to interconnect navigable waterways and provide continuous passage between major bodies of water. Lake Champlain is accessible from the upper reaches of the Hudson River only because of a 24-mile completely artificial waterway cut into the land. A dredged land cut is also found at the western end of the New York State Barge Canal to connect Lake Erie with rivers in the middle of the state.

Narrow land cuts pose problems of their own. A typical cross section of a dredged canal might have a surface width of, for example, 125 feet, but a bottom width of only 75 feet, with a depth of 12 feet. If normal cruising speeds were maintained through such portions of a canal, the bank would be quickly washed down into the channel with a consequent aggravation of maintenance problems. Thus, in such artificial waterways, speed limits are rigidly enforced. In New York State Canals, the limit is 6 mph in the land cuts and 10 mph in the canalized river and lake

FIG. 2736 Extreme caution is required when approaching a dam and lock from upstream. Check your chart carefully; watch for aids to navigation and direction signs. Keep at least 400 feet upstream from the guide wall until signaled to enter the lock.

Note: 1 foot = 0.305 m. 1 mile = 1.61 km. 1 mph = 1.61 km/h

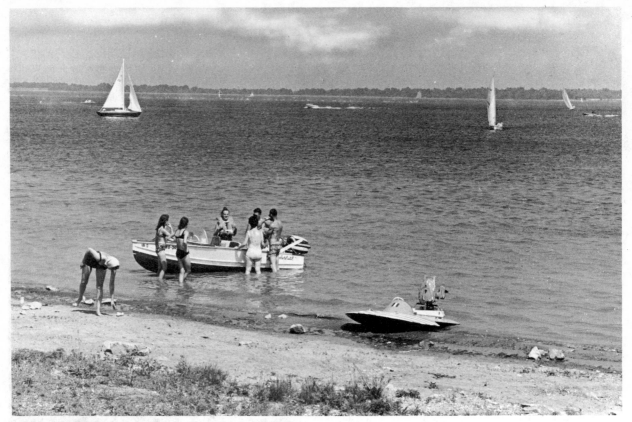

FIG. 2737 The many dams constructed for power and flood control purposes have created lakes ideal for inland boating. This is a typical scene showing many varied types of recreational activity on Lake Carlyle.

sections. A telephone network between the various locks enables lock tenders to know when a boat is due; speeders are quite easily caught! Some sets of locks also operate on time schedules and it serves no purpose to go too fast as one only has to wait when he reaches the next lock.

Some of the land sections are cut through solid rock, perhaps only 100 feet (30.5 m) or less in width. This makes a virtual trough with ragged walls of blasted rock. In a confined channel such as this, the wakes of a group of boats may combine and reinforce each other in a synchronized pattern, building up out of all proportion to the wakes of each craft individually. Unless speed is held down as required by the circumstances, regardless of the legal limit, small craft can get out of control, with the ultimate possibility of being thrown into the rock walls and suffering serious damage.

REGULATIONS

Lock permits, once required for non-commercial craft on the New York State Barge Canal, are no longer needed. On the Western Rivers, no special permission or clearance is necessary for passage through the locks. There are, however, regulations to be observed, and copies of these should be obtained from the Engineer District Offices at Chicago or St. Louis.

When craft are anchored at night along the side of the New York State Canals, authorities require the use of a red, rather than a white, anchor light.

Lake Boating

The term "lake boating" has extreme limits. The water area involved can range from the smallest of natural or man-made lakes and reservoirs to the Great Lakes, really inland seas. Some lakes are "protected waters" at all times; others can produce waves to hazard the largest of recreational craft and even ships of considerable size.

While it is true that an inland boatman can cruise hundreds of miles continuously on rivers and canals and never be more than a very short distance from shelter in case of bad weather, the larger lakes must be treated with considerable respect. Lake Superior, for example, is the largest body of fresh water in the world. Deep, with rock-lined coasts and subject to storms and fog as well, it can present a challenge to even the saltiest skipper. Lake Erie, although smaller than Lake Superior, is comparatively shallow. In a gale of wind, seas cannot shape up in the normal pattern of open ocean waves. Consequently, they are short and steep, frequently breaking in heavy squalls. Even Lake Oneida in mid-state New York on the Barge Canal route can build up seas that will test the abilities of an offshore boat.

Water levels

Lake levels vary from year to year and show a seasonal rise and fall as well, low in the winter and high in the summer. The Lake Survey Center, Detroit, publishes monthly bulletins during the navigation season showing current and projected levels of the Great Lakes, plus average and

FIG. 2738 Boatmen on some inland lakes encounter spectacular scenery. This is a view on Lake Powell in Utah, near the Arizona boundary.

Tom Bottomley photo

keeps track of where he is at all times. The very largest lakes will require the plotting of courses; the use of a compass; time, speed, and distance calucations; and even bearings and fixes.

Great Lakes charts

Charts of the Great Lakes, now published by the National Ocean Survey at Rockville, Maryland, are excellent, covering features of the navigable water in great detail. They show depths of water (the lesser depths in blue tint), safe channels, submerged reefs and shoals, aids to navigation, adjacent shorelines with topographic features and landmarks, types of bottom, and much related information. Scales of the charts vary from as large as 1:2,500 to 1:20,000 for harbor charts to 1:400,000 or 1:500,000 for general charts of individual lakes. The smallest scale used is for the general chart of all the Great Lakes at 1:1,500,000. The projection used for these charts is basically polyconic, but a few are additionally published with a Mercator projection; see Chapter 18.

On Great Lakes charts, a compass rose will be found, showing both true and magnetic directions with the variation stated. In parts of the Great Lakes, the variation reduces to zero. In some locations, great deposits of iron ore in the earth produce strong local effects; this is most pronounced along the north shore of Lake Superior where variation has been observed to change from 27° to 7° within a distance of 650 feet (200 meters)!

Many lake charts show some of the principal routes between major ports, giving the course in degrees (true)

record levels. More current information is contained in weekly reports released each Thursday to newspapers and radio and television stations.

In larger lakes, a steady, strong wind will lower levels to windward and pile up water on the leeward side. Barometric pressure can also exert an influence on lake levels, sometimes causing a sudden and temporary, but drastic, oscillation of considerable magnitude; this phenomenon is called a "seiche."

LAKE PILOTING

Many smaller lakes are not of a size to require "navigation" by the skipper; charts often do not exist for such bodies of water. On the larger lakes, however, shore lines may run to many miles of length and the prudent boatman

FIG. 2739 Reproduction (reduced more than half) of typical page from the Recreational Chart Series 14853 covering the Detroit River, Lake St. Clair, and the St. Clair River. Charts of this kind are prepared for the express purpose of providing the boatman with a maximum of navigation information in a convenient form. In these volumes, data are included which is not available on other chart series. In the original, Lake St. Clair, (below) is shown on a scale of 1:60,000; Belle Isle and a portion of the Detroit River 1:15,000. On the original, two tints of blue are used to define limits of the shoaler areas (up to one and two fathoms), thus emphasizing navigable deep-water channels which appear in white, with soundings in feet in black figures. Land areas are tinted light yellow.

and distance in statute miles. Comparative elevations are referred to mean tide as calculated at New York City. Local heights and depths are measured from an established datum for each lake.

The Great Lakes are partly Canadian waters and there are excellent charts available for these areas from the Canadian Hydrographic Survey, Ottawa.

Coast Pilot 6 (Great Lakes Pilot)

To supplement the information available on Great Lakes charts, boatmen should have a copy of the current edition of the Coast Pilot 6 published by the National Ocean Survey; see fig. 1712. This most useful volume provides detailed information that cannot be shown on charts. Included are full descriptions of the waters charted, laws and regulations governing navigation, bridge clearances, signals for locks and bridges, dimensions and capacities of marine railways, and weather information. Users of this Pilot should keep their copy corrected from Local Notices to Mariners issued by the 9th Coast Guard District.

Great Lakes Light List

The U.S. Coast Guard publishes the Light List, Volume IV, covering the Great Lakes; see page 331.

In this Light List, Canadian buoys and lights are identified by the letter "C"; except for minor differences in design, the system of buoyage used in Canadian waters is the same as used by the United States.

Caution along some shores

When cruising in some lakes, such as Lake Champlain, the depth becomes a factor. Along some shores, which may be particularly inviting because of their scenic attractions, the skipper may find depths of several hundred feet running right up to sheer cliff shores. If power fails, the anchor will be of little use in such deep water, and if the breeze is toward those cliffs, he is in danger of a lee shore.

RULES AND REGULATIONS

Many smaller inland lakes do not fall under federal jurisdiction and are regulated by the states or agencies thereof; see page 30. Others are, however, "navigable waters of the United States" where federal rules and reg-

FIG. 2740 Coast Guard Boating Safety Detachments bring their twin functions of advice and enforcement to inland boating areas under Federal jurisdiction. U. S. Coast Guard photo

ulations apply. Boatmen should check on the status of unfamiliar waters if there are any doubts.

Rules of the Road

The U.S. Inland Rules of the Road will apply to vessels on some of the waters covered in this chapter. Others will be governed by the Great Lakes Rules or the Western Rivers Rules; see page 38 for the boundaries of these sets of rules of the road, and remember that the "Western Rivers Rules" do not apply to rivers on the West (Pacific) Coast of the United States.

Pollution control regulations

Many inland lakes are used as sources of municipal water supplies or have their water quality maintained for other reasons. Boatmen visiting new bodies of water should check carefully for any special regulations regarding overboard discharges.

USCG BOATING SAFETY DETACHMENTS

The U.S. Coast Guard has jurisdiction on all "Navigable Waters of the United States" as defined on page 30. Coast Guard stations will be found on the Great Lakes, the larger rivers, and some other major bodies of water, but many of the smaller inland rivers and lakes do not have regular USCG facilities. On these waters, the Coast Guard meets its responsibilities and asserts its authority through mobile teams called *Boating Safety Detachments*, abbreviated *BOSDET*. During each boating season, these detachments travel thousands of miles and visit nearly every state; they will be seen in areas where one would hardly expect to note the presence of a *Coast* Guardsman.

Personnel and equipment

Each BOSDET normally consists of a Chief Petty Officer and two other enlisted men. These men have been carefully selected for such independent duty and have been given special schooling. Their equipment includes a 16 to 18 foot outboard or I-O boat together with a trailer for it pulled by a light pickup or carryall type of truck. The boats are clearly marked with the Coast Guard name and distinguishing stripe; many craft are equipped with the revolving blue light prescribed for law enforcement vessels.

Activities

The BOSDETs' function is educational and advisory as much as it is law enforcement. They would much rather counsel and assist boatmen, but in the event of flagrant violations they can, and do, issue citations. Team personnel are often seen at boat shows, boating or fishing club meetings, U.S. Power Squadrons and USCG Auxiliary classes, and similar functions—all on the basis that "an ounce of prevention is worth a pound of cure." Safety patrols on the water are a major activity of BOSDETs, with emphasis on the peak days of each weekend—their personal "days off" must come in the middle of the week!

The new authority to turn back boats in unsafe conditions, granted by the Federal Boat Safety Act of 1971, will undoubtedly be used more by BOSDETs than any other type of Coast Guard unit. Boats may be directed to return to port or may be escorted back if unsafe either in their condition, equipment, or loading, or if weather and sea conditions are hazardous for that size or type of craft.

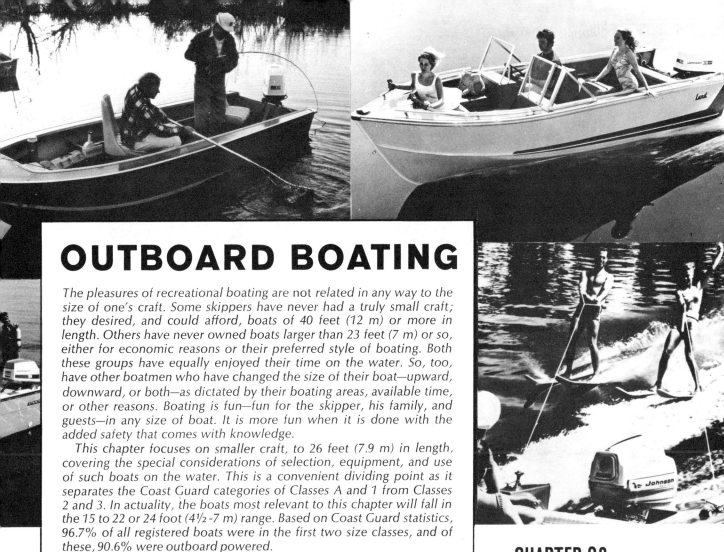

OUTBOARD BOATING

The pleasures of recreational boating are not related in any way to the size of one's craft. Some skippers have never had a truly small craft; they desired, and could afford, boats of 40 feet (12 m) or more in length. Others have never owned boats larger than 23 feet (7 m) or so, either for economic reasons or their preferred style of boating. Both these groups have equally enjoyed their time on the water. So, too, have other boatmen who have changed the size of their boat—upward, downward, or both—as dictated by their boating areas, available time, or other reasons. Boating is fun—fun for the skipper, his family, and guests—in any size of boat. It is more fun when it is done with the added safety that comes with knowledge.

This chapter focuses on smaller craft, to 26 feet (7.9 m) in length, covering the special considerations of selection, equipment, and use of such boats on the water. This is a convenient dividing point as it separates the Coast Guard categories of Classes A and 1 from Classes 2 and 3. In actuality, the boats most relevant to this chapter will fall in the 15 to 22 or 24 foot (4½-7 m) range. Based on Coast Guard statistics, 96.7% of all registered boats were in the first two size classes, and of these, 90.6% were outboard powered.

CHAPTER 28

Much that has preceded this chapter is applicable to outboard boating. The basics of aids to navigation, the compass, chart reading, weather, safety, seamanship, and many other topics are applicable as a whole or in large part to the outboard boatman. And here it might be pointed out that except for details of the motor, we include the skipper of the boat with inboard-outboard (out-drive, stern drive) propulsion.

The laws and regulations relating to outboard boats will be found with those relating to larger motorboats in Chapters 2 through 5 and they will not be repeated here. Outboard skippers should carefully study those applicable to the length of his craft.

For a great many outboard skippers this chapter might have been entitled "Trailer Boating," for their craft spend more time on land on trailers than they do in the water. Yet such would not be correct as a trailered boat is no different in its safe operation than any others once it is in the water—it is then just a "boat." The only differences are its land transportation and storage, both of which topics are covered in Chapter 29, "Boat Trailering."

The Boat

Outboard boats, those craft suitable for equipping with a detachable motor, come in an extremely wide range of design, size, construction material, and cost. They range from 8-foot (2.4-m) or smaller prams that can be "car-topped" or even used as a dinghy for a boat that it fits into the outboard category, to large hulls capable of carrying two motors of more than a hundred horsepower each. The craft that we will consider in this chapter may be of entirely open construction or have a small but comfortable cabin with bunks, galley, and a head.

THE USE OF THE BOAT

The key to the selection of the "right" boat for a particular skipper is the use or uses to which it will be put. No craft can do everything best—quite obviously the craft for water skiing is not the boat for fishing by trolling, the boat for an afternoon outing is not the craft for a weekend or week's cruise, the competitive racer is not a family boat. Probably no boating family will agree on just one or even

FIG. 2801 Outboard boating is not entirely "a world unto itself"—many of the basic aspects of boating covered in earlier chapters are applicable to smaller craft powered with an outboard motor, or an out-drive unit.

FIG. 2803 Many outboards are used for fishing in protected waters or, with due caution, offshore. These range from simple, displacement-type utility craft to complex and expensive "fishing machines."

FIG. 2802 Except for details of the motor, inboard-outboard craft are much like outboards. They are generally of the same size, handle alike, and are used for the same types of waterborne recreation.

FIG. 2804 Displacement hulls ride down in the water, while planing hulls derive lift from their forward motion and tend to ride "on" the water. Each type has its use and careful selection is advisable when choosing your boat.

two uses, and few families can afford a separate craft for each type of activity enjoyed by its members, so compromise is inevitable. If, however, all possible factors are considered in advance of selecting "the boat," the likelihood of disappointment will be lessened. Not to be overlooked, also, is the type of waters upon which it will be used, protected lakes and rivers, or coastal bays and off shore.

Hull designs

There are two basic hull types, displacement and planing—and many variations of the latter. Displacement boats cruise *through* the water; planing hulls lift and skim *over* the surface.

Often it is difficult to make a sharp distinction between "displacement" and "planing" types of hulls. Planing hulls receive a large part of their support at normal speeds from the dynamic reaction of the water against the bottom, and a lesser part from buoyancy which diminishes with increased speed, but never quite disappears at any speed. Generally, planing begins when the water breaks cleanly away at the chines and transom. In these days of high horsepower, many cruisers are actually planing hulls, and, of course, practically all runabouts are planing type.

Many boat designs for outboard motors have a single, rather conventional hull, but there is an increasing tendency toward wider craft which have greater horizontal stability and more interior space for passengers. Underwater, these have, in effect, two or three hull shapes although they are not catamarans or trimarans; a number of trade names are applied to patented hull designs of this type, often called "cathedral" hulls.

Flat bottom (displacement type) hulls. Usually rowboats or skiffs 14' to 18' (4.3-5.5 m); used for fishing or utility purposes on shallow streams and small protected lakes. They are not fast, are generally heavy and roomy. (Some light, flat-bottomed boats plane and are fast.)

Round bottom (displacement) hulls. Dinghies, tenders, car-top craft, occasionally runabouts 12' to 18' (3.7-5.5-m). These hulls at slow speeds are often more easily driven and maneuvered than the flat-bottomed craft. (Many fast, light, round-bottom boats will also plane.)

Vee-bottom hulls. Commonly used for runabouts, utilities, and cruisers when speed is a factor. Forward undersection is usually deep "V" in shape. Bottom flattens toward amidships, until at the stern it becomes broad and flat.

Hydroplane (planing) hulls. Generally used for racing. Bottom, which is flat, may be "stepped," i.e., divided into two levels, about amidships. The resultant notch reduces wetted surface, increasing speed.

Other terms that may be used are "utility" and "runabout." A utility and a runabout, in effect, are practically interchangeable terms. Both craft function about the same, are about the same size, take about the same horsepower, etc. The runabout, however, is generally considered to be a bit faster and more luxuriously equipped than a utility of comparable size.

FIG. 2805 Although this runabout demonstrates great carrying capacity, she should never carry so many passengers. Overloading is dangerous practice in small craft. No one should be permitted on forward deck while under way.

Size and loading

Economic considerations are, of course, a primary aspect in the choice of the size of an outboard boat, but its use and the typical number of persons to be aboard at any one time must also be considered. Coast Guard rules require that boats under 20' (6.1 m) (except sailboats and some special types) manufactured after 31 October 1972 *must* carry a "capacity plate" showing maximum allowable loads computed from complex formulas. Since August 1980, plates for outboard boats show a maximum horsepower for motor(s), maximum number of persons, and maximum weights both for persons only, and for motor, gear, *and persons;* see fig. 1023. Plates for inboard, I-O and unpowered craft omit maximum power rating.

Boats manufactured before this regulation *may* carry a capacity plate prepared from earlier formulas. If there is no such plate, there is a double check which, if properly used, will help prevent overloading.

First, a check of the *number* of persons:

$$\frac{L \times B}{15} = \text{_____ number of persons}$$

L = Overall Length
B = Maximum Width (Both dimensions in feet and tenths of feet)

The results, taken to the nearest whole number, gives the *number of persons* that can be put aboard without crowding in good weather conditions.

Second, one must *also* check the weight-carrying capacity to be certain the boat is adequate for that number of persons, taking into account their actual weight as well as the weight of engine, fuel, and equipment.

The *weight carrying capacity* of a small boat having a conventional hull can be checked by determining the allowable weight in pounds from the expression:

$$7.5 \times L \times B \times De = \text{_____ pounds for persons,}$$
engine, fuel and equipment

L is Overall Length
B is Maximum Width
De is *Minimum* Effective Depth of the Boat

Measure De at the *lowest point* that water can enter. This takes account of low transom cut-out or credits an acceptable engine well. All dimensions are in feet and tenths.

Having figured the total weight-carrying capacity of your boat by the above method, now use Table 28-1 to find the capacity that is available for *people.*

In any particular loading situation, the skipper should *obey whichever value,* from the number-of-persons formula or the weight capacity available for people, *sets the lower limit.*

Construction material

Small light boats are made of three basic materials: wood, metal, and fiber-reinforced plastics. Although "fiberglass" is now the leader in new boat construction for a number of reasons including lessened maintenance and adaptability to mass production, recent registration figures show that there are still significant numbers of small boats made of other materials. In round figures, there are 1.2 million craft of wood, 2.3 million of metal (almost entirely aluminum), and 2.6 million of fiberglass.

WEIGHT AND PERSON CAPACITY TABLE

(1)	Weight Carrying Capacity of Boat . . . . . . _____ lbs.	
	Add weight of:	
	—outboard motor . . . _____ lbs.	
	—battery . . . . . . _____ lbs.	
	—fuel tank and fuel (gas = 6 lbs. per gal.) . _____ lbs.	
	—equipment: anchor, oars, radio, etc. . _____ lbs.	
(2)	Total . . . . _____ lbs.	
(3)	Remaining Weight Available for Persons . . . _____ lbs. [Subtract (2) from (1)]	

Table 28-1 This table, used as described in the text, guides the skipper in determining the number of persons that can be safely carried, based on weight-capacity considerations.

Personal preferences and cost will undoubtedly be the controlling factor in the selection of a new or used craft, but the boatman will not go wrong with any of these materials if he purchases a well-designed and honestly-built craft.

Special design features

Many craft will have special design features for particular applications such as sport fishing. These invariably add to the cost of a boat and should be avoided unless that use will be made of the boat.

A design feature that can well be looked for on any outboard for the aspect of safety is the "motor well." Most craft have a transom that is "cut down" or lowered where

FIG. 2806 When the transom of a boat is cut down for the motor—and no full-height bulkhead is forward of the cut-down area—this reduced freeboard at the stern must be taken into consideration when figuring the craft's safe capacity.

FIG. 2807 A "motor well' is formed when there is a full-height transverse partition forward of the outboard motor. This is an important safety feature as it keeps the stern from being a low point for the entry of water into the hull.

FIG. 2808 Every small boat should have added buoyancy material to keep it, its motor, and its crew afloat if it swamps. It is extremely desirable that it float in an upright position; this is accomplished by placing the buoyant material high in the hull around the gunwales.

the motor or motors are to be attached; this is necessary so that the motor will be low enough that the lower unit and propeller will be well below the bottom of the hull. Such a mounting provides efficiency for the motor, but may seriously jeopardize the safety of the craft by providing an easier point of access for water into the hull. Safety can be maintained by an inner bulkhead forward of the motor that is not cut down, that is fully as high as the sides of the boat. The space aft of this bulkhead to the cut down transom is the motor well, and self-bailing drains should be provided at each corner; see fig. 2807.

Added buoyancy

Still another step can be taken to ensure the safety of your passengers and boating rig—built-in flotation. This can take the form of sealed air chambers or masses of plastic foam. In either case, there must be enough added buoyancy to support the weight of the boat and motor even though completely flooded.

It is very desirable that the added buoyance be located *high* in the hull so that the craft, if swamped, will float in any upright position and not capsize. Such a way of floating provides much greater safety for the skipper and his passengers. Persons in the water will be able to hold on more easily and it may be possible to recover some form of emergency signalling, bailing, or other needed equipment.

For boats less than 20 feet (6.1 m) in length, except sailboats and some special types, Coast Guard regulations specify flotation performance and materials. These are effective for craft manufactured after 31 July 1973.

The Motor and Accessories

An outboard motor is a *detachable* power plant of from one to six cylinders which is complete with drive shaft and propeller. The fuel tank and operating controls are usually separate, but may be integral on the smallest motors. It is a gasoline-fueled motor, nearly always of two-cycle design. It is normally raw-water cooled, and may be either manually or electrically started in the medium and larger size models.

Inboard-Outboards

A newer type of mechanical propulsion for small craft combines a conventional marine inboard engine with a drive unit that closely resembles the lower unit of an outboard motor. This is variously termed "inboard-outboard (I-O)," "outdrive," "stern drive," or other generally similar descriptive words or phrases. It seeks to combine the greater power and efficiency of an inboard engine (four-cycle) with the directed-thrust steering, tilt-up action, and other advantageous features of outboard propulsion.

Boats of I-O design can generally be included with outboards, except for matters directly relating to the engine. They are usually in the size category of medium and larger outboard craft, handle similarly, are used for the same general purposes, and can be trailered.

OUTBOARD MOTOR SELECTION

The first question *always* seems to be, "How much horsepower?" Such other factors as weight, electric starting, even price, seem to routinely come second to "horse-

FIG. 2809 An outboard motor offers many desirable features for smaller craft. It is detachable for storage and servicing; it gives great maneuverability with "power steering"; and it can tilt up if the lower unit strikes a submerged obstruction.

FIG. 2810 The inboard-outboard, or out-drive, type of propulsion offers the economy and power of an inboard engine without giving up outboard features such as directed-thrust steering and tiltability.

FIG. 2811 Use of an inboard-outboard drive unit will permit installation of diesel power in quite small craft. Cost may be greater than for a gasoline engine, but there are operating economy and safety features.

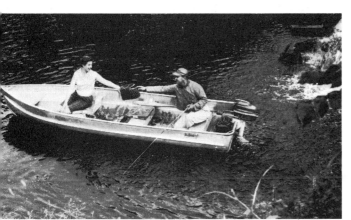

FIG. 2812 For use on protected inland waters with a utility type of craft, a motor of 10 horsepower is adequate. More power would be wasted on this displacement type of hull, and might be unsafe.

FIG. 2813 Water-skiing takes speed, and this requires horsepower. Typically, motors of 40 horsepower or more are used on planing types of hulls for this fast, exciting sport.

power." Outboard motors have been available for essentially all this century, with a slow rate of increase in horsepower until World War II, and a startlingly rapid rise in power ratings in recent years. The larger outboard motors have long ceased to be a *readily* detachable piece of machinery that one could walk up a pier with, carrying it by one hand. Power ratings of stock motors are now up to 200 hp, with weights over 375 pounds (170 kg).

Enough, but not too much!

The horsepower required for a boat will depend upon the size and weight of the craft (loaded), and the speed that it is desired to make. A displacement hull of 14 feet (4.3 m) or so will serve adequately for lake and river fishing with a 10 hp motor; any greater horsepower would be largely wasted in an attempt to drive the craft faster than "hull speed."

For water skiing behind a planing hull, typically a 16 to 18 footer (4.9-5.5 m), a skipper should consider 40 to 75 horsepower. A larger engine will make the boat go faster (provided the hull has the capacity for greater power), but not at all in proportion to the increase in engine power. Very roughly, horsepower must be tripled or even quadrupled to double speed.

For cruising about, either day trips or longer ventures, the typical outboard craft is a planing-type hull. It may not be operated at its maximum attainable speed, but "running on a plane" is both more enjoyable and economical

than pushing one's way through the water in the displacement mode. The size of motor must be considered from a consideration of the boat *and* its normal load of persons and equipment. No specific recommendation can be made — each situation is a case unto itself — but the boatman would be well-advised to make a trial run of any boat and motor combination prior to closing a purchase deal. These trials should be made *with load,* either actual or simulated with weights, and figuring a bit of excess for later additions. If at all possible, try the "rig" (outboarders' language for a boat and motor combination, sometimes also including a trailer) in various conditions of wind and water that are typical of how it is expected to be used.

FIG. 2814 Outboard motors have steadily grown in size until now the largest models produce 150 hp or more, and weigh over 350 pounds (160 kg)—a long way in both categories from the early models of only a few horsepower.

Rating plates

USCG regulations require that all outboard boats under 20 feet in length (except sailboats and certain special types) built after 31 October 1972 must show maximum horsepower on the required "capacity plate."

Lacking a rating plate, the maximum safe horsepower may be calculated from two dimensions of the boat, length and width *at the stern*. The product of these dimensions, in feet and tenths, taken to the nearest whole number, gives a "factor" which can be applied to Tables 28-2 and 28-3. These tables are illustrated graphically as fig. 2816 and 2817, respectively. For flat bottom, hard chine boats, the capacities of Tables 28-2 and fig. 2816 must be reduced by one increment. The horsepower ratings from Table 28-3 and fig. 2817 may be increased to the next greater multiple of 5 hp.

Both the tables and the figures referred to above are for outboard craft only. They give the maximum horsepower whether from one engine or two. Length is measured from the stem to the transom along a straight line parallel to the keel; do not include extensions such as outboard motor brackets in this measurement.*

A couple of examples may make these calculations a bit more clear. First, consider a round-bottom dinghy measuring 10 feet in length and 3 feet, 8 inches across its stern. The product of 10 x 3.7 gives a factor 37. From either Table 28-2 or fig. 2816, we can see that this craft should be limited to a 5 hp motor.

For a larger outboard boat with a length of 17 feet and a stern width of 5 feet, 2 inches, the factor would be 17 x 5.2 or 88.4, used as 88. *If* the craft had *both* remote steering and a 20-inch high transom, the horsepower capacity calculation would be (2 x 88) − 90 = 86, which can be rounded up to 90. This might be either a single 90 hp motor or twins of 45 hp each. If this craft lacked *either* remote steering or a transom height of 20 inches (or both), the horsepower capacity would be calculated as (¾ x 88) − 20 = 46, used as 50 hp, a significant reduction.

Recent research has shown that a series of carefully planned and instrumented tests can sometimes result in safe higher horsepower ratings than those produced by using the USCG calculations. The average skipper, however, should continue to use the above method unless he is satisfied that the manufacturer has responsibly established a higher rating.

Electric starting?

Early outboard motors were started by winding a short length of rope around the top of the flywheel for about two turns and then giving a strong pull—or perhaps several! This method, with refinements such as built-in pull cords that automatically retract and rewind themselves, remain in use for smaller and some medium horsepower motors. As the power ratings increased, it became necessary to go to electric starting motors to provide the required cranking power. This feature proved popular with boatmen, and their crews, and soon was extended downward to medium-power models, often as an optional accessory.

FIG. 2815 Before buying a combination of boat and motor, try it out under varying conditions of wind and water, and be sure to have a full normal load, live or simulated aboard.

BOAT HORSEPOWER CAPACITY CURVES

LENGTH X STERN WIDTH (FT) (FACTOR)

FIG. 2816 If the product of length and width at the stern is less than 52, the diagram (left) will graphically indicate the maximum safe horsepower.

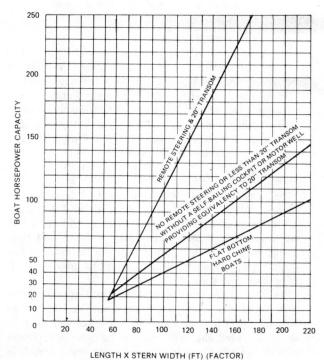

BOAT HORSEPOWER CAPACITY CURVES

LENGTH X STERN WIDTH (FT) (FACTOR)

FIG. 2817 For "factors" (product of length and width at the stern) greater than 52.5, the proper line on the above diagram is chosen as determined by such design characteristics as location of steering controls, presence of motor well, etc.

*Dimensions in metric units must be converted to English units to use these tables and diagrams; 1 meter = 3.18 feet, 1 cm = 0.39 inches.

Multiply overall length _____ x stern width _____ = factor _____ (nearest whole number)					
If this factor is	thru 35	36–39	40–42	43–45	46–52
H.P. capacity is	3	5	7-1/2	10	15

Table 28-2 The product of boat length times width at the stern gives a "factor" which can be used with this table to determine the maximum safe horsepower for the hull.

	Remote steering and 20" Transom or equivalent	No remote steering or Transom less than 20" or equivalent	
		Flat Bottom Hard Chine Boats	Other Boats
If this factor is	over 52.5	over 52.5	over 52.5
H.P. capacity is	(2 x factor) - 90	(1/2 factor) - 15	(0.8 factor) - 25
H.P. capacity = _____ (raise to next higher multiple of 5)			

Table 28-3 When the "factor" is greater than 52.5, multiplication and subtraction are used to determine the maximum safe horsepower for hulls in each of three general categories.

FIG. 2818 Twin outboard motors give a greater degree of security from complete loss of power, but only at the cost of greater investment, weight, and fuel consumption. Their use over a single, larger motor must be carefully considered.

Electric starting requires additional equipment — and weight and cost — the starting motor, a battery, control wiring, etc., but the considerable added convenience is usually greatly appreciated by all concerned. In general, motors under 10 hp will be manually started, and those over 40 hp will be electrically started; motors between these sizes may have either method of starting.

Nearly all electrically started outboard motors are also equipped with an *alternator* to supply electricity for battery charging and the operation of other accessories. This feature may not be automatically included on motors that have electric starting as an additional-cost option.

Single or twins?

Many outboard hulls are designed at the transom to allow the fitting of either one or two motors. There are definite advantages and disadvantages of each method for the same total horsepower. Some years ago, the largest available motors did not have enough power for larger craft or higher speeds; the use of multiple motors was the only solution. Now, a single large motor may well supply all the power that the hull can safely handle, and a choice must be made, one large single or smaller twins?

The reason most often advanced for twin motors rather than a single one of the total horsepower is added safety. Outboard motors are very reliable if given adequate care, but failures do occur, and many a boatman has made it home "on one" when the other was incapacitated.

The disadvantages, however, are many and must be considered. Greater initial cost (not twice as much but about 1⅓ times the price of a single large motor), a second battery or larger single one, more complex control systems, greater weight in the boat (about 50% more), greater underwater drag, and greater fuel consumption (again not doubled, but greater by ⅓ to ½); all these are negative factors that must not be overlooked. Twin motors, and their batteries and fuel tanks, will also take up greater space within the boat than that used for a single-motor installation.

A special case in the larger outboard cruiser where the use of two motors is required to meet horsepower needs, and where the weight and space penalties are less impor-

tant. Twin motors here will also allow the use of more efficient propellers with larger blade area.

The consideration above has been of the same total horsepower in a single or twin motors. Let us now look at a comparison of one motor with two of the same size (always assuming that the doubled horsepower is within the capacity of the hull). If a boat has performed to certain standards with one motor, what may be expected if a second, identical motor is added? First of all, the speed will *not* be doubled. The added weight and drag, combined with hydrodynamic factors, will hold the speed increase to roughly 25%, although this will vary widely with specific installations. Even if both motors are operated at the same rpms, fuel consumption will not be doubled as the second motor seems to "help" the first one; very roughly, the total fuel consumption will be about 1½ times that of the single motor rig.

A big one and a little one

A combination seen more and more often is that of a single large motor adequate for all normal operation, plus a smaller motor of 4 to 10 horsepower. The smaller motor is used for trolling while fishing—large motors do not like to run at idle speeds for extended periods of time—and for emergency back-up. A 6 hp motor will move a medium size outboard hull at 3 or 4 mph and get you home or to assistance if the main unit fails.

PROPELLORS

An outboard motor is sold complete with a propellor; this is a "stock" propellor, a suitable propellor for an average boat under average conditions. (Some outboard motors, especially the larger models—are offered with a choice of several propellors.) The stock propellor will undoubtedly be usable on your craft, but it probably will *not* be the optimum in pitch or diameter, or both Consideration should be given to changing to a more suitable

FIG. 2820 Light but very strong propellors are being made of stainless steel coated with Teflon. Much stronger than aluminum or bronze, these blades can be made thinner for higher efficiency and performance.

FIG. 2819 One of the advantages of outboard boating is ease with which a propeller can be changed in the case of damage or to have a more optimum diameter and pitch for a particular use of the boat.

propellor for *your* boat.

Manufacturers do publish tables of recommended propellor sizes for various applications, but these can serve as little more than initial guides. The answer lies in experimentation—unless you should be so lucky as to know another skipper who has an identical boat and motor combination, and whose style of boating matches yours.

The "right" propellor for any craft in a specific application is the one which allows the motor to turn up to its full rated rpm, but no more. It is necessary for the motor to turn up full rated rpm to develop full rated power; but if it will turn faster than that, the propellor is too small and full power is not being developed at the rated maximum rpm (which must not be exceeded except for brief tests).

If the craft is used for more than one type of activity, such as cruising, fishing, water skiing, etc., it may be that the same motor will require different propellors for the most efficient operation in each usage. As a spare propellor is an excellent safety item, the purchase of a more efficient propellor is not all "added expense"—the stock propellor becomes the spare.

Materials

Most stock propellors are aluminum, as are those normally purchased for more optimum performance. Propellors of bronze are also available; these are stronger and more easily repaired, but are more expensive.

Propellors of stainless steel and other high-strength alloys are advantageous for special applications, but are even more costly than bronze. Plastic is used for the propellors of some of the smaller motors, and a recent development is a teflon-coated steel propellor, said to be very strong and efficient yet light in weight.

Number of blades

For a stock propellor, most outboard motors are equipped with a three-blade type. For lighter loads, and faster speeds, a two-blade propellor may do a better job.

For lower rpm use on heavier craft, it may be desirable to install a four-blade propellor. The number of blades, is, of course, a factor closely inter-related to diameter and pitch.

Pitch

The pitch of a propellor determines its "bite" on the water, and thus the rpm which the motor can turn up, (this is also affected by propellor diameter). This in turn is related to the speed of the craft through the water—a lighter, faster boat will use a propellor of greater pitch, and a heavier, slower craft will use one of lesser pitch. Again, experimentation is really the only way of selecting the best match of propellor to the boat.

There are available on the market propellors for medium-size motors that allow an adjustment of pitch over a wide range. These are quite useful if load and speed conditions vary greatly, but this should not interfere with the carrying of a second, spare propellor.

If a single motor is "doubled up" with another similar to it, this will call for a change of propellor on the original motor. The faster speed obtained with the added horsepower will call for a greater pitch, probably one, but possibly two, inches more; again, only actual trials will tell for sure. (1 inch = 2.54 cm)

Shear pins and slip clutches

Somehow, outboard motors seem to run aground more than inboards, or at least the lower parts of the motor strike the bottom more often. To prevent damage to the

FIG. 2821 Having the correct propellor pitch is essential to optimum performance. Here the skipper is adjusting the dial which changes the pitch on this special propellor. If pitch is not adjustable, it may be a wise move to carry several propellors of different pitch for use under varying conditions.

FIG. 2822 Smaller outboard motors commonly use a "shear pin" to protect the drive shaft and other parts of the motor should the propellor strike a submerged obstruction. Driving power is transmitted through a pin of soft metal which will break if the propellor hits something. This pin must be replaced if sheared; several spares must be carried on board.

A shear pin is made of a relatively soft metal. It is installed so as to transmit the drive from the propellor shaft to the propellor, and is strong enough for this. Upon impact with a rock or other hard object by a propellor blade, this pin is broken, sheared off near each end, and the propellor is effectively disconnected from the motor. The outboard motor is then inoperative insofar as thrust is concerned until the propellor hub, and perhaps the propellor itself, is removed and a new pin installed.

To overcome the nuisance of having to replace sheared pins, manufacturers developed slip clutches in which a rubber inner hub is used to transmit the drive power. Under normal loads, there is no slippage, but upon impact with a hard object by a propellor blade (or even with the sudden load of a too-quick shift of gears), the rubber hub slips somewhat to absorb the strain. Obviously, there is here no internal component that need be replaced after impact, and yet it provides adequate protection for the motor, clearly an improvement over shear pins.

drive shaft and gears, and possibly other internal parts of the motor, these are equipped with either a *shear pin* (smaller motors) or a *slip clutch* (larger motors).

Equipment

The outboard boat must first of all meet legal requirements for equipment according to its size classification. The federal requirements have been spelled out in Chapter 3 and will not be repeated here. The craft must also carry any additional equipment required by state and/or local regulations. (The Federal Boat Safety Act of 1971 provides that no state or local jurisdiction can enforce regulations that are not identical with Federal regulations except as specifically authorized. This provision, however, has been suspended for all state and local regulations in effect as of 10 August 1971 pending the issuance of new and more detailed Federal regulations under the authority of the 1971 Act.) Boatmen venturing into new waters subject to other regulations than "at home" should check with a marina operator, park ranger, or other local authority to avoid inadvertant violations.

Navigation lights

Even if you plan absolutely never to use your boat at night, it should be equipped with navigation lights in accordance with the waters on which it *may* be found some evening after sunset. Engine trouble, fuel problems, unexpectedly good fishing, or other situations may keep you out longer than you intended. See Chapter 4 for details on the navigation lights for each class of boat or various waters.

Several items regarding legal requirements for navigation lights should be especially noted by the outboard skipper. Nearly all OB craft are delivered with a red-green combination light forward and an all-around white light aft. Such lights are legal, on U.S. waters *only,* if they are properly used *and meet the requirements of the regulations.* All too often the aft light is not high enough to meet the requirements for *all-around* visibility, especially when the craft is underway and the bow rises or when the canvas top is raised. Some lights are on a telescoping stem so that they may be lowered when not in use during daylight for convenience and to protect the mounting from accidental damage. Even when raised, these are usually too low to

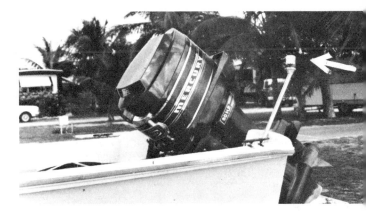

FIG. 2823 This stern light is too low to meet the legal requirements for all-around visibility—its beams will be blocked in some directions by the motor. For safety's sake, be sure that your white light can be seen from all directions when running or at anchor.

be seen from ahead. The prudent skipper will check his craft and make sure that he can be seen at night from *any* direction; the white light is even more important than the colored lights as it will be seen at a greater distance. These checks should be made both with the boat underway when the white light is a "running" light, and with the craft dead in the water simulating use of the white light as an anchor light.

Under the regulations of the old Motorboat Act of 1940 (which are continued in effect under the new Act until specifically superceded), boats up to 26 feet (7.9 m) in length *may* carry the white all-around light off the centerline of the craft as is sometimes made necessary by the positioning of an outboard motor or motors.

It should also be noted that the white all-around aft light described above does *not* meet the requirements of International Rules of the Road. These Rules require two separate white lights as described on pages 64(s) to 64(u).

No exception is made for outboards, although it is permissible for the after 12-point light to be located off the centerline for craft less than 26 feet (7.9 m) in length. If your fishing or cruising takes you beyond the boundary lines between Inland and International Rules, see page 31, then you must equip your boat with navigation lights to meet the requirements of those waters.

EQUIPMENT FOR SAFETY

Equipment for safety and convenience was also covered in Chapter 3 for boats in general. Here we will consider some of these, plus other, more specialized items specifically related to outboards.

Life saving devices

Outboards are more likely to capsize than are larger inboard craft, and consequently there is a greater possibility of the skipper and crew finding themselves in the water. The wise outboard skipper does not skimp on personal flotation devices. Although buoyant cushions are less expensive and are legally acceptable, life preservers or buoyant vests, see pages 52-56, offer substantially greater personal protection; they are worn rather than grasped and so provide greater safety for the injured or exhausted person. It should be an absolute "rule of the boat" that adult non-swimmers and all children *wear* a life preserver or buoyant vest *at all times* when the craft is underway. At the higher speeds of most outboards, there may not be time to locate and put on a life jacket when a sudden emergency occurs.

"Special purpose life saving devices" *approved by the Coast Guard,* such as some hunter's jackets and some water skiing *vests,* are legally acceptable items for smaller boats not carrying passengers for hire; ski *belts,* however, are not so approved and are not acceptable in meeting the legal requirements although their use is recommended while water skiing.

Paddle or oar

Required in some state and local jurisdictions, and by the Coast Guard Auxiliary for their courtesy examination decal, a paddle or pair of oars should be on all outboard boats. They could be the only way of reaching safety in the event of motor failure. Most outboard craft row or paddle quite clumsily and with considerable effort, but it can be done, and the means to do so should be on board.

Anchor and line

Every outboard should be equipped with a suitable anchor and line adequate in length for anchoring in es-

FIG. 2824 Regardless of the normal dependability of the outboard motor, small boats should be equipped with a paddle or two, or a pair of oars for emergency use. Some craft can be propelled manually more easily than others, but all can be so worked to safety, even tho slowly.

FIG. 2825 Every boat should carry at least one anchor and line of sufficient length for the waters cruised. The anchor may be used in a variety of situations, see text, and is essential in case of engine failure.

FIG. 2826 A scoop or hand bailer of some sort is a very desirable back-up to the pump or other means of removing rain and spray from the boat. These may be purchased inexpensively or home made easily. A large sponge is frequently useful for getting that last little bit of water out of the boat.

FIG. 2827 Every boat, even the smallest, should be equipped with distress signalling equipment. This should include an orange flag and orange smoke signals for day use, plus red flares for nighttime emergencies. All these should be kept dry in a waterproof container.

sentially all areas in which the boat is used. Obviously, this requirement must be applied with reason when the craft is used off very deep coasts, but do err on the side of having too much rather than too little when you decide on the length of your anchor line.

Anchors may be used in their normal manner, or specially in the case of outboards, when the craft is beached or nearly so. If the boat is fully beached, the anchor may be carried up on shore to keep the craft from drifting away on a rising tide or from the wake of passing vessels. If it is not desired to quite fully beach, the anchor may be used to hold the boat away from the shore, pulling against a line made fast to some object on the land.

Bailer

All small boats should be equipped with a manual bailer. This can be a scoop purchased or home-made from a household plastic jug; see fig. 2826. Transom drains are effective underway for many fast craft, but must have a means of closure when not in use. Manual or even electric pumps may be found on larger outboards. A large sponge is frequently convenient for getting that last little bit of water out of a small boat.

Distress signals

An outboard boat should be equipped with a distress signalling package consisting of several daytime orange

FIG. 2828 An electric lantern is an excellent item for any small boat whether or not operation after darkness is planned. If it will float, like the one shown that's an extra advantage for they do sometimes get dropped overboard.

FIG. 2829 A safety chain or cable is an excellent item for smaller boats on which the outboard motor is installed and removed at various times. It will prevent loss if the clamps work loose; it should be fastened just as soon as it will reach, and remain fastened as long as possible as the motor is being detached.

smoke signals, several nighttime red flares, and an orange flag (sea dye marker is also advisable for boats that will operate off-shore). Even though nighttime use of the craft is not contemplated, you may find yourself stranded out on the water after dark, so carry red flares. Do *not*, however, consider such flares a substitute for the orange smoke signals, which are much more effective for use in daylight.

Flashlight or lantern

Every outboard craft should be equipped with a flashlight or electric lantern whether or not it is ever intended to use the boat after dark. This item should be waterproof and it is desirable that it float if accidentally dropped into the water. Extra batteries, stored in a waterproof container, will often prove valuable in an emergency. Batteries in the flashlight or lantern, and the spares, should be renewed at the start of each boating season regardless of their apparent condition.

OPERATIONAL EQUIPMENT

A magnetic compass is an item of equipment that cannot be placed solely in either the safety or operational category; it fits both! Almost all outboards in their various applications can make good use of a compass. Select one of adequate size and quality, and install it properly. See Chapters 13 and 14 for additional information.

As most outboards are relatively open craft, it is particularly important that the compass be kept shielded from the sun's direct rays. When not in use, place a cover over its top; this should be completely light-tight, colored plastic or cloth will not do an adequate job.

Charts

One or more charts should be carried covering the waters being used. Learn to use a chart with your compass, and do use it under favorable conditions even where such use is not strictly necessary. This practice is excellent training and will prepare you for use with confidence and efficiency should an emergeny arise. Make a point of keeping track at all times of where you are on a body of water.

Tools

Every boat, no matter how small, should carry at least a few simple hand tools. The minimum should be a screwdriver, pair of pliers, and an adjustable open-end wrench. Consideration might be given to having two or more screwdrivers and wrenches in different sizes.

Safety chain

Most outboard motors are clamped to the craft's transom (a few of the larger ones may be through bolted). To protect against accidental loss overboard should the clamps loosen with vibration, a short *safety chain* (or cable) is often used between a connecting point on the motor and a ring securely fastened to the hull of the boat. Chains or lengths of steel cable, frequently plastic-coated to reduce rusting, may be inexpensively purchased for this purpose already equipped with snap fittings at each end; this is "cheap insurance" against an accidental dunking of an expensive motor, or its possible total loss in deep water.

Extra fuel tanks

The very smallest outboard motors have an integral fuel tank, but those of three or more horsepower now normally operate from external tanks which are more convenient with their larger capacity. Larger rigs, boats of 18 feet (5.5 m) or so in length with high horsepower motors, usually have built-in tanks.

It is often necessary to carry additional fuel in order to make long runs without stops. A skipper should carefully select any container or spare fuel tank; it must be made for that specific use. The material of the tank and its design must be satisfactory for containing gasoline in a marine (often salt water) environment. Homemade or converted tanks are very often hazardous.

Steering and other controls

The simplest outboard motors are directly controlled at the motor itself. A steering handle, or tiller, is used to turn the motor from side to side for steering the craft. A throttle to control motor speed may be incorporated into the tiller or may be a separate lever on the motor. A gear shift lever —for forward, neutral, and reverse—is located on the side of the motor. Controls for choking and carburetor jet adjustment are usually on the front of the motor.

In order to locate the skipper further forward than at the immediate stern next to the motor, *remote controls* are necessary. These are of two different kinds, a wheel for steering and a lever or levers for the throttle and gear shifting.

Steering controls may consist of a continuous loop of metallic cable (usually plastic covered) running from one side of the engine forward, around a drum on the shaft of the steering wheel, and back aft to the other side of the

FIG. 2830 The use of a steering wheel and remote motor controls will permit the operator of a small outboard boat to sit further forward. This improves the longitudinal trim and makes for safer operation; also, this usually make possible the use of motors of greater horsepower and weight.

motor. Pulleys are used to guide the cable, which may run forward on one side of the boat and aft on the other, or may run fore and aft on the same side. Another form of steering that gives excellent results is rod steering in which a stiff linkage is pushed back and forth in a protective sheath. Rack and pinion type of gearing at the steering wheel shaft imparts the push or pull which moves the motor from side to side around its central pivot. Rod steering gives smooth control and is free of the hazards of the exposed cables of the other type.

Hydraulic steering is feasible and quite good, but is rarely found on outboards. Likewise, automatic steering mechanisms, erroneously called "automatic pilots," are available for quite small boats, but are seldom found on outboards.

Throttle and gear shift controls also consist of a stiff cable within a sheath to transmit the back and forth motion required. With some equipment, the two controls are combined at the helm into a single lever which is pushed forward to go ahead faster and pulled backward, through a neutral center position, to go faster sternward. This mechanism is somewhat more complex than separate throttle and gear shift controls, and may give some troubles, but it does offer considerable operating convenience.

Tachometers

The need for an efficient propeller, and the importance of trials, have been mentioned above. The skipper must be able to measure engine rpm and boat speed; the former requires a *tachometer* and the latter is more easily done with a *speedometer*, both relatively inexpensive instruments.

An electronic tachometer can be fitted to essentially any outboard motor; it is a simple job requiring little technical know-how and only an hour or two of the skipper's time. This instrument, when properly calibrated, will indicate *motor* revolutions per minute and guide you in the selection of a propellor which will allow the motor to develop its full rated rpm and power.

Speedometers

Speed can be checked by timed runs over measured

distances, but a *speedometer* for an outboard boat is such a simple device that one should be considered. Direct-reading speed indicating devices for smaller craft normally operate from the pressure of the water on a pickup head as the craft moves forward. This, too, can be easily installed by the average outboard owner. Accuracy may be only moderate, but it can be calibrated by timed runs over known distances; see page 390. Even it not accurate in absolute terms, it can be adequately used to determine the relative speeds obtained with various motor and propeller combinations. Calibration is, however, necessary if it is to be used in navigation.

Electronic depth sounders

Many outboard craft can carry an electronic depth sounder and put it to good use. Special transom mounts are available for smaller boats where through-hull mounting may not be practical. More on this very useful item of electronic equipment will be found in Chapter 25.

Radiotelephones

Radios,—either VHF/FM or Citizens Band—are often installed on outboards that have a battery for electric-starting motors and an alternator to keep the battery charged. VHF equipment, with its smaller antennas, is especially suitable for smaller boats. Care should be taken to install equipment that is suitable for the craft and its intended operation; consult an expert (not just a salesman!) if you don't have the knowledge to make the choice yourself. In many applications, radios may fit into the "safety" rather than "operational" category; buy wisely. See also Chapter 25.

Boat covers

Many outboard boats have a cover of canvas or similar material. Some styles will cover the boat from the stem to and including the upper part of the motor; other designs will only cover the open parts of the craft. These are excellent for keeping rain and dirt out of the boat and will provide protection to any varnished or painted wood surfaces. Covers should, however, be used with caution as adequate ventilation of the interior of the boat is a *must* if mildew, "dry rot," and other forms of fungus growth are to be avoided; vents of proper design should be a part of the cover.

FIG. 2831 Outboard and inboard-outboard boats are especially suited for use on snorkeling or scuba-diving expeditions. Their shoal draft and the tiltability of the lower unit make them desirable for in-shore or over-reef work.

The cover must fit the boat it is used with, and must be capable of being adequately secured by means of snaps or a drawstring. (Snaps or other mechanical fasteners should be protected from corrosion by a non-staining lubricant; a silicone grease stick is excellent for this purpose.) Covers are of perhaps their greatest value when a boat is being trailered, but they must be fastened down adequately to prevent wind damage. In outdoor storage, a cover must also be adequately supported internally to prevent the formation of pools of rain water that will stretch and eventually tear the cover, dumping the water into the boat.

REGISTRATION AND NUMBERING

Boats are subject to the registration requirements of their "state of principal use" or the Coast Guard; see Chapter 2. Effective in 1974, the previous exemption from registration and numbering for boats with motors of less than 10 hp (or lesser specified horsepower in some states) was removed by the Federal Boat Safety Act of 1971. Now all "mechanically propelled" boats must be numbered if they are not documented. Additionally, some states have extended registration to cover "all watercraft," or "sailboats over 16 feet in length," or other categories of boats.*

Operation

As noted earlier in connection with considerations of selecting the boat, an outboard rig can be used for many, widely varied purposes—fishing, water skiing, cruising, skin diving, and others. In *each* of these applications, greater safety and enjoyment will result from knowing and using the proper boating practices.

Boarding

Before a boat can be used, one must get on board it. There is a right and a wrong way—perhaps several wrong ways—and the difference becomes increasingly important as the size of the boat decreases.

If you are boarding from a beach, climb in over the bow when practicable. When boarding from a float or low pier, step aboard as nearly amidships, both from side to side and stem to stern, as possible. Bend your body so that your weight is kept low, thus helping to keep the boat stable. Grasp the gunwale (the top of the boat's sides) for balance. In a small outboard, do *not* step on the gunwale or you will most likely flip the craft.

Do not carry bulky or heavy items of gear or supplies while boarding. If you are alone, place these items on the pier where you can reach them once you are safely aboard; or have someone ashore hand them to you.

MOTOR ADJUSTMENT

Begin your outboarding by installing the motor properly —the manufacturer's diagrams will help in doing this. Basically, the task is to seat the motor squarely on the center of the transom and securely tighten the bracket screws. Some motors come with special mounting plates; with others you may desire to use a rubber pad to reduce vibrations and prevent the transom from being marred. The safety chain mentioned above as desirable equipment should be connected between the motor and the hull.

If twin motors are to be used, they should be mounted with the proper spacing between them. The AB&YC rec-

*16 feet = 4.88 meters

FIG. 2832 Although the wide beam of a cathedral-hull craft gives it considerable lateral stability, a safer way to get aboard is with both hands free. Large or heavy objects should be left on the pier until you are safely aboard; then reach back for them, or have someone hand them to you.

FIG. 2833 The proper relationship between the motor and the boat's hull is very important. The anti-cavigation plate should be in line with the bottom of the hull at the stern for a proper flow of water to the propellor.

FIG. 2834 The AB&YC recommended dimensions for the sketch above are: "A" 33 inches for single motors, 54 inches for twins of less than 61hp each, and 60 inches for twins of 61 or more horsepower. The centerline spacing — "S" — should be 22 inches for under 61hp and 26 inches for larger motors. (1 inch = 2.54 cm)

ommended center-to-center separation is 22" (55.9 cm) for motors under 61 hp and 26" (66.0 cm) for larger motors. Standardized motor well dimensions are recommended to manufacturers which will allow this spacing.

If a combination of a large and small motor is used, the large unit is mounted on the craft's centerline, with the small "kicker" off to one side, usually on a bracket designed for such use. (Such brackets allow the small motor to be raised entirely clear of the water to reduce drag when it is not in use, yet keep it out of the boat.) The low horsepower of the small motor will prevent any significant steering problems from its off-center placement.

Motor height

Although there has been a high degree of standardization in the design of transom cut-outs for motor mounting, it is wise to check that the lower unit is correctly located with respect to the bottom of the hull. Motors are made in different shaft lengths, 15 and 20 inches (38 and 51 cm)* are common, and a transom can be modified if necessary to ensure proper motor positioning. The *anti-cavitation plate* on the lower unit should line up with the transom chine; see fig. 2833. If the motor is too high, a smooth flow of water will not reach the propellor and it will not be able to get a proper "grip" on the water. This may cause *cavitation* with definitely less efficient boat operation and possible damage to the propeller or motor through excessive rpm. If the motor is too low, drag will be increased due both to the greater area of the lower unit in the water and a distorted flow over and under the anti-cavitation plate. Attention to this detail of installation will provide both increased speed and decreased fuel consumption.

Thrust line adjustment

Most outboard motors have a tilt adjustment to vary the angle of thrust of the unit. For best performance, the drive of the propeller should be in a line parallel to the flat surface of the water at the boat's most efficient operating angle whether as a planing hull or in the displacement mode.

If the motor is too close in to the transom, the thrust line is upward from horizontal, pushing the stern up and the bow down making the boat "plow" through the water unnecessarily. On the other hand, if the motor is tilted too far out from the transom, the thrust line is below the horizontal and the bow is forced up to ride high while the stern "squats"; see fig. 2835.

Boats differ in design, and loading conditions vary widely with any specific craft, so manufacturers make the adjustment of the tilt angle as easy as possible. On inboard-outboards and some larger outboard motors, there is an electric or electro-hydraulic drive for powered adjustment of the tilt angle; just push the button for "up" or "down."

The wise skipper is aware of the inefficiency of an improper thrust angle and does not neglect to change the tilt adjustment to meet his current operating conditions.

The "best" tilt angle may vary with water conditions. On some craft, an adjustment with the motor a bit more out (bow up) for smooth water may give more speed, but this should be checked for your individual craft. A bit more in (bow down) may give a more "solid" ride in choppy waters, but again only actual trials will tell for sure.

FIG. 2836 Many hulls can be had in nearly identical form as either outboards or inboard-outboards. The prospective skipper should consider carefully the advantages and disadvantages of both these types of propulsion.

Special applications of tilt

While underway, the tilt feature of outboard motors and I-O lower units can be used to advantage for several special situations.

If the propellor becomes fouled with weeds, it is often easy to stop the motor, tilt it up, clear off the vegetation, lower the motor, restart it, and continue on your course. If a smaller motor shears its pin, this can frequently be replaced by tilting the motor and working on it in this position, rather than having to remove the whole unit and bring it into the boat.

It may be possible to partially tilt the motor or I-O lower unit so as to reduce the draft of the craft and get over shoal areas. Do this with caution, however; take care not to tilt so much that the cooling water intake comes above the surface, and watch out that the propellor does not strike rocks or other hard objects that might damage it; proceed slowly when using this technique.

Mixture controls

Many outboard motors will have controls for adjusting the fuel-air mixture ratios to obtain optimum performance at low and/high motor speeds. These are external to the motor cover so that they may be easily adjusted underway; see fig. 2837. Follow the manufacturer's instructions con-

MOTOR ANGLE ADJUSTMENT

FIG. 2835 It is most important for efficient operation of an outboard motor that its thrust be horizontal when the boat is in running trim. Motors are easily adjusted to secure the proper thrust line. Adjustment on smaller motors is made by moving pin (1) to different notches.

INCORRECT
CAUSES BOAT TO "PLOW"

INCORRECT
CAUSES BOAT TO "SQUAT"

CORRECT
GIVES MAXIMUM PERFORMANCE

*Some of the highest horsepower motors now have "extra long" shaft lengths, 25 inches (64 cm).

tained in the manual for the model being used in order to obtain the best results and to minimize the possibility of any damage to the motor from incorrect settings. Smaller motors will have adjustments for both low and high speed operation; medium size and larger motors will normally have only one adjustment, that for low rpm use, the high-speed carburetor jet being fixed.

Changes in fuel, air temperature, and altitude (such as going to mountain lakes from lower elevations or sea level, and vice versa) may require changes in mixture controls. Any adjustment should be made with the motor thoroughly warmed up and the boat loaded to its normal trim.

Essentially all motors will have a manual choke for use when starting.

FUELS AND OILS

Two-cycle outboard motors use a mixture of gasoline and lubricating oil. It is essential that both of these be of the correct type and that the mixture ratio be as specified by the manufacturer of the motor.

Fuels

The drive for a cleaner environment has resulted in the introduction of many gasolines in the "no-lead" and "low-lead" categories. In many of these, other chemicals have been added to maintain the octane rating and other desirable characteristics. These newer fuels have in numerous cases proven to be unsatisfactory, or even unsafe, in marine engines, especially in two-cycle outboard motors.

Automobile engines operate in circumstances of frequently changing speeds and loads. City driving is stop and go; highway driving has its up and down grades, of acceleration to pass another vehicle. On the other hand, marine use frequently involves sustained periods of heavy load at unvarying rpm. The differences in these two sets of operating conditions are significant to engines and their fuels.

Outboard motors are generally of relatively low compression ratios and can use fuels of quite modest octane rating. "Old fashioned" marine white gasoline (which is lead-free, but without the newer replacement additives) is satisfactory; regular leaded automotive fuel is also satisfactory. Do *not* use the modern *no-lead* car gasolines unless you have been advised by a responsible representative of the motor manufacturer that a specific fuel of this type is satisfactory for an outboard motor of your model and year; some low-lead gasolines may be used with adjustment of the ignition timing, but again seek *reliable* advice rather than risk extensive internal damage to your motor.

Oils

The typical outboard motor uses its lubricating oil mixed into the gasoline fuel supply; there is no separate crankcase for oil as there is in automotive and marine four-cycle engines. Thus special properties (low "ash" for example) are required of outboard oil, and many "normal" features such as detergents must be limited or avoided.

The best oil to use in a two-cycle motor is oil that is specifically made and sold for that purpose by oil companies or engine manufacturers. This oil will be certified as TC-W (two-cycle, water-cooled) and has no harmful compounds. It is not necessary to use oil bearing the label of the motor manufacturer—they don't make it, although presumably they do set the specifications for it—but such

FIG. 2837 Outboard motors will have one or more carburetor controls brought out to the front of the motor case for easy adjustment during use. Follow the manufacturer's instructions in the manual.

Pints of Oil per Gal. of Gas	GASOLINE TO OIL RATIO TABLE					
		Pints when applied to				
	ACTUAL RATIO	2 Gal	3 Gal	4 Gal	5 Gal	6 Gal
1/12	96:1	1/6	1/4	1/3	5/12	1/2
1/6	48:1	1/3	1/2	2/3	5/6	1
1/5	40:1	2/5	3/5	4/5	1	1-1/5
1/3	24:1	2/3	1	1-1/3	1-2/3	2
3/8	21:1	3/4	1-1/8	1-1/2	1-7/8	2-1/4
1/2	16:1	1	1-1/2	2	2-1/2	3
3/4	11:1	1-1/2	2-1/4	3	3-3/4	4-1/2

TABLE 28-4 This table shows the correct amount of oil to be used for different fuel-oil ratios and for various amounts of gasoline. Pints can be translated to ounces by multiplying by 16. Oil containers are frequently marked in fractions of a pint and in ounces. Ratios are easily calculated in metric units of liters and milliliters. (1 liter = 1,000 ml)

usage is an easy and sure way of ensuring compatibility between oil and motor.

If in an emergency, "two-cycle oil" cannot be obtained, use the least expensive grade of automotive oil (it is less likely to have additives!) in #30 weight, *not lighter*.

Oil-fuel mixture ratios

The outboard motor manufacturers specify the correct ratio of gasoline to oil for each of their motors. In past years the ratio was often 24 to 1, but technological advances have now moved this to 50 to 1 for most motors of U.S. manufacture. The amount of oil is frequently translated somewhat roughly to ounces or fractions of a pint per gallon of gasoline for partial tank fillings or for tanks of non-standard size.

"Pre-mix"

Many marinas now have special pumps dispensing a mixture of gasoline and oil. In some instances, the mixture is fixed, usually 50 to 1; at other pumps, controls can be set to deliver a mixture at any one of several standard ratios.

Fueling Procedures

There are two aspects of fueling an outboard that must be given careful consideration—safety and the proper mixing of the oil and gasoline. First of all, extinguish all flames and tell everyone nearby that there will be no smoking. Get all persons off the boat who are not participating in the fueling.

Fueling portable tanks

It is wise to remove portable fuel tanks from the boat whenever possible and take them ashore to be filled. Make

FIG. 2838 As a safety measure, portable tanks should be removed from a boat and filled on the pier. After filling, they should be wiped clean and dry before being put back on board.

sure that the gas pump hose nozzle is in contact with the rim of the tank fill opening to prevent the generation of a spark of static electricity which might cause an explosion.

Oil properly mixed with gasoline will *not* separate later, but the initial mixing procedure requires careful attention; follow these steps for a three or six gallon tank:

    (1) Put in approximately one gallon of gasoline.

    (2) Pour in *all* the oil that is to be added.

    (3) Replace the cap on the tank and shake *vigorously* —you can't shake it up too much!

    (4) Remove the filler cap, add the balance of the gasoline without delay, and replace the cap. It wouldn't hurt to shake the tank some more, but a full tank is much heavier and cannot be shaken as vigorously as one with only a gallon in it.

    (5) Wipe off the outside of the tank, and return it to the boat (if it has been removed for filling) *after* any odor of fumes has disappeared.

For the sake of safety, portable fuel tanks should be secured in the craft. A simple way is to provide wooden blocks on the hull or floor-boards to prevent sideways or endways movement of the tank, with a strap or straps over the top of the tank to hold it down in rough going.

Fueling larger tanks

If your outboard carries fuel tanks which would be impractical to remove for fueling—anything larger than a six-gallon tank would probably be so considered—or permanently installed fuel tanks, your fueling procedures will closely resemble those for inboards; see pages 205-206. Before taking on fuel, close all doors, hatches, windows, etc., to keep any gasoline vapors from getting below. After fueling, open them all and allow time for ventilation to clear these areas before starting the engine.

FIG. 2839 A proper mixing of the gasoline and oil is as important as the correct amounts of each. See text for procedures to be used with portable tanks and with installed tanks, as shown above.

The mixing of gasoline and oil for larger tanks that cannot be shaken up can be done in several ways—all of which are time-consuming but *very* important, even more so than getting the exact fuel-oil mixture ratio.

One method is to use a metal funnel that has a screen filter (metal so that a grounding connection can be made from hose nozzle to tank). This funnel is inserted in the tank or fill pipe and as gasoline flows thru it, oil is added at the same time, apportioning the oil flow rate and allowing the stream of gasoline to blend thoroughly with the oil.

A second method is to mix the fuel and oil in batches in a separate five- or six-gallon tank using the same procedures as for portable tanks described above. The mixed fuel is then poured into the larger tank. On tanks *not* larger than about 15 gallons, it is permissible to mix the total amount of oil in one five- or six-gallon tank of gasoline, pouring the mixture into the larger tank, and then adding the remainder of the gasoline directly. Do *not,* as should now be clear, pour oil directly into the tank—it will not mix properly! (1 U.S. gallon = 3.8 liters)

Check the fuel system now for leakage. Carefully wipe up any spillage (discard the rag, don't stow it in the boat), and hose down with fresh water if possible. Remember to thoroughly ventilate the boat before starting the motor; there is a hazard of an explosion even though the outboard with its motor external to the hull is safer in this respect than an inboard. It is essential that you be alert for gasoline vapors which are heavier than air and can sink into the lower parts of the hull just waiting for a spark or flame. A power bilge blower may be a wise investment, especially on an outboard cruiser.

BOAT HANDLING

The general principles of boat handling are covered in Chapter 8. It was noted there that outboards and I/Os handle differently than inboards in that they steer with a directed thrust of the propellor rather than by the flow of water past a rudder. This makes for easier and more positive steering in many situations, but it has a distinctly different "feel" and one must become accustomed to it if one is experienced in handling inboards. The reaction of the boat to a turning of the motor thrust line will be different at slow speeds and at planing speeds; it will vary with hulls of different design and with motors of widely different horsepower ratings. A wise skipper will handle an unfamiliar craft with considerable respect until he understands its reactions to his actions at the wheel and throttle.

FIG. 2840 Proper trim is important. In illustration above, boat lists heavily to port. Weight should be distributed to keep on even keel, as shown below.

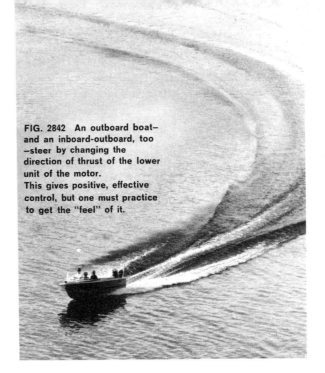

FIG. 2842 An outboard boat—and an inboard-outboard, too —steer by changing the direction of thrust of the lower unit of the motor. This gives positive, effective control, but one must practice to get the "feel" of it.

Trim

The number of seats in a boat is *no* indication of the number of persons she can carry safely. Overloading is a major cause of boating accidents—stay within the limits of your craft. The factors affecting trim become ever more critical as the load approaches the capacity, and as the boat's size decreases.

Have all weight evenly distributed so that the boat will trim properly—level from side to side and slightly down at the stern, never down at the bow. Passengers should be seated toward the centerline of the craft and not hanging over the sides; not too many forward or aft. It the load is concentrated near the bow or stern, the boat will plow or drag needlessly, reducing your safety margin and increasing your fuel consumption. Proper trim is essential to proper performance.

Trim your boat as well as possible *before* getting underway. In smaller craft, it is dangerous for passengers to attempt to change places or move about while she is scotting along briskly. If such movement becomes essential, slow or stop the boat first, remembering in rough weather to keep enough momentum to retain steerage control and to keep the craft headed into wind and waves. Have the person who must move keep low and near the boat's centerline.

Stability

Outboard craft are often operated at relatively high speeds and their stability becomes a matter of safety. Some hulls will run straight ahead quite steadily, but have a tendency to heel excessively, or even "flip over," when turned sharply.

The presence of an external keel, and its relative size has a major effect on the directional stability of a small boat. Smaller, faster craft have little need for much keel; larger, cruiser-type hulls which are slower will have a more pronounced keel. Greater directional stability naturally resists turning; attempting to make a sharp turn at too high a speed for the amount of keel carried may result in its broaching, flipping over sidewards. Conversely, a boat wilth little or no keel or skeg has little directional stability and may skid out sideways when a turn is attempted at excessive speed—initially the boat will point off in the new direction but actually continue to travel along essentially its old course.

FIG. 2843 An anti-tilt latch is found on most outboard motors. It prevents the lower unit from flipping up when the motor is put in reverse gear, but should be released while running forward normally so that the motor can tilt up if a submerged obstruction or shoal water is encountered.

INCORRECT

OVERLOAD FORWARD
CAUSES BOAT TO "PLOW"

INCORRECT

OVERLOAD AFT
CAUSES BOAT TO "SQUAT"

CORRECT

BALANCED LOAD
GIVES MAXIMUM PERFORMANCE

FIG. 2841 Fore-and-aft trim is also important for a comfortable ride and the most efficient operation.

FIG. 2844 The bow of a fast-moving outboard is not the safest place to ride! Never let an adult or small child ride with his or her feet dangling over the side—one slip and it's into the propellor!

The faster a boat goes, the less keel it requires, and the more important it is to reduce speed to a safe value before starting a turn; never turn more sharply than necessary; normal operation seldom requires a sudden, sharp, high-speed turn.

Reversing

Most outboard motors have a reverse gear that enables the boat to be backed. (Very small motors usually do not have such gears, but can be pivoted around 180° to give thrust in the opposite direction.) Unless restrained, an outboard motor has the tendency to tilt itself up and out of the water when the thrust is reversed. On many models, there is a manually-operated *reverse lock* that must be latched into place to keep the motor down while engaged in backing maneuvers. For normal running, however, it is important that this latch be released so that the lower unit will be free to tilt up if it strikes an underwater obstruction.

On some larger motors, especially those with electric shifting, anti-tilt latch operation is automatically interlocked with reverse operation.

SAFE OPERATION

Exercise your knowledge of the Rules of the Road, but also exercise good judgment, whether you have the right-of-way or not. Small craft should stand clear as far as possible from large yachts and commercial vessels. Watch their wakes carefully. Dont count on ships to look out for you; they need more, much more, room to stop, are more difficult to turn, and sometimes have "blind spots"—areas which are blocked to the helmsman's vision. Never assume that the pilot of a vessel sees you; keep well clear.

Stand clear of hazards

Should you come upon a tow in the bend of a river, or one maneuvering near shore, note whether the tow is swinging to starboard or port, and give it the room it needs.

You should not bring your boat near a moored vessel. If circumstances make this necessary, be exceedingly wary. Strong river currents moving under a moored barge can pull a small craft beneath the surface. A cross current—a current that is running at or about a right angle to your course—requires great caution. If you get into such a situation, give any object, floating free or made fast, an extra wide berth.

No one on the bow

It is extremely dangerous for anyone, especially children, to ride on the bow of a small boat with their legs dangling over the side. If one slipped off, it is very likely that he would be run over by the boat before the skipper could take any action—and a propellor easily makes hamburger of a human body, often with fatal or crippling results.

Watch the weather

Keep your mind on your course and boat handling, but keep an eye on the weather even of the morning forecast was for fair skies and gentle breezes. Weather is important to all boatmen, but especially so for the outboarder with his smaller craft. Learn to recognize threatening cloud formations. Train yourself to be sensitive to shifts in wind directions; a shift in the wind often is advance notice of a coming change in the weather. Know and observe official warnings.

Leave word behind

If you are going offshore or for a relatively long run on inland waters, or even just fishing some distance away from home, make someone ashore familiar with your plans in as much detail as possible. Should trouble develop, the Coast Guard will render all assistance possible on water where they operate; the more that they can be told of your plans, the more help they can be.

To help the Coast Guard assist you, the information left ashore should include: (a) where you plan to go, including any stops enroute; (b) list of persons aboard; (c) estimated time of return; (d) alternate plans in case of bad weather; (e) communications equipment on the boat; (f) a good description of the boat.

Distress-signals

Every outboard skipper should know the standard distress signals, see pages 87-88, and carry one or more types of emergency signalling equipment. These must be in good condition and ready for immediate use. If no distress equipment is on board, an outboard boatman in need of help can always signal this fact by slowly and repeatedly raising and lowering his arms outstretched to each side while he stands in his craft (or from a kneeling position if

FIG. 2845 When you go out fishing, leave word behind where you intend to go and when you plan to return. Be sure, also, that someone on shore has a complete and accurate description of your craft, including motor.

rough water conditions would make standing hazardous).

Never use "Mayday" on the radiotelephone unless there is a great danger and immediate assistance is required; don't use it for such a situation as running out of fuel.

Local knowledge

Whenever boating in unfamiliar waters, take advantage of "local knowledge"; watch the operation of boats piloted by skippers who are at home in these waters, and don't hesitate to ask questions about possible hazards.

A boat has no brakes!

Many persons who have not handled a small boat have the misconception that one can be maneuvered and stopped as easily as an automobile—'tain't so! But much can be done with a boat if one takes it slowly and easily. The new boat owner should practice the leaving from and returning to piers, and other maneuvers, until he has developed both skill and confidence; take it very cautiously and gently at first, and gradually build up to the procedures of experienced skippers.

Always slow down gradually rather than pulling the throttle back quickly. All boats have a stern wave that will catch up with and pass the craft if it comes to an abrupt stop. This can bring water into the boat, especially if it has a low-cut transom with no motor well.

Fuel consumption

An important aspect of outboarding safety is *not* running out of fuel! Each skipper should make tests and keep records to establish the rate of fuel consumption at various typically-used throttle settings (rpm as read on the tachometer). He should follow this up with a rough check on the number of hours run since last filling his tank. He should also know his fuel consumption on a per-mile basis to aid in planning cruises.

COURTEOUS OPERATION

Keep your boat's speed under control at all times—don't be a "show-off!" Respect the rights, and comforts, of others afloat; slow down not only when your craft is in danger, but also when it's a matter of courtesy to others. When passing other craft going in the same or opposite direction, give them a wide berth if possible, or drop

FIG. 2846 This 19-foot craft, with either outboard or I-O power, can provide overnight accommodations for two adults and a child; more could use sleeping bags in the cockpit. Cruising is quite feasible for weekends or other short trips.

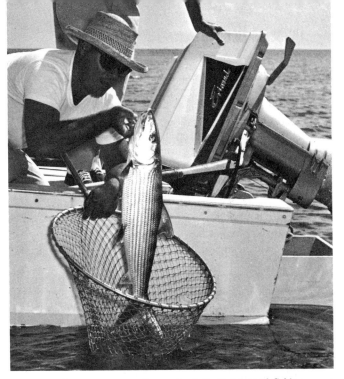

FIG. 2847 Keep an eye on the weather! Don't let good fishing take all your attention; watch out for thunderstorms building up or line squalls approaching. Head for home or a safe harbor in ample time—come back another day to catch that "bigger" one.

down to a slow speed. When passing through or by an anchorage, throttle down to your slowest speed and keep an alert lookout for mooring, swimmers, debris, etc.

It is courteous to keep down your wake and wash so as to not cause damage to other boats. It's a wise action, too, for you are legally responsible for any damage to other boats or persons from the waves you leave behind you.

EMERGENCIES

Various studies have shown the following to be the major causes of boating accidents:

(1) Overloading, overpowering, and improper trim.

(2) High speed turns, especially in rough water.

(3) Failure to keep a sharp lookout for obstructions.

(4) Going out in bad weather (or not starting for home soon enough when good weather turns bad).

(5) Standing in a moving boat.

(6) Having too much weight too high in the boat, as when someone sits on the deck of a small outboard.

(7) Leaks in the fuel system.

(8) Going too far offshore.

Each of these factors, and others not listed here, can and should be avoided. A carefully matched boat, motor, and propellor, operated in accordance with the law and with courtesy will go a long way toward eliminating accidents and even distressing moments. But some possibility of troubles always remains; be prepared to act in emergency.

Squalls and storms

If your boat gets caught in a squall or heavy seas, slow down immediately, maintaining only enough power to head her into or at a slight angle to the wind and waves. Have everyone put on life preservers, including yourself. Don't try to smash your boat through the waves at high speed in an attempt to get home sooner—that's inviting disaster. Instead, take the seas as gently as possible on the bow. The hull may pound, and the waves may toss up a lot of spray, but you will have your best control over the craft. If you don't run this way, you might get caught broadside in a trough and possibly capsize.

Keep enough weight at the stern in stormy weather to hold the propellor in the water. Since an outboard has no rudder, if the propellor comes out, control is lost. Should the motor quit, rig some sort of sea anchor, see pages 165-166, to hold the bow up to the seas.

Don't let water accumulate in the boat. If rain, spray, or waves bring water into the bilges, pump or bail it out immediately. Water inside a boat must not be allowed to build up to an amount that could affect the trim and stability of the craft.

Whenever safely possible, of course, get to a protected harbor rather than attempt to ride out a storm. But don't let your desire for a harbor upset your judgment. Avoid a course that will put large waves on your stern; they can swamp the boat, although self-bailing motor wells reduce this hazard. There is risk, too, of "pitchpolling" (turning end over end) in a heavy following sea by being driven too fast before it.

If you must turn in a heavy sea, watch for a lull in the wave formation in which to do it so that you won't get caught broadside in a trough by an approaching wave.. Always cross a large wave, or wake, at about a right angle; this lets you maintain the best control over your boat.

Capsizes

Stay with the boat if it capsizes! Almost invariably the temptation is to try to swim to shore if land is in sight, and almost always the shore is farther than it appears. Most outboard boats will remain afloat, even if filled with water; more and more are being designed so that they will not only float but will do so in an upright position. A boat is a much larger and more easily seen object than a person in the water; stay with the boat and you will receive help much more quickly than if you swim off on your own.

Rescuing a person in the water

One of the leading causes of death in boating accidents is drowning. Many of these fatalities result from people falling overboard. As the skipper of your craft, it is your responsibility to know how to rescue such a person. You

FIG. 2849 When anyone is in the water near an outboard or I-O craft, especially near its stern, the motor should be stopped, not just shifted into neutral. A boat's propellor can cause serious injuries—even fatal ones—to the human body. Be sure—stop that motor!

should practice the maneuvers necessary to accomplish this; a ring buoy or buoyant cushion can be used as the simulated victim. Practice enough so that you will be able to react instinctively and correctly; minutes saved may mean a life saved.

As soon as someone falls overboard, maneuver the boat's stern away from him. Shift into neutral immediately (kill the motor if you do not have a gearshift) and throw a buoyant cushion or life jacket near the victim—try to get it close, but don't try to hit him with it. Make sure that you are well clear of the person in the water before shifting into gear again.

Circle around quickly, selecting a course that will allow you to approach the person with the boat headed into the wind or waves. Approach him slowly, now, taking care to come alongside and not over him. Stop the motor before attempting to get the victim aboard.

When alongside, extend a paddle or boathook to him, or toss him one end of a line. *With the motor stopped,* lead him around to the stern, where the freeboard is the lowest, if there is enough space at the transom for him to get aboard without hurting himself on the motor. If it is not feasible, help the victim aboard over the side as far aft as possible. In either case, the use of a boarding ladder will be of help. To avoid a capsize while he is coming aboard, other passengers should shift their weight to the opposite side to maintain trim as much as possible. When helping a person aboard, hold him under the armpits and lift gently.

In case of an accident

If you are involved in a boating accident, you are required to stop and give whatever help you can without seriously endangering your boat or passengers. You must also identify yourself and your boat to any person injured or to the owner of any property damaged. See pages 36-37 for additional details.

If you see an accident without being a part of it, you may now render assistance without fear of liability. The Federal Boat Safety Act of 1971 contains a "good samaritan" section which provides that any person who renders assistance at the scene of a vessel accident will not be liable for civil damages from such action if he acts as a reasonably prudent man would have acted under the same circumstances.

FIG. 2848 Courteous boat operation is a mark of a knowledgable and safe skipper. Slow down when near other craft and yield to those that have the right of way.

FIG. 2850 A skipper who will take the time and trouble to learn can do much of his own motor maintenance work. He should have a copy of the manufacturer's service manual for the year and model of his unit.

Maintenance

Proper maintenance of an outboard rig pays off in many ways—increased safety, greater enjoyment through fewer breakdowns or other mechanical troubles, and increased pride in one's property as well as decreased depreciation. Careful attention to all aspects of maintenance, large and small, should be given to hull, motor, and equipment, and the trailer, too, if one is used.

HULL MAINTENANCE

The details of hull maintenance will, of course, depend upon the material of which it is made. Wood and metal are painted (a few aluminum craft are left bare), and fiberglass hulls are waxed. Whatever is required, do not neglect it, for the cost of materials and effort will be repaid well in beauty and resale value. On a wooden hull particularly, attention to the maintenance of paint and varnish will prevent deterioration of the structure itself. Pages 182-183 provide additional information on hull maintenance.

In any waters, but particularly salt, a boat should have a complete hosing down with fresh water after each use. Periodically, it should be washed down with soap or detergent rather than merely being hosed off.

Anti-fouling paints

In all but the cleanest of fresh waters, and in all salt water areas, a hull that is left afloat between periods of use will collect growth of marine grass, slime, and/or barnacles unless it is protected with *anti-fouling paint,* see pages 183-184.

Ventilation

Adequate ventilation of the interior of a boat is essential to a wooden hull, and is very advantageous for craft of other materials. Open drawers, side panels, etc., and let fresh air in when the boat is not in use. This will aid in the prevention of mildew and dry rot, and generally result in a "sweeter smelling" boat free of damp, musty odors.

MOTOR MAINTENANCE

The most important guide to outboard motor maintenance is the owner's manual furnished by the manufacturer. If you have lost yours, or bought a used motor without one, get a manual without delay; read it and carry out faithfully all its instructions. You will have greater reliability and lower repair bills.

The recommendations given above for hosing off and washing down the boat include the motor's exterior surfaces as well. Deposits of salt or pollution-laden water can quickly attack the unit's exterior finish. Although modern outboard motors are made of aluminum alloys that are designed to resist internal corrosion from salt water, an occasional flush-out with fresh water is desirable. Special fittings can be inexpensively purchased which clamp over the cooling water intake and allow the motor to be run "high and dry" with water being supplied through a hose from a nearby faucet.

On a boat that stays in the water between uses, the outboard motor (or I-O lower unit) should be tilted so that as much as possible of the lower unit—all of it if possible—is completely out of the water. This will lessen the possibility of any electrolytic action between the aluminum motor and dissimilar metals nearby, and will prevent the build-up of marine growth on the lower unit and propellor. Do not put a tight, airproof cover (a plastic bag is particularly bad) around the upper part of the motor; this will result in condensation and fast corrosion of metal parts. A loosely fitted cover to protect from dirt and rain is desirable, but ventilation should be provided.

Spark plugs

Much of the ignition system of an outboard motor should give no trouble if given normal care. Spark plugs, however, are "replaceable" items, ones that can be expected to "wear out" with use and require periodic replacement. A spare set should always be on board as that wear-out point just might come when least expected or convenient. The spare plugs should be in a sealed container to protect them from corrosion or breakage; plugs for marine use are normally sold in such packages.

Spark plugs for outboard motors are of a specific design for their application and the proper type should always be used. They come in various "heat" ranges and it is essential that the proper degree of heat be used for best results. Most motors are sold with a "normal heat" range set of plugs that will be satisfactory for average uses and loads. If the motor is to be lightly loaded (running cooler), a higher heat range ("hotter") plug may be desirable to prevent the build-up of deposits in the cylinders. If, on the other hand, the motor is to be heavily loaded (run hotter), a "colder" plug may be required. A plug type should be used that operates cleanly, without fouling at all engine speeds.

Spark plugs should be removed and replaced carefully lest the porcelain insulator be damaged; use a special spark plug wrench if possible. When installing or reinstalling a plug, the proper tightening is essential, too much can be as bad as too little. Unless specific instructions otherwise are furnished, install a plug finger tight and then give it one-half turn with a wrench, not more.

Used spark plugs can often provide a clue to any misoperation of the motor or incorrect selection of the plugs themselves. Specifics of diagnosis are beyond the scope of this book but will be found in specialized volumes.

FIG. 2851 Spark plugs are a vital part of an outboard motor. Two-cycle operation makes them susceptible to troubles. Take care to select the right type and heat range for your use; keep them cleaned and properly adjusted.

Fuel system

The most likely source of trouble with an outboard motor is the fuel system; here, too, the proper maintenance will forestall difficulties. The first precaution is to keep dirt and other foreign particles out of the fuel tank and lines; if in doubt as to the cleanliness of fuel, strain it through a funnel with a fine-screen filter. Secondly, fuel has a definite storage life and it is frequently more economical to discard old, unused fuel than to run the risk of gumming in the carburetor floats and jets.

In the event of apparent fuel starvation of an outboard motor when you know that your tank is not empty, first check the fuel filter on the motor. On most units, this is easily removed for inspection and cleaning.

Propellor

For smooth, vibration-free operation, the blades of a propellor must be free of distorting bends and major nicks and gouges on the edges; the propellor as a whole must have proper dynamic balance.

Minor nicks in blades can be filed smooth, at some risk of disturbing the balance of the propellor. More major damage will require the services of a properly outfitted shop. Often it is less expensive to replace an aluminum propellor than it is to repair it; bronze propellors are more "repairable."

FIG. 2852 Propellors should run without vibration. To do this, they must not have bent or warped blades, and each blade should be free of any major nicks or broken off pieces.

Motor overboard!

No, not "man overboard," but "motor overboard!" Despite the best of intentions and the availability of a safety chain, a motor sometimes does get dropped into the water, or perhaps the whole boat swamps and the motor gets dunked. Whatever the situation, prompt and correct "first aid" is essential.

Actually, less deterioration will occur underwater than when the motor is brought up and exposed to the air—so keep it down until you are fully prepared to take restorative actions. Ideally, once the motor is brought to the surface it should be again submerged in an oil bath; if this is not practicable, fresh water may be used to keep air from it until it can be rushed to a shop for disassembly, cleaning, and inspection. Don't attempt this work yourself unless you have done it before and have a maintenance manual.

EQUIPMENT MAINTENANCE

It is essential that all items of equipment aboard an outboard boat be given proper maintenance if they are going to have an economic life and be operable when needed. This is true of such simple items as buoyant cushions and such complex items as electronic depth sounders.

Basically, equipment needs to be kept clean and dry. If it is of the type that gets wet in use, it should periodically be washed off with fresh water to remove salt or other contaminants. Beyond these simple basics, details will be found in the manufacturer's instruction book on most pieces of equipment.

As an open outboard boat is more exposed to rain and spray than other craft, special attention should be given to electrical wiring and fittings such as the sockets for navigation and other lights. Movable mechanical parts, such as steering mechanisms and other control cables, should be kept lightly greased or protected by a spray-on coating. Batteries should be kept charged and the water level in the cells checked at least monthly.

FIG. 2853 Houseboats are frequently powered by inboard-outboard units, and sometimes by outboard motors. The same advantages and disadvantages of such types of propulsion apply to these craft as they do for runabouts and small cruisers.

FIG. 2900 The addition of a trailer can greatly widen a boatman's scope of operation. His craft can be taken to nearby or far-distant bodies of water. With this added capability comes a need for further knowledge—the proper selection, use, and care of the trailer itself.

Boat Trailering

CHAPTER 29

When an outboard boatman adds a trailer to his "rig" of hull and motor, or for his inboard-outboard craft, he adds a whole new dimension to his world of recreational boating. No longer is he confined to his local body of water—he can venture literally countless miles from his home port in search of new cruising areas or fishing grounds. Singly or in organized groups, the "trailer boatman" takes to the highway for day, week-end, or longer trips. Land journeys of hundreds of miles are not uncommon, and some skippers even travel thousands of miles for special boating adventures. Yet for others, trailering is merely a short haul from the local ramp to one's own backyard for storage and maintenance between uses on nearby waters. Trailering is whatever the skipper wants to make of it; the possibilities are limitless.

With this new dimension of boating comes a need for additional knowledge. When his craft is on the water, the trailer boatman is no different from any other skipper of a similar boat; but there is, however, a need for knowledge regarding the selection, use, and maintenance of his added major item of "equipment," the trailer itself. These matters are the concern of this chapter.

FIG. 2901 One advantage of trailer boating is that after use the craft can be taken home with the skipper for storage and minor maintenance. Frequently, it can be worked on in evening hours during the week, thus saving weekends for on-the-water use.

What a trailer provides

A boat trailer performs multiple functions and offers many advantages—probably more than you would think of on a quick review. Although a trailer is basically a means of transporting a boat across land distances, it also serves as the boat's "storage slip" when it is not in use, and its servicing "dry dock" when work is needed.

The "storage" aspects of boat trailering can be important. There is no need to pay rent for a slip at a marina (if you can find one, as space is steadily becoming more difficult to obtain in many boating areas). Many localities have free public ramps for launching, but even if a ramp or hoist fee must be paid for each use, these rarely approach the costs of regular slip rental. Dry storage on a trailer has a further advantage in that it eliminates the problems of fouling on the bottom of the hull—annual or semi-annual repainting is not required, nor is boat performance degraded as fouling accumulates between paintings. In coastal areas, there is the further advantage that often the boat will spend its non-working days in an environment much freer of salt air and spray, thus reducing inevitable corrosion and deterioration.

The secondary function of a trailer as a "dry dock" or "marine railway" can be very useful and money-saving. The craft and motor can be taken to the service facility, which always results in a smaller bill than if the repairmen has to come to the craft. Work gets done faster and better if the boat is at the shop, even though that may be only a short distance from the marina slip. Then, too, much work on small craft is often done by the skipper, with perhaps the aid of his family "crew." Consider the time saved if the boat is home in the driveway or backyard, as compared with being miles away at a marina; work can often be done on week days after work or dinner, rather than having to be put off until the weekend. Home workshop, tools, and other facilities can be used, and a boat in a stable position on shore is a more "workable" object than one that may bounce around in the water at its marina slip. Many items of work on the hull and external drive parts can only be

FIG. 2902 A trailer is of little use without a vehicle to pull it. The car-trailer combination must be considered as a whole, and each unit must match the other for safe and trouble-free operation.

done by an owner if he has his boat high and dry on his own property; financial savings can be significant.

The Car-Trailer Combination

An item essential for trailer boating that is often overlooked is the automobile that will pull the rig. As boats, and their trailers, get larger and heavier, just any car won't do. If you are considering pulling a new boat trailer with your present car, or if you have a rig now and are planning the purchase of a new car, it would be advisable to discuss the project with a knowledgable and responsible representative of the car dealer, or perhaps with several such persons.

It is quite possible that your present car, or a new one, will require modifications in order to be a trouble-free "tractor" for your boat trailer. These are discussed later in this chapter.

Trailer Selection and Equipping

As noted above, a trailer serves several functions, transportation and storage being the principal ones. The use to which it will be put will influence the selection of the trailer to be bought. If the trailer is to be used for short local hauls and home storage only, money can be saved by purchasing a light-duty unit. If, on the other hand, long, cross-country, high-speed trips are in the offing, the greater cost of a heavy-duty trailer is necessary to avoid time-consuming troubles and added expenses later.

Trailers, like boats and motors, come in many varieties. They are variously equipped with electric winches, adjustable keel rollers, finger-tip controls for loading and launching, etc. Your problem is to get the right combination, the right trailer for your boat and motor, and your type of trailering. There are many makes and models to choose from—take time to select wisely.

ADEQUACY

The trailer for your boat must be adequate in both weight-carrying capacity and length. Under-buy in either of these aspects and your craft will ultimately suffer.

You must have a trailer able to carry the weight of your boat, motor(s), *and the gear stowed in the boat*. This last factor is all-too-often overlooked in making calculations of

required trailer capacity. Having figured the total weight, check the prospective trailer's capacity, usually found on a plate affixed to the frame. If the load is to be carried within 100 pounds (45 kg) of the stated capacity, buy the *next larger* model. Don't underestimate; if possible, actually check the weight of the hull as some boat manufacturers seem to list the weight of their craft a bit on the light side. Make a detailed list of each item you plan to carry in the boat and its weight, and be sure to include a generous allowance for "miscellaneous"! It is wise to over-allow somewhat as experience always results in items being added to the equipment list, with few deletions. When all is done, it is advisable to get actual weight measurements on a truck scale; first the empty trailer and then the boat and trailer, preferably once without any gear, and finally with full load of items normally carried. You may be surprised at the final gross weight!

Length

The length of a trailer is critical as it is absolutely essential that the stern area, and especially the transom, be adequately supported. It must be possible to so position the boat on the trailer bed that the transom is *directly* over the aftermost supports; see fig. 2905. If there is *any* overhang, the hull will be distorted; this is true for outdrive craft, but it is particularly important for hulls with outboard motors which put their full weight on the transom.

There must not be a "sag" in the hull, or a "hook" (in the stern, from too short a trailer). Such things may change the shape of your boat permanently, affecting your speed in the water and the general handling characteristics of the craft.

Supports

A boat's natural environment is the water. Here the hull is uniformly supported and there are no concentrations of pressure on the hull. A trailer, like any dry-land cradle, is an unnatural place for a boat, so you must baby the craft all you can. Make the trailer bed as "comfortable" as possible. See that it fits the contours of the hull (special trailers are made for the modified catamaran or "cathederal" hull). Plenty of padding and bracing may be needed. Treat the boat right on the trailer and you'll get the sought-for results in the water.

Supports may take the form of rollers or of padded bars or stringers, or a combination of some of each. Each type has its advantages and disadvantages; the way that the boat will normally be launched and loaded must be considered.

Rollers of hard rubber are widely used on trailers that tilt and allow the craft to move backward into the water by gravity. Their disadvantage is in the very nearly point con-

FIG. 2903 Houseboats, too, can be trailered if their beam is not so great as to violate state highway restrictions. Their greater weight will require a multiple-axle trailer.

tact with the keel and the consequent high pressure on the hull there. The more rollers there are, the better the load is shared, *provided* that the height of each is adjusted properly; the depth of the indentation into the roller by the keel is a rough guide as to the weight being carried at that point.

Padded bar rests provide the maximum area in contact with the hull, and thus the minimum of point contact pressure. These are excellent for boats that normally are lifted from the trailer, as by slings from a crane. They have considerable surface friction, however, and are generally unsuitable for use where the boat must slide back from the trailer into the water unless special features are provided.

Some trailers of excellent design use a combination of these two forms of support. Rollers provide the basic support for the keel, and padded rests are levered into position to provide additional support for the transom after the craft has moved fully up the rollers and onto the trailer. The levering action allows the padded rests to be lowered out of contact with the hull just before launching so that their friction does not impede the movement of the hull under the force of gravity.

There should also be side supports to hold the boat firmly in position on the trailer and a bow chock into which the stem fits so as to prevent further forward movement of the craft on the trailer bed. All of these supports must be adjustable and so positioned that they carry out their intended function. The fore and aft location of the bow chock is especially critical as this is what ensures that the transom will be directly above its supports as it must be. This positioning of the boat on the trailer also directly affects the downward weight on the trailer tongue and coupling. Any unbalanced condition, once the hull is properly mated to the trailer bed, is properly corrected by shifting the location of the axle and wheels, *not* the bow chock.

SAFETY ASPECTS

Safety must be a primary consideration in the selection of a trailer—safety on one's investment in boat and motor, safety of personnel in its use, and the safety of other vehicles on the road. A few dollars more spent initially on the trailer may prevent much greater losses later.

Hitches and couplings

The American Boat & Yacht Council Safety Standard A-15 for boat trailers includes specifications for couplings (on the trailer) and hitches (on the car). These require a larger coupling ball for larger and heavier trailers. This may seem natural, but a Federal Highway Safety Standard proposed for use but not yet in effect would *reverse* the size requirement sequence; smaller (but still adequately strong) balls would be used on heavy-duty hitches, with larger balls on light-duty hitches, in a series of five gross-weight classes. The reasoning behind this inverse size sequence is that if a heavy-duty trailer had a *small* coupling, it could not be mated with a light-duty hitch which would have too large a ball to fit. Thus a hitch could not be overloaded, either inadvertently or by deliberate intent of risk.

A hitch on the rear end of a car should be secured to the

FIG. 2904 Care must be exercised when trailering that an excess weight of gear is not placed in the boat. Items that are heavy or which have sharp edges and corners must be securely fastened down so that they will not shift about while on the road.

FIG. 2905 As the full weight of an outboard motor is carried on the transom of a boat, it is essential that there be adequate support directly under this portion of the hull. The supports must be there and the boat must be properly positioned with respect to them.

FIG. 2906 Hull supports in the form of rollers provide for the greatest ease in launching and reloading, but do not distribute the contact pressure over a wide area as do padded bar rests. Each type thus has its own advantages, and many trailers use a combination of the two.

vehicle's frame either with bolts (using lock washers) or by welding. A light-duty hitch attached to the rear bumper should *not* be used. For heavier loads, there are available "weight distributing" or "equalizing" hitches which mechanically apply leverage to both the trailer and the towing vehicle. When properly adjusted, such a hitch lessens the load on the rear of the car and permits it to operate in a

FIG. 2907 The winch line alone should not be depended upon for keeping the bow of the boat in place. A separate chock should be on the front of the trailer into which the bow fits snugly. A separate hold-down lashing—in addition to the winch line—is desirable for maximum security of the boat on the trailer.

more level attitude. These are more expensive, but are necessary for trailers of more than 3,500 pounds (1588 kg) gross weight and are desirable for those in the 2,000 to 3,500 pound (907-1588 kg) category.

Safety chains

A safety chain between the trailer and the towing car is a must, and the use of two is desirable. The size of the chain must be adequate for the trailer with which it is used; its minimum breaking strength should be 1½ times the maximum gross trailer weight and any connecting hooks and attaching hardware should be of equivalent strength.

Brakes

The type and design of brakes on a boat trailer are often a matter of state or local regulations, the requirements of which must be met. In general, brakes are necessary for rigs of 1,500 pounds (680 kg) or more gross weight. It may be well to have even better brakes than the minimum legal requirement as they could be a key factor in the safety of the rig, car, and persons.

Many trailers have hydraulic "surge" brakes which act automatically as the towing vehicle slows. Although such brakes act *after* the car's brakes, the time lag is so brief there is no tendency for the rig to "jackknife."

There are electric trailer brakes which act automatically

as the car's brakes are activated, and also electric brakes that are manually controlled by the driver.

Automatic brakes are desirable as the driver does not have to remember each time to apply them, but manually-controlled brakes provide more flexible operation.

An excellent feature, required in some jurisdictions for larger trailers, is a "breakaway" device which will automatically apply the trailer's brakes if that unit becomes detached from the towing car, as in the case of a hitch failure.

Tie-downs

As determined by its design, every trailered boat should be held firmly in place with tie-downs. Starting at the bow —the winch cable should not be solely depended upon to hold the boat onto the trailer and the bow down into its chock. There should be an additional tie-down of a lashing and turnbuckle. Moving aft—straps may be fitted across the hull to hold the craft firmly against the supports of the trailer and prevent any bouncing up and down on rough road surfaces. To further prevent such up and down movement, there should be separate lashings with turnbuckles at each side of the transom. If a trailer as purchased does not have adequate hold-down straps and fittings, these should be added before any extensive trip is made.

FIG. 2909 Winches are used to gain added pull to get the boat back onto its trailer. Both manual and electrical models are available with gear ratios as required by the weight of the boat and motor.

Wheels and tires

Tire failures on the road are one of the most prevalent and annoying troubles of boat trailering, and one of the least necessary. An understanding of the differences between car and trailer tires, and proper selection and maintenance, will virtually eliminate tire troubles.

Usually trailer wheels are smaller in diameter than those of the car with which it is used, and with smaller tires to match. The smaller diameter means both heavier loading and faster turning. For higher-speed, long-distance highway trailering, favor a larger wheel diameter over a smaller one, and select a tire capable of meeting the service you will expect of it.

Electrical system

A boat trailer's electrical system powers its lights—tail, stop, license plate, marker, and turn signal—and in many cases, a braking system also. Good quality components and careful installation are essential for safety and long trouble-free operation. Wires should be protected from mechanical abrasion, road splash, and other physical damage. It is important that there be a ground wire as a part of the electrical system between the trailer and the car; do not depend upon the trailer coupling and hitch to provide a "return

FIG. 2908 When being transported, a boat must be firmly held down into its trailer bed so that it cannot shift about or rise and fall independently. When in storage at rest, the tie-downs may be slacked off a bit to reduce any distorting strains on the hull.

path'' for electrical currents. Connectors should be heavy-duty and waterproof.

Check carefully all state and local regulations regarding the number and placement of lights on a boat trailer of your size. Frequently, it is recommended that tail, stop, license plate, and turn signal lights be mounted high, either on the boat or on a bar placed across the boat's transom, but in some jurisdictions such a high and/or temporary location may not be legally acceptable.

Trailers will normally be sold equipped with several light reflectors. The Safety Standard for Boat Trailers issued by the American Boat & Yacht Council, see pages 192-193, calls for four amber and two red reflectors. Additional reflectors and/or reflector tape may be added as deemed necessary by the owner.

GENERAL FEATURES

There are a number of optional features for boat trailers, the selection of which will depend upon the craft and its owner.

Winch

A winch is used with all but the very smallest of trailered boats. Designs and capacity vary considerably; both manual and electrical models are available.

Two-speed manual winches have a low-speed, high mechanical advantage mode of operation for heavy pulls, with a faster operating mode for use once the pull becomes easier. Electrical winches are powered from the car's battery and the motor makes the work of loading a heavy boat onto a trailer more of a "push button" task than hard labor.

All winches should have a hand brake and an anti-reverse latch or lock for safety. The winch cable may be of synthetic line, but steel cable is frequently used. If you use the latter, also buy a pair of heavy gloves as a steel winch cable must never be touched with bare hands.

The winch should be mounted on a stand that can be adjusted fore and aft to match the positioning of the boat on the trailer bed. Vertically, the winch cable should come off the top of the drum level with (or slightly above, but never below) the eye in the stem of the boat into which the hook connects; the winch should be capable of adjustment on its stand to meet this requirement.

Tilting bed trailers

Many trailer designs feature a bed or frame that is hinged so that it can tilt up for easier launching and reloading. With such a model, it will not be necessary to back the trailer into the water, an action to be avoided if at all possible.

Walkway

Many trailers have a narrow walkway down one side of the frame inside the wheels. This permits a person to get out *over* the water to attach the hook of the winch cable rather than to wade out and get wet feet. It is a simple feature and can often be added by the purchaser if one is not a part of the basic trailer.

Accessories

In addition to the basic features and options of boat trailers, there are accessories which will make trailering both safer and more enjoyable.

Parking wheel

Some trailers include a front parking wheel, and one can be added in most cases where it is not standard equipment. A parking wheel should be on an adjustable shaft so that the height of the tongue of the trailer from ground level can be varied. The wheel will aid in maneuvering the trailer when it is detached from the car and will make hitching up an easier and safer job. The height can also be adjusted to give the proper angle to the boat when it is parked for storage.

Jack and lug wrench

Every over-the-road boat trailer rig should include a jack for the trailer; most automobile jacks are useless if the trailer should have a flat tire. The jack need not be elaborate, many simple designs are available, but it must fit the situation.

FIG. 2910 Many trailers employ a hinged bed that may be tilted up to facilitate launching and reloading. This normally makes it unnecessary to run the trailer into the water more than a few inches.

FIG. 2911 (Left) A walkway on a trailer is useful for attaching or releasing the winch line without getting one's feet wet. Such a walkway may go down either side of the trailer bed and should have a non-skid surface.

FIG. 2912 (Right) Every trailer should be equipped with a spare wheel and tire. Their availability will often prevent delays of hours or days if trouble is encountered on the road far from a source of repairs or replacement.

FIG. 2913 (Left) A small stand at the front end of the trailer will allow it to be parked in a level position. This is often equipped with a small wheel for greater maneuverability. The stand may or may not be adjustable, but must swing up to clear the road.

FIG. 2914 (Right) Many boats are of such beam that their width obstructs the driver's rearward vision unless special extended arms are used on the mirrors. These should be installed on both sides of the car for maximum rearward vision and safety.

As trailer wheels are generally smaller than those on automobiles, the size of the wheel lugs may be different. If the lug wrench for your car is not usable with your trailer wheels, be sure to purchase and carry one that will fit.

Spare wheel and tire

One of the best investments that a trailer boatman can make is a spare wheel and tire. Service for the smaller tire sizes usually used on trailers, or a replacement if one is ruined, is seldom available on a highway. The availability of your own spare might mean the saving of many hours, or even days, should trouble occur on a trip.

A related item for possible emergency replacement is a set of wheel bearings. These can cause trouble unexpectedly, and they, too, can be difficult to locate in out-of-the-way places.

Emergency signals

Every trailering rig should have highway flares, flags, reflectors, and similar equipment to set out if a flat tire, overheated bearing, or other trouble should cause an emergency stop along the shoulder of a road.

Wheel chocks

A pair of wheel chocks should be a part of every trailer rig; these are usually triangular in shape and made of wood. The chocks should be of a suitable size and shape for use with either the car's wheels (when launching or reloading) or the trailer's wheels (when parking on sloping ground).

Cover

Although a cover for the boat is not strictly an accessory for a trailer, it is a very desirable item in connection with road travel. One of these, properly fitted and secured for high-speed travel will keep dust and dirt, trash, rain, and other "undesirables" out of the boat when it is on the road. See Chapter 28 for further considerations regarding boat covers.

Insurance

Every trailer boatman should know *fully* the status of his insurance coverage when he is engaged in pulling a trailer with his car. It is quite possible that your policy allows for trailer operation, but it might not, or there might be limitations. Check your policy carefully and, if necessary, consult your insurance agent. If an endorsement is needed, don't delay or neglect to get it, even at the cost of a small additional premium—be protected, especially in your liability coverage.

CAR MODIFICATIONS

A car used with a trailer may require some modifications in the way of "beefing up" to give fully satisfactory performance. Rear springs and/or shock absorbers may have to be replaced with heavier duty units because of the added weight transferred from the tongue of the trailer. The turn signal flasher unit on many passenger cars is not satisfactory for the additional load of flashing the trailer's lights; a heavy duty unit can be quickly and easily substituted for the standard flasher.

Wide side mirrors

Driving with a boat trailer behind the car is not as easy as ordinary driving, especially when the craft is high and wide. A second external rear-view mirror on the right side of the car will make passing both safer and less nerve-straining. Where the boat is quite wide, consideration should be given to the installation of external mirrors specially designed to project out far enough to be effective, the type often seen on cars pulling house trailers.

Front bumper hitch

A hitch on the front end of a car is frequently useful in special launching situations. Where a ramp is slippery—such as at low water stages in tidal areas—or where the ramp is unsurfaced and soft, the use of a front hitch permits the car to be turned around so that the rear driving wheels will have better traction.

Other advantages of using a front hitch for launching or retrieving the boat include better maneuverability of the car-trailer combination in tight quarters, and the availability of the car's headlights for night illumination.

As the front hitch is used only for short distances and

FIG. 2915 A hitch on the front of the car can be very useful in some launching situations. As this hitch is used in only limited cases, a bumper mounting is acceptable rather than being secured to the frame as is necessary for rear, towing hitches.

FIG. 2916 When the load—boat, motor, gear, and trailer itself—gets too heavy to be shared between a single pair of tires, it is necessary to add a second axle and its pair of tires. For some of the heaviest loads, three axles are used.

special situations, a bumper-mounted hitch is acceptable, but heavy pulling strains should be avoided so as not to damage the car.

MULTIPLE-AXLE TRAILERS

As the length of a boat increases, so does its weight, and at an even greater rate. There is a definite upper limit to the weight-carrying capacity of trailer tires, and when the boat-plus-trailer gross weight exceeds the safe capacity of two tires, the only solution is the addition of another axle and pair of tires. Even with large tires such as 6.00-12 in a 6-ply rating, the gross weight limit for two is about 2500 pounds (1134 kg).

Characteristics

The general discussion of boat trailer features and characteristics mentioned above are applicable to trailers with two, or more, axles. These, because of their greater size and weight, more often will have electrical brakes, a front parking wheel, and weight-distributing hitches.

Trailering

Safety and freedom from troubles in boat trailering depends as much on proper preparations as on correct procedures while "underway" on the road. Preparations are not complicated or difficult, but even a single item overlooked can make for problems. It is an excellent idea to have a check list, *and to use it.* Such a list can be typed and then sealed in plastic; thus waterproofed, it can be attached to the trailer tongue where it cannot be overlooked in the hitching-up process. No standard check list can be given here; it is a matter of your own personalized list for your boat, trailer, and type of use.

GENERAL PREPARATIONS

Let's start properly with the "horse before the cart"—the car which pulls the trailer is, of course, a vital element in the trailering process. The vehicle should be in good mechanical condition and fully serviced prior to the trip; don't depend on stopping soon for fuel or water or other service once you're on your way.

Loading the Boat

The trailer, too, should have been lubricated and given any other service well ahead of the time for departure. All gear that is to be carried in the boat must be properly stowed. Soft and light items such as sleeping bags or cushions may be left loose, but heavy items or hard ones with sharp corners and projections, such as an anchor, must be secured firmly in place. If the motor is of the electric-starting type, the battery, although relatively small, is a particularly heavy item and must be firmly held in position, preferably in a fiberglass box.

Don't try to carry too much in a boat on a trailer, but don't overlook any essential items; use a checklist. Remember those items that you had aboard when you last checked your gross weight on those truck scales—don't let your gross weight creep up. Consider traveling with empty tanks and filling up at the other end—often 100 to 300 pounds (45-136 kg), or even more, can be saved as fuel weighs 6.6 pounds per gallon (0.8 kg/liter) and water is even heavier at 8.3 pounds per gallon (1 kg/liter).

Weight distribution

Consideration also must be given to the distribution of gear in the trailer, switching around light and heavy items to bring the trailer into proper balance. In extreme cases, such as with craft of unusual design, it may be necessary to relocate the axle and wheels with respect to the trailer frame to get a proper balance for the loaded trailer.

The optimum weight on the trailer coupling at the end of the tongue is approximately 7% of the gross weight, with any value between 5% and 10% being acceptable. For a larger boat-trailer combination of, say, 3,000 pounds, (1361 kg), this means 150 to 300 pounds (68-136 kg) at the coupling—here a parking wheel with screw-action adjustment is an obvious necessity.

For smaller, lighter rigs, the weight on the tongue can be estimated when it is picked up from the ground. A more accurate measurement, however, is desirable and can usually be easily made with the use of household bathroom scales. This method is really a necessity as tongue weights approach and exceed 100 pounds (45 kg).

Effects of improper tongue weight

The most readily apparent condition of maldistribution of weight on the trailer is a too-heavy tongue. Here the rear of the car sags excessively, the hitch is in danger of striking the road surface on bumps, and the trailer follows poorly because of faulty balance.

Too-light a tongue weight also can cause highway problems as there may even be an *upward* thrust on the hitch as the car moves along. This, too, makes driving difficult as the trailer will tend to sway and whip from side to side.

Check your tongue weight carefully before starting out, but also observe how your trailer follows. It may be that your particular rig or hitch will ride better with a tongue load toward either the high or low side of the allowable range.

Preparing the boat

The outboard motor should be tilted up and secured firmly in that position. If no travel latch is provided, a block of wood can be inserted between the motor and the transom and the motor lashed down against it to keep it in place. The lower unit of an outdrive may be in either the down or tilted position as recommended by the manufacturer of the craft, but if tilted, it must be secured in that position.

Tops and covers

A folding canvas top should be in the down position; these are not made to take the wind speeds of highway travel—50 mph (80 km/hr) on the highway will have the same effect as gale winds, or even more if moving into a natural head wind! Take down all flags; these, too, are not made to stand the whipping of such strong "winds."

The boat cover should be on and securely fastened so that the wind, and dust and dirt, will not get in under the edge. If the trip is to be made on dirt roads, a simple cover of canvas or plastic should be placed over the winch on the front of the trailer to keep out dirt and grit that might interfere with its smooth mechanical operation.

Securing the boat

All tie-downs must be correctly tightened—not too much, not too little. They should not be so tight as to compress or otherwise distort the hull, but they must be tight enough so that there is no relative movement between the boat and the trailer supports; all vertical motion should be as a single unit and absorbed by the springs of the trailer. Additional tie-downs, not needed for storage, may be added, especially at the bow and transom; the anti-reverse latch of the winch should be checked.

Tire Pressure

More trailering problems on the road develop from incorrect tire pressure than any other single cause. Trailer tires use higher pressures than regular passenger car tires, and the pressure used must be right for both the size of the tire and the load carried by it (gross weight less tongue weight, divided by the number of tires).

Trailer tires must not be overloaded; the "ply rating" of

FIG. 2917 When on the road trailering, a full boat cover will keep dirt, dust, and other undesirables out of the boat. The cover shown here protects from stem to stern, including the motor; other designs cover only the open areas of the hull.

the tire is an important factor to be considered in determining the maximum load capacity. Table 29-1 gives the tire load capacity for various size tires and inflations at highway speeds; the highest figure on each line is the maximum inflation pressure and load and *must not be exceeded*. Remember that these are "cold" pressures, readings taken before the trip is started. Tire pressures will increase during the trip due to heating, but do *not* bleed out air to reduce pressure as this is a normal change anticipated in the setting of the cold pressure.

Effects of incorrect inflation

Tires that are under-inflated tend to bulge at the area in contact with the ground. As the tire turns, this area changes with a resulting constant flexing of the sidewalls. This is an abnormal strain on the tire and will shorten its life, if actual failure doesn't occur on the road.

Excess tire pressure is equally bad. In the worst case, the pressure will rise during driving to such a point that the sidewalls burst and you have a "blow-out." At best, there will be excessive wear in the center of the tread and shortened tire life.

Know your loads; know your correct tire pressure—check tires *before* each trip; a special gauge may be needed.

Check wheel lugs

The lug nuts or bolts on each trailer wheel should be checked periodically for tightness; this is not necessary for every trip, but it should not be neglected. Looseness can cause uneven tread wear, and if a wheel should come off while driving, a serious accident is likely.

Tools and Spares

Before starting out on a trailering trip, make sure that you have in your boat (or car) all necessary spares and tools —especially the spare wheel and tire (properly inflated) for the trailer, and the jack and lug wrench to use if making a change becomes necessary. Spare wheel bearings and the proper grease could prevent delays if trouble develops.

Be sure that you carry a spare bulb or two for the trailer lights (at least one of each type if not all are the same)— these may burn out and should be replaced immediately for safety.

TABLE 29-1 This table gives load capacities per tire for various tire sizes and inflation pressures (measured cold before starting). The underlined value on each line is the maximum inflation-load value for that tire at highway speeds.

Tire Size	Ply Rating	30	35	40	45	50	55	60	65	70	75	80	85
		TIRE LOAD CAPACITY AT VARIOUS INFLATIONS											
4.80/4.00 x 8	2	_380_											
4.80/4.00 x 8	4	380	420	450	485	515	545	575	_600_				
5.70/5.00 x 8	4		575	625	665	_710_							
6.90/6.00 x 9*	6		785	850	915	970	1030	_1080_					
6.90/6.00 x 9*	8		785	850	915	970	1030	1080	1125	1175	1225	_1270_	
20 x 8.00-10	4	825	_900_										
20 x 8.00-10	6	825	900	965	1030	_1100_							
20 x 8.00-10	8	825	900	965	1030	1100	1155	1210	1270	_1325_			
20 x 8.00-10	10	825	900	965	1030	1100	1155	1210	1270	1325	1370	1420	_1475_
4.80/4.00 x 12	4	545	550	595	635	680	715	755	_790_				
5.30/4.50 x 12	4	640	700	760	810	865	_915_						
5.30/4.50 x 12	6	640	700	760	810	865	915	960	1005	1045	1090	_1135_	
6.00 x 12	4	855	935	_1010_									
6.00 x 12	6	855	935	1010	1090	1160	1230	_1290_					
6.50 x 13	6	895	980	1060	1130	1200	_1275_						

Note: 1 pound = 0.454 kilograms; 1 pound per square inch = 0.068 atmosphere.

Laws and Regulations

It is presumed that the prudent trailer-boating skipper is familiar with the laws and regulations of his state and local community regarding the use of his rig. If, however, you are venturing farther than normal from home base, don't assume that the requirements are the same everywhere. Check carefully into all requirements and restrictions before starting out. Information can usually be obtained from police departments, automobile clubs, or boating clubs, either locally or these in the new area.

HOOKING-UP

Before mating the trailer's coupling to the car's hitch, the ball may be lightly coated with grease to reduce friction. After joining the two units, make sure that the coupling is tightened properly and locked in accordance with its design. Now connect the safety chains *immediately* so that they won't be forgotten. Most trailers use "S" hooks, fig. 2918; a safer connection can be made with a "scissor" hook or a shackle or clevis. If a single chain is used, it should be long enough to go around the drawbar of the

WRONG   RIGHT

FIG. 2918 There is a right and a wrong way to hook up trailer safety chains. The open end of the hook should go up through the hole, never down into it. Two chains are better than one!

hitch and back to the trailer to fasten onto the frame or the chain itself near its beginning. *The chains must have no more slack than is necessary for making sharp turns; they should not be long enough to permit the coupling to fall to the road if the trailer should suddenly become unhitched.* Next, the parking wheel should be raised to its proper position for on-the-road travel, and the electrical connections made between the car and trailer. (A neat trick is to have the electrical cord on the trailer long enough so that the connector can be placed *inside* the car trunk to protect it from rain and road splash; the trunk lid will close easily over the wires without damage.)

A final check

Now you *should* be ready to move out—but are you? Make a final run-down of the check list. Check all lights with someone in the car depressing the brake pedal and operating the switches; check all functions, tail, license plate, stop, turn, and marker (if used). And don't forget to ask each member of the crew, "Have you forgotten anything?"

ON THE ROAD

Driving a car pulling a trailer can be quite different from driving the car only, especially if it is one of the lighter and less powerful models. There will be less acceleration ability, and more time and distance will be required to stop.

If this is your first experience in trailering, or if you are "moving up" in terms of size and weight of your rig, take time to learn the driving characteristics of your new combination—practice in light traffic before taking to crowded freeways and major roads on weekends.

FIG. 2919 In many areas, there may be a lower speed limit for cars pulling trailers than for those not so encumbered. This is in recognition of the greater weight and longer stopping distance of car-trailer combinations. Read and heed such signs.

Driving

The first principle to note in driving with a trailer behind is "No passengers in the trailer!" This is very unsafe and is illegal in nearly all jurisdictions. The rule should be applied liberally, and not even pets allowed to ride in the trailer.

Drive as smoothly as possible—no sudden jerks in starting, and well-anticipated, easy stops. Jerks and sudden stops put added loads on the trailer connection, the boat itself, and the gear stowed in it. Avoid quick turns and sudden swerves; these can make a car-trailer combination harder to handle.

Check your brakes

Just as soon as you start out towing a trailer—before you leave your own property if possible—test your brakes and those of the trailer if it is so equipped.

Look and listen

Watch the trailer in the rear-view mirrors as much as possible and keep an ear open for the development of unusual noises from that direction. If a car passes you making hand signals to you, pull off and make a check to see what might be wrong.

Drive carefully

Observe all speed limits; these are often slower for cars with trailers, and for good reasons. Don't "tail-gate"; re-

FIG. 2920 Even a small car can pull a boat and trailer combination of limited size. Whatever the weight of the rig, the car's driving characteristics will be changed while towing, and the driver must be constantly alert to the differences.

FIG. 2921 A thorough check should be made upon arrival at the ramp to detect any unsatisfactory conditions resulting from the trip. These may need correction before starting on the return journey.

member that your stopping distance is extended because of the trailer; leave more-than-normal space between your car and the vehicle ahead of you. Use added caution in passing; remember that your overall length is twice as much as normal, or more, and your car will have to be well ahead of the passed vehicle before there will be room for you to pull back into lane—and remember, too, that your acceleration to pass is going to be less than you normally have. Keep in the proper lane; on multi-lane highways, this will normally be the right-hand, or "truck," lane. If there is only one lane in each direction, and a pile-up of traffic begins to form behind you, it is courteous and a contribution to safety to pull off to the side (where you can safely do so) and let the faster cars get past you.

On city streets, and in other restricted areas, the driver of a car-trailer combination must swing a bit wider than usual in turns to allow for the trailer which will tend to "cut across the corner" slightly rather than following in the tracks of the towing car—it can be embarrassing to bump the trailer tires up over the curb when turning at a street intersection!

Stop and Check

On long highway hauls at relatively high speeds, it is important to stop occasionally and see how the rig is riding. This need not be overdone, but to neglect it is to invite troubles, if not a real disaster. A suggested plan for long trips is to pull off and make a thorough inspection after 5 to 10 miles (8–16 km) of open road speeds, again after about 50 miles (80 km), and then each 100 miles (160 km). The initial check should not be delayed too long after starting out lest an initial defect or human error build up to a problem before it is detected. Stopping intervals must of course, be adjusted to the availability of suitable locations, especially on heavily traveled roads.

Use a regular procedure

At each roadside check, the wise skipper has a regular procedure to follow to ensure that nothing is overlooked. The hitch should be checked for tightness and the safety chains for the right amount of slack. Check the tires visually; remember that a build-up of pressure is normal and don't bleed off air in the belief that it is excess. Feel all wheel bearings; warmth is ok, but if they are too hot to touch, you have a problem. Let them cool off and then drive as slowly as practicable to a service station for dis-

assembly and inspection. Be sure also to check all tie-downs and take a look inside the trailer at the stowed gear. Check all lights even though it is daytime, especially the stop and turn signals.

Check the car, too

At each stop, take the time, too, to check the car's tires and lights. Don't check radiator water unless there have been signs of overheating, and then do so with great caution if a pressure-type is used as on most cars.

When Conditions Are Bad

Driving in rain, fog, or other condition of reduced visibility is always somewhat more hazardous, but it is especially so when the added length of the car and trailer combination must be considered, and its less favorable acceleration and stopping characteristics. High winds, particularly cross winds, present added hazards to trailers and may exclude such vehicles from some roads and bridges at these times; be alert for caution or prohibition signs at toll booths and bridge aproaches.

Pulling Tandem-axle Trailers

It has been noted that the "following" characteristics of trailers with two axles can sometimes be improved by *not*

FIG. 2922 With a little ingenuity, a trailered small cruiser can be made to serve as your overnight accommodations on long overland trips by camping in authorized trailer parks.

FIG. 2923 Remember, trailer always backs in direction opposite to that of car. (a) Driver swings close to launching ramp, then cuts car away from ramp, placing trailer at angle to ramp and driveway. (b) He cuts wheels of car to left, backs slowly into ramp, as trailer moves to right. (c) Driver straightens wheel after "jackknifing" car-and-trailer until both are in line, then back slowly down ramp. Backing from the left gives the driver a better view of the trailer.

inflating all four tires equally. If you are experiencing any weaving back and forth of your boat trailer at highway speeds, try varying tire pressures by 5 or 10 pounds with the front wheels softer and the rear wheels harder than nominal pressure, or vice versa. No specific guidance can be given, except to try various combination of pressures and check for either improved or worsened handling characteristics.

ON ARRIVAL

When you reach your destination, make a final check just as you would have done at an intermediate stop. Even if the tie-downs are to be removed soon, for example, it is well to know whether or not they have tended to work loose, and similarly with the hitch and safety chains. Hot wheel bearings or even warm ones, must be allowed to cool down before launching; if they are too hot, it may be an indication that they will have to be serviced before starting out on the return trip.

Maneuvering the Trailer

Although the proper procedures for driving a car so as to maneuver a trailer in a desired manner will be described here, there is no substitute for experience and deliberate practice. A large shopping center parking lot on a Sunday or other day of light use makes an excellent practice ground; place some empty boxes or similar objects to mark limits for parking, backing, and other "precision" maneuvers.

Backing up

Learn how to back in a straight line and how to turn while backing so as to put your trailer just where you want

it. A trailer *always backs* in a direction *opposite* to that of the car! This causes much confusion to beginners, and can even embarrass experienced drivers if they forget this basic fact when hurrying or in the stress of an emergency. When backing, turn your car's steering wheel in the direction to which you wish the trailer to go—it's true that your car's front end will go in the opposite direction, but the trailer will head off just as you desired.

The key to success in backing a trailer is *slowness;* make all moves slowly and watch the results carefully. If things are not going well, if the trailer is tending to jack-knife on you, don't panic, just stop, pull *ahead* a few feet to straighten out the car-trailer combination, and then try again, *slowly* and with *less* turning of the car's wheels.

Practice, and practice again

Success will not normally come quickly or without some embarrassing moments, but backing a trailer is a skill that can be acquired. If ever the saying, "Practice makes perfect" were applicable, it is to the art of trailer maneuvering.

SPECIAL TIPS

When trailering a boat for any distance, it is a good idea to remove the fire extinguisher from the craft and carry it readily accessible in the car. All too often, a passing boat on a trailer is the target of a carelessly or deliberately discarded cigar or cigarette from a passing vehicle. The fire extinguisher may be unreachable if it is in the boat when a fire starts, so have it in the car, but don't forget to return it to the boat before the craft is used on the water.

The American Automobile Association has prepared a booklet, "Trailer Pointers and Driving Hints" check your local automobile club office for a copy.

Launching and Retrieving

The act of transferring a boat from its trailer to the water is *launching;* the reverse process is *retrieval,* or *loading.* Both of these actions must be planned and done with care to avoid troubles, either damage to the craft and its outboard motor or outdrive unit, or injuries to personnel.

USING A RAMP

A sloping surface extending both above and below the water surface, used for launching and retrieving trailered boats is called a *ramp.* Using a ramp is not the best way to get a craft into the water, but it is by far the most often

used method, and all trailer boatmen should be qualified in this technique.

Ramps vary widely in their characteristics, including their "quality." Many are surfaced with concrete or asphaltic paving; others are unsurfaced, hard packed dirt or sand, sometimes reinforced with wood or steel planking. Some ramps are only wide enough for one launching operation at a time; others are much wider and several trailers can be backed down side-by-side for simultaneous launching or retrieval.

The quality aspects of a ramp relate to its slope, extent

FIG. 2924 Ramps vary widely in size and nature of surface. This wide, paved launching ramp can handle six boats at a time. On busy days, one boat is launched every three minutes.

into the water, and condition of the surface. The angle of slope is not critical, but it must be steep enough that a trailer need not be backed down so far into the water that its wheel bearings get wet. On the other hand, it must not be so steep that an excessive pull is required to get a loaded trailer up and off the ramp. The ramp must extend far enough into the water that trailers can be backed down at any water level without running off the lower end. (Many surfaced ramps develop a sharp drop-off at the lower end where dirt washes away; serious problems can be encountered in getting trailer wheels back up over this "lip" if they are rolled too far down and off the hard surface.) A dirt or sand ramp must be firm enough to support the trailer and car wheels; a surfaced ramp must not have a coating of slippery slime that could make footing dangerous and provide inadequate traction for the car's driving wheels.

Preparations for Launching

First of all, remember to allow time for the wheel bearings to cool down if there is any chance of their getting wet. If a hot bearing is put into colder water, the sudden temperature change has the effect of creating a partial vacuum inside and sucking in water, a most undesirable circumstance.

While the bearings are cooling down, the boat cover can be removed, folded, and stowed in the car or boat. Tie-downs can be removed and stored in a safe place, but leave the winch line taut. If the outboard motor or out-drive unit has been in the down position during trailering —unlikely, but possible—it should now be tilted up.

At this time, it may be desired to remove or relocate some of the equipment that has been transported in the boat, remembering that it will take an up angle as it is launched. If the craft has been trailered with empty or only partially filled fuel and water containers, these may be filled at this time unless there is a pier to move the boat to after it is in the water.

Use two lines

Attach a both a bow and a stern line; a boat cannot adequately be controlled with only one line (you can't "push" on a line!), but it can be safely and accurately moved about with two. Put over the side any fenders that might be needed, such as if the boat will be moved to a pier or seawall once it is in the water.

"Preview" the launching

Study the launching ramp and surrounding water area; check for any hazardous conditions such as a slippery or too short ramp, estimate the wind and current effects.

In case of doubt, don't hesitate to ask another skipper who has just launched his boat or taken it out of the water. If you have the time, perhaps while waiting for your trailer's

FIG. 2925 A trailer should not be backed farther into the water than is shown above. Wheel bearings, especially, should not be submerged. A tilt-bed trailer will usually make this possible.

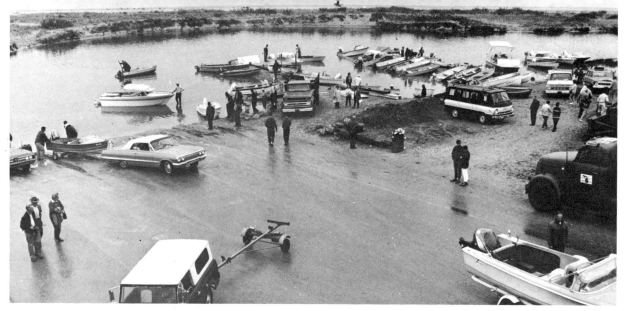

FIG. 2926 Especially on weekends and holidays, a popular ramp can be a very busy place with many boatmen waiting to launch or haul-out. The courteous skipper uses the ramp quickly and moves off promptly with both his boat and his car-trailer combination.

wheel bearings to cool off a bit, watch the launching operations of others, noting any peculiarities of this ramp which may be new to you.

Check and double-check

Now check the drain plug, if one is used; and as a final item, re-check the drain plug. It is quite embarrassing to launch your craft and have it start filling up with water, perhaps damaging gear placed on the floor boards. It can, and does, happen to experienced skippers who get careless about their preparations—don't let it happen to you. Look about, too, and see that no item of preparation has been forgotten.

The Actual Launching

Line up the car and trailer so that the backing process will be as straight and short as possible. On a wide ramp with multiple launching positions, give due regard to others and don't take up more than your share of the available space.

Back the car to the launching spot, preferably where the trailer's tires are just at the water's edge. (If ramp conditions are unfavorable, and you have a front bumper hitch, consider whether it is worthwhile to unhitch the trailer, turn the car around, and hook up again before spotting the trailer on the ramp.) Set the parking brake on the car and block a wheel on each side for added safety. Have one person man the winch controls and one, preferably two, others take the lines running from the bow and stern of the boat.

Release the tilt latch on the trailer if it is of this type. Tighten the winch brake and release the anti-reverse lock; do not disconnect the winch cable from the boat. The craft should then slide down and off the trailer easily, its speed controlled by the winch brake; a push or two might be needed to get it started. Be sure that the motor is tilted up so that the propeller and skeg will not dig into the bottom as the boat slides down.

When the boat is in the water, floating free of the trailer, unhook the winch line; move the boat aside and make it fast to a pier, beach it, or otherwise secure it temporarily. Return the tilted trailer bed to a horizontal position and

latch it in place. The winch line may be rewound on the drum if desired, but it can often be adequately secured by catching the hook on an after member of the trailer frame and taking up the slack.

Remove the car's wheel blocks and drive it to an authorized parking area—give consideration to others by clearing the ramp area promptly and selecting a parking spot that will not take up unnecessary space or block others. If at all possible, hose down with fresh water any parts of the trailer that got wet during the launching operation. Have a padlock on the coupling or safety chain to prevent theft of the trailer while you are enjoying your boating. Place chocks at its wheels if the trailer is detached from the car and the parking area has any slope.

At the boat, lower the motor or outdrive unit to its operating position and connect the fuel line if necessary. Make all other preparations for getting underway, such as transfer of gear from the car, load up your crew, and clear away from the launching area as rapidly as can be done with safety.

Reloading on the Trailer

Beach the boat or make it fast to a pier while someone goes to get the car and trailer from the parking area. If the outboard motor is not to be used further in the next day or so, it is an excellent idea to disconnect the fuel line with the motor still running at a fast idle. Let it run until all the fuel in the motor is used up; this will help prevent the formation of gum and deposits in the carburetor and fuel lines.

Back the trailer to the water's edge, again stopping, if possible, before the wheels and axles are submerged. Set the car brakes and block the wheels. (A front bumper hitch is even more useful in retrieval where the pull is harder than it is in launching). Release the trailer tilt latch and push the frame into the up position. Tilt the boat's motor and work the craft into position to move onto the first rollers with the keel of the boat straight with the centerline of the trailer; again, both a bow and stern line will make for easier handling unless conditions are favorable for someone to wade into the water and man-handle the craft into position. Run out enough winch cable and engage the hook

FIG. 2927 With the line attached to the eyebolt in the boat's stem, the winch is cranked so as to pull the craft up onto the trailer bed. If it is a two-speed winch, "low gear" may be used to start the boat up as this is the heaviest pull.

FIG. 2928 Cranes are often used to unload sailboats from their trailers and put them into the water, especially keel-boats that are not adaptable to the usual "slide-off" procedures.

in the eye in the stem of the boat; watch out for kinks in the cable and never handle a steel line except with gloves.

Crank in on the winch line and the boat should come easily onto the trailer bed; a tilted frame will come down to the horizontal position by itself as the boat moves up it. Often a winch has a lower-geared speed (higher mechanical advantage) which is useful for the initial pull to get the boat started up the trailer bed and a higher-speed mode to complete the loading when the pull gets easier.

Do not allow anyone to be in line with the winch cable, especially if a synthetic material is being used. A broken cable snaps like a broken rubber band and can throw a hook or fitting great distances. Serious injuries, even death, can result from being struck by a broken winch cable or fitting. *Keep clear!*

When the boat is fully onto the trailer, latch down the tilt mechanism (if it is of this type), remove the blocks from the car's wheels, and move the rig clear of the ramp so that others can use it. Don't overlook the other preparations that must be made for road travel, but do get away from the launching area to do them.

USING A CRANE

The use of a crane with padded slings is probably the launching method that is easiest on the craft. Done with care, this method puts a minimum of abnormal strains on the hull. Slings are normally provided by the crane operator, but should be checked for adequacy by the skipper before he entrusts his craft to them. The owner should know the proper placement of the slings for a safe balance of his boat.

Two lines, bow and stern, should always be used to control any swinging motion of the boat while it is hanging from the crane hoist between the trailer and the water.

Some cranes are fitted with hooks to engage in lifting eyes on the boat. This is generally not a good method as it concentrates the strains on the hull at two or three points. With proper planning and adequately installed eye bolts through the keel, however, it is possible to use this technique. Keep the boat light, removing loose gear, portable fuel tanks, and possibly the motor. Always use lines to control any swinging motion while the craft is up in the air.

Land Storage

A trailered boat is normally stored on land between uses, spending more time just sitting on its trailer bed than in the water or being hauled down a road. Thus for the sake of both the boat and trailer, land storage must be done properly.

Protection against theft of the boat and trailer can be at least partially achieved by installing one of the specially designed fittings that goes on the coupling of the trailer and is secured with a keyed lock—if they can't "hitch up," they can't haul it away!

As for the car when it is not pulling the trailer, the ball of the hitch can be covered with a small plastic bag secured

by a short length of cord or elastic. This will prevent any grease on the ball from rubbing off on clothing and will provide some protection from rusting.

Keep water out

Rainwater is undesirable in the boat for many reasons and a collection of it can rapidly increase the weight on the trailer, often beyond the trailer's capacity. A cover is desirable, but with or without one, the tongue of the trailer should be raised enough to cause rainwater to flow aft and run out through a drain hole. The tongue can be raised by the parking wheel, or lacking this, it can be kept elevated by securely blocking it up; the plug must, of course, be out.

If a cover is used, it must be adequately supported so that pockets of rainwater will not form, stretch the material, and possibly break through. Cross-supports under the cover and frequent fastening points around the edge will keep the cover sag-free; small sand bags in lieu of snap fasteners will ensure tautness but allow some "give" for shrinkage which occurs when the cover gets wet (such cover hold-downs, however, are not suitable for road travel).

Ease strains on the hull

A boat must be quite firmly held down to the trailer bed when it is being moved, particularly on rough roads or at high speeds. It need *not* be so tightly tied down when just sitting in storage, and the hull will be subjected to less strains and distortions if the tie-downs are slacked off a bit or some of them are removed.

Blocking up a trailer

If a rig is not going to be used for weeks or months, the trailer frame should be jacked up and placed on blocks to take the weight off the springs and tires. Blocking up must be adequate—at enough points to avoid distorting the frame which is undesirable in itself and which could transmit distortions to the boat's hull. The blocks need not be high, just enough to take the greater part of the load. If, however, the trailer wheels are clear of the ground, the air pressure in the tires should be reduced to 10 to 15 pounds. Remember that you must have means at hand to restore pressure when the blocks are taken out for the next trip; don't deflate tires unless you can pump them up again right there.

For long periods of land storage, consideration should

FIG. 2929 Folding canvas tops are subject to damage if the boat is towed at highway speeds. Be sure top is in the down position before starting on a trip, and take down all flags and pennants too.

also be given to removal of the battery, motor, and accessories, especially electrical ones, from the boat to more protected storage indoors. This may both prevent theft and provide for less deterioration.

Frequent checks

Don't forget the boat just because it is in land storage and out of regular use. Set up a schedule of weekly visits by yourself or someone else acting for you. Doing this at the same time each week will prevent forgetfulness or neglect.

On each visit to the craft, check for any signs of deterioration such as rust or peeling paint and don't let little problems grow into big ones before you take corrective action.

Maintenance

There is a need for regular maintenance on all items of boating equipment, and the trailer is no exception, especially if it is used around salt water. A bit of regular care and periodic major maintenance will protect your investment and ensure carefree use with a maximum of enjoyment and a minimum of "cussing."

Wheel bearings

The trailer's wheel bearings will need careful maintenance more than any other item. Basically, it is a problem of keeping water out and grease in. Use a proper grade of grease of high quality—if you didn't receive instructions with the trailer when you bought it, get guidance from the dealer or from an automotive mechanic familiar with trailer wheel bearings.

Bearings should be repacked at least annually, more often if adverse conditions are met. They should be inspected and repacked after *each* time that the trailer is submerged to such a depth that water reaches the bearings.

Tire maintenance

Whenever the trailer's wheels are removed for bearing lubrication, take advantage of this opportunity to carefully inspect each tire for imbedded objects in the tread, sidewall cracks or damage, or other signs of impending trou-

bles. Replace tires which have any serious damage or defects. When reinstalling the wheels on the trailer, switch the right side for the left so as to "rotate" the tires and even up tread wear.

Frame and mechanical parts

Rust and corrosion can quickly get a start and spread on a boat trailer. Hose it off with fresh water at every opportunity and keep painted surfaces intact. Touch up promptly wherever painted surfaces get scratched or scraped.

All bare metal surfaces, such as mating parts, latches, etc., should be protected by a light coat of grease. The winch should be lubricated regularly in accordance with its instruction book or with general good mechanical practices if no specific guidance is available.

Rollers on the trailer must be kept free of rust and well oiled so that they turn freely and added strains do not occur when the boat is moved on or off the trailer.

Electrical system

Water is a great enemy of electrical systems. Keep moisture out of light housings and connectors; drain holes help keep dampness from building up in such fixtures.

A light coat of grease or vaseline will fight off corrosion and lengthen the life of all electrical connectors.

FIG. 2930 Sailboats on trailers with their masts up and in the vicinity of overhead electric power lines present a very serious safety hazard—use extreme caution in these circumstances.

Sailboats, Too!

The attention of this chapter has been primarily focused on the trailering of outboard and I-O runabouts and fishing craft, as these predominate in numbers. But many small sailboats, too, are trailered from home parking areas to various bodies of water for racing or day-sailing. The same advantages of mobility, dry storage, "at home" maintenance, etc., apply here as well as for motorboats.

Much of what has been said earlier about trailers and their selection, use, and maintenance will be applicable to sailboat trailering. The selection of a sailboat trailer is just as critical and the supports must be just as carefully designed, perhaps even more so. Sailboats will usually be launched and reloaded using slings from a crane. For this reason, the supports will normally be of the padded-bar type, placed and adjusted to fit the contours of the hull; excellent support can be obtained if these are properly positioned.

The problem of the mast

Sailboats are trailered with their masts unstepped and carried in a horizontal position. Special holders for this must be mounted on the boat or the trailer. The mast will usually far overhang the hull and must be marked with warning flags and/or lights to meet local police regulations; extra care is required in driving a car pulling a trailer with such an extended length.

Maintenance

Sailboat trailers will rarely be immersed in the water and so wheel bearings will be less of a troublesome item, but all other maintenance will be required as for trailers in general. Padding on supports should be replaced when, due to its exposure to the weather, it begins to harden and lose its cushioning ability.

FIG. 2931 Sailboats can be "trailer boats"—and many are! Quite a few centerboard designs can be launched directly from trailers as shown above. Special provisions must be made for raising and lowering the mast, and for transporting it.

As with almost any form of modern-day human endeavor, there is a certain amount of "paperwork" involved with the ownership and operation of a boat. Although never really enjoyable, these necessary tasks and processes can be made less burdensome and more effective by an orderly and efficient approach.

A boat of almost any size larger than a dinghy or a sailboard is a relatively complex item that must be properly used and maintained for safety, efficient operation, maximum enjoyment, and the protection of one's investment in her. The use and maintenance of a craft might well be lumped together and termed "boat management"; the proper documents and records are a vital part of this function.

This chapter will offer broad guidance in connection with the paperwork of "boat management." It will remain the responsibility of each owner-skipper to work out the specific actions and records for his boat as every craft and its use are highly individualized matters. What is best for a cabin cruiser just won't be right for an outboard runabout or a sailboat—what is adequate for the weekend user of a Class 1 boat will fall short of meeting the needs of a cruising yachts-man. But in *all* cases, there is a re-quirement for a certain amount of

"BOAT MANAGEMENT"

Certificates and Documents

The term "ship's papers" has a long and honored history. Nearly all vessels, including the smallest of boats, have some official or legal papers relating to them. Even a rowing dinghy or a sailboat of any size completely without mechanical propulsion (and thus exempt from any requirement for registration and numbering) will have a bill of sale or purchase receipt.

Many items can be included in any listing of "ship's papers" for a recreational craft. Among these are the Certificate of Number or yacht document; radio licenses, both station and operator's; survey reports; insurance policies; personal certificates; etc.

REQUIRED PAPERS

The owner of a boat registered by the Coast Guard, or by a state under a numbering plan approved in accordance with the Federal Boat Safety Act of 1971, is issued a "Certificate of Number." This must be on board the craft whenever it is in use (with a few specified exceptions), and to facilitate this, the law prescribes that it shall be of "pocket size." If lost or destroyed, immediate action must be taken to obtain a duplicate, but use of the boat can continue while waiting for this to arrive.

In a number of states, a sticker or decal must be attached to the boat in a specified location. Broadly speaking, this small item can be considered a part of the ship's papers. It is visual evidence from a distance that the craft's registration is currently valid.

Documents

Boats over a specified minimum size *may* be "documented" by the Coast Guard in lieu of registration and numbering. Information on this procedure is given in Chapter 2.

Craft that are documented must carry this paper on board, and it must be renewed annually. These documents are valid for one year from date of issue or renewal; there is no calendar or other fixed year.

A Certificate of Number or document must be produced for inspection by a law-enforcement official upon his request.

Radio Licenses

A radio station aboard a boat must be licensed by the Federal Communications Commission. This includes VHF radiotelephones, single sideband (SSB) radios, and Citizen Band equipment, plus radar sets. No license is required for small "handitalkies" on CB frequencies provided that their power is not over 0.1 watt. No license is required for radio direction finders, loran receivers, electronic depth sounders, and other types of equipment that do not *transmit* radio signals.

For the operation of marine band and certain other radio transmitters, the individual must have an operator's license or permit. None is required for CB sets or radar equipment.

Posting of Licenses

The radio station license must be on board the boat, posted in a prominent location as near as practicable to the position from which the equipment is operated. A Restricted Radiotelephone Operator Permit may be carried on an individual's person; any higher class of license must be posted.

Copy of FCC Rules

Each boat radio station must have a copy of the current edition of Part 83 of the FCC Rules—or a copy of the new FCC pamphlet of simplified rules. This *should* be on board, but the regulations do allow for its being kept "in a suitable place on shore."

A radio log, required by the Rules, must be maintained;

this will be covered later in this chapter.

Additional information on the "paperwork" related to marine radio stations will be found in Chapter 25.

OPTIONAL BOAT PAPERS

Although not required by any law or regulation, an annual Courtesy Motorboat Examination by the Coast Guard Auxiliary is an excellent check on a craft's safety and "readiness for sea." If this examination is passed, a sticker will be awarded and the inspection form will be signed by the Auxiliarist and given to the Skipper. This signed form should be stowed safely away with the others of the ship's papers.

Personal certificates

If a motorboat is not carrying "passengers for hire," there is no requirement for the operator to have a Coast Guard license—state requirements may differ and should be checked. (The term "non-commercial operation" is often used in this connection, but it is not strictly correct as a person commercially fishing, crabbing, lobstering, etc., does not need a USCG operator's license provided he has no passengers for hire on board.)

The circumstances of when a guest aboard is, or is not, a "passenger for hire" have been examined in some detail in Chapter 2. It has also been held that a salesman, broker, or owner demonstrating a boat to a prospective buyer must have an operator's license or else place the craft under the command of a licensed individual.

Many skippers, however, do get a USCG license in one or more of the categories in which they are issued, just for the sake of having one rather than from any regular need for it. If so, it should be posted where it can readily be seen. If nothing more, it may serve to reassure any nervous "landlubber" guests aboard for a cruise!

Likewise, the Skipper's membership certificate in the United States Power Squadrons, with its endorsements for qualifications in Advanced Grades and Elective Courses is often posted on his boat rather than at home ashore. The same, too, is frequently done with one's certificate of membership in the United States Coast Guard Auxiliary. As with a USCG operator license, these documents all attest to the owner's established qualifications and abilities —they should be proudly displayed.

FIG. 3001 Every skipper should have a record aboard regarding the insurance coverages on his craft. He may keep the policy itself on board with the other "ship's papers," but if not, he must have at least a notation of the insurer, policy number, and other essential data.

Insurance Papers

Most boats are, or should be, covered by insurance policies; see page 64. The owner may either keep his policy on board, or ashore in a secure place such as a safe deposit box.

If the policy is not carried on board, there should at least be a memorandum of information in the ship's papers regarding it. It should list the insurance company, policy number, coverages, expiration date, and other pertinent information such as the agent's name, address, and telephone numbers, both office and residence.

Logs and Log Keeping

An important part of the paperwork of "boat management" is the maintenance of the legally required or otherwise desirable logs. The plural form of "log" is used as it is often convenient to keep separate records of navigational, engine, and radio operations. These, however, can be within the same covers or binder if such is desired.

Developing your log format

The first step in log-keeping is to have logs that fit your needs. It is useless to follow a format that provides space for recording many items of information that are not applicable to your style of boating—for example, the nature of the bottom as brought up by an "armed" lead, or true headings if you regularly use magnetic readings from the chart. Trying to use an unsuitable log format is a bad practice as it may lead to the neglect of making any entries at all. Many printed logs simply do not meet an individual's requirements—if they do, fine; but if they do not, then develop your own style for the data that you find necessary and useful at a later date. It is wasted effort to record information for which you have no future use.

A log should be kept in columnar form insofar as practicable, rather than in paragraph style, but columns should not be set up for data that are only occasionally entered as this would result in much wasted space.

Printed log books are available from *Motor Boating Books* and at most marine supply stores. These may be used as they are, or column headings may be modified. In general, the use of a loose-leaf notebook form of a log should be avoided as pages can get lost. Much more desirable is a bound, hard-cover book—often a "record" book, available from office supply stores, will do nicely for the boatman who rules his own columns. It is quite possible that *your* needs will be met by such a book ruled in just three columns—"Date," "Time," and "Remarks"—other entries may be many, but probably will not be so grouped as to make additional columns useful.

Determining needs

It may take some time to determine just what is needed and what is not. Your requirements for log data may not even "jell" until after you have made a second cruise over some of the same areas months or more later; then you will learn just what information you should have recorded on your first visit there.

In considering which form to use, or in designing one of your own, be systematic. List the items that you wish to enter; consider their relative value. Sort possible entries

FIG. 3002 A log is a most important document for any craft. Its format and contents will vary with the boat, its use, and its skipper's way of doing things. Develop a log to fit your needs and desires—but do have one. Log-keeping can be a pleasure rather than a chore!

into two categories—frequent and occasional. The first group will guide you in establishing columns; the second category can be put in a general column headed "Remarks." Once you have worked out your needs, reduce your log-keeping to those items only, and buy or prepare a form most convenient to record them. Be careful, however, that you don't overlook data for which you may have only infrequent use, but which would be invaluable in case of accident, breakdown, tax or insurance inquiry, etc. —don't be too brief!

DECK LOGS

A "deck log" is a record of navigational data—the time that you started a day's run and the time of reaching your destination, plus times of passing important navigational aids or landmarks and towns or cities. These latter items are particularly useful when cruising in inland waters where a constant speed cannot be maintained and you might later want to know the running time between such points. If your cruising takes you offshore, you will probably include your various headings and speeds, with the time of any change in either.

Other information that should be entered in the log are the names of any persons aboard other than the usual family "crew." Entries might be made of the weather—wind, visibility, sea conditions, etc.—at the start of the day's run and any significant changes. Entries should, of course, be made of any unusual events on board or seen; for example, engine trouble on your boat, or assistance rendered to another craft. These entries should be made in full detail so that reliance need not be placed on one's memory at a later date.

It is frequently useful to record in your log your operating expenses, such as fuel and dockage charges. Such records must, of course, be kept if you are able to take advantage of any business-related tax deductions. It is often of interest to record fuel prices at stops where no fuel is taken on, or dockage fees at brief daytime stops; this information may be of use in planning future cruises.

A log for every boat

A deck, or navigational, log should be kept by every boatowner and used for all activities—local outings, fishing trips, water skiing runs, etc., as well as "cruises." It is ad-

visable that a boat's log account for *every* day, in port or underway. The former may easily be done by such a simple entry as "8-12 June. In regular slip; no one aboard." This may later prove to be a useful and valuable record.

Validating the log

Regardless of format, certain essential elements should be entered. Each page should be numbered and the craft's name should appear somewhere on the page, usually at the top. Each day's entries, or a combined entry for several days in port, should be signed by the skipper as he completes them at the end of the day concerned. This authenticated record may be needed in connection with an insurance claim, a law suit, or other investigation. If a boat owner can state under oath that it is his practice to keep a daily log and then present a signed entry for the day involved, he has gone a long way toward legally establishing the situation as seen by him. Be sure that you *never* make erasures in a log—if you need to correct an item, rule out the old material without making it illegible, and then write in the correct entry if there is space, or make reference to where it will be found elsewhere in the log.

FIG. 3003 It is important that the log entries for each day's use, or period of time in port, be validated by the skipper with his signature. This may have important legal aspects if the log is ever needed to establish facts in a court of law.

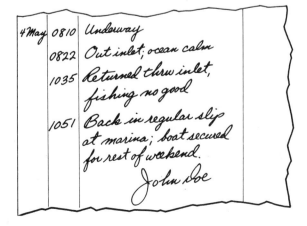

Initial the correction and add the date if it is made on a later day.

Why not an illustrated log?

With a bit of proper planning, log-keeping can be interesting and fun—and the log itself will be of interest and use long after a cruise is over. Why not consider an illustrated log? Use marginal sketches if you or your mate has the artistic ability; or put in photographs of scenes, events, and people.

ENGINE LOGS

An engine log is kept in terms of hours of operation and is valuable in timing oil changes and other items of preventive maintenance. Record all routine maintenance and other significant events such as any troubles, repairs, etc. If a record is kept in the engine log of the addition of crankcase oil to maintain the proper level, any increase will soon become apparent and consumption can be accurately computed. Any increase in the use of oil may be a valuable warning of internal engine troubles. Likewise, fuel consumption can be periodically figured in terms of engine hours and any unusual change noted.

Hours can be estimated, or roughly figured from the deck log, but the easiest and by far the best way is by use of an electric engine-hour meter. Such an instrument is not expensive, and a typical installation can be made in an hour or two by the average skipper. An engine log for the dinghy's outboard motor is not beyond reason, but here we confine ourselves to estimates of the running time if we remember to make an entry promptly after each use.

RADIO LOG

If your craft is equipped with a radio transmitter, a certain amount of log-keeping is required by the FCC Rules and Regulations. In recent years, the number of entries that are required has been greatly reduced, but there is no excuse accepted for a lack of these if your station is inspected. Refer to your copy of Part 83 of the FCC Rules and keep at least the minimum log. You may want to add more to your radio log relating to contacts with the Coast Guard, other boats, or the marine operator.

LOG-KEEPING TECHNIQUES

A most important feature of good log-keeping is the making of entries while the facts are fresh in your mind—the very best time is immediately after the occurrence of the event. On a small craft this may present problems—you may not be able to write neatly, or even legibly, due to the boat's motion; the cockpit of a sailboat may be far too wet for "paperwork." One solution to this is the use of a small portable tape recorder; some are now so small that they can easily be held in one hand, complete with built-in microphone. Thus the skipper can keep a running record of events and transcribe them later into the permanent log when he has reached a sheltered marina slip or a quiet anchorage. The use of a tape recorder will ensure that no event is overlooked, nor will the log be messy or unreadable at a later date. One caution however, watch your tape supply—don't get caught at the end of a day with no data because you ran to the end of a reel or cassette and didn't notice!

FIG. 3004 An excellent way to keep notes for logs —deck, engine, or radio, while underway is the use of a small hand-held tape recorder. Using this procedure, the actual log can be written up after the day's run and will be much more legible than one written at the helm while underway.

Retention of logs

Since the maintenance of a deck or engine log is voluntary on a recreational boat, its retention is at the owner's discretion. In any case, it should be kept in a safe place until any possibility of litigation has passed. Many skippers keep their logs permanently and read them with fond memories years later. A radio log *must be retained* for the period specified by the current regulations.

How about a "Fog"?

One further thought on log-keeping—the skipper's logs may well be supplemented by a "female's log," or "fog" for short. In this record, the skipper's wife records the names of boats seen, new friends made (and don't forget addresses), new recipes discovered, points of interest ashore, and any other bits of information that will aid her in planning for other cruises or will just bring back memories. If you are a "shutter-bug," here is the place to record enough information about your picture-taking so that months later you will not be wondering what in the world that particular photograph was intended to show.

Instruction Books

It is most important that a boat owner have instruction manuals or data sheets for all equipment installed on his craft. Such papers are of great value in the performance of routine maintenance to keep the equipment working properly, or whenever repairs are necessary. These instruction books will normally include a "parts list" which will help greatly in obtaining the correct replacement components when needed.

The prudent skipper ensures that he has a *complete* set of instruction books. He starts with the main engines and goes straight through the inventory to the smallest motor, pump, horn, etc. There should be no item categorized as "too small," "too insignificant," or "too dependable" for inclusion in this check-up.

Rare, indeed, is the craft that has a complete set of manuals when it is purchased, either new or used. Those that are not on board must be obtained—sometimes from a local dealer, but more often directly from the manufacturer of that particular item of equipment. The boat owner can usually determine the manufacturer's address from the name plate on the equipment or from advertising in *Motor Boating* or other publications.

Model and serial numbers

When making this check of equipment, it is wise to make a note of *both* model and serial numbers for all items. These can be recorded in a notebook set up for this purpose or in the back of a log book. The latter location is usually quite convenient, but it requires the transcribing of information when one volume of a log is filled and another is started.

When writing for an instruction book or a replacement part for any piece of equipment, be sure to include *both* model and serial numbers as often there are variations in design after a certain serial number without a change in model designation.

Parts lists

Parts lists must include as a minimum the identification of those units which normally wear out with the passage of time and whose replacement is a matter of routine maintenance, especially those whose replacement is within the capability of the skipper or crew.

Much more desirable is to have the instruction manual or parts book so complete that it shows the identification of *all* parts and sub-assemblies. This will facilitate the ordering of proper replacements in the event of any sort of breakdown, and much time may be saved thereby.

Names and addresses

Instruction manuals, parts lists, and the like should be annotated with the name, address, and telephone number of the nearest source of supply—the local dealer or his source, the area distributor. If service technicians must be obtained from a different firm, this, too, should be recorded with all necessary details.

Sailboats

Sailboats should have complete information on each sail carried—manufacturer, date made, cloth type and weight, and all dimensions, including those relating to battens, if these are used. It is so much easier to take measurements under ideal conditions at one's convenience, and then look up the information in a notebook or log when needed, than it is to have to measure under adverse conditions, perhaps in an emergency.

INFORMATION ON THE BOAT

Very few, if any, boats are delivered with what might be termed an instruction book on the craft itself. Such a document would typically include electrical wiring diagrams for each system of different voltage; a drawing of the fresh water system's pumps, lines, and valves; a diagram of the fuel lines and valves; information on the location of all seacocks and other through-hull fittings; and similar information regarding the boat and systems that are not a part of accessory equipment.

Unfortunately, some manufacturers consider that they have provided such a manual when they place on board each new boat a simple, generalized booklet of "safe boating tips," and nothing else.

If not found on board the boat when it is purchased, some or all of the above documents may possibly be obtained by writing to the manufacturer of the craft, being sure to include all available identification data including hull number. On a used boat, all such information, either coming with the boat or later obtained from the builder, should be verified as previous owners may have modified or added to one or more of the systems. In all probability, the owner will have to search out and record much of the information discussed above.

Docking plan

For craft larger than roughly 30 feet (9.1 m) or so in length, every skipper should have a "docking plan." This drawing shows where slings should be placed if the boat is to be lifted, or where shoring blocks must be placed if she is to be hauled on a marine railway. Close attention to this plan will prevent excessive stresses being placed on the hull when the craft is taken out of the water.

Safe stowage of books

It is important that all instruction books, parts lists, and similar publications be on board, but kept safe from damage or loss. Usually, it will be most convenient to place them in a waterproof plastic envelope and then put that in a secure place. On larger craft, where water damage is less likely, a large heavy-paper case with lettered or numbered subdividers makes an excellent means of filing these documents for the easiest retrieval when needed.

Check Lists

As the size of one's boat increases, its operation becomes more complex and there are more details to be remembered and executed at such times as getting underway or docking. While it should not be carried to extreme degrees that would complicate boat operation to the extent of decreasing enjoyment, the use of "check lists" can be valuable from a viewpoint of both safety and the avoidance of embarrassing situations. Their use can have real value in the prevention of expensive accidents and equipment damage.

Applications

The situations for which check lists can be prepared, and their level of detail, will, of course, vary with the size, type, and use of the craft. They may well vary, too, with the personality of the skipper. Typically, for a cruising Class 2 or 3 boat there will be check lists for:

1. Getting underway
2. Approaching a pier or mooring
3. Securing after a day's operations
4. Departure from the boat for a day or more
5. Periodic routine preventive maintenance

Importance for single-handed operation

Check lists are of particular importance and value for the person who is aboard by himself. Single-handed operation of a boat requires the maximum of thought and preplanning. Once underway, many tasks become much more difficult, if not impossible of accomplishment with safety, than if they had been performed before lines were cast off. A check list will minimize the reliance that must be placed on one's memory during the final minutes before casting off, and reduce the penalties for any forgetfulness.

DEVELOPMENT OF CHECK LISTS

The contents of any check list will vary so much with the individual craft and her skipper that it will not be possible here to give more than sample items which may or may not be applicable to another person's situation.

Probably the most significant single characteristic of any check list is that it is a "living" document—it is never "completed" and final; it must always be considered as being under review each time that it is used.

Getting underway

Before getting underway from a marina berth, many "disconnections" must be made—electric cords, water hose, possibly a telephone connection, and most certainly the lines which have held the craft fast to the pier or pilings. Forget just one of any of these and you're in trouble, but fast!

Even the most elementary "housekeeping" chores are candidates for a pre-departure check list. Trash and garbage should be put in proper containers ashore rather than being taken along for a day's cruise. Water tanks should be topped off, if appropriate, and certainly fuel tanks should be checked. Use of a check list helps prevent the omission of an item because each of two persons thought the other had done it.

Not too silly an item for family groups is a final head-count of all children and pets. Even if the individual is missed before the craft gets far away, it can mean another docking and undocking, an unnecessary waste of time.

For the single-hander, there are such matters as the proper setting of switches and valves, the raising or lowering of a radio antenna, or even the setting of the craft's colors. All of these are minor tasks, but they cannot be done underway without leaving the helm unattended.

Coming into port

When approaching a pier or wharf, a much better landing will be achieved, and embarrassment often avoided, if the proper lines are laid out where needed and fenders are placed ready for use if required. Once made fast to the shore, there will be switches to be turned and valves to be opened or closed. Notations must be made for log entries while the information is still fresh in one's mind. Supplies of fuel and water should be checked so that refills can be arranged as needed.

FIG. 3005 Larger craft should have on board diagrams of the electrical system—systems, if there is more than one voltage involved—and the network of tanks, valves, and lines of the fuel system. These will be of great value when troubles must be found and fixed.

FUEL SYSTEM, GASOLINE (SIMPLIFIED)

FIG. 3006 A "docking plan" is a sketch indicating where a craft's keel ends and where shoring blocks must be placed if she is to be hauled on a railway or elevator platform. It shows where slings must be located if the boat is to be lifted out.

Departure from the boat

This is a very important check list as items which are overlooked when leaving will often not be remembered until their execution is impracticable or even impossible. Primary choices for this list are items relating to the safety and security of the unattended craft—turning off fuel valves, the proper setting of electrical switches, pumping out the bilge and leaving the switch on automatic (if one trusts the switch) or making arrangements for such periodic pumping out as may be needed, and the physical security of ports, windows, hatches, and doors.

Routine maintenance check lists

Routine maintenance check lists will include both items based on use of the craft (usually in terms of engine hours) and on calendar dates (weekly, monthly, etc., checks). Typical of the former are crankcase oil level checks and oil changes, and oil and fuel filter changes.

On a calendar basis are such matters as checking the water in storage battery cells, pressure gauges on dry-chemical fire extinguishers, and all navigation lights. The proper operation on and off of automatic bilge alarms or pump switches should be checked by deliberately running water into the boat. Seacocks should be periodically operated closed and open several times to ensure their free and easy operation if needed quickly in an emergency. Equipment and supplies carried on board for emergency use should be inspected for any signs of deterioration.

CHECK LISTS MUST BE USED

The most important aspect of check lists is that they must be used *regularly*. They must be used if they are to be of any value to the skipper, and they must be used if they are to be kept up to date and increase in usefulness.

A pre-departure check list must be gone through *each* time the craft is gotten underway. A list prepared and filed away is of little value, and it may build up a false sense of security. For safety and to avoid any embarrassment, the boatman should train himself to automatically reach for the list when he is ready to start an operation for which a check list has been established. He should be like the aircraft pilot who goes through such a check list *every* time, no matter how many years experience he has or how many times he has taken off and landed that day.

The value of a check list lies in its use, not in its existence!

CHAPTER 31

"What's that odd-looking flag on that boat over there?"

"What flag? Oh, you mean the one with blue and white vertical stripes?"

"Yes, that one—it has a red union for the anchor and stars, rather than the usual blue field."

"That's the Ensign of the United States Power Squadrons."

"The United States . . . what? What's that?"

"The United States Power Squadrons—a volunteer organization dedicated to making boating safer through education rather than legislation. I took their free Boating Course—you should take it too."

"Perhaps I will; tell me more."

The United States Power Squadrons

FIG. 3101 The USPS Ensign is usually flown from the starboard spreader on a sailboat or a motorboat with a mast. On any craft, however, it can be displayed on a staff at the stern as shown above, and this is the normal procedure for smaller boats.

The United States Power Squadrons is a non-governmental, private membership organization, self-supporting in its efforts to enhance boating safety through education. Somewhat contrary to its name, which has more historical significance than current-day literal meaning, it is *not* limited to the owners of motorboats; many sailboat skippers belong, as well as some who do not own a boat at all.

Purposes

The purposes of USPS may be described by quoting in part from the "Objects" as stated in its constitution:

"To selectively associate congenial men of good character having a common love and appreciation of yachting as a nation-wide fraternity of boatmen. To encourage and promote a high amateur standard of skill in the handling and navigation of yachts, power and sail; to encourage and promote the study of the science and art of navigation, seamanship, and small boat handling; to develop and promote instructional programs for the benefit of members; and to stimulate members to increase their knowledge of and skill in yachting, through instruction, self-education, and participation in marine sports events and competitions."

The USPS Ensign

The Ensign of the United States Power Squadrons may be flown on boats only when they are skippered by members of the organization. Rules for where and when it can be flown are given on page 462 and V.

The USPS Ensign consists of seven *blue* and six white *vertical* stripes with a union of *red* on which is the same white fouled anchor and circle of stars as on the yacht ensign; see color illustration on pages Q, R.

In the form of decals and stickers, automobile emblems, boating cap insignia, etc., the USPS design can be worn or displayed only by members in good standing.

THE ENSIGN is the name of the USPS monthly publication.

HISTORICAL DEVELOPMENT

In 1912, the motorboat was beginning to challenge the sailboat for a place in the field of recreational boating. A group in the Boston Yacht Club felt that there was a serious lack of knowledge on the part of some who were taking up this new form of boating, and decided to inprove the situation by conducting classes. This program led to formation of the "Power Squadron of the Boston Yacht Club," and set the educational basis for the USPS which remains its primary function.

Formation of a national organization

On 2 February 1914, a meeting was held at the New York Yacht Club that resulted in the formation of the "United States Power Squadrons." Following World War I, the programs of the USPS were reorganized into a new format that emphasized instruction as a service to boatmen and boating in general. The old distinctions between "power" and "sail" faded, and the Squadrons began to have an appeal to all who used boats of any type. The word spread, and Squadrons were formed on the Great Lakes, in Florida, on the Pacific and Gulf Coasts, and on inland rivers and lakes.

Growth after World War II

During World War II, the USPS again provided training to thousands of men before their entry into military service or the Merchant Marine. With the end of this war, boating boomed, and with it, the USPS. Squadrons were formed in many new areas, including Japan and Okinawa, as well as Hawaii, Alaska, Puerto Rico, and the Canal Zone.

MEMBERSHIP

The USPS is a private organization and membership is by invitation. Members must be male U.S. citizens over 18 years of age who have met entrance qualifications set by the national organization and who have been elected by the local unit. As it is a volunteer organization depending upon its membership for support, an important aspect of a prospective member's qualifications is his willingness to "give" of his time and talents as well as "take" from the USPS of knowledge and improved skills.

There are also provisions for invitation to Apprentice status for male youths of U.S. citizenship who are at least 12 years of age; this status may be retained until their 21st birthday. Ladies and girls 12 years of age or older may be awarded a "Woman's Certificate."

Apprentices and Women Certificate Holders may take USPS Advanced Grades, Elective, and Instructor Qualification Courses, but have no other membership rights.

ORGANIZATION

The basic unit of the USPS is the local *Squadron*. These have names of geographic significance and may have as few as 20 to 30 members or as many as 1200 or more.

Squadrons are grouped into *Districts* which are numbered; this is the intermediate level between the local unit and the *National* organization.

FIG. 3102 The above organizational diagram is greatly simplified; there are 33 Districts and more than 440 Squadrons. The number of Squadrons in a District varies from 5 to more than 30. Each echelon is led by elected officers.

Officers

All levels of organization are led by elected officers. Squadrons and Districts have a *Commander,* plus several *Lieutenant Commanders* and *Lieutenants*. The USPS as a whole is directed by a *Chief Commander* and five department heads with the rank of *Vice Commander*. National Committee Chairmen and other staff officers hold the rank of *Rear Commander* or *Staff Commander*. All officers are unpaid volunteers; there is a small paid office staff at the National Headquarters at Raleigh, NC.

Uniforms, insignia, and flags

The USPS has a series of blue and white uniforms suitable for a wide variety of occasions and climates. The purchase of a uniform is optional for members, but is expected of officers. The various uniforms, plus insignia and flags of officers, are shown on pages 480-482, R, and S.

The USPS today

In 1978 the United States Power Squadrons were comprised of more than 65,000 members. There were more than 440 Squadrons assigned to 33 Districts.

FIG. 3103 USPS members may wear any one of a series of blue and white uniforms as determined by the nature of the Squadron activity and the climate. A blazer is available for informal occasions. The purchase of a uniform is not required of all members.

Educational Programs

The educational programs of the USPS are a major activity. There are four major areas of educational effort. One of these is for the general public. The other programs are for members only, and include two for further personal study and one for the internal training of the membership to improve their teaching abilities.

THE USPS BOATING COURSE

Each local Squadron is required to give each year at least one series of classes of the *USPS Boating Course* for the general public. Many Squadrons give the classes two or more times each year, varying the place and/or night of the week so as to reach the greatest number of boatmen and their families.

The USPS Boating Course is focused on the vast, and steadily growing, number of men and their families who go out on the water each year in small craft. The course covers the basic areas of piloting, seamanship, and small boat handling. The major topics are—

Handling Under Normal Conditions
Handling Under Adverse Conditions
Seamanship and Common Emergencies
Rules of the Road
Compass and Chart Familiarization
Aids to Navigation
Running Lights and Equipment
Inland Boating
Mariner's Compass and Piloting
Boat Trailering

The course material is prepared and distributed on a national basis, as is the end-of-course examination. Instruction is by local USPS members, supplemented in some instances by outside experts and specialists. The course is given free of charge by the local Squadron, although students will usually find it desirable to purchase a textbook, notebook binder, plotting instruments, etc., if they do not already have them. In some areas, the course is presented as a part of the adult education program of a local school system and a small registration fee is charged by that organization; no part of this money goes to the USPS or any member.

Family groups are encouraged to take the USPS Boating

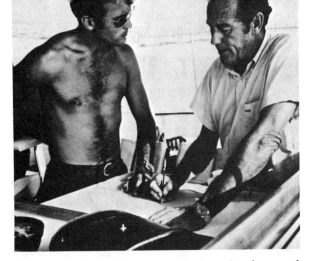

FIG. 3104 As a public service function, each Squadron annually presents the USPS Boating Course for the general public. This course covers all aspects of basic boating safety and is in furtherance of the aim of "safety through education, not legislation."

FIG. 3105 The USPS also has a progressive series of courses for its members. The initial courses are Seamanship and Advanced Piloting in which the basic material of the public course is studied in more detail and advanced aspects.

Course together; the minimum age is 12 years. Boating is widely enjoyed as family recreation, and both safety and pleasure are enhanced if all are knowledgeable.

THE ADVANCED GRADES PROGRAM

In keeping with its stated purpose of encouraging the study of the science of navigation, the USPS offers its members a progressive series of four courses.

The primary purpose of the *Seamanship Course* is to provide basic information about boating to people who have had little or no experience on the water. Knowledgeable boatmen, however, will find it quite valuable as a refresher course. The material covered in "S" applies to both motorboats and sailboats. The course includes instruction in "marlinespike seamanship" to develop a working knowledge of useful knots, bends, hitches, and splices.

The *Advanced Piloting Course* covers the basic principles and more important practices of pilotage, including modern electronic methods. The lessons will prove to be of great interest and practical value to the small boat skipper as much of the knowledge can be applied at once to the use of his own craft. This course includes a thorough study of the mariner's compass and its errors. The student is instructed in the use of government publications concerned with piloting. He learns how to determine the height of the tide or the strength of a tidal current at any specified time. Further instruction is given in the use of charts, in the laying of courses, and in the determination of position by bearings, angles, and soundings.

The *Junior Navigator Course* teaches the "sailings"— the mathematical counterpart of plotting. The practical use of the marine sextant is covered, including the taking and reduction of sights on the sun, moon, planets, and stars. A main objective of this course is to provide instruction sufficiently complete in itself that the graduate could navigate out of sight of land and bring his craft safely back to port.

The *Navigator Course* deals with alternative methods, special situations, and more advanced techniques. It aims to develop greater skill in the taking if sights and higher precision in position finding. Throughout the course, orderly methods for carrying out the day's work of a navigator at sea are emphasized. The grade of "N" is the

FIG. 3106 The Advanced Grades program of USPS education culminates in the Junior Navigator and Navigator Courses covering celestial navigation. The final grade of "N" is highly esteemed by members.

highest awarded by the USPS—its "PhD" in the field of boating study.

THE ELECTIVE COURSES PROGRAM

The USPS also offers to its members, apprentices, and woman's certificate holders four "elective" courses in speciality subjects; these do not constitute a series and may be taken in any sequence.

Engine Maintenance familiarizes students with the general construction, operating principles, and simple maintenance of marine gasoline and diesel engines, including outboard motors. As one of the major objectives of the course is to make the skipper a self-reliant and effective trouble-shooter, the diagnosis of all types of engine troubles is emphasized. EM is *not* intended to produce trained *mechanics,* only well-informed and resourceful *users* of marine engines.

Marine Electronics focuses on the legally proper and most effective *use* of marine radios and other electronic equipment that can be installed on boats for greater safety and convenience. This is *not* a technical course, and is well within the capabilities of the average USPS member. Students are prepared to take the FCC exam for a Third Class Radiotelephone Operator Permit.

The *Sail Course* is proof that the USPS is not just for the motorboat skipper! It covers sail terminology, types of rigs

FIG. 3107 At the Annual Meeting of the USPS there is a large exhibition of teaching aids developed by the local Squadrons. These are shown both for the recognition of achievement and for the mutual benefit gained from an exchange of ideas.

and hulls, the theory of sailing with emphasis on the balance of hull and sails, stability, and other related topics.

The *Weather Course* is concerned with what the weather is all about and how its many variations can be predicted. We may not be able to do anything about it, but we can boat more safely, and more comfortably, too, if we understand something about it. Throughout the course, the student is encouraged to make observations and predictions on his own, so that he may apply the principles learned in class to his activities on the water.

INSTRUCTOR QUALIFICATION

The USPS depends almost entirely upon its own membership as a source of instructors for all courses. For members who would like to teach, yet hesitate to do so for lack of experience, and for those now teaching who would like to increase their classroom effectiveness, the *Instructor Qualification* program can be of great value.

The *Instruction Techniques Course* covers such topic areas as the principles of teaching and the preparation of effective lesson plans. The new *Instructional Aids Course* guides the novice teacher in the availability and use of a

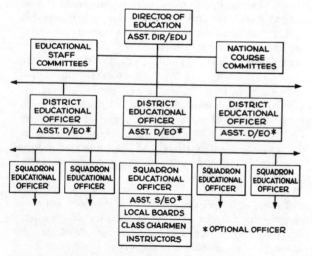

FIG. 3108 The Educational Department is the largest sub-unit of the USPS. Many members holding other offices or engaging in other tasks also teach on the local level or serve on national and district committees of the Department. At any time, approximately 80% of the membership is active in educational work.

wide range of teaching aids including films, slides, overhead projector transparencies, chalkboards, flip charts, and many others.

Topics to be covered will include such diverse subjects as the use and care of hand tools, predicted log racing, water skiing, the magnetic compass, and others.

SUPPLEMENTAL PROGRAMS

To provide further educational "packages" for members who have completed their basic boating education, the USPS is developing a series of *Supplemental Programs*. These generally are shorter and below the level of USPS courses.

FIG. 3109 The USPS also engages in other programs oriented toward increased boating safety. Squadrons and individual members assist in the Cooperative Charting Program for the correction and improvement of nautical charts issued by the Coast & Geodetic Survey and the Lake Survey.

Other Activities

The USPS participates in a *Cooperative Charting Program* with the Coast & Geodetic Survey and the Lake Survey. In this effort, the boating activities of thousands of USPS members are coordinated toward the reporting of errors, omissions, and changes for nautical charts and related publications. The limited field facilities of these federal agencies are thus much strengthened and expanded, and all boatmen are assured of more correct and accurate charts of the waters they use.

Many Squadrons also participate in events of a local nature such as boat shows and the annual observance of National Safe Boating Week.

Social Activities

It's not "all work and no play" in the USPS. Squadrons hold a wide variety of social activities both afloat and ashore. Each District has a Fall and a Spring Conference. These are working sessions, but they are usually preceded or followed by evening social gatherings. The national-level Annual Meeting each January combines both intense official events with those of a much lighter nature.

The Canadian Power Squadrons

In Canada, the Canadian Power Squadrons (CPS) is organized along lines generally similar to the USPS and conducts roughly equivalent education programs. There are close lines of communication and a well-developed sense of brotherhood between these two organizations.

FIG. 3201   The United States Coast Guard is a military service although it is not normally under the Department of Defense. It is unique in its dual roles of public service in time of peace and naval operations in time of war.   U.S. Coast Guard Photo

The never-ending work of the United States Coast Guard (USCG) touches upon the activities of the vast majority of U.S. boatmen. Even far from salt-water "coasts," far up the major rivers of this nation, the work of Coast Guardsmen assists and protects the boating public. In many of its functions, the Coast Guard is ably assisted by its civilian supporting organization, the Coast Guard Auxiliary (USCG Aux). (Note the correct abbreviation; it is *not* "USCGA," this stands for Coast Guard Academy.)

The principal activities of the Coast Guard relating to boating are in the areas of law enforcement and safety. These take many forms as will be discussed in this chapter. Auxiliarists do not have law-enforcement powers, but do engage in a wide variety of activities, afloat and ashore, that further the cause of safety on the water.

The United States Coast Guard

The **U.S. Coast Guard** is a military service and a branch of the Armed Forces. It is *not*, however, normally a part of the Department of Defense. In peacetime, the USCG functions as an agency of the Department of Transportation. In time of war or national emergency, though, the Coast Guard, or units thereof, may be transferred to the Navy.

The Coast Guard Ensign

The flag of the Coast Guard, its distinctive Ensign, is closely connected with its history. The red and white *vertical* stripes number *16,* the number of states in the Union when the flag was first authorized in 1799.

The Coast Guard Ensign is illustrated in color on plate T. It has the unusual feature that it is flown *day and night* on active USCG units afloat and ashore—a constant reminder that the Coast Guard is always on duty to render assistance.

Coast Guard cutters, ships, boats, aircraft, vehicles, etc., are easily identified by the distinctive red band with USCG emblem and blue stripe.

FUNCTIONS RELATING TO BOATING

Boatmen come into contact with the Coast Guard in both of its major areas of law enforcement and safety. Many of the federal laws relating to boating are implemented by regulations issued by the Commandant of the USCG.

Boating regulations

The Federal Boat Safety Act of 1971 is the basis for the registration and numbering of motorboats. Although the Coast Guard performs this task itself in only three states and two other jurisdictions, the boat registration systems of those states that carry out this function for themselves must be approved by the Commandant. Coast Guard patrol vessels may check the registration papers of boats on all U.S. waters.

Boats of more than a specified minimum size may be "documented" rather than registered and numbered. In

FIG. 3202   Coast Guard mobile boarding teams extend law enforcement and general boating safety activities to inland areas of navigable waters subject to federal jurisdiction. Such teams can also conduct limited rescue operations if an emergency arises.

FIG. 3203 Amphibious vehicles along the shore and helicopters in the air support the search and rescue operations of Coast Guard small craft and cutters. Every available means is used to save lives and property in times of emergency.

all states and territories, this function is performed by officials of the Coast Guard.

Coast Guard regulations also spell out the details of the safety equipment required by the Act of 1971. USCG personnel are authorized to make inspections of boats to determine the adequacy of such equipment.

Safety activities

Coast Guard craft make frequent patrols to keep a watchful eye for any reckless operation of boats and all hazards to navigation. They may make spot checks of boat registrations and required equipment. Races, regattas, and other marine events are patroled to ensure the safety of both participants and spectators.

Safe Boating Centers have been established in a number of major locations of small craft activity. At these, boatmen can get information, advice, and assistance on problems relating to safety on the water—the Coast Guard would much rather prevent an accident than to rescue one's victims!

Aids to navigation

The Coast Guard is responsible for the operation of many thousands of aids to navigation, from unlighted buoys and daybeacons to very large lighthouses. The USCG also operates hundreds of radiobeacons and many of the stations of the world-wide Loran-A and Loran-C systems.

This is a quiet and unspectacular, but most necessary, service to all who travel on the water. The installation and maintenance of lighted and unlighted aids to navigation is a major function of the Coast Guard and one that affects most boatmen every time that they leave their moorings.

Search and rescue

The rescue of mariners in distress is probably the most dramatic activity of the Coast Guard, the one that makes the headlines when a ship goes down at sea in a storm. Less publicized, but equally important, are the many instances when the USCG comes to the aid of the boatman who has lost his way at sea, gone aground, suffered dismasting or engine failure, or who has merely run out of fuel. Many boatmen, and especially their wives, venture out on the waters, offshore or inland, with a greater sense of security knowing that the Coast Guard is standing by to help, living up to its motto, "Semper Paratus"—"Always Ready."

Search and rescue units include amphibious vehicles, motorboats, and ships known as "cutters," a term with which historical reference for the Coast Guard. Fixed-

wing aircraft and helicopters both extend the search capabilities of surface vessels and in many cases perform rescue mission themselves when wind and sea conditions permit.

ORGANIZATION

The Commandant of the Coast Guard, an Admiral, and his staff are located at *USCG Headquarters* in Washington, D.C. Operational activities are geographically grouped into *Districts* each under its Commander, a Rear Admiral. Fig. 1502 shows the boundaries of the Districts of the contiguous 48 states; the 14th District is in Hawaii and the 17th District covers Alaskan waters. For better coordination of operational matters, primarily search and rescue, the Districts of the Atlantic/Gulf of Mexico and Pacific coasts have been placed under Atlantic and Pacific Area commands, respectively.

The operating units of the Coast Guard, the individual bases, stations, cutters, boats, aircraft units, etc., may be under the direct control of a District, or these may be under an intermediate level, the *Group*.

Officers and enlisted personnel

Personnel of the Coast Guard include commissioned officers, warrant officers, and enlisted men. Ranks are the same as in the U.S. Navy. To replace uniforms that were generally similar to those of the Navy, the Coast Guard has recently developed a new uniform of a distinctive new "Coast Guard Blue" color cloth. The distinguishing USCG device is a small shield worn above an officer's stripes and on the lower right sleeve of an enlisted man's uniform shirt or jacket.

There is a Coast Guard Reserve to support the regular establishment. Women now serve in both commissioned and enlisted ranks in the regular Coast Guard as well as the Reserves.

OTHER COAST GUARD FUNCTIONS

Functions of the Coast Guard not directly related to boating include the Merchant Marine Inspection Program that sets and enforces safety standards for vessels and crews, and oceanographic research. Icebreakers and cutters of reinforced construction keep harbors open for commercial navigation in winter, and each spring cutters and aircraft work with the International Ice Patrol tracking icebergs in the North Atlantic shipping lanes. In 1977 the Coast Guard became responsible for enforcement of offshore fishery laws out to 200 miles (370 km).

The final major function of the Coast Guard is to maintain at all times a high state of readiness to function as a specialized service in the Navy in time of war.

FIG. 3204 The Coast Guard Auxiliary includes both women and men as members. Many ladies have qualified in specialty subjects and participate actively in all aspects of Auxiliary work—education, examination, and operations.

FIG. 3205 Boats that are owned by members of the USCG Aux and have met the higher inspection standards of a "Facility" may fly the blue and white flag of the Auxiliary. If the owner is an officer, elected or appointed, he may also fly the pennant of his office.

FIG. 3206 Members of the Coast Guard Auxiliary make thousands of free voluntary courtesy checks each year on boats of all sizes and types. Deficiencies are brought to the attention of the owner, but are not reported to any law-enforcement officials.

The Coast Guard Auxiliary

The **Coast Guard Auxiliary** is a *civilian* organization functioning under the direction of the Commandant of the Coast Guard. It is composed of persons interested in the Coast Guard and its principles, dedicated to the interests of their country, and concerned about the safety and welfare of their fellow men. Despite its uniforms and insignia, the Auxiliary is a non-military body.

Eligibility for the Auxiliary extends to persons, male or female, U.S. citizens, who are at least 17 years old, and who own at least 25% of a boat, aircraft, or land fixed or mobile radio station (or who have some other needed special qualification). To become a Basically Qualified Member, one must meet the eligibility requirements and pass the BQ examination and practical demonstrations. Members are encouraged to take advanced training toward the highest membership status, AUXOP. The boat, aircraft, or radio station is termed a "Facility."

The Auxiliary flag

A boat that has qualified as a facility may fly the Coast Guard Auxiliary flag—popularly known as the "Blue Ensign." This is a rectangular blue flag with a white diagonal slash on which is the USCG Aux emblem; see color illustration on page T.

The Auxiliary flag shares with the regular USCG Ensign the distinction of being authorized to fly from boats *day and night*.

PURPOSES

The U.S. Coast Guard Auxiliary has several fundamental purposes which are stated as follows in the Act of Congress that established the organization—

To promote safety and effect rescues on and over the high seas and on the navigable waters.

To promote efficiency in the operation of motorboats and yachts.

To foster a wider knowledge of, and better compliance with, the laws, rules, and regulations, governing the operation of motorboats and yachts.

To facilitate other operations of the Coast Guard.

ACTIVITIES

In carrying out its stated purposes, the Auxiliary has three basic program areas—Education, Examinations, and Operations. All of these are focused on the objective of greater safety for those who go on the water in boats.

Education

The Auxiliary offers several courses to the boating public, tailored to meet the needs of various types of boatmen and their families: Courses consist of from one to thirteen lessons; classes are held in the evenings or on weekends. Constant attention is given to the improvement of these courses and the development of new lessons or courses as required.

Members of the Auxiliary are actively encouraged to take "specialty" courses to improve their knowledge and increase their value to the organization. Typical subjects include vessel examination, communications, search and rescue, patrol procedures, administration, and others.

Examinations

Many members of the Coast Guard Auxiliary are active in the "Courtesy Marine Examination" program. Boat owners are urged each year to request a "Courtesy Marine Examination." This purely voluntary action ensures that a thorough check is made of all safety-related equipment. Boats that pass are awarded the CME sticker for the current calendar year. Craft that do not pass are *not* reported to any authority—the owner is advised of the deficiencies and is encouraged to resubmit his boat for another check when they have been corrected.

Auxiliarists are also busy each year checking the craft of other members to determine their fitness for continued designation as "Facilities." Higher standards and equipment requirements are placed on such boats as they will be allowed to fly the Auxiliary flag. The highest standards are required for a craft that is designated an "Operational Facility" and will be used in operational programs under Coast Guard orders.

Operational programs

Personnel and craft of the Auxiliary are used to perform various missions in such fields as search and rescue and regatta patrols, where the resources of the regular Coast Guard are not sufficient to meet the demands placed upon them. This often occurs on weekends and during holiday periods. For such duties, orders are issued by a designated Coast Guard officer.

Auxiliary members have *no law enforcement powers.* In those cases where such is needed, a Coast Guard officer or petty officer will be embarked in the Auxiliary vessel and the craft will fly the regular Coast Guard Ensign.

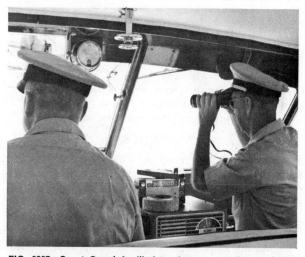

FIG. 3207 Coast Guard Auxiliarists give up many hours of their own family boating time to conduct search and rescue missions and safety patrols for the assistance and protection of their fellow boatmen. Such activities support and extend the efforts of regular Coast Guard units.

Auxiliary craft also conduct informal "Safety Patrols" without official orders. Other types of patrols include those to check on aids to navigation, or as a part of the Cooperative Charting Programs of the National Ocean Survey for the reporting of any errors and needed changes on charts.

Auxiliary operational facilities are often used to supplement regular Coast Guard units in search and rescue operations. Auxiliary aircraft aid in this work and are used

to make "twilight patrols" at the end of days of heavy boating activity to spot any craft that may need aid in reaching port safely.

Auxiliarists donate their time and abilities to the cause of safety on the water; there is no compensation for services rendered, except personal satisfaction, and only minor reimbursement of expenses, limited to activities under official orders.

Fellowship Activities

Units of the Auxiliary work hard at their basic responsibilities, but not to the complete exclusion of social activities. Rendezvous, parties, dances, and other events which tend to promote goodwill and fellowship are held on appropriate occasions.

ORGANIZATION

The basic unit of the Coast Guard Auxiliary is the *Flotilla*. This is a group of members and their facilities who work together in the various programs. Membership varies from the tens to the hundreds of individuals.

Flotillas are grouped geographically into *Divisions;* this is the normal intermediate level between the local flotilla and the District. In some cases, a District is divided into two or more Regions for better control.

Officers

All units of the Auxiliary are headed by their own elected officers—Flotilla Commander, Division Captain, or District Commodore. These are assisted by other elected and appointed officers. The USCG Aux as a whole is headed by a National Commodore, with a Vice Commodore, three Rear Commodores, and staff officers.

UNIFORMS, INSIGNIA, AND FLAGS

Although the Auxiliary is *not* a military or naval organization, its members are authorized to wear a series of blue or white uniforms quite similar to those of regular Coast Guard personnel. Uniforms are available for dress, ordinary service, and working situations, with raincoats and windbreakers for inclement weather. The purchase and maintenance of uniforms is optional for individuals but they are required for activities such as patrols and other duty under orders. See pages 483–484.

Officers' insignia

A series of "rank" insignia from one gold bar to three silver stars, each with the distinctive Auxiliary "A" superimposed, has been established for officers of the USCG Aux. These are shown on page U.

The boats of officers of the Auxiliary are identified by pennants of special design for each office or level of office. These are illustrated on page T. Past officers may fly a burgee of generally similar design, but of different shape from the pennants of active officers.

WHY NOT JOIN?

If you're an eligible boatman, or fit into one of the other categories, why not join the Auxiliary? You are sure to learn much for your boating safety and enjoyment, and there is nothing finer than the sense of satisfaction that comes from helping others. Ask any Coast Guard unit or Auxiliarist where *you* can "sign up."

UNITED STATES COAST GUARD AUXILIARY
FLAG CODE CONFIGURATIONS

A 2 STAFFS

NATIONAL ENSIGN

AUXILIARY ENSIGN OR AUXILIARY OFFICER

B 2 STAFFS AND RADIO ANTENNA

NATIONAL ENSIGN

AUXILIARY ENSIGN

YACHT CLUB OR AUXILIARY OFFICER

C 2 STAFFS AND MAST EXTENSION

NATIONAL ENSIGN

AUXILIARY ENSIGN

YACHT CLUB OR AUXILIARY OFFICER

D SIGNAL MAST WITH YARDARM

NATIONAL ENSIGN

AUXILIARY ENSIGN

OFFICER OR USPS ENSIGN

YACHT CLUB, DIVISION OR FLOTILLA

E 1 STAFF AND RADIO ANTENNA

NATIONAL ENSIGN

OPERATIONAL PENNANT

AUXILIARY ENSIGN

AUXILIARY OFFICER

F NATIONAL ENSIGN ON SPEAKER'S RIGHT
(whether or not the speaker is on a raised platform)

The information on page 602 has been drafted to show in tabular form what the United States Coast Guard Auxiliary has approved as a flag code for power vessels. The problem would be simplified if there were no diversification of sizes and types of boats, thus providing a uniform number and arrangement of positions at which the flags might be displayed. To illustrate typical configurations on small craft for the display of the national ensign, Auxiliary ensign, USPS ensign, yacht club or Auxiliary officer's flag, and division or flotilla pennant, the chart above provides a key for the respective types, depending on what staffs, yardarms and halyards may be available. In addition to configurations shown for boats, figure F illustrates correct procedure when the national and Auxiliary ensigns are displayed at meetings ashore.

THE METRIC SYSTEM

The Metric Conversion Act of 1975 declared the policy of the United States to increase the use of the metric system of measurement on a voluntary basis with the goal of "a nation predominantly, although not exclusively, metric." Accordingly, this Edition is including metric equivalents for all measurements in customary (English) units. (English) units.

The proper name is the International System of Units, abbreviated (from the French) as SI. This is a modernized version of the metric system which traces its origins back more than three centuries. SI provides a logical and inter-related framework for measurements in science, industry, commerce, and other forms of human endeavor.

The modern metric system is built upon a foundation of seven base units, plus two supplementary units. Multiples and submultiples are expressed in a decimal system using various prefixes.

The units

The base units and their symbols are:

Length	meter—m
Mass (weight)	kilogram—kg
Temperature	Kelvin—K*
Time	second—s
Electric current	Ampere—A
Amount of substance	mole—mol
Luminous intensity	candela—cd

The supplementary units and their symbols are:

Plane angle	radian—rad
Solid angle	steradian—sr

*The commonly-used unit of temperature is the degree Celsius, °C (formerly called "centigrade"); the size of the unit is the same, the zero point is different.

Note that the units for time and electric current are the same in both the customary and metric systems.

Most *symbols* (they are not abbreviations) are written in lower-case letters; exceptions are units named after persons for which the symbol is capitalized. Periods are *not* used with any symbols.

Derived units

Other units in the SI (metric) system are *derived* from the *base* units. Typical of those expressed in combinations of base units are

Area	square meter—m²
Volume	cubic meter—m³
Speed, veliocity	meter per second—m/s
Acceleration	meter per second squared—m/s²
Density	kilogram per cubic meter—kg/m³

Typical of derived units with special names are:

Frequency	hertz = Hz	s⁻¹
Force	newton = N	kg·m/s²
Pressure, stress	pascal = Pa	N/m²
Energy, work	Joule = J	N·m
Temperature	°Celsius = °C	K − 273.15

Multiples and submultiples

Units larger and smaller than the base units are formed by adding prefixes decimally to make multiples and sub-multiples. Symbols for the prefixes are added to the symbols for the base units.

1,000,000,000	10^9	giga	G
1,000,000	10^6	mega	M
1,000	10^3	kilo	k
100	10^2	hecto	h
10	10^1	deka	da
0.1	10^{-1}	deci	d
0.01	10^{-2}	centi	c
0.001	10^{-3}	milli	m
0.000,001	10^{-6}	micro	μ

There are others, both larger multiples and smaller sub-multiples, but those are of lesser interest to boatmen.

Retained customary units

Certain units that are not a part of the metric system are so widely used that it is impractical to abandon them.

> day, hour, minute (time)
> degree, minute, second (time)
> liter

Other customary units to be continued "for a limited time, subject to future review" include:

> nautical mile, knot
> bar, millibar (atmospheric pressure)

CONVERSION

The conversion factors given below have been rounded-off for practical use and do not, in most cases, yield exact results.

Customary units to metric

	Known value	Multiply by	To find	
in	inches	25.4	millimeters	mm
ft	feet	0.3048	meters	m
yd	yards	0.9144	meters	m
s mi	statute miles	1.609	kilometers	km
n mi	nautical miles	1.852	kilometers	km
oz	ounces (weight)	28.35	grams	g
lb	pounds	0.4536	kilograms	kg
oz	ounces (liquid)	30.28	milliliters	ml
qt	quarts	0.9464	liters	l
gal	gallons	3.785	liters	l
°F	Fahrenheit temperature	5/9 after subtracting 32	Celsius temperature	°C
°(angle)	degree	0.01745	radian	rad

Metric units to customary

cm	centimeters	0.3937	inches	in
m	meters	3.281	feet	ft
m	meters	1.094	yards	yd
km	kilometers	0.6214	statute miles	s mi
km	kilometers	0.5400	naut. miles	n mi
g	grams	0.03527	ounce (weight)	oz
kg	kilograms	2.205	pounds	lb
ml	milliliters	0.03302	ounces (liquid)	oz
l	liters	1.057	quarts	qt
l	liters	0.2642	gallon	gal
°C	Celsius temperature	9/5 then add 32	Fahrenheit temperature	°F
rad	radian	57.30	degree	°

Table I (right), boat speed over a measured 1-mile course can be picked out by inspection. For example, if it takes 4 minutes and 19 seconds to run a statute mile (5280-foot) course, the boat's speed is 13.9 statute miles per hour. If the course were a nautical mile (6076.1 feet), the speed is 13.9 knots (nautical miles per hour). The table is equally usable for distances in kilometers and speeds in km/h.

TABLE I—SPEED OVER A MEASURED MILE

Sec.	1 min.	2 min.	3 min.	4 min.	5 min.	6 min.	7 min.	8 min.	9 mid.	10 min.	11 min.	12 min.
0	60.000	30.000	20.000	15.000	12.000	10.000	8.571	7.500	6.667	6.000	5.455	5.000
1	59.016	29.752	19.890	14.938	11.960	9.972	8.551	7.484	6.654	5.990	5.446	4.993
2	58.064	29.508	19.780	14.876	11.921	9.945	8.531	7.469	6.642	5.980	5.438	4.986
3	57.143	29.268	19.672	14.815	11.881	9.917	8.511	7.453	6.630	5.970	5.430	4.979
4	56.250	29.032	19.565	14.754	11.842	9.890	8.491	7.438	6.618	5.960	5.422	4.972
5	55.384	28.800	19.459	14.694	11.803	9.863	8.471	7.423	6.606	5.950	5.414	4.965
6	54.545	28.571	19.355	14.634	11.765	9.836	8.451	7.407	6.593	5.941	5.405	4.959
7	53.731	28.346	19.251	14.575	11.726	9.809	8.431	7.392	6.581	5.931	5.397	4.952
8	52.941	28.125	19.149	14.516	11.688	9.783	8.411	7.377	6.569	5.921	5.389	4.945
9	52.174	27.907	19.048	14.458	11.650	9.756	8.392	7.362	6.557	5.911	5.381	4.938
10	51.428	27.692	18.947	14.400	11.613	9.730	8.372	7.347	6.545	5.902	5.373	4.931
11	50.704	27.481	18.848	14.343	11.576	9.704	8.363	7.332	6.534	5.892	5.365	4.925
12	50.000	27.273	18.750	14.286	11.538	9.677	8.333	7.317	6.522	5.882	5.357	4.918
13	49.315	27.068	18.653	14.229	11.502	9.651	8.314	7.302	6.510	5.873	5.349	4.911
14	48.648	26.866	18.557	14.173	11.465	9.626	8.287	7.287	6.498	5.863	5.341	4.905
15	48.000	26.667	18.461	14.118	11.429	9.600	8.276	7.273	6.486	5.854	5.333	4.898
16	47.368	26.471	18.367	14.062	11.392	9.574	8.257	7.258	6.475	5.844	5.325	4.891
17	46.753	26.277	18.274	14.008	11.356	9.549	8.238	7.243	6.463	5.835	5.318	4.885
18	46.154	26.087	18.182	13.953	11.321	9.524	8.219	7.229	6.452	5.825	5.310	4.878
19	45.570	25.899	18.090	13.900	11.285	9.499	8.200	7.214	6.440	5.816	5.302	4.871
20	45.000	25.714	18.000	13.846	11.250	9.474	8.182	7.200	6.429	5.806	5.294	4.865
21	44.444	25.532	17.910	13.793	11.215	9.449	8.163	7.186	6.417	5.797	5.286	4.858
22	43.902	25.352	17.822	13.740	11.180	9.424	8.145	7.171	6.406	5.788	5.278	4.852
23	43.373	25.175	17.734	13.688	11.146	9.399	8.126	7.157	6.394	5.778	5.270	4.845
24	42.857	25.000	17.647	13.636	11.111	9.375	8.108	7.143	6.383	5.769	5.263	4.839
25	42.353	24.828	17.561	13.585	11.077	9.351	8.090	7.129	6.372	5.760	5.255	4.832
26	41.860	24.658	17.476	13.534	11.043	9.326	8.072	7.115	6.360	5.751	5.248	4.826
27	41.379	24.490	17.391	13.483	11.009	9.302	8.054	7.101	6.349	5.742	5.240	4.819
28	40.909	24.324	17.308	13.433	10.976	9.278	8.037	7.087	6.338	5.732	5.233	4.813
29	40.450	24.161	17.225	13.383	10.942	9.254	8.018	7.073	6.327	5.723	5.225	4.806
30	40.000	24.000	17.143	13.333	10.909	9.231	8.000	7.059	6.316	5.714	5.217	4.800
31	39.561	23.841	17.062	13.284	10.876	9.207	7.982	7.045	6.305	5.705	5.210	4.794
32	39.130	23.684	16.981	13.235	10.843	9.184	7.965	7.031	6.294	5.696	5.202	4.787
33	38.710	23.529	16.901	13.187	10.811	9.160	7.947	7.018	6.283	5.687	5.195	4.781
34	38.298	23.377	16.822	13.139	10.778	9.137	7.930	7.004	6.272	5.678	5.187	4.774
35	37.895	23.226	16.744	13.091	10.746	9.114	7.912	6.990	6.261	5.669	5.180	4.768
36	37.500	23.077	16.667	13.043	10.714	9.091	7.895	6.977	6.250	5.660	5.172	4.762
37	37.113	22.930	16.590	12.996	10.682	9.068	7.877	6.963	6.239	5.651	5.165	4.756
38	36.735	22.785	16.514	12.950	10.651	9.045	7.860	6.950	6.228	5.643	5.158	4.749
39	36.364	22.642	16.438	12.903	10.619	9.023	7.843	6.936	6.218	5.634	5.150	4.743
40	36.000	22.500	16.364	12.857	10.588	9.000	7.826	6.923	6.207	5.625	5.143	4.737
41	35.644	22.360	16.290	12.811	10.557	8.978	7.809	6.910	6.196	5.616	5.136	4.731
42	35.294	22.222	16.216	12.766	10.526	8.955	7.792	6.897	6.186	5.607	5.128	4.724
43	34.951	22.086	16.143	12.721	10.496	8.933	7.775	6.883	6.175	5.599	5.121	4.718
44	34.615	21.951	16.071	12.676	10.465	8.911	7.759	6.870	6.164	5.590	5.114	4.712
45	34.286	21.818	16.000	12.632	10.435	8.889	7.742	6.857	6.154	5.581	5.106	4.706
46	33.962	21.687	15.929	12.587	10.405	8.867	7.725	6.844	6.143	5.573	5.099	4.700
47	33.644	21.557	15.859	12.544	10.375	8.845	7.709	6.831	6.133	5.564	5.092	4.693
48	33.333	21.429	15.789	12.500	10.345	8.824	7.692	6.818	6.122	5.556	5.085	4.687
49	33.028	21.302	15.721	12.457	10.315	8.802	7.676	6.805	6.112	5.547	5.078	4.681
50	32.727	21.176	15.652	12.414	10.286	8.780	7.660	6.792	6.102	5.538	5.070	4.675
51	32.432	21.053	15.584	12.371	10.256	8.759	7.643	6.780	6.091	5.530	5.063	4.669
52	32.143	20.930	15.517	12.329	10.227	8.738	7.627	6.767	6.081	5.531	5.056	4.663
53	31.858	20.809	15.451	12.287	10.198	8.717	7.611	6.754	6.071	5.513	5.049	4.657
54	31.579	20.690	15.385	12.245	10.169	8.696	7.595	6.742	6.061	5.505	5.042	4.651
55	31.304	20.571	15.319	12.203	10.141	8.675	7.579	6.729	6.050	5.496	5.035	4.645
56	31.034	20.455	15.254	12.162	10.112	8.654	7.563	6.716	6.040	5.488	5.028	4.639
57	30.769	20.339	16.190	12.121	10.084	8.633	7.547	6.704	6.030	5.479	5.021	4.633
58	30.508	20.225	15.126	12.081	10.056	8.612	7.531	6.691	6.020	5.471	5.014	4.627
59	30.202	20.112	15.063	12.040	10.028	8.592	7.516	6.679	6.010	5.463	5.007	4.621

TABLE II

Height (feet)	Distance (nautical miles)	Distance (statute miles)	Height (feet)	Distance (nautical miles)	Distance (statute miles)	Height (feet)	Distance (nautical miles)	Distance (statute miles)
5	2.6	2.9	70	9.6	11.0	250	18.1	20.8
10	3.6	4.2	75	9.9	11.4	300	19.8	22.8
15	4.4	5.1	80	10.2	11.8	350	21.4	24.6
20	5.1	5.9	85	10.5	12.1	400	22.9	26.3
25	5.7	6.6	90	10.9	12.5	450	24.3	27.9
30	6.3	7.2	95	1.2	12.8	500	25.6	29.4
35	6.8	7.8	100	11.4	13.2	550	26.8	30.9
40	7.2	8.3	110	12.0	13.8	600	28.0	32.3
45	7.7	8.8	120	12.5	14.4	650	29.1	33.5
50	8.1	9.3	130	13.0	15.0	700	30.3	34.8
55	8.5	9.8	140	13.5	15.6	800	32.4	37.3
60	8.9	10.2	150	14.0	16.1	900	34.3	39.5
65	9.2	10.6	200	16.2	18.6	1,000	36.2	41.6

TABLE II Distance to the horizon, or geographic range, for various heights of eye. To find the range to a distant object or light above the horizon, determine the distance separately for the height at each end and then add the two distances; do not add heights and make a single determination of range. Ranges given here are optical and may vary slightly with different conditions of refraction. Ranges for VHF radio and radar are about 15% greater, but also may vary with atmospheric conditions. (1 nautical mile = 1.85 km; 1 statute mile = 1.61 km)

Bilge Ventilation

Gasoline in its liquid and vapor states is potentially dangerous, but this fact need *not* make recreational boating hazardous. All that is required is a respect for its potential, combined with safe boat construction and sensible operating procedures. To enjoy safe boating, one need only follow Coast Guard regulations and good common sense.

VENTILATION FUNDAMENTALS

The "proper and efficient" ventilation of boat bilges was established as a requirement by the Motorboat Act of 1940 for all boats employing volatile fuels (gasoline) with certain limited exceptions, boats built before 25 April 1940 and those of "open" construction.

Now, however, mechanical ventilation blowers are specifically required for all boats built after 31 July 1980. Manufacturers must provide such equipment and no person may operate such a boat that has a gasoline engine for propulsion, electrical generation, or mechanical power unless it has an *operable* ventilation system that meets the new requirements.

Open construction defined

The Coast Guard has prepared a set of specifications to guide the boat owner as to whether his craft meets the definition of "open construction." To qualify for exemption from the bilge ventilation regulations, the boat must meet *all* of the following conditions.

(1) As a minimum, engine and fuel tank compartments must have 15 square inches of open area directly exposed to the atmosphere for each cubic foot of *net* compartment volume. (Net volume is found by determining total volume and then subtracting the volume occupied by the engine, tanks, other accessories, etc.)

(2) There must be no long or narrow unventilated spaces accessible from the engine or fuel tank compartments into which a fire could spread, unless the space meets requirements of item 4 below.

(3) Long, narrow compartments, such as side panels, if joining engine or fuel tank compartments and not serving as ducts, must have at least 15 square inches of open area per cubic foot through frequent openings along the compartment's full length.

Note: It was formerly required that all fuel and engine compartments have at least one square inch of open area per cubic foot within one inch of the bilge level or floor so that fuel vapors could drain out into open areas; this requirement has now been deleted.

Be safe—be sure

If your craft does not meet one or more of the specifications above, or if there is *any* doubt, *play it safe and provide an adequate ventilation system.* To err on the safe side will not be costly; it may save a great deal, perhaps even a life.

Diesel-powered boats

Diesel fuel does not come within the Coast Guard's definition of a "volatile" fuel, and thus bilge ventilation legal requirements are not applicable. It is, however, a sensible step to provide essentially the same ventilation system for your boat even if it is diesel-powered.

REQUIREMENTS FOR OLDER BOATS

A boat built on or before 31 July 1980 is subject to regulations derived from the Motorboat Act of 1940 as amended in December 1979. If it will entrap fumes, i.e., it is not an "open" boat, it is required to have at least two ventilation ducts fitted with cowls at their opening to the atmosphere for each engine and fuel tank compartment. An exception is made for fuel tank compartments if each electrical component therein is "ignition protected" in accordance with Coast Guard standards and fuel tanks are vented to the outside of the boat.

The ventilators, ducts, and cowls must be installed so that they provide for efficient removal of explosive or flammable gases from bilges of *each* engine and fuel tank compartment. Intake ducting must be installed to extend from the cowls to at least midway to the bilge or at least below the level of the carburetor air intake. Exhaust ducting must be installed to extend from the lower portion of the bilge to the cowls in the open atmosphere. Ducts should not be installed so low in the bilge that they could become obstructed by a normal accumulation of bilge water.

To create a flow through the ducting system, at least when underway or when there is a wind, cowls (scoops) or other fittings of equal effectiveness are needed on all ducts. A wind-actuated rotary exhauster or mechanical blower is considered equivalent to a cowl on an exhaust duct.

Lack of adequate bilge ventilation can result in an order from a Coast Guard Boarding Officer for "termination of unsafe use" of the craft; see page 36.

Ducts required

Ducts are a necessary part of a ventilation system. A mere hole in the hull won't do; that's a vent, not a ventilator. "Vents," the Coast Guard explains, "are openings that permit venting, or escape of gasses due to pressure differential. Ventilators are openings that must be fitted with *cowls* to direct the flow of air and vapors in or out of *ducts* that channel movement of air for the actual displacement of fumes from the space being ventilated."

Size of ducts

Ventilation must be adequate for the size and design of the craft. There should be no constriction in the ducting system that is smaller than the minimum cross-sectional area required for reasonable efficiency. Where a stated size of duct is not available, the next *larger* size should be used.

Small motorboats. To determine the minimum crosssectional area of the cowls and ducts for motorboats having small engine and/or fuel tank compartments, see Table 10-1, which is based on *net* compartment volume (as previously defined).

Cruisers and larger boats. For most cruisers and other large motorboats, Table 10-2, which is based on the craft's beam, is a practical guide for determination of the minimum size of ducts and cowls.

Ducting materials

For safety and long life, ducts should be made of non-ferrous, galvanized ferrous, or sturdy high-temperature-

Text continued on page 607

STERN-DRIVE RUNABOUT—Note that all engine and fuel tank compartments need to be efficiently ventilated. Hence, not only the engine area aft should be ducted, but the fuel compartment forward also. As on all installations, an electric exhaust blower is recommended, to be installed externally if it is not of the sealed or arcless type.

STERN-DRIVE INSTALLATION—Be sure the cowls are arranged to prevent the exhaust being picked up by the intake. If you can't spread them sufficiently apart horizontally (4 feet), to achieve this you probably can work it out by arranging one higher than the other. Where a power-driven exhaust blower is used in a *separate* duct, its duct may terminate in a flush fitting without a cowl. If the blower is in a natural ventilation duct, a cowl must be used and located so as to be in a normal suction situation.

INSTALLATION WHERE TRANSOM FUEL TANK IS USED—The requirements remain the same: at least two cowl-fitted ventilators properly ducted and of sufficient capacity.

INSTALLATION WHERE AFT SEAT IS USED—Where the fuel tank is under a stern seat, ventilate as illustrated in the diagram. It's a good idea to be sure you can get to the tank quickly, if for nothing else, to inspect it. Hinge the seat if it is not already so constructed.

Wind Activated Rotary
Exhauster Head

INBOARD CRUISER INSTALLATION—A wind-activated rotary exhauster head may be substituted for a cowl. Note the good practice of locating the inlet and exhaust ducts on *opposite* sides of the boat to aid in preventing recirculation of vapors back into the bilges.

Exhaust Duct

Fuel Tank

INBOARD CRUISER INSTALLATION—Note below the recommended practice for larger cruisers. Two intakes and two exhausts are shown, all cowled and ducted, with power exhaust outlet through the transom.

INTAKE COWL
AND DUCT

INTAKE COWL
AND DUCT

EXHAUST COWL
AND DUCT

Intake Cowl

Intake Duct

EXHAUST COWL
AND DUCT

Ventilation systems suitable for cruisers and larger boats

POWER EXHAUST
OUTLET

Intake Cowl

Wind Activated Rotary
Exhauster Head

Intake Duct

Exhaust Duct

Fuel Tank

AUXILIARY OR MOTOR SAILER INSTALLATION—Note that under any of the available industry standards the ducting should extend well down into the bilge; this is because gasoline vapors are heavier than air and so sink to the bottom of the hull. It is a good idea to always open the hatch to the engine compartment before starting the engine. This applies whether or not an exhaust blower is used.

WHEN AUXILIARIES ARE RACING
The U.S. Coast Guard has ruled that "sailboats used for pleasure purposes need not be ventilated when under sail alone and may block off cowls and ducts leading to engine and fuel compartments when under sail alone."

Intake Cowl

Exhaust Cowl or
Blower Motor Outlet

Exhaust Duct

Intake Duct

Fuel Tank

AUXILIARY OR MOTOR SAILER INSTALLATION—Another possible ventilation arrangement is the midship installation instead of the fore and aft one as above.

resistant non-metallic materials. Ducts should be routed clear of, and protected from, contact with hot engine surfaces.

Positioning of cowls

Normally, the intake cowl will face forward in an area of free airflow underway, and the exhaust cowl will face aft where a suction effect can be expected.

The two cowls, or sets of cowls, should be located with respect to each other, horizontally and/or vertically, so as to prevent return of fumes removed from any space to the same or any other space. Intake cowls should be positioned to avoid pick-up of vapors from fueling operations.

Air for carburetors

Openings into the engine compartment for entry of air to the carburetor are in addition to requirements of the ventilation system.

REQUIREMENTS FOR NEW BOATS

Boats built after 31 July 1980 are required to have mechanical bilge ventilation if they are fitted with a gasoline engine for propulsion, electrical generation, or mechanical power. Each compartment having a permanently installed gasoline engine must be ventilated by a powered exhaust blower system unless it is "open to the atmosphere" as defined in the regulations (see page 604). Each exhaust blower, or combination of blowers, must be rated at an air flow capacity not less than a value computed by formulas based on the net volume of the engine compartment plus other compartments open thereto. The installed blower or blowers must be tested to prove that they actually do move air at a rate determined by other formulas also based on compartment volume.

The engine compartment, and other compartments open to it where the aggregate area of openings exceeds 2% of the area between the compartments, must also have a natural ventilation system.

There must be a warning label as close as practicable to the ignition switch that advises of the danger of gasoline vapors and the need to run the exhaust blower for at least *four* minutes and then check the engine compartment for fuel vapors *before* starting the engine.

Natural ventilation systems are also required for any compartment containing both a permanently installed fuel tank and any electrical component that is not "ignition protected" in accordance with existing Coast Guard electrical standards for boats; or a compartment that contains a fuel tank that vents into that compartment (highly unlikely); or one having a non-metallic fuel tank that exceeds a specified permeability rate. The new regulations specify the required cross-sectional area of ducts for natural ventilation based on compartment net volume, and how ducts shall be installed.

The new regulations above concern the manufacturer of the boat, but there is also a requirement placed on the operator that these ventilation systems be operable any time that the craft is in use.

GENERAL SAFETY PRECAUTIONS

Ventilation systems are *not* designed to remove vapors in large quantities such as might be caused by breaks in fuel lines, leaking tanks, or dripping carburetors. If gas odors are detected, repairs are generally needed.

Before starting the engine, especially on calm days and on boats without a power ventilation system, the engine compartment should be opened to dissipate any vapors that may be present. The smaller the compartment, the quicker an explosive mixture of gasoline vapors can develop.

Regardless of the ventilation system installed, always open hatches and use your nose to detect any gasoline odors. Even the slightest trace should warn you to search for the cause and to ventilate the compartment thoroughly before pressing the starter switch.

PASSENGER-CARRYING VESSELS

Vessels that carry more than six passengers *for hire* are subject to special regulations. Consult the nearest Coast Guard Marine Inspection Office for details.

TABLE 10·1			
	One *intake and* One Exhaust System		Two *Intake and* Two Exhaust Systems
Net volume (cu. ft.)	Minimum inside diameter for each duct (inches)	Area sq. in. for cowl	Minimum inside diameter for each duct (inches)
Up to 8	2	3	
10	2¼	4	
12	2½	5	
14	3¾	6	
17	3	7	
20	3¼	8	2½
23	3½	10	2½
27	3¾	11	3
30	4	13	3
35	4¼	14	3
39	4½	16	3
43	4¾	19	3
48	5	20	3

TABLE 10·2—*Two* Intake and *Two* Exhaust Systems		
	Minimum inside	
Vessel beam (feet)	diameter for each duct (inches)	(Area square inches)
7	3	7
8	3¼	8
9	3½	9
10	3½	10
11	3¾	11
12	4	12
13	4¼	13
14	4¼	14
15	4½	15
16	4½	16
17	4½	17
18	5	18
19	5	19

Note: 1 inch = 2.54 cm; 1 sq. inch = 6.45 sq. cm; 1 foot = 0.305 m; 1 cu. foot = 0.028 cu. m.

Where To Obtain Charts, Cruising Information, And Other Publications

CHARTS OF VARIOUS WATERWAYS

Charts, U. S. Coastal Waters—Charts of coastal waters such as the Atlantic, Pacific and Gulf Coasts, the Hudson River as far north as Troy, and the Atlantic and Gulf Intracoastal Waterways, are published by the National Ocean Survey, Rockville, Md., 20852; they are available from local sales agents or directly from the Distribution Division (C44), National Ocean Survey, Riverdale, Md. 20840. Free catalogs are available.

Charts, Great Lakes—Charts of the Great Lakes and connecting rivers, Lake rivers, Lake Champlain, New York State Canals, and the Minnesota-Ontario Border Lakes are listed in N.O.S. Chart catalog No. 4; they can be purchased from local sales agents or the N.O.S. Distribution Division (address above).

Charts, New York State Canals—A bound booklet of charts of the New York State canals (Champlain, Erie, Oswego, and Cayuga-Seneca), east of Lyons, Chart 14786 (formerly 180), is available from the N.O.S. Distribution Division (address above).

Charts, Mississippi River and Tributaries—(*Middle & Upper Mississippi River; Cairo, Ill. to Minneapolis, Minn.*)
(*Middle Mississippi River; Cairo, Ill. to Grafton, Ill.*)
(*Mississippi River from Cairo, Ill. to Gulf of Mexico*)
(*Small Boat Navigation Chart; Alton, Ill. to Clarksville on the Mississippi River and Grafton, Ill., to LaGrange, Ill. on the Illinois River*)
(*Illinois Waterways; from Grafton, Ill. to Lake Michigan at Chicago and Calumet Harbors*)
U. S. Army Engineer District, 210 N. 12th Street, St. Louis, Missouri, 63101.

The offices listed below will supply exhaustive lists of available charts, detailing sources, prices, scales, and exact sections covered.
Mississippi River and connecting waterways, north of Ohio River—U. S. Army Engineer Division, North Central, 536 South Clark St., Chicago, Ill. 60605.
Mississippi River and tributaries, below Ohio River—Mississippi River Commission, P.O. Box 80, Vicksburg, Miss. 39180. This office also has a free booklet, "Mississippi River Navigation," discussing history, development and navigation of the river.
Ohio River and tributaries; Pittsburgh, Pa., to the Mississippi River—U. S. Army Engineer Division, P.O. Box 1159, Cincinnati, Ohio 45201.
Tennessee and Cumberland Rivers—U. S. Army Engineer District, P. O. Box 1070, Nashville, Tenn. 37202. Another general information source for the Tennessee is the Tennessee Valley Authority, Maps and Engineering Records Section, 102A Union Bldg., Knoxville, Tenn.
Missouri River and tributaries—U.S. Army Engineers, Missouri River Division, P.O. Box 103 DTS, Omaha, Nebraska 68101.

Charts, Canadian Waters—Charts of Canadian waters are available from Chart Distribution Office, Department of the Environment, P.O. Box 8080, 1675 Russel Road, Ottawa, Ontario, K1G 3H6, Canada. Those available include charts of Canadian coastal waters; Canadian sections of the Great Lakes including Georgian Bay; the St. Lawrence River; Richelieu River; Ottawa River; The Rideau Waterway; and other Canadian lakes, canals, etc.
Prices and details are given in a Coastal and Inland Waters Catalog; indexes of charts for any area in Canada are available free from the address above.

Charts, Foreign Waters—These are published by the Defense Mapping Agency Hydrographic/Topographic Center and are available from DMAHTC sales agents or by mail from the DMA Office of Distribution Services (DDCP), 6500 Brookes Lane, Washington, D.C. 20315. A general catalog (free) and nine regional catalogs (25¢) are available.

NOTICE TO MARINERS

Notice to Mariners—This is a weekly pamphlet published by the Defense Mapping Agency Hydrographic/Topographic Center, Washington, D. C. 20390 in cooperation with the U.S. Coast Guard and the National Ocean Survey. It contains announcements and corrections relative to charts, Light Lists, Coast Pilots, and other navigational publications. Notice No. 1 of each year additionally contains special announcements of standing interest plus administrative information such as the addresses of DMAHTC depots and regional representatives, N.O.S. regional offices, Army Corps of Engineers District Offices, and Coast Guard District Headquarters. (Lists of local sales agents for charts and publications are no longer included; see the applicable DMAHTC or N.O.S. catalog.)
Local Notices, of interest primarily within the limits of each of the Coast Guard Districts, are issued by Commanders of the respective districts, and are available from their district offices.

COAST PILOTS

Coast Pilots—For coastal waters, the Atlantic and Gulf Intracoastal Waterways, and the Great Lakes, these are published by the National Ocean Survey, Rockville, Md. 20852, and are available from them, their distribution offices, or sales agents as listed semi-annually in Notice to Mariners. These volumes supplement the information given on charts, with detailed descriptions of routes, courses, distances, depths, harbors, sources of supplies, tides, currents, weather, list of yacht clubs, facilities for repairs, etc.

For the Great Lakes and other waters covered by Lake Survey charts, the publication corresponding to the Coast Pilot is called the Great Lakes Pilot. This is an annual publication, kept up-to-date during the navigation season by seven monthly supplements issued from May to November. Coast Pilots and the Great Lakes Pilot can be obtained from local sales agents or the N.O.S. Distribution Division (address above).

For Canadian waters—available from the Chart Distribution Office, Department of the Environment, P.O. Box 8080, 1675 Russel Road, Ottawa, Ontario K1G 3H6, Canada. Details are given in the Coastal and Inland Waters Catalog available from the Chart Distribution Office at the address given above. A descriptive list of Pilots and Sailing Directions is also available.

LIGHT LISTS

Light Lists—These are published by the U. S. Coast Guard and are for sale by the Superintendent of Documents, Washington, D. C. 20402, or from many, but not all, of the local sales agents listed in each of the available N.O.S. Chart Catalogs. They describe lighted aids, radio beacons, fog signals, unlighted buoys, and daymarks. Vol. I covers Atlantic Coast from St. Croix River, Me., to Little River, S. C. Vol. II, Atlantic and Gulf Coasts from Little River, S. C., to Rio Grande River, Tex., and the Antilles. Vol. III, Pacific Coast and Islands. Vol. IV, Great Lakes. Vol. V, Mississippi River.

TIDE AND CURRENT TABLES

Tide Tables, Current Tables and Tidal Current Charts—These are also publications of the National Ocean Survey, Rockville, Md. 20852, and may be obtained from them, their distribution offices, or from many of the local sales agents listed in each N.O.S. Chart Catalog.

RULES OF THE ROAD

Rules of the Road—Rules of the Road for U.S. waters are published in three volumes. CG-169 covers Inland Waters, the Atlantic, Gulf of Mexico, and Pacific coasts and connecting rivers (CG-169 also includes the International Rules of the Road). CG-172 is for the Great Lakes and their connecting and tributary waters. CG-184 governs the Western Rivers (Mississippi River System) and the Red River of the North. Copies may be obtained from Coast Guard Marine Inspection Offices, or from the Commandant (G-WLE), U. S. Coast Guard, Washington, D.C. 20593.

Handbook of Boating Laws—in four editions for Southern, Northeastern, North Central and Western states. Lists state requirements for registering, numbering, equipment and small boat operation; fuel tax laws; boat trailer laws; and applicable federal regulations. Available from Outboard Boating Club, 333 N. Michigan Ave., Chicago, Ill. 60601.

NEW YORK STATE CANALS

Rules and Regulations Covering Navigation and Use of the New York State Canal System—A booklet by this title is published by and is available from New York State Dept. of Public Works, Division of Operation and Maintenance, Albany, N. Y. It contains a description of the New York Canal System, and regulations pertaining to use of the canal. Applications for free season permits to use the canals should be made to the same office.

Canal Guide Book for the New York State Barge Canal System and Connecting Navigable Waterways—A booklet of great value in cruising the Hudson River, Lake Champlain, New York State canals, and connecting Canadian waterways, including the St. Lawrence River and parts of Lake Erie and Lake Ontario. Lists sources of supplies such as fuel, oil, engine repairs, fresh water, provisions, anchorage and dockage. Available from Cruising Guide Book, 146 Sheridan Avenue, Albany, N. Y. 12210.

The Northwest Passage—Cruise kit and guide book, with charts, for Hudson River, Champlain Canal and Lake Champlain. Division of Motor Boats, New York Conservation Dept., Albany, N. Y. 12226.

The Grand Canal—Cruise kit and guide book, with charts, for Erie Canal, Oswego Canal, and the Cayuga Seneca Canals. Division of Motor Boats (address above).

INTRACOASTAL WATERWAYS

Waterway Guide—A publication detailing for the yachtsman a vast amount of information concerning the inland waterways. The Northern Edition covers the coast from Maine to New York; the Middle Atlantic Edition from New York to Sea Island, Ga.; the Southern Edition from Sea Island, Ga., to Florida and Gulf Coast to New Orleans; the Great Lakes Edition from New York to the Great Lakes with connecting Canadian canals and rivers. Available from Waterway Guide, Inc., 238 West St., Annapolis, Md. 21401.

Intracoastal Waterway Booklets—Comprehensive descriptions of the Intracoastal Waterway, with data on navigation, charts, distances, etc. Prepared by Corps of Engineers, U. S. Army, and sold by Superintendent of Documents, Washington, D. C. 20402. In two sections: (1) Atlantic Section, Boston to Key West, (2) Gulf Section, Key West to Brownsville, Tex.

Intracoastal Waterway Bulletins—Frequent bulletins giving latest information on the condition of the Intracoastal Waterway are published by the Corps of Engineers. These are available from the following District Offices of the Army Engineers: 803 Front St., Norfolk, Va. 23510; P. O. Box 1890, Wilmington, N. C. 28401; P. O. Box 919, Charleston, S. C. 29402; P. O. Box 889, Savannah, Ga. 31402; P. O. Box 4970, Jacksonville, Fla. 32201; P. O. Box 2288, Mobile, Ala. 36601; P. O. Box 1229, Galveston, Tex. 77551.

OTHER CRUISING PUBLICATIONS

Cruising Charts, Guides and Booklets—Although a number of major oil companies formerly provided various cruising services, in the summer of 1979 the only company still providing such services is the Texas Company. Write to Texaco Waterways Service, 133 E. 42nd St., New York, NY 10017.

Cruising Guide to the New England Coast—by R. F. Duncan and J. P. Ware. An updated version of Fessenden Blanchard's well-known descriptions of harbors, anchorages, and waterways, including the Hudson River, Long Island Sound and north to the New Brunswick coast. Dodd, Mead & Co. New York, NY.

Cruising Guide to the Southern Coast—by R. S. Roscoe and F. S. Blanchard. An updated "Blanchard's" for the Intracoastal Waterway from Norfolk to New Orleans. Dodd, Mead & Co.

Cruising Guide to the Chesapeake—by W. T. Stone and F. S. Blanchard. Extensive information on the waters and facilities of the Chesapeake Bay region. Dodd, Mead & Co.

Yachtsman's Guide to Northern Harbors—Harbors, boat basins and services around Long Island, and seacoast of New England. Seaport Publishing Co., 843 Delray Ave., S.E., Grand Rapids 6, Mich.

Guide for Cruising Maryland Waters—Prepared by Maryland Dept. of Tidewater Fisheries. Twenty full-color charts, with more than 200 courses and distances plotted. These are available from the same address is the booklet Maryland Marine Facilities.

Boating Atlas of Tidewater Virginia—An atlas of 53 charts in full color covering the ocean front, lower Chesapeake Bay, the James, York, Rappahannock and Potomac Rivers. Includes buoyage system, rules of the road, location of marine facilities, state and Coast Guard regulations, notes from the Coast Pilot, Tide Tables, safety suggestions, and a course protractor. Distributed by Paxton Co., Norfolk, Va.

Florida Boating—Pamphlet giving data on waterways, charts, Florida boat registration, and water safety regulations, fishing licenses, area maps and information, plus a directory of marine facilities throughout the state. Available from Florida Development Commission, Carlton Bldg., Tallahassee, Fla. 32304.

Yachtsman's Guide to the Great Lakes—Harbors, services, supplies on the Great Lakes, St. Lawrence, Richelieu and Hudson Rivers, Lake Champlain, and New York State Barge Canal. Seaport Publishing Co., 843 Delray Ave., S. E., Grand Rapids, Mich. 49506.

Cruising the Georgian Bay—Cruising information, with 23 pages of Ontario Government Aerial Survey Maps and tabulations of services and facilities at ports. Bellhaven House, 12 Dyas Road, Don Mills, Ontario.

Cruising the North Channel—Covers the waterway between Manitoulin Island and the north shore of Lake Huron. Bellhaven House, see address above.

Cruising the Trent-Severn Waterway—A cruising guide, including rules and regulations, supply points and services, mileages and general data. British Book Service, see address above.

Trailer Boating Where the North Begins—Written especially for the small boatman, and includes the Muskoka, Parry Sound, and Lake-of-Bays areas of Ontario. Bellhaven House, see address above.

Harbor Guide to the Upper Mississippi River—From Minneapolis to St. Louis, including St. Croix River. Covers harbors (services and location), cities and towns (population, transportation, shopping centers, tourist interest), locks and dams, mileage charts, source of navigation charts, history of river. Available from Mildred Quimby, Box 85, Prairie du Chien, Wisconsin 58321.

Yachtsman's Guide to the Greater Antilles—by Harry Kline. Virgin Islands, Puerto Rico, Dominican Republic, and Haiti. Tropic Isle Publishers, Inc., P. O. Box 340866, Coral Gables, Fla. 33134.

Cruising Guide to the Caribbean and the Bahamas—by J. C. Hart and W. T. Stone. Includes the North Coast of South America, Central America, and Yucatan. Dodd, Mead & Co.

Cruising the San Juan Islands—by Bruce Calhoun. Sea Publications, CBS, 1515 Broadway, New York, NY 10036.

Yachtsman's Guide to the Bermuda Islands—by Michael Voegeli, P. O. Box 1699, Hamilton 5, Bermuda.

Cruising Guide to the Hawaiian Islands—by G. T. Talbott. Cruising Guide, P. O. Box B, Honolulu, HI 96815.

Cruising the Pacific Coast, Acapulco to Skagway—by C. and J. West, W. W. Norton & Co., 500 Fifth Avenue, New York, NY.

Virgin Islands—Eggleston's descriptions of islands, harbors, people, history, passages, and facilities. Illustrated. Sailing Book Service, 34 Oak Avenue, Tuckahoe, N. Y. 10707.

U. S. COAST GUARD PUBLICATIONS

This Is the Seal of Safety . . . Get a Free Motorboat Examination—Aux-204. Flyer explains the Auxiliary Courtesy Motorboat Examination and the standards which must be met to be awarded a CME Decal. Commandant (BAE) U.S. Coast Guard, Washington, D.C. 20593.

Marine Aids to Navigation—CB-193. Brief explanation of the significance of colors of beacons and buoys, of the variety of light and fog signal characteristics, and of the system of electronic aids to navigation. Commandant (-CMA-3), U.S. Coast Guard, Washington, D.C. 20593.

Federal Requirements for Recreational Boats—CG-290. Digest of boating laws and regulations. Numbering. Boating accidents. Sales to aliens. Law enforcement. Documentation, C.G. approved equipment. Equipment requirements. Suggestions for safety. U.S. Coast Guard offices.

Emergency Repairs Afloat—CG-151. Pamphlet describes basic trouble-shooting, emergency repairs, and how to stay afloat if damage occurs. Commandant (G-BAE-2), U.S. Coast Guard, Washington, D.C. 20593.

Cold Water Drowning—CG-513. 13 pages, illustrated. A new lease on life, unusual outlook on drowning, explains how a youth survives 38 minutes under water, and what it can mean to you. Commandant, (G-BAE-2), U.S. Coast Guard, Washington, D.C. 20593.

Visual Distress Signals—CG-152. 16 pages, illustrated. Description and guidance for the use of many distress signals suitable for boats. Free from Coast Guard District offices, or Headquarters, U.S. Coast Guard, Washington, D.C. 20593.

The Skipper's Course—CG-433. Booklet is a "Do it Yourself" program in basic boating safety, informal text, with an exam offered at the end of the course. A Coast Guard certificate is awarded to all who pass. Bookstore #15, P.O. Box 713, Pueblo, CO 81002.

First Aid for the Boatman — AUX-206. 20 pages, illustrated, prepared with the assistance of the American National Red Cross. A basic manual of first aid information that will cover most injuries and illness afloat. Free.

Federal Marine Sanitation Device Regulations—CG-485. Flyer discusses the Environmental Protection Agency's federal standards of performance for marine sanitation devices (MSDs). Commandant (G-WEP), U.S. Coast Guard, Washington, D.C. 20593.

Hypothermia and Cold Water Survival—AUX-202. Pamphlet explains hypothermia, the cooling of the internal body temperature, and its first aid procedures. Commandant (G-BAE), U.S. Coast Guard, Washington, D.C. 20593.

Lightning—Cone of Protection—MICHU-SG-79-114. Pamphlet covers thunderstorms and lightning; and how boatmen can protect themselves and their vessels against lightning strikes. Commandant (G-BAE), U.S. Coast Guard, Washington, D.C. 20593.

Marine Communications for the Recreational Boater—

SSIC-16772. Informative and useful booklet clears up confusion about VHF radio communications. Commandant (G-BA-2), U.S. Coast Guard, Washington, D.C. 20593.

Trailer Boating—A Primer—

Introduction to trailerboating which covers the trailer and tow vehicle requirements along with the do's and don't's of trailering. Commandant (G-BAE), U.S. Coast Guard, Washington, D.C. 20593.

MISCELLANEOUS PUBLICATIONS OF THE DEFENSE

MAPPING AGENCY HYDROGRAPHIC/TOPOGRAPHIC CENTER

The Defense Mapping Agency Hydrographic/Topographic Center produces charts and Sailing Directions (Pilots) and lists of all oceans and seas, and of foreign coasts and islands and harbors, but only general charts of the coast of the United States.

Information on DMA Hydrographic/Topographic Center Charts and Publications. DMAHTC Pub. 1-N. Catalog listing some of the more popular index charts, world charts, general nautical charts, magnetic charts, pilot charts, bathymetric charts, special charts, plotting charts, oceanographic and bottom sediment charts, aeronautical charts, loran charts, published by the DMA Hydrographic/Topographic Center, with information on nautical, aeronautical and oceanographic publications.

Sailing Directions are books supplementing the nautical charts issued by the DMA Hydrographic/Topographic Center. They contain descriptions of coast lines, harbors, dangers, aids, port facilities, and other data which cannot be conveniently shown on charts.

Daily Memorandum carries a synopsis of the latest information relating to dangers and aids to navigation, including reports of drifting buoys, wreckage, and other hazards together with advance items that will appear in the Notice to Mariners. The Daily Memorandum is issued locally by the Branch Hydrographic Offices and the most urgent of the reports are also broadcast by radio under the title, Government Hydro All Ships and Stations, and are rebroadcast locally.

Pilot Charts of the North Atlantic Ocean, North Pacific Ocean are issued monthly. These present information on average winds and currents, percentages of gales and calms, and other hydrographic data of a varied nature.

Pilot Charts

#16 Pilot Chart of the North Atlantic Ocean (Monthly).

#55 Pilot Chart of the North Pacific Ocean (Monthly).

#106 Atlas of Pilot Charts—South Atlantic Ocean and Central American Waters.

#107 Atlas of Pilot Charts—South Pacific, Indian Ocean.

DMAHTC Lists of Lights and Fog Signals

Light Lists published by the DMA Hydrographic/Topographic Center give detailed descriptions of navigational lights and fog signals, and mention signals of various kinds operated at lighthouses.

Pub. 111A and 111B cover the Coast of North and South America (only the seacoast lights of the United States), the West Indies, and the Hawaiian Islands.

Pub. 112 covers islands of the Pacific and Indian Oceans, Australia, Asia, and the East Coast of Africa.

Pub. 113 covers the West Coasts of Europe and Africa, the Mediterranean Sea, Black Sea, and the Sea of Azov.

Pub. 114 covers the British Islands, English Channel, and North Sea.

Pub. 115 covers Norway, Iceland, and Arctic Ocean.

Pub. 116 covers the Baltic Sea with Kattegat, Belts and Sound, and Gulf of Bothnia.

Pub. 11A, 11B, 112, 113 are revised and reissued annually and Pub. 114, 115, 116 at less frequent intervals. Pub. 114, 115, 116 are corrected by annual supplements containing changes that have taken place during the years since the books were published. These supplements are mailed free of charge to purchasers of the books. Weekly corrections to the Light Lists, at the end of the Notice to Mariners. This section includes minor corrections not appearing in the main body of the Notice.

Other Publications of the DMA Hydrographic/Topographic Center

Chart #1 Nautical Chart Symbols and Abbreviations.

Pub. 9 American Practical Navigator. Originally by Nathaniel Bowditch, LL.D., etc. Revised (Including the Useful Tables).

Pub. 102 International Code of Signals.

Pub. 117A, 117B Radio Navigational Aids. Marine Direction-Finding Stations, Radio Beacons, Time Signals, Navigational Warnings, Distress Signals, Medical Advice and Quarantine Stations, Loran, and Regulations Governing the Use of Radio in Territorial Waters.

Pub. 150 World Port Index

Pub. 151 Tables of Distances Between Ports.

Pub. 217 Maneuvering Board Manual.

Pub. 226 Handbook of Magnetic Compass Adjustment and Compensation.

Pub. 234 Breakers and Surf: Principles in Forecasting.

Pub. 601 Wind, Sea and Swell: Theory of Relations in Forecasting.

Pub. 602 Wind Waves at Sea, Breakers and Surf.

Pub. 1310 Radar Navigation Manual.

WEATHER

Marine Weather Services Charts. A series of 15 charts containing broadcast schedules of radio stations, National Weather Service telephone numbers, and locations of warning display stations. The charts cover the Atlantic, Gulf, and Pacific coasts, and waters adjacent to Hawaii, Puerto Rico and the Virgin Islands, and Alaska. Price 25¢; obtained from Distribution Division .(C44), National Ocean Survey, Riverdale, MD 20854.

Marine Weather Services and **High Seas Storm Information Service.** Brochures containing marine weather information in capsule form. Price 25¢ Obtainable from: Distribution Division, C44, National Ocean Survey, 6501 Lafayette Avenue, Riverdale, MD 20854.

Worldwide Marine Weather Broadcasts. Broadcast schedules of marine weather information from all areas of the world where such service is available. Obtainable from: Superintendent of Documents, U.S. Government Printing Office, Washington, DC 20402—Price $2.65.

Hurricane, the Greatest Storm on Earth. Updated hurricane information, 34 pages. Price $1.25, Stock number 003-018-00018-1, Superintendent of Documents, Government Printing Office, Washington, DC 20402.

The Daily Weather Map, Weekly Series—National Weather Service. A complete explanation of the maps, including all symbols and tables used in plotting the data appears on the reverse side of the Sunday may only. Annual subscription, $16.50; airmail, add $5.20. Superintendent of Documents, Washington, DC 20402.

MISCELLANEOUS PUBLICATIONS

The American Nautical Almanac—United States Naval Observatory. Copies purchased from the Superintendent of Documents. A compact publication containing all the ephemeris material essential to the solution of problems of navigational position. Contains a Star Chart which shows the position of the stars used in navigation. Instructions for its use are included.

A Mariner's Guide to Rules of the Road, by William H. Tate. A concise and comprehensive presentation of the 1972 International Rules of the Road and current U.S. Inland Rules; extensively illustrated. Published by the U.S. Naval Institute, Annapolis, MD 21402.

First Aid—Superintendent of Documents, Washington, DC 20402. Illustrated. 160 pages. This is one of the best first aid manuals obtainable. Only first aid instruction is given.

Miscellaneous Publication No. 9 The Ship's Medicine Chest and First Aid at Sea—United States Public Health Service. Illustrated. 498 pages. Prepared especially for seafaring people. An excellent treatise. Sections included give special instruction for emergency treatment, and first aid by raido. (Superintendent of Documents, Washington, DC 20402.

GASOLINE TAX REFUNDS

Gasoline Tax Refunds—Some states allow a refund, in whole or in part, of the gasoline tax when the fuel is used for boat purposes. However, the regulations differ greatly and it would be well for the yachtsman to become familiar with these regulations in advance.

EXTRACTS FROM THE FEDERAL BOAT SAFETY ACT OF 1971
(Public Law 92-75, Approved 10 August 1971, as amended through 1977)

Be it enacted by the Senate and House of Representatives of the United States of America in Congress assembled, That this Act may be cited as the "Federal Boat Safety Act of 1971."

Declaration of policy and purpose

SEC. 2. It is hereby declared to be the policy of Congress and the purpose of this Act to improve boating safety and to foster greater development, use, and enjoyment of all the waters of the United States by encouraging and assisting participation by the several States, the boating industry, and the boating public in development of more comprehensive boating safety programs; by authorizing the establishment of national construction and performance standards for boats and associated equipment; and by creating more flexible regulatory authority concerning the use of boats and equipment. It is further declared to be the policy of Congress to encourage greater and continuing uniformity of boating laws and regulations as among the several States and the Federal Government, a higher degree of reciprocity and comity among the several jurisdictions, and closer cooperation and assistance between the Federal Government and the several States in developing, administering, and enforcing Federal and State laws and regulations pertaining to boating safety.

Definitions

SEC. 3. As used in this Act, and unless the context otherwise requires—

(1) "Boat" means any vessel—

(A) manufactured or used primarily for noncommercial use; or

(B) leased, rented, or chartered to another for the latter's noncommercial use; or

(C) engaged in the carrying of six or fewer passengers.

(2) "Vessel" includes every description of watercraft, other than a seaplane on the water, used or capable of being used as a means of transportation on the water.

(3) "Undocumented vessel" means a vessel which does not have and is not required to have a valid marine document as a vessel of the United States.

(4) "Use" means operate, navigate, or employ.

(5) "Passenger" means every person carried on board a vessel other than—

(A) the owner or his representative;

(B) the operator;

(C) bona fide members of the crew engaged in the business of the vessel who have contributed no consideration for their carriage and who are paid for their services; or

(D) any guest on board a vessel which is being used exclusively for pleasure purposes who has not contributed any consideration, directly, or indirectly, for his carriage.

(6) "Owner" means a person who claims lawful possession of a vessel by virtue of legal title or equitable interest therein which entitles him to such possession.

(7) "Manufacturer" means any person engaged in—

(A) the manufacture, construction, or assembly of boats or associated equipment; or

(B) the manufacture or construction of components for boats and associated equipment to be sold for subsequent assembly; or

(C) the importation into the United States for sale of boats, associated equipment, or components thereof.

(8) "Associated equipment" means—

(A) any system, part, or component of a boat as originally manufactured or any similar part or component manufactured or sold for replacement, repair, or improvement of such system, part, or component;

(B) any accessory or equipment for, or appurtenance to, a boat; and

(C) any marine safety article, accessory, or equipment intended for use by a person on board a boat; but

(D) excluding radio equipment.

(9) "Secretary" means the Secretary of the Department in which the Coast Guard is operating.

(10) "State" means a State of the United States, the Commonwealth of Puerto Rico, the Virgin Islands, Guam, American Samoa, and the District of Columbia.

(11) "Eligible State" means one that has a State boating safety program which has been accepted by the Secretary.

Applicability

SEC. 4. (a) This Act applies to vessels and associated equipment used, to be used, or carried in vessels used, on waters subject to the jurisdiction of the United States and on the high seas beyond the territorial seas for vessels owned in the United States.

(b) Sections 5 through 11 and subsections 12(a) and 12(b) of this Act are applicable also to boats moving or intended to be moved in interstate commerce.

(c) This Act, except those sections where the content expressly indicates otherwise, does not apply to—

(1) foreign vessels temporarily using waters subject to United States jurisdiction;

(2) military or public vessels of the United States, except recreational-type public vessels;

(3) a vessel whose owner is a State or subdivision thereof, which is used principally for governmental purposes, and which is clearly identifiable as such;

(4) ships' lifeboats.

Boat and Associated Equipment
Standards and Use

Safety regulations and standards

SEC. 5. (a) The Secretary may issue regulations—

(1) establishing minimum safety standards for boats and associated equipment, and establishing procedures and tests required to measure conformance with such standards. Each standard shall be reasonable, shall meet the need for boating safety, and shall be stated, insofar as practicable, in terms of performance;

(2) requiring the installation, carrying, or using of associated equipment on boats and classes of boats subject to this Act; and prohibiting the installation, carrying, or using of associated equipment which does not conform with safety standards established under this section. Equipment contemplated by this clause includes, but is not limited to, fuel systems, ventilation systems, electrical systems, navigational lights, sound producing devices, fire fighting equipment, lifesaving devices, signaling devices, ground tackle, life and grab rails, and navigational equipment.

(b) A regulation or standard issued under this section—

(1) shall specify an effective date which is not earlier than one hundred and eighty days from the date of issuance, except that this period shall be increased in the discretion of the Secretary to not more than twenty-four months in any case involving major product design, retooling, or major changes in the manufacturing process, unless the Secretary finds that there exists a boating safety hazard so critical as to require an earlier effective date; what constitutes major product redesign, retooling, or major changes shall be determined by the Secretary.

(2) may not compel substantial alteration of a boat or item of associated equipment which is in existence, or the construction or manufacture of which is commenced before the effective date of the regulation; but subject to that limitation may require compliance or performance to avoid a substantial risk of personal injury to the public that the Secretary considers appropriate in relation to the degree of hazard that the compliance will correct; and

(3) shall be consistent with laws and regulations governing the installation and maintenance of sanitation equipment.

Prescribing regulations and standards

SEC. 6. In establishing a need for formulating and prescribing regulations and standards under section 5 of this Act, the Secretary shall, among other things—

(1) consider the need for and the extent to which the regulations or standards will contribute to boating safety;

(2) consider relevant available boat safety standards, statistics and data, including public and private research, development, testing, and evaluation;

(3) consider whether any proposed regulation or standard is reasonable and appropriate for the particular type of boat or associated equipment for which it is prescribed;

(4) consult with the Boating Safety Advisory Council established pursuant to section 33 of this Act regarding all of the foregoing considerations.

Display of labels evidencing compliance

SEC. 7. The Secretary may require or permit the display of seals, labels, plates, insignia, or other devices for the purpose of certifying or evidencing compliance with Federal safety regulations and standards for boats and associated equipment.

Exemptions

SEC. 9. The Secretary may, if he considers that boating safety will not be adversely affected, issue exemptions from any provision of this Act or regulations and standards established thereunder, on terms and conditions as he considers appropriate.

Federal preemption

SEC. 10. Unless permitted by the Secretary under section 9 of this Act, no State or political subdivision thereof may establish, continue in effect, or enforce any provision of law or regulation which establishes any boat or associated equipment performance or other safety standard, or which imposes any requirement for associated equipment, except, unless disapproved by the Secretary, the carrying or using of marine safety articles to meet uniquely hazardous conditions or circumstances within the State, which is not identical to a Federal regulation issued under section 5 of this Act.

Prohibited acts

SEC. 12. (a) No person shall—

(1) manufacture, construct, assemble, introduce, or deliver for introduction in interstate commerce, or import into the United States, or if engaged in the business of selling or distributing boats or associated equipment, sell or offer for sale, any boat, associated equipment, or component thereof to be sold for subsequent assembly, unless—

(A) it conforms with regulations and standards prescribed under this Act, or

(B) it is intended solely for export, and so labeled, tagged, or marked on the boat or equipment and on the outside of the container, if any, which is exported.

(2) affix, attach, or display a seal, label, plate, insignia, or other device indicating or suggesting compliance with Federal safety standards, on, in, or with a boat or item of associated equipment, which is false or misleading;

(3) fail to furnish a notification as required by section 15 (a) or exercise reasonable diligence in fulfilling the undertaking given pursuant to section 15 (c) of this Act.

(b) No person shall be subject to any penalty contained in this section if he establishes that he did not have reason to know in the exercise of due care that a boat or associated equipment does not conform with applicable Federal boat safety standards, or who holds a certificate issued by the manufacturer of the boat or associated equipment to the effect that such boat or associated equipment conforms to all applicable Federal boat safety standards, unless such person knows or reasonably should have known that such boat or associated equipment does not so conform.

(c) No person may use a vessel in violation of this Act or regulations issued thereunder.

(d) No person may use a vessel, including one otherwise exempted by section 4(c) of this Act, in a negligent manner so as to endanger the life, limb, or property of any person. Violations of this subsection involving use which is grossly negligent, subject the violator, in addition to any other penalties prescribed in this Act, to the criminal penalties prescribed in section 34.

(e) No vessel equipped with propulsion machinery of any type and not subject to the manning requirements of the vessel inspection laws administered by the Coast Guard, may while carrying passengers for hire, be used except in the charge of a person

licensed for such service under regulations, prescribed by the Secretary, which pertain to qualifications, issuance, revocation, or suspension, and related matters.

(f) Section 12(e) of this Act shall not apply to any vessel being used for bona fide dealer demonstrations furnished without fee to business invitees. However, if on the basis of substantial evidence the Secretary determines, pursuant to section 6 hereof, that requiring vessels so used to be under the control of licensed persons is necessary to meet the need for boating safety, then the Secretary may promulgate regulations requiring the licensing of persons controlling such vessels in the same manner as provided in section 12(e) of this Act for persons in control of vessels carrying passengers for hire.

Termination of unsafe use

SEC. 13. If a Coast Guard boarding officer observes a boat being used without sufficient lifesaving or firefighting devices or in an overloaded or other unsafe condition as defined in regulations of the Secretary, and in his judgment such use creates an especially hazardous condition, he may direct the operator to take whatever immediate and reasonable steps would be necessary for the safety of those aboard the vessel, including directing the operator to return to mooring and to remain there until the situation creating the hazard is corrected or ended.

Notification of defects; repair or replacement

SEC. 15. (a) Every manufacturer who discovers or acquires information which he determines, in the exercise of reasonable and prudent judgment, indicates that a boat or associated equipment subject to an applicable standard or regulation prescribed pursuant to section 5 of this Act either fails to comply with such standard or regulation, or contains a defect which creates a substantial risk of personal injury to the public, shall, if such boat or associated equipment has left the place of manufacture, furnish notification of such defect or failure of compliance as provided in subsections (b) and (c) of this section, within a reasonable time after the manufacturer has discovered the defect.*

(b) The notification required by subsection (a) of this section shall be given to the following persons in the following manner—

(1) by certified mail to the first purchaser for purposes other than resale: *Provided,* That the requirement for notification of such first purchaser shall be satisfied if the manufacturer exercises reasonable diligence in creating and maintaining a list of such purchasers and their current addresses and sends the required notice to each person on said list at the address appearing thereon;

(2) by certified mail to subsequent purchasers, if known to the manufacturer;

(3) by certified mail or other more expeditious means to the dealers or distributors of such manufacturer to whom such boat or associated equipment was delivered.

(c) The notification required by subsection (a) of this section shall contain a clear description of such defect or failure to comply, an evaluation of the hazard reasonably related thereto, a statement of the measures to be taken to correct such defect or failure to comply, and an undertaking by the manufacturer to take such measures at his sole cost and expense.

Rendering of assistance in casualties

SEC. 16. (a) The operator of a vessel, including one otherwise exempted by subsection 4(c) of this Act, involved in a collision, accident, or other casualty, to the extent he can do so without serious danger to his own vessel, or persons aboard, shall render all practical and necessary assistance to persons affected by the collision, accident, or casualty to save them from danger caused by the collision, accident, or casualty. He shall also give his name, address, and the identification of his vessel to any person injured and to the owner of any property damaged. The duties imposed by this subsection are in addition to any duties otherwise imposed by law.

(b) Any person who complies with subsection (a) of this section or who gratuitously and in good faith renders assistance at the scene of a vessel collision, accident, or other casualty without objection of any person assisted, shall not be held liable for any civil damages as a result of the rendering of assistance or for any act or omission in providing or arranging salvage, towage, medi-

*(Amended in 1976 to limit the manufacturer's duty to five years from date of certification or manufacture.)

cal treatment, or other assistance where the assisting person acts as an ordinary, reasonably prudent man would have acted under the same or similar circumstances.

Numbering of Certain Vessels

Vessels requiring numbering

SEC. 17. An undocumented vessel equipped with propulsion machinery of any type shall have a number issued by the proper issuing authority in the State in which the vessel is principally used.

Standard numbering

SEC. 18. (a) The Secretary shall establish by regulation a standard numbering system for vessels. Upon application by a State the Secretary shall approve a State numbering system which is in accord with the standard numbering system and the provisions of this Act relating to numbering and casualty reporting.* A State with an approved system is the issuing authority under the Act. The Secretary is the issuing authority in States where a State numbering system has not been approved.

(b) If a State has a numbering system approved by the Secretary under the Act of September 2, 1958 (72 Stat. 1754), as amended, prior to enactment hereof, the system need not be immediately revised to conform with this Act and may continue in effect without change for a period not to exceed three years from the date of enactment of this Act.

(c) When a vessel is actually numbered in the State of principal use, it shall be considered as in compliance with the numbering system requirements of any State in which it is temporarily used.

(d) When a vessel is removed to a new State of principal use, the issuing authority of that State shall recognize the validity of a number awarded by any other issuing authority for a period of at least sixty days before requiring numbering in the new State.

(e) If a State has a numbering system approved after the effective date of this Act, that State must accept and recognize any certificate of number issued by the Secretary, as the previous issuing authority in that State, for one year from the date that State's system is approved, or until its expiration date, at the option of the State.

(f) Whenever the Secretary determines that a State is not administering its approved numbering system in accordance with the standard numbering system, or has altered its system without his approval, he may withdraw his approval after giving notice to the State, in writing, setting forth specifically wherein the State has failed to meet the standards required, and the State has not corrected such failures within a reasonable time after being notified by the Secretary.

Exemptions

SEC. 19. (a) The Secretary, when he is the issuing authority, may exempt a vessel or class of vessels from the numbering provisions of this Act under such conditions as he may prescribe.

(b) When a State is the issuing authority, it may exempt from the numbering provisions of this Act any vessel or class of vessels that has been exempted under subsection (a) of this section or otherwise as permitted by the Secretary.

Description of certificate of number

SEC. 20. (a) A certificate of number granted under this Act shall be pocket size, shall be at all times available for inspection on the vessel for which issued when the vessel is in use, and may not be valid for more than three years. The certificate of number for vessels less than twenty-six feet in length and leased or rented to another for the latter's noncommercial use of less than seven days may be retained on shore by the vessel's owner or his representative at the place from which the vessel departs or returns to the possession of the owner or his representative. A vessel which does not have the certificate of number on board shall be identified while in use, and comply with such other requirements, as the issuing authority prescribes.

(b) The owner of a vessel numbered under this Act shall furnish to the issuing authority notice of the transfer of all or part of his interest in the vessel, or of the destruction or abandonment of the vessel, within a reasonable time thereof, and shall furnish notice of any change of address within a reasonable time of the change, in accordance with prescribed regulations.

Display of number

SEC. 21. A number required by this Act shall be painted on, or attached to, each side of the forward half of the vessel for which it was issued, and shall be of the size, color, and type as may be prescribed by the Secretary. No other number may be carried on the forward half of the vessel.

Safety certificates

SEC. 22. When a State is the issuing authority it may require that the operator of a numbered vessel hold a valid safety certificate issued under terms and conditions set by the issuing authority.

Regulations

SEC. 23. The issuing authority may prescribe regulations and establish fees to carry out the intent of sections 17 through 24 and section 37 of this Act.† A State issuing authority may impose only terms and conditions for vessel numbering (1) which are prescribed by this Act or the regulations of the Secretary concerning the standard numbering system, or (2) which relate to proof of payment of State or local taxes.

State Boating Safety Programs

Establishment and acceptance

SEC. 25. In order to encourage greater State participation and consistency in boating safety efforts, and particularly greater safety patrol and enforcement activities, the Secretary may accept State boating safety programs directed at implementing and supplementing this Act. Acceptance is necessary for a State to receive full rather than partial Federal financial assistance under this Act. The Secretary may also make Federal funds available to an extent permitted by subsection 27(d) of this Act to national nonprofit public service organizations for national boating safety programs and activities which he considers to be in the public interest.

Boating safety program content

SEC. 26. (a) The Secretary shall accept a State boating safety program which—

(1) incorporates a State vessel numbering system previously approved under this Act or includes such a numbering system as part of the proposed boating safety program;

(2) includes generally the other substantive content of the Model State Boat Act as approved by the National Association of State Boating Law Administrators in conjunction with the Council of State Governments, or is in substantial conformity therewith, or conforms sufficiently to insure uniformity and promote comity among the several jurisdictions;

(3) provides for patrol and other activity to assure enforcement of the State boating safety laws and regulations;

(4) provides for boating safety education programs;

(5) designates the State authority or agency which will administer the boating safety program and the allocated Federal funds; and

(6) provides that the designated State authority or agency will submit reports in the form prescribed by the Secretary.

(b) The requirements of subparagraph (a) (2) of this section shall be liberally construed to permit acceptance where the general intent and purpose of such requirements are met and nothing contained therein is in any way intended to discourage a State program which is more extensive or comprehensive than suggested herein, particularly with the regard to safety patrol and enforcement activity commensurate with the amount and type of boating activity within the State, and with regard to public boat safety education, and experimental programs which could enhance boating safety.

Consultation and cooperation

SEC. 32. (a) In carrying out his responsibilities under this Act the Secretary may consult with State and local governments, public and private agencies, organizations and committees, private industry, and other persons having an interest in boating and boating safety.

(b) The Secretary may advise, assist, and cooperate with the States and other interested public and private agencies, in the planning, development, and execution of boating safety pro-

---

*In implementing and administering its numbering system, a State shall adopt any definitions of relevant terms, including, but not limited to, "model year" and "date of manufacture" established by the Secretary by regulation.

†The fees established pursuant to authority granted by this section shall apply equally to residents and nonresidents of the State.

grams. Acting under the authority of section 141 of title 14, United States Code, and consonant with the policy defined in section 2 of this Act, the Secretary shall insure the fullest cooperation between the State and Federal authorities in promoting boating safety by entering into agreements and other arrangements with the State whenever possible. Subject to the provisions of chapter 23, title 14, he may make available, upon request from a State, the services of members of the Coast Guard Auxiliary to assist the State in the promotion of boating safety on State waters.

Boating Safety Advisory Council

SEC. 33. (a) The Secretary shall establish a National Boating Safety Advisory Council (hereinafter referred to as "the Council"), which shall not exceed twenty-one members, whom the Secretary considers to have a particular expertise, knowledge, and experience in boating safety. Insofar as practical, to assure balanced representation, members shall be drawn equally from (1) State officials responsible for State boating safety programs, (2) boat and associated equipment manufacturers, and (3) boating organizations and members of the general public. Additional persons from those sources may be appointed to panels to the Council which will assist the Council in the performance of its functions.

(b) In addition to the consultation required by section 6 of this Act the Secretary shall consult with the Council on any other major boat safety matters related to this Act.

Criminal penalties

SEC. 34. Any person who willfully violates section 12(c) of this Act or the regulations issued thereunder shall be fined not more than $1,000 for each violation or imprisoned not more than one year, or both.

Civil penalties

SEC. 35. (a) In addition to any other penalty prescribed by law any person who violates subsection 12(a) of this Act shall be liable to a civil penalty of not more than $2,000 for each violation, except that the maximum civil penalty shall not exceed $100,000 for any related series of violations. Whenever any corporation violates section 12(a) of this Act, any director, officer, or executive employee of such corporation who knowingly and willfully ordered or knowingly and willfully authorized such violation shall be individually liable to the civil penalties contained herein, in addition to the corporation: *Provided, however,* That no such director, officer, or executive employee shall be individually liable under this subsection if he can demonstrate, by a preponderance of the evidence, (1) that said order or authorization was issued on the basis of a determination, in the exercise of reasonable and prudent judgment, that the nonconformity with standards and regulations constituting such violation would not cause or constitute a substantial risk of personal injury to the public, and (2) that at the time of said order or authorization he advised the Secretary in writing of his action under this proviso.

(b) In addition to any other penalty prescribed by law any person who violates any other provision of this Act or the regulations issued thereunder shall be liable to a civil penalty of not more than $500 for each violation. If the violation involves the use of a vessel, the vessel, except as exempted by subsection 4(c) of this Act, shall be liable and may be proceeded against in the district court of any district in which the vessel may be found.

(c) The Secretary may assess and collect any civil penalty incurred under this Act and, in his discretion, remit, mitigate, or compromise any penalty prior to referral to the Attorney General. Subject to approval by the Attorney General, the Secretary may engage in any proceeding in court for that purpose, including a proceeding under subsection (d) of this section. In determining the amount of any penalty to be assessed hereunder, or the amount agreed upon in any compromise, consideration shall be given to the appropriateness of such penalty in light of the size of the business of the person charged, the gravity of the violation and the extent to which the person charged has complied with the provisions of section 15 of this Act or has otherwise attempted to remedy the consequences of the said violation.

(d) When a civil penalty of not more than $200 has been assessed under this Act, the Secretary may refer the matter for collection of the penalty directly to the Federal magistrate of the jurisdiction wherein the person liable may be found for collection procedures under supervision of the district court and pursuant to order issued by the court delegating such authority under section 636(b) of title 28, United States Code.

Casualty reporting systems

SEC. 37. (a) The Secretary shall prescribe a uniform vessel casualty reporting system for vessels subject to this Act, including those otherwise exempted by paragraphs (1), (3), and (4) of section 4(c).

(b) A State vessel numbering system and boating safety program approved under this Act shall provide for the reporting of casualties and accidents involving vessels. A State shall compile and transmit to the Secretary reports, information, and statistics on casualties and accidents reported to it.

(c) A vessel casualty reporting system shall provide for the reporting of all marine casualties involving vessels indicated in subsection (a) of this section and resulting in the death of any person. Marine casualties which do not result in loss of life shall be classified according to the gravity thereof, giving consideration to the extent of the injuries to persons, the extent of property damage, the dangers which casualties create, and the size, occupation or use, and the means of propulsion of the boat involved. Regulations shall prescribe the casualties to be reported and the manner of reporting.

(d) The owner or operator of a boat or vessel indicated in subsection (a) of this section and involved in a casualty or accident shall report the casualty to the Secretary in accordance with regulations prescribed under this section unless he is required to report to a State under a State system approved under this Act.

(e) The Secretary shall collect, analyze, and publish reports, information, or statistics together with such findings and recommendations as he considers appropriate. If a State accident reporting system provides that information derived from accident reports, other than statistical, shall be unavailable for public disclosure, or otherwise prohibits use by the State or any person in any action or proceeding against an individual, the Secretary may utilize the information or material furnished by a State only in like manner.

General regulations

SEC. 39. The Secretary may issue regulations necessary or appropriate to carry out the purposes of this Act.

Savings provision

SEC. 40. Compliance with this Act or standards, regulations, or orders promulgated hereunder shall not relieve any person from liability at common law or under State law.

Miscellaneous provisions

SEC. 41. (a) The following are repealed:
(1) Section 7, as amended, and sections 13 and 14 of the Motorboat Act of 1940, Public Law 76–484, April 25, 1940 (54 Stat. 165);
(2) The Federal Boating Act of 1958, Public Law 85-911, September 2, 1958 (72 Stat. 1754), except subsections 6(b) and 6(c) thereof;
(3) The Act of March 28, 1960, Public Law 86-396 (74 Stat. 10); and
(4) The Act of August 30, 1961, Public Law 87-171 (75 Stat. 408).

(c) Any vessel, to the extent that it is subject to the Small Passenger Carrying Vessel Act, May 10, 1956 (70 Stat. 151), or to any other vessel inspection statute of the United States, is exempt from the provisions of this Act.

(e) Regulations previously issued under statutory provisions repealed, modified, or amended by this Act continue in effect as though promulgated under the authority of this Act until expressly abrogated, modified, or amended by the Secretary under the regulatory authority of this Act.

EXTRACTS FROM COAST GUARD REGULATIONS
RELATING TO THE MOTORBOAT ACT OF 1940

(These Regulations are retained in effect by the Federal Boat Safety Act of 1971 until specifically replaced by new regulations issued under the authority of that Act.)

24.01   Authority and Purpose

24.01–1   Purpose of regulations.

24.01–1(a)   The purpose of the regulations in this subchapter is to set forth uniform minimum requirements for motorboats, certain motor vessels, and barges carrying passengers when towed by motorboats or motor vessels in accordance with the intent of the Motorboat Act of April 25, 1940, as amended· (54 Stat. 163–167; 46 U.S.C. 526–526t). The regulations are necessary to carry out the provisions of the Motorboat Act of April 25, 1940, and such regulations have the force of law.

24.05   Application

24.05–1   Vessels subject to the requirements of this subchapter.

24.05–1(a)   This subchapter shall be applicable to all vessels indicated in column 6 of Table 24.05–1(a), and shall apply to all such United States flag vessels, and to all such foreign vessels, except as follows:

24.05–1(a)(1)   Any vessel operating exclusively on inland waters which are not navigable waters of the United States.

24.05–1(a)(2)   Any vessel while laid up and dismantled and out of commission.

24.05–1(a)(3)   With the exception of vessels of the U.S. Maritime Administration, any vessel with title vested in the United States and which is used for public purposes.

24.10   Definition of Terms Used in this Subchapter

24.10–1   Approved. This term means approved by the Commandant unless otherwise stated.

24.10–3   Carrying passengers for hire. The carriage of any person or persons by a vessel for a valuable consideration, whether directly or indirectly flowing to the owner, charterer, operator, agent or any other person interested in the vessel.

24.10–17   Motorboat.

24.10–17(a)   This term means any vessel indicated in column 6 of Table 24.-05–1(a), 65 feet in length or less which is equipped with propulsion machinery (including steam). The length shall be measured from end to end over the deck excluding sheer. This term includes a boat temporarily or permanently equipped with a detachable motor, since such a boat is also subject to the Act of April 25, 1940, as amended (46 U.S.C. 526–526u), and the regulations promulgated thereunder. For the purpose of this subchapter, motorboats are included under the term "vessel" unless specifically noted otherwise. The various classes of motorboats are as follows:

Class A—Any motorboat less than 16 feet in length.

Class 1—Any motorboat 16 feet or over and less than 26 feet in length.

Class 2—Any motorboat 26 feet or over and less than 40 feet in length.

Class 3—Any motorboat 40 feet or over and not more than 65 feet in length.

24.10–17(b)   The expression "length shall be measured from end to end over the deck excluding sheer" means a straight line measurement of the overall length from the foremost part of the vessel to the aftermost part of the vessel, measured parallel to the centerline. Bow sprits, bumpkins, rudders, outboard motor brackets, and similar fittings or attachments, are not to be included in the measurement. Length shall be stated in feet and inches.

24.10–19   Motor vessel. This term means any vessel more than 65 feet in length, which is propelled by machinery other than steam.

24.10–23   Passenger. A passenger is every person, other than the master and the members of the crew or other persons employed or engaged in any capacity on board a vessel in the business of that vessel. In the case of a vessel on an international voyage a child under one year of age is not counted as a passenger.

24.10–27   Vessel. Where the word "vessel" is used in this subchapter, it shall be considered to include all vessels indicated in column 6 of Table 24.05–1(a), except as otherwise noted in this subpart.

24.15   Equivalents

24.15–5   Canadian pleasure craft temporarily using navigable waters of the United States.

24.15–5(a)   Uninspected Canadian pleasure craft (uninspected vessels) temporarily using navigable waters of the United States may carry in lieu of the equipment required by the Motorboat Act of 1940 (46 U.S.C. 526–526u) and the regulations in this subchapter, the equipment as required by the laws of the Dominion of Canada and the regulations of the Department of Transport, Ottawa, Canada.

25.01   Application

25.01–   Applicable to all vessels.

25.01–1(a)   The provisions of this part shall apply to all vessels except as specifically noted.

25.05   Navigation Lights and Shapes, Whistles, Foghorns, Fog Bells, and Gongs

25.05–1   Vessels operating on waters governed by the International Rules of the Road.

25.05–1(a)   All vessels (including motorboats) operating on waters governed by the International Rules of the Road (33 U.S.C. 1051–1094) shall· be equipped with the navigation lights and shapes, whistles, foghorns, fog bells, and gongs as required by those rules.

25.05–10   Vessels operating on waters governed by the Inland, Great Lakes, or Western Rivers Rules of the Road.

25.05–10(a)   All vessels, other than motorboats, operating on waters governed by the Inland, Great Lakes, or Western Rivers Rules of the Road (33 U.S.C. 154–232, 241–295, 301–355) shall be equipped with the navigation lights and shapes, whistles, foghorns, fog bells, and gongs as required by the Rules of the Road applicable to the waters on which the vessel is navigated.

25.05–10(b)   All motorboats operating on waters governed by the Inland, Great Lakes, or Western Rivers Rules of the Road shall be equipped with the following:

25.05–10(b)(1)   Navigation lights as set forth in the Motorboat Act of April 25, 1940, as amended (46 U.S.C. 526–526u) or, in lieu thereof, the lights required by the International Rules of the Road.

25.05–10(b)(2)   An efficient whistle or other sound producing mechanical device as set forth in Table 25.05–10(b)(2), except:

25.05–10(b)(2)(i)   Motorboats engaged in a race which has been previously arranged or announced, or while engaged in such navigation as is incidental to the tuning up of the motorboat and engines for the race, need not carry the devices required by Table 25.05–10(b)(2).

25.05–10(b)(3)   An efficient fog bell, except that the following motorboats need not carry such a bell:

25.05–10(b)(3)(i)   Motorboats of less than 26 feet in length (Classes A and 1).

25.05–10(b)(3)(ii)   Motorboats engaged in a race previously arranged or announced, or while engaged in such navigation as is incidental to the tuning up of the motorboat and engines for the race.

25.05–15   Light intensity standards

25.05–15(a)   Navigation lights shall be of sufficient intensity so that the candlepower outside lens is not less than that amount corresponding to the required distance of visibility as specified in Table 25.05–15(a).

25.05–15(d)   The light intensity standards of this section shall apply to new navigation lights installed and replacements of existing lights made on or after January 1, 1973. Such lights shall be of an approved type.

25.30   Fire Extinguishing Equipment

25.30–1   Application.

25.30–1(a)   The provisions of this subpart, with the exception of section 25.-30–90, shall apply to all vessels contracted for on or after November 19, 1952. Vessels contracted for prior to that date shall meet the requirements of section 25.30–90.

25.30–5 General provisions.

25.30–5(a) Where equipment in this subpart is required to be of an approved type, such equipment requires the specific approval of the Commandant. Such approvals are published in the Federal Register, and in addition, are contained in Coast Guard publication CG–190,"Equipment Lists."

25.30–5(b) All hand protable fire extinguishers, semiportable fire extinguishing systems, and fixed fire extinguishing systems shall be of an approved type.

25.30–10 Hand portable fire extinguishers and semiportable fire extinguishing systems.

25.30–10(a) Hand portable fire extinguishers and semiportable fire extinguishing systems are classified by a combination letter and number symbol. The letter indicating the type of fire which the unit could be expected to extinguish, and the number indicating the relative size of the unit.

25.30–10(b) For the purpose of this subchapter, all required hand portable fire extinguishers and semiportable fire extinguishing systems are of the "B" type; i.e., suitable for extinguishing fires involving flammable liquids, greases, etc.

25.30–10(c) The number designations for size will start with "I" for the smallest to "V" for the largest. For the purpose of this subchapter, only sizes I through III will be considered. Sizes I and II are considered hand portable fire extinguishers and sizes III, IV,. and V are considered semiportable fire extinguishing systems which shall be fitted with suitable hose and nozzle or other practicable means so that all portions of the space concerned may be covered. Examples of size graduations for some of the typical hand portable fire extinguishers and semiportable fire extinguishing systems are set forth in Table 25.30–10(c).

25.30–10(d) All hand portable fire-extinguishers and semiportable fire extinguishing systems shall have permanently attached thereto a metallic nameplate giving the name of the item, the rated capacity in gallons, quarts, or pounds, the name and address of the person or firm for whom approved, and the identifying mark of the actual manufacturer.

25.30–10(e) Vaporizing-liquid type fire extinguishers containing carbon tetrachloride or chlorobromomethane or other toxic vaporizing liquids are not acceptable as equipment required by this subchapter.

25.30–10(f) Hand portable or semiportable extinguishers which are required on their nameplates to be protected from freezing shall not be located where freezing temperatures may be expected.

25.30–10(g) The use of dry chemical, stored pressure, fire extinguishers not fitted with pressure gauges or indicating devices, manufactured prior to January 1, 1965, may be permitted on motorboats and other vessels so long as such extinguishers are maintained in good and serviceable condition. The following maintenance and inspections are required for such extinguishers:

25.30–10(g)(1) When the date on the inspection record tag on the extinguisher shows that 6 months have elapsed since last weight check ashore, then such extinguisher is no longer accepted as meeting required maintenance conditions until reweighed ashore and found to be in a serviceable condition and within required weight conditions.

25.30–10(g)(2) If weight of the container is ¼ ounce less than stamped on container, it shall be serviced.

25.30–10(g)(3) If the outer seal or seals (which indicate tampering or use when broken) are not intact, the boarding officer or marine inspector will inspect such extinguisher to see that the frangible disc in neck of the container is intact; and if such disc is not intact, the container shall be serviced.

25.30–10(g)(4) If there is evidence of damage, use, or leakage, such as dry chemical powder observed in the nozzle or elsewhere on the extinguisher, the container shall be replaced with a new one and the extinguisher properly serviced or the extinguisher replaced with another approved extinguisher.

25.30–10(h) The dry chemical, stored pressure, fire extinguishers without pressure gauges or indicating devices manufactured after January 1, 1965, shall not be labeled with the marine type label described in Section 162.028–4 of this title nor shall such extinguishers manufactured after January 1, 1965, be carried on board motorboats or other vessels as required equipment.

25.30–15. Fixed fire extinguishing systems.

25.30–15(a) When a fixed fire extinguishing system is installed, it shall be of an approved carbon dioxide type, designed and installed in agreement with the applicable provisions of Subpart 76.15 of Subchapter H (Passenger Vessels) of this chapter.

25.30–20 Fire extinguishing equipment required.

25.30–20(a) Motorboats.

25.30–20(a)(1) All motorboats shall carry at least the minimum number of hand portable fire extinguishers set forth in Table 25.30–20(a)(1), except that motorboats less than 26 feet in length, propelled by outboard motors and not carrying passengers for hire, need not carry such portable fire extinguishers if the construction of such motorboats will not permit the entrapment of explosive or flammable gases or vapors.

25.30–20(a)(2) The intent of this regulation is illustrated in Figure 25.30–20 (a1) where fire extinguishers are required if any one or more of the specified conditions exist, and in Figure 25.30–20 (a2) where specified conditions do not, in themselves, require that fire extinguishers be carried.

25.35 Backfire Flame Control
25.35–1 Requirements

25.35–1(a) Every gasoline engine installed in a motorboat or motor vessel after April 25, 1940, except outboard motors, shall be equipped with an acceptable means of backfire flame control.

25.35–1(b) Installations made before November 19, 1952, need not meet the detailed requirements of this subpart and may be continued in use as long as they are serviceable and in good condition. Replacements shall meet the applicable conditions in this section.

25.35–1(c) Installations consisting of backfire flame arresters bearing basic Approval No. 162.015 may be continued in use as long as they are serviceable and in good condition. Replacements shall meet the applicable conditions in this section.

25.35–1(d) Installations consisting of engine air and fuel induction system and given a basic Approval No. 162.015 may be continued in use as long as they are serviceable and in good condition. Replacements shall meet the applicable conditions in this section.

25.35–1(e) The following are acceptable means of backfire flame control for gasoline engines:

25.35–1(e)(1) A backfire flame arrester constructed in accordance with the specification regulations contained in Subpart 162.041 of Subchapter Q (Specifications) of this chapter and it shall be specifically approved by the Commandant. The flame arrester shall be suitably secured to the air intake with flametight connection.

25.35–1(e)(2) An engine air and fuel induction system which provides adequate protection from propagation of backfire flame to the atmosphere equivalent to that provided by an approved backfire flame arrester. A gasoline engine utilizing an air and fuel induction system, and operated without an approved backfire flame arrester shall have such installation tested and labeled in accordance with the specifications contained in Subpart 162.042 of Subchapter Q (Specifications) of this chapter and such system shall be specifically approved by the Commandant.

25.35–1(e)(3) Any attachment to the carburetor or location of the engine air induction system by means of which flames caused by engine backfire will be dispersed to the atmosphere outside the vessel in such a manner that the flames will not endanger the vessel, persons on board, or nearby vessels and structures. All attachments shall be of metallic construction with flametight connections and firmly secured to withstand vibration, shock, and engine backfire. Such installations do not require formal approval and labeling, but will be accepted by Coast Guard law enforcement officers on the basis of compliance with this subpart.

25.40 Ventilation

25.40–1 Tanks and engine spaces.

(a) All motorboats or motor vessels, except open boats and as provided in paragraphs (d) and (e) of this section, paragraphs (d) and (e) of this section, the construction or decking over of which is commenced after April 25, 1940, and which use fuel having a flashpoint of 110°F, or less, shall have at least two ventilator ducts, fitted with cowls or their equivalent, for the efficient removal of explosive or flammable gasses from the bilges of every engine and fuel tank compartment. There shall be at least one exhaust duct installed so as to extend from the open atmosphere to the lower portion of the bilge and at least one intake duct installed so as to extend to a point at least midway to the bilge or at least below the level of the carburetor air intake. The cowls shall be located and trimmed for maximum effectiveness and in such a manner so as to prevent displaced fumes from being recirculated.

25.40–1(b) As used in this section, the term "open boats" means those motorboats or motor vessels with all engine and fuel tank compartments, and other spaces to which explosive or flammable gases and vapors from these compartments may flow, open to the atmosphere and so arranged as to prevent the entrapment of such gases and vapors within the vessel.

(d) Boats as defined in the Federal Boat Safety Act of 1971 built after July 31, 1980 or which are built in compliance with 33 CFR Part 183 are excepted from these requirements.

(e) Boats, as defined in the Federal Boat Safety Act of 1971, built after July 31, 1980 are excepted from the requirements of paragraph (a) for fuel tank compartments that—

(1) Contain a permanently installed fuel tank if each electrical component is ignition protected in accordance with 33 CFR 183.410(a); and

(2) Contain fuel tanks that vent to the outside of the boat.

26.15 Boarding
26.15–1 May board at any time.

26.15–1(a) In addition to any other authority provided by law, the boarding of vessels is authorized by subsection 8(c) of the Federal Boating Act of 1958 (46 U.S.C. 527e(c)), which reads as follows:

Commissioned, warrant, and petty officers of the Coast Guard may board any vessel required to be numbered under this Act at any time such vessel is found upon the navigable waters of the United States, the Commonwealth of Puerto Rico, the Virgin Islands, Guam, and the District of Columbia, or on the high seas, address inquiries to those on board, require appropriate proof of identification therefrom, examine the certificate of number issued under this Act, or in the absence of such certificate require appropriate proof of identification of the owner of the vessel, and, in addition, examine such vessel for compliance with this Act, the Act of April 25, 1940, as amended, and the applicable rules of the road.

26.15–1(b) To facilitate the boarding of vessels by the commissioned, warrant, and petty officers of the Coast Guard in the exercise of their authority, every vessel subject to the Federal Boating Act of 1958, or the Act of April 25, 1940, as amended (46 U.S.C. 526–526u), if under way and upon being hailed by a Coast Guard vessel or patrol boat, shall stop immediately and lay to, or shall maneuver in such a way as to permit the boarding officer to come aboard. Failure to stop or permit a boarding officer to board a vessel or refusal to comply will subject the operator or owner to penalties provided in these laws.

26.15–1(c) Coast Guard boarding vessels will be identified by the display of the Coast Guard ensign as a symbol of authority and the Coast Guard personnel

will be dressed in Coast Guard uniform. The Coast Guard boarding officer upon boarding a vessel will identify himself to the master, owner, or operator and explain his mission.

26.20 Exhibition of Motorboat Operator's License
26.20–1 Must Be Available.

26.20–1(a) Any person to whom a license as a motorboat operator has been issued shall have such license in his possession and available for immediate production to any Coast Guard boarding officer at all times during which any vessel which he is operating is carrying passengers for hire.

26.25 Crew Requirements
26.25–1 Licensed Personnel.

26.25–1(a) Every motorboat, as defined by the Act of April 25, 1940, as amended (46 U.S.C. 526), and any other vessel of fifteen gross tons or less propelled by machinery other than steam, while carrying passengers for hire, shall be operated or navigated by a person duly licensed for such service by the Coast Guard. This licensed operator shall be in charge of such motorboat or vessel, regardless of whether or not the passengers carried for hire are on such motorboat or vessel or are carried on a non-self-propelled vessel being towed or pushed by such motorboat or vessel. See Section 157.30–30 of Subchapter P (Manning of Vessels) for special provisions with regard to use of superior licenses for motorboat operator's license.

26.25–1(b) Certain uninspected vessels of 200 gross tons and upward are required to carry licensed officers. For details of these provisions see Subchapter P (Manning of Vessels) of this chapter, and the applicable law.

EXTRACTS FROM COAST GUARD REGULATIONS RELATING TO THE FEDERAL BOAT SAFETY ACT OF 1971

PART 173—VESSEL NUMBERING AND CASUALTY AND ACCIDENT REPORTING

Subpart A—General

173.1 Purpose. This part prescribes requirements for numbering vessels and for reporting casualties and accidents to implement sections 17, 18, and 37 of the Federal Boat Safety Act of 1971.

173.3 Definitions. As used in this part:

(a) "Act" means the Federal Boat Safety Act of 1971 (85 Stat. 213; 46 U.S.C. 1451, et seq.).

(b) "Issuing authority" means a State that has a numbering system approved by the Coast Guard or the Coast Guard where a number system has not been

approved. Issuing authorities are listed in Appendix A of this part.

(c) "Operator" means the person who is in control or in charge of a vessel while it is in use.

(d) "Owner" means a person who claims lawful possession of a vessel by virtue of legal title or equitable interest therein which entitles him to such possession.

(e) "Person" means an individual, firm, partnership, corporation, company, association, joint-stock association, or governmental entity and includes a trustee, receiver, assignee, or similar representative of any of them.

(f) "Reporting authority" means a State that has a numbering system approved by the Coast Guard or the Coast Guard where a numbering system has

not been approved. Reporting authorities are listed in Appendix A of this part.

(g) "State" means a State of the United States, the Commonwealth of Puerto Rico, the Virgin Islands, Guam, American Samoa, and the District of Columbia.

(h) "State of principal use" means the State on whose waters a vessel is used or to be used most during a calendar year.

(i) "Use" means operate, navigate, or employ.

Subpart B—Numbering

173.11 Applicability. This subpart applies to each vessel equipped with propulsion machinery of any type used on waters subject to the jurisdiction of the United States and on the high seas beyond the territorial seas for vessels owned in the United States except—

(a) Foreign vessels temporarily using waters subject to U.S. jurisdiction;

(b) Military or public vessels of the United States, except recreational-type public vessels;

(c) A vessel whose owner is a State or subdivision thereof, which is used principally for governmental purposes, and which is clearly identifiable as such;

(d) Ships' lifeboats;

(e) A vessel which has or is required to have a valid marine document as a vessel of the United States.

173.13 Exemptions. Where the Coast Guard issues numbers, the following classes of vessels are exempt, under section 19(a) of the Act, from the numbering provisions of the Act and this part:

(a) A vessel that is used exclusively for racing.

(b) A vessel equipped with propulsion machinery of less than 10 horsepower that—

(1) Is owned by the owner of a vessel for which a valid certificate of number has been issued;

(2) Displays the number of that numbered vessel followed by the suffix "1" in the manner prescribed in 173.27; and

(3) Is used as a tender for direct transportation between that vessel and the shore and for no other purpose.

173.15 Vessel number required.

(a) Except as provided in 173.17, no person may use a vessel to which this part applies unless—

(1) It has a number issued on a certificate of number by the issuing authority in the State in which the vessel is principally used; and

(2) The number is displayed as described in 173.27.

(b) This section does not apply to a vessel for which a valid temporary certificate has been issued to its owner by the issuing authority in the State in which the vessel is principally used.

173.17 Reciprocity.

(a) Subsection 18(c) of the Act states:

When a vessel is actually numbered in the State of principal use, it shall be considered as in compliance with the numbering system requirements of any State in which it is temporarily used.

(b) Subsection 18(d) of the Act states:

When a vessel is removed to a new State of principal use, the issuing authority of that State shall recognize the validity of a number awarded by any other issuing authority for a period of at least 60 days before requiring numbering in the new State.

173.19 Other numbers prohibited. No person may use a vessel to which this part applies that has any number that is not issued by an issuing authority for that vessel on its forward half.

173.21 Certificate of number required.

(a) Except as provided in 173.13 and 173.17, no person may use a vessel to which this part applies unless it has on board—

(1) A valid certificate of number or

temporary certificate for that vessel issued by the issuing authority in the State in which the vessel is principally used; or

(2) For the vessel described in paragraph (b) of this section, a copy of the lease or rental agreement, signed by the owner or his authorized representative and by the person leasing or renting the vessel, that contains at least—

(i) The vessel number that appears on the certificate of number; and

(ii) The period of time for which the vessel is leased or rented.

(b) Section 20(a) of the Act states in part:

The certificate of number for vessels less than 26 feet in length and leased or rented to another for the latter's noncommercial use of less than 24 hours may be retained on shore by the vessel's owner or his representative at the place from which the vessel departs or returns to the possession of the owner or his representative.

173.23 Inspection of certificate. Each person using a vessel to which this part applies shall present the certificate or lease or rental agreement required by 173.21 to any Federal, State, or local law enforcement officer for inspection at his request.

173.25 Location of certificate of number. No person may use a vessel to which this part applies unless the certificate or lease or rental agreement required by 173.21 is carried on board in such a manner that it can be handed to a person authorized under 173.23 to inspect it.

173.27 Numbers: Display; size; color.

(a) Each number required by 173.15 must—

(1) Be painted on or permanently attached to each side of the forward half of the vessel except as allowed by paragraph (b) or required by paragraph (c) of this section;

(2) Be in plain vertical block characters of not less than 3 inches in height;

(3) Contrast with the color of the background and be distinctly visible and legible;

(4) Have spaces or hyphens that are equal to the width of a letter other than "I" or a number other than "1" between the letter and number groupings (Example: DC 5678 EF or DC–5678–EF); and

(5) Read from left to right.

(b) When a vessel is used by a manufacturer or by a dealer for testing or demonstrating, the number may be painted on or attached to removable plates that are temporarily but firmly attached to each side of the forward half of the vessel.

(c) On vessels so configured that a number on the hull or superstructure would not be easily visible, the number must be painted on or attached to a backing plate that is attached to the forward half of the vessel so that the number is visible from each side of the vessel.

(d) Each number displayed on a tender exempted under 173.13 must meet the requirements of paragraph (a)

of this section and have a space or hyphen that is equal to the width of a letter other than "I" or a number other than "1" between the suffix and the number. (Example: DC 5678 EF 1 or DC–5678–EF–1.)

173.29 Notification to issuing authority. A person whose name appears as the owner of a vessel on a certificate of number shall, within 15 days, notify the issuing authority in a manner prescribed by the issuing authority of—

(a) Any change in his address;

(b) The theft or recovery of the vessel;

(c) The loss or destruction of a valid certificate of number;

(d) The transfer of all or part of his interest in the vessel; and

(e) The destruction or abandonment of the vessel.

173.31 Surrender of certificate of number. A person whose name appears as the owner of a vessel on a certificate of number shall surrender the certificate in a manner prescribed by the issuing authority within 15 days after it becomes invalid under paragraph (b), (c), (d), or (e) of 173.77.

173.33 Removal of number. The person whose name appears on a certificate of number as the owner of a vessel shall remove the number and validation sticker from the vessel when—

(a) The vessel is documented by the Coast Guard;

(b) The certificate of number is invalid under paragraph (c) of 173.77; or

(c) The vessel is no longer principally used in the State where the certificate was issued.

173.35 Coast Guard validation sticker. No person may use a vessel except a vessel exempted in 173.13 that has a number issued by the Coast Guard unless it has the validation sticker issued with the certificate of number displayed within 6 inches of the number.

Subpart C—Casualty and Accident Reporting

173.51 Applicability.

(a) This subpart applies to each vessel used on waters subject to the jurisdiction of the United States and on the high seas beyond the territorial seas for vessels owned in the United States that—

(1) Is used by its operator for recreational purposes; or

(2) Is required to be numbered under this part.

(b) This subpart does not apply to a vessel required to have a certificate of inspection under Chapter I of Title 46, Code of Federal Regulations.

173.53 Immediate notification of death or disappearance.

(a) When, as a result of an occurrence that involves a vessel or its equipment, a person dies or disappears from a vessel, the operator shall, without delay, by the quickest means available, notify the nearest reporting authority listed in Appendix A of this part of—

(1) The date, time, and exact location

of the occurrence;

(2) The name of each person who died or disappeared;

(3) The number and name of the vessel; and

(4) The names and addresses of the owner and operator.

(b) When the operator of a vessel cannot give the notice required by paragraph (a) of this section, each person on board the vessel shall notify the casualty reporting authority or determine that the notice has been given.

173.55 Report of casualty or accident.

(a) The operator of a vessel shall submit the casualty or accident report prescribed in 173.57 to the reporting authority prescribed in 173.59 when, as a result of an occurrence that involves the vessel or its equipment—

(1) A person dies;

(2) A person is injured and requires medical treatment beyond first aid;

(3) Damage to the vessel and other property totals more than $200 or there is a complete loss of a vessel; or

(4) A person disappears from the vessel under circumstances that indicate death or injury.

(b) A report required by this section must be made—

(1) Within 48 hours of the occurrence if a person dies within 24 hours of the occurrence;

(2) Within 48 hours of the occurrence if a person is injured and requires medical treatment beyond first aid, or disappears from a vessel; and

(3) Within 10 days of the occurrence or death if an earlier report is not required by this paragraph.

(c) When the operator of a vessel cannot submit the casualty or accident report required by paragraph (a) of this section, the owner shall submit the casualty or accident report.

173.57 Casualty or accident report. Each report required by 173.55 must be in writing, dated upon completion, and signed by the person who prepared it and must contain, if available, at least the following information about the casualty or accident:

(a) The numbers and names of each vessel involved.

(b) The name and address of each owner of each vessel involved.

(c) The name of the nearest city or town, the county, the State, and the body of water.

(d) The time and date the casualty or accident occurred.

(e) The location on the water.

(f) The visibility, weather, and water conditions.

(g) The estimated air and water temperatures.

(h) The name, address, age, or date of birth, telephone number, vessel operating experience, and boating safety training of the operator making the report.

(i) The name and address of each

operator of each vessel involved.

(j) The number of persons on board or towed on skiis by each vessel.

(k) The name, address, and date of birth of each person injured or killed.

(l) The cause of each death.

(m) Weather forecasts available to, and weather reports used by, the operator before and during the use of the vessel.

(n) The name and address of each owner of property involved.

(o) The availability and use of personal flotation devices.

(p) The type and amount of each fire extinguisher used.

(q) The nature and extent of each injury.

(r) A description of all property damage and vessel damage with an estimate of the cost of all repairs.

(s) A description of each equipment failure that caused or contributed to the cause of the casualty.

(t) A description of the vessel casualty or accident.

(u) The type of vessel operation (cruising, drifting, fishing, hunting, skiing, racing, or other), and the type of accident (capsizing, sinking, fire, or explosion or other).

(v) The opinion of the person making the report as to the cause of the casualty.

(w) The make, model, type (open, cabin, house, or other), beam width at widest point, length, depth from transom to keel, horsepower, propulsion (outboard, inboard, inboard outdrive, sail, or other), fuel (gas, diesel, or other), construction (wood, steel, aluminum, plastic, fiberglass, or other), and year built (model year), of the reporting operator's vessel.

(x) The name, address, and telephone number of each witness.

(y) The manufacturer's hull identification number, if any, of the reporting operator's vessel.

(z) The name, address, and telephone number of the person submitting the report.

173.59 Where to report. A report required by 173.55 must be submitted to—

(a) The reporting authority listed in Appendix A of this part where the vessel number was issued, or, if the vessel has no number, where the vessel is principally used; or

(b) The reporting authority where the casualty or accident occurred, if it occurred outside the State where the vessel is numbered or principally used.

Subpart D—Issue of Certificate of Number

173.71 Application for certificate of number. Any person who is the owner of a vessel to which 173.11 applies may apply for a certificate of number for that vessel by submitting to the issuing authority, listed in Appendix A of this part, where the vessel will principally be used—

(a) An application on a form and in a manner prescribed by the issuing au-

thority; and

(b) The fee required by the issuing authority.

173.73 Duplicate certificate of number. If a certificate of number is lost or destroyed, the person whose name appears on the certificate as the owner may apply for a duplicate certificate by submitting to the issuing authority that issued the certificate—

(a) An application on a form or in a manner prescribed by the issuing authority; and

(b) The fee required by the issuing authority, if any.

173.75 Temporary certificate. A temporary certificate valid for not more than 60 days after it is issued may be issued by an issuing authority pending the issue of a certificate of number. A temporary certificate is not valid after the date that the owner receives the certificate of number from the issuing authority.

173.77 Validity of certificate of number.

(a) Except as provided in paragraphs (b), (c), (d), and (e) of this section, a certificate of number is valid until the date of expiration prescribed by the issuing authority.

(b) A certificate of number issued by an issuing authority is invalid after the date upon which—

(1) The vessel is documented or required to be documented under Part 67 of Title 46, Code of Federal Regulations;

(2) The person whose name appears on the certificate of number as owner of the vessel transfers all of his ownership in the vessel; or

(3) The vessel is destroyed or abandoned.

(c) A certificate of number issued by an issuing authority is invalid if—

(1) The application for the certificate of number contains a false or fraudulent statement; or

(2) The fees for the issuance of the certificate of number are not paid.

(d) A certificate of number is invalid 60 days after the day on which the vessel is no longer principally used in the State where the certficate was issued.

(e) The certificate of number is invalid when the person whose name appears on the certificate involuntarily loses his interest in the numbered vessel by legal process.

173.79 Expiration of Coast Guard certificate of number. A certificate of number issued by the Coast Guard expires 3 years from the date it is issued.

173.85 Coast Guard fees.

(a) In a State where the Coast Guard is the issuing authority the fees for numbering are—

(1) Original number and two validation stickers—$6;

(2) Renewal of number and two validation stickers—$6;

(3) Duplicate certificate of number—$1; and

(4) Replacement of lost or destroyed validation sticker—$0.25 each.

(b) Fees must be paid by check or money order made payable to the "U.S. Coast Guard," except when the application is made in person by the owner, the fee may be paid in cash.

Appendix A—Issuing Authorities and Reporting Authorities

(a) The State is the issuing authority and reporting authority in:

STATE

Alabama—AL.	Nebraska—NB.
Arizona—AZ.	Nevada—NV.
Arkansas—AR.	New Jersey—NJ.
California—CF.	New Mexico—NM.
Colorado—CL.	New York—NY.
Connecticut—CT.	North Carolina—NC.
Delaware—DL.	North Dakota—ND.
Florida—FL.	Ohio—OH.
Georgia—GA.	Oklahoma—OK.
Hawaii—HA.	Oregon—OR.
Idaho—ID.	Pennsylvania—PA.
Illinois—IL.	Puerto Rico—PR.
Indiana—IN.	Rhode Island—RI.
Iowa—IA.	South Carolina—SC.
Kansas—KA.	South Dakota—SD.
Kentucky—KY.	Tennessee—TN.
Louisiana—LA.	Texas—TX.
Maine—ME.	Utah—UT.
Maryland—MD.	Vermont—VT.
Massachusetts—MS.	Virginia—VA.
Michigan—MC.	Virgin Islands—VI.
Minnesota—MN.	West Virginia—WV.
Mississippi—MI.	Wisconsin—WS.
Missouri—MO.	Wyoming—WY.
Montana—MT.	District of Columbia—DC.

(b) The Coast Guard is the issuing authority and reporting authority in:

STATE

Alaska—AK.	New Hampshire—NH.
American Samoa—AS.	
Guam—GM.	Washington—WN.

(c) The abbreviations following the names of the State listed in paragraphs (a) and (b) are the two capital letters that must be used in the number format to denote the State of principal use as prescribed in 174.23 of this chapter.

PART 174—STATE NUMBERING AND CASUALTY REPORTING SYSTEMS

Subpart A—General

174.1 Applicability. This part establishes a standard numbering system for vessels and a uniform vessel casualty reporting system for vessels by prescribing requirements applicable to the States for the approval of State numbering systems.

Subpart B—Numbering System Requirements

174.11 Applicability of State numbering system.

(a) Except as allowed in paragraph (c) of this section, a State numbering system must require the numbering of vessels to which 173.11 of this chapter applies.

(b) A State numbering system may require the numbering of any vessel subject to the jurisdiction of the State unless prohibited by the regulations in Part 173 of this chapter.

(c) A State numbering system may exempt from its numbering requirements any vessel or class of vessels to which 173.13 of this chapter applies.

174.13 Owner or operator requirements. A State numbering system must contain the requirements applicable to an owner or a person operating a vessel that are prescribed in the following sections of Part 173 of this chapter:

(a) Paragraph (a) of 173.15 *Vessel number required of this chapter.*

(b) Section 173.19 *Other numbers prohibited of this chapter.*

(c) Paragraph (a) of 173.21 *Certificate of number required of this chapter.*

(d) Section 173.23 *Inspection of certificate of this chapter.*

(e) Section 173.25 *Location of certificate of number of this chapter.*

(f) Section 173.29 *Notification to issuing authority of this chapter.*

(i) Section 173.71 *Application for certificate of number of this chapter.*

(j) Section 173.73 *Duplicate certificate of number of this chapter.*

(k) Section 173.77 *Validity of certificate of number of this chapter.*

174.14 State numbering system optional sections.

In addition to the requirements in §174.13, a State numbering system may contain any of the other requirements applicable to a boat owner or operator prescribed in Part 173.

174.15 Validation stickers.

(a) If a State issues validation stickers, its numbering system must contain the requirements that stickers must be displayed within 6 inches of the number and the stickers must meet the requirements in paragraphs (b) and (c) of this section.

(b) Validation stickers must be approximately 3 inches square.

(c) The year in which each validation sticker expires must be indicated by the colors, blue, international orange, green, and red, in rotation beginning with blue for stickers that expire in 1973.

174.17 Contents of application for certificate of number.

(a) Each form for application for a certificate of number must contain the following information:

(1) Name of the owner.

(2) Address of the owner, including ZIP code.

(3) Date of birth of the owner.

(4) Citizenship of the owner.

(5) State in which vessel is or will be principally used.

(6) The number previously issued by an issuing authority for the vessel, if any.

(7) Whether the application is for a new number, renewal of a number, or transfer of ownership.

(8) Whether the vessel is used for pleasure, rent or lease, dealer or manufacturer demonstration, commercial passenger carrying, commercial fishing, or other commercial use.

(9) Make of vessel.

(10) Year vessel was manufactured or model year.

(11) Manufacturer's hull identification number, if any.

(12) Overall length of vessel.

(13) Type of vessel (open, cabin, house, or other).

(14) Whether the hull is wood, steel, aluminum, fiberglass, plastic, or other.

(15) Whether the propulsion is inboard, outboard, inboard-outdrive, or sail and name of engine manufacturer if available.

(16) Whether the fuel is gasoline, diesel, or other.

(17) The signature of the owner.

(b) An application made by a manufacturer or dealer for a number that is to be temporarily affixed to a vessel for demonstration or test purposes may omit items 9 through 16 of paragraph (a) of this section.

(c) An application made by a person who intends to lease or rent the vessel without propulsion machinery may omit items 15 and 16 of paragraph (a) of this section.

174.19 Contents of a certificate of number.

(a) Except as allowed in paragraphs (b), (c), and (d) of this section, each certificate of number must contain the following information:

(1) Number issued to the vessel.

(2) Expiration date of the certificate.

(3) State of principal use.

(4) Name of the owner.

(5) Address of owner, including ZIP code.

(6) Whether the vessel is used for pleasure, rent or lease, dealer or manufacturer demonstration, commercial passenger carrying commercial fishing or other commercial use.

(7) Manufacturer's hull identification number (if any).

(8) Make of vessel.

(9) Year vessel was manufactured.

(10) Overall length of vessel.

(11) Whether the vessel is an open boat, cabin cruiser, houseboat, or other type.

(12) Hull material.

(13) Whether the propulsion is inboard, outboard, inboard-outdrive, or sail.

(14) Whether the fuel is gasoline, diesel, or other.

(b) A certificate of number issued to a vessel that has a manufacturer's hull identification number assigned, may omit items 8 through 14 of paragraph (a) of this section if the manufacturer's hull identification number is plainly marked on the certificate.

(d) A certificate of number issued to a vessel that is to be rented or leased without propulsion machinery may omit items 13 and 14 of paragraph (a) of this section if the words "livery vessel" are plainly marked on the certificate.

(e) An issuing authority may print on the certificate of number a quotation of the State regulations pertaining to change of ownership or address, documentation, loss, or recovery of vessel, carriage of the certificate of number on board when the vessel is in use, rendering aid in a boat accident, and reporting of vessel casualties and accidents.

174.21 Contents of temporary certificate. A temporary certificate issued pending the issuance of a certificate of number must contain the following information:

(a) Make of vessel.

(b) Length of vessel.

(c) Type of propulsion.

(d) State in which vessel is principally used.

(e) Name of owner.

(f) Address of owner, including ZIP code.

(g) Signature of owner.

(h) Date of issuance.

(i) Notice to the owner that the temporary certificate is invalid after 60 days from the date of issuance.

174.23 Form of number.

(a) Each number must consist of two capital letters denoting the State of the issuing authority, as specified in Appendix A of Part 173 of this chapter, followed by—

(1) Not more than four numerals followed by not more than two capital letters (example: NH 1234 BD); or

(2) Not more than three numerals followed by not more than three capital letters (example: WN 567 EFG).

(b) A number suffix must not include the letters "I," "O," or "Q," which may be mistaken for numerals.

174.25 Size of certificate of number. Each certificate of number must be approximately 2½ by 3½ inches.

174.27 Duration of certificate of number. A certificate of number must not be valid for more than 3 years.

174.29 Temporary certificate of number. A State may issue a temporary certificate of number that is effective for not more than 60 days.

174.31 Terms and conditions for vessel numbering. A State numbering system may condition the issuance of a certificate of number on—

(a) Title to, or other proof of ownership of a vessel except a recreational-type public vessel of the United States; or

(b) The payment of State or local taxes, except for a recreational-type public vessel of the United States.

Subpart C—Casualty Reporting System Requirements

174.101 Applicability of State casualty reporting system.

(a) A State casualty reporting system must require the reporting of vessel casualties and accidents involving vessels to which 173.51 of this chapter applies.

(b) The State casualty reporting system may require vessel casualty or accident reports resulting in property damage of less than $200.

174.105 Owner or operator casualty reporting requirements. A State vessel casualty reporting system must contain the following requirements of Part 173 of this chapter applicable to an owner or a person operating a vessel:

(a) Section 173.55 Report of casualty or accident.

(b) Section 173.57 Casualty or accident report.

(c) Section 173.59 Where to report.

174.106 State casualty reporting system optional sections.

In addition to the requirements in §174.105, a State casualty reporting system may contain any of the other requirements applicable to a boat owner or operator prescribed in Part 173.

Part 175—Equipment Requirements

Subpart A—General

175.1 Applicability.

This part prescribes rules governing the use of boats on waters subject to the jurisdiction of the United States and on the high seas beyond the territorial seas for boats owned in the United States except—

(a) Foreign boats temporarily using waters subject to U.S. jurisdiction;

(b) Military or public boats of the United States, except recreational-type public vessels;

(c) A boat whose owner is a State or subdivision thereof, which is used principally for governmental purposes, and which is clearly identifiable as such;

(d) Ship's lifeboats.

175.3 Definitions.

As used in this part:

(a) "Boat" means any vessel manufactured or used primarily for noncommercial use; leased, rented, or chartered to another for the latter's noncommercial use; or engaged in the carrying of six or fewer passengers.

(b) "Recreational boat" means any vessel manufactured or used primarily for non-comercial use; or leased, rented, or chartered to another for the latter's non-commercial use. It does not include a vessel engaged in the carrying of six or fewer passengers.

(c) "Vessel" includes every description of watercraft, other than a seaplane on the water, used or capable of being used as a means of transportation on the water.

(d) "Use" means operate, navigate, or employ.

(e) "Passenger" means every person carried on board a vessel other than—

(1) The owner or his representative;

(2) The operator;

(3) Bona fide members of the crew engaged in the business of the vessel who have contributed no consideration for their carriage and who are paid for their services; or

(4) Any guest on board a vessel which is being used exclusively for pleasure purposes who has not contributed any consideration, directly or indirectly, for his carriage.

(f) "Racing shell, rowing scull, and racing kyak," means a manually propelled boat that is recognized by national or international racing associations for use in competitive racing and one in which all occupants row, scull, or paddle, with the exception of a coxswain, if one is provided, and is not designed to carry and does not carry any equipment not solely for competitive racing.

Subpart B—Personal Flotation Devices

175.11 Applicability.

This subpart applies to all recreational boats that are propelled or controlled by machinery, sails, oars, paddles, poles, or another vessel except racing shells, rowing sculls, and racing kayaks.

175.13 Definitions.

As used in this subpart:

(a) "Personal flotation device" means a device that is approved by the Commandant under 46 CFR Part 160.

(b) "PFD" means "personal flotation device."

175.15 Personal flotation devices required.

(a) Except as provided in § 175.17, no person may use a recreational boat less than 16 feet in length or a canoe or kayak unless at least one PFD of the following types or their equivalents listed in Table 175.23 is on board for each person:

(1) Type I PFD.

(2) Type II PFD.

(3) Type III PFD.

(4) Type IV PFD.

(b) No person may use a recreational boat 16 feet or more in length, except a canoe or kayak, unless at least one PFD of the following types or their equivalents listed in Table 175.23 is on board for each person:

(1) Type I PFD.

(2) Type II PFD.

(3) Type III PFD.

(c) No person may use a recreational boat 16 feet or more in length, except a canoe or kayak, unless at least one Type IV PFD or its equivalent listed in Table 175.23 is on board in addition to the PFD's required in paragraph (b) of this section.

175.17 Exceptions.

(a) A person using a canoe or kayak that is enclosed by a deck and spray skirt need not comply with § 175.15 if he wears a vest-type lifesaving device that—

(1) Has no less than 150 separate permanently inflated air sacs made of not less than 12 mil polyvinylchloride film and has not less than 13 pounds of positive buoyancy in fresh water, if worn by a person who weighs more than 90 pounds; or

(2) Has no less than 120 separate permanently inflated air sacs made of not less than 12 mil polyvinylchloride film and has not less than 8½ pounds of positive buoyancy in fresh water, if worn by a person who weighs 90 pounds or less.

(b) A Type V PFD may be carried in lieu of any PFD required in § 175.15 if that Type V PFD is approved for the activity in which the recreational boat is being used.

175.19 Stowage.

(a) No person may use a recreational boat unless each Type I, Type II, Type III, or Type V PFD required by § 175.15 or § 175.17 is readily accessible.

(b) No person may use a recreational

boat unless each Type IV PFD required by § 175.15 is immediately available.

175.21 Conditions; approval; marking.

No person may use a recreational boat unless each device required by § 175.15, or each device allowed by § 175.17, is—

(a) In serviceable condition;

(b) Legibly marked with the approval number as specified in 46 CFR Part 160 for items subject to approval; and

(c) Of an appropriate size for the person for whom it is intended.

175.23. Personal flotation device equivalents.

Table 175.23 lists devices that are equivalent to personal flotation devices.

TABLE 175.23

Devices marked	Are equivalent to
160.002 Life preserver	Performance Type I personal flotation device
160.003 Life preserver	Performance Type I personal flotation device
160.004 Life preserver	Performance Type I personal flotation device
160.005 Life preserver	Performance Type I personal flotation device
160.009 Ring life buoy	Performance Type IV personal flotation device
160.047 Buoyant vest	Performance Type II personal flotation device
160.048 Buoyant cushion	Performance Type IV personal flotation device
160.049 Buoyant cushion	Performance Type IV personal flotation device
160.050 Ring life buoy	Performance Type IV personal flotation device
160.052 Buoyant vest	Performance Type II personal flotation device
160.053 Work vest	Performance Type V personal flotation device
160.055 Life preserver	Performance Type I personal flotation device
160.060 Buoyant vest	Performance Type II personal flotation device
160.064 Special purpose water safety buoyant devices.	A device intended to be worn may be equivalent to Type II or Type III. A device that is equivalent to Type III is marked "Type III Device—may not turn unconscious wearer." A device intended to be grasped is equivalent to Type IV.

Part 177—Correction of Especially Hazardous Conditions

Action to Correct Especially Hazardous Conditions

177.01 Purpose and applicability.

This part prescribes rules to implement section 13 of the Federal Boat Safety Act of 1971 which govern the correction of especially hazardous conditions on boats using waters subject to the jurisdiction of the United States and on the high seas beyond the territorial seas for boats owned in the United States, except operators of—

(a) Foreign boats temporarily using waters subject to United States jurisdiction;

(b) Military or public boats of the United States, except recreational-type public boats;

(c) A boat whose owner is a State or subdivision thereof, which is used principally for governmental purposes and which is clearly indentifiable as such;

(d) Ship's lifeboats.

177.03 Definitions.

As used in this part:

(a) "Act" means the Federal Boat Safety Act of 1971 (85 Stat. 213; 46 U.S.C. 1451, et seq.)

(b) "Boat" means any vessel—

(1) Manufactured or used primarily for noncommercial use; or

(2) Leased, rented, or chartered to another for the latter's noncommercial use; or

(3) Engaged in the carrying of six or fewer passengers.

(c) "Coast Guard Boarding Officer" means a commissioned, warrant, or petty officer of the Coast Guard having authority to board any vessel under the Act of August 4, 1949, 63 Stat. 502, as amended (14 U.S.C. 89).

(d) "Operator" means the person who is in control or in charge of a boat while it is in use.

(e) "Use" means operate, navigate, or employ.

(f) "Vessell" includes every description of watercraft, other than a seaplane on the water, used or capable of being used as a means of transportation on the water.

177.05 Action to correct an especially hazardous condition.

An operator of a boat who is directed by a Coast Guard Boarding Officer to take immediate and reasonable steps necessary for the safety of those aboard the vessel, under section 13 of the Act, shall follow the direction of the Boarding Officer, which may include direction to—

(a) Correct the especially hazardous condition immediately;

(b) Proceed to a mooring, dock, or anchorage; or

(c) Suspend further use of the boat until the especially hazardous condition is corrected.

177.07 Other unsafe conditions.

For the purpose of section 13 of the Act, "other unsafe condition" means a boat—

(a) Does not display the navigation lights prescribed by 46 CFR 25.05 between sunset and sunrise;

(b) Has fuel leakage from either the fuel system or engine;

(c) Has an accumulation of fuel in the bilges or a compartment other than a fuel tank;

(d) Does not meet the ventilation requirements for tanks and engine spaces prescribed by 46 CFR Subpart 25.40; or

(e) Does not meet the requirements for backfire flame control prescribed by 46 CFR Subpart 25.35.

(f) Is operated in a Regulated Boating Area as described in 177.08 when—

(1) The wave height within the Regulated Boating Area is 4 feet or greater; or

(2) The wave height within the Regulated Boating Area is equal to or greater than the wave height determined by the formula

$$\frac{L}{10} + F = W \text{ where:}$$

L=Overall length of a boat measured in feet in a straight horizontal line along and parallel with the centerline between the intersections of this line with the vertical planes of the stem and stern profiles excluding deckhouses and equipment.

F=The minimum freeboard when measured in feet from the lowest point along the upper strake edge to the surface of the water.

W=Maximum wave height in feet to the nearest highest whole number; or

(3) The surface current is 4 knots or greater within the Regulated Boating Area.

(g) Designated manifestly unsafe for a specific voyage on a specific body of water due to:

(1) Unsuitable design or configuration, or

(2) Improper construction or inadequate material condition, or

(3) Improper or inadequate operational or safety equipment, and set forth in a regulation issued by a District Commander under the authority of 33 CFR 1.05-1(d).

177.09 Penalties.

An operator of a boat who does not follow the directions of a Coast Guard Boarding Officer prescribed in § 177.05 is, in addition to any other penalty prescribed by law, subject to—

(a) The criminal penalties of section 34 of the Federal Boat Safety Act of 1971 which provides that "Any person who willfully violates section 12(c) of this Act or the regulations issued thereunder shall be fined not more than $1,000 for each violation or imprisoned not more than 1 year, or both," and

(b) The civil penalties of subsection 35(b) of the Federal Boat Safety Act of 1971 which provides "In addition to any other penalty prescribed by law any person who violates any other provision of this Act or the regulations issued thereunder shall be liable to a civil penalty of not more than $500 for each violation. If the violation involves the use of a vessel, the vessel, except as exempted by subsection 4(c) of this Act, shall be liable and may be proceeded against in the district court of any district in which the vessel may be found.

GENERAL INDEX

Note: All color plates are designated by the letters A through V, and placed in the following sequence:

A-D (Navigation Lights), between text pages 64(h) - 65
I-L (Buoyage Systems), between text pages 304-305.
O-V (Flags and Insignia), between text pages 464-465.

See also the Table of Contents, on page vii.

C

E

F

USPS

REFERENCES FOR INSTRUCTION COURSES

USCG

AUXILIARY REFERENCES FOR STUDY COURSE

WHERE TO APPLY FOR NUMBERING CERTIFICATES

The Federal Boat Safety Act of 1971 continued the pattern previously established by the Federal Boating Act of 1958 whereby powered craft could be registered and numbered by State authorities if the State had set up a program for such actions in accordance with Federal standards. Approval of the State system by the U.S. Coast Guard is required in each case for the sake of state-to-state uniformity.

The Coast Guard has officially approved the numbering systems of all states except New Hampshire and Washington. In these jurisdictions application forms for Coast Guard registration numbers may be obtained through local post offices or any Coast Guard facility. In Guam and U.S. Samoa application should be made to the Officer in Charge, Marine Inspection, U.S. Coast Guard.

Boats principally used in states having an approved number-ing law are numbered exclusively by the state; Coast Guard numbers are obsolete. In compliance with the Federal Act all of these state laws grant 60-day reciprocity to out-of-state boats awarded numbers pursuant to Federal law or a federally approved state numbering system.

The Outboard Boating Club of America (401 No. Michigan Ave., Chicago, Ill. 60611) has compiled all available information on state boating laws in handbooks for various regions of the country. These include not only the registration and numbering requirements, but also all related laws on equipment, operation, use of trailers, etc., which readers are urged to obtain.

Given below are extracts from OBC data, listing agencies responsible for boat numbering laws.

ALABAMA Department of Conservation, State Administrative Building, Montgomery, Alabama 36130.

ALASKA Department of Public Safety, P.O. Box 6188 Annex, Anchorage, Alaska 99502.

ARIZONA Game and Fish Department, 2222 W. Greenway Rd., Phoenix, Arizona 85023.

ARKANSAS Licensing Division, Department of Finance & Administration, P.O. Box 1272, Little Rock, Arkansas 72201

CALIFORNIA Vessel Registration Section, Department of Motor Vehicles, P.O. Box 780, Sacramento, California 95804

COLORADO Division of Parks & Outdoor Recreation, 13787 S. Highway 85, Littleton, Colorado 80215.

CONNECTICUT Department of Environmental Protection, State Office Building, Hartford, Connecticut 06115.

DELAWARE Department of Natural Resources & Environmental Control, P.O. Box 1401, Dover, Delaware 19901.

FLORIDA Department of Natural Resources, Crown Building, Tallahassee, Florida 32304.

GEORGIA Department of Natural Resources, Room 714, Trinity-Washington Bldg., Atlanta, Georgia 30334.

HAWAII Water Transportation Facilities Division, Department of Transportation, 79 S. Nimitz Highway, Honolulu, Hawaii 96813.

IDAHO Department of Parks & Recreation, 2177 Warm Springs Avenue, State House, Boise, Idaho 83720.

ILLINOIS Division of Law Enforcement, Conservation Department, 100 E. Washington Street, Springfield, Illinois 62706.

INDIANA Department of Natural Resources, 606 State Office Building, Indianapolis, Indiana 46204.

IOWA State Conservation Commission, Wallace Building, Des Moines, Iowa 50319.

KANSAS Forestry, Fish & Game Commission, R.R. #2, Box 54A, Pratt, Kansas 67124.

KENTUCKY Division of Water Enforcement, Department of Transportation, 114 W. Clinton Street, Frankfort, Kentucky 40601.

LOUISIANA Department of Wildlife & Fisheries, Wildlife & Fisheries Building, Quail Drive, Baton Rouge, Louisiana 70808.

MAINE Watercraft Section, Division of Recreational Safety & Registration, Department of Inland Fisheries & Wildlife, 284 State Street, Augusta, Maine 04333.

MARYLAND Department of Natural Resources, Tawes State Office Building, Annapolis, Maryland 21404.

MASSACHUSETTS Division of Marine & Recreational Vehicles, 150 Causeway Street, Boston, Massachusetts 02114.

MICHIGAN Bureau of Driver & Vehicle Services, Department of State, 7064 Crowner Drive, Lansing, Michigan 48918.

MINNESOTA Department of Natural Resources, Box 46, Centennial Office Building, St. Paul, Minnesota 55155.

MISSISSIPPI Boat and Water Safety Commission, Suite 240, 720 President St., Jackson, Mississippi 39202.

MISSOURI State Water Patrol, Department of Public Safety, P.O. Box 603, Jefferson City, Missouri 65101.

MONTANA Registrar's Bureau, Motor Vehicle Division, Department of Justice, Deer Lodge, Montana 59722.

NEBRASKA State Game & Parks Commission, P.O. Box 30370, Lincoln, Nebraska 68503.

NEVADA Division of Law Enforcement, Department of Fish & Game, Box 10678, Reno, Nevada 89520.

NEW HAMPSHIRE Division of Safety Services, Department of Safety, Hazen Drive, Concord, New Hampshire 03301. The State of New Hampshire registers power-boats operated on inland or non-tidal waters. As this registration system does not comply with the Federal Boating Act of 1958, the Coast Guard has retained the responsibility for registering and numbering undocumented vessels with more than 10 horsepower chiefly used on navigable waters of the United States within the territorial limits of New Hampshire.

NEW JERSEY Bureau of Marine Law Enforcement, Department of Environmental Protection, Box 1889, Trenton, New Jersey 08625.

NEW MEXICO Bureau of Boating Safety, State Park & Recreation Division, Natural Resources Department, P.O. Box 1147, Santa Fe, New Mexico 87503.

NEW YORK Marine & Recreational Vehicles Agency, Building No. 1, South Mall, Albany, New York 12238.

NORTH CAROLINA Division of Boating, Wildlife Resources Commission, Archdale Building, Raleigh, North Carolina 27611.

NORTH DAKOTA State Game & Fish Department, 2121 Lovett Avenue, Bismarck, North Dakota 58505.

OHIO Watercraft Division, Department of Natural Resources, Fountain Square, Columbus, Ohio 43224.

OKLAHOMA State Tax Commission, 2101 N. Lincoln Blvd., Oklahoma City, Oklahoma 73194

OREGON State Marine Board, No. 505, 3000 Market St. Plaza, N.E., Salem, Oregon 97310.

PENNSYLVANIA Pennsylvania Fish Commission, PO. Box 1673, Harrisburg, Pennsylvania 17120.

RHODE ISLAND Division of Boating Safety, Department of Environmental Management, Quonset Administration Building 7, Davisville, Rhode Island 02854.

SOUTH CAROLINA Division of Boating, Wildlife & Marine Resources Department, P.O. Box 12559, Charleston, South Carolina 29421.

SOUTH DAKOTA Department of Game, Fish & Parks, Anderson Building, Pierre, South Dakota 57501.

TENNESSEE Wildlife Resources Agency, P.O. Box 40747, Nashville, Tennessee 37204.

TEXAS Parks & Wildlife Department, 4200 Smith School Road, Austin, Texas 78744.

UTAH Division of Parks & Recreation, 1596 West North Temple Street, Salt Lake City, Utah 84116.

VERMONT Marine Division Department of Public Safety, Montpelier, Vermont 05602.

VIRGINIA Game & Inland Fisheries Commission, P.O. Box 11104, Richmond, Virginia 23230.

WASHINGTON The State of Washington does not have a boat registration and numbering law, but the Washington State Parks and Recreation Commission, 7150 Clearwater Lane (KY-11), Olympia, Wash. 98504, can furnish general information on boating in the state.

WEST VIRGINIA Department of Natural Resources, State Office Building, Charleston, West Virginia 25305.

WISCONSIN Bureau of Law Enforcement, Department of Natural Resources, P.O. Box 7921, Madison, Wisconsin 53707.

WYOMING Game & Fish Department, Cheyenne, Wyoming 82002.

DIST. OF COLUMBIA Harbor Precinct, Metropolitan Police Department, 550 Water St., S.W., Washington, D.C. 20024.

PUERTO RICO Maritime Department, Puerto Rico Ports Authority, GPO Box 2829, San Juan, Puerto Rico 00936.

VIRGIN ISLANDS Department of Conservation & Cultural Affairs, Lagoon Fishing Center, Estate Frydenhoj, St. Thomas, Virgin Islands 00801.

MARLINESPIKE SEAMANSHIP

Illustrated here are some common knots, bends, hitches, and splices. See Chapter 11, Pages 215-231 for details.

Overhand

The simple overhand knot is used to keep the end of a rope from unlaying.

Figure Eight

The figure eight knot. This does not jam.

Square or Reef Knot

The square or reef knot is a most useful and common knot. The rope manipulated by the right hand (this is the rope leading from the left side of the sketch and terminating in the arrow in A) is turned over the other rope in tying both the first and second half of the knot.

Sheet or Becket Bend

The sheet or becket bend is used for tying two lines together. It will not slip even if there is great difference in the sizes of the lines.

Clove Hitch

The clove hitch is used for making a line fast temporarily to a pile or a bollard.

Bowline

The bowline is considered a knot second in usefulness only to the square knot. The bowline will not slip, does not pinch or kink the rope as much as some other knots, and does not jam and become difficult to untie. By tying a bowline with a small loop and passing the line through the loop the running bowline is obtained. This is an excellent form of running noose.

Two Half Hitches

Two half hitches are used for making a line fast to a bollard, ring, timber, or stanchion. Note that the knot consists of a turn around the fixed object and a clove hitch around the standing part of the line.

Correct Method of Making Fast to a Cleat

Correct method for making fast to a cleat is shown. The half hitch which completes the fastening is taken with the free part of the line. The line can then be freed without taking up slack in the standing part.

Incorrect Method of Making Fast to a Cleat

Common incorrect method of making fast to a cleat is shown. The half hitch is taken with the standing part of the line and the line consequently can not be freed without taking up slack in the standing part. Accidents have been caused by the use of this type of fastening on lines which must be freed quickly.

Fisherman's Bend

The fisherman's bend, also called the anchor bend, is made by taking two round turns around the ring, then passing the end under both turns to form a half hitch around the standing part of the line. For further security, a second half hitch is taken around the standing part only.